1/91

Newsmakers®

ISSN 0899-0417

Newsmakers®

The People Behind Today's Headlines

Louise Mooney
Editor

1991
Cumulation

Includes Indexes to
1985 through 1991

 **Gale Research Inc.** · *DETROIT* · *LONDON*

STAFF

Louise Mooney, *Editor*

Julia M. Rubiner, *Associate Editor*

Marjorie Burgess, Victoria France Charabati, David Collins, John P. Cortez, Ellen Creager, Mary Lou De Blasi, Harvey Dickson, Simon Glickman, Joan Goldsworthy, Christine Ferran, Kelly King Howes, Anne Janette Johnson, Kyle Kevorkian, Virginia Curtin Knight, Mark Kram, Michael L. LaBlanc, Jeanne M. Lesinski, Glen Macnow, Carolyn March, Greg Mazurkiewicz, Nancy Rampson, Sharon Rose, Jon Saari, Susan Salter, Michael G. Sarafa, Warren Strugatch, Elizabeth Wenning, and David Wilkins, *Contributing Editors*

Peter M. Gareffa, *Senior Editor, Contemporary Biographies*

Jeanne Gough, *Permissions and Production Manager*
Margaret A. Chamberlain, *Permissions Supervisor (Pictures)*
Pamela A. Hayes, *Permissions Associate*
Karla Kulkis, Nancy Rattenbury, and Keith Reed, *Permissions Assistants*

Mary Beth Trimper, *Production Manager*
Shanna Philpott Heilveil, *External Production Assistant*
Arthur Chartow, *Art Director*
C. J. Jonik, *Keyliner*

Victoria B. Cariappa, *Research Manager*
Mary Rose Bonk, *Research Supervisor*
Jane Cousins Malonis, Andrew Guy Malonis, and Norma Sawaya, *Editorial Associates*
Mike Avolio, Patricia Bowen, Reginald A. Carlton, Clare Collins, Catherine A. Coulson, Theodore J. Dumbrigue, Shirley Gates, Sharon McGilvray, and Tracey Head Turbett, *Editorial Assistants*

Cover Photos: Julia Roberts and Norman Schwarzkopf (both AP/Wide World photos)

The paper used in this publication meets the minimum requirements of the American National Standard for Information Sciences—Permanence Paper for Printed Library Materials, ANSI Z39.48-1984. ∞™

Copyright © 1991
Gale Research Inc.
835 Penobscot Bldg.
Detroit, MI 48226-4094

ISBN 0-8103-7344-0 (this volume)
ISBN 0-8103-5452-7 (complete 1991 set)
ISSN 0899-0417

Printed in the United States of America

Published simultaneously in the United Kingdom
by Gale Research International Limited
(An affiliated company of Gale Research Inc.)

Contents

Obituaries

Introduction

Newsmakers provides informative profiles of the world's most interesting people in a crisp, concise, contemporary format. Make *Newsmakers* the first place you look for biographical information on the people making today's headlines.

Important Features

- **Attractive, modern page design** pleases the eye while making it easy to locate the information you need.

- **Coverage of all the newsmakers** you want to know about—people in business, education, technology, law, politics, religion, entertainment, labor, sports, medicine, and other fields.

- **Clearly labeled data sections** allow quick access to vital personal statistics, career information, major awards, and mailing addresses.

- **Informative sidelights essays** include the kind of in-depth analysis you're looking for.

- **Sources for additional information** provide lists of books, magazines, and newspapers where you can find out even more about *Newsmakers* listees.

- **Enlightening photographs** are specially selected to further enhance your knowledge of the subject.

- **Separate obituaries section** provides you with concise profiles of recently deceased newsmakers.

- **Publication schedule and price** fit your budget. *Newsmakers* is published in three paperback issues per year, each containing approximately 50 entries, and a hardcover cumulation, containing approximately 200 entries (those from the preceding three paperback issues *plus* an additional 50 entries), *all at a price you can afford!*

- And much, much more!

Indexes Provide Easy Access

Familiar and indispensable: The *Newsmakers* indexes! You can easily locate entries in a variety of ways through our four versatile, comprehensive indexes. The Nationality, Occupation, and Subject Indexes list names from the current year's *Newsmakers* issues. These are cumulated in the annual hardbound volume to include all names from the entire *Contemporary Newsmakers* and *Newsmakers* series. The Newsmakers Index is cumulated in all issues as well as the hardbound annuals to provide concise coverage of the entire series.

- **Cumulative Newsmaker Index**—Listee names, along with birth and death dates, when available, are arranged alphabetically followed by the year and issue number in which their entries appear.

- **Nationality Index**—Names of newsmakers are arranged alphabetically under their respective nationalities.

- **Occupation Index**—Names are listed alphabetically under broad occupational categories.

- **Subject Index**—Includes key subjects, topical issues, company names, products, organizations, etc., that are discussed in *Newsmakers*. Under each subject heading are listed names of newsmakers associated with that topic. So the unique Subject Index provides access to the information in *Newsmakers* even when readers are unable to connect a name with a particular topic. This index also invites browsing, allowing *Newsmakers* users to discover topics they may wish to explore further.

Suggestions Are Appreciated

The editors welcome your comments and suggestions. In fact, many popular *Newsmakers* features were implemented as a result of readers' suggestions. We will continue to shape the series to best meet the needs of the greatest number of users. Send comments or suggestions to:

The Editor
Newsmakers
Gale Research Inc.
835 Penobscot Bldg.
Detroit, MI 48226-4094

Or, call toll-free at 1-800-347-GALE

Newsmakers®

Spencer Abraham

Co-chairman of the National Republican Congressional Committee

F ull name, Edward Spencer Abraham; born June 12, 1952, in Lansing, MI; son of Edward Abraham and Julie Sears Abraham; married Jane Hershey (a Republican activist), January 27, 1990. *Education:* Michigan State University, B.A. in political science (with honors), 1974; Harvard Law School, J.D. (cum laude), 1979. *Politics:* Republican. *Religion:* Lebanese Orthodox.

Addresses: *Office*—National Republican Congressional Committee, 3201st Street, S.E., Washington, DC 20003.

Career

C o-founded *Harvard Journal of Law and Public Policy* while a student at Harvard Law School and continues to serve as publication's president; assistant professor of law at Thomas M. Cooley Law School and served as a consultant to the law firm of Denfield, Timmer & Taylor, 1981-83; served four terms as chairman of the Michigan Republican Party, 1983-91; chaired Michigan delegation to 1984 Republican National Convention; elected by Republican National Committee to chair Rules Committee, 1985; appointed by Vice-President Dan Quayle to position of deputy chief of staff, January, 1990, while simultaneously completing his tenure with Michigan Republican Party; left White House in March, 1990, to assume position of co-chairman of the National Republican Congressional Committee.

Member: Federalist Society for Law and Public Policy (co-founder and board member); State of Michigan Bar; District of Columbia Bar.

Sidelights

I n less than 15 months Spencer Abraham became deputy chief of staff to the vice-president of the United States, helped elect his close friend and political ally, John Engler, governor of Michigan, and was chosen for one of the top partisan political posts in Washington, D.C. At age 39, Abraham's quick ascension from state to national politics can be attributed to his keen intellect and political savvy. Abraham planted the seeds for his eventual national prominence with his many successes as chairman of the Michigan Republican Party.

First elected in 1983, the native Michigander became the youngest Republican state party chairman in the nation. Abraham moved quickly to modernize the state party apparatus. His emphasis on technical and organizational strength soon made the Michigan Republican party a model for other states and caught the attention of national Republicans. By 1984 Abraham had erased the $450,000 state party debt that he inherited, a frequently mentioned accomplishment.

Also in 1984 Abraham directed Republican victories in 11 of 13 statewide seats, all eight state board of education seats, and a state supreme court slot. On Abraham's watch, the Republicans gained eight seats in the Michigan House of Representatives and in

1985 took control (with a 20-to-18 majority) of the state Senate after two successful recall efforts and special elections. Engler, Abraham's friend and co-engineer of the Senate takeover became senate majority leader. Republicans also gained a congressional seat. Abraham is widely given credit for convincing William Lucas, a black and then-Wayne County Executive, to switch from the Democratic to Republican party. (Lucas ran unsuccessfully for Michigan governor in 1986.) Abraham was unanimously re-elected to the state's top party post in 1984 and 1986.

The May 1986 edition of *Detroit Monthly* magazine referred to Abraham as an "acknowledged organizational genius [who] has a genuine fondness for the nuts and bolts of professional politicking." And his early success caused *Detroit Free Press* columnist Hugh McDiarmid to dub Abraham "some kind of wunderkind" who "through a combination of brains, organizational skills, energy and good timing, seems to have made a roaring success out of the state chairmanship." His abilities were recognized when he was unanimously elected by the Republican National Committee to chair the powerful Rules Committee—the body that would set the parameters to govern the Party and its nominating process from 1988 through the 1992 election.

Abraham—and Michigan—gained further national prominence when he orchestrated a change in the presidential delegate selection process. This "early caucus" strategy brought Michigan to the forefront of the Republican nominating process and guaranteed the Michigan Republican Party a steady stream of visiting presidential hopefuls. It also ignited the fiercest political infighting of the year and posed a threat to Abraham's otherwise shining career.

The rift over choice of presidential candidates, which eventually gained national notoriety, was between the moderate supporters of then-Vice-President George Bush and the more conservative supporters of television evangelist Pat Robertson—both contenders for the Republican presidential nomination in 1988. The core of Congressman and presidential hopeful Jack Kemp's supporters sided with their philosophical ally Robertson, forcing more mainstream Kemp supporters to align with the Bush camp. The feud centered around control of the Party, hence the process and—given the early caucus system—the right to thrust one's respective candidates into the national front-runner position.

During the two-year prelude to the 1988 presidential election, the chairman took heat from all sides of the conflict. Headlines at the time read: "GOP's Abra-

ham faces threat to charmed career" (*Lansing State Journal*), "Abraham paid price for feud" (*Midland Daily News*), and "Abraham shares blame for GOP rift" (*Detroit News*). Pete Secchia, a close friend of Abraham's and a Bush loyalist who is now the ambassador to Italy said, "[Abraham] has tried so hard to please all the camps, I think he's lost most camps." Despite Secchia's complaints, Abraham was often accused of quietly favoring then vice-president Bush and, after a series of battles over arcane rules and processes, faced dual conventions at the 1988 state convention in Grand Rapids, Michigan—one chaired by Abraham and a "rump" convention called by supporters of Pat Robertson. Abraham was so frustrated he discussed stepping down if it would "heal" the Party. The process that had been hailed for expanding party involvement and focusing the national spotlight on Michigan left Abraham mired in a civil war.

Ironically, it was Abraham's neutrality along with sound judgment and steadfastness that allowed him not only to survive but to prosper. While Michigan's prominence in the Republican nominating process was somewhat diminished by the infighting, Abraham was quickly recognized as the only person who could keep the Republican party united. He had a strong record of inclusion and a deep faith in the power of pluralism. When tempers cooled, Abraham managed to rally Michigan Republicans around Vice-President Bush, the eventual nominee, and, following the election, Abraham was unanimously re-elected to a fourth term.

While Abraham considers himself a strong conservative, he practices a balanced blend of philosophy and practical management. In a *Lansing State Journal* article headlined "Abraham GOP's great conciliator," the 17th District Congressional chairman at the time put it this way: "With Spence, the center of gravity in Republican politics in Michigan is the party organization." Even in October of 1987 Abraham was being praised by *Detroit Monthly* magazine as "the major source of strength and unity within the Republican Party."

During the 1988 presidential election, Abraham traveled to Washington, D.C., many times to help Bush adviser Bob Teeter—also a Michigander—analyze and interpret polling data. Teeter had been the one who advised George Bush to select Dan Quayle as his running mate. Abraham shared credit for Bush's Michigan victory and by now was very well-known in Washington. So when an opening developed on the vice-president's staff, Abraham fit the part. Quayle praised the Michigan politician as a "valuable addition to my staff and the administration as a whole"; Teeter lauded Abraham for "melding political savvy with knowledge of issues and policy." David Beckwith, Quayle's press secretary, said, "What he brings . . . is his considerable reputation as an outstanding political operative, his national reputation and stature for dealing with sometimes conflicting elements within the Republican Party and just a good solid reputation for judgment and common sense." For a political junkie like Abraham, working in a corner office on the second-floor of the Old Executive Office Building was a dream come true.

During this time Abraham worked out a deal that allowed him to remain state party chairman that included giving up his chairman's salary and relinquishing the day-to-day operations. While some were skeptical about Abraham's ability to do both jobs, most Party activists were excited about the White House access the appointment would bring for Michigan. The White House opportunity would also keep Abraham based out of the same city as his fiancee, Jane Hershey, who had recently accepted a post at the Republican National Committee in Washington.

At the White House Abraham cemented his reputation as a political guru. His responsibilities included acting as Quayle's liaison with GOP leaders around the country and overseeing the day-to-day management and operations of the vice-president's office. Abraham would also take part in Republican political strategy sessions at the highest levels. He was still in charge of the Michigan Republican Party in November of 1990 when Republicans maintained their slim majority in the Michigan Senate and John Engler won the governorship. It was Abraham, a famed number-cruncher, who was tallying the votes for governor in the wee hours of the morning and who was first to know that his good friend would be Michigan's next governor.

Abraham did not run again for party chair but was soon recruited to fill the void at the National Republican Congressional Committee left by Ed Rollins. This high-profile position entails enormous responsibilities. Abraham is now charged with changing the partisan balance in the U.S. House of Representatives from Democrat to Republican—something that has not happened in over 30 years.

Abraham's interest in government and politics go back to his youth. At East Lansing High School he was elected junior class president and later student body president. At the age of 16 he began his political career as a volunteer in a race for Ingham County drain commissioner. Two years later he ran Nelson Rockefeller's presidential campaign in Michigan. In 1974 and 1976 he managed congressional campaigns for Clifford Taylor, who was Abraham's best man at his 1990 wedding. After graduating cum laude from Harvard Law School, where he co-founded a conservative alternative to the liberal Harvard Law Review called the *Harvard Journal of Law and Public Policy*, Abraham taught law at Thomas Cooley Law School in Lansing, Michigan. In conjunction with teaching, Abraham practiced law as a consultant to Denfield, Timmer & Taylor and did polling for the simultaneous campaigns of Richard Headlee for governor and L. Brooks Patterson for attorney general.

At every point in his career, Abraham has been ahead of his time in terms of accomplishments. While he has always been considered a wizard, Abraham has built a reputation as a powerful public personality, moving easily between crowds with a disarming combination of charm and stature. He has come a long way since the time that he once wore gym shorts to a brunch for Republican bigwigs. He has developed himself into a public speaker who commands an audience and projects a strong presence.

Abraham's success can also be attributed to his strong family upbringing. Abraham's grandparents were Lebanese immigrants. His father, affectionately known as "Eddie" by Abraham's friends and staff, was a regular at state party headquarters. Abraham's parents instilled in their son a strong sense of duty and patriotism that is common among second- and third-generation immigrant families. Abraham was very close with his parents. His mother died in 1982 and his father, who was able to watch his only son's tremendous achievements, died in 1991.

Abraham is proud of his ethnic heritage. He participates in major Arab-American conferences and maintains an extended network of Arab-American friends and relatives around Michigan—home to the largest concentration of people with Arab ancestry outside the Middle East. And Abraham enjoys dining on Middle Eastern food. But clearly his favorite pastime is baseball—not surprising for a statistical mastermind. When he has the time, Abraham has been known to immerse himself in the game—often citing obscure statistics from memory. In 1984 Hugh McDiarmid observed in the *Detroit Free Press* that Abraham had "sort of an ultimate dream—getting Ronald Reagan into Michigan during the campaign and sitting next to him in October at a Tiger Stadium World Series game."

Sources

Detroit Monthly, May 1986, October 1987.
Detroit Free Press, August 1984, December 1989.
Detroit News, December 1989.
Dowagiac Daily News (Michigan), March 1983.
Lansing State Journal, December 1986.

—*Michael G. Sarafa*

Isabelle Adjani

Actress

Full name, Isabelle Yasmine Adjani; born June 27, 1955, in Paris, France; daughter of Mohammed Cherif Adjani (a garage mechanic); children: a son, Barnabe Said, with film director Bruno Nuytten.

Addresses: *Office*—c/o Phonogram, 89 boulevard Auguste Blanqui, 75013 Paris, France.

Career

Began acting professionally at age 13 with film *Le Petit Bougnat* (*The Little Charcoal Dealer*), 1969; subsequent film appearances include *Faustine et le bel ete* (*Faustine and the Beautiful Summer*), 1971; *La gifle* (*The Gap*), 1974; *The Story of Adele H.*, 1975; *Le locataire* (*The Tenant*), 1976; *Barocco*, 1976; *Violette et Francois*, 1977; *The Driver*, 1977; *Nosferatu, Phantom der Nacht* (*Nosferatu the Vampyre*), 1978; *Les soeurs Bronte* (*The Bronte Sisters*), 1979; *Possession*, 1981; *Quartet*, 1981; *Clara et les chics types* (*Clara and the Nice Guys*), 1981; *L'annee prochaine si tout va bien* (*Next Year If All Goes Well*), 1981; *Tout feu tout flamme* (*Wild Enthusiasm*), 1982; *Antonieta*, 1983; *Motelle randonnee* (*Deadly Ramble*), 1983; *L'ete meurtrier* (*One Deadly Summer*), 1983; *Subway*, 1985; *Ishtar*, 1987; *Camille Claudel* (also co-producer), 1988. Stage appearances include Federico Garcia Lorca's *House of Bernarda Alba*, c. 1972; Moliere's *L'ecole des femmes* with the Comedie Francaise, 1973 (also appeared in television production of same, 1972); Jena Giraudoux's *Ondine*, c. 1973; August Strindberg's *Miss Julie*, 1983. Served as president of the Commission for Advances on Receipts, a funding agency for the French film industry, c. 1987-88.

Awards: Best actress awards from the National Society of Film Critics and the New York Critics Circle, both 1976, both for *The Story of Adele H.*; Oscar nomination for *The Story of Adele H.*; two Cannes Film Festival best actress awards, both 1981, for *Possession* and *Quartet*; Cesar awards for *Possession*, 1983, *L'ete Meurtrier*, c. 1984, and *Camille Claudel*, 1989; Academy Award nomination for best actress, 1990, for *Camille Claudel*.

Sidelights

To fans in her native France, Isabelle Adjani is considered "the greatest actress of her generation and probably the most beautiful woman in the world," according to *Vanity Fair*. Although American audiences know her primarily for her Oscar-nominated leading role in the 1988 film *Camille Claudel*, Adjani has rapidly gained attention in the United States not only for her extraordinary beauty, but as a creative, outspoken, and independent actress who spurns the trappings of conventional stardom. "Adjani's performances run on a dark, deep energy that makes her characters carry something larger than a story or a series of emotions," wrote Joan Juliet Buck in *Vanity Fair*. "Her work is complex and masterfully calibrated, yet always on the edge of a cataclysm, a terminal breakup. She is one of the greats."

Adjani was born in Paris in 1955 and raised in the working-class suburb of Gennevilliers. Her father was a native of Algeria—a French colony from 1848 to 1962 and thereafter an Arab nation. During World War II he joined the French army and fought with the Allies in the Italian campaign. After the war, in the West German (now German) state of Bavaria, he met and married Adjani's mother and settled in France. As a child Isabelle Adjani was precocious, theatrical, and domineering, with a voracious appetite for literature. In one of her first experiences in the dramatic arts, a 13-year-old Adjani directed her classmates in a production by the legendary French playwright Moliere. Also during this time the young actress was cast in supporting roles in two youth films. Up to this point she had not seriously considered an acting career—she had for a period entertained the idea of becoming a veterinarian—but the professional drive and attitude of her young film colleagues inspired her to audition for a place in the French National Conservatory. Adjani was not accepted but, at 15, she was invited to join the Comedie-Francaise, the home of French classical theater, without an audition.

With the Comedie-Francaise she found immediate acceptance. "She was called a phenomenon [and] received instantaneous acclaim . . . critics said that she had a great classical career in front of her," Buck reported. But Adjani abruptly severed her association with the repertory company after a few short years when filmmaker Francois Truffaut cast her in the starring role in *The Story of Adele H.* The actress had been offered a twenty-year contract by the Comedie-Francaise, with the condition that they hold the right to approve her film roles. Before Adjani signed the contract, however, the approval for *Adele H.* was flatly denied. Adjani summarily rejected her contract and left the Comedie-Francaise.

Not yet 20, the actress embarked upon a new phase of her already well-established dramatic career, devoting herself almost exclusively to film. Her following, however, was not pleased. As Buck noted, "When she turned her back on the austere opportunities of the French repertory to make movies, her audience, by now composed not only of theatergoers and readers of magazines, but of the entire population of France, turned its applause into a sour, critical watchfulness." The French, quite simply, took her actions as a slap in the face, and Adjani's reputation for rebellion and independent intensity had been born.

In *Adele H.*, Adjani played the daughter of poet and author Victor Hugo. Beset by obsessive romantic longing, Adele follows her love-interest, a soldier, to Nova Scotia, where she becomes so thoroughly engrossed in her own fantasies that she no longer recognizes him. Buck hailed the film as "a masterpiece, the most chilling and personal indictment of romantic obsession ever made." And despite national scorn, the accolades continued to roll in and her fans' opinions began to soften. Among her more noteworthy films were Werner Herzog's 1978 *Nosferatu, Phantom der Nacht* (*Nosferatu the Vampyre*), in which "she played Dracula's prey with an eerie, stylized passivity," according to *Interview*, and the 1983 thriller *L'ete meurtrier* (*One Deadly Summer*), in which Adjani appeared as "the baby-faced vamp, jiggling everything she had down the street of a small French town—Ruby Gentry crossed with Marilyn Monroe." Also, for her performances in the 1981 films *Possession* and *Quartet*, Adjani won best actress awards at the Cannes Film Festival.

In 1983 the actress's life took a bizarre turn when it was rumored that she was dying of acquired immune deficiency syndrome, or AIDS. After it was reported that she had died in a French provincial hospital, Adjani appeared on national television to prove the rumor false and present her doctor's statement attesting to her good health. The experience left Adjani hurt and angry. "It's offensive to turn illness into a weapon you point at someone," she told *Interview*, adding that she "was at the mercy of the nastiest imaginations."

Further controversy erupted when Adjani began to speak out, in the late 1980s—around the time of her father's death—against anti-Arab sentiment in France. Frustrated by an increasingly racist atmosphere in Paris, Adjani surprised her public by revealing her Algerian heritage. (She had previously been vaguely referred to as Turkish.) "To be Algerian in France," explained Buck in *Vanity Fair*, "is to be part of a feared and hated underclass—immigrants from a country that is a bad memory for the French, a mismanaged colony whose independence was accompanied by a war that split France in two." In another consciousness-raising incident, Adjani accepted a Cesar prize (the French equivalent of the American Oscar) by reading some lines of what "her audience took to be Romantic or French prose," Buck wrote; it turned out to be a passage from Salman Rushdie's *Satanic Verses*—a work which earned its author a death warrant from the Muslim world and sent him into hiding.

By 1985 Adjani had appeared in more than a dozen French films and was ready to launch one of her own pet projects, a film about Camille Claudel, sculptor and mistress of artist and sculptor Auguste Rodin. Adjani found Claudel's story compelling: While in her 40s, Claudel was committed to an insane asylum by her brother, the poet Paul Claudel. She languished there for thirty years, during which time she wrote many long and apparently clear-headed letters to her brother, pleading for her release. For the film Adjani chose as her director Bruno Nuytten, the father of her son Barnabe, and managed to secure rights to reproduce Claudel's original sculpture for the filming, as well as buy the rights to a biography by Reine-Marie Paris, Paul Claudel's granddaughter and Camille's great-niece. Adjani's performance in the title role (she also served as co-producer) garnered several honors, including a Cesar for best actress, a Golden Bear Award from Berlin, Germany, and an Academy Award nomination for best actress.

Adjani will no doubt continue to delight and surprise her ever-growing number of fans; she has proven her adaptability, creativity, and independence. This is particularly reflected in her personal lifestyle, of which she is fiercely protective. As Buck remarked, "She won't allow anyone to see where she really lives"; Adjani herself admits she has no permanent residence. "I'll always be a nomad, and I'm just beginning to accept it. I used to buy antiques, and had pretty Napoleon III things, and then—no!" she explained to Buck, adding: "What was the point of insisting on owning this universe of furniture that had nothing to do with me, my history, my ancestry." At one point Adjani sampled the domestic life by taking a two-year respite from her career at age 21, after son Barnabe was born. As she told Buck, "I wanted to be a housewife, a mother. I had an urge to simply feel good, not be glamorous or fascinating or on show . . . . It wasn't pleasant. It was a failure." She is philosophical about her role and the powerful force she exerts as an actress and public figure. "Your size scares people," she confided to Buck, "even though you're very careful not to crush any buildings or step on anyone. It's a Karma; you have to accept it, because it's not going to let you be."

Sources

Books

Dureau, Christian, *Isabelle Adjani: Biographie non autorisee* (unauthorized biography), 1987.
Roques-Briscard, Christian, *La Passion d'Adjani*, 1987.

Periodicals

Interview, January 1990.
New York, March 26, 1990.
Vanity Fair, October 1989.

—Louise Mooney

Lamar Alexander

AP/Wide World Photos

U.S. secretary of education

Born July 3, 1940, in Knox County, Tenn.; married; wife's name, Honey; children: four. *Education:* Vanderbilt University, B.A., 1962; New York University, LL.D. 1965. *Politics:* Republican. *Religion:* Presbyterian.

Addresses: *Office*—University of Tennessee, 831 Andy Holt Tower, Knoxville, TN, 37996.

Career

Law clerk to a U.S. Circuit Court of Appeals judge, 1966; legislative assistant to U.S. Senator Howard Baker, 1967-69; executive assistant to White House counselor on congressional relations, 1969; governor of Tennessee, 1979-87; president of University of Tennessee, 1988-91; U.S. secretary of education, 1991—. Served as chairman of Education Department commission to prepare national "report card," 1986; served on Southern Regional Education Board and Appalachian Regional Commission; has also worked in private law practice and as a political commentator for a Nashville TV station.

Member: National Governors Association (chairman, 1985-86), Tennessee Citizens for Revenue Sharing (founding member), Tennessee Council on Crime and Delinquency (founding member), Phi Beta Kappa.

Awards: Named one of 200 young U.S. leaders by *Time*, 1974; James B. Conant Award for education leadership, 1988.

Sidelights

Lamar Alexander is expected to put some punch in President George Bush's promise to be the education president. In December 1990, Bush made Alexander his choice as the nation's secretary of education, a move that could help protect the president from critics who say he has compiled a weak record on education issues during his first term. Alexander has received generally high marks for his education initiatives during two terms as the governor of Tennessee. After leaving the statehouse, he became president of the University of Tennessee.

In Washington, he has a big, politically volatile job ahead of him for at least two reasons. The first is that Lauro Cavazos, his genial but lackluster and ineffectual predecessor, was forced to resign in December. Cavazos, a holdover from the Reagan administration and one of two Hispanics in Bush's cabinet, "had long been the most visible symbol of the president's failure to make good on his 1988 campaign pledge to be the 'education president,'" *Time* said, adding that "Cavazos was handicapped further by Bush's desultory leadership. Since the president announced six national education goals [in early 1990] he, Congress, and the nation's governors have done little but squabble over who will assess whether the goals are being met.... The unceremonious dumping [of Cavazos] fuels suspicion that the White House is worried that voters will punish the president in 1992 unless he delivers on his promises."

Alexander's second challenge lies in the likelihood of his having to cope with the fallout from the recent federal flip-flop regarding scholarships for minorities—an issue that set the Bush administration and the Education Department reeling in late 1990. After Michael Williams, a mid-level education official, issued a ruling declaring college scholarships allocated for blacks and other minorities unconstitutional, loud protests arose nationwide. Coming on the heels of Bush's veto of the 1990 Civil Rights Act, the action "seemed to be yet another neoconservative attack on the legal foundations of affirmative action," *Time* said. The White House later shelved Williams's ruling and indicated that the whole issue was under review.

Not exactly the warmest Washington welcome for Alexander. But Washington is not totally new to him; neither is being cast in a clean-up role. He served as a legislative aide to former Senate majority leader Howard Baker and worked in the Richard Nixon White House in the late 1960s; Alexander entered the Tennessee governor's office following the scandal-tainted administration of Ray Blanton, who was convicted of selling pardons.

In a 1985 issue of *U.S. News & World Report*, Baker called his protege "the brightest young official in America—he's qualified to be president or anything else he wants to be." Indeed, Alexander is often mentioned as a future presidential contender and was seen as a potential GOP vice-presidential nominee in 1988, until Bush gave the nod to Indiana's Dan Quayle. In July 1988, *Conservative Digest* speculated that Alexander's position on abortion rights could alienate potential Republican supporters; "Party activists from [Alexander's] home state are quick to note that his wife is extremely active in Planned Parenthood, the nation's leading advocate of government-funded abortion and propagandizing school children about sex," a writer for the magazine noted. "[And] Alexander openly opposed the Home School Bill passed by the legislature, a red-flag issue for the millions of Christian activists, and he has been quoted as regarding social issues as not part of his agenda."

In a 1986 *Newsweek* poll the nation's governors selected Alexander as the most effective Republican state chief executive, ranking him second overall behind Democrat Michael Dukakis of Massachusetts. *Newsweek* cited Alexander for winning the high-stakes bidding war for General Motors' $3.5 billion

Saturn plant; for launching the national crusade for merit pay for teachers; and for generally capitalizing on the gubernatorial bread-and-butter issues of jobs and education. "Despite catcalls from the teachers' unions, Alexander in 1984 coaxed [Tennessee's] Democratic legislature into approving a $1.2 billion career-ladder plan that linked incentive pay with performance," *Newsweek* said.

> ## "Basic skills first, computer skills next, then job skills."

Before General Motors chose Tennessee over more than 30 other states seeking the Saturn plant, Alexander met three times with GM chairman Roger Smith. Alexander's winning argument, according to *U.S. News & World Report*, went this way: "If GM really wants to compete head-to-head with the Japanese, it should build its plant only 35 miles from the Nissan facility at Smyrna. Alexander said he gambled with that challenge, knowing it could be 'the hook—or the kiss of death.'"

Alexander is a political moderate, a classical pianist, a lawyer, and the son of teachers. He and his wife Honey are socially close to George and Barbara Bush. Alexander began playing the piano at the age of five and turned down a music scholarship offered by Converse College. He attended Vanderbilt University and studied law at New York University. After losing his first run for Tennessee's top job in 1974, Alexander hiked to the governorship via a 1,000-mile, 1978 campaign walk across the state. "It was so cold when I started that the television cameras froze, and it was so hot when I ended in Memphis that the sign on the bank said 106 degrees," Alexander said in a 1986 issue of *Southern Living*.

While governor, he routinely performed with Tennessee symphonies and orchestras to help raise money. "The most fun one was at Memphis' Sunset Symphony," he told *Southern Living*. "I did that once in '82. It was the closest I ever came to feeling like a Beatle, because the crowd was absolutely delighted with it. I wore the white suit and did some Chopin. I played a combination of classical and then Memphis music, and I ended up with a Jerry Lee Lewis routine. I had on the white suit, and I took off my coat and had on a red-and-black shirt. I kicked the piano bench over, and they had me come back and play it again."

During his two terms in the Tennessee statehouse—Tennessee law limits its governors from serving longer—Alexander became the leader among the nation's governors in calling for school reforms. He emphasized basic skills and implemented the nation's first statewide merit pay program for teachers. His caveat: "Basic skills first, computer skills next, then job skills." "[Alexander] is recognized around the country as the leading exponent of doing things in public education," University of North Carolina political scientist Thad Beyle told *Newsweek* in 1986. "And he's been able to do it in a bipartisan way."

In 1989 *Nation's Business* asked Alexander about his goals for schools: "What I hear from most businessmen is that they want people to have at least an eighth-grade education," Alexander replied. "Now that offends some people, because this is America and we're all supposed to be thinking higher than that. But an eighth-grade education—in case some people haven't checked lately—is a fairly significant set of skills." He continued: "If all Americans had an eighth-grade education today, we'd be leaving most of our worldwide competitors in the dust. We would still need Nobel Prize winners and our large number of higher educated people. But our most fundamental problem is with the bottom group—those who don't have eighth-grade skills."

Alexander devised the Better Schools Program for Tennessee, featuring a merit-day system for teachers, tougher standards for students, and more computer, science, and math instruction, according to *Time.* It has become a national model. "The ex-governor favors de-regulation of school bureaucracies to encourage innovation and strongly backs adult education to make U.S. workers competitive again," *Time* said. "Around the cabinet table, the new secretary can be expected to provide calm, deliberate counsel."

Alexander described the results of his Better Schools Program to *Nation's Business* in 1989: "The number of high school students enrolled in algebra I and II courses has increased 40 percent since 1985; the number taking advanced math is up 103 percent; the number taking science courses has risen 51 percent.

In that same period, total high school enrollment in Tennessee increased only 3 percent."

In his role as education secretary, Alexander is expected to select a few key issues—perhaps including Bush's proposal to give parents more choice in selecting their children's schools—and then drum up support for them. Albert Shanker, president of the American Federation of Teachers, said in the *Detroit Free Press* that he expects Alexander to help set goals and then "get rid of a lot of rules and regulations and let teachers and principals figure out how to get there."

That may be true, if Alexander follows the sentiment he expressed in an article he wrote for *Tennessee Education* in 1985 (reprinted in Education Digest in 1986): "We are getting where we are aiming; we get mediocrity because we are aiming for it," he wrote. "In my visits to Tennessee schools, I've found a lot more wrong with school goals, than with schools. There is nothing wrong with American public education that a few common-sense goals and a willingness to try something new won't fix." He added: "Some people would say I expect too much. I do expect a lot, and perhaps I am impatient. But the hard, honest truth is that we have not developed our brains as much as we can, and we haven't made our schools as good as they should be."

Sources

Conservative Digest, July 1988.
Detroit Free Press, December 18, 1990; December 19, 1990.
Education Digest, April 1986.
Nation's Business, April 1989.
Newsweek, March 24, 1986; December 4, 1990.
Reader's Digest, April 1988.
Phi Delta Kappan, November 1986.
Southern Living, October 1986.
U.S. News & World Report, August 12, 1985.
Time, December 24, 1990; December 31, 1990.

—David Wilkins

Joseph Antonini

Retail chain executive

Born July 13, 1941, in Morgantown, W. Va. *Education:* Graduated from the University of West Virginia, 1964.

Addresses: *Office*—K Mart Corp., 3100 West Big Beaver Rd., Troy, MI 48084; and K Mart Apparel Corp., 7373 Westside Ave. N., North Bergen, NJ 07047.

Career

Began with K Mart Corp. in 1964; served as president and director of K Mart Apparel Corp. in North Bergen, N.J., 1984-86; K Mart chief operating officer, 1986-87, chairman and chief executive officer, 1987—, president, 1988—. Member of board of directors of Michigan Bell Telephone Company.

Sidelights

In the 1980s it became fashionable for corporate executives to portray themselves, by way of marketing and advertising, as high-profile, high-energy patriarchs of the companies they ran. Just as Lee Iacocca's down-to-earth, no-nonsense image helped him sell a lot of cars for Chrysler Motors, so Joseph Antonini brought his own personal marketing touch to his revival of the K Mart Corp., America's leading discount chain and second-leading retail store overall. A genuine "company man," Antonini has never worked for anyone but K Mart; so when he took to the airwaves in the late 1980s espousing a more responsive, upscale, diverse store than the one

consumers had come to expect, the message evidently fell on receptive ears. "Mr. Antonini has spearheaded a mind-boggling list of new programs designed to help K Mart shed its 'junk' image," wrote Patricia Strand in *Advertising Age*.

Just a few years after he took the company reins in 1987, Antonini had solidified K Mart's solid position in the lucrative department store market and had the company more prepared for the ever-shifting demands of the fickle consumers of the 1990s. Just 46 years old when he was named CEO, Antonini's swift rise through the corporate ranks was due more to his personal enthusiasm and marketing expertise than to any shrewd political maneuvers or power plays.

After graduating from the University of West Virginia in 1964, Antonini did a seven-month stint with the U.S. Army before going to work as a stock boy with the Uniontown, Pennsylvania store of the S.S. Kresge Company, as K Mart was then called. He received sales training in the company's main offices in Detroit before getting his first store manager's job at a Buffalo outlet in 1970. In 1976 Antonini was placed in charge of a brand new store, where he was able to employ his aggressive promotion, bookkeeping, and ordering innovations from the ground up. The store began showing a profit in one year rather than the usual three, and Antonini's rise through sales management was speedy.

By the time he was named president of the K Mart Apparel Corp., the company's largest division, Antonini was not only the right man but was arriving at the right time. He was in an excellent position to make a strong impression on frustrated upper management. The rapid expansion of the 1970s, in which K Mart grew to over 2,000 stores, was beginning to take its toll on profits. Also, consumer tendencies were changing. Huge hypermarkets, such as the Wal-Mart chain, were chipping away at K Mart's discount appeal, while on the other end specialty stores selling faddish, brand-name items were, collectively, beating K Mart's selection. Antonini's idea was that K Mart could supply private-label lines of clothing that appealed to specialty store shoppers, while at the same time staying competitive with the hypermarkets by selling at a discount.

First, Antonini improved the quality of the product and began advertising in women's fashion magazines, something unheard of in the days when K Mart merchandise was considered "cheap." Second, he introduced full lines of private-label apparel, including the highly successful Jaclyn Smith line, which was vigorously promoted with television ads featuring the popular actress. The strategy worked. From 1983 to 1986, private-label sales jumped from 10 percent to 50 percent of total clothing sales. And while the rest of K Mart was still struggling, apparel's share of total K Mart sales rose from 20 to 24 percent and did a great deal to maintain the health of the entire corporation.

Because of his efforts, Antonini became the logical successor to chairman Bernard M. Fauber when he stepped down in 1987. Since that time, Antonini has intensified his push to make K Mart leaner, more diversified, and better able to keep up with changing consumer demands with more market research, faster sales-inventory response, better technology, and centralized bookkeeping. For instance, a $500 million, five-year push to introduce computerized scanners in checkout lanes will give instant data on what is selling and where. K Mart underwent another image enhancement in 1990, when its familiar red "K" and turquoise "Mart" logo was changed to a large red "K" with the word "mart" scripted in white within the letter.

If the numbers show that Antonini has helped shore up K Mart's weaknesses, they also show that competition is becoming increasingly tough. By the end of fiscal 1987, K Mart sales had risen to $25.6 billion, just $2.5 billion behind Sears, the number one retailer. And K Mart has strengthened its number one position among discount stores, a position which came under attack in the 1980s by the successful hypermarket chains like Wal-Mart and Target stores. "All of our competition is tough, and everybody's getting bigger and better," Antonini told *Advertising Age*. "Everybody's a threat to K Mart, just as we are a threat to everybody as well."

Sources

Advertising Age, July 25, 1988.
Business Week, September 8, 1986.
Detroit Free Press, October 11, 1989.
Forbes, May 27, 1991.
New York Times, December 21, 1986; September 15, 1987.

—*David Collins*

Jean-Bertrand Aristide

AP/Wide World Photos

President of Haiti

Born July 15, 1953, in Douyon, Haiti; orphaned; never married; no children. *Education:* Biblical study in Israel; studied in various countries, including Egypt, Great Britain, and Canada; earned graduate degree in psychology. *Politics:* Socialist-oriented. *Religion:* Roman Catholic.

Address: Presidential Palace, Port-au-Prince, Haiti.

Career

Ordained Roman Catholic priest in 1982; president of Haiti, 1991—. Clerical work primarily in helping the poor, running an orphanage and youth center.

Sidelights

An outspoken rebel priest from a ghetto parish deep in Port-au-Prince, Haiti, Jean-Bertrand Aristide helped liberate his country from three and a half decades of military rule, overcoming three assassination attempts to take office in 1991 as Haiti's first democratically elected president. Long an advocate of liberation theology—a movement within the Catholic Church that is particularly prevalent in Latin America, in which spiritual fulfillment is equated with social and political freedom—the Roman Catholic priest helped undermine the military dictatorship of the Jean-Claude Duvalier regime and its successor by breeding dissent among parishioners over years of violence and official intimidation. While clearly opposed to the methods of the regime he helped oust, he has offered few specific political or economic solutions.

Insisting that he held no interest in running for office himself, Aristide emerged as the only viable national leader in post-Duvalier politics and became the clear front–runner the moment he announced his candidacy. His election–day boast that he could have slept through the campaign was hardly an overstatement. A report in the *New York Times* compared his stature among his countrymen to that held by Nelson Mandela among South Africans, and Martin Luther King, Jr., among African-Americans.

Widely perceived as fervently nationalistic, anti-capitalist, and anti-Washington, as a presidential candidate Father Aristide cooled his heated appeals somewhat. His campaign rhetoric, as reported in the *Washington Post*, "stressed in somewhat messianic terms that his is the voice of the people, that his cause is the suffering of the poor, that his candidacy is at the masses' behest." Known as "the prophet" to his supporters, the young priest has done little to moderate the cult of personality that has swelled around him. Much of his popularity was earned during hours of service to the poor, running an orphanage and youth center in Port-au-Prince. Many of his supporters know him personally, from a time when he came to their aide at a moment of crisis. He has made the most of the bonds that tie him with the poor, however. "Jesus was not a priest," he declared to Mary Nemeth of *Maclean's*. "He was a lay worker."

Throughout the 1980s the charismatic priest preached his populist and frequently anti-government sermons at the Eglise de St.-Jean-Bosco, a Roman Catholic church of the Salesian order. In a small country where personal contacts are the primary basis of political action, he politicized thousands and thousands of individuals both in Port-au-Prince, the capital, and in the provinces. His highly politicized sermons attacked the Duvalier regime and its allies, the organized right-wing thugs known as the Tontons Macoutes, and the power of the United States. Even the Roman Catholic church was not exempt from his wrath.

> *"Along that hard and pitiless road toward life, death comes as an honor. But life in the charnel house is a disgrace, an affront to humankind."*

Described as "wispy" and "retiring" but also as "stirringly political" in a *New York Times* profile and as "a figure of exemplary courage" by American author Amy Wilentz, in sermon after sermon throughout the 1980s the priest incited the Haitian working man and woman to throw off the shackles of poverty and apathy. The squalor and indignity that define their lives need not continue, he declared. As he wrote in his book, *In the Parish of the Poor*, "I say: Disobey the rules. Ask for more. Leave your wretchedness behind. Organize with your brothers and sisters. Never accept the hand of fate. Keep hope alive. Refuse the squalor of the parishes of the poor. Escape the charnel house, and move toward life. Fill the parishes of the poor with hope and meaning and life. March out of the prison, down the hard and pitiless road toward life, and you will find the parishes of the poor gleaming and sparkling with joy and sunrise at the road's end. Children with strong bodies will run with platefuls of rice and beans to greet their starving saviors. That is your reward. Along that hard and pitiless road toward life, death

comes as an honor. But life in the charnel house is a disgrace, an affront to humankind."

Or, as the *New York Times* described his appeal: "His messianic pledge of redemptive justice for the victims of violence and persecution, and his own simplicity, coming just after the attempted entry into the race of a former leader of the Tontons Macoutes paramilitary squads, was received like a soothing balm by many Haitians. This lifted him onto a plane beyond the ordinarily political."

His election in December 1990 came in a landslide: He took 68 percent of the vote, compared to 13 percent drawn by his nearest rival. When election returns were announced the streets of cities and towns across the country were filled with supporters young and old, clogging the streets in a Mardi Gras atmosphere to celebrate his victory. According to news reports, the new president's support extended even to the Army—an important point, given Haiti's history of military takeovers of civilian-ruled governments.

Aristide's path to power had been threatened by three assassination attempts, apparently orchestrated by the government. The bloodiest such attempt occurred when armed thugs broke into his church during mass, shooting to death a dozen parishioners and hacking many more with machetes. And although he won the presidential election by two-thirds of the popular vote, in a plebiscite overseen by a 1000-member international overseeing committee, a last-minute coup attempt by his defeated rival nearly prevented him from taking office in February 1991.

The *Washington Post* reported that half of Aristide's campaign funds, a $.5–million budget that is minuscule by U.S. standards, was raised by Haitian exile groups in the United States. The majority of Haitian emigres seemed to support the priest's campaign. One who did not was Leo Joseph, publisher of *Haiti Observateur* in New York City. Joseph told the *New York Times*: "No doubt Aristide is a popular man. But we feel Aristide has very violent language and he is a divisive influence in Haitian society. Promoting justice in his own camp may mean resorting to violence to settle certain scores."

In Washington, state department officials have kept an attentive ear to the new president's public statements. Haiti is considered vital to U.S. interests, in part because it represents a source of low-cost manufacturing and exports, and serves as an anti-Communist stronghold in a volatile region where Communist sympathies run deep. As recently as

October 1990 the priest troubled state department observers by describing the United States as "a largely destructive, exploitative force in the world that is deeply implicated in Haiti's misery," according to the *New York Times*. Upon his election he began to tone down such comments in favor of conciliatory gestures towards Washington as well as trying to calm his own country's moneyed elite. He emphasized constitutional rule, telling numerous interviewers: "Those who would demand justice, must begin by respecting the law."

Respect for law, however, is something new in Haiti. The first threat to Aristide's administration came before the priest had even taken office. Weeks after the election, while the country was in the hands of a transition government, a Duvalier-era official tried to declare martial law, and headed a phalanx of army troops to storm the Presidential Palace early on the morning of January 6. The mutinous soldiers managed to seize the provisional president, but loyalist troops responded with a barrage of gunfire, freeing the president in 15 minutes.

It was hardly the last attempt by disgruntled right-wing forces to terrorize the new order. A couple of weeks later the orphanage and youth center that formed the core of Father Aristide's efforts on behalf of Port-au-Prince's poor caught fire, killing at least three children and a young employee. Although no arrests resulted, the Tontons Macoutes were widely believed to be responsible. "They aimed at my heart," Aristide told Howard French of the *New York Times* after the fire. "My heart will not become hard. The reign of the Macoutes is over."

The odyssey to the Presidential Palace was a most unlikely journey for the baby born 37 years earlier and orphaned in infancy. Aristide was raised by the Salesian order, a group whose main mission includes charity and spiritual instruction for impoverished children. The future priest benefitted from the educational opportunities the order offered him, and received an education that included biblical studies in Israel and scholarly trips to a number of other countries, including Egypt, Great Britain, and Canada. Ordained a priest in 1982, his education was not limited to the clerical. He also earned a graduate degree in psychology and speaks Creole, French, Spanish, English, Hebrew, Italian, German, and Portuguese. During the election campaign he impressed journalists by fielding questions in all these languages.

Aristide's relationship with the church, however, soured as he turned his pulpit into an agent of change, encouraging parishioners to rebel against the murderous Duvalier regime. The priest was expelled from the Salesian order in 1986, just two months after the attack on his church in which 13 parishioners were killed. The church was burned to the ground, never to be rebuilt. The Salesians announced that Father Aristide would be assigned to a suburban parish.

The transfer never happened. In an early indication of the priest's growing sway over the masses, the Salesian's efforts to remove and isolate Father Aristide were stymied by an orchestrated display of passive resistance. On the eve of the Feast of the Assumption, several thousand supporters filed into the cathedral of Port-au-Prince—"the very symbol of the Catholic hierarchy and its ties to the ruling class," reported Wilentz. A group of eight emerged to conduct a hunger strike in front of the altar. In fewer than 24 hours the church backed down.

Aristide, who had remained in an empty schoolhouse during the drama, now returned to address the crowd, which had grown to more than 4,000. His remarks, according to Wilentz, were "for once joyous and congratulatory . . . . The Salesian hierarchy, who denied acting upon Vatican orders, proved unable to squelch the priest's growing popularity. In 1987 the Church attempted to mute his voice by calling him to serve in Rome. What ensued thereafter was the largest street demonstration in Haiti's history, in which tens of thousands of supporters demonstrated at the airport and successfully blocked the priest's departure."

In a 1990 interview with Howard W. French of the *New York Times*, the priest spoke of his former order with mixed feelings. "I spent my whole life with them, and I still feel a great deal of love. There is a pain from our divorce, but there is a joy from my fidelity to the poor." His years of highly personalized service to the poor and downtrodden of Port-au-Prince earned the priest the fierce loyalty of many thousands. He helped mobilize them into political action by reminding them of their constitutional rights, advocating that every family keep "a little pile of bricks" to throw at soldiers who enter the slums.

As it became clear that the fiery young priest would become his country's new leader, Washington began to study the matter more closely. In official circles Father Aristide was regarded with suspicion, after years in which he had refused all contact with U.S. officials based in Haiti. He had publicly rebuked his government for accepting U.S. agricultural aid—a bizarre position, it might seem, in a country suffering from chronic starvation.

In an interview with Selden Rodman published in the *National Review*, Aristide elaborated on his position that U.S. aid merely aggravates the conditions of poverty. Haiti needs "not [economic] development, but change of structure: peasant communes, labor unions. Haitians are slaves. Better that they have no jobs at all! Let the factories go." He elaborated: "I make a distinction between the American government and its people. The government means imperialism. Food means death for us. When they give us food they destroy our agriculture." He illustrated this concept by describing the U.S. program that destroyed the island's population of black pigs and replaced them with white pigs, a controversial agricultural management program aimed at eliminating typhoid. When the white pigs failed to thrive in the alien surroundings, left-wing Haitians delightedly exploited the symbolism to rally anti-U.S. feelings.

A student who had been active several years earlier in the revolts against Duvalier told Marjorie Valbrun of Knight-Ridder newspapers on the election of the new president, "For me, Aristide as president represents a new era, an era of hope for change. But we cannot tell for sure, it depends on his collaborators and the cooperation of local and international sectors. So we will watch." Wilentz quoted the new president's election-night statements, a characteristic blend of political address and Sunday sermon: "The happiness we feel tonight after this historic victory is just a slice from the cake of contentment that we will one day share . . . . One day, we will reap the rewards of what we have done inside the church and inside our nation, so that this struggle will finally end, and we will be able to turn that slice into a whole cake of contentment and all sit down at God's table—at the table of brotherhood—and share that cake together as brothers and sisters. Amen."

Selected writings

In the Parish of the Poor.

Sources

Detroit Free Press, December 12, 1990; December 28, 1990; February 7, 1991.
Maclean's, December 31, 1990.
The Nation, September 12, 1987; October 3, 1988; January 23, 1989.
National Review, September 29, 1989.
Newsday, December 18, 1990; December 24, 1990.
New York Times, December 19, 1990; January 8, 1991; February 7, 1991.
Time, October 31, 1988; December 17, 1990.
Washington Post, December 14, 1990.

—Warren Strugatch

Giorgio Armani

© 1987 Piergiorgio Sclarandis/Black Star

Fashion designer

Born c. 1934 in Piacenza, Italy; son of Ugo (a transport executive) and Maria (a homemaker) Armani. *Education:* Attended pre-med university program for three years.

Addresses: *Home and office*—21 Via Borgonuovo, Milan, Italy.

Career

Joined Rinascente department store in Milan to work on window displays, became staff member in office of fashion and style for seven years; designer for Nino Cerruti until 1970; self-employed fashion designer, 1970—. Also served in the Italian military as a medical assistant.

Awards: Neiman Marcus Award for distinguished service; Fashion of the Year award from *Forbes* magazine for Emporio Armani label.

Sidelights

Characteristically clad in jeans, a white shirt opened at the neck, and a navy cotton pullover, Giorgio Armani designs new fashions in his 16th-century palazzo in Milan. He is a recipient of the coveted Neiman Marcus Award, and has built an international reputation—as well as a fortune—on his revolutionary, unstructured jacket for men. In April of 1982 *Time* magazine featured him on its cover.

Armani's first radically different blazer appeared in the fashion world under his own label between 1974 and 1975. His sartorial style exhibited a decidedly more relaxed, even rumpled look. The designer softened these new jackets by pulling out the padding and lining and leaving out stiffeners of any kind. He combined thinner lapels with baggier pockets and longer jackets. "Armani's unstructured look makes even his English wool suits feel as comfortable as silk pajamas," observed a writer for *People* magazine. And in *Esquire,* Rita Hamilton credited Armani's suit jackets with "the kind of shape that defied the proper Italian establishmentarian look and mirrored the defiant, angry mood of political and social unrest."

But, as American designer Donna Karan put it in the *New York Times Magazine,* "fashion evolves." And Armani's designs did change by the end of the 1970s. Creating what would eventually be known as the "wedge-shaped power suit," Armani extended the shoulders and even added padding to them. The lapels were widened, and the broadest point of the lapel, called the gorge, was lowered. The effect was similar to a style once worn by Hollywood sex symbols like Clark Gable. Still casual and comfortable, the new style was what the *New York Times* called a "second sartorial innovation" that endowed men with a "broad-shouldered, slim-hipped glamour."

In 1980 Giorgio Armani USA offered the American market a hybrid of the two styles. His more fluid sport coats of the first half of the decade could be compared to cardigan sweaters, with comfortable, sloping shoulders. These jackets were teamed up with T-shirts for a studied, informal look. The unmistakable Armani style evolved into an even more simplified version of the original groundbreaking blazer. In his spring 1990 women's collection, Armani "called attention to the generous flow of jackets by stripping them of superfluous detail," wrote Dan Lecca in the *New York Times Magazine*.

> *"The more you expose yourself, the more attentive you must be to details."*

Armani's feminine version of the menswear jacket looked like it was borrowed from Greta Garbo's closet, or so imply some fashion critics. "My first jackets for women were in fact men's jackets in women's sizes," he told *Time* magazine. But it's Armani's use of strategically modified menswear fabrics and tailoring in women's suit jackets that is his "special contribution," stated Geraldine Stutz, president of Henri Bendel department store in New York City, in the same publication. "No one had ever done that before."

While the jacket forms the foundation of the Armani empire, the Italian designer does create a variety of other garments as well. In 1982, for example, his fall collection featured felt hats, gaucho pants, and light suede hooded sweatshirts in what were described as "jelly bean" colors. Jackets were gold lame for evening and longer for daytime wear. Fabrics included silk-lined cotton and mixtures of velvet, silk, wool, and linen, in a plethora of patterns and stripes. Whatever Armani chooses to offer in a collection, he is praised for that sense of relaxed comfort. "It's the fit of the armhole," pinpointed Dawn Mello in *Vogue*. And "somehow his clothes never seem to wrinkle."

The man with the steel-blue eyes is not only a brilliant designer, he is also an astute business man. A writer for *Forbes* magazine noted that, in general, Armani "sets prices to maximize profits rather than minimize output." The company Giorgio Armani SpA made $350 million in the international market in 1988, $90 million of which came from the United States. The designer has targeted several different markets while maintaining high profit margins. In Italy, Vestimenta sells the priciest line for Giorgio Armani Via. In 1988 it was possible to spend $1,800 for one of Armani's best American suits for men. Blouses ran for between $300 and $400, and blazers ranged from $650 to $800, made by Gruppo GFT. Designed for the 20-years-old-and-up crowd, the Armani label appeared on less pricey suits and sport coats: $700 and $360 respectively.

To capture the younger market, Armani opened a line of stores called Emporio (or Emporium, in English), first in Italy, then in the United States. These boutiques debuted in 1981 to offer quality designs for slimmer pocketbooks. Local merchandise produced in quantity kept the prices low. For example, in 1982 a leather jacket could be purchased for between $250 to $300, skirts went for from $40 to $60, and blouses were priced at around $35. Jay Cocks wrote in *Time* magazine that "One would be hard put to tell the difference, in fact, between a leather jacket from the Emporium and one from the couture line, without resort to the price tag; an X ray would come in handy too."

Armani first stocked the Emporio with jeans, T-shirts, and brightly colored cotton bomber jackets. Many of these items were made of extra fabrics from the design studio. And despite the Armani eagle logo (i.e., his initials form an eagle), this clothing had a decided American flair to it: It was even referred to as "Rafaelo Laureno" after Ralph Lauren in the United States. But this style evolved, too, and became more truly Armani. He added dressier and more classic selections, borrowed from his couture line—but at a fraction of the cost. And the jackets alone became available in 250 fabrics and 25 styles by 1989. In that year, Armani opened an Emporio on New York City's Fifth Avenue offering many more items than just clothes. He added a wide selection of accessories, underwear, products for the home, and leather goods.

Well-organized and hard-working, Armani has also been described by some of his employees as a "maniac," noted the *New York Times Magazine*. He puts in 12-hour days at the design studio, devoting meticulous care to each phase of his work. In *New York* magazine, he explained, "The more you expose yourself, the more attentive you must be to details." Just before the showing of a new collection, for example, Armani can be found revamping a model's makeup and making other finishing touches. In Milan, he is known as "the Maestro." "A seemingly stoic man who is often silent with strangers," observed Charles Gandee in *House & Garden*, "he is compulsive about using time constructively."

A writer for *Vogue* magazine described Armani as "business class to the tips of his fingers," qualifying this by adding that that's the "class where all the action is." The designer had originally set out to become a doctor, but only studied for three years toward that goal. His mother has been credited with saying he couldn't take the sight of blood. But apparently Armani claims he simply couldn't sit still long enough to do all the reading required of him. If he could start his career all over again, Armani has said he would become a director of plays and films.

After leaving college, Armani fulfilled his requirements in the Italian army by serving as a medical assistant. Three years later, he took a job at the Rinascente department store (which has been described as the Sears of Italy) in Milan. There he gained experience as a window dresser and in the style office. And he got to know fashion buyers. From there he moved on to an experimental in-store boutique, where he tested new clothes for the store. Eventually he became acquainted with Nino Cerruti, who was looking for assistance in creating new menswear. Armani designed men's clothes for Cerruti for eight years. Then Sergio Galeotti, an architectural draftsman at a prestigious firm in Milan, convinced Armani to go into business with him. The two became equal partners in various ventures. By the mid-1970s, the team was ready to offer menswear under the now-famous black label of Giorgio Armani.

Armani has also done free-lance work on two menswear collections for Emanual Ungaro. This experience taught him the importance of fine tailoring. And he has designed fashions for Zegna, Sicons, Mario Valentino, and Erreuno. By 1984 Armani was designing 29 collections for himself annually. And supplemental to his lines of clothing, he has garnered licensees for a wide scope of accessories, jeans, and perfume.

The private life of Giorgio Armani is "absolutely banal," he told an interviewer in *Vogue*. Perhaps he was referring to the fact that he is a vegetarian who eschews smoking and alcoholic beverages. (He was once a bodybuilder, too.) It is still somewhat difficult to believe that Armani's life could have any commonplace aspect to it, considering that he lives and works in a 400-year-old palazzo (or palace) and owns two other Italian getaway homes (one in Forte dei Marmi and the other on an island near Sicily, called Pantelleria). The palazzo not only encompasses the design studio and Armani's bi-level apartment; it also has its own indoor pool, an apartment for Armani's widowed mother, and an apartment for his partner, Galeotti. And there is a columned amphitheater where Armani can show his latest collections. Now modernized, it was a ballroom in another era.

Twice a year Armani has his studio redecorated, "to suit the style, spirit, and coloring of the season's collection," Gloria Noda reported in *Vogue*. And after having his apartment redesigned by American architect Peter Marino, Armani still wanted to make some refinements. Describing his rooms, he shared these thoughts with *House & Garden* writer Charles Gandee: "I would like to have the time to fill them with personal objects, pictures, which can remove that aesthetically 'too perfect' look. And I would like as well to have the possibility of making some mistakes, thus bringing it closer to human nature."

This philosophy is inherent in Armani's clothing designs as well. He fosters a sense of individuality and human sensuousness in his collections. Talking about style, Armani told an interviewer in *Self* magazine that "Each face, each hair texture requires a personalized look." He went on to describe individual style as the "correct balance of knowing who you are, what works for you and how to develop your own character."

The 1991 spring collection of women's clothes by Armani seemed to be designed to enhance the wearer's sense of well-being. The collection included a softly tailored white silk and linen jacket with matching pants. There was also an off-the-shoulder dress paired with shorts, again in a combination of linen and silk, in a muted multiprint fabric design. For evening wear, Armani offered "molten dinner suits and dresses paved in sequins, small crystals and pearls," as described in the *New York Times Magazine*. Cap-sleeved dresses with A-line skirts were also part of the new collection. In another article for the same magazine, Armani told Carrie Donovan that his goal in 1991 was to offer a look that's "just a bit more modern and young."

Sources

Esquire, May 22, 1979.
Forbes, July 11, 1988.
Harper's Bazaar, May 1984.
House & Garden, January 1990.
New York, March 20, 1989.
New York Times Magazine, January 20, 1980; October 21, 1990; February 3, 1991.

People, July 30, 1979.
Self, February 1991.
Time, April 5, 1982.
Vogue, January 1984; August 1984; January 1985;
   August 1986.

—*Victoria France Charabati*

James A. Baker III

AP/Wide World Photos

U.S. secretary of state

Full name, James Addison Baker III; born April 28, 1930, in Houston, Tex.; son of James A. and Bonner (Means) Baker; married Mary Stuart McHenry, November, 1953 (died, 1970); married Susan Garrett Winston, August 6, 1973; children: (first marriage) four sons; (second marriage) three stepchildren, Mary Bonner. *Education:* Princeton University, B.A., 1952; University of Texas Law School, LL.B., 1957.

Addresses: *Office*—Office of the Secretary, Department of State, 1000 Pennsylvania Ave. NW, Washington, DC 20220.

Career

Admitted to the Texas Bar, 1957; member of Houston law firm Andrews, Kurth, Campbell & Jones, 1957-81; undersecretary of the Department of Commerce, Washington, D.C., 1975-76; deputy chairman of President Ford Committee, Washington, D.C., 1976; campaign chairman for George Bush, 1979-80; senior adviser, Reagan-Bush Committee, 1980-81; White House chief of staff, Washington, D.C., 1981-85; secretary of the U.S. Department of Treasury, 1985-88; secretary of the U.S. Department of State, 1988—. Trustee of the Smithsonian Institute Woodrow Wilson International Center for Scholars, 1977—. *Military service:* U.S. Marine Corps, 1952-54.

Member: American Bar Association, American Judicature Society, Houston Bar Association, Phi Delta Phi.

Sidelights

It can be assumed that for every politician there is at least one television reporter who watches eagerly for the signs of a scandal. Politics in America have been altered for this reason—many of the elected have developed an aptitude for frequent appearances on television, and their political careers depend on how they are portrayed. A whiff of scandal broadcast at home, and once-loyal constituents are gone forever. The effect on politicians is clear and the politics themselves have taken on a rushed quality: decisions are made and actions are taken in a less-than-considered fashion to make the six o'clock evening news.

One man unburdened by a constituency, yet mindful of American public opinion, is James A. Baker III (Jim Baker to most), the United States secretary of state. The overwhelming image in the media of Baker is of a quietly powerful man who can make a decision to meet a deadline, but will not be rushed. During his tenure in Washington, Baker has served as campaign manager, chief of staff, the secretary of the treasury, and secretary of state. Although several blunders in the past have marred his image, and have caught the critical eye of political analysts, Baker remains the picture of caution and diplomacy.

The designated duty of the secretary of state is to pursue the goals of American foreign policy through diplomacy. The five official concerns of foreign policy are: national security, international peace and stability, economic assistance, U.S. global interests, and the protection of human rights. "The executive branch has thirteen executive departments headed by presidentially appointed secretaries," according to Ronald E. Pym's *American Politics*. Each secretary is an administrator for his department and must balance the interests of the department with the interests of the president. Baker makes his loyalties very clear: "I want to be the President's man at the State Department, instead of the State Department's man at the White House," *Time* reported. And whether or not Baker was the best person for the job, President George Bush probably appointed him to keep a longtime adviser and friend at hand. Close friend Ben Love had thought Baker an ideal secretary of state, and called him, in the *Chicago Tribune Magazine*, "diplomatic and conciliatory, yet tough-minded, like lemon and sugar in iced tea." Some critics complain that the lines of power are drawn unclearly between the president and his secretary of state, but evidently the close partnership is crucial to the success of the Bush administration.

> *"I want to be the President's man at the State Department, instead of the State Department's man at the White House."*

The friendship between Jim Baker and George Bush goes back to the 1950s, and has roots in their similar backgrounds of privilege. Baker was born to a prominent Texas family whose wealth helped to build modern Houston. He was sent as a child to the prestigious Hill School near Philadelphia, and was raised to be a lawyer, not a politician. The Houston law firm Gray & Botts was altered to incorporate Jim Baker's great-grandfather in 1872, and today survives as the venerable Baker & Botts. While Jim Baker was not expected to join Baker & Botts because of an anti-nepotism rule, he was pointed toward judicature; his grandfather's admonition, according to the *New Yorker*, was to "work hard, study hard, and stay out of politics." Baker told the *New York Times Magazine* that he was brought up with a real distaste for politics—"That was sort of a creed in my family,

that politics was somehow a dirty business and really good lawyers didn't involve themselves in politics." Baker's cousin and friend Preston Moore expanded on the WASP-y family ideals in the *Washington Post Magazine:* "I think we were brought up to feel . . . that whatever mind you had, you ought to try to develop it; that you have a good body, and you ought to take care of it. But more than that, you had a good name, and you ought to remember that."

Baker became a corporate lawyer via Princeton and the University of Texas Law School, marrying between earning degrees and soon starting a family. Mary Stuart McHenry became his first wife, and the Bushes and the Bakers became friends largely because of Mary Stuart's Republican campaigning efforts for George Bush. Baker was nominally a Democrat at the time, reportedly going hunting on election day instead of voting. (Baker's hunting abilities are legendary. The *New Yorker* said that he is "widely known for his prowess in felling the furtive turkey.") His first wife was indirectly the cause for Baker's 1970 dive into politics, from which he would never return to practice law. While raising four sons, however, Mary Stuart died of leukemia at the age of 38. "Bush persuaded Baker to take the job of county chairman in his [Senate] campaign that year because it would be something different and so might relieve his pain," said the *New Yorker*. The widower was then pushed into the Undersecretary of Commerce job, then on to positions of power in the campaign to elect Gerald Ford. In 1978 Baker ran for attorney general of Texas, and lost in his only bid for election to a political post, but won a respectable 43 percent of the vote.

Baker has been a Bush man from that time forward; some would say that even during his time in Washington in the Reagan years he was looking out for his friend. The only serious rift between them came during Bush's 1980 campaign for president. Bush was showing poorly against Reagan in the primaries, and Baker, his eye on a vice-presidency for Bush, urged him to fold early. Bush rejected the idea. Baker held a press conference without Bush's knowledge and announced his candidate's intention to quit the race. Bush was reportedly furious, but Baker had thereby acquired the number-two spot for his friend. They remained close (though competitive) during the first phase of Bush's presidency. "They're these big, lanky, hot-as-a-pistol guys with ambition so strong it's like a steel rod sticking out of their heads," speechwriter Peggy Noonan (See *Newsmakers 90*) told the *New York Times Magazine*.

Despite their driving ambitions, pragmatism is the ruling force for both men; they adjust their actions to their surroundings and to current events. Neither wants to violate the ideas of his public persona and both are constantly weighing their decisions against the probable reactions in the White House and beyond. They work closely, in a way some call almost psychic, and their personalities complement each other in a "good cop/bad cop" way: "No one is scared of Bush. No one wants to cross Baker," reported the *New York Times Magazine*. The same source provided this brief summation of foreign policy under the two: "The Bush-Baker foreign policy is a series of ad hoc decisions, some of them based on creative strategies designed for a particular region, others on an intuitive sense of what seems right or reasonable . . . at the moment." Critics single out this lack of vision or sense of history as their most damaging flaw. William Safire, noted political commentator, wrote in a editorial for the *New York Times* that "our diplomacy is suddenly hip-deep in the molasses of multilateralism."

An example of how well the reserved characters of these two pragmatists may work for them occurred in the early days of 1991. While the world's attention was on the events leading up to the war in the Middle East, the Soviet Union's army invaded the Lithuanian capital of Vilnius and attempted to seize power from separatists, killing 13 people in the process. Later in the month, Soviet Black Berets invaded Latvia, again with fatalities, and threatened the other Baltic nations who had recently declared independence. Previously, Bush and Baker had not been as enthused as other world leaders when the Berlin Wall went down in 1990, when many hailed the end of the Cold War. Therefore, the pair did not seem as surprised as the rest of the globe when the Soviets back-pedaled. At the time their pragmatism translated to hesitation, and Bush's and Baker's hesitation made them appear wise—the solid, skeptical politicos who stood back as the others leapt in to congratulate the newly-evolved Soviet government.

Bush and Baker departed somewhat from their cautious methods in the events leading up to the Middle East crisis. Pym said in *American Politics* that "in foreign policies the two major groups of advisers are the National Security Council [NSC] and the State Department. . . . Composed of the vice-president, secretary of state, secretary of defense, and other personnel designated by the president, the NSC has an expert staff directed by the special assistant for national security affairs." While the secretary of state is involved with security matters through the NSC and as designated by the under-stood diplomatic foreign policy concerns of the United States, when war is declared, the secretary of state is replaced on center stage by military personnel. This pattern is exemplified by the events that developed into the war in the Middle East. When war was declared, Baker (who had been described as looking "exhausted") disappeared from the front pages of national newspapers.

In 1990, before the Iraqi invasion of Kuwait, the *New York Times Magazine* described the Bush-Baker stance in the Middle East this way: "Bush and Baker approach the region with identical gut feelings: no illusions about the Arabs, no illusions about the Israelis. Arab-Israel diplomacy for them is a snake pit, to be entered at one's peril and always wearing protective gear." Baker strongly encouraged the president to seek the approval of Congress (and lobbied for support there himself) before taking military action. Quite possibly Baker encouraged the president to take military action before Iraq did. When asked in 1989 about preemptive strikes against terrorists, the secretary of state told a *Time* correspondent, "I have absolutely no problems with that philosophically. Sometimes such strikes are not only justified but required."

The waging of war in the Middle East contains elements both of personal failure and of success for Baker. Failure, because he could not maintain international peace and security, a United States foreign policy objective. He was unable to reach an agreement with Iraqi foreign minister Tariq Aziz during talks in Geneva; some say Baker's hands were tied because he had no way to negotiate, and was only authorized to restate the position of the United States. Baker's efforts in the Middle East were front page news—the attention of the entire world was focused on him, and many said that he did not blink. TV journalist Sam Donaldson called him a "political poker player" on *Primetime Live* on January 3, 1991. Also, Baker was declared more powerful than Aziz because he had more influence on the leader of his nation. John McWethy, State Department correspondent for ABC News, gave Baker the credit for putting the international anti-Iraq coalition (also referred to as the Allied forces) together. Maintaining the coalition after the war is Baker's main diplomatic concern and responsibility. The American public might not have known who Jim Baker was before the crisis—they might not have known the functions of the secretary of state. But after the negotiations with Aziz and trips to Saudi Arabia accompanying the president, Baker has a very high profile, and Americans will probably associate him with the peace effort, not the war.

However successful, Baker did not perform flawlessly during his time at the White House, particularly while secretary of the treasury. In certain cases caution and pragmatism could not prevent major political flubs. Baker possibly helped to set the October 1987 stock market crash in motion by protesting loudly (*twice* on the weekend before "Black Monday," in televised interviews) about high West German interest rates. His later refusal to immediately divest his funds from banks presenting a possible conflict-of-interest case hurt his reputation for untarnished honesty. *Time* heard rare personal criticism from former New Hampshire governor Hugh Gregg, who said that "[Baker] is a consummate pragmatist and a very tough pol. But he'll stomp on anyone in his way, even a friend. Probe a bit, and you'll find that he doesn't really have much compassion for people."

There has been much speculation among the Baker watchers about his friendly competition with the president and his possible desire to take Bush's place. Baker has insisted throughout his time as a Bush adviser that he is not a "Southern Svengali," and that Bush has succeeded on his own merits. Baker's second wife, Susan Garrett, says that "he's never felt as if he wanted to run for president," according to the *New Yorker*, and Baker confirms this in every interview at every opportunity. And yet he is said to be "chafing at times," according to the *New York Times Magazine*. "The Secretary remarks humorously to friends that he prefers solo trips to trips with the President because on joint travels he is left with the role of 'the goddamn butler.'" Many sources agree that smooth-talking Secretary Baker is a confirmed leaker to the press, often enhancing his own image in the process. Yet his role in the Middle East crisis speaks for itself. The *New Yorker* predicted that "Baker might be very good in a crisis: the sharp instinct for action which he possesses would allow him to see all the possibilities open to the office of President in a dramatic, fast-breaking situation. Add to instinct his skills, experience, and energy, and one can imagine a Baker presidency more thematic and less rhetorical than Bush's." The country witnessed Baker's diplomatic skills in 1991, and may envision a Baker presidency in the 1990s. Doubtless his role in the resolution of the Persion Gulf Crisis will remain a critical factor in the minds of Americans.

Sources

Books

Pym, Ronald E., *American Politics*, Brooks/Cole, 1984.

Periodicals

Chicago Tribune Magazine, March 26, 1989.
New York Times Magazine, May 6, 1990.
New Yorker, May 7, 1990.
Time, February 13, 1989.
Washingtonian, August 1990.
Washington Post Magazine, January 29, 1989.

Television broadcasts

ABC News Special Report, January 16, 1991.
Primetime Live, January 3, 1991.

—*Christine Ferran*

Robert T. Bakker

Paleontologist and professor

Education: Studied as an undergraduate at Yale University, c. 1968, and as a graduate student at Harvard University, c. 1972.

Career

Taught at Johns Hopkins University, c. 1972; professor of paleontology, University of Colorado at Boulder.

Sidelights

Paleontologist Bob Bakker is considered both a maverick and a heretic, but he may nevertheless change the way the world thinks about dinosaurs. "Traditional dinosaur theory is full of short circuits," Bakker has written. "Like the antiquated wiring in an old house, the details sputter and burn out when specific parts are tested." A professor of paleontology—the study of fossil remains—at the University of Colorado at Boulder, Bakker sports long hair, an unkempt beard, a combative style and usually, cowboy boots. He has advanced often unpopular dinosaur theories since his student days at Yale and Harvard. Among Bakker's most controversial ideas is the contention that dinosaurs were not killed off by a cataclysmic event, like a sudden global climate change or a monumental meteor strike, as commonly believed. Instead, Bakker asserts, they died off in a series of extinctions triggered by the formation of land bridges that exposed particular dinosaur species to others that may have been enemies, necessitated competition for resources, or carried disease to which an area's original inhabitants were vulnerable.

Through his studies, Bakker has developed detailed profiles of the legendary "thunder lizards." Some dinosaurs fit the image of big "slow shufflers," but others would "gallop with all four huge feet off the ground in midstride," Bakker reported in *Reader's Digest.* "One can gauge the muscle power of a knee from the size of the cnemial crest (a bony ridge on the shinbone which anchors the knee tendons)," Bakker explained. "The biggest meat-eater, three-ton-plus Tyrannosaurus, had an absolutely huge cnemial crest, even by dinosaurian standards. A bull Tyrannosaurus could easily have overhauled a galloping white rhino—at speeds above 40 mph." Contrary to popular perception, many dinosaurs were actually warm-blooded, not cold and plodding. In fact, dinosaurs are believed by many scientists to have been the predecessors of birds.

While an undergraduate at Yale, Bakker "conducted an exhaustive study of dinosaur anatomy in a skeptical examination of the universally accepted theory that the giant beasts were coldblooded," *Discover* magazine reported. "Bakker studied dinosaurian skeletal structures, chest cavities and inferred heart size, and other features and found that the animals more closely resembled modern mammals like elephants and big birds like ostriches than lizards and other reptiles." As related by *Discover,* the paleontologist asked himself: "If so much of the dinosaurs' anatomy resembled that of warm-blooded animals, shouldn't their metabolism be similar also." Bakker published his theories, but they were rebuffed. "I took a lot of heat for that work," he admitted in *Discover.* "The papers were condemned as dangerous heresy. People didn't want to give up the image of dinosaurs as cold, slow and lumbering."

In 1972, as a Harvard graduate student in search of a pattern, Bakker decided to track the extinctions of various dinosaur species. "For more than five years, Bakker worked at the project, painstakingly following the development of 80 families of dinosaurs and all the families of mammals, frogs, turtles, and salamanders," *Discover* recounted. "By the time he had worked his way back to the earliest dinosaurs, a pattern indeed began to suggest itself. Massive die-offs among primitive species, it appeared, occurred at repeated but irregular intervals, separated by as little as five million years or as many as 60 million." While teaching at Johns Hopkins University in 1972, Bakker published a paper postulating a series of eight to 12 dinosaur die-offs over a 185-million year period—all connected to "some change in the state of the planet," related *Discover.* "Before this," Bakker pointed out in the science journal, "there had hardly been any talk about periodic extinctions among land critters. A lot of land-based paleontologists simply assumed that no serial die-offs had taken place. Frankly, I don't think they were paying enough attention to the fossil record."

Even so, Bakker's findings received little reaction. Subsequent work intended to nail down the serial die-off theory led Bakker to excavate in south-central Wyoming during the 1980s. This produced something unexpected: Fossils there indicated that 130 million years ago, at the border of the Jurassic and Cretaceous periods, many of the large dinosaurs were dying out, while small animals—turtles, crocodiles, lizards, salamanders, mammals, and a gull-sized pterodactyl—were thriving. Bakker knew the dramatic shift was not caused by a meteor strike or global climate change; both would cause falling temperatures, dark skies, and other changes more dangerous to the small animals than to the large ones.

Discover revealed that in his 1977 paper, Bakker *had* "observed that at each theorized extinction at least one land bridge appeared between continents." However, "back in 1977 Bakker had overlooked the

parallel .... With more bridges, a greater number of big animals could migrate and disperse, competing for one another's food and land .... Species would suddenly encounter diseases and parasites to which they hadn't evolved defenses .... " *Discover* elaborated on Bakker's findings, stating that "only two types of creatures would escape this epidemiological holocaust: aquatic creatures that were confined in freshwater lakes and marshes and smaller land dwelling creatures that did not have the size and stamina to wander far from home."

Bakker published his breakthrough in May of 1990; but, according to *Discover,* nearly a year later "the idea has not exactly taken the dinosaur world by storm." "People are so wedded to the idea of an asteroid or a climatic cataclysm," Bakker said, "they refuse to entertain anything else. It's tough to change minds when beliefs have become more a religion than a scientific hypothesis." In his 1986 book, *The Dinosaur Heresies,* quoted by *Reader's Digest,* Bakker described how he grew up hearing "the orthodoxy that relegates dinosaurs to an evolutionary sideshow." "This thinking must be wrong," he insisted, "since dinosaurs must rank as the No. 1 success story in the history of land life." After emerging an estimated 225 million years ago, "their control was complete," Bakker wrote. "Not only did dinosaurs exercise a monopoly as large land animals, they kept their commanding position for an extraordinary span of time"—more than 130 million years. Further discoveries may well bear him out. In the meantime, Bakker will undoubtedly continue to attract attention for his outspoken and far-reaching scientific opinions.

Writings

The Dinosaur Heresies, Morrow, 1986.

Sources

Reader's Digest, December 1989.
Discover, March 1991.
Earth Science, Fall 1988.

—David Wilkins

John Baldessari

©1990 Blake Little/Visages

Artist

Born c. 1931 in National City, CA; son of Antonio (a salvage dealer) and Hedvig Baldessari; married Carol Wixom (divorced, 1986); children: Tony, Annamarie. *Education:* B.A., San Diego State College, 1953, M.A., 1957.

Addresses: *Home*—Santa Monica, CA.

Career

Painter and art teacher in San Diego-area schools, c. 1959-70; art instructor, California Institute of the Arts, 1970—; students include David Salle and Eric Fischl; works displayed in major retrospective in Los Angeles, Washington, DC, San Francisco, Minneapolis, and New York City, 1990.

Sidelights

Akind of art world phoenix, John Baldessari has influenced a generation of new artists since literally rising from the ashes of his own work. The 60-year-old conceptual artist, whose long overdue day in the sun arrived in 1990 with a major nationwide retrospective of his work, had many years earlier abandoned the more traditional style of painting on canvas with a symbolic act, or "mercy killing" as he calls it. One afternoon in 1970, while looking around at a studio cluttered with more than 500 unsold paintings, Baldessari suddenly realized that he hated painting. So he called some friends, gathered up the canvases, and trucked the whole lot

over to a crematorium, where he watched the fruits of 13 years of labor go up in smoke.

Although this seems a horribly cruel renunciation of one's past, it was also for Baldessari a necessary psychic leap into a new future and a new style of art. "There was a lot of doubt and anxiety," he told *People* of the day he torched his work. "But I breathed a sigh of relief when the crematory door slammed shut. I felt liberated...I used to follow cultural standards about what was allowable in art. Then I decided that I was going to make up my own rules."

Starting over with a more conceptual approach, Baldessari began juxtaposing photographs and typewritten text in strange collages that seemed to float in space, presenting interesting contrasts and elusive messages. Irony was a key factor, and it needed to be for Baldessari to get out of what *Newsweek*'s Peter Plagens called "his own double bind: wanting to subvert modern art in a wasteland where nobody cared about modern art to begin with." Baldessari's aim was to create powerful, often haunting visual statements with ordinary, seemingly mundane words and images. Richard Koshalek, director of the Los Angeles Museum of Contemporary Art and organizer of the Baldessari retrospective, told *People* that the artist "made a breakthrough by using language and photos—culled from the mass culture—to express his personal ideas. He shows there are many ways of making art."

Growing up in the industrial Mexican border town of National City, California, Baldessari was a gawky outcast as a young man, already 6'4" by the time he was in junior high school. "An artist was like a social pariah in those years," he told *People*. After trying and failing to get into the Princeton Theological Seminary, Baldessari ended up at San Diego State College, from which he received his bachelor's degree in art in 1953 and his master's in 1957. He retreated to National City once more, where, he told *Newsweek*, he remembers "sitting in my studio nearly in a catatonic state, trying to figure out over and over again what was art and what wasn't."

Baldessari taught art classes in San Diego public schools and colleges while trying to sell his paintings, but it was not until his switch to conceptual art—post-cremation—that he caught the attention of Paul Brach, then the dean of CalArts, an experimental college near L.A., who hired Baldessari as an instructor. In his workshop-style classroom, Baldessari encouraged his students to try art forms alternative to painting, and with great success. Former students of

Baldessari include such prominent young artists as David Salle and Eric Fischl, and his own techniques echo the works of Jenny Holzer and Robert Longo (see *Newsmakers 90*).

It wasn't until the 1990 retrospective, however, that Baldessari's works finally received the attention that those of so many of his disciples had already enjoyed. With shows in Los Angeles, Washington, San Francisco, Minneapolis, and New York museums, and with his works selling well from $20,000 to $175,000 apiece, Baldessari can finally take some personal satisfaction from his work. "I'm happy now with the direction I've taken," he told *People*. "Of course, having some dissatisfaction keeps you working. You always try to get it right until the day you die."

Sources

California, April 1990.
Interview, March 1990.
New York Times, April 4, 1990.
Newsweek, April 23, 1990.
People, December 10, 1990.

—David Collins

Dave Barry

AP/Wide World Photos

Humorist and writer

Born c. 1947; grew up in New York State; son of a clergyman; married Beth Lenox; children: Robby. *Education:* Haverford College, Philadelphia, Pa., B.A. in English literature, 1969.

Addresses: *Home*—Miami, FL.

Career

Following graduation from college worked for the Episcopal Church; *Daily Local News,* West Chester, Pa., reporter and editor, 1971-75; worked for the Associated Press and taught business seminars; wrote humor column for the *Daily Local News* and other papers; syndicated columnist with the Miami *Herald,* 1983—. Author of several humor books.

Sidelights

As the latest in a treasured lineage of American humorists harking back to Mark Twain in the 19th century, Pulitzer Prize-winner Dave Barry rose to prominence in the 1980s with a weekly column that is now syndicated in more than 300 American newspapers. Dubbed "the funniest man in America" by the *New York Times,* Barry's unique, somewhat bent point of view has proved the perfect antidote for "baby boomers" who have abandoned their former idealism for a more practical approach to surviving in modern times. Indeed, Barry's sophomoricism almost seems proof of the old maxim "desperate measures for desperate times'—as if insanities like nuclear war, environmental destruc-

tion, and the Savings & Loan scandals can only be combatted by an equally ridiculous sense of humor. In the words of Peter Richmond in the *Times,* "it is Barry's special talent that he can take that back-of-the-classroom irreverence and layer it onto the mundane ingredients of his generation's everyday experience."

From his highly topical, weekly column to his numerous published books, Barry comments with authority and unbridled malice upon sweeping world events with all the tact of a sixth-grader snapping paper wads behind his teacher's back—and not caring if he gets caught. His imagery oozes like a kiddie B-flick: "duck spit," "rat saliva," "pig doots." At a wine tasting (Barry once wrote), where one friend said a certain wine tasted "much too woody" and another said it was "too heavily oxidized," Barry tastefully chimed in, "Bat urine." And when the Miami *Herald,* Barry's flagship newspaper, had a Dave Barry parody contest, the winning entry consisted of one word: "Boogers." Asked about his gift for the, say, *unusual* image, Barry told the *New York Times,* "Hey, I agonize over that stuff. What would Proust do?"

The son of a reverend with a social conscience and a mother who was "the funniest person" he has ever known, Barry grew up in New York State as a gawky, eccentric kid who developed a sense of humor to protect himself at school. "A geek with a real high forehead," Barry describes himself as a kid. "Real high. You could have rented out advertising up there." He earned a degree in English literature from Philadelphia's Haverford College, but spent more time smoking pot, playing the guitar, and protesting the Vietnam War, the draft, and anything else people felt like protesting in the 1960s. In fact, after graduating in 1969, Barry spent two years working for the Episcopal Church in New York as conscientious objector duty.

From 1971 to 1975, Barry worked as a reporter and editor for the *Daily Local News* in West Chester, Pennsylvania, where he met his wife, Beth Lenox. After a brief stint with the Associated Press in Philadelphia, however, Barry became disenchanted with the grind of daily reporting. When a neighbor offered him a job teaching business seminars, Barry took it instantly. The speaking engagements allowed Barry to loosen up a little more than journalism allows, and he discovered that his sense of humor struck a chord with middle-America business types. At the urging of his wife, Barry started writing a weekly humor column for the *Daily Local News,* and soon editors around the country were picking the columns up through syndication. The key to his early success, Barry told the *New York Times,* was that as a business seminar instructor he could avoid all the traps that everyday columnists fall into. "I was living a life so far removed from journalism it gave me a point of view about what was really worth writing about," Barry said. "It was deliberately irresponsible and non-journalistic." He continued writing the column on a free-lance basis until 1983, when he, Beth, and their son Robby moved to Miami, where Miami *Herald* editor Gene Weingarten cut Barry loose upon America through syndication.

Like many humorists and comedians, Barry admits to having an angry, sensitive side which feeds his sense of humor. Nor is he a stranger to tragedy, having gone through his father's death and his mother's subsequent suicide in the mid-1980s. In 1989 his wife began chemotherapy for cancer. "Sense of humor is a measurement of the extent to which you realize you are trapped in a world almost totally devoid of reason," Barry once wrote.

As far as the satirical, political edge latent beneath many of his bizarre musings, Barry told the *New York Times* that he does "get furious about politics. To write funny stuff you have to be outraged. If I weren't a humor columnist I'd have ulcers. Because I really do get angry." Barry's talent lies in his ability to translate common concerns and frustrations into rare humor. According to Barry, "I'm making people laugh because I'm receiving the same signals they are about the times we're living in, and rebroadcasting them at a slightly different frequency."

Selected writings

Taming of the Screw: Several Million Homeowner's Problems, Rodale Press, 1983.
Babies and Other Hazards of Sex, Rodale Press, 1984.
Stay Fit and Healthy Until You're Dead, Rodale Press, 1985.
Bad Habits, Holt, 1987.
Claw Your Way to the Top, Rodale Press, 1987.
Dave Barry's Guide to Marriage and/or Sex, Rodale Press, 1987.
Homes and Other Black Holes: The Happy Homeowner's Guide, Fawcett, 1988.
Dave Barry's Greatest Hits, Fawcett, 1989.
Dave Barry Slept Here: A Sort of History of the United States, Random, 1989.
Dave Barry Turns 40, Crown, 1990.

Sources

New York Times, April 1, 1988; September 23, 1990.

—*David Collins*

Marion Barry

AP/Wide World Photos

Former mayor of Washington, D.C.

Full name, Marion Shepilov Barry; born March 6, 1936, in Itta Bena, Miss.; son of Marion S. and Mattie B. Barry (sharecroppers); married Mary Treadwell, 1972 (divorced, 1977); married Effi Slaughter (a public relations agent), 1978; children: Marion Christopher. *Education:* LeMoyne College, B.S., 1958; Fisk University, M.S., 1960; postgraduate studies at University of Kansas and University of Tennessee.

Career

First national chairman of Student Non-violent Coordinating Committee, 1960; Director of Pride, Inc., 1967-74; member of Washington, D.C., school board, 1971-74; member of city council, 1974-78; mayor of Washington, D.C., 1978-90.

Sidelights

Marion Barry was elected mayor of Washington, D.C., as a black militant who promised—and delivered—economic and downtown development, as well as a full role for minorities. Twelve years later he was prepared to leave the office in shame. Barry was convicted in 1990 in a hotel-room cocaine sting that made headlines around the world. A now-famous FBI videotape caught Barry flirting with a former girlfriend and then smoking crack cocaine with her. In drug-ravaged Washington, the arrest of the mayor on cocaine charges was considered disastrous.

Barry was a country boy who fought his way out of poverty and segregation to become an educated man, a grassroots political activist, a powerful public official, and a champion of the rights of the powerless. He was born in tiny Itta Bena, Mississippi, the son of impoverished sharecroppers. His father died when Marion was four years old, and his mother soon moved her three children to a tenement duplex in Memphis, Tennessee. This difficult childhood, Barry told the *Washington Post,* affected him throughout life: "I grew up without a father. My mother worked a couple of jobs so I really didn't have any idea of what normal family life was. That was missing in my family. As a result of that, when I grew up I didn't know how to handle all this emotional lack of love. I believed I could go out and kick some doors down and I could sit in and I could take out a little frustration I had against the system, demonstrations, protests."

Growing up in the segregated South of the 1940s and 1950s, Barry struggled hard for money and respect. He often worked two or more jobs at a time. He picked and chopped cotton in the outlying areas. He had two paper routes and sold a third paper on the street corner. He bagged groceries, inspected soda pop bottles, waited tables. When white restaurant patrons would insult him with racial slurs, he told the *Los Angeles Times,* he would furtively spit on their food.

Barry was one of the first black Eagle Scouts in Memphis. Childhood friend William J. Hawkins told the *Washington Post,* "As a younger person, he was nondescript. He just collected merit badges." Barry went on to LeMoyne College, a predominantly black school in Memphis, where he narrowly escaped expulsion in 1958 when he criticized a college trustee for making patronizing remarks about blacks. He moved on to Fisk University in Nashville, where he grew more interested in the civil rights movement. In 1960, Barry helped organize the lunch counter sit-ins that were staged in Nashville and other Southern cities. Within months, he was catapulted into the political jet stream as the first national chairman of the Student Non-violent Coordinating Committee (SNCC), the civil rights group that played a pivotal role in the desegregation of the South. He traveled to the 1960 Democratic and Republican presidential conventions to address the party platform committees.

> "What was happening in
> the streets was more impor-
> tant than what I was doing
> in the classroom...I got
> caught up in other things."

Then, as quickly as he had been thrust into prominence, he all but walked away. Five months after he was chosen as a top student leader in the civil rights movement, Barry left the South to begin doctoral studies in chemistry at the University of Kansas. There, and later at the University of Tennessee, chemistry seemed a way to a professional career, a way out of poverty and discrimination. Barry's involvement in the civil rights movement became part-time; he conducted non-violent workshops, registered voters, and raised funds during the summers. In 1964, he quit school and a teaching job at Knoxville College to join SNCC full-time. "What was happening in the streets was more important than what I was doing in the classroom," he told the *Miami Herald.* "I figured I could always go back to school. But, as it turns out, I got caught up in larger things."

He moved to Washington in 1965 to lead SNCC's District of Columbia statehood drive in the "Free D.C. Movement." Within a year, black residents rated him fifth after four longtime Washingtonians in a poll that asked who had done the most for blacks in the area. Some whites also began to recognize him as a vigorous leader who was both firebrand and conciliator. In a flattering 1967 profile, the *Washington Post* credited him with cooling tempers during street disturbances and dubbed him "D.C.'s man for all stormy seasons."

In 1967 Barry co-founded Pride, Inc., a multimillion-dollar, federally funded youth training program which later became a national model in the so-called War on Poverty. The successful program, wrote the *Washington Post,* "was destined to make Barry an underclass hero." That same year, Barry resigned from SNCC, telling *Ebony,* "The civil rights direction of protest is dead. Now we must concentrate on control—economic and political power."

He plunged into politics in 1971, winning a seat on the D.C. Board of Education because, he later told the *Los Angeles Times,* "I felt that I could be more effective on the inside" of the political process than outside as a community organizer. He was twice re-elected to the board and served as president between 1972 and 1974. In 1973 Washington was awarded home rule (the district had been previously under Congressional control), and one year later Barry ran for city council president and won—in the first election of its kind in the city. He was easily reelected in 1976. Barry focused on economic issues and helped develop one of the nation's strongest municipal ordinances protecting the civil rights of homosexuals. One of the most notable moments of his council career came in March 1977, when Barry was shot by Hanafi Muslims during their siege of the District Building. A ricochet shotgun pellet struck him in the chest, and rescuers were unable to evacuate him promptly because of gunfire. The wound proved to be superficial, but Barry became a hero to many.

To others, however, he was gaining a reputation for arrogance and womanizing. He told *Newsday* that he was a "night owl," and that his private life was no one else's business. Barry's wife, Effi, told the *Los Angeles Times:* "Since the day we got married, he's always been involved with other women. It's difficult. And there is a caliber of female in this world [who] tends to gravitate toward a power figure."

In 1978, at age 42, the popular Barry announced his bid for mayor. He was regarded as the underdog among three candidates, but he received last-minute endorsements from the *Washington Post* and several city unions and scored an upset victory over incumbent Walter Washington. He built a diverse coalition among low-income blacks, labor activists, gay people, and middle-class whites. At his inauguration, Barry promised to make Washington "a capital city that works." "He was reaching his peak at this time," the *Washington Post*'s Arthur Brisbane later wrote. "He was Marion Barry—the brash, in-your-face mayor of Washington, who bristled with hard-earned power wrested from tired old elites who had learned not to underestimate this street-smart pol."

By most accounts, Barry's first term as mayor was a success. He promoted a downtown development and revitalization boom, restored the city's financial credibility on Wall Street, built roads, improved services, poured resources into poor neighborhoods. And he achieved his vow of turning Washington into a black city managed by the blacks who live in it, from top-level executive positions on down. "Barry was an effective and formidable chief executive," wrote the *Washington Post*'s R. H. Melton. "He could prod sluggish bureaucrats into action, articulate policy initiatives that brought sweeping changes, go face-to-face with powerful politicians and business leaders, besting them on their own terms." By his own account, Barry said hard work, rather than intrinsic intelligence, was responsible for his success. "Some people are destined and some are determined, and I am determined," he told *Newsweek*.

Barry easily won reelection in 1982, taking 60 percent of the vote in the Democratic primary against Patricia Roberts Harris, a former secretary of Health and Human Services. During his second term, progress continued in downtown and economic development. But new problems arose: the city's public housing stock deteriorated, the prison system grew dilapidated. And scandals touched the administration. Ten top city officials, including the mayor's top aide, were convicted of corruption or malfeasance, and the mayor's former wife, Mary Treadwell, was convicted of defrauding the government. And while Barry was accused of no crimes, his behavior came under question.

"Marion's always been a free spirit, he likes the ladies'-man image," Ivanhoe Donaldson, a deputy mayor who left after Barry's first term, told the *Los Angeles Times*. "But we'd get on his case, say: 'Hey, Marion, we got work to do.' Get him interested in other stuff. But now, we're gone, he's only got yes men around him."

In 1983, a woman with whom Barry was having a widely known affair was arrested and later convicted of selling cocaine. The incident started rumors that the mayor himself had a drug problem. Barry denied any problem. "I'm not going to tolerate this innuen-do," he told *Newsweek*. "I know about myself. I was trained as a scientist, and I know how dangerous this stuff is to your body. Plus, you can't be a good mayor high on alcohol or anything."

> *"I've had to look my human weaknesses straight in the eye."*

Despite the persistent rumors, Barry won 61 percent of the vote toward reelection in 1986. His opponent, a mother of three, tried to make an issue of Barry's sending his own son to private school. Things continued to get worse for the mayor. Critics accused him of losing focus, of bloating the bureaucracy for political purposes, at the expense of deteriorating city services. In a city of about 270,000 voters, 52,000 were on the city payroll—10,000 more than when Barry initially took office.

City councilman Curtis Wilson, a former ally of Barry's from SNCC, told the *Los Angeles Times*: "The mayor has bloated the bureaucracy for his own political purposes. We can't afford basic services, so the middle class is moving to the suburbs. We're turning into a city of the very rich and the very poor, and [the poor] don't pay any taxes. We're losing our tax base. Marion governs as if there is no tomorrow."

For his part, Barry said the complaints against him were part of a smear campaign run by the white power structure and the press. "I'm the most scrutinized politician in this country," he told the *Los Angeles Times*. "It's always open season on black mayors—look at L.A. and New York. But it's been open season on me for 10 years. Barry bashing's the biggest thing in town. . . . But I'm gonna be like that lion the Romans had. They can just keep throwing stuff at me. But I'll be kicking their asses, every time. In the end, I'll be sitting there, licking my paws."

In 1988, Barry was several times seen visiting a friend, Charles Lewis, at a downtown hotel known to be a center for drug trafficking. Lewis was later arrested, and told police that he sold Barry crack cocaine on several occasions. Barry denied the accusations. But discussion of the mayor's conduct continued. Barry had a highly publicized affair with a stripper in 1987, and his limousine was often seen cruising seedy parts of the city long after midnight. "I may be a poor role model," Barry told the *Post*, "but being a poor role model is not a crime." Then, on

January 18, 1990, Barry was caught in an FBI sting operation. In that incident, Barry responded to the invitation of an ex-girlfriend, former model Rasheeda Moore, to visit her at the Vista International Hotel; FBI agents then videotaped Barry smoking crack in Moore's room. He was arrested and charged with cocaine possession. Blood and urine tests confirmed that the mayor had ingested cocaine.

Barry called the arrest "a trap" and a "political lynching." Within days, however, he admitted to a substance abuse problem—specifically alcohol—and enrolled in a treatment program. "I've had to look my human weaknesses straight in the eye," Barry said in a press conference one week after his arrest. "I've had to realize that I spent so much time caring about and worrying about and doing for others, I've not worried about or cared enough for myself."

Many influential blacks felt that Barry was set up. "The white power cannot stand to see a black man making the decisions," the Reverend Louis Farrakhan told *Newsweek*. "So they set him up—try to kill him with cocaine—and then arrest him." But as Barry's trial opened in June 1990, others viewed things differently. An 85-minute FBI videotape of Barry's hotel room encounter with Moore was played at the trial, prompting *Newsday* columnist Sheryl McCarthy to write, "The tape reveals Barry's tremendous arrogance, even when he is caught red-handed. His denial of wrongdoing, even at this moment of discovery, is an echo of his behavior throughout this whole sorry affair." As the *Washington Post*'s Tony Kornheiser wrote, "they've got him cold as ice. He's already tried screaming entrapment, but the charges stretch over six years, not just one night at the Vista. Backed up to the shoreline, the water on his heels, Marion Barry pulled out the show-stopper."

As the trial continued, Barry announced that he would not seek a fourth term as mayor. "Accept my word that stepping aside now is good for our city," he said in a televised speech. "Tonight it's time to cast away." At the same time, he told the *Post* that he expected not to be convicted. "In this town," he said, "all it takes is one juror saying, 'I'm not going to convict Marion Barry, I don't care what you say.'" On August 10 a federal jury convicted Barry on one misdemeanor drug charge but failed to resolve 12 other charges. One day later, Barry apologized to the city, saying, "To young and old, black and white . . . rich and poor, I ask you to forgive me for any hurt I may have caused. Let us come together to heal ourselves and our city. I call upon the United States government, too, to join me in this healing." On August 14, Barry held a press conference to announce that he was changing his political registration from Democrat to Independent. The next day he announced plans to run for a city council seat. "They may think they're through with me," he told the *Post*, "but Marion Barry has a lot more left in him."

Sources

Ebony, December 1, 1967.
Los Angeles Times, January 7, 1990; January 22, 1990; February 16, 1990; August 12, 1990.
Miami Herald, January 14, 1990; January 25, 1990.
Newsday, July 2, 1990.
Newsweek, January 1, 1989; March 13, 1989; January 29, 1990; February 26, 1990.
Time, January 26, 1989; June 26, 1989.
Washington Post, December 10, 1978; April 26, 1987; December 24, 1989; January 14, 1990; January 21, 1990; March 16, 1990; May 13, 1990; June 1, 1990; June 14, 1990; July 1, 1990; July 2, 1990; August 22, 1990.

—*Glen Macnow*

Kathy Bates

AP/Wide World Photos

Actress

Born c. 1949 in Memphis, TN; daughter of Langdon (a mechanical engineer) and Bertye Bates. *Education:* Southern Methodist University, B.A., 1970.

Career

Actress, 1970—. Principal stage appearances include *Vanities, Frankie and Johnny in the Clair de Lune, Come Back to the Five and Dime, Jimmy Dean, Jimmy Dean* and *'night, Mother*. Principal film work includes *Come Back to the Five and Dime, Jimmy Dean, Jimmy Dean,* Cinecom Intl., 1982; *Men Don't Leave,* Warner Bros., 1990; *White Palace; Misery; At Play in the Fields of the Lord;* and *The Road to Mecca.*

Awards: Antoinette Perry (Tony) Award nomination, 1983, for *'night, Mother;* Academy Award, 1991, for *Misery.*

Sidelights

Kathy Bates is a gifted actress who happens to be middle-aged and somewhat overweight. She has had to fight typecasting all her life, but thanks to her Oscar-winning performance as a psychotic recluse in the 1990 chiller *Misery,* she has finally earned the attention of Hollywood's prominent producers and directors. *People* magazine contributor Mary H. J. Farrell described Bates as "frumpy, dumpy, and lumpy"; an artist who "hasn't had an easy time in Hollywood." The star herself hastens to agree. "I wish living in my own skin wasn't attached

to so many other things in Hollywood," she told *People.* "My body, my face, my hair are all fair game. I look at Marlon Brando and think, 'He does whatever the hell he wants to.'"

With starring roles in *Misery, At Play in the Fields of the Lord,* and *The Road to Mecca* now on her resume, Bates may be on the brink of Brando-type success. Although she has specialized in character roles of women who are eccentric, depressed, or outright bizarre, Bates is a versatile performer who can interpret many different parts. "All of us would just like to be real people," the actress told the *New York Times Magazine.* "But for women especially, somehow movies have gotten to be about glamour: either you're gorgeous or you're a dog. . . . So in some ways [my] future could be very limiting. But I keep thinking, well, Dustin Hoffman broke the mold for the guys. Although he's not an unattractive fellow, he certainly isn't your basic leading man. And maybe somebody can do it for the women."

Bates has been plagued with a weight problem all her life, and as she admits herself, "I never was an ingenue." She was raised in Memphis, Tennessee, the youngest of three daughters of a mechanical engineer. She remembers her childhood fondly, but by her teen years problems had developed; she felt stifled by the provinciality of Memphis and was plagued by bouts of depression. Bates told the *New York Times Magazine* that as a teenager she spent many hours alone, writing songs about death. "My mother used to ask, 'Why do you always write such sad songs?'" she recalled. "I don't know if I was different from a lot of adolescents in that respect."

After high school Bates attended Southern Methodist University in Dallas. As a freshman she studied English, but quickly changed her major to drama. While at SMU she became friends with playwright Jack Heifner, forming an association that would help to launch her professional career. Bates graduated in 1970 and announced her plans to move to New York City. Her parents objected strongly at first, but after seeing her perform in a play in Dallas, they gave her both financial and moral support. Her first part as an Actors Equity performer was as a duck in a children's play in Virginia.

Bates's break came in 1976, when Heifner brought a play called *Vanities* to Off-Broadway. A drama with only three roles, *Vanities* traces the fate of three cheerleaders as they emerge from high school and grow into mature women. The play drew appreciative notices and helped Bates land a role in the movie *Straight Time*, which starred Dustin Hoffman. Her Broadway debut came in 1980, in the short-lived Howard Sackler play *Goodbye, Fidel*.

Bates had also joined the prestigious Actors Theater of Louisville in Kentucky, an important proving ground for actors. Her first part there was a lead in *Crimes of the Heart*, a play that eventually went to Broadway and became a major film. "My first scene required me to cry on cue," Bates remembered in the *New York Times Magazine*. "At that age it was still a challenge for me to perform that way. And I used to go upstairs to the stage very early, like 7:45, and sit in the chair and think of horrible things, to get ready." Eventually, she said, this method drained her emotionally. "I learned...that I had to do all my preparation during the rehearsal period, and that when it came time to go onstage you had to just leave all that behind and walk to the edge of the cliff and throw yourself off. And trust that you would fly."

With enhanced professionalism, Bates returned to New York City and landed roles in several important plays, among them *Frankie and Johnny in the Clair de Lune* and *Come Back to the Five and Dime, Jimmy Dean, Jimmy Dean*. Her most important part, however, was that of the suicidal daughter in *'night, Mother*. Bates told the *New York Times Magazine* that her work as Jessie in that show intensified her own depression; at one point she had to take a break to preserve her

sanity. "My problem was that I couldn't separate what was happening to me onstage from what was happening in my life," she said. "My feelings of identification with the character were overwhelming, and I felt I was locked inside the mantra of that play every night." Bates entered therapy to help sort out the confusion and regain some personal balance. "That was when I began to learn my lesson about not dancing too close to the flame, and being able to leave things behind," she revealed. "To find that healthy balance between committing yourself 200 percent when you're there, and when you're not there just putting it away."

Her performance in *'night Mother* earned Bates a Tony Award nomination, but it did not guarantee her the role in the movie version. Nor did she land the lead in the film version of *Frankie and Johnny in the Clair de Lune*. In both cases the roles went to more conventionally pretty actresses—Sissy Spacek in the first, Michelle Pfeiffer in the latter. Bates told the *New York Times Magazine* that the news about the movie version of *'night Mother* brought her to a crossroads in her career. "On my bad days I got tired of developing material for Sissy Spacek and other stars," she said. "I started to think, 'Well, what am I up here bustin' *mah* hump for, while they're out there picking the gardenias off the bushes?' So I told myself, 'Let me see what I can do with this.'"

Clearly gambling with her future, Bates moved to California and tried to get more work in movies. She was no stranger to the screen, having appeared in everything from the film of *Come Back to the Five and Dime, Jimmy Dean, Jimmy Dean* to an episode of *The Love Boat*, but all of her work had been in small character roles. She was overjoyed in 1990 to receive the part of Annie Wilkes in *Misery*, even though the character was a murderous psychopath. Bates told *People* that she read the Stephen King book on which the film was based and saw the character as a great challenge. "I had to do the movie," she said. "My response to any material is through my stomach. If it grabs me there, I have to do it, and *Misery* did." *Misery* is a grimly realistic horror film about a best-selling author who is held hostage by a dangerously psychotic fan. David Sacks observed in the *New York Times Magazine* that the actress "plays Annie without apparent makeup—no fright wig, no false teeth. With the camera angled up at her full lips and chin's roll of flesh, she simply inhabits the character, making her both scary and pitiful." In fact, Bates arrived on the set with a full history imagined for Annie, dating back to the character's scarred childhood. This helped her infuse the part with a measure of sympathy. "Annie isn't a monster in a horror movie; she's a human being who is a psychopath," Bates said. "Her humanness comes from her inmost dreams and hopes, however crazy they may be."

Bates won an Academy Award for her work in *Misery* and the film did well at the box office, earning $20 million in its first two weeks in theaters. In the wake of that success, the actress has received plum roles in two major releases, *At Play in the Fields of the Lord,* in which she portrays a missionary's wife in the Amazon jungle, and *The Road to Mecca,* in which she plays a South African teacher. Bates told *People* that she is courting success, but not to the point where she will take substandard work. "There's a whole group of people out there who would like to see good films—no matter who is in them, who wrote them, who directs them," she said. "I want to come out of a theater feeling that someone has touched me . . . . The whole point is to have a revelatory experience, to be carried to the heights."

As for her figure and age, Bates admits that they still weigh against her in Hollywood, but far less than they once did. "I've always been a character actor," she told the *New York Times Magazine.* "When I was younger it was a real problem, because I was never pretty enough for the roles that other young women were being cast in. The roles I was lucky enough to get were real stretches for me: usually a character who was older, or a little weird, or whatever. And it was hard, not just for the lack of work but because you have to face up to how people are looking at you. And you think, well, y'know, *I'm* a real person."

Unlike those of some of her characters, Bates's personal life is stable. She has been involved in an ongoing relationship with actor Tony Campisi for almost fifteen years and plans to marry him some day. She lives primarily in Los Angeles, with occasional visits to New York and various far-flung locations for film shoots. The Academy Award-winning actress told the *New York Times Magazine:* "It matters to me, acting. It's what I do. It's what I've given up a lot to do. It's my life source. And I guess I'm too serious about it sometimes, but I want to treat it right."

Sources

Detroit Free Press, April 8, 1991.
Interview, August 1991.
New York Times Magazine, January 27, 1991.
People, December 24, 1990; Spring (special issue) 1991.

—*Anne Janette Johnson*

Ben & Jerry

Ice cream entrepreneurs

Full names, Bennett Cohen and Jerry Greenfield; Cohen born in 1950 in Brooklyn, N.Y.; son of an accountant; wife's name, Cindy (a psychologist); one daughter, Aretha; Greenfield born in 1951 in Brooklyn, N.Y.; son of a stockbroker; wife's name, Elizabeth; one son, Tyrone.

Addresses: *Home*—(Cohen) Jericho, VT. *Office*—Ben & Jerry's, Route 100, P.O. Box 240, Waterbury, VT 10676.

Career

Both Cohen and Greenfield worked a variety of jobs before founding Ben & Jerry's Homemade, Inc., in 1978; Cohen serves as chairperson of the board and Greenfield as president. They are also founders of Ben & Jerry's Foundation, established to benefit non-profit charities.

Awards: Corporate Giving Award from Council on Economic Priorities, 1988; both partners named U.S. Small Business Persons of the Year, 1988; Cohen has received an honorary degree from Hartwick College, Vt.

Sidelights

Ben Cohen and Jerry Greenfield, better known as Ben and Jerry, are best friends and founders of Ben & Jerry's Homemade, Inc., makers of super-premium ice cream, ice cream novelties, and ice milk. The company started small in 1978, with an ice cream parlor in a renovated gas station in Burlington, Vermont. By 1981 *Time* dubbed theirs "the best ice cream in the world."

Ben and Jerry became friends as children in Merrick, New York. Their common bond? A love of ice cream and the fact that they "were the two slowest, chubbiest guys in the seventh grade," Jerry told *People* magazine. "We were nerds." Nerds who would grow up to run a $58 million business empire.

Ben entered the ice cream business his senior year in high school, when he drove a truck, selling ice cream to neighborhood children. He graduated from Calhoun High School in Merrick in 1969, then enrolled in Colgate University. After only 18 months he dropped out and went back to being an ice cream vendor, and enrolled at Skidmore College to study pottery and jewelry-making. He also held odd jobs such as a cashier at McDonald's, a security guard, a janitor, taxi driver, hospital emergency room clerk, and art therapist. Ben dropped out of college in 1974 for good and moved to Paradox, New York, where he became a crafts teacher in a school for emotionally disturbed children. By 1977 he was experimenting with ice cream making, and decided to go into business with his childhood friend, Jerry Greenfield.

Jerry had a more conventional college career. After graduating from Calhoun High School he attended Oberlin College in Ohio on a National Merit Scholarship. He pursued pre-medical studies and worked as an ice cream scooper in the Oberlin college cafeteria. After graduating Jerry applied to medical school but wasn't accepted, so he toiled as a lab technician in New York. In 1976 he moved to upstate New York, and he and Ben decided to follow their dream of starting a food business. The problem, however, was that neither knew anything about such a venture. They signed up for a $5 correspondence course from Pennsylvania State University in ice cream making, and both got A's. They began experimenting with ice cream flavors, but often their trial flavors flopped. "I once made a batch of rum raisin that stretched and bounced," Jerry told *People*.

In May of 1978 they used $8,000 of their own money and borrowed an additional $4,000 to open their first Ben & Jerry's ice cream shop in Burlington, Vermont. Jerry made all the ice cream, inventing eclectic flavors such as Dastardly Mash, Heath Bar Crunch, Chunky Monkey (with bananas) and Tuskegee Chunk (with peanut butter). They named one flavor Cherry Garcia after the lead singer (Jerry Garcia) of the Grateful Dead.

The dense ice cream was a hit, but neither man was a financial wizard. "We actually closed one day to pay our bills. We put up a sign that said WE'RE CLOSED BECAUSE WE'RE TRYING TO FIGURE OUT WHAT'S GOING ON," Jerry told *People*. Finally,

they hired a local nightclub operator to be chief financial officer, and Ben & Jerry's took off.

But as the company soared, both men were uncomfortable. Having spent their working lives on the side of the have-nots, they suddenly found themselves amid prosperity. Jerry "retired" and moved to Arizona in 1982, and Ben contemplated selling the business. "I had this horrible feeling come over me that I had become a businessman. Worse, that now I was just some kind of mindless cog in the overall economy," he told *Inc.* magazine. After putting his company up for sale, Ben finally "decided to adapt it so we could feel proud to say we were the businessmen of Ben & Jerry's," Ben told *People*. So every step of the way, they built their company on a philosophy of dual purpose—profitability and social responsibility.

In 1984 Ben & Jerry's expanded its plant. The Ben & Jerry's Foundation was established one year later, and Jerry returned from Arizona to run it. The foundation uses 7.5 percent of Ben & Jerry's pre-tax income to support non-profit charities; in 1989 it helped 78 groups with grants of $288,971, including

Ben Cohen, left, and Jerry Greenfield. AP/Wide World Photos.

a $35,433 contribution to the 1% For Peace organization, in which both Ben and Jerry are active.

Back at the ice cream factory, they began dispensing free ice cream to the community. They developed the "Joy Committee" at work, to dream up employee perks, such as Halloween parties, massages, college tuition, free health club memberships, profit sharing and a day care center, not to mention the three free pints of ice cream each of the plant's 259 workers get each day. "This most certainly is the new model of the corporate form that we will see created in the 1990s and into the 21st Century," said trend tracker Patricia Aburdene, quoted in *USA Weekend*. The two founders "just might be the ultimate benign bosses in the friendliest of employee-friendly firms," the same article read. The company has been widely emulated as a leader in progressive American corporate culture.

Yet, Ben & Jerry's has had a few setbacks: in 1984, the company sued Pillsbury's Haagen-Dazs division for threatening to cut off suppliers who bought Ben & Jerry's products. The suit was settled out of court. In 1986 the two founders made a "marketing drive" in a "Cowmobile" across the country to publicize the company and hand out free ice cream. Outside Cleveland, the Cowmobile caught fire and burned; neither man was injured.

Perhaps most stressful of all, Ben and Jerry have tried to force a paradox to work: run a fast-growing multi-million dollar business and still "be weird."

"Once, Ben could be confident that everyone else at the company was just as weird as he, that everyone got off on the funk and adventure," wrote Erik Larson in *Inc*. "But lately, the company has gotten so businesslike . . . its explosive growth has stressed and eroded the Ben & Jerry's culture, diminished the fun, and brought strangers into the happy family." Their Waterbury, Vermont, ice cream factory is the second most popular tourist attraction in the state, with more than 30,000 visitors a year. Today "Jerry has the reputation as standard-bearer of the laid-back ethic," according to *USA Weekend* writer Carol Clurman. "Ben spends 95 percent of his time traveling around on company business—high stress work that shows in the sometimes sullen expression on his round, bearded face. Both understand that as the company continues to grow—the work force doubled in the past few years—the family atmosphere will be more difficult to sustain."

In 1988 Larson sat in on a company staff meeting, complete with birthday party and talk about the "joy" committee. At the meeting, "the dress is basic

woodchuck," he wrote in *Inc*. "Levis. Timberland boots. Nikes. Ben is absent, but Jerry is here, in weary slacks, a cow T-shirt, and a crumpled red flannel shirt, tails out, one button fastened . . . for all the fun, however, the Ben & Jerry's Way has a stressful side—a pervasive sense of crisis that has always lingered within the company. No one has ever been entirely sure where Ben & Jerry's was headed, or where it ought to head."

That year, the company hired a management consultant, who helped Ben & Jerry's define its mission. In the company's 1989 annual report, Ben Cohen reflected a new sense of purpose, mixing finances with funk: "We are becoming more comfortable and adept at functioning with a two-part bottom line where our company is measured by both our financial and our social performance," he wrote. "We are convinced that the two are intertwined. We will continue to refuse to run our business to make the short-term quarterly numbers 'look good.'" In spite of itself, the company continued to grow. Even with a recession in 1991, Ben & Jerry's had spread to 38 states, as well as to Canada and Israel. And Ben has been confident: "When you can't afford to buy a new house, a new car, or a new TV, you're still going to shell out two bucks for super premium ice cream," he told *Inc*.

In 1989 Ben founded a private company, Community Products, Inc., which makes a confection called "Rainforest Crunch," with 60 percent of profits going to Brazil's Rain Forest Preserve. Though Ben & Jerry's has a responsibility to stockholders to make a profit, this side company can make profit "the means to the goal" of social action, he told *Mother Jones* magazine.

In 1991 Ben & Jerry's received press for another instance of their unusual corporate social responsibility. According to *Fortune* writer Daniel Seligman, the ice cream makers insisted on paying Vermont dairy producers above-market prices for milk, even though there had been a steep decline in milk prices. Had Cohen and Greenfield taken advantage of the cheap milk, they could have passed the savings on to their customers and enhanced their profits. However, as Cohen told the *Wall Street Journal* (as quoted by Seligman), "We refuse to profit off the misfortune of our dairy suppliers due to some antiquated, misguided convoluted federal system." (The federal dairy-purchase program had, up to then, been artificially buoying milk prices.)

Still, can two ex-hippies keep the "weird" in Ben & Jerry's, no matter how big it gets? "The idea, I think, is to maintain the values of your culture and yet bring it along with you," said Jerry in an *Inc.* interview. "I mean, you don't want to stay stuck in the past. The gas station we started in was an amazing place, but it is there no longer. It's a parking lot. You can't tell wonderful stories about the place— but tell me the wonderful story about what happened at the plant last month. I think our company will be changed. I think there's no doubt about that. It will be changed. We just have to make it a good change."

Writings

(With Nancy Stevens) *Ben & Jerry's Homemade Ice Cream and Dessert Book,* Workman Publishing, 1987.

Sources

Fortune, June 3, 1991.
Harrowsmith, January-February 1990.
Inc., July 1988; March 1990; April 1990.
Mother Jones, January 1990.
New York Times, March 1, 1988.
People, September 10, 1990.
USA Weekend, January 19-20, 1990.
Village Voice, February 27, 1990.
Whole Earth Review, Winter 1988.

—*Ellen Creager*

Sarah and James S. Brady

Gun control activists

Sarah Brady: Born Sarah Jane Kemp, February 6, 1942, in Missouri; married James S. Brady, 1973; children: James Scott Brady, Jr. *Education:* College of William and Mary, B.A., 1964.

James S. Brady: Full name, James Scott Brady; born August 29, 1940, in Centralia, IL; son of Harold James (a railroad worker) and Dorothy Davidson Brady (a social worker); married Sue Beh, 1961 (divorced, 1970); married Sarah Jane Kemp, 1973; children: (first marriage) one daughter; (second marriage) James Scott Brady, Jr. *Education:* University of Illinois at Champaign-Urbana, B.S. in communications, 1962, attended law school, 1963.

Address: *Office*—Handgun Control, Inc., 1225 Bye St. NW, Suite 1100, Washington, DC 20005.

Career

Sarah Brady: public school teacher, 1964-68; assistant to campaign director, National Republican Congressional Committee, 1968-70; administrative aide to U.S. Representative Mike McKevitt, 1970-72; administrative aide to Congressman Joseph J. Mariti, 1972-74; Republican National Committee, 1974-81, director of administration and coordinator of field services, 1974-78; member of the board of Handgun Control, Inc., 1985, chairman, 1989. Member of the board for Easter Seals, College of William and Mary Society of the Alumni, National Head Injury Foundation, Arlington County Women's Club, Alexandria Hospital Corporation, and the League of Women Voters.

Awards: Washingtonian of the year, *Washingtonian* magazine, 1983; USO's woman of the year, 1984; one of *Ms.* magazine's women of the year, 1988; "Person of the Week," ABC-TV News, 1988; one of the "100 Most Powerful Women in Washington," *Washington* magazine, 1989; one of *Glamour* magazine's women of the year, 1990.

James Brady: Republican party congressional campaign manager, 1964-80; lobbyist for Illinois Medical Society, 1964-67; executive campaign director for Whitaker Baxter, 1967; James & Thomas (public relations firm), executive vice president, c. 1967; press secretary to the President of the United States, 1981-89.

Member: National Head Injury Foundation (honorary chairman), Sigma Chi.

Awards: Taft Young Republican Award, 1962; Sachem Award, 1962; Chicago's bachelor of the year, 1971; Lincoln Award of the Illinois Republican party, 1982; Will Rogers Humanitarian Award, 1985; *USA Today* Unity Award, 1985; Public Relations Society of America award for professional contributions, 1986; has also received various honorary degrees.

Sidelights

Jim Brady was a jovial man with many friends in the press and on Capitol Hill. He and his wife Sarah and son Scott enjoyed the social life that his 1981 appointment as press secretary to President Ronald Reagan afforded. In the less than three months that he held the job, Brady's wise cracks had gotten him in trouble on several occasions. Soon after the President had said that trees cause more pollution than cars and factories, Brady looked down from an airplane full of reporters at a small forest fire and yelled: "Killer trees, killer trees!" While he was chastised for those remarks, he wasn't in trouble for very long; his legendary charm profited him professionally as well as privately. Most friends agreed that Sarah was often Jim's best audience. The boisterous raconteur's huge frame earned him the nickname "Bear," while Sarah was "Raccoon," because of her quick, small hands and the dark circles under her eyes.

Sarah's true strength and perseverance only became obvious to all during the arduous period after Jim was shot during an attempt on President Reagan's life, on November 23, 1981. The assailant, John W. Hinckley, Jr., had purchased a handgun in Dallas and obtained Devastator bullets, which contain charges that explode after impact. Only one of the four bullets Hinckley fired actually exploded—the one that entered Brady's brain on the left side and came to rest on the right. During the tremendously stressful days full of risky medical procedures that followed, and the pursuant years of painful therapy and slow emotional and physical adjustment to the trauma, Sarah stayed by Jim's side. She was consumed by the full-time job of running the family's life for several years and did not become an advocate of gun control until four years after the attack. When asked about the implicit emotionalism a victim's wife brings to an issue like gun control, Sarah told *Vanity Fair*, "I did not get involved immediately [after Jim's injury]. I waited four or five years before I did. By that time I'd dealt with what happened, I'd grieved, gotten over it. My decision to get involved was a conscious effort to make a change. I had already dealt with the trauma and loss of Jim's shooting." Even in the first advertisements of gun control organization Handgun Control, Inc.—which featured Sarah's picture—the copy read: "I'm not asking for your sympathy. I'm asking for your help."

The Bradys apparently have no knee-jerk fear of guns: Sarah's father, who worked for the FBI, had taken her to the shooting range as a child, and Jim had hunted as a young man. They still plan to teach their son to shoot if he ever wants to, but an incident involving young Scott was decisive to the Bradys' activism. In 1985, while Sarah and Jim were visiting his relatives in Illinois, Sarah and Scott headed off to go swimming. They got into her brother-in-law's pickup truck, and her son picked a gun up from the front seat and pointed it at his mother. Sarah sternly told him never to point even a toy gun at anyone, and then took it away. She instantly realized that it was a real gun, a .22, the same sort Hinckley had used against the President. A crucial moment had arrived. Sarah had been approached by gun control advocates before, but never felt the moment was right. Now the issue of gun safety joined with her concerns about the availability of guns, and when the family returned home, she contacted Handgun Control, Inc. At the time, the McClure-Volkmer bill was in the congressional works: the bill, which had bi-partisan sponsorship and backing from the Natioal Rifle Association (NRA), compromised earlier gun control legislation, effectively "de-regulating" much of gun sales, import, and production. Soon Sarah became devoted to fighting it and fighting for stronger regulations and enforcement pertaining to gun imports, assembly, purchase, and use.

When the bill passed, the gun control law of 1968—the only federal law regulating the use of guns—was substantially weakened, and some felt that the patchwork quilt of conflicting state laws regarding guns was ineffectual. Criminals routinely cross state borders to purchase guns that might be illegal in their own state or in a way that is illegal elsewhere. Advocates of federal gun control laws believe that the ineffectiveness of the state's laws would be overcome by federal rulings on checks run before purchase, waiting periods, and restrictions of import and assembly of certain particularly lethal kinds of guns. Those who oppose these bills believe that they would be costly and impossible to implement. They also point to statistics, which indicate that most criminals buy their guns through middlemen with clean records, thereby rendering a check ineffective. Sarah Brady believes that a bill named after the Bradys has an excellent chance to at least curb, if not cure, the gun problem. She described the two-part Brady bill in an op-ed page in *Time*: "First we must require a national waiting period before the purchase of a handgun, to allow for a criminal-records check. Police know that waiting periods work. In the 20 years that New Jersey has required a background check, authorities have stopped more than 10,000 convicted felons from purchasing handguns. We must also stop the sale and domestic production of semiautomatic assault weapons. These killing machines clearly have no legitimate sporting purpose." Sarah claims that the license check mandated by the Brady bill would have stopped Hinckley.

The Brady bill is meant to be pragmatic and thoughtful, and no matter how much Sarah Brady insists that *she* is not emotional about it, many others are. A bill with this kind of sentimental impact could only expect an unsuccessful history in Congress in light of its opposition by a large and influential foe: the NRA. The NRA was founded in 1871 and has three million members and a budget of $86 million. Handgun Control, Inc., was founded by Pete Shields in 1974 after his son was murdered with a handgun in California. Handgun Control, Inc., has a membership of 250,000, but claims to be "one million strong," as it has the names of one million supporters in its computers. The NRA's pivotal argument against any gun restrictions concerns a reading of the Second Amendment in the Bill of Rights, which states: "A well-regulated militia being necessary to the security of a free state, the right of the people to keep and bear arms shall not be infringed." The NRA omits the section about militia and believes that the latter half of the sentence is independently meaningful, guaranteeing unrestricted availability of guns to Americans. A copy of this truncated version of the Second Amendment was found in John Hinckley's wallet after the assassination attempt. Sarah Brady and Handgun Control, Inc., find this defense paranoid. "You're hearing from people who are really panicky," she told *USA Weekend*. "They say they're going to have their rights taken away. That's poppycock."

That Sarah Brady is the group's most successful lobbyist makes her a special target of gun rights groups. "She has been very effective," Secretary of State James Baker, an NRA lobbyist, told the *New York Times Magazine*, "but in a large part because of her personal situation." "A pain in the neck" was how John Michael Snyder of the Citizens Committee

James S. Brady, seated, and his wife Sarah, right, greet the press after the June, 1991, Senate passage of a bill requiring a waiting period for handgun purchases. (Also pictured, from left: senators Herbert H. Kohl, Joseph A. Biden, Jr., and Robert Dole.) AP/Wide World Photos.

for the Right to Bear Arms, a gun owners group, referred to Sarah Brady in *USA Weekend*. The *USA Weekend* writer remarked that "Snyder insists she has appealed to the public's soft side—and that she has dragged her husband into the cause. 'He's being *used*,' Snyder says, 'to try to sway people emotionally rather than intellectually.'" Sarah enlisted Jim's help when visiting congresspeople in the 1990s. Jim was not able to join her sooner because as long as he worked for President Reagan he could not speak out on gun control and weaken his chief's position. He seems to many astonishingly in control when he travels with his wife to make appearances and give speeches. Despite his impaired speaking ability, he is a touching and direct lecturer. Jim spoke to Congress in 1990 about gun control, calling them "cowardly lions" and "gutless" for their apparent fear of NRA political retaliation. *Vanity Fair* quoted a part of his testimony: "I need help getting out of bed, help taking a shower, and help getting dressed, and—damn it—I need help going to the bathroom . . . . I guess I'm paying for their 'convenience,'" he said, referring to the complaint by potential gun buyers that a waiting period is inconvenient.

The Brady Bill has not had an easy history with such powerful opponents. Even with 104 congressional co-sponsors in 1988, and the support of all of the major law enforcement lobbies, the bill lost 228-182 in the House; in 1990, the bill never even made it to the House floor, though at that time co-sponsors numbered 151. (In 1991 Ronald Reagan reversed his position on gun control and spoke out in favor of the bill, which then passed in the House.) The Bradys fought their battle in state legislatures as well, and boosted precedent-setting laws. In 1988 Jim and Sarah threw their support behind Maryland's bur- geoning legislation to make illegal the manufacture and sale of Saturday-night specials, which are "cheap, concealable street guns that are the common currency of urban crime—and useless for almost any other purpose," according to *Vanity Fair*. It was their first real triumph, and the NRA spent approximately $6 million to overturn it. The landmark David-vs.-Goliath struggle inspired Sarah to say in *Ms.*: "Our side didn't have anywhere near their resources, but the people were behind us. Oh, it was a good victory. It'll show other states the NRA *can* be defeated." In *USA Weekend* Sarah revealed, "I really do enjoy the politics of it. I love the fight in a campaign. I want to *win*." Jim added, "You should see her chasing a congressman down the hall. She's yelling, 'Congressman!' and he's running as fast as he can go. 'Here comes that woman from gun control. We know what you want.'"

Sources

Books

Dickenson, Mollie, *Thumbs Up: The Life and Courageous Comeback of White House Press Secretary Jim Brady*, Morrow, 1987.

Periodicals

Ms., January/February 1989.
New York Times, April 24, 1991; April 29, 1991.
New York Times Magazine, December 9, 1990.
Newsweek, April 14, 1986; April 8, 1991.
Time, December 4, 1989; January 29, 1990.
USA Weekend, February 15, 1991.
U.S. News & World Report, December 4, 1989.
Vanity Fair, January 1991.

—*Christine Ferran*

Albert Brooks

Director, actor, and comedian

Born Albert Lawrence Einstein c. 1948, in Los Angeles, CA; son of Harry (a radio comic) and Thelma (an actress; maiden name Leeds) Einstein; changed name to Albert Brooks c. 1968. *Education:* Attended Los Angeles City College and Carnegie-Mellon University c. 1966-68.

Career

Comedian, 1968—; actor in feature films, 1970—, including *Taxi Driver*, Columbia, 1976; *Private Benjamin*, Warner Bros., 1980; *Twilight Zone: The Movie*, Warner Bros., 1983; and *Broadcast News*, Twentieth Century–Fox, 1987. Director, producer, and actor in films, including *Real Life*, Paramount, 1979; *Modern Romance*, Columbia, 1981; *Lost in America*, Warner Bros., 1985; and *Defending Your Life*, Warner Bros., 1991.

Awards: Academy Award nomination for best supporting actor, 1988, for *Broadcast News.*

Sidelights

Albert Brooks is slowly but surely gaining a mainstream audience for his quirky, ironic, and intensely personal humor. In the 1980s Brooks earned a cult following for films he directed, wrote, and starred in—including the popular *Lost in America*. More recently Brooks has moved into big-budget productions with *Defending Your Life*, a comic send-up of the afterlife and its day of judgment. *Chicago Tribune* correspondent Hilary de Vries called Brooks a "comic naysayer" who has "elevated whining to an art form." Continuing, de Vries stated, "Like Woody Allen, the other stand-up comedian turned auteur to whom he is most often compared, Brooks has become a moviemaker who transforms confessional comedy into social commentary."

Brooks has worn many caps in Hollywood since he decided to be a performer. He has written humorous essays for magazines like *Esquire*, contributed short films and comic material to *Saturday Night Live*, and created bizarre but hilarious stand-up routines. That much activity might satisfy some, but Brooks has gone further: He has starred in feature films—even earning an Academy Award nomination—and has brought his own satirical vision to the big screen. The common thread that unites all of Brooks's work is his excruciating self-awareness, portrayed in his films by a series of whiny neurotic characters. In the *New York Times* Bruce Weber wrote: "As writer and director and star of three feature films and as a featured actor in several others, Brooks has been probably the most self-consciously self-conscious of Hollywood's entertainers, a man whose mind seems permanently on rewind, considering over and over again the unanswerable comic questions: Where do I fit in? and Do I really want to?"

Brooks was born in Los Angeles into a family for whom radio comedy was the bread and butter. The youngest of four sons, he was named Albert, no doubt at the insistence of his father, Harry Einstein. Harry had enjoyed a long and profitable career as a comedian. His best known on-air character was an inept Greek businessman named "Parkyakarkus," who appeared regularly on singer and comedian Eddie Cantor's shows. While Albert was still young his father retired, but still rubbed elbows with Cantor, Milton Berle, Jack Benny, and other radio personalities.

Saddled with the name Albert Einstein, Brooks drifted in the direction of comedy himself. In high school he became best friends with Rob Reiner (also in *Newsmakers 91*), whose father, Carl, was also a comedian. Together Brooks and Reiner would mug for Carl Reiner until the older man was convulsed with laughter. As early as the 1960s, in fact, the senior Reiner predicted that Harry Einstein's youngest son might have a bright future as a performer.

"After high school, I knew I wanted to be an actor," Brooks told the *Chicago Tribune*. "But there were very few parts for people like myself.... You know, the part of the guy who the heroine likes but was too embarrassed to tell her friends." After a brief stint at Los Angeles City College, he transferred to Carnegie Mellon University in Pittsburgh, where he majored in drama. Midway through his four years he decided to quit college and return to Los Angeles. The first thing he did there was change his name. He told the *New York Times Magazine*: "When I was going to go into show business, I thought 'If I have any talent at all, I better not do this.' I tried a lot of names with Albert. I tried my middle name, which is Lawrence, but Albert Lawrence sounded like a Vegas singer." The name Brooks—culled from somewhere in his family tree—appealed to him, so he became Albert Brooks.

Although Brooks yearned to do drama, he made rapid strides as a stand-up comic. In 1968 he was booked at *The Hollywood Palace* as a mock ventriloquist act—as Brooks drank from a glass of water, the dummy gurgled. The following year he was chosen as guest host of *The Dean Martin Summer Special*; numerous appearances on *The Tonight Show* followed. Brooks told the *New York Times Magazine*: "When I started there weren't any Comedy Stores. There wasn't any place to go and try out material. I came up with bits while I was showering or sitting in front of a mirror. When I liked it I went out and did it on national television. I never once tried anything out. So I never used laughs as a barometer. Thought-provoking was more interesting to me than funny, and if it was funny too, then fantastic."

By the mid-1970s Brooks was a regular visitor to *The Tonight Show* and other television programs. He also served as the opening act for Neil Diamond's live concerts. Still, Brooks fought the idea of spending his life as a stand-up comic. He realized that his best

material came from self-parody, so he sought other outlets for his talents. In fact, he turned down a chance to be the regular host of *Saturday Night Live*, opting instead to provide comic short subject films for the zany television show. That experience paved the way for feature films—and the chance to do serious drama.

Weber wrote: "Brooks...garnered several acting roles, most of them small, but each distinguished by his half-charming, half annoying brand of self-involvement." In the award-winning movie *Taxi Driver*, Brooks appeared as a campaign worker with a crush on his pretty associate. He is better known, however, for his starring role in *Broadcast News*, a comedy-drama about network television. In *Broadcast News* Brooks plays Aaron Altman, an investigative reporter rich in wit but poor in looks, who vainly pursues an ambitious and lovely executive in vain. Brooks's performance earned him an Academy Award nomination and a high profile in Hollywood—a mixed blessing for someone who thrives on independence.

Long before he reached mass audiences with *Broadcast News*, Brooks had found a niche with aficionados

Actress Julie Hagerty, left, and Albert Brooks rehearse a scene from the film Lost in America. *AP/Wide World Photos.*

of highbrow comedy. He wrote and directed his first feature film, *Real Life*, in 1979. A scathing satire of suburban family life, *Real Life* follows the efforts of an egotistical and incompetent filmmaker—portrayed by Brooks—as he attempts to capture a family's day-to-day activities for a movie. Inevitably, all goes wrong, and the "typical American family" shatters in a mass of irrational hysteria. The humor in Brooks's second film, *Modern Romance*, is even blacker. In that work Brooks plays a neurotic boyfriend who alternately courts and rejects his longtime girlfriend. As Weber remarked, *Modern Romance* "got a polarized reaction from viewers and critics; many were unwilling to accept Brooks's portrayal of the obnoxious [character] as dark comic insecurity." The editors of *Playboy* commented on the strength of *Modern Romance* and dubbed Brooks "the funniest white man in America."

While *Real Life* and *Modern Romance* earned only modest returns at the box office, Brooks's 1985 movie, *Lost in America*, became a hit, especially on video. *Lost in America* concerns a yuppie couple living the good life in Los Angeles. Suddenly, the husband—Brooks again—loses his standing with his advertising firm. In a rush of old hippie spirit, he and his wife decide to cash in their assets and hit the road in a specially-outfitted mobile home. Their idyll soon becomes a nightmare, however, and they end up limping to New York City to beg for new yuppie jobs. "Much of Brooks's humor derives from such impossible dreams," Weber noted. "He's practiced at holding contradictory desires in his mind at the same time. You want everlasting love, but you want to be single. You want to be accepted, but you want to be extraordinary. . . . You want everything, but you can't have it. Of course, none of this makes him unusual, which he admits. In fact, he sees himself as something of a spokesman for the world's consciously divided selves."

This theme also filters into *Defending Your Life*, Brooks's 1991 comedy about an anxious businessman who meets his final reckoning after being hit by a bus in Los Angeles. Brooks's character finds himself in Judgment City, a tacky afterworld where souls are put on trial for their earthly behavior. "Generally, afterlife movies are about a dead person hanging around coaching a living person," Brooks told the *New York Times Magazine*. "This isn't like that. There are no earth people up there . . . . There are no harps, no angels. There are just prosecutors, defenders and this huge judgment center." *Defending Your Life* was Brooks's first big-budget, major box office release; it earned positive reviews and brisk business in the spring of 1991.

Although he admits that aspects of his personal life find their way into his films, Brooks is a private person who grants few interviews and says little about his relationships with women. He lives in Sherman Oaks, California, and has at one time or another been linked romantically with singer Linda Ronstadt and *Lost in America* co-star Julie Hagerty, but he has never married. Brooks has said he feels uncomfortable when critics claim he is a spokesman for an obsessive, self-conscious generation; but at the same time he is committed to what he calls "realistic comedy." He told the *Chicago Tribune:* "I could make a lot of people laugh—and I love to make people laugh—if I made up behavior that human beings never did. But I love to ring true and many [comedy] situations don't. You know, a car can fly off a hill and go over 17 mountains and land safely and the occupants wipe blueberry pie off their face, go 'Whew' and many people will laugh even though that could never happen. I like comedy that rings true."

Brooks expanded on this in the *New York Times Magazine*. "If the result of something I do is that someone feels 10 percent less crazy because they see someone else is thinking what they're thinking, then I provide a service," he said. "I know I've always felt better when other people were thinking about things that I thought I was the only one thinking about."

Sources

Chicago Tribune, April 11, 1988; March 31, 1991.
New York Times Magazine, March 17, 1991.
Rolling Stone, April 18, 1991.
Washington Post, April 5, 1991.

—*Mark Kram*

James Brown

Rhythm and blues singer and songwriter

Born June 17, 1928 (some sources say May 3; others say May 3, 1933) in Pulaski, TN (some sources say Augusta, GA); mother's name, Susie; married to fourth wife, Adrienne "Alfie" Rodriguez (a hair stylist and makeup artist).

Addresses: *Home*—Beech Island, SC. *Office*—Polygram Records, Worldwide Plaza, 825 Eighth Ave., New York, NY 10019.

Career

Boxer and semi-pro basketball player c. 1953-55; lead singer for the Gospel Starlighters c. 1955, group changed name to Famous Flames and format to rhythm and blues, 1956, then to James Brown and the Famous Flames c. 1956; appeared in motion pictures *Ski Party,* 1965, *The Blues Brothers,* 1980, and *Rocky IV,* 1986; formerly owned and was president of J.B. Broadcasting, Ltd., James Brown Network, James Brown Productions, and 17 publishing companies.

Awards: Grammy Awards for best rhythm and blues recording, 1965, for "Papa's Got a Brand New Bag," and for best male rhythm and blues performance, 1986, for "Living in America"; inducted into Rock and Roll Hall of Fame, 1986.

Sidelights

James Brown was more than 60 years old when he was paroled from prison for the second time in his life in February of 1991. If he were anybody

but James Brown, the Godfather of Soul, he would probably have been satisfied to live out the twilight of his life in peace and quiet and freedom.

But as he *was* James Brown—The Hardest Working Man in Show Business, The Sex Machine, The Minister of the New Super Heavy Funk, Soul Brother Number One, The King of the One Nighters—and as his popularity in the eyes of pop music lovers around the world had never been so great, the show most definitely had to go on. Publicity from his incarceration due to a confrontation with police after a speeding ticket, as well as the awareness slowly catching on in the music world that no pop, rock, R&B, funk, disco, or rap tune written over the past 30 years has not been directly or indirectly influenced by Brown's innovations, made the man who walked out of South Carolina's State Park Correctional Center that day nothing short of a living legend, refreshed, restored, and ready to breathe deeply of the second wind of his great career.

"James Brown's musical legacy will continue to provoke awe (as well as blatant imitation) for as long as music still matters," wrote *Spin's* Jim Greer in 1991, some 35 years after Brown's first recorded hit. "Even if he never sang another note, the stylistic innovations he brought into the vernacular of pop music will remain an influence and a source of inspiration.'' Indeed, many of pop music's greatest performers—Mick Jagger, Michael Jackson, Wilson Pickett, Otis Redding, Prince—all count Brown among their greatest inspirations.

If Brown's moment in the spotlight seems to be unfairly coming only years after he revolutionized the pop music world, perhaps this is the price the singer has paid for being so far ahead of his time. While Elvis Presley and Chuck Berry were cashing in on the relative popcorn and candy of simple, commercial pop tunes in the 1950s, Brown was coming to grips with the prime beef of a more energized, spiritual form of music. ''Mixing gospel and blues roots with the energy of his own aggressive personality, he created some of the most fervent records of the late Fifties and a dynamic road show that, by 1962, had made him America's leading R & B star,'' states Brown's entry in *The Encyclopedia of Rock*. ''Sidestepping the traditional fate of top black talent (limited rewards or compromise to mainstream, white-controlled showbiz) Brown then extended his music into an expression of defiant independence that was spiritually closer to the great jazz revolutionaries than to other 'soul' singers, but used compulsive dance rhythms to attract mass audiences, and brought about the polarization of jazz and soul in the form of Seventies street-funk.''

Born (according to most sources) in 1928 in Pulaski, Tennessee, Brown was raised in poverty near Augusta, Georgia. He worked at a variety of occupations as a youth, including field-hand, shoe-shine, boxer, and semi-pro basketball player, before being sentenced to an eight- to sixteen-year stint at the Alto Reform School in Toccoa, Georgia in 1949 for armed robbery. Three and one-half years later he was paroled and moved to Macon, Georgia to join his friend Bobby Byrd as a member of the singing group the Gospel Starlighters, which soon became known as the Flames and began dabbling in rhythm and blues.

Federal Records executive Ralph Bass discovered the group in Macon and brought them north to Cincinnati to sign with his label in January of 1956. Brown soon began to assume control and renamed the band—then featuring Don Terry, Syd Keels, Nash Knox, Floyd Scott, and Byrd—James Brown and the Famous Flames. That year they released their first single, ''Please, Please, Please.'' ''When Syd Nathan (of King Records, a subsidiary of Federal) heard 'Please, Please, Please,' he thought it was a piece of [crap],'' Bass told Arnold Shaw, according to Shaw's book *Honkers and Shouters*. ''He said that I was out of my mind to bring Brown from Macon to Cincinnati—

and pay his fare. We put out that first record on Federal, not King. But then after 'Please' began to sell and made the charts—that was in 1956—Syd sang a different tune . . . . Brown was way ahead of his time. He wasn't really singing R & B. He was singing gospel to an R & B combo with a real heavy feeling . . . . He wasn't singing or playing music—he was transmitting feeling, pure feeling.'' Two years later, the Flames hit the national charts with the reworked gospel tune ''Try Me,'' which attracted the attention of Ben Bart, owner of the Universal Attractions booking agency. Thus Bart became the first and probably most important in a long line of booking managers who helped shape Brown's career. With a list of show-stopping, high-energy songs like ''Good, Good Lovin','' ''Think,'' ''Night Train,'' and ''Baby You're Right,'' the Flames took their unique and powerful show on the road, selling out black venues from coast to coast and slowly building, by word of mouth, the Brown legend. A 1962 performance at the famous Apollo Theater in Harlem was captured on the album *Live at the Apollo*, which soared to Number Two on the Billboard album charts.

By then headlining the James Brown Revue, Brown had become the lynchpin of perhaps the tightest, most spectacular rhythm and blues act ever. Band members were fined for anything short of razor-sharp precision, while ''Mr. Dynamite'' himself virtually defined a new standard of showmanship. His wildly colored outfits, characteristic punctuating grunts, and totally original and joyous acrobatics and dance steps all contributed to the inimitable style of a man who seemed to be possessed by his own music each and every time he took the stage.

By the mid-1960s, with Bart's assistance, Brown moved further toward the center of the pop scene by forming his own production company, Fair Deal, and recording several of his new tunes for the more substantial Smash label, a subsidiary of Mercury Corporation. This gave him both more control over his sound and a chance for broader distribution of the finished product. The result was the 1964 hit ''Out of Sight,'' which scored with an international and bi-racial audience. King Records nonetheless eventually wooed Brown back to the fold with a promise of total artistic control over his career. Once back at King, Brown worked with band director Nat Jones to produce several new hits, including ''I Got You,'' ''Ain't That A Groove,'' and the classic ''Papa's Got a Brand New Bag.''

By the time racial and political tensions began to erupt into violence in the American black community of the late 1960s, Brown had become a role model for push it on your mind to drink a Pepsi Cola or drink a Budweiser or buy a Cadillac or a Lincoln or a Rolls. So let's use the same medium. Just give a man some stimulation, so he says I want to get an education and get a job.... We've got a bunch of people that are ignorant. Not fools, though."

During his stay in prison Brown also had time to recharge his musical batteries. His internment made his music more popular than ever, and at the same time, the public was finally catching on to the idea that many of the stylistic techniques Brown initiated years earlier were being used by contemporary musicians all over the world. Rap groups, particularly, have been known to borrow liberally from Brown riffs to provide the basic musical context for their lyrics. It is a situation that both flatters Brown and makes him angry when he is not compensated for his music. "We're working hard on that right now, trying to get some fair compensation from all these groups," Brown told *Spin.* "I think it's very flattering when someone uses, you know, whatever, a drumbeat or a melody of something, but they got to give something back. A lot of these guys are building their careers on my career—it's not right."

When Brown was finally paroled in February of 1991, he was prepared to capitalize on his regained career momentum in force. A pay-per-view television concert aired in June of 1991 featured Brown and several recording stars from both the past and present. Polydor released a four-CD boxed set, *Star Time,* chronicling Brown's entire career, and the singer eagerly returned to the studio to record a new album of songs, many of which he had written in prison. Brown promised that the new material, compiled for the 1991 summer release *Love Over–Due,* would deliver more of his unique, show-stopping music to an new generation of music-lovers. "I'm gonna make people feel like one family again," Brown told *Interview.* "I'm gonna bring 'em back together. Sports are good. But it don't touch music. Music is the master of the soul. I can play in a place, and thirty minutes after I play, everybody is brothers. You know, I love that."

Selected discography

Live at the Apollo: October 24, 1962. Polydor, 1990 (reissue).

Sex Machine, King, 1970.
Super Bad, King, 1970.
Sho Is Funky Down Here, King, 1971.
Hot Pants, Polydor, 1971.
Revolution of the Mind, Polydor, 1971.
Soul Classics, Polydor, 1972.
There It Is, Polydor, 1972.
Get on the Good Foot, Polydor, 1972.
Black Caesar, Polydor, 1973.
Slaughter's Big Rip-Off, Polydor, 1973.
Soul Classics Volume II, Polydor, 1973.
The Payback, Polydor, 1973.
Hell, Polydor, 1974.
Reality, Polydor, 1974.
Sex Machine Today, Polydor, 1975.
Everybody's Doin' the Hustle and Dead on the Double Bump, Polydor, 1975.
Hot, Polydor, 1975.
Get Up Offa That Thing, Polydor, 1976.
Bodyheat, Polydor, 1976.
Mutha's Nature, Polydor, 1977.
Jam/1980's, Polydor, 1978.
Take a Look at Those Cakes, Polydor, 1978.
The Original Disco Man, Polydor, 1979.
Gravity, CBS, 1986.
I'm Real, CBS, 1988.
Love Over–Due, Scotti Bros., 1991.

Sources

Books

Christgau, Robert, *Christgau's Record Guide,* Ticknor & Fields, 1981.
Dalton, David, and Lenny Kaye, *Rock 100,* Grosset & Dunlap, 1977.
Hardy, Phil, and Dave Laing, *Encyclopedia of Rock,* Schirmer Books, 1988.
The Illustrated Encyclopedia of Rock, compiled by Nick Logan and Bob Woffinden, Harmony Books, 1976.
The Rolling Stone Illustrated History of Rock and Roll, edited by Jim Miller, Random House/Rolling Stone Press, 1976.
Shaw, Arnold, *Honkers and Shouters,* Macmillan, 1978.

Periodicals

Entertainment Weekly, June 21, 1991.
Interview, December 1990.
People, April 15, 1991.
Rolling Stone, April 6, 1989.
Spin, June 1991.

—*David Collins*

many blacks, not simply as a successful musician but as an astute businessman who owned fast-food franchises, radio stations, a booking agency, a publishing company, and his own Lear jet. It was also significant that Brown managed his own career, rather than allowing himself to be directed by the white-dominated record industry. During this period Brown was working with producer Alfred Ellis, who helped shape another phase of the singer's career that included hits like "Cold Sweat," "Give It Up or Turn It Loose," and "Licking Stick."

Also recorded in these years were the black pride anthems "Don't Be a Dropout," "I Don't Want Nobody to Give Me Nothin'," and "Say It Loud—I'm Black and I'm Proud." Strong response to these works—both positive and negative—caused Brown to recoil from further political associations in his music. Nevertheless, he told Dimitri Ehrlich in *Interview*, songs like "Say It Loud—I'm Black and I'm Proud" had to be written: "That song was needed at that time, because the Afro-American didn't know who he was then. He was black, he was colored, he was 'boy', he was a nigger. He was all kinds of derogative things that didn't make sense." Brown's principal role during those troubled years was as a peacemaker. In fact, the singer received personal thanks from President Lyndon B. Johnson for performing a televised concert the day after Martin Luther King, Jr.'s assassination; the show was credited with helping to quell rioting across the country.

Brown's style continued to evolve into the early 1970s, when, calling himself the Minister of the New Super Heavy Funk, he helped to usher in a new music employing African rhythms. Several songs, including "Sex Machine," "Soul Power," "Superbad," and "I'm a Greedy Man," were recorded with young musicians who later went on to develop the pioneering group Funkadelic. Other groups like Sly and the Family Stone and Earth, Wind, & Fire, continued to move funk in a new direction, using high-tech instrumentation and pre-recorded backing tracks to produce a slick new sound.

Brown stayed with the scene as long as he could, producing such hits as "Get on the Good Foot" and "Make It Funky," but by the time disco arrived in full force in the mid-70s, Brown, though he continued to record prodigiously, seemed to be nearing the end of the line of his superstardom. Personal problems, including the death of his son, plagued him; his role seemed to move toward that of the fading legend. His mainstream public exposure in the 1980s was largely defined by a well-received cameo in the 1980 film *The Blues Brothers*, and his song "Living in

America," performed by the singer in the film *[Rocky] IV*. Despite his limited popularity at the time, "[Living] in America" in 1986 reached the Top Ten an[d won] Brown a Grammy Award for best male rhyth[m and] blues performance.

Brown's career, as well as his personal life, botto[med] out one September day in 1988. Police in A[iken] County, South Carolina, had already experienc[ed a] number of run-ins with Brown, who owns a 60-[acre] spread on South Carolina's Beech Island. Brow[n's] fourth wife, Adrienne, had complained of beatin[gs.] There were high-speed police chases involvi[ng] Brown, and rumors abounded of his abuse of t[he] drug PCP and of big trouble with the IRS. O[n] September 24th Brown's problems boiled over whe[n] he allegedly burst into an insurance seminar bein[g] conducted next-door to his offices in Augusta, carry[-]ing a shotgun and accusing the participants of using his restrooms.

Police arrived on the scene. Brown jumped into his pickup truck and started back for South Carolina. The chase lasted ten miles. Police say they cornered Brown once, but that the singer tried to run several officers over in his truck. Shots were fired at Brown's truck before it finally crashed into a ditch and the singer was arrested. Brown's version, as told to *People* magazine, is quite different. "In reality, it was only a speeding ticket. All the other stuff was fabrication. Me and the policeman, he asked me to stop, and when I stopped, this deputy sheriff, we're sittin' there laughin' and talkin'—and then these other cats came up at the last minute. They must have thought I just stopped there, and they shot the truck. Almost killed the deputy sheriff."

Concluding from the six-year sentence in a work-release program Brown incurred, the judge who heard the case put more weight in the police version of events. Ironically, the singer was never more famous than in those dark days. He used the time in prison to get clean of whatever substances he may have been abusing, and spent a great deal of time working with children and the poor and elderly. It was a period during which he reflected on the value of education. "I want a mandatory law that each young kid must have a high-school education and at least two years of tech," Brown told *Interview*. "If you started today, then you would see the difference in about four or five years." Expanding on this crusade in *Spin*, Brown likened education to a commodity that must be sold like any other. "You produce [the desire for education] the same way you produce a desire for Coke or Pepsi Cola—you advertise it . . . . You got to put it in their minds. They

Robin Burns

President of Estee Lauder

Born c. 1953 in Colorado; raised in that state in Cripple Creek; mother's name, Bettina. *Education:* Graduated from Syracuse University, 1974.

Addresses: *Office*—c/o Estee Lauder, New York, NY.

Career

Worked with Bloomingdale's executive training program beginning in 1974; by 1982 had joined Calvin Klein marketing department; appointed president and CEO of Estee Lauder, 1990.

Sidelights

One of New York City's most powerful business-women has been described as a "frontier girl," and indeed Robin Burns spent her formative years in the wide-open spaces of Cripple Creek, Colorado. But the fiercely independent Burns, who has worked since age 13, was destined to rule the boardrooms.

Upon graduating from Syracuse University, Burns had initially considered teaching as a career, but found "the kids were great; the red tape was horrible," as she told Martha Duffy in *Time.* As Duffy continued: "In 1974 there was pressure to hire women, and blue-chip firms recruited aggressively on campus." Though Burns says that these Wall Street types turned her off, she did accept a position at "Bloomingdale's state-of-the-art executive training program and burned up the syllabus," said Duffy, quoting Burns's memory of the time: "I worked 10

hours a day, seven days a week, but it was exhilarating."

Burns got off to a fast start at Bloomies, first in window coverings—"They wanted to get more aggressively into imports, so here I am, 23 or 24, on an eight-week trip to Europe, India, Japan. I truly thought I'd gone to heaven"—then pillows and lamps. But, as Duffy noted, Burns's "globe-trotting ended and her big-time career began when she was promoted into fragrances. Bloomingdale's vice president...was [he said],'astonished at the way she could handle people older and more sophisticated than she was. She put issues in front of people and never let the meeting wander.'" In 1982 the Calvin Klein cosmetics line was a faltering concern; when that company recruited Burns, she engineered a virtual turnaround. Even people who never heard of the young executive have "certainly heard of Obsession and Eternity, the two perfumes she launched with consummate marketing strategy and blatantly sexy ad campaigns," according to Duffy. To Burns, the Obsession launch "remains the high point of her professional life," Duffy reported, adding that at Calvin Klein, a business previously plagued by "no marketing strategy, wretched relations with stores, and a disgusted muse, Klein himself," Burns brought "as usual...a team that was superenergized and fanatically devoted." Burns, according to her Klein successor Kim Delsing, "had the ability to let her mind go—What if we did this? What if? What if?"

By 1989, with the Calvin Klein company sold to Unilever Group, Burns found herself increasingly attracted by the offers by Leonard Lauder, the president of the 44-year-old Estee Lauder cosmetics firm, established by Leonard's mother. When Burns finally agreed to sign on with Lauder as CEO and president, her salary of $1.5 million per year makes her "probably the nation's highest-paid woman executive," Duffy says.

"This is an incredible opportunity in our industry," Burns told Daniel F. Cuff in a *New York Times* article. "It's almost like going for your Ph.D. This is an opportunity to run probably the greatest and largest company in the prestige-cosmetics industry. It's too intriguing for anyone to turn down." As *Adweek*'s Laura Bird reported, the feeling at Estee Lauder is mutual: "I've admired everything she's been involved with," says Leonard Lauder. "There wasn't a single thing she ever did that I disagreed with."

Part of Burns' success in New York City, her former Bloomingdale's boss told Duffy, comes from the fact that "she is not a New Yorker, and she doesn't have their brashness, aggression and hostility." But she does have boundless energy, fueled by "a crazy appetite for this business," says fellow executive Carol Phillips in the *Time* article. One of Burns's pals from the Syracuse University days told Duffy that once on a vacation on Antigua, "every day at 1 o'clock [Burns] would go into town and spend two or three hours on the phone with the office."

Sources

Adweek, January 15, 1990.
New York Times, January 12, 1990.
Time, August 6, 1990.

—Susan Salter

Susan Butcher

Sled dog racer and breeder

Born December 26, 1954, in Boston, Mass.; daughter of Charles and Agnes (Young) Butcher; married David Lee Monson.

Addresses: *Home and Office*—Trail Breaker Kennel, 1 Eureka, Eureka, Alaska 99756.

Career

Dog kennel owner, 1977—; sled dog racer, 1979—; second place, Iditarod Race, Nome and Anchorage, Alaska, 1982, 1984; champion, 1986-88, 1990; world record holder, 1986-88, 1990.

Member: Iditarod Trail Commission, Iditarod Trail Blazers, Beargrease Race Commission, Kuskokwim 300 Race Commission, Interior Dog Mushers Club, Nome Kennel Club, Norton Sound Sled Dog Club.

Sidelights

A four-time winner of the grueling Iditarod Trail Sled Dog Race—in which competitors drive their twelve-dog teams over 1,137 miles of Alaska's coldest, windiest, and most forbidding terrain—Susan Butcher has helped to smash the commonly held notion that men are superior to women in performing feats of endurance and courage. Thanks to her, the Iditarod race, held annually on a trail first used in 1925 to transport diphtheria serum from Anchorage to Nome, is no longer the obscure sporting event it was when it began in the 1970s. Indeed, Butcher is not even the first four-time winner of the Iditarod; that honor belongs to Rick Swenson of Alaska. But

AP/Wide World Photos

since Butcher first won the race in 1986, each successive spring brings more interest in the race and the hardy, happy, driven woman who has become the world's greatest sled dog racer. In Butcher's home state of Alaska, the champion dogsledder, or "musher," has created a whole new cottage industry. Over one million t-shirts bearing the logo "Alaska—Where Men Are Men and Women Win the Iditarod" have been sold since Butcher first won what Alaskans refer to as "The Last Great Race."

Although the race takes place under the harshest of circumstances, forcing the mushers to battle wind chill temperatures of 140 degrees below zero and fatigue that often brings on hallucinations, the majority of the work is done by the rugged Alaskan huskies themselves. The dogs must be powerful, with great endurance, and they must be trained from the time they are pups to perform harmoniously with the other members of a team. It is Butcher's uncanny ability to breed and train her dogs that most sled dog experts agree is her greatest gift. From her home in the remote, tiny hamlet of Eureka, Butcher operates her Trail Breaker Kennel, where she breeds and trains up to 150 dogs. The best will eventually become part of her team, while the others, still fine specimens, will be sold at prices ranging from $1,000 to $10,000 each.

Growing up in a troubled home in Cambridge, Massachusetts, Butcher withdrew from human contact as a child, preferring instead the company of the family dog. "I used to say: 'My mother can die, my father can die and my sister can die. But if my dog died, I'd be very unhappy,'" she told the *Los Angeles Times.* "I was born with a particular ability with animals and a particular love for them." She grew up, she added, as "an individualist . . . hard core, big time tomboy, a real gambler who took dangers fairly lightly." After moving to Colorado to be with her father, Butcher visited the ranch of a woman musher who owned 50 huskies. "Ten minutes later I moved in," she said in the *Los Angeles Times.* "I lived with her for a couple of years, worked as a veterinary technician and mushed and was frustrated by every minute of it." Seeking the challenge of the remote wilderness, where life's essentials would come more into focus, Butcher made her way to Alaska, where she soon found herself spending the winter in a cabin in the Wrangell Mountains with a male companion. Snowbound for months with little provisions, Butcher said she quickly abandoned her vegetarian past. "If you were going to eat meat, you shot it. You saw its death. You caused its death and you ate it and you survived because of its death," Butcher told the *Los Angeles Times.* "And you hauled all your own water and everything was dependent on you."

In 1977 Butcher moved to Eureka with the idea of building the kennel that would one day become the Trail Breaker. The first years were difficult and lonely, but then in 1979 Butcher embarked with Joe Reddington, founder of the Iditarod race, on a 44-day sled dog trek to the foot of Mt. McKinley. The journey brought public attention to Butcher and, more importantly, to her struggling business. Meanwhile, her breeding and training methods became increasingly refined, more focused on creating a powerful bond between herself and her dogs that would one day carry her to victory in the Iditarod. By 1982 she had finished as high as second, and as her male competitors began to feel Butcher at their heels, the inevitable name-calling (she became known as Ayatollah Butcher for her stubbornness and risk-taking on the trail) and accusations (they said her dogs were drugged) became louder and more insistent.

But Butcher kept racing—and winning. Her 1986 Iditarod victory was followed by wins in 1987, 1988, and 1990, when she broke her own course record by covering the desolate trail in 11 days, 1 hour, and 53 minutes. Her dominance in the sport has become so complete that, of six races she entered in the 1990 sled dog racing season, Butcher won four and finished second in the others—and she did it by racing *three* different teams of dogs, a fact that further frustrates her male competitors. But rather than worry about that, Butcher prefers to think of the positive role model she has become for women, even those Eskimo and Indian women whose towns she rolls through along the Iditarod trail. "I have become a symbol to women across the country—and internationally, in fact—and I'm not going to say that there wasn't a lot of strength gained by that thought and by the support [from women] that I got," Butcher told the *Los Angeles Times.* "The Eskimo women, the Indian women literally giving me the physical support of saying as I came through the villages: 'Do this for us.'"

Sources

Detroit Free Press, March 18, 1988.
Los Angeles Times, April 29, 1990.
Newsweek, March 26, 1990.
New York Times, March 14, 1986; March 19, 1987.
Time, March 28, 1988.

—David Collins

Nicolas Cage

Actor

Real name, Nicolas Coppola; born January 7, 1964, in Long Beach, Calif.; son of a college professor and a ballet dancer. *Education:* Studied acting at American Conservatory Theater.

Career

Actor in feature films, 1983—. Movies include *Rumble Fish,* 1983, *Valley Girl,* 1983, *The Cotton Club,* 1984, *Racing with the Moon,* 1984, *Birdy,* 1984, *Peggy Sue Got Married,* 1986, *Raising Arizona,* 1986, *Moonstruck,* 1988, *Vampire's Kiss,* 1989, *Fire Birds,* 1990, and *Wild at Heart,* 1990.

Sidelights

Few actors under the age of thirty command more respect than Nicolas Cage, star of a dozen films since 1983. With his soulful eyes and offbeat good looks, Cage can carry any romantic lead, but he is equally gifted at comedy and is not afraid to play the buffoon. Hard-to-please *New Yorker* critic Pauline Kael called Cage "a wonderful romantic clown" who is "slack-jawed and Neanderthal and passionate." Kael added that Cage "may be the only young actor who can look stupefied while he smolders. And no one can yearn like Cage: his head empties out— there's nothing there but sheepeyed yearning." That ability to "smolder"—to project a heightened sensuality—has made Cage a top draw at the box office. Still he has resisted typecasting more successfully than any other star of his generation. *American Film* contributor Mark Rowland noted: "There aren't

many (any?)...actors with a resume this solid....[Cage] is a character actor whose presence is frequently so powerful, it becomes part of the film's signature. The movies, meanwhile, provide their own clues about Cage." *Los Angeles Times* correspondent Michael Wilmington sees Cage as a "great, elastic, soulful prankster, twisting himself endlessly into outlandish shapes....He may be the most playful and goofily inventive of young American movie leading men right now."

"Nicolas Cage" is in fact a stage name, appropriated to replace a more famous surname. Cage was born Nicolas Coppola in Long Beach, California, and is the nephew of director Francis Ford Coppola. As a youngster Cage lived with his two brothers in a middle-class home in Long Beach. His father was a college professor, so he was raised in an atmosphere of culture and serious study. His own serious nature occasionally exploded in a childhood prank—once he served egg salad with fried grasshoppers in it to his elementary school class. Cage told the *Los Angeles Times:* "As a child in Long Beach, I spent a lot of time pretending I was other people. I was into the whole concept of trying to disguise myself."

That fascination with fantasy and disguise continued as Cage grew older. When he was twelve, his parents divorced and his father moved the family to the outskirts of Beverly Hills. Cage attended high school at Beverly Hills High and remembers being shy with girls because he was not wealthy. His interest in acting was further heightened after seeing the film *East of Eden* in an old revival theater in Los Angeles. "It was the scene with James Dean breaking down in front of his father when he wouldn't accept the money," Cage remembered in *American Film*. "It really devastated me. That's when I thought, 'Yeah, I want to do *that*.'" At first glance it might seem a stroke of luck for a young would-be actor to have a famous uncle in the movie business. Indeed, Francis Ford Coppola was instrumental in bringing Cage to the screen, first in *Rumble Fish* (1983) and then in *The Cotton Club* (1984). Cage admits that he has learned a great deal from working with his uncle, but he realized that the name Coppola posed limitations for him as well. After giving it careful thought, he changed his name from Nicolas Coppola to Nicolas Cage, taking the surname of two of his heroes—comic book character Luke Cage and avant-garde composer John Cage. The actor explained in the *Los Angeles Times*: "When I first started going to auditions and was still using my real name, it was obvious that people were thinking about 20 years of someone else's history. I wanted to be able to go into an office and just do what I had to do, so I took the name Cage, and the first audition I did under that name was the best audition I'd ever had. That told me I'd done the right thing."

> "Cage's romanticism is his most attractive quality. Like the young Jimmy Stewart, he is unafraid of showing desire and passion on screen."

One of the first auditions Cage undertook with his new name was for a low-budget teen film called *Valley Girl*. Cage won the lead in the 1983 movie about a rich suburban girl who falls in love with a punk from Hollywood High. As the rough but tender Randy, Cage managed to pull the film from obscurity—most critics singled out his performance as the saving grace of the otherwise insubstantial movie. *Valley Girl* made Cage a star almost overnight. Offers for other film work came pouring in, and he chose only those that offered him a chance to stretch his talents. To quote Wilmington, "there's been something bracingly nutty about Cage's roles ever since."

Cage drew strong notices for his work as a psychotic hoodlum in his uncle's film *The Cotton Club* and for his role as a self-centered cad in *Racing with the Moon*. His best-known early performance, however, is his portrayal of a disfigured Vietnam veteran in *Birdy*. The film concerns the reaction of two young men to the horrors of war; Cage had to play many of his scenes with his face swathed in bandages. Although Cage would eventually come to call his performance in the film "emotional vomit," *Birdy* won the Jury prize at the Cannes Film Festival. Cage's deft interpretation of a demanding character proved, in Wilmington's words, that "he could do primal-man roles with the best of them."

At that point it seemed likely that Cage would opt for standard leading-man fare. Instead he took two daring comic roles that made a mockery of his sex appeal. In *Peggy Sue Got Married* (1986), he appeared as Charlie Bodell, a philandering huckster with few social graces, and in *Raising Arizona* (1986) he portrayed a luckless lowlife who steals a baby for his desperate, barren wife to raise. Kael called *Raising Arizona* a "monkeyshines burlesque" that revealed Cage "at his most winning." The critic commented: "Actors have made big reputations as farceurs on less talent than Cage shows here; his slapstick droopiness holds it all together."

In 1987 Cage won a role in the comedy-drama *Moonstruck*, a tale of May-September romance set in Brooklyn. As a finished work, *Moonstruck* is an ensemble performance of high quality, and Cage holds up his end as a romantic and dissatisfied baker who falls for his brother's fiancee. Wilmington wrote: "Cage's romanticism is his most attractive quality. Like the young Jimmy Stewart, he is unafraid of showing desire and passion on screen—and he doesn't mind looking nerdy or grotesque doing it. In *Moonstruck*, when, after a series of outrageous, self-pitying tantrums, he rises to confront his brother's fiancee (Cher) and then sweepingly tosses the table outside, grasps her in a ravenous clinch and carries her off to the bedroom, it's an ultimate post-Stanley Kowalski joke—and both Cage and Cher delightfully let us all in on it." Needless to say, his role in *Moonstruck* further endeared Cage to a legion of female fans.

Cage acknowledges that he is still learning his craft and that his earliest work could have been better. Wilmington has said that the actor has refined his style over time, sweetened it, and opened it out, showing "he can suggest the many opposing forces (good/evil, dark/light, hot/cold) that can beat within a single wild breast." Rowland concluded: "Nicolas Cage is not the star we expected, not from his generation, not in this day and age. Somebody forgot to blow-dry his hair, and the cowlick ended up in front. Somebody forgot to tell him that irony is hip, passion passe. Somebody forgot to smooth out that walk and that talk. Kathleen Turner had it right the first time in *Peggy Sue Got Married*—this guy is not the one. She had it right the second time, too. He is the one."

Cage's romantic air and rough exterior made him a perfect choice for the lead in the 1990 David Lynch film *Wild at Heart*. A twisted version of the all-American road movie, *Wild at Heart* follows the gothic/romantic adventures of Sailor Ripley and his sweetheart, Lula Pace Fortune. Wilmington called Cage's work in the movie "the latest in his recent string of ingenious, double-jointed performances.... He displays the lizard-lidded '50s cool of a rock 'n' roll rebel, murmuring lines in a smoky pastiche of Elvis' melodically gutteral, macho purr.... It's a multilayered turn with separate coatings of parody, pop tribute and poetic in-joke—and he delivers it with the lazy spontaneity of a Tupelo savage midwifed by a black leather jukebox out of a Chevy. It's a triumph.... And it may signal Cage's emergence as the ace—or, at the very least, joker—of his acting generation."

Wild at Heart garnered numerous honors at Cannes; prior to its American opening, it received a great deal of media attention for its bizarre, violent scenes, much as Lynch's television series *Twin Peaks* did when it was first broadcast in the summer of 1990. The film brought mixed—but by no means ambivalent—reviews; those who saw it either loved it or hated it. In any case, *Wild at Heart* did not fare as well as expected at the box office, and the hype that had preceded its debut died down quickly.

Cage, however, continues to sizzle. The common thread that unites all of his film work is his ability to portray—for laughs or thrills—a Romantic Man. As Rowland put it, in all his films Cage "pursues his loves with a resoluteness worthy of *Wuthering Heights*." One of the hardest-working actors in Hollywood, Cage admits that he can become consumed by romance—either in his personal life or in his films. "I really don't like working without some attachment to somebody," he told *American Film*. "It's all the trials and tribulations that get me wanting to do something. In fact, it's love that inspires me."

If Cage is inspired by love, it is not necessarily the easy, happy-ending variety that attracts him. In almost all of his films he portrays someone who reaches beyond his station for a seemingly impossible love and winds up paying all sorts of absurd or horrific consequences for daring to express himself. Even his funniest roles hint of the darker side of life, or as Wilmington termed it, "the beast in all of us." Cage told *American Film*: "I guess it's all open as to what's entertaining and what's not. I'm just more entertained with something that would give you bad dreams."

Cage regularly makes as many as three feature films each year. What little spare time he has is spent primarily in Los Angeles and San Francisco. Cage is unmarried and extremely reticent about his personal life. He told the *Los Angeles Times*: "I ... believe that an actor is someone you see playing a character and there's a danger in revealing too much about yourself because that gets in the way of whatever illusion you're trying to create on film." The actor is not so secretive about his success, however. He told *Playboy* that he is thrilled with the directions his career has taken and is excited about future projects. "I don't like it when people on the street say 'Smile' or 'Cheer up,'" he said. "It's a real cheap line. I'm feeling good. I'm feeling real grateful for everything. It's a solid time in my life. When people say I look sad, they're wrong."

Sources

American Film, June 1989; June 1990.
Los Angeles Times, February 21, 1988; August 12, 1990.
Maclean's, May 28, 1990.
New Yorker, April 20, 1987; January 25, 1988.
New York Times, March 23, 1984; December 23, 1984; October 5, 1986; June 2, 1989.
Playboy, June 1989.

—Anne Janette Johnson

Jane Campion

AP/Wide World Photos

Film and television director

Born in Wellington, New Zealand; daughter of Richard (a director) and Edith (an actress) Campion. *Education:* Attended art school in London and the Australian Film, Television, and Radio School.

Addresses: *Home*—Sydney, Australia.

Career

Attended art school in London before transferring to Australian Film, Television, and Radio School; directed *2 Friends* for Australian television, 1985; released first feature film, *Sweetie,* 1989; other films include *An Angel at My Table,* a miniseries for Australian television later released as a feature film, and *The Piano Lesson,* in progress.

Awards: Palme d'Or for best short film for *Peel,* at Cannes Film Festival, 1986; *An Angel at My Table* received seven prizes at the Venice Film Festival, c. 1991.

Sidelights

An offbeat young director from the Down Under, New Zealand-born Jane Campion arrived on the artfilm scene with resounding success in the late 1980s with two noteworthy debuts at the Cannes film festival. Her nine-minute short, *Peel,* won the Palme d'Or for Best Short Film at Cannes in 1986, and in 1989 her first feature-length film, *Sweetie,* made an equally strong impression on the stuffy Cannes audience. Actually, *Sweetie* was booed lustily

at its first international screening, but in artfilm circles a strongly negative reaction is infinitely more desirable than no reaction at all; the film has since come to be recognized as a minor masterpiece.

Focusing on a quirky, dysfunctional, middle-class Australian family, *Sweetie*'s protagonist is Kay, a depressed, repressed woman who is troubled by vague phobias dating back to her childhood, including a mysterious fear of trees. Bursting back into her life one day is her younger sister, nicknamed "Sweetie," and the audience soon learns the source of much of Kay's neurosis. "Sweetie is your nightmare of a sibling," wrote Carla Hall in the *Washington Post.* "She's a mess—she's fat, belligerent and bawdy. Emotionally unstable, she ricochets from violent overgrown child to lovable unschooled ham, obsessed with the idea that one day she will be a rock singer." Next to arrive on the scene is the girls' father, who has just been dumped by their mother. The rest of the film probes—in a troubling, sometimes grotesque, but nonetheless sympathetic manner—the interactions between the family members. "I'm interested in the transference between members of families, the way they compensate for each other and create the whole," Campion told *Premiere.*

Born in the New Zealand city of Wellington, Campion found herself lonely and uninspired as an art student in London, where she escaped her sorrows by slipping into movie houses. "I lived in a fog until I was about 25," Campion told the *Washington Post.* "I'm not a fast developer, and I just couldn't figure out what I was supposed to be doing; how to make my life more interesting." A short film she made at the school, however, entitled *Tissues,* was a great hit with her classmates and encouraged Campion to enroll in the Australian Film, Television, and Radio School. In the more stimulating environment of film school, Campion blossomed into a hardworking student and became enraptured with the works of surrealists like Luis Bunuel. "I just died when I saw his films," she said in the *New York Times.* "I thought, 'This guy is so wicked; I can't believe he's so naughty.'" Surrounded by more ambitious, male classmates, Campion still felt like an underachiever. "They . . . wanted to make big, exploitative movies immediately," she recalled in *Premiere.* "'Get the big Panavision camera, and we'll get the crane.' They thought they were on to something." But Campion timidly clung to her instinct that film can be simpler than that. "In the end, film is storytelling and communicating, and thoughts and characters, and that's what you have to have a feeling for," she continued. "People don't communicate with Elemack crane shots."

After her shorts were such a smash at Cannes in 1986, Campion sought funding for *Sweetie,* which eventually came in the amount of $1.3 million, a modest amount by Hollywood standards. Still, "I hyperventilated for a week when I heard I got the money," Campion said in the *Washington Post.* She saved money by co-writing the script and casting the movie herself, and though the oddly disjointed, quixotic, graphically imagistic final product left many viewers cold initially, *Sweetie* enjoyed wide critical success. "It is Miss Campion's gift to be able to record the commonplace in a way to make it seem as alien as life on another planet," wrote Vincent Canby in the *New York Times.* "Everything is strange. Nothing is taken for granted. She appreciates the precarious nature of our existence."

After *Sweetie* Campion made a conscious decision to try some more conventional projects. Her next effort was *An Angel at My Table,* a three-hour miniseries for Australian television which depicts the life of renowned New Zealand poet and novelist Janet Frame. After urgent prodding, Campion was convinced to release the miniseries as two and one-half hour feature film that claimed success at several international festivals and drew critical raves when released for general audiences in the summer of 1991. She then planned to start work on *The Piano Lesson,* a period piece in the true romantic tradition.

Sources

New York Times, January 14, 1990; February 4, 1990; May 19, 1991.
Mirabella, February 1990.
Premiere, February 1990, March 1990.
Washington Post, March 4, 1990.

—David Collins

Jennifer Capriati

AP/Wide World Photos

Professional tennis player

Born March 29, 1976, in Long Island, N.Y.; daughter of Stefano (a tennis pro) and Denise (a flight attendant). *Education:* Attending Palmer Academy, Wesley Chapel, Fla.

Career

Professional tennis player, 1990—.

Addresses: *Home*—c/o Saddlebrook Resort, Wesley Chapel, Fla.

Sidelights

In March of 1990, at only age 13, fresh-faced, black-haired Jennifer Capriati turned pro on the cutthroat women's professional tennis circuit. "Even though I'm going to be playing older ladies, when I'm out there playing, I'm as old as they are," she told the *New York Times*. "I have no fear. I guess I was just born with that kind of mind." And that kind of talent.

Capriati, the youngest tennis player ever to turn pro, was met with overwhelming expectations from both the tennis world and the public upon her debut at the Virginia Slims tournament in Boca Raton, Florida. The pressure was not just for her potential in tennis, but for her potential as the best charismatic draw for the U.S. women's circuit since Chris Evert. Headlines trumpeted Capriati as the "Teen Queen of Tennis," "Eighth Grade Wonder," and "The Next Chris Evert." Her own coach, Tom Gullikson of the U.S.

Tennis Association, said flatly to a *Los Angeles Times* reporter, "It's our viewpoint that [Capriati] is without question the most talented young pro in the world, man or woman." Interviewers scrounged for details of her life—she was five-foot-seven, 130 pounds, shoe size 8 1/2. Her favorite rap song: "Bust A Move." Favorite foods: hamburgers, chips, hot fudge sundaes. Favorite movie star: Johnny Depp. Favorite color: pink. Favorite pet: the family Shih Tzu, Bianca.

Meanwhile, the cool Capriati just hoped she wouldn't look "dorky" on television, and she told the *Los Angeles Times* she'd like to be remembered this way: "I'd like, you know, when I retire, like, you know, when I go down the street, people would say, 'There's Jennifer Capriati, the greatest tennis player who ever lived.'" The concept of a young, pretty teenager who could sigh over Twizzlers licorice, white leather mini skirts, and the baby on the TV show *The Simpsons*, while also blasting her way to the top of the tennis circuit, ignited thousands of new Capriati fans. One magazine writer wondered whether people wanted to see history in the making or really just had a weird fascination with seeing a player who might be a flash in the pan, used up, and burnt out by age 21. But those future anxieties were blotted out by the sheer talent and exuberance of Capriati's early play. In her first match she knocked off four seeded players and advanced to the finals before being beaten by Argentina's Gabriela Sabatini on March 11. With every later tournament, she showed her raw, powerful talent with booming ground strokes, a 94 m.p.h. overhead serve, and cool nerves that belied her young age.

In April, she reached the finals of the Family Circle Magazine Hilton Head Cup, finally losing to Martina Navratilova. Capriati was delighted, still, just to be there; she called Navratilova "a lege, you know, like, a legend." In June, seeded No. 17, she reached the quarterfinals of the French Open before she was beaten by No. 1 Monica Seles of Yugoslavia. In July, she made it to the quarterfinals of Wimbledon, ranked No. 12, before losing to Germany's Steffi Graff. On July 16, she won her first professional title, at the Mount Cranmore International tournament in New Hampshire. In August, she got beat in the early rounds at the U.S. Open, where she was ranked 16th. In September, as sixth seed, she made it to the quarterfinals of the Nichirei International Tennis Championship in Tokyo.

She hoped to make the New York Virginia Slims tournament in November. Though she didn't win any big matches, many believed Capriati had set the stage for her advancement to the pinnacle of women's tennis. It was a climb she was groomed for from infancy.

Jennifer Capriati was born in 1976 on Long Island, New York, to Stefano and Denise Capriati. Her Bronx-born mother, who is a Pan Am flight attendant, met her father in Spain in 1972. Stefano Capriati, a native of Milan, Italy, was a resident of Spain, where he was a movie stuntman and a self-taught tennis pro. They married and settled in Spain. Stefano Capriati knew Jennifer would be a tennis player when she was still in the womb, says Denise Capriati, who played recreational tennis until the day she went into labor with Jennifer. "Stefano knew she would be a tennis player . . . just by the way I carried her," she told *Sports Illustrated*. They moved to New York so Jennifer could be born in the United States, then moved back to Spain. Another child, Steven, was born three years later.

When Jennifer was a baby, her father did cribside calisthenics, propping her backside with a pillow and helping her do situps. When she was four years old, the family moved to Fort Lauderdale, Florida, to further Jennifer's tennis. By then, she could hold her own with a ball machine. "Already she could rally a hundred times on the court," her father said. He took her to see Jimmy Evert, tennis star Chris Evert's father. Evert did not want to even meet her since she

was only four, but when he saw her skill he agreed to take her as a student. He coached her from age four to age nine. Along the way, Jennifer became friends with Chris Evert. In 1987, the tennis star gave Jennifer a Christmas bracelet that reads, "Jennifer, Love Chris" that Jennifer Capriati wears in all her matches.

> *"When I'm on the court, I just block out everything I'm thinking about and bring out my tennis stuff. When I'm off, I'm just a kid."*

From age 10 to 13, Jennifer was coached by Rick Macci in Haines City, Florida, then went to the Hopman Tennis Academy at Saddlebrook resort in Wesley Chapel, where she got a third coach, Tom Gullickson. But the driving force in her budding career was her father, whom she called her main coach and whom the other members of her entourage called "the main boss." Stefano Capriati considers himself a tennis father, in the best sense of the term, noting that there is a difference between pushing and aiding. "You try to direct her in the right way, and you see she has the potential," he told the *Los Angeles Times*. "I see she enjoys it. After 9-10 years old, you cannot direct them anymore. They must want it."

As a junior tennis player, Jennifer wanted it. She ate up the competition. In 1988 at age 12, she won the U.S. 18-and-under championships on both hard and clay courts. In 1989 she won the 18-and-under French Open, made the quarterfinals at Wimbledon, and won the junior title at the U.S. Open. The rules said girls under 14 could not turn pro, but in 1989, her father, coaches, and tennis boosters thought she was ready. "People say she's only 13, but they miss the point. She's already put in 10 years," said tennis legend Billie Jean King, Jennifer's sometimes-doubles partner. "I'm telling you," said her former coach, Rick Macci, in *Sports Illustrated*. "She's scary."

The United States Tennis Federation was stubborn. It would not allow Jennifer to play until the month of her 14th birthday. Her father thought about challenging the rule in court, then changed his mind. Already, Jennifer Capriati was getting lucrative endorsement contracts. The Italian sportswear maker

Diadora of Caerano Di San Marco gave her $3 million to endorse their line and Prince gave her $1 million to endorse their tennis rackets. Later in the year, she made a commercial for Oil of Olay face cream. "First, immortality, then the SATs," joked *Newsweek*. But it was no joke: before even turning pro, Capriati was the third highest endorsed tennis player behind Chris Evert and Martina Navratilova. John Evert, Chris Evert's brother, became Capriati's business manager.

In between the relentless pace of tennis, Jennifer Capriati went through eighth grade at Palmer Academy in Wesley Chapel. When she couldn't go to school, she'd take her homework with her or have it sent to her on the road by fax machine. By March when she went pro, she still had to do homework in between matches. In September she started ninth grade at St. Andrew's School in Boca Raton, a 600-student private school. She was prepared to leave the Harry Hopman tennis facility of Saddlebrook and was offered a contract as touring pro at the Broken Sound Club in Boca Raton. But later that month, her parents changed their minds.

Uncomfortable in a temporary home in Boca Raton, the Capriatis went back to Saddlebrook and Jennifer returned to the Palmer Academy, where she had attended eighth grade. The family intended to move to Broken Sound in January, then realized it would be better to remain at Saddlebrook. "There is life besides tennis," said Denise Capriati. "Jennifer was so happy to see her friends again. Jennifer's emotional happiness is the bottom line."

Also in September, ranked 12th in the world, Jennifer traveled to Tokyo for the Nichirei tennis championship. The remainder of the year she planned to do an exhibition match for former first lady Nancy Reagan, one for Chris Evert, and then hoped to make the Virginia Slims Championships in New York in November. The pace was grueling, but her spirits were high. "I feel like a kid, kidwise. But tenniswise, I feel I guess I have talent, I guess," she told the *Los Angeles Times*. "When I'm on the court, I just block out everything I'm thinking about and bring out my tennis stuff. When I'm off, I'm just a kid."

Her tennis stuff continued to wow observers. One coach praised her aggressive style, unpredictability, and power: "She was strong before, but her movement wasn't very good. Now she covers the court as well as any of the men I can think of," said Tommy Thompson, head tennis pro at Saddlebrook, to the *New York Times*. "She's going to be different than most women, who tend to play very defensively, because she's very confident at net. She has no fear when she's going in there to volley. Said Thompson later in the *Washington Post*, "She's a kid off the court but a killer on it."

Whether the kid can continue life as a killer on the court without becoming overwhelmed is the question many had as her first six months on the circuit ended. While Capriati appeared to have a solid head on her shoulders, there were the inevitable comparisons with Andrea Jaeger and Tracy Austin, both of whom started tennis as young sensations but burned out from injuries and pressure. Jaeger won her first pro tournament at 14 but left the tour at 19 because of shoulder injuries. Austin, at 16, was the youngest player ever to win the U.S. Open, in 1979, but foot and back injuries sidelined her permanently at age 19. When asked about this by interviewers, Capriati sighs and replies wearily. "It's like, you know, it's not my fault," she says of Jaeger's and Austin's short-lived careers in the *Los Angeles Times*. "Why does everybody think it's going to happen to me? How do they know what my limit is?"

She would rather be compared to Chris Evert, who began tennis at 16 and finally left gracefully at 34. Or to Martina Navratilova, who is still is at top form in her thirties. Capriati says she plans to play to age 35, then quit. The experts wish her well, but keep their fingers crossed. "For every prospect that pans out, several get plowed under," is how one writer put it. In her first year of pro tennis, Capriati glittered and panned out like gold. Jimmy Evert predicted that by 1991, she would be among the world's top 10 women tennis players.

Sources

Detroit Free Press, June 6, 1990; June 8, 1990; June 30, 1990; July 3, 1990; July 16, 1990; August 31, 1990; September 4, 1990; September 14, 1990.
Fort Lauderdale News and Sun-Sentinel, September 16, 1990; September 25, 1990.
Los Angeles Times, May 27, 1990.
New York Times, March 5, 1990; May 20, 1990.
Newsweek, May 14, 1990.
Sports Illustrated, February 26, 1990: March 19, 1990; April 16, 1990.
Time, March 26, 1990.

—Ellen Creager

Mariah Carey

AP/Wide World Photos

Pop singer and songwriter

Born c. 1970; daughter of a vocal coach and former opera singer.

Addresses: *Record company*—Columbia/CBS Records, 51 West 52nd St., New York, NY 10019.

Career

Worked as a waitress and a back-up singer, c. 1987. Recording artist, 1988—.

Awards: Grammy Award for best new artist of 1990.

Sidelights

Pop vocalist and songwriter Mariah Carey set the music world ablaze when her self-titled debut album was released in 1990. Featuring the hit single "Vision of Love," the disc provoked critics to rave over Carey's seven-octave vocal range and gospel-toned voice. She has been compared to the late pop soprano Minnie Riperton, the Peruvian singer Yma Sumac, and, most often, to superstar Whitney Houston. As reviewer Ralph Novak asserted in *People*, Carey "sings with extraordinary control, driving power, lovely pitch, and wide range."

Carey was born to a mother who had sung with the New York City Opera and remained a vocal coach throughout Carey's childhood. Her mother influenced Carey a great deal, the singer revealed in *Seventeen*. "I knew from watching and listening to my mom that singing could and would be my profession." She recounted further that her mother

"had to tear me away from the radio each night just to get me to go to sleep." Carey also enjoyed listening to the record collection of her older brother and sister, especially those albums by such artists as Gladys Knight, Aretha Franklin, and Stevie Wonder.

When Carey was 17, she left her family home on Long Island, New York, to live in New York City. She shared rent with another aspiring musician, and waited on tables to earn her living while making demo tapes of her own songs to give to music executives. Carey eventually got a job as a back-up singer for a small record label. One of the vocalists she sang for, Brenda K. Starr, was sufficiently impressed with her abilities to introduce her at a party to Tommy Mottola of Columbia Records. At Starr's insistence, Carey gave him one of her demo tapes; Mottola listened to it in his car on the way home and called Carey to sign her the next day.

Carey worked on recording her debut album for the next two years. By the time she was twenty, *Mariah Carey* was released. Carey co-wrote and arranged all of the songs on the album, though critics have not been impressed by her non-vocal efforts. Novak called the tunes "uniformly forgettable, both melodically and lyrically"; Alanna Nash of *Stereo Review* commented that "none of the ten songs sticks in the mind." Nevertheless, Carey's single "Vision of Love" raced up the pop and adult contemporary charts, reaching number one. And she gained further exposure on national television by singing "America, the Beautiful" before the first game of the National Basketball Association finals at the Auburn Hills Palace in Michigan. Carey's debut album also contained the tracks "Someday" and "There's Got to Be a Way," which Nash described as "social-consciousness raising."

But "what you remember" about Carey, according to David Gates of *Newsweek*, "is the voice—all seven octaves or so of it, from purring alto to stratospheric shriek." Likewise, in spite of her criticisms of Carey's songwriting, Nash affirmed that *Mariah Carey* "is as exhilarating as a ride on the World's Tallest Roller Coaster." Amusement parks came to the mind of a *Seventeen* reporter as well, who noted that the "lissome diva carries the listener away on a riveting...roller coaster of sound." Not surprisingly, in light of such comments, Carey's efforts on the album

garnered her a Grammy Award for best new artist of 1990. As Novak concluded, "she is just about a lock to become pop music's biggest sensation since Whitney Houston."

Selected discography

Mariah Carey (includes "Vision of Love," "There's Got to Be a Way," "I Don't Wanna Cry," "Someday," "Vanishing," and "All in Your Mind"), Columbia, 1990.

Sources

Glamour, October 1990.
Newsweek, August 6, 1990.
People, July 16, 1990.
Rolling Stone, August 23, 1990.
Seventeen, October 1990.
Stereo Review, October 1990.

—*Elizabeth Wenning*

Fidel Castro

Reuters/Bettmann Newsphotos

Head of State of Cuba

Full name, Fidel Ruz Castro; born August 13, 1926, in Mayari, Oriente province, Cuba; son of Angel Castro y Argiz (a sugarcane planter) and Lina Ruz Gonzalez de Castro (a homemaker); married Mirta Diaz-Bilart, October 12, 1948 (divorced, 1955); children: Fidel. *Education:* University of Havana, doctor of laws, 1950.

Addresses: *Office*—Office of the President, Palacia del Gobierno, Havana, Cuba.

Career

Student leader at the University of Havana, 1945-50; founding member of Partido del Pueblo Cubano (Ortodoxos) in Havana, 1947; private practice of law in Havana, 1950-53; initiated armed rebellion against the Fulgencio Batista dictatorship by leading attack on Moncada army barracks in Santiago de Cuba, July 26, 1953; imprisoned in Santiago de Cuba, 1953-55; organized Cuban rebel force in Mexico, 1955-56, and landed force in December, 1956; commander-in-chief of the 26th of July Movement rebel army, Cuba, 1957-76; prime minister of Cuba, 1959-76; first secretary of the Cuban Communist Party and chairman of Agrarian Reform Institute, 1965—; head of state and president of Council of State and Council of Ministers of Cuba, 1976—.

Awards: Lenin Peace Prize, 1961, Hero of the Soviet Union award, 1963, Order of Lenin, 1972, and Order of the October Revolution, 1976, all from the U.S.S.R.; Somali Order (first class), 1977; Order of Jamaica, 1977; Dimitrov Prize from the People's Republic of Bulgaria, 1980; Gold Star from the Socialist Republic of Vietnam, 1982.

Sidelights

In the 1950s, Fidel Castro led the Cuban revolution that evolved into the Western hemisphere's introduction to Communism. Decades later, the powerful speaker still favors olive drab fatigues and a nearly all-white bushy beard. But even though this nationalist hero continues to have loyal followers, there is a spirit of unrest in his island country. The dramatic political changes in the Soviet bloc have adversely affected his regime.

In the late 1980s, Castro did not go along with Soviet leader Mikhail Gorbachev's reforms, known internationally as *perestroika*. According to *Time* magazine, these changes represented "warmed over capitalism" to Castro. The Cuban leader asserted in another *Time* article that "Nobody should dream that we are going toward capitalism." As Charles Lane put it in *Newsweek*, Castro "is defending what might be called the last bastion of Brezhnevism."

The Cuban economy has paid a high price for Castro's deteriorating relationship with the Soviet Union. Severe economic problems at home have also forced the Soviets to reassess subsidies to Cuba. The result was a reduction of the $5 billion per year given to that country in the form of aid and trade. And the U.S.S.R. insisted on hard currency, i.e., dollars, to replace bartering.

With only a reported 40 to 87 million dollars of hard currency in reserves in 1990 (reports vary), Castro was strapped for funds. He came up with a plan for his government to become more self-sufficient by saving energy and food. He cut back on production and reverted to using animals in the fields instead of tractors. Then he stepped up trade with China to about $500 million in 1990. And he sold Cuban-made vaccines to Brazil. Castro also laid the groundwork for promoting tourism from Canada and Europe, his only bow to capitalism.

Partly because of Castro's economic cutbacks, enthusiasm for the revolutionary and his ideology has waned among many of the people of Cuba. They are faced with the reality of shortages of almost everything but the barest of life's necessities. It is difficult to find toilet paper, bread, flour, razor blades, TV sets, and toothpaste, for example. And because of inefficiencies within the government, even tropical fruits and vegetables are hard to come by. A refrigerator manufactured in the East goes for the annual wage of an average Cuban: $2,000. And $500 will buy a Sanyo fan with a market value of $35 elsewhere. Long lines weave toward stores offering government surplus goods. People reportedly wait for as long as fifteen hours to purchase available items.

When Castro first came into power officially in 1959, he did bring about significant changes for the better. For one thing, food was rationed so that no one would go hungry. For another, everyone's rent was given a ceiling of 10 percent of the renter's income. That translated to about $10.00 per month even in the 1980s. Blacks and women have benefited from the stringent anti-discrimination laws. And Castro has kept infectious diseases at bay with his excellent free health care system. He also raised the literacy rate to a world-class 96 percent.

Castro grew up on his father's sugar cane plantation in Cuba's eastern province of Oriente. The elder Castro had earlier been a poor immigrant from Spain who married Fidel's mother sometime after the boy's birth. Determined to become educated at a time when formal schooling was accorded only to a select few, the strong-minded Fidel warned his parents he would burn down the house if they didn't let him have his way. The threat apparently worked, because he was able to attend a Christian Brothers elementary school and Jesuit junior and senior high schools. The younger Castro's considerable ambition and abilities took him through college to earn a doctoral degree in law at the University of Havana.

An active student political leader while at the university, Castro was still able to maintain high grades. This could not have been an easy task, considering the danger involved in campus politics in the 1940s. He carried a pistol, and thwarted various attempts on his life. Castro has described these years as more dangerous than later, when he fought as a guerrilla leader. His speaking gifts and personal magnetism won over the law student organization. Even then he was given to rousing speeches, many of which are in print.

In 1950 Castro went into a private law practice in Havana. There he was known to represent the poor and working-class—sometimes at no charge. Two years later, he ran for Congress until Fulgencio Batista changed the political climate by overthrowing the government in a coup. Castro attempted to oust Batista through legal measures, but was unsuccessful.

On July 26, 1953, the young revolutionary led a group of 165 rebels against dictator Fulgencio Batista. They attacked the Moncada barracks outside of the Oriente province capitol of Santiago de Cuba, hoping to arouse civil unrest. The plan did not work, but Castro was hailed by the masses for his bravery. He escaped execution only because the officer who arrested him was someone he'd known at the university. He was incarcerated in Isle of Pines prison until political amnesty was granted him in May of 1955.

Then in December of 1956, Castro, along with his brother Raul, led 82 guerrillas to the Sierra Maestra mountains on another dangerous mission against Batista, named the 26th of July Movement, commemorating the Moncada attack. This time, the insurgents received training in war tactics in Mexico and were supported financially by Carlos Prio Socarras, president in exile. Ernesto "Che" Guevara, the Argentine doctor and famous revolutionary, accompanied Castro and the other rebels on the yacht *Granma*. Soon after landing on Cuban soil, 52 of the fighters were killed by Batista's army. But Castro, his brother, and Guevara were among those who made it to the mountains, from which they launched their guerrilla insurgency against the corrupt ruler. On January 1, 1959, Batista was driven into exile by Castro's forces. Castro became Cuba's prime minister.

According to K. S. Karol in the *New Republic,* Castro did not have plans for a communistic Cuba in the late 1950s. Instead, it appeared that his "aim was to secure at last Cuba's full sovereignty with the help of the *humildes,* all those who suffered under a thinly disguised colonial regime imposed by the United States." At that time, the U.S. government could have been secretly intent on "toppling the barely established government in Cuba," put forth Karol. In January of 1961 diplomatic relations were broken between the two countries. The Bay of Pigs invasion followed that year, with CIA-trained Cuban exiles attempting, but failing, to overthrow Castro. An export embargo was then imposed by the U.S. in 1962. In the fall of that year, U.S. intelligence learned nuclear warheads from the Soviet Union had been taken to Cuba. The Soviets took back the missiles after President Kennedy sounded a serious warning.

Castro's relationship with the Soviet Union was far more promising than with the United States. It developed further when he endeavored to industrialize Cuba and free it from dependency on sugar sales. The United States had imposed economic sanctions against Cuba, so it was logical for Castro to turn to COMECON, the now-defunct Soviet-run trade group. The U.S.S.R. accepted Cuba, but as a principle sugar producer, with Soviet-built processing facilities. In return, Castro received annual aid and oil to resell on the world market at a profit. Under Soviet leader Leonid Brezhnev, these subsidies were considered cost-effective because of Cuba's strategic mili-

tary location in the West—it is just 90 miles off the coast of Florida.

How long Castro will stay in power remains to be seen. There has been much speculation and analysis in the media in the early 1990s. On the one hand, the Cuban leader runs the country as a police state. He and his brother Raul, who commands the armed forces, have quelled internal rebellion thus far. But in 1989 Cuba's human rights record had dropped alarmingly. Chris Lane observed in *Newsweek,* "In once admiring Latin America, Castro is increasingly compared, not to Simon Bolivar, the liberator he sought to emulate, but to Romania's Nicolae Ceaucescu." On the other hand, unlike Ceaucescu, Castro keeps in touch with the people and remains a nationalist hero to many. Even a detractor of the Cuban government remarked in *Time:* "The Bearded One is a good man. He understands everything. But the people around him are no good."

Sources

The Nation, May 9, 1987.
National Review, March 5, 1990.
The New Republic, January 19, 1987.
Newsweek, January 9, 1989; March 26, 1990; April 30, 1990; August 6, 1990.
Time, September 21, 1987; September 4, 1989; March 5, 1990; March 26, 1990; April 16, 1990.
Village Voice, May 1, 1990.

—*Victoria France Charabati*

Stockard Channing

AP/Wide World Photos

Actress

Real name, Susan Stockard; born c. 1946, in New York City; daughter of Leonard Stockard (in business); married Walter Channing (in business) c. 1965 (marriage dissolved); married Paul Schmidt (a professor of Slavic studies, actor, and playwright) c. 1971 (divorced, 1976); married David Debin (a screenwriter and producer), 1976 (divorced, 1981); married David Rawle (in business), 1982 (marriage dissolved). *Education:* Radcliffe College, B.A. (magna cum laude), 1965.

Address: *Agent*—International Creative Management, 8899 Beverly Blvd., Los Angeles, CA 90048.

Career

Actress. Performed with Theatre Co. of Boston, 1967; appeared in stage productions, including *Two Gentlemen of Verona,* 1972-73; *No Hard Feelings,* Martin Beck Theatre, New York City, 1973; *Vanities,* Mark Taper Forum, Los Angeles, 1976; *A Day in the Death of Joe Egg,* 1985; *The House of Blue Leaves,* 1986; *Woman in Mind,* 1988; *Love Letters,* 1989; *Jake's Women,* 1990, and *Six Degrees of Separation,* Lincoln Center, New York City, 1990-91. Appeared in films, including *Comforts of Home,* 1970; *Fortune,* 1975; *Sweet Revenge,* 1975; *The Big Bus,* 1976; *Grease,* 1978; *The Cheap Detective,* 1978; *The Fish That Saved Pittsburgh,* 1979; *Safari 3000,* 1983; *Without a Trace,* 1983; *Heartburn,* 1986; *The Men's Club,* 1986; *Married to It,* 1991; *Meet the Applegates,* 1991. Appeared in television movies, including *The Girl Most Likely To,* 1973; *Lucan,* 1977; *Silent Victory: The Kitty O'Neil Story,* 1979; *Not My Kid,* 1985; *Staying Together,* 1989;

starred in television series *Stockard Channing in Just Friends,* 1979, and *The Stockard Channing Show,* 1980.

Awards: Tony Award for best actress, 1985, for *A Day in the Death of Joe Egg;* Desk Award, 1988, for *Woman in Mind.*

Sidelights

Perpetually underrated, Stockard Channing has emerged from longtime sleeper status to receive substantial recognition as a dramatic stage actress. Channing was cast in a series of critical flops throughout the 1960s and 1970s—second-rate films, television movies, and series that usually flattered her gift for comedy, but failed in the ratings. Even in 1990, when she was cast in popular playwright Neil Simon's *Jake's Women,* the show closed before even reaching Broadway. Channing came out of these projects smelling like a rose, however, and was often distinguished by critics as the actress who propped up a lame script, or appeared bubbly or dynamic despite terrible plotting and direction.

Channing has developed her public persona from an all-American tradition—the spunky underdog who won't take no for an answer. Her perseverance finally rewarded, she was a critical and popular champ in John Guare's long-running Broadway play,

Six Degrees of Separation. The role that garnered Channing this success was dramatic *and* comedic. Robert Brustein, writing in the *New Republic,* raved: "Channing is that rare thing, a comic actress with genuine emotional depth. In this production, she is obliged to transform, in a matter of minutes, from a dizzy hostess into a woman of sympathy and sensibility, and the way she makes her mouth crumple and her cheeks sag is a signal demonstration of the actor's art." Channing's technical aptitude, seriousness, and tenacity have sustained her in a difficult industry for more than two decades.

Born Susan Stockard, Channing shone early as clever and a natural leader. Madeira boarding school chum Stuart Blue remembered Channing as "high-spirited and mischievous . . . but she was also president of the school. . . . Suzie was picked up in a long black limousine with two little white poodles in the back and driven to her riding lesson." Yet the actress told Celia McGee of *New York* that she feels removed from the traditions of East Coast money. "I'm not a preppy person, not a country club person, and I get sort of bristly when people think I am."

Channing married early; before she completed her undergraduate degree at Radcliffe she wed Walter Channing, Jr., a wealthy Bostonian. Diving into the world of collegiate theater, the young coed acted in both playful and thoughtful productions of Shakespeare before encountering a personal catalyst—Bertolt Brecht and his *Threepenny Opera.* Channing points to her role singing the Pirate Jenny song at Harvard's Agassiz Theatre as crucial to her decision to become a professional actress. "I've seen a lot of Pirate Jennys, and only Lotte Lenya sang it better than Stockard," said Boston *Herald* critic Arthur Friedman in *New York.* In *Interview* Channing told contributor William Wilson, "I couldn't sleep . . . . I was finding out that I had a talent! It was the most thrilling thing I'd ever experienced—the understanding that I had a knack for the process of acting, that my brain could follow it, like I suddenly realized I understood calculus or something."

After graduating from Radcliffe, Channing commuted from her Connecticut home to New York City auditions. She also joined the Theatre Company of Boston, to the apparent chagrin of her husband. She explained in *Working Woman* that he "wanted me to be a businessman's wife, and I simply couldn't be, so I left him. I am a very independent, stubborn person. Maybe too much so." Shortly thereafter Channing began living with Paul Schmidt, and though they were soon married, they rarely saw each other: He taught in Austin, Texas, and she was still working in New York. "It was a time of rebellion," Channing said in *New York.* "The theater was definitely tied in

with that for me, and with living a vaguely . . . alternative life style." *Savvy Woman* contributor Tim Appelo embellished the point, calling Channing an "erstwhile counter-culture rebel with the steely discipline of a traditionalist." Craft intact, she would soon take on Hollywood and the challenge of film and television.

> *"I couldn't sleep. . . . I was finding out that I had a talent! It was the most thrilling thing I'd ever experienced."*

After touring nationally in a prestigious version of Shakespeare's *Two Gentlemen of Verona,* Channing was cast in a comedy written by comedienne Joan Rivers, and in 1975's *The Fortune,* in which she co-starred with Warren Beatty and Jack Nicholson. *The Fortune* was supposed to make her a star, but was a box office bomb. Channing nonetheless received the first of what would be many excellent reviews for her work in bad productions. Then came the role which would make her a household name—Rizzo in the hit musical movie *Grease.* It seemed a bizarre twist of fate that an accomplished and serious actress would find fame in a musical comedy playing a girl gangleader. For years after *Grease* Channing was accosted in the street by kids who identified her with the smart-mouthed Rizzo.

The actress partly blames later failures, including that of her CBS television series, on the bittersweet success of *Grease.* "I was supposed to be the new Mary Tyler Moore," she told *Newsweek,* "but CBS did a survey and found that the demographics of [my] viewers were mostly between six and 12 years old." *Newsweek* reported in a piece exclusively about Channing's series that late CBS tycoon William Paley, after seeing the pilot of the sitcom, declared: "That is a star." Channing herself glowed with the prospect of a $2 million-dollar package including a series and five movies for CBS, but was somewhat wary of her new endeavor, saying, "I will not do 'Celebrity Challenge of the Sexes' . . . . Television is so draining and time-consuming [that] it's a bit like a room with no windows." Channing had two shots at sitcom fame, both produced by her then-husband, David Debin. *Stockard Channing in Just Friends* was form-fitting; Channing played Susan Hughes, a recently divorced woman fleeing Boston and a rich husband to take a job in a Hollywood health spa. A year later *The Stockard Channing Show* detailed the trials of another divorcee working for a selfish consumer advocate played by Ron Silver. Both the shows and Channing's marriage to Debin failed.

After the television programs were canceled, Channing took stock: "I realized I didn't really like my life," she told McGee. "I didn't like the way I was turning out, and I was grumpy because I was doing things that I didn't really want to do, and I had gotten this firsthand knowledge of the ebb and flow of the business. Also, it became all *about* the business. I hadn't really realized that you don't just take the next thing that comes along, that you had to take risks by not doing something. I wasn't behaving like a happy person, even toward myself. I didn't feel at ease in my skin. I wanted to change my life again." And so, in the 1980s the actress returned to the place of her ultimate professional victory—the Broadway stage.

Channing won a Tony Award for best actress in 1985 for her portrait of the mother of a handicapped child in *A Day in the Death of Joe Egg.* She also received good reviews for her role in a revival of John Guare's *The House of Blue Leaves.* Further dues were paid in several popular vehicles, including Neil Simon's *They're Playing Our Song.* The first real hint of genuine stardom, however, came with the lead in *Woman in Mind,* a 1988 play by Alan Ayckbourn that had opened to critical applause in London. Although Ayckbourn's work did not translate particularly well to American audiences, Channing's performance received solid notices. *New York* reviewer John Simon said of the rising star: "Stockard Channing makes Susan, for all her wit and superior imagination, irritating in her superiority even as she engages our complicity and compassion to the utmost. Her timing and inflections and befuddlement are splendid, and how expertly she glides or lurches from one world to another. She keeps us breathlessly guessing, but, right or wrong, crazy or sane, she has us rooting, cheering and grieving for her."

In 1990 actress Blythe Danner had to leave rehearsals of a play called *Six Degrees of Separation* several days into its schedule. When playwright Guare contacted Channing, who was then in Los Angeles, she agreed to take over for Danner. *Six Degrees of Separation* takes its material from a real event that occurred in New York in the late 1980s: A young black man made the rounds of a wealthy Manhattan neighborhood, conning wealthy people into believing that he was actor-director Sidney Poitier's son, saying that he could get them roles in his father's current project. "The common thread linking us all is an overwhelm-

ing need to be in the movie of [the Broadway sensation] *Cats,*" Channing's socialite character, Ouisa, tells the audience. Critics picked Channing out again and again for special praise in a cast of 17. And the play's serious look at American race relations boosted her credibility. This time the vehicle received high marks too; *Time* editors selected *Six Degrees of Separation* for its Best of 1990 issue.

In the wake of the play's success, one of Channing's former directors, John Tillinger, told *New York*'s McGee that Channing was "finally being recognized as one of the great actresses of the American stage." Jack Kroll of *Newsweek* crowed: "The spotlight that kindles Channing's face in the final glowing image of the play seems to anoint her as a major American actress." While *Six Degrees* was in production in 1990, and also during a brief hiatus that fall, Channing tackled roles in two films scheduled for release in 1991. One of them, *Married to It,* is about three unique Manhattan couples brought together by a New York private school. According to McGee, Channing plays Iris, a character fighting for her marriage, who "wisecracks her way through a lot of pain." The other film, *Meet the Applegates,* is a lighter endeavor; in it Channing plays a giant cockroach from Brazil masquerading as a typical suburban housewife.

A consummate theater person, Channing is still in touch with her Harvard acting buddies, and continues to network with directors and producers on both coasts. Split from her fourth husband, but settled with a longtime companion, she told *New York:* "It took me years to see that marriage isn't what I'm about. It's less about passion than about business and money and children and friendship." She later added tellingly, "I have this sense of being a late starter." The diversity and success of her professional projects in the 1990s would seem to bear her out.

Sources

Interview, July 1990.
New Republic, July 9, 1990; July 16, 1990.
New York, February 29, 1988; July 25, 1990; October 22, 1990.
New Yorker, February 22, 1988; June 25, 1990.
New York Times, July 1, 1990.
Newsweek, May 7, 1979; June 25, 1990; November 26, 1990.
Savvy Woman, May 1990.
Time, June 25, 1990; December 31, 1990; September 1986.

—*Christine Ferran*

Dick Cheney

U.S. secretary of defense

Full name, Richard Bruce Cheney; born January 30, 1941, in Lincoln, Neb.; son of Richard Herbert (a soil conservation agent with the U.S. Department of Agriculture) and Marjorie Lauraine (Dickey) Cheney; married Lynne Anne Vincent (chair of the National Endowment for the Humanities), August 29, 1964; children: Elizabeth, Mary. *Education:* Attended Yale University for three semesters; University of Wyoming, B.A., 1965, M.A., 1966, both in political science; University of Wisconsin, Ph.D. coursework.

Addresses: *Office*—Department of Defense, the Pentagon, Washington, D.C. 20301.

Career

Worked on power lines in Colorado, Arizona, and Wyoming, 1961-63; served as an intern in the Wyoming state legislature, 1964; worked on the staff of Wisconsin Governor Warren Knowles, 1965-68; American Political Science Association congressional fellow for Congressman William Steiger, 1968; special assistant to Office of Economic Opportunity director Donald Rumsfeld, 1969; deputy White House counselor, 1970; assistant director for operations at the White House, 1970-73; vice-president at Bradley, Woods, and Co., a Washington-based investment firm, 1973; deputy to the head of Gerald Ford's White House transition team, 1974; named Ford's chief of staff, 1975; worked in banking, 1978; U.S. congressman from Wyoming, 1978-88; chairman of the Republican Conference, 1987; Republican

party whip, 1988; appointed secretary of defense, 1989.

Sidelights

Many Americans were surprised when the relatively unknown civilian Dick Cheney was appointed to the post of secretary of defense. President George Bush, it was rumored, picked Cheney after the Senate rejected his first choice, the late John G. Tower. Once unanimously confirmed by the Senate, Cheney was expected to meet resistance in the Pentagon because he had not served in the military during the Vietnam era, having received several draft deferments. Cheney refuted the naysayers with aplomb, however, by taking decisive command immediately while faced with two major challenges: cutting the military's budget by $10 billion and managing the Defense Department during the Persian Gulf War. In fact, much of the credit for America's success in the Gulf can go to the understated Cheney, whose 22 years of experience in Washington and tight connections with White House staffers have made him a powerful asset to the Bush administration.

Cheney was born in Lincoln, Nebraska, but moved at a young age to Casper, Wyoming. In the rugged West Cheney became interested in hunting, fishing, and playing football and baseball. Cheney has kept up this active lifestyle and often adventures on backpacking and skiing trips for his vacations. The stocky Cheney became co-captain of his high school football team and was elected senior class president. After graduation he attended Yale University on a scholarship, but returned home after three semesters. He told Phil McCombs in the *Washington Post:* "I was not well organized in my youth . . . . I didn't like the East, I wasn't a good student . . . . I just wasn't prepared to buckle down."

"The White House staff jobs give you a broader opportunity to influence a variety of events, but you're ultimately a hired gun."

Back in Wyoming he worked on building power line transmission towers for a few years. Before long he felt the tug of matrimony and wanted to settle down. He remarked to McCombs: "It was clear that Lynne wasn't going to marry a lineman for the county. I had to go make something of myself if I was going to consummate the relationship, and so I went back to school at the University of Wyoming and finished up a B.A. and a master's there and then went to [the University of] Wisconsin and did all the work for my doctorate except the dissertation." Cheney's classwork earned him acclaim from his teachers and he is considered an authority in history—especially military history.

The Cheneys landed in Washington in 1968, where Dick had an internship with Wisconsin Republican Congressman William Steiger. Shortly thereafter Steiger loaned Cheney to the staff of Donald Rumsfield, a former congressman who had recently been appointed director of the Office of Economic Opportunity under President Richard Nixon. Rumsfield and Cheney hit it off almost immediately and worked closely together through the presidencies of Nixon and Gerald R. Ford. In 1975, at the tender age of 34, Cheney was named Ford's chief of staff. Ford commented wryly: "I'm so proud of him because I knew him when he was a young man."

Through his work for the Ford administration, Cheney made connections with two men who would figure prominently in his later management of the Gulf War. The first was Brent Scowcroft—Ford's, and later Bush's, national security adviser. The second was Jim Baker, Bush's secretary of state, whom Cheney had hired to chair Ford's 1976 presidential campaign. Cheney's well-established relationship with these power brokers made communication and decision-making much more fluent throughout the Gulf War.

After Ford's defeat in the 1976 presidential election, Cheney decided to move back to his home state. He worked briefly in banking before choosing to run for the U.S. Congress from Wyoming, a sparsely populated state boasting only one congressional seat. During the primary Cheney suffered a mild heart attack, but went on to win the nomination by 7,705 votes. "You become very much aware of your own mortality. When you're 37 years old and you have a heart attack, it's a total surprise . . . . It leads you to question what you're doing and why you're doing it," he explained to the *Washington Post.* Apparently he didn't question why he was running for Congress because he kept plugging on, resuming the campaign after only a six-week recovery period. He defeated the Democratic candidate in a landslide, earning 59 percent of the vote. He was easily re-elected from 1980 to 1988, when he left Congress to serve as secretary of defense.

Cheney immediately took to his job as congressman, enjoying a new kind of power. "The White House staff jobs give you a broader opportunity to influence a variety of events, but you're ultimately a hired gun. When you serve in the House, you may cast only one of 435 votes, but it's your decision to make," he said to Martin Tolchin of the *New York Times.* Cheney clearly impressed other House members with his decision-making; in his second term he was named head of the Republican Policy Committee, the number-four GOP post in the House.

It is easiest to identify Cheney's conservative political leanings by the programs he favored and opposed while in Congress. He supported all the domestic and foreign policy programs of President Ronald Reagan, especially when it came to strengthening the defense department. He also approved of funding for the multi-billion-dollar Strategic Defense Initiative ("Star Wars"), the MX missile, and production of new chemical weaponry. These choices made him a favorite among conservative political groups in Washington; he scored a 90 percent rating from the American Conservative Union while obtaining only a four percent rating from Americans for Democratic Action.

In domestic issues Cheney opposed the Equal Rights Amendment, busing, and abortion. He was in favor of prayer in schools and a law requiring Congress to balance its budget. McCombs wrote in the *Washington Post* that "during his decade on the Hill, Cheney was the congressman who never saw a welfare program he didn't hate" or "a weapons system he didn't love." Cheney also supported military aid to the Nicaraguan *contras* and related legislation. While Republicans generally saw Cheney as a "go-along, get-along guy," his Democratic opponents weren't quite so sure. A former congressional aide commented in McComb's *Post* article: "He's able to appear so cool and rational, but there's this other side. There was a harshness, that sneer he'd get, sort of attributing bad motives to his opponents, that you were suspect, that you were pro-Communist. There was venom—he made some very vicious remarks. He scares me."

In 1987 Cheney was appointed vice-chairman of a committee investigating the Iran-*contra* scandal. Just a few months later, he won the third-ranking post in the House Republican party—chairman of the Republican Conference. Not surprisingly, Cheney found that President Reagan had not committed the gross offenses of which he had been accused. In the report Cheney wrote: "There is no evidence that the president had any knowledge of the diversion of profits from the arms sale to the Nicaraguan democratic resistance . . . . There is also no evidence of any effort by the president or his senior advisers to cover up these events."

Late in 1988 Cheney became the Republican party whip, the number-two position in the House of Representatives. Cheney didn't get much time to enjoy this coveted post, however; four months later, in March of 1989, he was unanimously confirmed by the Senate to the position of secretary of defense. Cheney was questioned about his lack of knowledge of defense matters and about his health—by this time he had suffered three mild heart attacks and undergone bypass surgery. Cheney maneuvered through all the questions with skill, asserting that his experience in Ford's cabinet had given him the knowledge he needed to be secretary of defense.

Many expected Cheney to encounter problems with Pentagon staffers because of his lack of involvement in the Vietnam war. He was of draft age during the 1960s, but received five draft deferments and thus never served. The first four deferments were because of his student status; the fifth because he had

children. Cheney, however, commented that "I had other priorities in the '60s than military service." And he affirmed during his confirmation hearing that he "would have obviously been happy to serve had I been called."

Cheney took decisive action to show the Pentagon that he was in charge. He allowed only a few key assistants to advise him on critical matters, and surrounded himself with loyal friends and acquaintances. He asked David S. Addington, a trusted aide, to be his special assistant. His acumen demonstrated, Cheney was quickly accepted by the Pentagon establishment. He commented to the *Washington Post*: "In terms of the qualification for the current job, I'm the fourth civilian, the fourth secretary who has no prior military service. It's a civilian job, and so I've never felt it a hindrance of any kind."

Early in his tenure as secretary Cheney was faced with the difficult task of cutting the swollen defense budget by roughly $10 billion. In his typical style of low-key politicking, Cheney first asked the arms of the military what would happen if their budgets were indeed cut. The plan he ultimately proposed would slice $180 billion from Defense in the next five years. *The Economist* noted, however, that the proposal was actually "a lowering of future growth in the defense budget by that amount and a real cut of perhaps $50 billion—not much more than the defense budget has shrunk in the past five years." Members of the armed services, nonetheless, made these cuts appear drastic—the Army said that it would have to lay off 200,000 people. The Air Force warned that it would have to close 15 bases. Cheney's tactic was to aim low in his budget calculations so that Congress would not be inclined to look more deeply for further cuts.

Some critics have argued that the defense budget can and should be slashed drastically in light of the Soviet Union's waning influence in Eastern Europe, especially since Soviet Prime Minister Mikhail Gorbachev has softened his position toward the West. Characteristically, Cheney has objected to this kind of thinking, stating in the *New Republic* that the Soviet Union "is not about to give up its military superpower status." He is firm in his belief that the U.S.S.R. is still the greatest military force in the world and, as such, will continue to pose a threat to the United States. Cheney is also convinced that Gorbachev will be replaced by a leader more hostile to the West. He warned in the *New Yorker* that it would be unwise to plan for the United States's military future on "what fate may have in store for one man." In other defense spending matters Cheney has shown himself to be a moderate, practical man. He chose to stop production on the Navy's A-12 stealth bomber; "If we cannot spend the taxpayers' money wisely," he asserted in *The Economist*, "we will not spend it."

Cheney also flexed his skills by playing an intrinsic part in planning and implementing strategies for the Persian Gulf War. In August of 1990 he was sent to Saudi Arabia to persuade King Fahd to let the U.S. military deploy combat forces in that country. It was during this period that Cheney's ties with Scowcroft and Baker became particularly important. Baker, who by protocol would normally have made the trip to Saudi Arabia, was not disturbed that Cheney journeyed there instead. That communication between Cheney, Baker, and other key Washington personnel proceeded so smoothly can in large part be credited for winning the war. "We planned for a much worse eventuality than actually occurred," Cheney said of the ground war, which lasted roughly four days.

As a result of his high-profile participation in the war, Cheney has become a decidedly public figure, though his media exposure and mass popularity has not rivaled those of his more charismatic counterparts—General Norman Schwarzkopf (also in this volume) and Joint Chiefs of Staff Chairman Colin Powell (see *Newsmakers 90*); an aide commented that at one point there were 500 interview requests for Powell and only one for Cheney. Household-name status aside, Cheney's future appears bright. The ambitious, well-respected Republican has been viewed by some as a viable contender for the 1996 presidential campaign.

And just what is the real Cheney like? His wife Lynne claims that "what you've seen on television is what I've seen at home. He's calm, deliberate, not given to speechifying in an old-fashioned way, just says what he thinks the situation is. He's an unusual politician, not a back-slapping kind of guy." Morton Kondracke, writing in the *New Republic*, observed that Cheney "wins respect by observing keenly, speaking softly, inventing shrewd stratagems, and sticking to his guns." Whatever the whims of public opinion may have in store for him in years to come, Cheney must still battle Congress over the fate of the defense budget. Reflecting in the *Washington Post* on this challenge, he averred: "It helps to have just won a war."

Selected writings

(With wife, Lynne Cheney) *Kings of the Hill: Power and Personality in the House of Representatives*, 1983.

Sources

The Economist, November 25, 1989; March 31, 1990; January 19, 1991.
Harper's, July 1990.
New Republic, January 1, 1990.
New Yorker, February 12, 1990.
New York Times, April 6, 1982.
Washington Post (national weekly edition), April 15-21, 1991.

—Nancy Rampson

Andrew Dice Clay

Comic

Real name, Andrew Clay Silverstein; born in 1958 in Brooklyn, N.Y.; son of Fred (a real estate salesman) and Doris Silverstein; married Kathy Swanson, 1984, divorced, 1986.

Addresses: *Home*—Brooklyn, N.Y.

Career

Worked as a stand-up comedian in small New York City clubs, 1970-80; moved to Los Angeles in 1980, became a regular at the Comedy Store, 1980-88. Cast member of television show *Crime Story*, 1987-88; feature films include *Making the Grade*, 1984; *Pretty in Pink*, 1987, *Casual Sex?* 1988, and *The Adventures of Ford Fairlane*, 1990. Starred in HBO comedy special, *The Diceman Cometh*, 1988. Albums include *Dice*, 1989, and *The Day the Laughter Died*, 1990.

Sidelights

Andrew Dice Clay is the most profane comic in America—and one of the most popular. With an act that mixes filthy nursery rhymes with rude, X-rated remarks about women, "the Diceman" reached center spotlight in 1990. His act lampoons women, midgets, the disabled, gays, Arabs, Latinos, Pakistanis, and all other immigrant groups. It has incited protests, walkouts, and bans. And it has brought success to the mouthy, chain-smoking Brooklynite. "He is, simply, the antithesis of the '80s man," wrote *New York Daily News* critic Hank Gallo. "He stands

AP/Wide World Photos

on stage, hair slicked back, sideburns below the ear, a study in black interrupted only by a huge silver belt and sterling studs and chains that adorn his leather jacket. He is a hardened, chain smoking, lady-killing, biker misplaced somehow in this later, more sensitive decade. And the talk is dockside tough. He lectures women—whom he refers to as 'pigs,' 'sluts' and worse—on proper sexual technique. He takes hitherto harmless nursery rhymes and transforms them into raunchy chants. And he asks audience members for the most intimate boudoir details imaginable. And then he gets dirty."

The act, understandably, has sparked debate. Clay's supporters say he is in the tradition of Lenny Bruce and other cutting-edge comedians whose foul mouths made them controversial. Comedienne Joan Rivers told the *Lexington Herald-Leader*, "He's doing a parody, and anybody who doesn't see that is an idiot." On the flip side, comedian George Carlin, who became famous with his routine on the seven words that can't be spoken on television, told the *Washington Post:* "Andrew Clay is picking on underdogs—gays, women and immigrants. His audiences share his beliefs, so they cheer him on." And *New York Times* writer Lawrence Christon wrote that Clay "plays to the yahoo mentality of what is becoming an increasingly dysfunctional American culture."

Clay—born Andrew Clay Silverstein—was reared in the Sheepshead Bay section of Brooklyn. Even as a child, he wanted to become an entertainer. "I couldn't dribble a basketball, and that's why I turned to creative things that I found myself good at," he told *Vanity Fair*. "Music. Impressions. Seven, eight years old. I was already into drums. I watched more TV, and that's how the impressions started—Jerry Lewis, John Wayne, Louis Armstrong, the Beatles, Elvis—I used to dig them from watching them on TV."

"I thought I'd be the next Buddy Rich, but by the time I hit 18, 19 years old, I realized there were no big bands anymore. So I went into comedy."

His first goal was to become a jazz drummer, and he was playing professionally on the Catskills circuit at age 14 under the name Clay Silvers. "I thought I'd be the next Buddy Rich," he told *Playboy*, "but by the time I hit 18, 19 years old, I realized there were no big bands anymore. So I went into comedy." In high school, he hung out with a bunch of kids known as the Nostrand Avenue Schmucks. His heroes then were celebrities with macho images—Elvis Presley, John Travolta, Sylvester Stallone, and the Henry Winkler character of Fonzie, whom Clay told the *Los Angeles Times* was "a PG version of Dice."

In the fall of 1978 Clay was attending school at Kingsborough Community College in Brooklyn and drumming during the weekends for a local bar mitzvah band. On a whim, he decided to attend "open mike night" at a local comedy club. His debut, father Fred Silverstein later recalled to the *Chicago Tribune*, was clean—a five-minute set of impressions of Elvis, Travolta, and Jerry Lewis as "The Nutty Professor." Fred Silverstein subsequently became Andrew's unofficial manager, helping his son get bookings at showcase clubs around New York. In 1980 Fred called Mitzi Shore, owner of the Comedy Store in Los Angeles. He talked her into taking Clay sight unseen—as a regular— and sent his son west to Hollywood where he performed each night with the likes of Yakoff Smirnoff and Sam Kinison.

For two years, Clay struggled while working as an impressionist. "He was a guy we all teased at the Comedy Store, and didn't think he would go that far," comic Michael Binder told the *Washington Post*. Another comic from the Comedy Store, Linda Lyon, told *Vanity Fair:* "He always put his all into it. The sex stuff hadn't started yet, but he was extremely sexy and charismatic. And the audience responded to him right away. The girls did." After a year in Los Angeles, Clay decided he had to change his act to make it to the top. He told *Newsday* that the metamorphosis came largely by accident: "Someone wasn't able to go on at the Comedy Store one night and they asked me to fill in. I didn't have my Jerry Lewis stuff with me, so I just winged it, saying whatever popped in my head." That turned out to be the X-rated ramblings of a greaser in black leather, the kind of guy who sees women as whiny sex toys, foreigners as ugly misfits and gays as sickening perverts. The audience couldn't get enough. The Diceman—a street tough, cigarette-sucking Italian guy from Brooklyn—was born, soon to be dressed in studded leather jackets and topped by a ducktail haircut. "Andrew had been thinking about it for a while," Smirnoff told *Newsday*. "He saw how guys like Rodney Dangerfield and Richard Pryor did well using profanity. He used to watch a lot of Elvis movies on TV. Andrew wanted to be as radical as Elvis was, but as a comic. Still, he was a little uncomfortable about it. In real life, Andrew is a very nice, very polite guy."

The Diceman act was initially a moderate success. A 1984 review in the show business trade paper *Variety* said: "He stumbles onstage as the utterly inept 'Eugene Moskowitz' before metamorphosing into a black-leather-jacketed, obscenity-spouting hoodlum . . . . Easy on the eyes, but hard on the ears with a nonstop flow of X-rated subjects and vocabulary, he registers as a kind of four-letter Fonzie . . . Sample quips: 'Ever go on a blind date and wish you were actually blind?' 'Women are always on a diet—until you get 'em in the restaurant.' 'Why did I kill my first wife? I needed the phone.'" Clay's biggest frustration was being stuck in a late-night slot at the Comedy Store, performing in front of handfuls of people. So he entered what he would later call his "kamikaze comedy" period. Clay would buy a ticket to a movie, then stand up at the front of the theater before the show began and do his act. He'd cruise into all-night restaurants in Beverly Hills or on the Sunset Strip and run off a 20-minute routine at 3 in the morning. He was gaining a reputation around Los Angeles as a gutsy, if off-color, comic.

The Diceman persona landed Clay small parts in such movies as *Pretty in Pink* and *Casual Sex?*, in which he played what *New York Times* critic Michael

Wilmington described as "a macho bozo from New Jersey." He appeared on a Rodney Dangerfield cable television special in 1988. And he earned a recurring role as gangster Max Goldman in the television series *Crime Story.* The big break, however, came in November 1988 at a stag dinner at the Beverly Hills Hotel for the local chapter of Big Brothers of America. The elite of the film and TV industries were in attendance: Walter Matthau, Aaron Spelling, Carl Reiner, Sidney Poitier. The event was black tie, but Clay came in black leather. After most of the other acts had performed, Clay—unknown to most of the audience—was summoned onstage. "Carl Reiner brought me up and introduced me as a George Bush campaign adviser," Clay told the *Los Angeles Times.* "I remember walking by Jack Lemmon, who was on the dais, and I gave him a squeeze on the cheek and said, "You [expletive]. I love you!' I knew it was do or die, so I got up there, took the mike, looked across the room and said: 'So...'" Clay recited one of his obscene opening lines, which drew two minutes of raucous laughter. "By the time I was done," Clay told the *Los Angeles Times,* "Carl Reiner was saying, 'I don't know what just happened, but tonight, Andrew Dice Clay became a star in this room.' And it was true."

The next day, producer Joel Silver, who had been in the audience, called to offer Clay a three-picture multi-million-dollar deal with 20th Century-Fox. The first film turned out the be *The Adventures of Ford Fairlane.* Within days, a Clay concert was taped and turned into an HBO New Year's Eve comedy special. Another concert was recorded and turned into a live comedy album. By 1989, Clay was routinely attracting crowds of 20,000 eager to pay $20 per ticket. His second album, *The Day the Laughter Died,* sold 280,000 copies in the two months following its release in 1990, even though its distributor, Geffen Records, was so embarrassed that it didn't put its name on the album. "This is the realm of the king of bonzai comedy," wrote the *Chicago Tribune*'s David Silverman, "a land where there are no limits and the 'Diceman' rules. There's little doubt what lies in store: comedy's equivalent of the mobile 155-mm. howitzer."

Ford Fairlane was released in the summer of 1990 and flopped at the box office. Critics gave it mixed reviews. The *Boston Globe*'s Jim Sullivan wrote: "What has worked for Eddie Murphy, may well work for Clay.... For anyone who has loathed Clay and all he stands for throughout the last year or so, *The Adventures of Ford Fairlane* makes loathing a little harder." Among those who have loathed him are the executives at MTV. In September 1989, Clay earned

the distinction of being the first act banned for life from MTV. During the network's live music awards program, Clay delivered an impromptu and obscene monologue laced with lewd poetry and references to obese women and sex. In an on-air statement soon after Clay's segment, MTV vice-president Barry Kluger called Clay's monologue "reprehensible, distasteful and far out of line from our programming standards.... Based on this experience, Andrew Dice Clay will not be appearing on MTV in the future."

> "One of my aims in comedy is to make someone laugh harder than they have ever laughed at anyone before. In order to do that, you've got to hit them below the belt."

Clay continued to make waves in 1990. In May he was a guest host on *Saturday Night Live,* a show known for pressing the limits of censorship. His appearance prompted cast member Nora Dunn and musical guest Sinead O'Connor to withdraw from the program, citing his anti-feminist and anti-gay approach. "His work is hateful," Dunn told the *Washington Post.* "I know in my heart I can't work with him." NBC officials took the unusual step of putting the show on a 5-second time delay, a practice used only twice before in 15 years. The show was twice interrupted by protesters. Discussing the uproar preceding his appearance, Clay said during the show, "I couldn't get more PR if I took out my penis and wrapped it around a microphone stand."

In the end, the show was *Saturday Night Live*'s fourth-highest rated episode of the season. And A. Whitney Brown, a writer and cast member of the show, told the *Los Angeles Times,* "He's really no more sexist than Benny Hill. If racism is considered Andrew Dice Clay, then I'd say we're doing pretty good." For his part, Clay insists that the Diceman is just a character and not really him. "It's not me up there—it's an act," he told the *Los Angeles Times.* "I should win an Academy Award for Best [expletive] Acting performance for what I do on stage." And, he told *Gentlemen's Quarterly,* "If I really meant all the things onstage, there wouldn't be a person in the room, because they would just say this is just nasty, mean, violent humor. Anybody with a brain could see right through me."

Clay says that his humor works because of its bluntness. "I'm like a filthy Dr. Ruth, if she could bang some guy out with her fist," he told the *Chicago Tribune*. "It's just an attitude, a confidence, a guy that's not afraid to speak his mind, and people like that. One of my aims in comedy is to make someone laugh harder than they have laughed at anyone before. In order to do that, you've got to hit them below the belt." Indeed, Clay views himself in heroic terms. "I'm delivering a comedic hero to America," he told *Newsday*. "I'm giving people an image they've loved from the days of James Dean and Elvis and Marlon Brando when he was 'The Wild One'— only I'm doing it in comedy. It's only an act, for Christsake."

Sources

Boston Globe, October 22, 1989; November 10, 1989; July 8, 1990.

Chicago Tribune, January 4, 1989; September 14, 1989.
Detroit Free Press, May 15, 1990.
Gentlemen's Quarterly, August 1989.
Lexington Herald-Leader, July 16, 1990.
Los Angeles Times, May 11, 1990; May 14, 1990; June 3, 1990.
Newsday, September 3, 1989; May 14, 1990.
New York Daily News, July 15, 1990.
New York Times, January 8, 1989; September 10, 1989.
People, May 9, 1988.
Philadelphia Daily News, May 12, 1990.
Philadelphia Inquirer, July 28, 1990.
Playboy, January 1990.
Vanity Fair, June 1990.
Variety, November 20, 1984.
Washington Post, May 11, 1990; July 22, 1990.

—*Glen Macnow*

Roger Clemens

Professional baseball player

Full name, William Roger Clemens; born August 4, 1962, in Dayton, OH; son of Bill (a truck driver) and Bess Clemens; married wife, Debbie (a dance instructor), in 1983; children: Koby, Kory. *Education:* Attended San Jacinto Junior College, 1980-81; attended University of Texas, 1981-83.

Addresses: *Home*—Katy, TX. *Office*—Boston Red Sox, Fenway Park, 4 Yawkey Way, Boston, MA 02115. *Agent*—Randy Hendricks, Houston, TX.

Career

Professional baseball player in minor leagues in Winter Haven, FL, and New Britain, CT, 1983, and Pawtucket, RI, 1984. In major leagues with Boston Red Sox, 1984—.

Awards: Named American League most valuable player, 1986; Cy Young Award as best pitcher in the American League, 1986 and 1987; named to American League All-Star team, 1986, 1988 and 1990; named most valuable player of 1986 All-Star game.

Sidelights

In February of 1991, Boston Red Sox pitcher Roger Clemens signed a four-year, $21 million contract, becoming the highest-paid player in baseball history. For their money, the Red Sox secured the top right-handed pitcher in the major leagues, a hurler whose knee-high fastball, as Oakland Athletics outfielder Ricky Henderson told the *Providence Journal*, "is as difficult to hit as a marble shot out of a cannon." But

the Red Sox also invested millions in an intense, temperamental man whose judgment has several times been questioned.

"Who is Roger Clemens—a hothead who boiled over in the playoffs or an overgrown kid driven by obsessions?" asked *Sports Illustrated*'s Leigh Montville. "There is a steam that builds up in him and that he lets out when he pitches. A pressure." Sometimes the pressure serves Clemens well—his many awards and 116 pitching victories entering 1991 are testament to that. But sometimes it does not. Clemens boiled over before a national TV audience during a crucial 1990 American League playoff game and was ejected for cursing umpire Gerry Cooney. The volatile pitcher has tangled with Red Sox management, been portrayed as a pampered troublemaker by the Boston media, and has heard himself booed on Opening Day by hometown fans at Fenway Park.

"I don't want to be a superstar," Clemens told *Sports Illustrated*. "I just want to be a regular person. But it's getting harder and harder to do that. So I get angry inside. I'll just try to stomach it and show it's not bothering me. But I can't always do that."

Clemens was born in Dayton, Ohio, the youngest of five children of Bill Clemens, a truck driver, and his wife, Bess. When he was eight weeks old, Clemens's mother left his father. Two years later, she married Woody Booher, a tool-and-die maker 15 years her senior. Five years after that, Booher died of a heart attack. "I'm sure [his death] was hard on Roger, because Woody was the only father he ever knew," Bess Booher told *Sports Illustrated*. "But if he had any problems, he never showed it. When you have adversities in your life, you have to strive to overcome them."

To counteract the turmoil in his life, Clemens focused on baseball. At age seven, he was the star pitcher in a league of nine- and ten-year-olds. As a teenager, he dominated kids his age, prompting his family to seek tougher competition for him. During his freshman year of high school, Clemens left Ohio and moved to suburban Houston to live with his brother Randy, 10 years his senior; Randy Clemens and his wife lived in the Spring Woods School District, home of one of Texas's top high school baseball programs. "It was very intimidating for me," Clemens told the *Boston Globe*. "I was the best player I knew in Dayton. And then suddenly, as a junior at Spring Woods, I was just the third-best pitcher in the rotation. But I decided I wanted to make it to the top and I set certain rules to follow, and discipline just became a habit."

Clemens's wife, Debbie, who knew him in those days, told *Sports Illustrated*, "In high school he was always a good pitcher, but he was never considered the best. The thing was, though, he always felt he was the best. If someone told him he couldn't do something, it just became more of a challenge to him."

When he finished high school in 1980, Clemens was not offered a scholarship by the University of Texas, where he dreamed of playing for coach Cliff Gustafson, a legend for developing pitchers. Nor was he drafted by any major league team, though the Minnesota Twins offered him a contract. The Twins scout told Clemens that if he didn't sign then, he would never get another chance. Clemens ignored the threat and enrolled at San Jacinto Junior College. He was 18 years old at the time, 6'2" and 220 pounds. "I was a bit overweight and that kept me from having the strength to throw hard," he told the *Los Angeles Times*. "But I still had good control of my pitches."

At San Jacinto, Clemens put himself on a rigid exercise program—lifting weights and running miles each day—and lost 15 pounds. He played well enough as a freshman for the New York Mets to chose him in the 12th round of the 1981 draft. The Mets offered him $30,000 to sign, but he turned

them down when the University of Texas finally came through with a scholarship offer.

"I was very, very close to signing with the Mets," Clemens told the *Dallas Morning News*, "but I knew I could go to school for a couple of more years. Texas was where I'd really wanted to go. It was a national power and a great place to learn how to pitch. I figured if I went to Texas, my chances for becoming a pro would only improve."

Clemens pitched two years for the Longhorns, winning 25 games and losing just seven. More impressively, he struck out 241 batters in 275 innings, while walking just 56. In June of 1983, he was the winning pitcher in the final game of the College World Series. "He was an excellent pitcher in college, improving every year," college and pro teammate Spike Owen told *Sports Illustrated*. "But I don't think anybody could have looked at him then and known what was in store."

The Red Sox, plagued by disappointing pitching since they sold Babe Ruth in 1920, selected Clemens from the 19th pick of the first round of the 1983 draft. They sent him to Class-A Winter Haven, where he won three of four games and had a terrific 1.24 earned run average. He was quickly promoted to Double-A New Britain, where he won four of five decisions and rang up an equally phenomenal 1.38 ERA. In 81 minor-league innings that season, he struck out 95 batters. "I haven't seen anyone at the same stage who's got what he's got," New Britain manager Rac Slider told the *Boston Globe*. Bob Duffy, a reporter for the *Globe*, went to see Clemens pitch in New Britain and wrote: "His motion was as smooth as a seal's skin, his fastball was steaming at more than 90 miles an hour, his curveball was dropping in as if it had been rolled off a cliff."

By the 1984 spring training, Clemens, all of 21 years old, was the Red Sox's designated savior. That spring, Bob Ryan of the *Globe* wrote, "It's this simple: if a healthy Roger Clemens does not go on to become a major pitching star, then what's the sense of scouting? He has every ingredient needed to become a great major league pitcher. He has four pitches of above-average major league caliber and he throws strikes. He is mean out there. He is a young man of uncommon poise." Clemens chafed at the labels suddenly being applied to him, telling the *Globe*, "I'm not the one who started that phenom' business, I'm not a savior."

But clearly he was more than an average prospect. Fully grown to 6'4" and 220 pounds, Clemens combined one of baseball's best fastballs with pinpoint control. After joining the Red Sox midway through the 1984 season, he won nine games and lost four. He struck out close to one opposition hitter per inning.

The next season, Clemens lowered his ERA more than a run—from 4.32 to 3.29. Midway through the year, however, his shoulder began hurting so much that he could barely lift his pitching arm. Clemens underwent surgery, removing cartilage near his rotator cuff; some feared that his career might be over. In the end, however, Red Sox pitching coach Bill Fischer told *Newsday* that the injury may have been a blessing: "Maybe it's that arm injury that left him so determined to get the best out of himself. Maybe it scared him to work even harder. A lot of people have athletic ability. But very few make use of every ounce of it the way he does."

Clemens certainly made every use of it in 1986. He led the American League in wins (24 with just four losses), winning percentage (.857) and ERA (2.48). He started and won the All-Star game and was named its most valuable player. He won the Cy Young Award as the league's best pitcher and was voted most valuable player as the Red Sox won the pennant for the first time in 11 seasons. He pitched in two World Series games that October, but won neither.

One memorable night against the Seattle Mariners in May of that year, Clemens struck out 20 batters. No pitcher in 111 years of major league history had ever done that before. "It puts me in the Hall of Fame, at least in one sense," he told the *Boston Globe*. "Nobody can take that away from me. I just hope people don't think it's a misprint." If they did, it wasn't for long. Clemens came back in 1987 and defied the jinx that traditionally strikes Cy Young winners. He won the award for the second straight year—an accomplishment achieved just twice before. Overall, he won 20 games and lost just nine, struck out 256 batters, and had a 2.97 ERA.

The explosiveness of Clemens's fastball—usually clocked at between 95 and 97 miles per hour—earned him the nickname "Rocket Man." The sight of him on the mound is imposing. As *Sports Illustrated*'s Bruce Newman wrote, "Clemens looks down at hitters from his pitching promontory with the imperious air of a young liege lord inspecting his vassals. He is their master, they are there to do his bidding." Sometimes that attitude has gotten Clemens into trouble: He was tossed out of several games early in his career for arguing with umpires. And opposing hitters frequently complained that he had tried to show them up. "Everybody wants to

win, but it burns much deeper in [Clemens] than it does in other people," Red Sox catcher Rich Gedman told *Sports Illustrated*. "That's his edge. It's always like, 'I'll show you.' You look at him, he's got the eyes of a shark out there."

Clemens drew the ire of Red Sox fans in 1988 for leaving training camp in a salary dispute. Then he criticized team management for its treatment of players and their families; that criticism was largely interpreted as complaints about New England and its baseball fans. In 1988 Clemens heard boos for the first time. He also stopped talking to the press, except on days he pitched. "I only talk after games I pitch because I've been misunderstood," Clemens told *USA Today*. "The Boston papers turned into more like The Star or the National Enquirer. Off-the-field stuff became more important than what we did on the field."

In 1988 and 1989, Clemens sustained minor injuries that hurt his effectiveness. Still, he won 18 games in 1988 and 17 in 1989. He led the American League with 291 strikeouts in 1988. In 1990, he was back in top form: He won 21 games and lost just six, and led the league with a 1.93 ERA. *Sports Illustrated*'s Leigh Montville wrote, "When he is pitching well, when the control is good, when the speed is up, he is almost untouchable. The best pitcher in baseball. No debate. The evening sports news will be a collage of strikeouts, batters swinging at air, batters frozen in place, looking at pitches they can't see."

The 1990 Red Sox won the American League East and faced the Oakland Athletics in October for a chance to advance to the World Series. Boston lost the first three games and, on October 10th, faced potential elimination in a game Clemens started. In the second inning, down 2-0, Clemens stepped off the pitching mound and appeared to grumble something to home plate umpire Gerry Cooney. The ump later insisted that Clemens had cursed him; a photographer set up near the action said he heard Clemens question Cooney's parentage. Clemens insisted he was only talking to himself. Regardless, Cooney ejected Clemens from the game—the Red Sox went on to lose, 3-1—and the angered pitcher had to be restrained and carried off the field.

Ultimately, Clemens received a five-game suspension and a $10,000 fine, and his image suffered. The opposition pitcher, Dave Stewart, told the *Los Angeles Times*, "Who can think with Roger Clemens? There's just no excuse for what happened. Baseball was here long before Roger Clemens and the Red Sox, and it will be here long after they are gone." As *Baltimore Sun* writer John Eisenberg remarked, "Clemens had it coming. The guy has been acting like a jerk for a long time. He bullies his manager. He stomps his feet like a 2-year-old when he doesn't get his way. Clemens clearly thought he could get away with saying anything, that he would never get ejected in such a big game. That's classic Clemens. He's a terrific pitcher, but he believes he is above the rules."

Months after the incident Clemens admitted that his intensity had caused him to lose control. The Red Sox certainly forgave him. During a winter in which baseball salaries skyrocketed out of control, Boston signed Clemens to a pace-setting deal—four years for $21 million. The salary confirmed Clemens's standing at the top of his profession, but it raised new questions. Wrote Bill Parillo of the *Providence Journal:* "Clemens is going to be asked to do more than throw 95 mile-an-hour heaters for his $21 million. He's going to have to do more than win his 21 or 22 games a year. No longer can Clemens afford to get tossed out of playoff games in the second inning . . . He is going to have to grow up in a hurry now. No more temper-tantrums that can create chaos."

Clemens, while never apologizing for his actions, has said he wants to play the game long enough to leave a positive mark. "No doubt, I feel like I could be one of the best if I play long enough," he told the *Boston Globe.* "I want to take my family to the Hall of Fame and show them how I did. Besides winning a World Series, the next thing you strive for is to get into the Hall of Fame."

Sources

Atlanta Constitution, January 20, 1991.
Baltimore Sun, October 11, 1990.
Bergen Record (New Jersey), February 16, 1989.
Boston Globe, September 9, 1983; March 13, 1984; May 10, 1984; June 2, 1984; May 1, 1986; July 24, 1988; August 12, 1989; April 19, 1990; January 29, 1991.
Los Angeles Times, October 11, 1990; October 12, 1990.
Miami Herald, January 18, 1987.
Newsday (Long Island), February 16, 1987; May 22, 1988.
Philadelphia Inquirer, October 13, 1990.
Providence Journal, February 12, 1991.
Sports Illustrated, June 6, 1988; October 1, 1990; November 26, 1990; February 11, 1991.
USA Today, April 27, 1990.

—Mark Kram

Harry Connick, Jr.

AP/Wide World Photos

Jazz pianist, singer, and actor

Born in 1967 in New Orleans, La.; son of Harry, Jr. (an attorney) and Anita (a judge; deceased) Connick. *Education:* Attended New Orleans Center for the Creative Arts and Manhattan School of Music.

Addresses: *Home*—New York City. *Record company*—Columbia Records, Inc., 51 W. 52nd St., New York, NY 10019.

Career

Began playing with professional musicians on Bourbon Street, New Orleans, at age 6; tutored by jazz pianist James Booker; studied under Ellis Marsalis at New Orleans Center for the Creative Arts; moved to New York City at age 18 and performed in clubs and churches; signed recording contract with Columbia Records, 1986; performed music for film *When Harry Met Sally...,* 1989; actor in film *Memphis Belle,* 1990.

Sidelights

If jazz man Harry Connick, Jr. has a problem, it is that he is too young, too good, and his music is too old. The New Orleans-born Connick, who literally burst onto the American jazz scene at the age of just 22, has been compared to such stars of the golden era of American standards as Duke Ellington, Tony Bennett, and Frank Sinatra. But while his piano virtuosity is unquestioned, and his youth is obvious, Connick has caused some controversy by relying on a repertoire of great sounds from the past to make his musical statement. He is a throwback to another era, and yet that time is so long gone that Connick has been received by many jazz fans as a breath of fresh air.

And while some jazz sophisticates take a cool, wait-and-see attitude toward this upstart, those music lovers lucky enough to get a ticket to one of Connick's performances get something a little unexpected—an evening of genuine, old-time, saloon jazz with a Bourbon Street accent. "At first blush," writes *Newsweek*'s Cathleen McGuigan, "[Connick] looks too fresh-faced to have done so much growing up in saloons. But when he starts to sing, he assumes a grown-up golden glow. With his fast fingers and slow drawl, his slicked-back hair and laid-back glamour, the New Orleans pianist has been astonishing Yankee audiences with a jazz virtuosity far beyond his years."

Right down to his snakeskin shoes, Connick is already a polished showman. Tall, smooth, and handsome in his baggy suits and pomade hairstyle, he jokes, trades places with his drummer or bassist, does imitations, taps on his piano and occasionally performs an impromptu soft-shoe. Again, this is against the grain of modern jazz standards, which tend to call for a more sedate, laid-back style of performing. "What ever happened to a show, man?" Connick asked *Rolling Stone*'s Rob Tannenbaum. "You go to hear Louis Armstrong, and they were jitterbugging. Armstrong was a bigger goof-off than I am onstage. It's so staid now."

And behind this obvious glamour, which has already won him a film role in the acclaimed *Memphis Belle*, and promises of still more, Connick is a very serious musician. In fact, his musical upbringing reads like a pure jazz pedigree. His parents, both music lovers, put themselves through law school by running a record store in New Orleans, where Connick's late mother eventually became a judge. Connick was a piano prodigy who started playing the family piano at age 3. By the time he was 5 he was accomplished enough to play "The Star Spangled Banner" at his father's inauguration as the New Orleans district attorney.

> "All [I'm] trying to do is develop [my] own style, and the only way you can do that is by understanding the music of your predecessors."

It was his father's position as D.A. that got young Harry into many of the smoky saloons of Bourbon Street on weekends, where he learned to love the sounds of Dixieland, bebop, and rhythm and blues in their natural element. Many of the performers, including the legendary ragtime pianist Eubie Blake, even invited the boy wonder onstage. "Eubie was 96 at the time, and I was 9," Connick explained to Howard Reich in the *Chicago Tribune*. "To be able to play with a man who was born in 1883. My Lord—I still can hardly believe I touched him." Another strong influence was the talented pianist James Booker. Many believed that Booker was bound for greatness himself, but drugs destroyed his talent and Booker eventually died in 1983. Booker became so fond of Connick that he often came around the house to tutor the boy. Booker was "the only genius I ever met," Connick told *Rolling Stone*. But "he'd play a tune and throw up in the middle of the song. I didn't know what was wrong. I wasn't thinking about dope when I was eight."

But Connick's most complete musical education came at the New Orleans Center for the Creative Arts. There he was taught by Ellis Marsalis, a now-legendary jazz instructor who, more importantly, is also the father of current jazz stars Branford and Wynton Marsalis. By the time Connick was in high school, Wynton Marsalis had already become a star with his horn, and Connick idolized him. "I wanted to be Wynton," Connick told *Time*. "I wanted to be in his band. I dressed like him. I talked like him." Marsalis, too, made his mark by playing the music of the past and has also been roundly criticized for it. But Connick feels that a tip of the hat to the great masters is essential for young musicians. "It's a shame they criticize people like Wynton and me for going back, because all we're trying to do is develop our own style, and the only way you can do that is by understanding the music of your predecessors," he told the *Chicago Tribune*. "Everyone imitates when they start out. I'm not 40, I'm 22."

Connick's dream was to follow the footsteps of his friend Marsalis to stardom, and the sooner the better. He went to New York at the age of 18, telling his father that he wanted to study at the Manhattan School of Music. His real aim, however, was to sign a record deal with Marsalis's label, Columbia. After a couple of courses at the music school, Connick dropped out and began playing at churches, on street corners, and at small jazz clubs, anywhere he could play. "I'm a New Orleans performer," Connick told the *Chicago Tribune*, "and that means you'll do just about anything anywhere for the chance to perform, even if you have to tap dance out on the street. I simply have to perform all the time."

Eventually, the talent scouts at Columbia took notice, and Connick's first major-label album, a self-titled jazz collection, was followed by a second record titled *20* for Connick's age at the time. This second record featured Connick's Sinatra-style vocals, which he refers to as "swing." Connick's third collection was the immensely successful soundtrack to the 1989 hit film *When Harry Met Sally...*, which featured Connick on vocals, solo piano, and performing with a big band.

Despite his early success, Connick has no illusions about either the reasons for it or his place among the jazz elite. Referring to his record deal with Columbia, about which he expresses some guilt due to the lack of attention some of his friends in the industry have been getting, Connick knows that part of his appeal is his novelty. "I sing, and I'm young, and I wear baggy suits, and I play jazz, and I'm white," he told *Rolling Stone*'s Tannenbaum. "The sounds that come out of me shouldn't be coming out of someone so young. That's why I got signed." And when jazz critics begin to point out that Connick's playing is derivative of such legends as Ellington, Thelonius Monk, and Erroll Garner, Connick is quick to agree. "Shoot man," he quipped to *Rolling Stone* in 1989, "I'm twenty-one years old. Of course, I don't have a style." But he's got plenty of time.

Selected discography

Harry Connick, Jr., CBS, 1987.

20, CBS, 1987.
When Harry Met Sally... (film soundtrack), CBS, 1989.

Sources

Chicago Tribune, January 14, 1990.
New York, January 2, 1989.
Newsweek, February 20, 1989.
Rolling Stone, March 23, 1989.
Time, January 15, 1990.

—*David Collins*

Katherine Couric

AP/Wide World Photos

Television journalist

Born January 7, 1957, in Arlington, VA; daughter of John (a retired public relations executive) and Elinor Couric; married to attorney Jay Monahan; children: Elinor Tully Monahan. *Education:* Graduated with honors from University of Virginia with a degree in American Studies, 1979.

Addresses: *Home*—Washington, DC, and New York City. *Office*—NBC *Today*, 30 Rockefeller Plaza, Room 304, New York, NY 10112.

Career

News bureau desk assistant for American Broadcasting Companies, Inc. (ABC), in Washington, DC, 1979; joined the Cable News Network (CNN) as an assignment editor in 1980; moved to Atlanta as associate producer, later producer, then full-time political correspondent for CNN's *Take Two* news and information program; general assignment reporter at WTVJ in Miami, FL, 1984-86; general assignment reporter with WRC-TV, the National Broadcasting Company (NBC) station in Washington, DC, 1986-89; joined NBC News as deputy Pentagon correspondent, 1989; national correspondent for NBC News's *Today* show based in Washington, DC; named co-anchor of *Today*, 1991.

Awards: Couric wrote and produced an award-winning series on child pornography while at WTVJ in Miami, and earned a local Emmy and Associated Press award for her story on a dating service for the handicapped while at WRC-TV in Washington.

Sidelights

Katherine (Katie) Couric, newest co-anchor for the NBC News *Today* show, is having a professional identity crisis. "I still can't decide whether I'm Katherine or Katie," she laughingly admitted to her audience one morning. NBC execs don't care which name she sticks with, since her engaging personality is credited with helping *Today* recapture the top spot in a closely-watched morning show ratings contest.

In fact, she slips easily from Katherine-the-competent to Katie-the-cute, interviewing Pentagon brass with authority and poise, then submitting to an on-the-air cosmetic makeover with a giggle and grimace. When her quick peek in the mirror at the conclusion of the makeover results in shattering glass sound effects and off-stage laughs, it's clear that she's liked as much by her co-workers as by the fans at home. With her wholesome good looks and hundred-watt smile, she's the very approachable all-American cheerleader, girl-next-door, tag-along-kid-sister-type who's just what the doctor ordered for the troubled *Today* show.

When NBC replaced their very popular veteran hostess Jane Pauley with the very blonde and beautiful Deborah Norville (see *Newsmakers 90*) in

1989, fans were appalled. Reaction was swift and merciless. The longtime, number-one *Today* took a fast tumble in the ratings as viewers defected in droves. Couric was sympathetic. "I think that people have been too hard on Deborah," she told *TV Guide*. "She's smart and obviously does her homework and she's tough as nails. She's put up with a lot of criticism and she's carried herself with dignity." When Norville took a maternity leave in early 1991, Couric subbed as co-host with Bryant Gumbel and ratings perked up sharply. The *National Enquirer* dubbed her "KATIE CURE-IT" and NBC named Couric a permanent co-anchor as Norville opted for full-time mothering. "She's been terrific," Gumbel told *The Washington Post*. "Katie's easygoing, she's bright, she's curious, she's fun to be with. I've yet to hear someone say a bad thing about her."

Couric, 34, comes to *Today* with impressive journalistic credentials. After graduating with honors from University of Virginia in 1979, she was interested in reporting. Her father, John, a retired public relations executive and former news editor with United Press, advised her to try broadcasting because the money would be better. Couric took an entry level job as a desk assistant at ABC in Washington. "Basically I made coffee, answered phones and got [then ABC anchor] Frank Reynolds ham sandwiches," she told *TV Guide*. "It was the most humiliating job I ever had."

Within a year she jumped to CNN's Washington bureau as an assignment editor where she worked behind the scenes, learning the basics of broadcast journalism. Her early on-the-air reports were unappreciated by then-CNN president Reese Schonfeld, who informed producers that he never wanted to see her on the air again. Couric was discouraged but responded with characteristic pluck. She began working with a voice coach when she moved to Atlanta to be assistant producer for the CNN talk show *Take Two*. She continued doing occasional on-air features and was rewarded with a temporary reporting assignment as CNN's political correspondent during the 1984 presidential campaign. Her candidate profiles were praised, but after the election the job ended.

Couric still wanted to report, but was sidelined by a series of directors who felt her face was too fresh, her eyes too wide, and that she looked too young to be taken seriously. In 1984 she landed a job as cub reporter at WTVJ in Miami covering immigration and crime. She cut her hair for a more sophisticated look, hung around the federal courthouse developing leads, and learned to work on a fast deadline. She

honed her skills and wrote and produced an award-winning series on child pornography. Anchoring was not an issue. "I'm not glamorous," she told the *Chicago Tribune*. "I always thought of myself as the workhorse, street-reporter type. And besides, my bosses never encouraged me."

In 1986 she moved back to Washington to work as a late news reporter for WRC-Channel 4, an NBC affiliate, where she covered fires, murders, civic corruption, light features, and politics. Her story on a dating service for the handicapped won a local Emmy and an Associated Press award. She began to think about anchoring, but her news director advised her to look for a "really small market somewhere." Undaunted, she accepted a network job with NBC for the number-two spot at the Pentagon in the summer of 1989. NBC's Washington bureau chief Tim Russert was looking for a general-assignment reporter and had viewed dozens of tapes from all over the country, but kept noticing Katie Couric. "She was always so competent and unflustered," Russert told the *Chicago Tribune*, "whether she was covering hard news, soft news, the homeless or [former Washinton, DC mayor Marion] Barry."

Couric took some time out to marry Jay Monahan, a Washington, DC attorney whom she met at a party the year before. She studied military guides during their honeymoon in Italy, and hurried back to familiarize herself with her new beat and develop sources. In December of 1989 the hard work paid off. During the invasion of Panama, Couric gave live reports from the Pentagon. It was a measure of her progress and ability that her military updates now attracted positive attention. One week later, she was asked to fill in as week-end anchor of *NBC Nightly News*. In May of 1990 she was named national correspondent for *Today*, a newly-created position.

Assignments at *Today* turned her into a jetsetter. She took the shuttle to New York two or three times a week, covered gubernatorial elections in Massachusetts and Florida, reported on the savings and loan scandal from Indiana, then flew to Saudi Arabia to cover President Bush's Thanksgiving Day visit. She managed a victory of her own when granted an interview with commanding officer of U.S. troops, General H. Norman Schwarzkopf (also in *Newsmakers 91*). The war-seasoned general was charmed enough to later refer teasingly to her then-expected child as "little Norma or Norman."

According to her friends and family, Couric was a charmer even as a child. She and her three siblings, Emily, Clara, and John, were raised by parents John and Elinor in a pleasant Arlington, Virginia, neighborhood. The Couric children were good students at Jamestown Elementary, Williamsburg Junior High, and Yorktown High School. All three sisters were cheerleaders. Katie also found time for track, gymnastics, National Honor Society, and the school newspaper.

It's the normalcy that her viewers seem to like. "I'm just somebody who's not very different from a lot of thirty-four-year-old women working in America today," she told *Glamour*. "I think women think they could have me as a girlfriend; we could go out to lunch and talk about men and jobs . . . . I'm not into being ostentatious. The idea of having a $1,500 watch doesn't appeal to me very much. Neither does driving a Mercedes." Frugal Couric enjoys bargain hunts at Loehmann's and once rented a maternity gown for a White House dinner.

As new co-anchor of *Today*, Couric's schedule is hectic: a limousine picks her up from her temporary New York apartment for a 4:30 a.m. ride to her office where she typically works a 14-hour day. Friday nights she catches a shuttle home to Washington for the weekend. Husband Jay Monahan, an associate with the law firm Williams & Connolly, works equally demanding hours and is hoping to handle much of the firm's New York business so they can spend more future time in the same city. Their first child, daughter Elinor Tully Monahan, was born in July of 1991, and Couric took a two-month maternity leave.

"I'd like to say that I read [Jean] Cocteau and [Jean-Paul] Sartre on the weekends, but what I really do is veg out," she told *Glamour*. "I'm not a real whiz in the kitchen. I buy a head of lettuce and six weeks later it looks like a candidate for a science experiment." Couric also confesses to being disorganized. One interviewer described her as a well-groomed bag lady with a purse full of capless lipsticks, expired Pentagon passes, and an empty checkbook. Her best friend and former roommate, Wendy Walker, a producer at CNN, told a reporter, "About the worst thing I can say about her is that she's a total mess." Walker gave her a box full of cleaning supplies for a wedding shower gift. It's clear that Couric's husband takes a different view of her organizational skills. "It's amazing," Monahan told the *Chicago Tribune*. "She'll be lying on the couch, giving attention to our Persian cat, Frank, talking on the phone, watching the news on TV, reading *Newsweek* and *Time* and resting all at once."

Couric considers herself a feminist and hopes to work on stories about politics, women, the abortion debate, teen pregnancy, and the homeless, but is careful not to express her own opinions too freely on television. She believes that coming on strongly with a personal agenda might turn viewers off. However, there are some things about which she asserts herself. When NBC asked her to grow out her short hairstyle for a softer look, she refused, explaining that she preferred not to look like everyone else on TV. A compromise was achieved by adding blond highlights when even her mother called to complain that Katie could use some glitz.

"I think there's much more that goes into anchoring the *Today* show—not just the personality, the happy talk, the clever banter and all that," she told the *Washington Post*. "I feel that I'm using a lot of the skills that I honed when I was a reporter. I don't feel that I'm just throwing them out the window and doing Martha Stewart and rock gardens all the time."

Couric is looking for a nanny and a larger New York apartment while trying to keep a level head about all the attention and publicity her new position is attracting. "I appreciate that this is a capricious business," she told the *Chicago Tribune*. "As somebody said the other day, 'Today you may be drinking the wine. Tomorrow you may be picking the grapes.'" These days, it's safe to say, champagne could be her beverage of choice.

Sources

Broadcasting, April 8, 1991.
Chicago Tribune, May 5, 1991.
Glamour, July 1991.
Newsday, April 10, 1991.
New York Times, April 8, 1991.
People Weekly, April 22, 1991.
Saturday Evening Post, July/August 1991.
Time, April 15, 1991.
TV Guide, December 29, 1990.
Washington Post, May 21, 1991.

—Sharon Rose

Macaulay Culkin

AP/Wide World Photos

Actor

Born c. 1980; son of Kit (former actor and now Culkin's manager) and Pat.

Addresses: *Home*—New York, NY. *Agent*—Paul Feldsher, International Creative Management, 40 West 57th St., New York, NY 10019.

Career

Began acting at age four in off-Broadway shows; has appeared with the New York City Ballet in *The Nutcracker*, c. 1984, and on the New York stage in *AfterSchool Special*, 1987. Appeared in films, including *Rocket Gibraltar*, Columbia Pictures, 1988, *See You in the Morning*, Warner Bros., and *Uncle Buck*, Universal Studios, both 1989, and *Jacob's Ladder* and *Home Alone*, both 1990.

Sidelights

Macaulay Culkin is one of the most well-known child actors in America. His blonde-banged, mischievous grin has beamed brightly from billboards, magazine covers, newspaper pages, and television screens. And he had good reason to smile as the young star—with top billing—of the comedy smash *Home Alone*. Casting directors have lined up with offers for the fifth-grader and he reportedly earned $1 million for his work in *My Girl*, the film he made immediately after *Home Alone*.

Being cast as Kevin McCallister, the youngster whose frazzled family forgets to take him along on a Christmas trip to Paris, was a lucky and timely break for Culkin. Baby Boomer movie fans who had searched for suitable family viewing found a gem in *Home Alone*. The sleeper hit outdid considerable holiday competition and earned more than $246 million at the box office. Many believe that Macauley's talent and charm were responsible for luring fans back for second and third viewings.

As Kevin, Macaulay acts out every child's worst fear and biggest thrill: Left alone in his family's spacious suburban home, he revels in the absence of punitive parents and annoying siblings, ignores bedtime, watches TV all night, eats mountains of junk food, and freely explores previously off-limits areas. Comic reality sets in, however, when two bumbling burglars— played by Joe Pesci and Daniel Stern—target the McCallister home for a break-in. Feisty Kevin overcomes his fears in time to outwit the thieves in hilarious slapstick style; through a series of ingenious tricks employing toys and common household appliances, Kevin booby-traps his home. Then, satisfying sentimental audiences, he gives in to a bout of lonesome holiday blues just in time to welcome back his frantic family.

Writer-producer John Hughes wanted to do a movie that would appeal to all ages and received his inspiration while preparing to take his own family on a vacation. While making lists of things not to forget, he was struck by the funny thought that he'd better not forget his kids. He interrupted his packing to write pages of notes that later turned into *Home Alone*. Hughes suggested Culkin for the lead after watching the boy's stand-out performance as John Candy's precocious nephew in *Uncle Buck*. Director Chris Columbus auditioned more than 100 children before choosing Culkin. "Mack was very real and very honest. He seemed to be a real kid, one that you wouldn't be annoyed with if you had to spend two hours with," Columbus told *Time*. Still, the director was concerned that the then nine-year-old would have trouble learning so much dialogue. Macaulay convinced Columbus by memorizing two scenes for his callback interview.

"I had to do so many things at one time and I was like, 'Okay, what do I have to do first?' And I had to keep on doing lines over and over because I would keep on forgetting."

Hughes shared Columbus's anxiety over a youngster handling the lead in a $15-million film. In an interview with *Entertainment Weekly* he said, "The question was, could I get a 9-year-old to carry a whole film? The key is to get the real kid and not the actor kid who has a dialogue coach and parents reading him lines . . . . We really found that as a little kid, Mack's terrific. When he's jumping on a bed, he's not Kevin, he's Mack. He was having a great time in that scene. When we said, 'Okay, you have to stop now,' he said, 'Why?'" Hughes added, "Chris [Columbus] worked with him so well. He's sort of like a kid too." That may have been the reason Columbus and Culkin worked so well together; Culkin was impressed by Chris's habit of rocketing around the soundstage on roller skates, and since Columbus often directed scenes with his baby daughter in his arms, he tended to be sensitive to the behavior and needs of children.

Culkin admitted to *Entertainment Weekly* that he felt the pressure at times: "I had to do so many things at one time and I was like, 'Okay, what do I have to do first?' And I had to keep on doing lines over and over because I would keep on forgetting." Columbus

countered with a system of rewards. "During rehearsals, we had a deal," he told *Entertainment Weekly*. "Mack could play Nintendo if he'd memorized his lines. He'd show up and go through the entire script in about 15 minutes . . . . Mack is such an intelligent kid and so far advanced, it's like working with an adult." David Friendly, producer of *My Girl*, Culkin's follow-up to *Home Alone*, told *People:* "He had more presence than any child actor I can remember since Shirley Temple." In the same interview Friendly did concede, however, that "He does have a mischievous streak. Every time [director] Howard Zieff would ask him to do something, he'd say, 'Director, may I?' But then at the end he went around and thanked everybody—a real professional . . . . A Macaulay Culkin doesn't come along very often. It would be a mistake to think there are a lot of 10-year-olds who can do what he does."

Despite his mature on-set behavior, Culkin's interests are decidedly age appropriate; his list of favorites include skateboards, wrestling, Nintendo, Bart Simpson, video arcades, sleeping, eating, basketball, and summer. He's an accomplished mimic and managed to pocket about $50 playing liar's poker with teamsters on the *Home Alone* set. Stage presence, in fact, seems to run in the Culkin family. Macaulay's father is a former New York actor who has retired to manage his son's career. The boy's aunt is actress Bonnie Bedelia, and brothers Shane and Kieran have also acted on stage and screen.

Macaulay began his career at the age of four, appearing in off-Broadway shows. He danced the part of Fritz in *The Nutcracker* at New York City's Lincoln Center, was Burt Lancaster's favorite grandson in *Rocket Gibraltar*, and played Jeff Bridges and Farrah Fawcett's son in *See You in the Morning*. He learned to ride a two-wheeler for his role as Tim Robbins's son in *Jacob's Ladder*. His performance in *AfterSchool Special* at the Ensemble Studio Theatre was touted by the *New Yorker*, and he delighted audiences with his kitchen-table interrogation of John Candy in *Uncle Buck*.

Culkin lives with his family in a four-room apartment on Manhattan's upper East Side. There's not much space for large egos, or for that matter plain privacy, since Macaulay shares a bedroom with his six siblings. When he's not on location, he attends fifth grade at a New York parochial school. One of his parents accompanies him on all locations and interviews. While working on *Home Alone* in Illinois, Macaulay received the mandatory three hours of school instruction per day, and regularly spent ten-hour days working and studying and playing on the set.

Home Alone broke box-office records across the nation and established Culkin as a capable and reliable actor who appeals to all age groups. His salary for the film—in the low six figures—was modest by Hollywood standards, but the film's success has set the stage for higher earnings and a more prominent public profile for Culkin. He won an important role in *My Girl*, in which he co-stars with Dan Aykroyd and Jamie Lee Curtis; the young star is slated to receive his first screen kiss in the picture. *USA Weekend* reported that Culkin's agents asked $5 million for the actor's work in a *Home Alone* sequel tentatively titled *Alone Again.*

In the meantime Culkin, his parents, publicists, and assorted siblings cruise the streets of New York City in a limousine to keep up with their heavy schedule of press interviews and television appearances. Culkin made *Irish American* magazine's 1991 list of 100 top Irish Americans, was nominated as funniest lead actor in a motion picture for the 1991 American Comedy Awards, and appeared on the televised award show as a presenter. The downside of fame, however, has prompted the youngster to request a ski mask to hide from reporters and autograph-seekers.

Although it is difficult to predict the future of a child actor, industry observers believe Culkin has the ability to continue along the star track. "He could certainly continue acting if he doesn't get bored with it," Columbus told *Premiere.* "He was always really interested in the cameras and storyboards, so, who knows, maybe he'll be a director one day." Macaulay's reaction to all the fuss over whether he's enjoying his luminary status enough to continue to act is a matter-of-fact "Pretty much so." While he considers his options, his bank account and legions of fans continue to grow.

Sources

Detroit Free Press, February 11, 1991; March 4, 1991; March 9, 1991.
Entertainment Weekly, December 7, 1990.
Newsweek, September 4, 1989; December 3, 1990.
New Yorker, June 1, 1987.
New York Times, November 16, 1990; December 10, 1990; January 7, 1991.
People, September 12, 1988; December 17, 1990.
Premiere, December 1990; April 1991.
Time, December 10, 1990.
USA Weekend, April 5-7, 1991.

—Sharon Rose

Gerard Depardieu

AP/Wide World Photos

Actor

Born December 27, 1948, in Chateauroux, France; son of Rene (a sheet metal worker) and Eliette (Marillier) Depardieu; married Elisabeth Guignot (a psychoanalyst and actress), April 11, 1970; children: Guillaume, Julie. *Education:* Attended Cours d'art dramatique de Charles Dullin and Ecole d'art dramatique de Jean Laurent Cochet.

Addresses: *Home*—Bougival (near Paris), France; has second home on Normandy coast. *Agent*—Art Media, 10 Avenue George V, 75008 Paris, France.

Career

Made French film and television debut in 1965; appeared occasionally in dramas on French television and in plays in Paris, 1968-70; appeared in French television series *L'Inconnu*, 1974; made American debut in *Green Card*, 1990. Films include *Le Cri du cormoran, le soir au-dessus des jonques*, 1970; *Un peu de soleil dans l'eau froide*, 1971; *Le Tueur*, 1971; *Nathalie Granger*, 1971; *La Scoumoune*, 1972; *Au rendez-vous de la mort joyeuse*, 1972; *L'Affaire Dominici*, 1972; *Le Viager*, 1972; *Deux hommes dans la ville*, 1973; *Rude journee pour la reine*, 1973; *Les Gaspards* (released in English as *The Holes*), 1973; *Les Valseuses*, 1973 (*Going Places*, 1974); *Stavisky . . .*, 1973; *La Femme du Gange*, 1973; *Vincent, Francois, Paul, et les autres*, 1974; *Pas si mechant que ca* (The Wonderful Crook) 1974; *Maitresse*, 1975; *7 Morts sur ordonnance*, 1975; *Je t'aime, moi non plus*, 1975; *Bertolucci secondo il cinema*, 1974; *L'ultima donna* (in Italian; released in French as *La Derniere femme* and in English as *The Last Woman*), 1975; *1900* (or *Novecento*; in Italian),

1976; *Barocco*, 1976; *Baxter—Vera Baxter*, 1976; *Rene la Canne*, 1976; *Le Camion*, 1977; *Violanta*, 1977; *La Nuit tous les chats sont gris*, 1977; *Dites-lui que je l'aime*, 1977; *Ciao maschio*, 1977; *Dielinkshandige Frau* (*The Left-Handed Woman*), 1977; *Reve de singe*, 1977; *Preparez vos mouchoirs* (*Get Out Your Handkerchiefs*), 1978; *Bye Bye Monkey*, 1978; *Le Sucre*, 1978; *Les Chiens*, 1978; *Le Grand Embouteillage*, 1978; *L'Ingorgo* (*Traffic Jam*), 1979; *Rosy la Bourrasque*, 1979; *Buffet froid*, 1979; *Loulou*, 1979; *Mon Oncle d'Amerique*, 1980; *Le Dernier Metro* (*The Last Metro*), 1980; *Inspecteur la Bavure*, 1980; *Je vous aime*, 1980; *Loulou*, 1980; *Le Chevre*, 1981; *La Femme d'a cote* (*The Woman Next Door*), 1981; *Le Choix des armes* (*Choice of Arms*), 1981; *Le Retour de Martin Guerre* (*The Return of Martin Guerre*), 1981; *Danton*, 1982; *La Lune dans le caniveau* (*The Moon in the Gutter*), 1982; *Le Grand Frere*, 1982; (and co-producer) *Les Comperes*, 1983; *Fort Saganne*, 1983; (and director, co-writer) *Le Tartuffe*, 1984; *Rive droit, rive gauche*, 1984; *Police*, 1985; *One Woman or Two*, 1985; (and co-producer) *Menage*, 1986; *Rue du depart*, 1986; (and co-producer) *Jean de Florette*, 1986; (and co-producer) *Les Fugitifs*, 1986; (and co-producer) *Sous le soleil de Satan*, (*Under the Sun of Satan*) 1987; (and co-producer) *Drole d'endroit pour une rencontre*, 1988; (and co-producer) *Deux*, 1988; (and co-producer) *Camille Claudel*, 1988;

(and co-producer) *I Want to Go Home*, 1989; (and co-producer) *Too Beautiful for You*, 1989; (and co-producer) *Cyrano de Bergerac*, 1990; *Green Card*, 1990; *Merci la vie*, 1991.

Awards: Prix Gerard Philipe, 1973; Cesar Award for best actor, 1980, for *The Last Metro*; voted best actor of 1983 by the National Society of Film Critics for performances in *The Return of Martin Guerre*; voted best actor at Venice Film Festival for role in *Police*, 1985; Palme d'or Award at Cannes Film Festival, 1987, for *Under the Sun of Satan*; special jury prize at Cannes Film Festival, 1989, for *Too Beautiful for You*; best actor award at Cannes Film Festival for starring role in *Cyrano de Bergerac*; Academy Award nomination for best actor, 1991, for *Cyrano de Bergerac*; Golden Globe Award for role in *Green Card*.

Sidelights

Throughout Europe and in parts of the United States, French actor Gerard Depardieu has garnered a faithful following for his powerful performances in such diverse films as *The Last Metro*, *Danton*, *Jean de Florette*, *The Return of Martin Guerre*, and *Camille Claudel*. At six-foot-two-inches, Depardieu has rugged, irregular features that are not considered conventionally handsome. "Built like a house safe, he is a shambling mess of a man, and his face, with its skewered jaw and pronounced nose, looks as if it were put together with spare parts," Kitty Bowe Hearty remarked in *Premiere*. He is often compared to Marlon Brando and Robert De Niro for his on-screen presence, strength, and ability. At a young age he had already compiled a list of credits, many with important such important directors as Bernardo Bertolucci, Francois Truffaut, and Alain Resnais. His range includes classical and contemporary tragedies and slapstick and black comedies. A magnetic box-office draw, Depardieu makes three or four films a year with no plans to lighten his heavy schedule.

One of six children, Gerard was born to Eliette and Rene Depardieu on December 27, 1948, in Chateauroux in the central region of France known as Berri. Gerard lived a dismal life as the son of an illiterate sheet-metal worker who provided poorly for his family. By age eight Gerard was running the streets and trafficking in blue jeans and cigarettes at the nearby American Air Force base. When he quit school at age twelve he was a barely literate, hulking youth. He passed his time in bars with street gangs, working at various times as a dishwasher, traveling

salesman, beach attendant in southern France, and attendant at a home for the mentally retarded.

In his early teens, Depardieu mysteriously stopped talking completely and was mute for two years, until a prison psychologist—he had eventually ended up in jail—sent him to the leading French speech specialist Alfred Tomatis. Depardieu later credited Tomatis with helping discover his acting talent. At age fifteen Depardieu impulsively followed a friend to Paris and, like his friend, enrolled in acting classes at a school run by the Theatre National Populaire. At first he had trouble reading scripts but made quick progress. During these classes he met fellow student Elisabeth Guignot, a psychoanalyst six years his senior, whom he would marry in 1970.

> "I just work because I find some men I can follow. I don't follow the movie, I follow my friends."

While in his late teens, Depardieu made his film debut in Roger Leenhardt's *Le Beatnik et le minet* and his television debut in the series *Rendez-vous a Badenberg*. In 1968 he began to appear in plays at the Theatre National Populaire, one of which was Edward Bond's *Saved*. Looking for a threatening persona to play the evil traveling salesman in her film *Nathalie Granger*, Marguerite Duras cast Depardieu, whom she had first seen in *Saved*. The renowned French author remarked on the young actor's natural talent, intelligence, and unspoiled nature and selected him for later films, including *La Femme du Gange*, *Le Camion*, and *Baxter—Vera Baxter*.

Depardieu's leap to stardom came with Bertrand Blier's 1973 film *Les Valseuses*, which was screened in the United States the following year as *Going Places*. In this film, Depardieu plays one of two alienated young men who become involved in darkly comic misadventures as they travel throughout France. Since then Depardieu has repeatedly worked with Blier on such films as *Get Out Your Handkerchiefs*, *Buffet Froid*, *Menage*, *Too Beautiful for You*, and *Merci la vie*.

Depardieu often works with the same directors because, as he told Stephen Schaefer of the *Boston Herald*, "A feeling of family is what I like." He told *Premiere*'s Hearty: "I just work because I find some men I can follow. I don't follow the movie, I follow my friends." He did some of his best dramatic work under the direction of the celebrated Francois Truffaut (*The Last Metro* and *The Woman Next Door*) and was slated for at least three more films, but the relationship was ended by Truffaut's death in 1984. Directed by Francis Veber, Depardieu co-starred with Pierre Richard in the comic hits *Le Chevre* and *Les Comperes* and, under the direction of Alain Resnais, the films *Mon Oncle d'Amerique* and the English-language comedy *I Want to Go Home*. "I have never taken a script and just made the movie. We talk about it, dream the movie, the author and I, and one year later, we make the movie. So I have all the time [I want] to think and dream the movie. As soon as you dream your movie, what you want to do, even if you are acting in another one, you will make it so," Depardieu told Gary Susman of the *Newpaper*.

Commentators have remarked on Depardieu's staggering range as an actor. For example, Depardieu has portrayed Tartuffe in French playwright Moliere's seventeenth-century comedy *Le Tartuffe*, Cyrano in nineteenth-century author Edmond Rostand's *Cyrano de Bergerac*, the peasant Olmo in Bernardo Bertolucci's epic *1900*, the French revolutionary Danton in the film of the same name, the sculptor Auguste Rodin in *Camille Claudel*, and a homosexual burglar in the contemporary comedy *Menage*. As quoted in the *San Francisco Chronicle*, Depardieu prefers roles that allow him to be part of a male-female couple. "We've seen too much macho cinema. I don't care about my 'image'—what I look like onscreen. I love to be part of a couple with a woman—not for sex, but because too few men are strong enough to avoid competition with other men." As well as being able to play the sensitive romantic role, Depardieu is said to have a natural flair for comedy, even in such English-language films as *I Want to Go Home*, for which he learned his lines phonetically, and *Green Card*, the actor's American debut.

For an audience of Americans who avoid all movies with subtitles, *Green Card* served as their introduction to the French actor. In this film Depardieu and Andie Macdowell (of *sex, lies, and videotape* fame) play a pair who marry for convenience—he for an immigrant's green card, which will allow him to live permanently in the United States, and she for acceptance into a special apartment building for married couples only. When the immigration officials become suspicious, the two attempt to forge a history together (complete with staged snapshots), and in the process fall truly in love.

Some critics have compared Depardieu to Michael Caine or Gene Hackman as the best of the French treadmill artists. "Me, I'm not an actor. I'm a worker," Depardieu told Susman. "Acting is the last thing to do. The first thing is to work with the director, with the author, to find a crew, to find the energy, to push. Then acting, okay. But really, for me, acting is not the most important thing." Yet as an actor Depardieu is one of an elite few in France with enough stature to approve the choice of technicians to be used on a film. Depardieu has also become involved in directing and production efforts. While he directed himself in a film version of *Le Tartuffe*, he does not see directing as a new vocation. As for producing, Depardieu bought the French distribution rights to Indian director Satyajit Ray's film *Enemy of the People* and plans to produce a subsequent film by Ray; he has even set up a foundation for the preservation of the Ray's films.

Depardieu is broadening his horizons with successful business and writing efforts. His business activities include the ownership of a vineyard in Anjou and movie production and distribution efforts. Depardieu's book, *Lettres volees* ("Stolen Letters"), became a best-seller in France after its 1988 publication, a rather odd accomplishment for someone with little formal education. "I was grieved when my mother died and I realized I had never written to her," Depardieu explained to Schaefer. "So I started to write letters. And the first one I wrote was to someone dying in the hospital. That person was gone too far and could not read the letter and died also . . . . So over four months, while I was filming, I wrote letters to all these people as if I was going to mail them. There was one last letter, I realized. That was to my father. And my father died."

Writings

Lettres volees, 1988.

Sources

Boston Globe, April 22, 1990.
Film Comment, March 1978.
Los Angeles Herald Examiner, July 5, 1987.
Newpaper, January 10, 1991.
New York Times Magazine, June 14, 1987.
Premiere, February 1991.
San Francisco Examiner, April 15, 1990.
Vogue, December 1990.
Washington Post, April 11, 1990.

—*Jeanne M. Lesinski*

Johnny Depp

AP/Wide World Photos

Actor

Full name, John Christopher Depp II; born c. 1963 in Owensboro, Ky.; son of John (a city engineer) and Betty Sue (a waitress) Depp; married Lori Anne Allison (a musician), c. 1983 (divorced); engaged to Winona Ryder (an actress). *Education:* Attended high school in Miramar, Fla.

Career

Guitarist with band Flame, and later with the Kids, c. 1979-1985, and the Rock City Angels; actor, 1985—. Starred in television series *21 Jump Street;* films include *Nightmare on Elm Street, Platoon, Cry-Baby,* and *Edward Scissorhands.*

Sidelights

Johnny Depp's leading role in the television series *21 Jump Street* whisked him from obscurity to teen idol status in a remarkably short time. Within weeks of his first appearance on the show, he had become a staple of fan magazines such as *Sixteen* and *Tiger Beat,* despite his refusal to grant them interviews. Depp undoubtedly welcomed the opportunities that came with the excessive media exposure, but from the start, he was disturbed by the superficial nature of his fame. As soon as he could, he left *Jump Street* behind to search for roles that would challenge both his acting ability and his fans' two-dimensional image of him. "If Depp is anything, he is interesting," asserts *Rolling Stone* contributor Bill Zehme. "He takes the big risks."

Depp's rebellion against the commonplace began early. He was a troublemaker in school, fighting, smoking, drinking, and earning at least one suspension for dropping his pants in front of a teacher. Ironically, one of the most important influences in his young life came from an uncle who was a fundamentalist preacher. The influence was not of a religious nature, however. One of his services, featuring a gospel group, marked the first time Depp ever saw an electric guitar. "I got obsessed with the electric guitar," he told John Waters in *Interview.* "My mom bought me one from them for about twenty-five bucks.... Then I locked myself in a room for a year and taught myself how to play."

His dedication to music did nothing to improve his academic performance. He told Waters that after three years in high school, he had earned "no credits.... I didn't want to be there, and I was bored out of my mind, and I hated it." Not surprisingly, he dropped out when he was 16. For the next five years, he played guitar in rock clubs around Florida, first in a group called Flame and then in the Kids. The Kids eventually became a regional success; besides drawing large crowds at clubs, they also opened shows for the B-52s, Talking Heads, Iggy Pop, and others. Eventually they attracted the attention of Don Ray, a booking agent from Hollywood. He encouraged them to move to the West Coast and offered to manage them. The Kids saved some money, bought a car, and drove across the United States to what they hoped would be a new level of success.

The Kids were just one of many hungry bands in Los Angeles, however. Competition was fiercer than anything they'd experienced in Florida, and at first they found it impossible to make money. Depp endured a period of working miserable side jobs, struggling to find gigs, and watching his year-old marriage crumble. Eventually the Kids did attain a measure of success in Los Angeles, playing on bills with the Bus Boys and Billy Idol, but Depp's life was about to take a turn that would spell the end of the band. He had made the acquaintance of actor Nicolas Cage, whose agent felt that Depp might be right for a part in the film *Nightmare on Elm Street*. Depp told Waters that the part had been designed for "a big, blond, beach-jock, football-player guy. And I was sort of emaciated, with old hairspray and spiky hair, earrings.... Five hours later that agent called me and said, 'You're an actor.'"

> *"There were a lot of scripts where I would carry a gun, kiss a girl, and walk around corners and pose."*

The part was small—Depp played a boy who was eaten by a bed—but it was enough to let him know that he liked acting. The Kids were forced to disband because their guitarist was now spending most of his time studying drama at the Loft Studio and reading for parts. He played an interpreter in the Vietnam drama *Platoon*, and although he didn't have a lot of time onscreen in the completed film, the ten weeks spent in the jungle with director Oliver Stone were an important learning experience. *Platoon* sat unreleased for a few months and Depp went for some time without landing another acting job—long enough for him to begin playing guitar in another group, the Rock City Angels.

Hard up as he was for work, Depp still reacted negatively when his agent asked him to read for a television show about undercover high school cops. "I said, 'No, no, no, no, no,'" he told Waters. "I didn't want to sign some big contract that would bind me for years. So they hired somebody else to do it, and they fired him after about a month, and then

they called me and said, 'Would you please come in and do it?'" Depp relented, and was immediately cast as Tom Hanson in the Fox television series *21 Jump Street*. The show was one of the fledgling network's first big successes, running for four years, but Depp hated the whole project and claims to have seen only a half-dozen episodes. The hysterical hero-worship he now inspired in his fans was, to him, both embarrassing and frightening.

Filmmaker John Waters saw something more than a pinup boy when he looked at Johnny Depp—he saw something sinister as well. The combination of those qualities was exactly what he wanted for his work in progress, *Cry-Baby*. Waters, known for his classic underground films featuring 300-pound transvestite Divine, was putting together his own interpretation of the story behind *Romeo and Juliet*, *Grease*, and *West Side Story*: young lovers from different social strata struggle with society's disapproval. He wanted Depp to play Cry-Baby, the juvenile delinquent who falls in love with a high-society girl.

Depp was delighted with the casting and the tone of the whole venture. "There were a lot of scripts where I would carry a gun, kiss a girl, and walk around corners and pose, and things like that," he observed in *Interview*. *Cry-Baby* "makes fun of all the stuff I sort of hate. It makes fun of all the teen-idol stuff. It makes fun of all the screaming girls.... It gave me a chance not only to make fun of the whole situation but to do something really different. To be able to work with someone like [Waters], who's an outlaw in filmmaking and has always done his own thing." It also gave him an opportunity to work with an unusual array of fellow cast members, including Iggy Pop, Joey Heatherton, and Patty Hearst. *Cry-Baby* drew mixed reviews, with some critics praising Waters's bizarre, original vision and others dismissing the story as one told too often. But Depp's performance was well-received; Time's reviewer wrote that "the winsome tough from TV's *21 Jump Street* ... radiates big-screen grace and swagger."

His next film took him even farther from the pretty-boy image perpetuated by *21 Jump Street*. As the title character in Tim Burton's *Edward Scissorhands* he played a sort of modern-day Frankenstein's monster—a spectral, somber being created by a lonely inventor (Vincent Price) who dies before completing his work. Edward sports an unwieldy pair of blades in place of each finger, and his face is covered with small scars caused by his awkwardness with his own "hands." Taken in by the neighborhood Avon lady (Diane Weist), Edward struggles with society, his own creative and destructive powers, and his feelings for the Avon lady's pretty cheerleader daughter (played by Depp's real-life fiance, Winona Ryder; also in *Newsmakers 91*).

Edward was played "with touching gravity," according to Peter Travers, a reviewer for *Rolling Stone*. Depp had intense feelings for the Scissorhands character that came through in his performance. When making the film, he purposely remained in his uncomfortable costume all day, and even learned to smoke his cigarets while wearing his sharp-edged prostheses. Although his dialogue was minimal, he used his eyes and body language eloquently. He confided to *Rolling Stone*'s Bill Zehme that he based his performance on a dog he once owned. "He had this unconditional love," Depp explained. Edward "was this totally pure, completely open character, the sweetest thing in the world, whose appearance is incredibly dangerous—until you get a look at his eyes. I missed Edward when I was done. I really miss

him." Director Tim Burton drew parallels between Edward Scissorhands and the actor who portrayed him, telling Zehme: "Like Edward, Johnny really is perceived as something he is not. Before we met, I'd certainly read about him as the Difficult Heartthrob. But you look at him and you get a feeling. There is a lot of pain and humor and darkness and light."

Sources

Entertainment, December 7, 1990.
Interview, April 1990.
Mademoiselle, May 1990.
People, April 16, 1990.
Premiere, October 1990.
Rolling Stone, December 1, 1988; April 19, 1990; January 10, 1991.
Time, April 23, 1990.

—*Joan Goldsworthy*

Barry Diller

Movie and television executive

UPI/Bettmann Newsphotos

Born February 2, 1942, in San Francisco, Calif.; son of Michael (a real estate developer) and Reva (Addison) Diller. *Education:* Attended University of California at Los Angeles for four months.

Addresses: *Office*—Twentieth Century-Fox Film, 10201 W. Pico Blvd., Los Angeles, CA 90035.

Career

William Morris Agency, training program, 1961, became full talent agent, 1964; American Broadcasting Company (ABC), assistant to vice president in charge of programming, 1966-68, executive assistant to vice president in charge of programming and director of feature films, 1968-69, vice president of feature films and program development, east coast, 1969-71, vice president of feature films and Circle Entertainment (a unit of ABC Entertainment), 1971-73, vice president in charge of prime time television for ABC Entertainment, 1973-74; Paramount Pictures, board chairman and chief executive officer, 1974-84, president of Gulf + Western Entertainment and Communications Group, 1983-84; Twentieth Century-Fox, Inc., chairman and chief executive officer, 1984—; Fox, Inc. (comprising Twentieth Century-Fox Film Corp., Fox TV Stations and Fox Broadcasting Co.), chairman and chief executive officer, 1985—. Named to board of News Corp., Ltd, 1987.

Sidelights

With his successful business philosophy defined by the characteristics of risk-taking, creative decision-making, and tight control over financial strategies, Barry Diller has risen to become one of the most powerful studio managers in Hollywood. Couple that with his personality traits of bluntness, cunning, and intimidation, and you have the essence of Diller, a man who has brought financially troubled movie studios like Paramount and Twentieth Century-Fox from the verge of bankruptcy into solid profitability. He is the man who had the gall to start a fourth national television network—Fox—something which hadn't been attempted since Leonard Goldenson created ABC in 1951. Through daring and determination, Diller has brought the Fox television network through its formative years of mediocre shows and low profits to the point where it competes nationally with the other networks and offers unique alternatives to the usual bland prime time fare.

Diller was born in San Francisco in 1942, but he grew up in Beverly Hills. The son of a real estate developer who filled southern California with streets named "Barryvale" and "Barrydale," Diller didn't receive much formal education. He claims never to have attended classes at Beverly Hills High on Mondays or

Fridays and rarely on Wednesdays. He went to UCLA for four months before dropping out. Soon after he left the university, he took a job in the mailroom of the William Morris Agency. Diller read every piece of mail that went through the office and within three years, he was promoted to full talent agent, responsible for selling television talent to Universal and Warner Bros. studios.

At a party given by Diller's friend Marlo Thomas, Diller met ABC executive David Goldberg. The two men argued, but Goldberg liked Diller's style and energy, and he offered him a job as his assistant. Diller moved up through the corporate structure easily, eventually being put in charge of negotiating with external production companies for motion pictures rights. Undaunted by the studio salesmen, Diller became known for his strength and his ability to cut through their sophisticated story pitches and spot the ideas that were actually good. Commented Goldberg in the *New York Times*: "I used to hear the screams coming out of his office and see these chairmen who had their limousines waiting downstairs—Lew Wasserman, Charlie Bluhdorn, Joe Levine—eating egg salad sandwiches at his small desk and fighting with him. Here was this rough, tough kid who wasn't afraid of them and who had class and style."

Around 1969, Diller suggested that ABC produce more of their own films for air, rather than buy them from studios. The network liked this idea, and put him in charge of the project. In the fall of 1969, Diller presented *ABC's Movie of the Week*, the first series that gave a "world premiere" of a made-for-TV movie every week. It became a smashing success, winning 33 percent of U.S. viewership in that time slot for that season. The percentage rose to 38 in the coming years. Diller was promoted to vice-president in charge of Circle Entertainment in 1971. This division was in charge of selecting, producing, and scheduling most of the *Movies of the Week* on ABC. In 1973, he was promoted again, taking charge of all prime time entertainment and becoming responsible for inaugurating the first mini-series in television, *QBVII*. He eventually obtained the rights to *Roots*, which became the most-watched dramatic mini-series in history.

Charles Bluhdorn, one of the men who used to argue with Diller when he was a junior executive at ABC, lured him over to Paramount Pictures Corporation in 1974. Bluhdorn was the creator and chairman of Gulf + Western Industries, Inc., the parent company of Paramount. The studio was in a serious slump, and the energetic, bottom-line oriented Diller seemed

the perfect choice to turn it around. Although he was only 31 when he became chairman and chief executive officer of Paramount, Diller was not daunted by the difficult project at hand. He spent the first year of his reign making sweeping changes in management and reorganizing the functioning of the studio. The boy wonder moved the executive offices back to the Paramount lot and announced his commitment to make more movies—instead of purchasing ones from outside producers. Diller also worked with movie theater owners, conducted lavish advertising campaigns and had films released nationwide instead of choosing a few select theaters for a premiere.

Even with these changes, Paramount's recovery was slower than the dynamic Diller would have liked. It took the release of *Bad News Bears* in 1976 and the coming of Michael Eisner [see *Newsmakers* 89] to the executive fold to really make a difference in the fate of the studio. When he was still at ABC, Diller hired Eisner, who had been a low-ranking employee at CBS. Eisner and Diller complimented each other perfectly. Eisner had a boyish appreciation for adventure and comic movies and Diller had excellent taste, intelligence, and a die-hard pragmatism and bottom-line orientation. Diller's rule was to keep the budgets of his movies down to an average of $8.5 million per production—a total of $3.5 million less than that of his competing studios. He negated this rule only if he could make special financial arrangements.

In 1977 Paramount was still struggling—languishing at the bottom of the six major Hollywood studios in earnings. In 1978, it catapulted to first place with the releases of *Up in Smoke, Heaven Can Wait, Saturday Night Fever,* and *Grease*. Although they never recaptured first place again, Paramount consistently finished in the top three under Diller and Eisner with such releases as *Ordinary People* and *Elephant Man* in 1980. *Reds* and *Raiders of the Lost Ark* blossomed into the money makers of 1981. The next year delivered success with *Forty-Eight Hours, Trading Places, Staying Alive,* and *An Officer and a Gentleman. Flashdance* and *Terms of Endearment* brought home the bacon in 1983. Diller and Eisner were also responsible for quadrupling the number of high-rated television series at Paramount. Some of the most popular include *Mork and Mindy, Cheers, Taxi, Entertainment Tonight,* and the mini-series *Winds of War.*

In 1983 the Gulf + Western mogul Bluhdorn died. Martin Davis took charge of the company, consolidating it into three divisions and naming Diller the president of the newly-formed Entertainment and Communications group, which included Paramount

Pictures. Diller and Davis, however, differed on some major points. Relishing a new challenge, Diller decided to take an offer extended by another Davis, Marvin Davis, head of the financially troubled Twentieth Century-Fox Corporation (TCF). When he joined TCF in 1984, the studio was hundreds of millions of dollars in debt. For his role in fixing it, he commanded $3 million annual salary, and an ownership share in the studio of at least 5 percent. Diller ruthlessly cleaned house—reorganizing departments and laying off over 400 people. He also spent time negotiating with banks for delays in the repayment of loans and a greater line of credit. TCF's financial difficulties were allayed when publishing and broadcasting mogul Rupert Murdoch purchased a 50 percent stake in the studio for $250 million in 1985. With this infusion of capital, TCF purchased major independent television stations from around the country. By 1989, TCF affiliates numbered 125 stations—covering nearly every market in the United States.

"To the risk-taker, as always, comes the spoils."

With this turn of events, and with the movie end of TCF recuperating nicely (By 1985 it showed a small profit for the first time in 5 years), Diller began working on one of his most ambitious undertakings—starting a fourth national television network. It was an extremely risky proposition but, as he put it the *New York Times:* "To the risk-taker, as always, comes the spoils." This is an axiom that Diller's Friday night poker buddies have seen him carry out, game after game. Says producer Daniel Melnick: "Barry will take big chances looking for a big win and stay in a hand longer than he should, hoping to buy a card. He's fearless, and you can't bluff him out."

The gambler launched the Fox network in 1986 with his first program, *The Late Show Starring Joan Rivers.* To the delight of the skeptics, the show bombed, and the network lost $136 million in its first two fiscal years. In 1987, Diller made another strategic mistake when he filled the Fox schedule with high-priced sitcoms such as *Mr. President* starring George C. Scott ($475,000 per episode) and *Werewolf* ($375,000 per episode). "One of Mr. Diller's strong points is that he always learns from his mistakes," reported Aljean

Harmetz in the *New York Times.* This certainly was true of his choices for the Fox network.

He replaced the expensive shows with inexpensive, news-oriented programs like *America's Most Wanted*, produced by affiliate station WTTG, at a cost of only $125,000 per episode. He also added such hip shows as *21 Jump Street, Married...With Children, The Tracey Ullman Show, In Living Color,* and *The Simpsons,* programs that attracted an urban, 18- to 34-year-old crowd that advertisers adore. The programming has made the fledgling television network attain great popularity; the fact that Fox owns most of its affiliates, thereby profiting from advertising revenues, made it a modest financial success, too. "The naysayers, at least the gracious ones, are calling to say they were wrong," said Diller in *Business Week.* Also, TCF's movie studio was also making gains with such pictures as *Big, Die Hard, Young Guns,* and *Working Girl,* producing $35.8 million in operating earnings in the second half of 1988.

Diller continued to aggressively pursue the Fox television lineup in late 1990—adding more nights to the schedule as the network became more and more popular. Specifically, he had tried to obtain the rights to air *Monday Night Football* and seal a Monday evening schedule on Fox.

Although his professional life is high-profile, Diller prefers to keep his personal life out of the public eye. He occasionally finds time for skiing in Deer Valley, Utah, "where his skiing style is to bash headlong downhill," reports Harmetz. He has never married, but was rumored to have a romantic link with Diane Von Furstenberg. He reportedly socializes with a bicoastal set including Warren Beatty, Debra Winger, and Calvin Klein. Chevy Chase, Neil Simon, and Johnny Carson are among the show business pals who partake of his renowned poker games.

Because of his blunt and often ruthless business style, many people are intimidated by him. HBO's Michael Fuchs commented that "Barry's most valuable asset is his fearlessness in confronting. He's like a hot knife through butter. That's powerful if you face someone who doesn't like confrontation." But Eisner claims that Diller is not always as brusque as this description. "Barry is distant, and therefore many people think he's cold, but he is not cold. His bark is 20 times worse than his bite. He can be abrupt and impatient, but nobody is more honest, and in 16 years, he never once undermined me or changed directions on me in midstream."

Whatever his personal talents, Diller's talent for making troubled studios successful borders on genius. "Everybody in Hollywood knew Barry Diller was one of the real talents," commented David Londoner of the investment banking firm Wertheim Schroeder in the *New York Times*, "and it's finally showing up." With profitable returns coming from TCF movie studios and Fox television continuing to grow in profits and programming, Diller has tangible evidence of these real talents. Yet Diller knows that even with financial know-how, managers have to keep their eye on the bottom line in the entertainment business: "You can't fake it, hide from it or run away. In the movie and television business, everything depends on the programming."

Sources

Business Week, February 20, 1989.
The New York Times, September 12, 1984; October 5, 1986; September 29, 1988.

—Nancy Rampson

Jason Epstein

Editor and publishing executive

Born August 25, 1928, in Cambridge, Mass.; son of Robert and Gladys (Shapiro) Epstein; married Barbara Zimmerman, 1953 (divorced); children: Jacob, Helen. *Education:* Columbia College, B.A., 1949, Columbia University, M.A., 1950.

Addresses: *Home*—33 W. 67th St., New York, NY 10023. *Office*—201 E. 50th St., New York, NY 10022.

Career

Editor, Doubleday & Co., 1951-58; vice-president and editorial director, Random House, 1958—; director of New York Review of Books, Inc., 1963—.

Awards: National Book Award Medal for distinguished contribution in American letters (first recipient), 1988.

Sidelights

With the introduction of his innovative publication, *The Reader's Catalog*, in 1989, publisher Jason Epstein once again displayed the entrepreneurial savvy and marketing genius that has made him, for nearly five decades now, one of American publishing's leading and most admired figures. For the price of an ordinary hardbound book, book lovers can purchase *The Reader's Catalog*, scan its more than 40,000 titles of books under 208 different categories, and, after ordering the book from a bookstore—by mail, by fax, or by dialing the catalog's 800 number—have the copy in their hands in less than 48 hours. In summing up the significance of Epstein's latest venture for *New York* magazine, Dinitia Smith wrote, "Epstein, the inventor of the quality paperback and a co-founder of *The New York Review of Books*, has designed a system that could make it as easy to buy a book as it is to order a shirt from L.L. Bean."

But the catalog has not been a hit with all of America's booksellers, many of whom refuse to stock the volume for fear that their customers would buy only one book from them—*The Reader's Catalog*—and then buy the rest of their books directly through the catalog, thus eliminating much of the bookseller's business. Epstein disputes this theory, however. The primary reason he developed *The Reader's Catalog*, he maintains, is that the shelves in modern bookstores contain an overconcentration of bestsellers, to the exclusion of many excellent titles in diverse, important fields that might only sell a few copies. "The last thing I want to do is hurt bookstores or put them out of business," Epstein told *New York*. "I think this will increase book buying...I hope the catalog will encourage bookstores to maintain larger inventories." To appease the 5,000 members of the American Bookseller's Association, Epstein is developing a special, free edition of the catalog, without the 800 number, which he will allow bookstores to use as a ready reference.

A 1950 graduate of Columbia University, Epstein came to the Doubleday company in 1951 with a combined pedigree of high-brow bookishness and entrepreneurial spirit. He was a star pupil in Doubleday's advanced training program and by 1952 had convinced his superiors that there was a market, primarily among penny-pinching students, for quality—i.e., scholarly, sophisticated—paperback books. At the time, quality trade books were hardbound and sold in respectable bookstores at higher prices, while mass-market paperbacks were sold in drugstores and five-and-dimes. Doubleday responded by establishing a new subsidiary, Anchor Books, and placing Epstein in charge of the first line of what is now known as trade paperbacks.

After leaving Doubleday for Random House in 1958, Epstein began to gain recognition as the respected editor of such established writers as Philip Roth, Gore Vidal, and W. H. Auden. He also proved adept at recruiting new writers, many of whom exhibited a tendency toward left-wing politics. In 1960 Epstein agreed to publish Paul Goodman's *Growing Up Absurd: Problems of Youth in the Organized System* and Jane Jacobs's *The Death and Life of Great American Cities*, two books which won huge followings of disaffected students for their scathing indictments of modern society. Epstein's early support of these writers won him a great deal of respect among the decidedly liberal American literati. Thus, when the idea reached him that there was growing support for a new, intellectual American periodical, Epstein reportedly told an associate, "There's only one person in the country who could do it, and I'm busy."

In 1963 however, along with wife Barbara, poet Robert Lowell, Lowell's novelist wife Elizabeth Hardwick, and *Harper's* editor Robert Silvers, Epstein founded *The New York Review of Books*, primarily funding the new venture with $4,000 Lowell had taken from his trust fund. Many of the magazine's early contributors, including Susan Sontag, William Styron, and Robert Penn Warren, agreed to submit articles for free given the common financial struggles such publications usually experience in the early going. But *The New York Review of Books* was an instant and resounding success. The first edition sold more than 43,000 copies, and within eight years the magazine was considered the nation's most influential periodical, with a circulation of 95,000.

Furthermore, *The New York Review of Books* was the principal forum for writings protesting the increased United States presence in Southeast Asia during the 1960s. Although his duties at Random House kept Epstein away from the day-to-day business at the *Review,* he continued to contribute significant articles advancing the magazine's evolving political agenda. For instance, in 1968 Epstein himself covered the trial of the "Chicago Seven," a group of protesters accused of fomenting a riot at the Democratic National Convention. From the several bulletins he provided for the *Review,* Epstein compiled a book, *The Great Conspiracy Trial,* in which he advanced the view that the protesters—among them *Review* contributors like Abbie Hoffman and Tom Hayden—were merely exercising their constitutional right to dissent.

In the late 1970s Epstein again filled a hole in the American publishing canon when he co-founded the Library of America, a series of attractive, quality, hardbound editions of some of America's great writers from the past, among them Nathaniel Hawthorne, Herman Melville, and Walt Whitman. The venture proved to be an unqualified success and was greatly expanded in the 1980s. Epstein left the Library of America in 1989 after arguing with its board of directors, but with the launching of *The Reader's Catalog,* this first recipient of the National Book Award's Medal for distinguished contribution in American letters has once again turned up at the forefront of modern publishing.

Writings

The Great Conspiracy Trial, Random House, 1970.
(Co-author) *Easthampton, A History and Guide,* Random House, 1975.

Sources

Newsweek, March 7, 1988.
New York, August 7, 1989.
New York Times, September 13, 1987; November 23, 1988; August 13, 1989.

—*David Collins*

Boomer Esiason

AP/Wide World Photos

Professional football player

Real name, Norman Julius Esiason; born April 17, 1961, in East Islip, N.Y.; son of Norman and Irene Esiason; married; wife's name, Cheryl. *Education:* Attended University of Maryland, 1979-83.

Addresses: *Home*—Villa Hills, KY.

Career

Quarterback with the Cincinnati Bengals, 1984—. Picked in second round of 1984 draft; became starting quarterback in 1985.

Awards: Named Man of the Year by the Cincinnati Bengals in 1987 for his charity and community work; named NFL Most Valuable Player, 1988; selected to NFL Pro Bowl, 1989 and 1990.

Sidelights

Since 1984 the citizens of Cincinnati have been astonished to find in their midst one Boomer Esiason, a platinum-blonde quarterback with a strong arm and a gift of gab. Esiason has established himself as a dominant performer in professional football, where he is known for his swift and accurate passes and his skill at calling plays from the line. He is equally well known, however, for his outspokenness off the field—his theatrics during the strike-shortened 1987 season led the Bengals to affix a virtual gag order to his contract, and only a berth in Super Bowl XXIII saved him from the wrath of Cincinnati fans. It is hard to quarrel with success, so Esiason has ultimately earned praise from both his

home team fans and the Bengals front office. Still, he told the *San Francisco Chronicle*, "I'm like [Cincinnati's] bastard son. You either love to hate me or you hate to love me. Take your pick."

Norman Julius Esiason literally earned his nickname before he was born. He is the youngest of three children and the only boy, and he kicked in the womb so hard that his parents called him "boomer." The name stuck throughout childhood, high school, and college, and then followed Esiason to Cincinnati when he was drafted in 1984. Esiason was raised in the Long Island community of East Islip, New York. When he was only six, his mother died of cancer, leaving him and his two older sisters in the care of their father. The elder Esiason—also named Norman—was a responsible parent who has become quite proud of his children's accomplishments. "I never remarried, never even dated," Norman, Sr. told *Newsday*. "What woman could tolerate me running off to ballgames with Boomer all the time?"

Esiason attended East Islip High School, where he played baseball and football. A natural left-hander, he was gifted from the outset in both sports. His high school coach, Sal Ciampi, told *Newsday* that Esiason had talents beyond his years. "I saw something special in Boomer right away," Ciampi said. "When he came along, we were winning in football and baseball, but he wasn't intimidated at all. He wanted to play, and when he played he looked like he belonged." By his junior year Esiason was quarterbacking the East Islip football team. Ciampi describes the youngster as "somebody who had poise, huddle control and a take-charge attitude." Ironically, not many college coaches were interested in Esiason. The only Division I school that offered him a scholarship was the University of Maryland, never a football powerhouse.

Esiason signed his letter of intent for Maryland just prior to his senior year of high school. He went on that year to pitch for a 15-0 record in baseball, attracting the attention of a number of colleges and major league scouts. The many offers were tempting—the Seattle Mariners sent a representative right to the Esiason home—but Boomer decided to honor his decision to attend Maryland. He only did that, however, because he thought he would be allowed to play both football and baseball at Maryland. When he got to campus, he found out that he was restricted to football. He was bitterly disappointed, but he decided to make the best of the situation. How he did that was simple: he re wrote the record books for University of Maryland football, compiling the best passing record the school had ever seen (850 passes for 54.2 percent, 6259 yards, 42 touchdowns, and 27 interceptions). During his stay at Maryland he earned the Scholar-Athlete Award from the National Football Foundation.

Needless to say, Esiason assumed that he would be chosen high in the NFL draft when he announced his eligibility. Once again he was sorely disappointed—he was passed over entirely in the first round. What might have been mere expedience on the part of the NFL teams looked like a rank insult to Esiason. *Los Angeles Times* correspondent Michael Wilbon wrote that the player "was so angry at being passed over in the first round of the 1984 draft he vowed to show every club in the league how badly they had been mistaken." Since then, continued Wilbon, "Esiason has been almost obsessed with showing them how wrong they were." The disgruntled Esiason was chosen in the second round by the Bengals, and he reported to the team in the summer of 1984.

Esiason started four games in the 1984-85 season and became the full-time starting quarterback for the Bengals in 1985. His Cincinnati coach, Sam Wyche, was respected as a fine developer of quarterback talent—his previous experience included work with Joe Montana in San Francisco. Esiason may have resented being compared to Montana on almost

every throw, but he did learn from the experience. In 1985-86 the Bengals went 7-9 and narrowly missed the AFC Central playoffs. The following season—Esiason's first full year as quarterback—the team went 10-6, an impressive record but not quite good enough to make the playoffs from that division. Few outside the Bengals team circle knew of the level of strife between Esiason and Wyche during those years, but the tension escalated in the strike season of 1987-88.

Prior to 1987 Esiason was showing vast promise as a player who could throw more than twice as many touchdown passes as interceptions. The season of the strike, however, the Bengals went 4-11 and Esiason threw only sixteen touchdowns and nineteen interceptions. Esiason did not endear himself to Cincinnati fans during the strike, either. At one point he threw himself in front of a bus filled with strike-breaking players, and he was always a vocal supporter of the walkout. His position on the strike further alienated him from Wyche, who took the management's side in the dispute. *Detroit Free Press* contributor Curt Sylvester noted that as the Bengals compiled loss after loss, "the press and fans were ready to run them both out of town."

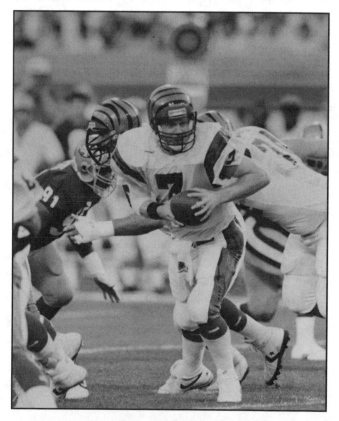

Cincinnati Bengals quarterback Boomer Esiason carries the ball in Super Bowl XXIII (1989) against the San Francisco 49ers. AP/Wide World Photos.

Sentiments were particularly bitter against Esiason, and the harassment began to be aimed at his personal life in the form of remarks about the health of his yet-unborn children. At season's end Esiason asked to be traded. His request was refused. Faced with a long-term stay in Cincinnati, he determined to do what he had done when he was drafted—prove himself with a vengeance. He mended fences with Wyche and the front office, resigned as team captain and player representative, and turned down some $100,000 in product endorsements, all in order to concentrate on his game. "My key word for . . . coming back was 'dignified,'" he told the *San Francisco Chronicle*. "The wounds will never be healed. I'll always remember. But the whole fact of the matter was, I consider myself an intelligent, logical person. For me to be able to put all that behind me, I had to forgive and forget. Now, for our fans, they had to forgive and forget, too." Esiason added: "Winning cures everything."

The Bengals certainly did win in 1988-89. Their 12-4 record carried them into the playoffs, where they won the AFC Championship. Such a spectacular year earned Esiason the fame—and respect—of not only Cincinnati's fans, but of fans nationwide. The colorful Boomer once again turned in a year where he threw twice as many touchdowns as interceptions, and his passing average of 9.21 yards was nothing short of phenomenal. Wyche gave Esiason a great deal of freedom to call his own plays, and the Bengals were able to threaten in both the passing and the running situations, often without a huddle. In the 1989 Super Bowl the Bengals met the San Francisco 49ers, and were beaten in a tough game by the veteran Joe Montana—Wyche's other protege.

By the time of the Super Bowl, Esiason was playing only with the aid of powerful pain relievers. He had not missed a start since 1985, and his shoulder and elbow joints were severely inflamed. To make matters worse, Esiason suffered an allergic reaction to an arthrogram in the off-season and was completely out of commission almost until the summer 1989 training camp began. Despite his injuries, Esiason turned in another Pro Bowl-caliber year in 1989-90, completing 258 of 455 passes for 3525 yards, with twenty-eight touchdowns and eleven interceptions. The team in general was plagued by injuries and only turned in an 8-8 season, but Esiason played in every game. He told the *Chicago Tribune:* "As football players, we've been geared to play with pain since we've been 9 years old. My whole thing is, I don't want to miss a game."

Boomer Esiason is not one of the highest paid players in the National Football League. His $1.2 million annual salary lags behind several in his division, and many in the league nationwide. This may change, though, as Esiason becomes a truly dominating quarterback. At a conservative estimate, he has five more good seasons left (he wants to play seven more), and that should give him ample time to bring Cincinnati to another Super Bowl. Esiason's strengths lie in his swift, accurate left-handed passing and his daunting no-huddle offense, run by coded calls at the line. While others sing his praises, however, Boomer wisely keeps his career in perspective. He told the *Chicago Tribune:* "I'm proud of the things I've accomplished. Also, I'm not hung up on thinking, 'I'm the best.' I feel I play for the best offense. I [play] a very important part in the offense, but 10 guys just as important give me the opportunity to do what I do."

Boomer Esiason and his wife Cheryl live in a custom-built home in Villa Hills, Kentucky. They are very active in charity and community work, donating time and money to cancer research and to the National Arthritis Foundation. Esiason told the *San Francisco Chronicle* that his years in the NFL have enriched his life, both personally and professionally. "It's a maturing process," he said. "I've grown up not only as a player but as a person. I'm better able to deal with human nature and with people's personalities." He added: "I'm not that controversial. I've always wanted people to be honest with me. I would want to be treated as I would treat somebody else."

Sources

Chicago Tribune, January 18, 1989; August 1, 1989.
Detroit Free Press, January 19, 1989.
Los Angeles Times, January 8, 1989; January 22, 1989.
Newsday (Long Island, N.Y.), January 17, 1989.
San Francisco Chronicle, January 17, 1989.

—*Mark Kram*

Gloria Estefan

AP/Wide World Photos

Pop singer and songwriter

Full name, Gloria Fajardo Estefan; born in Cuba; daughter of Jose Manuel Fajardo (a soldier and bodyguard); married Emilio Estefan (a keyboardist and record producer; also Gloria's manager), September 1, 1978; children: Nayib. *Education:* Attended University of Miami, B.A. in psychology.

Career

Lead singer for the group Miami Sound Machine c. 1978—.

Awards: Named *Billboard* magazine's best new pop artist, 1986; named Top Pop Singles Artist, 1986; named songwriter of the year by BMI, 1989; represented the United States at the Tokyo Music Festival and headlined the 1988 Olympic Games.

Sidelights

From Hispanic roots to the pop music mainstream, Gloria Estefan and the Miami Sound Machine are the embodiment of the immigrant's American dream come true. The Miami Sound Machine was originally a Cuban-American quartet that performed popular music with decidedly Hispanic influences. The band grew from being a sensation in Spanish-speaking countries to an international best-seller due to the talent and hard work of Estefan and the sound business sense of her husband Emilio, the band's onetime member and later its manager.

Gloria Fajardo was born in Cuba; as a toddler she fled Cuba with her family when Communist dictator Fidel Castro rose to power. Gloria's father, Jose Manuel Fajardo, had been a Cuban soldier and bodyguard of President Fulgencio Batista. After coming to the United States, Fajardo was recruited into the 2506 Brigade, a Central Intelligence Agency-funded band of Cuban refugees that was involved in the unsuccessful 1961 Bay of Pigs invasion. After President John F. Kennedy negotiated the release of the captured soldiers, Gloria's father rejoined his family. He eventually joined the U.S. Army and served for two years in Vietnam.

As a child Gloria liked to write poetry, and though she took classical guitar lessons, she found them tedious. She had no inkling that she would some day become a popular music star, but music played a very important role for her as a teenager. After her father's return from Vietnam, he was diagnosed as having multiple sclerosis, possibly as a result of having been exposed to the herbicide Agent Orange while serving in the army. His condition quickly deteriorated, though he did not die until 1980. While her mother worked and attended night school, Gloria took care of her father and younger sister. She had little social life, and because she felt the weight of such responsibilities she turned to music as a release.

"When my father was ill, music was my escape," Estefan told *Washington Post* reporter Richard Harrington. "I would lock myself up in my room for hours and just sing. I wouldn't cry—I refused to cry . . . . Music was the only way I had to just let go, so I sang—for fun and for emotional catharsis."

In 1975 keyboardist Emilio Estefan, a sales manager for the rum dealer Bacardi, led a band called the Miami Latin Boys, which played popular Latin music. As there was no lead singer, each quartet member took turns singing. A mutual friend of Gloria and Emilio asked Emilio to advise Gloria and some friends about organizing a band for a special event. Emilio heard Gloria sing, and when he met her again at a wedding at which the Miami Latin Boys were entertaining, he asked her to sit in with the band. A few weeks later Emilio asked Gloria to perform as lead singer with the band, which Gloria did on weekends because at that time she was still in school. A year and a half after Gloria joined the group, by then renamed the Miami Sound Machine, the band recorded its first album for a local label. *Renacer* was a collection of disco pop and original ballads sung in Spanish.

Although Gloria was somewhat plump and very shy when she joined the band, she slimmed down with a rigorous exercise program and worked to overcome her natural reticence. After several months on a professional level, Emilio and Gloria's professional relationship turned personal, and on September 1, 1978, they were married. Their son Nayib was born two years later, about the time that Emilio quit his job at Bacardi to work full time with the band, then made up of bassist Marcos Avila, drummer Kiki Garcia, keyboardist, arranger, and saxophonist Raul Murciano, keyboardist Emilio, and soprano Gloria.

By 1980 the group had signed a contract with Discos CBS International, the Miami-based Hispanic division of CBS Records. Between 1981 and 1983 Miami Sound Machine recorded four Spanish-language albums made up of ballads, disco, pop, and sambas. The Miami Sound Machine first met with success in Spanish-speaking countries. The group had dozens of hit songs around the world—particularly in Venezuela, Peru, Panama, and Honduras—but enjoyed little recognition in the United States.

The Miami Sound Machine's first North American hit was from the band's first English album, *Eyes of Innocence*. The disco single "Dr. Beat" went to the top of the European dance charts. The popularity of "Dr. Beat" prompted CBS to move the group to Epic, the parent label, and inspired group members to write songs in English, first with a couple of numbers

on the otherwise Hispanic record *Conga*. The rousing dance number "Conga" itself became the first single to crack *Billboard*'s pop, dance, black and Latin charts simultaneously. Estefan reminisced to Jesse Nash of the *New York Tribune*, "I'll never forget when we first did 'Conga.' A producer told us that the song was too Latin for the Americans and too American for the Latins. 'Well, thank you,' I said, 'because that's exactly what we are!'" Estefan and the group, the membership of which has changed over the years, pride themselves on the combination of Latin rhythms, rhythm and blues, and mainstream pop that makes up their hybrid sound.

In 1986 the album *Primitive Love*, the band's first recording entirely in English, set off a string of hit singles: "Bad Boy" and "Words Get in the Way" made their way onto *Billboard*'s Top 10 pop chart. Behind the scenes was the work of the trio known as the "Three Jerks"—producer-drummer Joe Galdo and his partners Rafael Vigil and Lawrence Dermer—who wrote, arranged, and performed the majority of the music on *Primitive Love* and the follow-up album, *Let It Loose*.

As a band, the Miami Sound Machine developed a split personality. In the studio the "Three Jerks" and session players made records, and for concerts the road band, which included Garcia and Avila, performed. Gloria was the common denominator. Extensive tours, concerts in 40,000-seat stadiums, and music videos on MTV and VH-1 made the Miami Sound Machine a leading American band. Estefan gradually became the star attraction, and the act has come to be billed as Gloria Estefan and the Miami Sound Machine or sometimes simply Gloria Estefan. Some commentators on the popular music scene called Estefan a demur, Hispanic version of Madonna.

After the *Let It Loose* album, Galdo and friends quit working with the Miami Sound Machine, so the band was on its own creatively. Early in its evolution, the band's biggest hits were the rousing dance numbers, but by the end of the 1980s it was Estefan's ballads that engendered its success. "Ballads are basically what I'm about," Estefan confessed to Dean Johnson of the *Boston Herald*. "I just feel you can express yourself more completely and eloquently in a ballad. It's easier to identify with someone else and form a closer bond with the audience." From the *Let It Loose* album the singles "Rhythm Is Gonna Get You," "Betcha Say That," and "1-2-3" made it to *Billboard*'s Top 10 list, but it was the ballad "Anything For You" that topped the charts.

Despite the group's popularity with English-speaking listeners, the Estefans did not forget their roots. There are always Spanish-language projects in the works, and the title of their 1989 album *Cuts Both Ways* attests to their intention to live up to their international reputation. Gloria contributed to *Cuts Both Ways* in more capacities than as just the lead singer. She was involved in its planning and production, composed some of the music, and wrote lyrics to most of the songs. The rollicking salsa finale "Oye Mi Canto" ("Hear My Song") rivaled "Conga" for its appeal.

Emilio Estefan relinquished his position as keyboardist with the Miami Sound Machine after the birth of son Nayib. He then devoted his considerable energy and managerial talent to promoting the band and the other enterprises that were to eventually make the Estefans producers of their own and others' records. While Gloria toured with the band, Emilio ensured that Nayib would have at least one parent at home. A close family, the Estefans would arrange to meet as often as possible during tours. While together on March 20, 1990, the band's bus was involved in an accident with a tractor-trailer on snowy I-380 near the Poconos Mountains of Pennsylvania. While Nayib suffered a fractured shoulder, and Emilio received minor head and hand injuries, Gloria suffered a broken vertebra in her back. In a four-hour operation several days later, surgeons realigned Gloria's spine and implanted steel rods to buttress the fracture. With a prognosis for complete recovery doubtful, Gloria retired to her home on Star Island, near Miami, to begin her long recovery.

Thanks to extensive physical therapy, intense determination, and the support of her family and fans, Gloria Estefan has made what many consider a miraculous comeback. She marked her return to performing with an appearance on television's *American Music Awards* in January of 1991, and beginning in March, she launched her year-long tour to tout her comeback album *Into the Light*. According to *People*, her "long, sometimes uncertain recovery" gave the singer-songwriter "a renewed feeling about life," as she told writer Steve Dougherty. "It's very hard to stress me out now. It's hard to get me in an uproar about anything because most things have little significance compared with what I almost lost." She added that "so many people got behind me and gave me a reason to want to come back fast and made me feel strong. Knowing how caring people can be, how much they gave me—that has changed me forever."

Selected discography

Primitive Love, Epic, 1986.
Let It Loose, Epic, 1987.
Cuts Both Ways, Columbia, 1989.
Into the Light, Epic, 1991.

Sources

Boston Herald, March 7, 1990; March 14, 1990.
Cleveland Plain Dealer, May 20, 1988.
Des Moines Register, August 21, 1987.
Honolulu Advertiser, May 27, 1987.
Las Vegas Review Journal, June 3, 1988.
Los Angeles Daily News, September 12, 1989.
Los Angeles Herald Examiner, January 29, 1989.
Miami Herald, September 30, 1988; May 7, 1989; July 9, 1989; May 27, 1990.
Newark Star-Ledger, March 6, 1990.
New York Post, July 25, 1988; February 28, 1990; March 21, 1990; March 22, 1990; March 23, 1990.
New York Tribune, September 14, 1988; December 13, 1989.
Palm Beach Post, July 13, 1989.
People, February 18, 1991.
Providence Journal, November 20, 1989.
Rolling Stone, June 14, 1990.
Union-News (Springfield, MA), November 9, 1987.
Washington Post, July 17, 1988.

—*Jeanne M. Lesinski*

Joni Evans

Courtesy of Joni Evans

Editor and publisher

Born Joni Goldfinger, April 10, 1942, in Washington Heights, NY; married Howard Evans (in business), 1967 (divorced, 1975); married Richard Snyder (Simon & Schuster publishing company chairman), 1978 (divorced c. 1991). *Education:* University of Pittsburgh, B.A. in English, 1963.

Career

Secretary at *McCall's* magazine, 1963; reader and reviewer for Book-of-the-Month Club c. 1964; aide to literary agent c. 1964; writer and editor for *Writer* magazine c. 1967; William Morrow & Company, New York City, manuscript reader, 1968; Simon & Schuster, New York City, director of subsidiary rights, 1974-76, associate publisher, 1976-79, publisher and editor in chief of imprint Linden Press, 1979-85, president of trade book division, 1985-87; Random House, New York City, executive vice-president and publisher of trade book division, 1987-90, head of imprint Turtle Bay, 1991—.

Sidelights

Joni Evans is dynamic, successful, and professionally driven, characteristics that make her undoubtedly the most famous and recognizable woman in the New York publishing world. Although she often appears in pictures of *Spy*'s and *Vanity Fair*'s party reportage, Evans confided to *Cosmopolitan* in 1987 that she doesn't care for fame. She said that "It's only in the last ten years that people started looking at the people behind publishing . . . . Editors or publishers should not be seen. It's our authors who should be seen." This concept and others like it reveal Evans's clear-eyed view of her profession; her boundless energy is applied to a savvy publishing philosophy; the combination is perhaps the secret to her success. Her demand for the best of everything may have been problematic in her private life, but it consistently makes her an amazingly productive publisher.

The professional versatility Evans has demonstrated has made her a sought-after employee: most say she is an efficient administrator, and it is generally agreed that her enthusiasm and drive make her a favorite among authors. She has often inspired her writers and fellow editors to accompany her when she makes career moves. *Entertainment Weekly* called her one of the world's most powerful people in entertainment (number 41 out of 100) in 1990, citing her powerhouse deal to get a new book by *Godfather* author Mario Puzo for Random House. She topped her competitor's bid for Puzo's book by $1 million.

In a way, Evans might have been seen as "trading down" by moving in 1987 from Simon & Schuster—the most financially successful American publisher, with $1,422 million in revenues in 1990—to Random House, which weighed in at roughly $850 million the same year. But at Random House Evans has the kind of sovereignty and freedom she has never had before. In 1991, with her own Random House imprint, Turtle Bay, Evans and her hand-picked assistants have the authority to pursue an eclectic title list, and the experience to make it pay. The *New York Times* declared that "at [Random House's] nucleus is Joni Evans, long one of the most visible, most prosperous and most voluble people in publishing, a business increasingly punctuated by the clashes of big egos, big dollars and big risks, a business that, even to its practitioners, often seems totally inchoate."

The native New Yorker got her true start in big-time publishing at Simon & Schuster. After years of working on magazines and reading manuscripts for smaller companies, she began there as a director of subsidiary rights in 1974. Interviewing her for that job was Richard Snyder—her future husband and the future chairman of Simon & Schuster—then a vice-president known for his imperious attitude, who was also saddled with a terminal 11-year marriage. Five weeks after the interview Evans called Snyder and told him that she needed an answer right away about the subsidiary rights job because her heart was breaking for it. He was impressed by her forthrightness and gave her the position.

Four years later, when she was promoted to associate publisher, Evans began reporting directly to Snyder. "So many people hate [Snyder]," gossip columnist Liz Smith told *New York*. "I think that she's the good cop and he's the bad one and I think it's quite deliberate, and they may accomplish a lot by squeezing people." The partnership thrived privately, too, as a romance developed despite office gossip; they married on a lunch break in 1978. Hard-driving Evans soon drove herself out of Snyder's office. He couldn't take her retaliation at home for not humoring her at work, so he created an imprint for Evans, taking her out of the direct chain of command.

In 1979, Evans became publisher and editor in chief of Linden Press, named after a glamourous chateau the couple had purchased together and were pouring great amounts of money into at the time. Friends of the couple said that Evans was not "attending to Snyder's needs" and that she was obsessed with her work. The marriage was always a "difficult" one, according to many. When *Cosmopolitan* asked Evans if she was a workaholic, she replied, "I'm not a workaholic, and it's important I say so every time I have the opportunity. I have a lot of energy, which may make people perceive me as a workaholic. I love what I do, so I don't see it as work. I have weekends and dogs and I cook and have a family and go on vacations and I'm perfectly happy."

Under Snyder's business tutelage, Evans turned Linden into an imprint that grossed $10 million in 1987. In retrospect, Linden and its quirky list were probably prototypes for Turtle Bay. Evans has admitted that Linden was not perfect—she faults herself for not establishing a backlist for the press. Meanwhile, all was not well with the editorial board at Simon & Schuster. Within a year, Snyder had hired and fired two trade book division heads who could not establish a rapport with the board. Despite his misgivings, Snyder offered Evans the position in 1985, and she accepted. As soon as she became chief of trade books at Simon & Schuster Evans went to work on streamlining and improving the editing and publishing process. "She promptly cut the editorial board from 21 members to 13," *New York* reported. "She trimmed the budget. She had contracts canceled on a slew of faulty copying machines. She ordered a new storage system built so manuscripts no longer had to be stacked up in the halls. She moved to computerize the house .... And she eased the company's tempo." Evans's versatile talents extended to creating a comfortable atmosphere where editors were invited to be innovative without fear of infighting and excessive competition.

Many believed that the Evans-Snyder match could not work because, while they were equally driven, Snyder put his work down when he left the office, where Evans was always at least thinking about it. They separated in the summer of 1986; while they managed to work together for almost a year, their professional relationship faltered when the animosity accompanying the division of their property climaxed. Evans resigned from Simon & Schuster in 1987 and was soon snapped up by Random House. Although she was hired to start her own imprint and utilize her in-house entrepreneurship, Evans was quickly offered the chance to exercise her organizational talents with a publisher position. The move to publisher at Random House was a coup; *Newsweek* said at the time that Evans was reluctant to take over from the previous trade books head, Howard Kaminsky, and that she particularly "had a tough time deciding to forgo plans to develop her own Random House imprint in favor of the new job." The prestige of the new job and the accompanying challenge made the offer irresistible.

When Evans was replaced in 1990 by Harold Evans (no relation), rumors flew that she had been moved out to make room for the Englishman who had run the London *Sunday Times*, the Atlantic Press, *U.S.*

News and World Report, and *Conde Nast Traveler,* and whose wife, Tina Brown, is the editor in chief of *Vanity Fair.* While *Time* ventured that Harold Evans would bring a "fresh dose of glamour" to the position, Joni Evans repeated that she had been brought to Random House to run her own imprint and was only claiming it after a pinch-hitting stint in the trade books division. *Time* reported that friends had allowed that she felt "crushed under the administrative responsibilities of her job and wanted to return to editing." The *New York Times* recounted a similar sentiment, saying that Evans was "discontent with the minutiae of overseeing a list of some 100 books." A more revealing statement was given to *Newsweek,* which reported that Evans was planning to write a book herself, about "her industry's ceaseless rumormongering."

No doubt Evans has found her niche in Turtle Bay Books, the Random House imprint that finally got off the ground in 1991, after four years of delay. Evans has the expertise to run the press herself, and at the same time, a free rein that she perhaps never had at Linden. The *New York Times* described the composition of the unique press this way: "The five women who comprise Turtle Bay hope to become something of a throwback to a bygone era, when publishers were small and lavished inordinate attention on their authors." Some who received this attention in the early 1990s were *Fear of Flying* author Erica Jong, who planned an unconventional portrait of Henry Miller; director Milos Forman, who set out on an autobiography with Jan Novak; and Mario Puzo, with most likely another bankable blockbuster.

The close consideration of manuscripts, and intimate rapport with authors, puts to use Evans's crackerjack—and famously direct—editorial skill. According to an unnamed author quoted in *New York,* "as Evans criticized portions of his manuscript, she ruthlessly used the word 'yuck.' To underline her point, she sometimes bent forward and stuck a finger down her throat like Joan Rivers. 'She doesn't mince at all.'" Yet, if she believes in a project, Evans will even cook veal parmigiana for an author if it is the thing she feels will be most persuasive or reassuring. Julia Phillips, author of the acid autobiography *You'll Never Eat Lunch in This Town Again,* told the *New York Times* that Evans "says these incredible sentences to you that cause you to walk around the house kicking lamps over and saying, 'What does she mean

by that?' and then it dawns on you that that's a brilliant insight." The sharp critical sense merges with ardent support that has been reinforced, time after time, with best-sellers. Evans's ability to pick winners no doubt lends credibility to her vehemence. In 1986 *New York* said that Evans's involvement with a book was so focused that "she usually read it and got back to the writer within 24 hours."

Business thrives under her supervision, authors rely on her vision, and editors follow her from house to house. Susan Kamil—who made the switch with Evans to Random House and in 1991 was one of the five women who formed the editorial board of Turtle Bay—described Evans's zeal to *New York* in 1986, saying that Evans "burst into the room and dropped [a] manuscript on Kamil's desk. 'I'm so excited I can hardly stand it!'... Kamil remembers Evans saying.... Kamil picked up the latest object of Joni Evans's passion. 'I started to get excited before I opened the page.... I mean, here I had this manuscript in my hand and it was almost humming.'" Another facet of Evans's publisher's philosophy may be prophetic: she believes the publishing industry lacks talent and drive like hers because of the lack of decent pay for beginners. Often the most promising people pursue a more highly-paid position, often in another field entirely. She told *Cosmopolitan* that publishers still "pay so little on the apprentice level," adding that if one really wants to make it in the book business, one should "live in New York City, where ninety percent of publishing goes on; on such a low salary, it shouldn't be hard to get a job." The fact remains, however, that even with a restructuring of salaries in the industry, publishing may not soon generate another editor of Joni Evans's caliber.

Sources

Cosmopolitan, April 1989.
Entertainment Weekly, November 2, 1990.
New York, March 10, 1986; December 14, 1987; August 13, 1990; December 3, 1990.
New York Times, March 17, 1991.
Newsweek, October 26, 1987; November 12, 1990.
People, November 16, 1987.
Publishers Weekly, November 9, 1990.
Spy, June 1991. *Time,* November 12, 1990.
Vanity Fair, June 1990, September 1990.

—Christine Ferran

Linda Fairstein

AP/Wide World Photos

New York City prosecuting attorney

Born c. 1948 and raised in Mt. Vernon, N.Y.; daughter of an anesthesiologist and a nurse; married Justin Feldman (an attorney), May, 1987. *Education:* Attended Vassar College and the University of Virginia Law School.

Career

Joined Manhattan district attorney's office in 1972; became director of the sex crimes prosecution unit, 1976.

Sidelights

As chief of the sex crimes unit of the Manhattan district attorney's office, Linda Fairstein's most celebrated hour to date came during her successful prosecution of Robert Chambers in the sensational "Preppie Murder" case of 1987. But one would be remiss, in discussing Fairstein's achievements since being appointed to her post in 1976, to focus merely on this one highly-publicized trial. Indeed, Fairstein has been a virtual pioneer in the difficult and still-evolving legal art of sex crimes prosecution—a field that has long been held back by both a legal system often insensitive to victims' rights and the inability or unwillingness of victims to prosecute their offenders. But as Fairstein explained to *Ms.* writer Maria Laurino, these difficulties are precisely what attract her to this demanding and often grim work. "What I like so much about the job is that most people come to the criminal justice system not anticipating help from the system," Fairstein said. "For me, part of the

process is exploding those myths and seeing that the person is well received here and that some kind of justice is done."

Born and raised in a comfortable suburban home and classically educated at Vassar College and the University of Virginia Law School, Fairstein credits the philanthropy practiced by her parents, an anesthesiologist and a nurse, as the driving force behind her strong dedication to public service. Directly after graduating from law school, Fairstein passed up lucrative offers from private law firms to join the Manhattan D.A.'s office in 1972. Under District Attorney Robert Morgenthau, New York was fast becoming a leader in progressive tactics for sex crimes prosecution, and in 1974 Morgenthau created the nation's first sex crimes prosecution unit, with Leslie Snyder as its first director. When Snyder left for a judgeship two years later, however, Morgenthau named Fairstein to the post. Fairstein was not happy with the move at first—her workload of major-felony cases was proving interesting—but she grudgingly took the new position. "I fell in love with the job to a degree I never imagined," she told *Ms.*

Under Fairstein's direction, the sex crimes unit grew to include 14 assistant district attorneys, two paralegals, a secretary, and a full-time detective by 1990, and the office was handling a caseload of between 500 and 700 cases of rape or other sexual abuse each year. The unit has had an 80 percent conviction rate, and Fairstein herself has won 31 of 33 cases she has tried personally. More importantly perhaps, Fairstein has attempted to make the legal system more receptive to victims both legally and emotionally, thus communicating to them, and hopefully the public at large, that rape is not in any way the victim's fault or that they had in some way led their assailant on, as is the archaic view of the crime. Until 1972, in fact, New York State required a corroborating witness—someone other than the victim—to confirm both the identity of the attacker and the nature of the crime, making rape virtually impossible to prove in many instances. Fairstein has also pressed successfully for the "rape shield law," which forbids, in most cases, the admissability of evidence of a victim's past sexual activity in a rape trial; and her unit has been at the forefront of using DNA genetic coding technology in helping to identify and verify sex offenders.

The most famous case Fairstein has tried was actually, in her mind, "a simple, straightforward murder case," although Robert Litman, defense attorney for the "preppie murderer" Robert Chambers, did indeed try to make sex an issue in the trial. Fairstein charged that Chambers, after meeting Jennifer Levin in a New York night club one evening in 1986, strangled and beat his 18-year-old acquaintance later that night in Central Park. Chambers claimed that Levin was killed in "rough sex" that got out of hand when the victim became violent. Litman attempted to back his client up by portraying Levin as sexually promiscuous, and by trying to introduce Levin's alleged "sex diary" as evidence (the judge deemed it irrelevant). Litman's defense was of the classic "blame the victim" variety that Fairstein had spent years fighting in her prosecution of sex offenders. After 13 weeks of testimony and 9 days of jury deliberation, Fairstein, fearing it would end in mistrial, agreed to a last-second plea bargain that reduced the charges on Chambers to first-degree manslaughter, provided he make a public pronouncement that his intention was to harm Levin. Chambers was sentenced to 5 to 15 years in prison, and though Fairstein had hoped for a murder conviction, she contended in *Ms.* that "for someone to be incarcerated from [age] 21 to 31 is no small victory."

Tall, blond, and impeccably dressed, Fairstein's striking physical appearance only adds to her courtroom aura. Opponents and colleagues alike describe her courtroom demeanor as forceful and persistent, but not theatrical. "The general sense is that she doesn't fight dirty, but she fights hard," said law professor Burt Neuborne in the *New York Times*. "She's so strongly moral, she so strongly wants the system to treat people equally. If there were more people like her it would be an infinitely juster system."

Sources

Detroit Free Press, June 21, 1990.
Interview, June 1989.
Ms., September 1987; June 1988.
New York Times Magazine, February 25, 1990.

—*David Collins*

Joseph Fernandez

AP/Wide World Photos

New York City public schools chancellor

Born December 13, 1935, in East Harlem, N.Y.; son of Angela and Joseph Fernandez Sr.; married Lily Pons, 1956; *Education:* Attended Columbia University; earned bachelor's degree from University of Miami.

Career

Coral Park High School, Miami, Fla., teacher, 1963; department chairman, 1964; superintendent of Dade County, Fla., 1987-89; chancellor of New York City public schools, 1990—. Has also worked as a labor negotiator and lobbyist in Tallahassee, Fla. *Military service:* Served in the U.S. Air Force in Japan and Korea.

Sidelights

In January 1990, Joseph Fernandez took over as chancellor of the troubled, 940,000-student New York City schools—and immediately made it clear who's in charge. *U.S. News & World Report* summed up Fernandez's first months as chancellor—sometimes called the toughest job in U.S. public education—this way: "After 27 years as a much heralded teacher and administrator in Dade County, Fla., Fernandez has taken public education's foundering, $6.7 billion behemoth by storm—earning by equal shares the admiration and enmity of many within the city's education establishment . . . [he has] slashed the school bureaucracy, strong-armed its nearly 1,000 principals into relinquishing building tenure and won

the abolition of the city's Board of Examiners, a notoriously bureaucratic teacher-licensing agency."

Born in East Harlem in 1935 to Puerto Rican parents, Fernandez was expelled from parochial school in the 10th grade and transferred to a public high school, where he later dropped out. "He hung out with heroin addicts and petty thieves," said *New York* magazine. "By 1953, Fernandez was just another 17-year-old dropout on the streets of Harlem." To escape the neighborhood he entered the Air Force, serving in Japan and Korea, and earned a high school equivalency degree. Back home in 1956, he married his high school sweetheart, Lily Pons, and enrolled at Columbia University on the GI Bill. Fernandez later earned a bachelor's degree from the University of Miami and, in 1963, got a job teaching math in Coral Park High School in Miami. A year later, he was department chairman.

"The fourth largest in the nation, the Dade County school system was an ideal training ground for Fernandez," said *U.S. News & World Report.* "He held a wide range of positions there—teacher, principal, labor negotiator and lobbyist in Tallahassee. Above all, he honed his skills as a political strategist."

In two years as superintendent at Dade County, from 1987 to 1989, "Joltin' Joe seemed to be everywhere,"

New York said. "He removed or transferred 48 principals.... He launched Saturday computer and music classes at many schools. He started magnet schools and preschool classes.... He had a knack for finding money. He talked 650 Miami businesses into sponsoring school activities and persuaded three companies to donate space for satellite schools.... Soon the new superintendent proposed a $980-million bond referendum for a huge school-construction program" and sold it to voters.

He also established the cornerstone for his school reform efforts in Miami—a school-based management system that puts more decision-making power in the hands of committees of teachers, parents, and building-level administrators. It is a system Fernandez intends to put in place in the New York City schools.

The New York job came with a basketful of perks and a $195,000 salary, which makes Fernandez the city's highest paid public official. And it came with the right bait for Fernandez's ego and ambition. "He understood from the beginning that New York would be the ultimate challenge," Stanley Litow, a longtime critic of the New York schools and Fernandez's deputy chancellor, told *New York*. "He knows this is a job that has eaten people up. But he also knows that if he succeeds here, it will send a message around the country. That was the ultimate lure."

New York magazine pointed out that "even Fernandez's friends say he is stubborn, egotistical, and hot-tempered, although they use these terms almost endearingly. His detractors see a darker side. 'He was the Joe Stalin of the Dade County public schools,' [said] Brian Peterson, a Florida college history instructor who had a run-in with Fernandez. 'The school system is in some ways a totalitarian system, and that was especially true under Joe Fernandez. He made things happen, but partly through terror.'" Fernandez, meanwhile, shows no lack of confidence in his ability to work magic on the New York City schools. "I'm very impatient with incompetence," he told *New York*. "I'm very impatient with people who don't want to try things differently, who say things can't be done because we've never tried it that way before. To move a large bureaucracy, sometimes you've got to kick people in the ass." Despite his detractors, Fernandez's approach may prove to be the right one: "People are so fed up with nothing happening that they're longing for someone larger than life to come along and do something," public education scholar Diane Ravitch was quoted in a lengthy cover story on Fernandez in the *New York Times Magazine*. "Ultimately," the article noted, "Fernandez and the moment seem supremely suited to one another."

Sources

New York, January 22, 1990.
New York Times Magazine, June 17, 1990.
Time, January 8, 1990; February 11, 1991.
U.S. News & World Report, October 1, 1990;

—*David Wilkins*

Carrie Fisher

Actress, writer

Full name, Carrie Frances Fisher; born October 21, 1956, in Beverly Hills, Calif.; daughter of Debbie Reynolds (an actress and singer) and Eddie Fisher (a singer); married Paul Simon (a singer), 1983 (divorced, 1984). *Education:* Attended London Central School of Speech and Drama.

Addresses: *Agent*—c/o Alan Loman, The Authors and Artists Group, 14 East 60th St., New York, NY 10022.

Career

Appeared on Broadway in the musical *Irene,* 1972, and *Censored Scenes from King Kong,* 1980; actress in films including *Shampoo,* 1975, *Star Wars,* 1977, *Mr. Mike's Mondo Video,* 1979, *The Blues Brothers,* 1980, *The Empire Strikes Back,* 1980, *Under the Rainbow,* 1981, *Return of the Jedi,* 1983, *Garbo Talks,* 1984, *The Man with One Red Shoe,* 1985, *Hannah and Her Sisters,* 1986, *The Time Guardian,* 1987, *Amazon Women on the Moon,* 1987, *Appointment With Death,* 1988, *Loverboy,* 1989, *The 'Burbs,* 1989, *When Harry Met Sally . . . ,* 1989, *Sibling Rivalry,* 1990, and *Drop Dead Fred,* 1990.

Sidelights

Carrie Fisher has turned personal misfortune into success through fortitude and wit. In the fall of 1990 Fisher found herself at the top of the Hollywood pyramid with the release of the Mike Nichols-directed *Postcards from the Edge* starring Meryl Streep

and Shirley MacLaine and the publication of her second novel, *Surrender the Pink.* Fisher wrote the screenplay for *Postcards* and introduced a central conflict between Doris Mann (MacLaine) and her daughter Suzanne Vale (Streep), a conflict that was not prominent in the novel and one that is essentially between the old and new Hollywood, leading to renewed speculation of the relationship between Fisher and her own mother, Debbie Reynolds. Fisher's new success did not seem to silence media questions about what it is like to be the daughter of America's most famous 1950s sweetheart couple, actress Debbie Reynolds and singer Eddie Fisher. Queries fly around the ex-wife of rock icon Paul Simon, a former Percodan-addicted actress best known for playing Princess Leia in George Lucas' *Star Wars* trilogy, which grossed over one-half billion dollars for Twentieth Century-Fox and made Fisher a millionaire.

Fisher is never at a loss for words and answers all questions with an ability to entertain and amuse, a combination that accounts for her success as a public personality and as a writer of novels and now screenplays. Describing *Surrender the Pink,* Margot Dougherty in *Entertainment Weekly* wrote: "Her novel is all talk—chaotic, out-of-control, idiosyncratically eloquent, consistently interesting. By nature she has what hordes of writing-school grad students would kill for: a voice of her own." Fisher's voice is marked by a sardonic and sarcastic power that penetrates to the core of a situation. She can direct her wit at the outside world or at herself; it makes her writing funny and truthful, producing laughter while capturing the pain of life. "There is the serious side and there is the sarcastic side and both are expressed in the same even voice, with a drop in pitch for a heavy goof," Anna Quindlen wrote in the *New York Times*. Fisher's grasp of the ever-changing symbols of popular culture gives her books and her interviews a sense of hip knowingness. Questions that Fisher feels invade her privacy or bore her because they have been asked repeatedly she disarms with her deadpan answers. She will not say anything negative about her parents or ex-husband Paul Simon. "Questions about my marriage are 'wire-hanger questions,' and no matter how I answer them they're wired to blow, no pun intended," she explained to *Esquire*.

> *"My family is really the epitome of an unfilmable Dynasty. I call us blue-blooded white trash, and there's an obsession in this country with that kind of thing."*

As the oldest daughter of a highly publicized Hollywood divorce in which Eddie Fisher left Debbie Reynolds to become Elizabeth Taylor's third husband, Fisher as a small child wondered how her mother earned a living and seldom saw her father. As an adult, she "discovered a lot of things I didn't know about" her parents' divorce through a set of scrapbooks a fan had sent her mother. She concluded that "it didn't seem to have much to do with them or with me." "My family is really the epitome of an unfilmable Dynasty. I call us blue-blooded white trash, and there's an obsession in this country with that kind of thing," she told *Esquire*. Like Michael Douglas and Jane and Peter Fonda, who also grew up with famous parents, Fisher has had to find a place for herself in a well-known public family history that invites media distortion.

Born on October 21, 1956, Fisher was raised by her mother. Reynolds's marriage to retail shoe magnate Harry Karl in 1960 provided economic stability until

he lost all of his money in 1972. As a child, Fisher was a voracious reader of serious literature, undertaking authors of the caliber of F. Scott Fitzgerald, Saul Bellow, and John Barth. Mike Nichols recalled that Fisher started writing stories and poems as a child: "She was a hilarious smartass kid. She was always asking questions . . . She was always searching for answers," he told *Time*. A student at the Professional Children's School in Los Angeles, Fisher at an early age wrote in diaries and journals and enjoyed watching old Hollywood films, which helps to account for her ability to write romantic comedy dialogue. Summing up the influence of her parents on her development, Fisher remarked to Chris Chase in a *New York Times* profile, "All they know to do is work . . . The values they handed down were show-business values, not basic life values. They don't teach it at school, either, how to have a great relationship, how to be a good parent; you learn how we won World War II."

The appeal of Hollywood had a powerful grip on Fisher at a young age. Fisher told Chase: "I'd visit my mother on the set, and it seemed to me that getting paid to dress up and goof around with stuntmen was a great job. By the time I was 13, I was part of her nightclub act. I was a good mimic, I could do a perfect Streisand, a perfect Garland. It was fun. Las Vegas was my summer camp." Fisher dropped out of Hollywood High School to join the chorus of *Irene*, a Broadway musical starring her mother. She made her film debut in the Hal Ashby-directed *Shampoo*, a Warren Beatty vehicle about a handsome hairdresser whose amorous escapades place him in various predicaments as he tries to balance his love interests against the backdrop of November 4, 1968, the date of Richard Nixon's election to the presidency. As Lorna, Fisher played a jaded Hollywood Lolita who brazenly seduces her mother's hairdresser, George (Beatty).

Fisher then studied at London's Central School of Speech and Drama for eighteen months, which she credits for providing a foundation to become an actor. "For the first time, I was with people my own age. Twelve hours a day of acting, fencing, voice, movement, everybody with one common interest. I was blessed. If it hadn't been for Central, I might have stayed a Hollywood kid, dressed in sequins and flinging mike cords for the rest of my life. I could have ended up in the Tropicana lounge."

Fisher auditioned for both Brian De Palma and George Lucas. She did not get the part of Carrie in the horror film of the same name, but as Princess Leia she appeared in *Star Wars* (1977), *The Empire*

Strikes Back (1980), and *Return of the Jedi* (1983). *Star Wars*, wrote Vincent Canby in the *New York Times*, "is the most elaborate, most expensive, most beautiful movie serial ever made." *Star Wars* introduced a new set of characters into the Hollywood myth-making lexicon—Luke Skywalker, Han Solo, Ben Obi-Wan Kenobi, C-3PO, Chewbacca, R2D2, Darth Vader, and Princess Leia, the love interest of Luke and Han. As Leia, Fisher wore her hair in distinctive coiled braids that covered her ears and exchanged snappy, sharp–tongued dialogue with the cowboy spaceship commando Han (Harrison Ford) while providing inspiration to the youthful Jedi-knight-in-training Luke (Mark Hamill). Lucas's masterful special effects pyrotechnics, coupled with an idealized fantasy space story, answered the need in the American movie-going public for larger-than-life story told in bright comic book colors and easy-to-follow dialogue; the *Star Wars* trilogy introduced the Hollywood mega-blockbuster concept to contemporary filmmaking. In promoting the *Star Wars* films, Fisher found it difficult to see a significance in them beyond their obvious entertainment value.

Fisher's life reached a crisis in 1985 when she came close to overdosing. She had a history of taking Percodan and frequent LSD trips. "I always wanted to blunt and blur what was painful. My idea was pain reduction and mind expansion, but I ended up with mind reduction and pain expansion," she explained in a *Time* profile. She then committed herself to a one-month detoxification program and continued outpatient and group counseling. After a seven-year friendship, her eleven-month marriage to Paul Simon had ended in 1984. Her career was supplanted by her association with *Saturday Night Live* actor-comedians Dan Ackroyd and John Belushi, appearing in *The Blues Brothers*, their most successful movie, in a small role. "The scariest thing Belushi ever said to me was, 'You're like me.' And then he died," she told John Gross of the *New York Times*. She confessed to Gross of being "world-weary at 20. I had unlimited access, money, fame and acceptance. ... How could I have felt I'd worked hard enough to achieve that? Something was missing. Something was off. I was never comfortable. Maybe that's what drugs did for me. Why drugs? They were there. I wanted to be accepted by people who did drugs. I thought I was too excited. I had this energy. Call it manic. Drugs put me where I perceived everyone else to be. They made me relax .... They made me comatose. Eventually, they eroded whatever coping skill I had. I let the drugs do the walking." She confessed to Jim Jerome of *People* that she would "celebrate not doing them [drugs] by doing them."

What Fisher discovered while trying to put her life back together was that she had a talent for writing. After the May 1985 *Esquire* interview where she displayed her obvious verbal wit and off-the-cuff intelligence, she was approached by New York publishers to attempt West coast versions of the kind of sociological essays Fran Liebowitz has written about the East coast. Fisher was assigned an editor to shape her prose but it became quickly apparent that she had the potential to become a fiction writer. Fisher has been able to use her comic perspective and experiences to write what Margot Dougherty, with appreciation, calls "literate trash." Fisher's novels are loosely autobiographical, but the interesting parts are not how she duplicates her own experience but how she uses it to write more broadly and comprehensively about Hollywood themes and conflicts. About those who think everything she writes is autobiographical, Fisher answers, in this case concerning *Postcards from the Edge*: "I'm not shocked that people think it's about me and my mother. It's easier for them to think I have no imagination for language, just a tape recorder with endless batteries."

> *"Something was missing. Something was off. I was never comfortable. Maybe that's what drugs did for me."*

"Writing pours out of her so easily and gives her such pleasure," says Mike Nichols. Dialogue comes easily to Fisher; she has an excellent ear for catching the way Hollywood celebrities talk about themselves, and she uses her own sensibility to filter conflicts and capture situations. "Carrie's jokes come out so fast and furiously, you can overlap them and layer them and get a wonderfully rich texture," Nichols elaborated in *Entertainment Weekly*. In describing Fisher's translation of her novel into a film, Vincent Canby of the *New York Times* wrote: "Kept firmly intact is the hilarious tone, though not the literary form, of the gutsy, merciless, sometimes self-deluding first-person monologues through which much of the novel speaks." Canby admired the "terrifically genial collaboration between the writer and the director, Miss Fisher's take of odd-ball woe being perfect material for Mr. Nichols's particular ability to discover the humane sensibility within the absurd."

Fisher has received kudos for her fiction. The *Washington Post* praised *Postcards* as "the most startling literary debut since Jay McInerney's *Bright Lights, Big City*." Editor Susan Kamil recognized Fisher's "natural narrative talent—she sees the world through stories. And she is an absolutely natural comedienne." Dougherty placed Fisher at the top of the Hollywood literary ladder. "Few people are sillier than movie stars with delusions of literature . . . But Carrie Fisher is the real thing: an actor of consequence who writes good novels—seriously, folks." Dougherty has admiration for *Surrender the Pink*, which has been purchased by Paramount and will be produced by Steven Spielberg. This roman a clef tells the story of Dinah Kaufman, a soap opera writer, and her failed marriage to playwright Rudy Gendler, who leaves Dinah for a younger woman. Kaufman-Gendler are stand-ins for Fisher-Simon. Oddly enough, Fisher credits her drug addiction and rehabilitation leading to her discovery of her talent as a writer.

Writing has also improved Fisher's acting. Her two best parts have been minor roles in Woody Allen's *Hannah and her Sisters* and Rob Reiner's *When Harry Met Sally . . .* As April, Diane Weist's Holly's friend in *Hannah*, Fisher had two memorable scenes in which she competes with Holly for the attention of a bachelor architect. And as Meg Ryan's girlfriend in *Harry*, Fisher reprised the *Hannah* role as the thirty-ish New York career woman wanting a decent, like-minded man to share her life. Working with Allen, Fisher learned "this Zen thing, freedom through limitation. He's the only Zen director we have."

Appearing on Broadway in *Censored Scenes from King Kong* in 1980, Fisher received a good review from Mel Gussow in the *New York Times*. "Wearing a smile as bright as satin—she can even grin through clenched teeth—Miss Fisher resembles her mother, Debbie Reynolds, while playing a pocket-sized version of Ethel Merman." In Steve Rash's 1981 film *Under the Rainbow*, a strange homage to *The Wizard of Oz*, Fisher was cast as Annie Clark, a talent scout who auditions 150 midgets for parts as Munchkins and gets romantically involved with Chevy Chase, a Secret Service agent. Janet Maslin wrote that "Miss Fisher looks great, and her manner is tough and spunky" in a film whose comedic focus was lacking.

But many of Fisher's films in the 1980s were off-target *Star Wars* imitations such as *Amazon Women on the Moon* (1987) and *The Time Guardian* (1989), or *Hollywood Vice Squad* (1986), a Penelope Spheeris police drama that Fisher obviously satirizes in the film, *Postcards*.

Fisher has a three-book contract with her publisher Simon & Schuster and her next novel is titled *Delusions of Grandma*. (Her own grandmother made this comment about *Postcards*: "I don't know how they made such a great movie out of such a lousy book.") She is turning *Pink* into a screenplay as well as her short story, "Christmas in Vegas." Her acting career includes two new films, Carl Reiner's *Sibling Rivalry*—"Carrie Fisher is enjoyable mean-spirited as a gynecologist married to a proctologist," wrote Maslin in the *New York Times*—and *Drop Dead Fred*.

Carrie Fisher lives in a cabin in Beverly Hills that she has decorated with accoutrements of popular culture such as a cutouts of the seven dwarfs and a large cow decoy on the lawn. She has been in analysis since 1972 and drug-free since 1985. Among her friends are Penny Marshall, Albert Brooks, Richard Dreyfuss, Don Henley, Jay McInerney, Buck Henry, George Lucas, and J. D. Souther.

Writings

Postcards From The Edge, Simon & Schuster, 1987.
Surrender the Pink, Simon & Schuster, 1990.
Delusions of Grandma, Simon & Schuster, forthcoming.

Sources

Entertainment Weekly, September 28, 1990.
Esquire, May 1985.
New York Times, May 26, 1977; July 13, 1977; March 7, 1980; May 21, 1980; July 31, 1981; June 3, 1983; October 30, 1984; February 2, 1986; February 7, 1986; August 14, 1987; August 16, 1987; August 30, 1990; September 2, 1990; October 26, 1990.
People, September 7, 1987.
Time, September 17, 1990; October 15, 1990.

—Jon Saari

James J. Florio

AP/Wide World Photos

Governor of New Jersey

Born August 29, 1937, in Brooklyn, N.Y.; son of Vincenzo (a painter) and Lillian Florio; married Maryanne Spaeth, 1960 (divorced); married Lucinda Coleman (a teacher), 1988; children: (first marriage) Christopher, Gregory, Catherine. *Education:* After earning high school equivalency while serving in the Navy, attended Trenton State College; graduated magna cum laude, 1962.

Addresses: *Office*—Office of the Governor, State House, Trenton, NJ 08625.

Career

Assistant director of urban redevelopment program in Glassboro, N.J., 1963; served on Camden County Council on Economic Opportunity; following admission to the New Jersey bar in 1967, set up practice in Camden; served as legislative assistant to state assembly, 1967-68; elected to New Jersey General Assembly, 1969; after unsuccessful bid for Congress seat as Democratic representative in 1972, won that seat in 1974 and biennially seven times after; elected governor of New Jersey, 1989.

Sidelights

Some people like to point to James J. Florio's left cheekbone as a symbol of the New Jersey Governor's tenacity: while serving in the Navy, Florio, who had defeated all the other boxers in his weight class, took on a much larger opponent. The result was a permanently sunken cheek and the reputation of not being afraid of big, intimidating issues.

Florio proved that most explicitly in 1990, when, after his election to the State House, he pushed through the legislature a $2.8 billion tax increase, levied on such everyday items as diapers, detergents, and even toilet paper. The resulting roar from residents of the Garden State culminated in a massive tax revolt, according to Lucille Beachy in *Newsweek.* "This was the last straw," an editor is quoted in that article. "There is a deep and abiding anger that is not going to go away."

Indeed, after years of Republican tax ethos, voters were perhaps unprepared for the staunch Democrat in Florio, an eight-time state representative, to come to the fore. "I'm in office six months," he said to *Newsweek.* "I have my shovel and I'm shoveling up the problems of the past." Meanwhile, in the wake of his tax increase, Florio saw his approval rating slide 19 points to 23 percent.

In other controversial actions, Florio "announced his plan to bring down automobile-insurance rates, a drastically pro-consumer move that would cost the insurance industry $1.4 billion a year," as Peter Kerr reported in a *New York Times Magazine* piece. "Then Florio assailed the Exxon Corporation as environmentally irresponsible, dismissed the powerful head of the State Police and endorsed a ban on assault rifles. Meanwhile, his band of policy experts, quickly dubbed Floriocrats, worked on plans to solve the state's health-care crisis, and debated how New Jersey could save the children of its inner cities."

"What Jim Florio has done is set up a test case for the Democratic party," said Representative Robert G. Torricelli, a fellow New Jersey Democrat. As Torricelli elaborated to Kerr: "For a decade, Democrats have been intimidated from offering substantive alternatives to the politics and rhetoric of Ronald Reagan. Now they are watching Jim Florio because he represents either the last defeat of a terrible decade, or our first success story in a new time when politics in America can be redefined."

Newsweek columnist George F. Will wonders if this massive redistribution of funds makes Florio a "Lenin in Trenton." As Will described it, the governor is "closing a $3 billion budget gap. He has cut the budget in a way Ronald Reagan never even tried, either as governor or president. Florio has cut $2 billion from a $12 billion budget cutting everything... except the departments of Corrections and Human Services. The latter, which covers welfare, is now bigger than the entire state budget was eight years ago."

Most significantly, Will added, "about 300 poor school districts will get more aid; about 150 wealthy districts will have their aid phased out." But do Florio's acts constitute "Bolshevism? Hardly," noted Will. "Florio did not raise corporate profits taxes because he considers those taxes high already."

Florio apparently approaches each of his projects with the enthusiasm he brought to the State House. He is "the only man I know who can talk passionately about sludge," Lucinda Florio told a reporter as her husband delivered an endorsement of recycling. And the Navy boxer pulls no verbal punches in getting his message across. As Kerr quoted Florio, after the announced crackdown on car-insurance rates brought a lawsuit from the insurance giant Allstate: "They call themselves the 'good hands people.' The question is, 'Which part of our anatomy do they have they have their good hands around?'"

Sources

New York Times, January 13, 1991.
New York Times Magazine, May 20, 1990.
Newsweek, June 18, 1990; July 16, 1990; August 6, 1990.

—Susan Salter

Shelby Foote

Civil War expert and writer

Born November 11, 1916, in Greenville, Miss.; son of Shelby Dade (a business executive) and Lillian (Rosenstock) Foote; married Gwyn Rainer, September 5, 1956; children: Margaret Shelby, Huger Lee. *Education:* Attended University of North Carolina, 1935-37.

Addresses: *Home*—542 East Parkway South, Memphis, TN 38104.

Career

Writer, 1949—; lecturer at University of Virginia, 1963; playwright in residence at the Arena Stage in Washington, D.C., 1963-64; writer in residence at Hollins College, Virginia, 1968.

Awards: Guggenheim fellow, 1955-57; Ford Foundation fellow, 1963-64; distinguished alumnus award from University of North Carolina, 1975; honorary degrees from University of the South, 1981, and Southwestern University, 1982.

Member: Society of American Historians.

Sidelights

Writer Shelby Foote is not one to seek the limelight. His working days are spent quietly, handwriting a goal of from 500 to 600 carefully chosen words per day in his Memphis, Tennessee home. The words have added up to six well-received novels and his magnum opus to date, a three-volume set entitled *The Civil War: A Narrative.* He is currently at work on another novel set in his home state of Mississippi.

As fate will have it, Foote has not been able to stay out of the public eye. In 1990, at the venerable age of 73, the author became recognizable across the nation. This is because he appeared no less than 80 times on public television, as he shared his keen observations in celebrated filmmaker Ken Burns's highly acclaimed documentary on the Civil War. Foote also served as a consultant for the film, which was aired on the Public Broadcasting System (PBS) over five consecutive evenings. "Getting Shelby Foote for my documentary was almost as good as getting Robert E. Lee," Burns said in *Newsweek.* In turn, Foote told the same publication, "Seeing the war presented in a different medium by a true genius was illuminating for me."

The two men share a sense of integrity; they are both interested more in telling how the Civil War really was—as scrupulously as possible with the information available—than portraying dramatic but questionable events. This became apparent when Burns was preparing to show that while Robert E. Lee's generals wanted to retreat, Lee ordered an advance. Although the scene was poignant, Foote told Burns that it wasn't based on fact. Burns listened and edited it out right away.

Such exacting standards paid off. Some historians called the documentary the best yet created about the Civil War. Foote observed in *U.S News & World Report* that there was no need to add drama to facts already colorful enough in the simple telling. "Even when everything slackens off and we're about to have this pitiful little ending where the war peters out," he said, "damned if John Wilkes Booth doesn't shoot Abraham Lincoln. God almighty is a great dramatist."

> "The novelist and the historian are seeking the same thing: the truth—not a different truth; the same truth—only they reach it ... by different routes."

Foote's fascination with the Civil War began in his youth. By the time he had five novels under his belt, the author was asked by Random House to put together a history of the Civil War. The year was 1954 and the publisher wanted a single-volume work. Foote soon realized that one book on the subject would not really add to the body of work already available on the War Between the States. He got the go-ahead, and twenty years and three volumes later, Foote had completed *The Civil War: A Narrative*. The work is looked upon "as one of the finest histories ever fashioned by an American—a narrative of over a million and a half words which recreates on a vast and brilliant canvas the events and personalities of an American epic," as noted on the book jacket.

Foote invested several years in meticulously researching and writing Volume I, entitled *Fort Sumter to Perryville*, which was published in 1958. He disciplined himself to put in eight-hour days, every day of the week. The result was a riveting account of the war between the Yankees and the Rebels from the participants' points of view. Foote covers major and minor battles, including Pea Ridge, Stonewall Jackson's Valley Campaign, Bull Run, Shiloh, Antietam, and Perryville. He begins the narrative with a vivid description of Jefferson Davis's voluntary departure from the Senate. The author goes on to describe Abraham Lincoln's move to Washington,

D.C., and then portrays the full cast of characters who lived the Civil War drama. The result is an unusual blending of scholarship with a gift for telling a story—a *true* story. At the end of the volume, Foote shares his observation that "the novelist and the historian are seeking the same thing: the truth—not a different truth; the same truth—only they reach it, or try to reach it, by different routes."

First appearing in 1963, *Fredericksburg to Meridian* is the second volume of the series. In it Foote continues the tale of the "ordinary" soldier—the one in the gray uniform (Confederate) and the one wearing blue (Union). The author's sympathies are for the South, where he was born, and he is described as a Southern gentleman. Yet Foote is not afraid to show his admiration for the outstanding Yankee leaders, just the same. Then, too, he is "unblinking about the dark side of the Confederacy and blessedly unromantic about the Lost Cause," stated Geoffrey C. Ward in *American Heritage*. Also treated throughout this volume is the abolition of slavery.

In Volume III, *Red River to Appomattox*, published in 1974, Foote leads off with the Ulysses S. Grant/Robert E. Lee conflict in Virginia. He tells how Joseph E. Johnston fought to hold back General William Tecumseh Sherman in Georgia, eventually losing Atlanta and Savannah. Foote goes on to explain how John Bell Hood moved courageously through central Tennessee, only to lose to George Henry Thomas in the final big battle near Nashville. Other events chronicled in Volume III include the sinking of the *Albemarle* by William Barker Cushing, Sherman's burning of Columbia on his way back north, and Lee's and Grant's movement to Appomattox. Foote captures the "dust and stench of war," states the book jacket, "a sort of Twilight of the Gods, with occasional lurid flare-ups, mass desertions, and the queasiness that accompanies the risk of being the last man to die." The book ends with Davis's escape after losing Richmond, the assassination of Lincoln, and the final surrender of the Confederacy.

Foote's Southern heritage has also guided him in his fiction writing. His first novel, *Tournament*, has been reissued as part of the Southern Literary Series by Summa Publications. "The novel is rife with glimpses of the writer he has since become," noted a reviewer in *Southern Living*. Both the South's William Faulkner and France's Marcel Proust are credited with having influenced this story about cotton planter Hugh Bart. Through his own abilities and hard work, Bart creates a small empire for himself, only to lose all that he's worked for when the bank holding his investments goes under. As he is dying he comes to realize the superficiality of his life and that the only lasting remnant of his existence will live on in his grandson.

Shiloh, probably Foote's best known novel, first appeared in print in 1952 and was highly praised by reviewers. Foote tells the story of this bloody two-day battle in plain language, from the point of view of the soldiers who fought in it. Each side—Yankee and Confederate—shares its viewpoint from the battlefield, giving the reader a feeling of being there. Quoted in the book's jacket text, *New York Times* contributor Orville Prescott called *Shiloh* "brilliant" and a "classic." He stated that every "section of this book is excellent in its own right—imaginative, powerful, filled with precise visual details." At least one other viewer compared it to the Stephen Crane classic, *Red Badge of Courage*.

As in his books, the facts of Foote's past are colorful in the sheer telling. As editor of his high school paper in Greenville, Mississippi, Foote and the principal did not always see eye-to-eye. After Foote had applied to the University of North Carolina in 1935, he discovered that his principal had effectively thwarted Foote's acceptance into the school. The undaunted young man showed up anyway, reportedly telling officials who asked why he was there, "I didn't think you meant it." He managed to take only those subjects that suited him for two years, then left the university for a larger world.

In 1939 Foote joined the National Guard and trained in northern Ireland as an artillery captain in the field. At one point an officer insulted one of Foote's men during an inspection, and Foote made him apologize. The officer ranked higher than Foote, and as a result the latter found himself court-martialed—for a mileage inaccuracy involving a military-owned vehicle. The official accusation was for "falsifying a government record," according to the *Durham Morning Herald*.

Back in the United States, Foote wrote for the Associated Press. The work didn't suit him, so he enlisted in the United States Marine Corps. World War II ended soon afterward, and Foote found himself back in Greenville. There he went to work for a local radio station as an advertising copywriter. By that time, he was also doing additional writing on the side, and before long he sold a story to the *Saturday Evening Post*. After that "I quit my job and haven't had another one since," he told the *Durham Morning Herald*.

Selected writings

Shiloh, Random, 1976.
Follow Me Down, Random, 1978.
September, September, Random, 1978.
Love in a Dry Season, Random, 1979.
The Civil War: A Narrative (three-volume set), Random, 1986.
Tournament, Summa Publications (2nd revised edition), 1987.

Sources

American Heritage, July-August 1987; December 1987.
Durham Morning Herald, September 28, 1990.
Newsweek, October 8, 1990.
Southern Living, April 1988; December 1989.
U.S. News & World Report, September 24, 1990.

—Victoria France Charabati

Robert Gallo

AIDS researcher

Full name, Robert Charles Gallo; born March 23, 1937, in Waterbury, Conn.; son of Francis Anton and Louise May (Ciancuilli) Gallo; married Mary Jane Hayes, July 1, 1961; children: Robert Charles, Marcus. *Education:* Providence College, B.A., 1959; Jefferson Medical College, M.D., 1963; postgraduate study at Jefferson University, 1987—.

Addresses: *Home*—8513 Thronden Terrace, Bethesda, MD 20034. *Office*—National Cancer Institute, 9000 Rockville Pike, Bethesda, MD 20205.

Career

Served internship and residency at University of Chicago; National Cancer Institute, Bethesda, Md., clinical associate, 1965-68, senior investigator in human tumor cell biology, 1968-69, head of section of cellular control mechanisms, 1969-72, chief of laboratory on tumor cell biology, 1972—. Served with United States Public Health Service, 1965-68. Adjunct professor of genetics at George Washington University, and of microbiology at Cornell University; consultant to Georgetown University Cancer Center; U.S. representative to world committee of International Comparative Leukemia and Lymphoma Association, 1981—. Served on board of governors of Franco American AIDS Foundation and World AIDS Foundation, both 1987.

Awards: Numerous honors in field include CIBA-GEIGY awards in biomedical sciences, 1977, 1988; superior service award from United States Public Health Service, 1979; Albert Lasker awards for basic biomedical research, 1982, 1986; Abraham White Award in biochemistry from George Washington University, 1983; General Motors Award in cancer research, 1984; Lucy Wortham Prize in cancer research from Society for Surgical Oncology, 1984; Hammer Prize, 1985; special award from American Society for Infectious Disease, 1986; Japan Prize in Preventive Medicine, 1988; and others.

Sidelights

Dr. Robert Gallo may be the nation's leading acquired immune deficiency syndrome (AIDS) researcher, co-discoverer of the AIDS virus, and a man driven to by an obsession for personal glory. Gallo and his chief rival, Dr. Luc Montagnier of the Pasteur Institute in France, spurred one of the nastiest scientific disputes in modern times when they battled over credit for discovering the AIDS virus in the 1980s. In 1987 the United States and French governments agreed to give Gallo and Montagnier equal billing for the discovery—and each side an equal share of royalties from the test that screens blood for the virus.

More recently however, Gallo found himself under investigation for allegedly misappropriating—either intentionally or inadvertently—the AIDS virus in his laboratory. It is the latest and potentially most serious turn in Gallo's long, flamboyant, and controversial career. *Spy* magazine, in July 1990, went so far as to say that "in the midst of the AIDS epidemic, Gallo's self-interested bid for glory has had a terrible human cost: by refusing to acknowledge the significance of the French scientists' earlier discoveries, he delayed the introduction of a widely available blood test for the AIDS virus by about a year. During that year thousands of hospital patients and hemophiliacs received tainted blood from blood banks and became infected, and many already infected unwittingly spread the virus."

Spy contended that Gallo further hindered AIDS research efforts by making it "difficult for the Centers for Disease Control and fellow researchers to obtain necessary supplies and samples of virus, and most damaging of all, as the [Chicago] *Tribune* showed, he published a vast amount of incorrect data and misleading conclusions." According to *Spy*, "interviews with 40 of Gallo's colleagues and peers indicate that his egomaniacal performance did not surprise those who know him well. As a scientist who once worked in his lab puts it, Gallo was known for 'this sort of unscrupulous behavior ten years before HIV [the AIDS virus] ever came along. When the stakes got higher, he was capable of doing anything. The stakes became too high."

Gallo, who grew up in Connecticut, was 13 when his sister contracted leukemia, a tragedy that determined his career choice in medical research over patient care, which he finds emotionally difficult. His sister's illness went into remission for a time after chemotherapy treatment, but she eventually succumbed to the disease. This experience profoundly influenced Gallo's interest in the *causes* of disease. Also influencing his future career choice was the pathologist who diagnosed his sister's illness; the doctor served as a mentor and sparked his imagination with tales of medical discovery.

Gallo is a lanky, hyperactive man noted for his rapid-fire speech and for sometimes referring to himself in the third person. He earned his bachelor's degree from Rhode Island's Providence College in 1959 and graduated from Jefferson Medical College in Philadelphia in 1963. From 1963 to 1965 he held an internship and residency at the University of Chicago. Gallo was then hired as a clinical associate at the National Cancer Institute, an arm of the National Institutes for Health (NIH). In later years, he would become head of a laboratory at the Cancer Institute, one of the world's leading AIDS researchers, and

recipient of scores of professional accolades and honors. He is a two-time winner of the prestigious Albert Lasker Award, often a precursor to the Nobel Prize.

In his early years at NIH, Gallo was intrigued by the notion that perhaps cancer in humans could be caused by viruses. By 1970, he had produced evidence of viral activity in leukocytes drawn from a leukemia sufferer. In 1975 Gallo announced that he had isolated a human leukemia virus, but the announcement proved premature; his laboratory's research could not be duplicated. After six years, Gallo again announced that he had linked cancer in humans to a virus, which he named human T-cell leukemia virus. Its two variants are known as HTLV-1 and HTLV-2.

Gallo continued his HTLV research; its importance became clear in 1981 when doctors began seeing great numbers of patients with complete and fatal immune system failure. The phenomenon, which they named acquired immune deficiency syndrome, or AIDS, was prevalent among homosexual men and intravenous drug users. Gallo noticed similarities between AIDS and HTLV: both were common in Africa and the Caribbean and both were transmitted through intimate contact such as sexual intercourse, breast feeding, and blood transfusions. In early 1982, he suggested that AIDS might be caused by an HTLV-related virus; later that year, the National Cancer Institute formed an AIDS task force, naming Gallo as its scientific director.

In a breakthrough, Gallo's colleague Mikulas Popovic found a way to grow the AIDS virus in the laboratory, a discovery which allowed the virus to be produced in large quantities and observed. The AIDS virus shared similarities with HTLV-1 and HTLV-2; Gallo named it HTLV-3. He and his colleagues described their discovery of the virus in four scientific papers published in the May 4, 1984, issue of *Science*. Also by this time, Gallo's lab had developed a test to screen blood for antibodies to the virus—a test designed to help keep the blood supply untainted by the AIDS virus. The U.S. government was awarded a patent for the test in May 1985 and a fiery dispute with the French researchers erupted.

Montagnier's team had published a paper in *Science* in May, 1983, identifying a new virus, lymphadenopathy-associated virus, or LAV, which later was found to be virtually identical to HTLV-3. Montagnier spent the next year "battling to convince his colleagues that AIDS was caused by a virus—and by *this* virus in particular," according to the December 1988 issue of *Omni* magazine. "Gallo held that a member of the leukemia-producing family of retroviruses that *he* had discovered caused AIDS. Montagnier . . . kept telling Gallo that the AIDS virus and his leukemia viruses had opposite effects. Instead of causing cells to multiply uncontrollably, as did the leukemia virus, the AIDS virus killed them.''

"Scientists in the United States are exposed to high pressure to produce results, and it sometimes warps their sense of ethics."
—Dr. Luc Montagnier

The French researchers had requested a patent from the U.S. Patent Office in December 1983 for an AIDS blood test—seven months before the United States asked for the patent for Gallo's blood screen. In December of 1984, the Pasteur Institute sued the United States government for a share of the credit in discovering the virus and a share of the royalties from the AIDS blood test. Three years later the two governments entered an agreement naming Gallo and Montagnier as co-discoverers of the AIDS virus and splitting the royalties, with 80 percent going to an AIDS research foundation. In the October 1988 issue of *Scientific American*, Gallo and Montagnier jointly published a paper recounting the virus's discovery.

While the heated dispute struck many as rather inappropriate for doctors of their stature, Lawrence K. Altman, writing in the *New York Times*, held that the argument demonstrated ''the very fabric of what makes scientists tick, their altruism as well as their egos, their fierce desire for independence, their yearning to gain respect from peers, and the competition for Nobel Prizes and other public recognition for themselves and their institutes.'' Prior to the dispute, ''Montagnier and Gallo were friendly rivals in the same research,'' *Omni* said. Twice in 1983 the French investigator sent samples of the new virus to his American colleague. Montagnier was dumbfounded when in April 1984, at a Washington press conference called by the U.S. Secretary of Health and Human Services, Gallo announced the discovery of the AIDS virus. ''Scientists quickly confirmed that Gallo's virus was virtually identical to Montagnier's,'' noted *Omni* article, which featured a lengthy interview with Montagnier. ''Gallo's claims to have

worked independently of the French laboratory were further compromised when he 'accidently' published Montagnier's photographs of the virus in a *Science* article announcing his findings. Montagnier was outraged when the U.S. patent for the AIDS blood test, which he had applied for in 1983, was awarded a year and a half later—to Robert Gallo.'' Montagnier told *Omni* that he ''was particularly furious that our patent for the blood test was ignored until Gallo's was accepted,'' and added that ''scientists in the United States are exposed to high pressure to produce results, and it sometimes warps their sense of ethics.'' In the same interview, Montagnier credited Gallo for developing the idea that AIDS is caused by a retrovirus and for discovering a method to grow the AIDS virus in continuous cell cultures—an important step in developing a sensitive AIDS blood test.

In early 1990, Congress asked the NIH to investigate allegations—raised in a book-length article published in the *Chicago Tribune* in November 1989—that Gallo used the virus isolated by the French researchers when he ''discovered'' the cause of AIDS. ''The evidence is compelling that [what happened in Gallo's lab] was either an accident or a theft,'' reporter John Crewdson wrote in the *Tribune*. In December 1989, U.S. Representative John Dingell, chairman of the House Energy and Commerce Committee, wrote to NIH and asked what the agency was doing in light of the *Tribune* article. NIH officials initially dismissed the *Tribune* report as a mere rehash of the dispute over the discovery of the AIDS virus. Later, the agency called on the National Academy of Sciences and the Institute of Medicine to ''nominate a slate of scientists who have no connection to the AIDS controversy or to Gallo to oversee the institutes' own review of events leading to the discovery of the AIDS virus,'' *Science* reported in February 1990.

''For most of his 30-year career as one of the National Cancer Institute's stars, Gallo has been a lightning rod for controversy, never more so than during the past six years when he has been the target of relentless accusations, often couched in innuendo, that he stole the AIDS virus from a French group headed by Luc Montagnier,'' *Science* wrote. Gallo told *Science* he welcomed the investigation. ''These allegations have been going on too long,'' he said. ''I have done nothing wrong and I have no apprehension or anxiety about the review. And, I'm confident the only chance I have is the help of independent colleagues.''

In March 1990, Crewdson reported in the *Tribune* that documents from a secret 1985 investigation by the United States government suggested that the virus Gallo isolated was probably the same as identified by Montagnier's virus which the Pasteur Institute had sent to the National Cancer Institute. In interviews dating back to 1984, Gallo has acknowledged that contamination could explain the similarities between the viruses isolated by his lab and the French investigators. As *Newsweek* put it, "thanks largely to a pair of articles published by the *Chicago Tribune*, history is again up for grabs."

After the second *Tribune* story was published, Montagnier urged Gallo to admit that he was mistaken. In March 1990 the *New York Times* said that Montagnier told the French newspaper *Le Monde:* "I think that Gallo should at last accept the evidence. I publicly make a new appeal to him to do so and I would be ready to salute his courage if he did so." The *Times* went on: "Dr. Montagnier was quoted as saying that he was not accusing Dr. Gallo of fraud. 'I stand by

the hypothesis of laboratory contamination. I've told Dr. Gallo many times that he should recognize there was contamination... The virus contained in one vial... contaminated other viral cultures in the laboratory, which are then identified as a new virus.'" In response, Gallo was quoted as saying: "I am really astonished and I find it shameful to hear such things.... If they want all the glory, that's fine, and I'll do the work. I don't understand what they want."

Sources

Newsweek, April 2, 1990.
New York Times, March 24, 1990.
Omni, December 1988.
Science, July 24, 1987; January 26, 1990; February 23, 1990; March 30, 1990.
Scientific American, October 1988.
Spy, July 1990.

—David Wilkins

Willie Gault

AP/Wide World Photos

Professional football player

Born September 5, 1960, in Griffin, Ga.; son of textile workers; married Dainnese Mathis, 1983; children: Shakari (daughter). *Education:* University of Tennessee, B.A., c. 1982.

Addresses: *Home*—Los Angeles, CA. *Agent*—William Morris Agency, 1350 Avenue of the Americas, New York, NY 10019.

Career

Sprinter, hurdler, and relay runner for the U.S. Olympic team, 1980; participated in World Games, 1982, winning silver medal in the 110-meter high hurdles. First-round draft choice of Chicago Bears, 1983; wide receiver for the Bears, 1983-88. As free agent, moved to Los Angeles Raiders, 1988, signing five-year contract. Alternate to the U.S. Olympic bobsled team, 1988. Made acting debut in television movie *Street of Dreams*, 1988.

Sidelights

Willie Gault is a talented all-around athlete who happens to make his living catching passes for the Los Angeles Raiders. A wide receiver in the NFL since 1983, Gault has blazed a controversial path across several sports—professional and amateur— earning almost equal amounts of praise and scorn from the media. Few observers have challenged Gault's speed and agility on the football field, but his attitude about the game is a source of constant contention. As Gault himself put it in the *Chicago*

Tribune: "Football is not the most important thing in my life . . . . I also think about my future . . . . I guess I'm a hustler. I like to say I have a diversified portfolio. I've been blessed with abilities and talent and I try to use them."

That "diversified portfolio" includes forays into ballet, modeling, and acting, pursuits not usually associated with professional football. Los Angeles *Daily News* columnist Ron Rapoport observed that Gault "is too busy to play football . . . . No matter where he happens to be he is already planning his next move." Rapoport added: "[Gault] has these chiseled features that belong on a movie poster and this all-purpose body that allows him to wear a leotard as easily as he does a football uniform. Nobody snickers when Gault puts a leotard on, either. He looks too much as if he was born in it for that." *Sports Illustrated* contributor Bruce Newman offered a bitter appraisal of the handsome young player. "In Gault's pin-up world," writes Newman, "looks are never deceiving, they are the only reality that truly matters. To see the gloss of his image is to know him the way he wants to be known."

Willie Gault is named after his mother, Willie Mae. He was born and raised in Griffin, Georgia, a town that calls itself the textile capital of the South. Both of

Gault's parents worked in Griffin's textile mills, earning modest but sufficient wages to support the family. Gault describes himself as "a very likable person" and a "teacher's pet" during his school years in Griffin. He was a star athlete in football and track, attended church regularly, and never touched drugs or alcohol. Newman wrote: "If Gault happened to be riding in a car when one of his classmates lit up a joint, he would stick his head out the car window for the rest of the trip so that he would remain pure of the drug peril."

Even as a youth, Gault's ambitions far exceeded what Griffin, Georgia had to offer. He was fully aware of the disadvantages black people faced in the South, but this awareness only deepened his determination to succeed. Gault told *Sports Illustrated:* "I want [my] children to be able to inherit millions of dollars when they're old enough to. It has to start somewhere; why can't it start with me, per se? Someone has to step out, someone has to start to accomplish what I want to see done. I'm willing to be that person.... You hear about dynasties and empires being built all the time. I want to build one. That's what drives me."

College seemed like the logical place to begin building a dynasty. Gault attended the University of Tennessee and earned a degree in business while playing football and running track. He gained his initial success as a runner and a hurdler, qualifying for the United States Olympic team in time for the 1980 games. Gault was one of many dedicated athletes who suffered when President Jimmy Carter announced a U.S. boycott of the 1980 summer games in objection to the Soviet Union's invasion of Afghanistan. The lost opportunity became especially poignant in 1982, when Gault won the silver medal in the 110-meter high hurdles at the World Games. By that time, however, the young athlete's talents as a wide receiver were winning the attention of football scouts. A career in the NFL, with its six-figure salaries and high visibility, would suit Willie Gault far better than a gold medal.

The Chicago Bears chose Gault in the first round of the 1983 draft. He reported to Chicago for the 1983-84 football season and quickly established himself as a dangerous receiver. In the space of three games during his rookie season he scored six touchdowns, and he consistently outran his defenders, even when he was double-teamed. Gault's honeymoon with the Bears was short-lived, however. "I caught everything my first year," he remembered in *Sports Illustrated*. "I was leading the league [in touchdown catches], then all of a sudden everything stopped. They just

stopped throwing the ball to me. I didn't know what was going on." Gault claims that the decision not to pass to him was based on racial prejudice. The Bears' coaches called it simple strategy: as the fawnlike Gault was being chased by two defensemen, other receivers were wide open and free to catch the ball.

In the off season of 1984, Gault instituted actions to regain a position on the U.S. track team. Having been denied a chance to compete in the 1980 Olympic games, he was anxious to try again in 1984. That decision brought an avalanche of controversy down upon the young star—Bears coach Mike Ditka publicly questioned Gault's dedication to football, and the Chicago media pointed out that the handsome and soft-spoken Gault hardly fit the image of a tough, nasty Bear. At any rate, Gault failed to win a berth on the Olympic team, and he returned to Chicago for the 1984 season having all but lost the respect of the Bears coach and the other players.

> *"You hear about dynasties and empires being built all the time. I want to build one. That's what drives me."*

"It wasn't until his second season with Chicago that Gault developed a reputation for having stone hands," Newman wrote. "He had gotten behind everybody in the first game of the year, then dropped a 50-yard pass for a sure touchdown. The Bears routed Tampa Bay 34-14 anyway that day, but nobody forgot." Gault was still a starter, but more and more he found himself being used as a decoy while the other receivers won the yardage. "From that point on I got the reputation that I couldn't catch the ball," Gault said. "I got more publicity off that one dropped pass than all the ones I caught. They were just waiting for me to make a mistake. It was a humbling experience. I was too perfect, I guess—the all-American kid who couldn't do anything wrong. Now they had found something they could criticize. Once that happened, all the players jumped on the bandwagon. I found out that year who my true friends were, and what I discovered was that I didn't have any. It opened my eyes. I spent the rest of that year fighting with the team. All the players didn't really understand me as a person, that I'm a humble and gentle guy. They didn't understand that I could have interests outside football."

Gault faced yet another round of controversy when it was suggested that he was afraid to be hit on the field. With so much criticism leveled against him, it became a point of pride for Gault to prove himself equal to the task of playing top-rate professional football. He effectively silenced his detractors in the 1985-86 season when he helped the Bears to advance to the Super Bowl and win it. Gault was particularly effective in the playoffs staged early in 1986. His eleven receptions for 253 yards, including a phenomenal 129 in the Super Bowl itself, brought him straight from the doghouse to the front parlor. In a busy post-Super Bowl off season, Gault made the most of his newfound popularity. He organized his fellow players for a charity video, "The Super Bowl Shuffle," he modeled clothing, he appeared on the *Today* show, he auditioned for a part on a television soap opera, and he even appeared in a charity ballet that received nationwide television and magazine coverage.

> *"You don't wait until your career is finally abruptly ended and then say, 'What am I going to do?'"*

Remembering his 1986 stint with the Chicago City Ballet, Gault told *Sports Illustrated:* "It took a lot of guts for me to do that. I second-guessed myself so many times. But I wanted to show that ballet wasn't a sissy sport, that a big football player could get up there in tights and not make a fool of himself." Gault's appearance with the ballet benefitted the Better Boys Foundation, a non-profit Chicago organization dedicated to the concerns of inner-city youth.

As the Bears began a new season in 1986, it quickly became apparent that Gault's troubles with the team had not ended. Some of the players accused him of financial impropriety for his management of the "Super Bowl Shuffle" video. (He was cleared.) Worse, he found himself thrown back into the role of decoy as the Bears offense geared up for a new year. Gault persisted doggedly, however, and in the 1987-88 season he led the Bears with 35 catches for 705 yards and seven touchdowns. Despite his fine statistics he was unable to secure the respect of either the team management or the fans.

The off season of 1988 saw Gault embroiled in yet another controversy. He arrived at the Winter Olym-

pics with the ambition of being named to the U.S. bobsled team. His interference infuriated a number of American bobsled athletes, who had labored in anonymity for years in order to be in Calgary, Alberta, Canada for the games. Suddenly, Gault was among them and was taking the lion's share of the publicity. In the end he was named an alternate, and the twelve-man team was actually extended to thirteen to accommodate him. Again he managed to alienate Chicago's football fans by claiming he was only at the Winter Games because then-Bears quarterback Jim McMahon hadn't thrown more passes to him in a playoff game against the Washington Redskins.

Gault's contract with the Bears expired in 1988, and talks toward a new one went badly. In the summer of that year the wide receiver accepted an offer from the Los Angeles Raiders that paid almost twice his $347,000 salary in Chicago. The Chicago media cited Gault's move to Los Angeles as proof that the athlete had his mind on Hollywood instead of football. "Gault was never a Bear," wrote Bernie Lincicome in the *Chicago Tribune.* "He was a ballet dancer and a bobsledder, but he was not a real Bear. He didn't growl, he hummed. He didn't stalk, he tiptoed. And he never said he was sorry for getting ordinary results out of extraordinary talent.... What he might have been will be missed more than anything he ever was."

For his part, Gault embraced the move to California as a professional milestone and vowed to give football his all as long as he possibly could. "I don't have any ill feelings about Chicago or their offense," he told the *Chicago Tribune.* "It was a learning experience, a great experience, one I'll always cherish. But life is full of crossroads, and this is one where I had to make a decision." Acting, he said, did not factor into the equation, even though he had signed for management by the William Morris Agency.

In Los Angeles Gault has found himself part of a team that has a number of talented receivers. He is therefore scrutinized less on the field and is certainly called to task less for his other ambitions. Gault made his acting debut in a 1988 television movie, *Street of Dreams,* and he is honest about wanting to be an entertainer when his football days are over. "Maybe I have another five [football] seasons left," he told the *Chicago Tribune.* "Then what is Willie Gault going to do after that? You have to start planning for your future ahead of time. You don't wait until your career is finally abruptly ended and then say, 'What am I going to do?'"

Gault, his wife Dainnese, and their daughter Shakari live in Los Angeles, the perfect location for a man dedicated to unconditional success. "I have tremendous energy," Gault told the *Chicago Tribune*. "I know where I'm going . . . . You try to go where you are going, but you don't try to hurt anyone in the process." He concluded: "Just so you can get up in the morning and look at yourself in the mirror and say, 'I've done my best' or 'I've done well' or 'I've tried.' That's all you can do. You can't ask for anything more and you can't satisfy everyone. You can't let anyone else control your destiny."

Sources

Chicago Tribune, September 7, 1986; September 29, 1986; September 30, 1986; February 18, 1988; July 29, 1988; August 17, 1988.
Daily News (Los Angeles), September 12, 1988; July 29, 1988.
Sports Illustrated, November 24, 1986.

—Mark Kram

Newt Gingrich

AP/Wide World Photos

Minority whip of the U.S. House of Representatives

Full name, Newton Leroy Gingrich; born June 17, 1943, in Harrisburg, Pa.; son of Robert Bruce and Kathleen (Daugherty) Gingrich; married Jacqueline Battley, June 19, 1952 (divorced, 1982); married, second wife, Marianne Ginther, August 1981; children: Linda Kathleen and Jacqueline Sue. *Education:* Emory University, B.A., 1965; Tulane University, M.A., 1968, Ph.D., 1971. *Politics:* Republican.

Addresses: *Office*—2438 Rayburn Bldg., Washington, D.C. 20515-0001.

Career

Professor of history, West Georgia College, 1970-78; U.S. Representative, Georgia's Sixth District, 1979—.

Member: GOPAC (general chairman), Conservative Opportunity Society (co-founder), World Futurist Society, Georgia Conservancy.

Sidelights

U.S. Representative Newt Gingrich is known as a Republican pit bull, a political guerrilla, Dennis the Menace of Capitol Hill, and the man who felled the former Speaker of the House Jim Wright for ethics violations. "When he arrived in Washington," the *National Review* wrote in 1988, "Gingrich proclaimed it is his mission to overhaul the Republican Party and, ultimately, to change American Society, if not life on earth. Since then, the chunky, mop-headed former history professor has elevated Democrat-bashing to an art form."

"One view is that Newt Gingrich is a bomb thrower," *Time* reported. "A fire-breathing Republican Congressman from Georgia, he is more interested in right-wing grandstanding than in fostering bipartisanship.... Another view is that Newt Gingrich is a visionary. An impassioned reformer... [who] brings innovative thinking and a respect for deeply felt American values to the House." In any case, Congress has not been quite the same since Gingrich was first elected to represent Georgia's Sixth Congressional District in 1978.

Gingrich, who holds his party's No. 2 job in the House of Representatives as minority whip, has gained a national reputation for his combative style and his leadership of a collection of young, aggressive, conservative House Republicans. "For his first five years in office," the *New York Times* said, "Mr. Gingrich, along with a band of young conservative Republicans, turned their junior status to advantage and waged guerrilla warfare against Democratic House leadership and even their own party's leaders. Under Mr. Gingrich's tutelage, about a dozen of the insurgents formed a group known as the Conservative Opportunity Society [COS]. Republicans, Mr.

Gingrich maintains, have become so accustomed to their minority status that they need to be prodded to challenge the status quo." (The Grand Old Party, or GOP, has not controlled the House since Dwight Eisenhower's first term as president.)

The tenets of Gingrich's philosophy are echoed by the COS—the antithesis of the "liberal welfare state," a state that he regularly criticizes. In 1984 "he turned preliminary sessions of the Republican national convention into a battleground until the Conservative Opportunity Society was inserted into the platform," the *Atlantic* said. "The number of congressman who have adopted their COS banner...has swelled from fewer than a dozen two years ago to more than forty today.... The COS is usually taken for hype and Gingrich for just an especially fast-talking member of the hard-line New Right.... The COS, as set forth in Gingrich's book, *Window of Opportunity*, is more systematic than Gingrich's critics might expect, however. It is a hawkish, limited government, growth- and future-oriented, traditional-values American utopia, which can come into being only if forces of the 'liberal welfare state' ...can be defeated."

Gingrich is well-known for his special taste for colleagues roasted on the moral spit of an ethics committee investigations. In 1979, during his first term, he called for the expulsion of Representative Charles Diggs, a Democrat from Michigan, who had been convicted of embezzlement. In 1983 he called for the expulsion of two representatives who allegedly had sexual relations with teenagers working as pages in the House. And later, of course, Gingrich spearheaded the movement to oust Jim Wright.

In the early 1980s Gingrich launched a new weapon, taking advantage of a rule allowing House members to read items into the record after Congressional sessions. He gave frequent speeches criticizing Democrats for their positions on a wide range of issues, from communism to school prayer to Central America—speeches which were given before an empty House chamber, but which were broadcast nationwide on the cable network C-SPAN. The tactic was also used by Gingrich's followers—a group of conservative Republicans elected mostly in the 1980s and labeled the party's "young Turks," in contrast to the GOP's less aggressive old guard.

In the spring of 1984 an angry Thomas P. "Tip" O'Neill, then speaker of the House, ordered the cable TV cameras to periodically pan the chamber to show that Gingrich was speaking to the empty House. O'Neill called Gingrich's tactic "the lowest thing I have seen in my 32 years in the House." The confrontation resulted in a rare House rebuke to the speaker and wide coverage for Gingrich—something he values highly. *Newsweek* defined what it called Gingrich's Newtonian law: conflict equals exposure equals power. "If you're in the newspaper every day and on TV often enough then you must be important."

Gingrich wrote in the *Conservative Digest:* "The Democratic Party is now controlled by a coalition of liberal activists, corrupt big city machines, labor union bosses and House incumbents who use gerrymandering, rigged election rules, and a million dollars from the taxpayers per election cycle to buy invulnerability. When Republicans have the courage to point out just how unrepresentative, and even weird, liberal values are, we gain votes.... Fear and corruption now stalk the House of Representatives in a way we've never witnessed before in our history." Gingrich further emphasized what he sees as moral discrepancies between the parties, saying that "Jim Wright as speaker of the House is the personification of this sick system in which rules are violated, pockets are filled with improper money, America's secrets are leaked—and nothing is done about it. That a man with so corrupt a record as Jim Wright is second in line to be president should frighten every decent American."

Gingrich's battle against Wright began in 1987 as a one-man crusade which few in Washington took seriously. Before Gingrich was through, however, more than 70 House Republicans signed his letter asking the House's ethics committee to investigate Wright. The accusations were related to Wright's links to a Texas developer, to his favors to savings and loan operators, and the way in which he published and sold a book of his speeches and writings, *Reflections of a Public Man*. Wright received unusually large royalties and sold the book to political contributors—an arrangement seemingly designed to circumvent ceilings on donations.

Gingrich was ruthless on the offensive. His dramatic contentions won him necessary Congressional allies, and his rhetorical skills made him eminently quotable, thus a media darling. "I'm so deeply frightened by the nature of the corrupt left-wing machine in the House that it would have been worse to do nothing," he was quoted in the *New York Times*. "Jim Wright has reached a point psychologically, in his ego, where there are no boundaries left." Following the investigation, the ethics committee said it had reason to believe Wright had violated House rules 69 times. Less than two months later, on June 6, 1989, Wright resigned as speaker.

In March 1989, in the midst of his war with Wright, Gingrich's Republican colleagues elected him to the post of minority whip by a narrow 87-85 margin. The vote signaled "a wakeup call to incumbent GOP leaders from younger members who want a more aggressive, activist party," said *Congressional Quarterly Weekly Report*. "Gingrich's promotion from backbench bomb thrower to minority whip was an expression of seething impatience among House Republicans with their seemingly permanent minority status." Gingrich's supporters pointed to his energy, communication skills, and commitment to capturing a majority of House seats by 1992—when congressional districts will be redrawn. "A year ago, no one would have predicted that this enfant terrible of the Republican Party could mount a credible bid for the leadership—let alone snag its No. 2 slot," the *Weekly Review* said, "But Republicans became particularly frustrated with their decades-old minority status in the house when the Reagan era came to an end: Even the eight-year reign of a president as popular as Reagan couldn't deliver them from their plight. Gingrich's call for radical change fell on receptive ears."

> *"There has been a conservative majority in America for at least 20 years, but the Republican Party has failed to capitalize on it."*

Gingrich's high-profile role has put his personal moral standards in the spotlight. "His foes point out that this 45-year-old Army brat and defense hawk never served in the military," *Newsweek* said. His opponents also have resurrected the contradiction between Gingrich's ethics-and-traditional-values stand and his messy divorce from his first wife, who was cancer stricken. Democrats, *Newsweek* said, also point out "his management of a political action committee that raised $200,000—and gave $900 to candidates." After Gingrich took on Wright, the Democratic Congressional Campaign Committee publicized a 1977 deal in which Gingrich received $13,000 from a group of friends to write a novel. He wasn't in Congress at the time, although he had run twice unsuccessfully for the seat which he eventually won in 1978. Democrats say the arrangement allowed Gingrich's backers to support him financially and get a tax shelter in the bargain. Gingrich said he

did research in Europe and wrote three chapters, but the book was rejected by publishers.

In addition to these charges, two days before Gingrich was elected minority whip, the *Washington Post* reported that he had persuaded 21 supporters to contribute $105,000 to promote *Window of Opportunity: A Blueprint for the Future*, which he co-authored in 1984 with his second wife, Marianne, and science fiction writer David Drake. The book sold only 12,000 hardcover copies; the investors reaped tax benefits and Gingrich and his wife made about $30,000. Gingrich acknowledged that the book deal was "as weird as Wright's," but was on the up-and-up because "we wrote a real book for a real [publisher] that was sold in real bookstores." The book deal remains a question mark in Gingrich's past, but does not seem to have stalled his political career in the 1990s.

In October of 1990 Gingrich gained headlines again when he opposed—and led 105 fellow Republicans in voting down—a proposed budget package. His defiance and disregard for the plan's presidential endorsement angered Senate Minority Leader Robert Dole, who was quoted in *Newsweek:* "You pay a price for leadership. If you don't want to pay the penalty, maybe you ought to find another line of work." Dole felt that Gingrich, fearful for his personal popularity, fought the budget in ignorance of the bi-partisan agreements that had been the fruit of hard work.

Some critics feel that Gingrich's in-House antics have won nothing for the Republican party itself, and have sometimes been counterproductive. The COS's oft-stated goal to wrest control of the House from the Democrats has yet to succeed. Even after eight years with Ronald Reagan in the White House and the subsequent election of George Bush, Democrats retain a strong hold on the House. "There has been a conservative majority in America for at least 20 years, but the Republican Party has failed to capitalize on it," Gingrich lamented in *Conservative Digest*.

At the November 1990 election, in fact, Democrats strengthened their hold on the House, picking up several seats. Ironically—despite his growing reputation on the national level—Gingrich had a scare in his home district at the election. He won by a narrow margin of 983 votes of the nearly 156,000 cast in Georgia's Sixth District. The root of Gingrich's trouble at home was his blockage of federal mediation in the 1989 strike at Eastern Airlines—the Atlanta airport is of great economic importance to the surrounding communities, and 6,000 employees of Eastern live in his district. This ill-considered move fostered a "Boot Newt" campaign, but he eventually defeated his Democratic challenger, 32-year-old lawyer David Worley, winning a seventh term in the House. Obviously shaken, Gingrich told his constituents that he had received their warning message in the close re-election, and will more closely carry out their mandate in his coming term in office.

Writings

Window of Opportunity: A Blueprint for the Future, with Marianne Gingrich and David Drake, St. Martin, 1984.

Sources

American Spectator, August 1989.

Atlantic, May 1985.
Business Week, August 14, 1989.
Conservative Digest, January/February 1989.
Esquire, October 1989.
Mother Jones, October 1989.
National Review, June 24, 1988; April 21, 1989; May 5, 1989; June 30, 1989; August 18, 1989.
New York Times, June 15, 1988.
Newsweek, April 3, 1989; October 15, 1990; October 22, 1990.
Time, April 3, 1989; June 12, 1989.
U.S. News and World Report, March 17, 1989.
Washington Post, November 11, 1990.

—*David Wilkins*

Philip Glass

AP/Wide World Photos

Composer

Born January 31, 1937, in Baltimore, MD; son of Benjamin (a record store owner) and Ida Gouline Glass; married Jo Anne Akalaitis (an actress and director; marriage dissolved); married Luba Burtyk (an internist), October, 1980; children: (first marriage) Zachary, Juliet. *Education:* Studied flute at Peabody Conservatory of Music, Baltimore; University of Chicago, B.A., 1956; Juilliard School of Music, M.S., 1962; studied counterpoint with Nadia Boulanger, Paris, 1964.

Career

Founder and director of Philip Glass Ensemble, 1968. Members have included Jon Gibson, Dickie Landry, Richard Peck and Jack Kripl—flutes and saxophones; Richard Prado—trumpet and flute; Iris Hiskey and Dora Orhenstein—sopranos; Glass, Steve Chambers, Arthur Murphy, and Michael Riesman—keyboards; Riesman also serves as conductor. In 1970, Kurt Munkacsi joined the ensemble as sound engineer.

Awards: BMI Award, 1960; Lado Prize, 1961; Benjamin Award, 1961; Ford Foundation Young Composer's Award, 1964-66; Fulbright scholarship, 1966-67; *Musical America* magazine's Musician of the Year, 1985; special jury prize, Cannes Film Festival for music for film *Mishima*.

Member: American Society of Composers, Authors and Publishers, SACEM of France.

Sidelights

Composer Philip Glass has made the long journey from avant-garde notoriety to mainstrean acceptance as one of the most popular composers of the twentieth century. Among his works are operas, orchestral pieces, film scores, dance works, and pieces written specifically for the Philip Glass Ensemble. Glass has worked with singer-songwriter Paul Simon, poet Allen Ginsberg, and avant-garde playwright Robert Wilson on a number of different projects.

Because his father was a record store owner, Glass was exposed to a wide variety of music at an early age. A precocious music student, he began flute lessons at the Peabody Conservatory in Baltimore at the age of eight. He went on to pass college entrance examinations at the age of fourteen and enrolled at the University of Chicago. There he took piano lessons and studied mathematics and philosophy, graduating with a B.A. in 1958. He then moved to New York City to study composition at the famous Julliard School of Music with Vincent Persichetti and William Bergsma. After earning his M.S. in 1962, Glass spent two years in Pittsburgh as a composer-in-residence on a Ford Foundation grant. In 1964 he was awarded a Fulbright fellowship that allowed him to study in Paris with the celebrated educator Nadia Boulanger, who had influenced three generations of American composers.

By the mid-1960s Glass had received many academic music awards, but he had not yet found his own voice. In 1965, he was hired to transcribe the Indian sitar music of Ravi Shankar and tabla player Alla Rahka for Conrad Rooks's film, *Chappaqua*. It proved to be a pivotal event for the young composer, who became avidly interested in Eastern music. Unlike Western music, the rhythmns of which are based on dividing large units, Eastern music is additive, based on gradually adding to small units or modules. Glass took Eastern music as his model. Depending on neither melody, theme, nor harmonic progression in any conventional way, Glass developed a music that is repetitive, tonal, and consonant, a latticework of shifting rhythmic figures that combine to create a shimmering and hypnotic effect. Some of his earliest works in this style were composed for the avant-garde Parisian theater ensemble Mabou Mines. After traveling in India, North Africa, and Central Asia for six months in 1965 and 1966, Glass returned to New York, where to support himself he worked a number of jobs, including driving a taxi. His works composed between 1965 and 1968 are experimental in nature and gained him the label "minimalist," which loosely describes a style that breaks music down into its rudimentary elements and uses them sparingly.

To insure the performance of his works, in 1968 Glass founded the Philip Glass Ensemble, which consisted mainly of amplified flutes and saxophones, electric organs, and synthesizers. His first concerts were performed in intimate New York City galleries and museums to small audiences; his first tours, in 1970, were sponsored by university art departments and museums in Europe.

While Glass gradually gained a following for his work, critics lambasted his music for its repetition and high amplification; purist classical composers ostracized him for rejecting twelve-tone music, the mainstay of twentieth-century classical music. "I always found serialism ugly and didactic. And so did many others. We rejected the idea of non-tonal music...the entire idea that music had to be an intellectual enterprise," Glass explained to Blake A. Samson of the *Kansas City Star*.

The year 1975 proved to be a watershed for Glass. He collaborated with the mixed-media artist and playwright Robert Wilson on the four-act opera *Einstein on the Beach*. For this non-narrative theater piece, Glass composed music that worked with the varied images representing the physicist Albert Einstein and the apocalyptic nuclear age. The soloists and chorus sing numbers and solfege syllables (do, re, mi). *Einstein* was first performed in Avignon, France, in 1976 and at other European locations before coming to New York's Metropolitan Opera for two performances later that year. It would be revived in 1984 and become the subject of a PBS special *The Changing Image of Opera*. Opinions of the work were widely divided. Though the music was more rhythmically and harmonically complicated than his previous works, detractors still faulted its repetitive nature; others found this effect mesmerizing.

Commissioned by the Dutch city of Rotterdam, *Satyagraha* is the second of what Glass calls his portrait operas. The text by Constance DeJong—which is written in Sanskrit and based on texts from the Hindu holy book the Bhagavad-Gita—deals with Mohandas K. (Mahatma) Gandhi's early days in South Africa, during which he formulated his ideas of nonviolent resistance. The title itself comes from two Hindu words "saty," meaning truth, and "agraha," meaning firmness. While imagistic like *Einstein*, the three-act *Satyagraha* is scored for orchestra, chorus, and soloists.

Akhnaten, another portrait opera, was commissioned by the Wurttemberg, Germany, State Theater. Glass and a group of collaborators assembled a series of scenes based on speculations about the life of Akhnaten, an Egyptian pharaoh who lived c. 1367 to 1350 B.C. Thought to be the first monotheist, Akhnaten outlawed the worshipping of the pantheon of Egyptian gods in favor of the sun god Aten. He and his wife, Nefertiti, ruled ancient Egypt until reactionary forces eventually overthrew them. *Akhnaten* uses a traditional orchestra, without the violins, and a synthesizer. It is sung in the ancient Accadian language, in Egyptian, and in Hebrew, with explanatory narration in English.

For *the CIVIL WarS: a tree is best measured when it is down*, Glass composed the score for the fifth act of co-librettists Robert Wilson and Maita di Niscemi's musical-dramatic work. The theater piece was being built in five different cities prior to its planned assembly at the Olympic Arts Festival in Los Angeles in 1984. However, the performance was canceled for lack of funds. The music for various scenes—which symbolize civil wars and are sung in different languages—was written by a number of composers. For Glass's two acts, called the Rome section, the topic was the American Civil War. The text by Niscemi in Latin and Italian is a compilation based largely on the poems of Roman statesman Seneca and letters written during the Civil War. The characters include a Snow Owl, Robert E. Lee, Abraham Lincoln, Mary Todd Lincoln, Italian patriot Giuseppe Garibaldi, and Hercules. Because the images combine to form a meditation on the end of the war and on rebirth and renewal, the music is much lighter and more lyrical than in Glass's previous operatic works. Though *CIVIL WarS* was not performed at the games, Glass was commissioned to compose music to accompany the lighting of the Olympic torch at the opening ceremonies: *The Olympian.*

With a commission from the Cambridge, Massachusetts, American Repertory Theatre, Glass worked with composer Robert Moran and children's author Arthur Yorinks on the two-act opera *The Juniper Tree.* Based on a Brothers Grimm fairy tale about a wealthy landowner and his wife who yearn to have a child, *The Juniper Tree* is scored for chamber orchestra, small chorus, and soloists. It is the first of Glass's dramatic works to be sung entirely in English.

Glass has long had an affinity for the writings of Edgar Allan Poe. Because he grew up in Baltimore, where Poe spent much of his life, Glass learned much about the author. Later, in France, where Poe's works are very popular, Glass rediscovered him. Commissioned by the Australian Dance Theatre, Glass created *Descent into the Maelstrom,* a dance piece based on Poe's short story of the same title. The Kentucky Opera and the American Repertory Theatre in Cambridge, Massachusetts, then commissioned a two-act opera based on Poe's *The Fall of the House of Usher.*

Other popular written works have also provided Glass with material for his music. Doris Lessing's science fiction novel *The Making of the Representative for Planet 8* is the basis of Glass's three-act drama with musical accompaniment of the same name. Lessing wrote the text, which treats the subject of a planet threatened by a new ice age. The music drama *1000 Airplanes on the Roof* also features a science-fiction theme: abduction by aliens. The single character "M"—portrayed by a man or woman—is abducted by aliens, experimented on, and returned with instructions to forget the experience, an experience that threatens to drive M crazy. The text by playwright David Henry Hwang is entirely spoken and the music, scored for synthesizers, amplified winds, and wordless soprano voice, follows the text closely. Slide projections also play an integral part of this drama, which was jointly commissioned by the Danube Festival of Lower Austria, the city of Berlin, and Philadelphia's American Music Theater Festival. When it was premiered in an airplane hangar at the

Vienna International Airport in 1987, Glass also performed directorial responsibilities.

The recording *Hydrogen Jukebox* is based on twenty-one poems by poet Allen Ginsberg, which examine American political and social issues. While some poems are spoken, others are sung. It is scored for six voices and a small chamber orchestra of two synthesizers, flute, saxophone, and percussion. "It's a return to non-narrative opera," Glass told Lynn Voedisch of the *Chicago Sun-Times.* "There is neither a story line nor a fixed character. It's a kaleidoscope...of America at the end of the twentieth century."

In addition to his operatic work, Glass has also composed music for several films and for dance companies. His scores for film include *Powaaqatsi,* Godfrey Reggio's *Koyaanisqatsi,* about environmental madness, Paul Schrader's *Mishima,* about the Japanese author and samurai, and *The Thin Blue Line.* Among his works for dance are *Dance* and *Glass Pieces.*

In the album *Songs from Liquid Days,* Glass decided to explore a musical form that he had yet to pursue—the song. Glass approached singers David Byrne, Paul Simon, Suzanne Vega, and performance artist Laurie Anderson, asking for lyrics that he could set to music and record. Unlike most albums by popular singers, Glass wanted to link the songs with a theme, like in a classical song cycle. The songs are performed not by their writers, but by other singers: the Roches, Linda Rondstadt, Bernard Fowler, and Janice Pendarvis. Glass told a *Newsday* reporter, "By just using their words and finding other singers, the focus of the record is really on myself as a composer, and that's what I was interested in." After the album was released, Glass persuaded the singers to perform the works live on a short U.S. tour to raise funds to support the expensive recording of *Satyagraha.*

In 1988 the Metropolitan Opera awarded Glass a $325,000 commission, the highest ever for an opera, to create a work for the October, 1992, commemoration of the 500th anniversary of Columbus's discovery of America. Glass plans a three-act allegory—with a libretto by Hwang—titled *The Voyage.*

Glass's works play to sell-out crowds, many of those in attendance drawn from the worlds of dance, opera, rock and roll, and film. Yet since the premier of his earliest works, Glass has not been taken seriously by the classical music establishment. Some detractors maintain that Glass's music lacks the substance, the staying power, of so-called serious music because of its static surface and underlying affinity to meditation. They find his scores excruciatingly boring and slick, overloud, artistically limited or merely trivial. Others consider Glass's commercial success a contradiction to his seriousness.

Glass, however, pays little attention to critics, maintaining that he is too busy to waste time reading reviews, and unlike many composers, openly admits his desire for success and recognition. "Music is a very social activity," Glass explained in an interview with Sally Vallongo of *The Blade*. "Music doesn't exist by itself; it exists when people play it for other people. It isn't a theory, it's a practice. When you know that your music is really part of the world you live in, I don't think a composer can really ask for much more than that."

Selected Works

String Quartet, 1966.
Music in the Shape of a Square (for two flutes), 1967.
In Again Out Again (for two pianos), 1967.
One Plus One (for amplified tabletop), 1967.
Music in Contrary Motion (for Philip Glass Ensemble), 1969.
Music in Fifths (for Philip Glass Ensemble), 1969.
Music in Similar Motion (for Philip Glass Ensemble), 1969.
Music in Eight Parts (for Philip Glass Ensemble), 1969.
Music for Voices (for the Mabou Mines Theater), 1970.
Music with Changing Parts (for Philip Glass Ensemble), 1970.
Music in Twelve Parts (for Philip Glass Ensemble), 1971-74.
Einstein on the Beach (four-act opera, vocal chorus, soloists, and Philip Glass Ensemble), 1975-76.
Dance (for Philip Glass Ensemble, in five parts combining film, live and recorded music; a collaboration with choreographer Lucinda Childs and sculptor-painter Sol LeWitt), 1979.
Satyagraha (three-act opera for orchestra, chorus and soloists), 1980.
Koyaanisqatsi (score for film directed by Godfrey Reggio for the Institute for Regional Education), 1982.
The Photographer (theater piece written with director-author Rob Malasch), 1982.
Akhnaten (three-act opera for orchestra, chorus and soloists), 1983.
the CIVIL WarS: a tree is best measured when it is down (Rome section of opera; with prologue and three scenes; with Robert Wilson), 1984.
Music for Mishima (for a film written by Paul and Leonard Schrader; directed by Paul Schrader), 1984.

The Juniper Tree (two-act opera for chamber orchestra, small chorus and soloists; written with composer Robert Moran and author Arthur Yorinks), 1984.
The Olympian (for chorus and orchestra), 1984.
Songs From Liquid Days (song cycle written with lyricists Laurie Anderson, David Byrne, Paul Simon, and Suzanne Vega), 1985.
A Descent into the Maelstrom (dance/theater work for Philip Glass Ensemble; with writer-director Matthew Maguire and choreographer Molissa Fenley), 1985.
The Making of the Representative for Planet 8 (three-act opera), 1985-86.
Concerto for Violin and Orchestra, 1987.
The Fall of the House of Usher (two-act opera), 1988.
1000 Airplanes on the Roof (opera), 1988.
Canyon (dramatic episode for orchestra), 1988.
Hydrogen Jukebox, with Allen Ginsberg, 1990.

Selected Discography

Glassworks, CBS Masterworks, 1982.
Koyaanisqatsi, Antilles, 1983.
Einstein on the Beach, CBS Masterworks, 1985.
Mishima, Nonesuch, 1985.
Songs From Liquid Days, 1986.
Akhnaten, CBS Masterworks, 1987.
Dancepieces, CBS Masterworks, 1988.
Mad Rush; Metamorphosis; Wichita Sutra Vortex, CBS Masterworks, 1989.
Music in Twelve Parts, Virgin Records America, 1990.

Sources

Books

Glass, Philip, *Music By Philip Glass*, edited and with supplementary material by Robert T. Jones, Harper, 1987.
Mertens, W., *American Minimal Music: LaMonte Young, Terry Riley, Steve Reich, Philip Glass*, [New York], 1983.

Periodicals

Ann Arbor News, October 2, 1988.
Atlanta Journal, April 7, 1985; May 4, 1990.
Chicago Sun Times, April 15, 1990.
Chicago Tribune, September 27, 1987.
Cincinnati Enquirer, February 12, 1987.
Cleveland Plain Dealer, October 18, 1987.
Detroit Free Press, October 6, 1988.
Detroit News, October 2, 1988.
Down Beat, December 1983.
Honolulu Advertiser, October 11, 1989.
Houston Post, October 7, 1984.
Kansas City Star, October 20, 1985.
Bucks County Courier Times (Levittown, PA) September 28, 1986.

Newsday, November 4, 1984; June 8, 1988.
Los Angeles Herald Examiner, June 22, 1983; November 26, 1984; November 21, 1986.
Courier-Journal (Louisville, KY), February 8, 1987.
Tennessean (Nashville), April 7, 1985.
New York Daily News, May 8, 1983.
New Yorker, November 19, 1984.
New York Times, April 20, 1986.
Ovation, February 1984.
Rolling Stone, January 21, 1982; April 10, 1986.
St. Louis Post-Dispatch, October 13, 1985.
Express News (San Antonio, TX), October 27, 1985.

San Diego Union, October 23, 1983.
San Francisco Examiner, November 23, 1986; November 13, 1988.
Marin Independent Journal (San Rafael, CA), November 23, 1986.
Saturday Review, May-June 1983.
The Blade (Toledo), June 14, 1987.
Washington Post, December 4, 1988.
Washington Times, May 9, 1990; October 25, 1990.

—*Jeanne M. Lesinski*

Jane Goodall

Ethologist and author

Full name, Jane van Lawick Goodall; born April 3, 1934, in London, England; daughter of Mortimer Herbert (a businessman and motor car racer) and Myfanwe (an author under name Vanne Goodall; maiden name Joseph) Goodall; married Hugo van Lawick (a photographer), March 28, 1964 (divorced); married Derek Bryceson (a member of Parliament and director of Tanzania National Parks), 1973 (died, 1980); children: (first marriage) Hugo Eric Louis. *Education:* Attended Uplands School, England; Cambridge University, Ph.D., 1965. *Religion:* Church of England.

Addresses: *Office*—Gombe Stream Research Centre, P.O. Box 185, Kigoma, Tanzania, East Africa; and The Jane Goodall Institute for Wildlife Research, Education and Conservation, Box 26846, Tucson, AZ 85726.

Career

After working briefly as a secretary and as an assistant film editor in England, left for Africa, and worked as assistant and secretary to Dr. Louis S. B. Leakey, curator of National Museum of Natural History in Nairobi, Kenya; returned to England, taking job as film librarian with Granada Television Ltd. while waiting for financial backing for proposed research project in Tanzania; Gombe Stream Research Centre, Tanzania, East Africa, researcher in animal behavior, particularly that of chimpanzees and other primates, and scientific director of center, 1960—. Visiting professor of psychiatry and human biology at Stanford University, 1970-75; honorary visiting professor of zoology, University of Dar Es Salaam, Tanzania, 1972—. Has been featured on numerous *National Geographic* television specials exploring her life and work.

Member: American Academy of Arts and Sciences (honorary foreign member, 1972—).

Awards: Two Franklin Burr prizes from National Geographic Society; gold medal for conservation from San Diego Zoological Society; conservation award from New York Zoological Society.

Sidelights

In her book *In the Shadow of Man*, Jane Goodall says that from the age of 8 she was determined to live with and study wild animals in Africa. She also notes that her favorite childhood toy was a stuffed chimpanzee named Jubilee, a fact that may be seen as a foreshadowing of much of her adult life. Goodall has dedicated more than 30 years to the study of chimpanzees in their natural environment and is now one of the world's most respected—and certainly best known—experts on the behavior of chimpanzees and other primates. She was one of the first people to conduct extensive research on wild chimps and is one of the few who have ever gotten close enough to them for a long enough period of time to make detailed observations of individual animals.

Goodall's story is a remarkable illustration of one woman's passionate adherence to her dream, a dream which began in England in 1939 when Goodall, then just 5 years old, moved along with her mother, father, and younger sister to a country home near the English Channel in Bournemouth. Goodall took immediately to the natural beauty surrounding her home, taking long rides on horseback into the countryside where she studied insects and animals. "Although I always did well in my studies, I never liked school," Goodall told *People*. "I just wanted to be outdoors, watching and learning. Once I disappeared for five hours to sit in a hen house to see how a chicken lays an egg. My mother was very worried, but when I came home—all bedraggled and my hair tangled with bits of straw—she never rebuked me. On the contrary, she recognized my patience with animals and encouraged me to study them."

> *"Although I always did well in my studies, I never liked school. I just wanted to be outdoors, watching and learning."*

Though her parents divorced when she was only 8, Goodall remained in Bournemouth with her mother and sister for several years before moving to London as a teenager to attend secretarial school. "Mum said secretaries could get jobs anywhere in the world," Goodall told *People*, "and I still knew my destiny lay in Africa." Fortunately, Goodall had a friend living on a farm in Kenya, and she was invited to visit. She worked as a waitress to finance the trip, then departed for Mombasa in 1957 at the age of 23. After working for a time as a secretary in Nairobi, Goodall met the famed paleontologist Dr. Louis S. B. Leakey who, she says, "must have sensed that my interest in animals was not just a passing phase, but was rooted deep, for on the spot he gave me a job as an assistant secretary."

Goodall subsequently accompanied Leakey and his wife on expeditions to the famous Olduvai Gorge site where, several years earlier, the discoveries of the prehistoric *zinjanthropus* and *homo habilis* had rocked the field of anthropology. As Leakey came to know her better, he felt that Goodall might be the right person to conduct a research project on a group of chimpanzees living in the Gombe Stream Chimpanzee Reserve located on the shore of Lake Tanganyika in Tanzania. The area was extremely rugged with steep mountains and dense jungles; the chimpanzees were totally wild, having had practically no contact with humans, and much patience and persistence would be required to study them. Leakey told her to expect to spend a minimum of two years on the project.

Although Goodall was thrilled with the prospect of observing wild chimps, she felt that she was not properly qualified to undertake a scientific study of animal behavior. But, as she says, Leakey "knew exactly what he was doing. Not only did he feel that a university training was unnecessary, but even that in some ways it might have been disadvantageous. He wanted someone with a mind uncluttered and unbiased by theory who would make the study for no other reason than a real desire for knowledge; and, in addition, someone with a sympathetic understanding of animals." Goodall agreed to undertake the project, and Leakey arranged funding and provided her with additional training. The study in the area that was to become the Gombe Stream Research Centre began in 1960 when Goodall was 26 years old. By 1990 the project was still going strong, although Goodall, who is scientific director of the Centre, was spending less time in the field studying chimps and more time lecturing around the world and raising more money for research.

But the cornerstone of the project was certainly laid down by Goodall herself, who spent years alone on the reserve making discovery after discovery that would change forever the way humans view their closest genetic relatives (chimps and humans share 99 percent of the same genetic material), and thus themselves. Of Goodall's greatest discoveries, two have proven the most startling and controversial. The first is her conclusive evidence that chimpanzees eat meat. It was generally thought that they were almost total vegetarians, occasionally supplementing their diet with a few insects or, less frequently, a small rodent. Goodall was the first to report that they regularly eat baby baboons, small monkeys, and baby bushpigs. And, she observed, not only did they eat these animals when they happened upon them by chance, but the chimps actually formed hunting parties in which they deliberately set out to capture game. Even more startling was Goodall's observance of cannibalism among the chimpanzees, particularly in the case of one female chimp, nicknamed Passion, who for a period of years went on a kind of terror spree, beating up other female chimps, stealing their infants, and then murdering and eating the baby chimps. Moreover she noted that meat-eating behavior in chimpanzees occurs in cycles. For about a month or two at a time they would concentrate on eating meat, then they would go back to a vegetarian diet for several months.

Goodall's other principal discovery was that chimpanzees fashion tools out of twigs or blades of grass. It had been recognized previously that chimps were able to use blades of grass to "fish" for termites by poking them into termite nests and withdrawing them with the insects clinging tightly with their mandibles. But Goodall was the first to observe the chimps bending blades of grass to a more suitable shape and stripping leaves from twigs—actually *making* rudimentary tools. She also saw chimps modify a number of twigs at the same time and pile them next to termite nests in order to have a supply of spares on hand while feeding. The chimpanzees, she found, also made sponges by chewing leaves to make them more absorbent and then pushing them into crevices of trees and rocks that held water. They would then lick the water from the leaves and repeat the process. Until Goodall made these observations, a common definition of the human being was "tool maker" or a creature who "made tools to a regular and set pattern." Goodall's research, as she writes, "convinced a number of scientists that it was necessary to redefine man in a more complex manner than before. Or else, as Louis Leakey put it, we should by definition have to accept chimpanzees as Man."

Goodall's observations came only after she had spent months gaining the trust of the animals she was studying, and her methods, though quite extraordinary, have come under fire as too emotional and unscientific. About one year after her arrival at Gombe, Goodall was approached by a male chimp she had nicknamed David Graybeard (her habit of naming the chimps has even been cited as proof that Goodall became too close to her subjects), who was followed by a female, Flo, who allowed Goodall to touch and play with her infant. She was soon welcomed by chimps all over the 30 square-mile reserve, and her tactic of offering bananas to chimps that wandered into her camp helped her to establish trust with certain animals, though this was a method she later rethought. As Goodall wrote in one of her many books on her experiences with the chimps, *The Chimpanzees of Gombe: Patterns of Behavior:* "In the early years of the research I actively encouraged social contact—play or grooming—with six different chimpanzees. For me personally, these contacts were a major breakthrough; they meant that I had won the trust of creatures who initially had fled when they

saw me in the distance. However, once it became evident that the research would continue into the future, it was necessary to discourage contacts of this sort."

> *"One of the ways we're different [from the animals] is that we have greater ability to be compassionate, we have the capacity to understand the suffering we inflict."*

Because chimpanzees are so humanlike in so many ways, there is a natural temptation, even for scientists, to anthropomorphize chimps—to place human values and judgments upon them. In the course of her research, Goodall became so emotionally attached to some of the chimps that some scientists have questioned the validity and objectivity of her deductions, suggesting that Goodall at times loses her grasp on the proper distance she must maintain between herself and the animals, and thus blurs the line that divides chimps from human beings. As Stephen Jay Gould writes in the *New York Review of Books:* "I was shaken by occasional statements in the worst tradition of the chain of being. 'It is evident that chimpanzees have made considerable progress along the road to humanlike love and compassion.' Or, comparing her chimps with their more sociable cousin, *Pan paniscus,* the pygmy chimp: 'It sounds like a utopian society—and viewed against this, it would seem that the Gombe chimpanzees have a long way to go.' But the Gombe chimps are not on any road, and the metaphor can only produce a biased itinerary."

But whatever criticism she may receive from the scientific community, Goodall has remained committed not only to her sometimes unorthodox research methods but also to her belief that humans not only can, but *must* bring an emotional element to any research conducted on animals. "If we're different from the animals, one of the ways we're different is that we have greater ability to be compassionate, we have the capacity to understand the suffering we inflict," Goodall told the *Cable Guide.* "Therefore we should be concerned about what we inflict on the rest of the animal kingdom. The fallacy that animals are machines that can be used in any way we like, don't have emotions and don't feel pain is not acceptable anymore, even by the scientists who use them in the labs."

Though she admits that her ideal situation would have her studying her chimpanzees in Gombe the year round, Goodall in recent years has decided that she can play a larger, less "selfish" role in helping the chimps and other animals by traveling and heightening world awareness about the endangered chimps. In 1990 there were about 175,000 chimps left in the world, and the numbers keep declining, mostly due to illegal poaching. Chimps are prized by poachers for numerous reasons, the most common being the top dollars paid for baby chimps sold as pets. Because the chimps are rarely left alone by their mothers, poachers will kill the mothers and steal the infants. "It's so distressing to see one of these infants after its mother has been shot." Goodall said in *The Cable Guide*. "A little chimp in the wild is always with the mother. The child will stay near the body of its mother, keep going back, listening for the heartbeat. They have the same emotional attachment to their mothers, the same need for reassurance, the same insecurities as we do."

Another of Goodall's educational missions involves a far more complex, and therefore thornier, problem. Although her affection for chimpanzees is obvious, Goodall, as a scientist, recognizes the great value chimps have to the scientific community as research subjects. Because they are so genetically similar to humans, chimpanzees make ideal stand-ins for humans in researching such diseases as acquired immune deficiency syndrome (AIDS) and hepatitis, as well as psychological studies and other areas of scientific exploration. Goodall's complaint with many researchers has not been their use of the chimpanzees, although she has pressed hard for more uses of computer modeling and tissue cultures that would allow research to go on without chimps, but rather the treatment the chimps receive by scientists who "use them as human surrogates yet have been very reluctant to admit the equally striking mental and emotional similarities."

At every lab she visits, Goodall discusses ways in which the chimps can be treated more humanely, such as allowing them contact with other chimpanzees so that they can play and groom one another— grooming being a very important aspect of chimp

socialization. "The suffering of chimps can be reduced by putting them in bigger cages, exposing them to the outdoors and allowing them more contact with each other. Toys and even simple video games can relieve the deadly boredom you see in all those empty stares," Goodall told *People*.

Despite her compassion for the chimpanzees, Goodall does not let her sentiment carry to the condescending conclusion that chimps are, in terms of evolution, a creature that humans have necessarily surpassed. Rather, she argues, they are simply different from us, certainly at a cruder stage in their development, but nevertheless progressing through time in their own unique fashion. "I think they've come to the very beginning of a cultural form of evolution, which is what characterized our explosive development since we began to talk," she told *The Cable Guide*. "Chimps are the beginning of that. I doubt that they would ever evolve into a human pattern. I don't think evolution repeats herself. They might turn into a more decent creature than us."

Writings

My Friends, the Wild Chimpanzees, National Geographic Society, 1967.
(With Hugo van Lawick) *Innocent Killers*, Collins, 1970.
In the Shadow of Man, Houghton, 1971.
(With van Lawick) *Grub: The Bush Baby*, Houghton, 1972.
Through a Window: My Thirty Years With the Chimpanzees of the Gombe, Houghton Mifflin, 1990.

Sources

Books

Green, Timothy, The Restless Spirit: Profiles in Adventure, Walker & Co., 1970.

Periodicals

The Cable Guide, May, 1990.
New York Review of Books, June 25, 1987.
New York Times Magazine, February 18, 1973.
People, May 14, 1990.
Saturday Review of Science, February, 1973.
Times Literary Supplement, November 20, 1970; November 19, 1971.

—*David Collins and Peter M. Gareffa*

Nicholas Graham

Mark Sennet/Onyx

Underwear designer

Born c. 1960; grew up in Calgary, Alberta, Canada; son of Ewen (an equestrian equipment salesman) and Nicky Graham; married Maria Goldinger, 1982 (divorced, 1985); married Margo Rosengren (a painter), 1987; children: (second marriage) Christopher. *Education:* Attended Trinity School, Ontario, Canada.

Addresses: *Home*—San Francisco, CA. *Office*—c/o Joe Boxer Corp., San Francisco, CA.

Career

Began designing ties in the early 1980s; created the Imperial Hoser line of boxer shorts; became founder and chief designer of Joe Boxer Corp., San Francisco, CA.

Sidelights

A few years after the end of the Second World War," wrote Robert E. Sullivan, Jr., in *Gentleman's Quarterly,* "a particularly imaginative anatomist ... proved boxer shorts to be the prudent choice of undergarment for the potent male." Some four decades later, boxer shorts have come out of the drawer as a fashion statement as well, and much of the credit goes to designer Nicholas Graham.

Graham, founder and chief designer of Joe Boxer Corp., a San Francisco-based manufacturer, made his mark during the late 1980s with a line of whimsical, wild, and just plain eccentric boxer shorts and other men's "sleepwear" choices. A Joe Boxer original

might be a pair of shorts festooned with toothbrushes, or happy-faces, or Statues of Liberty; it might be the eye-catching, polka-dotted "Bimbo Libido" robe; it might be pajamas that can be accessorized with a bow tie. "Our underwear lets people express themselves," Graham informed *People* reporter Tim Allis.

Graham, the son of equestrians who grew up on a Calgary ranch, learned early that expression can pay off: according to Allis's article, the designer "made his first foray into outer wear when he was 17, decked out as big-bosomed cowgirl Louise Disguise for a bar band called Disguise Da Limit. Then he spent a few bohemian years travelling through England, Greece and Sweden."

It was during his European sojourn that Graham met his first wife, Maria Goldinger, and together they lived and worked in San Francisco, designing ties. However, on a tip from a Macy's buyer who told Graham that boxer shorts would be tomorrow's hot ticket, Graham took a $1000 investment and launched the Imperial Hoser line. The shorts, "made of red plaid flannel, ... sported a detachable raccoon tail—and were an instant hit," as Allis wrote.

Graham had happened upon a revolution in the underwear business; as Sullivan elaborated in *GQ,* the propensity of boxers, as opposed to briefs, to allow their target area to "breathe," thus promoting a higher sperm count, inspired renewed interest during the "procreative 1980s" in what used to be dismissed as Army-issue undergarments. And Graham leaves little room for subtlety in his designs—as evidenced by a pair of boxers "that proclaim NO, NO, NO in the daylight and YES, YES, YES in the dark," as the *People* piece noted. Such innovations have boosted Joe Boxer Corp.'s sales to the point where it has trailed behind only Jockey and Calvin Klein. As for creativity, "Joe Boxer is the leader for the pack," as Tom Julian of the Men's Fashion Association told Allis.

Joe Boxer shorts have been publicly embraced by such diverse celebrities as Public Enemy rapper Flavor Flav (who wore a golf-ball pattern on an awards show) and actress Michelle Pfeiffer (who sported a boxer/tee-shirt set in the movie *The Fabulous Baker Boys*). The success of his company—which now has branches in Canada, Australia, and New Zealand—has had Graham thinking about expansion into linens, dinnerware, and even music, according to Allis. "We're in the entertainment business," Graham stated in the article. "We just happen to sell clothes."

Sources

Gentleman's Quarterly, February, 1989.
People, February 11, 1991.

—*Susan Salter*

Bob Guccione, Jr.

Courtesy of Spin magazine

Magazine publisher

Born in 1956; son of Bob Guccione (publisher and founder of *Penthouse* magazine).

Address: *Office—Spin* Magazine, 6 West 10th St., New York, NY 10011.

Career

Circulation director of the Penthouse group c. 1981; founder, editor, and publisher of *Spin* magazine, 1985—; author.

Sidelights

The name Guccione has been associated with magazine publishing ever since maverick publisher Bob Guccione founded *Penthouse*, an adult magazine, in direct competition with Hugh Hefner's successful *Playboy*. Guccione's oldest son, Bob Guccione, Jr., has followed in his father's footsteps. In 1985, Guccione, Jr., founded *Spin* magazine, a rock and roll publication, to directly compete with the popular *Rolling Stone*, which he called "boring, dull and obnoxious" in the *New York Times.*

The younger Guccione was raised in London and still has an accent that attests to those early years. Even though he grew up in the era of the Beatles and the British rock invasion, Guccione claims to not have cared a great deal about rock music in his early years, claiming in the *New York Times* that he "completely missed the Beatles when they broke"; he also does not play any kind of musical instrument. Commenting on his early years, he stated: "In those days, I wasn't into music, or girls or drugs, I was only into soccer. I was 15 before I really listened to a record." Even as an adult, Guccione feels no great affinity to the rock and roll world. The business, he feels, is filled with "boring people" and others "who have been sucked into the cyclone of somebody else's monstrously confused ago."

When he was in his late teens, Guccione had a big fight with his father. "He said that I would never be anything in this world without him. It offended me because it was probably true at the time." The fight, however, prompted young Guccione to move back to England and take a stab at something on his own. The result was that Guccione wrote and published a book titled *Step by Step Guide to Kung Fu* under the pseudonym Bob Hudson. The book sold out very quickly, and Guccione realized that he had done something important without his father's help.

For about a decade, Guccione worked for his father's Penthouse group, being promoted to circulation director when he was 24. Guccione, Sr., had urged his son to stay on and be groomed to take over a senior position. Guccione, however, had no desire to be like Christie Hefner, daughter of Playboy Enterprises Inc. president Hugh Hefner, who had taken over the company after her father retired. He declined his father's offer and a younger brother was coached on the family business instead. Guccione decided, at the age of 29, to found his own magazine.

The idea for the new magazine came to him while listening to Cyndi Lauper's song, "Girls Just Want to Have Fun." He realized that it was a normal human emotion to have fun and he didn't feel there were any magazines available that catered to this. "There seems to be a terrific guilt complex in publishing that forces people to become much more serious than they might be in regular life," he commented in the *New York Times.* "They can't reflect the sense of fun in their publications. *Rolling Stone* is a classic example." *Spin* was formed in direct competition with *Rolling Stone,* just as *Penthouse* had been formed to compete with *Playboy.* Guccione felt that the older publication had become rather staid. "I've started out wanting to kick *Rolling Stone*'s butt . . . . But it doesn't seem to be a very creative ambition just to want to beat somebody else. That's secondary to making this a great magazine."

Guccione borrowed $500,000 from his father to start up the magazine, and used the Guccione name to help him gain access to people who might help him in the venture. He went to work assembling a diverse and knowledgeable staff; editors from such areas as the Pacific News Service and *Interview* magazine were selected to provide an eclectic base for the fledgling publication. Guccione also made it a priority to cover new musicians and trends—beating *Rolling Stone* to the punch on more than one article. Articles on actors and athletes were also featured prominently. *Rolling Stone* general manager Kent Brownbridge commented that he was glad to have the competition from *Spin.* But he added that "I have to say we have not seen anything that gives us great cause for concern."

By 1991 *Spin* had reached a circulation of 300,000—not quite meeting Guccione's initial projections, or matching *Rolling Stone*'s 1,000,000. "Our objective will never be to sell more copies just to sell more copies," commented Guccione in an interview with Bob Talbert in the *Detroit Free Press.* "I feel with luck we can have a circulation of 700-750,000 over the next five years, but I don't intend to dilute the editorial material just to reach someone else's magic million in circulation."

Guccione has been able to establish *Spin* as a daring, cutting edge publication. He once turned over the editorship of *Spin* for a month to filmmaker Spike Lee, the producer of *Do the Right Thing* and *Jungle Fever,* among others. With the intention of promoting safe sex among his 18 to 30-year-old male audience, Guccione had a sealed condom put in every issue of *Spin* one month. In reaction, more that 60 percent of

the stores that sold the magazine banned it. "The mistake was not warning them. Most told us later that had we let them know it was coming they wouldn't have minded. The shock of seeing a condom in the magazine without prior notice got to them."

For the August, 1991, issue Guccione had another unique idea. He wanted to chronicle the soul of rock and roll across America. So he gave each of his reporters a round-trip plane ticket to some destination in the United States where they were to track down the soul of rock and roll and report on it. "I have no idea of what we'll find. But looking for it should be fun and that's part of the mood we intend to bring to the . . . issue."

Despite Guccione's threat in 1985 that he might not be able to keep his passion for music going long enough to edit *Spin* for ten years, he continues to work on making the publication the voice of the 18 to 30 generation. "The magazine is very much a reflection of me as a person," he commented in the *New York Times.* "I think all the best magazines reflect an individual personality. *Penthouse* is a reflection of my father, *Time* was a reflection of Henry Luce, *Playboy* is a reflection of Hefner." The reflection of Guccione that seems to come through in *Spin* is the commitment to the generation he represents. He will not pander to this audience through articles that patronize, rather than entertain or inform. *Spin*'s editorial content, according to Guccione, is half music and pop culture and half politics. He is especially proud of *Spin* articles on AIDS and the Bush administration. "These type of stories go against the mainstream media thinking today that dismisses the younger generation as vidiots who aren't interested in thinking or reading," he said to Talbert. Remembering back to the days when he had to prove himself to his father, he added: "Hey, my own generation was dismissed as a bunch of nonthinking rock heads who'd never amount to anything when we were growing up. We proved that wrong, didn't we?"

Writings

(Under name Bob Hudson) *Step by Step Guide to Kung Fu.*

Sources

Detroit Free Press, May 8, 1991.
New York Times, June 2, 1985.

—Nancy Rampson

M. C. Hammer

AP/Wide World Photos

Rap singer

Real name, Stanley Kirk Burrell; born in Oakland, Calif.; youngest of seven children; married; wife's name, Stephanie; children: Akeiba Monique. *Education:* High school graduate; took undergraduate classes in communications.

Addresses: *Home*—Fremont Hills, CA.

Career

Worked for the Oakland Athletics baseball team as a bat boy during high school years; served for three years in the U.S. Navy upon graduation from high school; formed first rap group, the Holy Ghost Boys, and founded music production company, Bust It Records; first debut single, "Ring 'Em," released in the mid-1980s; signed with Capitol Records, 1988. Performs in concerts worldwide.

Awards: Grammy Awards for best rap solo and for best rhythm and blues song, both 1991, both for "U Can't Touch This," and for best long form music video, 1991, for *Please Hammer Don't Hurt 'Em the Movie.*

Sidelights

Hailed by *Entertainment Weekly* as "rap's most pervasive, persuasive ambassador," M.C. Hammer has a reputation for pursuing his goals with remarkable energy and tenacity. His first dream in life eluded his grasp, however; if he had achieved it, he would be a professional baseball player today.

Instead, Hammer has had to settle for being the world's most successful rap artist.

Hammer was born Stanley Kirk Burrell in Oakland, California. He was the youngest of his parents' seven children. "We were definitely poor," he stated in describing his youth to *Rolling Stone* writer Jeffrey Ressner. "Welfare. Government-aided apartment building. Three bedrooms and six children living together at one time." Despite the rough neighborhood he grew up in, Hammer stayed out of trouble by immersing himself in his twin passions, baseball and music.

As a boy he'd be at the Oakland Coliseum to watch the Athletics play as often as possible. If he couldn't see the game, he'd hang around the parking lot hoping for a glimpse of one of his heroes, among them superstar pitcher Vida Blue. When the team was idle Hammer amused himself by copying the dance moves of James Brown, the O'Jays, and others. He showed the first glimmerings of his interest in business when he began writing commercial jingles for his favorite products.

One day his two interests collided in a way that would profoundly influence his life. He was dancing in the Coliseum's parking lot when the Athletics' owner, Charlie Finley, passed by. A comment by

Finley on the young dancer's style led to a conversation, and eventually to a job working in the team clubhouse and going on the road as bat boy. Hammer quickly became a sort of mascot for the team. Finley even gave him the honorary title of executive vice-president, while the ball players began calling the former Stanley Burrell "Hammer" because of his striking resemblance to batting great Henry "Hammerin' Hank" Aaron.

After graduating from high school, Hammer tried to break into the world of professional baseball as a player, but to no avail. He briefly pursued a communications degree, but was unsuccessful in that field too. Dejected and at loose ends, Hammer considered getting involved in the lucrative drug trade thriving in his old neighborhood. "I was a sharp businessman and could have joined up with a top dealer," he told Ressner. "I had friends making $5000 to $6000 a week, easy....I thought about that just like any other entrepreneur would." Hammer turned away from the fast money, however—making a moral choice that reverberates in his current image as a deeply religious, socially conscious performer—and joined the Navy for a three-year hitch in Japan and California.

> "I was a sharp businessman and could have joined up with a top [drug] dealer.... I thought about that just like any other entrepreneur would."

When his stint with the military ended, Hammer applied the discipline he'd acquired in the service to launching a career in music. His first musical venture was a rap duo he dubbed the Holy Ghost Boys. Religious rap might seem to have limited commercial appeal, but Hammer talked two record companies into taking a chance on producing a Holy Ghost Boys album. He and his partner went their separate ways before the project could be completed, however.

Two of Hammer's friends from the Oakland A's helped him make his next move. Mike Davis and Dwayne Murphy each invested $20,000 in Bust It Records, Hammer's own company. He hawked his debut single, "Ring 'Em," on the streets. At the same time, he was auditioning and working with musicians, dancers, and his female backup trio, known as

Oaktown's 3-5-7. Striving to put together a more sophisticated act, Hammer held rehearsals seven days a week, sometimes for fourteen hours at a time.

Shortly after the release of his second single, "Let's Get Started," Hammer teamed with Felton Pilate, a producer and musician from the group Con Funk Shun. The two worked long hours in Pilate's basement studio to bring out Hammer's first full-length album, *Feel My Power*. Produced on a shoestring budget and marketed without the tremendous resources of a major record company, *Feel My Power* nevertheless sold a remarkable 60,000 copies.

Early in 1988 Hammer was catching an act at an Oakland music club when he was spotted by Joy Bailey, an executive at Capitol Records. She didn't know who he was, but his presence and attitude impressed her. She introduced herself and later arranged for him to meet with some of the company's top people at Capitol's Los Angeles headquarters. With his music, dancing, and keen business sense, Hammer convinced Capitol that he was the man who could lead the company successfully into the booming rap music market. He walked away from the meeting with a multi-album contract and a $750,000 advance. The record company didn't have to wait long for proof that they'd made the right decision; a reworked version of *Feel My Power*, titled *Let's Get It Started* climbed to sales of more than 1.5 million records.

Touring and appearing at hip hop shows around the nation in the company of well-established rap performers Tone-Loc, N.W.A., and Heavy D and the Boyz didn't keep Hammer from working on his next album—he simply outfitted the back of his tour bus with recording equipment. Such methods enabled him to turn out the single "U Can't Touch This" for about $10,000, roughly the same cost of *Feel My Power*. He predicted to Capitol that the album would break all rap music sales records, and his boast was no idle one. Backed by a unique marketing campaign (which included sending cassettes to 100,000 children, along with personalized letters urging them to request Hammer's music on MTV), "U Can't Touch This" had already sold more than five million copies in late 1990, easily surpassing the record formerly held by the Beastie Boys' *Licensed to Ill*. The song also became the theme song for the Detroit Pistons basketball team during and after their second NBA championship campaign in 1990.

After the release of *Please Hammer Don't Hurt 'Em*, whose immensely popular "U Can't Touch This" was described by *Entertainment Weekly* as "shamelessly copp[ing] its propulsive riff from Rick James'

'Super Freak,'" James himself took legal action against Hammer. The two entertainers reached an out-of-court settlement, with Hammer paying James for "borrowing" James's early 1980s hit song. As reported in *Jet*, Hammer told James, "I felt good using music from a person I idolized. Ya'll used to come out and do a show. Then I'd do my thing at the club to *Super Freak*." According to *Jet*, the performers reconciled, with James telling Hammer, "Keep doing it."

Before each performance on his tour, Hammer leads his fifteen dancers, twelve backup singers, seven musicians, and two deejays in prayer, then puts on the most energetic show possible. His future ventures include an action-comedy film tentatively titled *Pressure*, an album to be produced by Prince, and a longform video for which 100,000 advance orders have already been placed. Furthermore, he has signed a contract uniting Bust It Records with Capitol in a $10 million joint-venture agreement. The rapper also makes commercial endorsements for Pepsi and British Knights athletic wear. Of his desire to pursue a film career, Hammer told *Rolling Stone*'s Steve Hochman: "I'm not a singer-want-to-turn movie star. I've always been an actor."

For now, however, it looks like M. C. Hammer will endure in his present field. "I'm on a mission," Hammer told Ressner. "The music is in me, and I have to get it out." As *Entertainment Weekly* phrased it, "Hammer is cultural evolution in fast action, the rapper as wheeler-dealer and sleek entertainer—and the next logical step for a form of music that is quickly becoming part of the fabric of American life."

Discography

Singles

"Ring 'Em," Bust It Records.
"Let's Get Started," Bust It Records.

LPs

Feel My Power, Bust It Records (revised version released as *Let's Get It Started*), Capitol, 1989.
Please Hammer Don't Hurt 'Em, Capitol, 1990.

Sources

Ebony, January 1989.
Entertainment Weekly, December 28, 1990.
Jet, November 5, 1990.
New York Times, April 15, 1990.
Rolling Stone, May 17, 1990; July 12, 1990; September 6, 1990.

—Joan Goldsworthy

Martin Handford

Author and illustrator

Career

Commercial artist and author; creator of the best-selling children's book series, "Where's Waldo?"

Sidelights

Where's Waldo? Everywhere. On the *New York Times* best-seller list. In millions of books. In more than 20 countries around the world. And mostly, in Martin Handford's head. Who's Waldo? Where have you been? Waldo is the biggest thing going in children's books. He's the fellow in the eyeglasses, jeans, red-striped sweater, and, of course, the stocking cap with the pom-pom.

Waldo grew out of a habit Handford carried from childhood to adulthood: drawing crowd scenes. As a child, Handford loved drawings of toy soldiers, historical comics, illustrated history books, and Hollywood swashbucklers with battle scenes and lots of extras. Crowds, in other words. "Handford would rush home after school to work on a densely populated battlefield sketch rather than play with other kids," *Newsweek* said. "He doted on the drawings of Cornelius DeWitt, who produced the 'Golden History of the World' and the work of American military illustrator H. Charles McBarron."

As Handford was quoted in *Entertainment Weekly*: "I liked to combine the excitement I'd experienced from books or comics or films, and then I'd try to carry on the adventure by adding to it in a picture that I did.

Ever since then, that's what I've spent all my spare time doing."

In Handford's books, the goal is to find Waldo in the crowds that crowd page after page of colorful illustrations. Each picture takes Handford a month to complete and includes 300 to 500 figures: vampires, mermaids, magic carpet riders, battling monks, even Waldo impostors. "Five years ago, Handford was just another struggling commercial artist in London," *Entertainment Weekly* said in December of 1990. "Now he's a publishing phenomenon. The first four Waldo books have sold an astounding 18.6 million books worldwide in the last four years [compared with 50,000 for a typical top-selling children's title] with the third, *The Great Waldo Search*, riding high on the *New York Times* best-seller list for a year.... The books—whose readership ranges from preschoolers to grownups who love sight gags—are printed in 22 countries and 16 languages, counting the forthcoming Basque, Hebrew and Korean editions. Coming soon to American stores: Waldo T-shirts, shoes, games and sleeping bags. And there's talk of a Waldo film or TV series." All because of kids' attraction to friendly, mild-mannered Waldo—or Ubaldo in Italy, Charlie in France, Valle in Sweden, Holger in Denmark.

In England, meanwhile, Martin Handford seems largely unaffected.

He still lives in a London suburb, still works through the night while listening to the Clash, the Bee Gees, and soundtracks of old Sergeant Bilko TV shows. He's been with his girlfriend for nine years. He has no plans for a bigger house, no desire to travel. He still talks about his real dream: to play in a pop band.

Handford says he is *not* the model for nerdish Waldo, as has been suggested. "It's a theory that's been put forward that rankles me a bit, I'm afraid," he said in *Entertainment Weekly*. And there's another part of his image he is battling: "Some journalists have tried to paint me as this owl, this nocturnal creature that doesn't like coming out in the daylight," he said in *Entertainment Weekly*. "It's true, I don't normally rise until after midday, but that's not uncommon amongst commercial artists. It worried me that I was being described as reclusive, because I'm not; I've got very good friends."

Sources

Entertainment Weekly, December 14, 1990.
Newsweek, August 13, 1990.
Publisher's Weekly, November 24, 1989.
Rolling Stone, May 17, 1990.

—David Wilkins

Emmylou Harris

AP/Wide World Photos

Country music singer and songwriter

Born April 2, 1947, in Birmingham, Ala.; daughter of a career Marine officer; married Tom Slocum (a songwriter) c. 1970 (divorced); married Brian Ahern (a record producer), January, 1975 (one source says 1977; divorced, 1983); married Paul Kennerley (a songwriter), 1985; children: (first marriage) Hallie, (second marriage) Meghann. *Education:* Attended University of North Carolina, 1965.

Career

Country singer-songwriter, 1967—; began career as solo folk singer in coffeehouses and nightclubs; sang backup with Gram Parsons band, 1971-73; signed with Warner Bros., 1974, cut first album, *Pieces of the Sky,* 1975. Has made numerous tours and concert appearances. President of the Country Music Foundation, 1983—.

Awards: Five Grammy awards; Country Music Association award for best album, 1980, for *Roses in the Snow;* named Female Vocalist of the Year by the Country Music Association, 1980; album of the year citation from Academy of Country Music, 1987, for *Trio;* nine gold albums; one platinum album.

Sidelights

Many country singers have achieved success by crossing over into the lucrative pop market. Dulcet-voiced Emmylou Harris has done just the opposite: she culls songs from pop and rock and transforms them into pure country fare. Harris, one of the most popular singers in Nashville, is praised on every side for the respect she holds for traditional country music. To quote Alanna Nash in *Esquire* magazine, the performer "has not only carried on the mission of taking pure, traditional country to a hip, pop audience, but through her own artistry and integrity has helped raise the music to a new position of respectability, carving an identity for herself unique in all of country music." Singer Holly Dunn, quoted in *People,* echoed Nash: "She has let major superstardom pass her by more than once because she's never sold out, taken the easier route. People revere her."

In *Country Music U.S.A.* Bill C. Malone observed that Harris seems dedicated to the preservation of older country music, the sound of the Carter Family, Hank Williams, and George Jones. Still, Malone remarked, "Harris is a true eclectic, borrowing from many styles. Her concerts and LPs contain a mixture of contemporary and traditional material, rock-flavored songs and Appalachian-sounding ballads, and modern country-and-western numbers." It is Harris's vocal abilities that guarantee her an audience, no matter the style of her presentation. A *Time* magazine correspondent characterized her singing as "more ...melancholy Appalachian bluegrass than... western swing," adding: "Despite its range, her voice is most telling because of its feathery delicacy, an almost tentative dying fall capable of stirring deep emotions.''

Harris was born in Alabama, but she grew up in the Maryland and Virginia suburbs of Washington, D.C. Her father was a decorated Marine Corps pilot who spent 16 months in Korea as a prisoner of war. Harris's family moved often, though never back to the deep South. She has recollected that her older brother liked country music much more than she did; her own musical preferences included folk and pop-rock. As a teenager she was a cheerleader and played saxophone in her high school marching band. She was also drawn to the theater. She told *Time:* "High schools are real hip now, but there was no counter-culture in Woodbridge [Virginia]."

After one year of studying drama at the University of North Carolina, Harris took off for New York City in search of the counterculture. Like so many other young people of the era, she drifted to Greenwich Village, where she sang country and folk music in coffeehouses and nightclubs, sometimes earning as little as ten dollars a night. In 1970 she and her first husband, songwriter Tom Slocum, moved to Nashville to try their luck in the country format. She failed to hit there and her marriage dissolved. With a newborn baby to care for, she returned to her parents' home in Maryland and began singing at clubs in Washington, D.C. Her performances at the Red Fox Inn and the Cellar Door were hailed by Washington audiences, which were already becoming known for a special receptivity to country-folk-bluegrass blends.

Harris met Gram Parsons in Washington in 1972. Parsons, formerly with the Byrds, was a primary force in the burgeoning country-rock movement. He was so impressed with Harris's voice and delivery that he invited her to join him in Los Angeles to sing backup on his first solo album. Harris was delighted by the offer, and over the ensuing two years she became Parson's protege, learning from him the special roots of country and honky-tonk music.

"It was an ear-opening period for me," Harris told *Newsweek.* "I'd always liked Hank Williams and Buck Owens, but with Gram I discovered that country music was a natural form of singing for me." "In Harris," wrote *People*'s Jim Jerome, "Parson's mournful twang found its harmonic soulmate; through Parsons, Harris discovered the aching, warbling world of George Jones and Bill Monroe and the timeless, intertwining duets of the Stanley Brothers, Louvin Brothers, and Everly Brothers." As Harris herself told Jerome of that time, "It's like I snapped. I

had been deaf and all of a sudden I could hear. Gram's music got past my intense, intellectual folk stuff and shot right into my heart." The two albums she cut with Parsons, *GP* and *Grievous Angel,* were hailed in *People* by country music's premier journalist Patrick Carr as "arguably the ultimate achievements in modern country music."

> *"It's like I snapped. I had been deaf and all of a sudden I could hear. [The] music got past my intense, intellectual folk stuff and shot right into my heart."*

In 1973 Parsons died of a heart attack, brought on by drug abuse. Left to her own resources, Harris formed a band and signed with Warner Bros. Records. There she was paired with Brian Ahern, a gifted producer who gladly followed her natural tendencies *not* to strive for a pop sound. In short order Harris was climbing the country charts with hits like the Louvin Brothers' 'If I Could Only Win Your Love," A. P. Carter's "Hello, Stranger," and Buck Owens's "Together Again." Harris and Ahern were married in 1977.

Harris may have shown an unusual dedication to country music, but her ear had also been honed by folk and rock; she and Ahern recorded a trove of offbeat songs like "Poncho and Lefty" by Townes Van Zandt, "The Boxer," by Paul Simon, and tunes by the Beatles and Bruce Springsteen. Her forte remained the ballad, however. Nash is one of many critics who suggests that Harris's best ballad work shows "a vulnerability rooted in the dark recesses of the soul."

Fueled by what *Newsweek* called the "plaintive, piney-woods feeling evoked by her sweet, sinewy soprano," Harris's albums went gold in America and Europe. Some of her best songs were written by members of her top-rate backup group, the Hot Band, whose membership included Ricky Scaggs and Rodney Crowell. From time to time she cut tracks with other country superstars, including Waylon Jennings, Dolly Parton, and Linda Ronstadt. By 1980, when she was voted Female Vocalist of the Year by the Country Music Association, Harris was among the most successful pure country performers in the nation. Unlike Parton and Ronstadt, she chose to adhere to the country format—and to singing in general.

Critics generally agree that Harris has recorded two "masterworks." The first is *Roses in the Snow*, an album from the early 1980s that is decidedly blue-grass in flavor. With its acoustic accompaniments and traditional songs, *Roses in the Snow* harks back to the work of the Carter Family, Ralph Stanley, and Flatt & Scruggs; it was a surprise commercial success for Harris. Her other outstanding accomplishment to date is the "country opera" album *The Ballad of Sally Rose*, a theme piece for which Harris wrote the lyrics herself. Based loosely on Harris's own life, *The Ballad of Sally Rose* follows a woman singer through the heights and depths of her career. In *Stereo Review* Nash observed that the work "carries a desperation, a smoldering, aching passion to connect with the poignant realities that live in the heart and not just the head."

For many years Harris worked out of Los Angeles in studios she built with Ahern. When that marriage ended in 1983 she returned to Nashville and based herself there. Today she is married to Paul Kennerley, a Grammy award-winning songwriter who helped her with *The Ballad of Sally Rose*. Harris has truly achieved success by following her own formula—by surrounding herself with a fine, distinctive backup band, by recording a quaint mixture of traditional, modern, and original tunes, and by presenting them all in a fine voice. As for her future, the singer's instincts seem sure. "I keep thinking at some point my excitement about music will go away and I can retire," Harris told Jerome. "But there's always that one song that you've got to sing, and then to record, and then, boy, you've got to sing it live. It just never stops—the songs just never stop coming."

Selected discography

With Gram Parsons

GP, 1972.

Grievous Angels, 1973.

Solo Albums

Gliding Bird, 1969.
Pieces of the Sky, Reprise, 1975.
Elite Hotel, Reprise.
Luxury Liner, Warner Bros.
Quarter Moon in a Ten-Cent Town, Warner Bros.
Blue Kentucky Girl, Warner Bros., 1980.
Roses in the Snow, Warner Bros., 1980.
Cimarron, Warner Bros.
Last Date, Warner Bros.
Evangeline, Warner Bros., 1981.
White Shoes, Warner Bros.
The Ballad of Sally Rose, Warner Bros., 1985.
Thirteen, Warner Bros., 1986.
Light From the Stable, Warner Bros.
Profile: The Best of Emmylou Harris, Warner Bros.
Profile II: The Best of Emmylou Harris, Warner Bros.
Angel Band, Warner Bros., 1987.
Bluebird, Reprise, 1989.

Other

(With Dolly Parton and Linda Ronstadt) *Trio*, Warner Bros., 1987.

Sources

Books

Malone, Bill C., *Country Music U.S.A.*, revised edition, University of Texas Press, 1985.
Nash, Alanna, *Behind Closed Doors: Talking with the Legends of Country Music*, Knopf, 1988.

Periodicals

Cosmopolitan, May 1989.
Esquire, September 1982.
High Fidelity, August 1980.
Newsweek, April 17, 1978.
People, November 15, 1982; January 14, 1991.
Stereo Review, May 1985.
Time, June 16, 1975.

—*Anne Janette Johnson*

Mickey Hart

Percussionist and author

Given name originally Michael; born c. 1944 in Brooklyn, N.Y.; son of Leonard (a businessman) and Leah (a bookkeeper) Hart; married; wife's name, Mary; children: Taro.

Career

Drummer with rock group The Grateful Dead, 1967—. Archivist/producer of music from around the world and author of two books on percussion; research associate at Smithsonian Institute's Folkways Records.

Sidelights

Exploring the spirit side of the drum has been the major venture of my adulthood, if not my whole life," confided percussionist Mickey Hart in his book *Drumming at the Edge of Magic.* "From the age of ten until forty, all I did was drum. Obsessively. Passionately. Painfully. For a long time the drum took everything I had; it had all my attention." Around 1980, however, he suddenly became obsessed with the history of his instrument. "To know the origin of the drum" is how he described his mission. "To know where it came from, how it was used. To know why, in particular, the tradition of drumming I inherited as a young American percussionist in the fifties had become devoid of the spirit or trance side of the drum, a side recognized by almost every culture on the planet."

Certainly it was a side recognized by the Grateful Dead, a rock band whose stadium concerts offer—at least for its fans—nothing short of a trip to "the other side." Since 1967 Hart has been one of the Dead's two drummers, a job that has given him wide latitude to explore the spiritual in music-making. Still, the Dead in no way represent American culture at large. There is no societal context, no tradition, for their "tripping out" approach to playing. And so the matter began to nag him. "How come we weren't given our musical legacy?" he asked *Mother Jones.* "I mean, how come we just wound up with music for entertainment purposes?"

The issue of America's lacking tradition led Hart to extraordinary discoveries in other cultures. For over ten years he immersed himself in the ethnomusicology of drumming throughout the ages. Two major projects have resulted. One is an ongoing compact disc series Hart titled "The World." Released on the Massachusetts label Rykodisc, the series features sounds ranging from Nigerian drumming to chanting by Tibetan monks to Jewish folk music to a 76-voice choir of Latvian women. All in all it is a set that highlights the richness of these distant traditions as well as the danger surrounding them, as much of the music comes from cultures threatened by technology. Hart's second project is a pair of books. *Drumming at the Edge of Magic,* published in 1990, presents the drum throughout history as a medium of transcendence, as well as his own life experience with that tradition. *Planet Drum,* following in 1991, picks up where the first left off, mostly through pictures and photographs.

"Suddenly, with two drums pounding away in the back, [the members of the Grateful Dead] had glimpsed the possibility of a groove so monstrous it would eat the audience."

Hart's bond with the drum seems to be partly hereditary. He was born around 1945 in Brooklyn to two rudimental (military) drummers, Lenny and Leah Hart, his father a world champion. Lenny Hart disappeared before his son's birth, leaving Mickey to be raised by his mother, a bookkeeper, and his grandparents. It wasn't until he was ten that he saw what his father looked like. As he recalled in *Drumming at the Edge,* he was watching a news clip about the 1939 World's Fair, "and for an instant I saw a tall, blonde man playing a drum. *World Champion Rudimental Drummer Leonard Hart.* Whether anyone talked about him or not, I was acutely aware that I was the son of a great drummer. That was my father's legacy to me, that and his drum pad and a pair of beautiful snakewood sticks he'd won in competition." As a young boy he would sit inside his closet—'my secret practice spot'—and play on the pad with the snakewood sticks. At night he slept with the sticks beneath his pillow, hoping "that I would absorb my father's drumming power."

Upon entering high school, Hart and his mother moved to Lawrence, Long Island. Hart joined the school band and then spent every possible moment practicing in the band room, suffering monthly lectures from the principal on his academic negligence. At home his practicing annoyed his truck-driver landlord. "My mother would hear him thundering up the stairs and bar the doorway with a broom," he recalled in *Drumming at the Edge,* "like a lioness protecting her cub." Twice a week his mother took him for private drum lessons. Jazz greats Gene Krupa and Buddy Rich and Latin legend Tito Puente became his heroes. "My most intense moments with

the drum were private ones," he wrote in *Drumming at the Edge.* "I would sit with my drums and slowly begin warming the traps up...I'd feel myself becoming lighter; I'd lose track of time. I realize now I was becoming entranced, but at the age of fifteen I had no idea what was going on."

Oddly enough, Hart learned more about the trance state in the Air Force, which he entered as a high school dropout. While stationed in Spain he met a young judo expert named Pogo, who trained him to become a lightweight champion. "Pogo taught me how to get into a zone of complete focus, a physical room that I could enter in my head," Hart recounted in *Drumming at the Edge.* After 18 months with Pogo, "I had the eye of the tiger...For me, the process involves consciously attempting to master your energy flows—the body flow, the mind flow, and the higher flow, the spirit side." The "eye of the tiger" technique of concentration would prove an invaluable gift to him over the course of his life, in playing music as well as other endeavors.

After leaving the Air Force in 1965, Hart got a letter from his father. Would he come to San Francisco and help run his new music store? Mickey worked there for two years. During slow business hours he taught himself to retool old drums. He also spent a few hours each day practicing the old rudimental solos his father used to play. "The only intimate times we shared were when we became master and student and Lenny showed me what he knew of the old techniques," he recalled in his book. "At night we'd stand at the glass counter and drum on our pads in perfect unison for hours, often attracting a crowd."

One night his world changed. He was introduced to Bill Kreutzmann, the drummer for the Grateful Dead, who turned him on to the psychedelic electricity of the California Bay Area rock scene. The two became "drum brothers," as Hart put it, hanging out and drumming together. On September 29, 1967, Hart attended a Dead rehearsal and was asked to join them for the second set. "I remember the feeling of being whipped into a jetstream," Hart wrote in *Drumming at the Edge,* "but I was so busy drumming that I didn't have time to think about what was happening until [the tune] ended some two hours later...I felt so calm, afterward, so *clean,* as if I'd taken a long steamy shower...At the end of the set we all embraced, wordlessly. [Guitarist Jerry] Garcia later told me that everyone had felt it when I finally synched up. Suddenly, with two drums pounding away in the back, they had glimpsed the possibility of a groove so monstrous it would eat the audience." His career with The Grateful Dead had begun.

Kreutzmann and Hart became known as the Rhythm Devils—'the best two-drummer team in the business," as Kreutzmann would later claim in *down beat*. In the early days, synchronizing their styles took hard work. "Sometimes we'd play for hours with our arms around each other, Billy handling one drumstick, me the other," Hart recalled in *Drumming at the Edge*. For the making of the album *Anthem of the Sun*, the Dead rented a castle in Hollywood Hills; into one room Hart and Kreutzmann moved their drum pads and stayed there for days, playing together for hours on end. "It was as if Kreutzmann and I had learned how to synchronize our hearts," he wrote in his book, "how to bond that basic physiological beat, so that, even though our styles of drumming were very different, there was now a rhythm linking us when we played."

In 1968 Hart moved to a sprawling communal ranch in Novato, California, about 30 miles north of San Francisco. On the ranch was an old cow barn commonly known as the Barn, most of which Hart turned into a private sanctuary. It was there that he would go to play or simply contemplate the drums in his collection, and just as often to record sounds in music and nature that intrigued him. "If the drum was my public instrument, the studio at the Barn became my private one," he wrote in *Drumming at the Edge*. "Dan Healy, the Grateful Dead's sound engineer, and I built it so it was always on; all I had to do was punch one button and I was ready to record." Late at night he often could be found in his favorite chair beside the Barn's old stove, playing the North African *tar* (a type of drum).

Around this time bandmate Phil Lesh handed Hart a recording by Alla Rakha, the master tabla player from India who played with the famous sitarist Ravi Shankar. Hart was floored. Alla Rakha, he wrote in *Drumming at the Edge*, was "a Mozart of my instrument, an Einstein of rhythm, and yet world music was arranged into such a rigid caste system that I had never heard of this man." A few weeks later, while in New York on tour with the Dead, Hart learned that Rakha was on tour there as well. Hart went to hear him and introduced himself afterward; Rakha invited him back to his hotel room, where he gave Hart an impromptu drumming lesson. "Alla Rakha destroyed my beliefs about rhythm," Hart wrote in *Drumming at the Edge*. 'Rhythm is just time, and time can be carved up any way you want. We played eleven over nine and twelve over eight and fifteen over thirteen . . . . He held my hand as I beat so I could feel how time was utterly elastic . . . I returned from that hotel room feeling as if I'd been shown the Golden Tablets."

Meanwhile, Hart's father was working as the Grateful Dead's business manager. In 1970 the band discovered he had been skimming off their profits, for which he want to jail. His son was affected profoundly. "I didn't want to play, didn't want to go out on the road," he confided in *Drumming at the Edge*. "Confused, unbalanced, I wanted to flee and hide, bury my head and cry. I stopped touring with the Grateful Dead in 1971 and went to ground at the Barn." During a three-year leave of absence Hart immersed himself in the rhythms of nature and began composing music from the sounds around him. One day he was visited by Joe Smith, president of Warner Bros. Records, who had been trying to arrange a record deal with him. "I talked about rhythm and noise," Hart recalled, "and about a theory I had concerning the mixing of environmental sounds—water, crickets—with a steady rock backbeat. Environmental rock." Smith gave him a contract for three records plus the money to build a good studio—for Hart, a dream come true.

> "The folk music of a people is a storehouse of their way of life, full of myths and experiences, joys, hopes and dreams."

At the same time Hart bought some recording equipment and, with the Dead's sound engineer, began taping unusual music in the Bay Area. "We recorded all the early Indian classicists who arrived in Alla Rakha's and Ravi Shankar's wake—masters of the sarod, the sitar, the tabla," he wrote in *Drumming at the Edge*. "I loved rolling tape. At night I'd play back my tapes and sit in the darkened Barn, sipping cognac. It was one of my greatest pleasures." Thus began a hobby of making field recordings that would grow more musically diverse and technologically sophisticated over the next two decades.

Toward the end of 1974, still holed up at the Barn, Hart was struck by rumors that the Grateful Dead were going to break up. On the night of what was suuposedly to be their farewell concert, Hart packed his drums and drove to San Francisco, joining them for their second set at Winterland. His old bandmates were happy to see him. "I was back on the bus," Hart wrote in his book, "for however long there was going to be a bus." (As it turns out, the "bus" is still going.)

As the 1970s drew to a close, Hart suddenly felt ignorant about the drums he had played for so many years. He began to read whatever ethnomusicology books on drumming he could find. On the walls of the Barn he started building a timeline that would present the drum's story—not just its evolution through time but the myths and practices that surrounded it in various cultures. He became obsessed. "People would ask me what I was up to," he reminisced in *Drumming at the Edge*, "and I'd hear myself saying things like, 'Did you know that the sacrificial drums of the Ashanti of Dhana were covered with a membrane of human skin and decorated with human skulls?'"

In 1987 he met his new idol, Joseph Campbell, the great comparative mythologist, and probed him for information on the relationship of drumming to shamans and animal powers. Later he hooked up with Betsy Cohen, a Ph.D. from Stanford University, who began feeding his handwritten timeline into the mainframe computer at "Karma," the Stanford Center for Computer Research in Music and Acoustics. "At Karma I used to sit at a terminal and make endless lists: *Supernatural Powers of drums/Consecration of drum/...Instruments associated with cosmologies/Use of drum as catalyst in metamorphosis.*" He assembled a research team at Karma, and the timeline—or "Anaconda," as he called it—took on a life of its own. "The Anaconda became a pulsing tree of data that I loved to climb around in, scanning for new growth," he wrote. Its final incarnation, as mentioned earlier, would take the form of two books.

One to juggle several projects, Hart continued all the while to make field recordings of indigenous musics. In 1989 he struck a deal with Rykodisc to remaster some of his private tapes for compact disc release as well as produce new recordings. "The World" is a series that has been lauded for the musical information gap it's helping to bridge. No longer are rare ethnic musics relegated to obscure, tinny field recordings. "There's a big world out there," Hart told *Rolling Stone*, "and wherever there's music going down, I've tried to roll my tapes. Much of this is endangered music, and I'm trying to tick them off one by one. Sometimes it's preservation, sometimes it's propelling the music into the next century. But part of it is to propagate the music and allow it to flower in its indigenous form."

Most if not all of "The World" series releases are embedded with personal meaning for Hart. *Hamza El Din: Eclipse*, a mesmerizing album of Sudanese folk music, has its origin in Hart's friendship with fellow musician Hamza El Din. "He taught me how to play the tar, a large Egyptian tambourine-like drum, and he took me to his village in the Sudan," Hart told the *Daily Californian.* "Since I could play the music, it was easy to interact with the people. Most of the music that interests me has a social or religious function, so you have to get to know people. You imbibe in whatever the local delicacy is, to get into the altered state that they want to achieve before they play. Sometimes it's a long conversation, sometimes it's hours of serious smoking or drinking before they'll even pick up an instrument. It's not cabaret music. When they got down it was a pretty raucous scene. The rhythms are relentless, like the desert, or the Nile. They go on and on."

Besides producing, Hart has assumed the role of crusader with this project. In 1988 he brought 21 Tibetan monks to the United States for a tour to foster awareness of their people's struggles. He also recorded them at George Lucas's Skywalker Ranch Soundstage in northern California, the results of which can be heard on the eerily beautiful *Freedom Chants From the Roof of the World: The Gyuto Monks.* An upcoming "World" release will feature music from the rain forests, where deforestation is destroying the culture as well as the trees—and very possibly the earth's climate as we know it. "It's not only a musical thing," Mickey told the *Arizona Republic.* "I'm concerned with the issues of the planet. This is how I scream. It's a consciousness-raising thing. I'm not into politics, I'm into social issues." Also included in "The World" series is *Music to Be Born By*, a meditative recording designed to help expectant mothers through the birthing process. Hart originally created it for his wife Mary, recording their son Taro's heartbeat within the womb and then overdubbing it with drums, bass harmonics, and wooden flute.

Toward the end of the 1980s, Hart became concerned about the impending demise of Folkways Records, a label that over the years had amassed over 2,000 titles in folk, blues, jazz, and ethnic music. To protect the Folkways catalog, Hart convinced the Smithsonian Institute in Washington D.C. to buy it. They did, and then appointed Hart, who is now a research associate there, to supervise the transfer of each recording to compact disc to preserve it for future generations. "Guys like ... [Folkways founder] Moe Asch were my heroes, going around and recording all this incredible music," he told the *Daily Californian,* "so when I got a chance to go through [the collection], it was like a dream. Moe never threw anything out, and I found tapes from Mongolia, the Baltics, everywhere ... The folk music of a people is a storehouse of their way of life, full of myths and experiences, joys, hopes and dreams. These sounds are very uplifting to the soul, and once they're gone they'll never return.''

Writings

(With Jay Stevens) *Drumming at the Edge of Magic: A Journey into the Spirit of Percussion*, HarperCollins, 1990.

Planet Drum, 1991.

Selected discography

As producer, solo artist—"The World" series

The Diga Rhythm Band, *Diga* (featuring Mickey Hart, Zakir Hussain, and Jerry Garcia).

Hamza El Din, *Eclipse*.

Dzintars, *Songs of Amber*.

The Golden Gate Gypsy Orchestra, *The Traveling Jewish Wedding*.

The Gyuto Monks, *Freedom Chants from the Roof of the World* (featuring Hart, Philip Glass, and Kitaro).

Hariprasad, Zakir Hussain, *Venu*.

Mickey Hart, *At the Edge* (companion album to the series).

Mickey Hart, Taro Hart, *Music to Be Born By*.

Mickey Hart, Airto Moreira, Flora Purim, *Dafos*.

Assorted artists, *The Music of Upper and Lower Egypt*.

Ustad Sultan Khan, *Sarangi: The Music of India*.

Olatunji, *Drums of Passion: The Invocation*.

Olatunji, *Drums of Passion: The Beat*.

The Rhythm Devils, *The Apocalypse Now Sessions* (featuring Hart, Bill Kreutzmann, Michael Hinton, and Airto Moreira).

Sources

Arizona Republic, March 4, 1989.

BAM, June 16, 1989.

Daily Californian, March 24, 1989.

Denver's News & Arts Weekly, December 14-20, 1988.

down beat, November 1987.

Elle, April 1989.

Mix, March 1989.

Mother Jones, January 1990.

New York Times, March 21, 1990.

People, August 14, 1989.

Rolling Stone, March 23, 1989.

Sound Choice, autumn 1989.

—*Kyle Kevorkian*

Katharine Hepburn

Actress

Full name, Katharine Houghton Hepburn; born November 9, 1909, in Hartford, Conn.; daughter of Thomas N. (a surgeon) and Katharine (a feminist; maiden name, Houghton) Hepburn; married Ludlow Ogden Smith, 1928 (divorced, 1934). *Education:* Bryn Mawr College, B.A., 1928.

Career

Actress on stage and in films, 1928—. Principal film appearances include *Christopher Strong,* 1933, *Morning Glory,* 1933, *Little Women,* 1934, *Spitfire,* 1934, *The Little Minister,* 1934, *Alice Adams,* 1935, *Mary of Scotland,* 1936, *Stage Door,* 1937, *Bringing Up Baby,* 1938, *Holiday,* 1938, *The Philadelphia Story,* 1940, *Woman of the Year,* 1942, *Keeper of the Flame,* 1942, *Without Love,* 1945, *The Sea of Grass,* 1947, *State of the Union,* 1948, *Adam's Rib,* 1949, *The African Queen,* 1951, *Pat and Mike,* 1952, *The Rainmaker,* 1956, *The Iron Petticoat,* 1956, *Desk Set,* 1957, *Suddenly Last Summer,* 1959, *Long Day's Journey into Night,* 1962, *Guess Who's Coming to Dinner,* 1968, *The Lion in Winter,* 1968, *The Madwoman of Chaillot,* 1969, *A Delicate Balance,* 1975, *Rooster Cogburn,* 1975, *On Golden Pond,* 1981, and *Grace Quigley,* 1984.

Principal stage appearances include *Holiday,* 1928, *The Warrior's Husband,* 1932, *The Lake,* 1933, *The Philadelphia Story,* 1939, *Without Love,* 1942, *As You Like It,* 1950, *The Millionairess,* 1952, *The Merchant of Venice,* 1957, *Antony and Cleopatra,* 1960, *Coco,* 1969, *A Matter of Gravity,* 1976, and *The West Side Waltz,* 1980.

Principal television appearances include *The Glass Menagerie,* 1973, *Love Among the Ruins,* 1975, *The Corn Is Green,* 1979, and *Mrs. Delafield Wants To Marry,* 1987.

Awards: *Hollywood Reporter* Gold Medal, 1933, and Academy Award for best actress, 1934, both for *Morning Glory;* Venice Film Festival award for best actress, 1934, for *Little Women;* Academy Award nomination, 1936, for *Alice Adams;* New York Film Critics Award for best actress, 1940, and Academy Award nomination, 1941, both for *The Philadelphia Story;* Academy Award nomination, 1943, for *Woman of the Year;* Academy Award nomination, 1952, for *The African Queen;* Academy Award nomination, 1956, for *Summertime;* Academy Award nomination, 1957, for *The Rainmaker;* Academy Award nomination, 1960, for *Suddenly Last Summer;* Cannes Film Festival award, 1962, and Academy Award nomination, 1963, for *Long Day's Journey into Night;* Academy Award for best actress, and British Academy Award for best actress, both 1968, both for *Guess Who's Coming to Dinner;* Academy Award for best actress, and British Academy Award for best actress, both 1969, both for *The Lion in Winter;* Antoinette Perry (Tony) Award nomination, 1970, for *Coco;* Academy Award for best actress, 1982, for *On Golden Pond.*

Sidelights

Katharine Hepburn is one of the nation's most admired and beloved screen actresses, a Hollywood "legend" who has performed to high acclaim for more than sixty years. The first woman ever to win four Academy Awards for best actress, Hepburn has made a fortune portraying characters who are at once strong-willed and blithely feminine. Her career on stage and screen has stretched over six decades, from her Broadway debut in 1928 to her last light television comedy, *Mrs. Delafield Wants To Marry*, in 1987. Few other actresses have been able to reap such admiration from earliest youth to advanced old age—and fewer still have earned the public's affection without sacrificing personal integrity.

In *Newsweek* Hubert Saal wrote: "Katharine Hepburn has always played herself. It is her virtues, her beliefs, which are projected on the screen—through the indomitable missionary in *The African Queen* or in the great expectations of Jo in *Little Women*. She is versatile as a woman rather than adaptable as an actress. Her roles are reflections of what she is rather than what she can pretend to be." Saal summed up the typical Hepburn heroine: "The key to almost all her interpretations is a gallant mixture of individuality and femininity, the ambivalence of the tomboy, the straight-from-the-shoulder gruffness expressing the soft, womanly sentiment, the female meeting the male on his own ground, the Atalanta whose sexuality is in her challenge." It is small wonder that the nation's film critics labeled Hepburn Hollywood's "iron butterfly'—the actress whose "glacial purr" gives way to "sudden dazzling flashes of girlishness."

Hepburn's upbringing in Hartford, Connecticut was genteel but decidedly eccentric. She was born in 1909 to parents who were passionately involved in the women's suffrage movement. Hepburn's father was a wealthy urologist who risked his career and social standing to bring the facts about venereal disease to a wider public. Her mother was a feminist who instilled self-discipline by requiring her children to take cold showers every morning. Remembering her childhood in the *Ladies' Home Journal*, Hepburn said: "My first public appearance was carrying a flag in one of those [suffrage] parades, and my first real, thrilling job was filling balloons with gas, then tying a string around them and making people buy them."

The oldest of five children, Hepburn grew up a tomboy who loved practical jokes. She nevertheless absorbed a certain air of gentility from her accomplished parents and their friends, a "to the manor born" hauteur that she would mine in numerous incarnations for her film work. She was educated by private tutors until her teen years and then attended the prestigious Hartford School for Girls and Bryn Mawr College. Hepburn at first wanted to study medicine, but she changed her mind after becoming involved with dramatics at Bryn Mawr. After receiving her bachelor's degree in 1928, she defied her parents and went to work with a Baltimore-based stock company. She made her professional debut there in 1928 as a lady-in-waiting in *The Czarina*.

Hepburn did not languish in Baltimore for long. By November of 1928 she had landed a part in a Broadway show, *These Days*, in which she appeared as a wealthy schoolgirl. A series of similar roles followed, each with more lines than the last, culminating in a starring role in *The Warrior's Husband* in 1932. By that time Hepburn had earned a reputation as a difficult artist who clashed with directors and crews. Her brief marriage to socialite Ludlow Ogden Smith ended when it became apparent that she valued her career more than the relationship. Several times she was fired from shows—including *The Warrior's Husband*—for arguing on the set. In that film's case however, she was rehired, and she carried the show. Her performance in that play earned her a contract with RKO Studios in Hollywood, and she set out for the West Coast determined to become a star.

In their book *The MGM Stock Company: The Golden Era*, James Robert Parish and Ronald L. Bowers noted that Hepburn hardly took Tinseltown by storm. "On July 4, 1932," they wrote, "a skinny, freckled, snooty typhoon Kate hit Hollywood. For eight years it kept hitting her back and almost knocked her out of the business." Romano V. Tozzi, in a 1957 *Films in Review* profile, also described the actress's early years in films: "Hepburn arrived in Hollywood determined to put the movie industry in its place. She immediately set out to break all the rules and was as unpleasant and uncooperative as possible. She fought senselessly with practically everyone, from top producer to lowest technician. She was insulting and abusive to the press and gave out ridiculous, inane interviews in which she deliberately distorted the facts of her personal life. She allowed herself to be photographed without makeup in all her freckles, and, even worse, dressed hideously in mannish garb—sloppy slacks, sweaters, and men's trousers and suits."

Her battles with the studio and the press notwithstanding, Hepburn immediately received hefty roles, such as the stage-struck tomboy in *Morning Glory*—for which she won her first Academy Award—as well as the title role in *Alice Adams* and the coveted part of Jo in *Little Women.* If her clothing and attitude seemed a bit unconventional, there were legions of Depression-era fans who appreciated it and even applauded her independence. In retrospect, Hepburn told the *World-Telegram and Sun* that she was never quite as sure of herself as she might have seemed. "Everyone thought I was bold and fearless and even arrogant," she said, "but inside I was always quaking." By 1937 Hepburn's relationship with RKO had deteriorated to the point that she bought out her contract and moved on, first to Columbia for a film version of the play *Holiday,* and then to Metro-Goldwyn-Mayer, where she turned in some of the finest work of her career.

> *"I chose to live as a man, and I'm very, very happy. I would not change any of the things I have done."*

Hepburn's association with MGM had its auspicious debut with the film *The Philadelphia Story.* The movie was based on a play that Hepburn had performed to great ovation in New York, and the title role was literally written for her. In *The Philadelphia Story* Hepburn appears as Tracy Lord, a socialite whose headstrong ways are challenged by her ex-husband (played by Cary Grant) and an equally headstrong newspaper reporter (played by Jimmy Stewart). Tozzi claimed that in *The Philadelphia Story* Hepburn "came of age as an actress. [The film] was practically a flawless vehicle for her. Every line, every gesture, and every scene had been tailored to her particular talents." That success was closely followed in 1942 by *Woman of the Year,* the first of eight films that paired Hepburn with Spencer Tracy, another MGM stock player.

Hollywood's golden years yielded a number of charismatic screen couples, but none endured longer than Spencer Tracy and Katharine Hepburn. Together they made such classic movies as *Keeper of the Flame, State of the Union, Adam's Rib, Pat and Mike,* and *Desk Set,* and their relationship offscreen was a matter of constant speculation. In a *Look* magazine profile, Hepburn herself summed up the chemistry that made her work with Tracy so memorable. In their movies, she said, "the woman is pretty sharp and she's needling the man, sort of slightly, like a mosquito. The man is always slow comin' along, and

she needles, and then he slowly puts out his big paw and slaps the lady down. He's the ultimate boss of the situation, but . . . it isn't an easy kingdom for him to maintain." As regards their intimate relations, Hepburn would only say: "I have had twenty years of perfect companionship with a man among men. He is a rock and a protection. I've never regretted it."

The films with Tracy helped Hepburn to make the delicate transition to mature roles, a transition she made easily on stage by appearing in Shakespearean dramas. At any rate, she found that mid-life offered her more challenging projects on both stage and screen, and she met those challenges with grace and wit. One of her enduring triumphs is *The African Queen,* in which she appears as Rose Sayer, a proper missionary woman who must escape war-torn Africa with a hard-drinking river boatman. Hepburn and co-star Humphrey Bogart endured hostile climatic conditions and the eccentricities of director John Huston to complete a film that has become an American classic.

In many respects, the 1960s offered Hepburn her most rewarding roles. Early in the decade she earned a best actress award from the Cannes Film Festival for her portrayal of Mary Tyrone, the heroine-addicted mother in Eugene O'Neill's *Long Day's Journey into Night.* She then retired briefly in order to care for the ailing Spencer Tracy. The duo made their final film together in 1967, *Guess Who's Coming to Dinner,* a comedy about a conventional family in which the daughter wishes to marry a black man. Tracy died shortly after the film was shot. After numerous nominations, Hepburn finally won her second Academy Award for her performance in that movie. Grief-stricken after the loss of her companion, she threw herself into work and turned in masterful performances in two serious films, *The Lion in Winter* and *The Mad Woman of Chaillot.* In *The Lion in Winter,* for which she won her third Academy Award, Hepburn played the hot-tempered Eleanor of Aquitaine, an imprisoned queen who manipulates her temperamental sons. *Time* magazine contributor Richard Corliss noted that roles in such movies as *Long Day's Journey* and *The Lion in Winter* gave the actress "an opportunity to soar, and she played each lovely chance to the hilt . . . . Hepburn fashioned a career as distinctive as any in screen acting."

Nor was Hepburn's career finished as she reached retirement age. In the 1970s and 1980s she gave a number of fine performances in films and plays such as *A Delicate Balance, Grace Quigley,* and *On Golden Pond.* The latter movie earned her another Academy Award, this time for her performance as the devoted wife and mother in a troubled family. Hepburn's most recent—and probably final—appearance was in a television movie titled *Mrs. Delafield Wants To Marry*, a light comedy about a love affair between two senior citizens.

Despite health problems and the inevitable changes brought about by age, Hepburn still makes public appearances and speaks out on a number of pertinent issues. The decades she has spent in the spotlight have not caused her to warm to the press, however—she still has little to say about her private life or her Hollywood acquaintances past and present. The actress told the *Ladies' Home Journal* that her work has been her life, and she has never regretted not having a husband or children. "I chose to live as a man, and I'm very, very happy," she said. "I would not change any of the things I have done."

Hepburn may have chosen to "live as a man," but her film work has given her fabulous opportunities to act like a woman. She has portrayed medieval queens, heiresses, and socialites with grace, has dragged boats through swamps and wrestled with cantankerous leopards, and has played lawyers, librarians, aspiring starlets, and devoted homemakers, all with warmth and dignity. As Richard Corliss concluded: "In Hepburn's case art and life have blended to create an actress and woman of spectacular integrity....Two dimensions couldn't hold her. The angular form, the tilted chin and cutting voice made her a secular Joan of Arc."

Writings

The Making of "The African Queen," or How I Went to Africa with Bogart, Bacall and Huston and Almost Lost My Mind, Knopf, 1987.

Sources

Books

Parish, James Robert and Ronald L. Bowers, *The MGM Stock Company: The Golden Era*, Arlington House, 1973.

Periodicals

Films in Review, December 1957.
Ladies' Home Journal, August 1975.
Life, January 22, 1940; January 5, 1968.
Look, July 11, 1967.
Newsweek, November 10, 1969.
New York, August 11, 1969.
New York Times, October 10, 1962; June 18, 1967; April 27, 1969.
Time, November 16, 1981.
Washington Post, February 10, 1968; September 1, 1969.
World-Telegram and Sun, May 16, 1957; September 27, 1962.

—*Anne Janette Johnson*

Lynn Hill

Professional rock climber

Born c. 1961 and grew up as one of seven children in Los Angeles, Calif.; married to Russ Raffa (an outdoor clothing sales representative). *Education:* College at New Paltz, New York, B.S. in biology, c. 1983.

Addresses: *Home*—New Paltz, NY.

Career

Began rock climbing at age 14; has traveled throughout the United States and Europe as a rock climber, participating in numerous competitions; has won more than a dozen contests in the women's division since 1986.

Sidelights

In the not-too-distant past, athletic contests of strength, skill, and endurance were limited strictly to male participants. Aside from the usual society-wide sexism of the time, which sought to keep women in the home and excluded them from sports entirely, there was also the notion, in a society which values absolute achievement above nearly everything else, it was silly for women to compete in the same arenas as men. Women could not possibly win, the argument went, and so they should concentrate on things they were good at. As the precepts of feminism began to gain more acceptance, however, these rigid controls were relaxed some, to the point where women were increasingly encouraged to participate in a variety of sports—though separately, of course, from men. Women could try as much as they liked, and enjoy it, the new argument went, but still they could not match the physical accomplishments of men. They were not big or strong enough, nor could they endure as much physical pain, and so their accomplishments were devalued simply because they were accomplished by a woman.

To this day, there remains an unspoken double standard toward the achievements of women in sports. Women are treated as equal, but separate, in everything from professional tennis to international Olympic competition. When a marathon is run, there is always a winner, presumably a man, and a *women's winner*. And although this situation is one based on "realistic" generalizations regarding the physical capabilities of the sexes, there are some women who are redefining just what is "realistic." Tennis legend Billie Jean King, after all, defeated Bobby Riggs, and Lynn Hill has literally scaled mountains as proof of what women athletes are capable of.

Hill is not only the world's foremost *women's* rock climber, she is simply one of the top five rock climbers in the world. "Hill's achievements have thrown into question old assumptions about the inequality of men's and women's abilities in rock climbing," wrote Trip Gabriel in the *New York Times*. "In a sport requiring extremely well-developed muscles, very low body fat and an appetite for boldness—all supposedly 'masculine' characteristics—how is it possible for a woman to achieve what men can?" This is a question that Hill has answered, not through political grandstanding but through sheer achievement. "Lynn is better than 95 percent of the men, and she'll continue to dominate the women for at least the next two or three years," rock climbing expert Michael Kennedy predicted in *Philip Morris* magazine. "She has a unique combination of competitiveness, experience, and natural talent. She's incredibly strong and her timing is impeccable."

But how does one come to be recognized as one of the world's top rock climbers? Surprisingly, competitive rock climbing is becoming increasingly popular in both the United States and Europe, and a world-wide governing body—the French-based Union Internationale des Associations d'Alpinisme—administers contests, ranks competitors, and further promotes the sport. Although rock climbing is still widely practiced in the traditional way, on lonely, wind-swept cliffs in natural settings, many competitions are held indoors, on elaborate synthetic walls pitted with artificial cracks, ledges, and crevices. Often, especially in Europe, climbers perform before thousands of screaming fans. When Jim McCarthy, then-president of the American Alpine Club, saw his first indoor competition in 1988, he was surprised by his own reaction to the new sport. "I expected to enjoy it," he told the *New York Times*. "I didn't know I'd be *riveted*."

Hill has become a fan-favorite at such competitions, where she has dominated the women's category over the years and made greater strides toward defeating her top male rivals. "[Climbing indoors is] such a different feeling than climbing on rock," Hill told the *New York Times*. "You're in front of all these people. They bring you on stage and start a little buzzer: *beep*. 'O.K., your warm-up is finished.' The time is now, you don't have a choice. You're there to *perform*."

At a World Cup competition in Lyon, France, in 1989, Hill delivered a performance that brought down the house. Long an advocate that women be allowed to compete on the same courses set up for the men, Hill got her wish in the event's final round, when she did indeed scale the same course as her top male competitors. Courses on the synthetic cliff-faces can be manipulated to increase the difficulty of a climb, and the course is made more difficult until only one climber can finish the route. On that particular day, only two men were able to finish the course. The second-place woman fell after the first move up from the stage. Then Hill, in a dramatic climb, made it to the very last move of the route before falling (restrained by a safety rope, of course). Finally, Hill was able to illustrate, for thousands of

people to see, that she was indeed among the top rock climbers in the world.

It is a standing toward which Hill, in a manner of speaking, has been climbing since her introduction to the sport as a teen. Even as a child growing up in a large family in suburban Los Angeles, Hill told *Philip Morris*'s Guy Garcia, she was a natural tomboy who enjoyed running, jumping, and climbing to the top of anything nearby. "I don't know why, but I was always climbing trees, telephone poles, even street-lights," Hill said. When her older sister began inviting her on trips to climbing areas in California's Joshua Tree National Monument and Yosemite National Park, Hill quickly fell in love with the sport. Soon, she was taking part in difficult three- and four-day climbs up faces like the legendary 3,600-foot El Capitan peak.

> *"I don't know why, but I was always climbing trees, telephone poles, even street-lights."*

Though she was also a top high school gymnast in her state, Hill soon found herself abandoning the more regimented sports and provincial suburban lifestyle, preferring instead the unexpected and varied challenges of her rock climbing excursions. "In California, everything is pavement, shopping malls, neighborhoods," Hill said in the *New York Times*. "Everything is very controlled and boring. This was an opportunity to be out in the desert by ourselves."

While Hill's pure love of climbing played a large part in her determination to master climbs of greater and greater difficulty, her compact, powerful build and intense training habits have certainly made her physically up to each new challenge. "I think it's part genetic," Hill said in the *New York Times* of her ideal climber's physique. "In sixth grade I did 14 pullups. That's not normal for a little girl. It also has to do with your sense of timing, your flexibility and the fluidity of your movements." As she began to get more serious about her sport and more competitions cropped up, Hill settled into a strict training regimen. Aside from plenty of practice climbs, she also runs and lifts free weights. At 5'2" and weighing about 100 pounds, Hill once nearly set a new world record for her body weight by bench-pressing 150 pounds.

And while Hill trains to be more competitive at her sport, she does not find it to be inconsistent with being a woman. Just as she does not accept different standards for judging men and women rock climbers, Hill also disputes society's old notions of femininity in general. "Society's contrived image of what a woman should and should not be is something I've never agreed with," she told Gabriel. "Developing muscles is something people look down upon . . . You look at the Miss America Pageant and all of them have pencil arms. There's just no definition. The classic American beauty has no muscle tone. What does she do all the time?"

"I'm always taking calculated risks. I decide whether it's reasonable or not and if it is, I don't think about it anymore."

Hill first realized her ultimate potential as a climber when, at the age of 19, she scaled a wall named Ophir Broke in Telluride, Colorado. Based on the somewhat arcane scale for rating the difficulty of each route—the easiest start at 5.0, then range upward to 5.9, and then to 5.10a, b, c, d, etc., based on rock angle and the number and size of hand and footholds—the Ophir Broke face was rated a 5.12d, and Hill was the first woman in the world to climb a route of that difficulty. She began to devote herself full time to climbing, while making ends meet in whatever way she could. In 1980 she even appeared on the televised junk sports program *Survival of the Fittest*, which ran competitors through various obstacle courses. Hill won the show's grand prize four straight years, and earned $30,000 in the process.

In 1983 Hill moved permanently to New Paltz, New York, to attend the College at New Paltz, where she eventually earned a degree in biology. Not coincidentally, perhaps, the college is located just a few minutes' drive from the Shawangunk cliffs, probably the best rock climbing region east of the Rocky Mountains. While training at the "Gunks," as they're called, Hill met Russ Raffa, a sales representative for the Patagonia outdoor clothing firm who became her climbing partner and, later, her husband.

With more economic security and Raffa's support ("He saw my other career choices as things anyone could do. Now I'm doing something I love," Hill told

Philip Morris), Hill has been free to lead the itinerant lifestyle necessary to stay competitive internationally. She travels often to Europe, where contests are held nearly every week and she can earn up to $5,000 per event. But as she gets older Hill foresees a time when climbing will not and should not be so all-consuming. She teaches the sport, and plans to write a book on outdoor physical fitness. And with her background in biology, Hill plans on a career in some health-related field. "I want to be productive in society," she told *Ms.* magazine. "Climbing is a self-serving thing, something I do for myself."

If Hill needed further proof that rock climbing is a career that is without a great deal of security, she found it the hard way in May of 1989. After finishing a routine climb on a limestone cliff in Buoux, France, Hill mistakenly neglected to tie a knot in her safety rope. Normally, after reaching the top of a climb, she would use the rope to rappell back down, but in this instance the rope slipped through its harness and Hill fell 85 feet to the ground. Miraculously, she emerged from the fall with just a dislocated elbow and a broken foot, and her desire to compete again was never really in question. She began rehabilitation, and within four months she won the women's division of a contest in Arco, Italy. "It took a lot out of me to get better again, physically and psychologically," Hill said in the *New York Times*. "We're all vulnerable. We could die any minute. People like to control all the things they can, but there's risk in everything. The accident made me look at that vulnerability that we all face, and I pulled myself together to try to come back."

Hill's comeback could not have been more complete. Indeed, by giving her a first-hand idea of the possible dangers of the sport, the accident almost seemed to double her concentration, and by the end of the same year Hill had more major wins than any other female climber. Then, in 1990 in Cimai, France, she again made rock climbing history by becoming the first woman to complete a grade 5.14 climb. Clearly, the near-fatal fall in France had not affected her competitive edge. In confronting such incredibly difficult challenges, Hill told Gabriel, she combats danger with experience and clear thinking. "I'm very aware of danger and potential danger," Hill said. "I'm always taking calculated risks. I decide whether it's reasonable or not and if it is, I don't think about it anymore. When you start to panic, you have to do what I call a mental shift. You don't think about the consequences of a fall, you think only of what you need to do to get through the moves."

The natural high that comes with each crisis averted is, thanks to superstar climbers like Hill, becoming less of a secret to American sporting men and women. The popularity of rock climbing in the United States, though not on the same level as in Europe, is definitely on the rise, with large synthetic walls being erected in urban recreation centers around the country. And although Hill competes for a living, she has not lost touch with the pure joy she discovered while climbing in Yosemite as a girl. "Climbing is a constant process of personal discovery," Hill told *Philip Morris*. "When things are going well, it can be an almost mystical experience, because you know that normally it would be hard to do what you're doing. But sometimes everything flows together perfectly. The rock is a tool for learning and understanding. When you get to the top, you've conquered something inside as well."

Sources

Ms., May 1987.
New York Times, December 31, 1989.
Philip Morris, September 1990.

—*David Collins*

Evander Holyfield

AP/Wide World Photos

Professional boxer

Born October, 1962, in Atlanta, Ga.; mother's name, Annie; wife's name, Paulette (divorce pending); children: four. *Education:* High school graduate. *Religion:* Christian.

Career

Amateur boxer c. 1972-84; professional boxer, 1984—. Fought as cruiserweight (190-pound division), 1984-88; won World Boxing Council, World Boxing Association, and International Boxing Federation championships; became undisputed cruiserweight champion, April, 1988; moved to heavyweight division, 1988; became undisputed heavyweight champion October 25, 1990, with third-round knockout of James "Buster" Douglas.

Awards: 1984 Olympic Games bronze medal.

Sidelights

Evander Holyfield has worked long and hard to earn his title of undisputed heavyweight boxing champion of the world. Superbly conditioned and brimming with determination, Holyfield has become boxing's most lethal practitioner simply by adhering to a punishing schedule and keeping his mind set on his goals. He rose steadily through the heavyweight ranks while a sea of 'doubting Thomases" claimed he could never beat the heavier—and therefore supposedly stronger—top contenders in his division. Now that he himself is poised at the top, Holyfield faces a challenge from another formidable fighter, Mike

Tyson. The champion told the *Philadelphia Inquirer* that he will enter that fight—and every title match—with the idea that he is the "little guy," the underdog, the one who has to fight harder because he is smaller. "All my life, I've been fighting people who didn't think I could make it," Holyfield told the *Inquirer.* "I've been waiting for this opportunity for a long time."

Holyfield, the youngest of eight children, was born and raised in Atlanta, Georgia. He credits his mother, Annie, with much of his success—she instilled a strong work ethic in him and provided him with Christian values. Holyfield's Christian faith kept him out of trouble as a youth and has sustained him throughout his career. He has favorite churches in his hometown as well as in Houston, where he trains.

At the tender age of eight Holyfield began to experiment with boxing techniques at the Warren Boys Club in Atlanta. "To tell you the truth, the only reason I got interested in boxing was the speed bag," he told the *Boston Globe.* "The speed bag made a lot of noise and I wanted to learn how to hit it. They had to stand me up on a chair at the Boys Club to reach it. It took about two months to get it down." Soon the youngster was participating in peewee boxing tournaments in Atlanta. "I always went out in the ring feeling I was the best," he said. "The only reason you fight is to prove it. As a kid, I loved to say, 'I'm a boxer.' But to tell you the truth, when the fights started I'd think, 'How'd I get myself into this?'"

Football was Holyfield's first love. He excelled as a linebacker on the Warren Boys Club team and hoped to have a stellar career for Fulton High School as well. He made the team as a sophomore, but at 5'4" and 115 pounds was hardly an imposing athlete. All season he warmed the bench, distraught because he was overlooked time after time. *Boston Globe* reporter Ron Borges wrote: "So little Evander Holyfield . . . sat on the bench. Game after humiliating game. He wanted to quit. Once he even suggested it to his mother, Annie, who had raised eight Holyfields with no intention of any of them quitting when troubled waters rose. She told him four simple words that ended their conversation: 'You finish it out.'"

Dutifully Holyfield rode out the season; when he was finally called into play during a regional championship game, he absolutely excelled at cornerback. The team lost the game, but the coaches had only praise for young Holyfield. Unfortunately for them, it was too little too late. Holyfield did not return to football, ever. "It kind of hurt my feelings when the coach said I was too small," he told the *Boston Globe*. "So I just gave up on football and told myself, 'Evander, stick to boxing. Football was important, but once I saw I wouldn't get a fair chance, I went back to what I did best."

Any doubts Holyfield might have had about boxing were laid to rest when the 1980 Olympic Trials were held in Atlanta. Borges noted that while watching those matches the young hopeful "saw . . . that he could fight with all the others standing between him and a gold medal." After graduating from high school Holyfield worked for minimum wage fueling planes at the Dekalb-Peachtree Airport. He trained in his off-hours, often rising at four in the morning to jog before catching a six o'clock bus to work. Then as now, he was almost obsessive about his training, rarely missing a workout and resting only on Sundays. Between 1980 and 1984 he compiled an impressive amateur record of 160-14, winning a Golden Gloves title and qualifying for the 1984 Olympic team.

The Olympics, however, proved Holyfield's first major disappointment. He knocked out his first three opponents to advance to the championship round against a New Zealander named Kevin Barry. During the fight Holyfield landed a punch just a split second after the referee ordered the fighters to break. He was disqualified for hitting late—a call that many observers still dispute. Holyfield was ultimately awarded the bronze medal, but he wore it not as an honor, but almost as a badge of shame. "I still use it as a motivating thing," he told the *Boston Globe*. "People aren't going to let me forget it anyway. No matter how many fights I win, they'll always ask about what happened at the Olympics."

"All my life, I've been fighting people who didn't think I could make it. I've been waiting for this opportunity for a long time."

Shortly after the games ended, Holyfield turned professional in the cruiserweight (190-pound) division. He became the first fighter of his Olympic class to win a championship when he unseated Dwight Muhammad Qawi in a grueling 15-round decision on July 20, 1986. That win brought him the cruiserweight titles of the World Boxing Association and the International Boxing Federation. Less than two years later he became the undisputed cruiserweight champion by unseating the World Boxing Council's top contender, Carlos DeLeon. Holyfield realized, however, that big money and stardom could only be found in the heavyweight division. With the support of his trainers—father-and-son team Lou and Dan Duva—he announced his intention to fight as a heavyweight beginning in 1989.

The decision was met with a chorus of disapproval. Many observers doubted that Holyfield, who rarely weighed more than a comfortable 212 pounds, could ever withstand the punishment meted out by opponents who entered the ring at 230 or more. Undaunted by the dire predictions, Holyfield and a massive team of trainers embarked on "Project Omega," a total-concept conditioning program. For more than a year Holyfield worked with an orthopedic surgeon, a former Olympic triathlete and swimmer, and even a former ballet dancer. He perfected his agility, his endurance, and his speed, but his most impressive gains were in the bench press and weightlifting departments. Month after month he endured three workouts a day, six days a week—workouts that included running, swimming, sparring, weight lifting, and aerobic exercise. *Philadelphia Inquirer* contributor Robert Seltzer concluded that Holyfield's punishing regimen "has given him the most impressive physique in the heavyweight division."

The doubters were silenced as Holyfield crushed his first six opponents, all of them heavier and supposedly stronger than "little Evander." Soon his trainers' assertions proved true: What Holyfield lacked in weight and stature he more than made up for in heart and desire. Holyfield himself told the *Boston Globe:* "You can't just fight for money because if you do, after the first round you can think you don't need to take all the punishment. You've got the money now. You fight for the belt plus the pride." He added: "If I was doing this in my backyard, I'd still want to win with nobody watching just because I don't want [my opponent] to have the bragging rights over me."

By late 1989 Holyfield was being touted as the only legitimate threat to the reign of Mike Tyson, then the undisputed heavyweight champion. Negotiations were under way for a Tyson-Holyfield bout when "Iron Mike" was defeated in a staggering upset by James "Buster" Douglas. Since Holyfield was the number-one ranked contender in the division, Douglas agreed to fight him, rather than take a rematch with Tyson. A Holyfield-Douglas showdown was set for October of 1990.

The outcome of that fight was almost a foregone conclusion; Douglas, pudgy and unmotivated, hardly mounted any opposition at all to the rigorously prepared, hungry Holyfield. When Holyfield knocked Douglas down during the third round, the champion chose not to regain his feet. A new undisputed heavyweight champion was crowned, one who added Bible verses to his autographs and preached values like Christian virtue, hard work, and determination. Asked what it felt like to be a star, champion Holyfield replied: "Ain't no stars except up in the sky." Holyfield was equally modest about his victory in his April, 1991 bout against George Foreman, which went for twelve rounds.

Holyfield pursues boxing the way a bricklayer builds a house; boxing is his job and he prepares for it every day. Unlike other contenders who let themselves get out of condition between matches, the champion works out habitually. "I'm always training, even when I don't have a fight scheduled," he told the *Philadelphia Inquirer.* "When you're training for a fight, you're all tired at the end of the day, and you sleep great. But, when the fight's over and you stop training, you don't have that tired feeling anymore,

and it's hard to sleep. That's why I keep training all the time. Sometimes, I go to the gym . . . and lift weights at one or two in the morning. Otherwise, I'd have insomnia." Needless to say, no one is calling Holyfield "little" or "scrawny" anymore—not even Mike Tyson, who faces the challenge of beating such a disciplined opponent.

Fame has also had its downside for Holyfield. The scandal sheets have made much of his divorce from wife Paulette—they have four children—and he is not quite as jovial with fans as he once was. Some observers have been amazed at the champion's ability to focus on his work and his goals even during the most difficult family crises. Holyfield says he sees the hard times through with his faith and his determination to succeed. "When I lost at anything, I was always able to go back and learn from those losses and then concentrate on the next fight," he told the *Boston Globe.* "By keeping focused I made the 1984 Olympic team not because I didn't lose any fights but because I was able to keep focused and I had a strong lady in my life, my mother. She taught me you have to live for today. Tomorrow is not always promising and not always promised. It's an attitude that comes from a lot of pride and a lot of faith."

Secure in his faith and proud of his accomplishments, Holyfield is a far cry from the nasty, snarling stereotype most boxers readily accept. "I don't believe that you have to be mean to be successful in the ring," the champion told the *Philadelphia Daily News.* "I don't understand why some boxers are motivated by hate. The way I see it, it's possible to be a good person and a good boxer at the same time, as long as you're able to master the technical skills that enable you to do your job well. And that's all boxing is, when you get right down to it. A job." He concluded: "Fighting is to the death, kill or be killed. In boxing, two athletes compete against one another. When it's over, you hug."

Sources

Boston Globe, December 9, 1988; October 24, 1990.
Philadelphia Daily News, July 27, 1989.
Philadelphia Inquirer, October 9, 1990.
Sports Illustrated, April 18, 1988; July 24, 1989; November 5, 1990.
Washington Post, October 23, 1990.

—Mark Kram

Brett Hull

Professional hockey player

AP/Wide World Photos

Full name, Brett Andrew Hull; Born August 8, 1964, in Belleville, Ontario, Canada; son of Bobby Hull (a former professional hockey player) and Joann Robinson (a figure skater); single. *Education:* Attended University of Minnesota at Duluth, 1984-86.

Addresses: *Home*—Duluth, MN. *Office*—c/o St. Louis Blues, 5700 Oakland Ave., St. Louis, MO 63110.

Career

Professional hockey player for the Moncton Flames (minor leagues), 1986-87; the Calgary Flames, 1987-88; the St. Louis Blues, 1988—.

Awards: Named to National Hockey League (NHL) all-star team, 1989, 1990, 1991; Lady Byng Trophy for excellence combined with gentlemanly play, 1990; named NHL most valuable player for the 1990-91 season.

Sidelights

Brett Hull inherited a famous surname and a famous slap shot, facts that make his emergence as a star in the National Hockey League seem unremarkable. Hull, the record-setting right winger for the St. Louis Blues, is the son of Bobby Hull, a member of the hockey Hall of Fame and one of the best players in the history of the NHL. Genetics aside, however, Hull's ascent to the NHL's elite is most remarkable considering his laid-back disposi-

tion. He described himself to the *St. Louis Post-Dispatch* as "naturally lazy and easygoing," saying he requires constant prodding from the Blues' coaching staff. His mother, Joann Robinson, told that newspaper that she worried that Hull "wouldn't graduate from grade 10 until he had a long gray beard and was in a wheelchair." Even as a teenaged player, Hull was considered too fat and lazy to be a professional prospect. A scouting report on him at age 17 said, "He is tubby, but he can score."

These days, Hull is slim and he can score. In the past three years, Hull has dedicated himself to converting fat to muscle. In the process, he has become one of the NHL's elite players, a man whose name can rightfully be used in the same sentence with those of Wayne Gretzky and Mario Lemieux. His nicknames—"The Incredible Hull," "The Golden Brett" and "The Great Brettsky"-show his status in the league.

In the 1989-90 season, Hull scored 72 goals, leading the NHL and breaking the all-time record for goals by a winger. To prove it was no fluke, he scored 86 goals in the 1990-91 season, becoming in the process just the fifth player ever to score 50 goals in the season's first 50 games. "He's a phenomenal player, a great shooter and one of those guys with a sixth sense about what to do on the ice," his father, Bobby Hull, told the *St. Paul Pioneer Press*. "He'll be far better than I was before he's through. Of course, I knew this about Brett long before anyone else had the chance."

As a young child growing up first in Chicago and then Winnipeg, Manitoba, Canada (cities where Bobby Hull played), Hull would stay after practice and play with the other hockey players' children. His father, Hull told *People*, "Never taught me anything directly. He just said, 'Watch me.' I figured out the game by watching what he did." Hull said that his parents never pushed him into the game, fearful of the inevitable comparisons. But those came anyway. "Kids would say, 'Oh, you're a hot dog, Hull, you're not as good as your father,'" his mother, told the *Los Angeles Times*. "He wouldn't even answer. He'd just say, 'Mom, the only way to get even with them is to put the puck in their net.'" When Hull was 12 his parents separated, divorcing two years later. Hull, the third of five children, went to live with his mother in Vancouver, British Columbia. For years after that, he lost contact with his father. "The man never came to see him at all," Robinson told the *Los Angeles Times*. "Never sent a Christmas card or a postcard or anything else. He seemed to wash his hands of the kids. We never heard from him." Only in the mid-1980s, as Hull embarked on his pro career, did father and son reconcile. Today they have a warm, if somewhat distant, relationship.

As a carefree teenager, Hull's nickname was "Huggy Bear," a needling reference to the 220 pounds he carried on his 5'9" frame. In those days he played hockey just for fun, without any real desire to follow in his father's NHL tracks. He quit the game at 18, but his mother—angry that he had already quit baseball after being considered a good prospect—talked him back into it. Still, the hockey scouts questioned his desire and his weight. They were impressed, however, with his booming slap shot. "Anyone who says they thought back then that Hull would be a 70-goal scorer is lying," Vancouver Canucks general manager Brian Burke told *USA Today*. Hull told *Sports Illustrated* that comparisons with his father caused him to shy away from exerting himself in hockey. "I learned very early that I was never going to be him. So I didn't even try. The sooner I figured out I was Brett, not Bobby, the better off I was gonna be."

When Hull finished midget hockey at age 17, no junior teams pursued him. He walked on to a lowly regarded Tier II junior team in Penticton, British Columbia in 1983. He scored a remarkable 105 goals and 83 assists for 188 points in only 56 games. This performance won him a scholarship to the University of Minnesota-Duluth, where as a freshman he scored 32 goals in 48 games and, as a sophomore, had 52 goals in 42 games. "He scared the hell out of every goaltender in college," New York Ranger scout David McNab told *Sports Illustrated*. "At every level he could get by on talent and that shot. The thought was that if he could get himself in shape and work hard, he'd be a star." Still, most pro scouts were so unimpressed that 116 players were chosen in the 1984 draft before the Calgary Flames picked him in the sixth round. Over his mother's objections, Hull quit college after his sophomore year to sign. The Flames sent him to their farm club in Moncton, New Brunswick, where he scored 50 goals and 92 points and made the American Hockey League All-Star team. There were problems, however. "Brett was continually in coach Terry Crisp's doghouse that first year in Moncton," teammate Perry Berezan told the *St. Paul Pioneer Press*. "I remember one game when Brett came off the ice after getting a hat trick [three goals by a player in a single game] and Crisp screamed, actually screamed, at him, 'You'd better get another goal because you've already cost us three.' Crisp tried to get Brett to play defense and couldn't."

The next season, 1987-88, Hull was promoted to Calgary, where to his chagrin, Crisp had been made coach. Hull played sparingly for the Flames, but still scored 26 goals and 50 points in 52 NHL games. "The more Brett scored, the madder it seemed to make Crisp," Berezan told the *Pioneer Press*. "He couldn't stand the idea that Brett wasn't a complete player." Much of Crisp's ire stemmed from Hull's lack of dedication. "I'm not like my dad," Hull told *People* magazine. "He was aggressive, with a quick temper. I'm a lazy person. I'd rather be sitting here watching TV than anything."

On March 7, 1988, Calgary general manager Cliff Fletcher traded Hull, then 23, to the St. Louis Blues in return for defenseman Bob Ramage and goalie Rick Wamsley. The Flames believed the trade would help them win the Stanley Cup, which they did the next season. At the time of the trade, St. Louis general manager Ron Caron told the *St. Louis Post-Dispatch*, "Brett Hull has the dimensions to be a franchise player. He is worth I don't know how many No. 1 draft picks. Checking is hard work; scoring is talent and skill. The game has changed quite a bit. You can't always win anymore by scoring four or five goals." In addition, no less an expert than Wayne Gretzky said that the Blues had made the better deal.

"It's a great trade for St. Louis. I wish we could have gotten him. He's going to score a ton of goals."

When Hull arrived, the Blues were near the bottom of the NHL, but attempting to build by acquiring good young players. Hull led the resurgence. In 1988-89, he made the all-star team by scoring 41 goals and adding 43 assists, but his labored skating and lack of attention in the defensive zone were liabilities. After the season, coach Brian Sutter took Hull aside and told him how important he was to the club and how much he could improve if he concentrated on it. It wasn't enough to blast slap shots at hapless goalies, the coach told Hull; he had to play defense, set up plays and become more of a leader. "It was a turning point for me," Hull told *People*. "My attitude up to that point was, 'Hey, I'm scoring, so they aren't going to get rid of me.' This helped wake me up." Sutter told the *St. Louis Post-Dispatch*, "He's a young man in a position to score a lot of goals in the NHL, and it was up to him whether he wanted to be an ordinary hockey player scoring 40 goals or be a damn good hockey player, improve in other areas of the game and score 55 to 65 goals."

After the lecture, Hull immediately cut back on his drinking and partying. He spent the off season running, doing aerobics, and skating with members of the U.S. Olympic team. Instead of red meat, he ate chicken; instead of a sour-cream-topped baked potato, he went for rice. He reported to camp for the 1989-90 season weighing 10 pounds less but carrying a new, muscular physique.

The results had an immediate impact on his game; Hull entered the 1989-90 season skating dramatically better and showing a new quickness in his shot. He dedicated himself to a conditioning regimen and, when he slumped, found himself being prodded by Sutter. The result was what Hull termed "a dream season": 72 goals and 41 assists. The goals were the most ever by an NHL winger and a number exceeded by just three players in the league's history—Gretzky, Lemieux, and Phil Esposito. Blues owner Michael Shanahan told the *Los Angeles Times*, "When Brett Hull came here in 1988, he had a great name. Now he's grown into it."

At the end of the season, Hull, who had just ten penalty minutes, was awarded the NHL's Lady Byng Trophy for excellence combined with gentlemanly play. The honor underscored the difference between Hull and his father, who was known to scuffle on the ice. Pointing up another difference between father and son, *Sports Illustrated*'s Paul Fichtenbaum wrote: "The most noticeable difference, other than Bobby's having a lefthanded shot and Brett a righthanded

one, is in physique. Bobby, now a cattle rancher in Ontario, looks like Popeye after a jolt of spinach, his chest stretching the seams of his sweater. Brett's build is less impressive."

Hull earned $160,000 for the 1989-90 season. Afterwards, as a free agent, he signed a four-year, $7.1 million contract that helped shake the salary structure of the league and upset some team owners. Still, the Blues knew that Hull was their franchise player. Their rise in the standings and increased popularity at the gate coincided exactly with his arrival. As *Sports Illustrated*'s Austin Murphy remarked, "Hull is the toast of St. Louis, the city's most popular sports figure since Stan Musial."

Hull started the 1990-91 season determined to live up to his contract. And in the season's 49th game, he joined Gretzky, Lemieux, Mike Bossy and Maurice Richard as the only players to score 50 goals within the season's first 50 games. "Being with those four names is something to be proud of," Hull told *Sports Illustrated* after scoring his 50th goal. "They all made a name in history. I have a lot of time ahead of me. Maybe I can, too."

Hull further made his name before the season ended. He scored 86 goals—35 more than anyone else in the league that season—within six of Gretzky's all-time one-season record. Hull declared that record his goal for the 1991-92 season. He was an odds-on favorite to be named NHL most valuable player when the voting was conducted in June 1991; when the votes were in, Hull walked away with the honor.

While comparisons to his famous father remain inevitable, Hull no longer shies away from them. Bobby Hull built his game on speed, strength, and a slap shot that petrified goalies. Hull is not fast and prefers open ice to the congestion of the corners, but he has the same frightening slap shot. Has Hull had enough success to make announcers and sportswriters call Bobby Hull his father, instead of calling Hull Bobby's son? "No way," he told *Sports Illustrated*. Then, rattling off his father's statistics he added, "Until I get 610 goals, 1,170 points and win a couple of Hart (most valuable) trophies and . . . get voted into the Hall of Fame, I'll still be Bobby Hull's son. Even if I did all that, I'd still be Bobby Hull's kid. I kind of like that."

Sources

Boston Globe, March 8, 1991.
Buffalo News, February 7, 1990.
Chicago Tribune, December 26, 1989; March 17, 1991.

Detroit Free Press, January 23, 1990.

Los Angeles Times, November 2, 1989; March 31, 1991.

People, April 9, 1990.

Philadelphia Daily News, March 17, 1989; February 22, 1990; March 1, 1991.

St. Louis Post-Dispatch, March 8, 1988; February 7, 1989; January 20, 1990; June 23, 1990; October 4, 1990; January 20, 1991.

St. Paul Pioneer Press, April 3, 1991.

St. Petersburg Times, March 27, 1991.

Seattle Times, January 27, 1991.

Sports Illustrated, December 25, 1990; February 4, 1991; March 18, 1991.

Sports Illustrated For Kids, November 1990.

USA Today, April 12, 1990.

Washington Post, February 27, 1990.

—*Glen Macnow*

Madeline Hunter

Education expert

Full name, Madeline Cheek Hunter; born c. 1916; married Robert Hunter (a retired Lockheed executive); children: Cheryl, Robin (son). *Education:* Attended University of California, Los Angeles, earning degrees in psychology and education.

Career

Began career working with terminally ill children at Children's Hospital in Los Angeles; worked briefly at the Los Angeles Juvenile Hall, c. 1936, and as a school psychologist; University Elementary School, Los Angeles, principal, 1963-82; professor of education at University of California, Los Angeles, 1982—. Has conducted workshops for teachers worldwide, 1967—; serves as consultant to school districts throughout the United States.

Sidelights

Known to many in the education field as "the teacher's teacher," Madeline Hunter has brought both tremendous influence and controversy to the troubled American education scene with her highly mechanized approach to education based on the tenets of behavioral psychology. As the American public education system continues to suffer the bad news of falling test scores, rising dropout rates, lack of discipline in the classroom, and frustrated parents, more and more administrators are looking to Hunter's theories for assistance. And what Hunter delivers is a message of empowerment to teachers. Teachers cannot change everything about a student's environment, she says, but they can control the environment of the classroom using her methods of positive reinforcement. "By changing nothing but the ability of the teacher to teach, we can bring about more dramatic change in the success of a child in learning than through the manipulation of any other factor," Hunter was quoted in the *Sacramento Bee.*

For more than twenty years, often bedecked in a white laboratory smock, Hunter has been espousing her theories at seminars and schools, in books and on instructional videotapes. She claims that sixteen state education departments have adopted her models in one way or another, and there are many schools who "do Madeline Hunter" as though it were a religion. As one school superintendent told the *Los Angeles Times,* "Every Friday at the end of another week, we pray to Madeline Hunter."

At the heart of Hunter's method is a simple seven-step approach to teaching a lesson: *Review* of the previous lesson, *introduction* of new material, *explanation* of the new lesson, *modeling* (or demonstration with engaging visual aids), *'dipsticking'* (or checking for understanding), *monitored practice,* and *independent study.* Hunter also strongly emphasizes what she calls "disciplining with dignity," a technique for maintaining order which draws disruptive students back into the lesson, rather than shutting them out. Before learning Hunter's methods in a special training school, one teacher told the *Los Angeles Times*, "I really knew nothing about teaching...all I got in college was theory. I don't know how any of us would survive without Madeline Hunter. She gives me a way to organize a classroom, to keep things under control."

And yet it is this highly controlled atmosphere of a typical "Hunterized" classroom that most disturbs her critics. They see Hunter's methods as too rigid and simplistic, a way of maintaining order and force-feeding information at the expense of children learning to think for themselves. "Mechanically applied, the method...treats students like answering machines, and this cuts off creativity," wrote David L. Kirp in the *Sacramento Bee*. Or, as California school administrator Bill Honig noted, "Maybe you can teach facts with Hunter's approach, but you can't teach 'What's Democracy?'" The reason so many teachers and administrators are sold on Hunter's methods, these critics argue, is that it provides a simplistic, quantifiable scale for gauging the progress of both students and teachers. But, as teacher Patrick Welsh asked in his book *Tales Out of School*, "Why should I be forced to go through a set of prescribed mechanistic procedures to satisfy the school system's need to document its seriousness about improving teaching?"

Growing up near Los Angeles, Hunter had decided on the study of psychology from the age of twelve. She attended University of California, Los Angeles (UCLA) in the mid-1930s to study under several eminent behavioral psychologists in the school's education and psychology departments. There, she researched ways in which the findings of modern psychology could be translated to effective language for teachers. In 1950, after years in other psychology professions, Hunter began working in the Los Angeles public schools as a psychologist and later as a principal. In the 1960s, she took a job as the principal and second-in-command to renowned UCLA scholar John Goodlad at Los Angeles's University Elementary School (UES), essentially a laboratory for the latest theories and practices of UCLA's education faculty. When Goodlad later became dean of the School of Education, Hunter was given enormous rein over the course of UES, and her methods were taught almost

exclusively. "Only Madeline Hunter's way went at UES," one UCLA professor told the *Los Angeles Times*. "She got in trouble with professors who were pushing methods that were less frontal, less dictatorial."

In 1982 Hunter left the post at UES under controversy that she was promoting her methods too strongly, almost religiously, and that she was spending more time on the lecture circuit than on running the school. Even well into her seventies, however, Hunter has remained a popular speaker at education seminars and conventions. She has appeared in every state and nearly fifty countries, sometimes at fees of $5,000 per day. She is also a partner in the firm Special Purpose Films and TIP Publications, which has produced eleven of her books, such as *Teach More—Faster!* and seventeen videotape collections that cost up to $3750 a set.

Selected writings

Motivation, TIP Publications, 1967.
Reinforcement, TIP Publications, 1967.
Retention, TIP Publications, 1967.
Teach More—Faster!, TIP Publications, 1969.
Transfer, TIP Publications, 1971.
Improved Instruction, TIP Publications, 1976.
(With Sally Breit) *Aide-ing in Teaching*, TIP Publications, 1976.
(With Paul V. Carlson) *Improving Your Child's Behavior*, TIP Publications, 1977.
Mastery Teaching, TIP Publications, 1982.
(With Doug Russell) *Mastering Coaching & Supervision*, TIP Publications, 1989.

Sources

Books

Welsh, Patrick, *Tales Out of School: A Candid Account from the Front Lines of the American High School Today*, Penguin, 1987.

Periodicals

Los Angeles Times, January 26, 1986; August 12, 1990.
Sacramento Bee, August 24, 1990.

—David Collins

Saddam Hussein

Reuters/Bettmann

President of Iraq

Full name, Saddam al-Tikriti Hussein (sometimes spelled Hossein, Husain, or Husayn); born April 28, 1937, in Tikrit, Iraq; married Sajida Khairallah Talfah (a primary school teacher), 1963; children: two sons, two daughters. *Education:* Attended Cairo University and Mustanseriya University, Baghdad.

Addresses: *Office*—Revolutionary Command Council, Baghdad, Iraq.

Career

Deputy secretary, Regional Leadership of Baath Party, 1966-79, secretary, 1979—; acting deputy chairman, Revolutionary Command Council, 1968-69; deputy chairman, Revolutionary Command Council, 1969-79, chair, 1979—; president of Iraq, 1979—. Member of Arab Baath Socialist Party, 1957—, 4th Regional Congress and 6th National Congress of Baath Party, 1963, 7th National Congress, Syria, 1964, and National Leadership of Party of 10th National Congress, 1970.

Awards: Order of Rafidain, 1st Class, 1976.

Sidelights

Beginning at 2 a.m. on August 2nd, 1990, Iraqi troops invaded the Arab oil sheikdom of Kuwait under orders from President Saddam Hussein. In just four hours the military had maneuvered the thirty-seven miles down Kuwait's six-lane highway to the capital, Kuwait City. It took twelve hours to seize the entire country.

Hussein apparently had several reasons for the abrupt annexation of this small Gulf emirate. One reason was that, according to Iraq, Kuwait owed its neighbor a great deal of money. For one thing, Kuwait had overproduced oil, in violation of quotas set up by OPEC (Organization of Petroleum Exporting Countries). The subsequent loss to Iraq was an estimated billion dollars a year for every dollar shaved off the price per barrel. At an OPEC meeting held in Geneva in July 1990, Kuwait and the United Arab Emirates (who had also produced in excess of their quotas) agreed to raise oil prices from $18 to $21 per barrel, and to keep a lid on production. But this was only after Hussein had positioned his best men, the 30,000 Republican Guard, at the Kuwait border. After the agreement Hussein added 70,000 troops to the buildup, although he had promised he would not attack Kuwait. At that point Egypt's President Hosni Mubarak still viewed the situation as "a cloud that will pass with the wind," quoted *Time*.

But the cloud didn't pass. There were more complaints. The Rumaila oil field represented another unresolved issue. This oil field reaches into a region that both Kuwait and Iraq claim as their own. Hussein's government accused Kuwait of moving the border about two and half miles further north into the disputed territory while Iraq was focused on war with Iran in 1980. Iraq calculated that Kuwait benefited from this move by $2.4 billion—and Hussein seems to believe he and his country are entitled to these profits.

Then, during the eight-year-long war between Iran and Iraq, Kuwait lent the latter billions of dollars. Apparently Hussein decided Kuwait should write off around $15 billion in loans, because Iraq had held back Iran's fundamentalism in the name of all Arabs—including Kuwaitis. But above and beyond looking for funds needed to help rebuild Iraq after the war with Iran, Saddam Hussein "seeks recognition as the pre-eminent Pan-Arab leader," stated Russell Watson in *Newsweek*. Or, as Lisa Beyer put it in *Time*, "Having won . . . the war against Iran, he is intent on making himself the new Gamal Abdel Nasser, master and hero of the entire Arab world."

> *Hussein "seeks recognition as the pre-eminent Pan Arab leader."*
> —*Russell Watson*

The world's major powers stood together in their condemnation of the Iraqi invasion. The United Nations Security Council responded to Hussein's expansionism by calling for his unconditional withdrawal from Kuwait. United States President George Bush described the acts of the Iraqi dictator as "naked aggression" and imposed economic sanctions against Iraq. He cut off all trade with that country and froze $30 billion of Kuwait's and Iraq's assets held in American banks. The European Community followed suit by imposing an embargo on oil from the two countries. Thanks to warmed relations between the West and Moscow, the Soviet Union cut off arms supplies to Iraq. Japan also froze assets. And the Arab League called for Iraq's immediate withdrawal from Kuwait and condemned the invasion, despite its reticence to allow Western involvement.

An array of fears surfaced as a result of Hussein's action. One of the biggest was that the Iraqi leader would not stop with Kuwait. Believing it might be next in line in Hussein's plan for hegemony, Saudi Arabia invited the United States to intervene. Considering that Hussein would control over 44 percent of the Earth's oil reserves should he take over that country, President Bush accepted the invitation. He began deployment of troops in Saudi Arabia, build-

ing up over several months under Operation Desert Shield. There was also concern that other countries bordering could be in jeopardy, such as Jordan and Syria. This possibility made Israel anxious as well.

Comparisons were drawn between Hussein's actions now and Adolf Hitler's actions in the 1930s. One similarity is Hussein's penchant for charismatic speeches against a country next door. And Hussein's takeover of Kuwait seems similar to how Hitler "began to gobble up Europe in pieces small enough not to provoke a military response by the other powers of the day," observed Beyer in *Time*.

Another fear was Hussein's inclination to engage in chemical warfare. He had no qualms about using chemical weapons to quell a Kurdish uprising in his own country in which many innocent civilians lost their lives. Chemicals were also used against Iran during the war. But according to William Dowell and others writing in *Time*, Iraq is well within a decade of obtaining a nuclear bomb. So, as a high ranking official in the U.S. State Department told Dowell, with "the mind-set of a person as ruthless as [Hussein] is, unless you meet this kind of aggressive behavior very firmly, he's encouraged to try again, and you'll pay a substantial price later."

Hussein's current status as president of Iraq belies his humble origins. He was born in Tikrit, a village located about 100 miles northwest of Baghdad. His father died before he was born, so Hussein went to live with his maternal uncle, Khairallah Talfah. Talfah, a devout Sunni Muslim, a nationalist, and an officer in the army, served as a role model for Hussein. And Talfah's son Adnan also influenced the young boy. It was Adnan who encouraged Hussein to seek an education. Eventually, Hussein married Talfah's daughter, Sajida.

During Hussein's high school years he joined the Baath Party, which promotes Arab nationalism (and is anti-Western). By the time he was 22 he was already involved in an assassination attempt on the life of Iraq's dictator at the time, Major General Abdel Karim Kassem. The major general was not killed, and Hussein was subsequently arrested. Hussein did manage to escape from prison, however, after which he traveled across the desert by donkey to Syria. Egyptian President Nasser heard of the young revolutionary, and summoned him to Cairo. Hussein answered the call and remained in Egypt to study law.

Then in 1968 the Baath Party took over Iraq in a bloodless coup. Major General Ahmed Hassan al-Bakr held the title of president, while Hussein was ostensibly his vice-president. But it was really Hussein who called the shots. In 1979 Hussein became president officially. He advertised his position throughout Iraq with posters twenty feet high, depicting himself in various roles. For example, he is portrayed as a young graduate in some; a desert horseman in others; a military man wearing a beret in still others.

President Hussein holds the titles of Secretary General of the Baath Party and Commander in Chief of the Armed Forces as well. He is a man with a reputation for brooking no opposition of any kind from anyone. One graphic illustration of this tendency is Hussein's purge of party officials and military officers just after he became president. These men were executed for the crime of treason against the Iraqi government as part of a Syrian plot. "Cassettes, distributed to senior officials of other Arab countries, show Hussein reading off the names of the supposed traitors, slowly and theatrically, pausing occasionally to light his cigar," Efraim Karsh stated in the New York Times Magazine. Then in 1982, 300 more officers were reportedly terminated for rebelling against Hussein's choice of strategic moves in the war with Iran. And, more recently, the major Egyptian newspaper Al Ahram reported that "120 Iraqi officers had been executed for questioning the wisdom of the invasion," as quoted in Newsweek.

To protect himself from possible internal threats to his regime, Hussein has created a coterie of relatives and friends. He has placed the people he can trust most in important government positions. But close blood relations are not even safe from Hussein's wrath, should it be incurred. For example, when Hussein had a much-publicized affair with Samira Shahbandar, his first-born son Uday attempted to defend his mother's honor. Uday elected to publicly club to death the official food taster and go-between in the affair. A livid Hussein had his son tossed into jail with a charge of murder. He eventually relented, exiling Uday to Switzerland.

But Hussein's desired public image of himself as a devoted father and husband had been shattered. His cousin and childhood companion, Minister of Defense Adnan Talfah, had stood with his sister (Hussein's wife) during the brouhaha. That decision cost Talfah dearly. In May of 1989, he perished in what the press called a "mysterious" helicopter crash. For the most part, however, disfavored members of Hussein's clique merely find themselves demoted.

But according to the U.S. State Department's 1989 report on human rights, Hussein's reputation in this area is "abysmal." He has himself survived many attempts on his life. And although he rules by intimidation, Hussein's regime has "brought Iraq, once a coup-plagued country, its longest period of stability," observed Elaine Sciolino in the New York Times.

Despite his reputation for ruthlessness and the almost worldwide condemnation of his takeover of Kuwait, Hussein still has proponents among some Arab peoples. There are several reasons for this. One is that believers in Islam are offended by the positioning of Western forces in their holy lands. Another reason is that the royal families ruling the Persian Gulf sheikdoms seem to control more than their fair share of oil-related wealth. Among the more poor in the Middle East, the Kuwaitis in general and their royalty in particular, are seen as "undeservedly rich, self-indulgent and spoiled," according to Time's Aileen Keeting. And the Palestinians applaud Hussein's attempt to bring more attention to the Israeli/Palestinian conflict in Israel. Hussein originally retained approximately 17,000 internationals, whom he called "guests." This is not unlike the Israelis, as some Arabs reason, who have been known to hold Palestinians at will.

A professor of Middle Eastern politics at the University of Paris explained Hussein's popularity among the average Arab in Time: "It's not that the man is personally charismatic. It's that he's viewed as someone who is shaking an unacceptable status quo." In another Time article, former United States President Jimmy Carter expressed his views on the ramifications of combat between U.S.-led international forces and Saddam Hussein's army. Carter wrote, "Armed conflict can exacerbate all these concerns and may unleash a violent grass-roots reaction."

Sources

Newsweek, August 13, 1990.
New York Times, August 5, 1990.
New York Times Magazine, September 30, 1990.
Time, August 13, 1990; October 22, 1990.
USA Today, September 28-30, 1990.

—Victoria France Charabati

Chrissie Hynde

AP/Wide World Photos

Singer and songwriter

Full name, Christine Ellen Hynde; born September 7, 1951, in Akron, Ohio; daughter of Bud (a telephone company employee) and Dee (a part-time secretary) Hynde; in the mid-1980s married Jim Kerr (leader of the rock band Simple Minds); divorced; children: Natalie (father is Ray Davies, leader/songwriter of the Kinks) and a second child. *Education:* Studied art at Kent State University, c. 1969-72.

Career

Began pursuing music career in London, 1973, and later in Paris; returned to the United States and joined R&B band Jack Rabbitt; again went to London and performed with members of the Clash, the Sex Pistols, and the Damned; signed by Real Records in 1978; formed Pretenders; recorded first single, "Stop Your Sobbing," 1978.

Addresses: *Home*—London, England.

Sidelights

When Chrissie Hynde finally pulled together her own band, she had little idea of the impact she'd make. The Pretenders reflected her own sensibility more than the late-1970s punk scene that surrounded them, and they scored an overnight success. But it was more than Hynde's spine-chilling vocals, incisive lyrics, and drop-dead look that grabbed fans and critics. Hynde, a *woman*, was a formidable rocker. *Creem* deemed her a "rarefied,

orchid presence" in the company of of such female rockers as Deborah Harry [see *Newsmakers 90*] and Pat Benatar. *The New Rolling Stone Record Guide* called Hynde "the only woman to make distinctions of sex nonexistent in rock," and asserted that "she has single-handedly reduced all other contemporary women in rock to any one of the number of cliches that abound about them." As the Pretenders built on their initial reputation, Chrissie Hynde became known as one of the first women to lead and shape a top band whose other members were men.

"In her sawn-off denims and black leather, hair tatted, cheeks chalked, pale mouth painted into a sneer," noted a writer for the *New York Times Magazine*, Hynde "comes on as the sort of girl mothers have always warned their sons against." Yet she's also a woman known to lavish herself with expensive perfumes, and she is an animal lover and vegetarian and a mother of two. Sexy but not a sex symbol, tough but not "butch," Hynde has always intrigued men and women alike. *Creem* wrote of "the Chrissie Myth," noting Hynde on *The Pretenders* album cover "looking like she'd just as soon hit you as sleep with you, *Jack,* . . . or maybe a little of both." Her music is imbued with a "psychosexual candor," as *Rolling Stone* put it, that's not part of an act but a projection of her offstage self. "Hynde doesn't pretend to be one of the boys or descend to hip-flipping," noted Jon Pareles in the book *The Year in Rock: 1981-1982.*

Indeed, her songs resist such one-dimensional stances so common in rock and instead address real-life issues, often through language and delivery that's shockingly blunt. Her famed gang-bang epic "Tattooed Love Boys," as *Rolling Stone* remarked, "erupts at a neck-cracking 7/4 pace, with Hynde slashing at her guitar and spitting out the cold, pitiless words like razor blades." During the Pretenders' first world tour she dedicated "Brass In Pocket," her hit song celebrating female sexual assertiveness, to "anyone who's worked as a waitress," as *Rolling Stone* reported. She also told her audiences that "Tattooed Love Boys" is "not about bikers. It's about girls who get beaten up by the same guy more than once."

Hynde was born in 1951 in Akron, Ohio's "rubber town," where she grew up. Her father, Bud Hynde, worked for the local telephone company, and her mother Dee Hynde was a part-time secretary. "I was Joe Normal," Chrissie told *Rolling Stone.* "But I was never too interested in high school. I mean, I never went to a dance, I never went out on a date, I never went steady. It became pretty awful for me. Except, of course, I could go see bands, and that was the kick. I used to go to Cleveland just to see any band. So I was in love a lot of the time, but mostly with guys in bands that I had never met. For me, knowing that Brian Jones was out there, and later that Iggy Pop was out there, made it kind of hard for me to get too interested in the guys that were around me." She took up the baritone ukulele at the age of sixteen and began writing songs. "I never had that kind of experience most guys in bands do," she told *Rolling Stone*, explaining that she was too shy to get involved with any of the local all-male garage bands. "I think that probably determined a lot of my style of playing. I still go by the dots on the guitar, you know? I have a very rudimentary knowledge of it."

As a junior high school student, Chrissie would watch the local train pass by and dream of the day she'd leave Ohio. "I know it sounds romantic, but it made me cry when I saw it," she told *Rolling Stone.* "I just knew that I had to be on that train someday." After high school she spent three years studying art at Kent State University, which brought little satisfaction. (She participated in the school's notorious 1970 National Guard riot—undoubtedly a high point.) By the start of 1973, though, she had her long-awaited ticket out of Akron—a thousand dollars she scraped together through waitressing and other odd jobs. She

split for London, which she'd been reading about in the British rock tabloid *New Musical Express.*

But while she went with hopes of playing music, she found herself doing everything else—office work, cleaning houses, working in a boutique (run by future punk god Malcolm McLaren)—to pay the bills. One of her jobs, incidentally, was writing for *New Musical Express*, which led to an interview with the innovative rock composer Brian Eno. The two ended up discussing pornography, and Hynde posed for the article dressed in high heels, a black leather mini-skirt, and bondage gear. After a while, she tried to put together a rock band in Paris. It didn't work out, however, and in 1975 she left for Cleveland, where she joined an R&B-based band called Jack Rabbitt. (One of its members was Mark Mothersbaugh, who would later earn fame in the group Devo.) "I had a terrible time," she recalled in *Rolling Stone.* "I was hitchhiking around, and I'd forgotten how dangerous it was. I had a few bad experiences, but the way I look at it now is, for every sort of act of sodomy I was forced to perform, I'm gettin' paid 10,000 pounds now. That's how I try to look at it, anyway."

In 1976, after another failed attempt to put together a band in France, she returned to London. It seemed like perfect timing: Punk rock was being born. Hynde tried to form a group with a young guitarist named Mick Jones, but as usual, had no luck. "He was really young and fresh, and here I was, already spent," she told *Rolling Stone.* "I didn't have his sort of fresh innocence. I wasn't like the young punk who had just gotten out of school." She then reconnected with Malcolm McLaren, who asked her to play guitar in a band he was putting together called Masters of the Backside. After several rehearsals, however, she was dumped; to make things worse, the group, renamed the Damned, became the first punk band to release an album. After joining another band and getting dumped again, Hynde was invited by Mick Jones to join his new band, the Clash, on their first British tour. "It was great," she told *Rolling Stone*, "but my heart was breaking. I wanted to be in a band so *bad.* And to go to all the gigs, to see it so close up, to be living in it and not to have a band was devastating to me. When I left, I said, 'Thanks a lot for lettin' me come along,' and I went back and went weeping on the underground throughout London. All the people I knew in town, they were all in bands. And there I was, like the real loser, you know? Really the loser."

But Hynde persisted. Early in 1978 she sent her demo tape to Dave Hill, a former promotions man who was looking for talent for his new label, Real

Records. Impressed, Hill decided to work with her and told her to put together a band. Meanwhile, Pete Farndon, an English bass player who had just returned from a stint in Sydney, Australia, was anxious to get back into a band. Through a friend he heard about Hynde—an American singer, he was told, with some great original tunes. Farndon was skeptical, but he arranged to meet with her. "As soon as we got down to her rehearsal room, which was the scummiest basement I'd ever been in my life, the first thing we played was 'Groove Me,' by King Floyd," he recalled in *Rolling Stone*. "The second thing we played was this *great* country & western song of hers called 'Tequila.' I was lookin' at this woman like . . . you know? . . . and then we did 'The Phone Call,' which is like the heaviest . . . punk-rocker you could do in 5/4 time. Impressed? I was *very* impressed." Farndon contacted his friend James Honeyman-Scott, a young, talented guitarist, and the two found Irish drummer Jerry Mcleduff to complete the lineup. Borrowing the title of an old Platters hit, they called themselves the Pretenders.

> "Because fame and success jumped on us so fast, we all had our own ways of dealing with it."

After several rehearsals, the group booked a small demo studio and recorded Hynde's "Precious" and "The Wait." Those two songs would become Pretenders classics, but the crucial cut on the tape turned out to be an obscure 1964 Kinks tune called "Stop Your Sobbing." Hynde's version was unique yet just as potent as the original, and she used it to grab the attention of top producer Nick Lowe. "I told him that there was a song on [the tape] that I thought he would particularly like," she recounted in *Relix*. Taken with the tune, Lowe agrred to produce it. "We were over the moon that he would do it. So he squeezed in a day between working with Elvis [Costello] and doing his own album." Released in early 1979, "Stop Your Sobbing" immediately entered the British Top 30 and caught on in the United States as an import. After replacing Mcleduff with Martin Chambers, more of a powerhouse drummer, the group recorded "Kid" and "Brass in Pocket," which also topped the singles charts, and played their first British gigs. The press raved, and the new band found themselves on the front pages of the London music papers. By spring they were ready to record again. Lowe had lost interest, so they turned to Chris Thomas, producer of Roxy Music and the Sex Pistols. Thus began a six-month project that yielded a stunning debut album called *The Pretenders*.

Amazingly, *The Pretenders* entered the English charts at Number 1, bumping Pink Floyd's *The Wall*, and it established the band faster in the U.S. than such other British acts as the Police, the Clash, and Elvis Costello. Calling it "one of the most brilliant debut records in rock," Debbie Geller in *The New Rolling Stone Record Guide* wrote, "From the Motown pleading on 'Brass in Pocket' to the unrestrained joyousness of 'Mystery Achievement' to the lovely 'Stop Your Sobbing,' the album holds endless delights. All the ambivalences of love, lust and hate are on display. There is no woman who loves rock who can't be thrilled by 'Precious,' when Chrissie wonders about getting pregnant against a backdrop of killer rock & roll—it just hasn't happened before." Following the LP's release, the Pretenders did their first extensive British tour, starting a tradition of promoting each album with a major tour.

The Pretenders impressed not only for its songs and overall sound but for the sheer distinctiveness of Hynde's singing. Her "voice combines the fluidity of jazz singing with the rawness of rock," observed *Rolling Stone*, praising her "full, uncaged alto." The *Village Voice* was even more taken. "Like a foreigner singing phonetically, Hynde divides words into discrete, equally weighted syllables—rushing them, in a burst, around a bit of melody, or hammering them on the beat like percussion," wrote Debra Rae Cohen. "Phrases and fragments, enticing and suggestive, leap out between swaths of guitar. But Hynde's capable of conveying enough shades of emotion with her voice that even when the words are obscured . . . the tone always comes through . . . . Hynde's knocking down barriers here: rock 'n' roll has a long tradition of dexterous incoherence, with all its overtones of erotic confidence, but I can't think of another woman who's pulled it off."

Less than two years later came *Pretenders II*, another smash success. But the band was struggling among themselves due to the drug problems of both Farndon and Honeyman-Scott. Farndon's problem was so bad, in fact, that Hynde had to fire him. He was "strung out and couldn't admit he was a junkie," she told *Time* about her former lover. Not long afterward Honeyman-Scott died of an overdose; Farndon later met the same fate. "Because fame and success jumped on us so fast," Hynde explained, "we all had our own ways of dealing with it." She last saw

Farndon at Honeyman-Scott's funeral. "He was terribly bitter and resentful. He felt like, 'You fired me, but Jim's the one who died from drugs.' Ten months later, [Farndon] had drowned in the bathtub with a needle sticking out of his arm." Hynde began to confront her own lifestyle—'I used to take any kind of drug, whatever was going on, but I always kept it in check'—and changed course. "I started drinking less, and I started to look less and less like a rock-'n'-roll personality. I didn't want to be recognized."

Meanwhile, she was sharing a London apartment with Kinks leader Ray Davies, who had been her idol during her teens. The tabloid music writers jumped on the story. "The couple has jammed together, gone to the movies together, even recorded together," reported *Circus*. "Ray has cooled Chrissie out a bit," a Warner Bros. employee told the magazine. "She doesn't drink that heavily anymore, and she's wearing really good clothing. Since they're both doing music all the time [when they're together] they just like to hang out." Hynde refused to comment on their relationship, but she did cite Davies as her favorite songwriter. "He writes these songs that leave absolutely nothing to be desired," she told the *New York Times Magazine*, "Right sentiments, right emotions, never *too* direct. He never wastes words."

After Farndon's firing and Honeyman-Scott's death, temporary replacements were found and the band recorded "Back on the Chain Gang," which became an instant hit. Then, with guitarist Robbie MacIntosh and bass player Malcolm Foster as the new members, the Pretenders recorded their third album. *Learning to Crawl* shot straight into the Top 10 and stayed there, having no rival, as *Time* asserted, "for tough rock and straight talk." At the same time it featured a gentler, more expressive Hynde. She was now the mother of a toddler named Natalie (born to her and Davies), and had been forced to "tame down," as she told *Time*. "Suddenly, you can't imagine sitting down and smoking a pack of fags or drinking whiskey. Being a mother's a real awakening." Through Natalie, she gained "a real feeling of humanity that I hadn't had before." *Learning to Crawl* reflected this depth. *New York Times* writer Robert Palmer wrote, "It is loving but without tears, and it is a chronicle of pain, separation and transcendence. Miss Hynde, always the group's focal point, has dramatically expanded the musical and emotional range of her singing." Interestingly, motherhood added to her music without making her any less of a rocker. Bringing Natalie with her on tour, she still took "a showwoman's pride in turning on an audience," as *Time* reported. "She is a current front-runner in all those fan-mag polls about 'sexiest woman in rock.'" *Get Close*, released in 1986, featured more personnel changes—T. M. Stevens on bass, Blair Cunningham on drums, and the addition of a fifth member, keyboardist Bernie Worrell, who added a soul/funk dimension. It also reflected further changes in Hynde. "I'm 35, and I can't keep pretending I have my head in a garbage can," the singer told the *New York Times*. "Punk music is 10 years old. I don't think the term 'punk' describes anything on the Pretenders' new album." Now the mother of two, ages 2 and 4, and married to Jim Kerr of the Scottish technopop band Simple Minds, she was writing songs that were "both deeper and more optimistic than the group's earlier music," as the *Times* commented. "Her songs address love and motherhood and the state of the world . . . . While she can still be feisty, Ms. Hynde now also writes touchingly about responsibility and commitment."

> *"Suddenly, you can't imagine sitting down and smoking a pack of fags or drinking whiskey. Being a mother's a real awakening."*

But like their earlier work, *Get Close* didn't lack for sarcasm and sharp social commentary. In "How Much Do You Get For Your Soul," a James Brown-style funk tune, Hynde criticized such black stars as Michael Jackson and Lionel Richie for using their music to endorse soft drinks. "How much did ya get?" Hynde sings. "Who's got soul? From the African nation/to the Pepsi generation?" Hynde commented on the song in the *New York Times*: "I'm sure that if Jimi Hendrix were here today, he would not be making soft-drink ads. Rock-and-roll used to be anti-establishment, but it has been overexposed in magazines and on television. In America, MTV has taken the excitement and magic out of rock-and-roll and turned it into the musical equivalent of McDonald's. The fact that musicians probably spend more time making a video for a song than working the song out musically says a lot about the condition of rock. I can remember exactly where I was sitting when the Beatles first appeared on TV. I felt plugged in to something that was totally from another world. Since then, the music and the culture have become completely domesticated."

After a four-year hiatus, the Pretenders came back—now with Billy Bremner and Dominic Miller on guitars, Blair Cunningham on drums, John McKenzie on bass, and producer Mitchell Froom (Los Lobos, Crowded House) on keys—with *Packed!*, their fifth and most understated release to date. "*Packed!* offers the Pretenders in soft focus. Even the production is toned down and muted," observed *New York* reviewer Elizabeth Wurtzel. "*Packed!* is not angry and it's not happy. Hynde's marriage to Jim Kerr of Simple Minds has fallen apart, and the songs are lost in some no man's land of sorrow and loneliness.... 'Empty me/Like a dustman rids a rubbish bin,' Hynde sings on 'Let's Make a Pact,' a title that underscores the irony of broken marriage vows." Featuring ten Hynde originals, as well as a heartfelt cover of Jimi Hendrix' 'May This Be Love,' *Packed!* is as eye-opening and original as any of her previous work.

In a press booklet released by Sire Records, Hynde commented on her song "Sense of Purpose": "It's not my motto, it's just an expression. Usually when I get ideas for songs, it's very much from the obvious. I pluck things off signs on a bus. It's just come full circle; in the sixties, the idea was to have no goals. People in the fifties were born to be so goal-oriented. We rejected them all, but you have to feel some purpose. You have to get your spiritual path in tune with your life.

"I'm not a workaholic," she continued. "If I don't have something to say, there's no point in being out there."

Selected discography

The Pretenders, Sire, 1979.

The Pretenders II, Sire, 1981.
Learning to Crawl, Sire, 1984.
Get Close, Sire, 1986.
Pretenders—The Singles (includes "Brass In Pocket," "Talk of the Town," "I Go To Sleep," "Message of Love," "Back on the Chain Gang," "Middle of the Road," "2000 Miles," "Show Me," "Thin Line Between Love and Hate," "Don't Get Me Wrong," "Hymn to Her," "My Baby," "I Got You Babe"), Sire, 1987.
Packed!, Sire (distributed by Warner Bros.), 1990.

Sources

Books

Marsh, Dave and John Swenson, editors, *The New Rolling Stone Record Guide*, Random House/Rolling Stone Press, 1983.
John Swenson, editor, *The Year in Rock: 1981-1982*, Amordian Press, 1981.

Periodicals

Circus, November 1, 1981.
Creem, August 1980; June 1983.
Los Angeles Times/Calendar, May 20, 1990.
Melody Maker, February 17, 1979; July 21, 1979; January 26, 1980; October 4, 1980; September 12, 1981.
Music and Sound Output, April 1983.
New York, May 28, 1990.
New York Times, April 18, 1984; May 3, 1984; November 19, 1986.
New York Times Magazine, June 8, 1980.
Relix, June 1980.
Rolling Stone, May 29, 1980.
San Francisco Weekly, May 16, 1990.
Time, April 30, 1984.
Village Voice, May 5, 1980.

—*Kyle Kevorkian*

Jeremy Irons

Actor

Full name, Jeremy John Irons; born September 19, 1948, in Cowes, Isle of Wight, England; son of Paul Dugan (an accountant) and Barbara Anne (Sharpe) Irons; married actress Julie Hallam, 1971 (divorced, 1971); married actress Sinead Cusack, March, 1978; children: (second marriage) Samuel James, Maximilian Paul. *Education:* Graduated from the Sherborne School, Dorset, England, 1965. Graduated from the Bristol Old Vic Theater School c. 1968.

Addresses: *Home*—Oxfordshire, England. *Office*—c/o Anne Hutton (personal manager), Hutton Management, 200 Fulham Rd., London, England SW1O 9PN.

Career

Stage, television, and film actor. Stage appearances include: in England, with the Bristol Old Vic Company (c.1968-1971), *Hay Fever, What the Butler Saw, The Winter's Tale;* on London's West End, *Godspell* (debut, 1971), *Much Ado About Nothing* (c. 1973), *The Caretaker* (1974), *The Taming of the Shrew* (1975), *Wild Oats* (1976), *The Rear Column* (1978); in Stratford-upon-Avon, with the Royal Shakespeare Company (c. 1984-87), *Richard II, The Winter's Tale, The Rover;* in the U.S., *The Real Thing* (Broadway debut, 1984). Television appearances include: in England, *The Pallisers, Notorious Woman, Love for Lydia, The Voysey Inheritance, Langrishe Go Down* (all c. 1971-1980), *Brideshead Revisited* (1981), *All the World's a Stage* (1982), *The Captain's Doll* (1982), *Danny, the Champion of the World* (c. 1986), *The*

Dream of a Ridiculous Man (1990); in the U.S., *Brideshead Revisited* (1982), *Saturday Night Live* (1991), and *The Barbara Walters Special* (1991). Film appearances include: *Nijinsky* (1980), *The French Lieutenant's Woman* (1981), *Moonlighting* (1982), *Betrayal* (1982), *The Wild Duck* (1983), *Swann in Love* (1984), *The Mission* (1986), *Dead Ringers* (1988), *A Chorus of Disapproval* (1989), *Australia* (1989), *Reversal of Fortune* (1990).

Awards: Clarence Derwent Award for best stage actor, 1978, for *The Rear Column;* Tony Award for best actor, 1984, for *The Real Thing;* New York Film Critics Circle Award for best actor, 1988, for *Dead Ringers;* National Society of Film Critics Award, Golden Globe Award, and Academy Award, 1991, all for best actor, for *Reversal of Fortune.*

Sidelights

His darkly handsome features first graced American screens in 1981, when he roamed the English countryside as the doomed Victorian lover obsessed with the mysterious title character in *The French Lieutenant's Woman.* His brooding, aristocratic presence further caught the fancy of Anglophiles when he starred in PBS-TV's landmark presentation of *Brideshead Revisited*. His Tony Award-winning portrayal of yet another suffering lover in Broadway's *The Real Thing* clinched his reputation as the quintessential romantic leading man, prompting *Glamour* magazine to dub dashing Brit Jeremy Irons "the thinking woman's sex symbol." A decade later, however, the as-ever attractive English actor has cast aside his romantic hero image, and reached the top of his dramatic form by playing demented villains and contemptible cads. Deliciously warping his debonair British charm, he has taken a successful descent into decadence, first earning rave notices as the deranged and sadistic twin gynecologists in *Dead Ringers*, then winning the 1991 Academy Award for his icy portrayal of Claus von Bulow, the sinister socialite convicted of trying to murder his wife, in *Reversal of Fortune*.

Always known as an intense performer in roles marked by their difficulty and substance, Irons has—over the course of his career—sharpened his edge by indulging his daring streak and stepping into controversial territory. In *Dead Ringers* he accepted the technically demanding task of playing the dual roles of identical twin gynecologists who are both psychopathic and repellent. It was a project no other actor would attempt; Robert De Niro and William Hurt were among the notables who turned it down. The extremely unsympathetic role of Claus von Bulow, whom *Newsweek* termed an "aristocreep," required Irons to ravage his leading man looks by balding and graying his full head of hair and adding three layers of middle-age paunch to his trim athletic frame. "I've always been very careful," Irons said, explaining his process of choosing roles to *Mademoiselle*, "but at the same time I always try to put my foot somewhere you're not expecting. I like to alter people's perceptions of me. Because I'm an actor."

For a man so dedicated to the craft of acting in public, Irons had quite an austere upbringing—certainly not the kind usually attributed to a budding thespian. The son of an accountant, Irons was born in the yachting resort town of Cowes on the Isle of Wight, an island off the southern coast of England. When he was just a boy of seven, he was shipped off to the first of a series of strict English boarding schools, eventually graduating from the rigid Sherborne School in Dorset when he was 17.

Irons explained that the seemingly cruel practice of sending so young a child away to school was simply traditional for upper-middle-class English lads of his generation. There he received training more appropriate for a future banker—learning to be a materialistic, emotionally repressed, stiff-upper-lipped En-

glish gentleman. It did help him years later, however, when he was cast as the snooty and distant Charles Ryder of *Brideshead Revisited*. "When I read *Brideshead*, I understood Ryder completely," he told the *New York Times*. "He was a man who kept his emotions deeply hidden and didn't give very much, who certainly didn't give any of his real self . . . . I really think Ryder is the man I was educated to be. He is everything an actor isn't or shouldn't be."

Actually, acting was not Irons's first, or even second, career choice. His love of animals and country life fueled his desire to become a veterinarian, but his poor academic performance in the physical sciences forced him to consider other options. After his graduation from the Sherborne School in 1965, he exchanged his upper-middle-class surroundings for a tough neighborhood in South London, where he became a social worker. Running a club for impoverished inner city youths "opened my eyes to the real world after a very privileged education, a life in a delightful Dorset town, a structured society," Irons told *New York*. "Suddenly I was thrown into this hoodlum land and had to make an evening at a youth club work when there were gangs coming in and trying to break the place up. There were guys selling drugs; there were girls on the game." After spending a frustrating six months getting beaten up one too many times by youth gangs, Irons thought he should seek a more pleasant way to interact with people.

It was when he started to supplement his social worker's salary by moonlighting as a busker—British slang for "street entertainer"—that he found his true calling. Singing and playing his guitar for the lines of movie- and theatergoers on the sidewalks of London's Leicester Square uncovered a latent exhibitionistic streak in Irons, and he was quickly seduced by the promise of a romantic life in the theater. Following his new resolve, he answered a newspaper ad and landed a position as an assistant stage manager with a theater repertory company in Canterbury. Within a year he gained acceptance into the Bristol Old Vic Theater School, where he underwent two years of rigorous classical training. He performed so well that he was one of only five students asked to join the Old Vic's touring repertory company, a prestigious troupe whose alumni include Peter O'Toole, Albert Finney, and later, Daniel Day-Lewis.

For three years Irons honed his craft with the Old Vic, progressing from bit butler parts to leading roles in plays ranging from Shakespeare to Noel Coward. In 1971, at age 23, however, he decided to pack his bags and head for the bright lights of London's West

End. During that time Irons began and ended a very brief marriage to Julie Hallam, an actress with the Bristol Old Vic, and, while waiting for his commercial big break, he survived by doing odd jobs as a bricklayer, house cleaner, and gardener.

The break arrived later in 1971 in a rather unexpected form: the man who confessed to *New York* that "I sing like an actor and dance like a duck" was cast as John the Baptist in the rock musical *Godspell*. A successful long run in *Godspell* brought Irons a plentiful supply of London stage and television work from then on. He distinguished himself on stage in classical roles with both the New and Royal Shakespeare Companies, and continued to display his versatility in contemporary works like Harold Pinter's *The Caretaker* and Simon Gray's *The Rear Column*. In the latter play, under Harold Pinter's direction—the playwright-director-actor who, Irons told *Film Comment*, "has done more to help my career than anyone else"—Irons gave a riveting performance that earned him London's Clarence Derwent Award for best stage actor of 1978. His work in such BBC television series as *Notorious Woman*, *Love for Lydia*, and *The Pallisers* made him a familiar figure across England.

Irons's career reached a major turning point in 1981. That was when two big-budget, long-awaited projects were unveiled in both England and America, making the actor an instant celebrity on both sides of the Atlantic. One was the eleven-part television adaptation of Evelyn Waugh's lush novel *Brideshead Revisited*; the other was the much-anticipated film version of John Fowles's 1969 best-selling Victorian romance, *The French Lieutenant's Woman*.

Brideshead Revisited chronicled the decline of a fabulously wealthy British family during the golden years between the two World Wars. The series was a historic television event; it was both the most expensive British television production and the all-time highest-rated series on America's PBS-TV to that date. More than holding his own among dramatic titans Laurence Olivier, John Gielgud, and Claire Bloom, Irons portrayed the hero-narrator Charles Ryder, a gentleman-painter bedazzled by and drawn into the decadent world of the aristocratic Marchmain family. *Newsweek*, which pronounced *Brideshead* "the most engrossing event of [the] television season," hailed Irons as "brilliant in the central role as a melancholy, obsessive snob."

The second half of the double bill introducing Irons to American audiences was the period romance *The French Lieutenant's Woman*, which *Newsweek*'s David Ansen termed "one of the most civilized and provoc-ative movies of the year." In his first major film, Irons—who was recommended for the leading role by the movie's screenwriter, his friend and mentor Harold Pinter—played a proper Victorian gentleman who gives up his fiancee, career, and respectable position in society for a tainted woman, played by Meryl Streep, who seduces and ultimately abandons him. His ardent performance reminded many critics of the young Laurence Olivier of *Wuthering Heights*, and the *New York Times* review of the film singled out Irons as "one of the few actors today who could be so completely convincing as the Victorian lover who thinks he's ahead of his time, being a follower of Darwin and a socially enlightened member of his privileged class, but who finds, ultimately, that he still has a long way to go."

After his initial film success, Irons turned down several lucrative offers which he considered "rubbish." "If you go for money and lose your integrity, you're lost," he told *Newsweek*. He chose instead a succession of high-minded movie projects that were confined to art-houses and little seen in the U.S.: the political *Moonlighting* saw him as a Polish laborer; Harold Pinter's cerebral *Betrayal* cast him in a deceitful love triangle; *The Wild Duck*, an adaptation of the Ibsen play, teamed him with Liv Ullmann; and he played another aristocrat obsessed with a scandalous woman in Marcel Proust's *Swann in Love*.

It was Irons's return to the stage that catapulted him back into the spotlight. His American stage debut—on Broadway no less—netted him the 1984 Tony Award for best actor. Irons's starring vehicle, Tom Stoppard's *The Real Thing*, which the *New York Times* called "the most bracing play that anyone has written about love and marriage in years," also won the Tony for best play and yielded best actress honors for Irons's co-star, Glenn Close. In Stoppard's highly articulate script, Irons has a passionate affair with his best friend's wife, marries her, then is in turn cheated on by his new spouse.

"It's a wonderful role, because it allows one to play a great range, from flippant comedy to deeply felt pain," Irons told the *Times*. The actor was more than equal to its demands. Critics hailed him as a master of nuance and emotional depth, and *Newsweek* predicted that his "strong and stylish performance will make him a big star." "The role of Henry, a brilliant, arrogant playwright of dazzling wit and verbal facility, has given Mr. Irons a tour-de-force part to mark a major milestone in his career," the *New York Times* wrote. *The Real Thing*, which became the biggest box-office hit of the 1984 Broadway season, elevated Irons to matinee idol status; countless magazines touted him as the new sex symbol, swooning over his exquisitely chiseled cheekbones, melancholy soft brown eyes, and seductive British accent, or as *Vogue* put it, his "luxuriant Shakespearean rumble."

Instead of capitalizing on his new-found Broadway stardom with more commercial ventures, Irons departed for England after *The Real Thing*'s run, returning to his classical roots for a two-year stint with the Royal Shakespeare Company. He subsequently filmed a few more scholarly projects for British television, as well as another classy, little-seen movie called *The Mission*, which costarred Robert De Niro and saw Irons as a Jesuit priest in the jungles of Brazil. These highbrow pursuits made his next move all the more shocking.

When he first read the bizarre plot to the psychological thriller *Dead Ringers*, Irons was "appalled," and he "couldn't find one woman who liked the script. Not one," he told *Mademoiselle*. "My wife read it and felt squeamish." Eventually the actor succumbed to the dramatic challenge of playing opposite himself in the lurid tale inspired by the real-life case of identical twin brothers Drs. Stewart and Cyril Marcus, two respected gynecologists whose partially nude and decomposed bodies were found among a clutter of garbage and barbituates in their posh New York City apartment in 1975. As interpreted by avant-garde director-writer David Cronenberg—whose past films include the sci-fi horror of *Videodrome* and *The Fly*— the brothers came to the gynecological profession with an underlying fear and hatred of females, and enjoyed humiliating their patients with psychological and physical abuse as the women lay helplessly suspended in stirrups on the examining table. The twins are both played by Irons; one is a suave swine, the other a paranoid introvert. They are pathologically dependent on one another, living together and enjoying the macabre game of substituting for each other in the examining room and in the bedroom, without their patients' or lovers' knowledge. In a frighteningly gripping performance, Irons takes the viewer on a harrowing journey that is at once repulsive, yet perversely fascinating, right up to the twins' demise by drug addiction, insanity, and a grisly suicide-murder pact.

"Irons is spectacular in his dual role, both haunted and haunting," declared *People*, while the *New York Times* pronounced his performance "seamless . . . a schizophrenic marvel." Citing his technically brilliant creation of two subtly distinct but eerily similar characters, coupled with the uncanny ease with which he played intensely emotional scenes with himself, many critics thought Irons's virtuosity merited an Academy Award. The horrific subject matter of the non-mainstream film, however, was thought to have alienated many conservative voters. Nevertheless, his superb work in *Dead Ringers* prompted the New York Film Critics Circle to name Irons best actor of 1988.

It was Irons's portrayal of another real-life unsavory character that earned him the prestigious Oscar. The 1990 film *Reversal of Fortune*, which chronicled the two most sensationalized criminal trials of the 1980s, starred Irons as Claus von Bulow, the arrogant, mistress-juggling socialite who was convicted, but later acquitted, of twice attempting to murder his $75 million-rich heiress wife with lethal injections of insulin. The movie teamed Irons with his good friend and *Real Thing* co-star, Glenn Close, who played the ill-fated wife, Sunny—the real Sunny von Bulow has remained in a coma since 1980.

Alan Dershowitz, the attorney who got von Bulow acquitted and wrote the book on which the film is based, was amazed at Irons's ability to transform himself into his infamous client. "Jeremy Irons," Dershowitz remarked to *Gentleman's Quarterly*, "is a better Claus von Bulow than Claus von Bulow." In preparing for his role, Irons could have arranged to meet the real von Bulow, but decided against it. "When you're playing a character, you are that character. And it isn't very helpful to meet someone who says they are also that character. It stultifies the imagination," Irons explained to *Interview*. "I watched Claus on video. I met a lot of people who knew him well, some not so well. I researched him very much as a fictional character so that I would be able to play him with freedom, without any feeling of trying to impersonate him."

The actor's method served him well: His finely-crafted characterization, complete with subtle body language and an upper-crusty accent dripping with sarcastic charm, won the superlative praise of critics. "Alternately sincere and sinister, droll and decadent, Irons makes an ambiguous figure vividly real and disturbing. It's a tricky, triumphant portrayal," declared *Rolling Stone*. The *New York Times* effused that "Claus von Bulow [is] played by Jeremy Irons within an inch of his professional life. It's a fine, devastating performance, affected, mannered, edgy, though seemingly ever in complete control. Mr. Irons comes very close to being too good to be true."

The man who so effortlessly embraces evil and menaces women on camera is quite the loving gentleman offscreen. Declaring himself a true family man with old-fashioned values, Irons is devoted to his wife of thirteen years, Irish actress Sinead Cusack—whom he met while performing in *Godspell*—and dotes on his two sons, Sam and Max. Reveling in the simple pleasures of country life, he resides in a 200-year-old Georgian farmhouse nestled on the banks of the Thames River in Oxfordshire, England, where he unwinds by boating, horseback riding, and romping with his dogs.

Often found dressed like the traditional English squire in an ascot, tweeds, and knee-high riding boots, Irons's views, particularly those on women, are decidedly unstuffy and enlightened. Declaring a general preference for female companionship, Irons expressed these thoughts to *Film Comment*: "Clearly, women are often badly done by, unfairly, but in so many ways that they are trying to overcome, they are superior beings. They're patient. They have less arrogance, less ego, more stamina and self-control, generally speaking. And nearly everyone admits that women are more interesting, and that's what really counts, not power." Irons's wife, an acclaimed stage actress best known for her work with the Royal Shakespeare Company, is often gone for long periods of time performing on tour. Proud of his talented wife, Irons accepts the sacrifice: "I want her to be fulfilled," he told *People*. "I think I would be bored by any woman fulfilled by doing dishes." Irons's cool and distant screen persona is further dispelled by the warmth he exhibits toward friends. Once when Glenn Close was mugged, Irons pursued the thief and pinned him to the wall until police arrived. "If I were in trouble," theater producer Emanuel Azenberg told *Gentleman's Quarterly*, "I wouldn't be

ashamed to call him, and he *would* show up. I'm lying under a truck, he'll fly in from England and lift it off me." Azenberg further recounted Irons's charitable work for an AIDS benefit, when the actor single-handedly raised over $100,000: "A lot of people give money. That's easy. He hustled, worked the phones. That's classy. And it wasn't for publicity. The cameras weren't rolling." Perhaps Jeremy Irons is best summed up by a remark he once made to *Vogue:* "As an actor, I am ballsy and slightly evil. But as a man, I am charm personified—and very soft."

Sources

Film Comment, March-April 1983; September-October 1988.
Gentleman's Quarterly, November 1990.
Glamour, June 1984.
Interview, June 1990.
Mademoiselle, October 1988.
Newsweek, September 21, 1981; January 18, 1982; January 16, 1984; October 3, 1988; November 5, 1990.
New York, January 23, 1984.
New York Times, September 18, 1981; January 6, 1984; January 9, 1984; September 23, 1988; October 17, 1990.
People, January 23, 1984; November 19, 1984; September 26, 1988.
Rolling Stone, November 15, 1990.
Time, January 18, 1982; January 16, 1984.
Vogue, January 1982; March 1984.

—*Mary Lou De Blasi*

Kevin Johnson

Professional basketball player

Born c. 1966 in Sacramento, Calif.; mother's name, Georgia; raised by grandparents George and Georgia Johnson. *Education:* Attended University of California, Berkeley.

Addresses: *Home*—Phoenix, AZ.

Career

Signed by Oakland Athletics baseball club, 1986; began career with NBA as a first-round draft selection by the Cleveland Cavaliers, 1987; point guard for the Phoenix Suns, 1988—.

Awards: Named NBA Player of the Month, February, 1989.

Sidelights

When he first entered the National Basketball Association (NBA), he was just another of seemingly dozens of men named Johnson. By the time he had completed his second pro season, he had come to be known as the *other* Johnson—in deference to Los Angeles Lakers guard Earvin "Magic" Johnson, who dominated the game as he revolutionized it during the 1980s. And finally, after helping the Phoenix Suns whip those same Lakers in five games in the 1989 Western Conference playoffs, he seemed ready to lead his young, talented team into the 1990s as *the* Johnson.

Who is this apparent heir to the NBA's Throne of Johnson? He's Kevin Johnson, the lightning-quick

Phoenix point guard whom Philadelphia 76ers forward Charles Barkley has said "might be the best pure point guard in the game," and who is otherwise widely considered to be in a class with the "Magic Man" of the Lakers, Mark Price of Cleveland, Isiah Thomas of Detroit, and Utah's John Stockton. As Phoenix coach Cotton Fitzsimmons explained in *Sports Illustrated*, it is difficult to describe Johnson because rarely does a player come along who can so thoroughly dominate a game as both a playmaker and a scorer the way Johnson can. "Special," Fitzsimmons said in trying to sum up his star player. "That's the only word that comes to mind. Special."

And special, too, seems an apt word to describe Kevin Johnson, the human being. In a day and age when star professional athletes are often nothing more than spoiled, pampered millionaires who would think nothing of charging a 6-year-old kid ten bucks for an autograph—and when, because of the prevalence of that kind of money-grubbing, other athletes are glorified as great guys because they occasionally sign for *free*—Johnson really does seem to be the genuine article. His acts of generous, spontaneous charity, often to people he doesn't even know, are well chronicled. Once, an old friend was lamenting the fact that he didn't own a car—so Johnson gave him his new Mazda RX-7. Another time, a down-on-his-luck security guard at Johnson's apartment complex received an unexpected donation of $5,000.

There are more stories, and a cynic could point out that, to a man who makes $1.5 million a year, such charities can hardly be called a sacrifice. But other quieter, less flamboyant gestures on the part of Johnson hint to a man genuinely trying to spread some of his good fortune around—and it doesn't always have to do with money. For instance, at each Phoenix home game there are ten fans present entirely on the good will of Johnson, who passes out tickets to people he comes across during his daily travels—the man who bags his groceries, for instance, or his hairdresser, or a shy kid who would have settled for a free autograph. And before that game the deeply religious Johnson could probably have been found leading several teammates—and even some members from the *opposing* team—in a chapel service. Even on the court, where winning is supposedly everything and the law of the jungle rules, Johnson never fully forgets the big picture. Once, when a ball flew off the court and the official didn't see who touched it last, Johnson admitted, "I did." As *Sports Illustrated*'s Rick Reilly fittingly asked, "Could Jimmy Stewart play this part or what?"

But what makes Johnson so refreshing is that his roots are anything but white-bread America. In fact, how such a sensitive, intelligent, talented human being emerged from the background Johnson did is anybody's guess. His beginnings were set against a lesser-known side of American life, but to fully understand his family tree, one must go back two generations to Grampy George, Johnson's grandfather and the most important influence in his life. George, a white sheet-metal worker from Sacramento, fell in love with Georgia, a white tavern manager who was pregnant with the child of a former black lover. George married Georgia, and they went on to raise Georgia's daughter, also named Georgia. The younger Georgia became pregnant at the age of 16 (the father, who never married her, drowned in the Sacramento River soon after). Kevin was Georgia's son, but he was raised by his grandparents. "Kevin had a couple of parents who were pretty hard to explain," Grampy George told *Sports Illustrated*. "But we were a happy family."

Though they struggled themselves in a poor section of Sacramento, the Johnson's house was where the children and the downtrodden of the neighborhood congregated to soak up some of the good will of Grampy, who played the part of the nice old man down the street with patience and generosity, but still plenty of street smarts. In fact, when his treasured grandson eventually became rich and offered to buy Grampy a new house, the elder Johnson refused the gift. Grampy didn't want to leave the neighborhood, so he settled for a new car instead. The house is still there, and Johnson returns every summer to live with the man who taught him

nothing about basketball but everything about being a man. "My grandfather was the one who taught me how to treat people, regardless of color, regardless of anything," Johnson told Reilly.

Growing up tall and athletic, Johnson was a natural in any sport, and he excelled in basketball and baseball particularly. But when he skipped over fifth grade and went right to sixth, it became obvious that his intellectual gift was equal to his athletic prowess. Thus when it came time for him to choose one college from the hundreds that offered scholarships (he was California's leading high school scorer his senior season), his decision was based more on academics than basketball. Johnson's choice, the University of California, Berkeley, may have had a weakling basketball team, but its political science department was one of the finest in the country, and once there Johnson thrived in the atmosphere of intense discussions of philosophy, theology, and politics. He also found time to star on the U-Cal baseball team, where as a switch-hitting shortstop he impressed the scouts enough to be signed by the Oakland Athletics in 1986. "In three years he would've been in the majors," Oakland's scouting director told *Sports Illustrated*.

Kevin Johnson, right, guards the ball from Patrick Ewing of the New York Knicks in a January 1990 game in New York's Madison Square Garden. AP/Wide World Photos.

But Johnson knew—and so, apparently, did the NBA scouts—that despite laboring under a mediocre basketball program at Berkeley, he was a can't-miss pro basketball prospect. "Johnson is one of those players who come along only a few times a decade," wrote Jack McCallum in *Sports Illustrated*, "a wunderkind whose talents are uniquely tailored to the pro game." The Cleveland Cavaliers made him their first-round selection in the 1987 draft, much to the chagrin of their rookie point guard, Mark Price, who had just finished a dismal first season. Going into training camp that fall, Price feared for his starting job, and Johnson (who, despite his nice-guy reputation, also has a tough, cocky court demeanor) came in fully intending to take it. But Johnson soon found how tough life can be in the NBA. "When we went to camp, I was playing the best defense I had ever played in my life," Johnson told the *Sporting News* of his first confrontations with Price. "I could not stop him. People were judging Mark on his rookie season, and he wasn't the same player. He was killing me every day, in every practice. I thought, 'Here is a less-than-average player, and he's murdering me every day.' That's when I had self-doubts."

> *"It happened so quickly. Before I knew it, I was at the top of the ladder. And I'm wondering: What happened to all those rungs on the ladder in between?"*

As Price embarked on an All-Star season, Johnson rode the pine until later that year when the Cavaliers' management, hoping to bolster their front line for the divisional race with Detroit, sent the rookie guard to Phoenix in a multi-player trade for Suns forward Larry Nance. The trade for Johnson was probably the key move in a rebuilding effort by Suns president Jerry Colangelo, which, on hindsight, can now be seen as nothing less than amazing. The Phoenix franchise had been almost totally decimated just two years earlier (1986-87) when several Suns players were implicated in a team drug scandal. Colangelo quickly cleaned the Suns house of that old regime, and by the start of the 1988-89 season, only one player—guard Jeff Hornacek—was left from the maligned 1986-87 squad.

When Johnson arrived later that same season, it took only three practices for then-coach John Wetzel to see Johnson had both the skills and the leadership qualities to take charge of the team. "This team's yours," Wetzel reportedly told Johnson—and the young, patchwork Phoenix team, also featuring star forwards Tom Chambers and Eddie Johnson along with "KJ," Hornacek, and a new coach, Cotton Fitzsimmons, completed the dramatic resurgence of Phoenix basketball by becoming a playoff team by the end of the 1988-89 season—just 1 1/2 years after Johnson's arrival. That quickly, Johnson had risen from the ashes of the Cleveland bench to a starring role in Phoenix, where he earned second team All-NBA honors after his first full season. "It happened so quickly," he told the *Sporting News*. "Before I knew it, I was at the top of the ladder. And I'm wondering: What happened to all those rungs on the ladder in between?"

In Johnson's case, he seemed to have just leapt over them. Indeed, in a league featuring some of the quickest human beings on the planet, Johnson can make many of them look slow. "He has the quickest first step I've ever seen," teammate Chambers told *Sports Illustrated*. "Nobody in the NBA can guard this kid," coach Fitzsimmons added. As for establishing oneself in a hurry: When the final statistics were tallied at the end of the 88-89 campaign, they showed a point guard who had moved up to a level with the NBA's elite. Johnson had become only the fifth player in the history of the league to average 20 points and 10 assists per game, joining his own boyhood heroes Magic Johnson, Isiah Thomas, Nate Archibald, and Oscar Robertson. Then, as if to prove it was no fluke, he did it again the following season. The double threat Johnson posed as a scorer and playmaker quickly made an impression on opposing defenses. "Every time he gets the ball, he has a chance to break your defense," Chicago Bulls' coach Doug Collins said in *Sports Illustrated*.

But every great NBA team of the 1980s had one thing in common, over and above great players: leadership. The Boston Celtics had the determination of Larry Bird; the Lakers had the enthusiasm and hustle of Magic Johnson; and the Pistons had the heart of Isiah Thomas. Other great players, such as the incomparable Michael Jordan of Chicago and Dominique Wilkins of Atlanta, had achieved great personal statistics but never won a championship. Clearly, for Phoenix to clear the last hurdle to a championship ring, they would need Kevin Johnson to become more than just a great player. They would need him to become the general on the court who would make all his teammates play better.

Fortunately, Johnson has proved himself as egocentric on the floor as he is selfless outside the arena. When the Suns management all but placed the history of the franchise on his shoulders with that declaration "this team is yours" (plans for a new domed stadium in downtown Phoenix were also hanging in the balance), the untested but heady rookie took his leadership role to heart. He moved his teammates around the court like chess pieces, and when they weren't *where* he wanted them *when* he wanted them there, a tongue lashing from the point guard was not far behind. "I considered the trade to Phoenix as my opportunity to be myself," Johnson told the *Sporting News*. "If I didn't yell at guys, then I couldn't be me. And I promised myself that if I failed or didn't last in this league, I would do it being myself. If I had to step on some toes, I'd do it."

But Johnson also found that with leadership comes responsibility—for failure as well as success. After that dream 1988-89 season, when he led the Suns to 55 victories and a spot in the Western Conference finals against the Lakers, and was named the NBA's Most Improved Player, the young star experienced a little of this flip side of glory. There was a protracted, sometimes bitter contract negotiation with Suns management that eventually yielded a seven-year pact worth between $15 million and $17 million (and, along with it, loads of pressure to perform). Then, the following season, Johnson started slowly, perhaps as a reaction to expectations or—more probably—due to his determination to say: "Look, we need *five* guys to win the game. I'm just this little point guard." "I forgot I was supposed to be this All-Star," Johnson told the *Sporting News*. "Probably everybody in Arizona had a talk with me about being aggressive. I wanted to get everybody else involved. I have to remind myself now who I'm supposed to be." KJ—and the Suns—eventually responded to their billing as one of the premier young teams in the league, ousting the Lakers in five games in the Western Conference playoffs later that year before losing in seven games to Portland in the conference finals. Against Los Angeles, KJ matched his hero, Magic, play for play, and one could say with a good deal of certainty that Phoenix would have beaten Portland as well if their star guard did not have to sit out the decisive seventh game with a pulled hamstring.

There is probably a trip to the NBA finals somewhere in Johnson's future, and possibly even an NBA championship. What will follow remains to be seen; political office, perhaps. Surely, Johnson's religious conviction, his continuing post-degree work at Berkeley, and his high profile will make him an attractive potential candidate. A particular concern of his is the struggle of his fellow African-Americans to reach new levels of economic independence and dignity, and his bookshelf, lined with the writings of Pascal, Martin Luther King, Malcolm X, Richard Wright, and Plato, are indicative of his seriousness. And he is realistic enough to know that the example he sets as a man, not as a basketball player, is what will ultimately prove his value as a leader in his community. "In the long run, it's the bus driver, the mailman, the clerk in the store, that are the role models, that will have the respect of the kids—not people like me in what I do. That's just a quick fix," Johnson told the *Sporting News*. "I would first say to them: 'Don't let your environment or your circumstances influence what kind of person you turn out to be.' They can't get caught up in comparing their lives to the Carringtons on *Dynasty*, or they'll never be happy."

Sources

Sporting News, March 6, 1989; May 29, 1989; November 20, 1989; April 23, 1990.
Sports Illustrated, August 31, 1987; October 12, 1987; December 28, 1987.

—*David Collins*

Bill T. Jones

Photograph by James Salzano

Dancer and choreographer

Raised in Wayland, NY, as the tenth of twelve children. *Education:* Attended State University of New York at Binghamton.

Career

Dancer, choreographer. Co-founder with Arnie Zane of American Dance Asylum, 1974-82, and Bill T. Jones/Arnie Zane & Company, 1982—.

Sidelights

A powerfully built dancer and innovative choreographer, Bill T. Jones has become one of the most influential figures on the American dance scene, particularly in the way his life and work reflect the continuing tragedy of AIDS. As co-founder of the Bill T. Jones/Arnie Zane & Company dance troupe, Jones saw both his personal and professional partnership shattered in 1988 when Arnie Zane, his companion and co-founder, succumbed finally to a long battle against the fatal disease. Since that time Jones has struggled to keep their dance company—which still bears Zane's name—afloat, and to exorcise his grief over the loss of his friend through powerful new dance compositions.

By most accounts Jones has met both of these challenges with resounding success. Critic Robert Jones said that Jones's *Absence*, a tribute to Zane in which he dances solo with an invisible partner, possesses "a shimmering, ecstatic quality that was euphoric and almost unbearably moving." As for

Jones's tightly-knit ten member company, *People*'s Michael Small saw beauty in its unique make-up. "It is their look as well as their grace that delights," Small wrote, "for the troupe is a striking study in contrasts. On a simply decorated stage, women both black and white spin and leap with such disparate partners as Arthur Aviles, a 5'4", 145-lb. Puerto Rican athlete with a shaved head, and Lawrence Goldhuber, a hulking white 6'1" former actor."

Dubbing Jones "a young black choreographer of immense talent," *Esquire*'s Guy Martin called the dancer's 1991 composition *Last Supper at Uncle Tom's Cabin/The Promised Land* "astonishing . . . . The piece sprawls, unafraid of itself. Slo-mo basketball, the Last Supper, excerpts from Lincoln's second inaugural address, snips of poetry from Amiri Baraka, minstrelsy, King's 'I Have A Dream' speech read in reverse; from a *very* strange grab bag of black political and cultural icons Jones and his dancers carve out a real, whole work of art." Jones took this unique work on a national tour, and in each town the troupe visited he hired some forty extra local dancers to perform in a final number that has the entire cast disrobe on stage. "You do see the rainbow coalition of bodies—all ages, shapes, colors, and sizes—and that, finally, is his message," Martin continued.

"History is our bodies moving through time, and this is what it looks like from God's perspective."

The tenth of twelve children of parents who worked on farms and later in factories, Jones was a high school track star and a promising actor as he grew up in rural Wayland, New York. His life took a permanent change of direction, he says, after he met Zane, an art and biology student, while attending the State University of New York at Binghamtom. "I didn't feel comfortable being a jock anymore, and the theater department was too conservative for me. So dance reared its beautiful head," Jones told *People*.

Jones and Zane met in 1973 when a mutual friend asked them to dance together in a student production. A year later they formed their own dance collective, the American Dance Asylum, and performed mostly together in imaginative duets. Though they were opposed to living in fast-paced New York City, rave reviews to one of their Manhattan performances convinced Jones and Zane to move to suburban Rockland County and to form the Bill T. Jones/Arnie Zane & Company in 1982. The initial success of the troupe was thwarted, however, when Zane developed the AIDS virus in the mid-1980s. Rather than keep his illness quiet, Zane went public with his disease in an attempt to educate people, a move that cost the troupe a number of investors and almost put them out of business.

The company continued to struggle after Zane's death, particularly as Zane was an energetic sort whose enthusiasm rubbed off on Jones and the other dancers. But in his grief over Zane, Jones told *People*, he finally found strength in the dance troupe they had created together. "[The troupe] saw me on the bathroom floor screaming like a baby when Arnie's body was taken away," Jones said. "And they kept me going. Right away, we went into rehearsal and started new pieces."

After Jones caught his stride, the company again took off to new levels of success, appearing on a PBS television special and with renowned dance theaters throughout the United States and Europe. And while Jones has known suffering, he told *People* that he has learned to channel his fears toward the creative medium of dance: "I just want this funky company to say, 'Yeah, life hurts like hell, but this is how I keep going. I have a sense of humor, I've got my brothers and sisters. I've got the ability to make something out of nothing. I can clap my hands and make magic.'"

Sources

Esquire, March 1991.
Interview, March 1989.
New York Times, October 29, 1990.
Newsweek, November 19, 1990.
People, July 31, 1989.

—*David Collins*

Frida Kahlo

The Bettmann Archive

Artist

Born July 6, 1907, in Mexico; died July 13, 1954, in Coyoacan, Mexico City, Mexico; daughter of Guillermo and Matilde Kahlo; married Diego Rivera (artist), August 21, 1929 (divorced in 1939 and remarried in 1940).

Sidelights

She lived only 47 years and has been deceased nearly 40 years, but Frida Kahlo is as popular today as she ever was during the 1930s and 1940s, when she produced the majority of her paintings. In fact, as Melissa Chessher suggested in an *American Way* cover story, a virtual "cult of Kahlo" has sprung up, fueled by interest in the artist by such celebrities as Madonna. At the auction house Sotheby's, a Kahlo painting recently sold for $1.43 million. And yet the artist remains an enigma to her followers and a stranger to the masses.

Born in Mexico in 1907 to a German-Jewish father and a Spanish-Indian mother, Kahlo later "changed her birthdate to July 7, 1910, the year of the outbreak of the Mexican revolution, so that she and modern Mexico would be born the same year," according to Chessher. Her middle-class upbringing (Guillermo Kahlo worked as a photographer for the Mexican government) suited a child described as a class cutup and prankster. But, as Chessher notes, Kahlo's life changed on September 17, 1925, when the teenager was riding a bus and "an electric trolley crashed into the center [of the vehicle], splitting it in half."

"Something strange had happened," as Hayden Herrera quoted a Kahlo intimate in his biography *Frida: A Biography of Frida Kahlo*. The young woman "was totally nude. The collision had unfastened her clothes. Someone in the bus, probably a house painter, had been carrying a packet of powdered gold. This package broke, and the gold fell all over the bleeding body of Frida. When people saw her they cried, 'La bailarina, la bailarina!' With the gold on her red, bloody body, they thought she was a dancer."

This bizarre incident carried lifelong ramifications: the injuries Kahlo suffered in that crash would result in several operations over the years, give her a permanently crippled right leg, and render her unable to have children. But the accident proved fateful in another way: it was while recuperating at her home in Mexico City that Kahlo produced her first self-portrait to present to her boyfriend. "Like all the self-portraits that followed, the painting was a gift meant to join the artist and a loved one, a kind of talisman against Frida's constant fear that people wouldn't remember her, that she was unloved," wrote Chessher.

Significantly, Kahlo has called her marriage to artist Diego Rivera her "second accident." As Salomon

Grimberg, a Kahlo scholar, related to *American Way*, the artist would openly cite "the first accident, the one that nearly destroyed her body, and the second accident, the one that nearly destroyed her emotionally." Rivera was already 37 and an established artist when the 16-year-old Kahlo first met him. "Frida would bring her work to show Diego, spending afternoons watching or teasing the muralist while he worked," notes Chessher.

The two married in 1929, and almost immediately established their unconventional relationship. Reportedly, Rivera carried on affairs during this, his third marriage; he even had one with Kahlo's sister. Kahlo, understandably, felt devastated, though she never showed it publicly; the two divorced in 1939, but even that lasted only a year. "As a manifestation of her loss, [Kahlo] cut off all her hair (just as she had done when she learned of Diego's affair with her sister)," Chessher continues, "and when the two remarried, she had a few conditions: She would provide for herself from the revenue of her own work; Diego would pay half of all household expenses; and there would be no sex. Frida said the images of Rivera with other women that flashed through her mind were too much of a psychological barrier."

During all these years, though in almost constant physical distress and mental anguish, Kahlo continued to produce her self-portraits, an often unrelenting array of psychic pain. One work, *The Broken Column*, refers to the spinal injury Kahlo received in that long-ago bus crash. "In the painting, the artist stares through her tears out at the viewer, her naked body strapped with bands and pierced by nails, her torso split in half, her spine a shattered Greek column," reported Jeff Spurrier in a *Connoisseur* article. This brand of art contrasted sharply with Rivera's, or as Spurrier put it, "Moving from Rivera's jazzy black-dancer series to Kahlo's *The Broken Column* is like stepping out of a warm tropical rain into a bone-chilling blizzard of pain." Another portrait shows her head grafted onto a doe's body; this human animal is pierced through with arrows.

During the summer of 1932, with the couple in Detroit so Diego could create his classic murals for the Detroit Institute of Arts, Kahlo, four months pregnant, miscarried. "Diego found her lying in a pool of her own clotted blood, and she was rushed to the Henry Ford Hospital," noted Chessher. "While recovering in the hospital, she pleaded with her doctor for medical books: she wanted to draw the fetus exactly as it should have looked when the baby was aborted. The doctor refused, and ultimately

Diego provided her with the books. The resulting painting is titled *Henry Ford Hospital*; in it, Frida lies nude in a hospital bed with a pool of blood beneath her and a large tear falling from her eye. Her stomach is swollen, and veinlike red ribbons stretch from her hand to six images: 'little Diego,' the fetus; a pinkish torso on a pedestal; an iron vise; pelvic bones; a lavender orchid; and a snail. Her bed floats between a dark-green earth and a blue sky. Detroit's skyline is visible." "Like all Kahlo's surrealistic images, it is haunting and hypnotic, powerful far beyond its physical size," Spurrier declared of the painting.

> *"Frida's many self-portraits pierce into the deepest layers of her being and express what she found there in a manner so direct and so physical that their message seems universal."*
> —Hayden Herrera

For years, art scholars and fans have struggled to fully understand the woman staring at them from the canvases. "Frida's many self-portraits pierce into the deepest layers of her being and express what she found there in a manner so direct and so physical that their message seems universal," Herrera, author of the Kahlo biography, remarked in the *New York Times*. He added that the paintings' "intensity prompted a London critic to warn that her exhibition walls should be covered with asbestos. The Surrealist poet and essayist Andre Breton called her art a 'ribbon around a bomb.' There is a peculiar urgency that radiates from Kahlo's self-portraits. Each painting is a bid for survival, perhaps a way to exorcise pain and to confirm the artist's hold on life."

Never one to go mainstream, Kahlo often pictured herself in colorful native Mexican dress, to advertise her heritage and hide her crippled leg. She defied other conventions, too—she made no secret of her bisexuality and expressed her feminist sensibility in her work. "When Kahlo painted herself," Herrera wrote, "she did not see a passive repository of a man's gaze; she saw an active perceiver, the female painter scrutinizing her own being, and that included her sexual being." Herrera quoted a modern feminist artist, Miriam Schapiro, who cited Kahlo's influence:

"Frida is a real feminist artist in the sense that during a period in history when the accepted modes of truth were truth seen through men's eyes, she gave us truth seen through the eyes of a woman. She painted the kinds of agonies women in particular suffer, and she had the capacity both to be feminine and to function with an iron will that we associate with masculinity."

The singer Madonna, a Kahlo fan, had this to say in Herrera's article: "Frida Kahlo used her accident, her crippledness and her pain to her advantage in her work. She had a lot of odds stacked against her—the Latin American culture in which men ruled and they still do. She played the role of the submissive female, but at the same time she was in control."

If the 1930s and 1940s saw Kahlo's peak production, the 1950s became the year she gained wider recognition than for being just Mrs. Diego Rivera. In 1953, a year before her death, Kahlo was granted her first one-woman show in her homeland; it was almost the only thing that lifted the woman from the depths of depression brought on by her debilitating physical condition. As Mexican photographer Lola Alvarez Bravo recalled in Chessher's article, by the time the show was scheduled to open, Kahlo was bedridden; many thought she would be unable to attend opening night. "The night of the opening, the gallery and the public began a vigil to see if Frida would show," Chessher wrote. Added Bravo: "We closed the street where the gallery [was] so it would be very clean and wouldn't have much traffic. It was filled with people.

"We had the door closed waiting for Frida and we were all getting nervous because [she] hadn't arrived," Bravo continued. "And people were knocking; they wanted to come in. Finally we heard sirens of the ambulance, and the people made way, and Frida arrived on a stretcher." The visitors, noted the article, lined up before the artist's bed, bearing gifts and song.

The successful opening, according to Chessher, "was one of [Kahlo's] last joyful moments. A few months later, and only a month before she anticipated celebrating her 25th wedding anniversary . . . , her leg was amputated. The operation was to remove her right leg, which had become gangrenous due to poor circulation. Although she continued to paint, her last year was a mixture of drugs and alcohol, emotional outbursts, hysteria and, as always, suffering."

Kahlo lived several more months in pain, ending her diary with the words, "I hope the exit is joyful—and I hope never to come back." On July 13, 1954, Kahlo died at her home in Mexico City. Although the diary "and her last drawings suggest suicide," noted Chessher, "the reason for her death was reported a pulmonary embolism, an obstruction of one of the heart's arteries by a blood clot or air bubble." At least one Kahlo scholar, Salomon Grimberg, believes that the artist indeed took her own life, that this act would be the ultimate answer to a life of misfortune.

Given a hero's funeral in Mexico City, with 500 people following her coffin as it was paraded through the streets to national anthems and funeral marches, Kahlo ultimately surprised her fans again. As her body was taken from the coffin and prepared to be placed in a cremation furnace, "a sight as mysterious and fantastic as the artist herself took place," reports Chessher. "The moment before Frida reached the furnace, the oven's blast caused her body to sit up, her burning hair standing on end and creating an aureole around her face. One of the mourners said her face looked as if to be smiling in the center of a large sunflower."

In the years since her death Kahlo's stock has risen, partly because of the emergence of a generation ready to accept the harsh messages the artist offered. Today, reported Herrera, "she has become an international cult figure. You can buy Frida Kahlo buttons, posters, postcards, T-shirts, comics and jewelry . . . . In 1984, in recognition of Kahlo's pre-eminence among Mexican women artists—indeed, in the opinion of many Frida is the greatest painter Mexico has produced—the Mexican Government decreed her art to be national patrimony." That honor put Kahlo in the company of a score of male artists—including Diego Rivera. Madonna, one of Kahlo's most ardent collectors, has even been rumored to be starring in a forthcoming movie about Kahlo's life and work.

Through her portraits Kahlo seemingly set out her life to be scrutinized, and to demonstrate that life "is full of contradictions," said Herrera. "Her festive, lace-bedecked exterior and her mask of control, for example, contrast with the turmoil we know to be raging inside her. Even as she presents herself as a heroine, she insists that we know her vulnerability. And although her self-portraits are both candid and seductive, they are also remote and withholding: they were in part a means to keep her emotions in check. Their aloofness, of course, adds to their attraction; it heightens their sexual charge."

Sources

Books

Herrera, Hayden, *Frida: A Biography of Frida Kahlo,* Harper & Row, 1983.

Periodicals

American Way, December 1, 1990.
Connoisseur, August 1990.
Newsweek, May 27, 1991.
New York Times, October 28, 1990.

Other

Frida Kahlo: Portrait of an Artist (television documentary), Public Broadcasting System, September 1989.
The Life and Death of Frida Kahlo (film documentary).

—*Susan Salter*

Nancy Kassebaum

AP/Wide World Photos

U.S. senator

Full name, Nancy Landon Kassebaum; born July 29, 1932, in Topeka, Kan.; daughter of Alfred M. and Theo Landon; married Philip Kassebaum (an attorney; separated); children: John Philip, Linda Josephine, Richard Landon, William Alfred. *Education:* University of Kansas, B.A. in political science, 1952; University of Michigan, M.A. in diplomatic history, 1956. *Religion:* Episcopalian.

Addresses: *Office*—U.S. Senate, 302 Russell Senate Bldg., Washington, DC 20510.

Career

Worked in radio and local politics early in career; member of Washington staff of Senator James B. Pearson of Kansas, 1975-76; member of U.S. Senate from Kansas, 1979—; has served as member of the Foreign Relations Committee, the Commerce, Science, and Transportation Committee, the Budget Committee, and the Select Committee on ethics.

Sidelights

Until 1978 women only became senators by following their husbands into office. But Republican Nancy Kassebaum changed that pattern when Kansans elected her to the Senate on the basis of her own experience and abilities. A slender, five-feet-two-inches tall, the diminutive politician has described herself as "Little Dorothy from Kansas."

While raising four children just outside of Wichita, Kansas, Kassebaum gained work experience as vice-

president of KFH and KBRA radio stations owned by Kassebaum Communications. She also participated in local politics by serving on the Kansas Committee on the Humanities and Kansas Governmental Ethics Commission. And she was elected to the local school board, eventually becoming its president.

Kassebaum's separation from attorney Philip Kassebaum provided the springboard for her move to Washington. "If it weren't for the change in my family life, I wouldn't have run" for office, she told Frank W. Martin of *People.* Yet Philip Kassebaum supported his wife's new ambitions. "We're still close," Nancy Kassebaum observed. She first became a caseworker for Kansan Senator James B. Pearson. In that capacity, Kassebaum assisted in solving problems Republicans had with federal agencies.

Senator Pearson did not run for reelection in 1978, so Kassebaum decided to campaign for the seat. She ran against eight other hopefuls for the Republican nomination, winning over even her closest rival by more than 7,000 votes. In the general election she found herself up against Bill Roy, a liberal physician and lawyer representing the Democratic party. Kassebaum pulled out all the stops, capitalizing on her father's political reputation and on her own years spent raising four children. (Alf Landon had been a governor of Kansas and was once the Republican candidate for the presidency.) Her slogan was, "A Fresh Face, A Trusted Kansas Name." And Kassebaum told *Parade* magazine, "It has been said I am riding on the coattails of my dad, but I can't think of any better coattails to ride on." Yet Kassebaum was able to help herself by contributing a whopping $115,000 to the campaign budget of $841,287. (Her personal assets came to about $2.5 million at that time.)

Opponent Bill Roy attacked Kassebaum for not disclosing all information about her personal finances. Because she still filed taxes jointly with her husband, she said she wanted to safeguard his privacy. Kassebaum did reveal she earned $92,000 a year, however, and paid a mere $5,075 in taxes. This issue resulted in a loss in popularity and a closing of her early lead over Roy. Still, Kassebaum came out ahead in the end—by 85,752 votes. A favorable climate for the Republican party in her state, coupled with backing from Kansas newspapers, helped her win the election.

While in office, Kassebaum has had to make difficult—and sometimes unpopular—decisions. In 1985, for example, she upheld President Ronald Reagan's veto of a farm bill designed to bail farmers out of financial trouble. Although she hails from farm country herself, as a member of the Senate Budget Committee Kassebaum was well aware of the $222 billion federal budget deficit. In the *Christian Science Monitor*, John Dillin observed that Kassebaum was faced with a choice between her conscience and her constituents. Her conscience apparently won out when it became clear the farm bailout would climb to over a billion dollars in a short time.

Later on that year Kassebaum reacted to South African President P. W. Botha's policy address by stating in the *Christian Science Monitor*, "We need to be very firm about the need for reform in South Africa." Racial violence in that country had reached its highest point since the early 1960s, making apartheid, the South African government policy of racial separation, a major national and international issue. But Botha stated that changes at that time would lead to South Africa's "abdication and suicide." Kassebaum, who was the Republican chairman of the Senate Foreign Relations Committee's African subcommittee then, observed, "What was terribly interesting was how fuzzy Botha made the crucial sections on reform." As a result, the United States was geared toward making economic sanctions against South Africa.

In 1986 Kassebaum became involved in a financial issue concerning the United Nations (UN). She was a principal proponent of a congressional amendment to a funding authorization bill that would limit the United States' contribution to the UN to 20 percent—that is, unless the voting power in financial areas related directly to the percentage paid. (Journalists dubbed it the "Kassebaum amendment" or "Kassebaum legislation.") As it was, each country was allowed one vote in UN matters, regardless of its financial input. At the heart of the issue was that the United States had handled 25 percent of the budget—the highest amount paid by any member. The Soviet Union was the next highest payer at 11.8 percent. At the low end was a combination of 78 third world countries which, together, paid only .01 per cent, according to Gertrude Samuels in the *New Leader*.

> "I've done the grocery shopping for a long time, and that's why women tend to see a budget in a different light from men."

UN sentiments against the United States, along with the ways in which the UN's finances were being handled, were what prompted Congress's action. Kassebaum's own focus was on budget reform. When asked by Samuels to discuss the amendment, she stated: "I feel very strongly that it would do a great deal to strengthen the UN. It has become a very flabby organization." Kassebaum also observed that the "tyranny of the Third World comes about because many of *us* are afraid to say, look, we do pay a large share of the budget, we should have some say in how that's spent."

Admittedly a feminist, albeit moderate, Kassebaum calls herself a humanist above all. But in the area of fiscal control, Kassebaum has implied that there is indeed a difference in viewpoints between the sexes. "I've done the grocery shopping for a long time, and that's why women tend to see a budget in a different light from men," she said the *New Leader*. She called for spending UN funds on health care and education. By 1987 the United States' contribution to the UN coffers was cut by both the Gramm-Rudman budget reduction and Kassebaum amendments.

Another political issue that involved Kassebaum in 1987 concerned American policy in Nicaragua. With fellow Republicans William S. Cohen of Maine and Warren B. Rudman of New Hampshire, Kassebaum sent a letter to the White House seeking support for keeping the rebel (contra) movement in Nicaragua together, along with full disclosure of earlier aid sent by the United States. The senators advocated aid to the contras and were against a movement to hold back the last $40 million of the $100 million promised to that group. The letter's authors pointed the finger at the United States government for getting in the way of peace in Nicaragua. The following excerpts from the letter appeared in the *New York Times:* "It is essential for the U.S. to support diplomatic initiatives currently underway in the region . . . . [The] disproportionate emphasis on the military aspect of the policy is counterproductive."

Also in 1987 Kassebaum focused on revisions to the Constitution. As co-chairman, with former White House counsel Lloyd Cutler, of the Reformist Committee to the Constitutional System, she encouraged what *Maclean's* described as "a closer collaboration between Congress and the presidency in making laws and treaties." The committee began as a study group under Cutler in 1982, with about 200 analysts and politicians from around the country. They proposed a more parliamentary style of government, with more unification of what is now the distinctly separate House of Representatives and Senate in the legislative branch, and President and cabinet and agencies in the executive branch. This form of government is similar to what is practiced in Canada. Kassebaum told *Maclean's* that some of the people she represents "view it as almost treason to be a member of this committee." But even to Kassebaum, the concept of the cabinet including Congress members was "way too far out."

Then, early in 1981, during a Senate Budget Committee meeting, Kassebaum moved to minimize budget constraints affecting the Export-Import Bank's lending power. The resolution was in support of big business, and most committee members went along with it, according to George J. Church in *Time*. In 1989 Kassebaum was in the news again, this time for proposing a capital-gains tax on profits derived from short-term investments of pension funds. This was one idea for making money during a time when Congress was considering giving workers a voice in what happens to the funds. Kassebaum has also supported legislation geared toward helping people whose spouses must be in a nursing home. The spouses still living at home often must spend all they have simply paying nursing home fees. She and Senator Barbara Mikulski of Maryland, a Democrat, worked together on this issue.

During the George Bush-Michael Dukakis race for the presidency in 1988, it was considered a possibility that Kassebaum would be asked to become Bush's running mate. Kassebaum was asked on NBC's *Meet the Press* what she would say if Bush called her to ask if she'd be the on the ticket. She answered, "I don't expect him to call," according to the *New York Times*. She also said she was not seeking the vice presidency that election year. Elaborating in *Ms.* magazine, she explained that while she didn't think gender per se was at issue, she thought that "Bush or Dukakis will be looking to what will add strength and balance." As for a woman becoming president, she stated, "I don't think the tea leaves are right." In Senator Mikulski's opinion, however, Kassebaum "is qualified to be President. She is a multiterm United States Senator, a businesswoman, she served on committees on both commerce and on . . . foreign relations," Mikulski told *Ms.*

On the subject of women, Kassebaum has said she is particularly interested in speaking to younger women's groups. She sees these women as eager to learn how to manage their family lives and careers, and keen on finding out how to become more involved in politics—involvement Kassebaum wants to encourage. As she stated in *Ms.*, "I'm such a strong believer that a person does make a difference."

Sources

Business Week, September 25, 1989.
Christian Science Monitor, March 7, 1985; August 19, 1985.
Economist, March 12, 1988.
Maclean's, February 9, 1987.
Ms., September 1988.
New Leader, May 5-19, 1986.
New York Times, July 11, 1983.
Parade, March 18, 1979.
People, January 8, 1979; December 24, 1979.
Time, March 30, 1981.

—*Victoria France Charabati*

Jim Kelly

Professional football player

Full name, James Edward Kelly; born February 14, 1960, in East Brady, PA; son of Joe (a machinist), and Alice Kelly. *Education:* Attended University of Miami, 1980-83.

Address: *Office*—c/o Buffalo Bills, One Bills Dr., Orchard Park, NY 14127.

Career

Professional football player with the USFL Houston Gamblers, 1983-85, and NFL Buffalo Bills, 1986—.

Sidelights

Buffalo Bills quarterback Jim Kelly has been described as "a Joe Namath with good knees." The comparison seems apt. Like Namath, Kelly is a strong-armed, strong-willed football player; like Namath, he comes from the quarterback-rich country of Western Pennsylvania; and like Namath, Kelly took a cellar-dwelling team, built it up, and took it to the Super Bowl. Kelly was named the American Football Conference player of the year in 1990 after leading the Bills to their first Super Bowl in the 25-year history of the game. Kelly led the club by both words and actions. With coach Marv Levy he developed a no-huddle, lightning-paced offense that opponents could not stop. Indeed, in the AFC title game against the Los Angeles Raiders, Kelly's Bills rolled up a record 31 points. "I knew Kelly was good," Raider coach Art Shell told the *Buffalo News*. "I didn't know he was Superman."

Kelly has not, however, always performed like Superman. He has been booed by hometown fans, squabbled with teammates, and questioned his coaches. Ultimately, in the 1991 Super Bowl, the Bills fell one point short, losing to the New York Giants 20-19. The previous year Kelly had signed a seven-year, $20 million contract, making him the second-highest-paid player in the NFL, trailing only Joe Montana. Shortly afterward he told the *Buffalo News*, "There are times when you stop and say, 'God, I can't believe how far I've come—from a little dinky town like East Brady, Pa., where my mother and father each worked a couple of jobs just to make ends meet, to where I am right now, being able to buy anything and do whatever I want to do.' I've busted my butt ever since I was eight years old to get to where I am now. But I'll never forget where I came from."

Kelly comes from the area around Pittsburgh that has produced a great line of quarterbacks: John Unitas, George Blanda, Joe Montana, Dan Marino and Namath, who was Kelly's childhood hero. According to Kelly, every boy in that part of the country grows up wanting to become a Super Bowl quarterback. "I came from East Brady, a town with 800 people," Kelly told the *Buffalo News*. "There were 23 people on my football team saying 'God, wouldn't it be great to have the feeling of playing in a Super Bowl and coming out in front of a national audience.' It's the common goal." Jim's father, Joe Kelly, was a machinist by trade, but the work was not steady. Jim was the fourth of six sons. "We went through hell while we were growing up," Kelly told the *St. Louis Post-Dispatch*. "Me and my brothers would be fighting over food at the dinner table. Many times we went to bed without much to eat. Sometimes the only thing we'd eat all day was peanut butter and jelly. But we learned that we had to work for everything we got."

Kelly now believes his upbringing—three boys to a room—helped form his mental approach. "When you grow up in a family like I did, where your brothers are bigger than you, you learn not to back down," he told the *Boston Globe*. "If you did, you got your butt kicked. That toughened me up. I learned to accept challenges." And, of course, there was sports. The six boys formed a gang, playing baseball or football or basketball every day, taking on all comers. Eventually, five of the six brothers would play college football and two, Pat and Jim, would make it to the NFL. "We were wild when we were growing up," Kelly told the *Post-Dispatch*. "We used to strap on the helmets, go into the living room and beat on each other. We'd take turns diving over the top of the sofa, with the other brothers seeing how hard they could body-slam you. We just liked hard contact."

His father was equally tough on Jim. Joe Kelly saw a talent in his fourth son that went beyond all the others. Every school day for years, Joe would order little Jim to come home for lunch, but instead of eating, Joe would take Jim out back and have him throw the football through a tire hanging from the wash line. As a ten-year-old, Jim came close to winning the national Punt, Pass and Kick competition. At East Brady High he became an all-state basketball player who led his tiny school to the state championship. He was so good in football that his efforts saw the team undefeated from the middle of his sophomore year until he graduated. "By Jim's senior year we were usually ahead of everybody 30-0 at halftime, so he didn't play much," East Brady coach Terry Henry told *Sports Illustrated*. "Normally, the only incompletions he had were drops. His senior year at East Brady he was the all-conference punter, place kicker, safety, quarterback and league player of the year." Even now, Kelly says, he thinks about his high school days to cope with the stress of being a professional. "I just tell myself, 'Don't let the pressure get to you. This is what you've always dreamed

about. This is everything you've wanted to do with your life, it's here, so you might as well enjoy it. Just pretend it's like a high school football game.'" After his high-school career, Kelly realized the dream of most Pennsylvania schoolboys when he was recruited by legendary Penn State coach Joe Paterno. But Paterno wanted the 6'3" 213-pounder to play linebacker, a plan that *Los Angeles Times* columnist Jim Murray would later call, "the most spectacular instance of miscasting since somebody thought Marilyn Monroe should play a nun." Kelly's older brother Pat, who had played linebacker in the NFL, convinced Jim to stay at quarterback, arguing that quarterbacks had the highest salaries. The argument worked. Kelly passed up Penn State, instead taking a scholarship offer at the University of Miami, which in those days, had a little-known and losing program.

Miami coach Howard Schnellenberger was attracted to Kelly's bravado. Schnellenberger, who had coached Joe Namath at Alabama, said the two were comparable in approach. "Joe was street-corner cocky," Schnellenberger told *Sports Illustrated*. "Jim is rural cocky. At Miami all the players called him Country—Country Jim Kelly." Schnellenberger first started Kelly in the eighth game of his freshman season against Penn State. Miami romped. From that point on, Kelly never left the lineup. He completed 62.8 percent of his passes over four years and, perhaps more importantly, helped set the Miami football program on its way to being the NCAA's dominant team of the 1980s.

The 1983 NFL draft has become known as the "Quarterback Class" draft. Its first round included superstars John Elway and Dan Marino, along with future starters Todd Blackledge, Tony Eason and Ken O'Brien. It also included Kelly, who was taken by the Buffalo Bills with the fourteenth pick. Kelly, who enjoyed playing at Miami and had no desire to return North, told the *Washington Post*, "I cried when I was drafted by Buffalo.... You can't be a great quarterback in snow and 30 mile-an-hour wind." Instead, he bypassed the Bills and the NFL, signing a five-year, $3.3 million contract with the Houston Gamblers of the upstart United States Football League. Houston owner Jerry Argovitz convinced Kelly that in the NFL he would just be another quarterback, but in the USFL he could become a legend, much like Kelly's childhood hero. "For a new league Kelly is the kind of guy you want," Argovitz told *Sports Illustrated*. "He's like Namath—working class, talented, anti-establishment."

In Houston Kelly found a league and a system made for him. Using the so-called run-and-shoot offense in a wide-open game, he shot plenty during his two seasons there. He passed for 83 touchdowns, including 44 in 1984. He set a professional record in 1985 by passing for 3,219 yards. Along with Herschel Walker of the New York Generals, he kept the USFL alive by bringing it national attention. In August 1986, however, the USFL died. For the Bills, who had stumbled through the two previous seasons, it meant a new chance to sign Kelly. Again, he was reluctant, and asked to be traded to a West Coast team. Bills officials, however, changed his mind by convincing him they were committed to building a winner and offering him a five-year, $8 million contract—at the time, the largest in the NFL. "When Jim didn't come here in 1983, it hurt this city more than just in losing a player," Bills general manager Bill Polian told the *Philadelphia Inquirer*. "It was another chance for people to laugh at Buffalo, to say, 'Here's another guy who won't play there.' In the end, signing Jim transcended football. It became a matter of civic pride."

When he finally did sign, Kelly was given a hero's welcome in Buffalo. He flew to the city in a private jet. Fans cheered and waved as his limousine passed by on its way from the airport to the hotel, where Kelly was officially welcomed by the mayor and New York Governor Mario Cuomo. Within weeks, the Bills season-ticket base jumped by nine thousand. The Bills' record improved just marginally during Kelly's first season, going from 2-14 to 4-12. But midway through the year, the Bills fired coach Hank Bullough and replaced him with Marv Levy. It quickly became apparent that Buffalo was a team on the rise and that Kelly was the key. He threw a club-record 22 touchdowns and ranked fourth among NFL quarterbacks. He followed that up in 1987 with 19 touchdowns in the strike-shortened season as the Bills improved to 7-8.

Kelly meant much more to Buffalo than other quarterbacks in other towns. Buffalo is the second-smallest city in the NFL and its citizens view their football team with possessive pride. Wrote *Newsday*'s George Willis, "Jim Kelly lives in a city where virtually his every move becomes tomorrow's news. In contrast to living in a huge metropolis such as New York, for Kelly, being in a smaller fish bowl just makes the fish easier to see." Sometimes that has worked in Kelly's favor, making him the city's number-one hero. "Since his arrival in Buffalo," wrote Jerry Sullivan of the *Buffalo News*, "Kelly has received the sort of attention and scrutiny usually reserved for world leaders. He has become the single most identifiable person in Western New York." But sometimes Kelly chafed under the attention. In 1987

a woman sued him for allegedly throwing a drink in her face at a local bar, but her suit was thrown out of court. In 1988, a local disc jockey started a false rumor by speculating on the air that Kelly had failed a drug test. Kelly's dates and public appearances became grist for radio talk shows. "In the Buffalo market, there's only one guy they like to pick on and that's Jim Kelly," he told *Newsday*. "Everybody wants to read what I do, and a lot of things aren't true. A lot of times, I'd like to throw a right hook at somebody. But in my situation you have to hold back . . . . I've learned to let a lot of stuff go in one ear and out the other."

The scrutiny tightened in 1988 as Kelly had his first mediocre season, passing for just 13 touchdowns and throwing 17 interceptions. For the first time in his career, Kelly was booed by hometown fans. Despite the heckling, the Bills were an improving club, thanks in large part to Kelly. They went 12-4 in 1988, their best record in a decade, and advanced to the American Football Conference championship, which they lost to the Cincinnati Bengals. Things grew tougher for Kelly in 1989. He offended teammates,

Jim Kelly winds up for a pass during an AFC divisional playoff game against the Miami Dolphins in January, 1991. AP/Wide World Photos.

coaches, and fans by blaming a lineman for allowing him to get injured, yelling at a receiver on Monday Night Football, and criticizing the team's "conservative" game plan. Kelly was injured for three games, all of which the Bills won. That prompted a television station to take a fan poll, in which 57 percent said backup Frank Reich should continue to start. After Kelly's return, the Bills lost four out of five games before taking the AFC East title with a final-game victory. Even so, Kelly was the NFL's sixth-rated passer in 1989, when he completed 228 of 391 passes—38.3 percent—for 3,130 yards and 23 touchdowns, and had 18 passes intercepted in the 13 regular season games he played. "I probably will never live up to the expectations of every fan," Kelly told the *Buffalo News* after the season. "When I throw four touchdowns and we win, it's going to be great. But when I throw two interceptions and we lose, then it's going to be my fault. When you get a big contract like mine, people expect Superman feats out of you. And sometimes, it just doesn't work that way."

Before the 1990 season, Kelly signed his $20 million contract extension, and vowed to change his approach to fans and teammates. As *Miami Herald* writer Linda Robertson wrote, "Jim Kelly, the Joan Rivers of the NFL last season, has transformed himself into Dale Carnegie." Teammate Jim Tasker told *Sports Illustrated*, "One of the hardest things for Jimmy seems to be to say he's sorry. It's like Fonzie, from Happy Days, trying to admit he was wrong. But he's trying."

It worked. The "Bickering Bills" of 1989 came together and Kelly was their leader. He and Levy devised a creative, unpredictable offense in which the Bills operated without a huddle and Kelly was freed to call his own plays—making him the first NFL quarterback in 15 years to direct his offense. Given the freedom of a no-huddle offense, an elite receiving corps and a superior runner in Thurman Thomas, Kelly had his finest pro season in 1990, leading the league in passing efficiency with a 101.2 rating. Then, just to show it wasn't a fluke, he performed even better in the Bills' two playoff games, completing nearly 70 percent of his throws and guiding the team to a record two-game playoff total of 95 points.

The Bills got into the Super Bowl and found themselves facing the New York Giants. Before the game,

Sports Illustrated's Paul Zimmerman wrote, "You're Jim Kelly and a nation of quarterbacks will be in your corner Sunday. If your Buffalo Bills beat the Giants, you will go down in history as the liberator, the man who set the QBs free. You run a no-huddle offense, you call your own plays. You represent the past, the pre-Paul Brown, pre-Tom Landry era when a signal-caller was a play-caller, too. And you also represent the future, NFL coaches being a breed of copycats." The Bills did not win. But Kelly had a great game, completing 18 of 30 passes for 212 yards. In perhaps the best-played, most exciting game in Super Bowl history, the Giants won, 20-19, as Bills kicker Scott Norwood missed—by inches—a 47-yard field goal with four seconds left.

Looking at Kelly's five-year career with the Bills, teammate Kent Hull told the *St. Petersburg Times,* "Jim pressed awfully hard those first few years. The expectations put on him by the media and the fans were tremendous. When Jim Kelly signed, people thought we'd immediately go to the Super Bowl. He was Buffalo's savior. There've been a lot of rocky roads for Jim since then. When we'd lose, the blame would go to him. It was very unfair. And now that we're winning, he deserves a lot of the credit."

Sources

Boston Globe, December 29, 1988; January 23, 1991; January 27, 1991.

Buffalo News, September 7, 1989; December 30, 1989; May 10, 1990; May 13, 1990; March 24, 1990; January 27, 1991.

Fort Lauderdale News and Sun-Sentinel, September 3, 1987.

Houston Post, December 29, 1988.

Los Angeles Times, December 10, 1988; January 7, 1989; January 27, 1991.

Miami Herald, September 19, 1989.

Newsday, September 4, 1988; January 7, 1989.

Philadelphia Inquirer, January 5, 1990.

St. Louis Post-Dispatch, January 25, 1991.

St. Petersburg Times, January 27, 1991.

Sports Illustrated, July 21, 1986; September 15, 1986; September 10, 1990; January 28, 1991.

USA Today, December 28, 1988.

Washington Post, November 1, 1987.

—*Glen Macnow*

Arthur Kent

AP/Wide World Photos

Journalist and television reporter

Born December 27, 1953, in Medicine Hat, Alberta, Canada; son of Parker (a newspaper editor) and Aileen Kent; married Vickie Lynn Mercy (divorced, 1983). *Education:* Earned B.A. from Carleton University.

Addresses: *Office*—c/o NBC, 30 Rockefeller Center, New York, NY.

Career

Began journalism career at age 19 at Ottawa affiliate of Canadian network CTV; at 21 became the Canadian Broadcasting Corp.'s youngest correspondent; currently network correspondent with NBC-TV based in Rome.

Awards: Two Emmy awards, both in 1989, for coverage of the revolution in Romania and for the NBC special *China in Crisis*.

Sidelights

The Scud Stud . . . the Desert Fox . . . the Satellite Dish—anyone needing evidence of television's ability to generate celebrities within any setting need look no further than the case of NBC foreign correspondent Arthur Kent, whose charismatic coverage of the Persian Gulf War earned him a sudden league of fans.

The Rome-based correspondent was a practiced, if not particularly well known, reporter until the evening of January 20, 1991, when NBC cut away from

an NFL playoff game to broadcast the image of Kent perched on a hotel roof in Dhahran, Saudi Arabia. "This is not a drill, New York," said Kent as the night sky glowed ominously behind him. It was a Scud attack on the city, and Kent, stalwart if somewhat shaky, stayed on live as long as possible, at one point donning a gas mask in response to the chemical warfare rumors.

As a *People* article put it, Kent—who filed several more live reports over the following days—"went out on the [hotel roof] a vaguely familiar face . . . and came back a star." Indeed, even before Kent's assignment in Dhahran ended, he was receiving "mash letters in the thousands and pleading faxes," as *People* noted; before long, Kent had become a bona fide celebrity, and one of the most well known media figures in the war.

As Kent would describe it later, the onslaught of stateside female attention—and the inevitable "Scud Stud" reputation—was almost as disorienting as a missile attack. In another *People* article, Maria Wilhelm, who interviewed Kent while he was still on assignment in Saudi Arabia, quoted the reporter as finding the fame "a mind-blower. I'll pay for it down the line. Even within our own happy little community, there will be a backlash." In that vein, Kent has borne the criticism of such writers as the *Washington Post*'s Tom Shales, who told *People* that "Kent may be a male Deborah Norville (see *Newsmakers 90*).... I would never say he is untalented, but he hasn't shown us yet the magnificent powers of communication that justify this hype." A spokesman from rival network CBS also took Kent to task for doing most of his field work from the hotel roof while other reporters "dodged sniper fire to get into Kuwait City an hour after the Iraqi troops left."

Still, Kent does have a respected and varied background to draw from. The youngest child of a veteran newspaper editor (two of his siblings also work as broadcasters), Kent has been on the scene during "Romanian dictator Nicolae Ceausescu's downfall,... the toppling of the Berlin Wall, and the massacre in Beijing's Tiannamen Square," Wilhelm noted. Other projects have been less lofty: "having learned to tap tax-shelter dollars, [Kent] raised the money to produce 'a pretty exploitative package called *The Class of 1984*,'" as he described the low-budget movie to Wilhelm.

In Kent's view, his sudden popularity (which, an *Entertainment Weekly* feature notes, he regards with degrees of "interest, gratitude, mystification, embarrassment, and scorn") will not stand in the way of his principles as a reporter—chief among them, the responsibility for gathering information within the confines of governmental censorship. "I find it bizarre to be on bended knee, begging for the rights guaranteed us by the U.S. Constitution and by previously accepted standards of press-government relations," the "Scud Stud" told Wilhelm. "We want all correspondents here to do what the troops and their parents want us to do—tell them directly and truthfully what is going on."

Sources

Entertainment Weekly, February 15, 1991.
People, February 18, 1991; special issue on the Gulf War (summer 1991).

—Susan Salter

Bob Kerrey

United States senator

Full name, J. Robert Kerrey; born August 27, 1943, in Lincoln, Neb.; son of James and Elinor Kerrey; divorced; children: Benjamin, Lindsey. *Education:* University of Nebraska, B.S. in pharmacy, 1966. *Religion:* Congregationalist.

Career

Former owner, founder, and developer of Grandmother's Skillet restaurants, and fitness enterprises, including Sun Valley Bowl and Wall-Bankers Racquetball Club and Fitness Center, Nebraska. Governor of Nebraska, 1983-87; U.S. senator from Nebraska, 1988—. *Military service:* U.S. Navy, 1967-69, served in Vietnam, earned Medal of Honor, Bronze Star, Purple Heart.

Member: American Legion, Veterans of Foreign Wars, Phi Gamma Delta.

Sidelights

He is a war hero and war protestor, a liberal Democrat who has wooed and won a Republican farm state, and a man both envisioned as a future president and remembered for quitting the Nebraska governorship after a single term. U.S. senator Bob Kerrey—who attracted the national spotlight with his relationship with actress Debra Winger and has been given the nickname "Cosmic Bob" for his nonchalance and New Age-isms is repeatedly paradoxical. Kerrey was clearly shaped by Vietnam, where he earned the Congressional Medal of Honor and lost his right leg below the knee. He has nevertheless long supported amnesty for Vietnam draft dodgers, was "outraged" by the U.S. invasion of Panama, and called U.S. involvement in Central America the "same old s--- again."

In late 1990 Kerrey was one of only three senators to vote against a resolution supporting President George Bush's policy in the Persian Gulf. "No American should die in the Persian Gulf in order to hold down the price of gasoline," Kerrey was quoted as saying in *Time* magazine. Earlier, during the summer of 1989, when most of his Senate colleagues had quickly condemned a Supreme Court decision that protected flag burning as a First Amendment right, Kerrey at first supported the decision, only to change his mind later. He blasted the dissenting opinion of Chief Justice William Rehnquist, saying, as quoted in a *New Republic* cover story, that it represented "a sentimental nationalism which imposes a . . . litmus test of loyalty before expression is permitted . . . . Chief Justice Rehnquist, in his disappointing dissent, asserts that men and women fought for our flag in Vietnam." Kerrey added, "In my case, I do not remember feeling that way."

Bob Kerrey grew up in a large, middle-class family in Lincoln, Nebraska, where he "received an early baptism in political discourse around the dinner table," *Time* said in a profile of the senator. "The younger Kerreys were taught by example to express and adhere to their beliefs. . . . Before the 1960 presidential election, a dinner guest argued heatedly that if John Kennedy won, the Pope in reality would be running the country. When James Kerrey, Bob's father, persistently rejected the notion, the angered guest bolted out of the house." "Despite the family sport of wrestling with issues, Kerrey gave no early indication that within him beat the heart of a skillful, if unorthodox, politician," *Time* said. "High school classmates remember him as bright, fun loving, outspoken and very competitive, but he was not a B[ig] M[an] O[n] C[ampus]. At the University of Nebraska he held a few minor student and fraternity offices, dated often and pursued a degree in pharmacy, which he was awarded in 1966."

"You bring people home, you clean them up, put a medal around their necks, and that's what everybody thinks war is about."

After graduation he enlisted in the Navy and volunteered for the Navy's elite special forces group, the SEALS. The *New Republic* described the incident that earned him the Congressional Medal of Honor: "Kerrey's seven-man platoon raided an island in the bay of Nha Trang in an effort to capture the leader of a Viet Cong 'sapper team,' a crack sabotage unit," the article recounted. "After scaling a cliff in the dead of night in order to launch a surprise attack at daybreak, Kerrey and his men split into two groups to take up positions. But the guerrilla camp was not where they thought it would be, and the SEALS found themselves in a confused firefight. A grenade exploded in front of Kerrey, blowing off his right foot and sprinkling his face and body with shrapnel. Somehow, he stayed conscious and directed his platoon's fire. After he was removed by Medivac, the others were able to escape by boat." Kerrey was nominated for the Medal of Honor for "conspicuous gallantry." Initially, he decided to refuse the award, feeling "you bring people home, you clean them up, put a medal around their necks, and that's what everybody thinks war is about," as he was quoted as saying in the *New Republic*. He later changed his mind and accepted the medal from President Richard Nixon in May of 1970.

"Kerrey went to Vietnam a beer-drinking, gung-ho fraternity boy and came home something quite different . . . bitter and humiliated," reported *Newsweek* in 1986. He returned to Lincoln, married, and went into the restaurant business with his brother-in-law, Dean Rasmussen. They worked hard and became wealthy. "There seemed no reason why Kerrey would not continue as a successful small businessman, but by 1981, he had grown restless," stated *Time*. "With small groups of family and close friends, the talk frequently had an 'Is this all there is?' theme. Maybe, Kerrey mused, he would try politics. Sure, everyone agreed. Mayor? The legislature? No, said Kerrey. He was thinking of running for governor. Rasmussen was astonished: 'Bob was not that well-known—some community involvement, businessman, war hero. But he didn't know politicians and they didn't know him.'" Kerrey had other liabilities entering the race: he was divorced, had switched political parties—from Republican to Democrat—only three years earlier, was a liberal in a conservative farm state, and incumbent Governor Charles Thone was heavily favored to win re-election. Even so, in November of 1982 Kerrey attracted enough Republican crossovers to upset Thone by 7,000 votes.

His successes as governor, the *New Republic* allowed, were small ones: he eliminated the state's $24-million debt, "deregulated telecommunications and branch banking, and settled disputes over water rights and state regulation of fundamentalist Christian schools." And, the magazine noted, Kerrey's inexperience showed: He was unable to make progress on a major goal—raising farm prices. He drafted educational reforms and the legislature passed them, but they were never funded. Two state-chartered savings institutions failed and Kerrey couldn't cover the cost of the bailout, so depositors lost their savings. Worse, Kerrey was involved in a real estate deal with a friend who was principal owner of one of the failed banks. "There is no evidence that he interfered on behalf of a friend, but he did create an appearance of impropriety by not putting his assets in a proper blind trust," the *New Republic* revealed.

On the other hand, as *Newsweek* pointed out, Kerrey "led a farm state through a time of economic crisis and emerged with his popularity intact." Said the *New Republic*: "Few Nebraskans . . . remember Kerrey's mixed record. What stands out is his affair with Debra Winger, which began when she went to Lincoln to film *Terms of Endearment* in 1983. With the exception of the odd Bible-thumper, few had any problem with the actress staying in the official residence. On one poll 76 percent said they thought the weekend sleepovers were 'all right' and another

12 percent thought it was 'nobody's business.' (With his own approval rating at 70 percent, Kerrey joked that more people thought it was OK for Winger to stay in the governor's mansion than it was for him.)"

Kerrey chose not to run for re-election, but in March of 1987 Nebraska senator Ed Zorinsky died and Kerrey saw an opportunity. He easily defeated Republican challenger David Karnes, who had been appointed to fill Zorinsky's vacant seat. Karnes botched things for himself by declaring that Nebraska needed fewer farmers and admitting that he was so inexperienced he viewed Dan Quayle as an elder statesman. With his victory Kerrey was among a handful of newly elected senators who, despite George Bush's easy victory, strengthened Democratic control of the Senate in 1988. "The charismatic Kerrey," *Time* said after the election, "has charm and spontaneity that seem to transcend the issues .... Self-effacing and willing to admit mistakes, Kerrey has the kind of appeal that has led women to ask him to autograph their T-shirts."

In Washington, even as a junior senator, Kerrey did not hesitate to go against the grain—on flag-burning, on the Persian Gulf War, on efforts to cope with the federal deficit. Kerrey vented his impatience with Congressional budget indecisiveness in *Time* when he tersely concluded, "We will pass a budget that will reduce the deficit by $34 billion, the economy will continue to weaken and the deficit will grow beyond $300 billion." Some feel his status as a decorated, disabled war veteran "shields him from some of the voter wrath that would rain down on other politicians if they dared to be equally outspoken," as *Time* put it. Others say Kerrey is helped by good looks and the ease with which he appears on television.

The senator loses his gift for candor, however, when it comes to talking about his war wound. In 1986 when he was a guest lecturer, discussing the impact of the Vietnam War before a 900-student class at the University of California at Santa Barbara, he declined to speak personally about his injury. Instructor Walter Capps described it in *Time*: "He gave a textbook lecture. It was almost as if he was going for tenure. A woman student complained, 'You haven't told us how you *felt*.' Kerrey looked at me helplessly, but I just stared at the floor. He told the class he couldn't tell them—he would have to do something

he usually only does in the shower—sing." Kerrey then sang *And the Band Played Waltzing Matilda*, an Australian song about a soldier who lost a leg in World War I. "And when I awoke in that hospital bed," the song goes, "I saw what it had done and I wished that I were dead. Never knew there were worse things than dying. No more waltzing Matilda for me." "When he turned and limped off the stage," Capps said, "nearly everyone wept."

"Kerrey's depth of feeling is impressive," seconded the *New Republic*. "What he has yet to demonstrate is an approach to foreign policy that consists of more than lessons derived from Vietnam. He has spoken out against support for the *contras* on the Vietnam analogy and opposes any settlement in Cambodia that involves the Khmer Rouge. But where his experience doesn't guide him, Kerrey seems lost. Nothing he has done in ... the Senate has shown much sophistication about the Soviet Union, Eastern Europe, the European community, China, the Mideast or South Africa .... Signs point to a career that will be distinguished more by sensibility than substance, more by leadership in selected issues of conscience than by legislative achievements."

As for the senator's future, the *New Republic* judged: "Before he goes anywhere, Kerrey has to demonstrate some staying power. [There is] the question of whether he will have the patience to stick with the drudgery of lawmaking .... He seems almost too detached and ambivalent to be in politics at all .... He might simply walk away ... if it all becomes too 'unreal' or if he feels he is compromising his beliefs." Still, Kerrey is seen as a leading dark horse presidential contender in 1992, or more likely 1996, or as a running mate for New York governor Mario Cuomo or New Jersey senator Bill Bradley. Although his ultimate impact on American politics remains to be seen, the forthright senator will no doubt continue to make news.

Sources

The Economist, September 10, 1988.
New Republic, December 18, 1989.
Newsweek, November 3, 1986; April 9, 1990; December 12, 1990.
Time, November 21, 1988; October 29, 1990.

—David Wilkins

Jack Kevorkian

AP/Wide World Photos

Physician

Born c. 1928 in Pontiac, Mich.; never married; no children.

Addresses: *Home*—Royal Oak, MI.

Career

Licensed to practice medicine in 1953; served residency in pathology at University of Michigan Hospital in Ann Arbor beginning in 1953; internship completed at Pontiac General Hospital in Michigan; associated with Pacific Hospital, Long Beach, Calif., until 1982. Contributor to medical journals, including *Medicine and Law*. Guest on talk shows, including *Donahue, Nightline, Geraldo, Good Morning America*, and *Crossfire*.

Sidelights

Dr. Jack Kevorkian considers himself an angel of mercy, but his detractors have dubbed him "Dr. Death." He is the inventor of a controversial suicide machine, which he used on June 4, 1990, to help end the life of a 54-year-old woman who had been in the early stages of Alzheimer's disease. His action raised a storm of debate over the rights of patients to choose the moment of death, and over what role doctors should play in that decision.

As a longtime euthanasia advocate, Kevorkian is well outside the medical mainstream. His unconventional views set him apart from his colleagues early in his career. While serving his residency as a pathologist at the University of Michigan hospital, he proposed that death-row prison inmates be rendered unconscious

so that their living bodies could be used as the subjects of medical experiments. His dedication to that plan resulted in his dismissal from the hospital, and he finished his internship at Pontiac General Hospital, also in Michigan. The last staff position he held was in 1982, at the Pacific Hospital in Long Beach, California. When that job ended, he was unable to find another. He told Isabel Wilkerson in the *New York Times* that this was because his revolutionary ideas were too frightening for hospitals to accept. "I don't apply anymore," he declared. "I've written off the medical profession. I'm an outsider. I'm the lowest in the profession." Despite his estrangement from the medical establishment, there were never any formal complaints filed or disciplinary actions taken against him.

After leaving Pacific Hospital, Kevorkian moved to a small apartment in Royal Oak, Michigan. For several years he occupied himself mainly with writing for European medical journals. Many of the articles he authored reflected his continuing preoccupation with euthanasia. In one issue of *Medicine and Law*, he suggested setting up suicide clinics, writing: "The acceptance of planned death implies the establishment of well-staffed and well-organized medical clinics ('obitoria') where terminally ill patients can opt for death under controlled circumstances of compassion and decorum." In the late 1980s, Kevorkian devoted more time to developing a working suicide device. In 1989 the prototype, built with about $45 worth of materials, was ready to be used. He tried to advertise his invention in medical journals, but was turned away. Frustrated, he sold his story to local newspapers.

The publicity earned him a guest appearance on the *Donahue* talk show in April, 1990. He suggested that death row inmates be allowed to use his device rather than waiting for execution; their organs could then be used for transplants. One person who saw the show was Janet Adkins of Portland, Oregon. She was a 54-year-old professor of English, an active, vital woman who enjoyed hang gliding, backpacking, world travel, and music. In 1987 she had begun experiencing slips in memory, along with difficulties in reading music and spelling. In 1989, an Oregon doctor diagnosed the onset of Alzheimer's disease, an incurable condition that causes progressive loss of memory, insight, and other mental functions. Adkins was horrified by the prospect of experiencing a decline in the quality of her life. Her husband recalled her response to the diagnosis in *People* magazine: "Right then Janet said, 'I want to exit'" Both the Adkinses were long-standing members of the Hemlock Society, which supports doctor-assisted suicide, so her reaction was not unexpected. Her three sons persuaded their mother to try experimental therapy for Alzheimer's, but it proved ineffective. Before long, Adkins and her husband boarded a plane for Detroit, determined to consult with Dr. Kevorkian.

Over a luncheon meeting, Kevorkian confirmed the diagnosis of Alzheimer's disease, judged Adkins lucid enough to make her fateful decision, and agreed to help her see it through. Characterized by friends and family as a zestful woman, Adkins enjoyed sightseeing and shopping while Kevorkian searched for an appropriate place to initiate the suicide machine. He first called the Paramed ambulance service of Pontiac, Michigan, requesting the use of one of their vehicles, which he wanted to park outside the Oakland County Medical Examiner's Office. Shocked, they refused. The doctor then began approaching hospitals, churches, hotels, funeral homes, and the owners of vacant office buildings, seeking permission to use their facilities, but he was refused by all. (He wanted their consent in order to avoid later lawsuits.) In the end he loaded his suicide device into his 1968 Volkswagen van, and in this, on June 4, he drove with Adkins and two assistants to Groveland Oaks County Park, some 20 miles south of Flint, Michigan.

Kevorkian's machine is a simple setup that mimics an execution by lethal injection. Three bottles are suspended from a metal framework. One contains a benign saline solution; one contains thiopental, a pain killer; the other, potassium chloride. In the van, Kevorkian hooked Adkins up to heart monitors, inserted the intravenous needle, and started the saline solution flowing into her body. Adkins herself then pushed a button on the machine that replaced the saline with the thiopental. Within 25 seconds she was unconscious. Within one minute, the thiopental was replaced by potassium chloride, which stopped her heart before five minutes had passed. When the monitors showed Adkins to be truly dead, Kevorkian unhooked her from the machine and called the police.

> "My ultimate aim is to make euthanasia a positive experience. I'm trying to knock the medical profession into accepting its responsibilities, and those responsibilities include assisting their patients with death."

When the authorities arrived they seized the van and the machine, but it was unclear what crime, if any, had been committed. Assisting suicide is a felony in most states, but Michigan law is vague regarding this question. There is no clear statement against it, and legal precedents only confuse the issue. In 1920, a Michigan man was convicted of first-degree murder and sentenced to life in prison after he placed poison within the reach of his wife, who suffered from multiple sclerosis. In 1983, however, the Michigan Court of Appeals dismissed murder charges against a man who had an affair with the wife of a friend, then gave a loaded gun to the depressed husband, who shot himself with it. While the legalities of Kevorkian's case were being sorted out, an injunction was filed forbidding him to use the suicide machine again.

Kevorkian's action drew swift, sharp criticism from the medical establishment. Although the American Medical Association does support "passive euthanasia," such as witholding food from a patient in an irreversible coma, it stands firmly against active euthanasia. The reasoning, supported by medical ethicists, is that killing on demand will inevitably lead to erosion of medicine's claim to be a moral profession. Judith W. Ross, professor of medical ethics at UCLA, explained in the *New York Times* that because of the trust factor vital to good physician-patient relations, "even if society wants something like this done, someone other than doctors should do it." Once the power to kill is legitimized, many doctors say, the chances for abuse and misuse skyrocket, leaving patients justifiably uneasy about where their physicians stand on the issue and what kind of value judgements might be made about the quality of their lives. Furthermore, doctor-assisted suicide seems to be in direct conflict with the Hippocratic oath, which states: "I will give no deadly drug if asked, nor will I make a suggestion to its effect."

Adkins's case struck many as particularly misguided. She was relatively young, in excellent physical shape, and able to carry on normal conversations. Condoning her suicide paves the way for society to abdicate its responsibility for improving conditions for the elderly and chronically ill, in the opinion of many ethicists. *Newsweek* quoted Dr. Robert Butler, head of geriatrics at Manhattan's Mt. Sinai Hospital: "It's very demoralizing to hear of a 54-year-old giving up life when you're in your 80s and have heart disease and arthritis and some dementia and are still surviving, maybe working and taking care of your spouse." Creighton Phelps, the National Alzheimer's Association's vice-president for medical and scientific affairs, stated in the *Chicago Tribune* that the association was "saddened by the tragic case" but did not approve of Adkins's suicide. "We believe hers was a very personal decision . . . . However, we also must affirm the right to dignity and life for every Alzheimer's patient . . . . We advocate life."

"Even the staunchest proponents of physician-assisted suicide should be horrified at this case," claimed biomedical ethicist Susan M. Wolf in the *New York Times*, "because there were no procedural protections." Death-with-dignity groups generally advocate a witnessed, legal, written suicide request, with two independent doctors verifying that the patient's condition is irreversible and unbearable. Alzheimer's disease is notoriously difficult to identify with absolute certainty, with doctors admitting a 30 percent margin of error, and as a pathologist, Kevorkian was not well-qualified to diagnose. Furthermore, because insight is one of the first things to be lost during the course of the disease, a diagnosis of Alzheimer's is inconsistent with the statement that Adkins was able to make decisions lucidly.

Dr. Lawrence K. Altman commented on the case in the *New York Times*: "Many physicians who criticized Dr. Kevorkian's action said it was not clear what kind of patient-doctor relationship the doctor had formed with Mrs. Adkins. They specifically questioned whether depression might have clouded Mrs. Adkins's judgement and whether she had been thoroughly examined for depression, which, unlike Alzheimer's, is a treatable disease. Dr. Leon J. Epstein, a specialist in geriatric psychiatry at the University of California at San Francisco, said it was common for patients with Alzheimer's and other degenerative diseases to become depressed and even suicidal after learning the diagnosis. But when depression is diagnosed and effectively treated, he said, most of them change their minds."

Adkins's family and friends insist that she was competent to make her decision and had every right to do so, and they defend Kevorkian's part in her death. "Quality of life was everything with her," stated her son, Neil, in the *New York Times*. "She wanted to die with her dignity intact." Kevorkian claimed in the *Chicago Tribune*: "She thanked me as she was going under . . . . She understood everything. She just couldn't live the life she wanted to live anymore." He has dismissed his critics as "brainwashed ethicists," "nonthinking physicians," and "religious nuts," and scoffed at the idea that his invention would encourage people to kill themselves. "They already do that," he pointed out to Lisa Belkin in the *New York Times*. "They jump out of buildings, they blow their brains out, they drink lye. Is that better? . . . My ultimate aim is to make euthanasia a positive experience. I'm trying to knock the medical profession into accepting its responsibilities, and those responsibilities include assisting their patients with death." Whether he is right or wrong in his convictions, Kevorkian has "dramatized the issue of the right to die in a way few physicians have in the past," according to Dr. Altman. "The publicity . . . is challenging more people to take public stands about the issue, to think about the way they want to die if they become chronically ill and to discuss those wishes with their families and friends."

Sources

Chicago Tribune, June 6, 1990.
Detroit Free Press, December 11, 1990.
Los Angeles Times, June 5, 1990; June 8, 1990.
Newsweek, June 18, 1990.
New York Times, June 6, 1990; June 7, 1990; June 10, 1990; June 12, 1990.
People, June 25, 1990.
Time, June 18, 1990.
Washington Post, June 6, 1990; June 8, 1990.

—Joan Goldsworthy

Val Kilmer

Actor

Married to Joanne Whalley-Kilmer (an actress). *Education:* Attended the Juilliard School.

Address: *Home*—Taos, New Mexico.

Career

At age 17 became youngest student ever admitted to drama division at the Juilliard School; made professional theatrical debut in Joseph Papp's *Henry IV, Part One;* made film debut in *Top Secret!* (1984); appeared in films *Real Genius, Willow, Top Gun, Kill Me Again,* and *The Doors;* has recorded one mini-album under name Nick Rivers (character from *Top Secret!*); writes poetry.

Sidelights

There is perhaps no more difficult role for any actor than that of re-creating the life of a person who actually lived, especially when that person's memory is still fresh in the minds of the audience. No matter how accurately the actor portrays the voice, gestures, and movements of the character, the expectations of the audience are so great that they are nearly always left unsatisfied. And then there is the temptation for the actor to give in to heavy demands for authenticity to the point of resorting to mimicry. "So-and-So's performance is a shabby imitation," the critics will inevitably cry. Often then, the challenge of a screen biography is a no-win proposition for an actor. The power of the viewer's memory is too great for the actor's illusion to overcome.

These were the almost insurmountable obstacles facing actor Val Kilmer as he prepared for the role of the rock legend Jim Morrison, lead singer for the group The Doors. Not only was Morrison a relative contemporary of most of the potential viewing audience (having died in 1970), he was also such a very distinct, outrageous character that at times he even seemed to be acting himself, making Kilmer's desire to avoid mimicry even more difficult.

The actor pulled it off. Kilmer's performance in the Oliver Stone film *The Doors* was considered one of the greatest portrayals of a music giant in the history of film, and will receive serious Oscar consideration in the spring of 1992. Film critics were dazzled. "Mr. Kilmer's performance...is so right it goes well beyond the uncanny," wrote Janet Maslin in the *New York Times.* "Leading dauntingly with his chin, projecting sexy insolence, never losing sight of the singer's magnetism, Mr. Kilmer captures all of Morrison's reckless, insinuating appeal."

When Jerry Hopkins, a Morrison confidante and author of the best-selling biography of the singer, *No One Here Gets Out Alive,* first met Kilmer in a restaurant prior to shooting of the film, he was momentarily shocked by Kilmer's likeness to Morrison: "Down the hall I saw Jim Morrison using the pay phone," Hopkins wrote in *American Film.* "I'd forgotten he was so tall. I laughed at myself. Morrison was dead, and this was Val Kilmer, the actor selected by [Oliver] Stone to play the sixties'

'Lizard King.' It was eerie. The start of principal photography was two months off, and Kilmer was already into the part: the wardrobe, the hair, the manner, the grin.''

Just 31 years old when he filmed *The Doors* (interestingly, he was playing Morrison between the ages of 19 and 27), Kilmer will be hard-pressed in the future to top this tour-de-force performance, despite the fact that it also represented his first real superstar turn, signaling his blossoming into a major-league leading man. So convincing was his performance that even two-thirds of the remaining Doors members, skeptical to the end because of the many stops and starts to the project over the years, have admitted that Kilmer was perfect for the part. "When I first met Val, I didn't think he was right," said former Doors guitarist Robby Krieger in *Rolling Stone.* "He didn't look the part, and his voice didn't sound like Jim's at all. But when he put on makeup and got into the part, he reminded me of Jim in everything from his voice to his manner. It was like having him back for a while. Spooky."

Of the surviving Doors, only keyboardist Ray Manzarek could not lend full acceptance to the film or the actor chosen to play Morrison. "It hurts me to disappoint someone who knows the truth," Kilmer told *Rolling Stone.* "But if you interviewed 100 people about Jim Morrison, you come away with 135 versions of the guy. The people I was directly involved with convinced me I was on the right track, and what else can you ask for as an actor?"

In a conversation with *Interview* magazine, Kilmer expounded further on the struggle he faced when trying to be true to Morrison and his family while still satisfying a director and an entire generation of rock fans. "You...come to realize that in playing this person, the people who actually knew him, the people whose lives he's still very important to, will be hurt, because you're not gonna do their version of him. And also, there are always things that you purposely want to adjust or change, because it'll make the story better or because that's your desire. But you feel a lot of pain because of it. You're torn between acting and obligation."

Growing up in the generation that came immediately after the huge baby-boom set that revolutionized rock music and society in the 1960s, Kilmer was not particularly attached to Morrison or the sixties scene as a youth. He was only just coming of age in California's San Fernando Valley when the 1960s era of turbulence and change was giving way to the more sedate, conservative seventies. But Kilmer and his two brothers did receive a somewhat vicarious

education of what the sixties were all about through the adventures of their male "nanny," Jan Dixon, a Vietnam veteran and art student who explained some of the mysteries of the boys' senior generation. "He was involved in the scene," Kilmer said of Dixon in *Interview.* "I remember years ago, driving in the Mustang on the freeway, and we passed the Hollywood Bowl. The Doors were playing—and the traffic jams! He had tickets, and he was rushing us home so he could go back and see this show. So we kind of had a peek into what was going on, even though we were too young, 'cause he was in my living room. He was the whole kit and kaboodle: an artist, and he had just got back from Vietnam maybe inside a year....It was a period when I was waking up to something right outside the neighborhood. There were all the deaths, peoples' older brothers and sisters who had OD'd or freaked out. And on the other hand, there was the grooviness of it all. Everything was so cool."

Kilmer says that while he was aware of the Doors growing up, and heard their hits on the radio, he never developed any sort of obsession about wanting to be like Jim Morrison. In fact, by age 17 he was already accomplished and serious enough about acting to become the youngest student ever admitted to the drama division at the Juilliard School.

At Juilliard he co-wrote and starred in a school play that attracted the attention of producer Joseph Papp, who cast Kilmer in his *Henry IV, Part One.* A Broadway run in the play *Slab Boys* with Sean Penn and Kevin Bacon led to Kilmer's motion picture debut in the 1984 movie *Top Secret!* Next came his role as a brilliant but irreverent physics student in *Real Genius,* then a turn as the wisecracking swashbuckler Madmartigan in *Willow,* a character *Newsweek's* David Ansen called "Han Solo in disguise." Kilmer made the difficult move to second fiddle appear easy when he played arch-rival to the enormously popular Tom Cruise in the showy Cruise vehicle *Top Gun.* His last role before *The Doors* came in the mystery-thriller *Kill Me Again,* which co-starred his wife, Joanne Whalley, whom Kilmer met on the *Willow* set.

By the time Kilmer had gotten wind of a possible movie on the Doors in the late 1980s, the idea had already been kicking around Hollywood for nine years. Hopkins and co-author Danny Sugerman had sold and then re-purchased the movie rights to *No One Here Gets Out Alive* four times during that period. Hopkins wrote in *American Film* of the "labyrinthine trail" of producers, directors, and actors who had at one time or another expressed interest in doing the movie. Among the producers and directors were such heavyweights as Jerry Weintraub, Brian DePalma, Francis Ford Coppola, Martin Scorsese, and William Freidkin; actors John Travolta, Michael O'Keefe, Richard Gere, and Tom Cruise, along with rock singers Michael Hutchence of INXS and Bono of U2, were all rumored at different times to be playing Morrison.

It took the energy and enthusiasm of Oliver Stone, arguably the hottest director in Hollywood and a man with a passionate interest in the 1960s, to write an acceptable script and get the project past the planning stages and into high gear. Stone considered several actors to portray Morrison, including Kilmer, whom he had seen in *Willow*. The two got together for an informal interview, the subject being how best to play Morrison, and then Stone asked Kilmer if he could sing. The actor said he could. After recording four Doors tunes, Kilmer then got the idea to perform the songs on videotape, like an MTV video, to give Stone a clear visual picture of how he would appear in the role. The further he got into the project, the more Kilmer became obsessed with playing the part, and the more he pestered Stone to let him do it.

Finally it was official. The production firm Carolco would produce the movie, Stone would direct using his own script, and Kilmer would play Jim Morrison. Although Kilmer, especially with a little make-up and his hair grown long, bears a striking physical resemblance to Morrison, it was probably his singing ability that eventually won him the part—and the praise of a majority of the critics. "Musically . . . Mr. Kilmer is unerringly good," wrote Maslin in the *New York Times*. "If anything he sounds even more like Morrison when singing a cappella, which he does in a couple of scenes, than when his extremely service-able new vocal readings are integrated into pre-existing Doors recordings." Kilmer was able to get the Morrison sound down by working closely with Paul Rothchild, who produced every album the Doors ever made, and with real-life Doors guitarist Krieger and drummer John Densmore, who assisted on site; he even went so far as to smoke a special cigarette for non-smokers to give his voice a harder edge.

Kilmer used other tricks to get into the Morrison character. He watched as much concert footage as he could of Doors shows and consulted choreographer Paula Abdul to get the hang of Morrison's distinctive stage prowl. He also located a pair of leather pants that Morrison actually wore—some say just about every day. "Some guy in San Diego had them," Kilmer told *Rolling Stone*. "They were used and pretty gamy. I put them on for fun, but they didn't fit. They came up to my kneecaps—he was riding them high. I don't know how the women of the world or the heavy-metal guys wear them that tight. It made me walk funny." Kilmer also beefed up to 190 pounds from his normal 155 to portray the singer in his later, more bloated years.

But the skill with which Kilmer pulled off his portrayal of the ultimate self-indulgent, excessive Bacchanalian was just that—the craft of an actor rather than the actual over-indulgence that a method actor might perhaps have employed to get fully into character. "Part of the beauty of doing a story about a famous drunk is that it gives you the chance to say, 'DON'T DO THIS,' in real big letters," Kilmer said in *Rolling Stone*.

Continuing on this same theme in *Interview*, the actor said that experiencing the decline of Morrison in the film taught him something about the importance of discipline in art. Since filming completed, "I've never been more religious or healthy," Kilmer said. "I believe you have to have this special kind of insanity to be insane while you're acting . . . I think I've found through playing this character an opportunity to reexperience some of my life, to reevaluate what may or may not have happened. It seems to have strengthened things I have always believed . . . to believe in God, and to believe in a reality that's a foundation for living. To believe and understand. To put yourself on the line, to confront that . . . that *fear*."

Sources

American Film, October 1990.
Interview, November 1990.
New York Times, March 1, 1991.
Rolling Stone, April 4, 1991.

—*David Collins*

John Kluge

Broadcasting and advertising entrepreneur

Full name, John Werner Kluge; surname pronounced KLOO-ghee; born September 21, 1914, in Chemnitz, Germany; came to United States, c. 1922; son of Fritz and Gertrude (Donj) Kluge; married third wife, Patricia Rose Gay, 1981 (divorced, June 1990); children: Samantha, Joseph B. *Education:* Attended Wayne State University; Columbia University, B.A., 1947.

Addresses: *Office*—Metromedia, Inc., 1 Harmon Plaza, Secaucus, NJ 07094.

Career

Otten Bros. Inc., Detroit, Mich., vice-president and sales manager, 1937-41; WGAY radio station, Silver Spring, Md., director, 1946-59; executive with numerous broadcasting companies, 1953-60, including St. Louis Broadcasting Corp., Pittsburgh Broadcasting Co., Capitol Broadcasting Co. (Nashville), Associated Broadcasters, Inc. (Fort Worth-Dallas), Western New York Broadcasting Co. (Buffalo), Washington Planagraph Co., Mid-Florida Radio Corp. (Orlando), and Mid-Florida Television Corp.; owner of Kluge Investment Co., 1959-60; Metromedia, Inc., New York City (including metropolitan broadcasting, worldwide broadcasting, Foster & Kleiser, and outdoor advertising divisions), chairman of the board, president, and director. Has served in executive capacities with numerous other companies, including Kluge, Finkelstein & Co. (food brokers), Tri-Suburban Broadcasting Corp., Marriott-Hot Shoppes, Inc., Chock Full O' Nuts Corp., National

Bank of Maryland, Waldorf Astoria Corp., Just One Break, Inc., Belding Heminway Co., Inc., and numerous others. Affiliated with numerous professional and civic associations.

Sidelights

John Kluge, the richest individual in the United States, got that way through a series of well-timed investments in industries ranging from broadcasting to computer software, restaurants to robotic painting, advertising media to entertainment properties. His 40-year track record of building empires from the ground up has earned him the reputation as the last great American entrepreneur.

Under his stewardship, the broadcasting company, Metromedia, grew into the largest independent television business in the United States. Although the tycoon sold Metromedia's seven lucrative local stations for an astounding $2 billion in 1985, he retained the Metromedia name and continued to develop interests in television and radio broadcasting, outdoor advertising, telecommunications, entertainment, and food wholesaling.

The list of business interests he has owned is an astoundingly diverse one. It includes the Ice Capades and the Harlem Globetrotters; music publishing companies holding such titles as *Fiddler on the Roof, Zorba the Greek,* and *Cabaret;* television production and syndication, including rights to the *Merv Griffin Show, Playbill* magazine, and advertising media including transit advertising and direct mail advertising. In recent years Mr. Kluge has raised his investment in the highly successful Orion Pictures, the movie production company, and bought the Ponderosa Steak chain and other restaurant interests.

Kluge is not especially articulate and does not enjoy bantering with reporters and talk show hosts; accordingly, the media tend to call him "reclusive." In a rare in-depth interview given to *Forbes* magazine in October 1990, he described his business philosophy to Vicki Contravespi: "I think the ability to take risks is crucial. I never ordinarily take on things that I can't see some end to, where you pile risks on risks. We are seeing a time where risks on risks are being liquidated. There's just an awful lot of excesses. I think when this period is over, the people who have gone through it will be a lot more seasoned. One is very fortunate if one learns that early." He went on, "My whole thrust has always been going into a business that I would like." Not only like, but understand. "Young entrepreneurs should spend an awful lot of time thinking about what they want to go into. The last thing you want to do, unless it's a very unusual situation, is to invest money. You should have a fund of knowledge of something and out of that you make your mind. Money is not a fund of knowledge."

That philosophy has not stopped him, however, from buying into deals that seemed instinctively right. Often those deals have paid off handsomely. As a young man in the dawn of television, Kluge became aware of the medium as an investment possibility when he ran into an acquaintance on a street in Washington, who conversationally mentioned the old Dumont Broadcasting network going up for sale. That led to his buying the Baltimore TV station. Some forty years later, he sold his interests in broadcasting for $2 billion based not on specific market research but because he "had the feeling" that the days of fast growth and high profitability in television were over.

Luck and gut feeling; two characteristics most tycoons would likely disavow. Not John Kluge. "The greatest factor in my life, and I know entrepreneurial people don't want to express it, they think it diminishes them, but luck plays a large part." Often described as "incredibly lucky" by business associates, Kluge happens to be a sharp card player: poker, bridge, blackjack are among his favorites. In

her *Forbes* profile, Vicki Contravespi proclaimed that "the essence of these games—the systematic weighing of risks against rewards against mathematical probabilities—is the essence of business itself." As an undergraduate student at Columbia, Kluge was a notorious money player, amassing a $7,000 pot by the time he graduated in 1937. The all-night gambling stopped only when a dean threatened him with expulsion.

> *"I think the ability to take risks is crucial....There's just an awful lot of excesses. I think when the period is over, the people who have gone through it will be a lot more seasoned."*

Born in Chemnitz, Germany, in 1914, Kluge grew up in Detroit where his mother resettled and remarried when he was 8. He left home in his teens and supported himself working on a Ford Motors assembly line, among other jobs. In 1933 he won a scholarship to Columbia, from which he earned a degree in economics. Kluge then went to work for a small paper company, where he helped increase sales, and left owning a third of the company. Serving Army intelligence during World War II, he returned with little taste for resuming a career in the employ of others. He bought a small Maryland radio station, sold it at a profit, and promptly invested in another radio station.

It was not glamour that lured Kluge into broadcasting, but the lure of profits. He has often branched out into more mundane enterprises. In 1951 he invested in a Baltimore food brokerage business, and set to work building that up. He succeeded dramatically. A few years later he sold a majority stake in the company, and sunk the profits into a brand new industry, television.

Forsaking the glamour of network TV, John Kluge was attracted to the opposite end of the spectrum, the independent broadcasters. There was less money to be made, perhaps, but the stakes were lower. He assembled an investment group and soon owned stations in New York, Baltimore/Washington, Los Angeles, and Houston. "He had the imagination to believe you could make it with independents if you got into the major markets," Albert P. Krivin, a retired industry consultant, told *Fortune* writer Strat Sherman in 1984.

The media magnate worked throughout the decade turning his chain of independents, which he renamed Metromedia, into a lucrative enterprise. He concentrated on cutting costs and maximizing revenues. First he moved Metromedia's operations across the Hudson River to Secaucus, New Jersey, where rents were lower. (He kept the chairman's office in Manhattan's fashionable Lincoln Center district, however.)

He was similarly tight-fisted in buying broadcast inventory. Metromedia's programming would win few awards for its schedule of network situation comedies, low budget movies, and shoestring local news coverage. Lacking the big audience shares that went to the network affiliates, Metromedia got smaller audiences at a fractional cost. In big cities, however, the numbers added up. As Sherman wrote in *Fortune*, "Cost control comes naturally to Kluge, who was a fiend for productivity long before it was chic. He knows how to trim fat from a payroll though he's a bit squeamish about firing executives: he tends to delegate the hatchet work, then offer a fat severance check and sometimes a hug. An avid reader of weekly profit & loss statements, he has never hesitated to pick up the phone and badger a free-spending subordinate, no matter how lowly."

But not every well struck oil. One disastrous misstep was Kluge's purchase of the niche magazine *Diplomat*. That soon folded. He also bought the advertising concession from New York's transit authority not realizing that the inevitable graffiti would render the ads unreadable. Envisioning the formation of a fourth network—impossible for Metromedia under Federal Communications Commission rules—he tried instead to arrange a sale to Transamerica for $300 million in stock. The sputtering economy prevented that deal, however, leaving Kluge stuck, momentarily, with Metromedia. It turned out to be a fortunate break for the tycoon.

After several years of poor advertising revenues industrywide, in 1976 the advertisers were back, and once again Kluge was prepared to seize the moment. In a good cash position, Metromedia bought syndication rights to *M*A*S*H* and other one-time hit network shows with proven audiences. Metromedia stations suddenly were offering a higher quality of programming; more people tuned in. With bigger audiences Kluge could raise advertising rates. More cash flowed in.

Not one to sit still, Kluge cooked up a deal to take the company private. It was the Wall Street deal of the year. By structuring a $1.3 billion leveraged buyout on unusually favorable terms in April 1984, Kluge astonished Wall Street observers. Starting out owning about a quarter of the company, he ended up owning three-quarters. Rather than spending money, he ended up pocketing $115 million in cash and securities. Kluge "once again is living up to his name: 'klug' means smart in German," quipped *Forbes* staff writer Allan Sloan.

Kluge was equally smart a year later when he completed another transaction, this time selling the seven stations outright to a partnership of Rupert Murdoch and Marvin Davis. The cost: just over $92 billion. Several cents over, that is. The extra change is "a matter of principle on Kluge's side," griped Murdoch lawyer Howard Squadron to Kluge-watcher Sloan. According to the standards of the broadcasting industry, Kluge had gotten top dollar.

Now, out of TV, with two billion dollars (and several cents) in his pockets, Kluge again took a qualified risk by sinking his fortune in a new industry. This time it was telecommunications. With his TV stations gone, Metromedia was stripped to several minor businesses, primarily the manufacture and distribution of paging devices—beepers and mobile telephones. Kluge turned his attention to this nascent industry. Both technologies had attracted early interest mainly as status symbols. As the decade progressed, however, they became pervasive business tools. In managing this new venture, Kluge retraced the steps he took in the early days of TV: buying a license in a major market at an affordable price, then waiting as the market evolved. Like broadcast frequencies, telecommunications frequencies are regulated—and limited—by Washington. Metromedia has also bought several long-distance telephone services and a satellite-based telephone service.

Once again, Kluge was either very lucky or very smart. Telecommunications suddenly got hot—very hot. It was hard to find a doctor, repairman, junior executive, or drug courier without a telephone beeper adorning his belt. And car phones became virtually standard equipment on Mercedes and BMWs. Even high school kids were buying private mobile phones. All of this benefitted John Kluge enormously. His wealth, which *Forbes* magazine estimated at $3.2 billion in 1988, swelled to "over $5.2 billion" in 1989. That was enough to land him atop the magazine's roster of the richest of the rich. The 1990 list estimated his wealth "conservatively" at $5.6 billion.

Privately, John Kluge lived rather inconspicuously until, in 1981, he wed his third wife, 32-year-old Patricia Rose Gay. The bride, born in Baghdad of a Scottish-Iraqi mother and British father, had moved to England at 16 and was last married to the publisher of *Knave*, the British skin magazine. She had appeared nude in the magazine, an indiscretion that her 67-year-old groom was prepared to overlook. The couple exchanged vows in New York City's St. Patrick's Cathedral.

The newlyweds soon moved above the store, so to speak, by converting the eighth floor of the Metromedia building into an ornate pied-a-terre. Trees are rooted in the marble floors, spreading out under the skylight; a waterfall runs down the wall of the outside balcony; the artwork decorating the doors of the private elevator are the work of Joan Miro. And so on. "The apartment of Patricia and John Kluge evokes a James Bondian luxe," gushed Francesca Stanfill, reviewing the apartment for *Vogue* magazine. The apartment is furnished with an array of Islamic and African pieces, Hellenic vases, and the canvasses of such contemporary modernists as Jackson Pollock, Man Ray, and Miro. A major design firm and an architecture firm were hired to make the place livable. "We felt very strongly that art and architecture should be combined," the former *Knave* model told Stanfill.

The real Kluge residence, however, is the 250-room Georgian mansion, Albemarle, situated on 10,000 acres in rural Virginia. Entertaining fellow moguls there nearly every weekend, John Kluge holds frequent shoots for his guests, handing out antique guns to aim at birds released by a large staff of British-born retainers. Neighbors began pressing charges when their household pets turned up dead or maimed, and local wildlife officials charged the staff with slaughtering hawks, a protected species. Staff members were found guilty in 1988.

Kluge divorced Patricia in June 1990, providing an estimated $80 million a year in alimony. Mansions and shoots aside, what John Kluge really likes best is going to the office. He told *Forbes*'s Contravespi: "Work isn't really work for me. I didn't think I've ever really 'worked' in my life, because 'work' to me means that you're really doing something that you don't like. I hate to tell you this, but I've never liked the weekend in my life. I was enthusiastic about Monday morning from the day I left college."

Sources

Business Week, July 8, 1985; July 14, 1986.
Forbes, April 1, 1971; June 8, 1981; December 17, 1984; June 2, 1985; March 21, 1988; August 7, 1989; October 22, 1990.
Fortune, June 4, 1990.
Newsweek, July 14, 1986.
Reader's Digest, November 1988.
U.S. News & World Report, June 27, 1988.
Vogue, January 1988.

—Warren Strugatch

Jeff Koons

Artist

Born c. 1955 in York, PA; son of a furniture salesman and a housewife. *Education:* Maryland Institute of Art, M.F.A., 1976.

Addresses: *Office*—c/o Jeff Koons Productions, New York, NY.

Career

Formerly a commodities broker on Wall Street; began gaining prominence displaying sculptures in mid-1980s. Founder of Lambert-Koons advertising agency, New York, NY.

Sidelights

A connoisseur of kitsch who has inspired indignation and delight" is how Mark Stevens, in a *Vanity Fair* article, described artist Jeff Koons, a most outspoken and outgoing sculptor. In the 1980s spirit of "deconstructionist" and "ironic" art forms, Koons uses the familiar as a stock in trade. At the same time, the artist has sought to make himself as familiar to the public as possible. In 1990 he announced his engagement to Cicciolina, the former porn star who got herself elected a deputy to the Italian Parliament. In Italy, at least, they have become a Couple of the Moment: "Whenever they appear in public, autograph seekers besiege her and paparazzi trample over one another in a rush to record their every move," reports *Vogue*'s Dodie Kazanjian.

As for Koons's professional life, it has been one of controversy mounted upon success. Comparing Koons to another pop artist, Andy Warhol, Stevens noted: "Like Warhol, he challenges sentimental expectations and behaves like a money-hungry operator. Every article written about him mentions that he once was a Wall Street commodities broker out for a buck. He makes no bones about his interest in celebrity; he says things intended to make you choke on their outrageousness. [Koons] has little use for literature and books, he says, reading only trendy magazines in order to keep up with what's hot. He does not aspire to the role of outsider, but instead takes pride in courting conventional success."

Celebrity is seldom accidental, and Koons makes no secret of his master plan. "My art and my life are totally one," he said in the *Vogue* piece. "I have everything at my disposal, and I'm doing exactly what I want to do. I have my platform; I have the attention, and my voice can be heard. This is the time for Jeff Koons." No shrinking violet, Koons uses self-promotion as aggressively as any artist ever has. "To promote his [1988] exhibition at New York's Sonnabend Gallery," remarked Stevens, "Koons created four different ads for the various art magazines. They were funny—schlock fantasies of self-importance and the good life that made the usual flattery and sexual innuendo of Madison Avenue look tame. In one, Koons surrounded himself with a bevy of bimbos bearing gifts and a dead, stuffed animal. In another, he sits cross-legged between two seals decked out in grotesque floral arrangements."

All this self-promotion might work against Koons if his art didn't live up to the hype. But according to Stevens, Koons' work deserves attention. The writer recalled seeing an early Koons sculpture called "Rabbit": "Made from a children's blow-up toy cast in stainless steel, it recalls in its reductive shape and otherworldly gleam several great Brancusis. By making a joke of one of the most elevated of modern sculptors, the Bunny is pretty offensive—it turns an art-world saint into Hugh Hefner." In subsequent sculptures, Stevens continued, Koons "makes use of cartoony characters—centerfold sirens, cute pigs, and sugary portrayals of childhood—all of which are turned into pricey porcelains and polychromed wood. In one recent piece...the Pink Panther is portrayed embracing a busty blonde; in another, [pop star] Michael Jackson and a chimp named Bubbles appear in whiteface."

In *Vogue*, a museum curator offered an assenting view: Though claiming that Koons is "straight from Mars...sort of an idiot savant," the curator also believes that "Koons must be taken seriously," as Kazanjian wrote. "There is a consensus that his work is strangely disturbing, undeniably powerful, and unlike anything else being done today."

"Art is communication, and that's the area that's really left for artists—communication," Koons told *Vogue*. "When a Picasso goes for $47 million, where's the value of money? The information in that painting has already been disseminated throughout the culture. The painting isn't a place of storage....This is why I think art has to compete and be more of a manipulator and a seducer, a propagandist tool. That's the only place it can really be effective today."

Sources

Vanity Fair, December 1989.
Vogue, September 1989, August, 1990.

—*Susan Salter*

Larry Kramer

Author and activist

Born June 25, 1935, in Bridgeport, Conn.; son of George L. (an attorney) and Rea W. (a social worker; maiden name, Wishengrad) Kramer. *Education:* Yale University, B.A., 1957.

Addresses: *Home and office*—New York, NY.

Career

Screenwriter, playwright, and novelist. Associated with training programs in New York, N.Y., for William Morris Agency, 1958, and for Columbia Pictures, 1958-59; Columbia Pictures, assistant story editor in New York City, 1960-61, and production executive in London, England, 1961-65; assistant to president of United Artists, 1965; associate producer of motion picture *Here We Go Round the Mulberry Bush*, 1967; producer of motion picture *Women in Love*, 1969. Co-founder of Gay Men's Health Crisis in New York City, 1981; founder of ACT-UP (AIDS Coalition to Unleash Power), 1987.

Awards: Academy Award nomination for best screenplay from Academy of Motion Picture Arts and Sciences, and nomination from the British Film Academy for best screenplay, both 1970, both for *Women in Love*; Dramatists Guild Marton Award, City Lights Award for best play of the year, Sarah Siddons Award for best play of the year, and Olivier Award nomination for best play, all 1986, all for *The Normal Heart*; Arts and Communication Award from the Human Rights Campaign Fund, 1987.

AP/Wide World Photos

Sidelights

Had Larry Kramer never become an activist, he would have been well enough remembered as a writer of such screenplays as the adaptation of D. H. Lawrence's *Women in Love* and such novels as the critically acclaimed *Faggots*. But Kramer's conscience, stirred by the government's slow response to the spread of AIDS in America, drove him to help found the Gay Men's Health Crisis (GMHC) in 1981.

By 1985, with the AIDS epidemic increasing and public empathy for many of its victims on the wane, Kramer wrote what is considered a premier political tract on the issue, his play *The Normal Heart*. The drama tells the story of how one man, gay activist Ned Weeks, rails at both community apathy and at political infighting among homosexual leaders in his attempt to curb the spread of the syndrome. Because Weeks is abrasive, even fanatical, he is rejected by his peers.

Many critics and audiences saw parallels between the protagonist and the author—both are outspoken in their condemnation of the Establishment, and both name names of those individuals (like New York's then-mayor, Ed Koch) they feel are hindering progress in the battle against AIDS. As a political piece more than a traditional drama, *The Normal Heart* received widespread praise and went on to be staged worldwide.

But while the play established its author as a writer of importance, and while the GMHC became one of the largest service agencies for AIDS patients in America, Kramer himself became "a lightning rod for straight and gay critics alike," as *People* reporter Ken Gross put it, "accused of exaggerating the AIDS crisis and of being antierotic for advocating a nonpromiscuous life-style." Kramer countered by calling the GMHC "a sad organization of sissies" in a *New York Times* article.

By 1987 Kramer had founded the activist group AIDS Coalition to Unleash Power (ACT-UP) to "call once again for riots in the streets to arouse what he regards as an indifferent and often hostile public," according to Gross. As *Rolling Stone* writer David Handleman described it, Kramer stirred up the first ACT-UP members during a lecture when he "told two-thirds of the room to stand up and said, 'At the rate we are going, you could be dead in five years. Two-thirds of this room . . . . If what you are hearing doesn't rouse you to anger, fury, rage and action, gay men will have no future here on earth.'"

Anger, fury, rage, and action have characterized ACT-UP's methods ever since. Their methods include, as Gross related, "a militant show of protest—taunting police, storming barricades, heckling government speakers and staging traffic-stopping 'die-ins' by lying in the street to symbolize AIDS deaths."

One of Kramer's prime targets is America's health system. It is through these organizations that Kramer discovered that "AZT—the only government-approved drug to fight the HIV virus—was egregiously overpriced," as Gross wrote. "There is also an aerosol treatment in London that costs $26," Kramer told Gross. "Here it costs up to $200. Same stuff. Same amount. Somebody's making big profits."

Despite his outspoken reputation, Kramer described himself to Gross as "a pussycat." He added that he fights so passionately because "we have nothing to lose; we've already lost the war. Soon we'll all be gone." This pronouncement hits home particularly for Kramer; he has been diagnosed with HIV, the AIDS-causing virus. "He is writing the novel that he believes will be his last," Gross noted. "It is called *Search for My Heart No Longer*, and it is autobiographical." "I need five more years to finish it," said Kramer. "I don't know if I have five more years. I'll just keep working as long as I have the energy."

Writings

(And producer) *Women in Love* (screenplay; adapted from the novel of the same title by D. H. Lawrence), United Artists, 1969.

Faggots (novel), Random House, 1978.

The Normal Heart (play), New American Library, c. 1985.

Just Say No (play), 1988.

Reports from the Holocaust: The Making of an AIDS Activist (nonfiction), St. Martin's, 1989.

Indecent Materials (play; partially based on Kramer's book *Reports from the Holocaust*), September, 1990.

Sources

New York Times, March 11, 1990.
People, July 9, 1990.
Rolling Stone, March 8, 1990.
Village Voice, September 11, 1990.

—*Susan Salter*

Lenny Kravitz

Rock/soul singer and songwriter

Born c. 1964 in New York, N.Y.; son of Sy Kravitz (a television news producer) and Roxie Roker (an actress); married Lisa Bonet (an actress), 1987; children: Zoe. *Education:* Attended Beverly Hills High School.

Addresses: *Home*—New York, NY. *Record company*—Virgin Records/CBS Records, 51 West 52nd St., New York, NY 10019.

Career

Solo recording artist, 1989, with debut album *Let Love Rule.*

Sidelights

When Lenny Kravitz, an unknown, unsigned, and unrecorded musician began showing up in gossip columns in 1987 as the new husband of actress Lisa Bonet (a.k.a. Cosby kid), celebrity-watchers understandably scoffed with skepticism. Here, they thought, was just another freeloader trying to advance his career by marrying somebody famous. As *People's* Steve Dougherty wrote of Kravitz, "Better known for his mate than his music—detractors called him Mr. Bonet—he seemed just the sort of dreadlocked ring-through-the-nose hipster who would take a merciless needling from playful Cliff Huxtable."

But that kind of sneering suddenly quieted in 1989 with the release of Kravitz's first album, *Let Love Rule,* a hard-rocking blend of soul and psychedelics that left critics and music fans comparing Kravitz to superstars like John Lennon and Prince. Ironically, at the same time Bonet's career seemed to be on the wane (questionable moves included a nude photo in *Rolling Stone* and an X-rated love scene with Mickey Rourke in the film *Angel Heart*), forcing her back to the relative safety of *The Cosby Show.* Suddenly, the dynamics of one of Hollywood's most glamorous young couples had done an about-face, leaving Kravitz as the partner most likely to succeed in the long term.

Though Kravitz's musical style is eclectic and ever-shifting, *Rolling Stone* reviewer Anthony DeCurtis aptly described it as symptomatic of a young generation "trying to capture the sound of young America sifting through the fragments of post-modern culture and creating childlike musical collages of no particular point . . . as if the world were a kind of shopping mall in which this kind of music can be blended with that regardless of the inherent integrity of any particular genre. The consolation for living in a time when social problems are pushing our nation to the point of collapse . . . is the freedom to play aimlessly among the ruins." Kravitz's approach, DeCurtis continued, is one that "courts artistic disaster by continually evoking his betters. But what saves him, oddly enough, in this brave, new postmodern world, is a tried-and-true rock & roll virtue: This boy can ignite a groove."

If Kravitz relies more heavily on any one style of music above all others, however, it is probably the psychedelic sounds of the late 1960s and early 70s. And if he is merely posing as a kind of throwback Love Child from that era, he has certainly fooled critics such as *Spin*'s Christian Wright, who speculates, "Maybe Lenny Kravitz is a new hippie with an old soul or maybe his neo-Bohemia is the supreme pretense. Either way he's convincing. He even uses crystals to cure his headache." The message that comes across in Kravitz's music, on songs like "Flower Child," "My Precious Love," and the title song, is so idealistic and upbeat that it almost sounds naive in an age run over by cynicism. "It *is* idealistic," Kravitz told *Spin*, "but you've got to try. I mean, why do the good things that you do? I believe in peace. I believe in getting along, all of us being as one, and looking at this place as a planet instead of separate little places. When you're up in a spaceship and look at the world, it's one place... I'm into the world coming together, if that ever happens. Maybe it'll take a great tragedy first."

The only child of actress Roxie Roker, who played Helen Willis on the TV sitcom *The Jeffersons*, and NBC news producer Sy Kravitz, Lenny Kravitz lived an idyllic city life while growing up in Manhattan's rich cultural atmosphere. In 1974 Kravitz's parents (now divorced) moved to Los Angeles, where Lenny got his first musical experience as a member of the California Boys' Choir. He also studied musical instruments diligently during these years, teaching himself to play guitar, bass, keyboards, and drums. As a student at the exclusive Beverly Hills High, Kravitz went through the typical phases of adolescence, assuming the role of a rich preppie before shucking it in favor of first punk, then hippie attitudes, before finally settling for a time on a new persona—that of the free-wheeling, hard-partying Romeo Blue. The period "was a phony time for me," Kravitz told *Spin*. "So I know what posing feels like. That was when I was really into my David Bowie phase. I wanted to be David Bowie more than anything in the world."

But there was also a different, more idealistic side of Kravitz evolving at this time. When he was just 17, Kravitz told *Spin*, he helped a young prostitute escape her pimp and her dreary street life by actually hiding her in his house, under his bed, where he fed her meals and kept the whole thing secret from even his parents. "She was so pretty and so sweet and we were talking and she started crying. She told me the whole thing. I was that kind of guy... My parents always said, 'You're always doing things for everybody except yourself.'" Kravitz's involvement with Bonet began with a chance meeting backstage at a New Edition concert in 1985. Though both were seeing other people, they immediately became fast friends, and then the relationship evolved slowly into something more. Finally, Kravitz's car broke down and he moved in with her so he could borrow hers. "If my car had been working during that time, I probably wouldn't be married to her," Kravitz told *Spin*. "It started to be this thing—every day, wake up, take her to work, pick her up. We'd have dinner and then I guess it was one day we realized like we couldn't be apart or something." They made a quick trip to Las Vegas to get married, and before long their first child, Zoe, was born.

Kravitz and Bonet then moved to a Manhattan loft, where she could continue taping for *Cosby* and he could continue working on his first album, which was taking shape at Henry Hirsch's Hoboken, New Jersey, studio. Hirsch described the rather unique recording session for *People*: "Lisa was there almost every day, sometimes with the baby," while Kravitz "took the subway out every morning. It was very unrock and roll." (The couple separated in 1991.) Even more unique was the fact that Kravitz alone recorded every musical and vocal track on *Let Love Rule*, a la Prince, though for his first tour he recruited a band that lived in his own home while they rehearsed. "It's like a commune. It's cool," Kravitz told *Spin*, adding that he tries to be as democratic as possible in leading other musicians. "Obviously there has to be a leader, a band leader, but I don't like that sort of—a lot of musicians get that tyranny attitude, you know, but it's really equal. When it comes to rehearsing music, obviously they're playing my music so it's got to be, but as far as living at home we're all equal." And judging by Kravitz's remarks to *People*'s Dougherty, he seems levelheaded enough to stay in it for the long haul. "I'm not in it for the stardom," Kravitz said. "I just want to continue to write great songs, make great records. This is only the beginning."

In March of 1991 Kravitz released his next album, *Mama Said*, to critical raves. The album spurred a new spate of publicity on the rising pop star, whose latest effort seemed to reinforce the messages of his earlier work. According to *Spin* writer David Samuels, *Mama Said* "sounds like it was recorded in a moving car somewhere between Detroit and New York in 1968." The album also hints at the pain Kravitz endured with the breakup of his marriage to Bonet. Explaining one of the album's songs to Samuels, he said, "I preached love and peace, and got lost inside it.... I end up losing the thing I'm singing about."

Another Kravitz project during this time was a collaboration with Sean Lennon on a re-recording of John Lennon's "Give Peace a Chance" released as a single and as a video during the buildup of the 1991 Perisan Gulf War. Produced quickly, with a host of popular singers and musicians, as well as updated lyrics and musical styles such as rap, the new version was both hailed—as a poignant, meaningful, and timely reworking of an old anthem—and criticized, for its oversimplification of the elder Lennon's original message. Somewhat baffled by the criticism, Kravitz told Samuels: "I think Sean did a great job. He's fifteen years old, and he wrote about the things that kids hear and talk about. It wasn't intended to save the world."

Selected discography

Let Love Rule, Virgin, 1989.
Mama Said, Virgin, 1991.

Sources

People, November 6, 1989.
Rolling Stone, September 7, 1989.
Spin, July 1990, May 1991.

—*David Collins*

Akira Kurosawa

AP/Wide World Photos

Japanese filmmaker

Born March 23, 1910, in Tokyo, Japan; son of a physical education teacher; married Yoko Yaguchi (an actress), 1945; children: Hisao (son), Kazuko (daughter). *Education:* Attended Tokyo Academy of Fine Arts, 1928.

Career

Director, screenwriter, and producer of motion pictures, 1937—. Served as assistant director to Kajiro Yamamoto, 1937-43, principal director associated with PCL Studios (now Toho Films), 1943—. Founder of Kurosawa Productions, 1960.

Director and co-writer of selected films, including *Sugato sanshiro* (title means "Judo Saga"), Toho Films, 1943; *Subarshiki nichiyobi* (title means "One Wonderful Sunday"), Toho Films, 1947; *Yoidore tenshi* (title means "Drunken Angel"), Toho Films, 1948; *Hikuchi* (title means "The Idiot"), Shochiku, 1951; *Rashomon,* Toho Films, 1950; *Ikiru* (title means "Living"), Toho Films, 1952; *Shichinin no samurai* (title means "Seven Samurai"), Toho Films, 1954; *Kakushi toride no san akunin* (released in the United States as *The Hidden Fortress*), Toho Films, 1958; *Warni yatsu hodo yoko nemuru* (title means "The Bad Sleep Well"), Toho Films, 1959; *Ran,* Toho Films, 1985; *Akiro Kurosawa's Dreams,* Kurosawa Productions, 1990.

Director of selected films, including *Ichiban utsukushiku* (title means "Most Beautiful"), Toho Films, 1944; *Shuban* (title means "Scandal"), Shochiku, 1950; *Kumonosu-jo* (released in the United States as *Throne of Blood*), Toho Films, 1957; *Donzoko* (released in the United States as *The Lower Depths*), Toho Films, 1957; *Yojimbo* (title means "The Bodyguard"), Toho Films, 1961; *Sanjuro,* Toho Films, 1962; *Aka hige* (released in the United States as *Red Beard*), 1965; *Dersu Uzala,* Soviet MosFilm, 1977; *Kagemusha* (title means "Shadow Warrior"), Toho Films, 1980.

Awards: Named best director in Japan, 1947, for *Subarshiki nichiyobi;* Gran Prix from Venice Film Festival and Academy Award for best foreign language film, both 1951, both for *Rashomon;* Silver Lion Award from Venice Film Festival, 1954, for *Shichinin no samurai;* Ramon Magsaysay Prize for journalism and literature, 1965; Academy Award for best foreign language film, 1976, and Donatello Prize (Italy), 1977, both for *Dersu Uzala;* award for "humanistic contribution to society in film production" from European Film Academy, 1978; co-recipient of Golden Palm from Cannes Film Festival, 1980, for *Kagemusha;* numerous other awards.

Sidelights

Some cinema critics regard Akira Kurosawa as the greatest filmmaker alive today. A native of Japan, Kurosawa was the first in his country to win international recognition for his films; his laurels include a Golden Palm Award from the Cannes Film Festival and two Academy Awards for best foreign language movies. As *Interview* contributor Ralph Rugoff noted, "It is difficult to discuss Akira Kurosawa without resorting to bleached cliches like 'genius' or 'giant of world cinema.'" *New York* magazine essayist William Wolf described Kurosawa as "among the few remaining craftsmen of his generation," an artist whose works reflect "the importance he places on the soul of a film." Wolf concluded: "The maturity, insight, intelligence, and sound judgment that [Kurosawa] brings to his work are not easy to emulate."

Kurosawa's influence on American cinema has been substantial—his admirers include Francis Ford Coppola, George Lucas, Paul Schrader, John Milius, and Steven Spielberg. A number of Kurosawa movies have been remade in America as well. *Shichinin no samurai* became *The Magnificent Seven; Rashomon* became *The Outrage;* and *Yojimbo* became the classic Clint Eastwood western, *A Fistful of Dollars.* Even individual characters in Kurosawa films have proven inspirational. George Lucas admitted in *People* that two comic peasants in Kurosawa's *The Hidden Fortress* were models for the robots C3PO and R2D2 in the popular futuristic film series *Star Wars.* Francis Ford Coppola told the *New Yorker:* "No one surpasses Kurosawa in the sense of humanity and the sincerity that mark his films."

Los Angeles Times correspondent Jim Bailey wrote: "Behind the tinted glasses Kurosawa has to wear after a lifetime under studio lights are the undimmed eyes of a perfectionist." Now in his eighties, with more than fifty years of filmmaking behind him, Kurosawa is still obsessed with quality and precise detail. His movies command budgets that are absolutely vast by Japanese standards (although modest when compared to the average American film), and they sometimes run far behind schedule as the director waits for perfect weather conditions or authentic costumes. Rugoff contended that upon close inspection of Kurosawa's films, "a portrait emerges of a director who knows exactly what he wants; how an actor should hold himself; where the fog should lie; the intonation of each word in a speech; how the moon should be lit."

Akira Kurosawa was born in Tokyo in 1910. He is a descendant of a prominent samurai family who lived in the north of Japan as far back as the eleventh century. Kurosawa's father, a physical education teacher, moved to Tokyo and raised his family there. According to Frank Gibney in the *New York Times*

Book Review, the Kurosawas' "big concession to modernity was a shared fondness for movies. Young Akira grew up watching Charlie Chaplin, William S. Hart and the other silent stars. His older brother, who later committed suicide, was a narrator at one of Tokyo's first movie houses." Kurosawa himself was more interested in painting than film when he first reached adulthood. He studied Western painting at the Doshusha School and the Tokyo Academy of Fine Arts, but was unable to support himself as an artist.

Kurosawa wandered into filmmaking almost by accident. He told *Show Business Illustrated:* "In 1937 I was a struggling young painter. I saw a newspaper advertisement. PCL, which later became Toho Studios, wanted an assistant director. They asked applicants to write essays on the basic weaknesses of Japanese films and what should be done about them. In my answer I suggested, humorously, that if weaknesses were basic, there could be no cure. I also said that films could always be made better." To his surprise, Kurosawa won a job as assistant to one of PCL's directors. At first he considered the position a temporary one, just so he could earn enough to return to painting. Then, quite fortuitously, he was made assistant to Kajiro Yamamoto, the most important director in Japanese cinema.

According to Gibney, the rigorous training Kurosawa received from Yamamoto inspired the young would-be painter to devote his life to films instead. "It was then," Gibney wrote, "that [Kurosawa] developed his own intense dedication and perfectionism, qualities which have made his movies great in the viewing but torturously difficult in the making." Under Yamamoto, Kurosawa mastered all the technical skills necessary for motion picture production, including screenwriting. When he began to direct his own films, he co-wrote many of the screenplays and made liberal changes in others. Kurosawa spent the years of World War II working with the movie studio. He was never drafted because one of his brothers had been killed in action, and the Japanese government felt that no family should lose more than one son.

National recognition as a film artist came to Kurosawa in the first postwar years. A full-fledged director from 1943 onward, he earned his first award—as best director of the year—in 1947 for a love story, *Subarshiki nichiyobi* ("One Wonderful Sunday"). The following year he introduced a dynamic young actor, Toshiro Mifune, in an intense drama called *Yoidore tenshi* ("Drunken Angel") that explored life among ghetto hoodlums and those who might try to redeem them. *Yoidore tenshi* was the first of many Kurosawa films to feature Toshiro Mifune; others include *Shichinin no samurai, Yojimbo,* and *Aka hige,* released in the United States as *Red Beard.*

In 1950 Kurosawa released *Rashomon,* the first Japanese film widely seen in the West. Set in feudal Japan, *Rashomon* recounts the murder (or suicide) of a nobleman and the rape (or seduction) of his wife by a bandit, played by Toshiro Mifune. Each of the principal characters recounts the incident differently, and a passing woodcutter adds his own questionable version of the event. *Rashomon* took first prize at the Venice Film Festival in 1951 and earned praise from critics all over the globe. *New York Times* reviewer Bosley Crowther, for instance, wrote: "Everyone seeing the picture will immediately be struck by the beauty and grace of the photography, by the deft use of forest light and shade to achieve a variety of powerful and delicate pictorial effects.... But only the most observant ... will fully perceive the clever details and devices by which the director reveals his characters, and, in this revelation, suggests the dark perversities of man."

The international response to *Rashomon* enhanced Kurosawa's reputation in his homeland. While Japanese cinema became known for its cheap monster movies and science fiction thrillers, Kurosawa was encouraged to produce artistic, serious films that won quite a following. Kurosawa adapted a number of Western stories for his films, including Dostoevsky's *The Idiot* and Shakespeare's *Macbeth,* but his best-known works of the 1950s and early 1960s are his samurai dramas such as *Yojimbo, Shichinin no samurai,* and *Sanjuro. New Yorker* critic Lillian Ross contended that in his samurai films Kurosawa was motivated by "the desire to have modern Japanese learn that the great old powerful samurai left a rich cultural heritage, which means much more than the physical strength and swordsmanship depicted in many Japanese movies. He feels it's important to show the high level of education, the sense of beauty, the spiritual training, and the mental sharpness of the samurai class. That is the spirit of the Japanese heritage." American audiences could not fail to notice the similarity between Kurosawa's samurai adventures and classic tales of the wild west. Before long, the Japanese director who had been influenced by John Ford and D. W. Griffith was himself being copied by a younger generation of American and Italian filmmakers.

Kurosawa's films present an eclectic body of work. Some are set in the present and deal with modern dilemmas. Others are historical dramas, and still others adaptations of classic plays and novels. Such a far-flung body of work is united by several themes, among them concern for the environment and the human race in a nuclear age, a preoccupation with death and violence, and the small gestures of compassion that allow hope to endure in a ruthless world. In the *New York Times Magazine* Ian Buruma wrote: "At his best, which is very often, Kurosawa's romantic idea that we can make things happen if only we try hard enough, merges with his sharp eye for the weakness of man, to produce great and compassionate art." William Wolf likewise observed: "Although rich in humanism and social consciousness, [Kurosawa's] films are not politically doctrinaire. He combines spectacle with depth of characterization, visual beauty with realism, action with intimacy. His hunger for perfectionism is evident."

> Kurosawa "combines spectacle with depth of characterization, visual beauty with realism, action with intimacy. His hunger for perfectionism is evident."
> —William Wolf

That "hunger for perfectionism" almost proved to be Kurosawa's downfall. As the 1960s progressed, his pictures began to run further and further over budget. Filming could take as much as a year as the director waited for perfect weather conditions. Kurosawa reached a low point in his career between 1965 and 1972. His 1965 film *Aka Hige (Red Beard)* was a box office flop that took so long to film that Mifune, its star, swore he would never work with Kurosawa again. And Kurosawa's first in-color movie, the 1970 *Dodes' ka-den,* was derided by critics everywhere and brought him to the brink of bankruptcy. Stung by the bad reviews and suffering from an undiagnosable illness, Kurosawa attempted suicide in 1971. He survived, but he did not return to work until 1975.

It was an offer from the Soviet Union that literally brought Kurosawa back to life. He was invited to make a film in Siberia about a simple wilderness man's first brush with civilization. The work, *Dersu Uzala,* won the Academy Award for best foreign language film in 1976. More importantly, the film suggested that Kurosawa could still exert his considerable powers if he received an adequate budget. For a number of years the director had found the going difficult in Japan—Toho Films, his home company since the 1930s, had all but closed its doors to him because of his extravagant spending. From the inception of *Dersu Uzala* to 1990, all of Kurosawa's films have been made with foreign financial support.

Several American directors, including Lucas and Coppola, came to Kurosawa's aid in the early 1980s. Lucas was able to secure a hefty advance for international distribution rights from Warner Bros. for a Kurosawa script, *Kagemusha*. This vote of confidence helped Kurosawa to secure funds from Toho, and *Kagemusha* was filmed with a record-setting (by Japanese standards) budget. The story of a condemned thief who extends his life by impersonating a slain warlord, *Kagemusha* won the Golden Palm award at the Cannes Film Festival and completely resurrected Kurosawa's career. The 1985 film *Ran*, a violent Japanese-dynasty adaptation of Shakespeare's *King Lear*, was also a critical and commercial success. As he neared his eightieth birthday—with his health restored—Kurosawa found himself once again admired for his quality films, old and new.

At eighty Kurosawa released one of his most personal films, known in America as *Akira Kurosawa's Dreams*. A pastiche of brief segments each representing a vivid dream, the work was funded almost entirely by Western sources and had a budget of $12 million. *Philadelphia Inquirer* contributor Desmond Ryan called *Dreams* a "unique and boundlessly imaginative work of genius" that "plays as a fully realized dream of an artist who wishes to push the limits and possibilities of his medium and share his deepest emotions and most profound concerns." Once again, the American directors who so admire Kurosawa stepped in to help with the film. The special effects were created at George Lucas's studios, and Martin Scorsese makes a brief personal appearance as the artist Vincent Van Gogh.

It rankles Kurosawa that he has had to seek financial assistance outside Japan. Ironically, although his films have always been popular with the Japanese public, the press and the young filmmakers in Japan all but ignore their most prominent director. *American Film* essayist Donald Richie wrote: "The Japanese have a very strong opinion that anyone who makes it in the West cannot be any good, and Kurosawa did make it. He has always had to pay for this appreciation from the West, although he himself has never wooed the West." Buruma states further that Kurosawa's strong views and blunt expression "make him stick out in Japan....He refuses to conform to a society that tends to celebrate the ordinary (*heibon*) as a virtue."

Asked if he feels at all indebted to the West for influences, Kurosawa responds with strong feeling. "I don't think I'm Western at all," he told *Film Comment*. "I don't understand how I could have that reputation. I feel that among Japanese directors today I must be the most Japanese....My interest in Japanese history is probably stronger than that of my colleagues of the younger generation. I'm a filmmaker who happens to live in Japan and I make movies according to what I see around me and my life experience." Of almost thirty films Kurosawa has produced in his lifetime, only one, *Dersu Uzala*, was shot outside his homeland.

On a recent trip to the United States, Kurosawa spoke about the international appeal of his many movies. "I am a filmmaker, and my greatest love is films," he told the *New Yorker*. "My whole life has been devoted to making films. All of them were made with my own Japanese people as their intended audience. Never once while I was making them did it occur to me that they might also come to be loved and appreciated by Americans and people all over the world. To me, it is almost like a dream, and I am profoundly moved that my films should be so well received. And yet—when you think about it—people everywhere share basic human sentiments that transcend all cultural differences and different ways of thought and social patterns. As human beings, we are the same, and our fundamental sympathy for one another as people is the same everywhere." He added: "I am often asked in Japan if I make films in some special way that will appeal to foreigners, or, at least, be understood by them. I do no such thing. As a Japanese, I can think only like a Japanese, and I can make only films that are honest and meaningful to Japanese."

Kurosawa still lives in Tokyo. He has been married for many years to actress Yoko Yaguchi and has two children and several grandchildren. His son Hisao has followed him into the film business and now helps him to secure financing for his ventures. Although he is now past eighty, Kurosawa plans to keep making movies as long as he can. He told *New York*: "There is nothing else that I enjoy that can replace filmmaking, so probably I'm going to keep doing it until they have to carry me off the set." He concluded: "My hope is that my films will be seen and understood by as many people as possible."

Writings

Something Like an Autobiography, translation by Audie E. Bock, Knopf, 1982.

Sources

American Film, April 1982.
Film Comment, November-December 1980.
Film Quarterly, Summer 1983.
Interview, September 1990.
Los Angeles Times, August 26, 1990.
Nation, January 28, 1978.
New York, October 20, 1980.
New Yorker, February 2, 1981; December 21, 1981.
New York Times, January 6, 1952; April 27, 1980.
New York Times Magazine, October 29, 1989.
People, October 27, 1980.
Philadelphia Inquirer, September 14, 1990.
Rolling Stone, September 20, 1990.
Show Business Illustrated, April 1962.
Time, September 10, 1990.
Village Voice, September 4, 1990.

—Anne Janette Johnson

Vytautas Landsbergis

AP/Wide World Photos

President of Lithuania

Born October 18, 1932, in Kaunas, Lithuanian S.S.R.; son of Vytautas Landsbergis-Zenkalnis; married; second wife's name, Grazina; three children. *Education:* Attended Vilnius Conservatoire. *Religion:* Protestant.

Addresses: *Home*—Vilnius, Lithuania. *Office*—Office of the President, Supreme Council of Lithuania, Vilnius, Lithuania.

Career

Pianist and teacher of musicology at Vilnius Conservatoire; served on the Congress of People's Deputies, Soviet Parliament; founder of Sajudis independence movement, 1988; elected President of the Supreme Council of Lithuania, March, 1990; has recorded two albums and published numerous scholarly books and articles.

Sidelights

As the move toward political independence from Moscow swept across Eastern Europe and many of the 15 republics comprising the Soviet Union in the late 1980s, an odd mix of political figures began to emerge from the rank and file of the long-oppressed citizenry of the Communist Bloc. Lech Walesa, for instance, a former laborer and union president, became president of Poland. In Czechoslovakia, Vaclav Havel, a poet and playwright whose writings strongly influenced the course of his country's revolution, became Czechoslovakia's first non-Communist president in more than 40 years. And when the tiny Soviet Republic of Lithuania made its courageous declaration of independence from the Soviet Union, it did so not under the direction of some charismatic, Napoleonic conqueror, but a quiet, aging music professor named Vytautas Landsbergis.

Landsbergis's selection by the newly formed Lithuanian parliament puzzled most outside observers and even some people in Lithuania. Many felt the three million-strong republic needed a more imposing figure to square off with the masterful Soviet leader Mikhail S. Gorbachev. "On the surface the two men would seem to be absurdly mismatched," wrote Michael S. Serrill in *Time* magazine. "Mikhail Gorbachev is a master politician who has pushed aside all competitors for power and won countless political battles in his struggle to reform the Soviet Union. He has an army of 4 million at his disposal, and has demonstrated his willingness to use it to crush civil disobedience in the Soviet Union's restive Transcaucasian republics. By contrast, Vytautas Landsbergis, the newly elected president of the tiny Baltic state of Lithuania, is a bookish, bespectacled musicologist who never before held political office. He presides over a breakaway government that has few laws, no army, no currency, no foreign recognition and a tenuous hold on its territory."

But with the break-up of the Warsaw pact community fully underway, a window of opportunity for Lithuania's formal break from Moscow had opened. And nobody knew for how long. There was no call—nor was there was time to wait—for a blown-dry candidate with personal magnetism and a public relations gift. Lithuania needed leadership, and Landsbergis had the intellectual credentials, courage, and willingness to assume the part in his country's daring escape from a half-century of Soviet domination. "He is not Ronald Reagan," Landsbergis supporter Romualdas Ozolas told the *New York Times.* "He is not handsome. He is not smooth. He is not especially articulate. But he is principled and firm in his convictions and morality. And right now we do not have the luxury to choose a president who can both put forth ideas and have a pretty face."

While Landsbergis may on the surface seem to be a colorless policy maker, his family history reveals a strong pedigree of courageous Lithuanian nationalism. His grandfather, Gabriclius Landsbergis, was exiled to Siberia by the Russian Czar for publishing an underground newspaper and writing plays in the banned Lithuanian language. Landsbergis's father, a prominent architect, played a key role in the Lithuanian struggle for independence following World War I and fought in the underground against the Nazis in World War II. His older brother was arrested by the Nazis in 1943 for organizing pro-independence rallies, and his uncle was executed by the Russians during the same period, when Eastern Europe was a battleground between the German and Russian armies.

Landsbergis was born in Kaunas, capital of the short-lived independent Lithuania, on October 18, 1932. As a boy and young man, he was an eyewitness to the Stalinist purges that saw an estimated 300,000 Lithuanians sent to labor camps. In the following years Landsbergis pursued his interest in music. He became an accomplished pianist (he has recorded two albums) and published numerous books and articles on nineteenth-century Lithuanian music, particularly the banned works of Mikolajus Ciurlionis.

In the late 1980s Landsbergis continued his teaching at the Lithuanian Conservatory in Vilnius, but his focus turned increasingly to politics. As the republic's delegate to the Congress of People's Deputies, the Soviet parliament, Landsbergis became known as *Gudri Lape,* the Clever Fox, for his deft political acumen. Thus he became an important writer of policy for Sajudis, or "the Movement," which convened in Vilnius on June 3, 1988, to present a united front of Lithuania's leading citizens against an increasingly unpalatable Communist rule. In February of 1989 Sajudis made its first public declaration distancing itself from Moscow, announcing that its chief aim was independence from Soviet control. As the man who had final editing for any policy issued forth from Sajudis, however, Landsbergis exercised his moderating influence by couching the declaration in nonconfrontational language. "The prevailing view," he told the *New York Times,* "which I suppose you could call utopian, is that Lithuania should help the Soviet Union by providing an intelligent economic model. The other view, which is the radical view, is to jump out of a sinking boat."

Despite Landsbergis's statesmanlike guidance, however, independence fever began to grip the country and the movement began to take on a life of its own, quite outside the control of any one man. Soon, ordinary citizens were in the streets protesting Communist rule, and the international press embraced the struggle of the tiny republic. Meanwhile, Gorbachev was faced with a monumental dilemma. Should he stand aside and let the individual Soviet provinces, such as Lithuania's independence-minded neighbors Latvia and Estonia, fall away from his rule, as he had done with so many Eastern European nations, or should he do whatever was necessary to keep the Soviet Union intact? And how far should he go to keep Lithuania in line? Should he use force?

The world was watching. Gorbachev at first made mild concessions, such as allowing the celebration of Christmas and reinstating the Lithuanian flag, but he found this only encouraged the determination of the people to gain total independence. In January, 1990, Gorbachev visited Vilnius in an attempt to reassert Moscow's intention to hold on to Lithuania. "Only calm and judicious work within the framework of the law," Gorbachev had announced repeatedly in those days, as quoted in *U.S. News and World Report,* "and not the separatist and extremist actions that we have come up against in the Baltic region . . . will give us a second wind to our great, multi-ethnic community." For a moment during welcoming ceremonies, Landsbergis stepped out of his low-key persona to daringly greet the Soviet leader as "the leader of a great neighboring state." The slight visibly angered Gorbachev, and Lithuania had instantly taken a decisive step toward a dangerous and uncertain destiny.

The following month Lithuania held the first multi-party elections in modern Soviet history, with Sajudis candidates overwhelmingly defeating those of Lithuania's breakaway Communist party. On March 11, 1990, the new Lithuanian parliament elected

Landsbergis president by a vote of 91 to 38 over Communist candidate Algirdas Brazauskas. Later that day Landsbergis led the vote formally declaring Lithuania's independence from Moscow, forcing Gorbachev's hand even further toward some sort of action.

A crackdown ensued almost immediately. Red Army troops and warplanes thundered in and around Vilnius as Gorbachev, with the enhanced powers he had just received from the Soviet parliament, moved to isolate Lithuania politically, even going so far as to expel all foreign journalists from the embattled republic, thus effectively removing the republic's most effective weapon—the watchful eye of the international community. Also looming, should Gorbachev decide to go that far, was an economic blockade which would easily cripple the Lithuanian economy within weeks. The tiny country depended on Moscow for virtually all of its raw materials.

> "Sooner or later, perhaps without cataclysm, [the Soviet] empire is collapsing. There's no guarantee that there won't be a cataclysm, but the process is under way."

Gorbachev clearly held all the cards. Landsbergis had only courage and defiance in his hand, but still he managed to confound both the Soviets *and* the Americans. Aware that Lithuania's bold break was upsetting the carefully planned public relations victories won by warming U.S.-Soviet relations, Landsbergis hit this common superpower soft spot. Gorbachev, long the darling of the international press for past reforms, was suddenly, with his hard-line stance on Lithuania, seen by the rest of the world to be sliding into the familiar role of Soviet dictator. And Landsbergis accused U.S. President George Bush of hypocrisy for ignoring Lithuania's fight for freedom in favor of the more strategically important Eastern European nations. "Can the freedom of one group of people be sold for another?" Landsbergis asked in *U.S. News and World Report.* "Of what value is freedom itself?" Landsbergis even went so far as to compare Bush's failure to support Lithuanian independence to former British Prime Minister Neville

Chamberlain's appeasement of Adolf Hitler at Munich prior to World War II.

In April, with Lithuania holding firm to its claim of independence, Gorbachev tightened the screws still further by shutting off the spigots to three of the four pipelines carrying natural gas into Lithuania and completely shutting off the flow of oil. The economy was brought quickly to its knees, but Landsbergis and a majority of Lithuanians maintained their resolve in hopes of putting more public relations pressure on Moscow. In late April a Lithuanian man set himself on fire in a Moscow square to protest Soviet domination, and Landsbergis was quick to pronounce the man a martyr for his country's struggle. During this difficult time, he was also often heard quoting a line from a favorite play by Henrik Ibsen: "The strongest man in the world is he who stands most alone."

This tension was diffused, at least temporarily, in June 1990, when Lithuania agreed to suspend its declaration of independence for 100 days upon the lifting of the blockade and commencement of talks to establish a new relationship with Moscow. But Gorbachev, facing internal pressure from hard-liners to crack down on dissident republics, was, Landsbergis sensed, only marking time. "Sooner or later," he predicted in the *New York Times*, "perhaps without cataclysm, this empire is collapsing. There's no guarantee that there won't be a cataclysm, but the process is under way."

By December 1990 Lithuania and its Baltic neighbors, Latvia and Estonia, were reaching a new boiling point as Moscow balked at making any real progress on talks with the republics. "We don't believe the Soviet Union wants real negotiations with Lithuania," Landsbergis told *U.S. News and World Report* at the time. "It wants either our total capitulation or some drawn-out procedure that leads nowhere but earns propaganda points for Moscow." But his words fell on deaf ears, primarily because Western powers were consumed with the escalating conflict in the Persian Gulf. "It doesn't frighten us that the Baltic problem is not a top priority in the West," Landsbergis continued. "Already, we have survived almost 50 years forgotten by most of the world ... but war in the Persian Gulf would be very dangerous for us, because then no one would notice a little war in the Baltic region ... it would be the most convenient time for the Soviets to intervene."

Landsbergis's words proved eerily prophetic. On January 13, 1991, two days before the United Nations deadline for the Iraqi withdrawal from Kuwait, Soviet Red Army tanks rumbled into Vilnius, seizing the city's television station and surrounding the Parliament Building. Unarmed protestors of the invasion could put up only a symbolic defense and 14 Lithuanians were killed, many crushed under the treads of the advancing tanks. More protestors took to the streets as news of the invasion spread. Many gathered outside the Parliament Building, where Landsbergis and other government officials defiantly stood their ground, even rigging a makeshift television antenna so they could continue to broadcast news of the crackdown throughout Lithuania. "Is it true Bush sold us?" Landsbergis asked a *New York Times* reporter just hours after the assault. The question alluded to speculation that the American President had in effect "traded" concern over the Baltics for Soviet cooperation in the U.S.-led alliance against Iraq.

Whether Lithuania had fallen victim to superpower dealing or not, the timing of the Soviet invasion recalled a similar move made against Hungary in 1956. That action took place in the context of the Suez Canal crisis. In this instance, Gorbachev's handling of Lithuania led to further speculation that he was coming increasingly under the control of hard-line Communists in the Soviet bureaucracy.

The politics leading up to January 13 were typical of past Soviet dictators—couched in deceit and double-talk. As part of the deal made with the republics in June 1990, Gorbachev had formed a new Federation Council of political leaders to give voice to the restive republics in the Soviet government. On January 12, the Federation Council had announced it was sending a delegation to Vilnius to search for a "political solution" to the Moscow-Vilnius standoff. When

asked of the significance of that upcoming meeting, Landsbergis expressed hope. "It means we are returning to civilized ways of solving problems," the Lithuanian president told the *New York Times*. "I would like to express a very cautious optimism." Four hours later, the boot of the Red Army once again smashed those hopes as Gorbachev napped in Moscow. Denying he had given the orders to shoot, the Soviet leader was quoted in *Time* as saying: "I learned about what happened when they woke me up the next morning."

Lithuania's future remains uncertain, even in the aftermath of the Persian Gulf War: much of the Western world continues to pore over the events and consequences of that conflict. Other factors that will determine Lithuania's fate include the political struggle between Gorbachev and his archrival Boris Yeltsin (also in *Newsmakers 91*), the Russian Federation president and tenacious economic reformer who has gained considerable popular support in the Soviet Union. And even as Lithuania strives for independence, along with the republics of Estonia, Latvia, Moldavia, Georgia, and Armenia, the entire Soviet nation writhes under harsh economic conditions—not exactly healthy soil for the seeds of democracy.

Sources

Christian Science Monitor, March 13, 1990.
New York Times, March 14, 1989; March 26, 1990; April 10, 1990; January 13, 1991.
Time, January 28, 1991.

—David Collins

Daniel Lanois

Photograph by Randy Allbritton

Record producer

Born in 1951 in Hull, Quebec, Canada; son of Guy (a carpenter and amateur musician) and Jill (an amateur musician) Lanois.

Addresses: *Home*—London, England. *Office*—Opal/Warner Bros., 3300 Warner Blvd., Burbank, CA 91510.

Career

Performed as a guitarist for several bands throughout Canada during the 1970s; started Grant Avenue Studio, with brother Bob, in Hamilton, Ontario, 1980; produced several albums with Brian Eno in the early 1980s; co-produced, with Brian Eno, U2's *The Unforgettable Fire*, 1984; co-produced, with Peter Gabriel, soundtrack for film *Birdy*, 1985, and album *So*, for Gabriel, 1986; co-produced, with Robbie Robertson, *Robbie Robertson*, 1987; produced *The Joshua Tree*, for U2, 1988; produced *Oh Mercy*, for Bob Dylan, 1989; produced *Yellow Moon*, for the Neville Brothers, 1989; recorded solo album, *Acadie*, 1989.

Sidelights

Daniel Lanois emerged in the 1980s as one of the most successful and innovative producers in the pop music industry. As the person responsible for overseeing the entire recording process—from sound mixing to helping with lyrics to directing the actual musicians themselves—the producer has always played an integral, albeit low-key, role in the music industry. But with the dizzying array of new technologies, instruments, and synthesizers increasingly available today, talented producers like Lanois have become more vital to musicians and record company executives trying to get the best possible sound quality for their recordings. Lanois, with his groundbreaking work on such albums as U2's *The Joshua Tree* and Bob Dylan's *Oh Mercy*, has proven himself a master at blending music's efficient new technologies with the more unique, human capabilities of individual artists. His work in the studio, said musician Brian Eno in *Rolling Stone*, strikes the "critical balance between professionalism and spontaneity."

A native French-Canadian, Lanois came from a musical family that broke up with his parents' divorce in 1963. He moved in with his mother in Hamilton, Ontario, where, along with his brother, Bob, he eventually opened the Grant Avenue Studio and recorded popular Canadian acts. By the late 1970s, Lanois's work had come to the attention of Eno, an avant-garde musician known for his experimentation with new musical forms and technologies. Eno at the time was creating what he called Ambient Music—light, quiet, instrumental pieces which many believe were the precursors to New Age music—and he hired Lanois to help him produce five albums at Grant Avenue. "Those years I spent with Brian are when I learned how to do the atmospheres, the moods," Lanois told *Rolling Stone*. "Those are still with me."

When Eno was asked to produce U2's 1984 LP *The Unforgettable Fire*, he asked Lanois to co-produce. The result was a memorable, pathbreaking album—and Lanois has been busy fielding offers ever since. Peter Gabriel asked Lanois to produce the soundtrack for the 1985 film *Birdy*, and in 1986 Lanois collaborated on Gabriel's enormously successful album, *So*. By this time, Lanois had sold his studio in Canada and had developed a "mobile" studio system, whereby he would have equipment and instruments flown in to wherever he wished to work. With Gabriel he worked in England; when Robbie Robertson, formerly of The Band, hired Lanois to produce his comeback solo record, they worked in Los Angeles; on the Dylan LP the recording was done with local musicians in New Orleans' French Quarter; and for U2's *The Joshua Tree* much of the work was done in a sixteenth-century castle in Ireland. "I prefer to be thrown into an unusual location because it seems to offer more interesting-sounding rooms, more surprises. It also strips away the formalities and the chilliness of the recording studio," Lanois told *Rolling Stone*.

In the late 1980s Lanois took a break from the studio to pursue a project he had been dreaming of for years—recording his own album. An accomplished guitarist and drummer in his own right, Lanois set to work writing 11 original songs that would eventually become *Acadie*, for the original name of the French-Canadian territory where he grew up. Among the many critical raves for the understated LP, the *New York Times* said it evoked "the slightly quaint, rustic feel of the Band's 1970s records but with a difference. A lot of the textures are electronically treated in a way that casts an ethereal glow over the songs." *Rolling Stone*'s Michael Goldberg compared Lanois's "untrained but appealing, almost sweet singing voice" to that of Neil Diamond and Robbie Robertson, and wrote that *Acadie* "sounds the way a great old pair of handmade moccasins feel. Subdued ballads are mixed with uptempo Cajun numbers." Speaking of the qualities that appeal most to him about Lanois, both as a producer and fellow musician, Robertson told *Rolling Stone*, "He has these extremes that I like. He's kind of sweet-and-sour. He's the kind of guy who can slay you with gentleness and then rip the phone out of the wall."

Sources

Maclean's, July 21, 1986; March 14, 1988.
New York Times, November 29, 1989; December 3, 1989.
Rolling Stone, December 12, 1987; November 30, 1989.

—*David Collins*

Rush Limbaugh

Christopher Little/Outline

Radio talk show host

Born in Cape Girardeau, Mo.; son of an attorney; married and divorced twice. *Education:* Attended Southeast Missouri State University.

Career

Began working in radio at age 16 at his hometown station; later held positions as radio disc jockey, newsreader, and commentator in various cities, including Pittsburgh, and at station KMBZ in Kansas City. Hosted talk show at station KFBK in Sacramento, 1984; moved to New York City station, 1988. Also worked as a marketing executive for the Kansas City Royals baseball club, c. early 1980s.

Sidelights

The self-proclaimed "number-one talk show host in America," possessing, in his own words, "talent on loan from God," Rush Limbaugh has become in just over two years, well, the number-one talk show host in America. His nationally syndicated radio call-in program, *The Rush Limbaugh Show*, has raised that peculiarly American, midday bastion of shut-ins to the level of pop art. That he has done so by sticking to a single, traditionally dry agenda—conservative politics—and with only one guest—himself—seems only to add to the broadcasting phenomenon Limbaugh has become. More than five million listeners tune in to his program each week on a growing network of more than 300 stations across the country. Whether his popularity is due more to his politics or his undeniable showmanship is not

clear; but for Limbaugh the two go hand in hand. "What makes me popular is that I do what the liberals don't do," Limbaugh declared in *Entertainment Weekly*. "They don't make people feel good about their country—they don't have fun."

But what is fun for Limbaugh only enrages his pet targets—namely, special interest groups, which Limbaugh characterizes in his inimitable lingo as "environmentalist wackos," "feminazis," "humaniacs," "arts and croissant people," and "pencil-neck geeks." Throughout his show, seemingly as the mood strikes him, Limbaugh will burst into his imitation of trumpet fanfare—dadalup! dadalup! dadalup!—announcing another of his many "updates" on what to him are the ongoing follies of some liberal group or another. Often these updates are preceded by a song befitting the issue at hand. For instance, the "animal rights update," a Limbaugh favorite, follows a recording of popular crooner Andy Williams singing "Born Free," only modified with the sounds of gunfire and screaming animals in the background. Similarly, the "homeless update" is launched with Clarence "Frogman" Henry's "Ain't Got No Home."

These bits are what set Limbaugh's show apart from the average radio talk programs that fill airspace on

AM stations across the country. Even his most vocal critics may recognize that Limbaugh's strident charisma seems to leap out of even the sleepiest of radios. From noon to 3:00 p.m. each weekday this bombastic champion of the right expounds in a booming voice upon the issues of the day, from New York City politics to those of the Persian Gulf. Each morning before his show begins, Limbaugh pores over seven newspapers from around the country, looking for items that will delight or outrage him, pique his interest, or provide new ammunition for his many updates. In this way he keeps his listeners on the cutting edge of current events, if not "the cutting edge of societal evolution" as he often boasts.

What makes Limbaugh's call-in show all the more entertaining is that there are mercifully few callers. Callers can be the weakness of radio shows; they are often inarticulate, nervous, misinformed, and overly emotional. Frequently callers are dull, and Limbaugh does not suffer fools gladly. Consequently his show is mostly Limbaugh, Limbaugh, and more Limbaugh, and why not? People tune in to hear Rush Limbaugh, not Larry from Tacoma complaining about taxes. "I wanted to be the reason people listened," Limbaugh told the *New York Times*.

Although he is polite to even the rare critic who gets through to his show, Limbaugh is also very good at making the caller get to the point. In the show's early days, Limbaugh tired of wasting precious time as each caller started with the usual "Rush, hi! I *love* your show and I've been trying to get on for the longest time...." So he instructed all his future callers holding the same sentiment to simply say "dittos," as in "Hi Rush, mega-dittos from the Sunshine State!" It saves time and, more importantly, the trademark greeting adds to the growing Rush cult by giving it the air of a secret society.

Limbaugh's intolerance of extremists, both liberal and conservative, further helps keep the show moving. While he is definitely conservative—the best free publicity the Republican party could ever hope for—he is also rational and articulate, pretty much towing a moderate conservative line. His bombast and self-promotion are a reaction, he says, to the inflamed and irresponsible rhetoric of special interest pariahs. "I demonstrate absurdity by being absurd," Limbaugh told the *New York Times*.

Limbaugh actually screens callers to weed out arch-conservatives who might seek to use his show as a soapbox. He looks upon these people, he explained in the *Los Angeles Times*, with as much disdain as animal rights activists and environmentalists who spike trees to prevent them from being felled: "I

don't want any John Birchers, no one-world-government theories. No UFOs, no abortion calls in the context of when life begins . . . people who are going to read anything [on the air], no Bible—faith is a personal and sacred thing. I don't want devout believers of any religion or cause because they don't *think*. I want people who think about things with a passion." As noble as this mission may sound, reasonable and serious political dialogue is merely the set-up blow in Limbaugh's one-two punch to radio success; it is humor that provides the knock-out. "So why has Rush Limbaugh become the new titan of talk?" asked Lewis Grossberger in the *New York Times*. "Maybe it is America's shock at discovering a new species: a funny right-winger."

> "This country is remarkably conservative. I travel it every week."

Indeed, since the 1960s—the decade of rock music, free love, and John F. Kennedy—conservatism has been widely considered not only closed-minded and wrong, but even more frightening, completely unhip—especially among young intellectuals. The core of Limbaugh's audience, however, is males aged 25 to 54 who respond as much to the *idea* of Limbaugh as to Limbaugh's ideas. In an era when even the most uneducated are growing wise to the slick, oversimplified sound-bites that often replace real political dialogue today, Limbaugh is refreshingly direct. He says exactly what he thinks; he is loud and he is funny. Suddenly liberals like Jesse Jackson, Ted Kennedy, and National Organization of Women president Molly Yard come off as humorless, occasionally downright sinister, and interested only in their own political survival—in a phrase, out of touch. Suddenly, with Rush Limbaugh, it's hip to be square. And Limbaugh maintains that conservatives have been lurking in the shadows all along; it simply took an irreverent, irrepressible, fearlessly committed big-mouth like himself to draw them out. "This country is remarkably conservative," he told Grossberger. "I travel it every week."

By this, Limbaugh was referring to the Rush to Excellence Tour. On most weekends he takes his one-man show on the road to cities across the country, where his ninety-minute monologue regularly sells out 3,000- to 4,000-seat auditoriums. The price to have this 320-pound gabber rant and rave onstage in your town: $15,000 to $20,000 per show. Like any pop star Limbaugh also cashes in on Rush t-shirts, caps, and coffee mugs, and his Rush to Excellence video sells briskly at $24.95. Rush has even embarked on a Rush to Excellence Caribbean Cruise. Some estimates place Limbaugh's 1990 income from radio and merchandising at $750,000. Critics who accuse him of exploiting his popularity, however, simply play right into the hands of this lampooning, capitalist king.

Limbaugh was born in the heart of America, in a small town called Cape Girardeau, Missouri, roughly 100 miles south of St. Louis. He has said that he is a perfect fusion of his stern, solidly conservative lawyer father, and his talkative, wisecracking mother, whom he calls the funniest person he has ever known. His love of radio began early, as did his boredom with school. When Limbaugh was 16 his somewhat exasperated father helped him get a job at a hometown radio station. Though Limbaugh eventually enrolled at nearby Southeast Missouri State University, his heart never really left radio and he quit school after only one year.

For the next several years Limbaugh lived the nomadic life of the radio-jock-for-hire, moving from city to city to work as a DJ, newsreader, and commentator, taking on different stage names and developing what would later become the Limbaugh style. After stints in Kansas City, Pittsburgh, and elsewhere, he returned to Kansas City determined to leave radio for good, and took a job as a marketing executive for the Kansas City Royals baseball club. He stuck with the Royals until 1983, when he was again lured back to radio, this time for a news commentator job at Kansas City's KMBZ. The job didn't last long, however; Limbaugh was fired for being too controversial. "Everything I did in Kansas City, I failed at," Limbaugh admitted to the *New York Times*. Though he was married twice there, both marriages ended in divorce.

But failure in Kansas City led to success in Sacramento, where Limbaugh latched on to KFBK as replacement for notorious talk show meteor Morton Downey, Jr. In his four years in California Limbaugh grew fully into his outrageous on-air persona, and the audience loved it; within a year he was the number-one radio host in Sacramento. In 1988 he caught the ear of independent producer-distributor Ed McLaughlin, whose company, EFM Media Management, signed Limbaugh to a two-year contract and brought him to New York City. McLaughlin's idea was to buck the trend by putting Limbaugh's show on nationwide, during the day, when most local markets run their own programs to take advantage of prime advertising rates. Though there were early problems, Limbaugh's ebullient personality quickly won out over, as he put it in the *New York Times*, the usual hometown jock "interviewing the sewage director or the latest carrot cake recipe expert." Word of mouth and Limbaugh's own relentless and shameless self-promotion quickly brought in new listeners and, more importantly, new stations around the country.

So what is the essence of the Limbaugh experience? What is it that keeps, at any given time, 1.3 million Americans tuned to his program in the middle of a weekday, when they should presumably be doing something else? The key seemingly lies in Limbaugh's absolute mastery of radio, a lost art in a world with 130 cable television channels. In the words of *New York Times* contributor Grossberger, "It is impossible to re-create in print the full Rush Limbaugh experience, as you get only a dry approximation lacking his exuberance, his energy, his volume, his sobs, giggles, sighs, coughs, snatches of song, simulated trumpet fanfares and other vocal effects." *Entertainment Weekly's* Giselle Benatar called Limbaugh a "consummate politicized comedian—a cross between George Bush with a sense of humor and Jackie Mason with a right-wing political agenda."

Limbaugh's voice is a truly remarkable instrument, filling the radio at one moment with an authoritative, voice-of-God proclamation on the economy and at the next with a hilarious, dead-on impression of sportscasting legend Howard Cosell or heavyweight Mike Tyson. Despite the fact that he spends more than three hours a day talking, Limbaugh appears to gain momentum as the show progresses, as he feeds off his own reactions to callers, his studio staff—all named, affectionately, "Snerdley"—and, of course, his own wit. To his unfailing amazement, with each program he finds that conservatism does indeed make strange bedfellows; a frequent caller is heavy-metal guitarist and outspoken hunting advocate Ted Nugent. And Limbaugh was very pleased one day to receive a call from two New York City fans who happened to be a gay man and a lesbian.

Perhaps what is most endearing about Limbaugh to his growing legions of listeners is that even as his fame skyrockets, he continues to be the same old Rush, a guy who could disagree with you vehemently about some political point one moment and buy you a beer the next. Despite boasts that he does his show "with half my brain tied behind my back, just to make it fair," or that he is "destined to have his own wing in the Museum of Modern Broadcasting,'' Limbaugh, the ''epitome of morality and virtue,'' is really just a regular guy who doesn't take himself or his beliefs too seriously, no matter how committed he is to them. ''Talk radio is perceived as being hosted by a bunch of irresponsible, uneducated, screaming loudmouths and insult jockeys,'' Limbaugh told *Entertainment Weekly*. ''I want people to respect what I do.''

Sources

Detroit Free Press, February 3, 1991.
Entertainment Weekly, February 8, 1991.
New York Times, December 16, 1990.

—*David Collins*

Tom and Ray Magliozzi

Car-repair experts

Tom Magliozzi born c. 1938; married; two children. *Education:* Graduated from Massachusetts Institute of Technology; has earned a Ph.D. Ray Magliozzi, born c. 1950; married; two children. *Education:* Graduated from Massachusetts Institute of Technology.

Addresses: *Home*—Cambridge, MA. *Office*—c/o National Public Radio, Washington, DC.

Career

Tom worked as a marketing and engineering expert for a manufacturing company for 12 years; Ray worked as a VISTA volunteer in San Antonio, TX., and was a junior-high teacher in Vermont. In 1971 Tom and Ray opened Hacker's Haven, a do-it-yourself car-repair shop in Cambridge, MA.; shop reopened as professional repair service under name Good News Garage; the pair made radio debut with car-repair advice show on public station WBUR, Boston, 1976; debut of weekly show called *Car Talk* on National Public Radio, 1987; they also write a newspaper column syndicated to some 70 publications. Ray still works at Good News Garage; Tom has become a marketing instructor at Suffolk University, Boston.

Sidelights

Tom and Ray Magliozzi—a.k.a. Click and Clack, the Tappet brothers—know things about people and cars that the rest of America merely wonders about. Like the kind of person who drives a Firebird. "Anytime you see a Camaro or a Firebird, especially red, driven by a female, that female is nine times out of 10 named Donna," declared Tom (who gallantly credits this revelation to "my brilliant wife") in an *Entertainment Weekly* article. Ray contributed this observation: "A BMW driver . . . , if it's a man, which it usually is, he's wearing suspenders and a bow tie, he works on Wall Street, and he drives on the sidewalk. Anything to get ahead."

To a growing audience of fans, the Magliozzi brothers—"the primal-scream therapists of the breakdown lane," as *USA Weekend* writer Jonathan Walters called them—are the last word in car-repair advice. With their weekly *Car Talk* show on National Public Radio a certified success, these former full-time mechanics (Ray still works at his Cambridge-based Good News Garage) dispense wisdom on most any auto ailment his nationwide listeners and letter-writers can lob their way. Their subject matter—on the air, in their syndicated newspaper column, or in interviews—can vary depending on the brothers' moods. While Ray, as quoted in *Rolling Stone*, may help a caller interpret the squealing of brake pads (it's dolphin language, Ray said, for "Replace me, replace me"), Tom can hold forth on the image of his contemporaries. One of the reasons many mechanics are considered incompetent, noted Tom in the *Entertainment Weekly* piece, comes right down to gender: "Most mechanics are men and men are all wrapped up in this machismo. They can't admit they're wrong. Rather than admit they put the wrong part in, they try to cover by making things up."

The brothers' from-the-hip style has endeared them to an audience that might not have necessarily tuned into a pair of garrulous mechanics. "In the strange world of public broadcasting, *Car Talk* is classified not as news and information but as an arts and performance broadcast," *Rolling Stone* writer Emily Yoffe reported. Yoffe quoted an NPR executive as saying: "A lot of [our] listeners don't even own cars. Even our classical stations are picking [the show] up, though Vivaldi and *Car Talk* don't seem to go together. Like most hit things [the show has run on some 230 NPR stations], it's just a phenomenon."

The brothers get some questions on how to buy a car. To that end, they provided some information for Walters's article. There are "two basics about buying cars," he writes. "Never pay more than $5 a pound—for your financial well-being. And never buy a car that weighs less than 3,000 pounds—for your physical well-being." "Do your homework, and it's easy to [deal]," added Ray. After checking though consumer magazines and manuals, "you go in and say, 'This is the car I want. This is how much *you* paid for it. I'll give you $200 more.' If they don't go for it, leave."

And once you have your dream car, as Walters reported, the Magliozzis remind you to keep a light touch on the clutch: "If you have a standard and you don't stall out at least once a day, you're wearing out the clutch by revving too high."

Given the Magliozzis' penchant for naming names— in a *Time* article they called Volvo the "poor man's Mercedes," emphasizing that its repair bills are what will keep you poor—they themselves drive surprisingly downscale models. In Yoffe's 1989 profile, Tom revealed he maintained a 1974 Chevy Caprice ("I had a Toyota once, but it was too reliable"), whereas Ray is the owner of a Dodge pickup if only because, as he told Walters, "Every man *must* own a pickup truck once in his life."

Sources

Entertainment Weekly, May 24, 1991.
Rolling Stone, November 16, 1989.
Time, April 30, 1990.
USA Weekend, January 5, 1990.

—*Susan Salter*

Tom, left, and Ray Magliozzi. Photograph by Richard Howard.

Maharishi Mahesh Yogi

Spiritual leader

Name originally Mahad Prasad Varma; born October 18, c. 1911, in Uttar Pradesh, India. *Education:* Graduated from Allahbad University, 1942, with a degree in physics; studied under Swami Brahmananda Saraswati Shankaracharya for 13 years.

Address: Maharishi International University, Fairfield, Iowa.

Career

Following 13-year study of Advaita Vedanta, a school of religious thought, became a missionary in southern India; moved to London, England, and founded Spiritual Regeneration Movement; moved to United States, 1959; founded Students' International Meditation Society, 1966; opened Maharishi International University in Los Angeles, 1971, moved it to Fairfield, Iowa, 1974; after spending a decade out of the public eye, announced plans to build Vedaland, a theme park in Orlando, Fla., 1990. Has also appeared on videos.

Sidelights

His name alone—Maharishi Mahesh Yogi—conjures up for many Americans visions of the "swinging sixties," of the Beatles, of sitar music and meditation, of flower children seeking a spiritual path. His peaceful countenance, and especially his long, snowy beard, have made the guru one of the most recognized among the spiritual leaders of the

world. Almost single-handedly, the Maharishi—the title means "great sage"—brought Eastern culture into Western consciousness. Yet this most influential figure, who combines his own spiritual impulses with the commercial instincts of a seasoned businessman, continues to elude easy definition.

There is, for instance, the low-key Maharishi who emerged in the late 1950s in London and the United States as a missionary in the cause of Hinduism, the philosophy of which is called Vedanta. In a *Life* article from 1968, a writer defined Vedanta as a belief that "holds that God is to be found in every creature and object, that the purpose of human life is to realize the godliness in oneself and that religious truths are universal."

Then there is the Maharishi of controversy, who emerged in 1967 to the bemusement of middle-class America as a leader among flower-children and an anti-drug advocate. Granted, the Maharishi's sudden popularity was helped along by such early fans as the Beatles, Mia Farrow, and the nascent spiritualist Shirley MacLaine. These people, and many others, practiced Transcendental Meditation (TM), a Hindu-influenced procedure that endures in America to this day. In 1967 *Life*'s Loudon Wainwright visited the guru and described his "grayish-white beard, mustache and long, dark, stringy hair . . . . [The Maharishi] sits cross-legged on his deer hide and chirps pleasantly from time to time as he delivers a point he considers of special importance. His brown eyes, except at moments when they darken with impatience at some member of the adoring group around him, positively glitter with good humor, and they should."

As Wainwright has told it, the Maharishi at that time was "in the middle of a flower-storming tour of West Germany and the Scandinavian countries. Before I saw him, I had made some effort to get a crude understanding of his teaching, and it seemed astonishingly—perhaps ridiculously—simple in outline and purpose. In the first place, [TM] . . . can be learned by anyone in normal health." To qualify as a meditator, Wainwright continued, "a prospective convert needs no preparation, no intellectual background and—now this is the kicker for anyone who has ever worried about sin—it requires no repudiation of the past and no promises to behave in the future. By meditating for one half hour morning and night, one is said to be able to achieve a deep understanding of the self, and a growing happiness, sense of well-being and success. The Maharishi's conviction about his technique is absolute; he thinks that its wide dissemination could utterly change the world and, in fact, leave it without problems."

Key to achieving TM success is "dwelling on a mantra, or repetitive sound, that induces a meditative state," as Douglas Starr explained in an *Omni* article. "This state, [the Maharishi has] told his followers, could open new horizons in consciousness."

In an America clashing over everything from the Vietnam War to the politics of LSD, the Maharishi's teachings resulted in "what may be the most wholesome mystique to attract a youthful following since Baron and Lady Baden-Powell founded the Boy Scout movement," as Jane Howard noted in *Life*. "To cautious suburbanites the gurus [for Maharishi Mahesh Yogi was not the only Indian spiritualist grabbing media attention at the time] may seem a little threatening, but the maxims they dispense are salutary: Don't be a chatterbox, the swamis say, and don't poison your system with cigarettes and drugs, don't feel sorry for yourself, avoid premarital sex, help others, and do things *right*, even little things like tossing paper into the wastebasket."

When the 1960s drew to a close, with the hedonistic 1970s nipping at its heels, the Maharishi began to fade from public view. Though TM remained popular, the other ministrations of restraint clashed with the credo of the "Me-Decade." The guru still had enough followers, though, to people the Maharishi International University, founded in 1971 in Los Angeles. By 1974 the institution moved to the site of the former Parsons College in Fairfield, Iowa, where it remains today.

One of the main draws of Maharishi International University was the study of TM-Sidha, "an exotic form of Transcendental Meditation," as Patricia King noted in *Newsweek*. "Sidhas believe that if enough disciples meditate at once, they create a 'maharishi effect,' a powerful force that can bring about anything from world peace to a rise in the stock market." This near-promise of affluence through spiritual concentration proved a magnet for a number of business people. "Call it karmic capitalism," said King, who reported that "nearly 300 disciple-owned businesses now operate [in Fairfield], bringing new life into the economically depressed region."

After noting how the non-disciples of the Iowa town have adjusted to an influx of TM advocates ("the local Hardee's sells herbal tea, and Easter Foods stocks Indian-style rice"), King revealed that the bustling businesses, including an ice cream manufacturer and a software company, have attracted some non-religious companies to Fairfield as well.

Though the Maharishi made few public appearances through the 1970s and 1980s, he still made his influence known. In 1989 the *New York Times* reported that the "Maharishi Heaven on Earth Development Center" was running workshops for investors looking to speculate into real estate. A representative of Heaven on Earth, which would supply peaceful havens for a city-stressed populace, used the Maharishi's reputation to promote the development, said the *Times*. As the article relates, the spokesman said "the Maharishi Mahesh Yogi came up with transcendental meditation more than 30 years ago to give meditating mortals the opportunity to create internal heavens. Then he told how in 1987 the Maharishi predicted the superpowers would make great strides toward peace. Presto! It happened. Now, he said, the Maharishi has turned his attention to creating utopian homes in idyllic communities for all earthlings at a cost of about $100 trillion, three times the estimated worth of the entire planet."

By 1990, wrote David Friend in *Life*, "The Maharishi is back—and now, his proponents will tell you, he's bigger than ever." Apparently having survived the acquisitive '80s and weathered becoming a pop-culture punch line in mainstream America, the Maharishi returned to the spotlight, after living for years in India, as a business executive to rival any.

"Aided by a largely volunteer staff of 25,000 world-wide and running a spiritual conglomerate with assets worth an estimated $3 billion, Maharishi is now bullishly diversifying his movement," Friend declared. "He has set up spas that cater to the body as well as the spirit.... His management team recently hired an ad agency to target would-be meditators in Seattle and Kansas City. By dialing 1-800-ALL-VEDA, customers can order the yogi's own music cassettes, herbal teas and cleansing bars. Indian workers are bottling Himalayan Bliss, the Maharishi's brand of mineral water."

"When you provide heat to boil milk, the milk puffs up. Even one cold drop immediately makes it settle down. Meditation is famous for producing coolness."

Also gaining some publicity was an aspect of TM that many found unusual, to put it mildly. As Starr observed in his *Omni* piece, some of the Maharishi's followers have purported to be able to use TM techniques to defy the law of gravity—to virtually fly. Starr visited Maharishi International University and found "two athletic-looking young men wearing T-shirts and karate pants [sitting] in lotus position, meditating." Gradually "they start wiggling gently, moving their shoulders, then their backs and heads. The gentle motion takes on intensity, expanding to include lower-back twitches and downward thrusts of the knee. One of the fliers starts laughing and then—boing!—they're off. They bound across the floor, cushioned by exercise mats, in short spurts, leaping from their knees like human frogs. The fliers stop to rest after every dozen or so hops, and after 15 minutes they stop for good." As skeptics would point out, these same movements can be imitated by non-meditating gymnasts.

"We don't actually call it flying anymore," a university spokesman told Friend. "We now call it hopping." But the underlying theories behind advanced TM still brought criticism from professionals, as the *Omni* article continued. "People with paranoia or schizophrenia may find that meditation exacerbates those preexisting problems, releasing suppressed conflict that the individual may not be able to address," a psychiatrist suggested to Friend. "This could cause a further loosening of their grip on reality."

Among the Maharishi's most recent ventures is his announcement of Vedaland, a theme park that is scheduled to open near Disney World in Orlando, Florida, in 1993. According to Friend's *Life* article, one of the Maharishi's better-known modern disciples, magician Doug Henning, remembers the guru telling him: "All theme parks are superficial. Create one that stimulates the intellect, stirs the emotions—and enlightens people." Friend calls the proposed Vedaland "a higher-than-high-tech amusement park, a sort of Six Flags on acid. A whole building will appear to levitate some 15 feet above a pond. A time tunnel will spirit riders from the Big Bang to Eternity's End. A chariot that can accommodate 120 passengers will alight on a colossal rose petal, then enter one of its cells, then its DNA, then the milky blue blur of its subatomic essence. In Vedaland, Henning warbles, audiences will not just be entertained, 'they will transcend.'" Attending a Maharishi lecture in 1990, Friend found "on a dais ablaze with roses, a dozen disciples perch on brocade chairs, rigid with rapture, a frieze of suits and ties. In their midst, on a couch of yellow silk, sits Maharishi, smiling. He holds a rose in his right hand, beside which sprouts a thicket of microphones." The guru, he went on to say, "seems to believe that every human being has the capacity to envision anything: What will life be like after death? Where are those damn car keys? The Destroyer of Ignorance thinks in millennial spans.... Yes, he is actually saying he can actually visualize what will happen in 11,990 A.D. The mind boggles. He might as well be saying that Neolithic man could have forecast fax machines. Yet as Maharishi sits there with a rose quivering subtly in his hand, his voice rising and falling hypnotically, reason fades. The man is thoroughly, confoundingly convincing. Another hour of this and a listener might believe anything."

"Everything has its place," the Maharishi said in an interview with Friend. "The sun during the day. The moon and the stars during the night. Comparing them is not of much value." Thus does the guru compare himself with current world leaders (Friend notes that prior to the interview the Maharishi had publicly stated that he deserves more credit for world peace than does Mikhail Gorbachev). The Maharishi also has advice for Iraqi leader Saddam Hussein, who at the time of the interview was engaging in terrorist activities against Kuwait, prior to the United States military action in the Persian Gulf. In a word, the Maharishi would advise Saddam to "meditate." How long? "One moment. When you provide heat to boil milk, the milk puffs up. Even one cold drop immediately makes it settle down. Meditation is famous for producing coolness."

For almost 25 years the Maharishi Mahesh Yogi has held in sway a number of devoted followers in America. Though the political and social climate has changed, Friend says, the guru's message never has. Even listening to him in 1990, he says, one is "seized by an eerie sensation that he's been caught in a time warp and it's going to be 1968 forever."

Sources

Life, November 10, 1967; February 9, 1968; November; 1990.
Newsweek, August 3, 1987.
New York Times, January 21, 1989.
Omni, May, 1990.

—Susan Salter

John Major

AP/Wide World Photos

Prime minister of Great Britain

Full name, John Roy Major; born March 29, 1943, in Wimbledon, England; father, Thomas Major, was a circus performer; mother was a singer; married Norma Johnson, 1970; children: Elizabeth, James. *Education:* Attended Rutlish Grammar School, a state school for gifted children; left school at age 16.

Addresses: *Office*—10 Downing St., London, England.

Career

Worked as a laborer for eight years after dropping out of school; worked for the Standard Chartered Bank, 1965-79, began as clerk, became bank's chief spokesman; elected to council, Lambeth section of London, 1968; Member of Parliament for Huntingdonshire, 1979-83, and Huntingdon, beginning in 1983; appointed junior minister for social security and the disabled, 1985, became full minister, 1986; chief secretary of the treasury, 1987-89; foreign secretary, July-October, 1989; chancellor of the exchequer, October 1989-November 1990; prime minister of Great Britain, November 1990—.

Sidelights

On the surface, John Major would seem an unlikely candidate to become prime minister of Great Britain. The son of a circus performer, raised in poverty, and a high school dropout who spent time on public welfare, Major was until 1990 a largely anonymous member of Parliament and minister in

the cabinet of former prime minister Margaret Thatcher. But Thatcher was impressed by Major and began grooming him to become her eventual successor. Many thought that by the end of the century Major could emerge as Great Britain's top leader.

They were wrong in one respect—it didn't take that long. On November 22, 1990, Thatcher resigned under pressure. Five days later Major, at 47, completed his meteoric rise. The son of a trapeze artist had made a stunning ascent to the high wire of British politics to become the nation's youngest prime minister in the 20th century. (Not long before her husband's election, Norma Major was asked what she thought his prospects were. "Not good," she told the *Los Angeles Times.* "That sort of thing doesn't happen to people like us.")

In fact, Major's life story could almost come from the pages of Charles Dickens or Horatio Alger. Major's father, Thomas, a former circus performer, was 67 when his youngest son was born in a middle-class neighborhood in Wimbledon. "When I was about 4 or 5, his sight began to fail, and I used to walk with him a lot, so that he wouldn't trip over curbs," Major told the London *Sunday Telegraph.* "He was a wonderful talker. And, there was this small boy who really enjoyed being an audience." When young John was 11, his father lost all his money in a business that manufactured ornamental gnomes for English gardens. This forced the family to move to a two-room flat in Brixton, a poor, racially mixed neighborhood in south London. "There was no difference in the way the family behaved or the way they treated me," Major told the *Sunday Telegraph*. "It was a good environment to be brought up in."

As a boy, he attended the Rutlish Grammar School, a state school considered a stepping stone to upward mobility. But he dropped out immediately after turning 16, vowing never to return. "Schools in those days were a good deal more authoritarian than they are now," he told the *Philadelphia Inquirer*. "I felt a little adrift from the mainstream, I think." He then began working to help out the family, first as a clerk in an insurance company, later mixing concrete for the London Electricity Board. He tried to get a job as a bus conductor but was rejected because of inadequate math skills. He bounced from one manual labor job to another, and, at the age of 19, spent eight months living on public assistance. Major said that experience made him a great believer in the welfare system. And he told the *Los Angeles Times* that he does not regret never attending college, saying, "It has been of immense value to me to have been on the other side of the fence and know what it is to face difficulties, and I don't regret any of that."

His life took a turn for the better in 1965 when, at age 22, he got a job as a clerk with the Standard Chartered Bank, where he worked his way up through the ranks. In the late 1960s, the bank sent Major to Nigeria to report on the Biafra War. Eventually, Major became the bank's chief spokesman and top aide to its chairman. Wrote the *New York Times*'s Craig R. Whitney: "To his admirers, he is the promise of Thatcherism come alive, proof that individual achievement means more than class privilege and is the best way of overcoming class disadvantage." Major's own life story has served as a foundation for his political positions. "I want a genuine classless society in which people can rise to whatever level their abilities take them regardless of their origins," he told the *Los Angeles Times*. "My goal is to make a classless society by the year 2000."

Major's political career began in 1968, when he was elected to the local council in the Lambeth section of London. He won with the support of blacks; housing and racism were his issues as he established a reputation as a progressive. He ran for Parliament twice in the mid-1970s, both times for a seat that was essentially unwinnable for any member of the Conservative party. Finally, loyal party work made him a candidate for the safe Conservative seat in Huntingdon. He was elected to Parliament in 1979, in the same general election in which Margaret Thatcher became prime minister.

As a junior member of Parliament, Major became a parliamentary aide in the Home Office. Later, he became a whip, keeping Thatcher's officials in touch with their back-bench Conservative supporters in the House of Commons and making sure they voted with her on crucial questions. It was in that capacity that he impressed Thatcher with his intellectual toughness. During a working dinner in 1983, Major attracted the prime minister's attention when he had the nerve to disagree with her in front of others in quite forceful terms. She was impressed, according to aides. In 1985 Thatcher appointed him junior social security minister, which was, not coincidentally, the first job of any rank she herself had held in government. She promoted him to minister of social security in 1980 and, a year later, moved him into the cabinet as chief secretary of the treasury, a job equivalent to that of director of the Office of Management and Budget in the United States.

> *"I want a genuine classless society in which people can rise to whatever level their abilities take them regardless of their origins."*

By 1989, it grew increasingly clear that Thatcher might be grooming Major as her successor. First, she made him foreign secretary, even though he had no experience in the field. He had been in the job for only 94 days when Nigel Lawson resigned as chancellor of the exchequer, a position equal to the U.S. Treasury Secretary. Thatcher immediately moved Major into that post, where he served for 13 months. He took Britain into the European exchange rate system, pegging the value of the British pound to other European currencies—despite Thatcher's misgivings—and he fashioned a tough anti-inflationary policy. Critics said that the policy managed only to bring the British economy to the brink of recession without lowering inflation.

Overall, Major was so closely aligned with Thatcher that members of the opposition Labor party jokingly dubbed him "Mrs. Thatcher's poodle." Major, however, basked in the role of protege. "I'm a proud

Thatcherite," he told the *Dallas Morning News.* "I'm honored to be working under the wing of one of the best leaders in this country's history." By all accounts, Major expected to be working for Thatcher for years to come. But in November 1990, Thatcher's government suddenly toppled after 11 and a half years.

The prime minister's downfall came after an encounter with a stretch of unpopularity—partly through her authoritarian manner, partly because of inflation and high interest rates, and partly because of her unpopular new "poll tax," which placed an equal tax on every person in Britain, regardless of income. Thatcher also appeared to take an anti-European attitude toward her 11 partners in the European Community, which caused her long-serving Cabinet colleague and deputy prime minister, Geoffrey Howe, to resign and deliver a witheringly critical resignation speech. That speech led Michael Heseltine, who had walked out of the Cabinet in 1984, to challenge Thatcher in a leadership vote in the Parliament. Shockingly, the prime minister failed to gain the necessary majority to hold her job. With support in the House of Commons eroding, Thatcher decided to resign rather than risk the humiliation of a defeat at the hands of one of her own colleagues.

At that point, three men sought leadership of the Conservative party, and thereby the title of prime minister. They were Major, Heseltine, and foreign secretary Douglas Hurd who, like Major, was a Thatcher loyalist. In the five-day campaign, Major tried to assert himself as his own man. "I am not running as 'Son of Thatcher,'" he told the *Los Angeles Times.* "I'm running as myself, with my own priorities and my own program." Still, Thatcher made it clear that Major was her preferred choice. She was quoted in the *New York Times* as telling Conservative party officials at a farewell event that she would be "a very good back-seat driver" in a Major administration. That did little to dissuade talk of Major as a Thatcher puppet.

On November 27, Major received 185 votes of support from Conservative members of Parliament—two short of the absolute majority needed. But before a second ballot could be taken, Hurd and Heseltine conceded the contest and threw their support behind Major. Even after his victory, Major remained a mystery to most of Great Britain. Even a member of his own party, member of Parliament Teddy Taylor, told *Newsday,* "I am not sure of his detailed positions. I am not sure where he stands on European issues. So it is a bit of a positive leap in the dark. But he is a decent chap, an honest chap." Neil Kinnock, leader of the opposition Labor party, called for a general election—an unlikely event until 1992. "John Major is a Thatcherette," Kinnock told the *Los Angeles Times.* "It means the policies that brought poll tax, recession, heavy mortgages and rising unemployment will go on."

For his own part, Major promised to give the nation more of what it had gotten used to—privatization, tax cuts, limited government spending, and high interest rates aimed at bringing down inflation. "I intend to build on the policies we have," he told the *Dallas Morning News.* If anything, Major figured to differ from Thatcher in tone rather than substance. Thatcher, a colorful and tough debater, had been dubbed "The Iron Lady." Major, wrote the *Washington Post*'s Glenn Frankel, is "a dry, wooden speaker." Michael Parks of the *Los Angeles Times* called him "very gray—a pleasant man but nearly featureless as a politician. He is invariably compared by Britons to their neighborhood bank manager or perhaps the chairman of the local school committee." And Larry Eichel of the *Philadelphia Inquirer* said that Major "is not highly experienced, well-educated or flamboyant. No one has ever accused him of being a visionary. He seems to have no clear ideology."

Major described himself to the *Los Angeles Times* as "not ideologically pure in any way. I plan to continue the economic and social revolution begun by Mrs. Thatcher, but we must move ahead. I am in the business of further change." The change he most wants to see is in how Britains treat each other. Major condemned the nation's social stratification, telling *Newsday:* "We must begin to treat all equally. I hope the general atmosphere we create will remove those old social attitudes."

On economic issues, Major is expected to carry on the policies of Thatcher, while taking a more sympathetic view toward Britain's role in the European community. Immediately after his election, he promised to review the controversial poll tax introduced by Thatcher. He also vowed to continue Great Britain's historically strong ties with the United States, including their implacable opposition to Iraqi leader Saddam Hussein's 1990 invasion of Kuwait. Britain committed about 30,000 military personnel to the Persian Gulf and backed a U.S. move for a United Nations Security Council resolution authorizing military action. "There will be no difference in policy in the Persian Gulf," he told the *Miami Herald.* "There is absolute unity that what has happened there is unforgivable and that it has to be reversed."

And, he told the *Washington Post:* "I want to see us build a country that is at ease with itself, a country that is confident, and a country that is prepared and willing to make the changes necessary to provide a better quality of life for all its citizens. I don't promise you that it will easy, and I don't promise you that it will be quick.''

Sources

Dallas Morning News, November 29, 1990.
Detroit Free Press, November 28, 1990.
Houston Post, November 28, 1990; November 29, 1990.
Los Angeles Times, November 23, 1990; November 28, 1990; December 4, 1990.
Miami Herald, November 28, 1990.
New York Times, December 1, 1990; December 2, 1990.
Newsday (Long Island), November 28, 1990.
Philadelphia Inquirer, November 28, 1990.
Press-Telegram (Long Beach), November 28, 1990.
Time, April 1, 1991.
Sunday Telegraph (London), November 25, 1990; December 1, 1990.
Washington Post, November 28, 1990; November 29, 1990; December 1, 1990.

—*Glen Macnow*

Diego Maradona

AP/Wide World Photos

Professional soccer player

B orn c. 1961; raised in Villa Fiorito, Buenos Aires, Argentina.

Career

G ave halftime exhibitions during professional matches starting at age ten; played with a junior club until age fifteen; became youngest-ever member of the Argentine national team at seventeen. Signed first professional contract, with the Boca Juniors, at age fifteen; signed with Barcelona of the Spanish League, 1980; sold to Naples of the Italian League, 1984.

Sidelights

A modern-day soccer legend, Diego Maradona is possibly the most recognizable athlete in the world. This would not be disputed in any country but America, where stars like Michael Jordan and Bo Jackson command huge personality cults, and where soccer is barely recognized as a sport. But soccer—or "football," as most of the world knows the game—is without question the most popular and passionately embraced sport worldwide; it is therefore not surprising that Maradona counts an adoring public probably three times the size of Jordan's and Jackson's together. Among even the most zealous soccer aficionados Maradona is recognized not just as a great player, but as one of the all-time greats. "About once in twenty years, a footballer of genius emerges," declared the London *Sunday Times* in 1980. "The last was Pele,

the great Brazilian player. Now there is another— Diego Maradona of Argentina."

If *Times* readers were unconvinced by that endorsement, they were certainly won over by Maradona's spectacular performance six years later in a 1986 World Cup quarterfinal match between England and Argentina. In leading Argentina's 2-1 victory, Maradona scored both of his team's goals—and fittingly, the two very different goals seemed to shed light on the corresponding dark and bright sides of this very controversial player's spectacular reputation. On the first, the stocky, 5'5" star leapt high into the air over the taller English goaltender, Peter Shilton, to head a lofting pass into the goal. England protested that Maradona had actually redirected the ball with his fist—an illegal move; television replays seemed to support this claim, but the referee awarded a goal nonetheless. After the game the cunning Maradona only fueled the debate when he credited "the hand of God" with the score. Maradona's second goal in that game seemed even more the work of an immortal, though in this instance the work was clearly all his. After dribbling the length of the field through the heart of England's rugged defense, Maradona deftly eluded Shilton and tapped the ball into an empty goal. "He changed gears like a fantastic sports car," said soccer observer Julio Mazzei in the *New York Times.* "It was unbelievable. The ball looked like it was glued to his feet."

Raised among seven siblings in the Buenos Aires barrio of Villa Fiorito, Maradona was a soccer prodigy who at age ten gave breathless halftime exhibitions of his skills during professional matches. His junior club won 140 straight games and he signed his first professional contract at 15. Two years later he became the youngest-ever member of the Argentine national team, which at the time was preparing to host the 1978 World Cup. Nonetheless, coach Cesar Luis Menotti made Maradona the last cut from that club, which went on to win the title. Maradona was so upset that he did not speak to Menotti for six months, a stance he softened when the two combined to bring the world junior title home to Argentina the following year. Maradona's reputation grew when he led his professional team, the Boca Juniors, to the Argentine national championship during the 1980-81 season.

As Maradona's star rose so did the controversy surrounding his career. In 1980 he signed a six-year, $12 million contract to play for Barcelona of the Spanish League; the move angered many Argentines, who had tired of seeing their best players bought away by wealthy European clubs. All the Argentine Football Association could do to hinder the move, however, was to bar Maradona from joining his new club until after the 1982 World Cup—which would feature Maradona's first appearance in the fabled "Mondiale."

Unfortunately, that tournament—held coincidentally in Spain—was a virtual catastrophe for Maradona and his team; not only was Argentina eliminated by arch-rival Brazil, but Maradona, in frustration over what seemed to stem partly from rough treatment received in an earlier game against Italy, was ejected from his team's final game for a vicious foul on a Brazilian player. Perhaps worse, his unsportsmanlike behavior put him in bad standing with the gentile Spanish fans, who were constantly at odds with the fitful Maradona over the next two years, even as he led his Barcelona team to a Spanish League championship.

In 1984 Barcelona sold the rights to Maradona's services to Naples of the Italian League for $10.8 million. With a new, nine-year contract for over $23 million under his belt, Maradona proceeded to take the top-flight Italian League by storm, raising his team's standing from 12th place to eighth to third in just two seasons and enthralling the blue-collar Naples fans in the process. The Argentine star would eventually lead his club to its first Italian League

championship, in 1987, and its first European title two years later.

But it was certainly at the 1986 World Cup in Mexico that Maradona sealed his legendary stature in the hearts of a generation of soccer fans the world over. In helping Argentina reclaim the Cup it had lost to Italy four years earlier, Maradona scored five goals in a seven-game crusade to vindicate his poor showing in 1982. Aside from the two tallies he had against England, Maradona also scored both goals in a 2-0 semifinal victory over Belgium—and he had the lone Argentine goal in a 1-1 tie with Italy, home of his professional team. When he was not scoring goals, Maradona was equally adept at setting up his teammates with passing that *Sports Illustrated*'s Clive Gammons wrote had "a precision that borders on the supernatural." In the dramatic final-game victory over West Germany, after Argentina had squandered a 2-0 lead, Maradona fed a pass through four German defenders to teammate Jorge Burruchaga, whose goal gave Argentina its second Cup in three tries.

> "They can say what they want about me. Fine me, withhold my salary, but I won't change. Remember, it's the players who bring 90,000 people to the stadium."

Injured, constantly harassed by opposing defenses, and possibly past his prime, Maradona did not make nearly as good a showing in the 1990 World Cup in Italy. Though Argentina once again returned to the finals against West Germany, this time the Germans dominated the game and held Maradona in check, eventually winning the title by a 1-0 score. Maradona returned the following season to honor his professional contract with Naples, which runs through 1993. With his career on the wane, however, the moody star found that his usual pranks—missing practices, insulting fans and teammates, and suffering mysterious injuries—were meeting with less tolerance from club officials. Still, his colorful exploits and musings on the idea of retiring made great copy for the Italian press. Through it all Maradona remained defiant. "They can say what they want about me," he said in *People*. "Fine me, withhold my salary, but I won't change. Remember, it's the players who bring 90,000 people to the stadium. I am Maradona, who makes goals, who makes mistakes. I can take it all, I have shoulders big enough for everybody.''

Probably Maradona's biggest mistake became evident in April of 1991, when he was suspended for 15 months after testing positive for cocaine. Also around that time he was arrested for possession of the drug in Buenos Aires. His future as a soccer star will most likely depend on his ability to get free of drugs; in the meantime, his fans can only hope that he will come clean and come back to the sport.

Sources

New York Times, May 27, 1990.
People, June 18, 1990.
Sports Illustrated, July 7, 1986.
Sunday Times (London), May 18, 1990.
Village Voice, July 3, 1990.

—*David Collins*

Penny Marshall

AP/Wide World Photos

Actress and film director

Born Carole Penny Marscharelli (family changed name to Marshall), October 15, 1942, in Bronx, N.Y.; daughter of Anthony W. (an industrial film-maker) and Marjorie Irene (a dance teacher; maiden name, Ward) Marshall; married Michael Henry (a football player) c. 1961 (divorced); married Rob Reiner (an actor and film director), April 19, 1971 (divorced); children: (from first marriage) Tracy Lee. *Education:* Attended the University of New Mexico.

Address: *Agent*—c/o Creative Artists Agency, 1888 Century Park E., Suite 1400, Los Angeles, CA 90067.

Career

Made television debut on *The Danny Thomas Hour;* also appeared on television in *The Odd Couple,* 1972-74; *Friends and Lovers* and *Let's Switch!,* both 1974; *Wives* (pilot), *Chico and the Man, The Mary Tyler Moore Show, Heaven Help Us,* and *Happy Days,* all 1975; *Saturday Night Live,* 1975-77; *Battle of the Network Stars,* and *The Barry Manilow Special,* both 1976; *The Tonight Show* and *Dinah,* both 1976-77; *The Mike Douglas Show,* 1975-77; *The Merv Griffin Show* and *$20,000 Pyramid,* both 1976-77; *Laverne and Shirley,* 1976-80; *Blansky's Beauties,* 1977; *Network Battle of the Sexes,* 1977; *More Than Friends,* 1978, *The Bob Newhart Show, Love, American Style,* and *The Couple Takes a Wife.* Appeared in films, including *How Sweet It Is* and *The Savage Seven,* both 1968; *The Grasshopper,* 1970; *1941,* 1979. Directed feature films, including *Jumpin' Jack Flash,* Twentieth Century–Fox, 1986; *Big,* Twentieth Century–Fox, 1988, and *Awakenings,* Columbia Pictures, 1990.

Sidelights

There was a time when Hollywood seemed ready to write Penny Marshall off as yet another one-hit wonder, an actress-comedienne with limited skills and narrow appeal. Instead Marshall has become a major film director with several highly acclaimed and profitable movies to her credit. "Penny Marshall got into directing the 'easy' way—by becoming a television superstar first," wrote Paula Dranov in *Cosmopolitan.* "Although a number of actors have directed movies . . . few actresses have made a similar transition successfully . . . . But with *Big,* starring Tom Hanks, Bronx-born Marshall became the first woman director of a box office bonanza."

Renown for her modesty, Marshall calls her success as a director "a crapshoot." Many disagree, however. Two Marshall projects, *Big* and *Awakenings,* have garnered Oscar nominations, proving that the former situation comedy star can tackle both lighthearted and heavy-duty material. "I'm used to comin' from under, so I get a little nervous about people liking something," Marshall told *People* magazine. "I just basically hope I don't get kicked out of this business . . . . I've just been lucky in some of the things that walked into my hands."

Carole Penny Marscharelli was born in New York City on October 15, 1942. The daughter of an industrial filmmaker and a dance teacher, she was raised in the Bronx. During her early youth her family decided to shorten their surname to Marshall. Penny practically grew up in her mother's studio, studying dance from the age of three. She also managed to find her way outside, into a colorful middle-class neighborhood populated by an ethnic mix of youngsters who would achieve fame in comedy, fashion design, stage production, and publishing. According to Marty Friedman in *New York* magazine, Marshall's former neighborhood "wasn't just any neighborhood. Although it was not rich, and its citizens were no more privileged than those of other working-class areas of the city, a formidable number of the kids who played together there in the fifties, all within a couple of years of one another in age, have names that are famous, important, or both today. Something was different about these people and this spot."

> *"I don't remember myself as funny. I was heartbroken for most of [my teenage] years, in love with everybody."*

Marshall remembers her youth in the Bronx with a great deal of fondness; once she even took her daughter on a tour of the old neighborhood, where her contemporaries included future fashion designer Ralph Lauren, comedian Robert Klein, and composer Stanley Silverman. It was customary for teens in that area to hang out together on the street, joking and playing games. Although she was an accomplished dancer, Marshall was ashamed of her looks. She saw comedy as an escape from her seemingly ordinary appearance. "I made fun of myself before anyone did," she told *New York*, "because I looked like a coconut and had bucked teeth, braces, and a ponytail. I wore a Davy Crockett T-shirt. I guess because I couldn't get the guys on a romantic level I took the friendship level.... I don't remember myself as funny. I was heartbroken for most of those years, in love with everybody. But I was always the character. Today people tell me, 'You were always fun to be around,' but did I have a different view of what I was doing! Still, I wouldn't trade that for anything. There

was a place you belonged. You just went out to the Parkway and found all your friends."

When Marshall was 14 her mother's dance troupe, the Marshalettes, appeared on Ted Mack's *Original Amateur Hour* and won. The group then went on to a one-time appearance on the *Jackie Gleason Show*. This early brush with television did not make Marshall yearn for the limelight, however. Instead she enrolled at the University of New Mexico as a math and psychology major. During her sophomore year there she dropped out to marry a football player. The couple soon had both a daughter and a divorce, and Marshall found herself teaching dance in Albuquerque and barely scraping by. In an interview with *TV Guide* Marshall revealed: "I had no future in New Mexico, and if I went back to New York my family would have treated me like a child. So I picked up a phone and called my brother in Hollywood."

By that time Marshall's brother Garry had made a name for himself as a television writer-producer. He encouraged Marshall to move to Los Angeles and take acting lessons at night while supporting herself as a secretary. He also helped Marshall get auditions and cast her in bit parts in movies he produced. In the late 1960s Marshall joined a Los Angeles repertory group known as The Committee, and there she met fellow Bronx native Rob Reiner (also in *Newsmakers 91*). In 1970 both Reiner and Marshall were invited to audition for a new television comedy, *All in the Family*. Reiner was cast in one of the lead roles; Marshall narrowly missed being cast as his wife. In real life they were married in 1971. While Reiner's career took off, Marshall struggled. A small part in an episode of *The Danny Thomas Hour* proved so traumatic that she almost quit the business. Her brother persuaded her to keep trying, however, and found her a recurring role on the popular situation comedy *The Odd Couple*. Between 1972 and 1974 Marshall appeared a number of times on *The Odd Couple* as Oscar Madison's secretary, Myrna. That part was the first in which Marshall exploited her poker-faced expressions and flat-toned voice. She also appeared on *The Bob Newhart Show*, the comedy *Friends and Lovers*, the *The Mary Tyler Moore Show*, *Chico and the Man*, and *Love, American Style*. Her made-for-television movies of this period included *The Couple Takes a Wife* and *Let's Switch!*

A bit part on yet another popular television show became the major catalyst for Marshall's career. In the fall of 1975 she showed up on *Happy Days* as a date for Arthur "The Fonz" Fonzarelli. Teamed with the sprightly Cindy Williams, Marshall helped forge a promising comic chemistry. Garry Marshall, who had a hand in the production of *Happy Days*, suggested a spin-off, and a new series, *Laverne and Shirley*, was born. Set in the late 1950s, *Laverne and Shirley* centered around the life of two working-class roommates, one a brash Italian—Marshall's Laverne—and the other a prim but perky WASP. The show aired in 1976, following *Happy Days* in the prime time lineup; it was an immediate ratings hit. Within weeks *Laverne and Shirley* had cracked the Nielsen Top Ten; it remained in the Top Twenty for three seasons. A *Cue* magazine reviewer offered one of many enthusiastic assessments of *Laverne and Shirley*: "Both Cindy Williams and Penny Marshall play their roles well, generating a great deal of magnetism. They manage the ponderous task of making gum-snapping an appealing art.... The show is fast-moving, and the writing is very good. The 1950's was a desperate time to adolesce in, yet Laverne and Shirley make it seem like a lot of fun."

Laverne and Shirley made Penny Marshall famous, but not necessarily happy. By 1980 the show had sunk to near-bottom in the ratings, Marshall's marriage had ended, and she was wearing herself out on the Los Angeles party scene. "The 1970s was a party period for most of the people I know," Marshall told *People.* "We couldn't deal with being famous. We were all holding onto each other. But the party's over now." After *Laverne and Shirley* was canceled Marshall found it difficult to find parts that did not echo Laverne. Worse, she found that many Hollywood insiders felt she had ridden to fame on the coattails of her brother and father, who had produced *Laverne and Shirley*. Marshall addressed herself to that charge in *People:* "This is a factory business; of course the sons and daughters of people in it are going to go in it."

During the last few seasons of *Laverne and Shirley* Marshall had directed several episodes. She found that she enjoyed working behind the camera, but it would be years before she was offered such work in films. Her first opportunity to direct a movie came in 1986, when she became a last-minute replacement on the Whoopi Goldberg comedy *Jumpin' Jack Flash*. The film was not terribly successful, but critics did not fault Marshall for its lack of focus. Producer Jim Brooks told *People*, in fact, that Marshall was able to make the best of a difficult project. "I believed in her," Brooks said. "She came into *Jumpin' Jack Flash* under the most insane conditions imaginable and showed a lot of imagination."

Big, Marshall's next project, held far more promise. The story follows the adventures of an adolescent boy who turns into an adult—overnight; while he looks grown up, the character remains a young teenager under his man's skin. Through a series of twists, the boy-man becomes a successful toy company executive and the love interest of a predatory businesswoman. *National Review* correspondent John Simon called *Big* "an accomplished, endearing, and by no means mindless fantasy," praising Marshall for her delicate treatment of the material. The film was one of the biggest box office draws of 1988, earning well in excess of $85 million in theaters. Dranov noted that the hit movie "has made Hollywood forget that once upon a time, Marshall's success was attributed solely to her family connections."

Marshall's subsequent work bore little resemblance to *Big*. A serious drama about a rare brain condition, *Awakenings* tells the story of a young doctor, played by Robin Williams, and his treatment of a catatonic patient, played by Robert De Niro. In the course of the film the doctor revives his dormant patient and helps him to experience the world again. "If anyone in the theater has a dry eye,... check them for a heartbeat," wrote Ralph Novak in *People.* The reviewer went on to praise Marshall for her "beautifully staged" sequences and her subtle control of difficult emotional territory. "The moments of anguish and triumph come so fast and furious that this movie is constantly threatening to turn into a medical soap opera," observed Novak. "But director Penny Marshall, De Niro, Williams and writer Steven Zaillian keep the emotions reined in just enough to create a moving, thoughtful film."

With two hit movies to her credit, Marshall is now in great demand in Hollywood. She divides her time between homes in Los Angeles and New York City. Her daughter, Tracy, is an actress with a few small film roles to her credit. Marshall spends little time socializing these days—much of her spare time is spent reading screenplays for future projects. "Some part of me must be ambitious because I keep doing things," she told *People.* She added: "I won't ever act in a movie I'm directing. I could never look at myself that long."

Sources

Cosmopolitan, November 1988.
Cue, February 21, 1976.
National Review, July 22, 1988.
New York, October 26, 1981.
People, April 28, 1980; August 15, 1988; December 24, 1990.
TV Guide, May 22, 1976.

—*Anne Janette Johnson*

Lynn Martin

U.S. secretary of labor

Born December 26, 1939, in Evanston, IL; daughter of Lawrence William and Helen Catherine (Hall) Morley; married second husband, Harry D. Leinenweber (a U.S. district judge), 1987; children: (first marriage) Julia Catherine, Caroline. *Education:* University of Illinois, B.A., 1960. *Religion:* Roman Catholic.

Career

Public school teacher in Illinois, c. 1961-75. Illinois House of Representatives, state congresswoman, 1977-79; Illinois Senate, state senator, 1979-81. United States Congress, representative from 16th Illinois district, 1981-90. National co-chairwoman, Bush-Quayle Presidential Campaign, 1988. Secretary of labor, 1991—.

Awards: Named one of the "outstanding young women in America" by the U.S. Jaycees; named Republican Woman of the Year, 1989.

Member: American Association of University Women, Junior League.

Sidelights

George Bush's new secretary of labor is a well-liked former congresswoman named Lynn Martin. Martin was appointed secretary of labor early in 1991, replacing Elizabeth Dole in the Bush cabinet. Martin's confirmation hearings—and her voting record in Congress—have helped to allay fears that she will do little more than play court to the Bush

AP/Wide World Photos

administration. The feisty and outspoken Martin told the *Chicago Tribune* that she wants to "make sure the 1990s are a time to be remembered as a pinnacle for chance and opportunity for the men and women who compose the working force for America."

Lynn Martin is no stranger to politics. A former public school teacher, she has worked her way through the ranks of the Republican party from local offices to positions in the Illinois state legislature and the U.S. Congress. Perhaps more important, Martin has been a friend and confidante to George Bush for more than a decade and has served as both an official and unofficial adviser to his administration. In announcing her nomination for labor secretary, Bush called Martin a "cherished friend." As the president was quoted in the *Chicago Tribune:* "She's a mother who knows the need for child care. She's a professional who understands the business-labor relationship. And as a congresswoman, she spent years dealing with the concerns and aspirations of the working Americans from every walk of life."

Martin was born in Evanston, Illinois, and grew up in Chicago. She earned a bachelor's degree at the University of Illinois and spent a number of years teaching high school English and economics in various Chicago suburbs. Her interest in politics dawned gradually, and she began her career in elected office with a position on the Winnebago County Board. She moved to the Illinois House of Representatives as a state congresswoman in 1977, and from there won a place in the Illinois Senate in 1979. Two years later, she won a seat in the United States Congress, taking the spot vacated by presidential candidate John Anderson. As congresswoman for the 16th Illinois district, Martin was considered virtually unbeatable. She won elections in 1983, 1985, 1987, and 1989 by comfortable margins. Martin told the *Chicago Tribune* that she never considered herself a sure winner, even as a well-entrenched incumbent in Congress. "Deep in my heart of hearts I never believed I was going to win any election," she admitted.

Washington Post staff writer Frank Swoboda noted that during her ten years in Congress Martin earned "a reputation for being very conservative on fiscal matters and more moderate on social issues. She supports abortion rights and has voted for the Equal Rights Amendment.... Martin has described herself to staff members of the House Budget Committee as conservative on economic issues, and she is an ardent supporter of the White House on key budget matters." Martin forged many friendships on Capitol Hill, among Republicans and Democrats alike, and she was considered a representative who would not always toe the Republican party line. She was nevertheless a conservative and therefore was not considered an ally of organized labor, either. Tracking her record on labor-related issues, the AFL-CIO (American Federation of Labor and Congress of Industrial Organizations) awarded her only 46 points on a scale of 100 in 1988.

Martin began her friendship with Bush over dinner in her Rockford, Illinois, home in 1980. As a Republican congresswoman, she quickly became an unofficial advisor to the president, helping him to keep abreast of congressional action and adding her candid counsel on the issues. In 1984 Martin served as a stand-in for Democratic vice-presidential candidate Geraldine Ferraro during practice debates, helping Bush to learn how to react in the debate format. In 1988 Bush named Martin national co-chairperson of his presidential campaign and conferred with her regularly on election matters. Martin assumed great power in the national Republican party, but she managed to do so without alienating House Democrats—and she still kept an open mind on several important public policy issues.

Unlike many Republicans, Martin has supported such issues as abortion rights and the Equal Rights Amendment. While still in Congress, she voted to override presidential vetoes of the Family and Medical Leave Act—which would require employers to give unpaid leaves to workers during times of illness, child care emergency, or parental care emergency—and the Civil Rights Act of 1990. She also voted to override Bush's veto of a bill raising the federal minimum wage. Some observers feel that Martin's actions on these particular pieces of legislation prove that she has an independent spirit and the verve to challenge Bush on his labor policy.

Others, however, are not so certain. After the announcement of Martin's nomination as secretary of labor, she was endorsed by the U.S. Chamber of Commerce and the National Association of Manufacturers, both business groups. On the other hand, AFL-CIO President Lane Kirkland told the *Washington Post* that organized labor questioned her commitment to workers and their families, "particularly when the economy is in recession and workers bear the brunt of hard times." Kirkland added: "Her voting record has not reflected a sensitivity to the needs of workers."

Ironically, Martin received consideration for a cabinet position only after losing an election for the first time in her career. In 1990 she decided to challenge Paul Simon, a Democrat, for his seat in the Senate. Simon defeated Martin handily, taking more than a million-vote lead on election day. At first Martin decided to retire from politics and spend more time at home with her husband, U.S. district court judge Harry Leinenweber. Friends began to dissuade her from early retirement, however, pointing to several openings in the Cabinet, including the job in Labor and one in the Department of Education. Martin let Bush know that she was interested in a job, and he responded that he was glad to hear it—he had one in mind for her.

Bush formally offered her the job of secretary of labor on December 14, 1990. Although her background was more education-oriented, Martin told the *Chicago Tribune* that she actually preferred the labor job. "Oddly enough, I thought the fit was best," she said. "I thought that what was done here [in the Department of Labor] was part of education, anyway. The part of labor that is growing the most is the part [involving training] after high school. Education is going to be done everywhere." She added that the opportunity to help working men and women was the attraction of the post. "I knew I hadn't articulated that well enough during the campaign," she said, "but if I could do some good here I might really be able to affect someone's life."

Martin's relatively easy confirmation was helped by the support she received from prominent Capitol Hill Democrats. Senate labor committee chairman Edward Kennedy told the *Chicago Tribune* that he hoped Martin would be "heard and heeded in the White House." Kennedy added that Martin "is the first and only secretary of labor ever to be nominated by a president after having voted in Congress to override the president's veto on a critical labor issue." On her part, Martin assured the legislators at her hearing that she would stand up for her beliefs in Cabinet meetings. "There are issues like civil rights and family leave where I have a legislative history," she said, as quoted in the *Chicago Tribune*. "I think it does say something about President Bush that he does want people around him ... not yes-women or yes-men ... but people willing to give him advice .... I assure you, I'm going to give him my best advice."

The Department of Labor is one of the largest regulatory agencies in the federal government, a massive enterprise employing 19,000 people in every part of the nation. The department sets safety standards, monitors labor-management relations, and enforces labor-related laws enacted by the government. As *Chicago Tribune* correspondent Mitchell Locin noted, the Department of Labor "affects almost every American worker and U.S. business." As head of this arm of the government, Martin will take a seat in a presidential cabinet of 14 members—a far cry from being one of 535 voices in Congress. Martin told the *Chicago Tribune:* "It's pretty wonderful to be asked to be in the Cabinet .... All you can say is what an incredible, incredible opportunity."

Sources

Chicago Tribune, December 15, 1990; December 18, 1990; January 31, 1991; May 19, 1991.
Newsweek, February 18, 1991.
Philadelphia Inquirer, December 15, 1990.
Washington Post, December 15, 1990; January 4, 1991; January 31, 1991.

—Anne Janette Johnson

Richard Misrach

Photographer

Born July 11, 1949, in Los Angeles, Calif.; son of a sporting-goods businessman and a homemaker; married; one son. *Education:* University of California, Berkeley, B.A., 1971.

Career

Professional photographer; instructor at Associated Students Studio, University of California, Berkeley, 1971-77, became visiting lecturer, 1982; visiting lecturer, department of art, University of California, Santa Barbara, 1984. Has had photographs collected in several books; exhibitions include solo shows at Georges Pompidou Center, Paris, Corcoran Gallery, Washington, D.C., and New York-based traveling exhibit, 1979—.

Awards: National Endowment for the Arts photography fellowships, 1973, 1977, 1984; Friends of Photography Ferguson Grant, 1976; Guggenheim fellowship, 1978.

Sidelights

Beautiful is an inadequate word to describe these photographs of the California desert," wrote Eric Levin in *People*, "but it won't go away." Levin was referring to the art of Richard Misrach. "Is a burning creosote bush beautiful?" continued Levin. "Is a flood beautiful? Are rampant tire tracks and graffiti-covered rocks and dying palm fronds and parched lake beds beautiful? As Misrach photographs them, yes, they are incomparably beautiful."

These works are included in Misrach's collection *Desert Cantos*, one of many art books the photographer has produced in his 20-plus-year career as "one of America's most distinctive and original nature photographers," as Sean Elder described him in the *Los Angeles Times Magazine*. "Among other things," Elder added, "he is not afraid to document the realities of the planet."

The realities of Misrach's vision include the effects of humankind on nature. In a Misrach vista, "power lines cut across the pristine scenery, satellite dishes wink in the distance, animals lie bloated, having drunk from toxic sumps," Elder remarked. "The images are formally beautiful, but the message is grim: Misrach considers humanity's assault on earth a 'failed stewardship.'" Misrach, the product of a southern California upbringing, enrolled in the University of California, Berkeley, in 1967. During that time of countercultural sensibilities, "Berkeley was going through tremendous upheaval," as the photographer told Elder. "I've never grown up as quickly as I did in that year; it sent me on a spiral of challenging a lot of the values my parents held." Though enrolled as a math major, Misrach "soon switched to psychology and began a thesis on 'altered states of consciousness,'" according to Elder. "He also fell in love with photography."

Like his inspirations, Dorothea Lange and Walker Evans, Misrach wanted to use his art as a vehicle for social reform. Said Elder: "He had a dream in which faces of burnt-out street-people who were overrunning the city appeared and disappeared." By age 24, the artist abandoned his graduate study in psychology to concentrate on his photographs. "Like many people in the counterculture nationwide, his concerns were turning mystical," Elder noted. "It sounds sort of hokey," Misrach admitted, "but I just sort of discovered the desert."

Early on, Misrach flouted the conventions of his field, primarily by employing artificial light. "At that point I was rebelling against traditional landscape photography, like Ansel Adams, and doing exactly the opposite of what he would do," Misrach recalled to Elder. "I was vandalizing with artificial light." During the 1970s Misrach's work began appearing in group shows, and by 1978, when he won his Guggenheim fellowship, the photographer was working in color, experimenting "in swamps, forests and the desert, using less artificial light and framing his shots less rigidly, letting nature claim its own definition," according to Elder.

Soon "a new quality began to creep into Misrach's work: a darker edge, a sense of things going awry in the natural world," Elder continued. As Misrach described it: "I became very future-conscious once my kid was born. Everywhere I looked, particularly in the desert, I started seeing these incredible symbols of our failed stewardship of the environment." Misrach was especially interested in the perilous marriage of civilization and nature: after shooting pictures of animals that had perished from toxic waste and industrial fire, "I felt like I'd developed a language and now I had something to say."

Art in America critic Mark Levy saw "a kind of Buddhist equation between man-made and natural objects in all of Misrach's photographs. Since, in his work, even junk seems to have a spiritual force, it is difficult to read his imagery as an unambiguous outcry against the evils of pollution, as some environmentalists would have it . . . . Although his style always maximizes the visual poetry of his chosen scenes, Misrach is a more objective and less sentimental observer of the landscape than [is Ansel Adams]." Levy concluded that Misrach's vision of "desertness" has meant "casting his eye on the tacky products of contemporary culture [that] litter the landscape as well as its majestic natural beauty. Both elements are transformed in his view."

Selected books

Desert Cantos, University of New Mexico Press, 1987.

Sources

Art in America, April 1988.
Los Angeles Times Magazine, November 4, 1990.
People, September 7, 1987.

—Susan Salter

Joni Mitchell

AP/Wide World Photos

Singer and songwriter

Born Roberta Joan Anderson, November 7, 1943, in Fort McLeod, Alberta, Canada; immigrated to United States, 1965, naturalized citizen; daughter of William A. (a grocery store manager) and Myrtle M. (a teacher; maiden name, McKee) Anderson; married Chuck Mitchell (a musician), June, 1965 (divorced, 1966); married Larry Klein (a musician), November 21, 1982. *Education:* Attended Alberta College of Art. *Religion:* Buddhist.

Addresses: *Home*—New York, NY; Malibu, CA; and Vancouver, British Columbia, Canada. *Agent*—Elliot Roberts, Lookout Management, 9120 Sunset Blvd., Los Angeles, CA 90096.

Career

Singer, songwriter, recording artist, and concert performer.

Awards: Grammy Award for best folk performance, 1970; *Playboy* Award for best female artist, 1974; Rocky Award for best female vocalist, 1975.

Sidelights

Since her emergence as a singer-songwriter in the late 1960s, Joni Mitchell has followed a curvy and highly personal path, exploring folk, rock and roll, and jazz. Her lyrics have influenced a generation of pop artists, and musicians as diverse as Stephen Stills and Prince have sung her praises. As a performer, she opened the door for many other independent-minded female musicians. Mitchell fol-

lowed her successful albums of the late 1960s and early 1970s with a series of experimental projects that alienated many critics and often sold poorly, but she returned to a more mainstream sound during the 1980s and to critical acclaim with her 1991 release, *Night Ride Home.*

Mitchell was born Roberta Joan Anderson in 1943 in Fort McLeod, Alberta, Canada. Her mother was a schoolteacher who read her Shakespeare; her father was a former Air Force officer turned grocery store manager. At age nine she contracted polio, which attacked the muscles in her back and leg. Though doctors predicted she would never walk again, Mitchell recovered, thanks in part to her artistic spirit. "I drew like crazy and sang Christmas carols," she recalled in an interview with Steve Matteo in *CD Review.* "I think that the creative process was an urgency then, that it was a survival instinct."

Although she took piano lessons in her youth, Mitchell later switched to the guitar, teaching herself with the help of a Pete Seeger instruction book. Exposure to the songs of Bob Dylan strongly influenced her lyric-writing. "I wrote poetry," she told David Wild in *Rolling Stone,* "and I always wanted to make music. But I never put the two things together. Just a simple thing like being a singer-songwriter—

that was a new idea. It used to take three people to do that job. And when I heard [Dylan's song] 'Positively Fourth Street,' I realized that this was a whole new ballgame; now you could make your songs literature." At the same time she explored the visual arts, and though painting remained a secondary career for her, she has produced the cover art for several of her albums and shown her work in galleries.

After high school, Mitchell attended the Alberta College of Art in Calgary, but left a year later to play music in Toronto's folk clubs. There she met Chuck Mitchell, a folk singer from Detroit, whom she married some thirty-six hours after their introduction. She returned with him to Detroit, forming her stage name from his last name and an alteration of her middle name. The couple were divorced about a year later; Joni Mitchell moved to New York in 1966.

After a year and a half of struggling in the extremely competitive Manhattan folk scene, Mitchell caught the attention of rock musician David Crosby and scored a record deal with Reprise. In 1968 she released *Joni Mitchell*, later retitled *Songs to a Seagull*, produced by Crosby and featuring the songs "I Had a King" and "Michael from the Mountains." Despite her strong debut, Mitchell at first gained more attention as a songwriter than as a performer or recording artist. Her song "Both Sides, Now," which she performed on her second album *Clouds*, has been recorded by 45 artists, including Judy Collins—who scored a hit with it—Buffy Sainte-Marie, and crooners Frank Sinatra and Bing Crosby.

Clouds appeared in 1969; the following year Mitchell received a Grammy Award for the album. By this time, of course, recognition of her talents as a performer had grown. Upon the release of *Clouds*, a writer for *Time* remarked that Mitchell "has a fluty, vanilla-fresh voice with a haunting, pastoral quality." Jacoba Allas asserted in *Melody Maker* that the singer-songwriter "has emerged as a major force in music." Praise for *Clouds* was not unanimous, however; according to *Newsweek*'s Hubert Saal, "The artless folk singer has become dark-voiced and professional, with the folk idiom diluted. This isn't bad in itself. But the songs themselves are thin in subject, nebulous in form, and self-conscious in their poetic effects."

In the midst of the political and social turmoil of 1969, Mitchell was a soft-voiced advocate rather than a radical. Her anti-war song "The Fiddle and the Drum," Susan Donoghue noted in *Jazz & Pop*, "seems to chide gently, rather than 'protest.'" Mitchell herself told *Newsweek* that "when I think of [the

war in] Vietnam or [student unrest at California's University of] Berkeley, I feel so helpless. I've never been political. I still haven't made my own moral decisions of what I feel is right for man and for the world." Even so, her next album, *Ladies of the Canyon*, featured the song "Woodstock," inspired by the famous rock music festival that marked the high point of the youth movement of the late 1960s. The song became an anthem; the rock group Crosby, Stills, Nash and Young scored a hit with the upbeat version on their album *Deja Vu*. Composed after Mitchell moved to a home on Laurel Canyon in Los Angeles, *Ladies* also contained "Big Yellow Taxi," which combined Mitchell's familiar theme of lost romance with larger social concerns: "Don't it always seem to go that you don't know what you've got 'till it's gone? / They paved paradise and put up a parking lot."

Mitchell achieved an artistic breakthrough with her next effort, *Blue*, which was released in 1971. The LP contains some of her most memorable songs, among them "Carey," "Case of You," "California," and "The Last Time I Saw Richard." While the songs on *Blue* explore many of the personal issues touched on in Mitchell's earlier work, they demonstrate a songwriting craft and breadth of vision that mark the album as a turning point. In "California" she sings about missing her adopted home while visiting Europe: "I'm gonna see the folks I dig / I'll even kiss a Sunset pig / California, coming home." By 1971 Mitchell sensed the disappointment that followed the excitement and turmoil of the previous decade: "Sitting in a park in Paris, France / Reading the news and it sure looks bad / They won't give peace a chance / That was just a dream some of us had."

After *Blue*, Mitchell left Reprise and recorded a series of albums for David Geffen's Asylum label, beginning with *For the Roses* in 1972. While not as ambitious as its predecessor, *For the Roses* featured several songs that would become favorites among Mitchell fans, including "You Turn me On (I'm a Radio)" and "See You Sometime." *Creem*'s Lester Bangs called the record "the best album Joni Mitchell has ever made."

With *Court and Spark*, released in 1974, Mitchell began exploring rock and pop song styles more aggressively. She enlisted an impressive group of musicians to play on the album, including horn player Tom Scott, guitarists Larry Carlton, Robbie Robertson, and Jose Feliciano, drummer John Guerin, and vocalists David Crosby and Graham Nash. *Court and Spark* represented another substantial leap forward for Mitchell's songwriting, but also for her popularity: "Help Me" was a hit and "Raised on Robbery" received considerable radio airplay. Arthur Schmidt in *Melody Maker* referred to the album as "her most mature piece of work yet, and one in which she deepens the complexities of her art, both in a lyric and musical sense, as well as [taking] off in a new direction."

In November of 1974 Mitchell took the L.A. Express, the band she had assembled for *Court and Spark*, on a concert tour, and released a double live album, *Miles of Aisles*. It quickly became a gold record. The following month she appeared on the cover of *Time* in a story titled "Rock 'n' Roll's Leading Lady." The article called her "a creative force of unrivaled stature in the mercurial world of rock." *Miles of Aisles* produced another hit single, this time a rocking new version of "Big Yellow Taxi." In 1974 she received the *Playboy* Award for best female artist and in 1975 the Rocky Award for best female vocalist. Mitchell reached the very peak of her commercial success during this period.

Her next effort, however, marked the beginning of a long downturn. *The Hissing of Summer Lawns* appeared in 1975, evidently engaging in more musical experimentation than critics and fans could appreciate. The LP was rated *Rolling Stone*'s worst album of the year; even critics who spoke highly of its lyrics disliked the music. Perry Meisel, writing for the *Village Voice*, called it "aimless" and *Rolling Stone*'s Ariel Swartley referred to its "self-conscious artiness." The jazzy textures in her music had deepened and become more complex just when Mitchell had been dubbed a "Queen of Rock." Retrospectively, however, many writers and fans have come to appreciate the album, particularly since it anticipated by some time the use of similar musical styles on popular albums by Paul Simon, Sting, and many others. Songs like "In France They Kiss on Main Street," a nostalgic but upbeat picture of sex, rebellion, and music in the 1950s, and "Edith and the Kingpin," a tense love story filled with compelling images, further demonstrated Mitchell's range as a lyricist. The album contains several other strong songs, including "Don't Interrupt the Sorrow," "Shadows and Light," and a haunting piece called "The Jungle Line," which features African drumming.

1976 saw the release of *Hejira*, a musically spare but lyrically packed collection of songs featuring contributions by several prominent jazz musicians, most notably bassist Jaco Pastorius of the group Weather Report. *Hejira*'s title refers to the prophet Mohammed's flight from the city of Mecca, portrayed in the Koran, the Bible of Islam. Flight and exploration are dominant themes in many of the songs. In "Coyote," the singer refers to herself as "a prisoner of the white lines on the freeway"; "Amelia" calls upon the spirit of vanished aviatrix Amelia Earhart and speaks of sleeping "on the strange pillows of my wanderlust"; the restless "Black Crow," like the narrator of the song, swoops down on "every shiny thing." "Refuge of the Roads," the last cut on the album, contains some of Mitchell's most powerful observations about her place in the world: "In a highway service station / Over the month of June / Was a photograph of the earth / Taken coming back from the moon / And you couldn't see the city / On that marbled bowling ball / Or a forest or a highway / Or me here least of all."

Critics responded to *Hejira* with ambivalence. Meisel, in an article for the *Village Voice* titled "An End to Innocence: How Joni Mitchell Fails," concluded that "Mitchell clearly lacks any real understanding of what her work is and how it behaves." Swartley, however, claimed in *Rolling Stone* that on *Hejira* Mitchell "redefines the elements of her music with as much courage as when she scrutinizes her aims and motivations."

Reviews of 1977's *Don Juan's Reckless Daughter*, however, were almost universally negative. Mitchell continued using jazz elements on this two-record set, and despite the inclusion of strong songs like "Dreamland," "Off Night Backstreet," and the title track, critics seemed to agree that Mitchell had clearly overreached on this project. Janet Maslin, in a *Rolling Stone* review, called the album "sapped of emotion and full of ideas that should have remained whims, melodies that should have been riffs, songs that should have been fragments." "Having concentrated on herself for so long," wrote Jon Pareles in *Crawdaddy*, "she can't separate out the trivia anymore." *Circus* magazine's Ray Sturgeon remarked that "Mitchell fans tell me it's an excellent album. But I wonder if the rest of us have the patience for the serious listening it requires."

In 1979 Mitchell released *Mingus*, the result of a collaboration with famous jazz bassist and composer Charles Mingus. Mitchell wrote lyrics to several Mingus compositions; unfortunately the jazz legend died before its release. Although Mingus sent for Mitchell and proposed the project, many jazz fans accused her of using Mingus and black music for the sake of her own career. "With that album," Mitchell later told *Rolling Stone*, "I became a person without a country. I was considered an expatriate from pop music. Meanwhile, the jazz folks thought, 'Who is this white chick?' They saw me as an opportunist come to exploit Charles, whereas, in fact, Charles sent for me. In jazz circles they still complain about it, that what we did was not Mingus's music. Well, of course it wasn't; it was a collaboration. It was not mine either. We had to meet somewhere in the middle with integrity.''

Shadows and Light, another double live set comprised primarily of songs from *Hissing, Hejira, Don Juan,* and *Mingus,* appeared in 1980. Featuring musical contributions from Pastorius, guitarist Pat Metheny, saxophonist Michael Brecker and the singing group The Persuasions, *Shadows and Light* is an engaging mixture of intimate playing—demonstrated in Mitchell's haunting solo rendition of "Woodstock"—and showbiz flamboyance, best exemplified by a rollicking version of the 1950s classic "Why Do Fools Fall in Love." The album was moderately successful, though Mitchell was still a long way from her mid-seventies peak. In 1991 she looked back on this period without regret. "I started working in a genre that was neither this nor that," she remarked to *Rolling Stone's* David Wild. "People didn't know where I fit in anymore, so they didn't play me at all. And so I disappeared. I lost my ability to broadcast, my public access. It was worth it. I would do it all over again in a minute for the musical education.

In 1982 Mitchell released *Wild Things Run Fast,* the first of a series of albums for David Geffen's new label. A return to pop-oriented songs, *Wild Things* includes a charming medley of Mitchell's original song "Chinese Cafe" and the 1950s ballad "Unchained Melody." The effect of the combination is nostalgic and bittersweet; in the song the singer describes being "caught in the middle"—no longer part of the wild generation of rock and roll, but belonging instead to a bland middle class. That year Mitchell married bassist and producer Larry Klein, who played on *Wild Things* and her next three albums. (Mitchell remarked in a *Rolling Stone* interview that she prayed at the time for "a real good kisser who likes to play pinball," and that Klein invited her out to a video arcade shortly thereafter. "We've been together ever since," she said. "So I look at it as divine intervention.")

Mitchell's next LP, *Dog Eat Dog,* released in 1985, used electronic textures and a variety of sound effects; co-produced by British rock artist Thomas Dolby, the album reflected the emergence of a new political anger in Mitchell. *Stereo Review's* Alanna Nash called the record "a beautifully crafted and intelligent appraisal of American culture in decline" but also "an angry album, one that fairly seethes

with outrage as Mitchell surveys the general state of things and finds rampant moral decay." Mitchell had come a long way from her apolitical stance of the late 1960s. The album includes a duet with singer Michael MacDonald titled "Good Friends," and "Tax Free," a song about a right-wing television evangelist portrayed on the record by actor Rod Steiger.

Mitchell's 1988 follow-up, *Chalk Mark in a Rain Storm,* featured a diverse group of guest artists, among them rock vocalists Peter Gabriel, Billy Idol, and Tom Petty, country star Willie Nelson, and Native American actor Iron Eyes Cody. Although more delicate in its themes than *Dog Eat Dog, Chalk Mark* pursued a number of social issues, including Native American land rights on "Lakota" and capitalist ambition on "Number One." The album garnered largely favorable reviews and marked the beginning of Mitchell's critical resurgence. "Subtle, sophisticated, musical, and accessible, *Chalk Mark* is an amalgam of the different strains and voices that this underappreciated, extraordinary musician has been experimenting with in the last decade," wrote Rory O'Connor in *Vogue.* Nicholas Jennings of *Maclean's* called it "her best album in years." Although several critics noted flaws in the album, *Rolling Stone's* J. D. Considine was probably most severe: "Alluring as its surface is...this album doesn't invite repeated listenings; in that sense, *Chalk Mark in a Rain Storm* is all too aptly named, for its pleasures simply wash away with time."

1991 saw the release of *Night Ride Home,* which inspired even better reviews and a flurry of new interest in Mitchell's career. The album emphasizes simple, guitar-driven song stylings; its first single, "Come in From the Cold" fared well on radio. Other songs include "Cherokee Louise," which deals with a young incest survivor, "The Only Joy in Town," in which the singer admires the "Botticelli black boy" she sees in Spain, and a musical interpretation of William Butler Yeats's famous poem "The Second Coming" called "Slouching Towards Bethlehem." Michael Small noted in *People* that on this album "she swirls all her styles into one collage." "While some may interpret *Night Ride Home* as a return to Mitchell's earlier, more musically sparse sounds," Steve Matteo pointed out in *CD Review,* "the recording is actually a refinement, both lyrically and musically, that involved long years of searching for new sounds, melodies, vocal arrangements, and poetry." In fact, as Matteo saw it, the exploration of Mitchell's late seventies records laid the groundwork for her later success. *Rolling Stone's* Tom Sinclair concluded that "Old-time Mitchell fans may well prefer the incandescence of her *Blue* period or even the abstract expressionism of *Mingus* or *Shadows and Light*. Still, *Night Ride Home*, if not the masterpiece some might have hoped for, is a convincing demonstration of her continuing validity as an artist."

In a 1991 interview in *CD Review*, Mitchell suggested that she might tour in support of *Night Ride Home*, though the physical strain of the road has limited her in the past. Even so, she felt that "we should tour, really, because *Night Ride Home* has got a tail-wind, and people tend to like it." Her consideration of the tour, like her unusually thorough participation in the publicizing of the album, suggested that with her latest album, at age 47, Joni Mitchell had re-entered the popular music scene with determination. Though no longer the "Queen of Rock 'n' Roll," she has proven herself an artist with staying power and boundless creative energy, the same combination that got her on her feet in her childhood and into the public eye in her folk-music days. "Miles Davis and Picasso have always been my major heroes," she commented in *Rolling Stone*, "because we have this one thing in common: They were restless."

Selected discography

Joni Mitchell (later retitled *Song to a Seagull*,) Reprise, 1968.
Clouds, Reprise, 1969.
Ladies of the Canyon, Reprise, 1970.
Blue, Reprise, 1971.
For the Roses, Asylum, 1972.
Court and Spark, Asylum, 1974.
Miles of Aisles (live), Asylum, 1975.
The Hissing of Summer Lawns, Asylum, 1975.
Hejira, Asylum, 1975.
Don Juan's Reckless Daughter, Asylum, 1977.
Mingus, Asylum, 1979.
Shadows and Light (live), Asylum, 1980.
Wild Things Run Fast, Geffen, 1982.
Dog Eat Dog, Geffen, 1985.
Chalk Mark in a Rain Storm, Geffen, 1988.
Night Ride Home, Geffen, 1991.

Sources

Books

The Rolling Stone Illustrated History of Rock and Roll, edited by Jim Miller, Random House, 1976.

Periodicals

Audio, August 1988.
CD Review, July 1991.
Circus, February 16, 1978.
Crawdaddy, February 1978.
Creem, February 1973.
Interview, April 1991.
Jazz & Pop, September 1969, July 1970.
Maclean's, April 4, 1988.
Melody Maker, September 28, 1968; June 20, 1970; July 10, 1971; January 26, 1974.
Newsweek, July 14, 1969.
People, March 28, 1988; February 11, 1991.
Rolling Stone, February 10, 1977; March 9, 1978; April 21, 1988; March 21, 1991; May 30, 1991.
Saturday Review, July 26, 1969.
Stereo Review, April 1976; March 1986; July 1988.
Time, April 4, 1969; December 16, 1974.
Video Review, December 1990.
Village Voice, January 24, 1977.
Vogue, August 1988.

—Simon Glickman

Isaac Mizrahi

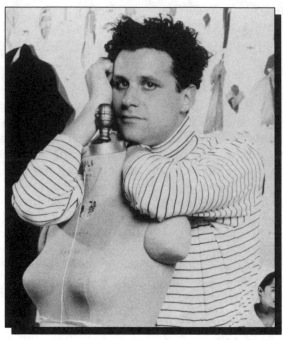

© *Benno Friedman/Outline Press*

Fashion designer

Born October, 1961, in Brooklyn, N.Y.; son of a children's wear manufacturer. *Education:* Attended Performing Arts High School; graduated from Parsons School of Design, 1982.

Career

Began creating and selling own designs under label IS by age 15; worked for fashion designers Perry Ellis, 1980-84, Jeffrey Banks, and Calvin Klein; began own design house, c. 1987; first fashion show, 1988.

Awards: Named best newcomer, 1988, and best women's designer, 1989, by the Council of Fashion Designers of America.

Sidelights

A true overnight success, even by fashion world standards, Isaac Mizrahi recalled in *New York* magazine the day of the first triumphant unveiling of his designs in April 1988 as "the most emotionally wrenching experience I can remember." Surely, the possibility of failure must have haunted him, but Mizrahi might also have had some prophetic sense of the chaotic uproar that would soon take over the life of fashion's newest golden boy. The show reportedly opened slowly with a few conservative designs, but soon those press luminaries who had even bothered to show up for the supposedly minor event knew something extraordinary was happening. After a model in a jacket of brilliant orange came down the runway, a young *Vogue* editor named Elizabeth Saltzman knew she had a major discovery before her. "It was like opening a dam. I gushed. I no longer had to be dressed in black," Saltzman told *New York.*

Seemingly from out of nowhere, with at once a renegade spirit and firm allegiance to classical American design, Mizrahi was able to deliver what the fashion industry clamors for—bold, imaginative, but wearable new designs. "The heart of the Mizrahi style is simple but fresh," wrote the *Washington Post*'s Martha Sherrill Dailey. "An American look that's sophisticated without being scary." *Elle*'s John Howell applauded Mizrahi's willingness to experiment with odd patterns, prints, and colors. "Making the unsightly beautiful is one of Mizrahi's most admired adventures. Many of his trademark patterns . . . have less than chic reputations, and Mizrahi has been dubbed 'the prince of prints' for his consistent use of bold, slightly questionable motifs," Howell remarked, adding: "Like a mad mixmaster turned loose in a Magic Marker factory, Mizrahi puts together 'off' colors in unexpected combinations that should only emphasize their 'offness'—but somehow don't." And *New York*'s Michael Gross wrote simply: "Serious clothes are hardly ever this much fun anymore."

Mizrahi, born in Brooklyn to Syrian-Jewish parents in 1961, grew up in a fashion-conscious household. His father was a manufacturer of children's clothes, and his mother used to take her son on her frequent shopping trips to New York's finest boutiques. Mizrahi traces his love of fashion to those early years. "It's fetishistic," he told *New York*. "I am maniacal about clothes." His father bought him a sewing machine and Mizrahi was making his own clothes by age ten. Overweight, withdrawn, and precocious as an adolescent, Mizrahi got the feeling of acceptance he really needed when he enrolled at New York's Performing Arts High School. He weighed 250 pounds when he got to school, but after a semester and a winter on the Scarsdale diet, he had lost 75 pounds. "It was a very big adjustment, but by my sophomore year I was really swinging," Mizrahi said. "I had become sort of, like, accepted, and I had found my whole personality."

A friend of Mizrahi's father recommended that Isaac enter the prestigious Parsons School of Design, where he soon proved to be light years ahead of his classmates. Before graduating he had already won a part-time job with Perry Ellis, and from there he moved to Jeffrey Banks and finally to Calvin Klein before setting out on his own. Along with his business partner, longtime family friend Sarah Haddad Cheney, Mizrahi rented a SoHo loft and began making deliveries out of Cheney's Jaguar for his first spring line. Though Mizrahi downplays the quality of that line, he quickly garnered attention from several key editors, models, and financiers. He and Cheney succeeded in arranging more monetary support from such skeptical investors as Haim Dabah and Jack Dushey, and the fateful spring '88 show was arranged. That night, Mizrahi's mother reportedly sobbed tears of joy, saying, "I don't believe what I just saw!" While the accolades came pouring in— Mizrahi was named best newcomer in 1988 and best women's designer in 1989 by the Council of Fashion Designers of America—he was determined not to grow too quickly and burn out, as has happened to other young designers. In 1990 he moved his offices and 50 employees to a relatively modest, 27,000 square foot office building in New York City's SoHo, and sales for that year were expected to top $8 million. Mizrahi credits his years working under Perry Ellis for his conservative business sense and merchandising sensibilities. "He's got his head screwed on straight," said fellow designer Peter Speliopoulos in *New York*. "He has an incredible mother who has handled his success well, a partner he can trust, and he's surrounded by devoted young people, which is so rare." Though Mizrahi dreams of someday moving uptown to the heart of New York's fashion district with a house that rivals Yves Saint Laurent and Calvin Klein, he is content to take his time getting there. "Slow is the key, I think," Mizrahi told the *Washington Post*.

Sources

Elle, June 1990.
Interview, March 1988.
New York, October 1, 1990.
New York Times, June 21, 1988; November 5, 1988; April 15, 1989.
People, Special Spring Issue, 1990.
Washington Post, May 8, 1988.

—*David Collins*

Warren Moon

AP/Wide World Photos

Professional football player

Full name, Harold Warren Moon; born November 18, 1956, in Los Angeles, Calif.; son of Harold (a laborer; deceased); mother was a nurse; married wife, Felicia, March 8, 1981; children: Joshua, Chelsea, Blair, Jeffrey. *Education:* Attended West Los Angeles Junior College, 1974-75; University of Washington, B.S. in communications, 1978.

Addresses: *Home*—Sugarland, TX. *Office*—c/o Houston Oilers, P.O. Box 1516, Houston, TX 77251. *Agent*—Leigh Steinberg, Berkeley, CA.

Career

Quarterback for the Edmonton Eskimos, 1978-83; quarterback for the Houston Oilers, 1984—.

Awards: Named Pacific-8 Conference Player of the Year, 1977; named Most Valuable Player in the Canadian Football League (CFL), 1983; named National Football League (NFL) Rookie of the Year, 1984, and NFL Man of the Year, 1989; named Associated Press NFL Offensive Player of the Year, 1990.

Sidelights

In 1990 Warren Moon achieved one of the greatest seasons ever by an NFL quarterback. Despite missing all of one game and most of another, he threw for 4,689 yards—the fifth highest total ever in the NFL. He was named the league's top offensive performer of the year and named to his third straight Pro Bowl team.

Seven years earlier, however, Moon was not even considered a candidate to play in the NFL. Coming out of the University of Washington, he was considered non-prospect. It was not the first time he had been passed over. And coming out of high school, Moon was not considered a legitimate collegiate recruit. "I've had to kind of take that extra step at every level just to show what I can do, whether it be junior college or Canada before I got a chance to play in the NFL," Moon told the *Rocky Mountain News.* "I've been told all my life that I didn't have what it took. It was the people who told me I couldn't do things that kept me going. I have a lot of confidence in myself."

A native of Los Angeles, Moon was the middle child and only boy of seven children. Warren was seven when his father died while waiting for a liver transplant. His mother, a nurse, raised the family by herself. Like his sisters, Moon had to help cook and clean. He also held jobs after school to help support the family. He grew up in a rough neighborhood, but steered clear of rough activities. His mother repeatedly lectured him about staying away from drugs and crime, and Moon was determined to obey. Gertrude Peoples, a University of Washington academic adviser who has known Moon since 1975, told the *Seattle Times* that his upbringing "made him very caring, kind and sensitive. Maybe it is because he was the only boy in a household of women. But there's no pretentiousness. There never was."

Realizing the temptations of the neighborhood he lived in, Moon transferred to Hamilton High School in Los Angeles, which had a better academic and athletic program. Brought in to mop up in his first game on the freshman team, he launched an 80-yard pass, overthrowing his receiver but impressing varsity coach Jack Epstein, who was watching from the stands. "I'll remember that pass until the day I die," Epstein told the *Houston Post.* "He was just a little skinny kid and he threw that ball so hard there was smoke coming off the back of the ball. The ball went about a mile over the receiver's head. I knew then he would be a great one."

After taking over as varsity quarterback, Moon led Hamilton to the 1973 city playoffs as a senior and was named to the all-city team. But college recruiters showed little interest in him because he was only 5'11" and 165 pounds. Eventually Moon followed Epstein, who had become offensive coordinator at West Los Angeles Junior College. Moon flourished at the school and was named the Western State Conference Player of the Year as a freshman. His strong performance caught the attention of University of Washington coach Don James, who offered Moon a chance to transfer to a school playing big-time football. Moon went, despite his apprehension about attending a college that had experienced racial tension under a previous coach and where fewer than four percent of the students were black.

As a sophomore, Moon warmed the bench. As a junior, he was a starter and the University of Washington Huskies stumbled to a 5-6 record, prompting fans to boo the quarterback. "There's always a big question whether they were booing the guy because he was the quarterback and we weren't winning, or whether they were booing him because he was black," James told the *Seattle Times.* "I'm sure they were tough times for Warren to go through. I'm sure it did bother him. It was really grim at times. But Warren was a real gentleman. He didn't lash out at any of the fans publicly. He took everything he got and he turned around and got more determined to prove that he was a good quarterback."

Moon went on to prove that in 1977. After a slow 2-2 start and more calls for the coach to change quarterbacks, Moon led the Huskies to the conference championship and a win over the University of Michigan in the 1978 Rose Bowl game. He was named the Rose Bowl's Most Valuable Player and the Pacific-8 Player of the Year after passing for 1,584

yards and 11 touchdowns. Overall, Moon passed for 3,277 yards and 19 touchdowns in his collegiate career.

Although Moon managed to win over Washington's fans, he failed to win over skeptical NFL scouts. He was rated just the 10th best quarterback in the 1978 draft. "The stereotype was that he was a black quarterback and he was going to run around like a madman, but he wouldn't be able to throw very well," former Edmonton Eskimos and Houston Oilers coach Hugh Campbell told the *Los Angeles Times.* So, once again, Moon decided to prove himself elsewhere, signing with the Eskimos of the Canadian Football League. During his six seasons there, he put up some stunning numbers—21,228 yards passing and 1,700 yards rushing. He had back-to-back 5,000-yard passing seasons. His 5,648 yards passing over 16 games in 1983 remains an all-time high for pro football. In addition, the Eskimos won five straight

Warren Moon (number 1) launches a pass during an October 1990 game against the Cincinnati Bengals in Houston. AP/Wide World Photos.

Grey Cup trophies as champions of the CFL, from 1978 to 1982.

By 1984 Moon had nothing left to prove to NFL scouts. When his contract with Edmonton expired, seven NFL teams sought to sign him as a free agent. Moon initially leaned toward the Seattle Seahawks, which would allow him to return to his college town, but he eventually chose the Houston Oilers for two reasons. First, it offered a chance to rejoin his Edmonton coach, Campbell, whom Houston had hired a month earlier. Second, the Oilers tendered a five-year, $5.5 million contract which, at the time, made Moon the highest paid player in the NFL before he even played in a league game. "It would have been the natural thing for me to stay [in Seattle]," Moon told the *Houston Post*, "but I was thinking that Seattle was where I would make my permanent home, and sometimes playing where you're going to live isn't the best situation. This way people there will remember me as the University of Washington quarterback ... just well enough for me to get a seat at a table."

"As I improved, you started not to hear the word black put in front of quarterback all the time."

When Moon joined Houston, it was the sorriest franchise in the NFL, a team that had won a total of three games the previous two seasons. "One of the challenges of Houston was to be part of a growing situation," Moon's agent, Leigh Steinberg, told the *Houston Post*. "He knew it would take longer [to be on a championship team], but when it came, he knew he would be an instrumental part of the building process."

In 1984 Moon was a rookie sensation. His six years in the CFL gave him a head start on the guys just out of college, and he threw for a then-club-record of 3,338 yards. Still, the Oilers went 3-13, finishing last in the AFC Central Division. The next season, after the club won just five of its first 14 games, Campbell was fired and a defensive-oriented coach, Jerry Glanville, took over. Glanville then drafted top college quarterback Jim Everett of Purdue, who threatened to take Moon's job, until the Oilers traded Everett over contractual differences. "Those early years [in Houston] were really hard for me to deal with at first,"

Moon told the *St. Louis Post-Dispatch*. "There were some uncertainties about my career here because of the coaching change. That left me disenchanted.... Plus, I think most of the people looked at the amount of money I was paid and just decided I must be a star all of a sudden. I didn't respond well to it."

Moon also faced the pressures then of being the only black starting quarterback in the NFL (a situation which has changed in more recent years). "The stereotypes are there," he told the *Los Angeles Times*. "The opportunities haven't been given. But I think I've been accepted pretty well throughout the league. As I improved, you started not to hear the word black put in front of quarterback all the time. And now I'm pretty much recognized as just another quarterback in the league."

In 1986 the Oilers played what coach Glanville called "smash-mouth football," a game plan built around a punishing running game. The Oilers won their opener and then lost eight consecutive games, prompting a usually self-controlled Moon to publicly complain about the lack of offensive ingenuity. After a meeting with Glanville, the Oilers opened things up, and Moon ended up eclipsing his single-season passing mark with 3,489 yards. As *Houston Post* columnist Ray Buck wrote after the 1986 season: "Forget George Blanda, who set records against marginal competition. Dismiss Dan Pastorini, who had the right arm but the wrong temperament. Ignore Kenny Stabler, who was a has-been when he landed in Houston. Trust me on this: Warren Moon is the best quarterback ever to wear an Oiler uniform. With him, no matter what happens against Seattle, the Oilers have a future."

Eventually, a more pass-oriented offense began to evolve, and predictably, so did Moon. Between 1987 and 1989, the Oilers made the playoffs all three seasons as Moon threw for 61 touchdowns. Twice he was rated among the NFL's top five quarterbacks and twice he started in the Pro Bowl, the league's all-star game. Still, the Oilers never advanced to the Super Bowl and Glanville was fired following the 1989 season. His replacement was Jack Pardee, a college coach known for helping design the "run-and-shoot" offense, a system based on speedy receivers and a strong-armed quarterback. Moon was thrilled, knowing he would finally have a chance to show his talents. "They have finally found an offense for Warren Moon in Houston, the run-and-shoot, and if ever a player was born for a system, that player is Moon," *Sports Illustrated*'s Paul Zimmerman wrote midway through the 1990 season. "First they told him, you had better keep your arm healthy, because you're going to throw, maybe more than any quarterback has ever thrown in one year. Throwing? No problem. Whip it or dink it or gun it deep or throw the touch pass—Moon can do it all. Always has."

Indeed, Moon responded in 1990 by evolving from a good NFL quarterback into a great one. In 15 games he led the league with completions in 584 attempts for 4,689 yards and 33 touchdowns. At the end of the season, Moon was voted NFL Offensive Player of the Year by the Associated Press. In the season's 14th game, against the Kansas City Chiefs, Moon threw for 527 yards. The figure fell just 27 yards short of Norm Van Brocklin's all-time NFL record, which Moon almost certainly would have broken had he not removed himself from the 27-10 game midway through the fourth quarter. "People tend to say Super Bowl quarterbacks are the great ones," Moon told *Sports Illustrated* after the game. "If I get there, I don't think anyone could argue with my play." The Oilers seemed to have a chance of getting there in 1990 until Moon was injured in the next-to-last game of the season. He sat on the sidelines during the playoffs as the Oilers lost to the Cincinnati Bengals.

In a 1990 poll by the *Houston Post*, Moon was voted the most popular athlete in Texas, even beating out baseball legend Nolan Ryan. Certainly, Moon's success on the field has much to do with that, but so too does his off-field demeanor. "Warren is the kindest, most sincere person I've ever met," Judy Riley, executive director of the Crescent Moon Foundation, told the *Akron Beacon-Journal*. The foundation is a non-profit corporation that Moon established to help underprivileged kids in the Houston area. Moon was chosen NFL Man of the Year in 1989 for his involvement in charitable causes, such as the United Negro College Fund, the Special Olympics, the March of Dimes, the Cystic Fibrosis Foundation, the Cerebral Palsy Foundation, and the American Heart Association. In 1989 he donated $200,000 to the Windsor Village Methodist Church in southwest Houston. The money was used to convert the old sanctuary into a sparkling neighborhood community center.

"It's really flattering to me to be thought of the way I am in this state," Moon told the *St. Louis Post-Dispatch*. "Hopefully, it's more out of respect than popularity. I hope people respect me more than they think I'm just a popular guy. I hope people see more into me than just football.... I just want to be looked at as a guy who is trying to help as many people as he can. I definitely want to excel in my sport, and I think I do."

Sources

Akron Beacon Journal, November 1, 1990; January 10, 1991.

Houston Post, December 25, 1987; March 13, 1988; November 13, 1988; April 8, 1989; July 29, 1990.

Los Angeles Times, November 18, 1989; November 3, 1990.

Rocky Mountain News, November 18, 1990.

St. Louis Post-Dispatch, October 28, 1990.

San Jose Mercury News, November 8, 1987.

Seattle Times, December 2, 1990.

Sports Illustrated, November 5, 1990; December 24, 1990.

—Mark Kram

Demi Moore

Actress

Full name, Demetria Gene Guynes Moore; born in Roswell, New Mexico, c. 1963; stepdaughter of Danny (a newspaper reporter) and daughter of Virginia (King) Guynes; married Freddy (some sources say Rick) Moore (a musician), c. 1981 (divorced, 1983); married Bruce Willis (an actor), November 21, 1987; children: (second marriage) Rumer Glenn, Scout La Rue (daughters).

Career

File clerk for a collection agency, 1979; modeled, including posing on the cover of *Oui* magazine; appeared on television as Jackie Templeton in daytime drama series *General Hospital*, 1982-84; actress in films, including *Blame It On Rio, St. Elmo's Fire, About Last Night, The Seventh Sign, No Small Affair, Parasite, One Crazy Summer, Wisdom, Ghost, Mortal Thoughts, Valkenvania*, and *The Butcher's Wife*.

Sidelights

Best known as the gravelly-voiced actress from the top-grossing 1990 movie *Ghost*, Demi Moore has a personal and professional life that exceeds her young age. When she was 19, with no previous acting experience, Moore won a regular spot on the popular daytime drama, *General Hospital*. In the next few years, Moore was to land parts in many major motion pictures, get engaged to and break up with actor Emilio Estevez, marry television and movie star Bruce Willis, and have a baby ten months later. Much of the recent publicity about Moore has

AP/Wide World Photos

focused on her Hollywood marriage, a factor which has not kept the actress from winning a spate of leading roles in major films.

Moore was born in the small town of Roswell, New Mexico. Until the time she turned seven, her life was relatively quiet and stable. Moore spent a lot of time with her cousins, largely because her aunt, Marjorie Bramlet, was her primary babysitter. Moore's lifestyle changed radically when her mother, whose earlier teen marriage had ended in divorce, married David Guynes. When Moore was seven, Guynes had to move to look for work. The moves ultimately totaled 48 in all, and young Demi never went to one school for more than a year at a stretch.

"I made the best of what little time I had anywhere," Moore commented to Nancy Anderson in *Good Housekeeping*. "I wanted to meet everyone, to really see people's lives for what they were. And having to move so often, I created a game for myself to play—I became the character who could fit in. I'd pick out a group I wanted to get in with, and I'd say 'Let's see how fast I can do it.'" Despite this attitude, the family's transient lifestyle took its toll on her personality. Each move seemed to reinforce Moore's insecurity. She never knew if she would be popular or a loner in the new school. Every summer, however,

Moore would return to her hometown, where her relatives gave her complete acceptance.

Also when she was a teen, Moore underwent an operation to correct crossed eyes. Her first husband commented to Audrey Lavin in *Redbook* that "Demi told me she grew up with people telling her how stupid and ugly she looked, cross-eyed. A major inferiority complex stemmed from insults about her odd gaze. I think that's why she is so nice to people today, because she remembers how cruelly she was abused by others." The last place Moore's well-traveled family moved was California. There, her parents separated and she stayed with her mother. Shortly after, Moore's stepfather died of asphyxiation—he left his car running in a garage.

Moore decided to live on her own, and she moved out and began working for a collection agency. Because of her voice, the agency soon had her talking to people about their past due bills. She started doing a little modeling and acting to supplement her income. "It just seemed right," said Moore in *Good Housekeeping* about her decision to go into acting. "I took a good year figuring out what I needed to do. Then I got an agent and started working." Moore was afraid, however, that she didn't have the talent or the looks to really make it.

Then she met Freddy Moore, a musician who played in a local band. They got married right after Moore's eighteenth birthday and moved to New York. Demi did some modeling there, but lack of opportunities led the couple back to California. In 1982 Demi got a coveted part on the popular daytime drama, *General Hospital*. She was only nineteen. The instant fame affected Demi right away. "Toward the end of our relationship, Demi started having a problem with drinking," her ex-husband was quoted as saying in *Redbook*. "She would have just one beer and turn into a completely different person." Demi explained in the same publication: "I had no sense of who I was or what my ideas really were. I got involved with drugs because I was young and not sure how to deal with my sudden burst of fame. I didn't know how to cope, and didn't know how to say no. I just wanted to belong."

Soon after, the Moores split and Demi headed for a rehabilitation program. Her stint on *General Hospital* also came to an end. This gave Moore a chance to make her first film, *Blame It On Rio*. Although the picture was not first-rate, it gave her the exposure she needed to launch her movie career.

Two years later she was cast as a neurotic in the movie *St. Elmo's Fire*. There she met Emilio Estevez, son of actor Martin Sheen and one of the infamous Hollywood "Brat Pack" of young actors. They fell instantly in love and became engaged. The wedding was postponed numerous times, and in 1987 the couple split permanently. Ironically, at a screening for Estevez's film *Stakeout*, Moore met Bruce Willis, the wise-cracking star of television's *Moonlighting* and the popular motion picture *Die Hard*. At the time, Willis was known for his womanizing, late-night partying, and heavy drinking. (In fact, after a three-day party at his house, Willis was arrested for assaulting a policeman who had come to stop the fracas.)

Moore was uncertain about Willis's reputation, and called a friend to check up on him. Willis phoned her during this conversation, and every day after that. They were together virtually every day for four months, and were married close to midnight in a Las Vegas ceremony on November 21, 1987. The ceremony was held at the Golden Nugget Hotel on a day Moore felt was lucky. Moore was so determined to have her wedding on this particular day that she lied when filling out the marriage license about her previous marriage. "I thought it was going to take longer if I put it on there," Moore stated in *Redbook*. "I wasn't hiding it—it's been in print . . . but I wanted to be married before midnight because I wanted that day to be the day." Shortly thereafter, the couple had a big wedding ceremony at the Burbank Studio—a present from Tri-Star pictures. It was officiated by Little Richard, with actress Ally Sheedy as a bridesmaid.

Rumors started circulating soon after the couple was wed. Some people in the Hollywood community found it hard to believe that Willis would give up his drinking and carousing for his newfound bride. Yet domestic bliss seemed to dominate the couple's relationship. Willis gave up drinking and settled down into married life, seemingly without looking back. Moore commented in *Good Housekeeping:* "Bruce and I communicate very well and he is fun to be with. I hope I am as easy to live with as he is. I've been with him a long time and I've seen nothing of the wild, crazy guy he's supposed to be."

A few months after their wedding the couple announced that Moore was expecting their first child. She delivered Rumer Glenn Willis at Western Baptist Hospital in Paducah, Kentucky, where Willis was filming *In Country*. The couple left the hospital a few hours after the birth. "Bruce helped pull this baby out of me," Moore told *People* magazine. "He's as passionate and as excited and as driven with being a father as he is with anything else that he does."

Despite the obvious happiness the couple felt about the birth of their child, rumors persisted that the Willis-Moore marriage was on the rocks.

It was hinted that Willis was jealous of Moore's success in the hit film *Ghost.* Both stars denied the rumors. "We have problems. We argue, but we both understand marriage takes care and nurturing, and we're both prepared to do that," Willis told *Vanity Fair.* Moore's second pregnancy quelled some of the rumors (although her appearance in a photo spread for *Vanity Fair* at a very advanced stage in her pregnancy caused quite a bit of controversy). Moore gave birth to the couple's second daughter, Scout La Rue, on July 21, 1991.

Already quite advanced in her career at an early age, Moore has continued to work through her marriage and motherhood. Asked whether she was afraid of taking certain roles for fear of not performing well in them, Moore commented in *Time:* "I'm not as afraid to fail as I used to be, because I'm learning to accept myself for who I am."

Sources

Good Housekeeping, November 1988.
People, December 7, 1987; November 12,1990.
Redbook, August 1988.
Rolling Stone, September 26, 1985.
Teen, July 1982, March 1987.
Time, May 26, 1986.
Vanity Fair, August 1991.

—Nancy Rampson

Robin Morgan

AP/Wide World Photos

Editor, journalist, poet, and novelist

Born January 29, 1941, in Lake Worth, Fla.; daughter of Faith Berkley Morgan; married Kenneth Pitchford (poet, novelist, and playwright), September 19, 1962; children: Blake Ariel Morgan. *Education:* Attended Columbia University.

Addresses: *Home*—New York, NY.

Career

Curtis Brown Ltd., New York City, associate literary agent, 1960-62; free-lance editor, 1964-70; writer, 1970—; *Ms.* magazine, New York City, editor in chief, 1990—. National and international lecturer on feminism, 1970-76; guest professor at New College, Sarasota, Fla., 1972; has given poetry readings throughout the United States.

Member: Authors Guild of Authors League of America, Women's Anti-Defamation League, Susan B. Anthony National Memorial Association.

Sidelights

Robin Morgan is perhaps the last, best hope for *Ms.* magazine. At a time when rising conservatism has threatened to undermine many of the hard-won tenets of feminist ideology and *Ms.* has slowly choked on a shrinking diet of advertising revenues, the new owners of the pathbreaking feminist publication decided in 1989 that a sharp change of direction was in order. Thus Lang Communications, owners of *Ms.*, along with Gloria Steinem, founder and consulting editor, suspended publication in

November of that year with the idea of revamping *Ms.* and bringing it more into line with the spirit of its original mission: to present a vital, original forum for the cutting edge of international feminist thought.

Enter Morgan, the fiery, determined, self-described "radical feminist" brought in to serve the new *Ms.: The World of Women* (the subtitle was added to stress the editors' renewed dedication to international issues) as its editor in chief. A poet, novelist, and journalist, Morgan has published 12 books, including her best known, *Sisterhood is Powerful.* Her poetry has been called "frankly militant, didactic, and functional" by feminist poet and writer Adrienne Rich in the *Washington Post,* containing a "savage elegance, a richness of vocabulary, a thrust and steely polish." Morgan will need to instill that kind of vibrancy into her new effort to save *Ms.*, a magazine that has lost money since its founding by Steinem and partner Pat Carbine in 1972. "With Robin in charge," said Steinem in the *Chicago Tribune,* "I know that *Ms.* will give readers all the best, unique traditions of its past, plus a new depth and breadth of coverage."

Under Morgan, the new *Ms.* definitely has a new look—there is no advertising. The magazine, Steinem says, labored for years under the constant strain of trying to sell space to advertisers who either rejected or sought to manipulate the editorial message the publication was trying to present. Throughout the 1980s, advertising revenues began shrinking even though readership rose slightly. As Steinem told the *New York Times*, "If you don't have recipes, you don't get food ads, and if you don't have beauty editorials, you don't get beauty ads." Thus when the first issue of the new, advertisement-free *Ms.* debuted in July 1990, under Morgan's new editorship, Steinem submitted an editorial blasting the way advertisers such as Revlon and Estee Lauder influence the content of magazines. The magazine also ran an apologetic item, illustrated by past examples of sexist ads they had run which may have betrayed the magazine's editorial mission—a kind of act of contrition for stooping to the whims of advertisers. The new *Ms.* costs more (it opened on newsstands at $4 a copy and $40 a year for six bi-monthly issues, as opposed to the old $2.50 and $15 for twelve monthly issues) but Lang believes the magazine can break even with a circulation of 200,000—substantially fewer readers than before the overhaul.

The obvious benefit to Morgan and her staff is that they now have no one to answer to but themselves and their readers. Morgan says the new format, which has the appearance of an academic journal, will contain roughly 100 pages of entirely editorial material, including longer articles, wider coverage of international issues of interest to women, six pages of photos, comic strips, fiction, poetry, health, and new, cutting-edge feature topics. "But substantial will not mean dull. It will be funny and lively as well," Morgan told the *New York Times*. In her debut issue as editor, Morgan sounded the reinvigorated commitment of *Ms.* with a defiant editorial entitled "*Ms.* Lives," writing: "Here we are, stubborn as hell, committed to helping you feel validated, informed, furious, joyous, argumentative, and hopeful . . . welcome to liberated territory—where we defiantly proclaim the beginning of the postpatriarchal era. The 'magabook' you hold in your hands at this moment is a piece of future history."

Selected writings

(Editor with Charlotte Bunch and Joanne Cooke) *The New Women*, Bobbs-Merrill, 1970.
(Editor) *Sisterhood is Powerful*, Random House, 1970.
Monster: Poems, Random House, 1972.
Lady of the Beasts: Poems, Random House, 1976.
Going Too Far: The Personal Chronicle of a Feminist, Random House, 1977.

Sources

Chicago Tribune, January 7, 1990; June 10, 1990.
Mother Jones, November/December 1990.
Ms., July/August 1990.
New York Times, March 5, 1990.
Time, August 6, 1990.
Washington Post, December 31, 1972.

—*David Collins*

Mark Morris

Dancer and choreographer

Born August 26, 1956, in Seattle, Wash.; son of William (a high school music teacher) and Maxine (an amateur dancer) Morris. *Education:* Studied flamenco dancing in Madrid, Spain; studied ballet with Perry Brunson.

Career

Began performing with semiprofessional dance troupe, Koleda Balkan Dance Ensemble, c. 1969, and with First Chamber Dance Quartet in Seattle, Wash., c. 1975; free-lance dancer with choreographers including Eliot Feld, Twyla Tharp, Lar Lubovitch, Laura Dean, and Hannah Kahn; formed Mark Morris Dance Group, 1981. Also taught at University of Washington, Seattle.

Awards: Bessie Award for choreographic achievement, 1984.

Sidelights

Imaginative, prolific, and witty, modern dancer and choreographer Mark Morris has become a central figure on the American dance scene. As early as 1985, New York dance critics were lavishly praising his efforts. In the *New York Times*, Jennifer Dunning wrote that Morris "is now considered one of the most gifted choreographers of his era," and Arlene Croce of the *New Yorker* maintained that "he's the clearest illustration we have, at the moment, of the principle of succession and how it works in dance: each new master assimilates the past in all

its variety and becomes our guide to the future." With his move to Brussels, Belgium, in 1980, Morris became a prominent, though often outrageous and baffling, international dance figure.

The youngest child and only son of William and Maxine Morris was born in 1956 in Seattle, Washington. Mark's interest in music and dance developed early, and he was encouraged by his father, a high school music teacher, and his mother, an amateur of flamenco dancing. "My mother took me to see the Jose Limon Company in Seattle when I was nine, and I knew, I actually knew, that I had to make dances," he told Charles Siebert of *Esquire.* Later, under the tutelage of Verla Flowers, Morris learned the basics of flamenco, folk, modern dance, and ballet, and in his early teens he began choreographing. At age thirteen Morris also joined a semiprofessional dance group called Koleda Balkan Dance Ensemble, which performed Bulgarian and Yugoslavian folk dances.

After graduating from high school at age sixteen, Morris traveled in Europe and studied flamenco dancing for five months in Madrid, Spain. He decided against a career as a flamenco dancer, however, and in 1975 he returned to Seattle, where he studied ballet with Perry Brunson and occasionally performed with the First Chamber Dance Quartet.

A year later Morris moved to New York, where he spent a number of years involved in the dance scene, working on a free-lance basis with such prominent choreographers as Eliot Feld, Twyla Tharp, Lar Lubovitch, Laura Dean, and Hannah Kahn.

In 1980 Morris assembled some friends and rented choreographer Merce Cunningham's Manhattan studio for two nights to perform his own works. The following year he formed the Mark Morris Dance Group and that December gave a series of performances at the Dance Theater Workshop's Bessie Schoenberg Theater. The public and critics took notice of Morris's advent on the dance scene, and opportunities to perform his work publicly increased steadily.

By 1982 Morris had tired of the political nature of the New York City dance scene and returned to Seattle, where in addition to his choreography work he taught dance at the University of Washington. In 1984, a pivotal year, Morris won a Bessie Award for choreographic achievement and was invited to the Brooklyn Academy of Music (BAM)'s prestigious New Wave Festival, at which he was asked to participate again in later years. In 1986 seven of Morris's dances were televised on Public Broadcasting Services' *Great Performances/Dance in America* series, and he was the central draw of BAM's Next Wave Festival. While generally considered a choreographer of modern dance, Morris has also delved into the realm of ballet choreography with a work for the Joffrey Ballet, *Esteemed Guests*, which was not well received by critics, and *Drink to Me Only With Thine Eyes* for the American Ballet Theater, which fared better at the hands of reviewers.

In his choreography Morris draws on years of experience dancing with other troupes and exposure to dances of many cultures, an eclecticism that does not please all viewers. Morris initially thinks of numerous steps for each dance work, more than he can possibly use. Running and falling backward, and moving in a whirlwind are prominent to his personal style, and his other sources of movement include sculpture, folk dance, literature, and American sign language. He does not use a set system of dance notation or analysis, but he depends on his dancers to be the archives of his works-in-progress. Frequently first inspired by a piece of music, Morris often closely associates the steps with the emotive content of the music, in direct contrast to much dance of his era and in what his detractors call "mere musical visualization." Morris, however, believes otherwise. "Postmodern dance, whatever that means, has been about how it feels to dance or the theories of

dancing, and I don't buy that," Morris told Joan Dupont in an interview for the *New York Times*. "There's also the dramatic, emotional element which is not acting or mime, but it's real emotion, and you have to make those emotions happen. It's pretend, in that it's bigger in a shorter period of time than real life is, but all of that has to happen."

> *"Postmodern dance, whatever that means, has been about how it feels to dance or the theories of dancing, and I don't buy that."*

By conventional standards, Morris is taller and larger-boned than many male dancers, and while most dance companies employ anorexically thin female dancers, Morris prefers robustly featured women. Another Morris trait is a lack of gender typing among members of his troupe: gender has nothing to do with dominance or who may dance with whom—women may partner women, men may partner men. Morris, himself, is a militant homosexual and thinks nothing of portraying a female character if the part suits him.

Both the music and the subject matter of Morris's works varies widely. He has choreographed works to music ranging from the Baroque, to country and western, to punk rock. The subject matter has run the gamut from what has been called by some critics his pornographic ballets (*Lovey* and *Striptease*), to religious works (*Sabat Mater*) to his most unconventional comments on modern society (*Love Song Waltzes, Championship Wrestling,* and *Strict Songs*). *Lovey,* set to music by the new wave rock group Violent Femmes, is a study of sexual perversity in which the dancers manipulate naked baby dolls. *Sabat Mater,* set to Baroque music, choreographically deals with how young people experience religious faith. *Love Song Waltzes* are dances set to the songs of the 1950s country and western singers the Louvin Brothers, and *Strict Songs* is set to Hopi Indian chants sung by an all-male chorus.

In fall 1988 the Morris dance troupe became the official dance company of the Theatre Royal de la Monnaie in Brussels, Belgium, replacing the famous dancer/choreographer Maurice Bejart and his Ballet of the Twentieth Century whose home it had been for more than 25 years. With total artistic control, a generous budget, twenty state-salaried dancers, several rehearsal studios, live music, Belgium's most prestigious national opera house, and freedom to tour widely in Europe and the United States, Morris was in his element. "We came here because this is the absolutely perfect thing," he told Dupont. "Just the studio thing alone is phenomenal, and the live music thing, having a resident orchestra. We came to stop the one-night stands. But I wouldn't have come if I had to make up stupid dances for opera or perform with tape or not get paid much or if I had a quota of Belgian dancers."

Morris demonstrates a predilection for music of the Baroque period. Among his many pieces set to Baroque music are *One Charming Night*, which, first inspired by a literary work—*Interview with a Vampire*—is a vampire seduction duet performed to the music of English composer Henry Purcell. Morris's *Dido and Aeneas* is a choreographic version of Purcell's opera by the same name, in which the opera is performed by dancers with singers off to the side.

Likewise, the choreographer's creation *L'Allegro, il penseroso, ed il moderato* is based on a seventeenth-century allegorical work by the British author John Milton, set to the eighteenth-century music of George Frederick Handel. According to a writer for the *New Yorker*, "You see boys and girls responding to the beat, leaping, holding themselves in the air, becoming stages or birds, and rushing on. At different times, you see fleeting allegorical figures—Attic Grace, Melancholia—and lively, real little persons: shepherds, knights and ladies." Local reviews of *L'Allegro* were mixed, with the French generally favorable, the Flemish hostile. When the Monnaie Dance Group/Mark Morris performed *Dido and Aeneas* in Brussels, it also shocked some members of the public and media. While Morris is still treasured in America for his inventiveness, daring, and musicality, there has been much speculation about whether or not his contract with the Theatre Royal de la Monnaie will be renewed when it expires in June 1991.

Sources

Esquire, December 1985.
Interview, May 1989; October 1990.
Mirabella, June 1990.
New York, December 11, 1989; July 16, 1990.
New Yorker, December 1, 1986; January 16, 1989.
New York Times, January 22, 1989.
Time, September 17, 1990.
Village Voice, July 10, 1990.

—*Jeanne M. Lesinski*

Bill Moyers

AP/Wide World Photos

Television journalist

Given name legally changed from Billy Don; born June 5, 1934, in Hugo, OK; son of John Henry (a laborer) and Ruby (Johnson) Moyers; married Judith Suzanne Davidson, December 18, 1954; children: William Cope, Alice Suzanne, John Davidson. *Education:* Attended North Texas State University, 1952-54, and University of Edinburgh, 1956-57; University of Texas, Austin, B.J. (with honors), 1956; Southwestern Baptist Theological Seminary, B.D., 1959.

Addresses: *Home*—76 Fourth Street, Garden City, Long Island, NY 11530.

Career

News Messenger, Marshall, TX, reporter and sports editor, 1949-54; KTBC Radio and Television, Austin, TX, assistant news editor, 1954-56; served as student minister at two churches in Austin, 1954-56, and at a rural Oklahoma church, 1957-59; special assistant to Senator Lyndon B. Johnson, 1959-60, executive assistant during vice-presidential campaign, 1960, and early 1961; associate director in charge of public affairs for the Peace Corps, 1961, deputy director, 1962-63; special assistant to President Lyndon B. Johnson, 1963-65, press secretary to the president, 1965-67; *Newsday,* Garden City, NY, publisher, 1967-70; host of *This Week,* a public affairs broadcast, for National Educational Television, 1970; Educational Broadcasting Corp., New York City, editor-in-chief of *Bill Moyers' Journal,* 1971-76, 1978-81; editor and chief reporter for *CBS Reports,* for Columbia Broadcasting System, 1976-79, senior news analyst

for *CBS Evening News,* 1981-86, also did *Our Times* and *Crossroads* series for CBS during the 1980s; returned to public television to do several series of documentaries, 1986—. Contributing editor for *Newsweek* magazine.

Awards: Rotary International Fellowship, 1956; numerous Emmy Awards, including one for outstanding broadcaster of 1974; ABA Gavel Award for distinguished service to the American system of law, 1974; Lowell Medal, 1975; ABA Certificate of Merit, 1975; Peabody Award, 1977, 1981, 1986, and 1987; Monte Carlo TV Festival Grand Prize, Jurors Prize, and Nymph Award, all 1977, all for documentary *The Fire Next Door;* Robert F. Kennedy Journalism Grand Prize, 1978; Christopher Award, 1978; Sidney Hillman Prize for Distinguished Service, 1978, 1981, 1987; Distinguished Urban Journalism Award from the National Urban Coalition, 1978; George Polk Award, 1981, 1987; Columbia-DuPont Award, 1981, 1987; Overseas Press Award, 1986.

Sidelights

Bill Moyers has been lauded as "perhaps the most insightful broadcast journalist of our day," in the words of *People* magazine's Jane Hall. Critics almost universally hold similar opinions of him, and constantly compare him to broadcasting legend Edward R. Murrow. Publications as ideologically diverse as the liberal *Village Voice* and the ultra-conservative *Christian Alert* have praised his impartiality. After such varied career choices as Baptist minister and press secretary to President Lyndon Johnson, Moyers began his stint as a television journalist in the early 1970s, and has since been responsible for such acclaimed documentaries as *The Vanishing Family: Crisis in Black America, The Secret Government, A World of Ideas, In Search of the Constitution,* and *Joseph Campbell and the Power of Myth.* As Tony Schwartz concluded in the *New York Times:* "In a medium more effective at communicating images and impressions than ideas and insights, Mr. Moyers has emerged as the broadcast journalist who consistently wrestles with ideas, in areas such as history, literature, philosophy and politics."

Moyers was born in 1934 in Hugo, Oklahoma, but shortly afterwards his parents relocated to the small town of Marshall, Texas, where the future journalist spent the remainder of his youth. From his parents Moyers gained his qualities of objectivity and fairness; he recalled for Lisa E. Smith in another *People* article that "my father never knew the difference between black and white except in color, and to this day I cannot remember his saying an ugly thing about anybody." He was also deeply influenced as a child by the broadcasts of Murrow, whom he described to Smith as "this stout voice coming across the ocean night after night, describing the horrors of [World War II]. He brought history alive for me." By the time he was a teenager, Moyers had a job as a beginning reporter for the local paper, the Marshall *News Messenger.* At roughly the same point in his life, he also had the pivotal experience of seeing future employer Lyndon Johnson for the first time. Moyers reminisced for David Zurawik of *Esquire:* "It was 1948. Johnson was speaking on the courthouse square in Marshall, Texas. No microphone. No loudspeaker. Took his coat off. His tie was pulled back. His white shirt was glinting in the sun. And he was literally forcing himself physically on that audience of three thousand to four thousand people there on the east side of the square. I couldn't really hear him. I was in the back row. Fourteen years old. But I remember the sheer presence of the man. And I thought, 'That's what power is. And this man is reaching this audience. And he's got this audience. And he's telling this audience something that's very important.'" After graduating fifth in his high school class, Moyers entered North Texas State University to study journalism. While there, he

worked on the student newspaper and was active in student government and in the Baptist Student Union. Moyers continued to work for the Marshall *News Messenger* during the summers. He also managed to find time to seek a job in Washington, DC, on then Senator Johnson's staff. He started out merely addressing envelopes, but rose to the job of handling all of the senator's mail. Johnson took an interest in Moyers, too, and persuaded him to transfer to the University of Texas at Austin, where he was able to work as assistant news editor for KTBC Radio and Television, which was owned by Mrs. Johnson.

Though Moyers continued his interest in both politics and journalism, he began to feel a call toward the Baptist ministry—or, as he later admitted to Zurawik: "I thought it was a call to the ministry. But actually it was a wrong number." Nevertheless, at the time he was convinced, and preached part time at two local Austin churches as he worked toward his degree. After completing his bachelor's in journalism, Moyers studied both at the University of Edinburgh in Scotland and at the Southwestern Baptist Theological Seminary to earn his degree in divinity. He then accepted a lectureship in Christian ethics at Baylor University. But at about the same time "Moyers found that his Baptist faith was insufficiently orthodox" to continue in this course, in Smith's words, Johnson asked Moyers to rejoin his staff for his upcoming bid for the vice-presidency as John F. Kennedy's running mate. Moyers did so, and served as Johnson's executive assistant during the campaign of 1960.

By 1961, however, Moyers had become so enthusiastic about President Kennedy's proposed Peace Corps that he left Johnson's staff to serve as the new organization's associate director in charge of public affairs. After he helped drum up support for the Peace Corps from both the U.S. Congress and the American public, Kennedy nominated Moyers for the post of Peace Corps deputy director. While in this post Moyers happened to be in Texas on the day Kennedy was assassinated, and rushed to Johnson's side to offer his support to the new president. Thus Moyers left the Peace Corps to return to Johnson's service as his special assistant.

In this capacity Moyers helped organize Johnson's 1964 campaign to retain the presidency. He was responsible for the Johnson camp's aggressive stance toward the Republican nominee Barry Goldwater, and influenced the development of the infamous campaign commercial that implied Goldwater would, if elected, start a nuclear war—it featured a little girl plucking petals from a flower while a countdown to an atomic explosion went on in the background. Moyers also supervised the task forces which produced Johnson's Great Society legislation, and, when Johnson's press secretary George E. Reedy, Jr., resigned in 1965, Moyers filled the vacancy.

But as Johnson escalated the war in Vietnam, Moyers grew disillusioned with his work, and despite the president's displeasure, resigned from his staff in 1966. Since then, many publishers have asked Moyers to write memoirs of his years under Johnson, but he told Smith that he has always refused, saying: "That would make me a thief of his confidence. Johnson spent hours and hours with me in unguarded moments. He could not have done so had he ever thought I would write what he was saying."

After leaving Johnson's staff Moyers became the publisher of *Newsday*, a large daily newspaper. Moyers recruited the best writers for the paper and added more features, analysis, and investigative reporting. Under his leadership *Newsday* abandoned its traditional conservative stance and came out in support of the peace demonstrators of the late 1960s. The paper took on a more sophisticated tone, and, by the time Moyers had been in command for three years, it had won several journalism awards, including two Pulitzer Prizes. But *Newsday*'s owner, Harry F. Guggenheim, was offended by what he saw as Moyers' liberal views and, despite Moyers and associates' offer to buy the paper, sold it to a publishing conglomerate for less money than Moyers offered.

Moyers promptly resigned from *Newsday* and went on a cross-country tour of the United States. He wrote about what he found on the trip in his first book, *Listening to America: A Traveler Rediscovers His Country*, which was published in 1971 to much critical acclaim. From this success, Moyers went on to host a show for New York City's public television channel, WNET. The program eventually evolved into the nationwide public television success *Bill Moyers' Journal*. On his *Journal* Moyers interviewed famous writers, historians, economists, and other public figures; or devoted shows to issues and ideas, including the Watergate scandal of 1973. In 1974 Moyers took a hiatus from television and wrote a weekly column for *Newsweek* magazine. When he returned to public television the following year, his program became known as *Bill Moyers' Journal: International Report*, and, as might be expected, it took on a more international focus. Moyers interviewed world leaders and journalists from many different countries to gain perspectives on interna-

tional issues such as the earth's environment and worldwide human rights.

Frustrated by the lack of funding for projects available in the realm of public television, Moyers moved to CBS in 1976. For three years he served the commercial network as editor and chief reporter of *CBS Reports*. For this show Moyers made many well-received documentaries, including *The Fire Next Door*, a hard-hitting look at arson and crime in the Bronx region of New York City that won him several awards, including the Monte Carlo TV Festival Grand Prize, the Jurors Prize, and the Nymph Award in 1977. He also did a feature on the problems of selling baby formula to third world countries which was particularly devastating to corporations who encouraged this practice, and which CBS felt was too harsh to attract advertisers. Moyers was ordered to tone it down, and, according to Smith, he complained to the network executives: "Congratulations. You've just turned *Jaws* into *Gums*." Nevertheless, Moyers' scathing tone came through. In another tangle with CBS's executives, Moyers won a clearer victory. In the course of filming *The Vanishing Family: Crisis in Black America*, Zurawik reported, "Some of the teenage mothers in Newark" that Moyers was interviewing for the program, "started really opening up. Moyers put the word in the CBS News management pipeline that he was going to need ninety minutes instead of one hour of airtime for the show." When he was told they could not give it to him, Moyers threatened to quit. He got his ninety minutes, and the result, according to Ken Burns in the *New York Times*, was "perhaps Mr. Moyers's single best work."

Complaining of lack of freedom and perhaps recognizing the early warning signs of the death of the documentary on commercial television, Moyers went back to PBS in 1979, only to return to CBS again in 1981. During this stint with the commercial network, Moyers served as a commentator on the *CBS Evening News*, in addition to being featured in the unsuccessful magazine shows *Our Times* and *Crossroads*. Under his contract with CBS, Moyers also retained the freedom to do independent documentaries and series for PBS, notably the *Creativity* series, which featured interviews with such diverse talents as poet Maya Angelou and entrepreneur Fred Smith, the founder of the Federal Express messenger service. But when Moyers broke with CBS in 1986, he cited the commercial network's news department's shift in emphasis to entertainment rather than hard news in order to maintain ratings as his reason for leaving. He lamented to a *Newsweek* reporter: "Pretty soon, tax policy had to compete with stories about three-legged sheep, and the three-legged sheep won. There were periods when I thought the British royal family had signed on as correspondents, so frequent were their appearances. And now we're trapped. Once you decide to titillate instead of illuminate, you're on a slippery slope, you create a climate of expectation that requires a higher and higher level of intensity all the time until you become a video version of the drug culture, and your viewers become junkies."

Since Moyers's second return to public television, he has been able to concentrate on the idea-filled, thought-provoking kind of documentary he prefers. Examples include *The Secret Government*, an expose of the Iran-Contra scandal of President Ronald Reagan's administration; the 41-part series *A World of Ideas with Bill Moyers*, in which the journalist interviews thinkers and philosophers such as Carlos Fuentes, Barbara Tuchman, Noam Chomsky, Joseph Heller, and Leon Kass; and, what Burns described as "the most improbable series of all, the sleeper of all sleepers, what no one wanted to show, 'Joseph Campbell and the Power of Myth,' six one-hour conversations with the late student of religions and mythologies." The last series proved extremely popular, attracting an audience of 30 million. Burns explained further: "Viewers saw a strange and wonderful sight: There, in prime time, was a mesmerizing look at the question of the soul's survival." The series represents precisely the sort of programming that the spiritual Moyers wishes to present to people, for Moyers explained to Zurawik that he offers viewers "companionship on a pilgrimage. I think I am looked to by viewers as a sojourner, a reporter who takes them with me on assignment.... It's all connected: journalist, journal, journey."

Selected writings

Listening to America: A Traveler Rediscovers His Country, Harper Magazine Press, 1971.
Report from Philadelphia, 1987.
The Secret Government, 1988.
Joseph Campbell and the Power of Myth, 1988.

Sources

Christian Century, December 23, 1987.
Esquire, October 1989.
Mirabella, June 1990.
National Review, March 10, 1989.
Newsweek, July 4, 1983; September 15, 1986.
New York Times, February 4, 1979; January 3, 1982; April 26, 1984; September 20, 1984; August 14, 1985; September 9, 1986; May 14, 1989; September 13, 1989.
People, February 22, 1982; August 1, 1983.
Time, May 3, 1982.

—Elizabeth Wenning

Hosni Mubarak

AP/Wide World Photos

President of the Arab Republic of Egypt

Full name, Mohamed Hosni Mubarak; born May 4, 1928, in Kafr-El Meselha, Menoufiya, Egypt; son of a Ministry of Justice inspector; wife's name, Suzanne; children: Alaa, Gamal (sons). *Education:* Graduated from Egypt's National Military Academy, 1949; graduated from Egypt's Air Force Academy c. 1952; attended the Frunze General Staff Academy in Moscow, U.S.S.R. *Politics:* National Democratic Party of Egypt.

Addresses: *Home*—Heliopolis, Egypt. *Office*—Office of the President, Cairo, Arab Republic of Egypt.

Career

Flight instructor at the Egyptian Air Force Academy, 1952-59; commander of several Egyptian Air Force bases, 1965-67; commander of the Egyptian Air Force Academy, 1967-69; chief of staff of the Egyptian Air Force, 1969-72; commander in chief of the Egyptian Air Force and Deputy Minister of War, 1972-75; vice-president of the Arab Republic of Egypt, 1975-81; president of the Arab Republic of Egypt, 1981—.

Awards: Several Egyptian military and civilian awards, including the Order of the Republic, the Sinai Star, and the Military Star of Honor.

Sidelights

Hosni Mubarak became President of the Arab Republic of Egypt following the assassination of President Anwar Sadat in 1981. Since then, he has continued his predecessor's policy of peace with Israel, but he has also won back diplomatic relations with the Arab states that cut themselves off from Egypt after Sadat decided to recognize the Jewish state's right to exist. Although for the most part Mubarak has remained steadfast in working for peace in the Middle East, he did join the United States-led coalition in the Persian Gulf War of 1991 and sent Egyptian troops to aid in the liberation of Kuwait. With the subsequent defeat of Iraq and its president, Saddam Hussein (also in *Newsmakers 91*), Mubarak—as president of the most populous Arab nation—became in the minds of many analysts the most powerful leader in the Arab world.

Mubarak was born in 1928 in Kafr-El Meselha, a small village near the Nile River Delta region of Egypt. His father was an inspector for the Ministry of Justice; on finishing secondary school the younger Mubarak opted for a government career as well, studying at Egypt's Military Academy. He finished the usual three-year course in only two years by omitting the vacation leave that was his due, and graduated in 1949. From there Mubarak went on to the Air Force Academy, where he became a pilot; part of his training was spent in the Soviet Union learning to fly Soviet war planes provided to Egypt during this period. After graduation, Mubarak became a flight instructor for his nation's Air Force Academy.

Mubarak worked his way up through the Egyptian Air Force and by 1965 was in command of several air force bases. Two years later he returned to the Air Force Academy, this time serving as its commander. In 1969 Mubarak became chief of staff of the Air Force; in 1972, he came to the attention of then-President Anwar Sadat, who named him commander in chief of the Air Force and Deputy Minister of War. In this capacity Mubarak helped mastermind the 1973 Egyptian air attack on Israel. With inferior equipment, his pilots managed to destroy 90 percent of their targets within a span of 20 minutes; after the battle, Mubarak was perceived by his fellow Egyptians as a national hero.

This popularity made Mubarak a good choice when in 1975 Sadat decided to replace his vice-president, Hussein el-Shafei. After accepting the post, Mubarak was sent on many foreign diplomatic missions, including trips to Syria, Iraq, the United States, and the People's Republic of China. As the 1970s wore on, Mubarak was increasingly involved in negotiations with Israel that would lead to the 1978 Camp David Peace Accords. But Sadat was also grooming Mubarak for the handling of his country's internal affairs. Because Sadat wished to devote more time to following his vision of peace in the Middle East, he placed more and more of his domestic duties in Mubarak's hands. As vice-president, Mubarak controlled Cabinet meetings—with full authority to act in Sadat's place—and performed the day-to day operations of the president's office. Mubarak also supervised Egypt's nuclear energy program, its armament purchases, and its intelligence work. He took Sadat's place at many official ceremonies as well.

One such ceremony, at which Mubarak joined Sadat rather than filling in for him, was an October 6, 1981 military parade in honor of Egypt's 1973 victory over Israel. Mubarak sat next to the president in the reviewing stand; when Sadat was fired upon and killed by a squad of Islamic fundamentalists, Mubarak was thrown to the ground, but escaped the attack with only a hand injury. He calmly appeared on television a few hours later to reassure the Egyptian people. Although Mubarak, as vice-president, took over in the wake of the assassination, Egyptian law required that he be confirmed as president by an

election. The election took place the following week; Mubarak ran unopposed and received over 98 percent of the vote.

As president, Mubarak fell heir to the task of combatting Egypt's many problems. The greatest, throughout the 1980s, were unemployment and a struggling economy. Mubarak's administration tried to increase the production of affordable housing, clothing, furniture, and medicine, and the president encouraged foreign investment to help further these ends. He also urged greater discussion of birth control issues, crucial to helping stem the tide of Egypt's alarming population explosion. Noting that the increasing gap between Egypt's upper and lower classes was threatening unrest, Mubarak had several of the country's luxury retreats—symbolic of the abuses of the rich—destroyed. What Richard Z. Chesnoff and Gordon R. Robison described in *U.S. News & World Report* as a "network of industrial and agricultural 'desert cities,'" was constructed during the 1980s; the cities, however, were only partially successful in providing Egyptians with needed jobs. In order to reschedule foreign debts, Mubarak has reluctantly cut government subsidies of consumer goods, but expressed his reservations to Chesnoff and Robison: "If I overload the people [by making them pay full price for necessities]...it will be another disaster." The new president also tried to increase the efficiency of his government by firing ministers at the first hint of scandal, and fining parliamentary legislators for unnecessary absences.

One of Mubarak's greatest concerns immediately after taking office was dealing with the religious unrest that had led to Sadat's assassination. Referring in his inaugural address to the radical Islamic fundamentalists behind the crime, Mubarak was quoted in *Time*, saying that "anyone who thinks he can mess about with the rights of the people, not one of them will escape ruthless measures." Soon afterwards he ordered the arrest of many fundamentalists, a policy that has continued and has brought Mubarak's administration under fire by groups like Amnesty International, which abhor the taking of political prisoners. According to Mubarak in an article by Mortimer B. Zuckerman of *U.S. News & World Report*, by 1990 Egypt's problem with Islamic extremists had greatly decreased: "We have some [extremists]...we can't deny it," he confessed. "But it's exaggerated in the media. We know where they are, we know them by name, and we have full control." Despite this confidence, Mubarak admitted that in his Egypt, "no religious political parties are allowed, and I'm not going to change the laws.... I don't want headaches. I would like to build a country, not cause reasonable people to fight one another."

As he promised he would on taking office, Mubarak has continued Egypt's policy of good relations with Israel. He almost immediately resumed negotiations with that country on the issue of autonomy for Palestinians; he has since been instrumental in most of the progress towards a peaceful resolution of this matter. As Barbara Slavin in *Business Week* pointed out, "It was . . . Mubarak who prodded Palestine Liberation Organization [PLO] Chairman Yasser Arafat to recognize Israel's right to exist." The Egyptian president was also an important factor in the U.S. decision to reverse its policy of not talking to the PLO. At the same time, Mubarak has succeeded in mending fences with the Arab states that cut off diplomatic ties with Egypt in anger over the 1978 Camp David Peace Accords with Israel. By 1982 he was talking with Saudi Arabia; by 1989 he had reopened relations with all of the Arab nations except for Syria, Lebanon, and Libya; by 1990 even these three hold-outs had softened their stance toward Egypt.

When Iraq invaded Kuwait in August of 1990, Mubarak expressed surprise and dismay in a *Time* interview with Dean Fischer. "I didn't have even the slightest thought that one Arab country would swallow another," he said. "I thought President Saddam [Hussein] was very reasonable." As of September, 1990, Mubarak thought the Gulf War could still be avoided, but, as he told Fischer, he placed the responsibility solely on the shoulders of "President Saddam Hussein. He should respond to the pressures to save his country and his people. War is a tragedy, a disaster. I can't understand why he doesn't realize what would happen if war broke out." Mubarak also defended the decision on the part of Saudi Arabia—controversial in the Arab world— to invite troops from Western nations, including the United States, to help defend it against the Iraqis. "What could the Saudis do?" he asked Fischer. "When your country is threatened, you have to protect yourself. Many nations over the years have called for help from foreign armies. Even Egypt brought in Soviet troops after the 1967 defeat by Israel." Mubarak sent approximately 45,000 Egyptian troops to the allied coalition effort in the Gulf War, even though, as Jane Mayer pointed out in *Barron's*, "if the Gulf war [had been] transformed into an Arab-Israeli war by Iraq's rocket attack on Israel, no country [would have had] more to lose than Egypt." Mayer further explained that "Mubarak [was] in an enormously delicate position, balancing two separate and not necessarily compatible goals of becoming the West's most important Arab ally, and also the most powerful force in the Arab world. . . . Too strong a reaction from Israel [to the Iraqi rocket attack on Tel Aviv] could [have shattered] both Egypt's ambitions, and in the bargain, the allied coalition."

The years of work Mubarak had invested in regaining the trust of his fellow Arab leaders could easily have been erased. As it turned out, due to Israeli restraint, this did not occur. And, unlike many of his fellow Arab coalition leaders, Mubarak enjoyed the almost unanimous backing of his people for Egypt's contribution to the Gulf War. As David Aikman reported in *Time*, only a few Egyptians protested their country's involvement in the war: "When a small band of demonstrators assembled in Cairo . . . for a march on the presidential palace," Aikman related, "bystanders watched approvingly as police broke up the protest with nightsticks." He concluded that "most of Mubarak's 56 million countrymen support his stance on the war and have not fallen sway to Saddam's attempts to turn the conflict into a battle of Arab vs. West." With the Allied coalition's victory in the Gulf War, Mubarak's gamble in aiding the West has paid off—as a *Business Week* reporter put it, "Saddam's humiliation boosts Cairo's [and thus Mubarak's] claim to lead the Arab world."

Mubarak puts in an average of 16 hours a day presiding over the business of his country, but when he finds time for hobbies he likes to participate in field hockey and squash. He also enjoys reading on a wide variety of subjects. Mubarak and his wife, Suzanne, have two sons, Alaa and Gamal.

Sources

Barron's, January 21, 1991.
Business Week, January 9, 1989; March 11, 1991.
People, February 8, 1982.
Time, October 19, 1981; September 10, 1990; February 25, 1991.
U.S. News & World Report, April 10, 1989; April 16, 1990.

—Elizabeth Wenning

New Kids on the Block

Pop singing group

Born in Boston, Mass., the members of the group and their birth dates are: Jonathan Knight, November 29, 1968; Jordan Knight, May 17, 1971; Joseph McIntyre, December 31, 1972; Donnie Wahlberg, August 17, 1969; and Daniel Wood, May 14, 1969.

Address: P.O. Box 39, Boston, MA 02122.

Career

New Kids on the Block was formed in 1985 when Boston composer Maurice Starr launched a city-wide talent search. Knight brothers Jon (backup vocals) and Jordan (lead vocals), Joe McIntyre (back-up vocals), Donnie Wahlberg (lead vocals), and Danny Wood (backup vocals and keyboards) were the lucky recruits whose best-selling albums, videos, and sell-out concerts have earned them top spots on pop/rock charts and millions of fans. The group signed with Columbia Records in 1986; marketing follow-ups include videos, a cartoon series, television specials, and lucrative product endorsements.

Sidelights

New Kids on the Block have captured pre-teen hearts and pop music charts with their catchy tunes, wholesome looks, clean reputations, and sexy style. They've combined a street-wise attitude with an energetic, upbeat, anti-drug message which appeals to parents as well. All this popularity adds up to major marketing opportunities and escalating income for the five young men from Boston.

Their lives in the limelight are far removed from the middle-class, blue-collar Boston neighborhood of Dorchester where promoter-composer Maurice Starr discovered them. Starr had already masterminded the debut of New Edition, a successful group of five black teens with similar talents and appeal. When he lost New Edition to a larger record company in an unpleasant contract dispute, Starr, who is black, bounced back with his idea to create a "white New Edition" with soul. He launched a city-wide talent search with agent Mary Alford, to find street-wise kids with break-dance, rapping, and singing skills.

Alford discovered 15-year-old Donnie Wahlberg in Dorchester, and talked him into an audition. One of nine siblings whose divorced parents were a working mother and a bus driver father, Wahlberg almost missed his big chance because of family responsibilities. "[Alford] came to my house, but I couldn't talk because my father said I had to mow the lawn," Donnie told *People*. "But she came back, and two hours later, I was at Maurice Starr's. When I told him I needed some music, he started clapping his hands. I did one of my best spontaneous raps ever. I swore in it and in the next line, made up a line apologizing for swearing. Then here's Maurice Starr, this famous guy, telling me, Don Wahlberg, a goof-off kid on food stamps, that I was one of the best rappers he ever heard. I mean, it was like, 'Are you serious?'"

Wahlberg introduced Starr to former classmates Jon and Jordan Knight and Danny Wood. The four were bussed to school at Trotter Elementary in Roxbury, the mostly black neighborhood where Starr lived. Joe McIntyre, a community theater veteran, was added when another performer's parents wanted him out of show business. Starr dubbed the group Nynuk, wrote their songs, choreographed slick dance routines, and began intense rehearsals.

Stardom, however, wasn't instant. The group worked their share of low bills and small gigs, but developed an increasingly smooth stage style and synchronized, energetic dances. In 1986, Starr negotiated a contract with Columbia Records and the group changed its name to New Kids on the Block to match the title song of their first album. The album received a lukewarm response, but a 1988 single, "Please Don't Go Girl" attracted enough attention to earn them a national tour opening for teen pop star, Tiffany. America's adolescents saw the New Kids and loved them. Within a year, Tiffany did a stint as *their* opening act.

Hangin' Tough, the New Kids' second album, took off like a rocket in 1988, eventually selling more than eight million copies and generating five hit singles.

Suddenly the New Kids' blocky logo and smiling faces were everywhere—on teen magazine covers, T-shirts, posters, jewelry, hats, and key chains. They've been compared to the Jackson 5, the Osmond Brothers, the Beatles, and the Temptations, but their marketing strategy surpasses anything their predecessors ever dreamed of. Dell Furano, merchandising manager for the Kids, expected their products, not including books, videos, concert-ticket and record sales, to gross $400 million in 1990 alone.

The Kids tour the country in their well-stocked, home-away-from-home bus, playing to sell-out crowds of screaming youngsters. They're having a great time and the fun is contagious. The smiles seem genuine, and when they sing "I'll be loving only you," and point into the audience, every adolescent girl is convinced they're singing directly to her. Fans keep all-night vigils outside hotels where the Kids stay, send 30,000 fan letters a week, and dial 400,000 calls a month to the New Kids' 900 phone line to listen to pre-recorded, upbeat messages. The group has crossed the lines of racial preference with their funky music, a toe-tapping mixture of rhythm and

New Kids on the Block at the 1990 American Music Awards, where they were honored for favorite pop album. (Left to right: Jordan Knight, Daniel Wood, Joe McIntyre, and Donnie Wahlberg. Not pictured: Jonathan Knight.) AP/Wide World Photos.

blues, smooth harmonies, and drum-beat rap. Starr claims their white skins cover black souls, an attribute which some credit to Boston's controversial school-busing program.

"This is the biggest thing in rock, ever," Furano told *People*. "For comparison, you'd have to go back to the Beatles. They created this kind of intense lifestyle euphoria. These are young girls falling in love with the performers. In England, where the Kids' new album [*Step by Step*] is No. 1, it's the Beatles invasion in reverse."

Several best-selling, fluffy biographies have been published about the group, to the enjoyment of their fans. The young men are fast friends, who present a united front on most issues. They all come from large families with whom they keep in close touch; their mothers serve as last-word consultants to their fan club. The media tends to treat them as a unit rather than individuals, but the careful observer can see flashes of distinct personality escape on occasion.

Donnie Wahlberg is the most outspoken of the Kids. He's the self-confident, onstage emcee who sports a slightly scruffy look, sometimes a small growth of beard and mustache. Even with five brothers and three sisters, mother Alma says he always stood out. He loved music and drums, demanded attention, and was a devoted Michael Jackson fan who amused siblings as he moonwalked through the house. He's the creative one who earned recognition in high school for his painting and an essay on friendship, and has co-written several of the group's hit songs. "We do have talent to produce and write and play, and we will do more of it," he told *Rolling Stone*. "We've done some on the records already. But right now, we're still learning, still growing. We're proud of our past, and we're confident about our future. We know people are going to try and stick drugs in our faces—do something to trip us up. But we're not worried. We know who we are, and we're not puppets. There are no strings."

Jonathan Knight is the oldest member, the big brother of the group, and perhaps the quietest. He and brother Jordan both sang in their church choir before they joined New Kids. "I almost never sing lead vocals, and it doesn't bother me," Jon told *People*. "With us knowing each other so long, we're more a family than a business." Extended families are the norm for the Knights. Mother Marlene Knight is a former social worker who's squeezed foster children and disabled adults into a home that already includes six offspring. Her famous sons have bought her a new home and, she says, turned her life into a fairy tale.

Jordan Knight is the lead singer that *Rolling Stone* described as "the gorgeous Tom Cruise look-alike with the dreamy highflying falsetto." He started the tour with plastic braces on his teeth and worried that fans would think him gay because of his three pierced earrings. Since those early days, all the New Kids are sporting earrings in a typical show of solidarity. Jordan is the heartthrob who confidently works a crowd like he was born to the stage. "I expected exactly what came," he told *People*. "Even when that first album died, I went around and told people, 'Yeah, man, we're gonna be famous. I probably won't be in school next year. I'll probably have a tutor.' They must have thought I was arrogant as hell."

"Why is it such a crime that we're 'only singers'? Did Frank Sinatra write his own songs or play an instrument?"

Danny Wood is the muscle-bound break-dancer who enjoys a good workout in the hotel gym and has energy to spare. He sometimes plays keyboards for the group, and is most interested in the behind-the-scenes action of recording. He has five siblings and hopes to become an engineer someday. He told Anne Raso, author of *New Kids on the Block Scrapbook*, "I feel a strong responsibility to fans. Sometimes in the press, you hear jokes that we're squeaky clean. We're drug-free but it's not like we're wimps. Anyway, I do think it's important to set an example for teenagers because at that point in your life, you're dealing with some mega-heavy peer pressures."

Joe McIntyre is the "baby" of the group and the youngest of eight siblings in a talent-packed family. He performed with them in community theater productions before he joined New Kids. He names Frank Sinatra as a favorite singer and was chosen to be a Michael-Jackson-type lead singer for the group, but slipped into backup when his voice changed. He was a reluctant Kid, at first, who had to complete high school on the road with a tutor. "The others were all buddies," he told *People*. "I didn't want to do it [join the group]. It was like going to camp or something. It was hard getting accepted. I would go home crying. Mary [Alford] would try to talk me out of quitting. One day she asked me to stay long enough to find a replacement. Then she had Donnie call me. Donnie can talk a dog off a chuck wagon . . . . After that it was all right."

In spite of all the adoration the New Kids have inspired they're not without their critics. The music industry views them with a wait-and-see attitude, apparently expecting them to disappear as quickly as they came when their young fans turn to other interests. Their music, it's said, is too safe, their reputations are too clean, their message too positive. They're just too good to be true. When Wahlberg was involved in a minor scuffle with another passenger on a plane, the media turned on the group with near relief to report the negative news.

Still, nobody denies that the fivesome work hard to please their fans. *Rolling Stone*'s David Wild wrote in a concert review that "despite their audience's low standards, the Kids still actually bothered to put on quite a good show. They sang—live, if not always very well—and danced and even managed to work up an old-fashioned sweat as they offered up piece after piece of tasty pop-soul ear candy. Call them the hardest-working . . . Kids in showbiz, if you will."

This kind of grudging, reluctant respect has had its effect on the New Kids, who have developed a defensive edge and a tougher line. "Our first album was a Svengali-type situation," Jordan Knight told *Time*, referring to Starr's influence. "But on the second," brother Jon added, "we told him stuff we wanted. We're from the streets. We like music that is funky, with heavy bass."

"We're getting lynched, man," Donnie told *People*. "Why is it such a crime that we're 'only singers'? Did Frank Sinatra write his own songs or play an instrument?" Wahlberg and Starr co-wrote a strong rap piece for *Step by Step*, their 1990 hit album, entitled "Games" which offers some sassy backtalk to their critics: "Somebody said somebody wouldn't last too long/ Somebody keeps going strong/Somebody said somebody was all a front/ Somebody's still talking junk." The group performed a hard-hitting, defiant version of the song at the 1991 American Music Awards, to the delight of their supporters.

Although the New Kids may still be struggling for recognition with the critics, their fans need no convincing. They faithfully buy the merchandise, attend the concerts, and read the fan magazines to learn their heroes' vital statistics, favorite foods, and life ambitions. Teens group outside their houses, ring their doorbells, peek in their windows and collect leaves from their lawns. Coping with all this intrusive success has its drawbacks, but the New Kids and their families aren't complaining much. "At home I cannot walk down my own little street," Jordan Knight told *People*. "On the road, I can't even go out in the hallway of a hotel. Some days it gets to me pretty bad. If I want to go out at night, I go to a punk club where they don't care who I am . . . . I really feel lucky that there are five of us. If one of us was solo and it got this big, it would be very, very hard to handle. I can see now why Elvis killed himself with drugs and why so many people have turned to drugs and committed suicide. Because it can really, really get to you if you're alone. Thank God we have each other."

Later Jordan admitted in the same interview, "The weird thing is, I love it. I could complain about it all day, but when it's gone, I'll be like, 'Where'd it go?'" It's hard to tell how long the New Kids can continue to be so popular. Some say they're already fading. If so, each Kid would admit it was fun while it lasted.

Selected discography

New Kids on the Block, 1986.
Hangin' Tough, 1988.
Merry, Merry Christmas, 1989.
Step by Step, 1990.

Sources

Books

New Kids on The Block, Modern Publishing, 1990.
Raso, Anne, *New Kids on the Block Scrapbook,* Modern Publishing, 1990.

Periodicals

Forbes, May 28, 1990.
New York Times, May 17, 1990; June 6, 1990.
People, June 19, 1989; October 23, 1989; February 5, 1990; August 13, 1990; September 24, 1990.
Publishers Weekly, May 18, 1990.
Rolling Stone, November 2, 1989; August 9, 1990; September 6, 1990.
Time, November 20, 1989; July 30, 1990.

—Sharon Rose

Harrison Ngau

AP/Wide World Photos

Environmental activist

Surname is pronounced "En-*gow*."

Address: *Home*—Sarawak, Borneo, Malaysia.

Career

Became environmental activist in opposition to the deforestation of his homeland, c. 1970s; works closely with Malaysia's Penan, Kenyah, and Kayan tribespeople.

Sidelights

While world awareness of the earth's mounting environmental problems has increased in the wake of the Exxon oil spill in Alaska and media events like Earth Day, grass roots movements toward practical solutions to these concerns have been quietly building for years through the work of local activists like Harrison Ngau. A Kayan tribesman from the Sarawak province of Malaysian Borneo, Ngau has been working since the 1970s to build a strong local and international opposition to large-scale logging operations that are wiping out the old-growth tropical forests of his homeland. Although his success in this complex task has been limited, Ngau has nonetheless become a living example of what individual citizens can accomplish in making politicians and multi-national corporations accountable to environmental issues. As Ngau told *Time* magazine, "It is our time to look after our place so that it will have a future."

Working closely with Malaysia's Penan, Kenyah, and Kayan tribespeople—who have seen their numbers drop significantly due to problems compounded by the soil erosion and pollution that accompany the harvesting of timber essential to their existence—Ngau has organized petitions and letter-writing campaigns, marches on the Malaysian capital of Kuala Lumpur, and even blockades of logging roads to call attention to the plight of the tribes. Ngau has also enlisted the help of Sahabat Alam Malaysia (SAM), the Malaysian chapter of the international environmental organization Friends of the Earth, to help expose those corporations—principally Japanese—and politicians who most directly benefit from the logging.

By the late 1980s Ngau's strategy of combining highly visible local activism with international media pressure met with some attention. In June of 1987 Ngau and 12 native tribesmen from Sarawak traveled to Kuala Lumpur to meet with government ministers about deforestation, which, at its peak in 1983, was consuming 75 acres per hour to provide 39% of Malaysia's total tropical log exports; this figure accounted for more than 50% of the world's total. That same year, Ngau and members of several tribes stepped up a campaign to frustrate loggers by invading logging camps and blocking roads in more than 20 areas. One of the primary targets of these activities was the Limbang Trading Company, owned by Malaysian Minister for Environment and Tourism James Wong. Although this intervention had little direct effect on policy, the publicity Ngau and his supporters generated left Kuala Lumpur reeling with embarrassment.

Ngau became such a burden to his government, in fact, that in October of 1987 he and dozens of tribals were arrested after a police crackdown on several blockades. Ngau was then held without trial or indictment for 60 days, in solitary confinement, under the auspices of Malaysia's Internal Security Act. Even after his release the activist remained under restriction orders for two years; he was unable to leave his house at night without permission. He nevertheless continued even more determinedly to stop logging in Sarawak. In 1988, due largely to the efforts of Ngau and SAM founder Mohamed Idris, SAM was awarded a $100,000 Right Livelihood Award—the so-called "Alternative Nobel Prize"—which was established by Swedish baron Jakob von Uexkull to encourage practical solutions to everyday problems. Although the trucks and chainsaws were far from silenced, by 1990 the provincial government of Sarawak was finally brought to the bargaining table to discuss environmental issues affecting tribal homelands.

Sources

Boston Sunday Globe, November 15, 1987.
Time, April 23, 1990.

—*David Collins*

Malgorzata Niezabitowska

AP/Wide World Photos

Polish government spokeswoman

Born c. 1949 in Poland; daughter of an economist and a television newscaster; married Tomasz Tomaszewski (a photographer); children: Maryna. *Education:* Warsaw University, degrees in law and journalism.

Addresses: *Home*—Warsaw, Poland.

Career

A former model and journalist; also wrote television plays and song lyrics. After publishing several underground political pieces, was appointed spokeswoman for Poland's Solidary-run government, 1989.

Sidelights

We were watching *Miami Vice* while I was preparing dinner when I got the call that the Prime Minister wanted to see me." That's how Malgorzata Niezabitowska describes the moment she became the official spokeswoman of Poland's historic Solidarity-run government in 1989.

This appointment is the culmination of an active and varied career. Born into a solidly middle-class Warsaw family under the Communist rule—Niezabitowska's father, an economist, "was imprisoned briefly during the Stalinist roundups of the early 1950s," according to a *People* article. Her mother, the piece relates, became "Poland's first television newscaster," though she died when Malgorzata was only nine.

Malgorzata herself attended Warsaw University, where "her striking looks and ebullient spirit brought her not only a reputation as a girl-about-town but also modeling assignments that brought in money to pay bills," as Bill Hewitt continued in the *People* profile.

After graduation Niezabitowska worked as a magazine reporter, but found herself at odds with governmental censorship. So she opted instead to write television plays and song lyrics, telling Hewitt, "With fiction, it was a bit easier." Meanwhile, she had married photographer Tomasz Tomaszewski and together they produced *Remnants: The Last Jews of Poland.* This book chronicles a five-year period in recent history of the vanishing Jewish population— "nearly all sickly and elderly, they remained in the country after the last mass exodus, in 1968, which was prompted by a savage anti-Semitic campaign," as Abraham Brumberg describes it in the *New York Times Book Review.*

In that same article, Brumberg noted that Tomaszewski and Niezabitowska, who are both gentile, were "fascinated by a number of young Jews who in the past few years have rediscovered their Jewish roots, and have taken to 'praying and keeping the Sabbath and learning Yiddish and even organizing lectures'"

(Niezabitowska's text was translated by William Brand and Hanna Dobosiewicz).

By 1980, Niezabitowska's energy had been directed toward the emerging Solidarity movement, and she contributed to a pro-Solidarity journal "edited by a rumpled intellectual named Tadeusz Mazowiecki," as Hewitt wrote. When in 1981 the Communist regime began to repress Solidarity, Niezabitowska was forced to publish her political tracts through Western Europe and the Polish underground press, as *People* noted.

"In August [1989], with the remarkable energy of a Solidarity-dominated government, the still-rumpled Mazowiecki became the first non-Communist leader in the Soviet bloc," Hewitt reported. One of the new prime minister's first duties was to contact Niezabitowska, who herself is fluent in English, to become official spokeswoman.

"Some in Warsaw say Niezabitowska owes her position to her stunning looks and the new government's shrewd sense of public relations, but she shrugs off both the criticism and her lack of experience," a *Time* article by Johanna McGeary stated. As Niezabitowska is quoted: "I think I'm one of the Prime Minister's closest advisers. I discuss all the issues with him, try to convince him of my ideas, keep him informed about what is happening in the country. That is influence."

Writings

Remnants: The Last Jews of Poland (photographs by Tomasz Tomaszewski; translated from the Polish by William Brand and Hanna Dobosiewicz), Friendly Press (New York), 1986.

Sources

New York Times Book Review, October 19, 1986.
People, November 13, 1989.
Time (special report on women), fall, 1990.

—*Susan Salter*

Antonia Novello

Surgeon general of the United States

Full name, Antonia Coello Novello; born August 23, 1944, in Fajardo, Puerto Rico; daughter of Antonio and Ana D. (a schoolteacher and principal) Coello; married Joseph R. Novello (a psychiatrist, author, and medical journalist), June 30, 1970. *Education:* University of Puerto Rico, Rio Peidras, B.S., 1965; University of Puerto Rico, San Juan, M.D., 1970; Johns Hopkins University, master's degree in public health, 1982.

Addresses: *Home*—1315 31st St. NW, Washington, DC 20007. *Office*—200 Independence Ave. SW, Washington, DC 20201.

Career

University of Michigan Medical Center, Ann Arbor, Mich., intern and resident in pediatrics, 1970-73, pediatric nephrology fellow, 1973-74; associated with Georgetown University Hospital, Washington, D.C., 1974-75; project officer at the National Institute of Arthritis, Metabolism, and Digestive Diseases (under the National Institutes for Health [NIH]), 1978-79; NIH staff physician, 1979-80; executive secretary in the division of research grants at NIH, 1981-86; deputy director of the National Institute of Child Health and Human Development (under NIH), 1986-90; clinical professor of pediatrics at Georgetown University Hospital, 1986—; Surgeon General of the United States, 1990—.

Member: International Society of Nephrology, American Academy of Pediatrics (fellow), American Medical Association, American Society of Artificial Internal Organs, American Society of Pediatric Nephrology, Pan American Medical and Dental Society, Society of Pediatric Research, Association of Military Surgery (United States), Virginia State Medical Society, District of Columbia State Medical Society, Alpha Omega Alpha.

Sidelights

When C. Everett Koop (see *Newsmakers 89*) announced in late 1989 that he would retire from the post of United States Surgeon General, speculation about who his predecessor would be was particularly lively. During his eight-year tenure, Dr. Koop played an unusually prominent role in American public life, elevating the previously softspoken voice of the Surgeon General to a forceful, opinionated one that people paid attention to. Koop gained national prominence and respect by speaking out on controversial issues, sometimes colliding openly with the views of the administrations of presidents Ronald Reagan and George Bush on such topics as sex education and the use of condoms to prevent the spread of AIDS.

When Dr. Antonia Novello, the deputy director of the National Institute of Child Health and Human

Development at the National Institutes of Health (NIH), was chosen for the Surgeon General post, many observers noted that following in the illustrious footsteps of Dr. Koop would not be easy. The first woman and the first Hispanic to hold the position, Dr. Novello brought with her a reputation for hard work and dedication, but her ability to fight for her convictions was unproven. Both Novello and administration officials admitted that questions about her views on abortion—she opposes it—had been a part of the selection process. This so-called "litmus test," allegedly applied to candidates for this and other high-level health care appointments, was a subject of widespread controversy. But Novello claimed, as reported in the *Washington Post* several months after she was sworn in, "I'm for the people who deserve help...how I vote is not relevant. I think that as a woman, as a Hispanic, as a member of a minority...I bring a lot of sensitivity to the job." Voicing a concern that echoed in other quarters, California Democratic Representative Henry Waxman told the *Post*, "I hope she's a fighter, because it's a bad time for infant mortality, for AIDS, for the homeless, for the uninsured, and this administration hasn't shown much interest in these problems...she can do a lot."

> *"I'm for the people who deserve help ... I think that as a woman, as a Hispanic, as a member of a minority ... I bring a lot of sensitivity to the job."*

Antonia Coello Novello was born in Fajardo, Puerto Rico, in 1943. She and her brother were raised by their mother, a schoolteacher, after their parents' divorce. Novello suffered from a painful congenital colon condition until she was 18 years old, when it was corrected. She has said that one of the reasons she became a doctor was to help others who were suffering as she had. Novello received both her B.S. and M.D. degrees from the University of Puerto Rico, where she was—as described by her teacher Dr. Ivan Pelegrina in the *Detroit Free Press*—"one of our brightest students." Ana Flores Coello appears to have been a major motivating force in her daughter's life at this stage; Novello told *Glamour*: "I wasn't allowed to work until I graduated from medical school because my mother felt that once I earned

money I might be sidetracked by material rewards before I got to my real work."

Novello did get to her "real work," beginning with an internship and residency in pediatrics from 1970 through 1973 at the University of Michigan (UM) Medical Center in Ann Arbor. She served as a fellow in pediatric nephrology at UM in 1973 and 1974, and she remembered this "first job" in *Glamour* as germinal in her eventual decision to enter government work; she "learned how many people slip through the cracks." Monitoring the progress of patients waiting for kidney transplants, Novello was dismayed at the number who could not be helped. Those cases in which she, personally, was powerless to help were especially affecting: "You become a true caring physician when you're able to share the pain."

In 1971 Novello was the first woman to receive the UM Pediatrics Department's Intern of the Year award. Classmate Dr. Samuel Sefton, who is now a neonatologist in Kalamazoo, Michigan, told the *Detroit Free Press*, "It was difficult for women to be accepted [in the medical field] then, and I always was impressed with the way she handled situations." Barbara Lanese, head nurse (then and now) of the UM perinatal unit, concurred with Sefton: "[Antonia] was a resident when female physicians weren't as readily accepted as they are today.... She was a wonderful physician, and she was warm, friendly and well-respected. She was able to break the tension just by the kind of person she is."

In 1974 Novello joined the staff of Georgetown University Hospital in Washington, D.C. as a pediatric nephrology fellow. She served as a project officer at the NIH's National Institute of Arthritis, Metabolism and Digestive Diseases in 1978 and 1979, a staff physician at NIH from 1979 through 1980, and the executive secretary in the Division of Research Grants at NIH from 1981 through 1986. She earned a master's degree in public health from Johns Hopkins University in 1982.

From 1986 until her appointment as Surgeon General, Novello served as deputy director of the National Institute of Child Health and Human Development, where she nurtured a special interest in children with AIDS. Concurrently, Novello was a clinical professor of pediatrics at Georgetown University Hospital. Her colleague there, pediatric department chairman Dr. Owen Rennert, told the *New York Times* that Novello "is tremendously concerned about the medical and social problems of children and she has a way of drawing others into that concern." In 1982 and 1983 Novello was a Congressional fellow on the staff of the Labor and Human Resources Committee chaired by Senator Orrin Hatch, a Republican from Utah. As reported in the *Washington Post*, Hatch later commented that she had "given good advice on several bills...including legislation on organ transplants and cigarette warning labels."

Novello's appointment to the post of Surgeon General came at a time of controversy and hostility between some scientists involved in public health issues and the Bush administration. Several candidates for top jobs at such organizations as the NIH, the Center for Disease Control, and the Health Care Financing Administration had withdrawn their names from consideration, complaining that their interviews had included questions about their views on abortion and on the use of fetal tissue in research (another controversial practice opposed by the Bush White House). Dr. Burton Lee, the President's personal physician, might have been a contender for Surgeon General, but took himself out of the running because his views on abortion did not coincide with Bush's. In so doing, he echoed the administration's contention that it is important and appropriate that the appointee defend Bush's positions with conviction.

During Novello's two-hour interview, she was able to convince administration officials that her view on abortion was the approved one. Some observers speculated that Novello's reputation for cooperative, dedicated and essentially low-key work made her a particularly desirable choice after the outspoken reign of Dr. Koop. Yet Novello claimed at a press conference covered in the *Washington Post* that "as long as the data can be trusted and is not just hearsay, I'll say it like it is....I was never told I have to keep a low profile. I really intend to be like Dr. Koop when the data is there."

As head of the 5,700 commissioned officers of the Public Health Service, Novello promised to focus her energies on AIDS-infected children, smoking (she opposes particularly the glamorous portrayal of smoking in advertisements) and such women's health issues as breast cancer and heterosexual AIDS. Other areas of concern for Novello include teenage drinking, drinking and driving, and finding ways to diminish the stigma of mental illness.

The Surgeon General's is an essentially public role, and Novello—who receives several hundred invitations to speak per month—spends much of her time on the road, promoting the cause of better health. She talks with Louis Sullivan, Secretary of Health and Human Services, three or four times a week and meets with him monthly. Sullivan, with whom Novello has pledged to work closely, described her (as quoted in the *Detroit Free Press*) as "a very commanding woman who has a tremendous ability to reach out to communities." To what extent and to what ends she will put that ability to use is a subject of concern for some, like the Congressional official (a Democrat) quoted in the *Washington Post* who said, "Toni Novello is a nice, talented, hard-working woman. But she has never stood up and shouted for the programs she directs....If she wants to play anything like the role Koop did, she is going to have to learn to speak up."

Novello's own perception of the potential power and impact of her new job became more sharply defined, she told the *Washington Post*, when she visited her birthplace, Puerto Rico, shortly after becoming Surgeon General: "When I got off the plane, kids from my mother's school lined both sides of the road handing me flowers....I went to the VA hospital to speak. When the veterans saw my gold braid [she is a Vice Admiral in the Public Health Service] they all stood and saluted....I realized that for these people, for women, I have to be good as a doctor, I have to be good as a Surgeon General, I have to be everything."

Sources

Detroit Free Press, October 30, 1990.
Glamour, August 1990.
New York Times, November 2, 1989.
Newsweek, October 30, 1989.
Parade, November 11, 1990.
People, December 17, 1990.
Washington Post, October 18, 1989; October 24, 1989; May 8, 1990.

—*Kelly King Howes*

Sandra Day O'Connor

Supreme Court justice

Born March 26, 1930, in El Paso, Tex.; daughter of Harry A. (a cattle rancher) and Ada Mae (Wilkey) Day; married John Jay O'Connor III (an attorney), December, 1952; children: Scott, Brian, Jay. *Education:* Stanford University, A.B. in economics (magna cum laude), 1950, LL.B., 1952. *Politics:* Republican. *Religion:* Episcopalian.

Addresses: *Home*—Chevy Chase, Md. *Office*—Supreme Court Bldg., 1 First St., N.E., Washington, DC 20543.

Career

San Mateo County, California, deputy county attorney, 1952-53; Quartermaster Market Center, U.S. Army, Frankfurt, West Germany, civil attorney, 1954-57; private law practice in Phoenix, Ariz., 1959-60; homemaker and volunteer worker for the Phoenix Junior League, juvenile court, state bar exams, and the Republican party, 1960-65; State of Arizona, assistant attorney general, 1965-69; senator in the state legislature of Arizona, 1969-75; Maricopa County Superior Court, Maricopa County, Ariz., judge, 1975-79; Arizona Court of Appeals, judge, 1979-81; United States Supreme Court, Washington, D.C., associate justice, 1981—. Member of national board of directors for the Smithsonian Associations.

AP/Wide World Photos

Sidelights

The most influential woman in America," according to Marjorie Williams and Al Kamen in the *Washington Post Magazine*, is Sandra Day O'Connor. In 1981, President Ronald Reagan appointed her associate justice to the United States Supreme Court, making her the first woman ever to serve on the highest court in the land. Since her confirmation by the U.S. Senate later that year, O'Connor has played a major role in deciding cases dealing with controversial issues such as the death penalty, affirmative action, separation of church and state, and abortion, thus permanently affecting the way lower courts throughout the country may view these concerns in the future. By most accounts, O'Connor has surprised people on both sides of the political spectrum; though she often sides with fellow conservative justices on the court, she frequently issues separate, more moderate opinions, and occasionally casts her vote with her more liberal colleagues. As Tamar Jacoby said of O'Connor in *Savvy* magazine, "she has made amply clear" that "she is not a knee-jerk conservative."

Though most court observers do not classify O'Connor as a feminist, she has from early childhood been used to work and activities not traditionally accorded to women. Born Sandra Day on March 26, 1930, in El Paso, Texas, she was raised on a large ranch—the Lazy B—that ranged from southeastern Arizona to southwestern New Mexico. There O'Connor learned to perform such rough chores as mending fences and branding cattle; even so, she told a *Time* interviewer, she "didn't do all the things boys did." Though this rural environment instilled in her a love of the outdoors and of physical exercise, it also led O'Connor to good study habits and a great enjoyment of reading because the secluded ranch lifestyle did not allow her much opportunity to play with other children. Indirectly, it also helped form her sense of independence. Because her parents did not trust the academic reputation of the ranch area schools, they sent her back to her birthplace, El Paso, where her maternal grandmother lived. There O'Connor attended Radford, a private school for girls, returning to the Lazy B for holidays and summer vacations.

Despite intense homesickness, O'Connor learned to like El Paso and made good grades at Radford. When she was thirteen, however, her siblings were just toddlers and she missed feeling part of the family and being able to watch them grow. O'Connor returned to the Lazy B, but she had to ride a school bus every day to Lordsburg, New Mexico, which was thirty-two miles from the Days' ranch house. Thus she still did not get much time with her family, because she had to catch the bus before the sun rose and it was dark by the time she got home. She returned to El Paso the following year. (O'Connor later cited this experience as having greatly influenced her distaste for busing as a solution to the problem of school segregation.)

O'Connor completed high school and matriculated at Stanford University when she was only sixteen years old. She majored in economics, graduating magna cum laude in 1950 before going on to law school, earning her LL.B. two years later. O'Connor graduated third in her Stanford law school class, behind first-ranked William Renquist, who would later be one of her colleagues on the Supreme Court and rise to the position of Chief Justice. She also made the acquaintance of John Jay O'Connor III while earning her law degree; they married upon her graduation.

Despite her excellent academic record, O'Connor experienced sexual discrimination in her job search. She interviewed for positions with major law firms in San Francisco and Los Angeles, but, as Williams and Kamen reported, none of them were willing to hire a woman, no matter how well-qualified. One firm, however, did offer her a job as a legal secretary.

Undaunted, O'Connor sought work with the government and was hired by California's San Mateo County as deputy county attorney. She stayed in this capacity only briefly, however, because her husband was sent to West Germany as part of his military service. O'Connor accompanied him, and became a civilian attorney for the U.S. Army Quartermaster Corps. After the couple returned to the United States they settled in Phoenix, Arizona, where O'Connor started her own small practice with another lawyer.

Meanwhile, the O'Connors had begun to have their three sons. In 1960 O'Connor took a hiatus from law—or at least from being paid for her efforts—to concentrate on motherhood. But she remained active in several volunteer capacities, and began her political efforts during this period, helping with the 1964 presidential campaign of Arizona Senator Barry M. Goldwater. When she returned to professional legal work in 1965, it was in the office of assistant attorney general of Arizona. From there, O'Connor was chosen to serve out the term of a Republican Arizona state senator who left office in 1969 for a position in the administration of President Richard Nixon. She eventually campaigned successfully for two terms in the state legislature, and in 1973 she was elected majority leader of the Arizona Senate—the first woman in the United States to hold such a position.

O'Connor's approach as a state senator was similar to her approach to law in general—no nonsense. She consistently refused to pass bills with unrelated riders attached to them; one such involved a restriction of abortion rights tacked on to a bill proposing funding for building a stadium. This action on her part was later interpreted by anti-abortion forces as sympathy towards the pro-choice movement, but O'Connor explained during her Supreme Court confirmation hearings that it merely represented her antagonism towards unconnected riders. Williams and Kamen quoted former Arizona state senator Ray Rottas on her impartiality: "She was strictly an issue-oriented person . . . If the program was good for the state, it didn't make a whole lot of difference to her which side initiated the issue." Despite this seeming disregard for party politics, O'Connor showed herself in the Arizona Senate as more or less a moderate Republican. She tended toward fiscal conservatism, but supported the ill-fated Equal Rights Amendment (ERA) to the U.S. Constitution. She fought a 1974 state resolution asking the U.S. Congress to amend the Constitution to ban abortions, and supported a measure to spread contraceptive information, but voted for restrictions on state funding of abortion for poor women, and for a bill giving hospital employees the right not to help with abortions if they so desired.

Commenting on O'Connor's time in the state senate was Democratic governor of Arizona Bruce Babbitt, who was quoted in the *Washington Post Magazine:* "She was not a clubhouse politician. She was a little incongruous at a political rally, standing in front of the troops—much more at home in a committee room than at a rally." O'Connor also tended to get frustrated with her fellow state senators, rewriting their bills when they did not satisfy her legal sensibilities. Perhaps this helps explain why she left the senate after her second full term to run for a judgeship in Maricopa County, Arizona's Superior Court. She was elected, and as a superior court judge O'Connor began practices she would carry with her to the highest court in the land. She was strict with the lawyers who tried cases before her, frequently urging them to come to the point of their argument. As Phoenix attorney Hattie Babbitt recalled in the *Post Magazine,* O'Connor "didn't have much use for lawyers who came and said, 'This is the right thing to do.' She wanted a lawyer to say 'This is the right thing to do, and here are 25 pieces of precedent to support it.'" Though O'Connor at this time was perceived as a good judge by most observers, she received low bar evaluation marks in the category of courtesy to litigants and attorneys.

"There will be time enough to examine Roe *[vs. Wade] and to do so carefully."*

O'Connor enjoyed being a judge, and turned down the requests of prominent Arizona Republicans, including Goldwater, to run for governor in 1978. Bruce Babbitt, the man elected to the office that year, appointed O'Connor to the Arizona Court of Appeals in 1979. Though, as might be expected, she dealt with more abstract issues on the Court of Appeals than she had with the Maricopa County Superior court, the cases she considered concerned matters of divorces, tenant disputes, bankruptcies, workman's compensation, and criminal appeals—as a rule, they did not bear much relevance to the problems she would have to iron out as a U.S. Supreme Court justice.

Fulfilling a campaign promise to appoint the most qualified woman he could find, President Reagan nominated O'Connor to the Supreme Court in 1981. During her U.S. Senate confirmation hearings in September of that year, she was grilled by both liberals and conservatives about her views on social issues such as busing and affirmative action, but especially on the subject of abortion. Members of the religious right opposed her confirmation because of her state senate support for the ERA and because of her occasional votes in favor of abortion rights. Despite much pressure, O'Connor declined to tell her Senate examiners how she would vote on any particular issue, deeming such revelations inappropriate. She carefully maintained her neutrality on the abortion issue, citing her personal distaste for the practice but also citing her recognition of opposing viewpoints. She was confirmed as the first female associate justice of the U.S. Supreme Court by a wide margin.

As she began her new duties on the Supreme Court, O'Connor seemed to have become more conservative and seemed intent on laying to rest any right-wing reservations about her confirmation, voting consistently with then-Chief Justice Warren E. Burger's conservative decisions. But by the mid-1980s, she was increasingly viewed by court observers as the swing vote, the one who would determine whether the liberal or the conservative view would decide the outcome of a case. Depending on the issue, O'Connor would side with her four fellow conservatives, or with the four more liberal judges. But, according to Williams and Kamen, "she seems suspicious of bold solutions from either the left or the right." Whichever side she takes, "she often writes a concurring opinion that shows a different reasoning—trying to find a middle ground and attempting to narrow the scope of the ruling." For instance, in a 1988 decision, she cast her vote with the court's liberals to ban executions of murderers under the age of sixteen, but her separately issued opinion was written in such a way as not to exclude this kind of execution in the future. In cases involving separation of church and state, O'Connor has generally sided with conservatives in allowing government funds to be used for purposes that aid certain religious groups, but in her written opinion of one such case she differed from her colleagues in stating that "the test of the constitutionality of government actions should be whether the government was 'endorsing' a religion, not simply whether it was doing something that might aid religion in some way," Williams and Kamen reported.

On controversial cases involving restrictive state abortion laws, O'Connor has satisfied neither anti-abortion nor pro-choice activists. She voted to uphold a Missouri statute barring abortion in state-supported medical facilities, but, though critical of the legal analysis used in the 1973 ruling, has refused to overturn *Roe vs. Wade*, the Supreme Court decision that made abortion legal throughout the United States. Richard Lacayo quoted part of her written opinion on the Missouri case in *Time*: "There will be time enough to re-examine *Roe*, and to do so carefully." O'Connor also helped strike down a Minnesota law requiring notification of both parents before a minor obtains an abortion, and contributed to the approval of the same state's law allowing a minor to get permission from a judge to waive parental notification.

O'Connor's sometimes contradictory rulings on abortion can perhaps be better understood in light of her strong views in favor of state's rights. The restrictive laws that she has upheld come to her, of course, approved by the highest courts of the states that have passed them. While O'Connor was still serving on the Arizona Court of Appeals, she wrote an essay for the *William and Mary Law Review* in which she asserted that "it is a step in the right direction to defer to the state courts . . . on federal Constitutional questions when a *full* and *fair* adjudication has been given in the state court." She declared further that "when the state-court judge puts on his or her federal-court robe, he or she does not become immediately better equipped intellectually to do the job." Also, according to Williams and Kamen,

O'Connor "has been especially impatient with federal judges intervening to release state prisoners who claim their constitutional rights have been violated. For her, this is a double sin—letting guilty criminals go free, and stepping on state judicial turf."

Regardless of O'Connor's decisions on individual cases to come before the Supreme Court in the future, her continued ability to sway the outcome for the entire court depends on the nature and opinions of David Souter, the conservative associate justice confirmed to replace retiring Justice William J. Brennan, a liberal, in October 1990. Now O'Connor's role is reduced to being part of either a six-to-three majority or a four-to-five minority in court decisions. Despite Souter's leanings, however, O'Connor retains her vital part in deciding the United States' important issues.

Sources

Savvy, October 1988.
Time, July 20, 1981; July 9, 1990.
Washington Post Magazine, June 11, 1989.
William and Mary Law Review, summer 1981.

—*Elizabeth Wenning*

Lena Olin

AP/Wide World Photos

Actress

Born in 1956 in Stockholm, Sweden; father's name, Stig; both parents were actors; Olin has one son, August. *Education:* Graduated from Royal Dramatic Theater School.

Career

Actress, c. 1980—. Began career in plays at the Royal Dramatic Theater of Sweden. Films include *The Unbearable Lightness of Being*, 1988; *Enemies: A Love Story*, 1990; *Havana*, 1990.

Awards: New York Film Critics Circle Award for best supporting actress and Academy Award nomination for best supporting actress, both 1990, both for *Enemies: A Love Story*.

Sidelights

Likened to such compatriots and film star icons as Ingrid Bergman and Greta Garbo, Swedish actress Lena Olin recalls the haunting beauty of the former and has the kind of aura of reserve that elevated the latter to legendary status. While she has made only three films in the United States—*The Unbearable Lightness of Being, Enemies: A Love Story*, and *Havana*—Olin has nevertheless left an indelible mark on American filmgoers, movie critics, and colleagues alike. Yet least impressed by her growing celebrity is Olin herself, who dismisses the overzealous attention of the press and benefits awarded by her blossoming film career as excessive. Called by *Premiere* magazine "the thinking man's beauty," Olin

also remains detached from her newfound stature as a sex symbol. "I definitely don't see myself that way," she told *Rolling Stone*. "Although it's nice. It's wonderful. But I don't take part in what people think about me, write about me. I have enough problems in my own life without getting involved in how people see me."

Born in Stockholm, Sweden, in 1956, Olin grew up in a theatrical family; her mother was an actress before raising Olin and her two siblings, and her father, Stig, appeared in some early Ingmar Bergman films. As a girl, Olin dreamed of being an actress but felt her acute shyness to be a hindrance. In *Rolling Stone*, she remarked, "Somebody would have said, 'Try to speak to the people around you before you think about getting up on stage.'" Her love of theater prevailed, however, and at age 20 she entered the Royal Dramatic Theater School of Sweden. It was there that Olin learned to use her physical rather than mental energy in acting.

"What was important was how you showed your feelings with your body and the sound of your voice," she told *Premiere*, "how different it was if you are 90 years old living in the country or 9 years old in the city, in a state of love or grief—it was all very *practical.''* Some training sessions entailed masking her face to force her body to work harder.

After graduation Olin began performing at the Royal Dramatic Theater in such classical roles as created by William Shakespeare, August Strindberg, and Anton Chekhov. She was playing Cordelia in a production of *King Lear* directed by Ingmar Bergman when producer Philip Kaufman discovered her. Their meeting resulted in Olin's initiation into American film, and Kaufman cast her, along with Daniel Day-Lewis and newcomer Juliette Binoche, in *The Unbearable Lightness of Being*, based on Czechoslovakian author Milan Kundera's 1984 novel of the same name. Nearly three hours long, the film wrestles with the complex and compelling interplay between personal relations and politics, in effect, according to *People,* showing ''an uncanny knack for pitting sexual heat against the dark chill of despotism.''

As the free-wheeling artist Sabina, Olin comes off in this film, in the words of *People,* as ''sensuous and intoxicating.'' Her character is but one of many mistresses to Tomas, a Czech physician, and the two seem a likely match for one another in their mutual propensity toward ''lightness''—interpreted by *New Yorker* critic Pauline Kael as retaining ''some of its happy, buoyant associations but . . . also [referring] to being cut off from your history, your culture, your memory.'' Completing this love triangle is Tomas's wife, Tereza, who repeatedly feels jealous and hurt by her husband's extramarital trysts and thus represents the antithesis of ''lightness'—she is ''weight,'' or commitment.

As the personal drama unfolds against the backdrop of the Soviet invasion of Prague in 1968, each character is tested in yet a larger sense. Tereza finds her life's work snapping front-line photographs of the invasion and thereby strengthens her identity; barred from his medical practice, Tomas experiments with other occupations, and other women, finally trading the ''lightness'' of freedom for the ''weight'' of his marriage vow; and Sabina, ever the whimsical independent in the black bowler hat, ultimately betrays her lover, her family, and her country to remain free, eventually retreating to the United States. The film received critical acclaim, and, with it, came high praise for its actors. *Time* called Olin ''a marvel'' whose ''grand witty gestures have a theatricality that underlines Sabina's desperate assertion of her independence,'' while Kael pronounced her ''glorious,'' encompassing ''the many meanings tucked away in the phrase 'the unbearable lightness of being'—the freedom and the elusive sadness.''

But if Olin's American film debut left a lasting impression on those who witnessed it, her prior success as a stage actress in her native country seems to have inured her against the hoopla of Hollywood stardom. In *Rolling Stone* Kaufman observed that ''[Olin is] not part of the syndrome . . . of arriving to work with a personal manager and entourage . . . . She's not concerned with a lot of the *trappings* of movie actresses.'' While Olin values what she terms the ''perks'' available on American movie sets, such as food, drivers, and stand-ins, in that they free her up to concentrate on the actual work, she maintains that she could just as easily do without and exercises caution in using them to fuel her ego ''as some actors do.'' Again, the difference appears cultural. As Olin told *Rolling Stone,* ''In Sweden you go to the set any way you want. No one cares. And when you're done, you take the subway home.''

> ***"In Sweden you go to the set any way you want. No one cares. And when you're done, you take the subway home."***

Another pitfall that Olin steels herself against are offers that want to capitalize on her sex appeal alone. With a candor that is at once refreshing and characteristic, she commented in *Rolling Stone,* ''If someone offers me a character with just sex, I'll say no. I don't need the American film business.'' Thus, while her sexy performance in *The Unbearable Lightness of Being* inspired an abundance of new script possibilities, Olin had little interest in any until the one for *Enemies: A Love Story* came her way. Apparently, the story continued to haunt her even after she had distanced herself from the manuscript, and the idea of playing Masha, a Holocaust survivor, captured both her heart and imagination. *American Film* pronounced it ''the sexiest, the most volatile and probably the most difficult to play of the three [female] roles,'' and it became the only one for which director Paul Mazursky interviewed more than one actress. Evidence that he found the answer in Olin came later, when, according to *American Film,* he deemed her a ''revelation.''

Based on Isaac Bashevis Singer's novel of 1972, *Enemies: A Love Story* is about four Holocaust survivors who unite in New York in 1949. Owing his survival to a Gentile peasant woman who hid him in a hayloft for three years, Polish Jew Herman Broder, played by Ron Silver, marries his savior (Margaret Stein) and brings her to New York after the war. There Herman discovers that his first wife, played by Anjelica Huston, was not killed in the Holocaust as he had thought, but survived her shooting and also lives in New York. Heightening the dramatic tension is Olin's character, Masha, Herman's mistress and a veteran of the death camps as well.

Co-written with Roger Simon, Mazursky's screenplay captures the story's humorous moments without glossing over the book's dark undercurrents, epitomized in the description of Herman as "without belief in the human race; a fatalistic hedonist who lived in presuicidal gloom." By the end of *Enemies: A Love Story*, one character commits suicide, another disappears, and it is clear that the lives of the two remaining, survivors in the truest sense of the word, will be haunted by their tortured pasts.

It may come as little surprise that none of the major studios ventured to tackle such a sensitive project, but it was perhaps this very sensitivity that prompted little-known Morgan Creek Productions to finally accept it and piqued Olin's offbeat interest as well. She agrees with painting an uncompromised picture of existence both on screen and off, telling *Rolling Stone*, "I can't imagine how someone can be content on this earth . . . . Some say we have to make movies like that [lightly entertaining] to give people a break. I don't think that's true. It's a relief to go to movies or theater that give a real sense of life." So important was this realism to Mazursky that he discarded a more conclusive, if not happier, ending for Singer's original one and even reshot lovemaking scenes between Olin and Silver that looked too beautiful, too staged. As testimony to Olin's magnetism, the enamored Silver told *Rolling Stone*, "If anyone is lucky enough to work with Lena, you don't have to try very hard to get that passion." For her efforts in *Enemies*, Olin received a New York Film Critics Award for best supporting actress and an Oscar nomination in the same category.

For Olin, dedication to her craft at times invokes a private struggle, as she tends to internalize the roles she plays to the degree that it threatens her identity. "[My] character is some kind of shadow that's always following me," she told *American Film*. "So my life is not terrific, because I have so little left of myself, of my own life . . . . when people ask me about my life, I really don't know what that is." What does constitute her personal life the naturally reticent Olin prefers to keep from the hawkish public eye. She never married

and no longer lives with the Swedish actor with whom she had her young son, who divides his time between joining her on the set and staying in Sweden with his grandmother and nanny. For inspiration in her dual role as parent and actress, Olin looks to fellow countrywoman Ingrid Bergman. "She was a very courageous woman," Olin explained in *American Film*. "She managed to work and cope with all the demands, and to have children."

But if Olin finds it a challenge to balance her multifaceted life, maintaining residences in both her homeland and America, what repeatedly draws her to Hollywood is what she sees as its limitless potential in filmmaking. "I've fallen in love with the ability of American movies to do anything—the wardrobe, the makeup, the sets," she told *American Film*. "When it's good, it's better than anywhere else." Her next film, *Havana*, directed by Sydney Pollack and co-starring Robert Redford, took full advantage of such technology and is considered a "big" movie—on a par with such grand-scale films as *Dr. Zhivago* and *Out of Africa*. According to *Premiere*, the $40-million-dollar project portrays "the decadence-flavored, end-of-an-era Havana—that bygone city of sloe-gin fizzes, gangsters, whores, and all-girl bands . . . the real La Florida."

Given such a polished and expansive product, it would not be expected that the shooting of *Havana* adhered to an extremely tight schedule nor that there were any casting dilemmas. Unable to find an appropriate American actress to play Bobby, the female lead, Pollack, who had seen Olin in *The Unbearable Lightness of Being*, revised the script with Judith Rascoe to transform Bobby into a Swede. According to *Premiere*, Pollack found that his choice of Olin "worked beautifully," and Redford, expounding on her presence and permanence on screen, summed it up this way: "There is somebody there, with something." In the 1990 film Redford plays American gambler Jack Weil, with whom Olin's character—married to a Cuban aristocrat played by Raul Julia—falls in love.

With three American films behind her, Olin is in no hurry to work again until the perfect script comes along. Meanwhile, she is growing accustomed to her new lifestyle, and even New York City, whose crime rate and crowds at first seemed overwhelming, has since grown on her. Perhaps best characterizing Olin's philosophy on life is the response she gave to *Rolling Stone*, when asked why she named her son, August, after Swedish playwright and novelist August Strindberg. "[Strindberg's] *exactly* what I love. He sees life as black as you can, but he sees the humor in it. I never laugh as much as when I watch Strindberg.''

Sources

American Film, November 1989.
New Yorker, February 8, 1988.
People, February 15, 1988.
Premiere, January 1991.
Rolling Stone, March 8, 1990.
Time, February 8, 1988.

—*Carolyn C. March*

Jim Palmer

AP/Wide World Photos

Former professional baseball player, sports broadcaster

Full name, James Alvin Palmer; born October 15, 1945, in New York, N.Y.; adopted son of Moe (a garment manufacturer) and Polly Wiesen; married Susan Ryan, c. 1964 (divorced, c. 1984); married Joni Pearlstone, April 7, 1990; children (first marriage): Jamie, Kelly.

Career

Pitcher for the Baltimore Orioles, 1963-84. Play-by-play broadcaster for network television and ESPN sports network, 1984—. Also serves as spokes-man/model for Jockey International, Inc.

Awards: Four Gold Gloves for defense; American League Cy Young Award, 1973, 1975, and 1976; named American League pitcher of the year by the *Sporting News*, 1973, 1975, and 1976; named to Baseball Hall of Fame in first year of eligibility, 1990.

Sidelights

Jim Palmer was the Baltimore Orioles' finest all-time pitcher and one of the purest hurlers in American League history. Palmer was only the twentieth player in major league baseball to be voted into the Hall of Fame in his first year of eligibility—an honor that reflects his superb ability on the mound. *Baltimore Sun* columnist Mike Littwin claimed that Palmer "set a rather disturbing standard for the rest of us. He was perfect. So, now he is immortal, too." In a *Playboy* feature, Thomas Boswell

called Palmer "as glamorous, as bright, as gifted and as public a figure as baseball has had to offer . . . . To the public eye, a glance at Palmer is a glimpse of the all-American ideal made manifest."

Palmer won three Cy Young awards and pitched in six World Series games. Since he was released from the Orioles in 1984 he has forged a new and equally successful career as a television announcer. What has brought Palmer his greatest fame (or infamy), however, is his work with Jockey, International, modeling men's underwear. Boswell maintained that Palmer's work with Jockey has made him a "national sex symbol," recognized by Americans who have never even visited a ball park. Boswell concluded that the Jim Palmer of the Jockey ads and the sportscasting booth "stands for elegance and sophistication: the embodiment of natural gifts, both athletic and personal."

James Alvin Palmer was born in New York City in 1945. When he was only a week old he was adopted by a wealthy clothing manufacturer named Moe Wiesen and his wife, Polly. Palmer grew up in a posh Park Avenue apartment with servants and every luxury. To this day he expresses no curiosity about his natural parents—he always knew he was adopted and accepted the fact without anxiety. Palmer's first adoptive father died when he was nine. His mother moved the family—Palmer and a sister, also adopted—to Los Angeles, where they lived in a modest but upscale bungalow. Palmer's mother remarried in 1956, this time to a character actor named Max Palmer. Max and Jim formed a close relationship, and when he was twelve Jim changed his name to that of his new dad. The change was announced, to Max's surprise, at a Little League awards dinner in Beverly Hills. Palmer's father told the *Sun:* "I have had some thrills in my life. But nothing, ever, like hearing those words."

It was Max Palmer who encouraged his stepson to sign with the Baltimore Orioles and play professional baseball. A gifted all-around athlete, Palmer was offered a basketball scholarship to UCLA at the same time that the Orioles were pursuing him. After a summer of semi-pro ball, he decided to try his luck with the Orioles. Ironically, he almost missed the contract-signing session. Driving home from his summer baseball league in South Dakota, he and a friend were involved in a one-car accident. The automobile was demolished, but miraculously Palmer and his friend—who was driving at the time—walked away with minor injuries. Palmer joined the Orioles in August of 1963 and began his career as a professional the following spring. The club had such confidence in him that he was awarded a $50,000 signing bonus.

With the Aberdeen (South Dakota) Pheasants (the Orioles farm team) in 1964, the eighteen-year-old Palmer earned an 11-3 record that included a shutout and a no-hitter. The team management thought he should stay in the minors perhaps one more year, but in those times minor league players could be drafted to fight in the Vietnam War. Palmer was therefore promoted to the Orioles in 1965 and placed under the tutelage of fellow pitchers Dick Hall and Robin Roberts. His work in 1965 came mostly in relief, and he compiled an unimpressive 5-4 record. In the off-season he worked with Orioles pitching coach George Bamberger, and he came to spring training in 1966 determined to move out of the bullpen permanently.

He did just that, and more. By July 30, 1966 he had twelve wins, including eight of his last nine starts. Surrounded by Oriole greats such as Brooks Robinson, Frank Robinson, and Luis Aparicio, Palmer seemed nearly invincible. He helped guide the team to its first World Series appearance by winning the pennant-clinching game against the Kansas City A's. It was the 1966 World Series, however, that introduced the baseball world to Jim Palmer. At twenty,

he was too young to vote, drink alcohol, or buy a house, but he went to the mound facing pitching giant Sandy Koufax and threw a shutout. The Orioles won the game 6-0, and subsequently took the Series with four straight.

> *"It was easy to pitch for the Orioles, because there was a constant goal. We were always trying to do something collectively—win a pennant."*

Just as real fame beckoned, Palmer found himself afflicted with a sore back and shoulder, the first of many serious injuries that would dog his career. Between June 8, 1967 and the beginning of the 1969 season Palmer worked in only two major league games. For a time it even looked like he would have to retire. A stint with the winter Puerto Rican league helped him to regain his form, and he returned to the parent club in time for the 1969 season. There he pitched to a 16-4 record with six shutouts, a doubly impressive achievement considering he spent six weeks of that season on the disabled list.

With Palmer's help, the Orioles appeared in the World Series in 1969, 1970, and 1971. The club had exceptional all-around talent in those years, and Palmer became famous for positioning his teammates from the mound—a practice he continued throughout the rest of his career. In 1970 Palmer had his first twenty-game season (he had eight in all), and most observers felt that he had finally hit his stride. Palmer is quick to acknowledge that his teammates on the Orioles helped to assure him victory after victory. As Littwin noted, the pitcher "played on good to great teams for his entire career. And, in those 19 years, he pitched with some of the best in the game. But the Orioles were never better than when Palmer was on the mound, no matter who was winning the Cy Young that year."

Palmer won his share of Cy Young awards as well, earning the honors in 1973 (with a 22-9 record), 1975 (23-11), and 1976 (22-13). In fact, his only off-year in the 1970s was 1974, when a sore elbow led to a 7-12 record. On May 29, 1978 he became the 75th pitcher in history to capture two hundred victories. Palmer shrugged off the milestone as if it were inconsequential. "I hate to belittle 200," he said, "but I have my eye on 300. If I can stay healthy and play on good clubs, and if I can pitch until I'm 36 or 37, I've got a good shot."

Unfortunately, Palmer did not stay healthy. Multiple injuries in the shoulder, elbow, and back began to affect his performance as early as 1979, and as the 1980s progressed he declined still further. Manager Earl Weaver and some of his teammates suggested—sometimes bluntly—that Palmer was a hypochondriac. Weaver, who had always quarreled openly with Palmer, told the media: "The Chinese tell time by the Year of the Dragon, the Year of the Horse. I tell time by the Year of the Shoulder, the Year of the Elbow, the Year of the Ulnar Nerve." Weaver's claims did little to endear Palmer to the fans in Baltimore, many of whom called for a trade. Despite his troubles, Palmer managed to turn in a fine year in 1982, going 15-5. The following season found him in rehabilitation, but he did earn a relief victory in the 1983 World Series.

The Orioles released Palmer on May 23, 1984, at an emotional press conference that ended when Palmer fled in tears. "A lot of things had gone wrong, the team wasn't pitching, hitting, playing defense, or winning," Palmer told the *Sun.* "The handwriting was on the wall and I knew my days were numbered. It might not have been right, but there was nothing you could do about it . . . . To go to another team just to try and win 300 games wasn't worth it, and it was totally contrary to what I had been used to. It was easy to pitch for the Orioles, because there was a constant goal. We were always trying to do something collectively—win a pennant."

Palmer finished his career with 268 victories, all for the Orioles. A "thinking fan's pitcher," he could draw upon a dizzying array of pitches, especially the curve and—early in his career—the fastball, to confound his opponents. He was also an able defensive player, earning four Gold Gloves for his work in the field. Possibly the most astonishing feat of Palmer's career is the fact that he never gave up a single grand slam in nineteen years of major league ball. After his release by the Orioles, Palmer put his encyclopedic baseball expertise to use as a sportscaster, first for the networks and more recently for cable television. Today he brings a welcome perspective to the game as he provides color commentary for both the American and the National Leagues.

Jockey International hired Jim Palmer to model its bikini briefs in 1975. At first Palmer was one of a group of athletes from baseball, basketball, and football, who were all featured in Jockey ads. Gradually Jockey came to realize that women (the major purchasers of men's underwear) preferred Palmer to the other models. Jockey preferred him too—he was punctual, polite, and willing to sign autographs for his thousands of new female fans. The company's vice president for advertising told the *Sun:* "I classify Jim as an advertising man's dream. He's got the looks and the body. He's a professional." Palmer still appears in an occasional Jockey ad, and he still wears the same size brief he wore in 1975. When he was inducted into the Hall of Fame in 1990, Jockey honored him with an eighteen-by-ninety-six billboard in New York's Times Square that read "Congratulations, Jim. Hall of Fame."

In 1991 Palmer surprised observers of the game when he announced his intention to return to the game. The Orioles management invited him to attend the team's spring training camp as a non-roster player. No Hall of Famer had ever resumed a major league career and there was a good deal of speculation over how a successful comeback would affect his Hall of Fame status (eligibility for induction into the Hall begins five years *after* officially leaving the sport). The point became moot, however, when Palmer tore his right hamstring during his first appearance on the mound, a two-inning stint against the Boston Red Sox in which he allowed two runs and five hits. Palmer called off his comeback attempt the following day, citing the lengthy recovery time required for such an injury, and indicated he planned to resume his modeling and broadcast careers.

Sources

Baltimore Sun, July 26, 1989; January 11, 1990; August 2, 1990.
Baltimore Evening Sun, August 2, 1990.
Detroit Free Press, February 20, 1991.
Playboy, May 1983.

—*Mark Kram*

Octavio Paz

AP/Wide World Photos

Poet, author, and educator

Born March 31, 1914, in Mexico City, Mexico; son of Octavio Paz Sr. (a lawyer) and Josefina Lozano; married Marie Jose Tramini; children: one daughter. *Education:* Attended National University of Mexico. *Politics:* Once considered himself a Marxist, but today Communists consider him a conservative because he said he rejects the "simplistic and simplifying ideologies of the left." He also has angered the far right in his homeland, leaving him ostracized by both extremes. *Religion:* Raised Catholic.

Address: c/o Revista Vuelta, Leonardo da Vinci 17, Mexico City 03910, Mexico.

Career

Poet, essayist, diplomat, professor, and critic. Author of more than 21 books; best known work includes essay *The Labyrinth of Solitude* (1952), and poem *Sun Stone* (1957). Also founder of several literary magazines, including Mexico's most prestigious intellectual magazine, *Vuelta*. Served in the Mexican diplomatic corps, 1944-62, in such countries as the United States, Japan, France, Switzerland, and India. Taught at Cambridge University, 1970; Charles Eliot Norton professor of poetry at Harvard University, 1971-72; lectured at University of Texas.

Awards: Guggenheim fellow, 1944; International Poetry Grand Prix, 1963; Jerusalem Prize, 1977; T. S. Eliot Award from the Ingersoll Foundation, 1987; Nobel Prize for literature, October 1990.

Sidelights

Octavio Paz is a poet, yet he is not a gentle man. His poetry and essays have been described as phosphorescent, political, passionate, complicated, moral, and hauntingly lonely. His writing is surreal, sensuous, and intense, like a bright sun burning into the heart and soul of Mexico itself. Here is a passage from *Sun Stone*, his most famous poem: "a bright hallucination of many wings/when they all open at the height of the sky/the sun has forced an entrance through my forehead/has opened my eyelids at last that were kept closed." To understand the depths of Paz's poetry, which won the Nobel Prize for Literature in 1990, one must understand the background of the man, now in his late 70s, who has been described by fellow Latin American author Mario Vargas Llosa as "one of the greatest poets that the Spanish language world has produced."

Paz was born in 1914 in Mexico City. His father was a lawyer whose ancestors were Mexican and Indian; his mother's parents were immigrants from Andalusia, Spain. Paz's well-off family lost all its money in the Mexican Civil War, and Paz grew up poor in Mixcoac, a village outside of Mexico City. But Paz remembers his childhood through an artist's eyes: "One day, while on a picnic with my friends, we found a small pyramid . . . this was the Mexico of my childhood—a Mexico rich in pre-Columbian art, the art of the colonialists, and the flowering of modern Mexican art," he recalled in *New Perspectives Quarterly.*

Paz attended Catholic schools, but questioned their teachings. He enrolled at the National University of Mexico, but left without getting a degree. Instead, he began writing—prolifically. At age 19, in 1933, he published his first book of poetry, *Luna silvestre* ("Forest Moon"). That and other volumes established him as a promising writer. He first came to the United States in 1944 on a Guggenheim fellowship, but soon ran out of money. In 1945 he joined the Mexican diplomatic corps. During the next 23 years, he was posted to France, Switzerland, the United States, Japan, and India.

> *"Poetry is not a very popular art form these days, but it's an essential part of human life.... Without poetry, people can't even talk well."*

In each country Paz visited he embraced the cultures and writers, taking most delight from oriental traditions, which he called "my discovery of the other." All this time he was writing. In 1952 his essay *The Labyrinth of Solitude* became the platform for great philosophical change in Mexico; it was published in English in 1957. The essay penetrated what Paz called the "underneath" of Mexico: "The Mexican seems to me to be a person who shuts himself away to protect himself; his face is a mask and [he] is always remote," he wrote in his attempt to illuminate the "indecipherable anguish of a race born in violence and obsessed with the past."

In 1957 he published *Sun Stone*, a lyrical poem inspired by an ancient Aztec calendar stone. Between 1950 and 1960 Paz synthesized his world experience and travels into a clear vision; this he transmitted to paper. Yet he remained relatively unknown outside of Latin America until many of his works were translated into English in the 1960s and 1970s.

Paz was posted to India by the diplomatic corps in 1962. There he met Marie-Jose Tramini, who would become his wife. But his career in the service of his country ended abruptly when government troops massacred 300 student rebels at the National University of Mexico. He resigned his ambassadorship in protest. Since then, Paz has lived around the world. He taught at England's Cambridge University in 1970, lectured at the University of Texas, and was the Charles Eliot Norton professor of poetry at Harvard University from 1971 to 1972.

Paz, who now lives back in Mexico, has been critized by the political left as being too sympathetic to Mexican President Carlos Salinas de Gortari and hypocritical for advocating free-market economic reforms in his homeland—contrary to his *The Labyrinth of Solitude* warning that Mexico cannot thrive unless it becomes a "really just society." Yet politics are not the primary focus of Paz's overridingly artistic, deeply personal worldview. He is above all things an interpreter of the world. He does not enjoy writing, he confessed to Rita Guibert, author of the book *Seven Voices*, but he enjoys the results. He told Guibert that he writes by hand, never typewriter. Paz works a little each day and also reads poetry and the dictionary, which he calls "his adviser, his elder brother."

In the summer of 1990 Paz served as curator of "The Privileges of Vision"—an exhibit at Mexico City's Museum of Contemporary Art which was mounted as a sort of autobiography of his life and work. The purpose of the program was the same as Paz's poetry—to make connections between cultures, times, and languages through art. "Baudelaire said that poets are the universal translators because they translate the language of the universe—stars, water, trees—into the language of man. Though it was not my goal, in some ways it has been my destiny as a poet to be a translator," he told *New Perspectives Quarterly* magazine. "Sometimes the artist seems not to be in tune with the art tendencies of his epoch, but this remoteness, in some cases, helps him penetrate his own time more deeply." The artist's goal, he said, should be to "transcend the time in which the artist lives." In the Paz poem "This Side," for example, he describes the poet's struggle with this transcendence: "With shadows I draw worlds/I scatter worlds with shadows/I hear the light beat on the other side."

It was for his ability to see both light and shadows that Octavio Paz received the Nobel Prize for literature in October 1990. The academy praised Paz for "exquisite love poetry," especially *Sun Stone*, which was "at the same time sensuous and visual" and for his "intractable but fruitful union of cultures, pre-Columbian Indian, the Spanish conquistadors and Western modernism." Paz, who happened to be in New York for an exhibit of Mexican art on the day his Nobel Prize was announced, was astonished. He did not expect to win, but he was delighted. "Poetry is not a very popular art form these days, but it's an essential part of human life," he was quoted in several newspapers. "Poetry is the memory of a country, of language. Without poetry, people can't even talk well."

While Paz believes that modern culture and communication can lead to bland artistic sameness around the world, he is not pessimistic. "I do not believe we are at the end of the arts. We are at the end of some kind of art, that's all," he told *New Perspectives Quarterly*. "True, this end of a century has seen a tendency toward uniformity in the arts culture generally. But it has also, just as strongly, seen a return of times and of language... Universality in the 20th century is not the monologue of Reason, but the dialogue between human beings and cultures."

Selected writings

In English translation

The Labyrinth of Solitude, 1961.
Sun Stone, 1962.
Selected Poems, 1963.
Marcel Duchamp; or, The Castle of Purity, 1970.
Claude Levi-Strauss: An Introduction, 1970.
Eagle or Sun? 1970.
Configurations, 1971.
Renga: A Chain of Poems by Octavio Paz et al, 1972.
Alternating Current, 1973.
The Bow and the Lyre, 1973.
Children of the Mire: Poetry from Romanticism to the Avant-Garde, 1974.
Conjunctions and Disjunctions, 1974.
Blanco, 1974.
The Siren and the Seashell, and Other Essays of Poets and Poetry, 1976.
A Draft of Shadows and Other Poems, 1979.
Selected Poems, 1979.
Marcel Duchamp: Appearances Stripped Bare, 1979.
The Monkey Grammarian, 1981.
Airborn: Hijos del aire, 1981.
Selected Poems, 1984.
One Earth, Four or Five Worlds: Reflections on Contemporary History, 1985.
The Collected Poems of Octavio Paz, 1957-1987, 1987.
On Poets and Others, 1987.
Convergences: Essays on Art and Literature, 1987.
Sor Juana; or, the Traps of Faith, 1988.
A Tree Within, 1988.

Sources

Books

Guibert, Rita, *Seven Voices,* 1972.

Periodicals

Detroit Free Press, October 12, 1990.
Esquire, March 1991.
New Perspectives Quarterly, summer 1990.
Newsweek, October 22, 1990.
Time, October 22, 1990.

—Ellen Creager

Cesar Pelli

UPI/Bettmann

Architect

Born c. 1927, in Argentina.

Addresses: *Office*—New Haven, CN.

Career

Came to the United States in the 1950s and worked under architect Eero Saarinen. Designer for Gruen Associates, and Daniel, Mann, Johnson & Mendenhall, both of Los Angeles. Founded own practice in New Haven, CN, 1977, and became dean of architecture at Yale University.

Sidelights

In the past few months," Douglas Davis wrote in a 1986 *Newsweek* article, "the most visible name in architecture has not been that of I. M. Pei or Philip Johnson—the expected stars—but Cesar Pelli." For the Argentina-born designer, the 1980s brought a new recognition of his gleaming modern skyscrapers and Art Deco-inspired towers.

Among Pelli's most famous buildings are New York's Battery Park series, which line up in increasing height and sport glass arches near the entrances, and his Carnegie Hall tower—a slim, Deco homage soaring over the famous concert hall. Then there is what Davis called a "Pelli coup"—a 57-story tower that, "clad in a rose-beige Kasota stone, topped by a sparkling white and gold crown, . . . [glistens] like a jewel in Minneapolis."

Pelli began his U.S. career working under one of the 1950s' most influential architects, Eero Saarinen. And Pelli "was touched—if not convinced—by the postmodern counterrevolution that flourished in the '70s, which revived the past as a source of inspiration," noted Davis. "For much of his career," wrote Paul Gapp in the *Chicago Tribune*, "Pelli demonstrated an almost obsessive fondness for taut, practically seamless, wet-look glass skins. He has since turned to often stone-clad buildings of greater sculptural quality and livelier, carved-out profiles."

Not everyone, though, is a Pelli fan. Referring to the architect's designs for London's Canary Wharf—a waterfront metropolis on the Thames River that will include the tallest skyscraper in Britain—no less a critic than Prince Charles, quoted in *Maclean's*, said Pelli's project "will cast its shadow over generations of Londoners who have suffered enough from towers of architectural arrogance."

But for the most part, Pelli is respected as a consummate professional, a "mature practitioner unencumbered by the kind of blazing ego that marks some design stars," as Gapp wrote. "He is known as a solidly pragmatic sort of fellow who is comfortable with tight construction budgets and timetables." Pelli's dedication extends to the staff of his New

Haven design studio. As Davis described it, the "large, active office...spews out a stream of lyrical, technically sophisticated buildings that are neither 'modern' nor 'postmodern.' Each attempts to please on many levels at once, captivating clients and public but frustrating critics."

A typical building of that description is Chicago's 181 West Madison, a huge edifice of an office tower that Gapp interpreted as recollective of Art Moderne. "From considerable distances, 181 W. Madison presents itself as a steel-framed building which in silhouette, surface detail and other respects projects a visual message of strength as well as delicacy," Gapp remarked. "Pelli eschewed the polychromic and geometric overkill that blemishes too many of today's tall buildings done by architects who don't know when to turn off their computer-driven drawing machines." Concluding, Gapp noted that despite some internal distractions, like a lack of any place to sit down, 181 W. Madison shows that Pelli "has driven his personal guidon into the soil of Chicago,

mostly to splendid effect. Overall, he has again demonstrated his propensity of quiet good taste, which is a relatively scarce commodity in our time."

And to Davis, the secret of the architect's success is that, whatever else may be said about the details and flourishes, a Pelli design like the Carnegie Hall tower simply "'fits' its place and purpose so well. Despite the vast discrepancy in their sizes, the new skyscraper and the earthbound 95-year-old [concert] hall seem of a piece. Over and again, Pelli's buildings defer—despite their ingenuity—to their sites and to their context. His architecture is unfailingly humane and courtly."

Sources

Chicago Tribune, July 1, 1990.
Maclean's, July 9, 1990.
Newsweek, August 4, 1986.

—*Susan Salter*

Roger Penrose

Physicist and mathematician

Born August 8, 1931, in Colchester, Essex, England; son of Lionel Sharples Penrose; married Joan Isabel Wedge, 1959 (marriage dissolved, 1981); children: three sons. *Education:* University College, University of London, BSc spec. 1st class in mathematics; St. John's College, Cambridge, Ph.D.

Addresses: *Office*—Mathematical Institute, 24-29 St. Giles, Oxford OX1 3LB.

Career

Assistant lecturer in pure mathematics at Bedford College, London, 1956-57; research fellow at St. John's College, Cambridge, 1957-60; NATO Research Fellow at Princeton and Syracuse universities, 1959-61; research associate at King's College, London, 1961-63; visiting associate professor at University of Texas, Austin, 1963-64; reader, 1964-66, and professor of applied mathematics, 1966-73, at Birkbeck College, London; Rouse Ball Professor of Mathematics at Oxford University, 1973—. Visiting posts include those at Yeshiva, Princeton, and Cornell universities, 1966-67 and 1969; Lovett Professor at Rice University, Houston, TX, 1983—.

Awards: Adams Prize from Cambridge University, 1966-67; Dannie Heineman Prize from the American Physics Association and American Institute of Physics, 1971; recipient, with physicist Stephen W. Hawking, of the Eddington Medal, 1975; Royal Medal from the Royal Society, 1985.

Member: International Society for General Relativity and Gravitation; London Mathematical Society; Cambridge Philosophical Society; Institute for Mathematics and its Applications.

Sidelights

Like many of the world's greatest scientists and thinkers, Roger Penrose, a mathematician and physicist who teaches at Oxford University, has worked most of his life in relative obscurity, despite his impressive contributions to science. All of that changed, however, in 1989 with the publication of Penrose's groundbreaking book, *The Emperor's New Mind*, which fueled public fascination with the interrelationship between artificial intelligence and the human mind—and touched off controversy in the scientific community as well. Though complex and, at times, highly speculative, Penrose's book was so thought-provoking, so sweeping in its attempt to draw a picture of the contemporary state of scientific research, that Timothy Ferris of the *New York Times Book Review* was obliged to rank it "among the most innovative and exciting science books to have been published in the last 40 years."

Among Penrose's major contentions in *The Emperor's New Mind* is that computers will never be able to think as humans do, a point that angers many researchers in artificial intelligence, who believe they are well on their way to developing super-computers that will one day think as well, if not better, than humans. But Penrose points to two well-known mathematical laws as proof that the mind can think in ways that computers, which compute only according to strict rules, or algorithms, cannot possibly duplicate. "The very fact that the mind leads us to truths that are not computable convinces me that a computer can never duplicate the mind," Penrose states.

Having established this limitation on artificial intelligence, Penrose went on to attempt an explanation of the human thought process by conjecturing that it may be linked to the two great polar opposites of physics theory—relativity, which explains gravity, and quantum mechanics, which concern the laws governing subatomic particles. Since the establishment in the 20th century of these two awesome but mysteriously contradictory guideposts, physicists have been working diligently to develop a superunified theory, or so-called theory of everything, to tie the two theories together into one grand explanation of the physical laws governing the universe. Quantum mechanics state that charged particles in an atom can "jump" from one place to another without traversing the space between—the so-called "quantum leap." Penrose postulates in his book that human intuition may be the result of a similar "jump" occurring between individual cells and neurons within the brain.

Since computers are unable to operate by these mysterious quantum rules, Penrose argues, they will never be able to think creatively or have insight; in short, they will not have consciousness. Writing in *Time*, reviewer Michael D. Lemonick ascertained that "Penrose believes human creativity and consciousness are nothing less than the perceptible workings of the most basic laws of the universe"— laws which, when someday discovered, will bring physics to a profound understanding of the way matter has evolved to its most complex orientation— that of human consciousness.

Although his field is sometimes misunderstood as a haven for rigid thinkers who deal only in formulae

and numbers, Penrose has a well-established reputation for making great discoveries through creative, highly abstract thought that is almost playful. As a child, he developed with his father the impossible "Penrose staircase," which spirals around and around without going higher or lower. A famous lithograph by Dutch artist M. C. Escher, called *Ascending and Descending*, employs this concept by showing figures going both up and down the stairway simultaneously.

In the early 1970s, through a characteristically frolicsome experiment in geometry with triangular tiles, Penrose unknowingly discovered the architecture of a new class of crystals the existence of which was unheard of then. These "aperiodic tiles" also helped to prove the mathematical concept of random order. "In fact, their symmetry is of a type that physicists thought simply couldn't exist in the natural world," wrote *Discover* editor Paul Hoffman. "[Penrose's] tiling patterns, they believed, along with similar structures in three dimensions called quasicrystals, were intriguing but ultimately fantastic mathematical toys. Then they found the patterns in nature, and suddenly a whole new field of physics was born." Penrose's research was also of great benefit to Stephen W. Hawking (see *Newsmakers 90*), perhaps the most influential physicist of the modern era, in establishing the plausibility of black holes in space and providing new insights into research of the Big Bang, the great explosion that is believed to have created the universe.

Selected writings

The Emperor's New Mind: Concerning Computers, Minds, and the Laws of Physics, Oxford University Press, 1989.

Sources

Discover, February 1990.
New York Times Book Review, November 11, 1989.
Time, June 25, 1990.

—*David Collins*

Javier Perez de Cuellar

AP/Wide World Photos

United Nations secretary-general

Born January 19, 1920, in Lima, Peru; wife's name, Marcela (Temple); children: two. *Education:* Studied law at Catholic University, Lima. *Religion:* Catholic.

Addresses: *Office*—United Nations Secretariat, New York, NY 10017.

Career

In Peruvian diplomatic service, 1944-66; secretary-general of Foreign Office, 1966-69; ambassador to the Soviet Union and Poland, 1969-71; permanent representative to the United Nations (UN), 1971-75; representative to UN Security Council, 1973-74; special representative of UN secretary-general to Cyprus, 1975-77; ambassador to Venezuela, 1978-81; UN under-secretary, 1979-81; personal representative of the UN secretary-general to Afghanistan, 1980-82; UN secretary-general, 1982—.

Sidelights

Charisma is not usually a quality sought in a secretary-general of the United Nations. Javier Perez de Cuellar is no exception. The London *Sunday Times*, editorializing on the occasion of his appointment in 1981, observed: "Any secretary-general for the 1980s would have to be a lowest-common denominator man, grey, two-dimensional and without a sharp edge to his character. Mr. de Cuellar from Peru is all of that." Perez de Cuellar has, however, tried to attain that third dimension—impact on the

world stage—and is perhaps best known for his efforts to preserve peace between the United States and Iraq in the days leading up to the Persian Gulf War. Sometimes dogged by serious illness during his two terms as head of the United Nations, sometimes confounded by difficult geopoliticians, de Cuellar will likely leave the world organization as he entered it: a man with a grey flannel, but respected, reputation.

Perez de Cuellar has certainly benefitted by comparison to his most recent predecessor, Kurt Waldheim, who somehow alienated both the United States and the Soviet Union, as well as most of Europe and the Third World. Soon after leaving the United Nations Waldheim was accused of fabricating his military activities during World War II. "Compared with Waldheim, who has been described by one of his former senior officials as a 'scheming, ambitious egomaniac,' Perez de Cuellar is self-effacing, friendly and sincere," said the *Sunday Times*. Waldheim had lobbied frantically for an unprecedented third term as secretary-general; de Cuellar went home to Peru during the voting. The London *Times* revealed that "the news [that de Cuellar had been selected] was telephoned to him at a beach house outside Lima and he was dumbfounded." He nonetheless announced that he would stay for only one term. The Associated

Press quoted de Cuellar in 1983, a year after his election: "If I say that I will run for another mandate, then I will have to start pleasing the Soviets, the Americans, the French, the British and Chinese in order to have their votes at the end of my [first] mandate." Five years later, however, the secretary-general opted for a second term.

Despite his tireless shuttle efforts, none of the great issues of his day—the Soviet invasion of Afghanistan, Apartheid in South Africa, violence in the Middle East, the Falkland Islands War, superpower confrontations—have really carried the de Cuellar stamp. This can be blamed in part on the inherent limitations of his office, which carries no real power, not even a vote in the United Nations General Assembly. "It has been said," wrote the *Sunday Times*, "that previous occupants of the post of secretary-general have had to choose between being secretaries or generals." Dag Hammarskjold, a dynamic and tireless Swede who held the post from 1953 until 1961, when he was killed in a plane crash, could be characterized as a general. U Thant, the quiet Burmese diplomat who held the post from 1961 to 1971, took the role of secretary. De Cuellar wanted none of the trappings of a general. Until 1982, wrote the *Los Angeles Times*, "one elevator in the 38-floor [United Nations] secretariat building has always been held in readiness by a white-gloved attendant whenever the secretary-general has been in the building. De Cuellar has ended the custom, taking elevators as they come and sharing the ride with others."

De Cuellar would be the first to admit he is no Hammarskjold. He told the London *Times*, "The secretary-general cannot be compared to the president of a country. The secretary-general has to respond to the demands of 157 countries. Governments and people want concrete results. They don't appreciate 'drop of water' progress. I don't complain. This is normal. The secretary-general should be a constant inspirer." "His favorite word," wrote the *New York Times*, "is 'caution.'" And the London *Times* commented of his low profile: "He lacks ... strong political beliefs—a qualification that has certainly endeared him to the big powers. When ... he was eased without fuss into a second five-year term, Margaret Thatcher supposedly remarked that he had not caused any trouble first time around."

Still, Perez de Cuellar does not shy from the good fight. Throughout the 1980s he attempted to mediate between two of the world's most fanatical enemies, Iran and Iraq, which were locked in a monstrous war for eight years. In 1984 he managed a short-lived, partial truce. But that soon collapsed and the conflict,

including Iraq's deadly use of chemical weapons, lasted another four years, eventually costing a million or more lives on both sides. Then, with Iraq's invasion of Kuwait on August 2, 1990, de Cuellar again tried to insert himself and the United Nations into the volatile Middle East, hoping to negotiate an end to the crisis. But it was the member countries, led by the United States, which ultimately generated UN policy. Their efforts resulted in a string of United Nations resolutions demanding Iraq's withdrawal, and imposing sanctions and a deadline by which Iraqi leader Saddam Hussein's forces were to be out of Kuwait. De Cuellar was left to attempt an eleventh-hour mission to Baghdad, during which he apparently beseeched Saddam to withdraw from Kuwait before the January 15 deadline. The mission failed, however; just hours after de Cuellar's plea the anti-Iraq coalition began its devastating bombing campaign.

"The secretary-general cannot be compared to the president of a country. The secretary-general has to respond to the demands of 157 countries."

Though he was unable to prevent war in the Persian Gulf, Perez de Cuellar has logged some victories during his international career. He is credited with bringing together the late President Makarios of Cyprus and Turkish Cypriot leader Rauf Denktash, in 1977—the first meeting of the two sides in 14 years. The issue was tricky. according to the *Boston Globe*, a 30,000-strong Turkish army confronted a nearly defenseless Greek population across a no-man's-land patrolled by United Nations forces. After de Cuellar's initial progress, the talks collapsed, in part "because of [then-Secretary General] Waldheim's insistence on intervening personally, with attendant wide publicity. Perez de Cuellar was not part of this whispering campaign, but in a moment of petulance Waldheim exploded in the presence of aides: 'I invented Perez de Cuellar.'"

Even more indicative of his skills, de Cuellar made himself a major player during the Falkland Islands War in 1982 after the Argentine invasion of that British concern. For two weeks de Cuellar held twice-daily but separate meetings with Argentine and

British diplomats at United Nations headquarters in New York City. Although the South American secretary-general found himself in negotiations with a South American nation, he won praise from Britons for his unbiased handling of the affair. According to the Associated Press, British negotiator Sir Anthony Parsons said, "I can't imagine anyone who could have handled this better." Unfortunately, the rival claims of the two countries eventually nullified de Cuellar's effort and Britain reconquered the islands by force. The *Boston Globe* nevertheless reported that "the secretary general employed classical diplomatic methods, concentrating on the less difficult aspects of the problem, hoping to narrow the gaps there to the point where a substantive dialogue might follow and tempers might cool, while leaving the really tough issues for later."

Perez de Cuellar was born in 1920 in the Peruvian capital of Lima. The family's roots, however, lay in the town of Cuellar in Spain. De Cuellar's father was a successful businessman and amateur pianist. The secretary-general received a law degree from Catholic University in Lima. The *New York Times* summed up his early career thus: "He stumbled into diplomacy by accident. As a law student at the Catholic University of Lima, he looked for a job to earn pocket money and found one as a $50-a-month clerk in the Foreign Ministry. By the time he graduated he decided that the foreign service was a good life—'It helps you to know countries and at someone else's expense'—and he signed on as First Secretary in the Paris Mission." Other early foreign postings included serving as counsellor in Britain, Bolivia, and Brazil, and as ambassador to Switzerland, Poland, Venezuela, and the Soviet Union.

De Cuellar's impact on Peru's international relations is easier to quantify than his stewardship of the United Nations. As the London *Times* revealed, "He was instrumental in breaking Peru of a provincially Latin mentality and steering it to a full-bodied membership of the non-aligned movement." He helped normalize Peru's relations with the Soviet Union and became his country's first ambassador there. Those efforts perhaps helped insure his election as secretary-general of the United Nations several years later. Eventually, following the Soviet invasion of Afghanistan, de Cuellar was able to use his ties and a working knowledge of Russian to help soften the crisis and nurture a dialogue between the Soviet Union and Pakistan without alienating either nation. Upon leaving Moscow he was named Peru's chief delegate to the United Nations. After a brief foray into academia at home, de Cuellar was named

Waldheim's special representative to Cyprus in 1975 and spent two years on the Mediterranean island.

When he was chosen as the fifth secretary-general of the United Nations—taking office on January 1, 1982—blandness seemed to be the most important attribute he brought to the job. De Cuellar was a compromise candidate, selected after nearly two months of rancorous debate in late 1981. The *Los Angeles Times* called him a "talented but bland Peruvian diplomat ... a highly regarded but colorless negotiator." The paper added, "The key to the Peruvian's election appears to have been his inoffensiveness. He was the only one of seven candidates considered ... who failed to draw a veto from one of the five permanent members of the Security Council." China, a prominent member of the Council, blocked the Austrian Waldheim's election to a third term 16 times, insisting instead on a candidate from the Third World. De Cuellar earns $200,000 a year for running the 14,000-employee United Nations and administering its $1 billion annual budget.

Once chosen de Cuellar quickly articulated his worldview. In his acceptance speech he told the UN General Assembly, "I cannot separate myself from my origins in a developing country." He has also always been insistent on the "need for quiet diplomacy. If I want to be effective, I have to be discreet. I am not running for a Nobel Prize." With de Cuellar at the helm, however, the United Nations did win the prize and new respect in 1988 for its peacekeeping efforts. Under Waldheim the United Nations had actually seemed to lose control of its peacekeeping machinery. But de Cuellar, stated the Associated Press, "engaged in a low-pressure campaign to sell the idea of the UN as an ideal negotiating forum and a 'very good device for saving face.' It was, he reasoned, 'much easier for a government to make concessions to the United Nations than to make concessions to one another or to a bigger power.'"

De Cuellar's tastes have understandably been influenced by his foreign postings. The *New York Times* described his "quiet love affair with French literature, Gothic cathedrals, French cooking, and Bordeaux wines." He is intimate with the early twentieth-century Spanish philosophers Unamuno and Ortega y Gasset, and the works of Colombian novelist Gabriel Garcia Marquez and Argentine author Jorge Luis Borges. De Cuellar is himself the author of two books on diplomacy: *Recognition of States and Governments* and *Diplomatic Law;* both are used as texts at the Diplomatic Academy in Peru. He favors classical music—Schubert is a favorite—playing the piano, stamp collecting, and writing poetry. "He is," according to the London *Times,* "a model of old-world cultivation and charm. His manner is courtly, his humor dry. He likes quiet dinners at home with friends." Despite quadruple heart bypass surgery in 1985, de Cuellar has maintained a full work schedule. The *Sunday Times* in 1987 alluded to an earlier health crisis, observing that de Cuellar's face holds "a rigid, stern, almost haunted look. It is not necessarily a guide to his inner feelings. The immobile features of the United Nations secretary-general are the result of a stroke suffered ten years ago that left his face partially paralysed."

In the final analysis de Cuellar's legacy is defined less by splashy success than by careful avoidance of out-and-out disaster. The *Los Angeles Times* termed him "an international bureaucrat whose past successes owe more to persistence and patience than to brilliance and leadership." The London *Times* echoed this sentiment, concluding, "Perhaps Senor Perez de Cuellar has not been able to call his...efforts successful, but he has kept the crises within well-defined bounds."

Selected writings

Recognition of States and Governments.
Diplomatic Law.

Sources

Periodicals

Boston Globe, May 21, 1982.
Los Angeles Times, December 12, 1981; December 16, 1981; April 2, 1982; August 14, 1988; November 4, 1989.
New York Times, December 12, 1981.
Sunday Times (London), December 13, 1981; September 13, 1987.
Times (London), December 12, 1981; July 28, 1988.

Other

Associated Press Biographical Service, June 1983.

—*Harvey Dickson*

Paloma Picasso

AP/Wide World Photos

Fashion designer

Born April 19, 1949, in Paris, France; daughter of Pablo Picasso (an artist) and Francoise Gilot (an artist); married Argentinean playwright and businessman Rafael Lopez-Cambil (pen name is Rafael Lopez-Sanchez) in 1978.

Addresses: *Home*—New York City and Paris, France. *Office*—Lopez-Cambil Ltd., 37 West 57th Street, New York, N.Y. 10019.

Career

Designed costume jewelry for Yves St. Laurent, early 1970s; actress in the film *Immoral Tales*, 1974; began designing fine jewelry for Tiffany & Company, 1980; launched her own fragrance line, 1984; introduced accessories collection, 1988; designed china for Villeroy & Boch, 1989; introduced By Paloma Picasso, an accessories line, and opened boutiques in Paris and Tokyo, 1990.

Sidelights

Paloma Picasso is a uniquely talented woman with firm and stylish designs on success. Far from fading in her famous father's artistic shadow, she has established a reputation and presence in the highly competitive world of fashion design, and launched a multi-million-dollar international accessories company. Picasso's distinctive signature can now be found on her own jewelry, china, perfume, cosmetics, eyewear, leather goods, and scarves. Her designs are whimsical and modern, the craftswom-

an's use of color is dramatic and bold, a reflection of her own personality and style. Despite her small size (five feet, four inches) and soft voice, she makes a striking impression with her pale skin, dark, shoulder-length hair, and deep-set, expressive eyes. Her photogenic good looks are enhanced by her own deep red trademark lipstick (only one color available—*Mon Rouge*), and her face is familiar to the public because she often models her own fashions in glossy, close-up magazine advertisements. The simple black clothes she favors make a theatrical backdrop for her oversized jewelry and colorful accessories.

As the daughter of two artists, the Spanish Pablo Picasso and French Francoise Gilot, it is hardly surprising that Paloma chose a career in the arts. Born in April of 1949, she was named Paloma (which is Spanish for dove) as a reference to the peace symbol which her father designed for an International Peace Conference just opening in Paris. When her parents met, Pablo was 62 and Francoise was 21. The celebrated and unconventional couple lived together for ten years and had two children, Paloma and her older brother, Claude. Pablo Picasso had long been separated from his first wife, but because Spanish law did not permit divorce, he and Gilot never married. Picasso legally gave the children his name and legitimized their status in 1961, though he and Gilot were no longer together.

In 1963 Gilot wrote a bitter account of their relationship entitled *Life with Picasso* and the resulting publicity caused the father to withdraw from his children. Paloma's mother is an accomplished artist and lives in the United States with her husband, Dr. Jonas Salk, inventor of the polio vaccine. The years have softened her memories, and in 1990 she wrote a gentler book, *Matisse and Picasso: A Friendship in Art*, published by Doubleday. In his later years, when Picasso married Jacqueline Roque and became estranged from his children, Paloma sustained herself with memories and says that she never doubted his love.

Paloma has happy memories of her early years with Picasso. Their home in southern France often included her stepbrother Paulo and stepsister Maya, (Picasso's children, respectively, by his first wife, Olga, and Marie Therese Walter, one of his models) a variety of pets, and other artists. Photographs show the children playing and drawing in his studio as he sketched them—their stylized faces peek from many of his canvases. Her father's genius and fame were an inescapable fact of life. Crowds of autograph seekers surrounded their every outing. Even young Paloma understood he was someone very special. She related an incident to *Newsweek* that occurred when she was a 6-year-old. Paloma was modeling new shoes for her father when suddenly "he couldn't resist the clean, white canvas of my espadrilles," she said. "He took them from my feet, picked up his crayons and did drawings all over them. I was so depressed, because I was proud of my shoes. At the same time, I was aware that he *was* Picasso, and that anybody else would be thrilled."

Her childhood impressions of her father's importance were again described during Paloma's televised interview with Maria Shriver: "When I was about seven years old, a man came to see my father and when the meeting was over, he walked backwards. And you could see that the man just couldn't imagine turning his back on Picasso, and I thought, this is something, this is really incredible."

At first, the larger-than-life legacy of her father was an obstacle. She was drawn to a career in art, but feared the inevitable comparisons. In the same interview with Shriver she explained, "The minute I take a pencil in my hand, I get a little afraid, thinking of my father. I wouldn't even doodle on my notebooks, I was so afraid I might become something like a painter. But by the time I was about 18 or 19 it started coming back into my life and I thought, well,

I'd better not go to an art school or people will be laughing at me and driving me crazy all the time."

> *"The minute I take a pencil in my hand, I get a little afraid, thinking of my father. I wouldn't even doodle on my notebooks, I was so afraid I might become something like a painter."*

Picasso's decision was to concentrate on style, and she studied jewelry design and fabrication at a school in France. During the late sixties, she had already made an impression on the French fashion scene with her trendsetting clothes, often salvaged from flea markets or antique stores. Paloma's breakthrough was made during a stint as a stage designer assistant. She was asked to find a necklace for the leading lady, and transformed a "bejeweled bikini from a Folies Bergere costume" into a choker, according to *Mirabella*. Designer Yves St. Laurent is a fan, and helped launch her career with a commission to design fashion jewelry for sale in his Rive Gauche boutique.

Pablo Picasso died in 1973, leaving no will for his enormous estate which included a fortune in art, a tangled domestic scene involving his wife, ex-mistresses, illegitimate offspring, and a mountain of inheritance taxes. Fortunately the French government was quite pleased to accept works of art in lieu of payment. Picasso's heirs turned over $50 million worth of his work and other pieces from his private collection, and Paloma Picasso assisted in the establishment of a new Musee Picasso in Paris. Since Picasso himself hated to part with anything, there were still plenty of treasures for his family. Paloma's personal choices included a set of dolls whose faces her father painted to resemble her own, and a whimsical sculpture of a *Girl Jumping Rope* which Picasso assembled from a basket, cake pans, and other odd pieces he found along the road near his home.

Along with her work on museum exhibitions and costume jewelry, Paloma Picasso continued her association with theatrical design. Her interest in theater extended to a notable acting stint. She starred in the 1974 film *Immoral Tales* (or *Contes Immorreaux*) which won the Prix de l'Age d'Or and was released in the United States in 1976. Picasso received favorable reviews for her colorful portrayal of a seventeenth-century Hungarian countess whose evil interests ranged from orgies to bloodbaths. She enjoyed the experience and said she would someday like to star in a film about French designer Coco Chanel.

In the early 1970s, Picasso met Rafael Lopez-Cambil, a playwright and director whose work she admired. They began a relationship which included her design of costumes and sets for two of his productions. The association was so satisfactory that it became personal. The two were married in 1978, (Picasso wore a red, white, and black Saint Laurent design for the ceremony and celebrated afterwards at a disco reception), and Lopez-Cambil left the theater to become Picasso's business partner. "I became the main character in his next play," Picasso jokingly told *Working Woman*. She supplies the creative inspiration and he provides the business acumen. "I'm not disciplined at all," she admitted to *Harper's Bazaar*. "I'm very messy, yet I manage to do a great deal. I'm a terrible businesswoman, but Rafael, as a playwright, can envision all the parts and how to make them work together."

Paloma Picasso introduced her first collection of fine jewelry for New York's Tiffany & Company in 1980. Her simple, offbeat creations were an immediate hit, characterized by their large size (chunky necklaces of marble-sized gemstones, sculptured bracelets, and a fan ring that spread over three fingers), bright colors, and hefty prices ($145 to $42,000). Her "hugs and kisses" jewelry, stylized 0s and Xs in gold and silver pins, bracelets, and necklaces are especially popular and often copied. "They have the spontaneous look of a love note scribbled on a steamed-up bathroom mirror, a playful tweak on the notion that gold is a serious investment," *Mirabella* reported. "I like big jewelry even though I am small; little jewelry doesn't work for me," she told *Vogue*. "It's a question of bones and proportion rather than being small or tall. I've always been rather surprised; but, when I put a hat or a jewel on, it's the bigger the better."

Four years after launching her jewelry interest, Picasso introduced her own fragrance, which is logical considering that her maternal grandfather, Emile Gilot, was a chemist and perfume manufacturer. The process of defining a scent was time-consuming and exacting. "It's hard to have a precise idea of what you want," she told *Harper's Bazaar*. "In a way it's like explaining music. At first, when I talked to the chemists, I used words that sounded stupid, and then I asked them what words they used to describe things." There were months of trial and error, but the result was sophisticated and heady, a marketing success enhanced by eye-catching red and black packaging and the distinctive circle-within-a-circle crystal flask which she designed. "My designs are very bold, very straightforward," she explained to *Vogue*. "What you see is what you get. I wanted my fragrance to be like that, too."

The success of Picasso's jewelry and fragrance encouraged her to branch out into the crowded and competitive accessories market. Where other firms manufacture some of her products (Tiffany does her jewelry, Cosmair markets her perfume and cosmetics, Villeroy & Boch sells her china, and her eyewear is made by Optyl), Paloma and Rafael created their own company, Lopez-Cambil Ltd., to manufacture and market her handbags, scarves, belts, and gloves. Lopez-Cambil Ltd. has offices and an elaborate showroom in New York City, and their products are manufactured in Italy.

The accessories resemble the well-bred designer: simple and understated, but with a playful, sometimes hidden splash of color. Sleek, angular leather handbags are discreetly studded with gems, or conceal a bright red lining, or have bracelet-style handles. "Most evening bags you have to hold or put under your arm," Picasso explained to *Vogue*, "and maybe it's more of French woman's preoccupation, wondering how to hold your drink and your bag, and then shake hands. Nobody's thought of this, because no one's had the connection in their mind. Nobody's been a jewelry designer and then a designer of handbags."

Picasso's china designs marked her entry into the lucrative home furnishings market. Her porcelain and ceramic place settings and tiles, manufactured by Villeroy & Boch, are classically contemporary in design with colored crystal accents. "It's an opportunity to stretch yourself," she told *Savvy Woman* magazine. "The ideas I get from one medium I can bring to the other. You learn, you develop another background, a new approach. And that's how you come up with things that are different—like trying to combine ceramic with crystal."

In 1990, By Paloma Picasso, a lower-priced accessories line of "masterworks for women who work" was launched with a dramatic, million-dollar advertising campaign. Picasso's compelling, bejeweled portrait gazes from the glossy pages of thousands of high-fashion magazines. Her products are sold in a nearly worldwide market, she opened her first free-standing stores in Paris and Tokyo, and aggressive expansion is planned. Also in 1990 she presented her tenth anniversary collection for Tiffany and Company; *Mirabella* described these pieces as having the "raw power of just-cut stones an just-mined minerals. Her gems are deep pools of color hung on thick veins of gold."

The ultra-modern Picasso makes frequent promotional appearances on behalf of her businesses, maintains art-filled, meticulously decorated homes in New York City and Paris, and travels at least month to Italy to supervise production. The Concorde speeds her travel between continents, her schedule is computerized, and she uses fax machines to send design ideas ahead to her office from wherever creativity strikes. "I think by concentrating on my work I have been able to gain a sense of security and self, and that's been my way of dealing with the fact that I am the daughter of Picasso," she told *Harper's Bazaar*. "I thought that by making something I can be proud of, it would be easier for me also to be the daughter of Picasso. Because it is *also*, not *just*, the daughter of Picasso. People want to create a name for themselves. But I had to make them forget my name first, before I could start building my own."

Sources

Atlantic, June 1988.
First Person with Maria Shriver, (television broadcast), October 21, 1990.
Harper's Bazaar, October 1984; December 1989.
House and Garden, December 1982.
House Beautiful, February 1989.
Lear's, November 1990.
Mirabella, November 1990; December 1990.
Newsweek, October 20, 1989.
People, July 8, 1985; July 25, 1988.
Product Marketing, February 1984.
Savvy Woman, June 1989.
Vogue, April 1981; April 1984; December 1985; August 1987; July 1988; January 1990.
Women's Wear Daily, April 28, 1989; February 9, 1990; February 23, 1990; June 22, 1990.
Working Woman, October 1990.

—*Sharon Rose*

Robert Rauschenberg

AP/Wide World Photos

Artist

Name originally Milton Rauschenberg; born October 22, 1925, in Port Arthur, Tex.; son of Ernest (a utilities company employee) and Dora (Matson) Rauschenberg; married Sue Weil, 1950 (divorced, 1952); children: Christopher. *Education:* Attended University of Texas at Austin, Kansas City Art Institute and School of Design, Academie Julian (Paris), Black Mountain College (North Carolina), and Art Students League (New York City).

Addresses: *Home*—381 Lafayette St., New York, NY 10003. *Office*—Leo Castelli Gallery, 420 W. Broadway, New York, NY 10012.

Career

Painter, sculptor, collage artist, performance artist, and dancer, 1946—. First solo exhibit at Parsons Gallery, New York City, 1951; has exhibited subsequent work in numerous shows worldwide and at museums in the United States, Europe, the Soviet Union, and Japan. Stage and costume designer for Merce Cunningham Dance Company, 1955—, technical director, 1960—. Director of Rauschenberg Overseas Cultural Exchange (ROCI), 1985-90.

Awards: First prize, V International Exhibition of Prints, Galerija Moderna, Ljubljana, Yugoslavia, 1963; first prize, XXXII Biennale de Venezia, Venice, Italy, 1964; first prize, Corcoran Biennial Exhibition of Contemporary American Painters, 1965; Art Institute of Chicago Award, 1966; Skowhegan School Painting and Sculpture Medal, 1982; Grammy Award, 1984; honorary degrees from Grinnell College, 1967, and the University of South Florida, 1976.

Member: American Academy and Institute of Arts and Letters, Royal Academy of Fine Arts (Stockholm, Sweden).

Sidelights

At a time when most men are ready to retire, Robert Rauschenberg continues to exert an enormous influence in the world of modern art. Rauschenberg is one of America's most famous painters, a pioneer whose work has embraced sculpture, collage, lithography, photography, and even dance and performance art. Walter Hopps, curator of the National Collection of Fine Arts, told *Newsweek* that Rauschenberg "embodies the notion of citizen and artist, involved in secular life through politics and philanthropy, with an insatiable curiosity." Once considered the *enfant terrible* of American modernism, the eclectic artist has lived long enough to become a venerable elder statesman in his field, praised by critics, sought after by collectors, and admired for both his work and his interest in world affairs.

Many critics feel that Rauschenberg's enormous output has set the tone for much of the American art of the 1960s and 1970s. As a *Time* magazine reporter put it, "There has not been much antiformalist American art that Rauschenberg's prancing, careless and fecund talent did not either hint at or directly provoke. It is to him that is owed much of the basic cultural assumption that a work of art can exist for any length of time, in any material (from a stuffed goat to a live human body), anywhere (on a stage, in front of a television camera, underwater, on the surface of the moon, or in a sealed envelope), for any purpose (turn-on, contemplation, amusement, invocation, threat), and any destination it chooses, from the museum to the trash can." The reporter continued: "Rauschenberg did not give a fig for the times of high seriousness imposed by the hard-core New York art world. His reputation would look after itself; he would not tend it." In fact, Rauschenberg did not need to tend his reputation—his successful challenge to the seriousness of abstract expressionism and his prolific mingling of media made him a hero among the younger generation of artists. Davis concluded: "For sheer energy—artistic and social—[Rauschenberg] is probably without peer in the art world. Indeed, Rauschenberg's only serious flaw may be that his is an act impossible to follow."

Rauschenberg was born October 22, 1925, in Port Arthur, Texas, an oil refinery town on the gulf of Mexico. He was christened Milton Rauschenberg and was the grandson of German immigrants. Neither of Rauschenberg's parents had any particular interest in the fine arts—his father worked as a utilities company employee and trained pedigreed bird dogs in his spare time. The *Time* reporter wrote: "Port Arthur was no cultural center. Its symphony orchestra was the jukebox, the comics its museum. The nearest thing to art one could see was the cheap chromo-litho holy cards pinned up in the Rauschenberg living room (the whole family was devoutly active in the local Church of Christ)." As a student Rauschenberg was plagued with nearsightedness and dyslexia, but he did manage to qualify for entry into the University of Texas at Austin after graduating from high school.

Rauschenberg studied pharmacy at the University of Texas, but he was expelled in 1943 after he refused to dissect a frog. Shortly thereafter he was drafted into the U.S. Navy, where he boldly declared that he had no intention of killing anyone. This assertion led to a two-and-a-half-year stint as a neuropsychiatric technician at various naval hospitals in California. "This is where I learned how little difference there is between sanity and madness," Rauschenberg told *Time*, "and realized that a combination of both is what everyone needs."

"I learned how little difference there is between sanity and madness, and realized that a combination of both is what everyone needs."

In his brief moments of spare time, Rauschenberg would thumb rides to nearby California towns and visit the local libraries and museums. He admitted in *Time* that he actually wandered into the Huntington Library in San Marino on a whim and was immediately struck by the paintings housed there. Viewing the paintings, he said, he became aware "that someone had thought these things out and made them. Behind each of them was a man whose profession it was to make them. That just never occurred to me before." Rauschenberg had been drawing since he was ten, and quietly—almost in secrecy—he decided to become an artist.

After his discharge from the Navy, Rauschenberg used the G.I. Bill of Rights to pay his tuition at the Kansas City Art Institute. He studied there through 1946 and 1947, earning spare money by doing store window displays. It was during this period that he changed his first name from Milton to Robert, entirely for professional reasons. In 1948 he set out for Paris, in order to study at the Academie Julian. His tenure there was brief, however, because he did not speak French and therefore could not communicate effectively with his instructors. The *Time* reporter contended that in Paris, the young artist "felt unfocused, self-indulgent and queasy, surrounded by an already academized modern tradition that he could not grasp."

In France Rauschenberg met Susan Weil, another American painter who would become his wife. Together Rauschenberg and Weil returned to the United States and enrolled at the Black Mountain College in North Carolina, where they studied with the pioneer abstractionist Josef Albers. Although Albers simply loathed Rauschenberg's work, Rauschenberg still calls him "the most important teacher" he ever had. "Albers had a marvelous system," the artist told *Time*. "Facts plus intimidation. I felt crushed. I would have done anything to please him; that was where the pain lay. Albers disliked my work exceedingly. I felt I could never do anything worthwhile. I had no background and no damn foreground either." Rauschenberg admitted, however, that Albers did provide him with a valuable sense of discipline and accomplishment. During his time at Black Mountain Rauschenberg also forged close friendships with composer John Cage and dancer Merce Cunningham, ties that would lead to collaborative projects in the 1950s and 1960s.

In 1949 Rauschenberg moved to New York City and continued his studies at the Art Students League. In 1950 he married Weil, with whom he had collaborated on a series of pictures made by running a sun lamp over blueprint paper. Oddly enough, these prints of miscellaneous objects, rendered eerily transparent by the process, became part of a window display at the Bonwit Teller department store. Thereafter Rauschenberg was able to support himself through lean times by doing window displays at the major department stores in Manhattan. With Cage and Cunningham, the young artist became part of a community of dancers, musicians, and painters who were all experimenting with a multimedia approach to art. Rauschenberg remembered that period in *Time:* "Cage and I used to sell our books to eat. There were times when I felt miserable. But having to decide, 'Is this what you want to do?' each day—that put a lot of joy into the work too."

Rauschenberg's first solo exhibition was held in May of 1951 at the Parsons Gallery. The exhibition featured the predecessors to Rauschenberg's famous all-white, all-black, and all-red canvases, created with the idea that the changing reflections of viewer, lights, and other objects complete the work. Rauschenberg also displayed grass paintings—bundles of soil and seedlings, held together with chicken wire. These early efforts were not received with great enthusiasm, but the underlying philosophy of the works—that a painting's surface could be an impartial collector of images—would become central to Rauschenberg's mature output. Having divorced his wife in 1952, the artist traveled through Italy, Spain, and North Africa, finding inspiration in the collages of German Dadaist Kurt Schwitters and sculptor-painter Marcel Duchamp.

By the mid-1950s Rauschenberg had begun to create innovative works that he called "combines." These collages of cast-off junk, parts of animals and household utensils, and drips of paint were half-painting and half-sculpture, and they created quite a stir among New York's staid art critics. Two works from this period have become particularly famous. *Bed* (1955) features a patchwork quilt and pillow stretched on a frame and spattered with red paint. The suggested violence of the red spatters led Italian critics to ban the work from exhibition at the Festival of Two Worlds. *Monogram* (1959) consists of the head of a stuffed Angora goat, an automobile tire, and a collaged base that incorporates a tennis ball, a shirtsleeve, a rubber heel, and footprints. Critics attached a sexual connotation to *Monogram* because the goat's head protruded from the tire. Whatever their perceived connotations may have been (Rauschenberg never claimed any), the works certainly broke new ground. *New York Times* art critic Grace Glueck noted that the "messy, outlandish tableaux... brought the jaded art world to full attention and were later credited with providing a bridge from Abstract Expressionism to Pop."

Between 1955 and 1962 Rauschenberg cultivated a close friendship with Jasper Johns, the other leading artist of the 1950s avant-garde. Rauschenberg and Johns worked together on window displays for department stores, but their most important work was done in the studio, where they critiqued and inspired one another. As his "combines" began to attract attention, Rauschenberg continued to experiment, using everything from lighter fluid to cardboard to newspaper headlines in streams of juxtaposed, fragmentary images. Rauschenberg was also one of the first American artists to turn to the silk screen image. "The silk-screen paintings that Rauschenberg made between 1962 and '65 had a brilliantly heightened documentary flavor," the *Time* reporter remarked. "The canvas trapped images, accumulating them. One was reminded of the shuttle and flicker of a TV set as the dial is clicked: rocket eagle, Kennedy, dancer, oranges, box all registered with the peacock-hued, aniline-sharp intensity of electronic color. The subject was glut."

The once-vilified experimenter found himself, by 1964, at the pinnacle of success in the international art world. Rauschenberg won the prestigious first prize at the Venice Biennale in 1964 and the gold medal at the Corcoran Biennial Exhibition of Contemporary American Painters in 1965. "Rauschenberg was now a celebrity," the *Time* reporter observed, "almost the Most Famous artist in the World." Some wide-eyed critics even dared to compare the painter to Picasso, while the old-school dissenters blamed him for the crass and facile quality of Pop art. Rauschenberg responded to all this attention by returning to collaborative work. He served as an adviser and dancer with Merce Cunningham's company and he started a nonprofit foundation named E.A.T. (Experiments in Art and

Technology) that produced multimedia happenings in America and Japan.

In the 1970s Rauschenberg returned to the studio, this time involving himself primarily with lithographs and prints. The best known of these works are the *Stoned Moon* series (1970) and the delicate *Hoarfrost* series (1974), done on descending layers of silk, chiffon, taffeta, and cheesecloth. Rauschenberg also escalated his creative use of photography as the decade wore on; in 1979 some six hundred slides he had taken were projected as a backdrop for *Glacial Decoy*, a dance created by choreographer Trisha Brown. Some of Rauschenberg's photographs are collected in *Robert Rauschenberg Photographs*, published by Pantheon in 1981.

His fame assured, Rauschenberg visited a number of foreign countries through the 1970s and 1980s, including China, India, and Japan. Each country he visited offered him new inspirations and a wealth of local artifacts from which he could create art. These travels culminated in the creation of a foundation, the Rauschenberg Overseas Cultural Interchange (ROCI). Under the aegis of ROCI, Rauschenberg has traveled to more than a dozen countries—including the Soviet Union and other Iron Curtain nations—in order to develop an "international artistic communication." By 1989, some critics estimate, more than two million people had seen themselves and their global neighbors through the idiosyncratic prism of Rauschenberg's art. Initially, Rauschenberg had hoped for corporate sponsorship of ROCI, but with few exceptions he wound up paying for the project himself.

Retrospectives of Rauschenberg's work were already popular in the 1970s. More recently, however, new exhibitions have been staged that more accurately reflect the long and many-faceted career of the dedicated artist. Early in 1991 three major Rauschenberg shows were held—one at the Whitney Museum in New York, one at the National Gallery of Art in Washington, D.C., and another at Washington's Corcoran Gallery. Even as critics chart his career, Rauschenberg continues to create new art. In 1990 he showed a series of works on brass, steel, and anodized aluminum. In an *ARTnews* review of the exhibition, critic Ruth Bass wrote: "The use of a reflective ground recalls Rauschenberg's early all-white paintings.... Here, sections of metal were so polished that the room, viewer, and other works became inextricably bound up with the work, confusing and enriching the imagery, creating new kinds of space, and seeming to dissolve the material itself.... The poignancy of Rauschenberg's pictorial juxtapositions is undercut by the visual splendor of his medium, allowing the artist to explore his characteristic imagery in a new context, brilliantly preempting the contemporary taste for the spectacular and making it something that is totally his own."

Rauschenberg divides his time between a property on Captiva Island in the Florida keys and a home in New York City. At 65 he is still actively engaged in his craft and has no plans to retire or even scale back his working hours. The artist told the *New York Times*: "What's exciting is that I don't know what's next. For so many years, I've had a plan as to where I was going, but now I don't. And there's no one more anxious than I am to find out what I'm going to do."

Sources

Books

Kotz, Mary Lynn, *Rauschenberg/Art and Life*, Harry N. Abrams, 1990.
Tomkins, Calvin, *Off the Wall: Robert Rauschenberg and the Art World of Our Time*, 1980.

Periodicals

Art in America, March 1989.
ARTnews, March 1990; May 1990; summer 1990.
Newsweek, October 25, 1976; January 7, 1991.
New York Times, December 16, 1990.
Time, November 29, 1976.

—*Anne Janette Johnson*

Rob Reiner

Director, actor, and writer

Born March 6, 1947, in New York, N.Y.; son of Carl (a comedian, actor, writer, and director) and Estelle (Lebost) Reiner; married Penny Marshall (an actor and director), 1971 (divorced, 1981); children: Tracy (stepdaughter). *Education:* Attended University of California at Los Angeles, 1965-68.

Addresses: *Agent*—Creative Artists Agency, Inc., 1888 Century Park E., Suite 1400, Los Angeles, CA 90067.

Career

Worked as an actor with regional theater and improvisational comedy troupes, 1965-68; TV comedy writer for *The Glen Campbell Show* and *The Smothers Brothers Comedy Hour*, both 1968; writer, with Phil Mishkin, of TV series *The Super*, 1972, and *Free Country*, 1978. Actor with appearances in TV comedy series, including *That Girl, Gomer Pyle, The Beverly Hillbillies,* and *Free Country,* 1967-78; landed small roles in movies *Where's Poppa?*, 1970, *Halls of Anger*, 1970, and *Summertree*, 1971; appeared regularly on TV series *All in the Family*, 1971-78. Appearances in television movies include *Thursday's Game*, 1974, *More Than Friends*, 1978, and *Million Dollar Infield*, 1982. Director of films, including *This is Spinal Tap*, 1984, *The Sure Thing*, 1985, *Stand By Me*, 1986, *The Princess Bride*, 1987, *When Harry Met Sally...*, 1989, and *Misery*, 1990. Also appeared in film *Postcards from the Edge*, 1990. Creator of television series *Morton & Hayes*, 1991.

Awards: Emmy awards for best supporting actor in a comedy series for *All in the Family*, 1974 and 1978.

AP/Wide World Photos

Sidelights

For many years during his show business career Rob Reiner struggled to emerge from the shadow of his famous father, comedian Carl Reiner. His father was a well-known and well-regarded comedy writer and actor on television, and the younger Reiner was not sure if he could ever measure up to his dad's talents, even after his own TV career began to take off. Finally, after establishing himself as a popular movie director during the 1980s, Rob Reiner is very definitely his own man. And as Myra Forsberg of the *New York Times* noted, Reiner is much more recognizable to today's generation of TV and movie viewers. "It's funny, I talked to my father the other day," he told Forsberg. "And he was out exercising in Venice and somebody yelled at him, 'Rob, Rob.' But that's O.K., I still get 'Carl, Carl' now and then."

Reiner was born in 1947 in New York City. The oldest of three children, his family lived in an apartment building in the Bronx. When he was 7 years old, they moved to suburban New Rochelle. In the 1950s his father became a writer and performer on the pioneering TV comedy *Your Show of Shows*, and the other comic writers would often gather at his house. The lineup now sounds like a comedy hall-of-fame—Sid Caesar, Mel Brooks, Neil Simon, Larry Gelbart, and Norman Lear. Reiner told April Bernard of *Interview*, "I'd sit there and be in awe of what was going on. I mean, the parties they had... Very funny people hanging around the house."

In 1959 the family moved to Beverly Hills and Carl Reiner began writing for the *Dinah Shore Show* and the *Dick Van Dyke Show*. The latter program was another acclaimed TV show and Carl again both wrote and appeared in it. Rob Reiner often accompanied his dad to the set and it was then that he began to have mixed feelings—idolizing and feeling jealous of his father, wondering if he could ever live up to him. "I just thought, Jesus, there's no way I'm going to be able to be like him," Reiner said to David Rosenthal of *Playboy*. "I was in awe of him; he was like a god to me. I remember when I went over to the 'Van Dyke' show with him.... And I used to look around and think, God, look at all this! He's creating these TV shows, he's winning Emmys, he's a genius—and I'm inadequate."

Being around comics and comic writers so much, and trying to emulate his father, Reiner made his first foray into comedy writing at the age of 16. Carl and Mel Brooks were working at the Reiner home on some new material for their 2000 Year-Old-Man act. And young Rob came up with a routine that they actually incorporated into the act. It was "one of the biggest thrills in my life," Reiner proclaimed to Rosenthal.

In his senior year at Beverly Hills High School, Reiner won a role in the school play and his success led him to try his hand at an acting career after graduation. He spent two summers working in regional theater back East, and enrolled at University of California, Los Angeles (UCLA), majoring in theater arts. While at UCLA in 1967 Reiner helped form an improvisational comedy troupe called The Session. The group played clubs in Los Angeles and New York, but broke up after a year. Reiner dropped out of UCLA during his junior year and later joined the comedy group The Committee. While doing his comedy troupe work, Reiner was able to land some TV acting jobs on various comedy shows. "I was hired to play every TV hippie you can imagine.... I did two 'Beverly Hillbillies,' a 'Gomer Pyle,' a 'That Girl'—I played hippies in all of them," he told *Playboy*.

In 1968 Reiner got his first break. He was discovered by Tommy Smothers during one of his Committee shows and hired as a TV comedy writer. Smothers was producing *The Glen Campbell Show* and Reiner worked on that show first, then wrote for the popular *Smothers Brothers Comedy Hour*. Reiner also landed some small movie roles. He was in the 1970 movie *Where's Poppa?*, directed by his father. He also appeared in *Halls of Anger*, released in 1970, and *Summertree*, released in 1971.

> *"What was more fascinating to me than my acting on* [All in the Family] *was structuring the scripts, working out the stories, looking at the staging and watching the other actors."*

In 1971 Reiner won a TV acting role that brought him immense and lasting fame. He became a regular on Norman Lear's smash-hit comedy series *All in the Family*, playing Mike "Meathead" Stivic, a radical-thinking "voice of reason" who served as a constant annoyance to father-in-law Archie Bunker, played by Carroll O'Connor. Although Lear was a friend of the family, Reiner had to audition for the role and was initially turned down—twice—before finally winning the part. The controversial show entered previously uncharted waters for television, exploring racial divisions and engaging in pointed political humor. *All in the Family* soon became the number-one-rated show on TV for several years. Reiner's acting won him Emmy awards in 1974 and 1978 for best supporting actor in a comedy series.

During his stint on *All in the Family*, Reiner was able to get involved in the writing of the show. "What was more fascinating to me than my acting on that show was structuring the scripts, working out the stories, looking at the staging and watching the other actors," he told Forsberg. "My mind was always drifting to the overall scheme even then, and I was fortunate enough that they let me in on the script rewriting and editing." The show was "one of my two apprenticeships" for later becoming a director. (The other had been watching his father on the *Dick Van Dyke Show*.)

Reiner signed a long-term contract with ABC-TV in the fall of 1978 to write, produce, and act in shows for the network. In the spring of 1978 he left *All in the Family*, but his next several projects were far from successful. Reiner put together a TV series with Phil Mishkin called *Free Country*, a comedy-drama which also featured Reiner as an actor. After that show's brief run as a summer series in 1978, he starred with then-wife Penny Marshall (also in *Newsmakers 91) in the TV movie More Than Friends*. Reiner appeared in a Broadway comedy in 1980 called *The Roast*, which closed after just two days, and in 1982 he produced, co-wrote, and acted in a coolly received TV movie called *The Million Dollar Infield*.

In 1981 Reiner went through a painful divorce and began to reevaluate his life. As an actor, he told Rosenthal, he was trying to prove himself. "I think a lot of what I did with my acting career was, in a way, to show people—show my father—'Look, I can do this, too; I'm good at this.'" But through the *All in the Family* years up to his divorce, he told Betsy Borns of *Interview*, "I never felt, during any of that time, that I was living my own life. I thought I was an extension of my father's life." And so the younger Reiner decided to find his own way.

Being typecast as "Meathead," his *All in the Family* character, also led Reiner to look beyond acting. That image of him as the socially conscious radical liberal was very strong "but I certainly didn't want to keep doing what I was doing. You get typed, though, and no one wants to see you do anything else," he said to Borns. His interests in the "overall scheme" that he developed while working on *All in the Family* brought him to pursue directing.

Back in 1977, Reiner and friends Christopher Guest, Michael McKean, and Harry Shearer had done an ABC comedy special called *The TV Show*. Later they tried to develop one of the skits, a rock 'n' roll parody, into a feature film. Unfortunately, Reiner recalled to *Playboy*, "It took four and a half years from the time we began working on it until the time it got on screen." They took a demo reel and showed it to studio after studio but could not stir any interest. Finally, Norman Lear provided the financing for the film. Reiner directed the movie, called *This Is Spinal Tap*, which was released in 1984.

This Is Spinal Tap was critically praised. Stanley Kauffmann of the *New Republic* called it a "slyly witty mock-documentary." Harlan Jacobson of *Film Comment* wrote that it "satirizes more than rock-'n-roll culture. It goes on to wipe out documentary filmmaking for its pretentiousness." The movie, which wryly chronicles a once-popular (and fictional) rock band's slide into obscurity, cost only $2.2 million to make but, although it made money, it only brought in $7 million at the box office. Reiner felt that the film "went over most people's heads," he remarked to Forsberg. "The vast majority who saw it thought it was about a real group, and couldn't understand why anybody would make a movie about a band that was this bad."

The fact that his first film made money gave Reiner the opportunity to do another, and Lear continued to provide the financing. Reiner's second movie, released in 1985, was a teenage romantic comedy called *The Sure Thing*. Again, the reviews were good. Kauffmann stated that Reiner "directed 'The Sure Thing' buoyantly and brightly," adding that "this film is pleasant, is credible in character without being either candied or consciously candid." Forsberg wrote that the movie "recalled vintage [director] Frank Capra." This film cost $4.5 million to make and was a moderate success at the box office, bringing in $20 million.

In 1986 Reiner came out with his next film, *Stand By Me*. Based on a Stephen King story, it was about adolescent boys coming of age. Critical reviews continued to be generally favorable. David Ansen of *Newsweek* said that the movie "owes some of its appeal to sheer nostalgia, an easy enough emotion to evoke. But there is more here as well: sweetness of spirit, and comedy that comes from a well-remembered vision of the way we were." This film was a genuine hit, an $8 million movie that pulled in $53 million at the box office.

Robert Lloyd of *American Film* noted that each of Reiner's movies "draws extensively on what he happens to be feeling inside at the time he makes them." As Reiner told the *New York Times*, "'This Is Spinal Tap' was about people who are frightened of leaving the nest, and cling to each other.... 'The Sure Thing' is about discovering that love and sex can be one and the same, which, although I was 37 then, I was just figuring out. 'Stand By Me' is about liking yourself, which started happening to me at that time in my life." Lloyd stated that "part of the appeal of Reiner's films, part of what sets them apart, is precisely the element of psychological autobiography he brings to material that, under less compulsively self-analytical direction, might produce fairly routine genre pieces."

Reiner based his next movie on a novel by William Goldman called *The Princess Bride*. Goldman wrote the screenplay himself and this time Reiner received a good-sized budget of $17 million and a cast with several stars including Mandy Patinkin, Billy Crystal, and Carol Kane. Lloyd described the 1987 movie as "a crazy-quilt fantasy that eschews bravura special effects in favor of elementary pyrotechnics, some old fashioned swordplay...and a lot of William Goldman's repartee." The film received widespread critical acclaim. Rita Kempley of the *Washington Post* said that it is "a lively, fun-loving, but nevertheless epic look at the nature of true love." Jacobson wrote that the film contains "lots of good Garment District shtick... with curtsies to Mel Brooks here and there. Everything, even the Dread Pirate Roberts, is a franchise."

1989 saw Reiner's release of a romantic comedy titled *When Harry Met Sally*... Reiner again added a personal flavor to the movie, basing it partly on his life after his divorce. The film turned out to be immensely popular, and a number of reviewers praised the film. Richard Corliss of *Time* labeled it "terrific," saying it was one of the "season's smartest, funniest real-love films." Kauffmann called it "very entertaining." Ansen, however, disagreed, stating that although the movie "can be explosively funny, as in the soon-to-be-famous scene when Sally fakes an orgasm in the middle of a crowded deli... for all its wit and knowing details, the movie is strangely unsatisfying." Despite being "a movie of wonderful parts," Ansen concluded, "it doesn't quite add up."

Late in 1990 Reiner came out with a film that represented a change in direction for him—a thriller. Adapted from a Stephen King novel, *Misery* relates the story of a serial romance novelist who yearns to write serious fiction. The writer (James Caan) is injured in a snowy car accident in the remote Colorado mountains while on his way to deliver the last of his romance novels—in which his famed heroine, Misery, dies—to his publisher. He is rescued by a maniacal fan (Kathy Bates), who literally holds him hostage until he rewrites the novel. At the Hollywood premiere, Reiner joked, "Welcome to the birth of what might be the Jewish Hitchcock," reported *People*. Once again, the film "strikes the familiar note of the psycho-personal," said Lloyd. Reiner told him, "The allegory is that he's battling with his own demons to force himself to grow, to move on to different areas, and this psychotic fan represents the demons inside him."

Reviews of "Misery" ran the gamut from great to dreadful. Susan Stark of the *Detroit News* said: "Rob Reiner can do no wrong and he never does right the same way twice. Here, he follows 'When Harry Met Sally' with a screen version of a Stephen King thriller that just crackles with intelligence and wit." Richard Schickel of *Time* wrote: "Popular moviemaking—elegantly economical, artlessly artful—doesn't get much better than this." On the other side of the fence, Brian D. Johnson of *Maclean's* said that with screenwriter William Goldman, "Reiner tempers shock with an edge of black humor. But it is as if Reiner and Goldman are slumming in a genre that does not suit them. For a while, they get the better of it; eventually, however, it gets the better of them. By the end of the movie, they are wielding the blunt instrument of cliche with senseless abandon." Ralph Novak of *People* opined: "Stretched as it is over 105 minutes, the plot of this movie wears thinner and thinner until holes start popping out all over." He added that "the graphically violent final fight is clumsily staged, and there's a silly epilogue that recalls the laziest cheapo chillers." Despite the mixed reviews, the film soared at the box office, rolling up $20.1 million in receipts in just its first two weeks.

Explaining his affinity for directing, Reiner said to Jacobson: "I'm not great at anything, but I'm real good at a lot of things. I'm a pretty good actor, a pretty good writer, I have pretty good music abilities, pretty good visual and color and costume sense. I'm not great at any of these things, but as a director I have the opportunity to utilize all these things in one job." As far as future projects are concerned, Reiner is collaborating with Goldman on a movie musical that they would like to make with Stephen Sondheim. It will mark another step in a new direction for Reiner. And regarding his relationship with his father, "it's nicer now," Reiner told Forsberg. "It was difficult for a long time, but I think you start maturing and the fact that I'm now established takes a lot of the tension and angst away. We both love each other and we're both proud of each other. We've gone our own separate ways careerwise—basically, he comes to see my films when they're finished and says, 'I love this! I love this film!'"

Sources

American Film, July/August 1989.
Christian Science Monitor, December 14, 1990.
Detroit News, December 7, 1990.
Esquire, June 1988.
Film Comment, September/October 1987.
Interview, October 1986; July 1989.
Maclean's, December 3, 1990.
New Republic, April 8, 1985; August 21, 1989.
Newsweek, August 25, 1986; July 17, 1989.
New Yorker, October 19, 1987.
New York Times, October 18, 1987.
People, December 10, 1990; December 17, 1990; December 24, 1990.
Playboy, July 1985.
Time, July 31, 1989; December 10, 1990.
Washington Post, October 9, 1987.

—*Greg Mazurkiewicz*

Ann Richards

AP/Wide World Photos

Governor of Texas

Full name, Dorothy Ann Richards; born in 1933 in Lakeview, Tex.; daughter of Cecil (a salesman) and Iona (a homemaker; maiden name, Warren) Willis; married David Richards (a lawyer), May, 1953 (divorced, 1984); children: Cecile, Dan, Clark, Ellen. *Education:* Baylor University, B.A., 1954; attended the University of Texas for a professional teaching certificate. *Politics:* Democrat. *Religion:* Baptist.

Addresses: *Home*—Austin, TX.

Career

Taught junior high school in Austin, Tex., 1954; volunteered as precinct headquarters worker and in civil rights groups; formed auxiliary women's political group; campaign adviser for Sarah Weddington and Wilhelmina Delco; administrative assistant to Representative Sarah Weddington; elected Travis county commissioner, 1976, reelected, 1980; elected treasurer of the State of Texas, 1982, reelected, 1986; elected governor of the State of Texas, 1990. Served on Jimmy Carter's Advisory Committee for Women.

Sidelights

Ann Richards's spunk, savvy, and speaking ability are legendary in Texas, a state that values all these things—but preferably from its tough male citizens. Richards, currently the governor of the Lone Star State, has a down to earth, "Good Ole' Girl" quality that plays well in a state founded on macho cowboy ethics. Born to a poor family, she attended college on a debate scholarship, raised four children, got involved in local politics, tirelessly campaigned for state office, and through determination and her keen political skills, ended up in the governor's mansion. Richards has also taken some hard knocks that have added to her character: She was divorced from her high school sweetheart in 1984, confronted with a growing alcohol problem by her family and friends, and involved in what may be one of the dirtiest campaigns in the history of the Texas governor's race. Richards, however, is still considered to be one of the most influential women in the democratic party today—perhaps poised on the way to becoming the first woman in the White House.

Richards was born during the Depression to working-class parents in the small town of Lakeview, Texas, eight miles from Waco. She was an only child, a fact on which she speculated in her autobiography, *Straight From the Heart:* "I believe Mama would have liked to have had more children, but times were hard and I was the only one. Daddy had the fear—maybe that fear is indigenous to the Depression generation—that he wouldn't be able to afford all the things he wanted to give me, and he wanted to give me everything he'd never had. So they never had another child." During World War II, the family left

Texas and moved to San Diego, where her father was stationed in the military. It was there that Richards was exposed to children of different racial backgrounds. She commented that she "was never able to understand prejudice after that." This experience had a lasting influence on her life and she later became very involved in the civil rights movement.

After Richards finished junior high school, her parents insisted on moving to the larger city of Waco so that their daughter could have a first-class education. Intimidated by the new school system and her parents' high standards for her, she decided to try to change herself, dropping her first name, Dorothy, and going by her middle name, Ann. About her high school years, Richards commented in the *Washington Post*: "I was going to take the world by storm, I remember thinking clearly; 'This is your big chance now, going to Waco High School. Striving for acceptance.'" In Waco, Richards excelled in the debate class, because it used one of her best skills—the ability to speak well. Richards's debating soon won her acclaim in her school, and as a junior she was asked to attend Girls State, a gathering of students from each Texas high school who went to the Texas capital of Austin for a week to set up a mock government. Richards loved her first taste of government. She was then asked to continue on to Girls Nation, the same type of event that was held in Washington, D.C. Richards came away loving the experience, but thinking it would have no real impact on her career: "Even though no one told me, there were certain things that you knew, and the world knew, that women and girls couldn't do. Running the government was one of them."

During Richards's senior year she met David Richards, the man she would eventually marry in 1953. She also won a debating scholarship and chose to go to Baylor, a nearby university that allowed her to live with her parents and save money. After graduating from college in 1954, the couple moved to Austin, where David attended law school and Richards taught junior high. She commented in her autobiography that "teaching was the hardest work I had ever done, and it remains the hardest work I have done to date." On Friday nights the Richardses would head out to the Scholz Beer Garden, a local drinking place where Austin's politically-minded came to socialize and debate. The couple fraternized with a group of mostly Democratic local politicians and their friends.

When David finished law school, he secured a job in Dallas with a firm that specialized in labor relations, and the Richardses moved there with their first child. Ann started work on a political campaign for gubernatorial candidate Henry Gonzales, a Hispanic. It was her first acquaintance with interracial campaigning. She also worked for the John F. Kennedy-Lyndon B. Johnson election shortly before David got a job in Washington. They lived in the nation's capital for a year but soon tired of the Washington bureaucracy and returned to Dallas, where Ann became a founder of the North Dallas Democratic Women. Moving again, they settled in Austin, where Richards vowed she would never have anything to do with politics. "Women, it was painfully clear," she commented, "weren't going to be allowed to use their brains and I certainly wanted to use mine."

> "Women, it was painfully clear, weren't going to be allowed to use their brains and I certainly wanted to use mine."

Richards reconsidered her vow when a promising young woman named Sarah Weddington asked for Richards's help in running her campaign for the Texas legislature. Richards worked tirelessly on the campaign, drawing on her grass roots political style and organizational ability. Her efforts paid off and Weddington won her bid for state congress. Soon after, Weddington asked Richards to be her administrative assistant—a job Richards held for a full legislative term. In 1974 Richards advised Wilhelmina Delco in her run for Texas legislature. Delco also won, becoming the first black to be elected to the legislature from Travis county.

After David Richards declined to run for the position of county commissioner in 1975, the local Democratic party approached Ann Richards. Flattered, she was concerned that a female candidate wouldn't have a chance at such a traditionally male position. (The job included supervising building works and highway construction.) After analyzing precinct statistics that indicated she could win, she accepted the offer. She organized a superb grass roots campaign and was elected handily.

Richards's new success began to cause a strain in her marriage, and her drinking was increasing. In 1980 a group of her friends staged an intervention where each of them shared a story with her about how her drinking had affected their lives adversely. Richards immediately checked into St. Mary's Hospital in

Minneapolis for treatment. When she returned home, however, problems between her and her husband only worsened. They separated twice, eventually divorcing in 1984.

A year after her release from the hospital, gubernatorial candidate Bob Armstrong asked Richards to run for Texas state treasurer. Once again, she was skeptical, thinking the populace wouldn't support a female candidate for a job that involved public money. She ran, however, and won with 61.4 percent of the vote, becoming the first woman to hold state office in Texas in over 50 years.

The treasurer's office was a mess, with antiquated procedures that were causing the state to lose a great deal of money. Richards took action immediately, asking the legislature for money needed to modernize the system. By the time Richards completed her second term of office in the treasury, the state had made more money during her two terms than was made during the terms of all the previous treasurers combined.

During the 1988 presidential campaign, Richards got a call from Paul Kirk, national chairman of the Democratic party, who advised her that she was about to be asked to deliver the keynote speech at the Democratic National Convention. When she accepted, her life was thrown into a whirlwind of activity and she became an overnight celebrity. After long hours of crafting the perfect speech and employing a team of speechwriters to tie it together, the final version was eaten by a computer only hours before she left Texas for the convention. But instead of getting ruffled by this turn of events, Richards continued to plug away at the speech until all the elements she wanted were in it.

Delivered in the casual, down-home Texas style Richards is known for, the speech was an amazing success. Jody Becker wrote in *McCall's* that "Ann Richards became the darling of the Democratic Party with her dazzling keynote speech at the Democratic National Convention." She was especially quoted for her witty remark that George Bush "was born with a silver foot in his mouth."

Richards next set her political sights on the Texas governor's mansion for the 1990 election. The campaign was characterized by mudslinging on both sides. During the primary runoff, Jim Mattox, the state's attorney general, asked in a debate whether Richards had ever taken illegal drugs, and she refused to answer. Many considered her silence to be an admission of guilt. Later, articles speculating that *Mattox* had used illegal drugs sprung up. Richards

won the primary, but with the *Houston Post* blazoning the headline: "It's Richards in a Mudslide." About the messy race, Richards claimed in her inimitable style in *Newsweek* that she'd "been tested by fire and the fire lost."

As she prepared to square off with Republican opponent Clayton Williams, a millionaire rancher and the epitome of a Texas Good Ole' Boy, Richards looked like she was a lost woman in the land of macho politics. Nor did her liberal politics help in a state that bends toward the conservative. Ironically, it was Williams who defeated himself. When Richards claimed to be catching up to Williams in the polls, he suggested that "she must be drinking again," as quoted in the *Washington Post*. Later, Williams stuck his foot in his mouth when he compared rape to bad weather, saying that if it was inevitable, one should just "sit back, relax and enjoy it." Williams also launched a media blitz in Texas where he actually oversaturated the constituency—it was estimated that the average Texan had seen him on television over 80 times.

Even with Richards's political savvy and campaigning ability, her success in this race had very little to do with such virtues. Political scientist Jerry Polenard commented during the race that "the polls really don't show her gaining any strength at all, just Williams losing . . . The other day some people down here were saying that if you could get on the ballot and change your name to 'None of the Above' you'd win in a walk." Richards eventually won the muddy battle, becoming the governor of the nation's third most populous state.

"Ann Richards is genuine populist Texas: exuberant, shrewd, earthy, blunt and often hilarious," commented Emily W. Sunstein in the *New York Times Book Review*. She has a personality that plays well in a state founded on cowboy individualism. "She's sort of the female good old boy," Jill Buckley was quoted as saying in *McCall's*. Some have speculated that Richards may also have what it takes personally and politically to make a positive impression on people outside her state. If so, she stands in a good spot to head for the White House in her next career move.

Writings

(With Peter Knobler) *Straight From the Heart: My Life in Politics and Other Places,* Simon & Schuster, 1989.

Sources

McCall's, June 1990.
National Review, May 14, 1990.
Newsweek, March 19, 1990; April 23, 1990.
New York Times Book Review, December 10, 1989.
People, April 30, 1990.
Time, September 10, 1990.
Washington Post, October 22, 1990.

—Nancy Rampson

Julia Roberts

AP/Wide World Photos

Actress

Real name, Julie Roberts (she took the name Julia when she found a Julie Roberts was already a member of the Screen Actors Guild); born October, 1967, in Smyrna, Ga.; son of Walter and Betty Roberts.

Addresses: *Home*—Hollywood Hills, CA.

Career

Film and television actress. TV appearances include an episode of *Crime Story*, 1986, and HBO movie *Baja, Oklahoma*, 1987. Films include *Blood Red*, 1986 (unreleased), *Satisfaction*, 1988, *Mystic Pizza*, 1988, *Steel Magnolias*, 1989, *Pretty Woman*, 1990, *Flatliners*, 1990, *Sleeping With the Enemy*, 1991, and *Dying Young*, 1991.

Awards: Golden Globe Award and Academy Award nomination for best supporting actress, both 1990, both for *Steel Magnolias*; Golden Globe Award and Academy Award nomination for best actress, both 1991, both for *Pretty Woman.*

Sidelights

The breathtaking ease with which Julia Roberts has seduced Hollywood and legions of lovesick fans is a throwback to that Golden Age of Clark Gable and Vivien Leigh—a time when movie stars had that unmistakable star quality that could light up the screen with a larger-than-life glamour. Many actors today have either one or the other—a predominant beauty or talent—but Roberts has that rare and formidable combination of both drop-dead gorgeous looks and an instinctive and versatile dramatic ability which perhaps explains her meteoric rise to the pinnacles of both popular and critical success. Ever since the completion of only her third major film, *Pretty Woman*—the blockbuster that pulled in sales of over $400 million worldwide—Roberts now wields the power of being the number-one female box office draw. Her subsequent films have garnered their star highest respect from critics and peers alike; she has been honored with two Golden Globe Awards and two prestigious Academy Award nominations—all this achieved at the tender age of 22.

In *Pretty Woman* Roberts plays a down-on-her-luck prostitute who is whisked off the streets into the lap of luxury by a wealthy Prince Charming, played by Richard Gere. This modern-day Cinderella story has parallels to Roberts' real-life rocket to fame—a rather swift trip accomplished with a minimum of dues-paying and no formal training. Three days after her high school graduation, Roberts left her hometown of Smyrna, Georgia for New York City. Almost immediately she was offered a modeling contract by the famous Click agency, and shortly thereafter secured a role in her first feature film. Never mind that prior to this her sole acting credits were a couple of high school plays.

Having family connections didn't hurt. Roberts's older siblings, brother Eric and sister Lisa, are actors as well. It was Lisa's apartment in New York where Roberts made her home-away-from-home at age 17, and it was Eric who secured the neophyte actress her first movie role playing his on-screen sister in the still unreleased 1986 western, *Blood Red*.

The theatrical seeds were sown early in Roberts's childhood. In the 1960s, her parents operated a workshop for actors and writers in Atlanta, and young Julia spent her toddler years taking in family productions of Shakespeare-in-the-park. Although the theatrical workshop was a financial disaster and disbanded after her parents' divorce in 1971 (her father subsequently sold vacuum cleaners until his death five years later, and her mother became a church secretary), it served to infect all the Roberts children with what matriarch Betty calls "the family disease." While siblings Eric and Lisa pursued acting more single-mindedly throughout their growing-up years, Julia's acting bug remained latent until later. She long harbored the dream of becoming a veterinarian, but remarked to *Rolling Stone* that the interest in acting was, all the same, "just kind of there in my mind all the time." Of the three adult Roberts children (there is also a younger sister, 14-year-old Nancy), Eric has had the most formal training. He studied at London's prestigious Royal Academy of Dramatic Art and finished up at New York's American Academy of Dramatic Arts, while Lisa trained at the Neighborhood Playhouse in New York.

When Julia Roberts moved to New York, her initial plan was to study acting. However, she soon found that the academic route just didn't work for her. As she told *American Film*, "I never really made it to acting school. I went to acting classes a few times, but it never seemed very conducive to what I wanted to do, somehow. I never really decided, I'll go to school, I won't go to school—things just sort of happened. Sometimes people seem kind of disappointed by that; they want to hear about all these grueling years." She did bounce around for a year, on the one hand enjoying the bohemian life in Greenwich Village with her sister Lisa, and on the other, plunging herself into auditions for commercials, film, and TV work, but coming up empty. As she reflected on that time in *American Film*, "I don't think I really impressed anyone. I didn't get called back a lot, just enough to keep on going." That's when her brother Eric stepped in to pave the way for her film debut—her first professional job. As *Blood Red*'s director Peter Masterson recalled in *People*: Eric "just said,

'I've got this sister. Is it okay if she *plays* my sister?' He just said that she was good."

That was just the push Julia Roberts needed to get her career rolling. Shortly after *Blood Red,* she landed a role in an episode of TV's *Crime Story;* then, in the summer of 1987 she had the good fortune of shooting three movies back-to-back. The first two were rather inconsequential: the shallow teen dud *Satisfaction* (co-starring *Family Ties'* Justine Bateman and *Darkman's* Liam Neeson), in which Roberts portrayed a bass player in an all-girl rock band; and the little-seen HBO movie *Baja, Oklahoma,* where she played Lesley Ann Warren's free-spirited daughter. But it was the coming-of-age, girl-buddy feature *Mystic Pizza* that finally provided the showcase for Roberts's star presence to shine. Well-received upon its release in 1988, this unpretentious, gentle little film became the beginning of the big-time for the actress. Portraying a feisty Portuguese-American waitress in a performance charged with sexuality, Roberts became a darling of the critics and the new find atop every casting director's list. As good as the other actresses were who shared the screen with her, they tended to fade from view—all eyes were hypnotically focused on Roberts as she proceeded to single-handedly steal every scene. As Nancy Mills wrote in *Cosmopolitan,* "Her gutsy, sultry Daisy Araujo, eager to escape the confines of a Connecticut fishing village, struck many as a reminder of those forties sirens who had oomph as well as intelligence."

> *"I never really made it to acting school. I went to acting classes a few times, but it never seemed very conducive to what I wanted to do, somehow."*

Among those taking notice of her magnetic *Mystic Pizza* performance was director Herbert Ross, who sought out Roberts to join the star-studded cast of his *Steel Magnolias.* Working alongside such stellar company as Sally Field, Shirley MacLaine, Olympia Dukakis, Daryl Hannah, and Dolly Parton—on only Roberts's second major film—was a heady and enlightening experience for Roberts. "I learned so much from those women," she told *American Film.* "I owe them a lot more than I could ever articulate. Just watching five tremendous women do what they do close to perfectly." With her intensely moving portrayal of Shelby, Sally Field's dying, diabetic daughter, Roberts demonstrated remarkable range for someone so new to film acting. The understated sweetness and sorrow of *Steel Magnolias'* Shelby was worlds away from the lusty, wise-cracking bombshell of *Mystic Pizza*. With *Steel Magnolias* Roberts secured her place among Hollywood's elite. In a cast filled with Oscar-winning veterans, it was only newcomer Roberts who walked away with accolades—a Golden Globe Award and an Academy Award nomination.

With her next film—the enormously successful *Pretty Woman*—Roberts became a household name and picked up best actress honors with an additional Golden Globe Award and another Oscar nomination in the process. Although zealous fans made it the number-two box office smash of 1990 and the highest grossing romantic comedy in cinematic history, *Pretty Woman* was more often than not condemned by the critics for being insultingly simplistic and sexist. Richard Corliss of *Time* felt that it came "close to finding the least admirable characters [a prostitute and a greedy tycoon] to build a feel-good movie around," and that it pandered to the lowest common denominator with its "mechanical titillation and predictable twists." Many critics, however, were quite smitten by Roberts's sexy comedic charm, and shelved their objections to the ho-hum script. "As a sexy, free-lance hooker who wins the heart of a cool and powerful corporate raider . . . Roberts exudes a melting warmth, a well-honed wit and a smile so disarming it's dangerous," extolled *Newsweek's* David Ansen, declaring that her "delectable comic performance in *Pretty Woman* turns an all-too-familiar romantic formula into a surprising treat." Even the *New York Times* gushed that Roberts "is so enchantingly beautiful, so funny, so natural and such an absolute delight that it is hard to hold anything against the movie." The *Times* further pronounced that Roberts "is a complete knockout, and this performance will make her a major star."

That it did. A tremendous publicity storm descended upon Roberts when *Pretty Woman* was released in the spring of 1990, and her phone rang off the hook with endless requests for photo sessions and interviews. Her comely image was splashed across countless magazine covers (she even became the first woman to grace *Gentleman's Quarterly*), and she made every most-beautiful-women-in-the-world list that was compiled that year. For while *Pretty Woman* displayed the actress's comedic flair, it trumpeted her sex appeal to full advantage. The movie never could have reached the heady heights it did without the considerable aesthetic attributes of its star. Audiences and critics alike fell in love with a unique beauty marked by its enormity of features—the huge, mile-wide smile set off by a pair of supple, voluptuous lips, deep, cocoa-brown eyes framed by a set of expansively arched eyebrows, a wild mane of auburn hair, and what *Pretty Woman* director Garry Marshall described in *Rolling Stone* as "possibly the longest legs since Wilt Chamberlain."

Her box office appeal assured, Roberts became a hot property with a jam-packed schedule. Ever honing her versatility, she immediately switched gears from romantic comedy to shoot two films in the thriller genre, *Flatliners* and *Sleeping With the Enemy*, both of which went on to enjoy financial success. *Flatliners*, released in the summer of 1990, saw Roberts as a cerebral medical school student intent on experiencing temporary lab-induced death, while *Sleeping With the Enemy*, released the following winter, proved Roberts's ability as a serious dramatic actress with her portrayal of a housewife seeking refuge from an abusive husband. The directors of both films had nothing but praise for Roberts. *Flatliners'* director Joel Schumacher was particularly impressed with her complexity, remarking to *Rolling Stone* that "There's this wonderful dichotomy with Julia. There's this woman, this little girl, this shitkicker, this very innocent lady. There's a *My Fair Lady* thing in there, and I think the reason she can pull it off is that all those people are inside her." "It's as if she has the thinnest skin imaginable," commented *Sleeping With the Enemy's* Joseph Ruben in the same *Rolling Stone* profile. "There's a vulnerability there that knocks you out. She's got two things going. There's something that happens photographically with her, that star quality you hear about. And she's got this emotional vulnerability that lets you see and feel everything that's going on with her. And the two of them together—*bam*." New projects in the works for the busy star include another serious film about death, as well as one which takes her into never-never land. The first, *Dying Young* (which reunites her with *Flatliners'* Schumacher), casts Roberts as a hired companion to a terminally ill leukemia patient with whom she falls in love. Her second project will have her suspended in wires as Tinkerbell in *Hook*, Steven Spielberg's big-budget adaptation of *Peter Pan*.

Considering her reigning superstar status in Hollywood, one would think Roberts would play it to full advantage by becoming a fast-lane party regular, partaking of the attentions of her many male admirers. Surprising for someone of her youth and beauty, however, she prefers a quiet and monogamous private life. Celebrity makes her uncomfortable, and she shuns the glamorous Hollywood nightlife. "I'm home so little that, when I'm home, I prefer to stay there. That scene can be a little exploitive. Whenever possible, it's better to lay low," she explained to *USA Weekend*. Not one with a heavy dating calendar, her romantic life has been limited to a few serious and exclusive relationships with co-stars. When filming *Satisfaction*, she met and began living with co-star Liam Neeson, who was 16 years her senior. The set of *Steel Magnolias* teamed her with Dylan McDermott, who played her husband on-screen, her fiance off-screen. She then dated and became engaged to her *Flatliners* co-star Keifer Sutherland; their plans to marry in 1991 fell through, and the couple broke up. She was reportedly seeing actor and Sutherland friend Jason Patric shortly thereafter.

Although Roberts takes her work very seriously, cultivating a close, supportive base of family and friends is the top priority for her. "I mean, acting is a true love of mine," she told *Rolling Stone*, "but it's not *the* true love. There are times when I get so bogged down by the politics of this business that I just have these great domestic fantasies. Being at home, and being quiet, and reading, and having a garden, and doing all that stuff. Taking care of a family. Those are the most important things. Movies will come and go, but family is a real kind of rich consistency." She went on to compare the rewards of movie-making and family life: "It's funny, because I've spent the last year and a half making movies and giving and giving and giving. There would be nothing left, and I'd find one more thing, so I'd give that. But there comes a point where you're losing sleep, and it takes a long time to get anything back from all that giving. It's a great thing to have the opportunity to give like that—but at the same time, you know, when you have family, friends, and there's love in your life, and you give to that, you can see instant gratification. You can see somebody smile or just pick somebody up or something. And it's easier to give that way than it is to just be giving to this . . . *black machinery*."

When asked about specific long-term career goals, Roberts remains fairly low-key—she just expresses the hope that she'll keep on working. Her longevity in Hollywood, however, seems assured. As her *Flatliners* director Joel Schumacher proclaimed: "She has the kind of talent and the kind of screen presence," he told *Rolling Stone*, "where she can have a career for as long as she wants to."

Sources

American Film, July 1990.
Cosmopolitan, November 1989.
Harper's Bazaar, February 1989; September 1989.
Newsweek, March 26, 1990.
New York Times, March 18, 1990; March 23, 1990.
Parade, February 24, 1991.
People, Special Summer Issue, 1990; September 17, 1990, December 31, 1990–January 7, 1991; February 25, 1991; March 4, 1991.
Premiere, December 1990.
Rolling Stone, August 9, 1990.
Star-Ledger (Newark, NJ), February 24, 1991.
Teen, December 1990.
Time, April 2, 1990; February 18, 1991.
USA Weekend, February 8-10, 1991.
Vogue, September 1988; April 1990.

—Mary Lou De Blasi

Dennis Rodman

AP/Wide World Photos

Professional basketball player

Born c. 1961 and raised in Texas; two sisters; children: Alexis (by former fiancee, model Annie Bakes). *Education:* Briefly attended Cooke County College (junior college) in Gainesville, Tex., on scholarship; attended Southeastern Oklahoma University, beginning in 1983.

Addresses: *Home*—Detroit, MI, and Bokchito, OK.

Career

Worked briefly as a janitor at the Dallas-Fort Worth Airport, c. 1978; 2nd-round NBA draft choice, 1986; forward for the Detroit Pistons, 1986—.

Awards: Named to NBA Eastern Conference All-Star team, 1989; Defensive Player of the Year award, 1990.

Sidelights

Basketball purists and old-time observers of the game sometimes like to call Detroit Pistons forward Dennis Rodman a throwback to another era—a player whose hustle, enthusiasm, defensive intensity, and dedication to team goals all recall the days of basketball before multi-million dollar salaries, superstar cults, and the modern obsession with personal statistics. It is a common ploy for connoisseurs of any sport to claim such rare and unheralded players as one of their own and thus draw attention to their "enhanced" understanding of the subtleties of the game. But in reality no era, not even the

current one, could rightly claim Rodman. He plays basketball in a different world, in a different time, and the truth is that there has *never* been a player quite like him.

Rodman is an original—not so much a throwback as a quirk. In fact, as basketball has evolved in America on urban playgrounds and country driveways, in colleges, and in the National Basketball Association (NBA), it has produced perhaps its first superman in the multi-talented Chicago Bulls forward Michael Jordan, widely considered to be the finest player in the history of the game. In the context of that progression, then, Rodman could be considered basketball's mutant gene—a one-in-a-million player who sort of happened by accident. "I hope people realize," said Rodman's teammate Isiah Thomas in the *Detroit News*, "that they will never see a player like him again."

Rodman is such a unique player that in trying to describe him it is difficult to know where to begin. But what is perhaps most immediately striking about him, and what in many ways is the source of his original style of play, is his physique. If he could be an animal, he would probably be a gazelle—lean, wiry, and solidly packed with strident muscles that seem to bounce and stretch like elastic as he prances up and down the court. At 6'8" tall and 210 pounds, Rodman is a "between-size" player who does not physically match up at any position in any conventional sense. He is too short to play center, too slight to play power forward; he is not blessed with the great offensive skills normally required from the small forward, nor with the ball-handling duties of a guard. So, rather than try to place a square peg in a round hole, Pistons coach Chuck Daly learned early in Rodman's professional career that the best way to coach him was to *not* coach him—just turn him loose. "Dennis is at his best when he doesn't think," Daly told the *Detroit News*.

The result of Daly's hands-off approach to Rodman is a grown man who plays the game with the completely unbridled, unstructured joy of a 12-year-old kid. While the average NBA player is serious, intense, and focused on the job that his coach has defined for him over and over, Rodman on the court is a loose, gangly free spirit, bounding around with barely contained ecstasy as though he were playing all by himself on a driveway in Texas. His mannerisms and odd twitches are the result of a boyish energy that is too pure to be kept inside. "He is full of nervous tics," wrote Joe LaPointe in the *New York Times*, "tucking and untucking his shirt, taking his shoes off while resting on the bench. When he runs, Rodman prances with a stiff-backed gait, elbows pumping, knees high. He hand-checks his foes, bumps them with his flat belly, pats them on the back when the whistle stops play. More than most players, he is liable to end up in Row 2 after diving after a loose ball."

Earlier in his career, such antics were interpreted by opposing fans and players as showboating, but as Rodman's reputation in the league has been solidified by two world championship rings, an appearance in the NBA All-Star Game, and a Defensive Player of the Year award, he gets more respect. "People used to say, 'He's just a hot dog. Why doesn't somebody just lay him on his butt?'" Rodman told the *New York Times*. "Now, people are coming to grips with it's just the way I play. I don't go to other teams' benches and point at them. I don't point fingers in their faces. I would never do that. Why should I talk trash to a player? I think I get more people more mad by playing good defense. I'm always on their butts. I try to keep it in my mind: 'Work hard, keep going, keep going. Eventually, one of you is going to wear down and it damn sure isn't going to be me.'" As a player who, in many games, compiles more offensive rebounds than points, his selection to the 1989 Eastern Conference All-Star team was indicative of the way Rodman, and the

Pistons in general, revolutionized the pro game en route to their back-to-back championships in 1989 and 1990. Though they had plenty of talented scorers, the Pistons prided themselves on their ability to stop other teams' scorers with a smothering brand of team defense. Whereas during the 1980s the pro game had become known for flashy offensive players like Magic Johnson and Larry Bird, and for the high-flying slam dunks of Jordan and Dominique Wilkins, the Pistons, nicknamed the "Bad Boys," brought defense back in style with their physical, hard-nosed play.

> *"People used to say, 'He's just a hot dog. Why doesn't somebody just lay him on his butt?"*

And nobody was better at it than Rodman. Whether he was taking a charge, grabbing a key rebound, blocking a shot, or helping out a teammate who had been beaten, Rodman made himself an utter nuisance to opponents at the defensive end of the court, often switching effortlessly, in the middle of games, from covering smaller, lightning-quick guards to bigger, punishingly physical centers and forwards. He would guard anyone, and no challenge was too great. In one two-game stretch during the 1989-90 season, Rodman shut down New York's 7'2" center Patrick Ewing one night, then came back the next night to stop Houston's 7' center Hakeem Olajuwon during a fourth-quarter comeback by the Pistons. In a 1989 playoff game with the Chicago Bulls, Rodman, who periodically spelled teammate Joe Dumars in the thankless task of covering Jordan, perfectly anticipated a Jordan move and drew a charging call to foul out the Bulls' superstar. "I was trying the whole game to get an offensive foul on him," Rodman told the *New York Times*. "He had five fouls. He came down with the ball. He made a move and I anticipated it just perfect and got the charge. He fouled out! . . . And that was one of the best plays of my career."

One of the best plays of his career? Taking a charge? Is this guy for real? He must be, because even kids on the playgrounds are starting to appreciate Rodman's enthusiasm for doing the dirty work. A friend of Rodman's once told him that his son had recently come home from a schoolyard game with a black eye, courtesy of a guy on the other team. When his father asked him why the other boy had punched him, his son replied, "Because I was playing defense like Dennis Rodman."

If Rodman seems to play the game as though he is living on borrowed time, it is because he knows that without plenty of good fortune and the help of a very special family in Oklahoma, he would more than likely be sweeping floors in Dallas these days—or shooting baskets in a prison yard. Born in Texas, Rodman grew up in what his mother, Shirley, has called a "female family." His father left town when Dennis was three, never to return, leaving Rodman in the shadow of his two younger sisters, Kim and Debra, who were doted on by their mother.

The consummate late bloomer, Rodman was still only 5'9" when he graduated from high school. In fact, he is probably the only player in the NBA who never even *played* high school basketball, much less starred for the team. "I couldn't even make a layup right," Rodman told *Sports Illustrated* of his game in those days. He did try out for the football team once, but was cut for being too small. All the talent in the family, it seemed, went to Rodman's sisters—6'3" Debra was an All-American forward for Louisiana Tech's national championship team, and 6'1" Kim

Dennis Rodman drives for two points in a 1989 game against the Los Angeles Lakers. AP/Wide World Photos.

was an All-American at Stephen F. Austin. As a teenager, Dennis was teased by friends for tagging along with his sisters.

After graduating from high school, Rodman appeared to be heading nowhere fast. While working as a janitor at Dallas-Fort Worth Airport, he was arrested for stealing watches from an airport boutique. It was also around that time, however, that somewhere in Rodman's body a hormonal floodgate opened. He began to grow so fast that his clothes wouldn't fit; he felt so awkward that he would literally hide inside the house. The two-year growth spurt raised Rodman's height nearly a full foot, to 6'8", and he began to play basketball again. At his new height the game suddenly became a little easier. But while his body had matured, Rodman still had plenty of growing up to do. He won a two-year scholarship to play basketball at Cooke County (junior) College in Gainesville, Texas, but he blew the chance. He tired of the structured lifestyle of classes and practice and quit the team after half a season.

Rodman headed back to the Dallas streets. "The way I was going I would've ended up in jail for sure," he told *Sports Illustrated.* Things got worse, or so it seemed, when Shirley Rodman kicked her son out of the house. But perhaps it was time to leave the nest, learn some self-reliance. Rodman moved from one friend's house to another, which made things difficult for Jack Hedden, coach of the Southeastern Oklahoma University basketball team, to locate him. Hedden had somehow heard of Rodman and wanted him to try out for his NAIA division team. The year was 1983. Rodman was 22 years old when he headed north with Hedden to Durant, Oklahoma, for what he knew would be his last chance to make something of his life.

What unfolded next is a strange, wonderful story that seems destined to someday be played out on the ABC Movie of the Week with an improbable story line: A young black man at a crossroads and a white, country boy in a terrible depression somehow find one another and become great friends. In 1983, 14 year-old Bryne Rich's parents, Pat and James, sent their son to a basketball camp at Southeastern Oklahoma in hopes he might somehow get away from his troubles for awhile. The year before, Bryne had accidentally killed his best friend in a hunting accident and became entrenched in a deep depression. One day during the camp, Bryne was shooting baskets when Rodman, with a shiny quarter placed in each of his rather oddly-shaped, prominent ears, walked up and started rebounding for Bryne.

Bryne was so taken with his goofy new buddy that he drove the 15 miles back to his family's farm in Bokchito that night and asked if he could invite a friend to dinner. To put it mildly, Pat Rich was a little shocked to hear that not only was Bryne's new friend eight years older, he was also black. "I almost swallered my tongue when I heard," she told *Sports Illustrated*. "It's hard to believe a family like ours could love a black boy like Worm." ("Worm" being Rodman: "He kind of puts you in mind of a worm, the way he wriggles around and all," Mrs. Rich said.) It took a while for a large, young black man to break down the fears and prejudices of a white farm family from Oklahoma, but eventually Rodman accomplished the task and soon was living on the Rich's farm, doing chores and sleeping in Bryne's room. "All of a sudden, I'm driving a tractor and messing with cows," Rodman told *Sports Illustrated*. "But I never went back to Dallas, I never did. I figured if I was going to make it, if I was going to clear that street crap out of my life, I couldn't go back there."

Meanwhile, Rodman was also in the process of becoming an NAIA All-American forward at Southeastern. Incredibly, in his first year of organized basketball, Rodman averaged 26 points and 13.1 rebounds per game. The next two years he led the NAIA in rebounding, averaging 15.9 and 17.8 per game. Still, Southeastern Oklahoma and the NAIA have never been considered fertile training grounds for future pro basketball players, so it was somewhat of a shock when the Pistons made Rodman their second-round choice in the 1986 NBA draft.

It became clear very soon, however, that Detroit general manager Jack McCloskey had pulled off a major coup in landing Rodman, despite the rookie's misadventures at his first pro training camp. During that session Rodman was rushed to the hospital once for hyperventilating; another time he alarmed doctors during a physical when his heart began beating wildly. But this hyperdrive energy was something that Coach Daly soon grew to appreciate in Rodman. With his happy-go-lucky, just-glad-to-be-here attitude, Rodman was a coach's dream, more than willing to dive for loose balls or play hard-nosed defense, tasks that most pros look upon with disdain. He quickly established himself as a key player off the bench, as part of Detroit's vaunted second unit. Rodman and 7' teammate John Salley came to be called the "X-Factor," for the decisive way they could turn a game around with their defense, shot-blocking, and fast-breaking offensive assaults. Rodman's playing time and statistical outputs improved each season also; by late in the 1990-91 season he was challenging San Antonio center David Robinson for the league rebounding title.

But Rodman's growth into one of the most versatile and respected players in the NBA did not come without some pain. The most infamous moment in his career came at the end of his rookie season in 1987. The Pistons had just lost a heart-breaking, seven-game playoff to the Boston Celtics in the Eastern Conference finals, and Rodman was cornered by some reporters after the game. A very emotional person (he has been known to break down in sobs at Pistons championship celebrations, and he choked up at the press conference when he won his Defensive Player of the Year award), Rodman lashed out with rookie impulsiveness when a reporter mentioned the name of Larry Bird, Boston's great forward. "He's way overrated," Rodman snapped. "Because he's white. You never hear about a black player being the greatest." Fortunately for Rodman, Pistons captain Isiah Thomas overheard this exchange and bailed Rodman out by starting an even larger controversy. "If Bird were black, he'd be just another good guy," Thomas reportedly said. The controversy boiled in the newspapers for a week, with Thomas taking most of the blame. Rodman, meanwhile, slipped out of town and headed south for the off-season to stay with his adopted family, the Riches, who, as mentioned earlier, are white. The irony became that much more apparent when piles of hate mail, labeling Rodman a racist and worse, started arriving in Bokchito. It was a lesson Rodman will not forget. "If we had won the game, I wouldn't have said anything like that," he later told *Sports Illustrated*. "I was hurting, and I wanted to hurt those people back. But I shouldn't have said what I said. Larry Bird proved to me he's one of the best, and they were the better team that day. I made a mistake."

When he's not playing basketball, Rodman approaches daily life with the same manic energy. A free spirit, he is often sighted dancing the night away in some Detroit nightclub, or testing his skills against eight-year-old kids in the local video arcade. Rodman was once engaged to Sacramento model Annie Bakes, the mother of his daughter, Alexis; though the engagement was broken, Rodman and Bakes maintain an amicable relationship. As for Alexis, her father is known to spoil her with extravagant gifts, and during the 1990 playoffs he even had the message "I Love Alexis" shaved into the short-cropped hair on the back of his head. During the off-season, Rodman gets away from the crowds by taking long, solo excursions on country roads in his big Ford pickup truck. "It makes you feel so good,"

Rodman told the *New York Times*. ''Just ride down the road and be in your own world''—sort of the way he plays basketball.

Sources

Detroit News, March 28, 1991.
New York Times, May 20, 1990.
Sports Illustrated, May 2, 1988.

—David Collins

Buddy Roemer

AP/Wide World Photos

Governor of Louisiana

Real name, Charles Elson Roemer III; born October 4, 1943, in Bossier City, LA; son of Charles (a cotton farmer and businessman) and Adeline Roemer; second wife's name, Patti Crocker Roemer (separated); children: (first marriage) two; (second marriage) Dakota Frost. *Education:* Harvard University, B.A., M.B.A. *Politics:* Republican (formerly Democrat). *Religion:* Methodist.

Career

Worked as a banker in Shreveport, LA, and ran family computer business Innovative Data Systems (IDS) during the 1970s; Louisiana delegate to the U.S. House of Representatives, Washington, D.C., 1980-88; governor of Louisiana, 1987—.

Sidelights

Since the days of post-Civil War Reconstruction, Louisiana politics have been marked with corruption that often runs as deep as the oil wells drilled into the state's bayous. From the heyday of freewheeling populist governor Huey Long, who was assassinated in the 1930s, to the high-living regime of Edwin Edwards in the 1970s and 1980s, the state capitol of Baton Rouge has seen more than its share of controversy. In 1987 Louisiana voters elected to the state's top political post Charles Elson "Buddy" Roemer III, who promised to rid the governor's mansion of graft and cure the Bayou State's social and economic ills.

The "Roemer Revolution," as it has been called, inched Louisiana along on its road to recovery, but not without a price. Since taking office three years ago, Roemer has separated from his second wife, jumped political parties, and come to blows time and again with the Louisiana legislature, which in 1991 finally pushed a strict anti-abortion bill past Roemer's veto. As the 1991 gubernatorial election drew near, political pundits pointed to Louisiana to generate interest in an otherwise lean election year. As a *U.S. News & World Report* headline declared: "As usual, Louisiana politics will provide great theater in '91."

Charles Elson Roemer III was born in 1943 and grew up one of five children at Scopena, the Roemer family cotton plantation near Bossier City in northwestern Louisiana. Family discussions around the dinner table over a wide variety of social, political, and practical topics helped young Buddy hone the verbal and analytical skills that have marked his political career. His mother, Adeline, regularly conducted chalkboard drills in Latin and geography after school; his father, Charlie, led lively roundtable discussions in the Socratic manner. Such an instructive upbringing inside a wealthy compound like Scopena, along with the family's keen interest in

Democratic politics, led to comparisons that labeled the Roemers "Louisiana Kennedys."

Like his lifelong idol John F. Kennedy, Roemer attended Harvard University, leaving the bayou behind and traveling north for his education. He entered Harvard at the tender age of 16 and used his considerable powers of communication to ease an otherwise awkward college tenure. Roemer earned a master's degree from the Harvard School of Business, then returned to Louisiana to enter politics. "I don't like Louisiana politics," he said in one of his political ads. "I *love* Louisiana. I love Louisiana enough to make some people angry."

In the 1970s Roemer wet his feet in the Louisiana political scene while working as a banker in Shreveport. He also ran Innovative Data Systems (IDS), the family computer business. Roemer's father turned IDS over to his son when the younger Roemer assumed a top advisory post to then-Governor Edwards. A series of alleged improprieties in dealings between IDS and the state brought conflict-of-interest charges from political opponents and more than one appearance before federal grand juries for Buddy Roemer.

Although no charges were filed against Roemer, his opponents gained substantial political ammunition from the transactions, particularly when his father was indicted in an FBI undercover investigation. In 1982 Charlie Roemer received a three-year prison sentence for charges involving insurance contract bribes and kickbacks. He served 15 months; the conviction was later overturned, but not before Buddy Roemer had effectively distanced himself politically from his father and family.

In 1973 Roemer, divorced from his high-school sweetheart—with whom he'd had two children—married Patti Crocker. He was a 29-year-old delegate to the 1972 constitutional convention in Baton Rouge when they met; she was a 19-year-old page. In 1979 they had a son, Dakota Frost. The couple separated in 1989.

After an unsuccessful congressional run in 1978, Roemer won a seat in the House in 1980, where he quickly gained a reputation as a financial whiz and a boll-weevil Democrat who consistently voted with the Republican Reagan administration. He was known as a tireless worker, despite being a diabetic who must inject himself with insulin twice a day. During his four two-year terms in the House of Representatives, Roemer's voting record displayed "a decidedly right-wing bent," according to *The Nation,* though his supporters maintained their man was a social-issue liberal. His social legislation record while

in Congress included opposition to abortion rights, the Equal Rights Amendment, and a variety of consumer-protection acts. He was, however, a strong backer of environmental legislation, a path he would continue to travel back home in Louisiana.

In 1987 Roemer set his sights on the governor's mansion; the *New Republic* quipped that the tragedy of his campaign was that he won. Louisiana was in a quagmire; it led the nation in unemployment, illiteracy and high-school dropouts. It had the worst teacher salaries and lowest bond rating. Oil and petrochemical companies had pockmarked the state's countryside with 40,000 hazardous waste sites and eroded wetlands through offshore drilling methods. To make matters worse, Roemer inherited a budget operating at nearly a billion-dollar deficit and a state teetering on the verge of bankruptcy.

Roemer based his campaign on promises to cut state government employee rolls by 25 percent, revamp the education system, clean up the environment and restructure the tax system to encourage new business investment and diversification. Unlike Texas, which had invested its share of oil boom dollars to diversify its economy, Louisiana was devastated when the bottom fell out of the oil and gas market in the early and mid-1980s. "Louisiana had made 'a deal with the devil,' he preached," according to *Esquire,* "swapping jobs for America's worst pollution and some of its highest cancer rates. He painted incumbent Edwin Edwards as a Great Satan who had winked at corruption while squandering the state's oil windfall. He, Buddy Roemer, was going to deliver the state from its disgrace." That, in essence, represented the nuts and bolts of the Roemer Revolution.

Under Louisiana law all candidates for governor run against one another in a non-partisan primary. If no one candidate gets more than half the vote, the top two go to a November runoff election. Three weeks before the primary, the state's eight largest newspapers endorsed Roemer. He won the primary with 33 percent of the vote. Edwards, who ran second with 28 percent, conceded rather than face an embarrassing loss in a runoff.

Once in office Roemer moved quickly, persuading a reluctant legislature to reform campaign laws and raise teacher pay by five percent. But reluctance soon turned to hostility; a bill designed to reduce the size of state government was defeated. Louisiana state government, according to the *New Republic,* is teeming with boards and commissions that corrupt governors have long used for payback appointments, including a State Board of Watchmakers and a State Board of Embalmers. A Roemer bill to eliminate 150 of the 2,300 governing bodies was defeated in the legislature. "It was a classic Louisiana paradox," appraised the *New Republic*. "To get the legislators' votes, Roemer needed to promise them they could appoint their friends to the very jobs they'd be voting to eliminate." Roemer then made an appointment of his own, further infuriating the legislative branch: New Orleans *Times-Picayune* investigative reporter Bill Lynch was made the state's first inspector general. Lynch revealed enough improprieties to prompt Roemer to replace all members of the state racing and real estate commissions. "If I had known as a reporter what I have learned in my first three days here, I could have won five Pulitzer Prizes," Lynch told *Time*, explaining why he had increased his staff from 12 to 35.

Roemer's major defeat came at the hands of voters, who rejected his tax reform proposals. According to *Business Week*, Louisiana's tax structure allows 90 percent of the state's homeowners to avoid paying property taxes. A Depression-era homestead exemption frees people from paying any taxes on homes assessed at less than $70,000, "which, under the state's archaic tax structure, includes most of the homes in Louisiana." After Roemer cajoled his tax reforms through the state legislature, 55 percent of voters soundly defeated the Roemer tax referendum. "By the time the battered tax plan reached the voters, they were in no mood to hear that they should tax themselves because it was the right thing to do," explained *Esquire*.

The tax fight was but one of Roemer's troubles. By the time the legislature recessed for the summer of 1990, it had passed a measure outlawing the sale of record albums with "obscene" lyrics, nearly passed a law instituting a $25 fine for anyone who assaults a flag-burner, and put through a bill that outlawed abortion except in cases of rape or incest, which Roemer vetoed. "The legislature threw a party and I get to clean it up," said Roemer in *U.S. News & World Report*. The ensuing furor over abortion, an intensely emotional issue ablaze in an intensely emotional political state, cost the state's economy millions of dollars in revenue when the Democratic party dropped New Orleans from contention as a site for its 1992 convention, choosing instead to meet in New York. After two successive Roemer vetoes, a revised version of the restrictive abortion bill earned enough votes to override the veto in June of 1991.

With a 59 percent approval rating, Roemer entered the 1991 campaign. The state's unemployment rate has been cut in half from when he took over in 1988. As a result of the Persian Gulf War, the oil-rich state saw a $400 million budget surplus, just three years after coming within 48 hours of declaring bankruptcy. Roemer's two chief adversaries going into the primary were David Duke—a former Ku Klux Klansman running as an independent who garnered 43 percent of the vote as a Republican candidate for the U.S. Senate in 1990—and Democrat populist and former governor Edwards, who had been indicted and acquitted twice for bribery and corruption. Edwards has a strong core support in the traditional Democratic party, and Duke has support among white supremacists. The Republicans had also planned to run a candidate in the primary. According to the *Economist*, "If Roemer and a Republican were to split the rest of the vote between them, there might be a run-off between Edwards and Duke."

On March 11, 1991, Buddy Roemer announced that he was switching parties, the first sitting governor ever to do so. In one swift political move, Roemer eliminated any Republican opponent who might siphon votes from him in the primary. Roemer told *U.S. News & World Report* that the Republican party was "more open to new ideas, new thinking, new people." Two months previously, however, he had told the same magazine, "I just think the Republican party is not sensitive at all to people who look different, to another opinion and to helping those who by circumstance don't have a level playing field."

The state's rank of 47 in graduation rates is but one indication that the Roemer Revolution is unfinished, but according to *U.S. News & World Report*, most political experts predict it will continue with Roemer's re-election in 1991. As related in *Esquire*, "One columnist pointed out, 'You have to understand that a successful term for a governor here means he hasn't stolen and he hasn't been indicted.' By that standard Roemer is a raging success...If the price of oil holds, he could well become Louisiana's first reform governor in memory to get himself reelected."

Sources

Economist, March 16, 1991.
Esquire, March 1991.
The Nation, March 12, 1988.
Newsweek, August 13, 1990.
New Republic, March 20, 1989.
Time, June 13, 1988.
U.S. News & World Report, July 30, 1990; January 14, 1991; March 25, 1991.
Business Week, July 23, 1990.

—*John P. Cortez*

Pete Rose

AP/Wide World Photos

Former baseball player and manager

Full name, Peter Edward Rose; born April 14, 1941, in Anderson Ferry, Ohio; son of Harry Francis (a banker) and LaVerne Rose. Married Karolyn Ann Engelhardt, January 25, 1964 (divorced, 1979); married Carol Woliung, 1979; children: (first marriage) Pete, Jr., Fawn; (second marriage) Tyler, Cara. *Education:* High school graduate.

Career

Professional baseball player, 1960-86; player-manager of the Cincinnati Reds, 1984-89. Signed with the Cincinnati Reds, 1960, made the majors in 1963. Moved to the Philadelphia Phillies, 1979, to the Montreal Expos, 1984, and back to the Reds, 1984. Named to the All-Star Team, 1965, 1967-71, 1973-82; named Sportsman of the Year by *Sports Illustrated,* 1975; holds major league all-time records for most career hits (4,256), most games played, most singles, most 200-hit seasons (10), most consecutive 100-hit seasons (23), highest fielding percentage by an outfielder, most positions played, most doubles in the National League (746), and longest hitting streak in the National League (44 games).

Sidelights

Pete Rose was one of the finest baseball players of his—or any other—generation. Rose broke so many records during his 25 years as a major league player that he will never *ever* be outclassed in every category. Certainly his most spectacular achievement

came in 1985, when he surpassed the legendary Ty Cobb to become the man with the most hits in the history of the game. *Gentleman's Quarterly* contributor Pat Jordan described Rose as "the athlete from an ordinary background who achieved great success not from an abundance of talent but from an abundance of boyish desire and hard work." Jordan added that Rose "played his game the way young boys played it when Norman Rockwell was painting covers for *The Saturday Evening Post.* He slid headfirst into third base. He ran to first on a walk. His uniform was perpetually caked with dirt and ripped from his fearless style of play. His fans read into that style of play a host of qualities—courage, discipline, desire, perseverance—that have little to do with him or his success. The secret is much simpler than that. He devoted his life to one thing—baseball—at the exclusion of almost everything else."

His spectacular achievements on the diamond have not insulated Rose from the harsher realities of life, however. In 1989 a series of allegations about his excessive gambling—including the assertion that he bet on baseball games—caused him to be banished from baseball for the rest of his life. The following year he pleaded guilty to income tax evasion and served five months in a minimum security prison, where he vowed he would pay for his mistakes. As

Pat Calabria noted in *Newsday*, Rose is no stranger to scandal. "Behind the gleaming All-America smile and the irrepressible charm," wrote Calabria, "Pete Rose has spent much of his career putting out one brushfire after another. Until now, he always managed to escape unharmed.... Rose was a remarkable hitter and enormously popular—his face was on the front of a Wheaties box. But the public image never did square with the private reality." That "private reality" has now become a matter of public record, and Rose—one of baseball's greats—now faces the possibility that he may never reach the Hall of Fame.

Peter Edward Rose was born and raised in the tiny Ohio River town of Anderson Ferry. His father, Harry, was a bank teller who spent his weekends playing rough semi-pro football. Young Pete, who served as waterboy for his father's teams, learned a number of lessons from his years spent beside a football field. The elder Rose played football until well into his forties, he hustled on every play, and he had little patience for those who did not do the same. Pete followed his father into sports, but he was not what one would call a natural athlete. Although he never had trouble making local baseball teams, he was not invited to try out for the high school football team until he was a junior. Rose himself admits that he should have spent more time worrying about his studies and less about sports when he was a teen. In his book *Pete Rose: My Story*, he said: "I'll tell this to every person who listens. There is nothing more important for a young person than getting educated. One thing in my life, if I could do differently, I would have concentrated more on getting educated."

In high school Rose was small and light. He played with every ounce of determination and spirit that he would later show as a pro, but baseball scouts were reluctant to court him all the same. Luckily, Rose's uncle, Buddy Bloebaum, had connections with the Cincinnati Reds organization. Bloebaum put in a good word for Rose and got him a contract in 1960 that gave him a $7000 signing bonus, a $400-per-month salary, and an incentive clause of $5000 if he made the majors. In the summer of 1960 Rose left for New York, where he reported to the Geneva Red Legs. He was ecstatic.

Rose climbed through the minor leagues at a reasonable pace, playing winter baseball in Florida and spending some time on a Macon, Georgia, team before finally making the Reds in 1963. During spring training of his rookie year Rose earned the nickname "Charlie Hustle," a title that would stick throughout his career. By then he had grown several inches and put on some weight, so he was an altogether more formidable athlete. But it was that "hustle"—that dogged, almost maniacal determination to give his all—that began to characterize Pete Rose as superstar material. Calabria wrote: "Rose's appeal, in fact, always was rooted in the blue-collar upbringing he carried into the clubhouse, as if he'd packed a lunchpail. He wasn't spoiled and he didn't duck autographs. Above all, all the fans knew that he earned his paycheck." By 1965 Rose was hitting better than .300 and was chalking up more than two hundred hits per season, a great many of them singles and doubles.

> "I'll tell this to every person who listens. There is nothing more important for a young person than getting educated."

The 1970s were great years for the Cincinnati Reds and spectacular years for Pete Rose. As part of Cincinnati's "Big Red Machine," Rose helped the Reds advance to the league playoffs five times and the World Series four times. In the 1975 World Series—considered by some to be the best series ever—he batted a phenomenal .370 and had ten hits as the Reds beat the Boston Red Sox. Rose was also a perennial favorite at the All-Star game, making the starting roster every year from 1965 to 1985 except 1966, 1972, and 1984. Rose played his whole career in the National League, so he was never allowed the relative ease of working as a designated hitter. Instead he became a solid defensive player, the only one ever to work more than five hundred games at five different positions. At various times in his career Rose played first base, second base, third base, left field, and right field.

Rose was named Sportsman of the Year in 1975 by *Sports Illustrated*, and at the end of the 1970s he was one of the top vote-getters for sportsman of the decade in every sporting publication. He batted better than .300 every year except 1974 and even turned in a 44-game hitting streak in 1978. Nevertheless, the Cincinnati management did not stop Rose from turning free agent in 1978 and peddling his wares elsewhere. Reds fans were shocked to learn that their superstar would begin the 1979 season not in Cincinnati but in Philadelphia, with the Phillies.

True to his reputation, Rose turned in several good years with the Phillies, helping the team to advance to the World Series in 1980 and 1983. At the end of the 1983 season he moved to Montreal, playing most of 1984 with the Expos. Late in the 1984 season he was given an offer that must have seemed like a godsend—he could return to Cincinnati as a player-manager and possibly break the daunting all-time hits record with the team that had given him his start. Needless to say, Rose accepted the offer.

On September 11, 1985, Pete Rose captured the attention of the nation when he smacked hit number 4,192 to become the all-time leading hitter in the history of baseball. Rose lost all control of his emotions as the crowd roared around him. Hugging his son, Pete, Jr., who was batboy at the time, he looked at the sky. Later he told Roger Kahn, "I saw clear in the sky my dad and Ty Cobb. Ty Cobb was in the second row. Dad was in the first. With Dad in the sky and Petey in my arms, you had three generations of Rose men together that night. So that's what it was that made me cry." Rose terminated his playing career in 1986 and managed the Reds until allegations of compulsive gambling sidelined him in 1989.

Rose had always enjoyed betting on horse races, but as his career advanced, so—the allegations contend—did his penchant for gambling. Although the testimony against him from a former bookmaker can certainly be questioned, some hard evidence of Rose's habits did surface in 1989. He still swears that he never bet on professional baseball games, but it was that charge that drew him a lifetime ban from baseball, imposed by the late commissioner A. Bartlett Giamatti [See *Newsmakers 88*]. (Rose is currently eligible to appeal for reinstatement.) What Rose *did* eventually admit was that he failed to report some $300,000 in income from card shows and personal appearances to the Internal Revenue Service. In 1990 he served a term in federal prison and paid a steep fine, becoming the most celebrated inmate the Marion Federal Prison Camp in Illinois had ever seen.

The taint of scandal has serious implications for Rose in years to come. Had the tales of gambling and tax evasion never surfaced, Rose was a certain early choice for the Hall of Fame. Now, despite his fabulous statistics, his long list of records, and his historic "hustle," he may face the humiliation of

being voted down for a place in the Hall. It is this possibility—and the possibility that he may forever be denied access to his profession—that has forced Rose to examine his faults.

Rose told the *Boston Globe*: "I have felt bottomed out. A game that was dear to me was taken from me. I'm financially secure. And I'm strong emotionally. The most important thing in my life now is not to be seen forever in the light that I have been shown.... It took a lot of waking up to get me into therapy. I was gambling, and that created problems. They took baseball away from me.... I realized I had to find out why I was gambling. This decision is one of the most important decisions of my life. If I'd kept going, I'd have destroyed myself. Material destruction is one thing. Destroying the love and respect I have from the people, well, that's another thing."

It remains to be seen whether Rose can rebound in the public eye. If baseball were a mere matter of numbers, a science so to speak, he would be assured a high rank among the superstars. The game has a moral aspect too, however, and there, despite his heart and hustle, Pete Rose has been found wanting. After his sentencing in July of 1990, Rose told the press: "I think I'm perceived as a very aggressive, arrogant type of individual. But I want people to know that I do have emotion, I do have feelings, and I can be hurt like everybody else." Rose added: "I hope no one has to go through what I went through the last year and a half. I lost my dignity, I lost my self-respect, I lost a lot of dear fans and almost lost some very dear friends."

Writings

(With Roger Kahn) *Pete Rose: My Story*, Macmillan, 1989.

Sources

Boston Globe, November 22, 1989.
Chicago Tribune, August 25, 1989.
Detroit Free Press, July 20, 1990.
Gentlemen's Quarterly, April 1989.
Los Angeles Times, July 29, 1990.
Newsday, August 25, 1989.

—*Mark Kram*

Winona Ryder

AP/Wide World Photos

Actress

Surname originally Horowitz; born October, 1971, in Winona, Minn.; daughter of Michael and Cindy Horowitz; grew up in San Francisco, Mendocino, and Petaluma, Calif. *Education:* Attended high school in Petaluma; attended classes at the American Conservatory Theater, San Francisco.

Career

Actress in films, including *Lucas,* 1986, *Square Dance,* 1987, *1969,* 1988, *Beetlejuice,* 1988, *Heathers,* 1989, *Great Balls of Fire,* 1989, *Welcome Home, Roxy Carmichael,* 1990, *Edward Scissorhands,* 1990, *Mermaids,* 1990.

Sidelights

Premiere called Winona Ryder "the witty, wondrous sweetheart of hip America." For *Esquire,* Ryder's beauty "makes you want to consume—to devour its innocence in a mad chase to recapture your own." And for *Newsweek,* "an actress with subtleties beyond her years." Ryder has combined an atypical personal background and a strong desire to perform in film as major influences in fashioning a screen presence captured by these descriptions. 1990 was a particularly productive year for Ryder. She appeared as Dinky Bossetti in *Welcome Home, Roxy Carmichael* and was not satisfied with the film whose reviews were largely negative, save those praising her performance. Assessing the film in the *New York Times,* Caryn James wrote: "Its most certain feature is Winona Ryder's delicate mature performance"; "Ry-

der deftly explores the teenager's desperate and fearful emotions." By year's end, Ryder was in two of the Christmas season's hottest films, *Edward Scissorhands* and *Mermaids,* and would have been in a third, *The Godfather, Part III* had it not been for an illness—brought on by exhaustion—that kept her from fulfilling her commitment to play Michael Corleone's daughter. (Ryder's sudden departure left director Francis Ford Coppola in the position of finding a substitute quickly, with Coppola turning to his inexperienced daughter Sofia to play the part—leaving forever unanswered what difference Ryder's appearance would have made in the film.)

Ryder cites her unorthodox childhood as particularly influential on her outlook on life and acting. Named after a small town in Minnesota, Ryder, called "Noni" by her family and friends, moved with her family to San Francisco when she was ten years old. Her parents, Cynthia and Michael Horowitz, who do not subscribe to middle-class values and habits, raised Winona, the third oldest of four children (she has an older half-sister named Sunyata, an older half-brother, Jubal, and a younger brother, Uri), in an unstructured, free environment. Her godfather is the counterculture guru Timothy Leary, who describes Ryder's parents as "hippie intellectuals and psychedelic scholars." A frequent family visitor during her childhood was the poet Allen Ginsburg. Her parents are the editors of *Moksha,* a book about Aldous Huxley's psychedelic experiences, and *Shaman Woman, Mainline Lady,* a book of readings on the spiritual life of women throughout history.

For one year the Horowitzes lived in a semi-commune with seven other families in Mendocino, California. Leary has described the site as "one of the most successful, upscale hippie communities in the country." In *Rolling Stone,* Ryder clarified this part of her childhood: "It wasn't as hippie as it sounds . . . A lot of people, when they hear the word commune, connect it with, like, everyone's on acid and running around naked. This was more like this weird suburb . . . It was just a bunch of houses on this chunk of land; we had horses and gardens. You have so much freedom, you can go roaming anywhere. We didn't have electricity, which was weird, but it was great to grow up that way. We didn't have TV, so you'd have to do stuff. My friends' names were Tatonka, Gulliver and Rio. We'd had hammock contests, sit around and make up stories, make up weird games. I don't know—it was a weird, weird childhood. I mean, it was great."

The Horowitzes then moved to Petaluma where Michael Horowitz runs Flashback Books, specializing in counterculture publications, and Cynthia Horowitz makes educational videos. An excellent student, Ryder reads avidly and regards J. D. Salinger's *Catcher in the Rye* as her favorite book, one that she has read innumerable times. Her mother once ran a movie theater in an old barn where Winona, watching from atop an old mattress on the floor, saw films usually unavailable to youngsters in the days before video rental stores. Winona developed a fondness for the late director John Cassavetes. "I was too young to understand the movies, but I felt like I was there, like he [Cassavetes] invited me into his world, and it was wonderful to be invited. I thought, 'I want to make people feel this way,'" Ryder told Aljean Harmetz of the *New York Times.* About her parents, Ryder told Harmetz, "They're great people to hang around . . . they're both incredibly smart and intellectual and they could have become very wealthy but they struggled to pay the bills and stuck to what they want. That has to do with how I make my decisions. If they taught me anything, it's to trust myself and go with what my gut tells me. When I ask people for advice, that's when I get confused."

As a child, Ryder felt she was an outsider living in Petaluma and even suffered the indignity of being beaten up by classmates in the seventh grade. Explaining the effects of the assault to Harmetz,

Ryder said: "That was kind of great in a way. I was so into movies it seemed dramatic. I felt like a gangster." She then sought out children "who were more like me," and enrolled in acting classes at the American Conservatory Theater in San Francisco. There she experienced for the first time what it means to be an actor. "I asked," she told *Rolling Stone,* "if I could find my own monologue to perform. I read from J. D. Salinger's *Franny & Zooey.* I made it like [Franny] was sitting, talking to her boyfriend. I had a connection with Salinger-speak; the way she talked made sense. It was the first time that I felt that feeling you get when you're acting—that sort of yeah! feeling."

Ryder eventually made a videotaped audition for a leading part in *Desert Bloom,* which starred Jon Voight, Christine Lahti, and Ellen Barkin, but lost out to another actress. A year later Twentieth Century-Fox producers saw the videotape and cast Ryder in *Lucas,* a movie about teenage love and good intentions written and directed by David Seltzer and starring Corey Haim, Kerri Green, and Charlie Sheen. Ryder played Rina, a shy, poetically inclined girl who has a crush on Lucas. Seltzer was the first Hollywood director to see Ryder's screen power; he told *Rolling Stone:* "There was Winona, this little frail bird. She had the kind of presence I had never seen—an inner life. Whatever message was being said by her mouth was being contradicted by the eyes." In the critically panned *1969* Ryder again played a minor part that she turned to her advantage. As Beth, the younger sister of Robert Downey Jr., Ryder, wrote Janet Maslin in the *New York Times,* is a "beautiful young actress who . . . has such fascinatingly offbeat timing that she becomes a lot more interesting than her role." but she doesn't look 13."

In her next film, Tim Burton's *Beetlejuice,* yuppies Adam and Barbara (Alec Baldwin and Geena Davis) die in an accident and as ghosts are appalled by the eccentric new owners of their country dream home. They try to scare the new owners but to no avail. In desperation the two turn to Betelgeuse (Michael Keaton), a bio-exorcist who is comically horrifying. As the teenage Lydia, "Ryder makes a good impression as the new owners' daughter, a girl much creepier than the ghosts themselves," concluded Janet Maslin in the *New York Times.*

The film that established Ryder's diverse acting gifts, however, was *Heathers,* the 1989 black humor satire of teenage cruelty and snobbism. First-time screenwriter Daniel Waters and director Michael Lehmann showcased the obnoxious materialism of teenagers in the Reagan 1980s through three high school students, each named Heather, who pass judgment on their classmates' taste in clothes and physical appearance, treating anyone outside their narrow circle with malicious nastiness. They use their friend Veronica (Ryder) to embarrass and ridicule their classmates, who both fear and loath the Heathers. But when Veronica, who has begun to question the Heathers' tactics, does not live up to Heather Chandler's (Kim Walker) expectations at a fraternity party, Veronica sees her position in the group jeopardized. Veronica teams up with J.D. (Christian Slater), a transfer student with a personal agenda more deadly than the effete elitism of the Heathers. J.D., without Veronica's knowledge, gives Heather a drink spiked with kitchen cleaner, and then he and Veronica, who is an expert forger, concoct a suicide note. Suicide panic sets in at the school, with the administrators and teachers ineptly dealing with two subsequent copycat suicides. J.D. next plots to kill two obnoxious football players who have harassed Veronica, making it appear that the two jocks were homosexual lovers. Veronica becomes troubled by her complicity in the faked suicides and confronts J.D. in what proves to be a deadly battle with Veronica winning out.

Ryder showed a remarkably impressive sense of satiric calculation turning to humanistic decency in her interpretation of Veronica. *Heathers*, Ryder told *Rolling Stone*, "taught me a lot about what I want to do with my life, my career...which is never do anything I don't feel 100 percent about. I don't have any big floor plan, but I wouldn't do a movie where I thought I'd influence anybody in a bad way."

Ryder also starred in the 1989 *Great Balls of Fire*, a film biography of rock 'n' roll pianist-singer Jerry Lee Lewis. At the height of his success, Lewis married his 13-year-old cousin, Myra Gale, which resulted in scandal when he took his young bride on tour to England. Dennis Quaid as Jerry Lee Lewis offered a larger-than-life interpretation of the singer whose success as a rock 'n' roll artist came from a raw, sexual energy emanating from his hunched presence over a piano keyboard. "The key to the film's innocent tone is that Winona Ryder, as Myra, looks like a very young woman of 16 and not a little girl," wrote Caryn James in the *New York Times*. "Ms. Ryder's enormously poised performance balances Mr. Quaid's wild one. With her ponytail, saddle shoes and doll house, Myra looks naive, but she doesn't look 13."

In the acclaimed 1990 picture *Edward Scissorhands*, Ryder reteamed with *Beetlejuice* director Tim Burton who also directed *Batman* and is known for his rich visual style. Burton's *Scissorhands* was praised as an imaginative, original story of a boy whose creator died before he was able to make hands for his creation. Edward (Johnny Depp; also in *Newsmakers 91*) lives alone in a castle until he is discovered by Avon Lady Peg (Diane Weist), who takes Edward home with her to suburbia, where he becomes a curious oddity who sculpts hedges, creates new hair looks for the neighborhood women and their dogs, and falls in love with Peg's daughter Kim (Ryder), who is less accepting of Edward than others are. Depp, star of the Fox network's *21 Jump Street*—and Ryder's fiance, who sports a "Forever Winona" tattoo—"gives a sensitive reading of Edward as a sad, funny clown with a Chaplinesque shuffle," according to *Variety*. Ryder donned a blond wig to play Kim and transformed herself into her opposite. "Kim was like the girls in eighth grade who called me a weirdo and threw Cheetos at me. I had a crew cut, and I liked the Sex Pistols," Ryder told Harmetz. Of Ryder's portrayal of Kim, *New York Times* critic Janet Maslin remarked: "As lovely as she is diffident, she makes an enchanting Beauty to Mr. Depp's poignant, bashful Beast."

> "I don't have any big floor plan, but I wouldn't do a movie where I thought I'd influence anybody in a bad way."

Next Ryder became close friends with actress-singer Cher in the filming of *Mermaids*, Cher's first film since her Academy Award-winning performance in *Moonstruck*. While filming in Boston, Cher had Ryder move into Cher's apartment. Cher saw the story of Mrs. Flax and her two daughters, Charlotte (Ryder) and Kate (Christina Ricci), as a comedy much like her own relationship with her mother and sister; she had Lasse Hallstrom, the director of *My Life as a Dog*, dismissed after he wanted a darker, less comedic vision for the film. When Frank Oz was hired in Hallstrom's place, Cher and Ryder became dissatisfied with him, and Cher had Oz dismissed as well. Richard Benjamin finally directed the script by English writer June Roberts that was adapted from a novel by Patty Dann. Set in 1963, *Mermaids* tells the story of Mrs. Flax, a free spirit who depends upon no man for support. Her sexuality is unrestrained while her daughter, Charlotte, is torn by the need to be perfect and free of impure thoughts. Charlotte longs to be a Catholic nun and studies the lives of the female saints and martyrs. "As played by Miss Ryder, who is enchanting and funny, and firmly in control of every scene not handed to Cher, Charlotte is a potentially rich character," wrote Vincent Canby in the *New York Times*. "Miss Ryder is so good, in fact, that "Mermaids" might have dared to be a tougher, more satisfying movie than the stylish sitcom it is."

With the fruits of success that would seem phenomenal to some, Ryder has purchased a new home in Beverly Hills and has a loft in New York City, but does not like New York because of the high crime rate and the distance from her parents. Her favorite city is San Francisco, while she is an avid Los Angeles Dodgers fan. In capturing the young actress's power as an actor, her friend Robert Downey Jr. has said: "She's a pure-at-heart person who knows that the darkness is all around her. She brings to light that there is truth and love even in the darkest impulses."

Sources

Dayton Daily News, December 9, 1990; December 14, 1990.

Esquire, April 1990.

Newsweek, April 3, 1989.

New York Times, March 28, 1986; January 20, 1987; March 30, 1988; November, 18, 1988; March 31, 1989; June 30, 1989; September 3, 1989; December 9, 1990.

New Yorker, April 18, 1988; April 17, 1989.

Premiere, November 1990.

Rolling Stone, May 18, 1989; December 4, 1990; December 7, 1990; May 16, 1991.

Time, April 17, 1989.

Variety, December 10, 1990.

—*Jon Saari*

Bernie Sanders

AP/Wide World Photos

U.S. congressman from Vermont

Born c. 1941; son of a paint salesman; married. *Education:* Attended Brooklyn College, 1960-61, and University of Chicago.

Career

Has worked as a civil rights activist, carpenter, and videomaker. Mayor of Burlington, VT, 1981-89; U.S. congressman, 1990—.

Awards: Selected as one of the top twenty mayors in the country by *U.S. News & World Report.*

Sidelights

Elected by an overwhelming margin to Vermont's lone seat in the U.S. Congress in 1990, maverick Bernie Sanders established himself as one of America's most intriguing political figures by becoming the first socialist to serve that body in 40 years. The election of this fiery straightshooter, who ran as an independent candidate, reflected probably as much upon the tattered, confused state of the Democratic party as it did upon any perceived rise in socialist sentiment in Vermont. That Sanders was better able to voice the concerns of Vermont's small, economically-strapped, mostly rural population—an electorate traditionally thought to be a stronghold for the Democrats—gave rise throughout the country to renewed calls for a third national party to address the plight of farmers, women, minorities, the elderly, and the poor. "Some folks want to scare both the Democrats and the Republicans," said Eleanor

Smeal, former head of the National Organization for Women, in the *Village Voice,* "because they're fed up with a one-party system with two names. They're fed up with women and minorities being locked out of the decision-making of the nation." And University of Vermont political analyst Garrison Nelson added, "there are going to be 100 Bernie Sanders running for Congress in 1992."

A child of the tough streets of Brooklyn and the son of a paint salesman, Sanders became active in politics as a student at the University of Chicago in the 1960s, where he led student protests as a member of the Young Socialist League and applied for conscientious objector status during the Vietnam War. He moved to Vermont in 1968, presumably as part of a growing movement of hippies seeking a lifestyle closer to nature, and started his own video production business making educational films. Sanders joined the Liberty Union Party and quickly moved to a leadership position, running and losing four times in state races until 1981 when, as an independent backed by college students, blue-collar workers, and the poor, he burst onto the national scene by winning the Burlington mayoral race by 10 votes.

Sanders was extremely popular in his eight years on that job, proving himself a capable administrator and creating a political organization, the Progressive Coalition, which still dominates Burlington politics today. As mayor, Sanders worked to provide state-run day care centers, shifted away from property taxes toward corporate and hotel/restaurant taxes as means of revenue, and was named by *U.S. News & World Report* as one of the country's top 20 mayors. In 1986 Sanders ran for governor, only to lose, and then in 1988 he again lost his bid for the state's congressional seat, although by only three percent of the vote. He left his job in Burlington in 1989 to concentrate on a second run for Congress in 1990 against incumbent Republican Peter Smith and Democrat Dolores Sandoval. The race essentially boiled down to Sanders, who had become extremely popular with Vermont's independent thinkers, dairy farmers, farmers, loggers, and the poor, against Smith, identified more as a yuppie candidate. Sanders swept the election, winning by 16 percentage points over Smith, and in an otherwise uneventful election year, the socialist congressman from Vermont was suddenly a media darling.

Still, there is some skepticism as to whether Sanders's victory will have any kind of far-ranging impact on national politics. "Is Sanders's election a mandate for strident class politics and third-party candidates?" asked Alexis Jetter in the *Village Voice.* "Or could it happen only in a state whose tiny population commands just one congressional seat, and where diversity is largely limited to the flavors of Ben & Jerry's ice cream?" Quoted in the same magazine, Sanders, an inspired orator with a firm belief that he is at the forefront of a larger wave, had a question of his own: "At a time when the country is $4 trillion in debt, when the people have experienced one enormous scandal after another, when you have a president who's itching to go to war, an enormously growing gap between the rich and the poor, 3 million people sleeping out on the street, and a health-care situation in absolute chaos—how is it conceivable that the left is not making enormous gains from one end of this country to the other?"

Sources

Economist, September 24, 1988; September 22, 1990.
Nation, June 11, 1990.
Newsweek, February 27, 1989.
Village Voice, January 8, 1991.
Washington Post, March 12, 1989; April 1, 1989; September 1, 1990.

—*David Collins*

Arnold Schwarzen-egger

Actor and bodybuilder

AP/Wide World Photos

Full name, Arnold Alois Schwarzenegger; born July 30, 1947, in Graz, Austria; came to U.S., 1968, naturalized, 1983; son of Gustav (a policeman) and Aurelia Schwarzenegger; married Maria Owings Shriver (a television news anchor), April 26, 1986; children: Katherine Eunice. *Education:* B A. in business and international economics from University of Wisconsin-Superior.

Addresses: *Office*—Oak Productions, 321 Hampton Dr., Suite 203, Venice, CA 90291.

Career

Actor; feature films include: (under the pseud-onym Arnold Strong) *Hercules Goes to New York*; (as Schwarzenegger) *Stay Hungry*, 1976, *Pumping Iron*, 1977, *The Villain*, 1979, *The Jayne Mansfield Story*, 1980, *Conan. The Barbarian*, 1982, *Conan, The Destroyer*, 1983, *The Terminator*, 1984, *Commando*, 1985, *Raw Deal*, 1986, *Predator*, 1987, *Running Man*, 1987, *Red Heat*, 1988, *Twins*, 1989, *Total Recall*, 1990, *Kindergarten Cop*, 1990, and *Terminator 2*, 1991. Producer of bodybuilding video tape. Owner of a production company and real estate in Denver and southern California.

Bodybuilding champion from 1965-80; titles include: Jr. Mr. Europe, 1965, Best Built Man of Europe, 1966, Mr. Europe, 1966, International Powerlifting Championship, 1966, German Powerlifting Championship, 1968, International Federation of Body Builders Mr. International, 1968, Mr. Universe (amateur), 1969, National Association of Body Builders Mr. Universe (amateur), 1967, National Association of Body Builders Mr. Universe (professional), 1968-70, Mr. World, 1970, International Federation of Bodybuilders Mr. Olympia, 1970-75, 1980. Chairman of the President's Council for Physical Fitness.

Awards: Golden Globe Award for best newcomer in films, 1976; voted International Star of 1984 by ShoWest.

Sidelights

With a heavy accent and a distinctive bodybuild-er's physique, Arnold Schwarzenegger seemed an unlikely candidate for box office superstardom. But that is exactly the position Schwarzenegger has achieved since his humble beginnings in the movie *Hercules Goes to New York*, where he used the pseudonym Arnold Strong to mask his identity. Although he was already known for his bodybuild-ing titles such as Mr. Universe, and in the documen-tary *Pumping Iron*, Schwarzenegger did not become a success in feature films until he landed the lead role in *Conan, The Barbarian* in 1982. That movie, which grossed more than $100 million worldwide, pro-pelled him into international stardom. During the 1980s, his films grossed more than $1 billion, earning him the title "Superhero to the World." Schwarzenegger's success has not been limited to the movie world, however; he is also a real estate tycoon, owning property in southern California and Denver; he married Maria Shriver, a successful national TV news anchor and one of the Kennedy clan; and he was appointed Chairman of the President's Council on Physical Fitness by President George Bush.

Schwarzenegger came from very humble beginnings. He was born in a small village outside of Graz, Austria, where his house was not equipped with a telephone, flush toilet, or refrigerator until he was fourteen years old. "With that kind of upbringing," commented Schwarzenegger in *Vanity Fair*, "you learn not to take anything for granted." Schwarzenegger's father was a policeman, and his only sibling, a brother, died in an auto accident.

> "*The whole thing was to make bodybuilding hip, to take it out of the sports page or circus page or whatever and have it covered in the regular press.*"

Schwarzenegger claims that it was precisely this lack of material goods that served as his motivation to be successful. He began to look for a way out of his village when he was very young. Schwarzenegger would "daydream about success when I was ten years old. I would dream about America." At age fifteen, he committed himself to bodybuilding. He was soon winning competitions throughout Europe, and by age twenty he won his first Mr. Universe title.

In 1968 Schwarzenegger realized it was time to make a move on his dreams, and he came to America to participate in a Miami Beach bodybuilding contest. He was disappointed to lose in a contest he thought he could win easily, but the trip turned out to have a positive result. The well-known bodybuilder Joe Weider was impressed by Schwarzenegger, and asked him to come to Los Angeles. "I decided to move," said Schwarzenegger. "There was no alternative. The thought of going back to Austria or Germany was not an option. My vision of where I wanted to be in life was *forward*, and Austria would have been backward."

The move marked a turning point in his career. Schwarzenegger, who was already known for his strictness and self-discipline, began to increase his training regimen. He attended school and studied English and business. Weider encouraged him to write articles on bodybuilding and pose for photographs. In the years from 1968 to 1980 Schwarzenegger climbed to the peak of his professional bodybuilding career, eventually accumulating an unheard-of seven Mr. Olympia titles.

Schwarzenegger, however, had his eyes on a bigger goal—he wanted to reach a larger audience, a movie audience. At a Mr. America contest in 1972, he met George Butler and Charles Gaines, who were interested in making a bodybuilding documentary called *Pumping Iron*. They were duly impressed with Schwarzenegger's physique. "Arnold is like the Matterhorn," Gaines commented. "We didn't discover him, we just noticed him first."

The notoriety he gained in *Pumping Iron* had an unusual side effect—it put Schwarzenegger at the forefront of the high society crowd. He posed for artist Jamie Wyeth; was part of a living-art exhibit at the Whitney Museum; and he modeled for Andy Warhol pieces. Schwarzenegger used his increased visibility to promote his sport. "The whole thing was to make bodybuilding hip," he claimed, "to take it out of the sports page or the circus page or whatever and have it covered in the regular press."

Popularizing bodybuilding wasn't the only goal in Schwarzenegger's career. Before *Pumping Iron*, he had made a disastrous feature movie called *Hercules Goes to New York* under a pseudonym. Despite the movie's poor showing, the experience had an effect on defining Schwarzenegger's career goals. "Everyone in the business told me to lose my name, my accent and my shape," he commented in the *Chicago Tribune*. "But, far from limiting me, I think all that helped me to be unique. No one could ever tell me I looked just like another actor or sounded like someone else. So after using another name in my first movie, I decided to just go with my real name and be myself. I wanted to be successful on my own terms."

Not wanting to star in another flop, Schwarzenegger got to know Dino De Laurentiis and was eventually cast in De Laurentiis's adaptation of the comic-book hero, Conan, The Barbarian. *Conan* became a bit hit, making $100 million around the world. Schwarzenegger's successive action/adventure movies—*The Terminator, Conan, The Destroyer, Commando,* and *Raw Deal*—were also hugely popular, marketing the Schwarzenegger image and propelling him into international superstardom in the course of a few years.

As a departure from the strong man role, Schwarzenegger starred in the film *Twins*, a comedy adventure that paired him with diminutive actor Danny De Vito, with whom he formed a couple of mismatched and misplaced twin brothers. The film was a big success, proving that Schwarzenegger could be just as popular in lighter roles as he was playing superheroes. Schwarzenegger admits that this kind of role may be more in tune with his real personality: "I feel much more comfortable with gentle scenes than violent ones," he said in *Premiere*. "When I studied with [acting coach] Eric Morris, I was always much better with lovey-dovey talk than with dialogue when I'm mad and angry. I had the most trouble where I had to scream and hit everyone, because I'm not that way myself."

Since *Twins*, Schwarzenegger claims to have retired from one-dimensional strongman parts. In *Total Recall* he plays instead an interesting dual role: that of a simple construction worker with a hidden identity in this science fiction psychological thriller. About the film, Schwarzenegger commented in the *Chicago Tribune*: "It's very strange and bizarre, and as much about the nature of reality and dreams as it is an action film. It's definitely got a Hitchcock feel to it, and having to play two totally different characters was a big challenge for me."

It was Schwarzenegger's hard work, spanning the course of several years, that got *Total Recall* released. He purchased the script from Dino De Laurentiis and found the right production team and cast. He did most of this simply because he liked the plot and was intrigued by the lead role. About Schwarzenegger's performance, Georgia Brown wrote in the *Village Voice* that his portrayal of the character was well-intentioned, if flawed: "In the beginning, when he's supposed to be a slightly thick, memory-erased construction worker, Schwarzenegger conveys a gen-

Arnold Schwarzenegger, in his role as president of the President's Council on Physical Fitness and Sports, meets with President George Bush at the White House in January 1990. AP/Wide World Photos.

tle, passive pathos. But as his character expands and grows potent, there's need for interior growth."

Schwarzenegger's discipline and hard work showed during the production of this movie, which was made under difficult conditions in Mexico. The star expressed his feelings about the hard work involved in movie-making in *Premiere:* "I don't care what it takes. You can scream at me, call me for a shot at midnight, keep me waiting for four hours. As long as what ends up on the screen is perfect." This is an attitude Schwarzenegger learned from sports: "You go back to the gym and you just do it again and again until you get it right," he said in *Vanity Fair.*

Schwarzenegger's personal life has been as high-profile as his career. In 1986 he married television news anchor Maria Shriver, and became part of the Kennedy clan, "America's putative royalty," commented Iain Blair in the *Chicago Tribune.* He and Shriver frequently appear at charity functions near their Pacific Palisades, California, home. "I love to schmooze," said Schwarzenegger in *Vanity Fair* about his many social appearances. In 1990, the couple's first child, Katherine, was born. "Becoming a father for the first time has definitely changed me, and for the better," he admitted in the *Chicago Tribune:* "Having a baby really does make you aware of how others depend and rely on you. A new baby is so helpless and so vulnerable and you feel protective and want to make sure it grows up the right way and is well loved and looked after."

Schwarzenegger's non-movie pursuits include real estate investing and politics. He has parlayed his movie income and some shrewd real estate speculating into a fortune of over $50 million. He campaigned for Republican presidential candidate George Bush during the 1988 elections, in spite of his relationship with the Democratic Kennedy clan. Bush named him chairman of the President's Council on Physical Fitness for his help, a position Schwarzenegger calls "a fun challenge." Schwarzenegger has tackled this appointed post with the tireless zeal and salesmanship that he displays in the rest of his career.

Rejecting claims that his work on the Council is simply a launch pad for a future political career, Schwarzenegger said: "Right now, I'd be crazy to go into politics. I've got my movie career, my businesses, and most of all my wife and baby daughter to look after. That's quite enough—even for me." In his work on the Council, he has traveled to schools around the country, posing for pictures, signing autographs, and generally spreading the message that fitness is good. "Fitness has to be marketed like a vehicle or a TV set or a movie," he said in *Vanity Fair.* "We have to say, 'It's hip to be fit. That's it. Read my hips. No more fat.'" Overall, Schwarzenegger seems to be the embodiment of the American Dream ideal that if you work hard and are disciplined, you will be successful. He wakes up every morning at six a.m. and goes to the gym. "I do not miss a day. It keeps me in check," Schwarzenegger indicated. "Bench-pressing three hundred pounds will always be bench-pressing three hundred pounds. That will never change, no matter how much money I have or how famous I am." The actor is also supremely self-confident, and kind and tolerant of his adoring fans. "Arnold's confidence is not surprising, if you consider what he's accomplished," said *Total Recall* director Verhoeven. "After all, he did what seemed impossible. He was not a logical choice for fame. But Arnold's drive and his charm made him different. It made him a star."

Writings

Arnold: The Education of a Bodybuilder, 1977.
Arnold's Bodyshaping for Women, 1979.
Arnold's Bodybuilding for Men, 1981.
Arnold's Encyclopedia of Modern Bodybuilding, 1985.

Sources

Chicago Tribune, May 27, 1990.
Premiere, June 1990.
Vanity Fair, June 1990.
Village Voice, June 12, 1990.

—*Nancy Rampson*

Norman Schwarzkopf

AP/Wide World Photos

United States Army general

Full name, H. Norman Schwarzkopf; born August 22, 1934, in Trenton, N.J.; son of H. Norman Schwarzkopf Sr. (a career military officer); married Brenda Holsinger (a flight attendant), 1968; children: Jessica, Christian, Cynthia. *Education:* U.S. Military Academy at West Point, B.S. in engineering, 1956; attended United States Army War College, Carlisle Barracks, Pa., 1972-73.

Addresses: *Office*—U.S. Army Central Command Center, MacDill Air Force Base, Tampa, FL.

Career

Joined the U.S. Army in 1956; major assignments include: two tours of duty in Vietnam, 1965-66, with an airborne infantry unit, and 1969-70, as executive officer to the chief of staff at United States Army headquarters and as commander, First Battalion, 6th Infantry, 198th Infantry Brigade, 23nd Infantry division; Office of Personnel Operations, Washington, D.C., chief of Professional Development Section, Infantry Branch, 1970-72; Office of the Assistant Secretary of the Army, Washington, D.C., military assistant, 1973-74; deputy commander, 172nd Infantry Brigade, Fort Richardson, Alaska, 1974-76; commander, 1st Brigade, 9th Infantry Division, Fort Lewis, Wash., 1976-78; deputy director for Plans, United States Pacific Command, Camp H. M. Smith, Hawaii, 1978-80; assistant division commander, 8th Infantry Division (Mechanized), in Europe, 1980-82; director of military personnel management, Office of the Deputy Chief of Staff for Personnel in Washington, D.C., 1982-83; command-

ing general, 24th Infantry Division (Mechanized) and Fort Stewart, Fort Stewart, Ga., 1983-85; assistant deputy chief of staff for Operations and Plans, Washington, D.C., 1985-86; commanding general, I Corps, Fort Lewis, Wash., 1986-87; deputy chief of staff for operations and plans/army senior member of Military Staff Committee, United Nations, Washington, D.C., 1987-88; promoted to general in November 1988; general, U.S. Army Central Command Center, MacDill Air Force Base, Tampa, Fla., 1988—.

Awards: Numerous military decorations include two Distinguished Service Medals, three Silver Stars, Distinguished Flying Cross, three Bronze Star Medals, two Purple Hearts, and three Meritorious Service Medals; honorary knighthood conferred by Queen Elizabeth II, 1991.

Sidelights

As a commander you have to walk that difficult balance between accomplishing your mission and taking care of the men and women whose lives have been entrusted to you,'' said the four-star army general who led allied forces to victory in the Persian Gulf, becoming the first bona fide U.S. military hero since the era of General and President Dwight D.

Eisenhower. At 6'3" and 240 pounds, the general is a grizzly bear of a man with a teddy bear side, a rare blend, as *People* magazine (who quoted him above) put it, of "martial mastery and human sensitivity."

"I don't consider myself dovish and I certainly don't consider myself hawkish," General Schwarzkopf told Eric Schmitt of the *New York Times*. "Maybe I would describe myself as owlish—that is, wise enough to understand that you want to do everything possible to avoid war then be ferocious enough to do whatever is necessary to get it over with as quickly as possible in victory."

> *"I gotta tell you, a soldier doesn't fight very hard for a leader who is going to shoot him on a whim."*

As he commanded an allied force of over 500,000 troops in a quick mop-up of Iraqi forces, the commander emerged as a TV-ready hero perfect for the nightly news—a smooth composite of traditional and contemporary concepts of masculinity and leadership. "Norman Schwarzkopf is America's hero," trumpeted *20/20*, ABC-TV's news magazine show. Described in appearance as a "fatherly meatpacker" by *Newsweek*, a "230 pound pussy cat" by one supermarket tabloid, and "Stormin' Norman" by innumerable headline writers, the General seemed to spend most of his time in the aftermath of the Persian Gulf war explaining himself to America. "I've been scared in every war I've ever been in," he told Barbara Walters, who interviewed him on *20/20*. "Any man who doesn't cry scares me a little." A second-generation general, he told *Insight* magazine's Richard Mackenzie that his first priority in the war was protecting the well-being of his troops: "I have loved soldiers since my first platoon, the first I ever commanded."

Although Iraqi resistance crumbled faster than expected, the general did not claim tactical genius in orchestrating the victory. Although he was able to keep the enemy in the dark about allied troop position, he attributed victory largely to the poor quality of Iraqi military leadership, training, and morale. The enemy's forces, he said to *Newsweek*'s Tom Mathers, simply were inadequate. "This was a lousy outfit. Lousy." His famous one-word answer

when asked his opinion of Iraqi dictator Saddam Hussein? "Hah."

After the war ended Schwarzkopf had a more elaborate description. Ticking off Saddam's deficiencies on the fingers of one hand, the general declared the Iraqi commander was "neither a strategist, nor is he schooled in the operational art, nor is he a tactician, nor is he a general, nor is he a soldier." Having run out of fingers, he added sarcastically, "Other than that he is a great military man." Schwarzkopf also blamed Saddam's penchant for shooting his own soldiers. "I gotta tell you," he remarked to *Newsweek*, "a soldier doesn't fight very hard for a leader who is going to shoot him on a whim."

Earlier in the war, especially at moments when the United States' victory seemed less than certain, the general displayed the four-star temper he tried to keep under wraps. Reporters who wrote stories he thought were less than favorable suddenly found their access to sources had dried up as fast as rainfall in the desert sand. One reporter who questioned Schwarzkopf's battlefield tactics got his answer fired back in the form of a question; "You ever been in a minefield?" Despite his thin skin for bad press, and little taste for what he saw as an argumentative and ill-informed media disdainful of security issues, he displayed a sure touch when he did see a use for the media. Dramatically dropping to his knees when he arrived to liberate Kuwait and bottling Kuwaiti sand to take home to his family, Schwarzkopf set a new definition of photo opportunity. On network prime-time TV he told Barbara Walters he would not rule out running for President: "Never say never."

> *"The outcome of the Vietnam War was a political, but it was not a military defeat."*

Born in Trenton, New Jersey, in 1934, the future war hero grew up an army brat, the only son of World War I general Herbert Norman Schwarzkopf (his father decided against passing on the name Herbert). The elder Schwarzkopf was between army stints when his son was born, serving as the founding commander of the New Jersey state police. In this capacity he had tracked down and arrested Bruno Richard Hauptmann, convicted of murder in the celebrated Charles Lindbergh baby kidnapping case, and the notoriety had brought him a weekly spot as narrator of a popular radio program, *Gangbusters*. One of his son's earliest memories is staying up late to listen to the broadcasts.

When world war broke out again, his father rejoined the Army. The remaining Schwarzkopf household was predominantly female, a fact the future general recalls as bearing no small impact on his developing personality. "I wasn't your normal, tough, macho young boy," he told *Insight*. "Maybe it was the influence of my mother and my sisters, the fact that I had this responsibility on my shoulders. I can remember being pushed around a lot. I can't really say why. I learned to hate the bully. I learned to hate the playground group that went around pushing other people around. I never ran with that bunch as a young boy." Later on he boarded at the Bordentown Military Institute near his hometown.

After the war ended his father was shipped out to Iran to establish a police force for the Shah, a strong ally. Young Norman went over to join his father in Teheran, and stayed several months before the rest of the family came over. He recalls being impressed by the admiration his father received from his subordinates. He himself admired his father as a war hero, much like General Eisenhower. "My father was a very honorable man," he told *Insight*. "He epitomized the best [West] Point graduate of his day that's totally committed to a sense of duty, totally committed to a sense of honor, totally dedicated to his country, and a selfless servant."

He did have another role model: Alexander the Great. He told Charlayne Hunter-Gault of public television's *MacNeil/Lehrer NewsHour*, "When I was a young man, everything was shades of black and white, and Alexander the Great was one of my heroes, because he conquered all the known world by the time he was twenty-eight." (His more enduring role models are two later generals, Ulysses S. Grant and Creighton Abrams, the latter his Vietnam commander, "because they didn't worry about who got the credit. They just got the job done.")

Schwarzkopf followed his father on other assignments. The military was helping to rebuild Europe under the Marshall Plan, and the general was shuttled from country to country for the next five years; first Italy, then Germany, then Switzerland. His classmates included Iranians, displaced Jews, Germans, Italians, Yugoslavians, and various other ethnic groups and nationalities. The experience permanently broadened his mind, he recalled years later to *Insight*. "I came to understand that you judge a person as an individual. I also learned that the American way is great, but it's not the only way. There are a lot of other ways things are done that are just as good, and some of them are better."

He eventually returned to the United States and entered West Point, as his father had done before him. He graduated 42nd out of 485 in the class of 1956. Upon graduation he joined the army as a second lieutenant in the infantry, attending the Infantry Officer Basic course and Airborne School at the Army's Infantry School at Fort Benning, Georgia. In March 1957 he was sent to Fort Campbell, Kentucky, where he served as a platoon leader and later as an executive officer in the 2nd Airborne Battle Group, the 187th. That assignment lasted about two years.

In July 1959 Schwarzkopf was sent to Germany for a year to serve as a platoon leader in the 6th Infantry. The following year he was named aide-de-camp to the commanding general of the Berlin Command. In September 1961 he shipped back to Fort Benning to

General Norman Schwarzkopf and Saudi Arabian King Fahd stand at attention during the king's visit to review U.S. and allied troops in Saudi Arabia in January of 1991. AP/Wide World Photos.

continue advanced infantry officer training, then enrolled at the University of Southern California in Los Angeles and pursued a master's program in guided missile engineering, graduating in June 1964. He returned to West Point and taught in the department of Mechanics for a year.

Then came the Vietnam War. In June 1965 he was sent over with an airborne brigade and served his 300 days' duty in what the army calls an "advisory capacity." He returned to a staff job in Washington, then returned to West Point to resume teaching there. He was back in the classroom as a student the next year, this time at General Staff College at Fort Leavenworth, Kansas. He returned to army headquarters for another staff job supporting efforts in Vietnam, then in December 1969 shipped over there for a second tour of duty as commander of the 1st Battalion, 6th Infantry, 198th Infantry Brigade of the 23rd Infantry Division. During this stint he was awarded two Purple Hearts and three Silver Stars.

His reputation, however, was tarnished by casualties, including eight deaths, that occurred as a result of "friendly fire" from U.S. artillery. The callous way the army handled the incidents gave rise to a public sense that the army had lost control over the situation. Form letters that went out under the name of Lt. Colonel Schwarzkopf implicated him in the debacle. The incidents were recounted in the book *Friendly Fire*, published in 1976, and fictionalized by Hollywood in a feature film that appeared soon thereafter.

Schwarzkopf returned home from Vietnam livid over the way Washington had handled its part of the entire war effort. The war, he felt, had been lost by the politicians on the battlegrounds of the media. He told *Insight*'s Richard Mackenzie, "The United States military did not lose the war in Vietnam period. In the two years I was in Vietnam I was in many battles. I was never in a defeat—came pretty close a couple of times, but we were never defeated. The outcome of the Vietnam War was a political defeat, but it was not a military defeat."

Back in Washington, the soldier alternated administrative work and advanced military and technical training for several years. In October 1974 the lieutenant colonel was made deputy commander of the 172nd Infantry Brigade in Fort Richardson, Alaska, was appointed a full colonel in 1975, and made commander of the First Brigade, 9th Infantry Division, in Fort Lewis, Washington. He retained that post nearly two years.

In July 1978 he was sent to Hawaii to serve two years at the Pacific Command post at Camp H. M. Smith; when he returned to Washington he was made a general. In August 1980 he shipped out to Europe for two years, as assistant division commander of the 8th Infantry Division. Back in Washington he handled administrative work for a year, then was assigned to Fort Stewart, Georgia, as deputy commanding general of the 24th Infantry Division. From this post he served as deputy commander of the U.S. invasion of Grenada.

Schwarzkopf's high-visibility performance in Grenada did not escape attention from the Pentagon. After another year of staff work he was assigned to I Corps at Fort Lewis, as commanding general. Then, in August 1987, he returned to the capitol as senior army member of the Military Staff Committee of the United Nations. In November 1988 he was appointed full general and moved to the top of the U.S. Central Command. In this capacity he began planning U.S. military strategies in the event of a Persian Gulf showdown.

Much of the general's popularity rests on his family-man image. The general is married to the former Brenda Holsinger, whom he met at a West Point football game in 1967, when she was a 26-year-old TWA flight attendant. The couple married in 1968; they have three children plus a sizable household menagerie: a black Labrador retriever, a cat, a gerbil, and two parakeets. According to an account in *People*, the General's hobbies include hunting and fishing; dining on a thick cut of steak, rare, followed by Breyer's mint-chocolate chip ice cream. He likes to watch TV, tuning in *Jeopardy!* and *Cheers* as well as Clint Eastwood westerns and Charles Bronson flicks. To this list, he says, you can add opera. (During his senior year at West Point he conducted the academy choir.) The difference between conducting music and troops, he quipped to a *People* reporter, is that in war "the orchestra starts playing, and some son of a bitch climbs out of the orchestra pit with a bayonet and starts chasing you around the stage."

Sources

Periodicals

Insight, March 18, 1991.
New York Times, January 28, 1991.
People, March 11, 1991.
The Progressive, January 1991.

Television broadcasts

MacNeil/Lehrer NewsHour, PBS, October 10, 1991.
20/20, ABC-TV, March 17, 1991.

—Warren Strugatch

Monica Seles

AP/Wide World Photos

Professional tennis player

Surname is pronounced "*Sell*-iss"; born c. 1974, in Novi Sad, Yugoslavia; daughter of Xarolj Seles (a former cartoonist and documentary filmmaker; now Seles's coach).

Address: *Home*—Bradenton, Florida.

Career

Won Yugoslav 12-and-under girls championship at age nine, and European 12-and-under championship at ten; named Yugoslavia's sportswoman of the year, 1985. Turned pro in 1989; won Italian and German opens, and first Grand Slam title, French Open, all 1990; ranked Number One female tennis player by the Women's International Tennis Association, 1991.

Sidelights

Monica Seles is finally getting more attention for her tennis playing than for her on-court grunts and off-court giggles. The teenager, a native of Novi Sad, Yugoslavia, is part of a fresh breeze invigorating women's tennis; she is often grouped with two other up-and-comers—Arantxa Sanchez-Vicario and Gabriela Sabatini. "The three S's have shown they have the gumption to go after [top-ranked Steffi] Graf relentlessly.... Clearly, Seles looms as the single greatest threat to Graf," said Steve Flink in *World Tennis.* "The lefty, with two-fisted strokes off both sides, overflows with confidence and a sense of limitless possibilities. Her ground game is devastatingly potent and her will to win is almost tangible."

Seles's celebrated noises of exertion have been compared to the squawk of a goose having its neck wrung, a hyena's screech, a pig, and a monstrous, unfinished sneeze. In June of 1989 *Sports Illustrated* analyzed her trademark sound effects thus: "Her strokes are accompanied by a bewildering array of guttural yowls that seem to vary in timbre according to the situation. For a lob she employs the basic gasping, quick whoosh cry, while a lunging backhand drive requires a four-syllable jungle squeal." The magazine later compared Seles's laugh to Woody Woodpecker's.

Sports Illustrated also recounted that at the age of nine Seles won the Yugoslav 12-and-under girls championship; a year later she won the 12-and-under European championship, and in 1985 was named Yugoslavia's sportswoman of the year. By then she had caught the eye of Nick Bollettieri, coach to, among others, American phenomenon Andre Agassi. Seles enrolled in Bollettieri's tennis academy in Bradenton, Florida, on scholarships. Her parents soon gave up their jobs in Yugoslavia and relocated to a Bradenton apartment.

In May of 1990 Seles beat superstar Martina Navratilova in the Italian Open and Graf in the German Open. A month later she defeated Graf in the French Open to become, at 16, the youngest player to win a Grand Slam event since Lottie Dod won Wimbledon in 1887. According to *Sports Illustrated*, Seles then had a bitter parting with Bollettieri. Her father, Xarolj, a former cartoonist and documentary filmmaker, took over as her coach. The Seles family claimed that Bollettieri had neglected Monica to concentrate on Agassi; they also insisted that Xarolj had been coaching Monica all along. Bollettieri countered the Seles' accusations with assertions that he had turned down an offer to coach American rising star Jennifer Capriati because he felt an obligation to Seles.

From the time she turned pro—in early 1989—to June of 1990, Seles climbed from Number 88 to Number 3 and grew roughly six inches to 5'9". Although this growth spurt added to her power, it required her to relearn the game from a "lofty vantage point [that] gave her new angles from which to sight her shots," observed *Sports Illustrated*. Seles ended 1990 with a 54-6 record—second only to Graf—and winnings totaling $1.63 million. This accomplished, it seems she need not worry about her legacy. After her 1990 Grand Slam win she fretted: "I didn't want to go into the history books 20 years from now and have people read, "She was a great grunter, a great giggler and had a lot of hair."" In February of 1991 Seles became the number-one-ranked female tennis player in the world.

Sources

People, July 2, 1990.
The Sporting News, August 17, 1990.
Sports Illustrated, August 22, 1988; June 19, 1988; June 18, 1990; May 27, 1991.
Tennis, April 1990.
World Tennis, March 1990.

—*David Wilkins*

Ayrton Senna

Race car driver

Full name, Ayrton Senna da Silva; born c. 1960 in Sao Paulo, Brazil; son of an industrialist; married and divorced c. 1980.

Career

Race car driver, 1981—. Formula Ford driver in Europe, 1981-82; Formula Three driver, 1983-84. Joined Formula One circuit, 1984, racing with Toleman in 1984, Lotus in 1985, and McLaren Honda in 1988. Currently star racer with McLaren Honda. Formula One World Champion, 1988 and 1990; has achieved pole position in Grand Prix races more than 53 times.

Sidelights

Ayrton Senna is the fastest driver in the history of Formula One racing. An intense competitor who has dominated the pole position over the past three years, Senna is a constant winner in a deadly sport where a mistake of a fraction of an inch can mean disaster. Senna was the Formula One World Champion in 1988 and 1990, earning a reputation for aggression on the track and obsessive concern for his vehicles off the track. Not one to indulge in small talk with the media, he told *Sports Illustrated* that his success can be credited to "good chassis, good engine, good manager, good mechanics, good organization, . . . good work."

Few competitions of any kind are more dangerous than Formula One racing. The sport follows a

AP/Wide World Photos

worldwide circuit, with stops in America—in Detroit and Phoenix—Japan, Australia, and, of course, the famous Monaco Grand Prix. Unlike the standard speedway races more popular in the United States, the Formula One races follow crazy courses—sometimes through city streets—with blind corners, fast curves, hairpin turns, hills, tunnels, and even the occasional manhole cover. It is not uncommon for a Formula One driver to shift gears more than fifty times during one lap. Formula One drivers can average speeds of up to 80 miles per hour, and sometimes faster, in high-powered, computerized machines that can reach 140 degrees in the cockpit. Drivers must concentrate at every moment on the road ahead of them, the performance of their cars, and the moves of their opponents. Formula One competitors can lose eight pounds in the course of a race.

Sports Illustrated contributor Sam Moses wrote: "Senna, 30, is probably the most complex world champion in the history of Grand Prix racing. Certainly he is the most obsessed . . . . Senna is a concentration machine. So dedicated is he to his pursuit of speed that he seemingly rejects all else, including consideration of others. Rude and arrogant are adjectives that are often applied to him. He seems to have no time for anyone who can't show him how to go faster."

An obsession with speed has been part of Senna's life almost since he was born. The son of a millionaire industrialist, he was raised in Sao Paulo, Brazil. His indulgent parents gave him his first motor-powered vehicle at the age of four. "I was actually driving when I was 4," Senna told *Gentleman's Quarterly.* "Braking, putting my foot on the throttle—it's still that feeling of speed and pushing the limit that I like most."

As long as he kept his grades high in school, Senna was allowed to race go-karts. In his late teens he qualified for the World Karting Championships in Europe, competing in 1979, 1980, and 1981. Twice he finished second and once fourth, but he was not satisfied with anything but absolute victory. He almost gave up racing entirely when he married in 1980, but the marriage soon dissolved, and he returned to Europe to muscle his way into Formula One.

Senna began his professional career in Great Britain in Formula Ford races. He won 13 of 18 starts in 1981 and absolutely dominated Formula Ford in 1982. He spent 1983 on the British Formula Three circuit, blazing such a spectacular path that he was courted by Formula One the following year. He signed with Toleman, a lesser-known sponsor trying to make inroads into the competitive field. *Car and Driver* correspondent David Phipps noted: "At that stage, people were just beginning to take Toleman seriously. They took Toleman and Senna *very* seriously when Senna finished second . . . at Monaco." In fact, Senna almost won the Monaco Grand Prix that year, and might have done so if the race had not been halted by rain.

At the end of 1984 Senna moved to the Lotus team. He won his first Grand Prix in April, 1985. Most observers agree that Senna would have had more success with Lotus had he not been plagued with car trouble so often. Despite his close collaboration with designer Gerard Ducarouge, Senna found himself in a sophisticated machine that somehow never seemed to make the most of its powerful engine. Still, Senna

Ayrton Senna steers his McLaren-Honda while leading the 49th Monaco Formula One Grand Prix in May of 1991. AP/Wide World Photos.

won two races each year for Lotus and took 16 pole positions between 1985 and 1987.

In 1988 Senna faced the most important decision of his career. He chose to move to the McLaren Honda team, one of Formula One's strongest. Doing so, however, put him on the same team with Alain Prost, the Formula One World Champion in 1985 and 1986 and the driver with the most victories in the history of Formula One. Even before they became teammates, little love was lost between Prost and Senna. Close association only deepened their animosity, and in the late 1980s many Formula One races became duels between the two McLaren superstars. Phipps wrote: "In deciding to move to McLaren for 1988, Senna knew he was facing the ultimate examination. Prost was well established there, well liked, and acknowledged by many as the world's best driver, so anything less than the championship for Senna would constitute failure. Like Prost, Senna is clearly not one to avoid challenges." Senna and Prost clashed constantly, but not often with more spectacular results than in the 1988 Grand Prix of Monaco. In that race, Senna carried a commanding lead into the final laps. Rather than acknowledging his sure defeat, Prost turned up the heat and posted the fastest lap time of the race on the fifty-seventh lap. Taking up the challenge, Senna pulled off two record-breaking laps before his pit crew begged him to relax and cruise to the victory. Finally Senna did pull back, but a split-second lapse caused him to catch a rail with his tire and crash. Prost won the race.

"It was my fault," Senna remembered in *Car and Driver*. "I knew from the pits that Alain would not push. I was not concentrating and I just touched the barrier on the inside. I lost grip of the wheel, and before I could catch it back I had hit the barrier on the outside. There was nothing I could do about it." Despite this disappointing loss, Senna came back to win the Formula One World Championship in 1988, earning more points than any other Formula One driver. Between them, Prost and Senna won 15 of a possible 16 victories on the Formula One circuit that year.

"Perhaps the most remarkable thing about Senna's championship year is the fact that Prost allowed him to join the McLaren team in the first place," Phipps declared. "As the most successful Grand Prix driver of all time, Prost could justifiably have demanded that he be given unchallengeable number-one status—guaranteed in writing and enforced by a journeyman number-two trailing behind into a series of second places—in which circumstance Prost could possibly have won all sixteen races! Instead, he accepted Senna's presence on the team as a challenge, and still came very close to beating him."

Eventually, however, that challenge began to wear thin. In 1989 at the San Marino Grand Prix, Senna sucker-passed Prost in the first lap and went on to win the race. Afterwards, Prost charged his teammate with violating an agreement they had reached not to pass each other on the first lap. Later that year, at the Suzuki Grand Prix in Japan, Senna jammed his car into Prost's, knocking the Frenchman out of the race. Senna finished, but was later disqualified and fined $100,000 for bad-mouthing the judges' decision. McLaren paid the fine, and Senna released a retraction of his remarks, but Prost was not satisfied. Prost quit McLaren and moved to Ferrari, convinced that his former sponsor had begun to favor the more aggressive Senna.

Senna has won far more races than friends on the Formula One circuit. Some of his fellow drivers have characterized him as ruthless and threatening. Michele Alboreto of the Ferrari team told *Gentleman's Quarterly*: "Get alongside [Senna] and he'll drive straight into you. This business is dangerous enough as it is. All he's doing is making enemies. I might forgive him if I liked him. But I don't." Sam Moses summed up the general opinion on Senna: "In the selfish world of Formula One drivers, Senna is far the most selfish on the track. He believes that other drivers should give way, simply because he is who he is. They should know he will be there. Such an attitude is blindly self-centered and unrealistic, yet it has undoubtedly been a key factor in what is a brilliant career."

Having knocked Prost from the McLaren team and having won the World Championship in 1988 and 1990, Senna offered no apologies for his tactics. "You can win a race fighting fairly or unfairly," he told *Gentleman's Quarterly*. "It's whatever ground rules you and the other drivers decide to play by."

Senna is certainly a risk-taker who constantly pushes himself and his machine to the very limits. He is also single-minded in his pursuit of victories. Few drivers in the history of the sport have spent more time conferring with mechanics, engineers, and designers than Senna does. He arrives early at the track and stays late, paying few visits to the glittering parties along the Formula One circuit. McBride concluded: "While some drivers . . . are laid back to the point of snoozing in the pit lane, Senna is coiled tight as a clock spring. Force him to ease off and his skin crawls."

This attitude—combined with a visible reluctance to speak to the press—has made Senna an unpopular champion everywhere but in his native Brazil. One of his fellow drivers even went so far as to suggest that Senna's lack of interest in women meant that he was gay, a charge the champion emphatically denies. In fact Senna is a devout Catholic who claims that he has seen Jesus during races. When he does relax, he prefers to return to Sao Paulo and the company of his family.

With the backing of Formula One's strongest sponsor and a string of daring victories behind him, Senna now commands more than one million dollars per race. He has no plans to leave the sport any time soon. Senna told *Car and Driver:* "I will retire when I no longer enjoy it, but obviously I do not know when that will be." He added: "You know I don't need the money!"

Sources

Car and Driver, February 1989.
Gentleman's Quarterly, November 1988.
Motor Trend, August 1987.
Road and Track, April 1989; August 1989; February 1990.
Sports Illustrated, June 29, 1987; June 27, 1988; March 19, 1990; March 18, 1991.

—Mark Kram

Al Sharpton

AP/Wide World Photos

Civil rights leader and minister

Full name, Alfred Sharpton; born in 1954 in Brooklyn, N.Y.; mother's name, Josephine; married Kathy Jordan (a civilian employee of the U.S. Army), 1983; children: two daughters. *Education:* Graduate of Tilden High School; attended Brooklyn College.

Addresses: *Home*—116 St. Marks Place, Brooklyn, NY. *Office*—Slave Theatre, Brooklyn, NY.

Career

Ordained minister at age 13; youth director of Operation Breadbasket, 1969-70; director of National Youth Movement, later renamed United African Movement, 1970-c.86.

Sidelights

To critics, he is known as "Al Charlatan" or "Rev. Soundbite," a rabble-rousing racial ambulance chaser who never met a video camera he didn't like. To others he is a voice for the disenfranchised, an intelligent, articulate activist who knows how to play the media to get his point across for the underclass. Either way, the Reverend Al Sharpton has emerged as a voice that people listen to—even if they don't like what they hear. Sharpton, a Pentecostal minister without a parish, uses his theatrical style and inflammatory rhetoric to make himself as familiar a front-page figure as New York City residents Donald Trump and Leona Helmsley. The self-declared civil rights leader injected himself into many of the city's stickiest issues—the Tawana Brawley case, the Bensonhurst racial murder trial, the Bernhard Goetz shooting—often making himself part of the controversy.

Even Sharpton's harshest critics admit he touches a nerve by tapping into a vein of black discontent with white society. Revelations that would devastate other leaders, such as the news that Sharpton secretly worked as an FBI informant and tape-recorded conversations with blacks, rarely stick to Sharpton because they merely confirm the view of his supporters that the white media and the white criminal justice system are out to get him.

Sharpton is "a creature of the New York media," Wilbert Tatum, publisher of New York's black newspaper, the *Amsterdam News*, told *Newsday*. "When they saw Al Sharpton, who was articulate, fat and wore jogging suits, with a medallion around his neck and processed hair, they thought that he would be the kind of caricature of black leadership they could use effectively to editorialize without editorializing at all . . . While white media were using Al as a caricature, he was organizing the troops to do what respected black leadership could not do: speak to the issues without fear or favor, and use media in the process. Media thought they were using Al, and Al was using media."

On January 12, 1991 Sharpton was stabbed in the chest minutes before he was to lead a protest march through a predominantly white Brooklyn neighborhood where a black teenager was slain by a mob of white youths two years earlier. In stable condition at the hospital the next day, he did something typical—he called a press conference. As *Esquire*'s Mike Sager wrote, "Sharpton has been defined by his sound bites, nine or 10 seconds of the most explosive rhetoric the reporter or TV producer can find. Of course, Sharpton comes from a tradition of hyperbole; he started preaching in the Pentecostal church at age four."

Born in the Brownsville section of Brooklyn where he still lives, Sharpton was drawn to the spotlight at a young age. He says that he decided early on to become a preacher, and began delivering sermons before entering kindergarten. By 13, he had become an ordained Pentecostal minister and was known as "the boy wonder," preaching gospel in local churches and accompanying entertainers such as Mahalia Jackson on national religious tours.

Sharpton graduated from Brooklyn's Tilden High School, a classmate and friend of longtime major league baseball player Willie Randolph. He briefly attended Brooklyn College before dropping out. Sharpton's father was a well-off contractor who bought a new car each year. But when Al was 10, he told the *Los Angeles Times*, his father deserted the family, forcing his mother to work as a cleaning woman and go on welfare. After his father left, Sharpton attached himself to a series of father figures, from U.S. Congressman Adam Clayton Powell to Jesse Jackson to singer James Brown.

In 1969 Jackson, then a young Chicago minister, named the 14-year-old Sharpton as youth director of his group, Operation Breadbasket. Around the same time, Sharpton grew close to Brown, whose son, a friend of Sharpton's, had been killed in a car accident. "He sort of adopted me," Sharpton told the *Washington Post*. "He lost a son, didn't have a father, so he made me his godson." Brown hired the stout teenager as a bodyguard, and introduced him to his business agents. Before he even finished high school, Sharpton was working in the concert promotion business.

Brown introduced Sharpton to two other people who would figure prominently in his life. One was backup singer Kathy Jordan, whom Sharpton met in 1972 and married in 1983. (Together they have two daughters, and Jordan now works for the U.S. Army.) The other was boxing promoter Don King, whom Sharpton met in 1974 while promoting a Brown concert that coincided with the Muhammad Ali-George Foreman heavyweight title fight. Soon, Sharpton was seen at the ringside of major prize fights. Years later, Sharpton and King would team up to win a $500,000 contract to promote Michael Jackson after threatening to organize a boycott of Jackson's concert tour because of lack of minority involvement.

> *"How did [Martin Luther King, Jr.] establish his leadership? By marching, by putting people in the streets. Tell me when in the history of the civil rights movement the goal wasn't to stir things up."*

In the early 1970s Sharpton founded the National Youth Movement, an organization with the stated purpose of fighting drugs and raising money for ghetto youth. As the 16-year-old director of the organization, Sharpton made his first newspaper headlines in 1971 by urging black children in Harlem to participate in the African celebration of Kwanza instead of traditional Christmas events. The organization was later renamed the United African Movement, which Sharpton touted as a charitable anti-drug group with 30,000 members in 16 cities. But Victor Genecin, a New York state prosecutor, told the *Washington Post* that the group was "never anything more than a one-room office in Brooklyn with a telephone and an ever-changing handful of staffers who took Al Sharpton's messages and ran his errands."

In 1974 Sharpton again made headlines when he led a group of older black leaders into a meeting with New York City's deputy mayor to protest the police shooting and death of a 14-year-old black youth. The meeting was prompted by a Sharpton-led demonstration of 500 people at City Hall. Later in the decade Sharpton began experimenting with protest tactics of disorderly conduct. He was arrested for the first time in 1970 after a sit-in at New York City Hall to demand more summer jobs for teenagers. Later, he was ejected from a Board of Education meeting after sitting in front of the board president during a protest. Another time, he led a group along Wall Street, painting red X marks on office buildings he claimed were fronts for drug dealing. Sharpton told the *Washington Post* he borrowed such tactics from Martin Luther King, Jr. "How did King establish his leadership? By marching, by putting people in the streets. Tell me when in the history of the civil rights movement the goal wasn't to stir things up."

By and large, however, Sharpton was not known beyond his Brooklyn neighborhood. That changed in 1984, when he led the demands for a murder indictment for white subway gunman Bernhard Goetz, who shot four unarmed black teenagers he said were trying to rob him. Goetz was indicted on a murder charge but acquitted on all but minor gun charges. As Goetz's trial unfolded, Sharpton led daily protests on the courthouse steps, often finding his way onto the nightly news.

Sharpton gained national prominence with his tactics in the 1986 Howard Beach racial killing. In that case, three black men leaving a pizza parlor in the community were assaulted by a group of bat-wielding white youths. One black man died when he was chased into traffic and run over by a car. Sharpton led a "Days of Outrage" protest that shut down traffic on the Brooklyn Bridge and halted subway service in Brooklyn and Manhattan. A year later, he tied himself to the case of 15-year-old Tawana Brawley, an upstate New York girl who claimed she was raped by five or six white men, one of whom had a police officer's badge. Sharpton, as one of Brawley's three "advisers," publicly accused several officers of the crime and persuaded Brawley not to cooperate with the state investigation. Eventually, several inquiries strongly indicated Brawley had fabricated the entire incident.

Sharpton "seemed utterly out of control, likening the state attorney general to Adolph Hitler and demanding the arrest of Duchess County officials without a shred of proof," wrote the *Philadelphia Inquirer*'s Claude Lewis. "Both Brawley and Sharpton proved to be among the saddest of figures, using their talents at deceit to fool the public. They thought that by merely being mysterious they could bamboozle us. They refused to speak specifics about the case and employed mysticism to enhance charges of racism to put the authorities in a defensive position. Both proved to be virtuosos at distorting reality. They are brazen people with no scruples." Sharpton remains unrepentant about his role in the Brawley case. "We don't let nothing slip through the cracks, and that case is still unresolved," he told the *Los Angeles Times*. "We've only won when we hit the streets and stay out in the streets and keep this town in disruption."

To the amazement of many, Sharpton survived his curious role in the Brawley affair, as well as revelations in 1988 that he was an informant for the FBI. Sharpton confirmed that for five years he secretly supplied federal law enforcement agencies with information on Don King, reputed organized crime figures, black leaders, and elected officials.

In 1989 and 1990 Sharpton again beat the odds, prompting *Newsday* columnist Murray Kempton to compare him to "a cat who has nine lives. He just keeps surviving." First, Sharpton beat a tax evasion rap, which he called a government vendetta. Then, in 1990, he was acquitted on charges that he pocketed more than half of the $250,000 he raised through the National Youth Movement. At the beginning of the case, Sharpton wrote to the grand jury: "Since I was a young child, I was a minister. I know no other life than serving others and allowing God to take care of me. I never owned a car, house, jewelry, etc. My intent is my causes, not wealth."

Sharpton's most recent cause was Yusef Hawkins, a black 16-year-old who was killed by a bat-wielding mob in Bensonhurst in August 1989. The murder stunned New York, which was already beset by spiraling racial tensions. To many New Yorkers it symbolized a breakdown in racial civility that had no quick explanation or readily available cure. Hawkins's father, Moses Stewart, called Sharpton for help the day after the murder. "I wanted someone who was going to take my plight and scream for justice," Stewart told the *Washington Post*. "I didn't want anyone to come to me with a compromise. I wanted the world to know that my son was murdered because he was black. This is what Sharpton does. He brings it to the forefront."

Sharpton led protest marches through Bensonhurst and led a group standing a noisy vigil outside the courtroom where two white teens were being tried for Hawkins's murder. Not-guilty verdicts, Sharpton told *Time* magazine, would be "telling us to burn down the city." Eventually, one of the teens was convicted for the murder.

On January 12, 1991, while preparing to lead a march in that same Bensonhurst neighborhood to protest the light sentence given to Hawkins's killer, Sharpton was attacked by a man who stabbed him in the chest. The attack occurred in front of more than 15 supporters and 100 police officers. Sharpton was hospitalized, but officials said his wound was not serious. Michael Riccardi, 27, of Bensonhurst, was immediately arrested and charged with the stabbing.

If Sharpton is a hero to angry young blacks, he is also an embarrassment to some middle-class blacks and a reviled figure in much of the white community. A *New York Daily News* poll found that 90 percent of whites, and 73 percent of blacks, believe Sharpton is harming race relations in New York. Overall, fewer than 15 percent of New Yorkers citywide had a good thing to say about him. Such surveys do not bother Sharpton, however. "My detractors have pulled every trick in the book to try to discredit us," he told the *Washington Post*. "You go through what I call a baptism of fire when you emerge," he said. "If you survive that, you have the possibility of becoming a positive force. If you don't, you wasn't equipped anyway. If I can't take the heat, I have no business in the kitchen."

Sources

Albany Times-Union, April 11, 1990.
Atlanta Constitution, May 12, 1989.
Buffalo News, August 26, 1990; October 15, 1990.
Esquire, January 1990.
Los Angeles Times, September 27, 1989; January 13, 1991.
Miami Herald, July 14, 1989.
Newark Star-Ledger, August 26, 1990.
Newsday (Long Island), January 20, 1988; January 22, 1988; June 22, 1988; January 6, 1989; April 27, 1989; June 30, 1989; May 21, 1990; August 12, 1990; January 13, 1991; January 18, 1991.
Orlando Sentinel, May 25, 1990.
Philadelphia Inquirer, May 24, 1990.
Time, May 28, 1990.
Washington Post, July 14, 1988; September 5, 1990.

—*Glen Macnow*

Jeff Smith

Chef and television personality

Born c. 1939 in Seattle, WA; son of a salesman; married Patty Dailey, c. 1964; children: Channing, Jason. *Education:* Drew University Divinity School, M. Div., 1965. *Religion:* United Methodist.

Career

Ordained United Methodist minister, 1965. Pastor of a church in Tacoma, Washington, 1965-67; University of Puget Sound, Tacoma, campus minister, 1967, university chaplain, 1967-72; owner of a restaurant and cooking school in Tacoma, 1972-83. Host of *The Frugal Gourmet* on Public Broadcasting System (originates from WTTW Chicago), 1983—.

Sidelights

Jeff Smith is arguably the most famous chef in America. Better known as "The Frugal Gourmet," Smith stirs up new concoctions each week on the Public Broadcasting System and has become known worldwide for his nonstop friendly chatter. Smith is an ordained minister who turned a hobby into a livelihood when he began to teach cooking in Tacoma, Washington. Today, through his television show and his bestselling cookbooks, he spreads more than good recipes to the public. *Christian Century* correspondent Pamela Payne Allen noted that on his show, Smith has fun with food, theology, and people. "His watchers may be drawn not just to his witty theologizing, but also to his warm and welcoming countenance," Allen wrote. "His camera person-

Photograph by Mark Ricketts

ality is congenial, chatty and pastoral. His physical presence is beckoning, ingratiating. Both Jeff Smith's personality and his demeanor indicate his commitment to the inclusiveness of the kitchen. He constantly encourages anyone of any age to take up spatula and garlic press."

The name "Frugal Gourmet" is somewhat misleading. In Smith's case, "frugal" doesn't necessarily mean cheap—rather, it indicates a wise use of precious resources. Smith told *People* magazine that, to him, frugal means "you use everything and are careful with your time as well as with your food products. Fresh foods, prepared with care and concern, will result in terrific meals with lower costs." Smith usually uses common ingredients and chooses dishes that can be prepared quickly. He told *Newsweek:* "I attempt to set up situations where you can cook with your family and enjoy it. For the most part these are fun dishes, and they're easy dishes and they're not going to intimidate even junior-high kids."

Smith's earliest experiences with cooking date back to his youth during the World War II. He was born and raised in Seattle, Washington, the son of a salesman. Times were often hard for the Smith family—Smith's parents were divorced when he was a teen, and he describes his father as a "Willy Loman type," referring to the luckless hero of the Arthur Miller play, *Death of a Salesman*. Smith's mother, on the other hand, was industrious—and frugal. Smith told *Christian Century:* "My mother would stand at the counter and argue with herself over a particular piece of meat, or whether she could afford some desired item. She would pick up vegetables that the supermarket decided they couldn't sell (and of course they'd throw them out, they wouldn't give them to people to eat). I remember being mortified!" He added: "As a child I would watch her peel a potato until the thing was damn near nonexistent. Finally, when she had something acceptable, she would set it down and go on to the next one. And she never served us anything except delightful, charming and gorgeous food. But she never threw anything away. That's frugality: you don't feed your garbage disposal better than you feed your children!"

Smith went to college in 1958 and earned his bachelor's degree in 1962. He was accepted at Drew University Divinity School and received his master's degree in 1965. Shortly before graduating he married Patty Dailey, a student from Brooklyn, New York. The couple have two grown sons. Also in 1965, Smith was ordained as a United Methodist minister, and he became pastor of a church in Tacoma, Washington. After two years there, he moved to the University of Puget Sound, where he became university chaplain. A dual interest in cooking and theology followed in short order.

Smith told the *Philadelphia Inquirer:* "When I was a chaplain at the University of Puget Sound—a lot of this was during the late sixties, during the Vietnam War—I realized a lot of my students were starving to death because they were pumping their money into the peace movement. And so I began having feasts regularly at the house and after church on Sunday. Pretty soon, they started coming early, you know, the minute the service was over, they would beat me to the house. And I realized what they wanted was to learn to cook, so we began offering cooking classes along with my regular faculty load." One of Smith's most popular classes was "Food as Sacrament and Celebration," a combination cooking and theology seminar.

Eventually the work load became oppressive, so Smith quit his job as university chaplain and opened a restaurant called The Chaplain's Pantry in Tacoma. There his menus offered scripture verses about food along with the items on sale, and he continued to teach cooking locally. In the late 1970s, the public television station in Tacoma filmed a series on cooking, featuring Smith as "the Frugal Gourmet." The show was immensely popular in Washington state, and it was picked up by the larger and better-funded WTTW-TV in Chicago. The ratings in Chicago were equally impressive, so WTTW took a gamble and hired Smith to do a yearly thirteen-week series of programs. Even though he was recovering from serious heart surgery—and was determined to cut back on his schedule—Smith accepted the opportunity to do the show.

By 1987 *The Frugal Gourmet* was airing nationwide on public television stations and was among the top five most-watched PBS shows. Smith's airy manner drew viewers—many of them men—who never cared for the stuffy Julia Child. "The food snobs put too much pain into food," Smith told *Newsweek*. "I don't use truffles, and I don't buy good caviar. I don't want us to use food products for the sake of snobbery and separation. That's what the Bible means by sin." He added: "My audience goes across the board. Half of it is male, and there are old people, young people, low-income, high-income all over the country. Everybody finds some kind of appeasement to their appetite."

At first Smith brought his viewers simple dishes from many origins, but as his show became more popular he branched into theme series. These allowed him to visit every state in the nation for programs on American cuisine, and more recently he completed a long series of episodes on international cookery. Some of these segments included location shoots at restaurants in such locales as Hong Kong and New Orleans, but they always returned to the now-familiar WTTW set with its dizzying variety of utensils and neat bowls of ingredients prepared ahead of time. Smith has compiled his recipes into several bestselling cookbooks, including *The Frugal Gourmet* and *The Frugal Gourmet Cooks with Wine*.

Payne Allen noted: "Jeff Smith seeks not merely to fulfill our physical hunger—that has for most of us always come readily—but rather to sate our spiritual hunger, the hunger for meaning, through our physical consumption of food. This hunger needs sating *as* we deal with the more complex issues, and doesn't need to hinder our involvement in the latter."

In his own jovial way, Smith admits that he uses his show as a storefront ministry. Food, for him, becomes a classic device for discussing theology. He has been known to express wonder at the Creator's bounty in the form of mushrooms, onions, and herbs, and he constantly stresses the celebratory function of feasting with friends and family. Smith told the *Chicago Tribune:* "The cooking is a front, and

I'm glad it is so blatant. My calling is to relate to families. I keep preaching as best I can about the big problem of our times, the need for family unity. The kids talk to their parents about the stories I tell and the dishes I cook. I encourage the whole family to get involved in cooking and enjoy eating what they cooked together."

In *Christian Century*, Smith even suggested that any ordinary meal can become grace-filled, a time for thanksgiving and relating to God. "One expresses thanks for food," he said, "not because one is happy with the food. That's bad theology. That would mean that you would pray over a beautiful prime rib and Yorkshire pudding, but not over macaroni and cheese. That's cheap theology! We pray to give thanks for the fact that each time we sit down we realize again that we are totally dependent upon the King of the universe."

Most of Smith's shows look entirely spontaneous, if somewhat hectic and giddy. Although he has a substantial technical staff—and a number of aides who help him prepare the food for each shoot— Smith works without a script, improvising comments as he proceeds. In many cases, mistakes and hesitations are left in the episodes, because Smith likes his work to be alive and anxiety-relieving. *Chicago Tribune* contributor William Rice wrote: "As far as one can tell, for all the technical talent on hand, Jeff Smith truly is the Frugal Gourmet, both on camera and off. There is no entourage of managers, writers, hand-holders. It is his concept, his recipes. He selects many of the props, organizes the set and suggests shots and even camera angles.... The shows look fresh, real and unrehearsed because they are."

Smith admits that he has had the time of his life being "the Frugal Gourmet." Fans accost him on the street everywhere in America, his cookbooks regularly top the bestseller lists, and his work for WTTW leaves him with precious spare time to spend with his family. "My ego's the size of a moving van with a trailer," he said. "If Heaven is any more agreeable than this, I wouldn't be able to deal with it." He told the *Philadelphia Inquirer* that even though his professional path has been unusual, he feels he has remained faithful to his ordination as a cleric. "We talk about theology a great deal," he said of his shows. "I do it kind of, if you'll pardon the expression, under the table! But everyone knows what I'm up to, and they really seem to appreciate this."

Writings

The Frugal Gourmet, Morrow, 1985.
The Frugal Gourmet Cooks with Wine, Morrow, 1986.
The Frugal Gourmet Cooks American, Morrow, 1987.
The Frugal Gourmet Cooks Three Ancient Cuisines: China, Greece, and Rome, Morrow, 1989.
The Frugal Gourmet Desk Diary, Morrow, 1989.
The Frugal Gourmet Cooks Your Immigrant Heritage: Recipes You Should Have Gotten from Your Grandmother, Morrow, 1990.

Sources

Chicago Tribune, January 29, 1987; February 28, 1988.
Christian Century, December 2, 1987.
Newsweek, March 9, 1987.
People, February 23, 1987.
Philadelphia Inquirer, January 17, 1988; February 22, 1989.

—*Mark Kram*

David Souter

U.S. Supreme Court judge

Full name, David Hackett Souter; born September 17, 1939, In Melrose, Mass.; son of Joseph Alexander (a bank manager) and Helen Adams (a gift shop clerk; maiden name, Hackett) Souter; single; no children. *Education:* Harvard University, B.A., 1961, LL.B., 1966; Rhodes Scholar at Oxford University, 1961-63. *Politics:* Republican. *Religion:* Episcopalian.

Addresses: *Home*—34 Cilley Hill Rd., Weare, NH 03281. *Office*—Supreme Court Building, Washington, DC.

Career

Orr & Reno (law firm), Concord, N.H., associate, 1966-68; State of New Hampshire, assistant attorney general, 1968-71, deputy attorney general, 1971-76, attorney general, 1976-78; associate justice of the Superior Court of New Hampshire, 1978-83; New Hampshire Supreme Court justice, 1983-90; judge on the United States First Circuit Court of Appeals for New Hampshire, 1990; United States Supreme Court justice, 1990—.

Awards: Honorary master's degree from Oxford University, 1989.

Member: Phi Beta Kappa.

Sidelights

David Souter, the most recent addition to the United States Supreme Court, is an enigma to friends and foes alike. Dubbed the "Stealth candi-

date" when he was nominated for a vacant seat on the nation's highest court, Souter came from a relatively obscure background and offered little evidence—in writings or statements—of how he might vote on crucial Supreme court cases. Nevertheless, the unpretentious federal judge was placed onto the high court by an impressive 90 to 9 Senate vote. All constitutional scholars agree that the Harvard-trained Souter could exercise great power over the country's laws for the next quarter century.

Time magazine correspondent Margaret Carlson wrote: "No one knows quite what to make of a man who has a life, not a lifestyle, who lives modestly, works hard, spends inconspicuously, attends church, enjoys solitude, honors his mother, and helps his neighbors." Carlson added that with such a background, Souter "may be the answer to [President George Bush's] secret moderate dreams: someone conservative enough to allay right-wing suspicions that he has been insufficiently sympathetic to their causes but at the same time unknown enough to keep liberals from finding anything on which to hang another bruising confirmation fight." Indeed, liberals and conservatives alike will wait anxiously to see how Souter votes on such crucial issues as abortion rights and affirmative action. *Time* contributor Richard Lacayo commented that Souter "has said and written so little about major constitutional issues that it is almost impossible to determine how he might rule on them."

Souter was born in Massachusetts in 1939, but he considers New Hampshire his home. His family moved there when he was 11, settling in tiny Weare, a town near the state capital of Concord. Both of Souter's parents held jobs—his father was an assistant bank manager, his mother a clerk in a gift shop—and Souter attended public schools. Carlson noted that in high school the future justice "managed to be well liked despite being something of a grind—voraciously studious, fastidiously neat, with no time for organized sports." In his senior year, Souter served as president of the National Honor Society and co-editor of the yearbook. He was also voted "most likely to succeed."

> "I am glad that I can have an aspiration for America which is as good as the circumstances that I came from."

During his confirmation hearings in September of 1990, Souter told the Senate panel that growing up in a small town made him "intimately aware of other lives . . . lives that were easy and . . . lives that were very hard." *U.S. News and World Report* further quoted the justice on his personal feelings about race relations. "Never once . . . did I ever hear my mother or my father refer to any human being in terms of racial or ethnic identity," Souter said. "I am glad that I can have an aspiration for America which is as good as the circumstances that I came from." Those modest circumstances may seem obscure to the country at large, but Souter has always had a warm following in his home state. *Newsweek* correspondent Aric Press stated: "In his part of the New Hampshire outback, Souter has been a source of local pride for decades."

After high school Souter attended Harvard University, where he majored in philosophy. His senior thesis explored the judicial theories of justice Oliver Wendell Holmes, especially the jurist's belief that a judge should not be influenced by either politics or ideology. Souter graduated *magna cum laude* and was made a member of Phi Beta Kappa. He also won a prestigious Rhodes Scholarship for study at Oxford University in England. There he continued to study philosophy, history, and sociology. Classmates remember him as quite studious but nonetheless friendly and adventurous.

In 1963 Souter returned to the United States and enrolled at Harvard Law School. *Time* reporter Dan Goodgame wrote that while reading for a law degree, "Souter played the role of courtly gentleman, wearing a three-piece suit to parties and telling stories in his strong New England accent." He did not make the law review, but he did graduate with impressive credentials.

Good Harvard-trained attorneys rarely have trouble finding jobs. Souter chose to return to Weare, and was hired as an associate to the firm of Orr & Reno. He soon discovered that he did not care for private practice, so in 1968 he joined the New Hampshire attorney general's staff in Concord. His quiet scholarship and thoroughness soon earned him the attention of Warren Rudman, who became New Hampshire's attorney general in 1970. Rudman promoted Souter to deputy attorney general in 1971—in effect making him a top aide—and when Rudman won a Senate seat in 1976, Souter replaced his mentor and became attorney general himself. He was 37 at the time.

Press noted in *Newsweek* that as New Hampshire's attorney general, Souter "ran a respectable, meticulous office." Armed with a wealth of legal information—some of it dating back into the 17th century—Souter mounted powerful arguments, often at the behest of the governor. He won a case for the state when the federal government tried to claim jurisdiction over an inland lake, but he was unsuccessful in his attempts to prosecute New Hampshire residents who for religious reasons covered up the state motto—'Live Free or Die'—on their license plates. What Souter did manage to do as attorney general was to provide a very slim profile of his own ideological bent. A *Nation* editorial contended that his record shows "complete support for the reactionary Governor Meldrim Thomson, an almost unvarying hostility to the rights of the accused and no sign of sympathy for women or other groups on society's short end." On the other hand, Goodgame claimed that Souter "seems to have been acting as a lawyer putting forth the best argument he could on behalf of his client."

Souter served as New Hampshire's attorney general from 1976 until 1978, and was then appointed to the state's Superior Court. There too he remained relatively non-controversial—Press claimed that as a trial judge "his record suggests that he sees the judiciary as an institution with limited powers." This tendency not to "legislate from the bench" is a standard conservative view. From the Superior Court Souter moved to the New Hampshire Supreme Court in 1983. He sat on that bench for six years, but few of his opinions allowed insight into how he might decide in a case such as *Roe vs. Wade*, the controversial case that legalized abortion in the United States.

Souter had only recently been promoted to the U.S. First Circuit Court of Appeals when U.S. Supreme Court justice William Brennan announced his retirement. As always, the sitting president nominates a successor to the high court, so George Bush quickly began to consider eligible candidates. *People* magazine suggests that president Bush was alerted to Souter by White House chief of staff John Sununu, himself a New Hampshire native. Officials of the Bush administration found Souter attractive because he was "virtually unknown, a man without tracks [who] couldn't be hunted down by Senate Democrats," to quote Press.

A "virtual unknown" may prove to be a surprise even to his backers, however. Some observers feel that Bush and Sununu have acted more or less on a hunch where Souter is concerned. Some doubt remains, however—especially on the touchy abortion issue. One White House staff member told *Newsweek:* "Neither side can find anything to support their pre-beliefs, so they're all nervous." Throughout his confirmation hearings, Souter refused to reveal his personal feelings about issues such as a woman's right to choose an abortion. He did say that personal experience counseling a fellow Harvard student faced with that dilemma taught him "what is at stake on both sides" of the debate.

One source of controversy in Souter's case is his marital status. Women's groups in particular have suggested that the solitary, bookish Souter lacks experience with the everyday problems of ordinary people, since he himself is a bachelor. Several women who have dated Souter have spoken in his defense on that matter, however. Former girlfriend Ellanor Fink told *Time:* "Having never married, I know everyone is wondering does he have the empathy to understand women's issues. He's not all brain. He's a friendly, warm person and extremely considerate."

Souter showed little of that warmth during his confirmation hearings, but he did handle the tough and often personal questions with great dignity. *Newsweek* correspondent Bob Cohn claimed that throughout a barrage of questions on civil rights, the First Amendment, abortion rights, and the right to privacy, Souter "retained his composure and impressed the committee members as gracious, thoughtful and modest." Cohn continued: "Sitting ramrod-straight and staring earnestly at each senator in turn, Souter spoke without notes on dozens of issues, displaying an impressive knowledge of constitutional law and an uncanny memory for the dates and details of events in his own past." In the end, Souter practically sailed through his confirmation, satisfying both liberals and conservatives with his quiet intelligence.

Souter was sworn in as a Supreme Court justice in October of 1990. Cohn contended that the newest justice is a "studiously enigmatic man" who is now in a position "to reshape the law and the court." The startling change in his career has led Souter to move his modest belongings—and mounds of books—from his family home in Weare to an apartment near the Supreme Court building in Washington, D.C. While the nation awaits his important votes on cases that could overturn abortion rights and curb affirmative action, Souter maintains that he will exercise every ounce of his heart and mind to get his rulings right. He told *Newsweek* that all judges realize the gravity of their missions. "At the end of our task," he said, "some human being is going to be affected, some human life is doing to be changed."

Sources

Nation, October 8, 1990.
Newsweek, August 6, 1990; September 24, 1990.
People, August 6, 1990.
Time, August 6, 1990; September 24, 1990; October 15, 1990.
U.S. News and World Report, September 24, 1990.

—*Anne Janette Johnson*

James Spader

AP/Wide World Photos

Actor

Born in 1960 in Boston, Mass.; son of Todd and Jean Spader (both teachers); married wife, Victoria (a set designer), 1987; children: Sebastian. *Education:* Attended Phillips Academy preparatory school.

Addresses: *Home*—Cape Cod, MA, and Hollywood, CA. *Agent*—Interantional Creative Management, 40 West 57th St., New York, NY 10019.

Career

Began studying acting in New York City, c. 1977; worked at numerous odd jobs, including those of busboy, messenger, stablehand, and yoga instructor; landed role in first feature film, *Endless Love,* 1981; subsequent films include *Tuff Turf, The New Kids, Pretty in Pink, Mannequin, Baby Boom, Wall Street, Less Than Zero, Jack's Back, sex, lies, and videotape, Bad Influence,* and *White Palace.*

Awards: Named best actor at the Cannes Film Festival, 1989, for performance in *sex, lies, and videotape.*

Sidelights

Atalented, resourceful character actor, James Spader emerged in the 1980s as part of a group of young film stars that the Hollywood press—in many ways unfairly—dubbed the "Brat Pack." All handsome, charming, and seemingly self-absorbed, such actors as Spader, Rob Lowe, Charlie Sheen, Andrew McCarthy, Robert Downey Jr., and to a lesser extent Sean Penn and Michael J. Fox, were frequently cast in roles that accentuated the greed and shallowness of the typical 1980s "yuppie." Often, the films they appeared in were poorly written, badly directed, and indeed performed without depth or subtlety. Almost always, the films were blasted by critics and yet successful at the box office, a fact which confounded the critics and sharpened their attacks against the upstart stars, whose every boyish prank, all-night party, and temper tantrum made great fodder for the gossip columns.

But the "brat" stigma never quite stuck to Spader, and as his career moved into a new phase in the 1990s with more mature, leading roles, it became apparent that what the critics had missed in all those sophomoric movies Spader appeared in was that he was actually *acting.* Which is not to say Spader could not be convincing as a spoiled, shallow punk—only that by 1989 his work was finally being recognized for its craft rather than its content. "There was a time in James Spader's career when he portrayed the excesses of yuppie scum more regularly and with more bravado than did any other actor in the movies," wrote Trip Gabriel in *Gentlemen's Quarterly (GQ).* "In *Baby Boom,* he was a smarmy young exec who stole Diane Keaton's job. In *Wall Street,* he was a corporate lawyer who succumbed to insider trading.

Even when he wasn't wearing a yellow tie, Spader managed, in *Less Than Zero*, to suggest the eerie parallels between a Machiavellian yuppie and a predatory coke dealer. His roles were a catalogue of the worst sins of the 1980s."

And if the 1990s are to be, as many predict, the deserved hangover of that decadent, booming decade presided over by President Ronald Reagan, then Spader's breakthrough role in the lauded 1989 film *sex, lies, and videotape* may have helped to sound the wake-up bell. In fact, it is interesting to note that director Steven Soderbergh was just 30 years old himself when this, his first feature film, debuted at the prestigious Cannes Film Festival. Soderbergh's penetrating psychological drama won the Golden Palm Award as best film that year, and Spader was sprung into fame when he walked away with the festival's best actor award for his portrayal of Graham, a detached, impotent drifter who could only become sexually aroused while watching women talk about sex on videotape. As *Los Angeles Times* critic Sheila Benson wrote of Spader's performance in the film: "Blond and quiet spoken, Spader is open, disingenuously inquiring, almost a '60s throwback—the sort who takes pride in his lack of possessions . . . If there is something intense about him that puts people off-balance, there is an equal quality that makes them trust him. Especially women."

Here was a character quite unlike anything that had appeared on the screen for some time; and equally unlikely was Spader in that particular role—up to this point he had almost become typecast as a sneering California punk in a pastel suit. It is almost as if Spader the snake had shed his skin, revealing a new, more vulnerable surface. Even *Esquire* magazine, itself a significant contributor to the self-absorbed, orgiastic mentality of the 1980s, could not help but notice that something different was going on. "Spader's Graham is a sharing-caring kinda guy, a sex symbol for the Michael Steadman [a character on TV's *Thirtysomething*] crowd," *Esquire* reported. "The movie is about communicating and not communicating, about how people will do anything to avoid touching each other . . . with both Graham and the movie finally leaving the stultifying Eighties behind, the film will strike a chord with those suffering from an excess of postmodern anomie and brat-pack films." In many ways Spader's Graham seemed to hold up a mirror to an entire generation. He is full of realizations about himself that for a long time had escaped him. "I'm a pathological liar," Graham admits, and later, when the brunt of his pathetic delusions and disaffectedness finally reach home, Graham offers, almost in disbelief, "I have a

lot of problems." The revelation is so subtly ironic that Spader almost seems to be awakening from a dream—an apt image for Soderbergh's metaphor.

In many ways, Spader's own personal maturation and development as an actor followed the same path as his screen persona. Although by 1990 the actor had become a mysterious recluse, even retreating to his Massachusetts hometown to live in his grandparents' old house, Spader was in many ways a guru for the young Hollywood film-star crowd and hangers-on that became so prevalent in the 1980s. By most accounts he was wilder than any of them, but with one important distinction—for Spader the binge years seem to have paid off with a corresponding level of experience, while for many of his crowd it was a time of shallow posing. "It was a strange period in my life," Spader told *GQ*. "And I . . . indulged the strangeness to great lengths . . . . Everybody goes through periods where they're experimenting in their dark corners." Many of Spader's high times during those years revolved around an apartment house on Hollywood Boulevard, where he lived with, among many others, fellow actor Eric Stoltz. "Jimmy used to play the role of older brother to a lot of us," Stoltz told *Playboy*. "Jimmy's a very peaceful man. He's the sweetest, nicest man in the world. He's just a tad eccentric."

For the most part, Spader avoided other "brat-packers," choosing instead to run with a select, tight-knit group of friends that included Stoltz and agent Gerald Harrington. A blues music fan (he has a collection of over 1,000 albums), Spader would lead his crew into the raunchiest blues clubs from Greenwich Village to West Los Angeles, or to the Seventh Veil, a seedy Hollywood strip joint he liked to frequent. He was also known for taking off in his 1969 Porsche Targa for long road trips, sometimes for weeks at a time, to points all over the United States; and among his more bizarre indulgences was a collection of strange and varied weapons.

While filming *The New Kids* with Spader in Florida, Stoltz recalled for *Playboy*, "Jimmy was at his wildest. We'd take road trips to the Keys or up the coast, and he'd insist on having weapons in the trunk. He'd drive like a maniac—fast, with the music blaring—and I was always living in fear that we'd be pulled over and some officer would find his crossbow, his lance, his twelve-inch knife, his whip." One morning Stoltz woke up to find Spader out in the motel courtyard wearing nothing but his underwear and a leather jacket, firing his crossbow at a palm tree. But according to actress Jennifer Jason Leigh, Spader could be as gracious and magnanimous as he was spontaneous. A perfect evening for Spader, Leigh told *Playboy*, usually involved long, long hours of conversation (which he often tried to dominate), at "great, huge, decadent dinners at the Ivy or Dan Tana's. They last five hours and you leave feeling sick. Jimmy's great at hanging out—not always having to be on the move. He can sit five hours and just talk."

Indeed, by most accounts from those who know him, behind the reclusive public Spader who avoids talk shows, the press, and increasingly nearly everyone else, there is a man who loves to talk. To understand that aspect of Spader, one needs to hearken back to his true-blue Yankee roots in Boston. Both of Spader's parents were private school teachers who encouraged their son and his two sisters to explore whatever they liked—and to *talk* about it. "I think the wonderful thing about his parents is they really allowed all the children to become individuals and choose their own course," Stoltz told *GQ*. "It's a very loving and supportive family. And *loud*. I was there at Christmas one time, and you have to fight for conversation time, and it has to be *loud*. Jimmy's the worst; he's always trying to upstage everyone."

"Spader's hard-boiled atti-tude toward his work echoes that of such person-al heroes as John Huston, Charles Laughton, and es-pecially Humphrey Bogart."

—Trip Gabriel

As a student at the prestigious Phillips Academy prep school in Andover, Spader immediately took to acting; he even performed in a one-act play written by fellow student and now internationally famous stage director Peter Sellars. Acting soon became an obsession for Spader, so much so that he decided another year of high school would be a waste of time. At age 17 he dropped out and moved to New York to study acting, only to go through the usual string of manual labor jobs that most actors must endure before getting a break. He worked as a busboy, a stable hand, a messenger, a janitor, and a yoga instructor at a health club—a job he conned his way into after reading a book on yoga.

It was this last job that brought him in touch with the woman who would become his wife, Victoria; she taught the class immediately after Spader's. As Spader told *Cosmopolitan*, "I think it was just luck that we finally got together—we both just wanted something physical and then we turned out to be the right people for each other." The two became virtually inseparable, and as Spader's career blossomed, he defied the cliche of the typical Hollywood relationship and drew even closer to Victoria, as if further intimacy could keep the press-hounds at bay. "Jimmy and Vickey are this incredibly close couple; they really don't do much without each other," observed friend Harley Peyton in *Playboy*. "They're one of those couples who are completely joined at the heart and the hip. It's not one of those relationships that are based on a kind of odd dependence; I think they just prefer it that way. They nurture each other." The couple lived together for eight years before finally marrying in 1987. In 1989, their first child, Sebastian, was born. The two events, along with Spader's increased public exposure, say friends, served to drive the actor still further into the shelter of domestic life. The partying days have ended; Spader would now rather spend his time alone with his family or with one or two friends. He splits his time between a house in the Hollywood Hills and the one on Cape Cod formerly owned by his grandparents. "It's like pulling teeth trying to get him to leave the house," Stoltz lamented in *GQ*.

But for Spader, his withdrawal from the wild side of life seems to be a composite reaction *away* from the illusory nature of fame and *toward* the more grounded responsibilities of wife, child, and home. It is, in a way, an effective strategy, giving him the protection of family while at the same time adding mystery and romance to his image as a star. Much like Robert De Niro, Spader disassociates his true self from his screen persona by downplaying the importance of his work. "If I don't need the money, I don't work," Spader told *GQ*. "I'm going to spend time with my family and friends, and I'm going to travel and read and listen to music and try to learn a little bit more about how to be a human being, as opposed to learning how to be somebody else."

If this is an affected attitude, as *GQ*'s Trip Gabriel points out, it is not without precedent among past Hollywood stars. "Spader's hard-boiled attitude toward his work echoes that of such personal heroes as John Huston, Charles Laughton, and especially Humphrey Bogart. Like Bogie, Spader affects a grand-scale romantic cynicism," Gabriel writes. But, he adds, "It's hard to know how much of this is a pose. On the one hand, Spader was obsessed enough with making it as an actor to drop out of prep school. On the other hand, he has fled Hollywood and New York to be near his family, in a corner of America where the last thing he's likely to be taken for is a movie star."

What seems to work for Spader is this constant maintenance of an identity separate from what is commonly known as the "movie star," and it works because that distance allows him to inhabit the characters he plays with even more imagination and creativity. He doesn't have to worry about what kind of image he's projecting, or whether his acceptance of a certain role will endanger his delicate star status. He talks about his work in a film as simply a job, to the point where he told Gabriel "every single film I've ever done I've taken because of the money." And this retro-ego trip seems to add validity to his performances. Spader knows that his acting is fresher, more honest, when he treats each role specifically, without pretense and without one eye calculating his next step up the Hollywood ladder.

Even his groundbreaking, award-winning role in *sex, lies, and videotape*, Spader told *GQ*, was a surprise to him. In fact, as the film was being made he confided to friends that he didn't think it would work. Even after the accolades started pouring in he still remained distant from the film's success. "It's a film. It's not the answer to life," Spader told *Esquire*. "I took the film because I was interested in doing that part," Spader added in *GQ*. "Looking at work as stepping stones is something I don't have any time or energy for. It seems a shame to look at your work as some sort of means to an end, because the end is death, you know? The means is the flesh and blood, so you'd better enjoy it. F— the end."

Sources

Cosmopolitan, August 1988.
Esquire, September 1989.
Gentlemen's Quarterly, October 1990.
Los Angeles Times, August 4, 1989.
Playboy, April 1990.

—*David Collins*

John Spong

Episcopal bishop

AP/Wide World Photos

Full name, John Shelby Spong; born June 16, 1931, in Charlotte, N.C.; son of John Shelby and Doolie Boyce (Griffith) Spong.

Career

After entering Episcopal clergy served several parishes in the South; ordained bishop of Newark, N.J., in 1976.

Sidelights

Controversy has followed John Shelby Spong since his election as an Episcopal bishop in 1976. At that time, 70 conservatives argued that Spong was unfit to serve as bishop, *Time* magazine reported, "because he had written, among other things: 'The simplistic claim that Jesus is God is nowhere made in the Biblical story. Nowhere!'" Most of the uproar has surrounded the Newark bishop's views on sex and gender—he advocates for women and homosexual clergy, says sex outside marriage can be holy, and believes monogamous homosexual relationships should be affirmed by the church.

Spong's 1988 book *Living in Sin?* is "probably the most radical pronouncement on sex ever issued by a bishop," *Time* said. "Spong interprets traditional morality as the product of a patriarchal bias. 'Sex outside of marriage can be holy and life-giving under some circumstances,' he writes. Spong argues that most people are likely to break the traditional rules anyway, what with the advent of birth control and modern lifestyles. Since the church wants to counter-act promiscuity, he reasons, it should encourage unmarried people to at least establish committed sexual relationships, while retaining lifelong monogamy as the ideal." And regarding homosexuals, *Time* added, "Spong spurns the biblical literalism of his youth, explaining that St. Paul (who wrote of 'dishonorable passions') did not realize that the inclination is inborn. Spong declares that the church should repent of past 'ignorance and prejudice' and perform ritual blessings of same-sex couples."

In the *National Review*, Richard John Neuhaus said of Spong and his book: "More than most who succumb to the clerical conceit of being prophetically avant-garde, John Spong is dreadfully mean-spirited toward those who disagree with him. His pages are chock-full of exhortations to be loving, sensitive, accepting and open—except to those of a different view. Not once does he seriously address the argument counter to his. In his comfortable narrow-mindedness, he dismisses those who differ as superstitious, tradition-bound, fearful, and captive to the sexist, homophobic, and patriarchal patterns of the past. The most bitter venom is reserved for believing Jews, Roman Catholics, evangelicals, and fundamentalists."

Spong was raised in Charlotte, North Carolina, and decided early to enter the clergy. He completed seminary studies in Virginia and served several parishes in the South. "Spong privately started to rethink sexual morality," *Time* said, "when a parishioner who did not want to divorce his paralyzed wife decided to take up with a widow." "For the first time," Spong is quoted in the magazine, "I faced the fact that it might be more loving and life-giving to have a relationship outside marriage than to be moralistic."

At the 69th General Convention of the Episcopal Church in 1988, Spong was involved in a fray in which conservatives were called legalistic, homophobic, and moralistic, and liberals were accused of trying to redefine sin, said *Christianity Today*. And early in 1989, the Episcopal Church dismissed a set of charges brought against Spong for the second time in two years. "The charges, known as presentments, contended that Spong violated church law in a column he wrote for his diocesan newspaper," said *Christianity Today*. "The column reads in part: 'I covet for all people the joy of being sustained in the fullness of a relationship that unites two persons in mind, body, and spirit, even when that relationship has not been blessed with a service called holy matrimony.' Spong's opponents maintain that this statement violates consecration vows, which call for the denial of 'all ungodliness and worldly lust.'" The presentments were dropped because they were not filed according to proper church procedure.

In February 1991, *Time* said Spong's latest book, *Rescuing the Bible from Fundamentalism*, asserts that some New Testament passages portray Jesus as narrow-minded and vindictive, Gospel writers twisted the facts about Christ's resurrection, the virgin birth is unthinkable, and St. Paul was a repressed homosexual. Spong countered with a letter to the editor calling the *Time* article an inaccurate and misleading account that distorted his words.

"Since he joined the hierarchy," *Time* said in June 1988, "Spong has continued to be a china-breaker in the tradition of the late bishop James A. Pike, the 1960s scourge of Episcopal tradition. Unlike Pike, who underwent a heresy trial and eventually resigned as a bishop, Spong has got little hierarchical heat. He has, however, prompted the creation of Episcopalians United, a 20,000-strong organization of priests and lay people dedicated to maintaining older Episcopal teachings."

Selected writings

Into the Whirlwind: The Future of the Church, Harper, 1983.
(With Denise Haines) *Beyond Moralism*, Harper, 1986.
Living in Sin? A Bishop Rethinks Human Sexuality, Abingdon, 1988.
Rescuing the Bible from Fundamentalism, c. 1990.

Sources

Christian Century, October 24, 1990.
Christianity Today, September 1, 1988; March 3, 1989.
National Review, July 8, 1988.
Newsweek, February 12, 1990.
Time, June 13, 1988; February 18, 1991.

—David Wilkins

Shelby Steele

Ed Kashi/TIME Magazine

Social critic, author, and educator

Born in 1946 and raised in a suburb of Chicago, Ill.; mother was a social worker and father was a truck driver (both parents were also activists); married wife, Rita; children: two. *Education:* Graduated from Coe College, Iowa; attended night school to earn master's degree in sociology; Ph.D. in English literature from University of Utah.

Career

Taught high school in East St. Louis until earning doctorate in English literature; has taught English at San Jose State University since 1969. Author of book of essays, *The Content of Our Character: A New Vision of Race in America*; television appearances include those on *Good Morning America* and *This Morning*. Writer and narrator of public television documentary *Seven Days in Bensonhurst.*

Awards: *The Content of Our Character* was nominated for a National Book Award in January, 1991.

Sidelights

If the crucial American issue of the 20th century is truly the color line, as W. E. B. Dubois pronounced in *The Souls of Black Folks*, then Shelby Steele's controversial observations on racism will continue to impact relations between blacks and whites as the century gives way to the 21st without having yet resolved the very same issues that originally preoccupied Dubois. And that, essentially, is Steele's point. Americans—blacks and white both—are suffering

from what the California professor calls "race fatigue." Blacks, Steele asserts, must begin to define themselves in other than racial ways in order to free themselves from the prison of racism. They must struggle for individual identity rather than inheriting a prepackaged "black" identity defined by white society.

As racial issues emerged in the late 1980s into the nation's consciousness with an urgency missing since the heyday of the civil rights movement, Shelby Steele himself emerged from academic obscurity to become a very audible voice in America's ongoing racial debate. The publication of several provocative Steele essays in leading magazines achieved high visibility among the American reading public. Television watchers discovered the tweedy, cigarette-smoking English professor as he turned up on their TV screens proclaiming that "black need not be the color of entitlement."

Steele's challenge is to what he calls the black establishment's "party line": the view that white society is inherently racist, that all blacks are thereby victimized by racism, and that (white) society must continuously redress these grievances—politically, through giveaways such as affirmative action and minority contract set-asides, and socially by individually acknowledging this guilt in every interracial personal encounter. These policies and attitudes, he says, have outlived their initial usefulness. He writes, "Such policies have the effect of transforming whites from victimizers into patrons and keeping blacks where they have always been—dependent on the largesse of whites."

His essays first reached national audiences through the *New York Times Magazine* and *Harper's*. In the summer of 1990 they and other essays were collected and published by St. Martin's Press under the title *The Content of Our Character: A New Vision of Race in America*. Steele hit the talk show circuit, touting his book and his ideas on ABC's *Good Morning America* and CBS's *This Morning*. He was invited to write and narrate a PBS documentary on the murder of a young black man in Brooklyn, called *Seven Days in Bensonhurst*.

Steele found a supportive audience among the nation's conservative and neo-conservative opinion makers, who were delighted to find an articulate black man—actually, a mulatto—whose own life illustrated that a black could become successful without needing special privileges. Predictably, many black leaders in civil rights, politics, and the arts derided his viewpoint. They dug in at his mixed-race background, sneered at his Silicon Valley lifestyle, and questioned his credentials to generalize about black life. His arguments were dismissed as "slick sophistry" by Martin Wilson, Harvard's first tenured black professor; and "nothing but a conservative viewpoint in black skin," by NAACP executive director Benjamin Hooks, according to *Time*. Roger Wilkins, a Justice Department civil rights lawyer in the 1960s, told the *Washington Post* Steele lacked "intellectual candle-power" and merely provided "comfortable" ideas to the white establishment. Poet/activist Amiri Baraka dismissed him as "a basket case" in a *Newsday* article.

Those adversaries, clearly, have the most to lose from a civil rights "perestroika." Walter Williams, professor of economics at George Mason University in Virginia, defended Steele to *Newsday:* "At least [he is] saying some of the things that have needed to be said for a long time."

Steele, as even his critics acknowledge, defends his viewpoint in a style that is graceful and articulate. Reviewers have already enshrined him in the pantheon of black essayists that includes Dubois, James Baldwin, Martin Luther King Jr., and Frederick Douglass. In the introduction to *The Content of Our Character* he writes: "To retrieve our individuality and find opportunity, blacks today must—conscious-

ly or unconsciously—disregard the prevailing victim-focused black identity. Though it espouses black pride, it is actually a repressive identity that generates a victimized self-image, curbs individualism and initiative, diminishes our sense of possibility, and contributes to our demoralization and inertia. It is a skin that needs shedding."

> *"I have had both to remember and forget that I am black. The forgetting was to see the human universals within the memory of the racial specifics."*

He urges each black to build a personal identity not circumscribed by blackness. The black citizen, "supported by a massive body of law and the not inconsiderable goodwill of his fellow citizens, is basically as free as he or she wants to be. For every white I have met who is racist, I have met 20 more who have seen me as an equal. And of those 20, 10 have only wished me the best as an individual."

Recalling the process of writing the essays, Steele told Paul Pintarich of the *Portland Oregonian:* "I have had both to remember and forget that I am black. The forgetting was to see the human universals within the memory of the racial specifics. One of the least-noted facts in this era when racial, ethnic and gender differences are often embraced as sacred is that being black in no way spares one from being human. Whatever I do or think as a black can never be more than a variant of what all people do and think." He added, "I believe it is time for blacks to begin the shift from a wartime to a peacetime identity, from fighting for opportunity to the seizing of it. The immutable fact of late 20th century life is that it is there for blacks to seize."

Steele's book was widely reviewed in the national media through late summer and fall, 1990. Reaction was mixed. The *New York Times* chose to assign the review to an associate professor at a small midwestern law school who offered the volume a chilly reception. Reviewer Patricia Williams scoffed at Steele's "psychology as politics" and suggested his own experiences, unsupplemented by outside corroboration, offered flimsy proof of his theories. She cites the author's anecdotal evidence of the well-dressed black woman in the predominately white-patronized supermarket in his neighborhood who regularly passes him by without comment. The author interprets her distance as an implied insistence that mutual blackness is in itself insufficient reason to speak. Professor Williams, however, thinks otherwise: "It never occurs to him that maybe she just doesn't like him."

Steele has often encountered strong personal criticism from television and radio panels. Generally he takes a puff from his cigarette and responds in a calm manner. "You can insult me all you want," he told Eleanor Holmes Norton when the former Carter administration Civil Rights Department chief lashed out personally during a National Public Radio debate in 1989. "I find it flattering that people attack me as a middle-class, middle-American because it indicates people who don't like me really do have trouble criticizing [my ideas]," he told *Newsday*'s Gene Seymour.

Shelby Steele and his twin brother Claude, a social psychologist, were born in 1946 to a mixed-race couple steeped in the civil rights movement. His mother, a social worker, and his father, a truck driver, were founding members of the Congress of Racial Equality (CORE). They raised their family in Phoenix, a blue-collar suburb of Chicago, in a household that placed high value on reading and education. Their father, although a high school dropout, was an autodidact and voracious reader. Steele recalled to *Washington Post* staff writer E. J. Dionne Jr., "I grew up in that ethos of CORE—high principled Gandhian activism." When an elementary school teacher's consistently negative comments began to demoralize Shelby, his parents organized a parents' campaign against the teacher.

> ## "I'm not a very political person. Politics bore me to tears."

The brothers attended a segregated school. Steele traces back his racial self-awareness to an incident in which the white mother of a friend criticized his grammar and speech. Steele, then 14, answered that she must be racist to make such a comment. She retorted angrily that she wanted to make him aware of the importance of good speech "so he would not sweat [his] life away in a steel mill." In his book Steele writes: "I was shocked to realize that my comment had genuinely hurt her and that her motive

in correcting my English had been no more than simple human kindness. If she had been black, I might have seen this more easily. But she was white and this fact alone set off a very specific response pattern in which vulnerability to racial shame was the trigger, denial and recomposition the reaction, and a distorted view of the situation the result." In another incident several years later he discovered how easy it was to race-bait whites for financial advantage. He and a friend manipulated a $20 tip for a black custodian by making a white patron feel personally guilty for the custodian's lot in life.

Steele went on to attend Coe College, a small school in Iowa, where he was one of just 18 blacks. With his sheepskin still fresh he set out to teach high school in the slums of East St. Louis. "It's the best teaching experience I've had, in the worst ghetto I've ever been in," he told Dionne. Studying nights he was able to earn a master's degree in sociology. The degree convinced him his true vocation was literature and he went to the University of Utah, where he obtained a doctoral degree in that subject. There he met his future wife, Rita, a psychology graduate student. Upon graduation he obtained a position with the English department of San Jose State; there he has taught since 1969 a section called "Literature and Personality," whose syllabus includes such writers as Primo Levi, Toni Morrison, Ernest Hemingway and Fedor Dostoevski. He also teaches a course in essay writing called "Creative Non Fiction." The essayists he most admires, he told *San Jose Mercury News* book critic Constance Casey, include William Gass, Annie Dillard, Philip Lopate, and James Baldwin.

Steele professes to have little use for more polemical thinkers. "I'm not a very political person," he told Dionne of the *Washington Post*. "Politics bore me to tears." He describes himself as a continued admirer of both Martin Luther King Jr. and Malcolm X, although he thinks the latter's confrontational ideology is no longer suited to advancing the black cause today. He acknowledges voting for presidential candidate Jesse Jackson in 1988, and boasts he's never cast a vote for a Republican. "All I do now is spend my energy saying I'm not a conservative," he chuckles. He says he supports such "liberal" concepts as more early intervention programs for infants, an expansion of Head Start programs, and improved education programs.

Nevertheless Steele continues to face widespread criticism, especially from blacks, that he is "isolated" from the black mainstream, both intellectually and physically. He responds wryly to this in *The Content* of Our Character: "We are the only black family in our suburban neighborhood, and even this claim to specialness is diminished by the fact that my wife is white. For me to be among large numbers of blacks requires conscientiousness and a long car ride, and in truth I have not been very conscientious lately. I only occasionally feel nostalgia [for an all-black environment]. Trips to the barbershop now and then usually satisfy this need, though recently, in the interest of convenience, I've taken to letting my wife cut my hair."

Steele lives with his wife and their two children in what he describes as a bicultural home. Their offspring "know about their Jewish heritage and they know about their black heritage. They know a great deal about black American culture," he told Dionne. As for his own motivations in writing the essays in *The Content of Our Character*, he added, "The reason I write is because I believe in black people. I believe

they can do anything. I believe they can overcome any obstacle. I write out of love."

Sources

Business Week, October 1, 1990.
Chicago Tribune, September 16, 1990.
Emerge, September 1990.
National Review, September 17, 1990.
Newsday (Long Island), October 10, 1990.
Newsweek, September 24, 1990.
New York, May 14, 1990.
New York Times, September 16, 1990.
New York Times Magazine, May 13, 1990.
Portland Oregonian, September 16, 1990.
San Jose Mercury News, August 19, 1990.
Time, August 13, 1990.
Village Voice, May 15, 1990.
Washington Post, December 10, 1990.

—*Warren Strugatch*

George Steinbrenner

New York Yankees co-owner, businessman

Full name, George Michael Steinbrenner III; born July 4, 1930, in Rocky River, Ohio; son of Henry G. (an engineer and shipping industrialist) and Rita (Haley) Steinbrenner; married Elizabeth Joan Zieg, May 12, 1956; children: Henry G. III, Jennifer Lynn, Jessica Joan, and Harold Zieg; *Education:* Williams College, Williamstown, Mass., B.A. in English, 1952; *Religion:* Christian Scientist.

Addresses: *Home*—Tampa, Fla. *Office*—Am Ship Building Co., 2502 Rocky Point Rd., Tampa, FL 33607.

Career

Assistant football coach at Northwestern University, 1955, and Purdue University, 1956-67; Kinsman Transit Co. (became Kinsman Marine Transit Co.), treasurer, 1957-63, president, 1963-67, director, 1965—; president, American Ship (Am Ship) Building Co., president and chairman of the board, 1967-78, chairman of the board, 1978—; principal owner of the New York Yankees, 1973—; owner of Bay Harbor Inn, Tampa, Florida, 1988—. Member of the board of directors of Great Lakes International Corp., Great Lakes Associations, Greater Cleveland Growth Association, Cincinnati Sheet Metal & Roofing Co., Nashville Bridge Co., Nederlander-Steinbrenner Productions.

Awards: Named Man of the Year by Cleveland Press Club, 1968.

Sidelights

On July 30, 1990, Baseball Commissioner Fay Vincent ended a tumultuous era in the recent history of the game with the decree, "Mr. Steinbrenner will have no further involvement in the management of the New York Yankees." After 17 years, 19 managers, 15 general managers, 32 pitching coaches, and 10 public relations directors, George M. Steinbrenner III was finally himself whisked out the perpetually revolving door of the Yankees' front office. The man whom *Newsweek*'s August 6, 1990 cover trumpeted as "The Most Hated Man in Baseball" was in baseball no more. Back in 1973 Steinbrenner had taken control of sport's most storied franchise and quickly returned it to greatness. But after winning four American League pennants and two world championships by 1981, the franchise saw its decline begin anew, crashing to baseball's bottom in 1990, when the team posted its worst record since 1912. As team management prepares to address its present problems, it does so without Steinbrenner, banished from the Yankees' day-to-day operations because of payments made to an alleged gambler.

A Yankee from the start, George Michael Steinbrenner III was born on the fourth of July, 1930, in Rocky River, Ohio, a few miles west of Cleveland. His parents' personalities were quite opposite, and each consequently had a different effect on his development. His mother, Rita, a devout Christian Scientist of Irish descent, was a caring, compassionate woman to whom George was very close. Dick Schaap, in his biography *Steinbrenner!*, writes that from his mother "George acquired a sense of compassion, a feeling for the underdog." But it was his father whose values dominated.

Henry M. Steinbrenner was a strict disciplinarian who demanded the best from his son and two daughters. Once when George was running track in high school he finished first in two events and second in a third, his father angrily asked, "How could you let that guy beat you?" In 1981 Maury Allen of the *New York Post* asked a psychiatrist friend for an instant analysis of Steinbrenner. "It seems a classic case of a filial relationship with a strong father," the psychiatrist opined. "His aggressiveness, toughness and meanness to his employees all come from his inability ever to please his father." The elder Steinbrenner instilled in his son a tremendous work ethic and a huge drive to succeed—at any cost. George often quotes his father's credo: "Always work as hard as, or harder than, anyone who works for you."

Although Henry Steinbrenner had built a comfortable living at the helm of the Kinsman Marine Transit Company in Cleveland, he did not give young George an allowance; instead he gave him chickens. At the age of nine, George started the George Company, selling eggs door to door for spending money. It became the S & J Company five years later when George went off to military school and passed the fledgling dairy business on to his sisters Susan and Judy. George attended the Culver Military Academy near South Bend, Indiana, and was involved in many sports there, baseball not among them.

After graduating from Culver, Steinbrenner enrolled at Williams College in Massachusetts. At Williams, Steinbrenner was a C student, but was an active one. He was captain of the track and field squad, served as sports editor of the paper, played in the band, and ran the glee club. In the summers, Steinbrenner learned his father's shipping business from the bottom up. After graduating with an English degree in 1952, Steinbrenner joined the Air Force, was commissioned a second lieutenant, and assigned to Lockbourne Air Force Base near Columbus. He headed the sports program at Lockbourne and fed his entrepreneurial appetite, setting up a coffee-cart stand that grew to six pick-up trucks serving about 16,000 military and civilian personnel daily. After his 1954 discharge came what Steinbrenner told *New York* was "my happiest time"—the football years.

Following a year of postgraduate study in physical education at Ohio State University, where he met future wife Joan Zieg, Steinbrenner began a brief career as an assistant football coach, much to his father's dismay. He spent a year each at Northwestern and Purdue, then moved back to Cleveland and the shipping business in 1957 with his new bride. But he didn't lose his zeal for the sporting business. In 1960, against his father's advice and wishes, Steinbrenner led a group of investors in the $125,000 purchase of the Cleveland Pipers, an AAU basketball team playing in an industrial league. As he would later with the Yankees, Steinbrenner took his basketball team extremely seriously, ranting after losses, and blasting newspaper editors who gave the team scant coverage. In just two years the league and the Pipers had folded and Steinbrenner lost over a quarter of a million dollars.

By 1967 Steinbrenner and Kinsman Marine Transit were successful again, despite Henry Steinbrenner's predictions that the best days of Great Lakes shipping were over. The younger Steinbrenner assembled a group of investors that bought a third of the shares of the American Ship Building Company, and he was named president. Under Steinbrenner's leadership, the Am Ship fleet grew in size and scope and soon became the dominant grain carrier on the Great Lakes. Steinbrenner bought Kinsman and merged it with Am Ship and, more significantly, purchased an old shipyard in Tampa that within a decade became a $23 million drydock capable of handling 85 percent of the world's bulk cargo fleet. In ten years, Am Ship tripled its revenues and net worth, and quadrupled its assets. Steinbrenner's personal wealth grew such that he was able to buy back Kinsman and restore it to the family, temporarily talking his father out of retirement to run it. "Finally," writes Dick Schaap, "he had his father working for him."

As Steinbrenner's power and wealth grew, so did his reputation for being a tough boss and a generous benefactor to charities, particularly in helping underprivileged students get through college. One of Steinbrenner's contributions turned out to be the blackest mark on his record until the scandal which resulted in his 1990 ouster from baseball. In 1972 he illegally contributed to Richard Nixon's reelection campaign using corporate funds and bogus employee bonuses. In 1974, he pleaded guilty to two felony counts and was fined $15,000—seemingly a slap on the wrist. But then-commissioner Bowie Kuhn slapped harder, suspending him from baseball for 15 months.

Through his financial rise of the late 1960s and early 1970s, Steinbrenner maintained his interest in sports ownership. He purchased an 860-acre horse farm in Ocala, Florida, and formed a syndicate to race horses called Kinsman Stables. But he had his sights set higher. After a failed 1972 attempt to buy his hometown Cleveland Indians, Steinbrenner headed a 12-member group who purchased the New York Yankees on January 3, 1973, at a bargain price of $10 million. Henry Steinbrenner was finally impressed with his son. "It's the first smart thing he's ever done," Henry said. It was smart—the franchise today is valued between $200 million and $250 million, according to *Newsweek.*

Back in 1964 CBS had purchased the Yankees for $13.2 million. The franchise was a gold mine on the field and at the box office; it won 29 pennants and 20 world championships in 45 years, hadn't had a losing season in 39 years, and drew more than 1.3 million fans for 19 consecutive years. In just eight seasons, CBS ran the most successful franchise in the league into the ground: no pennants, four losing seasons, a last place finish, declining attendance, and the team's worst record in 53 years. Steinbrenner arrived in 1973 and, as general partner, began the rebuilding process.

Steinbrenner spent millions to restore the pride of the Yankees and bring the fans back to the Bronx. The spending spree began New Year's Eve, 1974, when the Yankees signed free agent pitcher James "Catfish" Hunter to a five-year pact for the then-unheard of price of $3.35 million. Hunter, who had just pitched the Oakland Athletics to three consecutive world championships, brought a new winning attitude that the Yankees had lacked. In August 1975, another proven winner arrived, manager Billy Martin [see *Newsmakers* 89, 90], thus beginning the furious love/hate relationship between the fiery manager and the domineering owner who hired him and fired him five different times, and was rumored to have been on the verge of hiring him again when Martin was killed in a traffic accident on Christmas Day in 1989.

Martin led a scrappy Yankee team to its first American League pennant in 12 years in 1976, only to be swept in the World Series by the Cincinnati Reds. That off-season witnessed a revolution that would change the game of baseball; the first free-agent reentry draft was held. Veteran ballplayers, many of them superstars, could now play out their contracts and offer their services to the highest bidders, and George Steinbrenner was prepared to bid as highly as anyone. Over the next several years, Steinbrenner's fat checkbook lured dozens of free agents to don pinstripes and play ball in what was quickly becoming known as "The Bronx Zoo'— among them Rich Gossage, Oscar Gamble, Tommy John, Luis Tiant, Dave Collins, and Ken Griffey. But two free-agent signings loom as large in Steinbrenner-era Yankee fortunes as the hiring of Billy Martin: Reggie Jackson and Dave Winfield.

Jackson was the cream of the first free-agent crop in 1976, and Steinbrenner stopped at nothing to make him a Yankee, even though Martin did not want him on the team. Martin and Jackson simply could not co-exist; combined with Steinbrenner, they formed a trio of volatile egos. And the sparks often flew. Martin and Jackson squared off on national television and had to be restrained from each other after the manager pulled the rightfielder from a game for not hustling after a flyball. The three were often at one another's throats in the press, and Martin's job was in constant jeopardy. There came a brief respite from the turmoil in October, 1977, when the Yankees trounced the Dodgers to capture the World Series, with Jackson scoring three homers in the clinching game.

By the next season, the tension was back. It boiled over in July when, after a tough week and a few drinks, Martin told reporters that Jackson and Steinbrenner "deserve each other. One's a born liar and the other's convicted." With that, Martin's first stint as manager of the Yankees was over. Bob Lemon took over and calmly brought the team from 14-1/2 games behind in August to defeat Boston in a one-game playoff for the East Division title, and eventually to win its second straight world championship over Los Angeles. Martin returned to manage in 1979, but was fired after a barroom brawl. Martin, Lemon, Gene Michael, Dick Howser, and Lou Piniella would all manage the team on more than one occasion during Steinbrenner's tenure, and all would complain of his meddling with the team.

Steinbrenner's penchant for making incessant locker room speeches, shuttling players back and forth to the minors, phoning the dugout with instructions during games, and publicly humiliating his players, coaches, and front office people alienated his team and infuriated fans. Once he arrived at an airport and found that a ticket was not awaiting him. He called his office and fired his secretary. Later, he recapitulated and called her back, telling her he wanted to send her children to summer camp to make up for the sudden sacking. And the public berating of his players are legendary. When a young pitcher named Jim Beattie was shelled by the Red Sox in an important 1978 game, Steinbrenner steamed to reporters that Beattie looked "scared stiff out there," and sent him immediately to the minors. Beattie, crushed, left the ballpark before the game ended. Steinbrenner later said he was trying to toughen Beattie, according to Dick Schaap.

One player under Steinbrenner's mental microscope for nearly a decade was Dave Winfield, whom Steinbrenner signed as a free agent in 1980, giving him a precedent-setting contract to the chagrin of the rest of baseball's owners: a ten-year pact worth over $23 million. The owner and his new star were at odds almost from the beginning, with Winfield going 1-for-22 in the 1981 World Series loss to Los Angeles. In a bit of sarcastic deference to Reggie Jackson's title of "Mr. October," Steinbrenner labeled Winfield "Mr. May," attacking his failure to come through in the clutch. Winfield and his boss frequently sparred over the David M. Winfield Foundation, a charity aiding poor children, to which both annually donated.

The two disagreed on how funds at the Foundation were to be used, and the dispute turned into a convoluted court battle that dragged on, eventually being settled out of court. But the war of words was not settled, and egos were wounded in both camps. Steinbrenner charged Winfield with misappropriating funds, using them for administrative perks such as limousines. In early 1990 Steinbrenner made a $40,000 payment to former Foundation employee and confessed gambler Howard Spira, allegedly to obtain "dirt" on Winfield.

Baseball, still in a state of 70-year-shock after the 1919 Black Sox Scandal, frowns upon nothing more than it frowns upon gamblers, employing gamblers, consorting with gamblers, and especially *paying* gamblers, for whatever reason. So none of Steinbren-

ner's excuses—which, according to *New York,* included threats from Spira on Steinbrenner's family, threats to smear former Yankee employees, and even a tale about Spira's sick mother needing the money for treatment—carried any weight with Commissioner Fay Vincent. Steinbrenner was done for, to the delight of Yankee fans who cheered the stadium announcement of his banishment.

Although Vincent declared that he was banned permanently, Steinbrenner's first question after learning his fate was to ask, "How long does this last?" Steinbrenner retains his partnership in the Yankees, although he must reduce it to less than 50 percent, but he must stay out of the owner's box, and away from the day-to-day operations of the ballclub. He has other responsibilities, with his shipping company and as vice president of the U.S. Olympic Committee. And he has stated that he was preparing to turn the Yankees over to his sons and sons-in-law. But, as George Steinbrenner plots his next move, he draws inspiration from a gift he once received, a cigarette box inscribed with the words of English poet John Dryden: "I am wounded / But I am not slain. / I shall lay me down and bleed awhile / Then I shall rise and fight again."

Sources

Books

Schaap, Dick, and Jerry Kramer, *Steinbrenner!*, Putnam, 1981.

Periodicals

New York, April 13, 1990; August 6, 1990.
New York Times, July 31, 1990; August 22, 1990.
Newsweek, April 23, 1990; August 6, 1990.
Sports Illustrated, May 10, 1990; August 6, 1990.
Sporting News, August 13, 1990.
Time, August 13, 1990.

—*John Cortez*

Robert Stempel

AP/Wide World Photos

Automobile manufacturing company executive

Born in 1933 in New Jersey; son of a banker; wife's name, Pat; children: three. *Education:* Worcester Polytechnic Institute, B.S.M.E., 1955, Ph.D., 1977; Michigan State University, M.B.A., 1970.

Addresses: *Home* — Bloomfield Hills, MI. *Office* — General Motors Corp., General Motors Building, 3044 W. Grand Blvd., Detroit, MI 48202.

Career

Worked summers during high school and college as an automobile mechanic; General Motors Corp. (GM), Detroit, Mich., Oldsmobile division, senior detailer in chassis design department, 1958-62, senior designer, 1962-64, transmission design engineer, 1964-69, motor engineer, 1969-72, assistant chief engineer, 1972-73, special assistant to president, 1973-74, Chevrolet division, chief engines and components engineer, 1974-75, director of engineering, 1975-78, Pontiac division, corporate vice-president and general manager, 1978-80, European passenger car operations, West Germany, corporate vice-president and general manager, 1980-82, Chevrolet division, corporate vice-president and general manager, 1982-84, Buick-Oldsmobile-Cadillac Group, corporate vice-president and group executive, 1984-86, Worldwide truck and bus group, and Overseas group, corporate executive vice-president, 1986-87, corporate president and chief operating officer, 1987-90, chairman and chief executive officer, 1990—. *Military service:* U.S. Army, 1956-58.

Sidelights

After working his way up through many divisions of the company in engineering and executive capacities, Robert Stempel became CEO of General Motors Corporation (GM) on August 1, 1990. Replacing controversial former CEO Roger Smith, (see *Newsmakers 90*), Stempel faced many challenges. Though still the world's largest industrial corporation, GM's car sales slumped during the 1980s, from 46.3 percent of the market in 1979 to 34.7 percent at the end of 1989. The company's production costs per car were significantly higher than those of competitors such as Ford and Chrysler, and product quality had suffered during the early 1980s. But in spite of the 1991 recession, hopes have remained high that Stempel—gifted with both technical know-how and communication skills—can provide the impetus to put GM back on the road to regaining some of its previous market share.

Born in New Jersey in 1933, Stempel worked summers as an automobile mechanic while earning his bachelor's degree in engineering from Worcester Polytechnic Institute. He also won a few drag racing trophies in his youth. After a few years' service in the U.S. Army, Stempel was hired at GM in Detroit, Michigan as a senior detailer in the chassis design department of the Oldsmobile division. He was steadily promoted, and by 1966 was responsible for developing the front suspension and transmission for that year's Oldsmobile Toronado, GM's first front-wheel drive automobile since before World War II. Stempel's admirers point to this experience as presaging his most valuable talents as chairman: "When a prototype flunked preliminary tests," reported James B. Treece in *Business Week*, Stempel "invited himself over to the GM Technical Center. [He] brought along a design that he admitted wasn't too great and asked the staff to smooth it out. This was an early sign of his willingness to ignore organizational barriers, form alliances with others, and then listen to what they advised."

Eventually the quality of Stempel's work brought him to the attention of GM's then-president, Edward N. Cole, who named him his special assistant in 1973. In this position, Stempel helped keep track of changes in emission regulations and was instrumental in the development of the revolutionary pollution control device, the catalytic converter. According to Treece, Stempel "impressed Cole with his capacious memory and...talent for sorting through huge amounts of data." The engineer went from special assistant to the president to many other executive positions in GM's various divisions, astounding other co-workers with what S. C. Gwynne lauded in *Time* as "a photographic memory for both faces and statistics." Gwynne further reported that "while Stempel was general manager of Chevrolet in the early 1980s, he gave a detailed presentation of 17 different vehicles, ranging from the subcompact Chevette to medium-duty trucks—all without referring to notes."

Another of Stempel's triumphs came in his position as corporate vice-president of European passenger car operations from 1980 to 1982. Working primarily with the General Motors division Opel, located in West Germany, he gained a reputation as a diplomat, smoothing over troubled labor relations. Treece quoted Stempel's then-secretary as saying that Stempel "loved going into the plant to listen to what the workers had to say. He didn't speak German, but he understood it and he listened attentively and knew what they said." In addition, Treece said, "Stempel...modernized plants to turn those operations around"; he also began work on the Opel Kadett, which would later become Europe's car of the year. Stempel returned briefly to Europe in 1986 as corporate executive vice-president of GM's Overseas Group and was a major factor in that division's becoming one of the company's most successful, turning in profits of $1.88 million in 1987.

In addition to charming the German workers at Opel, Stempel had meanwhile gained the trust of his co-workers in various other divisions of General Motors. Treece quoted former Oldsmobile engineer Thomas R. Leonard: "I've had some bosses who took my ideas. But with Bob you never thought, 'I'll keep this to myself or he'll steal it.'" Stempel's reputation as a team player was further enhanced when he was named corporation president and chief operating officer of GM in 1987. While doing his best to improve the troubled company, he was still careful not to come into conflict with Roger Smith, then CEO. But GM's dealership owners noticed a big change from the corporation's previous close-mouthed president F. James McDonald; Treece quoted Donald R. Mann on the subject of a dealer's meeting in Detroit: "We didn't ask Stempel a question that wasn't answered with sincerity, honesty, empathy, and intelligence." Similarly, when dealers complained to Stempel about advertisements for GM cars that focused too much on special accessories and not enough on the cars themselves, the ads were pulled within a month. Stempel as president also became one of GM's most enthusiastic spokesmen for company car quality. In another *Business Week* article, Treece quoted Stempel as frequently proclaiming, "Look us over. Drive the car. Touch the car." This hands-on approach has won Stempel the approval of the company's engineering staff. One of them, according to Treece, pointed out that when Stempel views a new model, "where most GM executives will be looking at the instrument panel and the controls, he'll look under the hood like a real engineer."

> "Look us over. Drive the car. Touch the car."

Under Stempel's presidency, the average number of defects per 100 cars—defects defined in *Fortune* magazine by Alex Taylor III as "problems that customers notice, such as poorly fitted body panels, squeaks and rattles, and broken parts"—came down to 168 in 1989 from the 1980s high of 740. Adding this to his previous performance within the company, no one was particularly surprised when Stempel was chosen to replace retiring CEO Roger Smith in 1990. Once Stempel had ascended to this lofty position, he had greater freedom to begin implementing his plans to increase GM's efficiency and profitability. Though, like Smith, Stempel has had to argue with the United Auto Workers (UAW) on the subjects of plant closings and providing jobs for the average assembly line worker, he has also trimmed many white collar, executive-level jobs. Speaking of his plans to Taylor, Stempel proclaimed: "We need to delayer the organization and restructure to eliminate redundancies. In our plants we've had seven layers from the plant floor to the manager, and in some plants we are now down to four. We're looking at our staff operations to see if they are duplicating our operating activities. Blending them will take out some people. In the case of our engine plants, we're looking at bringing the engineering staff functions in with the operating guys. If it is better in the personnel area to have a central personnel function serving five or six plants as opposed to each one having its own, then we will probably centralize that."

Stempel also has plans to make the automobiles themselves simpler to make, thus cutting production costs. He explained to Taylor: "After we converted to front-wheel drive in our small-car lines, lo and behold, we wound up with 14 or 15 different kinds of drive shafts, a half-dozen rear suspensions, and so on. Now it's time to say, 'Okay, guys, among that array of components, which ones are best for what we're trying to do?' Drive shafts on one particular car line will come down from over a dozen to two. That's where the economies of scale start to go up."

During both Stempel's presidency and chairmanship, GM has come out with several revamped car models, hoping to cause the car buying public to forget its criticism during the 1980s of the company's look-alike models—the various GM divisions' models were not sufficiently differentiated in their stylings to offer much variety. Predicted to be big money-makers, not all have fared as well as Stempel and others hoped. The Pontiac Turbo Grand Prix and the Oldsmobile Cutlass Calais, despite GM's trimming efforts, reported Taylor, still "suffer from production inefficiencies." And the idea behind the Cadillac Allante and the Buick Reatta—that of a luxurious, two-seater car—has not caught on with consumers.

On the other hand, under Stempel's leadership, other models *have* proved money makers. The 1990 Cadillac Brougham was both popular enough and efficiently produced to provide high profit margins, as was the same year's Oldsmobile Touring Sedan. As of 1991, Buick Park Avenue sales were "running 34 percent ahead of the last model year with no rebates," according to Jerry Flint in *Forbes*. In 1990 GM's Cadillac division won the prestigious Malcolm Baldrige National Quality Award, which, as Patricia Sellers put it in *Fortune*, "has become *the* standard for U.S. manufacturing and service excellence." During

the same year, GM's Cadillac and Buick divisions "were the only domestic manufacturers to rank in the top 10 of a recent J.D. Power survey of customer satisfaction," revealed Annetta Miller and Frank Washington in *Newsweek*. Predictions are favorable as well for many 1992 models, including the Pontiac Bonneville and Grand Am, and the Cadillac Seville and Eldorado. The latter two cars, Flint noted, will be less expensive to produce than in previous years because "the number of parts on the front and rear . . . will be 45 percent fewer." By January of 1991 GM's market share had moved up to 36.1 percent and, Flint added, "pushing to 37 percent or 38 percent is not out of the question this year."

But Stempel and GM feel "Saturn is the company's strongest hope for reinventing itself," according to Miller and Washington. Saturn, the much publicized compact car GM has designed to compete favorably with the small Japanese cars that have gained such popularity in North America, began rolling off the assembly lines just before Smith retired in 1990. Saturn was due to arrive at dealerships in October of 1990, but "the company told dealers it is slowing down shipments in order to make sure the car is defect-free," reported Miller and Washington. Manufactured in GM's most modern, efficient plant, by some of its best factory employees, Saturn has had favorable reviews in automobile publications, and Miller and Washington quoted an unidentified Honda executive as admitting: "We think it will be very competitive."

Stempel lives with his wife, Pat, in Bloomfield Hills, Michigan. They have three children, two grown and one in college. He maintains a fleet of old cars that he enjoys tinkering with in his free time. He also likes to read car magazines and remains in touch with friends who race automobiles professionally. Aside from car-related activities, he enjoys skiing and surf casting. Stempel has been known to commute to work in a Pontiac Bonneville SSE because, he told Treece, "it's black, it's good-looking, and it's fast."

Sources

Business Week, April 15, 1988; May 9, 1988; January 22, 1990; February 4, 1991.
Forbes, March 4, 1991.
Fortune, April 9, 1990; November 5, 1990.
Money, May, 1990.
Newsweek, October 22, 1990.
Time, November 14, 1988; April 16, 1990; August 13, 1990; October 29, 1990.
U.S. News and World Report, April 16, 1990.

—*Elizabeth Wenning*

David Stern

Commissioner of the National Basketball Association

Full name, David Joel Stern; born September 22, 1942, in New York City; son of William (a deli owner) and Anna (Bronstein) Stern; married Dianne Bock, November 27, 1963; children: Andrew, Eric. *Education:* Rutgers University, B.S., 1963; Columbia Law School, LL.B., 1966. *Religion:* Jewish.

Addresses: *Home*—Scarsdale, NY. *Office*—National Basketball Association, Olympic Tower, 645 Fifth Ave., New York, NY 10022.

Career

Joined law firm of Proskauer, Rose, Goetz & Mendelsohn in New York City, 1967, became partner, 1973; joined National Basketball Association (NBA) as its first general counsel, 1975, overseeing all aspects of the league's litigation, negotiations, and Congressional relations; named NBA vice-president for business and legal affairs, 1980; elected NBA commissioner, February 1, 1984. Adjunct professor of law at Cardoza Law School, New York City; member of board of trustees of Beth Israel Medical Center.

Member: American Bar Association.

Sidelights

While superstars Michael Jordan, Magic Johnson, and Charles Barkley battle for the honor of being the best player in the National Basketball League (NBA), there is little doubt as to who is really

the NBA's Most Valuable Person—a 5'9" lawyer who can neither dunk nor dribble. David J. Stern, as commissioner of the NBA, is the biggest man in a land of giants. Since becoming commissioner in 1984, he has reshaped a floundering, financially strapped league into an entity that is the envy of professional sports—an innovative, multifaceted, billion-dollar global marketing and entertainment company.

Under Stern's guidance the NBA has set the standard other sports leagues are trying to reach. The NBA has the best substance abuse treatment program, the best collective bargaining agreement, the most liberal free agent policy, and a salary system that assures stability for the owners and wealth for the players. "David has taken us to another level," Magic Johnson told *USA Today*. "He's a great commissioner but also a mastermind at marketing, and that's where he's passed everyone else in sports. He deserves what he's earning. We're the hottest league in the world, not just the United States, but the world, and he's the reason why." Indeed, Stern has been so successful that no one disputes that he is now the best commissioner in sports, the best in the history of basketball and perhaps the equal of the best commissioners of all time, such as the National Football League's Pete Rozelle and baseball's Kenesaw Mountain Landis. One indication of Stern's reputation: in recent years, when baseball and football searched for new commissioners, both sports started their search by asking Stern if he would take the job.

For David Stern, however, basketball is the only sport. As a child, Stern dreamed of playing for the New York Knicks and was a regular visitor to Madison Square Garden, marveling at the feats of Carl Braun and Jimmy Baechtold.

Stern grew up in the racially mixed Chelsea section of Manhattan. The son of second-generation Russian immigrants, David spent his childhood hanging around and working at the family's delicatessen on Eighth Avenue and 23rd Street. From the start, his parents told him that his future would involve professional school, not 40 years' worth of seven-days-a-week work at the deli.

In 1956 Stern's family moved to northern New Jersey. Stern earned a varsity letter in tennis at Teaneck High School "out of the goodness of the coach's heart," he told USA Today. "I was undefeated in my only match. I always played recreation league basketball and softball." His first love, even then, was basketball, but he described himself as too small, too slow and too uncoordinated to play beyond the level of intramurals. Plus, he stopped growing when he was 13. "I was competitive when I did play, but I wasn't very good," he told USA Today. "I was a pretty good rebounder, but the idea was to pass the ball as soon as I got it, so I wouldn't lose it on the dribble." Washington D.C. attorney Edward Norton, who has known Stern since they were both teenagers, told the Washington Post, "What I remember about him is he was as good as you can be without any physical talent. He understood the game; he knew where to go. But he couldn't run and he couldn't jump."

Stern worked at the family deli to put himself through Rutgers University, from which he graduated with a degree in history in 1963. He subsequently entered Columbia Law School, earning his law degree in 1966. Stern then joined the law firm of Proskauer, Rose, Goetz & Mendelsohn in New York City. Initially, his responsibility was providing legal support and guidance to the Fair Housing Operation in Bergen County, New Jersey. "David's sense of racial justice is deep," Norton told the Post, "which is why I trust him on anything he does in the league on those issues."

In 1968 the law firm assigned him to work full-time on cases concerning its largest client—the NBA. One of the first was Connie Hawkins's suit that charged

the NBA with blackballing him for alleged involvement in the college point-shaving scandals of the 1960s. Hawkins won an out-of-court settlement and joined the Phoenix Suns in 1969. "I'm not even sure that I knew the firm represented the NBA," Stern told the Bergen Record, "but as soon as I learned that the NBA was a client, I was available to work on anything they had related to the NBA. Basically I was a young litigator doing antitrust advisory work and commercial litigation, just normal run-of-the-mill corporate litigation."

In 1974, at age 32, Stern became the firm's youngest partner ever. Since then, he has been involved in nearly every important case involving the NBA. In 1976 he found himself in charge of the landmark antitrust case pitting legendary player Oscar Robertson against the league. Stern helped negotiate a settlement that paved the way for free agency and ended nearly a decade of confrontation between the owners and players. That same year he guided the merger with the American Basketball Association, which led to absorption of four teams into the NBA.

The work gave Stern a knowledge of the inner workings of the league and a familiarity of its politics and its owners. "I think he was always well liked by the owners when he was a lawyer representing the NBA," Russ Granik, the league's executive vice president, told the Los Angeles Times. "But now he's gone beyond the relationship with owners and is just well liked by everyone. He has to be viewed as invaluable."

In 1978 then-commissioner Larry O'Brien hired Stern as the league's first general counsel, overseeing all legal affairs. Two years later, the league created the position of executive vice-president for business and legal affairs for him. At the time, NBA attendance was shrinking, all but a few of the 23 franchises were losing money, the league's TV contract was threatened, and the NBA had a severe image problem, caused most notably by several highly publicized drug cases. Wrote Sports Illustrated's E. M. Swift, "Essentially, Stern was being given the opportunity to revamp the ravaged image of the league. But he took his stated charge a step further. By focusing the owners' attention on the proper ways to market their product, he actually revamped the way the league did business." "Before David joined the league there was no coordination," former NBA Team Services director Bob King told Sports Illustrated. "All the teams were islands unto themselves. What Stern did was take the islands and turn them into a continent."

As the NBA's number-two man under O'Brien, Stern led the push for two landmark agreements. The first was the joint drug agreement of 1983, which enables players to seek treatment without losing their jobs, yet prescribes strict penalties, including banishment for life, for offenders who do not seek help. "I think the drug agreement played more in changing people's attitude about us than I thought was ever likely," Stern told the *Bergen Record*. "People greatly appreciated the fact that we and our players sat down together and addressed one of the enduring problems, one that is continuing to grow greatly in our society." Wrote *Newsday's* Jan Hubbard: "Stern was the first to come to the conclusion that the best way to implement a drug policy is to cooperate with the players, not try to browbeat them. The result was an intelligent drug policy that may not be perfect, but is the best in professional sports."

The second landmark agreement was a salary cap, which established a ceiling on team salaries while guaranteeing a percentage of league revenues (53 percent) to the players. Stern negotiated the agreement with Players Union chief Larry Fleischer in 1983. "We were on the precipice," Stern told *Newsday*, "and we managed to sit down with our players and make a deal that made us partners of a type, and you can't overemphasize the importance of that. And in the face of a previous strike by baseball, and by football, we managed to avoid one . . . There was a great sense of appreciation all around when we said 'Okay, here's a percentage of the gross and if business is good, you'll do really well. We're in this together.'" In 1984 O'Brien, in ill health, stepped down. The NBA owners, with hardly a search, unanimously voted Stern as the league's fourth commissioner. At the time, the league's annual revenues were $200 million; in 1990-91 they topped $600 billion. In 1983, fewer than half of the teams managed a profit; today nearly all of them do. And franchise values have soared: the Portland Trail Blazers, which paid $3.7 million to join the NBA in 1970, fetched $72 million in 1989.

Stern's greatest accomplishment has been marketing and selling the NBA as an entertainment product. For example, in 1954 he took the moribund NBA All-Star game and transformed it into a weekend carnival with slam-dunk and three-point-shooting contests that have proven popular with players and fans. These days, the NBA All-Star Weekend has become the league's showcase event. In 1985 Stern devised the NBA lottery to determine which of the league's seven bottom nine teams get to draft first. Not only did the lottery create a popular TV event, it marked the first time a sports league did anything to discourage bad teams from playing to lose at the end of the season in order to improve their draft posi-

tions. "Nobody, including me, envisioned that this young, bright attorney would have such marketing genius," *Washington Bullets* owner Abe Pollin told *Sports Illustrated*. "We used to think it was a big deal if we broke even. David thought that attitude was ridiculous, and he told us so. Then he showed us how to start making money at it."

In recent years, Stern has positioned the NBA to became a global league, scheduling games in Europe and the Orient. Each has been a sellout and, these days, wrote *Sports Illustrated's* Swift, "Isiah, Magic and Michael are as well known on a first-name basis in Rome and Barcelona as they are in Detroit, L.A. and Chicago." Stern and the league's owners have talked—in the long-term—about adding a few foreign teams. In the short run, the NBA figures to sponsor an international championship to be played in a different country each year. Already, Stern has convinced the International Olympic Committee to allow NBA players to play in the 1992 Games.

"David Stern can sell an anvil to a drowning man. He can sell a pogo stick to a kangaroo," Orlando Magic general manager Pat Williams told the *New York Times*. Stern has also been able to sell NBA merchandise and clothing. Two years ago he devoted himself to increasing sales at NBA Properties, the league's licensing and marketing arm. In 1990, NBA Properties was expected to generate $1 billion in retail sales—up ten-fold from five years earlier. Wrote *Newsday's* Jerry Sullivan: "What NBA Properties has done, in essence, is sell the league to the public. Think about the "Fan-tastic" ads shown during national telecasts, and how they end with shots of people in the stands going wild over a great move. The league is affirming the relationship between the game and the people in the stands. They also do it by pushing team products through their slick NBA catalogs.

The approach, Stern says, is modeled after Disney World. "I'm the chief executive officer of an entertainment company," he told the *New York Times*. "And so I have to sell and sell and sell . . . . Disney has theme parks, and we have theme parks. Only we call them arenas. They have characters: Mickey Mouse, Goofy. Our characters are named Magic and Michael. Disney sells apparel; we sell apparel. They make home videos; we make home videos."

Stern's good work has not gone unrewarded by NBA owners. In February 1990, they gave him a five-year, $27.5 million contract. Including a $10 million signing bonus, the deal pays him an average of $5.5 million per year. As far as the NBA's future goes, Stern told *Sports Illustrated*, "We see ourselves moving into areas that ordinary fans don't associate with us. I've been telling our owners for years that we're becoming a mature industry. What else is there? Publishing, events, licensing, home entertainment—all on a global basis. It's how you conceptualize your corporate goals." And as far as his own future goes, Stern told the *Los Angeles Daily News*, "Right now, I'm having a very good time. I can't imagine anything else I'd rather be doing. I like this job. Besides, I get great seats to any game I want to attend."

Sources

Atlanta Journal, February 11, 1990.

Bergen (New Jersey) *Record*, June 2, 1991.
Charlotte Observer, March 20, 1988.
Detroit Free Press, June 17, 1988.
Fort Lauderdale News and Sun-Sentinel, February 9, 1990.
Fortune, August 28, 1989.
Los Angeles Daily News, March 11, 1990.
Los Angeles Times, February 12, 1989; November 2, 1990.
Newsday, February 8, 1987; February 18, 1990.
New York Times, March 10, 1990.
Orlando Sentinel, January 28, 1990.
Sports Illustrated, June 3, 1991.
USA Today, February 20, 1990.
Washington Post, June 5, 1990.

—*Glen Macnow*

Dave Stewart

Professional baseball player

Full name, David Keith Stewart; born February 19, 1957, in Oakland, Calif.; son of David (a longshoreman) and Nathalie Stewart. *Education:* Attended St. Elizabeth High School in Oakland.

Addresses: *Office*—Oakland Athletics, Oakland Alameda Coliseum Complex, Oakland, CA 94603.

Career

Pitcher for the Los Angeles Dodgers, 1982-83; pitcher for the Texas Rangers, 1983-85; pitcher for the Philadelphia Phillies, 1985-86; pitcher for the Oakland Athletics, 1986—.

Sidelights

It was 4:30 a.m. one day in late October, 1989, and Dave Stewart, who had just the night before pitched the Oakland Athletics (A's) to their third consecutive victory over the San Francisco Giants in the World Series, could not sleep. No, it was not a post-game adrenalin rush that was bothering Stewart, though he had every right to be excited by the increasingly likely notion that the A's would go on to sweep the Series—and assure Stewart the honor of being named its most valuable player. To the contrary, Stewart at that time was having difficulty even thinking about baseball in the wake of the tragedy that was unfolding in his beloved hometown of Oakland. One week before, on the night of October 17, a devastating earthquake measuring 7.1 on the Richter Scale had brought the sister cities of Oakland

and San Francisco, in the midst of their proudest hour and with the eyes of the country upon them, abruptly to their knees.

In a matter of a few seconds, these two communities, which for years have waged an often bitter civic rivalry that had become even more intense with their World Series match-up, were suddenly forced to confront a common calamity. Baseball didn't seem to matter anymore. The World Series was put on hold, the two northern California cities turned to the grim task of assessing both the human and structural damage brought on by the quake—and right in the middle of it all was Dave Stewart.

At the wreckage of the collapsed, two-tiered Nimitz Freeway, Stewart could be found day after day, night after night throughout the crisis, providing encouragement to the rescue workers who dug through piles of concrete and twisted steel in the search for survivors. "I just stand and watch and try to boost the spirits of these people working all night, the people trying to find bodies and cleaning up the rubble," Stewart told *Sports Illustrated*'s Peter Gammons at the time. "Some nights I didn't plan to be here, but when I couldn't get to sleep, I'd drive over and stand for an hour or two, then go home and go right to sleep. I haven't figured out why I'm drawn here, except for me this isn't something to gawk at like a tourist. This is part of my life."

A child of Oakland's tough, blue-collar neighborhoods, Stewart has become more than a great ballplayer in the eyes of the people of his city; he has become a symbol of what they, individually and collectively, can become. Stewart has proven that it is indeed possible to go home again, and certainly in his case Oakland has meant as much to him as he has given back. It is the place that has seen the revival of both his once-struggling pitching career and his once-wavering idea of the kind of man he wants to be. For while many modern athletes, with all of their riches and with the understanding that the children and downtrodden of their communities look up to them as heroes or even gods, have been known to lend their names and dollars to charitable causes, none approaches the extent to which Stewart goes to champion the rebirth of Oakland. And he does it with a philosophical graciousness that makes his efforts all the more sincere—and effective. "I'm probably the only big leaguer who's actually playing for his hometown team," Stewart explained to *Sports Illustrated.* "A lot of people are ashamed of what's happened to my city. They call it Cokeland. I want kids today to have the same chance I had growing up."

> "It wasn't hard staying away from drugs or trouble. I had the Boys' Club and sports. There was a heck of a lot more good available to me than there was bad."

While Stewart has certainly made his chances pay off—in 1990 he signed a contract extension that will make him baseball's highest paid player at $3.5 million a season—he has not forgotten where he came from. Stewart has given his time, name, and money to such groups as the Oakland Boys' Clubs (where he also serves on the board of directors), the Just Say No anti-drug campaign, the Multiple Sclerosis Society, the Oakland Library, and several youth recreation leagues. And those are just his "official" charities. "There are hundreds of groups he helps that we don't know about," said Dave Perron, the A's director of community affairs, in *Sports Illustrated.* "They're run by people who come up to Stew

on the street to ask for help, and he just can't say no to caring."

In 1987, along with his childhood friend, financial analyst Wornel Simpson, Stewart founded the nonprofit organization, Stewart's Corporations for Kids ("Kidscorps"), which provides a platform for soliciting corporate grants to fund Stewart's various neighborhood restoration projects. "When we were in high school, we used to sit at home and dream about the future," Simpson told *Sports Illustrated.* "I was prone to the books, he was the athlete, but we had a shared dream—to make a lot of money, then use it to help others from our community. Little did we know that someday he'd be a superstar pitcher and I'd be a financial planner, doing just what we always dreamed." For Stewart, the Kidscorps project provides the ultimate opportunity for him, as a famous athlete respected by rich and poor alike, to act as a bridge between wealthy corporations and the needy. "The days of government financing are over," Stewart told *Sports Illustrated,* "so we have to rebuild ourselves. I provide all the legwork. With the exception of the day I pitch, I have plenty of time before I get to the park."

It is indeed at the ballpark where all of Stewart's worthy acts of charity must begin, if only because a star pitcher and World Series hero carries much more clout with corporate benefactors than the troubled, middle-of-the-road relief pitcher Stewart was when he joined the A's in May 1986. At that time, his career was foundering, and his personal life was checkered with past indiscretions that embarrassed him. It was, he knew, probably his last chance to save both, and the fact that he was in Oakland only seemed to further intensify the pressure placed upon him by both himself and others.

The difficult circumstances besieging the city of Oakland during Stewart's upbringing in the turbulent 1960s were so intense that the place became a breeding ground for some of the country's most extreme revolutionary political groups. The Black Panthers had their original clubhouse in Stewart's neighborhood; Stewart's grandmother's home was once riddled with bullets by police who mistakenly believed that Panther leader Bobby Seale was hiding out there. The Hell's Angels also had headquarters in the area, as did the Symbionese Liberation Army. "I was tempted by the street life," Stewart told *Sports Illustrated.* "But it wasn't hard staying away from drugs or trouble. I had the Boys' Club and sports. There was a heck of a lot more good available to me than there was bad."

Stewart's primary role models were his parents. His father, David, was a hardworking longshoreman who, ironically, told his son to forget about baseball because he couldn't "make a living hitting a ball with a broomstick." The elder Stewart died in 1972, but Stewart's mother, Nathalie, has steadfastly remained in the family's old Havenscourt Boulevard home, even though her now-wealthy son has offered to build her a new house.

Despite the efforts of David and Nathalie Stewart and Simpson, who, Stewart says, "was as good as I was bad," it was not until Stewart came under the influence of a physical education teacher named Bob Howard at St. Elizabeth High School that he began to channel his energies and skills into something positive. Noting Stewart's prowess in football, basketball, and baseball, Howard pressed Stewart to take advantage of his skills by trying harder to make something of himself. By his senior year Stewart had received 26 scholarship offers to play college football, but he chose instead to take the offer of baseball's Los Angeles Dodgers, who drafted the strong-armed catcher with the idea of converting him to a pitcher.

Boasting a 95-m.p.h. fastball upon his arrival to the Dodgers big league club in 1982, Stewart soon found that relying solely upon his overpowering arm would not be good enough in the majors. Hitters started waiting on his fastball, and the result was a 1-8 record for Stewart over his first two professional seasons. Late in the 1983 season, the Dodgers traded Stewart to the Texas Rangers, and the switch paid off for Stewart in the short run; he finished the 1983 season with a 5-2 record and a 2.14 ERA for the Rangers.

But the 1984 season saw the beginning of a string of personal and professional problems that threatened to destroy Stewart's hard-earned reputation as a caring community leader and, possibly, even end his baseball career. The first mark against his name came when he admitted to reporters that, during his years with the Dodgers, he had on several occasions withheld information from Dodgers manager Tommy Lasorda regarding the personal habits of teammate Steve Howe. Howe, with Stewart's knowledge, had developed a cocaine addiction that would effectively ruin Howe's career, and Stewart's subsequent admission that he protected Howe was not taken lightly in an era when drug-use among athletes was making national headlines.

On the field, Stewart's record dropped to 7-14 in 1984, and to make matters worse, he feuded with Rangers' manager Doug Rader over Stewart's use of a new pitch—the forkball. Rader did not like the pitch, which, when thrown properly, fools hitters into thinking it is a fastball until the ball drops suddenly when it reaches the plate. Stewart felt that the forkball would be a good compliment to his excellent fastball and would keep hitters offstride. Stewart and Rader never settled the issue, and by September of 1985, with Stewart mired in the Texas bullpen with a 0-6 record, the pitcher was traded to the Philadelphia Phillies.

Despite his baseball problems, however, Stewart had always been able to stand proud with regard to his charitable activities off the field, no matter where he was playing. After the 1984 season, Stewart was justifiably awarded the Good Guy award by the Dallas-Fort Worth baseball writers, but two days before he was to accept the award, he was arrested in Los Angeles for soliciting a prostitute, who, to his surprise and further humiliation, turned out to be a transvestite. Under the circumstances, Stewart could understandably have ducked the award presentation or even declined to accept it. But to the surprise of the Dallas media, Stewart showed up for the ceremony and answered every question thrown his way, taking the situation as a kind of bitter pill to swallow for his past transgressions. "I was going through a period where one bad thing after another seemed to be happening to me. I've learned a lesson," Stewart told *Sports Illustrated*. "Now I try to do what's right, knowing that sometimes I'll fall short. Some people might think of me as a hypocrite when I speak against drugs, since I'm the guy who protected Howe. And if I'm talking to a class, they can say, 'Hey, he was the one with the prostitute.' The thing is, I know I'm a sinner. But I do try. I also know you never finish growing."

In order to turn his life entirely around, however, Stewart had one more major hurdle to clear. Shortly after his trade to the Phillies, he learned that he would need surgery during the off-season to remove bone chips from the elbow of his pitching arm— potentially a career-ending operation. Stewart went ahead with the surgery and rejoined the Phillies to start the 1986 season, but just two months into the season Philadelphia management gave up on the right-hander and released him. Now unemployed, Stewart had only one place to go—home. The struggling Oakland A's signed Stewart to pitch for their minor league team in Tacoma, and after only one Triple A start the pitcher was called up to help arm the A's depleted bullpen. For the next month, however, Stewart continued to pitch poorly, so poorly that any day could conceivably have been his last in baseball. In fact, the only reason he stuck with the club at all was that the A's were in last place. On June 26, manager Jackie Moore was fired. Then, on July 2, in a move that would prove equally beneficial to Dave Stewart and to the ballclub itself, the A's hired Tony LaRussa to manage the team.

A lawyer by trade and known as one of baseball's more cerebral, sophisticated managers, LaRussa, in assessing the sad state of the Oakland pitching staff, knew he could afford to gamble a little in his first game as the new manager. Seeing in Stewart a man with enormous potential and hungry for a break, LaRussa called the pitcher on July 4 at the A's hotel in Milwaukee and asked him if he would like to be the starting pitcher for LaRussa's debut two nights later in Boston. Stewart readily accepted, and in that game, before a national television audience, he went nose to nose with Red Sox ace Roger Clemens and won 6-4. It was a game that would have enormous significance for the futures of Stewart, LaRussa, and the entire A's organization. Over the next two years the team would add sluggers Mark McGwire, Jose Canseco, and Dave Parker, as well as pitchers Bob Welch and Dennis Eckersley. By the end of the decade the A's were the dominant team in baseball, with a nucleus of star players that could make them a dynasty for years to come.

The A's will all point to Stewart as the most indispensable man in their line-up. With the vote of confidence provided by LaRussa, Stewart suddenly seemed to discover the delicate blend of temperament and poise to go along with his blazing fastball. LaRussa also encouraged Stewart to continue working with the forkball, a pitch that has now become the ideal strikeout pitch he envisioned when he began working with it in Texas. But the most valuable quality Stewart brings to the ballpark each day is his consistency, both on the field and in the clubhouse. It is almost as if the many trials and difficulties he faced earlier in his career were necessary to give him the proper frame of mind with which to play the game. It is a quality that is not lost on his teammates. "Respect is the first word anyone uses about Stew," Eckersley told *Sports Illustrated.* "There's just a different feeling when he walks out to pitch. He makes everyone feel good about himself." Adds pitching coach Dave Duncan: "David Stewart is a leader; he gives the other players so much confidence that they play better." LaRussa himself refers to Stewart as "the backbone" of the A's.

With his newfound control, and with Oakland's potent offensive attack backing him up, Stewart was the only pitcher in the 1980s to win 20 games in three consecutive seasons (1987-89). Though Stewart has never received the American League's Cy Young Award, the ultimate honor for a pitcher, it is something that ceased bothering him as the A's began having so much success as a team. Though Oakland was upset in the 1988 World Series by a gritty Los Angeles Dodgers team, the A's bounced back in 1989 even more determined to get the job done right. Stewart finally started getting the recognition he deserved in the 1989 post season when he won two games in the American League Championship Series against the Toronto Blue Jays. He then pitched the opening game victory over San Francisco in the World Series, and was available to pitch game 3 only because the earthquake delayed the game for one week. The Series victory was especially sweet to Stewart because it came at the hands of San Francisco, a town that has long cast its glamorous shadow over blue-collar Oakland's undistinguished streets. In the hype leading up to the series, San Francisco mayor Art Agnos, in a display of snootiness that the people of Oakland have come to expect from their sister city to the south, rejected a wager from Oakland mayor Lionel Wilson by saying: "There's nothing in Oakland that I'd want." After World Series MVP Stewart and the rest of the A's finished dusting off the Giants in four games, Wilson seemed to size up the feeling of the whole community of Oakland. "The A's winning the Series really means something to Oakland," Wilson said, "whereas had the Giants won, it wouldn't really have meant much to San Francisco. And the fact that David Stewart won it for his hometown makes it most important, because David Stewart is the symbol of what Oakland can—and will—be."

Sources

Jet, February 5, 1990.
Newsweek, May 20, 1988.
Sports Illustrated, October 5, 1987; May 30, 1988; October 24, 1988; July 9, 1989; October 23, 1989; November 6, 1989.

—David Collins

Sting

Musician, singer, and songwriter

Real name, Gordon Matthew Sumner; born October 2, 1951, in Newcastle upon Tyne, England; son of Ernest Matthew (a milkman) and Audrey (a hairdresser; maiden name, Cowell) Sumner; married Frances Eleanor Tomelty (an actress), May 1, 1976 (divorced, March 1984); longtime companion (one source says wife): Trudy Styler (an actress/model); children: (first marriage) Joseph, Katherine; (with Styler) three.

Addresses: *Office*—IRL, the Bugle House, 21 A Noel St., London WI, England; and, c/o Frontier Booking International, 1776 Broadway, New York, NY 10019.

Career

Worked as a schoolteacher in Newcastle upon Tyne, England, 1975-77; singer, songwriter, and bass player in rock group the Police, 1976-83; solo performer, 1985—. Actor in films, including *Quadrophenia*, 1980, *The Secret Policeman's Other Ball*, 1982, *Brimstone and Treacle*, 1982, *Dune*, 1984, *The Bride*, 1985, *Plenty*, 1985, *Julia and Julia*, 1988, and *Stormy Monday*, 1988; founded record label, Pangaea, 1988.

Awards: Winner of five Grammy Awards with the Police and four Grammy Awards as a solo artist; (with the Police) named best new artist in *Rolling Stone* Critics' Poll, 1979; received numerous awards, as a member of the Police and as a solo artist from *Down Beat* magazine's readers' and critics' polls.

Sidelights

Sting is a star with substance, "the pop idol adults can admire," according to *Rolling Stone* writer Anthony DeCurtis. "His infallible instinct for hooks made the Police one of the world's biggest bands, but his ventures into jazz-inflected rock . . . made him an acceptable figure even to the most recalcitrant members of a thirtysomething generation that has turned its back on the adolescent excesses of much rock & roll." Yet Sting's appeal goes well beyond his music, or the effective dramatic performances he has given on stage and screen. His dedicated work to preserve the Amazon's vanishing rain forest make him an inspirational figure for anyone concerned about the pressing environmental problems facing the world today.

Growing up in the bleak English industrial town of Newcastle, Sting—then known as Gordon Sumner—was primarily concerned with breaking free from the dead-end life that most of the people around him seemed resigned to living. "I come from a family of losers," he told Kristine McKenna in a 1980 issue of *Rolling Stone.* "Part of my egocentric drive is an attempt to transcend my family . . . . I've rejected my family as something I don't want to be like. My father delivered milk for a living and my mother was a hairdresser. Those are respectable occupations, but my family failed as a family." He would later regret the harshness of his remarks, which hurt his relatives deeply; but Sting still maintains that Newcastle "wasn't a great place to grow up in. What did we have? There certainly wasn't any work. I wanted to get the f--- out and I was given the means to escape: by education, by having some sort of talent and, also, by having the *desire* to leave. But that sets up all kinds of pressure and turmoil within a family, knowing that someone wants to break out."

To make music was Sting's greatest ambition. He never had formal lessons, but by the age of 17 he was working semi-professionally in local jazz clubs, where he had learned from older players to play bass guitar and read music. He also pursued his education, however, and worked as a schoolteacher by day. Later as a member of the Police, he would project a rebel image, but during this earlier stage in his life, Sting immersed himself in the system in order to ensure that he would move a little farther along in it than anyone else in his family had.

By the time he was 20, he felt he'd progressed enough musically to make a break for London and take a shot at a professional career. He hadn't been in London long when he met Stewart Copeland, a drummer who was combing the club scene for members of a new band. In 1976 Copeland, Sting, and Andy Summers began performing as the Police. It was the heyday of the punk/new wave movement. The Police were frequently referred to as a new wave group, but their music was more complex than that of most in that genre. Sting contributed highly literate lyrics, and their music utilized polyrhythmic structures and lush chordal work to create a truly unique sound. Stewart Copeland's brother owned a small record label, Illegal Records, and the Police recorded a single for him. "Fall Out" sold about 10,000 copies and led to a contract with A & M Records.

Elated over signing with a major label, the band members decided that they had to conquer America *immediately*. Despite strenuous protests from A & M, they began planning a club tour of the States, where no one had heard of them and they hadn't released any music. "It was right in the middle of corporate rock & roll, where to tour in America you had to support Foreigner," Sting recalled in *Rolling Stone*. "You'd go on as the doors opened, people would be eating popcorn or whatever and would hate you. Instead, we *headlined* every night—but sometimes to three people. We played to three people in Pough-keepsie, New York . . . It was a *great* show . . . . We did

four or five encores for those three people." That sort of energy and dedication saw them through the many rough moments of their first American tour.

Proof of their success came with the release of the haunting single "Roxanne." Suddenly, the Police were a bigger hit than any of the already-established new wave groups they were associated with in the record business. A & M rushed to release their debut LP, *Outlandos d'Amour*, which had been recorded for a mere $6000. *Reggatta De Blanc* was released that same year (1979), and *Zenyatta Mondatta* followed early in 1980. The three albums made them the superstars of the music world. In 1980 they embarked on a tour that included many Third World venues. Sting credits that tour as really opening up his world view. Shortly after the tour, he told *Guitar Player*: "I've developed my songwriting away from the subjects of love, alienation, and devotion to a more political, socially aware viewpoint." The evolution was evident in the songs on the group's fourth and fifth albums: *Ghost in the Machine* and *Synchronicity*.

Copeland, Summers, and Sting had hung together through the rigors of their rise to the top, but by 1983 their three admittedly huge egos could no longer be contained within one group. "In our final year, it was very clear to me that for the sake of sanity, for the sake of *dignity*, we should end it," Sting told DeCurtis. "We had the big song of the year, the big album of the year, the big tour of the year. We were *it*. We'd made it—everything we attempted, we'd achieved to the power of ten." And so the group disbanded at the height of their popularity. For Sting at least, there are no regrets. "I'm very proud of the legend of the Police—I think it's intact. And I want to keep it intact. I'm very proud of the work we did, and I'm proud of my association with Andy and Stewart . . . . But it's in the past. I don't want to return to the Police for nostalgic reasons or for money. That would spoil it."

One of Sting's first priorities after the breakup of the Police was to devote time to one of his longtime interests, acting. His first role had been that of the hypocritical rebel Ace Face in the Who's 1980 rock film *Quadrophenia*, and he'd also appeared in *The Secret Policeman's Other Ball* and *Brimstone and Treacle* in 1982. Now he devoted himself to bigger parts, in the science fiction epic *Dune*; the Frankenstein remake *The Bride*; and the war drama *Plenty*, which starred Meryl Streep. More recently, he appeared on Broadway in the role of Macheath in Bertolt Brecht's *Threepenny Opera*. His performances, according to DeCurtis, "attest to a range of talents that is increasingly rare in what often seems the increasingly one-dimensional world of pop culture." Sting released his first solo album in 1985. *The Dream of the Blue Turtles* combined Sting's intelligent lyrics and the Police's rhythmic sophistication with a fresh jazz sound. Backing Sting were jazz musicians Branford Marsalis (See *Newsmakers 88*), Darryl Jones, Kenny Kirkland, and Omar Hakim. Sting was pleased with the album, but when it was nominated for a Grammy in the jazz category, he was "horrified and dismayed," and relieved not to win. . . . *Nothing Like the Sun*, released in 1987, had a sound much like *Blue Turtles*, and was equally popular. Sting dedicated the album to his mother, who died suddenly while he was recording it.

Six months later Sting's father also died. "I was told about it just before I went onstage in front of about 250,000 people in Rio for the first gig of the world tour," Sting told Phil Sutcliffe of *Us* magazine. "I had to do the show. I *wanted* to. In a way, it was a wake for my father. It was great—seething with energy. But I never cried for him." He told DeCurtis: "I figured the modern way to cope with death is to ignore it, just work through it. It's the modern thing to do–you go to work. Really, I think, it's fear. You're scared to actually deal with the enormity of what's happened and you try to pretend it *hasn't* happened. So I did that. I worked my butt off . . . . I just didn't stop. I didn't want to think about it."

Sting paid a high price for his emotional denial. The once-prolific writer found himself unable to write a word for three years. When at last he confronted this frightening block, he realized he was "going to have to write a record about death," he told DeCurtis. "I didn't really want to." Once he sat down to do it, *The Soul Cages* poured forth in about two weeks. "It was quite painful, a bit overwhelming," he told Sutcliffe. "But I'm glad I did it." Sting dedicated *The Soul Cages* to his father, and has said that the album has reconciled him with the family and background he once rejected so violently. "It's the old pingpong of wanting to escape and then having go back and face it," he commented. "Wanting to escape the idea of death, yet having to go back and face it. Wanting to escape where I came from, yet having to come back and face it . . . . My relationship with my father was complex, and it wasn't resolved . . . . I think now, through some psychic working, it seems to be resolved."

Sting devotes a great deal of time and money to human rights and ecological causes. His activism might seem to be at odds with the apolitical stance his lyrics often seem to take, but as he explained to DeCurtis: "I'm still, in a sense, a believer in transcendent cures for various problems . . . . But it's getting a bit late, unfortunately. I feel that with certain issues, like the environment, for example, you *have* to be active. You can't just sit there with your legs crossed and hope that the air is going to be fit to breathe tomorrow. I think we don't have very long left, frankly."

In trying to do his part for the environment, Sting has focused on the preservation of the Amazon rain forest, which is vital to the health of the earth's atmosphere. To that end, he founded the Rain Forest Foundation. It originated in 1987, after he went deep into the jungle to meet with the Indians there. He developed a close friendship with one of the chiefs, Raoni, and the two traveled to Rio de Janiero to appeal to the government to stop the forests' destruction. Then-president Jose Sarney promised that if Sting raised the necessary $1,000,000 to cover expenses, an area the size of England—including Raoni's homeland—would be demarcated as Xingo Park. Sting agreed to do so, generating much favorable publicity for Sarney. But when the money was produced, Sarney backed down. It was a painful lesson in politics for both Sting and the Indians, and led to some criticism of the Rain Forest Foundation. Sarney's successor, Collor De Mello, seems to be more favorably disposed to actually doing something for the rain forest, but in light of his experience with Sarney, Sting is now directing part of the Rain Forest Foundation's money into programs to educate and empower the Indians in their rights and the workings of politics.

Sting told DeCurtis: "I've tried very consciously to break the mold, to do things that rock stars don't normally do or aspire to . . . . Of course, you end up being called pretentious. I'm not pretentious. I'm just willing to take a lot of risks, to the extent where I don't mind being ridiculed and I don't mind failing, because I think the process of trying to burst out of the stereotypes is worth doing. The standard you measure yourself by is, Have you learned something? Often you learn more from failures than you do from success; they're often more interesting experiences in retrospect. You learn to obey your instincts."

Selected discography

With the Police; released by A & M

Outlandos d'Amour, 1979.
Reggatta de Blanc, 1979.
Zenyatta Mondatta, 1980.
Ghost in the Machine, c. 1981.

Synchronicity, c. 1983.

Solo releases

Bring on the Night (live recording), A & M, 1985.
The Dream of the Blue Turtles, A & M, 1985.
Nothing Like the Sun, A & M, 1987.
The Soul Cages, A & M, 1991.

Sources

Down Beat, December 1983, May 1984, August 1984, December 1984, May 1985, November 1986, December 1987, December 1988.

Guitar Player, September 1982.
Guitar World, April 1988, October 1988.
Musician, September 1987.
Rolling Stone, June 14, 1979; December 13, 1979; November 16, 1980; December 25, 1980; February 19, 1981; September 1, 1983; September 25, 1986; November 5, 1987; February 7, 1991.
Spin, May 1991.
Us, May 16, 1991.

—*Joan Goldsworthy*

Robert Strauss

UPI/Bettmann

United States ambassador to Moscow

Full name, Robert Schwarz Strauss; born October 19, 1918, in Lockhart, TX; son of Charles H. and Edith V. (Schwarz) Strauss; married Helen Jacobs, 1941; children: Robert A., Richard C., Susan. *Education:* University of Texas, LL.B., 1941.

Addresses: *Office*—1333 New Hampshire Ave. NW, Suite 400, Washington, DC 20036.

Career

Admitted to the Texas State Bar, 1941, and to the District of Columbia Bar, 1971. Special agent with the Federal Bureau of Investigation (FBI), 1941-45; partner with law firm Akin, Gump, Strauss, Hauer & Feld, 1945-77, 1981-91; member of the Democratic National Committee from Texas, 1968-72; member of executive committee of the Democratic National Committee, 1969-77, treasurer, 1970-72, chairman, 1972-77; special representative for trade negotiations with rank of ambassador for the Office of the President, 1977-79; chairman of President Jimmy Carter's reelection campaign, 1978-81; served as Carter's personal representative for Middle East negotiations, 1979-81; appointed ambassador to Moscow, 1991.

Awards: Presidential Medal of Freedom, 1980.

Sidelights

"I don't know who the next president is going to be, but I know who his best friend will be," quipped former House speaker Jim Wright of fellow Texan Robert Strauss. A presence in national politics since the late 1960s, Strauss is the walking definition of the garrulous, back-slapping, high-stakes power broker who never forgets a name nor makes a permanent enemy. Dubbed "Mr. Democrat" by the media in the 1970s, Strauss has actually been a confidant of Republicans and Democrats alike: power interests him, not politics.

In 1991 President George Bush named his old Texas friend ambassador to Moscow. The post is considered especially vital at a time when U.S.-Soviet relations are being restructured along friendlier, post-Cold War lines. And his work takes on added importance in light of the world-jolting 63-hour coup by right-wing Communists, the KGB, and the Soviet military that occured in August of 1991. The man who has raised millions of dollars for the Democrats was clearly selected to give the Soviets a first-hand glimpse into big-time wheeling and dealing. Influential *Washington Post* columnist Nary McGrory observed: "President Bush had a choice. Either he could have tried to explain capitalism to Mikhail Gorbachev or he could send him Robert Strauss, who embodies it. He chose the latter."

Known for his Dallas poker games, afternoons at the race track and a high-spirited work-the-crowd style, the Texan ambassador made it clear from the first what Moscow could expect from someone who speaks Texan, not Russian. "It ain't an easy job and it's not comfortable surroundings, but the President and [Secretary of State] Jim Baker talked me into it and I'm going to give it the best shot I got," Strauss said at a Washington press conference, as reported by *New York Times* correspondent Maureen Dowd. "If they want a Soviet expert, they made a mistake picking me. I'm as poor an example of a Soviet expert as they could find. But if they want a winner who's been successful at a lot of different things and understands relationships and how to help the Soviets with their economic problems, then I was the right choice." Commented Strauss's old friend John White, also a former Democratic party chairman, to Dowd: "This is where American capitalism meets Soviet Communism. Strauss is the ultimate capitalist if there ever was one. Just look at his client list, a page and a half of Fortune 500 companies. He'll teach 'em about making money."

Indeed, making money—"being a winner"—is what Strauss most enjoys, and has plied his skills for many years as a key financial player of the Democratic party. After helping reunite the organization after the major party setbacks of the 1970s, Strauss has increasingly taken a public role in Washington. Named United States trade representative by President Jimmy Carter in 1977, he handled a long round of trade negotiations with the Japanese that culminated in major trade legislation and continues to shape U.S. trade policy. He also served Carter as a special Middle East envoy and campaign fundraiser. Yet it was clear the pragmatic Texan was no Carterite. After losing his reelection campaign Carter joked, "Bob is a very loyal friend: he waited a whole week after the election before he had dinner with Ronald Reagan."

Upon leaving the government Strauss returned to his highly successful law firm, whose role was increasingly expanding into a global one. In 1990 he was hired by Japan's third-largest company, Matsushita Electric Industrial Company, to help it acquire Hollywood entertainment giant MCA. In a virtuoso bit of lawyering, Strauss—who also sits on the board of MCA—got himself hired by MCA as well to complete the friendly deal, which carried a sales tag of $7.5 billion. From MCA he collected a $8 million fee; what Matsushita paid him was secret.

Reminded that lawyers typically represent only one side of a deal, Strauss explained away the unusual double-dip: "The transaction was my client," he told the *Washington Post*. "I was trying to bring the parties together." As for his hourly fee for that transaction, it would no doubt be astronomical. However, as he informed the *Post*, he hasn't charged by the hour for over 20 years. "I don't work by the hour anymore," he sniffed, in an uncharacteristic snit. "I don't do windows. There are a lot of things I don't do I used to have to do. I don't take $25 divorce cases and traffic ticket cases, which I started doing 45 years ago."

Robert Strauss was born in 1918 in Lockhart, a small town in south central Texas, the elder of two sons of Charles H. and Edith Strauss. Charles Strauss was a Jewish emigree from Germany who married into an established Texas Jewish family and ran a dry goods store; in later years his son remembered him as a "gentle man" with a taste for classical music but little for business. Helping out from behind the counter, the future power-broker would run the store while his father would sometimes sit out back listening to radio broadcasts of faraway symphony orchestra recitals.

During his student years at the University of Texas, Strauss pledged a Jewish fraternity. After classes he clerked at the state capital in Austin, an experience that provided a youthful grounding in Lone Star State politics. "My employer had a little problem with alcohol and he was socially active," Strauss recalled to columnist McGrory. "So at age 16 I did about half his voting for him." During this time he struck up a friendship with a classmate, John B. Connally, a future Texas governor and presidential hopeful. In 1937 Strauss approached the Congressional campaign committee of a young Texan New Dealer named Lyndon Johnson, and volunteered his services to the campaign.

University classwork, political legwork, legislative gruntwork: It was the beginning of a lifelong work ethic. Strauss is known for working whatever hours are necessary to accomplish his goal, and for making whatever friends and allies are necessary to do this. "A poor Jewish kid from West Texas learns early how to survive," he told *Time* magazine. He stayed in Austin another three years and acquired a law degree, in 1941, then joined the Federal Bureau of Investigation (FBI) as an alternative to military service. He was assigned posts in Des Moines, Iowa; Columbus, Ohio; and finally Dallas, Texas, where he made his home. He has never been more specific about his duties as a special agent other than to describe his job as "watching out for Communists." "I would catch a spy nearly every other day," he joked to Maureen Dowd. "I would come home at night and my wife Helen would say, 'Did you catch any spies today, dear?'"

Leaving FBI service, the young man hung out a legal shingle in Dallas, along with several partners. The firm, today known as Akin, Gump, Strauss, Hauer & Feld, became increasingly prominent in both Dallas and Washington. During the start-up years of his law firm, Strauss also invested substantially in a number of deals in both real estate and broadcasting enterprises, often taking a management position. Many have since been sold at substantial profits.

When Connally ran for governor in 1962, he tapped his old classmate to raise money. Strauss raised a bundle, Connally won handily, and Strauss was rewarded with a six-year state banking board term. In 1968 Connally, clearly holding presidential aspirations, got his friend named to the Democratic National Committee. The appointment served to highlight Strauss's two key talents—fundraising and conciliatory politics. Strauss was asked to handle fundraising for Lyndon Johnson's former White House mate, Hubert Humphrey, now running his own presidential campaign. The ticket lost; the campaign finished in the black. This fiscal feat did not go unnoticed by the party's hierarchy; nor did Strauss's coup in forging a campaign alliance between his chum Connally and the governor's political opposite, liberal senator Ralph Yarborough.

By this time the political bug was beginning to nip at Strauss, who considered throwing his own hat in the ring during the 1972 Texas Senate campaign. Eventually he bowed to the argument that he was more valuable as a fundraiser, and accepted an appointment as party treasurer. In taking the post, Strauss was looking at a $9.3 million holdover debt remaining from the 1968 campaign, as well as the fast-approaching deadline to raise $2 million to finance the 1974 party convention. Strauss undertook an intensive campaign of private solicitations, fundraising dinners, and his own innovation—a television marathon—that carved the debt in half and ensured the party convention would take place as planned.

The party, however, was changing. A new generation of Democrats, many young and members of minorities, waved the banner for presidential hopeful George McGovern and saw themselves not as party regulars but as outsiders forcing change on the "old boy network" personified by people like Strauss. The Texan yielded the treasurer's post to a McGovern choice, and transferred his fundraising efforts to benefit Democratic congressional campaigns. After the 1972 landslide defeat of the McGovern campaign, Strauss and the other old-line Democrats pushed to regain control. So closely was Strauss associated with the old guard that McGovern's National Committee chair, Jean Westwood, announced she was ready to step down provided someone other than Strauss replace her. The issue was put to a vote and Strauss emerged as the new chair of the National Committee, a post he held through 1977.

It was a historic low moment in terms of party unity: the incoming chair "came to power disliked, mistrusted and feared by the liberals and reformers, and suspected of racism by the blacks," reported *Time.* Strauss began a long process of reconciliation, reaching out to both left and right. He called on Alabama governor George Wallace, long-standing symbol of the party's right wing, and to black caucus leaders on the left. His professed goal was to establish a tone of neutrality, and bring the party back together. When the party convened in Kansas City in 1974, Strauss gave his backing to some proposals from the left, like affirmative action, that clearly angered the labor unions and other long-standing bastions of Democratic support. Long-term losses, however, appeared minimal.

After two years Strauss assessed his first tenure as party chairman to *Time:* "I'm going to have more and more trouble with the hard-liners on the left and right. I'm going to have to take the 15 [percent] at the fringes and keep them in the position of a halfway mean dog that goes grr a lot and that you hope doesn't bite you. If I do that, and I'm fair about it, I'll be the kind of chairman that the majority of the party wants."

The Democrats regained control of the White House in 1976, and President Jimmy Carter appointed the party fundraiser a special trade representative, a position newly elevated to Cabinet status. Over the next two and a half years Strauss handled the Tokyo Round of the Multilateral Trade Negotiations and directed its passage through Congress which culminated in the Trade Act of 1979. Following completion of the trade agreements, Carter asked Strauss to serve as his personal representative in the Middle East peace negotiations, overseeing follow-up to the historic Camp David Peace Accord.

It was a difficult task to assign a diplomatic neophyte, and the results were not impressive. "Mr. Strauss was dealing with unfamiliar terrain and a hopeless issue as he tried to work out an agreement on Palestinian authority in the West Bank," sympathized the Maureen Dowd in the *New York Times*. Lacking diplomatic training, and indulging a tendency to keep the press rather well informed, his opportunity quickly soured. When Carter offered him the chief fundraising position for his 1978 reelection campaign, Strauss was quick to accept and jet back to Washington.

The Carter campaign proved a losing effort. But unlike others whose careers were closely associated with the Carter administration, Strauss was in no hurry to pick up and leave Washington. Throughout the decade he remained the consummate political insider, and was the first to get through to George Bush—in 1974 Strauss's opposite as chair of the Republican National Committee—and offer congratulations on his 1988 electoral victory. (The Bushes and Strausses are frequent dining companions, sharing a taste for Chinese restaurants).

If anyone in Washington wields power without lugging the baggage of ideology, it is this Texan. In December 1973 he explained his non-partisan stance to *Nation's Business* magazine: "Some people might think I am on the radical right but most people know I am a middle-of-the-road Texas Democrat...a Texas corporation lawyer with the image of a conservative. I kid my friends that I'm too liberal for Texas and too conservative for Washington. So I must be just right."

In addition to his legal work and, now, his overseas diplomatic mission, Strauss serves on the directors' boards of numerous corporations and public institutions. He is also busy as a lecturer and author. He and his wife, the former Helen Jacobs, have raised three children: Robert, Richard, and Susan. He is prominent in a local Dallas reform synagogue, and is active in the Dallas social scene. "One of the difficulties with writing about Bob Strauss is that the printed word does not convey the whole flavor of the man," complained *New Republic* scribe John Osborne in January of 1978. "He cusses, he swigs within reason, he speaks with remarkable frankness to reporters whom he trusts, and he mostly talks on the record...[with a] modulated Texas drawl."

Sources

Nation's Business, December 1973.
New Republic, January 7, 1978.
New York Times, June 5, 1991; December 10, 1990.
Time, December 16, 1974.
Washington Post, June 5, 1991; June 6, 1991.

—*Warren Strugatch*

Oliver Tambo

President-general of the African National Congress

Full name, Oliver Reginald Tambo; born October 27, 1917, in Bizana, Cape Province, South Africa; married Adelaide Tsukudu (a nurse) in 1956; children: Dudulani, Dalindlcla, Tambi. *Education:* Fort Hare University, B.S., 1941. *Religion:* Christian.

Career

Science and mathematics teacher at St. Peter's Secondary School, Johannesburg, South Africa, 1943-47; practiced law in Johannesburg, 1952-60; founder, with Nelson Mandela, of the African National Congress (ANC) Youth League in 1944; elected to ANC national executive, 1949; became acting secretary general, 1954; appointed acting president, 1967; president general, 1977—.

Awards: Honorary degrees from Jawaharlal Nehru University of New Delhi, University of Atlanta, University of the West Indies, and Cambridge College.

Sidelights

On December 13, 1991, Oliver Tambo, president-general of the African National Congress (ANC), returned home after nearly 31 years in exile from his native South Africa. Oliver Tambo, or "O.R." as his followers affectionately call him, along with Nelson Mandela (see *Newsmakers 90*) and Walter Sisulu, are the most prominent founding members of the ANC Youth League and senior

officials of the ANC's national executive committee. Through the strength of his integrity and perseverance, Tambo countered the image of the ANC as a terrorist organization that the Pretoria regime promoted. Tambo's reputation as a devout Christian (Anglican), his anti-Communist stance, and his deliberate and informed style helped change the Western world's perception of the ANC to one of a genuine liberation organization. The jubilant welcome he received from thousands of supporters and official dignitaries was mixed with sadness at his failing health and weakened condition, the result of a partially paralyzing stroke the 73-year-old suffered in August of 1989. Tambo's poor health and lack of strength is a loss to his long-time friend and confidante, ANC deputy president Mandela.

Tambo first met Mandela when they were students at Fort Hare University College in the late 1930s. Tambo graduated in 1941 but stayed on to pursue a masters degree in education. He was expelled in 1942 for organizing a student strike. Nevertheless, he took a teaching post at his alma mater, the Anglican Secondary School of St. Peter's in Johannesburg, and resumed his friendship with Mandela and other political activists. In 1957, Tambo introduced his cousin, Nomzamo Zaniewe Winnifred (Winnie; see *Newsmakers 89*) to her future husband, Nelson

Mandela. Tambo's wife, Adelaide, and Winnie Mandela became good friends and shared the same political concerns as their husbands.

In 1944 Tambo, Mandela, Walter Sisulu, and others formed the ANC Youth League. Tambo began studying law in 1948 and in 1952 he and Mandela set up the first black legal practice in South Africa. In 1949 Tambo and seven other Youth Leaguers were elected to the ANC national executive. Tambo became acting secretary general in 1954 when Sisulu was banned. In 1955 he was formally elected to the post. In 1967, on the death of ANC president Chief Albert Luthuli, Tambo was appointed acting president; he took the full title of president-general in 1977.

The Youth League pressed to have its "Programme of Action" adopted as ANC policy, thus injecting the ANC with fresh ideas and a vigorous program. The Youth League paved the way for the civil disobedience campaign, directed the Defiance Campaign in 1952, and steered through adoption of the Freedom Charter in 1954. In 1956 Tambo was accepted as a candidate for ordination in the ministry by Anglican Bishop Ambrose Reeves. However, in December of that year he was arrested and charged with high treason. Although charges against Tambo were withdrawn the following December, he was never ordained. The final 30 accused of treason were acquitted on all counts after a trial that lasted more than four years.

Tambo began his years in exile in 1960, a week after the shootings in Sharpeville in which authorities killed 67 blacks and wounded 187 others, and just days before the government outlawed the major anti-apartheid organizations. The ANC leadership instructed Tambo to flee the country to set up an externally based organization. The nature of the movement changed the following year, when the ANC decided it had no alternative but to take up arms against the government. The increasing use of violence by the South African government persuaded the ANC leadership to revoke its basic principal of non-violence, determined at the organization's founding in 1912, and wage a guerrilla war against the regime of apartheid.

Tracing the roots of this change in policy, Tambo observed in his autobiography, *Preparing for Power: Oliver Tambo Speaks:* "For decades we did not think violence had a role to play in the ANC's struggle: not until the National Party came into power in 1948 and was physically violent. The obvious thing was to respond with violence, but then we thought that perhaps that was what they wanted—that they

would use our violence to rally whites around them .... But as the years went by, violence increased. We saw more armed police—with pistols at first, then sten guns. Then the tanks came.... Then we had the Sharpeville shootings...Even after that we decided to continue with non-violence. In 1961 we called a strike to protest against the formation of a republic in South Africa.... But the army was mobilised on a scale not seen since the Second World War—against a peaceful strike.... The police were no longer sufficient. It was a new situation. We decide then to embrace violence as a method of struggle."

When the ANC began its campaign of violence the countries adjacent to South Africa formed what was then known as a *cordon sanitaire*, so called because they were still under white colonial rule. Tanzania, more than a thousand miles from South Africa's borders, was the nearest country where the ANC could set up its military bases and headquarters. Tambo oversaw the establishment of these bases and arranged for young men and women to be sent for political and military training to Algeria and other African countries, as well as to Cuba, Eastern Europe, and the Soviet Union.

In South Africa the government arrested and detained thousands of suspected ANC members, severely crippling the internal movement. Most of the other internal leaders, including Mandela and Sisulu, were sentenced to long prison terms. Many of those who fled joined Tambo in exile in the early 1960s. With the vacuum created within the country, ANC leaders in exile had to coordinate both the underground within South Africa as well as train fighters and wage the guerrilla war outside country.

In 1969 the ANC held a national consultative congress at its party headquarters in Morogoro, Tanzania. The national leadership received harsh criticism from the rank and file for its poor performance in running both the guerrilla war and the internal political wing. The entire executive membership resigned; some, including Tambo, were reelected. Others were replaced by more radical members. The Morogoro conference also set up a Revolutionary Council to run the military wing, Umkhonto we Sizwe (the Spear of the Nation), and voted to allow non-Africans to join the external ANC. The decisions made at Morogoro gave the hardliners—people who were both members of the ANC and the South African Communist Party (banned in South Africa in 1950)—access to positions of power within the movement. Although non-Africans could not be elected to the national executive committee, Communist party members, many of whom were whites or Indians, nevertheless came to dominate the leadership. They took positions with authority within the structure.

Tambo, a moderate, was elevated to a role that kept him out of the day-to-day operations of the organization. He began to travel extensively, setting up missions abroad and raising revenue and support for the ANC. He spent most of his time away from headquarters, petitioning the United Nations, addressing the Organization of African Unity, and winning support from sympathetic governments.

In 1975, in protest over the domination of the ANC by Communists, eight senior ANC members formed a breakaway faction called ANC-African Nationalist. They joined the staunchly anti-Communist, black nationalist movement, the Pan Africanist Congress (PAC), which had broken away from the ANC in 1958 because the PAC opposed a membership that included non-Africans and Communists.

Under the direction of the South African Communist Party the ANC emphasized the importance of the urban working class but seemed to neglect the role of the rural poor. In the 1960s and 1970s the ANC encouraged Inkatha leader Mangosuthu Gatsha Buthelezi (see *Newsmakers 89*) to work within the Nationalist party's homelands system in order to politicize the rural poor. Buthelezi was thus able to build up a large political following, with which he later challenged the ANC. Buthelezi had been sharply criticized by the ANC for working with the government, but at the 1985 ANC conference held at Kabwe, Zambia, Tambo admitted for the first time that the ANC had encouraged Buthelezi to accept the role of leader of the Kwazulu homeland.

In 1976 thousands of young people fled South Africa after the crackdown that followed the Soweto uprising. To accommodate these new recruits, the ANC set up camps in newly independent Angola. There they were given military training and ideological indoctrination. Many of the radical township youths became Marxists, and today some of them are among the ANC's most influential people. A substantial majority of the 36 members of the national executive committee of the ANC, as of its unbanning in February 1990, were members of the Communist party. Tambo and several others are not.

The inclusion of the young radicals transformed the democratic traditions of the ANC. According to *Africa Confidential*, "among the rich array of Stalinist methods which gained currency was the practice of discrediting dissenters by sending them into internal exile." Any ANC members who dissented or challenged the new leadership were punished or expelled by decree. The ANC's research director, Dr. Pallo Jordon, was detained in 1983 for eight weeks for criticizing the excesses of the security branch. (Tambo, who had been away at the time of the incident, rescued him on his return.) Shortly after Jordan's detention, others in the Angola camps protested the repressiveness of the security branch. The mutiny was quashed, its leaders were executed, and some of those detained are in ANC detention centers in Tanzania and Uganda today.

> *"We have to make apartheid unworkable and our country ungovernable."*

For fear of losing control of the more radical elements, Tambo seldom spoke out against the excesses. However, in 1988 he publicly refuted Umkhonto we Sizwe chief of staff Chris Hani's statement on the need to carry war to white civilians. But when it came to the practice of "necklacing" (the township style of execution by setting alight a gasoline-filled tire hung around a person's neck), Tambo was quoted by Alistair Sparks in *The Mind of South Africa* as saying, "We disapprove, though we understand what drove them to it."

In 1984 the uprisings in the South African townships began again, sparked by new local council decisions to raise rents. The violence escalated. The exiled ANC leaders met in Kabwe, Zambia. In response to the South African government's declaration of a state of emergency, Tambo called on the people "to break down and destroy the old order." He said in *Preparing for Power:* "We have to make apartheid unworkable and our country ungovernable. The accomplishment of these tasks will create the situation for us to overthrow the apartheid regime and for power to pass into the hands of the people as a whole."

The high visibility of the government's repression on television and in newspapers brought loud international condemnation. Tambo took the opportunity to travel widely to explain the policies of the ANC and to press demands for sanctions against the white-controlled government. An investigation sponsored by the Commonwealth nations resulted in a report from its team of "Eminent Persons" that was highly critical of so-called reform in South Africa. The report made it clear that dialogue with the government of then-President P. W. Botha was futile.

When the Western powers and the United Nations decided to take economic action against the South African government, the ANC in exile was consulted as a source of leadership for any future order. White South African businessmen, executives of international corporations, and government leaders sought out Tambo and other ANC leaders. Through his tireless efforts and consistency in explaining ANC policy and structures and its vision for a post-apartheid society, Tambo won wide international respect for himself and the organization.

On Tambo's return to South Africa in December 1990, he addressed a consultative congress of the ANC. He urged the movement to reconsider sanctions as a weapon against apartheid. He said in *Preparing for Power:* "It is no longer enough for us to repeat the tried slogans. We should therefore carefully re-evaluate the advisability of insisting on the retention of the sanctions, given the new developments in the country and abroad." However, the ANC rank and file was so opposed to his suggestion that on the following day Tambo backtracked and proposed that "existing sanctions be maintained." The second proposal was approved by a standing ovation.

In June 1991 the ANC held its first national congress to elect members to the national executive council since the 1969 Morogoro Conference. The results of this congress remain to be seen. Although Tambo is planning to return to South Africa to live, his physical condition will probably necessitate that he be given an honorary position on the executive council. He was recently appointed chancellor of Fort Hare University.

Oliver Tambo led the ANC through some of its darkest times—the failure of the armed struggle, internal disputes and wrangling, and the South African government's successful destabilization of countries allied to the ANC. But he also witnessed the glory days of international support against the apartheid system, the release of Nelson Mandela from prison after 27 years, and the unbanning of the ANC. He and Mandela were reunited in March 1990 in Stockholm, Sweden, where Tambo was recuperating from his stroke. He has lived long enough to see the end of the apartheid legislation and the promise of a multi-party democratic system in his native land. The *Weekly Mail* quoted an ANC veteran, who spent years in guerrilla camps doing very little, recalling those grim days: "They were very confusing, very difficult times. But O.R. led us through them, and so he became the father and mother of us all."

Sources

Books

Meli, Francis, *South Africa Belongs to Us: A History of the ANC,* Zimbabwe Publishing House, 1988.
Sparks, Alistair, *The Mind of South Africa,* Heinemann, 1990.
Tambo, Adelaide, compiler, *Preparing for Power: Oliver Tambo Speaks,* Braziller, 1980.

Periodicals

Africa Confidential, January 12, 1990; March 8, 1991.
New York Times, December 16, 1990.
Weekly Mail, October 23-October 29, 1987.

—*Virginia Curtin Knight*

Randall Terry

Anti-abortion activist

Son of two public school teachers; wife's name, Cindy. *Education:* Attended Elim Bible Institute.

Sidelights

As leader of the crusading anti-abortion group Operation Rescue, Randall Terry, a youthful, zealous, born-again Christian, has become the field general for the increasingly militant far right wing of abortion protest organizations that is attempting to disrupt activities around the country at clinics where abortions are performed. "In the war to outlaw abortion, Terry is the chief guerrilla leader," wrote *People*'s Montgomery Brower. "The group's principal tactic is to strike without warning, surrounding an abortion clinic. Operation Rescue counselors then confront women patients, pleading with them not to enter. For every woman who approaches a clinic and turns back—no matter what her intentions—Operation Rescue assumes it has 'rescued' an unborn child. If police show up, the demonstrators simply go limp and are carted off."

Since Operation Rescue's inception in the late 1980s, Terry claims that more than 35,000 people have been arrested at these demonstrations. Terry himself has been arrested dozens of times, and in 1989 he was sentenced to 24 months in prison for criminal assembly and unlawful trespassing at an Atlanta clinic. Still, though abortion is legal in the United States, Terry says that he will continue his unlawful activities, citing adherence to biblical law. "If you think abortion is murder," he reasoned in *Rolling Stone*, "then *act* like it's murder." However one views

Terry's stance on the highly volatile abortion issue, the intensity of his commitment cannot be denied. Indeed, Terry's prison sentence could have been suspended had he paid a $1,000 fine and agreed to stay away from Atlanta for two years, but he refused. "Number one . . . , I am not guilty of a crime," he was quoted as saying in *People*. "It is not a crime to save a child from murder. Two, if at all possible I do not want to give money to a system that is protecting murderers and jailing people trying to save babies."

The son of two public school teachers, Terry lived a fairly secular childhood in upstate New York, playing in a rock band as a teenager and occasionally smoking marijuana. At age 17 he dropped out of school for a time and roamed the country with a friend. He discovered religion while working at an ice cream parlor back in Rochester, New York, around that time after befriending a young couple who attended the nearby college, Elim Bible Institute. He enrolled in the school himself in 1978 and soon met his future wife, Cindy. The two studied Spanish and planned to become missionaries in Central America after graduation.

But in 1983 Terry found himself becoming increasingly embroiled in the struggle over abortion rights in this country. What started as a one-man picket of a

Binghamton, New York, abortion clinic soon grew to include Cindy, who began joining her husband, and then several members of Terry's church. Terry was arrested for the first time in 1985, and since then Operation Rescue has grown into a nationwide, somewhat clandestine, highly sophisticated organization that prides itself in being able to strike in large numbers, seemingly from out of nowhere, to block entrances to clinics anywhere in the country.

The organization is operated as a for-profit business with Terry as sole proprietor, drawing a salary of about $30,000, because the group's unlawful activities make it unable to accept tax-exempt contributions. Donations, which run well into six figures annually, come in the form of checks, but Terry cashes only those checks he will need immediately for payroll and other expenses through bank accounts he continues to move from state to state. Uncashed checks are kept hidden until needed, and can be destroyed if a lien is placed on Operation Rescue's assets, which are few—office equipment, cars, etc. are all rented so that anyone trying to seize the group's assets will come away with nothing.

How long Terry and Operation Rescue will continue to operate with such effectiveness is anybody's guess. The group has become so well-known to pro-choice activists that their "target" clinics are often discovered before the group has a chance to move, making for some semi-comical chess games between walkie-talkie wielding organizers on both sides trying to outmaneuver the other. But Terry seems more than willing to continue to do whatever is necessary to keep up the fight, including raise foster children. He and Cindy adopted three mixed-race children, the youngest of which was born to a woman whom Terry talked out of having an abortion. Terry told *People* magazine that the country can find a way to care for the additional 1.6 million children that would be born each year if abortion were outlawed: "If abortion ended tomorrow, we'd have our work cut out for us," he said. "But we could do it."

Sources

Ms., April 1989.
People, November 20, 1989.
Rolling Stone, October 5, 1989.
Time, May 1, 1989.

—*David Collins*

Wayne Thiebaud

Artist

Full name, Wayne Morton Thiebaud; born November 15, 1920, in Mesa, Ariz.; son of Morton J. (an inventor and engineer) and Alice Eugenia (Le Baron) Thiebaud; married Patricia Patterson, 1943 (divorced, 1959); married Betty Jean Carr (a filmmaker), 1959; children: (first marriage) Twinka, Mallary Ann; (second marriage) Matthew Bult Carr (adopted), Paul Le Baron. *Education:* Attended Frank Wiggins Trade School, Los Angeles, 1938, Long Beach Junior College, 1940-41, and San Jose State College (now San Jose State University), 1949-50; California State College (now California State University), Sacramento, B.A., 1951, M.A. 1953.

Addresses: *Office*—Department of Art, University of California, Davis, Davis, CA 95616. *Agent*—Allan Stone Gallery, 48 E. 86th St., New York, NY 10028.

Career

Animator for Walt Disney Studios, 1936-37; stage technician, usher, free-lance cartoonist, and illustrator, 1938-40; cartoonist for military newspaper and muralist, 1942-45; layout designer, free-lance cartoonist, and illustrator, 1945-46; illustrator and art director at Rexall Drug Company, 1946-49; Sacramento Junior College (now Sacramento City College), art instructor, 1951-54, chairman of art department, 1954-56, 1958-60; producer of educational art films with own company, Patrician Films, 1954-59; advertising art director at Deutsch & Shea Advertising Agency and Frederick A. Richardson Advertising Agency, New York, 1956-57; University of California, Davis, assistant professor 1960-63, associate professor, 1963-67, professor, 1967—.

Individual exhibitions include those at E. B. Crocker Art Gallery, Sacramento, 1970; Whitney Museum of American Art, New York, 1971; Artists Contemporary Gallery, Sacramento, 1973; Colorado State University, Fort Collins, 1975; Mary Porter Sesnon Art Gallery, University of California, 1976; San Francisco Museum of Modern Art, 1978; Walker Art Center, Minneapolis, 1981; Crocker Art Museum, Sacramento, 1983; Van Stavern Fine Art Gallery, Sacramento, 1985; Newport Harbor, Newport, California, 1986; Richard R. Nelson Gallery, 1988; numerous traveling exhibits.

Awards: Chicago Golden Reel Award and first prize at California State Fair Art Film Festival, Sacramento, both for the film *Space*, 1956; Osborn Cunningham Award, 1958; University of California Faculty Fellowship, 1961; Golden Apple Award for distinguished teaching from University of California, Davis, 1973; citation from College Art Association of America as most distinguished studio teacher of the year, 1980-81; Faculty Research Lecture medal from University of California, Davis, award of distinction from National Art Schools Association, and special citation award from the National Association of Schools of Art and Design, all 1984; Cyril Magnin Award and Golden Plate Award from American Academy of Achievement, both 1987; many honorary degrees and visiting professorships.

Member: American Academy and Institute of Arts and Letters, National Academy of Design.

Sidelights

Realist painter Wayne Thiebaud enjoys a career that has already spanned 30 years. His paintings and prints, which range in subject from still lifes to figures to urban landscapes, can be found in major collections in the United States and Europe, including the Museum of Modern Art, the Metropolitan Museum of Art, the Whitney Museum of American Art, the Chicago Art Institute, and the San Francisco Museum of Modern Art. Also a dedicated teacher, Thiebaud has received numerous academic honors and served as a visiting professor or artist-in-residence at institutions throughout North America.

The elder of two children, Thiebaud was born in 1920 in Mesa, Arizona, to Morton J. and Alice Eugenia Le Baron Thiebaud. Within a year of Wayne's birth the Thiebaud family had moved to Long Beach, California, where Morton Thiebaud was an inventor and engineer working at a creamery and a Ford Motor Company distribution center. After the onset of the Great Depression in 1931, the Thiebaud family moved to a southern Utah ranch, but by 1933 they had returned to Long Beach.

Wayne Thiebaud was active with the Mormon church and with various extracurricular events at Long Beach Polytechnic High School, including basketball and serving on the stage crew for plays. At age sixteen, Thiebaud broke his back while participating in sports and turned his attention from sports to drawing, particularly cartooning. His talent was such that though he was inexperienced he was hired by Walt Disney Studios' animation department, where he worked as an "in-betweener": After a principal animator would draw the first and last cartoons of a strip, Thiebaud would draw the middle frames. Thiebaud was fired from this position six months later because of his pro-union sympathies, but the experience turned his attention toward commercial art. While finishing high school, Thiebaud also took commercial art courses at the Frank Wiggins Trade School in Los Angeles.

Following graduation Thiebaud worked at various jobs: stage technician, usher, free-lance cartoonist, and occasional illustrator of movie posters for the Rivoli movie theater in Long Beach. In 1941 he worked as a shipfitter on Terminal Island near Long Beach, and a year later he joined the U.S. Army Air Force. While he initially wanted to be a pilot, he quickly realized that his talent as an illustrator could be useful in the military. In less than a year he was transferred to Mather Army Air Force Base near Sacramento, where he worked as an artist and cartoonist with the Special Services Department. His duties included creating a cartoon strip for the base newspaper, designing posters, and executing murals. In 1945 he was transferred to Culver City in southern California, where he worked in the first Air Force Motion Picture Unit under the command of Ronald Reagan. After his discharge from the military, Thiebaud worked for a year as a free-lance illustrator and cartoonist before going to work for a short stint at Universal-International Studios in the San Fernando Valley, north of Los Angeles. From 1946 to 1949 he worked as art director and cartoonist with the Rexall Drug Company in Los Angeles. During his tenure at Rexall, Thiebaud met sculptor Robert Mallary, who inspired Thiebaud to paint seriously.

In 1943 Thiebaud married Patricia Patterson and by 1952 they had two daughters, Twinka and Mallary Ann. Family responsibilities, however, did not prevent Thiebaud from—at age twenty-nine—enrolling at what is now San Jose State University in northern California. A year later he transferred to California State University in Sacramento, where in 1951 he earned his undergraduate degree in art. Immediately following graduation he began teaching at what is now Sacramento City College while working on a master's degree in art, which he completed in 1953. From 1956 to 1957, while on sabbatical leave from his teaching position, Thiebaud worked as an advertising agency director for a New York agency and met other painters of his era.

He was soon back in the West. Because the artistic community in 1950s Sacramento was limited, Thiebaud tried to inspire cultural vitality through his teaching, creating public murals and sculptures, and designing sets for local theater productions. From 1954 to 1959 he also established a small film production company in his home to produce educational art films. In 1959 the Thiebauds divorced and Wayne married filmmaker Betty Jean Carr. Thiebaud adopted Betty's son Matthew and a year later their son Paul Le Baron Thiebaud was born.

During the 1950s Thiebaud worked in oils, exploring various styles—particularly the colorful and loose brush stroke styles of abstract impressionism. By mid-decade he had simplified his paintings and made the object the central focus. He had also become attracted to the displays of commercial merchandising, finding himself intrigued by such things as bakery and candy counters, gumball machines, and ice cream cones. In the film *A Piece of Cake* Thiebaud reflected on his early work: "[In] the midfifties . . . I began to try to formulate and synthesize the information I had and began to work on a number of things that I felt were interesting to me, like painting objects I hadn't seen painted, like gumball machines and store window fronts. They were an attempt to try and say something, to try and do something about those things, which somehow I felt strangely attracted to, the fascination with things like display counters, the way we light them, the insistent reverie inherent in something like a toy, what toys meant, the way in which objects stood as kind of a melancholy of loss, dealing with a kind of bright pathos." Thiebaud paints from memory and the objects are set off from plain backgrounds by bright lighting from an indeterminate source that causes the edges of shapes to emanate brilliant color. He tries to create a sense of energy by allowing vigorous brush strokes to remain.

Thiebaud found at first that he was somewhat embarrassed to be painting such objects. "I could imagine myself frosting cake, squeezing cream. Matter of fact, when I painted those damn pies I said to myself, 'This is ridiculous, painting pies. I'm a respectable painter; I can't do pies.' But they were very physical, and I couldn't stop," he told Dorothy Burkhart of the *San Jose Mercury News*. During a visit to New York in 1956, while on sabbatical leave from his teaching position, Thiebaud learned that other artists were also very much interested in depicting such banal objects.

Thiebaud's paintings attracted little critical or public attention until 1961 when, during a visit to New York City, Thiebaud met gallery owner Allan Stone. In April 1962 Stone held the first one-person exhibit of Thiebaud's work on the east coast. Thiebaud was pleasantly surprised to discover that all of the paintings in the show were sold. Such noteworthy artists as Andy Warhol, Roy Lichtenstein, and Claes Oldenburg were then painting similar objects in what was latter to become known as Pop Art, a style in which artists depicted everyday objects as an indictment of consumerism and mass culture.

With such works as *Pies, Pies, Pies, Toy Counter, Jawbreaker Machine, Three Lipsticks*, and *Wedding Cake*, critics erroneously labeled Thiebaud a Pop artist because of the similar subject matter, but Thiebaud has always been more interested in the particular set of technical problems a painting poses—composition, light, and paint handling—than trying to make a social statement. Unlike the works of Pop artists, in which the hand of the artist is minimized by using flat paint and stencils, Thiebaud's works abound with his personal touch—brush strokes. Thiebaud once told Donald Hoffmann, art critic of the *Kansas City Star*, "What

painters do, is to develop alternative ways of knowing things—things that we've overlooked, or haven't looked deeply enough at, or haven't really examined with concentrated uninterrupted consciousness: those quiet corners of life, those things which are terribly important but often don't seem so in light of an active, electronic society." Thiebaud believes that if he can charge common objects with grandeur or eloquence by painting them, they can take on a life of their own, become something more than what they appear to be.

> *"When I painted those damn pies I said to myself, 'This is ridiculous, painting pies. I'm a respectable painter; I can't do pies.'"*

While many artists support themselves from teaching early in their careers, only to leave teaching after they are established financially, Thiebaud has, despite his success, taught throughout his career. Since 1960 he has been on the faculty at the University of California at Davis. "I'm not doing it out of missionary zeal," explained Thiebaud to *Sacramento Bee* art correspondent Ellen Schlesinger. "I get a lot from teaching. It's satisfying to be around young people who are just beginning to get a sense of themselves. I try to get them to declare their artistic intentions. Of course, I think in the end we are all self-taught, but it I can help them to find something that they feel passionate about, something gripping, then I've done my job." A rigorous formalist, Thiebaud teaches his students the techniques needed to realistically depict a subject. With these skills learned, the students are then able to consciously decide which rules, if any, they want to break in arriving at an personal style.

Thiebaud has often referred to himself as an unabashed thief who borrows easily from the styles of many artists: eighteen-century French still life painter Jean Baptiste Chardin, twentieth-century Italian still life painter Giorgio Morandi, seventeenth-century Spanish master Deigo Velazquez, and twentieth-century American realists Edward Hopper and Richard Diebenkorn of the Bay Area figurative school.

Less well known than his still lifes are Thiebaud's figure paintings. From 1963 to 1966 Thiebaud concentrated on depicting the human form; figures have remained in his array of subjects since then. For him the capacity of an artist to deal with the figure is a device to measure the painter's skill. In 1964 Thiebaud received a fellowship from the University of California that freed him from teaching for a year and thus allowed him to focus on painting the human form. Since this time, Thiebaud has regularly attended life drawing sessions as he sees the figure as his greatest personal challenge. Unlike his still lifes, Thiebaud's figures are painted from live models, often his children or wife Betty Jean. "The figures . . . are not supposed to reveal anything," Thiebaud told *Sacramento Bee* reporter William C. Glackin. "It's like seeing a stranger in some place like an air terminal for the first time. You look at him, you notice his shoes, his suit, the pin in his lapel, but you don't have any particular feelings about him." To prevent his paintings from having any narrative content, Thiebaud asks the models to move around until at random he chooses a pose, often one with little action, and when there are multiple figures in a Thiebaud painting, they do not interact with one another.

Landscapes form the third major topic of Thiebaud's work, which he added to his repertoire in the mid- and late-1960s. With his drawings and paintings of rural scenes of the San Fernando Valley, Thiebaud changed from using oils to stained acrylics or a combination of oils, pastel, and charcoal. After making sketches at the site, Thiebaud executed these pastoral landscapes in the studio, where he could manipulate the elements, freeing himself from the desire to picture the scene with camera-like exactness.

In 1973 Thiebaud bought a small second home in San Francisco on Potrero Hill, south of the downtown financial district. The dramatic contrasts of the city quickly caught his attention. He became interested in the problems of depicting the roller coaster character of the city's terrain. He painted many cityscapes on site, later using some smaller paintings to inspire larger works done in the studio. While details abound—cars, crosswalks, street lamps, trees—Thiebaud seldom depicts people in these works. Again, once inside the studio, Thiebaud rearranged elements of the scene, sometimes distort-

ing the perspective, to interpret a scene rather than portray it directly.

While Thiebaud is regular in his work habits and often depicts the commonplace, his aspirations are for a result much less common. For Thiebaud, painting is a continual learning process which involves approaching and solving, or failing to solve, the same problems of composition, light, and paint handling. "As far as I can sort of ascertain from the work I do, fifteen or twenty, maybe—one out of those may have some chance of staying. I'm sure I don't destroy enough of them, but that's what it's about, for me at least, doing a lot of work, making lots of mistakes, making lots of terrible paintings which are awful or confused, out of that often you build surprises," he said in the film *A Piece of Cake*. "If we're looking . . . in our hopes and dreams at least . . . [to achieve] some sort of rareness, some sort of extraordinariness, then it only stands to reason that there has to be risk taking. You have to push to extremes or try to, to do things which are a little crazy, a little strange, unusual in the hope that that thing might be made extraordinary."

Sources

Books

Tsujimoto, Karen, *Wayne Thiebaud*, University of Washington Press, 1985.

Periodicals

Kansas City Star, October 5, 1986.
Mirabella, July 1990.
Sacramento Bee, October 3, 1965; February 13, 1983; September 13, 1985.
San Diego Union, September 22, 1985.
San Francisco Examiner, September 15, 1985.
San Jose Mercury News, September 8, 1985.
Tribune (Oakland, California), September 8, 1985.

Films

A Piece of Cake and Other Paintings by Wayne Thiebaud, written and produced by Louise Lo for KQED, Inc., 1983.

—*Jeanne M. Lesinski*

Garry Trudeau

Cartoonist

Full name, Garretson Beekman Trudeau; born in 1948 in New York, N.Y.; son of Robert (a physician) and Jean Amory Trudeau; married Jane Pauley (a television journalist), June 14, 1980; children: Rachel, Ross, Tommy. *Education:* Yale University, M.F.A., 1970.

Addresses: *Office*—c/o Universal Press Syndicate, 44 Johnson Dr., Fairway, KS 66209. *Home*—New York City.

Awards: Pulitzer Prize for editorial cartooning, 1975; Academy Award nomination for animated film, *A Doonesbury Special*, 1977; several honorary degrees from colleges and universities.

Career

Cartoonist for *Yale Daily News*, 1969-70; operator of a graphic arts studio in New Haven, Conn., 1970; writer and illustrator of *Doonesbury*, a comic strip currently running in more than 900 newspapers, 1970—. Has also published more than 60 books (mostly compilations of his comic strips); written several television specials; and co-authored two plays, a stage musical, *Doonesbury*, and *Rap Master Ronnie*, a satire aimed at former President Ronald Reagan. Also wrote the HBO television series *Tanner '88*.

Sidelights

Garry Trudeau's comic strip *Doonesbury* has taken readers on a tour through former President Ronald Reagan's brain. It has portrayed President George Bush as a man with no visible image and Vice President Dan Quayle as a feather. It has questioned the foreign policy of five presidents and called Frank Sinatra a member-in-good-standing of organized crime. It has boldly tackled issues such as abortion, AIDS, and premarital sex.

Along the way, *Doonesbury* achieved two distinctions: It is both the most controversial and most widely acclaimed comic strip in the United States. In many papers, Trudeau's work appears on the opinion pages. In some papers, his more caustic works have been pulled when editors accused him of crossing the boundaries of good taste. On the other hand, social critics praise Trudeau for harpooning popular figures and using his medium to raise questions. Trudeau even won a Pulitzer Prize in 1975 for editorial cartooning, the first time a seven-day-a-week comic strip received such an honor.

"Neither radicals nor reactionaries are safe from his artillery," a *Time* reporter wrote in a 1976 profile of Trudeau. "Stuffed shirts of Oxford broadcloth or frayed denim receive the same impudent deflation. Yet Trudeau attacks with such gentle humor that even hard-nosed presidential aides can occasionally be heard chuckling over the daily White House news summary—when it includes a *Doonesbury*.

Not everyone in the White House shares that feeling. In 1987, Bush told the *Miami Herald* that he resented Trudeau since the cartoonist showed him placing his "manhood in a blind trust" to be Reagan's loyal running mate. "My first reaction was anger, testiness, getting upset," Bush said. "I thought, what the hell? Who is this elitist who never ran for sheriff, never [took] his case to the people? Who is this little guy that comes out of some of the same background as me? So I had that personal feeling that I wanted to go up and kick the hell out of him, frankly."

> *"Criticizing a political satirist for being unfair is like criticizing a 260-pound noseguard for being too physical."*

Many of Trudeau's targets have probably felt the same way since he began writing the strip *Bull Tales* in 1968 while a student at Yale University. The strip centered on campus life and included many of the characters—B.D., Michael Doonesbury, Zonker Harris, and Mark Slackmeyer among them—who remain mainstays. Within a month Trudeau was discovered by a syndicate. From the time the strip debuted in 29 papers in October 1970, it was a hit.

Trudeau was born into a well-to-do family and raised in the small town of Saranac Lake, New York. His background includes five generations of doctors on his father's side and politicians, clerics, and businessmen on his mother's. His great-grandfather discovered the "rest cure" for tuberculosis, and Trudeau is a distant relative of former Canadian Prime Minister Pierre Trudeau. Garry Trudeau's earliest passion was theater. "I was a single-interest kid. I mounted basement productions and organized a local theater group. I was more attracted to the impresario aspects than to performance. I was not extroverted by nature. When I was 12 I made the decision I wanted to be behind the scenes and write and compose and direct," he told *Newsweek*. Trudeau's childhood theater group, The Acting Corp., produced plays complete with tickets, scripts and programs. It stayed

in business until he was 17. Later, at Yale, Trudeau designed sets for university productions.

Trudeau's parents divorced when he was 12. That year he developed an ulcer, which went undiagnosed until his military induction entrance physical ten years later. (The condition kept him out of the service.) Trudeau spent his adolescence at prep schools, where he was teased for his lack of athletic ability. "I didn't like being a teenager. I didn't like teenagers when I was one. And I still don't like them. It's a very selfish time of life."

Trudeau did earn some popularity by drawing his first cartoon character, "Weenie Man," on posters selling hot dogs for football games. "Weenie Man was the prototype for Mike Doonesbury," he told the *Washington Post*. "He was very [Jules] Feifferesque in look and in temperament."

At Yale, Trudeau co-edited a humor magazine and, during his junior year, launched *Bull Tales*. He told the *Washington Post* that becoming a cartoonist seemed at the time to be "the perfect profession for somebody with quintessential '60s sensibilities. . . . Because, in effect, I was being permitted to do the same things I was doing when I was in college—which was to act on my social concerns and to share my view of the absurdity of society."

Trudeau's cartooning heroes were satirist Feiffer and the late Walt Kelley, creator of "Pogo." He told the *Philadelphia Inquirer*: "'Doonesbury' has never been a gag strip in the traditional sense. I have always tried to create a sense of the four-panel smile as opposed to the last-panel laugh. People should feel that they're simply visiting this world for a few moments. I get it from 'Pogo.' Walt Kelley never told a joke in his life. It's all texture, it's all situations, and it's all characterizations."

And frequently it plays off politics and the news. In the early years, *Doonesbury* centered on life at the Walden Puddle Commune, a haven for 1960s throwbacks. It explored issues such as the Vietnam War, women's rights, and Watergate. To those who felt stung by Trudeau's barbs, former Secretary of State Henry Kissinger told the *Akron Beacon Journal*, "The only thing worse than being in it would be not to be in it." And while *Doonesbury* strips are frequently attacked for their unfairness, Trudeau insists that political cartoons aren't supposed to be fair. "Criticizing a political satirist for being unfair is like criticizing a 260-pound noseguard for being too physical," he told *Newsweek*.

In January 1983, weary of 12 years of meeting daily deadlines, Trudeau suspended the strip and began a leave of absence, which ended up lasting 21 months. During that time he wrote two screenplays—on campaign reporters and right-wing activists—which sold but were never produced as films. He also co-authored (with Elizabeth Swados) and produced the Broadway musical *Doonesbury*, based on his work. The show had a brief run and was not a critical success. As reviewer Benedict Nightingale of the *New York Times* wrote: "Even the most astringent passages don't seem ideally suited to that extrovert medium, the musical theater. Often you can see the drawings in your mind's eye." Trudeau, whose heart remained in the theater from his childhood, was bothered by the reviews.

When he returned to cartooning, Trudeau changed *Doonesbury*. The characters left Walden Puddle, moved out into the post-college world and began exploring life issues. The strip's wit, however, remained caustic and political. "One way to judge a political cartoonist is by the controversy he keeps," wrote the *Chicago Tribune*'s Chris Lamb. "And no American cartoonist—perhaps no American satirist—has created more controversy than Garry Trudeau.... And through the 1970s, 1980s and into the 1990s, no caricaturist or cartoonist has captured our society or chronicled its change better than *Doonesbury*.

A complete list of *Doonesbury* greatest hits would require pages. But a partial list of its victims includes former House Speaker Tip O'Neill, former California Governor Jerry Brown, Henry Kissinger, the anti-abortion movement, the city of Palm Beach, Florida, and Frank Sinatra. After a 1989 sequence lampooning Reagan's decision to award Sinatra the Medal of Freedom and lumping him with various organized crime figures, Trudeau was the target of legal action brought by Sinatra. "He's about as funny as a tumor," Sinatra told the *Washington Post*.

Other controversial episodes have been pulled by the editors of various newspapers. They include strips picturing two unmarried characters sleeping together (1976), criticizing the anti-abortion film *Silent Scream* (1985), and portraying presidential candidate Pat Robertson taking campaign orders from God (1988). Trudeau's rendering of President Bush—partially rooted in their common privileged, prep-school heritage—has never been censored, but has embarrassed the cartoonist's mother, who told him to lay off Bush's family. Trudeau has said he is not bothered when papers pull his work, telling the *Akron Beacon Journal*, "It's not censorship, it's editing.... That's their call." Nor does he see himself, or other members of his profession, as being particular-

ly forceful. "I don't think the media has any power," he told *Newsweek*. "They have influence, which is not the same. The lowliest functionary in the federal government has more actual power over people's lives."

Most often, Trudeau stays away from public debate, letting his opinions come out through his work. He has avoided all but a handful of interviews over the years and not been on television since an appearance on *To Tell the Truth* in 1971. His marriage to well-known television journalist Jane Pauley, however, has made it difficult for Trudeau to remain a recluse. The two met in 1979 at a dinner party hosted by newsman Tom Brokaw. They married the next year. The couple and their three children now live in New York City and try to keep their home life private. Also not publicly discussed is the half-day each week he volunteers at a homeless shelter. "What Jane and I have in common," Trudeau told the *Washington Post*, "is that we are both professional generalists. Which is why, perhaps, we are role models, to the extent that we are, to a generation of college students. Because we know very little about a great many things. It's a bizarre way to conduct your life, no question about it."

In recent years Trudeau has strived to branch out. He and Swados teamed up again to produce *Rap Master Ronnie*, a satirical musical revue of the Reagan administration. The show, which played in major cities and later was shown on cable television, took shots at the president's policies and ethics and what Trudeau viewed as a moral deterioration of the political system. The *Philadelphia Inquirer*'s Steven Salisbury called it a "tour through the glimmering highlights of the Reagan years, a song-filled assault down memory lane." In 1988 Trudeau and renowned film director Robert Altman teamed up to produce *Tanner '88*, a deft HBO series chronicling the fictional presidential campaign of Jack Tanner of Michigan. "This show's target is not an individual, but the process by which America perhaps forces the creation or invention of presidents who are more creatures of media, more technocratic myth, than anything else," wrote the *Miami Herald*'s Steve Sonsky. "That could be Ronald Reagan—and it could be every president since John Kennedy."

As the 1990s began, Trudeau was working on a new project. He and film director Alan Pakula teamed up to write a black comedy about AIDS researchers. The subject is one that Trudeau finds fascinating. Recent *Doonesbury* episodes have centered on AIDS, and have proven to be among his most controversial. In 1989 Trudeau introduced character Andy Lipincott, a wise-cracking AIDS victim who would later die in the comic strip. Trudeau came under fire for his humorous treatment of the sensitive issue, but told the *St. Paul Pioneer Press:* "In order to understand and come to terms with it, I had to strip it of its taboos, to attack the fear and ignorance by laughing in its face. It's an outlet for despair, a means to quell the terror. As a satirist, I am trying to make it easier to look into the abyss as all of us will have to do. These [AIDS patients] are fellow human beings with mothers, fathers, friends. It's time to come to terms with that."

Trudeau also plans to continue writing *Doonesbury,* he told the *Philadelphia Inquirer,* "for as long as people want to read it. And I'll always take the position I think any satirist does: insist that we do better." From his own perspective, Trudeau believes he needs to learn to become a better illustrator of his comic strip. "I'm still working on it," he told the *Washington Post.* "I have always felt that I'm not much of a writer and I'm not much of an artist but I reside at the intersection of those two disciplines and that's where I make my contribution."

Selected writings

But This War Had Such Promise, Holt, 1973.
Call Me When You Find America, Holt, 1973.
The President is a Lot Smarter Than You Think, Holt, 1973.
The Doonesbury Chronicles, Holt, 1975.
Dare to Be Great, Ms. Caucus, Holt, 1975.
As the Kid Goes for Broke, Holt, 1977.
Stalking the Perfect Tan, Holt, 1978.
But the Pension Fund Was Just Sitting There, Holt, 1979.
And That's My Final Offer!, Holt, 1980.
In Search of Reagan's Brain, Holt, 1981.
The People's Doonesbury: Notes from Underfoot, Holt, 1981.

Ask for May, Settle for June, Holt, 1982.
You Give Great Meeting, Sid, Holt, 1983.
Check Your Egos at the Door, Holt, 1985.
Death of a Party Animal, Holt, 1986.
That's Doctor Sinatra, You Little Bimbo!, Holt, 1986.
Downtown Doonesbury, Holt, 1987.
Calling Dr. Whoopee, Holt, 1987.
Talkin' About My G-G-Generation, Holt, 1988.
We're Eating More Beets!, Holt, 1988.
Give Those Nymphs Some Hooters! A Doonesbury Book, Holt, 1989.
Read My Lips, Make My Day, Eat Quiche and Die! A Doonesbury Collection, Andrews & McMeel, 1989.
Recycled Doonesbury: Thoughts on a Gilded Age, Andrews & McMeel, 1990.
You're Smokin' Now, Mr. Butts! A Doonesbury Book, Andrews & McMeel, 1990.

Sources

Akron Beacon Journal, October 29, 1987; February 11, 1988.
Charlotte Observer, April 6, 1989.
Chicago Tribune, April 9, 1989; October 26, 1990.
Detroit Free Press, September 7, 1987; January 22, 1988.
Gary Post-Tribune, December 4, 1988.
Houston Post, October 30, 1990.
Miami Herald, October 16, 1987; February 13, 1988; October 26, 1990.
New Republic, August 1, 1988.
Newsweek, June 24, 1989; September 24, 1987; October 10, 1990.
New York Times, November 22, 1983; September 30, 1984; October 7, 1984.
Philadelphia Inquirer, July 19, 1987.
St. Paul Pioneer Press, April 2, 1989; August 19, 1990; October 13, 1990.
Time, February 9, 1976; December 8, 1986.
Washington Post, May 14, 1986; November 12, 1986; October 9, 1990.

—*Glen Macnow*

Dawn Upshaw

AP/Wide World Photos

Opera singer

Born July 17, 1960, in Nashville, Tenn.; daughter of a psychotherapist and a teacher; married Michael Nott, 1986; one daughter. *Education:* Wesleyan University, B.A., 1982; Manhattan School of Music, M.A., 1984.

Addresses: *Agent*—c/o Columbia Artists Management, Inc., 165 West 57th St., New York, NY 10019.

Career

Upon graduating from Manhattan School of Music, began apprenticeship with the New York Metropolitan Opera; made debut during 1984-85 season in *Rigoletto;* went on to perform in *Simon Boccanegra, Carmen, Clemency of Titus,* and other productions. While continuing work with the Met, has also performed at Wolf Trap Festival, Washington, D.C., and with other companies in the United States and Europe; has made several recordings.

Awards: Shared first prize in Naumburg Competition, 1985; Grammy Award, 1990, for *Knoxville: Summer of 1915.*

Sidelights

Dawn Upshaw joins the ranks of what *Newsweek* labeled "the divine new divas"—opera singers including emeritus member Kathleen Battle, and up-and-comers like Carol Vaness and June Anderson. Of this group, Upshaw is the youngest and among the most popular as far as star power is concerned, having appeared with some of the major opera

companies in the United States and Europe. At the same time, Upshaw pursues a side career as a soloist in recitals she arranges herself.

Such ambition is not unusual for a classical artist; what distinguishes Upshaw from many of her peers, according to *New York* magazine's Peter G. Davis, is her temperament. She combines modesty and integrity with what Davis calls "a rare blend of voice, values, and musical independence." In a review of one of her recordings, Davis lauded Upshaw's "secure and confident lyric soprano" voice, with its "sensual appeal, youthful freshness, clarity, and purity throughout its whole range."

Unlike many of the divas of the past, Upshaw did not grow up with a classical education, or even the early drive to perform. Born in Nashville, the young girl was more accustomed to folk music; her parents, who played guitar and piano, toured as the Upshaw Family Singers, singing "Peter, Paul & Mary, Bob Dylan, 1960s stuff," as Dawn related in an interview.

Even the first time Upshaw was exposed to an opera, Rossini's *Barber of Seville,* which she saw as a senior in high school, it left her less than enthused. "I just could not sit still," she told *Wall Street Journal* writer Barbara Jepson. "Even now, I sometimes have trouble sitting still at the opera."

Still, Upshaw, with designs on singing advertising jingles and pop songs, enrolled as a music major at Wesleyan University. There, under the tutelage of her classical music professor, David Nott, she began venturing onto the university's operatic stage. (At the same time, Upshaw had become romantically involved with Nott's son, musicologist Michael Nott; they married in 1986.) After earning her B.A. at Wesleyan, Upshaw moved to New York City, to pursue graduate work with the prestigious Manhattan School of Music.

By 1984, with her M.A. assured, Upshaw began garnering attention from the professional stage. She won the Young Concert Artists international auditions, which secured Upshaw a place with the Metropolitan Opera's apprenticeship program. Her professional debut, in the 1984-85 season, was three lines in Verdi's *Rigoletto.* A handful of small and growing roles followed, with the young artist scoring a major victory by sharing first prize in the Naumburg Competition in 1985.

While serving her Met apprenticeship, Upshaw occasionally understudied the major roles; a proverbial "big break" came in February 1988, when diva Kathleen Battle called in sick, and Upshaw took her place as Adina in Donizetti's *L'eliser d'amore.* Her reviews were ecstatic, and the success foresaw Upshaw's move into leading roles.

Upshaw "doesn't look like a diva," said *Newsweek*'s Katrine Ames. "Success came almost instantly to her. She has an aching, crystalline sound, flawless diction, and a natural stage presence." Noting Upshaw's interest in the non-classical fields of lieder (German folk) and contemporary music, Ames described the artist's interpretation of Samuel Barber's *Knoxville: Summer of 1915* as "a ravishing, offbeat disc of 20th-century music."

"I don't want to be tied up with what other people think," Upshaw told Ames. "I hope I don't need to be someone I'm not." And the restless high-schooler still comes forth from the acclaimed diva. "Opera is ridiculous," Upshaw proclaimed in *Newsweek.* "I sometimes wonder, 'Oh, please, am I supposed to believe *he* loves *her?*'"

Sources

Newsweek, April 16, 1990.
New York, May 22, 1989.
Wall Street Journal, December 10, 1987.

—Susan Salter

Vanilla Ice

AP/Wide World Photos

Rap singer

Full name, Robert Matthew Van Winkle; nickname, Vanilla; born October 31, 1967 (one source says 1968), in Miami, Fla.; son of Beth Mino (a music teacher and classical pianist). *Education:* Attended R. L. Turner High School, received high school diploma through correspondence course from the American School.

Career

Discovered in 1987 at the City Lights Talent Show, Dallas, Tex.; opened for City Lights opening acts, including Tone-Loc, Public Enemy, and Paula Abdul; City Lights owner Tommy Quon became his talent manager in 1988; formed Vanilla Ice Posse (VIP) with City Lights disc jockey Earthquake (Floyd Brown) and dancers Hi-Tec (Jay Huffman), E-Rock (Everett Fitzgerald), and Juice (Marc Grinage). Recording artist and touring performer; film appearances include cameo role in *Teenage Mutant Ninja Turtles: The Secret of the Green Ooze*; television appearances include *Into the Night with Rick Dees, Friday Night Videos, Saturday Morning Videos, MTV's Hot Seat, Saturday Night Live, American Music Awards, The Arsenio Hall Show*, and *MTV Tailgate Party for the Superbowl*; has made endorsements for Nike and Coke.

Awards: Three regional motocross biking titles, including fourth place in the Florida Winter National Olympics, 1985; won regional contest of the Grand National Championships in motocross three times. Album *To the Extreme* certified gold, platinum, double-platinum, and triple-platinum, November 19,

1990, and quadruple-platinum, November 20, 1990; favorite new artist award from the American Music Awards, 1991.

Sidelights

Vanilla Ice, the white boy who recorded the first rap single to hit Number One on Billboard's Hot 100 pop chart, was controversial from the moment he arrived on the music scene. Accused of inventing his image as an urban rapper, the Iceman, whose real name is Robby Van Winkle, lowered his pants on Rick Dees's TV show to display scars he claims he received in a knife fight. He informed his critics in his acceptance speech as favorite new artist at the 1991 American Music Awards Ceremony that they could kiss his white posterior. With a hit single, "Ice, Ice Baby," that catapulted sales of his first album, *To The Extreme*, to five million in three months, Vanilla Ice is a hot new performer who seems to defy categorization. "So who is he," questioned *People*, among others, "fibber or phenom, street kid or star . . . ?" Ice answered them all in *Newsweek:* "I'm 100 percent original."

Robert Matthew Van Winkle was born on Halloween in 1967 (one source says 1968) in Miami, Florida. His father left his mother, a music teacher and classical pianist, while she was pregnant with Van Winkle. "I will not say anything about my father. Period," Ice told *People*. "I don't have a dad." His mother raised him and an older half-brother in culturally and ethnically mixed neighborhoods of Miami. When Van Winkle was five years old he became interested in music and dance. "I picked up the dance steps from what I saw the black kids doing in the streets," he related in his autobiography *Ice By Ice*. "The streets of Miami—that was my dance school." As a youngster Van Winkle shunned formal music lessons, never learning to play an instrument. His childhood dream was to become a motocross champion. Eventually he won a few amateur regional motocross titles; at one point in late adolescence he broke his ankles in a race.

> "I picked up the dance steps from what I saw the black kids doing in the streets."

Van Winkle was a difficult child, moody and temperamental, who used to play truant from grade school. His mother tried in vain to modify his behavior by seeking counseling and changing addresses frequently. When Van Winkle was eight his mother married Ecuadorean Byron Mino, whom she met when he sold her a car. Although family economics improved, the marriage broke up after three years. The couple got back together for a time after the divorce, but did not remarry. In his teens Van Winkle moved with his family, which now included a younger sister, to a middle-class suburb of Dallas where Mino had landed a better auto sales position. Van Winkle continued to rap and dance; he was also hanging out on weekends with gang members who took joy rides and picked fights. At a hospital after one skirmish in which he was stabbed several times, Van Winkle found God and gave up gang life. Dropping out of suburban R. L. Turner High School in his second year, he worked as a lot attendant at the car dealership where his stepfather was employed.

An IROC Camaro Z28 became Van Winkle's next obsession. When he parked his car under the marquee one evening in 1987 at City Lights, a 2,000-seat club in Dallas, the owner of the club, Tommy Quon, went out to tell Van Winkle to park elsewhere. "He looked like a rich white kid—and he looked like a

star," Quon told Dave Handelman in *Rolling Stone*. After Van Winkle convinced Quon to let him keep his parking place, he won the club's talent show. Quon confessed to Handelman, "He wasn't that great as a rapper, but he had that charisma, style." Quon signed him to a contract at City Lights where he performed before the club's opening acts, which included rap and pop acts Tone-Loc, Public Enemy, and Paula Abdul. When Quon became the rapper's talent agent in 1988 he backed Van Winkle with all black, male dancers to make him stand out. Dubbed "Vanilla" in seventh grade because he was the only white boy around rapping with blacks, Van Winkle became Vanilla Ice—purportedly because he was smooth as ice—and named his back-up group VIP, or Vanilla Ice Posse.

The group included Ice, writer-DJ Earthquake (Floyd Brown), and dancers Hi-Tec (Jay Huffman), E-Rock (Everett Fitzgerald), and Juice (Marc Grinage). When Quon could not interest record companies, he independently made the album *Hooked*, which featured "Ice, Ice Baby." To promote the group Quon released the single "Play That Funky Music" with "Ice, Ice Baby" on the B-side. DJ Darrell Jaye in Columbus, Georgia, meant to air Ice's "Play That Funky Music" when he flipped the record over accidentally. Overnight the song went to Number One on Southern stations and became a top request on pay-per-view *Video Jukebox*. Consequently the album was remixed and reissued by SBK Records in October of 1990 under its new title, *To the Extreme*. Ice had unprecedented success with the single "Ice, Ice Baby." When the song topped Billboard's pop chart, SBK executives made the single available only on the album. The strategy worked; *To the Extreme* was the first album to reach all five certification levels in one month, and Ice was handed gold, platinum, double-platinum, and triple-platinum album awards on November 19, 1990. The next day he received a quadruple-platinum award, and subsequently, a multi-fold persona problem with his SBK bio.

A skeptical press hooted at the discrepancies in his stories—especially over those concerning the loss of half his blood when he was stabbed five times and resultant religious conviction. When they discovered that Ice had given three different locales for the incident, they intimated that the singer—with his Z28 and home in a Texan suburb—was a rich kid who fibbed. Critics of *To the Extreme* wrote scathing reviews accusing the model-handsome rapper of creating a street-wise background to more effectively appropriate a black art form. "Rap lite," *Newsweek* called Ice's work, summing up reviewers' response to the lack of profanity and political substance in his lyrics. The magazine questioned whether a black rapper "with little vocal technique or rhythmic sense, largely inarticulate and devoid of wit" could sell millions of records, unless like Ice, he had "the right clothes, the right look and the right moves, and the right recycled hits to rap to." *People* reported that the album "mostly thumps on mindlessly," but John Rockwell defended "the looker with attitude" in the *New York Times*. Interpreting *To the Extreme* as a new, mainstream musical style, Rockwell called the album "a triumph for Vanilla Ice, a triumph for rap." Proof of Ice's "street" past and some vindication came with the warrant issued for his arrest in 1991 by Dallas police—which dated back to a 1988 unpaid fine for a parking lot incident where Ice had maced a kid and beat him over the head—and the publication of his autobiography *Ice By Ice*.

Despite that legal entanglement, the future is bright for the star who maintains that he allowed the press to be misled to protect his family's privacy. His cameo role in the sequel to the movie *Teenage Mutant Ninja Turtles* has led to a film project about a motorcycle gang, entitled *Cool as Ice*. Though he opened the M. C. Hammer 1990 fall tour, he went solo on his own world tour in 1991. A new album, *Ice Capades*, is in the works for the bad boy-turned-role-model, who will be endorsing Coke and Nike. "I always set new goals," Vanilla Ice told Sanders, emphasizing that his success is no novelty, "and that's my new goal, to be here, keep it goin'! The media can try and break me all they want, but the bottom line is it's *up...to...me.*"

Writings

Ice by Ice, Avon, 1991.

Selected discography

To the Extreme, SBK Records, 1990.

Sources

Billboard, November 3, 1990; December 15, 1990; December 22, 1990.
Entertainment Weekly, March 15, 1991.
Newsweek, December 3, 1990.
New York Times, November 18, 1990.
People, November 26, 1990; December 3, 1990.
Rolling Stone, January 10, 1991.
Variety, November 12, 1990.

—*Marjorie Burgess*

Lech Walesa

AP/Wide World Photos

President of Poland

Born September 29, 1943, in Popowo, Poland; son of Boleslaw (a carpenter) and Fela (Kaminska) Walesa; married Miroslawa Danuta, November 8, 1969; children: Bogdan, Slawomir, Przemyslaw, Jaroslaw, Magdalena, Anna, Maria Wiktoria, Brygida. *Education:* Attended Technical State Vocational School in Lipno, Poland, 1961. *Religion:* Catholic.

Career

Electrician at Lenin Shipyard, Gdansk, Poland, 1967-76 and 1980-1990; activist with the Constituent Committee of Free Trade Unions of the Baltic, Gdansk, 1978-80; co-founder of National Coordinating Committee of independent trade union Solidarity (Solidarnosc un Grunwaldzska), 1980, became national chairman, 1981; elected president of Poland, December 1990.

Awards: Free World Prize from the Kingdom of Norway, 1982; International Democracy Award from Greece, 1982; Nobel Peace Prize, 1983; numerous other awards and honorary doctoral degrees.

Sidelights

An unemployed shipyard electrician in Gdansk, Poland, when the decade began, Lech Walesa had been elected his country's president when it ended, the powerhouse Solidarity trade union he founded having not only toppled the Communist government in Warsaw but also having inspired prodemocracy revolutions in East Germany, Hungary,

and throughout the Eastern bloc. The key role he played in liberalizing Eastern Europe has earned him a long list of honors, not least of which was the Nobel Peace Prize in 1983; his rumpled appearance, handlebar mustache, and air of undeniable authenticity—that here indeed stands a true leader—makes him among the most prominent world statesmen of the present day.

As a young electrician employed by Poland's biggest shipyard, the Gdansk Lenin Shipyard, Walesa soon became active in the worker's underground reform movement. Blacklisted as a labor troublemaker he was fired well before the now-legendary Gdansk shipyard strike in summer 1980. According to his often-told account, Walesa was watching the strike from outside the shipyard gates when, seized by emotion, he vaulted the wall and joined his comrades. He soon was coordinating the strike activities across Poland as unrest spread from factory to factory.

The strikers negotiated recognition of their union, called Solidarnosc, or Solidarity, the first non-government union in the Eastern bloc. The government retrenched almost immediately, however, outlawing the union, then imposing martial law on the populace. Repressive political conditions and enduring economic turmoil followed the lifting of martial law a year later. During that period Walesa was often detained in jail or kept under house arrest.

Western attention spotlighted the charismatic electrician as the leader of Polish anticommunism, but in reality the union was losing its power even as Walesa was losing his grip on its leadership. Nevertheless Solidarity was ultimately able to force the Communists to share power in Parliament, and finally to allow free elections—the first in Eastern Europe since 1945. As the union moved from revolutionary force to governing entity, Walesa acted behind the scenes, denying any interest in elected office. He changed his mind and, manipulating an election five years ahead of time, ran successfully for the presidency in December 1990.

Despite the accolades, awards, and private papal audiences, Walesa remains the plain-spoken workingman from Gdansk who ogles attractive women, disdains political ideologies and university "eggheads," and whose grammar would make a schoolteacher wince. His reasoning appeals to common sense and an unschooled sense of justice, articulated in a mix of folk wisdom and more high-toned reasoning and vocabulary learned from his ideological Solidarity colleagues. "We are fed up with being the paupers of Europe. So it is in everyone's interest, especially Europe's, to help Poland reform itself away from this absurd system—the economy, law and politics—a labyrinth of the absurd that we have to escape from," he told Nicholas Bethel, a European Parliamentarian writing in *New Republic*.

On the world stage Walesa cuts a curious figure. He is short and of late grown paunchy, his beer hall mustache grown grey. He speaks calmly yet imbues his words with urgency. Having never set forth a vision of a specific political system for his country, he relies rather on personal charisma for his authority and his ability to gauge the popular mood. He manages to change his mind regularly without appearing contradictory or confused to the public. "Walesa is not one, but 10 men: Solidarity leader, electrician, father, husband, actor, negotiator, and more," Adam Michnik, scholar and Solidarity activist, told *New York Times* writer John Tagliabue in 1988. "He's a worker, with intellectuals around him. He's very nationalistic, without being chauvinistic; very Catholic, without being clerical. A kind of Polish synthesis."

Walesa began working at the Gdansk Lenin Shipyard in May 1967 soon after completing his military requirements. An apprentice electrician, he lay cables through freighters and repaired electrical caddies.

Lacking a home base he moved throughout the sprawling plant as needed, meeting many different co-workers each day. Not coincidentally, most of Solidarity's core leadership were also electricians who circulated widely among the work force.

> *"We are fed up with being the paupers of Europe. So it is in everybody's interest, especially Europe's, to help Poland reform itself."*

Although all workers were enrolled in a government-run union, dissent began to spread throughout the country, which erupted in riots over escalating food prices in 1970. More than 100 were killed in the Gdansk shipyard by police. Workers rioted again in 1976, and many were fired afterwards. One of them was Walesa. Doing odd jobs around Gdansk for several years, in 1979 he joined other disgruntled workers comprising the underground Baltic Free Trade Union. This collective helped foment the riots of the summer of 1980, in Gdansk and other large shipyards. More than 300,000 workers took part in the unrest, shaking up the government and causing the dismissal of the prime minister.

Walesa and the other fired workers were reinstated, but they had more than soldering and circuits on their minds. Walesa was recognized by his co-workers as the strike's leader, and as such signed an accord August 31, 1980, gaining workers the right to organize an independent union. This was the first non-government union in post-war Poland. The accord also provided for higher wages, new social benefits, increased freedom of expression, and the release of jailed activists. Also provided for was the Roman Catholic Church, which could now broadcast mass on Sunday over the state airwaves.

A staff writer from the *New Yorker* visiting Poland in 1981 wrote: "It is clear that almost from the start Walesa served as a charismatic leader, calm but firm in negotiations, making flamboyant and inspirational public speeches; that he had a particularly fine sense of the mood of the crowd and a conviction that it was necessary for the leadership never to vault too far ahead of that mood; and that his abrupt, ironic personal style utterly captivated both the Poles and the western press."

The freedom was short-lived, however. General Wojciech Jaruzelski, the head of state in Warsaw, soon banned Solidarity again, imposed martial law on the country, and placed a number of activists, including Walesa, in detention. Walesa continued to speak out from jail, however, sending messages to the western media through the parish priest of St. Brigida, the church serving the shipyard workers and their families. Walesa spent nearly all of 1982 in jail.

The repression merely increased his heroism in the eyes of the West, and in October 1983 the Nobel Peace Prize committee named Walesa as its 1983 laureate. The union leader sent his wife to collect the prize, reportedly fearing exile if he left Poland. He promised to donate the $194,000 prize to a church charity for needy farmers.

As Walesa's star continued to rise on the world firmament, it clearly flickered in Poland. The country was mired in economic chaos, the people's spirit low from long months of martial law and continuing repression. The ranks of Solidarity continued to

Lech Walesa greets a crowd at Chicago's Daley Center Plaza in November, 1989. AP/Wide World Photos.

shrink, down to several million from the 10 million who claimed membership in 1980. Younger men, more militant than Walesa, were at the union's helm now, calling for the government's immediate overthrow; Walesa, more conciliatory by nature, already seemed a relic of the movement's past. That he still had the authority to call a strike was in doubt. Observers commented that the Nobel Prize came two years too late.

Walesa, however, remained influential. In 1984 he and thousands of supporters infiltrated the official May Day celebrations, chanting "Sol-i-dar-nosc" over and over until police came swinging clubs. Demonstrations followed in other cities. Choosing dates that carried emotional resonance for the Poles, Walesa was able to rally thousands for street demonstrations: observance of the anniversary of Poland's 1791 Constitution; the defeat of Nazi Germany; and the one-year anniversary of a freedom protestor's death at the hands of police.

The popular mood clearly demanded change. Store shelves were nearly empty; factories were working only two days a week. Facing massive popular resistance, Jaruzelski sought Solidarity's participation in a coalition government that might soften opposition. He released all political prisoners, and proffered several cabinet posts to Walesa's representatives. Walesa was ready to go along, but this time failed to gain the support of Solidarity's more radical leadership. The union resisted participation in the government, continuing to press for its overthrow. Walesa was personally less intransigent. "I cannot say that everything the authorities are doing is wrong," he told *U.S. News & World Report* in late 1986. "Many are in the right direction. I am afraid that we will see the effects only in 200 or 300 years, but at least the direction is right."

With the Soviet Union suffering economic woes of its own, Jaruzelski turned increasingly to the West for trade. The price for this was allowing for greater domestic plurality. The general announced free elections to be held in the summer of 1989, and the Poles voted into office the first non-Communist government in Eastern Europe in four decades. Ironically, Jaruzelski remained in office as a compromise, running the government as president. Choosing not to run himself, Walesa nominated protege Tadeusz Mazowiecki as prime minister.

In October Walesa traveled abroad, officially representing Solidarity but in fact symbolizing the entire democratic movement sweeping Eastern Europe. He made an astonishing appearance before the U.S. Congress as a private citizen of a foreign country—a virtually unprecedented event. The speech, televised to an international audience, was a canny blend of self-effacement, coy flattery, and moral finger-wagging. Walesa poked fun at his own expanding waistline. He cited the U.S. Constitution, spoke reverently of American ideals, quoted the Polish Pope, and invoked a Polish folk saying; he chided the United States for allowing Poland to be overlooked in the meting out of Marshall Plan funds that rebuilt the rest of post-war Europe; and he finished by requesting economic aid. "We have heard many beautiful words of encouragement," he declared. "These are appreciated. But being a worker and a man of concrete work, I must tell you that the supply of words on the world market is plentiful, but the demand is falling. Let deeds follow words now."

After his successful fund-raising he returned to Poland and dire economic straights as the country struggled to convert from a managed economy to a free market system. He continued to affirm his confidence in Mazowiecki, perhaps more often than was necessary. His activities in Gdansk, nominally limited to Solidarity activities, assumed the character of a shadow government. He began testing the waters that summer, calling for a new presidential election some five years ahead of schedule. That accomplished, he finally announced his candidacy.

It would be an uphill campaign. Despite his international stature, at home Walesa was viewed with some suspicion, having long been outside the movement's leading edge. Campaigning as an underdog, he barnstormed the country as an advocate of worker's rights, opposing the "eggheads" and their useless theorizing. Walesa made promises to keep everyone working, shrugging off critics who wanted to know how he planned to accomplish this. On December 9, 1990 he was elected Poland's president.

Leaning out the window of his Gdansk headquarters on election night he seemed the Walesa of old, vague yet inspirational, declaring to his admirers (as quoted in the *Washington Post*): "I will be your servant, I will work for all of you. We have to work together, and I will not play around—I will work hard every day."

Poland's most famous labor leader grew up one of four children in a family ravaged by the loss of their father, Boleslaw, amidst the general desolation of postwar Europe. In his autobiography, *Lech Walesa: A Way of Hope*, published in 1987, he describes the deprivation of German occupation. His father, a peasant carpenter, suffered imprisonment by the Nazis. Strangely, Walesa recalls his father returning home "dressed like a Gestapo"; neighbors assumed he was a collaborator until he was imprisoned a

second time. He died of the effects of the harsh treatment in 1945.

After the war his mother, the former Fela Kaminska, married her husband's brother, Stanislaw, with whom she had four more children. Walesa describes an impoverished rural childhood, farming a seven-acre subsistence tract. School was a four-mile walk, made "usually barefoot" after completing morning chores. After school, chores resumed until 11 p.m. All children worked hard, he recalled, except those who "pretended" to like school and books. He left Popowo in 1959 and enrolled in a two-year vocational program in nearby Lipno.

After working two years at his first job, as an electrician in Lochochino, Walesa was called up for two years' mandatory military service; he was decommissioned a corporal. He returned to civilian life and found work in a town not far from Popowo, then moved to Gdansk in 1969. He and his wife Miroslawa have raised seven children in a seven-room apartment on a tree-lined street in Gdansk. Observers often describe the Polish president's small stature—he stands 5'7"—and his distinctive features: a drooping mustache, his rumpled clothing, his "twinkling" or "impish" eyes, and the pipe he usually keeps lit. He is often described as a devout Catholic, wearing a devotional pin of the madonna of Czestochowa prominently on his lapel. An aide hangs a large crucifix on the wall behind the podium whenever he is to address an audience.

As Solidarity's efforts to bring democracy to Poland crested in October 1988, Walesa told *Time* magazine: "Even the biggest battles in history have ended sitting down at a table. What is better—to be a boxing champion or a chess champion? I prefer chess. And I don't have any doubt that eventually we will win."

Selected writings

The Book of Lech Walesa, Simon & Schuster, 1982.
Birth of Solidarity: The Gdansk Negotiations, St. Martin's, 1983.
Lech Walesa: A Way of Hope, Holt, 1987.

Sources

Business Week, August 20, 1990.
Christian Century, June 4-11, 1986.
The Nation, October 29, 1983.
New Republic, November 2, 1987.

Newsweek, December 8, 1980; April 6, 1981; February 15, 1982; November 22, 1982; November 29, 1982; June 20, 1983; October 17, 1983; May 14, 1984; September 12, 1988; November 20, 1989; November 27, 1989; April 23, 1990.

New Yorker, November 16, 1981.

New York Times Magazine, December 14, 1981; October 23,1988.

Time, January 5, 1981; May 4, 1987; October 3, 1988; August 7, 1989; April 23, 1990; November 19, 1990.

U.S. News & World Report, December 1, 1986; November 27, 1989; September 10, 1990.

Vital Speeches of the Day, December 15, 1989.

Washington Post, December 10, 1990.

World Press Review, November 1988; August 1990.

—Warren Strugatch

Wendy Wasserstein

AP/Wide World Photos

Playwright and screenwriter

Born October 18, 1950, in Brooklyn, N.Y.; daughter of Morris W. (a textile manufacturer) and Lola (Schleifer) Wasserstein. *Education:* Mount Holyoke College, B.A., 1971; City College of the City University of New York, M.A., 1973, Yale University, M.F.A., 1976.

Addresses: *Home*—New York, NY. *Agent*—International Creative Management, 40 West 57th St., New York, NY 10019.

Career

Dramatist and screenwriter. Teacher at Columbia University; actress in plays, including *The Hotel Play*, 1981; member of artistic board of Playwrights Horizons; contributor to *New York Times* and *New York Woman*.

Awards: Joseph Jefferson Award, Dramalogue Award, and Inner Boston Critics Award, all for *Uncommon Women and Others*; grant for playwriting from Playwrights Commissioning Program of Phoenix Theater, c. 1970s; Hale Matthews Foundation Award; Guggenheim fellowship, 1983; grant for writing and studying theater in England from American Playwrights Project, 1988; Pulitzer Prize for drama, Antoinette Perry (Tony) Award, and award for best new play from New York Drama Critics Circle, all 1989, all for *The Heidi Chronicles.*

Member: Dramatists Guild, Dramatists Guild for Young Playwrights.

Sidelights

Tragic, funny, serious, and insightful—playwright Wendy Wasserstein's work is praised for being all of these things. Beginning in the late 1970s with her first major work, *Uncommon Women and Others,* she has explored the choices, compromises, and frustrations of modern women struggling with the opportunities and pitfalls of feminism. In *The Heidi Chronicles* she used a series of flashbacks to illuminate the life of an art history professor who is successful and independent, yet increasingly disillusioned with her life. "Serious issues and serious people can be quite funny," Wasserstein once told the *New York Times;* in *The Heidi Chronicles* she created a mix of wit and wisdom that resulted in one of the longest-running hit plays on Broadway—one which earned both a Pulitzer Prize and a Tony Award for its author.

Not surprisingly, in many respects Wasserstein's life closely reflects that of her protagonists. She was the youngest child in a family that placed a high premium on traditional achievement. Two of her siblings went on to lucrative careers in finance, but Wendy was a mediocre student (she now believes she was affected by dyslexia). As a child her strengths were making friends and making people laugh. Her parents frequently took her to Broadway shows, which she loved, but it never occurred to her that one could make a career in theater. Unsure of what to do with herself after high school, she applied to elite Mount Holyoke College because, as she told Kim Hubbard in *People*, "I thought if I went to a Seven Sisters school [one of a constellation of prestigious New England colleges] my parents would leave me alone for the rest of my life."

> "I was ... a very serious writer all along. I just didn't realize it."

In 1969 she went to nearby Amherst College as an exchange student. It was a pivotal year, when she was first exposed to the burgeoning feminist movement and began attending consciousness-raising groups. After graduation from Mount Holyoke she opted for further study at New York's City University. Writing still didn't seem like an acceptably realistic career choice; nonetheless, her graduate work was in creative writing. Among her teachers were the illustrious playwright Israel Horovitz and novelist Joseph Heller. In 1973 she earned her master's degree and saw the production of her first play, *Any Woman Can't*. This bitter farce about a woman's struggle for success in a male-dominated field was presented by the experimental theater group Playwrights Horizons.

Despite the thrill of having a play professionally produced, Wasserstein still felt compelled to seek out a more traditional career. She considered medicine, but trouble with physics ruled that out. She applied to law school, business school—and to the Yale Drama School. Accepted to Columbia Business School and Yale, she finally acknowledged her inner desires and chose the precarious life of a dramatist. At the time, Yale Drama was headed by Robert Brustein, who, Wasserstein told the *New York Times*, "felt that theater was as important as law or medicine." His attitude "gave you high standards to maintain." Her classmates included writers Christopher Durang and Albert Innaurato and actress Meryl Streep, all of whom went on to successful careers. Durang and Wasserstein became close friends, and he influenced her greatly by piquing her interest in the works of Anton Chekhov. The Russian writer's ability to create characters that were at once comic and tragic became a lasting inspiration to her. In a

New York Times tribute to him she would later declare: "There is no better reason to write than to attempt to barely touch where he succeeded."

While at Yale, Wasserstein's work evolved from broad mockery to a more subtle form of satire. Her first effort, *Happy Birthday, Montpelier Pizzazz*, lampooned the social games common to college parties; the next, *When Dinah Shore Ruled the Earth*, ridiculed beauty pageants. Her thesis play, *Uncommon Women and Others*, was different; it was more complex, with greater tension underlying the low-key humor. The drama revolved around the fears and aspirations of eight Mount Holyoke students coming of age at the height of the women's movement. Rita, a brash aspiring novelist, dominates the play. "When we're thirty we're going to be pretty amazing," Rita states confidently to her friends. But when the eight women meet for lunch several years later, they are for the most part confused and unfulfilled, and Rita has to revise her prediction. She suggests that perhaps by the time they are 45, they'll be "amazing."

After *Uncommon Women* was presented as a one-act at Yale, Wasserstein rewrote it as a two-act, with an eye toward professional production. She sent it to several theaters and was rejected by all but Playwrights Horizons. The small off-Broadway theater was now under the direction of Andre Bishop, who remembered in *People*: "What drew me to Wendy's work was its underlying seriousness and sadness.... I think in the early days she was thought of as funny and goofy, with some talent. People didn't take her seriously. But I thought *Uncommon Women* was funny and touching. I knew she had the gift." The association between Bishop and Wasserstein has proven to be a long-lasting one. Reviewers responded favorably to *Uncommon Women*; Edith Oliver wrote in the *New Yorker* that it was a "wonderful, original comedy" in which "every moment is theatrical," noting that "for all [the characters'] funny talk and behavior, they are sympathetically drawn." The play got national exposure when it was filmed for the Public Broadcasting System's (PBS) Theater in America series, with Meryl Streep in one of the lead roles. *Uncommon Women* is still performed frequently at colleges across the United States.

Like *Uncommon Women*, Wasserstein's next play was inspired by her own life. As she approached 30 she witnessed "biological time bombs going off all over Manhattan," as she described it in the *Washington Post*; many of her contemporaries were giving up their romantic ideals of the perfect mate and suddenly marrying. "It was like, it's not wild and passionate, but it's *time*," she explained. *Isn't It Romantic* featured Janie Blumberg, a bright, sophisticated 30-year-old who comes close to marrying a sincere but dull suitor, finally rejecting the compromise at the last minute. When the play opened Wasserstein was criticized for letting her comedic flair obscure the serious moral issues involved. In response she began an ambitious rewrite. Seven versions later *Isn't It Romantic* returned to the stage, 45 minutes shorter and much more tightly focused. Oliver applauded its increased "momentum and . . . sense of purpose," and declared that "the troubling emotions that were an undercurrent the first time around have now been brought to the surface, and without any loss of humor." The success of *Isn't It Romantic* led to its development as a film.

Wasserstein next broadened her horizons beyond the theater by writing adaptations and original works for PBS, doing some teaching, and writing articles for the *New York Times* and *New York Woman* magazine. In a *Contemporary Authors* interview she commented: "A play for me is a three-year commitment, a large commitment. Not everything you do are you going to care about that much or take that kind of time on. The articles, to me, are like sketches in a way. They're small and they're contained. And that's nice. It's more like craft. I like writing them, I like polishing them, and they don't take three years to get produced." *New York Woman* editor Betsy Carter told *People* that Wasserstein's articles generated strong reader response: "Wendy is more emotionally naked than most writers, and she gets a lot of mail. Readers write to her as if they know her." In 1990 many of Wasserstein's magazine pieces were collected in book form under the title *Bachelor Girls*.

Wasserstein's least autobiographical—and least successful—theater production was *Miami*, a musical comedy about a teenaged boy vacationing with his family in the 1950s. It was commissioned by Playwrights Horizons and had a limited run there in 1986. In 1988 that same venue saw the premier of what is by far Wasserstein's most acclaimed play to date, *The Heidi Chronicles*. "When I wrote *Heidi* I was 35, I had just written a movie for [director Steven] Spielberg that didn't work out, I wasn't married, and I was beginning to feel like the odd man out at baby showers," she commented. "I didn't know whether the sacrifices I had made were worth the road I was taking. So I decided to write a play about all that." In the play Heidi Holland is a highly successful woman who nonetheless feels stranded by the choices she has made in life, and alienated from both men and other women. Flashbacks take the audience through Heidi's high-school years, her involvement with

1960s political activism, her transformation through feminism, and the hardening of her character in the career-oriented 1980s. In the climactic scene she addresses alumni from an elite women's school and unexpectedly confesses her dissatisfaction with her life. Happiness appears to come only at the end of the play when she adopts a child.

This conclusion sparked criticism from many commentators, who believed that Wasserstein had become a traitor to the feminist cause. "That's silly," the author told Hubbard. "The women's movement, the movement that said, 'Your voice is worthwhile,' is the only reason I feel like a person. But what still needs to change is that women shouldn't beat themselves up for their choices—for being a mother or a single mother, or being a playwright, or being beautiful or not being beautiful. It's important that there isn't one woman slot that puts you all in competition with each other." Moralizing concerns aside, reviewers found Wasserstein's script to be her most effective yet. "Heidi's search for self is both mirthful and touching," wrote Mel Gussow in the *New York Times*. "[Wasserstein] has been exceedingly careful about not settling for easy laughter, and the result is a more penetrating play." Ironically, the play that arose from Wasserstein's feelings of dissatisfaction with her life helped to resolve those emotions. Hubbard reported that the writer felt much "less stranded" after winning the Pulitzer Prize and Tony Award. "The acceptance of *Heidi*, the respect from my peers while we were staging it, made me feel that," Wasserstein affirmed. "I was . . . a very serious writer all along. I just didn't realize it."

Selected writings

Bachelor Girls, Knopf, 1990.
The Heidi Chronicles and Other Plays, Harbrace, 1990.

Sources

Books

Contemporary Authors, Volume 129, Gale, 1990.
Contemporary Literary Criticism, Volume 32, Gale, 1985.

Periodicals

Chicago Tribune, October 12, 1985; November 10, 1985; October 21, 1990.
Christian Science Monitor, April 30, 1986.
Daily News (New York), December 16, 1983; April 23, 1986.
Horizon, February 1978.

Los Angeles Times, January 31, 1984; October 28, 1984; October 30, 1984; December 17, 1988; October 7, 1990.

Nation, December 17, 1977; February 18, 1984.

New York, June 29, 1981; January 2, 1989.

New Yorker, December 5, 1977; June 22, 1981; June 13, 1983; December 26, 1983; December 26, 1988.

New York Post, November 22, 1977; December 16, 1983; April 23, 1986.

New York Times, November 22, 1977; May 24, 1978; June 23, 1978; December 27, 1978; June 8, 1979; February 15, 1981; May 24, 1981; June 15, 1981; June 28, 1981; July 17, 1983; December 16, 1983; January 1, 1984; January 3, 1984; February 26, 1984; June 13, 1984; January 3, 1986; March 28, 1986; April 23, 1986; January 11, 1987; August 30, 1987; January 24, 1988; June 8, 1988; December 11, 1988; December 12, 1988; February 19, 1989; March 12, 1989.

New York Woman, April 1988.

People, March 26, 1984; June 25, 1990.

Time, December 5, 1977; December 26, 1983; April 16, 1990.

Variety, June 17, 1981.

Village Voice, December 20, 1988.

Washington Post, May 3, 1985; May 6, 1985.

Women's Wear Daily, December 16, 1983; April 23, 1986.

—Joan Goldsworthy

Elizabeth Watson

AP/Wide World Photos

Houston police chief

Born August 25, 1949, in Philadelphia, Pa.; daughter of John (a physicist) and Elizabeth Herrmann; married Robert Watson (a sergeant in the Houston Police Department), 1976; children: Susan, Mark, David. *Education:* B.S., Texas Tech University, 1971.

Addresses: *Home*—Clear Lake, TX. *Office*—c/o Houston Police Department, Houston, TX.

Career

After graduating from Houston (Texas) Police Academy, became officer, 1972-76, promoted to detective, 1976-81; named lieutenant, 1981; became captain and commander of inspections division, 1984; worked as commander of west patrol bureau, 1987; appointed chief of police, 1990.

Sidelights

When in January 1990 Kathy Whitmire, the first female mayor of Houston, Texas, announced her most recent appointment, few were surprised that it would be Elizabeth Watson as Houston's chief of police—the first female police chief of a major American city.

No token designee, Watson was an 18-year veteran of the force at the time of her promotion. She had come up through the ranks of officer, detective, lieutenant, captain, and commander. Still, Watson's appointment drew national attention. Dr. Susan Martin, who studied women in the police field,

likened the news to "the first woman in Congress, the first woman in the state legislature, or the first woman C.E.O. of a Fortune 500 company." As Martin explained to *New York Times* reporter Lisa Belkin: "Police work is typically one of the most male-dominated occupations. For a woman to achieve position of Chief in one of the largest departments in the country is a major event."

Those close to Watson might well have seen her rise as one that follows a family tradition. Her grandfather was a police officer, as were her uncles and several cousins. Born Elizabeth Herrmann, she married fellow officer Robert Watson in 1976; their third child, David, was born eleven months after Elizabeth became chief. On taking office, Watson vowed to maintain and uphold the department's standards. High on her list was continuing to heighten public awareness of the force. "We have done some tremendous work in the past years opening channels of communication," Watson was quoted in a *Houston Post* article, "and I am committed to keeping them open to effect real input and dialogue with the community."

Still, the officer known in her department as "By-the-Book Betsy," for her no-nonsense management style, has had her share of critics. As a *Houston Post* piece related, when Watson took over the city's auto theft division in 1985, her "first move was to make her officers account for their time in 15-minute increments, which frustrated many in that division." An unnamed officer told Andrew Kirtzman in that same article that Watson "follows theory a lot," adding that time will tell "if she deals with people instead of theory. It's just now getting interesting."

Three months into her administration, Watson became the centerpiece of controversy when Justo Garcia, a Houston police sergeant and president of the Organization of Spanish-Speaking Officers, took the chief to task for bypassing several Hispanic officers for the post of assistant chief. Under a *Houston Post* headline proclaiming the "honeymoon [is] over for Watson," reporter Kirtzman quoted Houston City Councilman Ben Reyes calling Watson someone who is "totally insensitive and doesn't understand our community" (the city of Houston has a heavily Hispanic population; Watson lives some 40 miles outside the city in Clear Lake). Watson responded by agreeing that Hispanic officers should be a part of the command staff, and "as we reorganize, I will see that that is done."

Among Watson's indelible memories of her early years on the force, according to a *Time* special edition on women, is "being handed a dress pattern and told to sew her own uniform." Eighteen years later, asked by a *Houston Post* writer which role—cop or wife and mother—was more important, she replied, "My family is extremely important to me, and I get my relaxation and my recharge of the batteries from [them]. My children are extremely important to me. My husband and I just like the quiet time at home." But at the same time, "I stand here a product of the Houston Police Department, proud to be a member and to have the opportunity to lead an organization [that] I deeply believe is the finest police department in the greatest city in America."

Sources

Houston Post, January 20, 1990; January 21, 1990; March 8, 1990; May 13, 1990; December 16, 1990.
New York Times, January 20, 1990.
Time (special edition on women), fall 1990.

—Susan Salter

Keenen Ivory Wayans

AP/Wide World Photos

Comedian, filmmaker, writer, and actor

B orn c. 1958 in New York, N.Y.; son of Howell (a salesman) and Elvira (a social worker) Wayans. *Education:* Attended Tuskegee Institute.

Career

W orked as a standup comic at clubs in New York City and Los Angeles; co-author of screenplay for film *Hollywood Shuffle,* 1988; writer and producer of film *Eddie Murphy Raw,* 1989; writer, director, and star of film *I'm Gonna Git You Sucka!,* 1989; creator, executive producer, and writer/performer of television series *In Living Color,* Fox Television, 1990—.

Awards: Emmy Award for Outstanding Comedy/Variety series, 1990, for *In Living Color.*

Sidelights

B efore 1990, if Keenen Ivory Wayans's name was known at all, it was as a behind-the-scenes talent: co-writer, co-star, producer. The former stand-up comic had found cinematic success with such projects as Robert Townsend's acclaimed feature *Hollywood Shuffle,* which skewered the white Hollywood establishment by showing the tribulations of black actors who could get cast mostly as "movie muggers," "TV pimps," and "street punks."

Wayans also worked on the Eddie Murphy feature *Raw,* which ended up as the world's highest-grossing concert film. But Wayans's own comic vision finally broke through with his self-written and -directed

farce *I'm Gonna Git You Sucka!* Wayans also starred in the story, which not only sent up such 1970s "blaxploitation" films as *Superfly* and *Shaft,* but also corralled some of those movies' stars (like Richard Roundtree and Isaac Hayes) as co-stars. In this sometimes bad-taste comedy, "I'm not satirizing black people but bad moviemaking," as the Wayans explained to Kevin Sessums in *Interview.* "The inspiration came from [the 1980 farce] *Airplane!* I'm a big fan of that movie. I was sitting around watching old *Superfly* movies, and I realized they were ripe for humor."

Despite favorable advance notice, *I'm Gonna Git You Sucka!* received only limited release in larger cities. Nevertheless, the film, which cost $3 million, grossed some $12 million domestically. Wayans, in an *American Film* interview, thinks his movie could have done even better with more promotion. "A black film is a funny animal," he told Betsy Sharkey. "If a movie is so self-indulgent, or so specific [regarding black subject matter], then you have a black film. Otherwise, I think you have to sell the content. With *Sucka,* [production studio United Artists] never got beyond the fact that it was black."

As Sharkey went on to say, the comedy "illustrates how the same marketing data can mean diametrically different things to filmmaker and film-marketer. Wayans thought *Sucka* might first attract a black audience but eventually would have crossover potential. UA saw it as a film whose core audience would be young black males." At *Sucka* screenings, Sharkey added "black audiences laughed, but white audiences did not, according to UA. Exit-card comments from the white audiences said they thought the movie would offend blacks. Black audiences said they would recommend it to their friends."

> *"[Being called racist is] a racist criticism because it limits the kind of work that I can do. When Woody Allen makes a movie, no one says, 'He's making fun of Jews.'"*

To Wayans, the schism reflected already strained race relations in action. "People just need to know its OK to laugh," he said to Sharkey. "Having standup comedy as my base at the Improv or Comedy Store, where most of the audience is white, I know my material will translate." When UA executives didn't agree with him, choosing to release *Sucka* only to the larger urban venues, Wayans felt resentful. "I could have set myself on fire, and it wouldn't have changed their minds," he related. "I think [the studio was] unfair and that we were treated with a lot of callousness. There are times when you ask yourself, 'What does a black man have to do?' But you have to channel those feelings into something productive. Bitterness will kill you."

That "something productive" came about in an unusual way. In 1989 an executive of the fledgling Fox Television network took in an advance screening of *I'm Gonna Git You Sucka!* and was taken enough with Wayans's comic style to offer the writer/actor his own television series. But Wayans was not immediately interested. "I hate TV," he told Daniel Cerone in a *Los Angeles Times* interview. "I don't watch TV. It seems like everybody has their own version of each other's shows. I didn't think TV was the arena for what I do, because what I do is *out there*. But Fox was pretty persistent. They told me this was a place I could do anything I wanted to."

Sketch comedy as a series format is a risky venture— not since *Saturday Night Live* and *SCTV* had a sketch-

comedy show gained strong notices. But Wayans presented Fox with his own sketch show, called *In Living Color*. The differences in this show, which premiered in late spring of 1990, were immediately apparent. Though it has an interracial cast, headed by Wayans, the show's focus is definitely African-American, with the material poking sometimes caustic fun at such black cultural figureheads as Jesse Jackson, Mike Tyson, Oprah Winfrey, Washington D.C.'s former mayor Marion Barry, and talk-show favorite Arsenio Hall.

As host of *In Living Color*, Wayans introduces each week's installment. Those viewers who wonder if there are any more at home like Keenen need only check the comedic cast: Wayans's brother Damon and sister Kim are featured players; another brother, Shawn, acts as deejay for Keenen's Fly Girls, a dance troupe that segues between breaks in the sketches. "We're a very tight family, almost like the Osmonds," explained Wayans to Charles E. Cohen in a *People* article.

From the beginning, *In Living Color*'s distinctive attitude caught the eyes of critics and public alike. The show boasts "a wicked political edge," as Andrew Feinberg remarked in *TV Guide*. "In one of its boldest sketches ('The Equity Express Card: Helping the Right Sort of People'), a successful black man is treated like a criminal when he attempts to use a charge card." Fox executive Harris Katleman, quoted in the same article, thinks that "two years ago, no one would have aired *In Living Color*. It's too different, too ethnic, and brings up too many issues that standards and practices [the network term for the censors] has never had to deal with before."

Not everyone was initially pleased with the series, however. Wayans and company were cited for homophobia (especially concerning a recurring segment called "Men on ... "—the topics vary from week to week and have included art, literature, and travel—hosted by two characters who perpetuate a swishy stereotype). Charges of racism have also surfaced. But Wayans defended such sketches as "Homeboy Shopping Network" (the hucksters peddle hot merchandise from the back of a truck) in the *Los Angeles Times*: He feels being called racist is "a racist criticism because it limits the kind of work that I can do. When Woody Allen makes a movie, no one says, 'He's making fun of Jews.' Why shouldn't he be able to talk about his culture? Why shouldn't I be able to talk about mine? Why shouldn't I be able to find the humor in it and share it with people?"

"The program is also catching heat from feminists," noted *Newsweek*'s Harry F. Waters. "A parody of a talk show for women ended with a shrieking cat-fight; sketches have snickered at underarm shaving, sagging breasts and tampon ads." Even a musical group, Living Colour, accused *In Living Color* of logo infringement. Wayans has acknowledged the charges of sexism. "It's possible," he told Waters and Lynda Wright in the *Newsweek* piece. "I'll admit my sensitivities probably are slanted toward a more male point of view." He added: "If the show picked only on one group, I could understand people being uptight. But we get *everybody*." The comic does draw the line at "AIDS or crack jokes," he told in *TV Guide*. And he holds no ill will toward organized protest groups rallying against his series. "That's just people who want their voices heard," Wayans remarked to Feinberg.

In the face of his rocketing success, Wayans finds at least one drawback. For this performer, described by Sharkey as "well over six feet tall, with the body of a weightlifter," finding time for a personal life has proven more than a little difficult. First, there is the stigma of being a comedian. "Comics don't know how to relate to people," he noted in *TV Guide*. This has had a predictable effect on his relationships with women. "I start dating someone and I realize I don't want any physical contact. There's a certain expectation, and rather than be brutal or callous, I'd rather not start," Wayans said. "I'm an affectionate, cuddly kind of guy, but I don't like to have it demanded from me."

Then there is the pressure of living up to his reputation as a charter member of Hollywood's "Black Pack," a group of comics and writers that includes Eddie Murphy, Arsenio Hall (whom Wayans himself has parodied in *In Living Color* as a hyperactive sycophant), Robert Townsend—and, according to Sessums in *Interview*, writer/director Spike Lee, whose work is as dramatically controversial as Wayans's is comedically. But Wayans sees no reason to emulate Lee. "Spike Lee likes to dance on people's nerves," he told Cerone in the *Los Angeles Times*. "I like to tickle their funny bones."

Sessums reported that the "Black Pack" meets on occasion to network and hone their material. Wayans described the arrangement as "a group of friends who hang together and have a good time. Sometimes the term can get manipulated a bit to sound as if we might be scary—you know, like a youth gang that's going to attack you. I can't worry about that, though—these guys are my comrades."

The "Black Pack" has been heralded by some as evidence of the new black influence in Hollywood.

But to Wayans the celebration may be premature. "This town still has not embraced the black creator," he commented in *People*. To the Cerone he remarked: "How can I explain this? You can't look at four or five guys as a wave, you know? That's not even a ripple in the water. Compared to the days when there were zero, that's a significant step. But it's only been a step. It's not like we're off and running. It's not like Hollywood is going [here Wayans does an impression of a game-show announcer] 'Come on down!'" Wayans offered ideas for a solution to Les Payne in a *Detroit Free Press* interview. "In order to see images black people are yearning to see, blacks must be in control. We need more black creative writers, more black directors, producers, etc.... I don't think it's fair to rely on studios to represent [us]. They are all owned by corporations, not individuals like [top box-office draw] Eddie Murphy."

Until then, Wayans seems happy to keep producing his brand of entertainment. It's the culmination of a lifelong desire to be the funny center of attention. As he recalled in *People*, "When I was 6 and saw Richard Pryor on TV, I said, 'That's what I want to do.' Damon and I used to do things like go out in character as the homeboys. It would flip people out." And although the Wayans household was a large one—Howell and Elvira Wayans raised ten children—it was a supportive one. "I could draw a circle on a piece of paper and my mother made me feel like Van Gogh," Wayans said.

As for Wayans's approach to life, he likes to cite a scene in the 1980 film *Raging Bull*, about boxer Jake LaMotta. "[It's when] LaMotta is fighting Sugar Ray Robinson, and he's just getting beaten to a pulp," as he recalled in *People*. "At the end of the round, he walks over and his face is bloody and he says, 'I never went down, Ray. I never went down.' He knew he couldn't win, but he wasn't going to let this guy beat him. His objective was to stay on his feet. As far as his attitude was concerned, he was victorious. That's the kind of attitude I have."

Sources

American Film, July/August 1989.
Detroit Free Press, August 10, 1990.
Interview, December 1988.
Los Angeles Times, April 15, 1990.
Newsweek, May 21, 1990.
People, June 11, 1990.
TV Guide, June 2, 1990.

—*Susan Salter*

William Wegman

Artist

Full name, William George Wegman; born February 12, 1942 (some sources say December 2, 1943), in Holyoke, Mass.; son of George W. and Eleanor (Vezina) Wegman. *Education:* Massachusetts College of Art, B.F.A. in painting, 1965; University of Illinois, M.F.A., 1967.

Addresses: *Home*—New York City and York County, Maine. *Dealer*—Holly Solomon Gallery, 724 Fifth Ave., New York, NY 10019. *Other*—431 E. 6th St., New York, NY 10009.

Career

Instructor at University of Wisconsin at Wausau, 1967, and at Waukesha, 1968-69; assistant professor at University of Wisconsin—Madison, 1969-70; lecturer, 1970-71, and visiting artist, 1978, California State University at Long Beach. Numerous individual photography, painting, and videotape exhibitions, including a retrospective at the Holly Solomon Gallery, 1979; included in group exhibitions such as *The Animal in Photography 1843-1985* at the Photographers' Gallery, London, 1986, and *Photography and Art 1946-1986* at the Los Angeles County Museum of Art, 1987. Collections in several museums, including the Whitney Museum of Modern Art, New York, and International Museum of Photography at George Eastman House, Rochester, New York.

Awards: Guggenheim fellowship, 1976 and 1987; grant from National Endowment for the Arts, 1982; Creative Artists Public Service Award, 1979.

© *Benno Friedman/Outline Press*

Sidelights

William Wegman's love affair with dogs is probably the most craftily documented since American humorist James Thurber's in *Thurber's Dogs*. The photographs Wegman takes of the Weimaraners Man Ray, Fay Ray, and Fay Ray's puppies, are captivating regardless of the viewer's age, art training, or personal appreciation of canines. Icons of human consumerism coexist with the soulful dignity of the dog in these deceptively simple 20-by-24-inch Polaroids. Seeming to be one-line jokes, Wegman's photos examine the capriciousness of human desire and how it effects the ever-patient dog without comedic overstatement—he gets just enough material out of a subject, then abandons it. Faulted for favoring style over substance to widen his appeal, Wegman responded in the *New York Times,* "It's exciting when your own parents like your work." In the same article, Holly Solomon, Wegman's longtime dealer, elaborated on his attitude, describing some of the artist's earlier video work: "Video before Wegman was Andy Warhol recording a man sleeping for 24 hours. It was art about art. [He] felt a real responsibility to engage an audience, and not just art people." Evidence of his widespread popularity is found in two successful books of his photographs, *Man's Best Friend* (1983) and *William Wegman* (1990).

The versatile artist made a music video for the band New Order in 1988, which contained what *Rolling Stone* called "the world's most artful Stupid Pet Trick." His best known video short is called *Dog Baseball* (featured on the television program *Saturday Night Live* in 1986) in which Wegman thwacks tennis balls around his backyard to the delight of Fay Ray (the "pitcher") and other assorted outfield hounds. Aside from his video work, Wegman is best known for his photographic prints, though his college degrees are both in painting. After years of concentrating on photos, Wegman told Martin Filler of *Vanity Fair* that he has been focusing on his painting in the early 1990s, the medium he calls "my neglected child." "Dog photography is a fraction of what I do, but a compassionate one," he told the *New York Times*.

While the charm of Wegman's work is obvious, the nuances are probing without being aggressive. For instance, a 1979 photograph of Man Ray (called *Fey Ray*) shows the dog lifting one paw replete with nail polish, the bottle at his side. The color of Man Ray's short, glossy coat is black and the background is black; the photograph's only other tint is the muted red of the nail polish. The subtlety of the color keeps the joke from being exaggerated, an effect enhanced by Man's expression of woeful endurance. The portrait would be less than gentle if, for instance, Man was shown (with the same expression) in a gaudy 1950s-style beauty salon, with a bulky iron hairdryer over his head and a woman at his side giving him a pedicure. The same criticism of human vanity would be evident, but would seem more biting.

Man Ray was Wegman's first dog model. The Weimaraner is well-suited to posing, as it was originally bred for attentiveness to hunting commands. A mere tennis ball can still the model for minutes at a time; the dogs's docile natures (as adults) allows Wegman to pose them easily. Noting that Wegman believed that Man Ray sulked if he was not being photographed, Filler described the ascent of the dog-muse: "During the next dozen years, Wegman transformed the blue-gray short-haired hound into an international art-world celebrity, one of the most famous contemporary portrait subjects since Alex Katz [see *Newsmakers 90*]'s Ada and David Hockney [see *Newsmakers 88*]'s Celia. [Man] Ray

submitted to being wrapped in yards of tinsel garland for the photo *Airedale* and being sprayed green and made to wear flippers and fake pop eyes for *Frog*. He was doused with a bag of flour for the memorable shot *Dusted* and donned a tasseled pantaloon getup for *Louis XIV*."

Some critics believe that the artifice of such disguises points to a subject *behind* the camera rather than in front of it. Obviously, the dog isn't interested in being spray-painted green; the viewer wonders about the twisted humor of the photographer. The dog functions as a straight man for the human photographer. Targeting the humans-only vice of cigarette smoking, Wegman poked fun at both species in a video quoted in the *New York Times*—"Don't just puff—*in*hale. C'mon, you promised. How do you *know* you won't like it if you don't try it." Wegman is the real subject of this gag, as dogs surely know better than to take up smoking. Man Ray was so popular that he appeared on the cover of the *Village Voice* after his death from cancer in 1982. Fay Ray, Man's successor, was discovered in Memphis several years later. After being shown a litter of puppies and deciding against buying a new dog, Wegman could not forget about Fay in particular: "I got on the plane, and it was like a perfume ad—I couldn't get one dog's face out of my mind." The *New York Times* quoted Wegman rhapsodizing about Miss Ray, saying that "the best thing about Fay isn't visible in a photo. It's her voice. You say, 'Fay, *speak*,' and she sounds like a distant thunderstorm."

Fay's puppies, born in 1989, were like "a small herd like a nomadic tribe in perpetual search of new olfactory sensations," according to *Vanity Fair*'s Filler. "Feeding time sets off a virtual stampede." Wegman's patience with the herd has been known to reach an end; "Sometimes they totally took over," he told Filler. "One day I couldn't take it anymore, and started shouting...and turned the hose on them." The Weimaraner dynasty is bound to carry on, however. Fay Ray's almost full-grown son Batty has shown a knack for posing.

Sources

New York Times, November 29, 1987.
Rolling Stone, April 6, 1989.
Vanity Fair, July 1990.

—*Christine Ferran*

Bob Welch

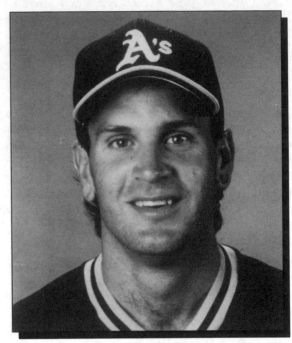

Courtesy of the Oakland Athletics Baseball Company

Professional baseball player

Born November 3, 1956, in Detroit, Mich.; married to Mary Ellen Wilson; children: Dylan, Riley. *Education:* Attended Eastern Michigan University.

Addresses: *Home*—San Francisco, CA.

Career

Signed as first round draft choice with the Los Angeles Dodgers, 1977, became pitcher, June, 1978; traded to Oakland Athletics as part of a multi-player deal, 1987.

Awards: Cy Young Award, 1990.

Sidelights

Oakland Athletics (A's) pitcher Bob Welch has risen through personal and professional tragedies to become one of baseball's biggest stars. Since moving to the Athletics in 1987, Welch has been an essential element in a dominant, championship caliber team—a fact not lost on his coaches, fellow players, or fans. In fact, the winner of the 1990 Cy Young Award has brought his game to whole new heights since he married, became a father, and came to terms with his addiction to alcohol. Oakland pitching coach Dave Duncan told the *New York Times:* "A lot of guys wouldn't even be in the game today if they'd gone through what [Welch] went through. It took a lot of inner strength, especially to overcome the alcoholism problem to the point he has. And on top of that, he's been able to bring

himself to a level high above a large percentage of pitchers who play the game."

To say that Welch's level of play is higher than average is putting it mildly. In a game where pitchers consider themselves blessed when they turn in 15-win seasons, a player who can win 27 games finds himself in great demand. Such pitching talent is rare, but rarer still is a sense of dedication to a region or to a particular team. Welch turned free agent after his first year with the A's and was offered fabulous deals with a number of the nation's baseball clubs. In a move reminiscent of another era, the celebrated pitcher left several tempting offers on the table and re-signed with the A's for another four years. "You think of a lot of things at these times, not just dollars and cents," he told the *Akron Beacon Journal.* "You go where you want to play and where your heart is. Things came into focus and there was no doubt: it was Oakland."

Life has not always been so focused for Welch. He grew up in a blue-collar community just outside Detroit, the son of a machinist in an airplane parts factory. His childhood was happy, and he enjoyed warm relations with both of his parents, but he began drinking heavily during his junior year of high school. "I did what everybody else did," he says regretfully of his younger days. Fortunately, the onset of Welch's problem was slow enough that it did not affect his ability as an athlete. He was a star pitcher at Hazel Park High and a heavily-scouted prospect during his three years at Eastern Michigan University. After his third year of college he signed with the Los Angeles Dodgers organization. He was chosen high in the first round of the 1977 June draft and was posted to the minor league farm team in Albuquerque, New Mexico.

Welch joined the parent club as a 21-year-old rookie in June, 1978. Within three months he found himself in the starting rotation as a replacement for the injured pitcher Rick Rhoden. On August 5, in his first game as a rotation starter, he shut out the San Francisco Giants to halt a six-game Dodger losing streak. He pitched yet another shutout on September 24 in a game that clinched the division crown. The Dodger management found his 7-4 record and 2.03 earned run average quite promising. Welch went on to distinguish himself in the 1978 World Series against the New York Yankees. Working in relief in the ninth inning, the young pitcher faced the legendary Reggie Jackson with two men on base. A Jackson hit would erase the Dodgers's slim 4-3 lead and virtually assure a Yankee victory. After running up a tense 3-2 count with a series of foul tips, Jackson struck out on a Welch fastball, and the Dodgers won the game.

"It was all downhill after that," Welch remembered in *Sports Illustrated*. Welch took a loss in the sixth game of that series, and the Yankees won the crown. The following season, the young pitcher was plagued by a sore arm and by a more serious, deep-seated problem—binge drinking. By the autumn of 1979 Welch found himself heading for a crisis. His pitching record of 5-6 was an enormous disappointment, and his relationship with his fiancee, Mary Ellen Wilson, was stormy. He began spending many late nights at bars and often had several drinks at lunch on game days. *Sports Illustrated* contributor Ron Fimrite writes: "[Welch's] teammates noticed that he got drunk too easily and too often. He was an embarrassment at team social functions." On one occasion late in 1979, he tried to pick a fight with a member of the San Francisco Giants team during batting practice. His friends had to restrain him, and later he had no memory of the event.

"If I had continued in that direction, I was going to die," Welch said in the *Fresno Bee*. Fortunately, the Dodgers had a functioning drug and alcohol abuse program, headed by Don Newcombe—himself a former professional athlete and recovering alcoholic.

Persuaded that he needed help, Welch admitted himself to a rehabilitation facility in Arizona in January of 1980. He stayed there almost five weeks and has been a member of Alcoholics Anonymous ever since. Having come to terms with his disability, Welch improved as a pitcher, although his statistics gave no indication that he would ever reach top-level greatness. His best year with the Dodgers was 1982, when he went 16-11 with a 3.36 earned run average and 176 strikeouts. That same year he published a candid account of his struggle with substance abuse, *Five O'Clock Comes Early: A Young Man's Battle with Alcoholism.*

> *"If I had continued [to drink], I was going to die."*

Welch was traded to the Oakland A's as part of a multi-player deal in 1987. He brought an 80-62 record with him from Los Angeles, and the A's coaching staff thought they might be able to improve him. Pitching coach Dave Duncan noted several weaknesses in Welch's game: he had command of only two pitches, the fastball and an overhand curve, and he sometimes lost his cool on the mound. "I don't know whether it was nerves or what, but Bobby would respond to adversity by rearing back and trying to overpower the opposition," Duncan told *Sports Illustrated*. "He has recognized that as a drawback. Now he'll step back, collect his thoughts and return to the game plan....Now he neither looks back nor forward."

Duncan also tutored Welch on the split-finger fastball, a pitch particularly devastating to left-handed hitters. Welch was an apt pupil, and he soon added the split-finger to his arsenal. Just as Welch joined the A's the team exploded as a major power in the American League. Welch's 1988 record of 17-9 with a 3.64 earned run average contributed significantly to Oakland's strong showing. The A's finished the season as American League champions, although they lost the World Series to the Dodgers.

Welch faced many difficult tests on and off the field in 1989. His first son was born on July 27, and less than 24 hours later, his mother died of pancreatitis. "My mother was the type of woman who would trade her life to know we had a healthy baby," Welch told *Sports Illustrated*. "She fought a hard battle to stay alive long enough to have that happen. I told [manager] Tony [La Russa] I was leaving that day, and my father-in-law drove me to the airport for a 3 p.m. flight. But we got there too late. So I rescheduled my flight for midnight and went back to the ballpark and pitched." Welch worked seven innings in the game, leaving it with a comfortable 6-3 lead. The A's eventually won, 8-7.

"My mother was buried on Sunday," Welch added. "I had some pictures of my baby boy with me, and in the funeral home I lifted up her hands and placed those pictures with her. I've never experienced anything in my life like what I went through at that moment." The mingled moments of joy and grief brought new strength and maturity to Welch, and once again he helped the A's advance to the 1989 World Series.

Welch was scheduled to start Game Three of the 1989 Series against the San Francisco Giants in Candlestick Park. He was warming up on the field—and was more than a little concerned about a painful groin pull—when the area was hit by a devastating earthquake. Welch and his wife had recently bought a condominium in San Francisco's prestigious Marina neighborhood and were planning to move when the Series was over. Many of the homes in that area were levelled by the quake and fires in its aftermath. The Welchs's condo was spared, but it did sustain damage.

Strangely enough, when the World Series resumed after the earthquake, the A's beat the Giants in four straight games, and Welch did not get a start. After the season ended, he and his family moved into their Marina condominium as the area began to rebuild. Even two years later, Welch told the *Akron Beacon Journal* that memories of the quake still linger. At home, he said, "I can go out on the deck in back and see the San Francisco Bay, the bridge, Alcatraz. But you walk out the front door and there's still construction going on. You can reconstruct houses, but a lot of people lost their lives, and that was the greatest loss."

Had Welch's entire 1990 season mirrored his performance in spring training, he would probably be out of work now. His 17.72 earned run average had the entire clubhouse on alert for a poor showing during the regulation games. Fortunately, Welch pulled himself together and settled into a pace that would provide him with his best year ever. His 27-6 regular season record—the most wins by a major-league pitcher since 1972—brought the A's into the World Series for a third straight year. This time the A's lost the Series to the Cincinnati Reds, but Welch was still awarded the Cy Young trophy—the highest honor a pitcher can earn.

Now in his 30s, Welch is hitting a stride that may take him through several more distinguished seasons. He is still primarily a fastball pitcher, but he is constantly experimenting with other pitches and working on the demanding split-finger move. "I haven't come close to perfecting it yet," Welch told the *New York Times*. "None of my pitches have been perfected. If they were, you'd never have to continually practice and improve." Ironically, Welch has yet to pitch a season opener. So strong is the A's organization that he still comes second in the rotation behind All-Star Dave Stewart.

Married since 1983, Welch is the only professional baseball player who lives within the city limits of San Francisco. He has two young sons, Dylan and Riley, and he is more than ever dedicated to a life free of addiction. "Today, I'm doing well, yes, but sobriety is something I must deal with every day," he told *Sports Illustrated*. "The problem will never go away." Welch will play at least four more years in Oakland under a contract worth $13.8 million plus bonuses. He told the *Fresno Bee* that he is both proud of his accomplishments and happy with the outcome of his once troubled life. 'The biggest joy I get now," he concluded, "is when I leave the ballpark and there's my family."

Writings

(With George Vescey) *Five O'Clock Comes Early: A Young Man's Battle with Alcoholism,* 1982.

Sources

Akron Beacon Journal, October 7, 1990; December 18, 1990.
Fresno Bee, February 24, 1991.
New York Times, October 7, 1990.
Sacramento Bee, March 12, 1991.
Sports Illustrated, September 17, 1990.

—*Mark Kram*

Marianne Williamson

©David Strick/Onyx

Spiritual therapist

Born c. 1953; grew up in Houston, TX; daughter of Alan (Vishnevetsky) Williamson (a lawyer who immigrated to the United States from the Soviet Union); children: India Emmaline. *Education:* Attended Pomona College.

Addresses: *Home*—Southern California. *Office*—c/o Los Angeles Center for Living, Los Angeles, CA.

Career

Lecturer; founder of Los Angeles Center for Living, and Manhattan Center for Living, 1987—.

Sidelights

Though she's not yet as well known as Werner Erhard, Jim Bakker, or Jimmy Swaggart, Marianne Williamson is still a rising star on the spirituality circuit—her lectures command increasingly greater audiences in her two base cities, New York City and Los Angeles. And like her contemporaries, Erhard, Bakker, and Swaggart, the dynamic native Texan is as controversial as she is popular.

Williamson "is not only the guru of the moment," noted a *Vanity Fair* article, "but also a leading spokeswoman for a quasi-religious phenomenon that is making waves around the country." Williamson's lectures, tapes, and classes are based on a book called *A Course in Miracles*. Though not the author of the book—psychologist Helen Schucman takes that credit—Williamson espouses the tenets of this vol-

ume, which some have summed up as "a correction to Christianity."

Williamson is seldom forthright about her past, but she did admit, according to *Vanity Fair*, that while in her twenties she "went from relationship to relationship, job to job, city to city, looking for anything that would give me some sense of identity or purpose.... My pain deepened, and so did my interest in philosophy.... I always sensed there was some mysterious cosmic order to things, but I could never figure out how it applied to my life." Reading *A Course in Miracles* in the late 1970s, she reported, gave her direction. When she decided in the early 1980s to give a lecture on the teachings, the former drama student drew fifteen people. Then, as word got out, attendance grew.

Many of Williamson's fans and followers fit her demographic description: upper middle class, liberal Baby Boomers rethinking their traditional Judeo/Christian upbringing, looking for a kind of no-fault spirituality. To that end, the lecturer covers topics like "Fear of Abandonment," "Forgiving Your Parents," and "Death Does Not Exist." Those who think Williamson's brand of preaching is anti-God will find that she mentions the Supreme Being often. "God is definitely out of the closet," Williamson told

Vanity Fair. "I refuse to pretend we don't pray here." Elaborating, she noted that "one of the reasons the political right wing in this country has had such an upsurge in popularity is because they have at least acknowledged the idea of God, and the so-called liberals have lost by default. The left wing is too cool to even mention God, so Middle America thinks, Well, I guess God's in the Republican Party."

One of Williamson's most important projects is the founding of the bi-coastal Centers for Living. The Los Angeles Center opened first, as a nonprofit organization that provides "meals, housecleaning, counseling, and even massage to people dealing with what both centers call 'life-challenging' illnesses," according to the *Vanity Fair* article. Thousands of those life-challenged are AIDS patients, who know they can appeal to the Centers for non-judgmental support.

"In accomplishing all this, however, Williamson has also attracted a lot of scrutiny from cynics who wonder what she's really up to," the *Vanity Fair* article continued. Williamson's philosophy is "complete gibberish," stated one critic in the article. "It's typical Southern California New Age bullshit." And as for its self-made missionary, "She's playing a win-win game for herself," said another Williamson critic.

"Here she's preaching the gospel of giving and love and goodness, and what she's getting out of it is fame. She wanted to be a nightclub singer; she wanted to be needed, to be powerful, to be recognized, to be fawned over. She's getting what she wanted: she's a star."

Indeed, even her most ardent fans would admit that Williamson is no Mother Teresa—as evidenced by the lecturer's flamboyant lifestyle and out-of-wedlock daughter. But to follower David Geffen, the record producer who has become one of the richest men in America, "there's no question Marianne is genuine, and she does a lot of good work. She's not some new version of [old-time evangelist] Aimee Semple McPherson. She doesn't hold herself out to be a perfect person, but she takes care of people who are in trouble and who are dying. She's also able to articulate things that are valuable for people to hear. People are alienated from their families, from religion, and she's found a way to bring them together."

Sources

Vanity Fair, June 1991.

—*Susan Salter*

Katarina Witt

Olympic figure skater

Born c. 1966 in Karl-Marx-Stadt, East Germany (now Germany); daughter of Manfred (a departmental director at a plant and seed cooperative) and Kathe (a physical therapist) Witt. *Education:* Post-secondary study in the arts. *Politics:* Socialist Unity party/Communist.

Addresses: *Home*—Karl-Marx-Stadt, Germany. *Agent*—Jefferson Pilot Sports and Entertainment, Charlotte, NC.

Career

World class amateur figure skater until 1988; professional figure skater, 1988—. Olympic contender in 1984 and 1988.

Awards: Olympic gold medals, 1984, 1988; has earned four world titles and six European titles; Emmy Award for outstanding individual achievement in classical music dance programming, 1990.

Sidelights

Representing her native country of Germany (then East Germany), svelte figure skater Katarina Witt went for the gold at the 1988 Winter Olympics in Calgary, Alberta, Canada. A spellbinding performance on the ice won Witt the title of Olympic champion—for the second time. Witt went home with a gold medal in 1984, as well, and has come out on top in four world figure skating championships. She surpassed Peggy Fleming's rec-

ord of winning three consecutive world championships. And Witt has won the European title six times.

Witt was awarded her first gold medal at the 1984 Winter Olympics in Sarajevo, Yugoslavia. Her performance there "was the first to hit the perfect blend of art and athletics, pirouettes and panache," wrote Rick Reilly in *Sports Illustrated*. In 1987 Witt skated against defender Debi Thomas at the World Championships in Cincinnati. They couldn't have asked for a more enthusiastic crowd—even workouts were sold out. A controversial issue arose around these practice sessions. Witt, who "skates for the crowds," according to a German friend, received many standing ovations. Thomas's coach, Alex McGowan, reportedly observed that when Witt smiled and waved at the audience during workouts, she was "milking the crowd." In response, Witt's coach Jutta Mueller stated that Witt wins public approval with her caliber of skating. "Katarina does not need to draw the public to her side by any other means," she told E. M. Swift in *Sports Illustrated*.

Over 15,000 onlookers viewed Thomas's and Witt's spirited skating in the long program. Representing the United States, Thomas competed brilliantly just prior to Witt. This was perhaps the toughest act Witt ever had to follow in competition up until then. In

Sports Illustrated, Thomas recalled what went through her mind as she observed Witt's sparkling performance: "This girl's amazing." Witt's own point of view, expressed in the same publication, was: "It was uncommonly difficult to skate after Debi. The crowd was in such ecstasy." But Witt was still able to psyche herself up when Thomas left the ice.

Skating to tunes from the musical *West Side Story,* Witt executed two successful double axels and five flawless triple jumps. Of the nine judges, seven put Witt in first place. Previously, however, the compulsory figure skating competition had been a different story. While Witt is gifted with versatility, she had not been considered among the best; her figure skating alone was described as "mediocre" by Swift. As a result, she found herself in fifth place in that category—to Thomas's second positioning. The writing was on the wall. To win the world title, Thomas only needed to come in second in the upcoming long and short programs. Even if Witt won first place in both programs, she would be in second place overall. Faced with these odds, Witt's tears reportedly flowed when she went back to the locker room. But as luck would have it, Witt need not have worried. The 115-pound beauty performed with pizzazz to the Glenn Miller tune "In the Mood" and won the short program. Thomas had problems executing the required double axel, which eventually put her in third place.

> *"You can skate to the music, or you can interpret the music."*

The tables had turned in Witt's favor, but the excitement and pressure were not over yet. Thomas then redeemed herself in the free-skating program by completing five successful triple jumps along with two additional double axels for good measure. A crowd of over 15,000 spectators were on their feet in support of the United States's defender of the title.

Despite the standing ovation for her potential nemesis, Witt steeled herself and skated onto the ice to perform to the hilt. Her self-talk was, "You are the best. Do it," she confided to *Sports Illustrated.* And she did, skating her way past all contenders to win the title of World Champion. Carlo Fassi, coach for former Olympic skating greats Peggy Fleming and Dorothy Hamill, said in the *Chicago Tribune* that it was the "best I have ever seen a woman skate."

A highlight of the 1988 Winter Olympics in Calgary was the women's singles figure skating competition. For the freestyle program, Witt selected a dramatic scene from the Georges Bizet opera *Carmen.* As Carmen, Witt dressed in a frilly black and red costume, with her hair pulled back and adorned with a Spanish-style fan. Her routine featured a triple jump and double jump combination triple salchow. "Carmen" then landed after a double axel jump, was "stabbed," went into a camel spin, and "died" on the ice to bells tolling. Witt's superlative performance was rewarded with a gold medal. "You can skate to the music, or you can interpret the music," she told Phil Hersh in the *Chicago Tribune.* JoJo Starbuck, former U.S. pairs champion, commented on ESPN-TV, "Watch the style, the grace, the sensuality and the way she pulls you right out on the ice with her."

Witt's training as a world-class ice skater began at the Kuechwald rink, in the neighborhood of her kindergarten in Karl-Marx-Stadt, East Germany (now Germany). The local sports and education experts saw enough promise in the little girl to hand her over to Jutta Mueller by the time Witt was ten years old. Nearly half of the 48 international class medals won by Mueller's proteges have been Olympic gold. Rick Reilly described Mueller as the former German Democratic Republic's "most famous, fearsome skating coach," in *Sports Illustrated.*

Six-hour practice sessions were not unusual for Witt under Mueller's watchful eye. But the ice princess's training did not end there. Imparting a sense of style to her proteges is also part of the coach's technique. So she taught Witt the most effective way to wear her hair, makeup, and skating costumes. As Reilly put it, Mueller spent "hundreds of hours teaching smiles, contact, glitz and sass." And given Witt's reputation for enchanting the crowd, the training paid off.

Certain types of behavior were strictly forbidden in Mueller's training program. For example, Witt was not allowed to give in to her weakness for ice cream. "I want the skater's figure to have absolutely no fault," Mueller told *Sports Illustrated.* And there was no dancing at discos (another Witt favorite) or playing around with friends at all hours of the night. Nor was there time for boyfriends, no doubt much to the chagrin of the thousands of males who penned love letters to the 5'5" blue-eyed skater. Witt was apparently able to follow these rules philosophically (other than perhaps sneaking a bite of ice cream here and there).

In *Maclean's,* Witt compared the sports system of Germany (specifically the German Democratic Republic before unification between East and West) to the business opportunities in the United States. "The best person goes forward," she explained. As a sports success in her own country, Witt enjoys government perquisites, such as expenses for coaching, for ballet instruction, and for renting rink time, to name a few. Her U.S. counterparts have been known to run up a tab of $1 million in training fees. And unlike most of her countrymen, Witt did not have to wait ten years for an apartment. (She lives in a house.) She also owns a car (the pricey Soviet-made Lada has been traded in for a German Golf)—again without having to put in the typical waiting time of about twelve years. Moreover, most people could not travel beyond the Iron Curtain until the age of 65. Witt has traveled extensively.

When she turned 20, Witt applied for membership in the exclusive Socialist Unity Party (an honor extended to only 13 percent of the population). Witt was criticized for supporting communism, after the Berlin Wall separating East Germany from West came tumbling down in 1989. She told Richard Regen in *Interview:* "I didn't do anything wrong. I was living in my own little sports world and I was proud to represent my country."

Now Witt can be proud to represent herself. After the 1988 World Competition in Budapest, she went from amateur status to professional. At first it was difficult. The government wanted Witt to continue her education in the arts, so it limited her professional opportunities somewhat and occasionally withheld visas. But since 1989, Witt has been able to travel freely. Discussing freedom in *Maclean's,* she observed, "You get used to it so fast that you can't imagine life was different before."

Witt starred in several ice shows after the Olympics in Calgary. She created KW Arts and Entertainment, a company based in Frankfurt. And she hired Jefferson Pilot Sports and Entertainment, of Charlotte, N.C., to work on product endorsements. She also teamed up with the 1988 male gold medalist in figure skating, American Brian Boitano. The two joined forces in two television specials and began touring the United States in the spring of 1990.

While Witt and Boitano enjoy a close professional relationship, Witt insists they are not more personally involved. "I have no boyfriends at the moment," she told D'Arcy Jenish in *Maclean's.* "Now, I am too busy to do anything but skate." But the two have been friends since the 1988 "Tour of World Figure Skating Champions," which followed the Olympics. They got to know each other while touring 30 cities.

Canvas of Ice, a 1988 ABC-TV hour-long special, was the first professional project Witt and Boitano embarked on together. At that time, it still took six months to talk the East German government into allowing Witt to perform in the show. When the two did perform, they realized, "We love it so much that we decided to do other projects together," Boitano told Jenish.

Witt then came up with the idea of elaborating on her earlier performance of "Carmen." She conceived of a film titled *Carmen on Ice,* in which Boitano plays the part of Carmen's jealous lover Don Jose and Canadian skater Brian Orser plays her new lover, the matador Escamillo. Witt, of course, skated in the role of the gypsy cigarette girl Carmen. HBO, the pay-cable television network, aired the film in 1990. Later on that year, the three actor/skaters won Emmy awards for outstanding individual achievement in their category of classical music-dance.

Then came the ice show *Katarina Witt and Brian Boitano—Skating.* Despite entanglement in more bureaucratic red tape, the two-hour show was free to tour a season late, beginning in spring 1990. This led to *Katarina Witt and Brian Boitano—Skating II,* which began its North American tour of 23 cities in January 1991. Thirteen additional skaters from Canada, the U.S., Spain, and the U.S.S.R. round out the cast. With this gifted group, the two stars "have created a show that is athletic and artistic, hip and sexy," stated Jenish.

Witt and Boitano have chosen a career path that is both bold and innovative. Before them, the world's best skaters most often ended up in already established organizations like the Ice Capades, based in Hollywood. Their decision to do otherwise opened up more doors for the two, and allowed them to perform to their own standards. For example, they preferred to focus on excellent individual skating rather than the more traditional group performances. And they wanted to come up with a show that will go on to star the brilliant skaters who come after them.

Still, success is never guaranteed—especially in such a competitive glamour sport as ice skating. But Witt is taking the risk. Michael Burg, program director for Jefferson Pilot Sports and Entertainment, envisions Witt as the anchor for a "triple crown of skating." Three competitive events open to professional skaters will make up the competition. The prize money is to be around $100,000, more than twice the current purse offered by the NutraSweet World Professional Figure Skating Championships. The new event is slated to take place in the United States, Europe,

Canada, and Japan in winter 1991-92. Part of the overall plan is for Witt to endorse various products. Witt's promoters are optimistic about her professional career. As Jenish put it, the glamorous "skater still has the beauty, talent and charm to become an international star as a professional."

Sources

Chicago Tribune, February 21, 1988.
Interview, March 1991.
Maclean's, January 14, 1991.
New York Times, February 2, 1986.
Sports Illustrated, March 23, 1987; January 20, 1986.

—*Victoria France Charabati*

James Worthy

Professional basketball player

Full name, James Ager Worthy; born February 27, 1961, in Gastonia, N.C.; son of Ervin (a Baptist minister) and Gladys Worthy; married Angela Wilder (an actress), c. 1984; children: Sable Alexandria. *Education:* Attended University of North Carolina, 1979-82.

Career

Number-one pick in the National Basketball Association (NBA) draft, 1982; chosen by the Los Angeles Lakers; forward for the Lakers, 1982—.

Awards: Numerous honors include Most Valuable Player of the NBA Finals, 1988.

Sidelights

James Worthy may be one of the most aptly named athletes ever. The poker-faced Worthy is an indispensable component of the powerful Los Angeles Lakers, arguably the finest professional basketball team of the last decade. Worthy's contributions as a forward for the Lakers have been formidable almost since the moment he joined the team in 1982. "The thing about James Worthy is, you don't know whether that's a name or a description," wrote Jim Murray in the *Los Angeles Times.* "You don't know whether he's James the Worthy—like one of those old-time kings who were Charles the Great, or John the Good, or Richard the Lion-Hearted." Murray continued: "Whatever he is, he's basket-ball royalty . . . . He is like a guy stealing a pie when he gets the ball."

On any other squad Worthy would be the reigning superstar, the hometown hero who reaps all the laurels. Worthy plays for the Lakers, however, and he has spent most of his career in the shadows of the likes of Magic Johnson and Kareem Abdul-Jabbar. Only in the last few years has he begun to earn the praise and recognition his stellar play deserves. Murray noted that the talented forward "didn't exactly come into the league with banners waving and trumpets blaring. He wasn't 'Magic' or 'Air Jordan' or 'the Mailman.' He was just James . . . . James Worthy didn't explode into a whole bunch of 50- or 60-point nights. He didn't spend half his game flying through the air like a Wallenda. He didn't win any slam-dunk contests. He was just, well, Worthy. He never showed elation when he won. He never showed frustration when he didn't . . . . He was as dependable as sunrise, as unflappable as a cigar store Indian." That determination and dignity—learned through eight tough NBA seasons and countless championship playoffs—has become Worthy's signature style as he enters his prime years of play.

Worthy told the *Los Angeles Times* that he began to play basketball at the ripe age of four. The son of a Baptist minister, he grew up in a large family in the town of Gastonia, North Carolina. Even as a youngster Worthy refused to answer to the names "Jimmy" or "Jim." His family and friends called him by his middle name, Ager, and by high school he was demanding to be called James. Worthy grew up in a religious environment with parents who stressed study and good behavior. He spent most of his spare time playing ball, and by high school he had developed many of the skills that he took with him to the NBA. Eric "Sleepy" Floyd, a guard for the Golden State Warriors, also hails from Gastonia and often found himself opposing Worthy on the court. "James was just like he is now," Floyd told the Los Angeles *Daily News.* "Getting out on the wing. Good low-post moves. Basically the same."

In Sleepy Floyd, Worthy found a near-perfect opponent. The two young men attended rival high schools (Worthy attended Ashbrook High) and often met in closely contested games. Both were quality players who were aggressively recruited by colleges all over the East. Nor did their friendship off-court and rivalry on-court end after high school. Floyd enrolled at Georgetown University and played basketball for coach John Thompson. Worthy chose to stay in his home state, attending the University of North Carolina. The two players met only once during their college years—in, of all places, the 1982 NCAA

James Worthy heads down center court in a 1988 NBA playoffs game against the Dallas Mavericks. AP/Wide World Photos.

championship game. There, Worthy's Tar Heels pulled off a thrilling 63-62 victory. Worthy noted that these days, Gastonia's residents are proud of the success that both he and Floyd have achieved.

Worthy's years as a Tar Heel were some of the most difficult he has faced. During his freshman season he injured his ankle so severely that two screws and a six-inch metal rod were implanted to repair the damage. The pain was so intense that he was placed under heavy sedation for two weeks after the operation. Remarkably, he returned the next season—with the screws still in his leg—and helped lead North Carolina to the 1981 NCAA championship game. The Tar Heels lost that contest to the Indiana Hoosiers, but Worthy and his teammates returned the following year to beat Georgetown for the national title. The 1982 North Carolina team also featured another future NBA star, Michael Jordan.

Shortly after winning the 1982 NCAA championship, Worthy decided to turn pro, and he offered his name for consideration in the draft. Injuries notwithstanding, he was a tempting prospect, considered by many the best athlete eligible for the draft that year. He was chosen first in the first round by the Los Angeles Lakers, a team already heavy with proven talent. Had Worthy been picked by a struggling franchise, he would no doubt have been made a starter immediately. Instead, he found himself playing a substitute role in Los Angeles, where he averaged only about twenty-five minutes of court time per game. Midway through Worthy's rookie season, *Sports Illustrated* reporter Bruce Newman called him "one of the best players to come into the NBA in the last decade." Newman added that Worthy was "having a year to match his name, and only an idiot would say the Los Angeles Lakers erred in making him the draft's No. 1 choice."

A broken leg kept Worthy on the sidelines through the 1983 playoffs, and he was slow to regain his form during the regular season of 1983-84. By the time of the 1984 playoffs he had recovered, however, and he played like one inspired in the championship series against the Boston Celtics. Ironically, Worthy is remembered less for his spectacular showing in the first three games of that series than he is for missing an important foul shot that led to a Lakers loss in Game Four. Los Angeles went on to lose the championship to Boston, and some suggested that the arrogant Celtics were able to rattle Worthy and break the momentum of his play.

Subsequent years have seen a meaner, tougher Worthy, a player who cannot be intimidated by word or action. Lakers coach Pat Riley told the *Los Angeles*

Times that Worthy "used to get mad . . . . His first two years, everyone would take their shots. He'd get all upset, it would take him out of the game." Since then Worthy has adopted a "game face" that never varies, characterized by a stone-cold expression that borders on mild boredom. It is also worth noting that Worthy incurs few penalties and has hardly ever been ejected from a game.

Incredibly, Worthy was in his fourth season before he was named a permanent starter. As the Lakers began the 1985 season—having retaken the championship from the Celtics that spring—Worthy was finally about to come into his own as a certified star. His talents were no secret to the Lakers' staff, but despite his fabulous post-season play he had yet to win a fan following. That would begin to change in the 1985-86 season, as Worthy and the Lakers contended to repeat as champions. In 1986 Worthy was chosen as an NBA All-Star for the first time. He also became the NBA's all-time leader in career playoff field-goal percentage (.600) and averaged twenty points per game. Slowly Worthy began to emerge from the shadows of his more famous—and more personable—teammates. Talk of trading him to Dallas was acceptable to the Lakers' fans in 1986, but it was absolutely forbidden by the team's general manager, Jerry West, who has since been lauded for his foresight.

Jim Murray wrote that Worthy's moment of truth arrived when Kareem Abdul-Jabbar retired. "Now, the smart money said, the Laker franchise would turn back into a pumpkin," claimed Murray. "Its lineup would just be an orphan asylum. The 'orphans' only posted the league's best won-lost record, 63-19. As the [1987-88] season wore on, Magic Johnson-James Worthy became as effective a combination as a ballroom dance team—or the Lone Ranger and Tonto. They moved in tandem. Whenever Johnson was double-teamed, which was most of the time, Worthy was like a man who had just been let out of a cage. 'W-o-o-r-t-h-y!' rang through the Forum night after night as he flipped, shoveled, arced or tapped in 1,685 points, including 711 field goals, and took down 478 rebounds, praise-Worthy statistics." With Worthy and Johnson both in prime physical condition, the Lakers have been a championship-caliber team without pause.

Despite the fact that he shuns the media and keeps a low profile, Worthy has become "a major in-your-face force and Laker leader," to quote Scott Ostler of the *Los Angeles Times*. Always a post player with quick feet and brilliant, defense-defying moves, Worthy has evolved into a consummate strategist and a scoring threat with the long jump shot. Worthy's greatest asset, however, is his grace under pressure. He is often at his finest in playoff situations, raising his game to an even higher level. "There's more pressure during the playoffs," Worthy conceded in the *Daily News*, "but you're more stable too. You're not traveling as much and you're concentrating on one team. You're able to hone in against it the way you can't when you're playing against different teams." Magic Johnson summed up Worthy's talents best when he told the *Daily News*: "[James] wants the ball. And he's doing something with it when he gets it."

> *"There's more pressure in the playoffs, but you're more stable too. You're not traveling as much and you're concentrating on one team."*

Late in 1990 Worthy found himself in the public eye for quite a different reason. He was arrested in Houston for allegedly attempting to solicit sex from two undercover police officers posing as prostitutes. In court Worthy pleaded no contest on two counts of soliciting prostitution and was fined $1000 and ordered to perform 40 hours of community service. Worthy is married and the father of an infant daughter; he has said very little about the incident and its effect on his immediate family. Shortly after his arrest, he released a statement, saying: "I made a major mistake. I can't dwell on it. It's a tough problem, but it's not going to go away. I know I've hurt some people badly and I've got to address that. I'm just going to go out and play. I'm not looking for sympathy."

Worthy has indeed gone on with his career in a "business as usual" sense. The adverse publicity has in fact actually endeared him to basketball fans, many of whom regard him highly for his apology and his professional attitude. Still in his early 30s, Worthy can look ahead to several more productive years in the NBA, years in which he may wrest the limelight from Magic Johnson. "Let us now praise James Worthy," wrote Ron Rapoport in the *Daily News*. "Neither rain nor snow nor gloom of night can keep him from his appointed rounds. Neither flying elbows nor fatigue nor 14,000 people screaming unpleasant things in his ear, either. Rapoport concluded: "There should be one on every team."

Sources

Daily News (Los Angeles), February 9, 1986; May 7, 1987; May 22, 1987; May 24, 1987; June 22, 1988; May 27, 1989; December 15, 1990.
Jet, December 10, 1990.
Los Angeles Times, May 24, 1987; June 8, 1987; June 15, 1987; May 13, 1990; November 21, 1990.
Sports Illustrated, February 21, 1983; May 19, 1986.

—Mark Kram

Molly Yard

AP/Wide World Photos

Former president of the National Organization for Women

Born in Shanghai, China; daughter of James (a Methodist missionary) and Mabelle Hickcox (an import business owner) Yard; married Sylvester Garrett (an attorney and labor arbiter), 1933; children: James, John, Joan. *Education:* Swarthmore College, B.S., 1933.

Addresses: *Homes*—Washington, DC; and Ligonier, PA.

Career

Social worker for the Pennsylvania Department of Public Welfare, c. 1933-37; then served as national secretary and chair of the American Student Union (formerly the Student League of Industrial Democracy); co-founder of the Washington Student Service Bureau; director of Citizen's Council on City Planning in Philadelphia, 1944-47; served on the Philadelphia zoning board, 1951-53; served during the 1960s on the Leadership Conference on Civil Rights; membership and activism in the National Organization for Women (NOW) began in 1974, served on senior staff, 1978-84, became political director, 1985, elected president, 1987; stepped down after suffering a stroke, 1991.

Sidelights

Dubbed the "unsinkable Molly Yard" by the *Washington Post*, the former president of the National Organization for Women (NOW) played a critical role in revitalizing the women's movement for the 1990s. Yard was at the forefront of such issues as abortion rights and the Equal Rights Amendment (ERA), most recently advocating what she terms the "feminization of power"—the election of more women to political office. While her trademark hair bun and feisty demeanor have been targeted by adversaries as symbols of feminist radicalism, her supporters have attested to her limitless energy and commitment to change while in office. The *Hyannis Daily* stressed Yard's "graciousness and warmth," adding that "her voice is soft, though there is no mistaking a resonance of firm resolve." It is with this resolve that Yard has assisted NOW in attaining its ultimate and her personal goal—equality between the sexes. "NOW is an organization of both men and women who believe in women's rights," she told the *Hyannis Daily*. "We believe what is good for women is also good for everybody—for the whole human race."

An unfortunate stroke in May of 1991 and subsequent prolonged hospitalization, however, has prevented Yard from fulfilling her duties as president and effectively brought her term to an end. (Patricia Ireland, a Miami attorney, officially took over for Yard in late 1991). Still, Yard's impact on the organization and on feminism in the 1990's will surely continue to be felt.

Yard's interest in equal rights was sparked long before her involvement in NOW; according to the Bloomsburg, Pennsylvania *Press-Enterprise,* she claims to have been "born a feminist" because she was surrounded by the "devaluation of girls from birth." The third of four daughters born to Methodist missionaries, Yard spent her first 13 years living with her family in China. She recalls that after she was born, the town leaders in Shanghai gave her father, James, a brass wash basin as consolation for having another daughter. When the family returned to the United States, settling in Connecticut, Yard found that the treatment of women was little better than in China. Though more subtle, sexism was still rampant, and Yard notes that although she loved sports, girls had few opportunities to participate in competitive athletics. She told the *Press-Enterprise* that in high school "girls only got to use the gym when the boys were finished."

Yard's mother, Mabelle Hickcox Yard, who had been denied a college education herself as a young woman, used the income from her business of importing jewelry and linen from China to put all four of her daughters through Swarthmore, a small liberal arts college in Pennsylvania. While Yard would have liked to attend law school following college, her parents were unable to finance it, and her chances of getting accepted were unlikely. "Women were just not admitted," Yard told the *Press-Enterprise,* regarding the law school admissions policies in the 1930s. At Swarthmore she majored in political science and took her first action against discrimination. A member of the sorority Kappa Alpha Theta, she led a campus-wide campaign to abolish the Greek system on the grounds that her own and other sororities would not pledge Jewish women. "It left a handful of women totally out of the whole system and it was cruel," she commented in the *Swarthmore College Bulletin.* Yard graduated in 1933, having left an indelible mark on the college.

Her first job out of college was as a social worker for the Pennsylvania Department of Public Welfare until, reports the *Swarthmore College Bulletin,* she became "very disgruntled by the whole public relief system because it was so clearly inadequate." Yet the seeds for political activism had been sown, and one of her final gestures before leaving the welfare department was to urge—in direct violation of the rules of her job—an impoverished client to organize other unemployed people to pressure state legislators for more benefits. She then began working for the

Student League of Industrial Democracy, whose members formed a new organization called the American Student Union in 1937. Yard served as both national secretary and chair of this student movement during the early years of her marriage in 1938 to Sylvester Garrett, who worked with the National Labor Relations Board (NLRB) in Washington, DC.

But if joining her husband in Washington seemed uncharacteristic of Yard, her insistence on keeping her own name certainly was not. To Yard, this symbolized her intent to preserve her independence, and she told the *Hyannis Daily* that their marriage, which has lasted more than fifty years, has been a "continual learning process" for Garrett. Yard helped found the Washington Student Service Bureau, which enabled students to observe the government in action and has since evolved into an expansive student intern program. She also worked to reelect Franklin Delano Roosevelt in the 1944 presidential campaign and became an ardent supporter of the New Deal (Roosevelt's post-Depression economic restructuring plan), even though the American Student Union had been critical of it. "Eleanor Roosevelt, who really was the eyes and ears of the president, invited us to meet with her," Yard told the *Knoxville News-Sentinel.* The two women developed a strong friendship and working relationship that continued until Eleanor Roosevelt's death in 1962.

The late 1940s brought a career change for Garrett, who became chair of the War Labor Board's regional office in Philadelphia, and Yard plunged immediately into local politics. "Working in Philadelphia politics naturally introduced me to the long-entrenched and corrupt Republican city machine," Yard explained in the *Swarthmore College Bulletin.* She ran the Citizens Council on City Planning and worked with the Democratic team of Joseph Clark and Richardson Dilworth to oust the Republican party from office, precipitating what she told the *Philadelphia Sunday Bulletin* was "one of the most famous episodes of my life." As chair of the Republican City Committee, William Meade made a radio address in 1949 in which he called Yard and three others Communists. Yard filed a libel suit, and Eleanor Roosevelt spoke out publicly on her behalf. "I undertook the unpleasant job of suing Meade because he had done a reprehensible thing," Yard stated in the *Philadelphia Evening Bulletin.* "[He] debased the democratic practice of free elections by making the fear-inspiring charge of communism." Her efforts were rewarded by a payment of $1,500 and a public retraction by Meade.

Her resolve hardly dampened, Yard continued to be active in the Democratic party throughout the 1950s and 1960s. She worked on Helen Gahagan Douglas's Senate campaign against Richard Nixon in 1952 and on the 1960 Citizens for Kennedy campaign. In 1951 Joseph Clark was elected mayor of Philadelphia and appointed Yard to the zoning board where she remained until her husband became a labor arbitrator for the U.S. Steel Corporation in 1953. "The steel workers and U.S. Steel were headquartered in Pittsburgh so out to Pittsburgh I went," she explained in the *Swarthmore College Bulletin*, adding, "This is the fate of women." The move marked the beginning of what Yard's daughter, Joan Garrett-Goodyear, wryly calls her mother's "domestic period," in which she combined her work in local and national politics with raising Joan and sons James and John.

Civil rights became Yard's primary focus in the 1960s, and she served in the Leadership Conference on Civil Rights, which fought for national civil rights legislation. In 1963 she was a key organizer of the western Pennsylvania contingent of the civil rights march on Washington, and led a march to the Pittsburgh post office armed with thousands of letters to senators and representatives urging the passage of the Civil Rights Act of 1964. That same year Yard took her own advice to women to seek office and ran for a seat on the Pennsylvania state legislature. Although she won the Democratic nomination, she lost the general election, later telling the *Syracuse Herald-Journal*, "What I really wanted to do was run for Congress."

It was not until the early 1970s that Yard began devoting her energy full time to the women's movement. She became a member of the Pittsburgh chapter of NOW in 1974, and her first task was to help obtain a time extension for the ratification of the Equal Rights Amendment. Her stance on the ERA has not wavered since then, and despite its defeat resulting from a narrowly missed deadline in 1982, Yard maintained in the *Knoxville News-Sentinel*, "ERA is bottom line. Until we pass it, we're not going to be taken seriously by the courts. If you want a guarantee for your rights . . . you have to be in the Constitution." In 1978 Yard accompanied friend and colleague Eleanor Smeal, who had recently been elected president of NOW, to NOW's headquarters in Washington, where she worked tirelessly on the ERA Ratification Drive, serving as an influential lobbyist in Congress.

The key to passing the ERA, in Yard's view, is to get more women elected to state legislatures—a strategy called "feminizing power"—as she believes that the amendment will have passed in Congress by 1992 and will be ready for state ratification. In her public addresses, according to the *Hyannis Daily*, she would urge women: "Get yourself elected . . . . Help other women get elected." In 1987 she and Smeal organized the Women's Trust, a political committee with the long-range purpose of helping women run for public office. Yard also endeavored to accentuate what she and her colleagues have referred to as the "gender gap," particularly evident in the presidential election of 1980. "In the 1980 campaign women were 8 percent less supportive of [Ronald] Reagan than men were . . . on issues of nuclear arms, foreign policy, confrontations in Central America, [and] the business in Lebanon," Yard told the *Swarthmore College Bulletin*. "Our belief was that . . . if we could intensify [the difference] enough, it would make a difference in the election." While this plan failed in practice, awareness of the gender gap piqued Yard's interest in women's potential power in politics, and she has looked forward to the day when legislatures contain 30 to 35 percent women, particularly at the state level.

As a prime architect of NOW's political and legislative agenda, Yard served on the senior staff of NOW/PAC from 1978 to 1984. She became NOW's political director in 1985 and was instrumental in coordinating its successful campaign the following year to defeat anti-abortion referenda in Massachusetts, Rhode Island, Oregon, and Arkansas. Yard has voiced the belief that abortion should remain a federal issue and fervently opposed the recent Supreme Court decision on *Webster v. Reproductive Health Services* that gives states more power to restrict abortion laws. A very real threat is that the Supreme Court will eventually overturn its landmark *Roe v. Wade* decision of 1973, which recognized abortion as a constitutional right, and many fear a huge step backward for women because, as Yard told the *Swarthmorean*, "if you can't control your reproductive life, you have no freedom at all." One of the many ways that Yard battled to keep abortion legal is by speaking from NOW's Freedom Caravan for Women's Lives, which travels throughout the United States galvanizing pro-choice votes. She also made it a top priority to visit a number of college campuses, encouraging students to become active in the fight for equality.

Elected president of NOW in July 1987, Yard helped rekindle the women's movement. NOW experienced a dynamic revitalization under her administration. Its membership grew from 140,000 to 250,000, and the annual budget increased 70 percent to over $10 million. One of Yard's less publicized campaigns before her stroke was the effort to win import approval for RU 486, a French pill that is said to produce safe abortions, in the United States. The pill may be a treatment for such diseases as breast cancer, endometriosis, glaucoma, and prostate cancer, and Yard told the *Wall Street Journal* that she could not "understand why the medical community isn't outraged by the failure to bring this drug to this country." During Pope John II's visit to the United States in September 1987, Yard organized and participated in a demonstration at the Vatican Embassy in Washington, protesting what she called, according to the *Press-Enterprise*, "the Roman Catholic Church's betrayal of women." For her efforts, Yard was honored in Paris in February 1990 by the Alliance des Femmes pour la Democratisation as an international leader on reproductive rights.

Throughout her NOW career Yard refused to disclose her exact age because she found that age tends to be the first question that male reporters ask women. When pressed on the issue, according to the *Hyannis Daily*, Yard has replied, "I'm old enough to know what I'm doing and I have the energy to do it. What else do you want to know?" Thus, Yard found no age barrier between herself and women coming of age in recent years, confident of the fact that the newcomers will not forget the struggle of their forebears and will continue to wage the equal rights battle. "I have total faith that the young feminists of this country are alive and well and ready to do battle," she told the *Plain Dealer*. On the heels of the Persian Gulf War, one issue that particularly effects younger women is their role in combat. While NOW opposes war on principle, it asserts that women are entitled to combat pay and should not be barred from any position in the military for which they are qualified. "Our position is that women should not be excluded from combat," Yard asserted in the *Plain Dealer*. "When you make exclusion provisions you keep women from the best jobs." This issue has specific ramifications for the ERA, as Yard noted that men in the state legislatures who do not believe that women should be in combat seize it as a reason not to vote for equal rights.

Prior to her stroke Yard expressed the desire to explore the possibility of a third political party in the United States—one that primarily serves women and minorities. Whether or not she will recover sufficiently to become involved once again in her cause, it would seem that Molly Yard has done much toward her goal: to see, according to the *Hyannis Daily*, "the world we all want—one of equality, hope and justice for all people."

Sources

Cleveland Plain Dealer, February 3, 1991.
Hyannis Daily (Massachusetts), June 20, 1988.
Knoxville News-Sentinel, May 8, 1988.
Newsweek, July 22, 1991.
New York Times, July 1, 1990.
Philadelphia Evening Bulletin, July 25, 1950.
Pittsburgh Press, May 14, 1989.
Press-Enterprise (Bloomsburg, PA), July 7, 1989.
Swarthmore College Bulletin, January 1988.
The Swarthmorean, February 16, 1990.
Syracuse Herald-Journal, July 7, 1987.
Wall Street Journal, September 5, 1989.
Washington Post, July 22, 1987.

—*Carolyn March*

Boris Yeltsin

AP/Wide World Photos

Soviet politician

Full name, Boris Nikolayevich Yeltsin; born February 1, 1931, in Butka, U.S.S.R.; *Education:* Graduated from the Urals M. Kirov Polytechnic Institute with a degree in engineering, 1955.

Addresses: *Office*—The Kremlin, Moscow, U.S.S.R.

Career

Joined the Communist party in 1961. Worked in various positions for the party, 1968-76. Appointed first secretary of the Sverdlovsk District Central Committee, 1976; secretary of the national Central Committee for Construction, 1985; first secretary of the Moscow City Party Committee, (mayor of Moscow), 1985; named as non-voting member of the Politburo, 1986; resigned Politburo seat, October, 1987, and fired by Mikhail Gorbachev from post as mayor, November, 1987; elected to Congress of People's Deputies (new Soviet Parliament), 1989, quit Communist party, July, 1990; elected president of the Russian Federation, November, 1990.

Sidelights

If I did not exist," Boris Yeltsin told the *Washington Post* in 1989, "[Mikhail] Gorbachev would have to invent me." Indeed, as the Soviet Union entered the post-Cold War era, Yeltsin—the maverick populist and president of the Russian Federation, the largest most powerful republic in the Soviet Union—served a crucial role to the Communist party leader. While the U.S.S.R.'s right-wing political establishment ac-

cused Gorbachev of moving too far, too fast with his policies of *glasnost* (openness) and *perestroika* (economic restructuring), Yeltsin provided a counter-balance, complaining from the left that Gorbachev was too much talk and too little action. Throughout 1990 and 1991, amid harsh economic conditions and the strident clamoring of a number of Soviet republics for independence from the Soviet Union, Yeltsin's increasing popularity made him Gorbachev's foremost political rival. The tense 63-hour coup attempt of August, 1991, in which Gorbachev was temporarily deposed by hard-line Communists, the KGB, and the Soviet military, only served to bolster Yeltsin's stature worldwide: In a courageous gesture of resistance, the Russian Federation president and 100 legislators remained barricaded in the republic headquarters, while outside thousands of Soviet citizens clashed with troops until Gorbachev's reinstatement was announced.

In the immediate aftermath of the coup, Yeltsin's role as a national hero was greatly enhanced, and his status as an international force changed dramatically. He was publicly thanked by Gorbachev, his rival, for thwarting what the Soviet premier called "this shady enterprise." President George Bush, who had formerly appeared uncomfortable about Yeltsin in light of

Yeltsin's threat to Gorbachev, also expressed gratitude and pledged his support.

Yeltsin was elected president of the Russian Federation in May of 1990. He quickly called for sovereignty for the Russian state from the rest of the Soviet Union. And in July he shocked the nation by publicly quitting the Communist party and leading fellow radicals toward formation of an alternative party. The move seemed designed to end communism's 72-year stranglehold on Soviet politics.

Speaking to the 28th Communist Party Congress on July 12, 1990, Yeltsin told stunned delegates that he was leaving the party because he could no longer blindly obey its policies. "As the highest elected figure in the republic, I can only subordinate myself to the will of the people and its elected representatives," he said. "I therefore announce my resignation from the Communist Party of the Soviet Union." That Yeltsin could survive such a move seemed testimony to Gorbachev's policies of openness. "Under Josef Stalin and Fidel Castro, Yeltsin would have already been executed," Jiri Valenta, director of the University of Miami Institute for Soviet and East European Studies, wrote in the *Miami Herald*. "Under [Premier Nikita] Khrushchev, he would have been jailed, and under [successor Leonid] Brezhnev, committed to a mental institution for political deviants."

But rather than disappearing, Yeltsin appeared poised to challenge Gorbachev for Soviet leadership. Already a folk hero of the nation, he had used popular pressure to propel a three-year odyssey of political revenge and rehabilitation. First promoted by Gorbachev and then purged by him in 1987, Yeltsin continued to attack Gorbachev's leadership and the privileges of power in the U.S.S.R.

> "As long as no one can build his own dacha, as long as we continue to live in such relative poverty, I refuse to eat caviar followed by sturgeon."

Throughout his life, Yeltsin has loudly questioned authority. At his eighth-grade graduation ceremonies, Yeltsin grabbed the microphone and announced before all the parents and teachers that the head teacher was "harming the kids" and should be dismissed. "After that," he told the *Washington Post*,

"I was thrown out of school and disallowed to continue. But I managed to get reinstated." Two years later, he and a friend cut school for two months to go hiking in the Siberian forests.

Yeltsin was born the son of peasants in the industrial Ural Mountain city of Sverdlovsk. In his autobiography, *Against the Grain*, Yeltsin says he had a love-hate relationship with his abusive father. He also describes himself in the book as having been "a little bit of a hooligan" in his youth and recounts losing two fingers on his left hand when he was 11; he and two friends had stolen two hand grenades from an arms storehouse; one of the grenades exploded when Yeltsin tried to disassemble it.

He was trained as a construction engineer and directed various building projects from 1955 to 1968. At age 30, in 1961, he joined the Communist party because he was inspired by Khrushchev's anti-Stalinist reforms. From 1968 to 1976, Yeltsin worked for the party, mostly in construction and planning positions. In 1976 Yeltsin was named first secretary of the Sverdlovsk District Central Committee, a position akin to an American mayor. He earned a reputation as a creative leader and a man intent on rooting out bureaucratic malignancy and profiteering.

In time, Yeltsin had become a protege to Gorbachev, who was looking for new leadership to push the Soviet Union forward. In 1985 Gorbachev brought him to Moscow, first as secretary of the Central Committee for Construction. Within months Yeltsin was promoted to first secretary of the Moscow City Party Committee (mayor of Moscow), with a mandate to clear out corruption and streamline the bureaucracy. In 1986, Gorbachev gave Yeltsin a non-voting seat on the ruling Communist party Politburo, then the highest governing body in the U.S.S.R. The promotion put Yeltsin on track for a top national post.

Initially, Yeltsin was regarded in Moscow as just another of Gorbachev's new reformers, but it didn't take him long to start making waves. He became known for firing dozens of corrupt officials and encouraging a freer press and private markets in the capital. He campaigned in stores and on TV to improve food supplies and spoke out against special privileges for the government and the party elite. He rode the subway and managed to cut through bureaucracy to bring fresh new fruits and vegetables to Moscow supermarkets.

At the 1986 Communist Party Congress, just three months after taking the Moscow post, Yeltsin already was taking shots at the party bureaucracy, demanding an end to the perquisites top officials enjoy and saying that no leader—including Gorbachev—should be above criticism. Wrote the Associated Press's Andrew Katell, "For many Muscovites, who watch their leaders rocket by in sleek limousines while they stand in line to buy soap, sugar and countless other scarce items, Yeltsin's borscht-in-every-pot message has immediate appeal."

In his autobiography, Yeltsin wrote that a key moment in his life occurred in 1986 when, as Moscow party chief, he was offered Gorbachev's old dacha, or country vacation home. Yeltsin wrote that he was "shattered by the senselessness" of all the luxury—the crystal, the movie theater, the 30-foot-long dining room table. "As long as no one can build or buy his own dacha, as long as we continue to live in such relative poverty, I refuse to eat caviar followed by sturgeon. I will not race through the streets in a car that can ignore traffic lights. I cannot swallow excellent imported medicine knowing that my neighbor's wife can't get an aspirin for her child. Because to do so is shameful."

Quickly, Yeltsin's criticisms grew bolder. In a political memoir published in the Soviet Union, he lashed out at the Soviet Council of Ministers as "a disorganized, confused gathering of dunderheads." In October 1987 he made a stinging speech to the Communist party's Central Committee that defied the unwritten rules of political etiquette. He made scathing personal comments about conservative leader Yegor Ligachev and denounced party leaders for what he called their native tendency to "idolize" Gorbachev. "What made Yeltsin different from most of his Politburo colleagues was that he took perestroika seriously," Dimitri Simes, a senior associate at the Carnegie Endowment for International Peace, wrote in the *Washington Post*. "Frustrated with the empty sloganeering that covered up the lack of any real change, he became increasingly bold both at Politburo meetings and in his periodic purges of deadwood accumulated in the Moscow party apparatus." Gorbachev was enraged by Yeltsin's remarks. A few weeks after his attacks on the party Yeltsin was forced to quit as Moscow party boss, and several months later he was thrown out of the Politburo.

On November 8, 1987, Yeltsin was hospitalized for heart trouble. The word went out that he was finished politically. Three days later he was pulled out of the hospital while heavily sedated to deliver a so-called confession at the plenum of the Moscow party organization. "While this treatment, in some respects, resembled the show trials of [Communist leader Joseph] Stalin's purges in the 1930s, these were milder times," wrote the *Los Angeles Times*.

"Therefore, Gorbachev offered Yeltsin the post of deputy chairman at the State Construction Committee—a prestigious but powerless job. Moreover, Gorbachev informed Yeltsin that he would not let him return to politics."

Gorbachev and Yeltsin never did patch things up, and Yeltsin remained on the outs with top leaders. But he made the rift work for him. Thanks to Gorbachev's own efforts, perestroika had changed the rules of Soviet politics. Students and intellectuals protested on his behalf and texts of his now-famous October speech began spreading across the Soviet Union. Yeltsin began to wear his conflict with the party establishment as a badge of honor. On every possible occasion, he reminded the people that he too was a victim of the corrupt and repressive system.

As public opinion became a factor on the political scene, Yeltsin's career began to flourish again. In his March 1989 campaign for a seat on the Soviet Congress of People's Deputies, the new national parliament, he linked his call for immediate improvements in the average Soviet's living standard with daring denunciations of the privileges granted top state and party officials. Yeltsin won 90 percent of the popular vote in a direct election—crushing the establishment candidate and garnering more votes (5 million) than any other candidate in seven decades of communism.

"People identify with Yeltsin," the weekly *Moscow News* wrote in April 1989. "He's a victim of dislike on the part of higher-ups—who of us hasn't been in the same position? And he is being slighted for refusing to seek their approval—who hasn't dreamed of doing that?" The *Washington Post*'s David Remnick compared Yeltsin with a historical American populist: "Moscow doesn't much resemble the political culture of Baton Rouge in the '40s, but in Boris Yeltsin there is certainly more than an ounce of [former Louisiana governor] Huey Long. In his rhetoric, Yeltsin seems ready at times to break out in Long's theme song of individual entitlement: 'Every man a king.'" In September 1989, Yeltsin toured the United States, giving lectures and meeting with American political and business leaders, including President George Bush. In speeches and interviews he criticized Gorbachev for moving too slowly, telling *Newsweek* that Gorbachev "had not more than one year and probably about six months" to get his reform plan moving. Gorbachev, he said, "is a man who loves half-measures and semi-decisions."

Yeltsin's American tour made news in the U.S.S.R. for other reasons. When he gave a slurred and erratic performance in a speech in Baltimore, Soviet television was quick to put it on the air. Yeltsin was accused of drunkenness, and later of spending his American royalties on alcohol and blue jeans. Soon after returning to the Soviet Union, Yeltsin showed up at a police station after midnight, charging that hooded government agents had thrown him off a bridge into a river, and warning that the KGB may yet try to kill him with a mysterious ray gun that stuns the heart.

His public behavior did nothing to slow his growing popularity. In March 1990 Yeltsin was elected to the Supreme Soviet of the Russian Republic (the national legislature) by 85 percent of the voters in his native Sverdlovsk. On May 29, that body elected him—against Gorbachev's wishes—as president of the Russian Federation, the largest of the 15 Soviet republics and home of half of the nation's residents.

That victory immediately cast Yeltsin as a powerful rival to Gorbachev. *Newsday* Moscow correspondent Allison Mitchell called Yeltsin's election "a potentially crippling political blow to Gorbachev.... He won even though Gorbachev had staked his own prestige in the battle by openly campaigning against Yeltsin." For his part, Yeltsin told *Newsday* that his election marked "the beginning of the road to Russia's social, economic and spiritual rebirth, the way out of the crisis and toward the blossoming of Russia as a sovereign, independent government in the framework of our union."

Yeltsin vowed to assert the sovereignty of Russia, the republic that holds the Soviet Union together. Depending on how far he goes, his pledge to make Russia autonomous could cause as much of a crisis as Lithuania's declaration of independence—by raising the price of Russia's vast oil resources to other republics, reconfiguring trade relations within the Soviet Union, and providing an alternative to Gorbachev's own economic policies.

If anyone doubted Yeltsin's bravado, that doubt was erased on July 12, 1990, when he publicly resigned from the Communist party. The nearly 4,700 usually raucous Communist delegates sat still and stunned. Within hours, several leaders of the radical-reform faction called Democratic Platform announced that they, too, would leave the party, with the intention of launching a rival left-wing party and convening a fall congress of all "democratic forces" opposed to Communist party rule.

Yeltsin's actions have in no doubt helped reshape the Soviet political scene. His resolve and bravado demonstrated during the August, 1991 coup made him an international hero, giving rise to hopes that perhaps *both* Yeltsin and Gorbachev could now work together to speed economic and political reforms.

Gorbachev, necessarily absent during the coup (he was held under house arrest with his family in his vacation home in the Crimea), was unable to demonstrate any command of the situation, while Yeltsin, calling for his fellow Soviets to resist the takeover from within the walls of the barricaded parliament building, appeared firmly, if not officially, in control of the situation. In the aftermath of the coup, President Bush was quoted in numerous news sources as saying that U.S. relations with Yeltsin "have taken a quantum leap forward now by this man's displayed courage and by his commitment to democracy." As Sergei Zamascikov, a Soviet consultant to the independent think tank Rand Corporation, told the *Detroit Free Press*, "Everybody can see who the real savior of democracy in Russia was. It was Yeltsin."

Yeltsin himself told the *Washington Post* in 1989: "The time of compromise and half-measures is past. We are sitting on top of a volcano, and very soon neither Gorbachev nor anyone else will be able to control the events. The people will take their fate in their own hands, as it happened in Eastern Europe. If we are lucky, everything will happen orderly, as in East Germany, Czechoslovakia and Bulgaria. But what happens if the situation develops in the Rumanian pattern? Bloodshed? Tragedy?" And asked if he would like to be president of the Soviet Union some day, Yeltsin told the *Post*, "It's a possibility if I am not too old and have strength."

Writings

Against the Grain: An Autobiography, Summit Books, 1990.

Sources

Akron Beacon Journal, May 31, 1990.
Business Week, March 5, 1990.
Detroit Free Press, July 14, 1990; August 22, 1991.
Los Angeles Times, April 8, 1990; May 29, 1990; June 11, 1990.
Miami Herald, September 17, 1989.
Moscow News, April 23, 1989.
Newsday, May 30, 1990; July 1, 1990; July 13, 1990.
Newsweek, September 25, 1989.
Philadelphia Inquirer, February 18, 1989; June 2, 1989; June 10, 1990.
Time, March 20, 1989; September 25, 1989.
Washington Post, February 18, 1989; May 21, 1989; May 13, 1990; May 30, 1990; June 3, 1990; July 13, 1990.

—Glen Macnow

Neil Young

Guitarist, singer, and songwriter

Born November 12, 1945, in Toronto, Ontario, Canada; came to U.S., 1966; son of Scott Young (a sports journalist); married first wife, Susan; married second wife, Pegi Morton, in 1978; children: Zeke (by Carrie Snodgress, companion from 1971-75); Ben, Amber (with Pegi Morton Young).

Addresses: *Office*—Warner Bros./Reprise Records, 3300 Warner Blvd., Burbank, CA 91510.

Career

Formed first band, Neil Young and the Squires, early 1960s; moved to Los Angeles, Calif., in 1966 and formed band Buffalo Springfield; also played solo and with band Crazy Horse; joined David Crosby, Stephen Stills, and Graham Nash to form Crosby, Stills, Nash & Young, 1969. Throughout career has recorded and toured extensively. Cofounder, with wife Pegi, of the Bridge School for handicapped children in San Francisco.

Awards: Named Artist of the Decade by the *Village Voice* for the 1970s.

Sidelights

As the graying of the Age of Aquarius approaches, many of the voices leading rock 'n' roll into its maturity are the same ones who guided it through the formidable teenage wasteland years of the 1960s and early '70s. One of those voices belongs to Neil Young. His distinctive nasal tones, shrill guitar work and casually quirky style have earned him fans from two generations.

At the end of the 1980s Young climbed back to prominence in the music world after a disjointed decade of diverging musical styles and personas that left even his most ardent fans puzzled. His 1989 LP *Freedom* brought him back into the rock mainstream after earlier forays into blues, country, rockabilly and computerized techno-rock. In 1990, Young reunited with his favorite backing band, Crazy Horse, and released the raw, rocking *Ragged Glory* to the delight of most rock critics, not to mention his legions of fans. Critical acclaim is nothing new to Young; nor is critical crucifixion—he's seen plenty of both extremes.

In 25 years in the recording industry, dating back to his days in the seminal folk-rock band Buffalo Springfield, Young has experienced three critical and commercial peaks, and at least that many valleys. In the early 1970s Young rode a huge crest of popularity generated by big-selling albums like *After the Gold Rush* and *Harvest*, and "Heart of Gold," his only number-one single. Scorning fame and its trappings, Young retreated to his northern California ranch in the middle of that decade, releasing a string of introspective, mildly successful albums. In 1978-79

Young released *Rust Never Sleeps* and embarked on a major tour that resulted in a live LP and film, vaulting him again into public acclaim. The *Village Voice* subsequently named him Artist of the Decade for the 1970s. With the passage of another decade, Young emerged again in 1990 as a vital force in rock and roll. His appearances as musical guest on *Saturday Night Live* and at "Farm Aid" and other benefits placed him back in the public eye, and, as Young prepared to begin a 1991 American tour, *Ragged Glory* was turning up on "Best of 1990" lists everywhere.

Born in 1945 in Toronto, Ontario, Neil Young is the son of Scott Young, a well-known Canadian sportswriter. Young's parents were divorced when he was still a child, and he moved with his mother to Winnipeg, Manitoba. In the mid-1950s, Young became enamored of the new rock 'n' roll sounds of Bill Haley and Elvis Presley. In his early teens, he taught himself to play an Arthur Godfrey-style ukelele and eventually progressed to acoustic guitar. He formed a band, Neil Young and the Squires, in the early 1960s, and it became a local favorite in Winnipeg. About the same time, Bob Dylan was leading a folk music explosion in the States, and Young packed his acoustic guitar and left Winnipeg for the folk club circuit of Toronto.

In 1966 Young and bassist Bruce Palmer deserted Toronto and set their sights on the musical promised land of the time, Los Angeles. There they hooked up with another pair of musicians, Stephen Stills and Richie Furay. Along with drummer Dewey Martin, the five formed Buffalo Springfield, and played their first gig in March 1966. Buffalo Springfield based its sound around swirling three-part harmonies and the dueling electric guitars of Stills and Young. Its 1966-67 live performances are legendary, including a six-week stay at L.A.'s famed Whiskey-A-Go-Go, and an opening stint for the Rolling Stones at the Hollywood Bowl.

Musically, the band was solid, releasing a string of crisp cuts like their biggest hit, "For What It's Worth," and "Mr. Soul," "Bluebird," "Rock 'n' Roll Woman," and "Sit Down, I Think I Love You." But the tension between Stills and Young for control of the group's direction boiled, particularly during stage shows where each would step on the other's toes frequently. After quitting the band once and returning, Young left Buffalo Springfield for good in 1968, and the band itself splintered shortly thereafter.

Young then went to work on his eponymously titled solo album, which followed the same path he set out on with his Buffalo Springfield work—fluent, melod-ic guitars, innovative experimental arrangements, and ambiguous lyrics filled with dark, childlike wonder. It was Young's second album that established his prowess as a solo artist. *Everybody Knows This Is Nowhere* was recorded in 1969 with a Los Angeles band called Crazy Horse, with whom Young would form a lasting musical partnership. The album was a collection of churning guitars and driving rhythms, and yielded such Neil Young standards as "Cinnamon Girl," "Down by the River," and "Cowgirl in the Sand."

By 1969 Stephen Stills had formed a new band with David Crosby, who had split with the Byrds, and Graham Nash, who had quit the Hollies. The trio recorded an immensely successful album and were putting together a band to take on the road. Neil Young's name came up. Though Young was engrossed in his own music, the vocals on the Crosby, Stills & Nash album impressed him and he was intrigued with the idea of joining the outfit. Crosby and Nash were hesitant to add such a big name to their cozy trio, but after Stills took them out to Young's place, they changed their minds. Crosby told *Crawdaddy*, "Neil played 'Helpless,' and by the time he finished, we were asking him if we could join *his* band."

The first live performance of Crosby, Stills, Nash & Young was August 16, 1969, at Chicago Auditorium. The second came the following weekend at Woodstock. Their legendary appearance was indicative of how most of their shows went: some acoustic material sung solo or in duos, then, after a break, a raucous electric set that reunited the searing guitars of Stills and Young. Within a month, the four were being referred to as a "supergroup" and "the American Beatles." In October 1969 the group began recording its masterpiece album, *Deja Vu*. The often stormy sessions resulted in a groundbreaking LP showcasing each member's talents. Young's contributions to the album included the touching medley "Country Girl" and the classic "Helpless," of which he later wrote on his *Decade* liner notes, "Recorded in San Francisco at 4 a.m. when everybody got tired enough to play at my speed."

A tour took CSN&Y around the world and into 1970. On May 4, National Guardsmen murdered four students at an anti-Vietnam War rally at Kent State University in Kent, Ohio. Young went off by himself and wrote "Ohio," which CSN&Y recorded in one emotional session that saw David Crosby burst into tears at the end of the take. Of "Ohio," Young wrote, "It's still hard to believe I had to write this song. It's ironic that I capitalized on the deaths of these

American students. Probably the biggest lesson ever learned at an American place of learning. My best CSN&Y cut."

In 1970 Crosby, Stills, Nash & Young had the world's ear, but they were often at each other's throats. Among other disagreements, the old Stills-Young guitar feud was heating up again, with Stills accusing Young of playing better on his own songs, and Young accusing Stills of overarranging. The summer tour yielded a double live album, *4-Way Street*. The four then went separate ways and worked on solo albums.

Young released *After the Gold Rush*, recorded with Crazy Horse, Stephen Stills, and a 19-year-old Nils Lofgren. The sound they established, said *Rolling Stone*, was "unmistakable, a combination of dense, muscular rock and world-weary innocence that has made Neil Young one of the most important rock artists of his generation." The album's highlights include the longing title track, "Tell Me Why," and the attack on the conscience of the American South, "Southern Man." Southern band Lynyrd Skynyrd responded to the latter with "Sweet Home Alabama," which asserted: "I hope Neil Young will remember / Southern man don't need him around anyhow." Later Young characteristically remarked, "I'd rather play 'Sweet Home Alabama' than 'Southern Man' anytime. I first heard it and I really liked the way [Lynyrd Skynyrd] played their guitars. Then I heard my own name in it and thought, 'Now *this* is pretty great.'" (Young subsequently wrote the song "Powderfinger" for Lynyrd Skynyrd, who declined to record it.)

Young's 1972 release, *Harvest*, brought him to the forefront of American music with such hits as "Heart of Gold," "Old Man," and "Needle and the Damage Done." A commercially accessible mix of folk, rock, and country, *Harvest* featured everyone from Crosby, Stills & Nash to the London Symphony Orchestra. Young's next two releases were considered disappointments by rock critics and many fans. 1973's *Time Fades Away* is a country-rock-flavored live album that lacked the commercial appeal of *Harvest*, and his 1974 *On the Beach* told bleak, brooding tales of despair against a California backdrop.

1974 saw a brief reunion of Crosby, Stills, Nash & Young as the foursome hit the road for a massive stadium tour. *Rolling Stone* reviewer Ben Fong-Torres captured the moment in rock history when he wrote: "Minutes after Crosby, Stills, Nash & Young hit the stage for the first concert of their reunion tour, it was clear that no other group ever had a chance of replacing them while they were apart—not America,

not Bread, not Poco, not the Eagles, not Seals and Crofts, not Loggins and Messina." CSN&Y finished a triumphant world tour by entering the studio, but again personality conflicts led to the demise of the sessions, with Young walking out.

> *"I have a real bad habit where, like a snake changing skins, I'll do something and I'll be completely into it, be possessed by it. And then at a certain point I crack, and then I don't want to have anything to do with it at all."*

Young then walked into a creative and productive period with Crazy Horse. Devastated by the drug overdose deaths of Crazy Horse guitarist Danny Whitten and CSN&Y roadie Bruce Berry, Young released the dark, dreary, drunken *Tonight's the Night*. Roundly criticized upon its release, the LP is now considered a classic. The sloppy, haunting album is definitely mood music, Young told *Rolling Stone*. "If you're going to put a record on at 11 in the morning, don't put on 'Tonight's the Night.' Put on the Doobie Brothers."

Young and Crazy Horse cut the rocking *Zuma* in 1975, which featured the epic "Cortez the Killer" and the ballad "Through My Sails." The following year Young reunited with Stills and recorded *Long May You Run* with a configuration known as the Stills-Young Band. The album went gold, and the band went on tour, in the middle of which Young left Stills, claiming a throat ailment. The pattern of Young quitting something he'd started perhaps foreshadowed the rapid stylistic changes he would undergo in the approaching decade. Later, Young would explain to *Creem*, "I have a real bad habit where, like a snake changing skins, I'll do something and I'll be completely into it, be possessed by it. And then at a certain point I crack, and then I don't want to have anything to do with it at all. It's over. The next thing is what's happening."

The "next thing happening" for Young was releasing *American Stars 'n' Bars*, a collection of country and rock songs recorded over two years' time that included the airy jam, "Like a Hurricane." He also compiled a three-record greatest hits package called *Decade* that firmly documented his importance in rock history. (In 1990 Young was hard at work compiling *Decade II*, a comprehensive look at his work since.) In 1978 Young produced *Comes a Time*, an easy-going collection of folk-rock.

Young again assaulted the national rock 'n' roll scene in 1979, this time with the loud, raunchy guitars of Crazy Horse and a platinum album, *Rust Never Sleeps*. The record is comprised of an acoustic side and an electric side, recorded live in arena shows that also became a film of the same name, directed by Young. The tour was also documented in a double live LP, *Live Rust*. The live shows, taped in the fall of 1978, were filled with theatrics illustrating a young boy's rock 'n' roll fantasies. Young awoke from an oversized sleeping bag to start each show, strummed his acoustic guitar, and declared, "Hey, hey, my, my, rock 'n' roll will never die." The spectacle was initially lost on some critics, but the music was too powerful to ignore.

Whatever commercial momentum Young had rolling from *Rust* disappeared with 1980's *Hawks and Doves*, an enigmatic collection of acoustic ballads and straight-ahead, fiddle-filled country tunes. No hits here, nor on 1981's furious frenzy of shrieking electric guitars, *Re-ac-tor*. During the recording of this album, Young and wife Pegi were struggling with a rigorous program to reach out to their severely handicapped son, and the distraction and frustration shows in the music. Young left his longtime record label, Warner/Reprise, to begin a stormy six-year relationship with Geffen Records, which ended up suing him for not making "Neil Young-type" records.

The first non-Neil-type record to get him into trouble was 1982's *Trans*, on which Young experimented with voice synthesizers and computer technology, inspired by his desperate efforts to communicate with his non-oral son. The critics who were at a loss to understand *Rust Never Sleeps* had a field day panning *Trans*. When Geffen rejected a countryish album Young put together called *Old Ways*, Young was furious. He greased his hair back and recorded an almost comical collection of rockabilly tunes and hit the road with a '50s outfit called the Shocking Pinks. "I almost vindictively gave Geffen 'Everybody's Rockin,'" he told the *Village Voice*. When Young then went back to recording country music, Geffen hit him with a $3 million lawsuit.

The suit was settled with the release of a repackaged *Old Ways* in 1985. The finished product went over the country deep end, more than the original *Old Ways* two years earlier. "It was much more of a country record—a direct result of being sued for playing country music," Young said. "The more they tried to stop me the more I did it." The album is laced with fiddles, pedal steels and mouth harps. Young found himself at odds with his record company and virtually gone from the rock scene he had ruled five years earlier.

Two lackluster rock LPs (1986's *Landing on Water* and 1987's *Life*) and subsequent tours marked Young's return to rock. A reunion album with Crosby, Stills, Nash & Young, *American Dream*, was disappointing. Suddenly, however, in 1988, Young became a bluesman. He put together a horn section, recorded *This Note's for You* and hit the road with the Bluenotes. In the title track, Young sneered sarcastically at rock colleagues who lend themselves to product promotion: "Ain't singin' for Pepsi / Ain't singin' for Coke / Don't sing for nobody / Makes me look like a joke / This note's for you." The song's video landed Young in the national spotlight again, with its lampooning of rock's commercial underbelly—a Michael Jackson look-alike's hair catches fire and is doused with a Pepsi poured by a Whitney Houston look-alike. The controversial video was first banned by MTV, then given "Best Video" at the network's annual awards.

By the time Young's video had captured praise, Young was already into his next project, 1989's *Freedom*. An amalgam of the styles that made Young a star, the album was widely hailed as a great comeback. "Rockin' in the Free World" was hailed as an anthem in a year when freedom broke out around the globe. But Young was saving the real comeback for 1990: In August of that year Young and Crazy Horse reunited for a quick but fiery jam session in a barn on Young's ranch. The quartet rocked the free world so hard they failed to notice a mild earthquake that shook the grounds. The result of the taping was the aptly titled *Ragged Glory*, a collection of raw, spontaneous sounds that rival anything Young has done in years. *Rolling Stone* called it "a great one from one of the greats."

Ragged Glory comes as close as anything to capturing the essence of Neil Young playing live. The live abilities of his first recorded band, Buffalo Springfield, were never done justice on vinyl, and it's a trap that Young has fallen into many times since. The raw power and bottled energy of Young in concert is riveting. Bill Flanagan of *Musician* captured Young in a "Performance of the Month" piece describing a *Saturday Night Live* rehearsal: "As television staffers stood with their mouths hanging open, Young stamped his foot on the stage, whirled around and played a guitar solo to rival his very best . . . . When he was done the crew burst into applause and cheers."

Selected discography

(With Crazy Horse) *Everybody Knows This Is Nowhere,* 1969.
(With Crosby, Stills, Nash & Young) *Deja Vu,* 1970.
After the Gold Rush, 1970.
(With Crosby, Stills, Nash & Young) *4-Way Street,* 1971.
Harvest, 1972.
Journey Through the Past, 1972.
Time Fades Away, 1973.
(With Crosby, Stills, Nash & Young) *So Far,* 1974.
On the Beach, 1974.
(With Crazy Horse) *Tonight's the Night,* 1975.
(With Crazy Horse) *Zuma,* 1975.
(With the Stills-Young Band) *Long May You Run,* 1976.
American Stars 'n' Bars, 1977.
Decade, 1977.
Comes a Time, 1978.
(With Crazy Horse) *Rust Never Sleeps,* 1979.
(With Crazy Horse) *Live Rust,* 1979.
Hawks and Doves, 1980.
(With Crazy Horse) *Re-ac-tor,* 1981.
Trans, 1982.
(With the Shocking Pinks) *Everybody's Rockin',* 1983.
(With the International Harvesters) *Old Ways,* 1985.
Landing on Water, 1986.
(With Crazy Horse) *Life,* 1987.
(With the Bluenotes) *This Note's For You,* 1988.
(With Crosby, Stills, Nash & Young) *American Dream,* 1988.
Freedom, 1989.
(With Crazy Horse) *Ragged Glory,* 1990.

Sources

Books

Hardy, Phil and Dave Laing, *The Encyclopedia of Rock,* Schirmer Books, 1988.
The Rolling Stone Encyclopedia of Rock, Rolling Stone Press, 1983.
Stambler, Irwin, *The Encyclopedia of Pop, Rock and Soul,* St. Martin's, 1989.
Zimmer, Dave, *Crosby, Stills & Nash: The Authorized Biography,* St. Martin's, 1984.

Periodicals

Creem, December 1990-January 1991.
Detroit Free Press, September 9, 1990.
Musician, December 1989.
Newsweek, January 14, 1991.
Rolling Stone, June 4, 1987; August 27, 1987; June 2, 1988; December 15, 1988; March 8, 1990; September 20, 1990; October 4, 1990.
Spin, December 1990.
Village Voice Rock 'n' Roll Quarterly, winter 1989.

—*John P. Cortez*

Steve Yzerman

Professional hockey player

Surname pronounced EYE-zer-man; born May 9, 1965, in Cranbrook, British Columbia, Canada; came to United States, 1983; son of a Canadian government official; married Lisa Brennan, 1989. *Education:* High school graduate.

Addresses: *Home*—Grosse Pointe, MI. *Office*—Detroit Red Wings, Joe Louis Arena, Detroit, MI.

Career

Played two seasons with Peterborough in Ontario Hockey League; chosen in first round of 1983 draft by Detroit Red Wings; team captain, 1986—.

Awards: Member of National Hockey League All-Star team, l984—.

Sidelights

The Detroit Red Wings have become a winning hockey team in recent years thanks largely to the work of center Steve Yzerman. Still in his mid-twenties, Yzerman offers strong scoring on the ice while also serving as the team's official captain. He is adored by Detroit's media and fans alike and is the rare professional athlete who has expressed allegiance to his team *and* town. *Detroit Free Press* columnist Mitch Albom called Yzerman "a skating wizard who is hockey's answer to the deer: graceful, elusive and smart.... His passing is deft, his aim is true...he is as mature as they come." Albom continued: "We are talking about a guy here who could become legendary. He could become (gulp) this

era's Gordie Howe. He is already the star on a team that is on the lip of excellence.... And he is on his way."

Few observers of the National Hockey League (NHL) have failed to be impressed by Yzerman's performance. He is a cool operator in a hot-headed sport who has blossomed since being named the Red Wings' youngest-ever captain. Red Wings general manager Jimmy Devellano told the *Detroit Free Press* that knowing Steve Yzerman "is one of the nicest things that has happened to me since I've been in Detroit." Devellano added: "He's been a shining light for us, an absolute gem."

Yzerman was born in British Columbia and raised in Neapean, a suburb of the Canadian capital of Ottawa. His father was a high-ranking official in the Canadian government's social services department. Although Yzerman grew up in a scholarly family, he showed little interest in school. His only love was sports, and he gravitated to hockey at a very young age. "I know it's not good advice to kids," he told the *Detroit Free Press,* "but all I ever thought about was playing hockey. School took a back seat when I started moving up. I just played hockey. I did what I had to do, nothing else." Yzerman did manage to graduate from high school, however, and he has even taken some college-level courses in accounting and finance.

Yzerman progressed quickly through Canada's many ranks of midget and peewee hockey. By age 14 he was skating for Cornwall, a highly-ranked amateur team that also featured future Chicago Blackhawks goaltender Darren Pang. Pang and Yzerman were both shy of sixteen when they led Cornwall to a victory in the Air Canada Cup tournament. Both players were being scouted vigorously at that point by executives of the NHL. "Everyone knew about [Steve]," Pang told the *Detroit Free Press.* "He was pretty sharp on his skates. Everybody compared him to Denis Savard then. And we didn't do too bad in that Air Canada Cup. Steve led our team in scoring." Asked about Yzerman's personality as a teen, Pang replied: "He was very similar then as he is now. He has a real sense of humor, kind of dry at times. He's kind of reserved, the kind of guy who doesn't make harsh judgments. Even at a young age, he was real mature. It seems like he always said and did the right things."

Devellano first saw Yzerman skate when the young athlete was playing junior hockey with a team out of Peterborough, Ontario. "When [Steve] was on the ice, you could tell he had a whole lot of ability," Devellano remembered. "He was a very good skater. He had good balance and good hockey sense." Although Yzerman didn't get very much playing time, his modest statistics did not mask his talent from the scouts. He was chosen fourth in the first round of the 1983 draft. Devellano feels that Yzerman may have been the very first choice in 1983 had he skated more in Peterborough. "If he had played all the power plays and gotten the ice time other players like him get, his stats would have been so great he would have gone one, two or three," the general manager said.

Yzerman signed a seven-year contract with the Red Wings and reported to Detroit at the tender age of 18. Most hockey players spend at least a year in the minor leagues, but the talent on the Red Wings was so sparse that Yzerman quickly earned a spot with the parent club. Yzerman's debut as a rookie was

Steve Yzerman slips past New York Rangers defender Darren Turcotte (number 8) in a March, 1990 game at New York's Madison Square Garden. AP/Wide World Photos.

nothing less than splendid. In 80 games he scored 39 goals and earned 48 assists, a performance that helped the Wings to advance to the playoffs. Nor was his success Detroit's secret. At season's end he finished second in rookie-of-the-year voting, and in 1984 he became the youngest player ever selected to the NHL All-Star game. Yzerman's second season was almost a carbon copy of the first, with 30 goals and 59 assists in 80 games.

> *"I was on the edge of becoming a run-of-the-mill player.... Never a day went by when I didn't think, 'Geez, If I'm not careful, in a couple of years I could be out of hockey.'"*

All was not rosy for the young star, however. By the 1985-86 season it had become obvious that Yzerman was struggling, both on the ice and off. *Detroit Free Press* correspondent Keith Gave wrote: "Yzerman was a loner, unable to find his niche with the club. He seldom went on a road trip without his Walkman. Through his earphones, he listened to music and sang along to himself. In both a literal and a figurative sense, it seemed as though only he knew the words to the songs. It was an unhappy time." Yzerman's gloom was deepened by interference from the front office. His two best friends on the team, Lane Lambert and Claude Loiselle, were demoted to the minors. Worse, management leaned on him when his name began to appear in gossip columns with references to barroom antics.

"When Claude and Lane got sent down, I lived alone," Yzerman told the *Detroit Free Press*. "And I stayed home and did nothing. I played poorly, but I wasn't running around.... I wasn't having too much fun at the rink, but I sure wasn't having any fun away from the rink, either.... I didn't fit in anywhere. I didn't feel comfortable. It was a tough position to be in. But I couldn't say anything, because I was one of the major reasons the team didn't do well." The Red Wings did in fact finish last in the league in 1986, with Yzerman sitting out part of the season with a broken collar bone.

In the off-season the Wings hired a new coach, Jacques Demers. Faced with the task of rebuilding a last-place team, Demers went straight to the club's strength: he named Yzerman captain. At the time, Yzerman was consumed with doubts about his ability and shame at the abysmal season the Wings turned in in 1986. "All summer I worried about it," he told the *Detroit Free Press*. "I was on the edge of becoming a run-of-the-mill player.... Never a day went by when I didn't think, 'Geez, if I'm not careful, in a couple of years I could be out of hockey.' It worried me every day." Demers's faith in Yzerman helped to restore the young man's confidence and forced him to mingle more effectively with his teammates. Through the summer of 1986 Yzerman added fifteen pounds to his slender frame and consequently became, in the pivotal year of 1987, an even more aggressive player.

Keith Gave called 1987 the year "Steve Yzerman led the Detroit Red Wings back to glory." Yzerman did indeed turn in another superstar-caliber season in 1986-87, scoring 31 goals with 59 assists, but he was helped by Demers's coaching and other talented and determined teammates. From a last-place finish in 1986 the Wings moved straight into the playoffs in 1987 and eventually won the Stanley Cup. Yzerman still calls his moments of holding the Cup and skating around in victory with his teammates the high point of his career. In the post-season bliss following the championship, Demers told the *Detroit Free Press* that he had never doubted either Yzerman's talent or his leadership ability. "He's handling the captaincy as well as anyone could," the coach said. "You can talk about him being a superstar, a rich kid, good-looking and all that. But he's handling it as classy as anybody can handle it.... Let me put it this way. Steve Yzerman is a Red Wing."

To this day Yzerman is a Red Wing. Even a career-threatening knee injury in 1987 has done little to curb his dominance on the ice. *Detroit Free Press* contributor Corky Meinecke remarked: "More and more, experts are putting Yzerman... in a class with Wayne Gretzky and Mario Lemieux, perhaps the most dominant hockey players of all time. All around the NHL, objective observers rave about Yzerman's playmaking, his skating, his marksmanship, his toughness in the clutch.... Perfect, is how he comes across."

Few fans in Detroit would dispute that assessment. Yzerman has married and settled down in Detroit as if he had been born to the place. He openly admires other Detroit athletes who have played their entire careers in the town and has told the press that he hopes to do the same. "I'd like to stay in Detroit," he told the *Free Press*. "I don't know what's going to happen, whether they want me or not, but I know I don't want to go anywhere else. It's very rare, I know, but when you look at a lot of the greats in sports, they all played in one city . . . . I think you lose a little something when you move. You can always move for more money, but I don't believe in that."

Yzerman can look forward to at least a few more productive years in the NHL, and the Red Wings have made great efforts to keep him in the club. The unassuming Yzerman has only added to his popularity by remaining modest about his success. He told the *Detroit Free Press* that he can never understand why everyone makes such a fuss over professional athletes. "When I was a kid," he said, "I used to think that hockey players were like God or something. I thought it would be great to be a hero like that. Then, I got there and it's no big deal. It's really no different than playing midget or peewee. It's still just playing the game. Sure, you want to make money, but the guys here are still out there trying hard and playing to win."

Sources

Detroit Free Press, February 3, 1987; October 6, 1988; December 9, 1988; December 25, 1988.

—*Mark Kram*

Franco Zeffirelli

AP/Wide World Photos

Film director and producer

Real name, Gianfranco Zeffirelli; born February 12, 1923, near Florence, Italy; son of Ottorino Corsi (a merchant) and Alaide Garosi (a fashion designer). *Education:* Studied architecture during the 1940s. *Religion:* Roman Catholic.

Addresses: *Home*—Rome and Positano, Italy.

Career

Began as a set designer for films by director Luchino Visconti; made directorial debut in 1955 with opera *Il turco in Italia*; subsequent opera directorships include *L'elisir d'amore*, *Cavalleria rusticana*, *Pagliacci*, and *Tosca*; directed the play *Romeo and Juliet* in 1960 at the Old Vic Theater in London, England; made filmmaking debut in 1965 with *The Taming of the Shrew*; subsequent films include *Romeo and Juliet*, 1968; *Brother Sun, Sister Moon*, 1972; *Jesus of Nazareth*, 1976; *The Champ*, c. 1978; *Endless Love*, 1981; *La Traviata* (filmed opera), 1982; *Otello* (filmed opera), 1986; *Young Toscanini*, 1988 (unreleased); and *Hamlet*, 1991.

Military service: Fought with the Italian Resistance during World War II.

Sidelights

Throughout the history of filmmaking, some of the finest actors to grace the screen have played the title role in Shakespeare's classic tragedy, *Hamlet*, from John Barrymore to Laurence Olivier to Daniel Day-Lewis. When celebrated Italian director Franco

Zeffirelli, a Shakespeare veteran, selected the cast for his 1991 remake of *Hamlet*, his choice for the ill-fated Danish prince was Mel Gibson, known chiefly for portraying macho heroes in such action films as *Road Warrior* and *Lethal Weapon*. Zeffirelli's calculated risk paid off—Gibson received mostly favorable reviews, as did the film. *Time* said the role of Hamlet was "almost perfect for Gibson," and added that Zeffirelli's direction made "*Hamlet* so vigorous that the kids will forget it's poetry." Almost a quarter-century ago Zeffirelli achieved international stardom by taking another of Shakespeare's tragedies, *Romeo and Juliet*, and making it accessible to young movie-goers. In more than 40 years in show business, Zeffirelli has produced and directed opera, theater and cinema. His personal life has had its share of drama as well; he has survived three encounters with death—two in World War II, and a serious auto accident in 1969. His traumatic experiences, he says, have only increased his zest for living, which shows up in the intensity and immediacy of his work.

Franco Zeffirelli was born February 12, 1923, in a small clinic outside of Florence, Italy. His mother, Alaide Garosi, was a successful fashion designer in Florence, and his father, Ottorino Corsi, a merchant who supplied her with fabrics. The child of two lovers married to others, Zeffirelli was scarred with an identity crisis as a young boy that affected him for many years. "Gradually, I pieced together the whole story," he wrote in his 1986 autobiography, *Zeffirelli*, "though it always seemed quite unreal, as if I was hearing about someone else's life."

His mother's husband died just before young Franco was born, following a long bout with tuberculosis. The man's family refused to believe that Franco was his posthumous son, since they knew the man had been too ill to father a child. Equally adamant, the Corsi family refused to accept young Franco. Of the two families, only his father's cousin Lide stood by Zeffirelli's mother, aided her and counseled her, convincing her to keep the baby when she considered abortion during pregnancy. "Maybe that's why I'm such a strict anti-abortionist," Zeffirelli remarked in his book. "My mother defied so much of the existing social structure to have me." After he was born, a name had to be invented for him. His mother's married name and his father's name were both off-limits. His mother was fond of a Mozart aria in *Cosi fan tutte* that mentions the *zeffiretti,* the little breezes. In the birth register, it was misspelled as "Zeffirelli."

His mother left him in the care of a wet nurse for two years before taking him back. She passed away when Zeffirelli was six and he was taken in by his Aunt Lide. The turmoil of his childhood, and the confusion of going from mother-figure to mother-figure took its toll on his psyche, he says in his book: "Every time I offered love to one of these women I was forced to take it back and give it to another . . . I still have difficulty in trusting love when it is offered. I still search, but even when love is given to me, I seldom manage to fully absorb it or to believe that it will last."

As a child Zeffirelli spent his summers in a peasant village in the Italian countryside with the family of the woman who nursed him. He was fascinated with the traveling theatrical troupes that would occasionally visit, saying, "I've never believed anything at the theater as much as the fantasies that those storytellers brought us." Back in Florence by summer's end, Franco built little stages and created his own world of theater using puppets, props, and special toys. His aunt's lover fed young Franco's affection for the theater by taking him to his first opera, *Die Walkure*, at age nine. "I was riveted by the incredible sounds . . . the metal helmets with horns, the forest of rocks, the fire, the smoke, the Valkyries galloping everywhere. It was hardly a refined appreciation, more like a child of today gawping at Star Wars." Young Franco was hooked; he immediately began

the arduous task of reconstructing the production's set in miniature. "While most of the other children were out playing after school, I was buried in my own cardboard Ring of the Nibelungs."

Zeffirelli was 17 and headed for college when World War II came to Italy in 1940. As the war progressed Zeffirelli knew he would either have to join the Italian Fascist Army or face conscription. Instead, he spurned the Fascists and joined the Italian Resistance. He was ordered to infiltrate an Italian Fascist faction by joining it undercover. The Fascists discovered his true identity and political persuasion and prepared to send him to the firing squad. When a Fascist officer learned that Zeffirelli was the son of Ottorino Corsi, he spared his life and assigned him to a labor camp—the officer was another of Corsi's bastard sons.

> "While most of the other children were out playing after school, I was buried in my own cardboard Ring of the Nibelungs."

Zeffirelli managed to escape the Fascists and later linked up with a Scottish battalion as an interpreter. He traveled with them and helped them find their way around his hometown of Florence in the days before its liberation. In 1944, after the British and Americans had effectively liberated much of Italy, a lone Zeffirelli was picked up by a local militia in a remote mountain town as he was making his way home. They arrested him on charges of being a Fascist and he again found himself facing a firing squad. On the way to the field where others were being executed, Zeffirelli made one final emotional plea to one of his captors, showing his papers and recounting his story of helping the British. He finally persuaded them of his innocence and he was released, free to return to post-war Florence.

Once back in Florence Zeffirelli was a confused 21-year-old, unsure about his future—"It was as if the war continued, not in the world, but in my head." In September of 1945 Florence was treated to a showing of Laurence Olivier's film, *Henry V*. The beauty and spectacle of the film gave Zeffirelli direction. "I wanted to do something like the production I was witnessing," he recounted. "When the lights went up my head was clearer than it had been for months. I knew that at last my war was over."

In the late 1940s, Zeffirelli abandoned his architecture studies and entered the world of theater, his first love. Taking a cue from his hobby as a youngster, he became a set designer. He landed some bit acting roles in plays and a few films and eventually caught the attention of the famed Italian director Luchino Visconti, with whom he formed a long-lasting companionship. From Visconti, Zeffirelli learned to pay uncanny attention to detail in cinematography, to direct by acting out examples, and to throw "a well-timed tantrum." Zeffirelli made a name for himself designing sets for Visconti productions of *Troilus and Cressida* and *A Streetcar Named Desire*. He gained more experience working in productions in Florence, Rome, Milan, and throughout Italy. In 1955 he directed the renowned diva Maria Callas in *Il turco in Italia*. He also directed *L'elisir d'amore* at the Milan opera house La Scala, but, despite his success, Zeffirelli was looking to move his career in a new direction: "Even after directing at La Scala I still couldn't think of opera as anything other than something to do until a break in films came along." By the end of the 1950s Zeffirelli had directed operas in such places as Israel, Dallas, and London.

The London performances of *Cavalleria rusticana* and *Pagliacci* in 1959 were destined to change Zeffirelli's life. The general manager of London's Old Vic Theater was impressed with Zeffirelli's work and wanted him to direct *Romeo and Juliet* there in 1960. Zeffirelli was stunned that one of the most prestigious theaters in Great Britain wished an Italian to direct Shakespeare, and agreed, though not without reservation: "I'd never done Shakespeare in my own language, and the thought of tackling the great poetry in English for all those guardians of the true flame was terrifying." Zeffirelli was hired to give the production a Mediterranean feel, to change the Victorian interpretation that still dominated the English stage.

Franco Zeffirelli attends the premiere of his 1990 film Hamlet *at New York City's Museum of Modern Art with two of the film's stars, Glenn Close, left, and Helena Bonham-Carter. AP/Wide World Photos.*

His *Romeo and Juliet* opened at the Old Vic in autumn of 1960. The set was gray, dark, and Italian-influenced. The actors were young newcomers, for the most part. The reviews of the opening performance were dismal, but the second night's show was better. London's leading reviewer of the time, Kenneth Tynan of the *Observer*, was cited in Zeffirelli's book as calling the play "a revelation, perhaps a revolution . . . a masterly production . . . a glorious evening." The show then caught like a brushfire, drawing crowds from across Europe and even America. It especially appealed to younger audiences, and "slotted neatly into the world of the Beatles, of flower-power and peace-and-love," Zeffirelli wrote. He was subsequently invited to direct *Othello* at Stratford for the Royal Shakespeare Company.

After directing a few more operas in the early '60s, including *Tosca* in London with Maria Callas starring and *Falstaff* in New York with Leonard Bernstein conducting, Zeffirelli cemented his solid reputation in filmmaking by directing Elizabeth Taylor and Richard Burton in *The Taming of the Shrew*. They filmed in Rome in the spring of 1965. Zeffirelli recounts an incident when the three were invited to the home of an Italian princess to meet Robert and Ethel Kennedy. "Burton and Kennedy began to compete as to who could out-recite the other in Shakespeare's sonnets . . . they continued reciting as they got out of the car and walked into the hotel lobby and it was then that Richard delivered the coup de grace—he threw back his head and . . . recited the fifteenth sonnet backwards, starting at the last word and ending on the first. We all stood dumbfounded at this insane achievement and Robert Kennedy graciously conceded defeat."

Both Burton and Taylor, along with Zeffirelli, agreed that the next logical step was a film version of *Romeo and Juliet*. Three months after the 1967 release of *The Taming of the Shrew*, work began on the new film. Zeffirelli cast Leonard Whiting and Olivia Hussey in the title roles, both relative unknowns. Filming just outside of Rome from June to October, Zeffirelli finished the picture for about $1.5 million. The film eventually grossed over $50 million and helped keep Paramount Studios in business, and pushing ahead to make such films as *Love Story* and *The Godfather*.

Zeffirelli's autobiography provides an interesting aside to *Romeo and Juliet*: While Zeffirelli and crew were filming, Laurence Olivier was on an adjacent soundstage making *The Shoes of the Fisherman*. Never one to pass up a contribution to Shakespeare, Olivier wanted to help with *Romeo and Juliet*. Zeffirelli asked him to voice the prologue, but Olivier wished to do

more. So Zeffirelli had him overdub the voice of Lord Montague. "By now unstoppable, Larry insisted on dubbing all sorts of small parts and crowd noises in a hilarious variety of assumed voices. The audiences never knew just how much of Laurence Olivier they were getting on the soundtrack of that film."

Zeffirelli had pulled off the unthinkable: "From the Bronx to Bali, Shakespeare was a box-office hit. The effect on me was stunning. It made me a lot of money," the director declared in his autobiography. The success resulted in international stardom, press tours, interviews and all the accompaniments of fame. But the good times were short-lived. In October, 1968, a month after the American debut of *Romeo and Juliet*, Zeffirelli's Aunt Lide lost a brief battle with cancer—"I have never fully recovered from the blow," he said. The following January, on the way to a football match in Florence, Zeffirelli suffered life-threatening injuries in an accident while riding in a car driven by actress Gina Lollobrigida. He went headfirst through the windshield and suffered 18 different facial bone fractures. He was in the hospital for three months, and left feeling weak after numerous facial operations. He didn't fully recover until the end of the summer, he recounted, annoyed that he missed the "ballyhoo" at the Oscars, where *Romeo and Juliet* won only two of the slew of awards for which it had been nominated. But he was rewarded with a five-year contract by Paramount.

> *"I'd never done Shakespeare in my own language, and the thought of tackling the great poetry in English for all those guardians of the true flame was terrifying."*

His survival of the terrible accident strengthened Zeffirelli's deep religious beliefs. His next major project was *Brother Sun, Sister Moon*, a film based on the life of St. Francis. By the time the film debuted in 1972, much of its inspiration had come from an era gone by. "I realized how much the film was rooted in the '60s, yet now that the 1970s were unfolding it was clear that a massive change had taken place. Young people were no longer espousing peace and love . . . . Just as *Romeo and Juliet* had struck the right note at a time when young people were creating a cultural revolution, so *Brother Sun* went totally against the grain of the new cynicism." Critics were merciless in attacking the naive innocence of the film, in a world so rife with war and violence. So began a period of incomplete programs for Zeffirelli, "a weary succession of collapsing projects."

In 1974 Zeffirelli began what was to be his biggest undertaking, two years in the making: the six-hour made-for-television epic, *Jesus of Nazareth*. Before even assembling his all-star cast, Zeffirelli concentrated on the monumental task of siting locations and, above all, getting a screenplay completed. Author Anthony Burgess produced a masterful script, Zeffirelli recalled, and locations were sought in the Holy Land and in Morocco and Tunisia. For the title role, Zeffirelli selected Robert Powell, and Olivia Hussey as Mary. Other notables in the cast included Laurence Olivier, Rod Steiger, Ann Bancroft, James Mason, and Anthony Quinn.

Jesus of Nazareth was enormously successful worldwide and has since become a television perennial. It enabled Zeffirelli to write his own ticket for his next film. While watching television one afternoon he came across King Vidor's 1931 *The Champ*, a movie that had reduced young Franco to tears when he saw it as a boy—and again as a 55-year-old: "I cried so much that, when I took a mouthful of spaghetti, it was salty with tears." As he did by bringing Shakespeare to the screen, by filming the life of St. Francis, and by directing an all-star cast of egos in a six-hour film about Christ, Zeffirelli took a chance. The risk was a remake of a tear-jerker that could easily be written off as sappy. He made the film in Hollywood, his first experience working in there. As expected, critics bashed the film for its oversentimentality, but the $9 million movie raked about $146 million for Metro-Goldwyn-Mayer.

Zeffirelli remained in Hollywood to make another film, 1981's *Endless Love* with actress-model Brooke Shields. Zeffirelli made a three-hour production that was subsequently edited down to under two hours, at the expense of a great deal of plot and ideas, which infuriated him: "How on earth could I have allowed this to happen, I, who had directed Callas . . . Taylor and Burton . . . who had made a hit out of Shakespeare? I finished the film in a way that can only be described as a total compromise, if not a complete surrender." Critics assailed *Endless Love*, too: "The critical reception made that for *Brother Sun, Sister Moon* seem positively jovial," he remarked in his autobiography.

After putting two operas on film, *La Traviata* in 1982 and *Otello* in 1986, Zeffirelli made *Young Toscanini* in 1988, as yet unreleased. He also produced a number of productions at New York's Metropolitan Opera House. Then came *Hamlet*. Again, Zeffirelli took a risk, casting Gibson as Hamlet and cutting the five-hour play down to a two-hour film without ending up with a "Highlights from Hamlet" production. Critics, for the most part, are finally back in his corner. The picture was filmed in England and Scotland for $15.5 million, modest by today's standards. Now Zeffirelli is looking ahead to a new project called *The Florentines* about the rivalry between Leonardo da Vinci and Michelangelo. He recently told *Premiere* that he plans to keep working, but "I'm quite ready to pass away, you know, quite ready to die. I've been more afraid to live badly—to live as an artichoke, or live making people unhappy around me, living without contributing something."

Selected writings

Zeffirelli: An Autobiography, Weidenfeld, 1986.

Sources

New York Times, December 14, 1986.
Premiere, February 1991.
Time, January 7, 1991.

—*John P. Cortez*

Obituaries

Eve Arden

Real name, Eunice Quedens; born April 30, 1912 (some sources say 1908), in Mill Valley, Calif., died of cancer, November 12, 1990, in Beverly Hills, Calif. Actress. Eve Arden was always cast as a certain kind of comedic character—one full of sarcasm. Those who knew her said that she was sweet-tempered, a devoted mother and wife, and a loyal friend. Yet her eyebrows were seemingly meant for a caustic arch, and so it is no wonder that her successful radio show, *Our Miss Brooks*, translated to 1950s television as well as it did. "Greetings, fairest of all possible English teachers," Richard Crenna (as Walter, a student) would say. "Well, good morning, most observant of all possible pupils," Arden (as salty English teacher Miss Brooks) would reply. The country was constantly absorbed with the trials of Miss Brooks, including her battles with the stuffy principal, Osgood Conklin, and her romance with biology teacher Philip Boynton. In 1953 Arden's triumph was officially recognized with an Emmy for best actress in a regular series. A favorite in films as well, with more than 70 to her credit, Arden made her last professional appearance in the 1983 made-for-television movie *Alice in Wonderland*. "She never really got over the [1984] death of her husband," her manager, Glenn Rose, told the *Los Angeles Times*. "She was never really the same after it."

Arden's career was inspired by her mother, an actress, who eventually traded in her stage career for a millinery in San Francisco. She encouraged her daughter in acting, and after a grammar school recitation, Arden was hooked. "From then on," she was quoted in the London *Times*, "you couldn't keep me out of the school plays, the song and dance skits and anything else." In the early 1930s she was discovered by producer Lee Schubert in the Pasadena Community Playhouse; soon she was whisked into the show biz life as the most famous sort of New York chorus girl—a Ziegfeld Follies performer. Legend has it that the former Eunice Quedens picked her professional name from two cosmetics: Evening in Paris perfume and Elizabeth Arden makeup. That name became famous enough to merit the actress her own series, *The Eve Arden Show* (which ran from 1957 to 1958), and her renown was long-lived enough to see a 1985 autobiography, *The Three Phases of Eve*, published.

Originality and creativity were Arden's hallmarks from the start; the daring young actress wore a live cat, "boalike around her neck in the movie *Stage Door*," according to *People*. The same magazine quoted a critic who once said that Arden could "brighten even the most banal lines." Her Miss Brooks-like role in the 1978 movie *Grease*, and her reprise in 1982's *Grease II* bear out the assessment—she made even the hackneyed character of an aging, straight-laced principal seem original. The London *Times* remembered her in a better movie, and quoted with relish her delivery of these immortal lines about parenthood in the 1945 movie *Mildred Pierce*; "Vida's convinced me that alligators have the right idea. They eat their young." As supporting actress in *Mildred Pierce* (supporting the famously difficult star Joan Crawford), Arden was nominated for an Academy Award in 1945. In 1968 she received a Sarah Siddons award as actress of the year for her role in the stage production of *Hello, Dolly!* Other stage conquests included the lead roles in *Butterflies are Free* and *Auntie Mame*.

The London *Times* said of the comedienne: "As Eve Arden she was seen in films as the best friend or big sister of the female lead, offering wisecracks in a dead-pan, throwaway manner that ultimately became her public persona." Privately, she was the consummate family person, adopting three children and having one of her own, and was reportedly devoted to her second husband, to whom she was married for 33 years before his death. While she called her mother a beauty, Arden didn't regret her own less-than classic features, according to the *Los Angeles Times*. "I've worked with a lot of great, glamorous girls in movies and the theater. They would always give their last ounce to get where they wanted to be. And I'll admit I've often thought it would be wonderful to be a *femme fatale* . . . . But then I'd always come back to thinking that if they only had what I've had— a family, real love, and anchor—they would have been happier during all the hours when the marquees and the footlights are dark." **Sources:** *Los Angeles Times*, November 13, 1990; *People*, November 26, 1990; London *Times*, November 14, 1990.

Lee Atwater

Full name, Harvey LeRoy Atwater; born February 27, 1951, in Atlanta, GA; died of cancer, March 29, 1991, in Washington, DC. Political strategist. Lee Atwater's untimely death at age 40 left a gap in the Republican party and put an end to a promising political career. He had been named chairman of the Republican National Committee at 37, a reward for managing George Bush's successful 1988 presidential campaign. When Atwater was diagnosed with a brain tumor a year before his death, he reassessed some of his tactics during the campaign, and eventually apologized to Bush's opponent, Michael S. Dukakis. The *New York Times* quoted Atwater as having said, "In 1988, fighting off Dukakis, I said that I 'would strip the bark off the little bastard' and 'make Willie Horton his running mate.' [Horton was a Massachusetts convicted murderer who committed other felonies while participating in a Dukakis-sponsored furlough program] . . . I am sorry for both statements: the first for its naked cruelty, the second because it makes me sound like a racist, which I am not." His love of music with black roots (Atwater had been a blues guitar player at one time) was held up as proof of his equanimity. He said in the *Chicago Tribune*, "My hero of all time is Otis Redding," the legendary rhythm and blues singer.

Atwater developed his self-avowed political techniques in largely Democratic South Carolina, where he was raised. "Republicans in the South could not win elections by talking about the issues," he said in the *New York Times*. "You had to make the case that the other guy, the other candidate, is a bad guy." Atwater and Bush first met when the former was 22 years old and the head of the College Republicans, and the latter was the chairman of the Republican National Committee, which seems to suggest that Atwater's political prowess could have led him to the White House. After working on former President Ronald Reagan's 1980 presidential campaign, Atwater worked for a Washington consulting firm until recruited by Bush in 1987. Soon after the 1988 campaign, Atwater decided to improve his image. He made speeches about attracting blacks to the Repub-

lican party, but after being nominated to the board of the reputable "black" Howard University, students protested, calling "devious" Atwater's involvement in the use of Willie Horton "sinister"; the students then staged a takeover of the university's administration building. Atwater declined the nomination to the board.

Atwater wrote about his struggle with cancer and the resulting chemotherapy in *Life* magazine and reported that "my campaign-honed strategies of political warfare were simply no match for this dogged opponent. Cancer is no Democrat," he playfully added. He kept the title of chairman of the Republican National Committee until two months before his death. When President Bush learned of Atwater's death, he stated, "I am very saddened . . . . Lee practiced the art of politics with zeal and vigor." Atwater is survived by his wife, the former Sally Dunbar, and three daughters, one of whom was born after Atwater's fatal disease was diagnosed. **Sources:** *Chicago Tribune*, March 30, 1991; *New York Times*, March 30, 1991, March 31, 1991.

Pete Axthelm

Born c. 1943; died of acute hepatitis, February 2, 1991, in Pittsburgh, Pa. Sportswriter. Enthusiastic and hospitable, Pete Axthelm lived only briefly, but by most accounts, fully. A sporting and betting enthusiast, Axthelm wrote in his time for many popular magazines and papers, and was a sports columnist for several television networks. His diseased liver cut his life short as he continued drinking despite the warnings of his doctors; several sources say the writer was awaiting a liver transplant. Andrew Beyer of the *Washington Post* reported this conversation at Axthelm's favorite racetrack, Gulfstream Park: "The conviviality of the gambling world was his favorite environment, and he said to a friend recently, 'If I had to live any other way I'd rather be dead.'" Beyer added that Axthelm had made several "half-hearted and short-lived" attempts to quit drinking. Axthelm made his choice and effectively ended his life, within the apparently intertwined fundamentals of writing, sport, gambling, and drinking.

Axthelm started his career as a writer while an undergraduate at Yale University, where he wrote his first book, an analysis of the confessional novel. After graduation he went to work covering horse racing for the *New York Herald Tribune*. He then wrote for *Sports Illustrated*. Axthelm began writing for *Newsweek* in 1968 and at age 24 covered the Olympic Games in Mexico City. Melvin Durslag of the *Los Angeles Times* claimed that "it was never noised about, but Pete played a role in one of the most celebrated affairs of the modern Olympics—the black-fist incident [involving two black sprinters, Tommie Smith and John Carlos] on the victory stand." Axthelm occasionally functioned as a political commentator, and Beyer stated that "he might moralize in print about the Soviet invasion of Afghanistan, or about the propriety of playing the Super Bowl in the midst of the war with Iraq, but he'd never condemn a con man or a hustler."

After working 20 years with *Newsweek*, Axthelm worked for the *Washington Post*. A popular television horse racing and pro football commentator as well, he worked with NBC from 1980 until 1985, then transfered to ESPN in 1987. His unpolished looks and clever characterization of the "Goddess of Wagering"—who made appearances in his books on gambling—made him a favorite. Beyer considered "his book about basketball, *The City Game*..., a classic."

Apparently, Axthelm was not especially proud of his own writing abilities—what made life worth living to him was being at the track and betting on horses. While some felt that Axthelm's lack of self-appreciation led him to throw his talents away, friends theorized that he wanted to live his own way or not at all. "It is simply that guys who gamble go nuts," Durslag opined. **Sources:** *Los Angeles Times*, February 5, 1991; *Washington Post*, February 3, 1991, February 4, 1991.

Pearl Bailey

Born March 29, 1918, in Newport News, Va.; died of heart disease, August 17, 1990, in Philadelphia, Pa. Singer, actress, author. Fans and critics agree that Pearl Bailey's immense appeal was not just her warm and sultry voice, her elegant gestures, her stage presence, and all of her charms in performance, but also her exuberance and compassion in all areas of her life. As a special representative to the United Nations, and in all aspects of her existence, Bailey worked to promote interracial understanding, and before her death was concentrating on promoting acquired immune deficiency syndrome (AIDS) research. She entertained U.S. troops overseas as recently as 1988 and toured widely besides. Bailey wrote six books, the first two of which are autobiographical: *The Raw Pearl*, and later *Talking to Myself*,

which *Publishers Weekly* called "affectionate homilies laced with recollections of her life and travels." In addition to theater and movie work, Bailey performed on many variety shows for ABC-TV, and had her own syndicated cooking show, *Pearl's Kitchen*, in 1970. Her personable and straightforward nature made her a favorite on the talk show circuit.

Bailey sang and danced for the first time at age 3 in the Pentecostal church that her father administered. At the age of 15, she won a talent show (and the $5 prize) in Washington, D.C.'s Pearl Theater for singing "Talk of the Town," and "Poor Butterfly." Before blossoming into popularity on the 1940s New York nightclub circuit, Bailey paid her dues as a chorus girl in Philadelphia. Her singing voice was most often described as throaty and lusty, with a suggestive growl; her renditions of such songs as "Toot Toot Tootsie (Goodbye)," "St. Louis Blues," and "Bill Bailey, Won't You Please Come Home," garnered her the most fame. The London *Times* described her singing as "seemingly haphazard but in fact cunningly controlled lapses of vocal concentration causing the lyrics to disappear under a groundswell of mumbled monologue which always slipped back into the rhythmic pattern of the song with unerring accuracy."

The unique style of her delivery was not to be ignored, as her graceful gestures made her a natural for stage and screen. *Entertainment Weekly* quoted her saying, "Tie my hands and I wouldn't be able to sing a note." Her Broadway debut was in the musical *St. Louis Woman*, and her performance won the Donaldson Award for best newcomer to Broadway. Her best known performances were as Dolly in a 1960s Broadway production of *Hello Dolly* (for which she won a special Tony Award), and Maria in the 1959 movie *Porgy and Bess*.

Survived by her fourth husband (of 39 years), Louis Bellson, a jazz drummer who sometimes backed Bailey, and their two adopted children, Bailey suffered her first heart attack at 54. Recovering after having been pronounced dead she wryly but thankfully commented at her 61st birthday party that it was "not bad for a lady who died seven years ago," according to *Maclean's*. Bailey often quoted blues singer extraordinaire Sophie Tucker's motto: "It ain't how good you are. It's how long you last." In her career of 57 years she entertained her fans in every possible medium and showed her concern for the human race with her diplomatic work: she had been scheduled to address the United Nations on the 24th of August when she died. **Sources:** *Entertainment Weekly*, August 31, 1990; London *Times*, August 20,

1990; *Maclean's* August 27, 1990; *Publishers Weekly*, August 23, 1971.

Joan Bennett

Born February 27, 1910, in Palisades, N.J.; died of a heart attack, December 7, 1990, in Scarsdale, N.Y. Actress. Though she appeared in more than 70 movies, held starring roles in several television series, and toured nationally in successful plays, Bennett probably never attained the kind of stardom she deserved. Bennett's career in Hollywood was solid, but not illustrious. She co-starred with many of the popular male leads of the time (like Spencer Tracy in the *Father of the Bride* movies) and was guided by some excellent directors, yet most critics agree that these actors and directors did less than their best work with her.

Born to a family of actors, Bennett's mother, Adrienne Morrison, traced her ancestry back five generations to "strolling players in 18th-century England," reported the *New York Times*. Bennett's father, matinee idol and stage actor Richard Bennett, was her co-star in the play *Jarnegan* the first time she acted professionally. Richard played a temperamental movie director, and Joan played a young ingenue. Before the well-received five-month run of that play however, Bennett's life had been anything but child's play. Her family had sent her to finishing schools in New England and France, and at 16 she married John Marion Fox, the son of a millionaire, whom Bennett would later describe as a playboy and a drunk. She was a mother at 17 and a divorcee at 18, the year she appeared in *Jarnegan*. Her father helped her land her first Hollywood contract and Bennett, at 19, starred in *Bulldog Drummond*, opposite Ronald Colman.

Bennett was briefly married to film writer and producer Gene Markey, then in 1940 married Walter Wanger, a producer who had introduced Viennese brunette Hedy Lamarr to the United States. Until then, Bennett had appeared on film as a blond, but Wanger convinced her that she would be more successful with her original dark color; the *New York Times* elaborated: "Combined with her sultry eyes and husky voice, the new look gave her an earthier, more arresting personality." As Bennett was quoted in *People*, "My change of hair color made a definite difference in my career. My voice dropped, and I smoldered all the way from the South Seas to Manhattan, [but] I got awfully sick of it." The busiest and most artistically substantial portion of her career

followed, but another obstacle reared up. In 1951 Wanger, apparently depressed about his finances, shot Bennett's longtime agent, Jennings Lang, calling him a homewrecker. Scandal was not the money-making vehicle in Hollywood in the 1950s that it is in the 1990s. Bennett was only offered a handful of film roles after the shooting, though her husband served only three months in prison. They were divorced In 1965.

Bennett sustained her acting career with theater and television roles after the shooting incident. Most notably, she appeared in the cult television series *Dark Shadows* from 1966 to 1971. Personally, she was well-liked; the *Washington Post* said that "Miss Bennett gained a reputation as a consummate, good-natured professional who also was glamorous." Despite her treatment at the hands of the studios, Bennett revealed no bitterness. The *New York Times* reported that she missed the old ways: "The industry held a combination of nuts, talents, charlatans and geniuses, all of whom were learning, bumbling and creating with fury and innocence. The colorful types had a passionate love for the business, not lust for the money. Today, it seems to me, it's strictly a big business, based on dollars and cents." **Sources:** *New York Times*, December 9, 1990; *People*, December 24, 1990; *Washington Post*, December 10, 1990.

Leonard Bernstein

Born August 25, 1918, in Lawrence, Mass.; died of a heart attack, October 14, 1990, in New York City. Pianist, conductor, composer. Bernstein's popular compositions, operettas, choral pieces, and ballet scores attest to the variety and substance of his musical talents and his charisma and appeal were as legendary. *New York Times Book Review* contributor Leon Botstein said in his review of a 1987 Bernstein biography: "He was more than musical. He was a star at Boston Latin School and Harvard University. His talents as a speaker and writer are considerable. Gregarious, energetic and charming, he has been the center of attention since his boyhood. As early as his Harvard years, he demonstrated a knack for connecting with the right people and demonstrating to them his fabulous musical talent, enthusiasm, insight and memory."

Many music critics believe that a critical combination of his talents and their applications altered the way Americans listen to music and the way the world listens to Americans: Bernstein's conducting of famous European orchestras gave him an international reputation for aesthetic excellence, his educational work on television increased his populist currency in the States, and his compositions gave him a quasi-academic prestige. Many would call this versatility genius, but Bernstein detractors found him "vulgar and mannered," according to *Time*. Bernstein fans, however, savored his unabashed enthusiasm as the perfect American antidote to stuffy, traditional approaches to classical music.

As a young man, Bernstein was pressured by his father (who was a Russian Jewish immigrant) to enter the profitable family business in beauty supplies, but his mother had encouraged his piano lessons and supported his career choice. His father admitted that "you don't expect your child to be a Moses, a Maimonides or a Leonard Bernstein," according to *Time*. The young musician went on to Boston's competitive Latin School and then Harvard, taught along the way by legendary pianists and conductors. His true mentor was conductor Serge Koussevitsky of the Berkshire Music Center at Tanglewood, who recognized his talent and in 1942 made him his assistant. In the 1940s Bernstein built a following with his interpretations of twentieth century works and proved an effective proponent of American music.

The 1950s were his most dynamic and successful composing years, bringing to life such works as the one-act opera *Trouble in Tahiti*, the operetta *Candide*, the ballet *Fancy Free*, and the musical *On the Town*. Bernstein often collaborated with choreographer Jerome Robbins, and their masterwork was *West Side Story*, for which they both won many awards. Botstein suggested that the success of the musical was two-bladed: "It is probable that Mr. Bernstein would prefer to be remembered as a composer of great serious concert music than as a conductor or composer of theater and popular music. Nonetheless, it is on his reputation as the creator of *West Side Story* that his mass popularity rests."

Bernstein did battle with his success of the fifties for the rest of his life. His later choral works and compositions would never have the same popularity or reveal the same genius. Some critics believed that his diversity took him in too many directions, and that he could never properly concentrate on any one of his pursuits. Others charged that he lapsed into self-parody with his conducting; *Maclean's* reported that "some concertgoers found his podium antics—jiving, manic twitching and the occassional airborne leap—disconcerting."

The appeal of Bernstein the Conductor was put succinctly by Botstein, who said in the *New York Times Book Review* that "his greatness as a conductor does not stem from his personal relationship to a particular tradition of music-making or from a profound study of specific styles and periods. His ease with musical language in general, from the popular song and jazz to serial music, has made his own compositions too susceptible to external influences; his work sounds skillful, but derivative and eclectic. However, this chameleonlike quality—the ability to absorb the essence of divergent styles—has enabled him, as a conductor, to range over the entire repertory with unrivaled success. Mr. Bernstein is . . . America's first native-born conductor to reach the ranks of great."

Bernstein's private life was subject to much public scrutiny—author and social critic Tom Wolfe lampooned his chic charity causes (such as the Black Panthers) and rumors circulated for years regarding his sexual preference. He left his wife in the early 1970s and surrounded himself with young male admirers for the rest of his life. His death had a profound impact on the music world, and *Newsweek* described several commemorations: "The New York Philharmonic and the Boston and Chicago Symphony orchestras added the elegiac Adagietto of Mahler's Fifth Symphony (which Bernstein had chosen to conduct, for its 'great solemnity,' at Robert Kennedy's funeral) to their programs." Bernstein's musical signatures will always be a part of American music. **Sources:** *Maclean's*, October 29, 1990; *New York Times Book Review*, May 10, 1987; *Newsweek*, October 29, 1990; *Time*, October 29, 1990.

Art Blakey

Born October 11, 1919, in Pittsburgh, Pa.; died of cancer, October 16, 1990, in New York City. Jazz drummer, band leader. Blakey's creative influence on the development of jazz is difficult to measure—his midwifery brought many young talents into the spotlight, while his own performances inspired many musicians. Nat Hentoff, writer and critic, said that Blakey was "perhaps the most emotionally unbridled drummer in jazz, and there are times when his backgrounds resemble a brush fire," as the *Los Angeles Times* reported. The subject of a film and jazz festival retrospectives, and the recipient of a 1984 Grammy Award and countless other honors, Blakey enjoyed the reflected glory of his younger band members, saying in the *Chicago Tribune* that "when I take these 18-year-old kids out on tour, it makes most of the pros feel like cutting their wrists . . . they're going to take the music farther than it has been."

The self-taught drummer started out on the piano; at age 15 he was leading a band, but was discouraged by the talent of pianist Erroll Garner. Blakey moved over to the drums, where his originality and inventiveness showed even in the seemingly awkward way he held his sticks. Blakey graduated from the tutorship of pianist Mary Lou Williams and the big band of Fletcher Henderson to the groundbreaking Billy Eckstein band. From 1944 to 1947, this band (including Dexter Gordon [see *Newsmakers* 89, 90] and Charlie Parker on saxophone, Dizzy Gillespie on trumpet, and Sarah Vaughan [see *Newsmakers* 90] sharing vocals with Eckstein) revolutionized jazz with bebop, an explosive and unpredictable form of jazz. Gillespie said of Blakey in the *New York Times,* "He had the knack of knowing when to play loud or soft, and when he played the whole band would lift right off the bandstand. He'd shout like somebody in a sanctified church. He was truly one of our greats." Drummer Max Roach added that "we used to call him 'Thunder.'" In 1947, after Eckstein's band broke up, Blakey traveled to Africa to study and converted to Islam, taking the name Abdullah Ibn Buhaina. Many musicians called him by the nickname "Bu."

Blakey's group, the Jazz Messengers, was formed in 1954 with tenor saxophonist Hank Mobley, trumpet player Kenny Dorham, and bassist Doug Watkins. The *New York Times*'s Peter Watrous said that Blakey "acted as a one-man university for young musicians." Graduates include Wynton and Branford Marsalis [see *Newsmakers* 88], Wayne Shorter, Chuck Mangione, and Freddie Hubbard [see *Newsmakers* 88]. Wynton Marsalis said in the *New York Times* that Blakey "came up with a new way to interpret the blues and another way of building the ensemble, where the drums are more orchestrated. That sound is the sound you hear today, particularly with many of the younger musicians. And he had his own particular brand of swing, which makes him important by itself."

Stubborn and vital, Blakey performed until two months before his death. Blakey played drums through vibrations in the stage because he was almost completely deaf in his later years. He refused to wear a hearing aid as he thought it would throw off his time. Married four times, Blakey adopted six children and fathered nine, including a child born in 1986. "There's snow on the roof but a fire in the furnace," he would tell his audiences. **Sources:** *Chicago Tribune,* October 17, 1990; *Los Angeles Times,* October 17, 1990; *New York Times,* October 17, 1990.

Gordon Bunshaft

Born May 9, 1909, in Buffalo, N.Y.; died of cardiovascular arrest, August 6, 1990, in New York City. Architect. An urban architect, Bunshaft was known for building designs that eventually changed the shape, tenor, and spirit of cities in the 1950s and 1960s, and his work continues to be an influence on new architects. Because of a timeless quality—the result of elegant lines, thoughtful proportions, and a light touch verging on anonymity—Bunshaft's buildings comfortably link the old and the new in such metropolises as New York City, Jeddah in Saudi Arabia, and Belgium's city of Brussels. According to the *New York Times,* Lewis Mumford [see *Newsmakers* 90], the feared and respected architectural critic, called the Pepsi-Cola Building of Manhattan "an impeccable achievement . . . . It says all that can be said, delicately, accurately, elegantly, with surfaces of glass." Bunshaft's preferred materials of glass, metal, and stone were the elements of the International Style. He defended this style as the only acceptable architectural language of the twentieth century, all others, according to Bunshaft, being self-indulgent and whimsical.

The son of Russian Jewish immigrants, Bunshaft studied architecture at the Massachusetts Institute of Technology. Shortly after earning his master's degree, he won a Rotch Traveling Fellowship, which he used to tour Europe and North Africa. He met with one of the founders of the Bauhaus school, Walter Gropius, who, according to the *New York Times,* "queried him about the readiness of the United States to accept the cool, crisp architecture of the International Style." He returned to the United States in 1937 and entered the New York architectural firm of Skidmore, Owings & Merrill, of which he was soon the chief designer. Married in 1943, he left the firm briefly (between 1942 and 1946) to serve in the U.S. Army Corps of Engineers. Soon after his return, he was assigned the now-famous Lever House of New York City.

Paul Goldberger, an architecture critic of the *New York Times,* wrote admiringly of the qualities of the Lever House and Bunshaft's early designs, especially his "magnificent balances between sensuality and restraint." The Lever House's most famous characteristics are those of moderation; it was built well within the New York City zoning permit, thus allowing light and air through to the street. While much of modern urban architecture is excessively self-referential (each mirrored to reflect the surrounding buildings, ad infinitum), Goldberger said that Bunshaft treated

Lever House as an object, "a piece of minimalist sculpture that treated the city as a podium."

"His knowledge and appreciation of sculpture was outstanding," said the London *Times*. "Several monumental works of sculpture, notably by Isamu Noguchi and Henry Moore [see *Newsmakers* 86], adorn his buildings, a prominent example being the bronze figure by Moore outside the Banque Lambert at Brussels." The *Times* also noted that Moore and Bunshaft became close friends before the sculptor's death in 1986. The influence of sculpture on his buildings is most strongly exemplified in his designs of the 1960s and 1970s; a 27-story triangular office tower for the National Commercial Bank in Jeddah was appointed with huge loggia that Bunshaft called "gardens in the air," according to the *New York Times*. Most critics, however, fault his work in this period for flaws in proportion and a lack of sympathy for the surrounding buildings and community.

Bunshaft retired from the architecture firm in 1979, but was occupied with such responsibilities as trusteeship and membership of the international council of the Museum of Modern Art. He was a member of the American Academy and Institute of Arts and Letters, a fellow of the American Institute of Architects, and an academician of the National Academy of Design. When the Lever House was threatened by a developer in 1983, it was declared a New York City monument, one of the first modern buildings the city so honored. Despite debate that surrounded his late works, Bunshaft was presented the Pritzker Prize in 1988, architecture's most coveted award. **Sources:** London *Times*, August 9, 1990; *New York Times*, August 8, 1990; August 19, 1990.

James Cleveland

Born c. 1932 in Chicago, Ill.; died of heart failure, February 9, 1991, in Los Angeles, Calif. Gospel singer and Baptist minister. The "King of Gospel" Reverend James Cleveland had not been able to sing for a year before his death due to respiratory ailments. But the last Sunday of his life, he faced his congregation at the Cornerstone Institutional Baptist Church (which he had founded) and told them, "If I don't see you again and if I don't sing again, I'm a witness to the fact that the Lord answers prayer. He let my voice come back to me this morning," the *Los Angeles Times* reported. A self-described "fog horn," Cleveland, like the late entertainer Sammy Davis, Jr., had received shortly before his death a huge show business tribute which had been billed as a golden

anniversary celebration but turned out to be a fond farewell from those he had assisted, inspired, and entertained. The *Los Angeles Times* described those attending as "dozens of African-American music legends...[who paid] their respects directly to the man who cleared their path instead of saving their flowers for his headstone."

A gifted pop artist might dream of the recognition and honors Cleveland received; Cleveland's glory was to see *gospel* music skyrocket in popularity and acceptance. The *Los Angeles Times* declared that "Cleveland's star burned brightest when he was helping others shine, and his contribution will be remembered more in terms of influence than in gold records or Grammy nominations." The recipient of 16 gold records, Cleveland also saw three works bring in Grammys—the 1974 single "In the Ghetto," 1977's *James Cleveland Live at Carnegie Hall*, and the 1980 *Lord, Let Me Be an Instrument*. According to legend, he taught 9-year-old Aretha Franklin how to sing gospel while living in her minister father's home in Detroit, Michigan. Later Cleveland would produce Franklin's 1970 hit album *Amazing Grace*—a mainstream breakthrough for gospel. In Detroit in 1968 Cleveland created the Gospel Music Workshop of America, his proudest personal achievement. It began as a small group of musicians and swelled to 200 chapters and 20,000 members throughout the United States.

The prestige Cleveland accrued in life was reflected in his memorial service. The *Detroit Free Press* reported that "rhythmic clapping and gospel music honored the King of Gospel, whose body, cloaked in white, lay on a bier in front of the stage. 'We come to salute an honorable life, a life that was filled with accomplishment and the spirit of the Lord,' said California state Senator Diane Watson." The *Los Angeles Times* reverently opined that Cleveland had been "not just...a record maker, but a mentor, producer, primary source of new material and fountainhead of artistic recognition for the form." **Sources:** *Chicago Tribune*, February 17, 1991; *Detroit Free Press*, February 18, 1991; *Los Angeles Times*, February 10, 1991, February 15, 1991; *Washington Post*, February 11, 1991.

Aaron Copland

Born November 14, 1900, in Brooklyn, N.Y; died of pneumonia, December 2, 1990, in North Tarrytown, N.Y. Composer. Aaron Copland taught Americans about themselves through his music. By thematically weaving the folk melodies of the 19th century throughout his popular works, and echoing their simple brilliance in his other pieces, Copland immortalized the American musical personality. "I had studied in France, where the composers were all distinctively French," he told the *New York Times* in 1985; "it was their manner of composing. We had nothing like that here, and so it became important to me to establish a naturally American strain of so-called American music." Though the lifelong bachelor cut short his composition work 20 years before his death, Copland produced a prolific and widely varied body of work, including academic experiments with modernism, and his popular masterpieces such as *Appalachian Spring.* When in the academic vein, he was criticized by a few scholars for use of jazz rhythms. When in his popular mode, some accused him of selling out his true complex nature for fame. Generally, it can be said that all of Copland's phases were carefully scrutinized and uniformly gained widespread acclamation and acceptance. Recognized internationally with practically every kind of musical award, Copland received a Pulitzer Prize, a Presidential Medal of Freedom, the Guggenheim Foundation's first music fellowship, and, in 1948, an Oscar for the score of *The Heiress.*

Copland was the youngest of five children—his parents were immigrants from Eastern Europe and owned a neighborhood department store in Brooklyn. A precocious musician, Copland wrote his first song for his mother at 8. At 16 he convinced his parents to pay for lessons in harmony, counterpoint, and sonata form with Rubin Goldmark (who had also taught George Gershwin), and they assented, despite their initial reluctance. The *Detroit Free Press* quoted Copland's explanation: "My parents were of the opinion that enough money had been invested in the musical training of the four older children, with meager results."

In his early twenties, Copland grew to musical prodigy in Paris, partially under the tutelage of Nadia Boulanger, "the most influential composition teacher of the century," according to *Time.* "It was where the action seemed to be," Copland recalled in 1985, according to the *New York Times.* "Stravinsky was living there, and the whole new 'group of six' with Milhaud and Poulenc. And so I went to study at a new summer music school at the Palace of Fontainebleau. It's always said that I went to France to study with Nadia Boulanger, but I had never heard of her before I arrived."

Not only did Copland become her pupil, but Boulanger gave him his first big break by giving Copland's first symphony (for organ and orchestra) to conductor Serge Koussevitzky, who was also crucial in the development of the late Leonard Bernstein's career. Like Bernstein in the 1960s, Copland in the 1930s and 1940s was a supporter of left-wing ideals—his populism was reflected in the wide appeal of such compositions as *Fanfare for the Common Man.* This 1942 composition exemplified the artistic change of direction he took, away from academic compositions to more easily understood and appreciated works. In his 1941 book *Our New Music,* Copland said, "It seemed to me that we composers were in danger of working in a vacuum. Moreover, an entirely new public for music had grown up around the radio and phonograph. It made no more sense to ignore them and to continue writing as if they did not exist. I felt it was worth the effort to see if I couldn't say what I had to say in the simplest possible terms." He achieved this with rousing themes, memorable phrasing, and American folk music roots.

Throughout the 1950s and until he stopped composing, Copland experimented with a 12-tone system. These experiments lost him his popular audience and engendered a public debate with Leonard Bernstein—an anomalous one, as the composer was "unflappable . . . [with] almost no enemies," the London *Times* claimed. Bernstein whined in 1970 (as quoted in the *New York Times*) that Copland had jumped aboard the 12-tone ship "just as it, too, was becoming old-fashioned to the young . . . . How sad for him. How awful for us." Copland angrily replied to *New York Times* writer Donal Henahan that "it was rather naive of him to imagine that you can just happily go on doing what you always had been doing and get away with it." Unfortunately, Copland's composing trickled to a standstill, though he stayed active as a conductor and lecturer until the mid-1980s. He suffered from diabetes and had suffered two strokes in the three weeks before his death. **Sources:** *Detroit Free Press,* December 3, 1990; *New York Times,* December 3, 1990; *Time,* December 17, 1990; *Times* (London), December 4, 1990.

Carmine Coppola

Born June 11, 1910, in New York City (some sources say Italy); died of a stroke, April 26, 1991, in Northridge, CA. Composer, conductor, and flutist. A classical flutist who spent years playing with such groups as the Detroit Symphony Orchestra, the Los Angeles Civic Opera, and the NBC Orchestra in New York City, Carmine Coppola received the most recognition for the music he wrote for motion pictures, specifically those produced or directed by his son, Francis Ford Coppola. Before migrating to Hollywood, Coppola played and arranged music for the Radio City Music Hall Orchestra, and conducted Broadway musicals including *Kismet* and *Once upon a Mattress*. His first Hollywood project was at his son's urging—the score for his son's adaptation of the 1968 Broadway musical *Finian's Rainbow*. Coppola settled into California and composing for movies for the rest of his life.

Coppola once told the *Los Angeles Times* that he "always felt the public hadn't heard my music until I started writing for the films a little bit." That little bit included an Oscar, which he shared with Nino Rota for the score of 1974's *Godfather II*. Coppola had composed the music for the original *Godfather* movie, and went on to score his son's films *Apocalypse Now*, *The Outsiders*, *Gardens of Stone*, *The Black Stallion*, and *Godfather III*. One of his most impressive accomplishments of musical composition was a 3,112-hour score for *Napoleon*, a 4-hour French silent epic made by Abel Gance. The movie was reconstructed by Francis Ford Coppola in 1981—the original music by Arthur Honegger was lost, with only a few bars remaining. The music that Carmine Coppola then "composed for *Napoleon* may just be the ticket for popular acceptance," said Vincent Canby of the *New York Times*. Although the movie never became popular, Coppola toured with an orchestra and conducted his music at special showings of the film; however, he did not play the flute himself: "I don't have the chops left," he told the *Los Angeles Times* during the *Napoleon* tour, "I haven't been practicing." His daughter, actress Talia Shire, broke into the movies with the *Godfather* sagas, and then achieved fame as boxer Rocky Balboa's wife in the *Rocky* movies. Coppola is survived by both children and his wife, lyricist Italia Pennino, with whom he made cameo appearances in the *Godfather* movies. **Sources:** *Los Angeles Times*, April 27, 1991; *New York Times*, April 28, 1991; *Washington Post*, April 28, 1991.

Nancy Cruzan

Born c. 1957; died of dehydration, December 26, 1990, in Mount Vernon, Mo. Subject of right-to-die debate. Nancy Cruzan's death after eight years in a coma became a powerful symbol and lesson in the national right-to-die controversy. In 1983 Cruzan survived a car accident in which she suffered irreversible brain damage and which left her breathing, but insensate. Five years later, Cruzan's parents began a legal battle to free her from the artificial life support system she depended on for her physical survival. Despite the fact that former co-workers testified that Nancy would not have wanted to live "like a vegetable," according to *Time*, and that doctors offered no hope for her recovery, the fight to remove Cruzan's feeding tube took three years and went to the U.S. Supreme Court. Besides expensive legal maneuvering, the Cruzans dealt with protestors and countersuits. Demonstrators picketed the hospital after Cruzan's feeding tube had been removed—their apparent concern for the young woman's life led them to camp out in pup tents and carry placards appealing to Nancy's parents. "How would you like to be starved to death?" read one sign during the protest, which *Washington Post* reporter Paul Hendrickson called "a vulgar circus come to town."

Thankful for what he felt to be Nancy's release from life, her father, Joe Cruzan, told *People*: "Hundreds of thousands of people can rest free, knowing that when death beckons, they can meet it face-to-face with dignity. I think this is quite an accomplishment [for Nancy], and I'm damn proud of her." As a result of the Cruzans' crusade, consciousness has been raised about the issue of euthanasia. The Society for the Right to Die, based in New York City, received 800,000 requests for living-will forms when Nancy Cruzan's case was being decided in the Supreme Court. *Time* reported that Congress passed a law requiring Medicare- and Medicaid-funded institutions to inform patients of their right-to-die options.

The person at the middle of the controversy was remembered as a lively outdoorswoman. Nancy was coming home from her night shift job at a cheese factory on January 11, 1983, when her car went out of control on a patch of ice and she was thrown from her vehicle about 33 feet. She did not breathe for approximately 20 minutes, which caused brain damage. Some who supported Nancy Cruzan's right to die said that had technology not interfered, Nancy would have died that day anyway, instead of eight years later. Others, anti-euthanasia protestors, claimed that having saved her life, the technology had to be allowed to extend it. Don Lumkins, director of the Missouri Rehabilitation Center in which Cruzan lived for eight years, believed the latter, but felt he had to enforce the court decision. He told the *Washington Post* that "it wasn't the protestors on the outside who were against this thing. *We* were against it. *I* was against it. But I had to uphold the law. I was caught. I felt locked in. And then, when you went out that door, there were these people from Operation Rescue or wherever yelling 'murderer' at us."

There were plans afoot to "rescue" Nancy, to reinsert her feeding tube or take her from the hospital, but all were checked by the presence of the police. Joe Cruzan felt no hostility towards the protestors who held signs that read "Feed Nancy." He told the *Chicago Tribune*, "To the ones who maybe didn't understand or didn't agree, we did what we felt we had to. We appreciate their prayers." Even taking coffee outside to the protestors, Mr. Cruzan told them that he, too, was praying for a miracle. Nancy Cruzan died twelve days after being disconnected from her life support system.

The U.S. Supreme Court had ruled that "medical treatment and food can be withdrawn from a patient, even an incompetent one, if there is 'clear and convincing evidence' that doing so conforms with the patient's wishes," as *Time* phrased it. Nancy Cruzan's case is similar to that of Karen Ann Quinlan (see *Newsmakers 85*); both lived in comas during court battles that decided their fates, and the moral arguments among the press and the public struck all of the same chords. But the removal of life support was allowed for different legal reasons—Quinlan's father was eventually granted the right to detach her respirator because the New Jersey Supreme Court ruled that a person's right to privacy allowed it. Quinlan remained alive for ten years after the respirator was removed, and died of pneumonia in 1985. All sides agree that the euthanasia question is far from solved by Cruzan's case, and it seems that while more people will insure themselves against Nancy's fate by writing living wills, there will no doubt be more Nancy Cruzans and Karen Ann Quinlans, as long as medical technology makes artificial life support possible. **Sources:** *Chicago Tribune*, December 30, 1990; *Los Angeles Times*, January 10, 1991; *People*, December 31, 1990; *Time*, January 7, 1991; *Washington Post*, December 28, 1990.

Xavier Cugat

Born January 1, 1900, in Barcelona, Spain; died of arteriosclerosis, October 27, 1990, in Barcelona. Bandleader. Xavier Cugat and his dance band, the Gigolos, popularized Latin rhythms with Americans through movie appearances, radio programs, and famous longtime gigs at such legendary clubs as the Coconut Grove of the Ambassador Hotel in Los Angeles, and the Waldorf-Astoria in New York. Although he was called the "Rumba King," Cugat

also conducted tangos and congas with the bow of his violin.

The prodigious violinist began his music career at the age of 6 with the Cuban Symphony before studying in Berlin, Paris, and New York (where he was instructed by Franz Kniedel and Damrosch), then playing at age 12 with the Havana Symphony. The boy moved to New York with his parents in 1912, and became a citizen of the United States in 1915. After spending five years as a violinist for tenor Enrico Caruso, Cugat could not find enough work as a musician, so he drew caricatures (a skill he learned from Caruso, who was reputed to be a wicked satirist) for the *Los Angeles Times*.

The true calling for Cugat was the dance band, however. He never felt an obligation to apologize for giving up his classical music career, saying instead: "I play music, make an atmosphere that people enjoy. It makes them happy. They smile. They dance. Feel good—who be sorry for that?" as his former employer, the *Los Angeles Times*, recalled. Cugat worked hard paying his dues as a bandleader at the Coconut Grove, filling in the breaks between the featured artists' sets. According to the *Los Angeles Times*, Cugat's "big break came when he was booked into the Starlight Roof of the Waldorf-Astoria . . . . His music was a big hit there, and became known as the 'Cugat Room' of the Waldorf for nearly a decade."

The 1930s and 1940s saw a wave of Latin-influence fads born of artists such as Cugat, Carmen Miranda, and Desi Arnaz. Cugat's bands were featured in many movies, beginning with 1942's *You Were Never Lovelier*, which starred the late Rita Hayworth. Usually appearing as himself, he "led his orchestra in several MGM musicals of the 1940s, including *Bathing Beauty*," according to the *Washington Post*. "It was his splashy, tropical Hollywood films, such as *Neptune's Daughter*, in which he starred with Esther Williams and Red Skelton in 1949, that made him a household name."

Cugat's personal life was equally famous. Married and divorced many times, his extramarital affairs made headlines—one Mrs. Cugat broke into a hotel room (with several private detectives) and caught her husband with Abbe Lane, who would later marry Cugat. Cugat himself broke into another hotel room to catch Lane with another man. Many of these antics Cugat would chalk up to his fiery temper. His most famous wife was the Spanish dancer Charo Baeza, known best as simply Charo. The *Washington Post* quoted a piece of his self-explanation: "If I had it to do all over, I'd marry the same ones. We always divorced for our careers. You cannot play the violin in Philadelphia when your wife is in Rome making a movie with Marcello Mastroianni." Though his heart ailments prompted an early retirement to Barcelona at age 78, Cugat formed a new band ten years later and toured Spain. **Sources:** *Los Angeles Times*, October 28, 1990; *Washington Post*, October 28, 1990.

Roald Dahl

Born September 13, 1916, in Llandaff, Wales; died of an infection, November 24, 1990, in Oxford, England. Author. The distinctive element about the best-selling children's book, *Charlie and the Chocolate Factory*, and its author, Roald Dahl, is a twist of cruelty. Naughty children in *Charlie* are turned into giant blueberries, or sucked into chocolate rivers, never to be heard from again. The iconoclastic Dahl rarely did or said what was expected from him; in 1990 he denounced *Satanic Verses* writer Salman Rushdie as a "dangerous opportunist," according to *Entertainment Weekly*, which also noted Dahl's "paranoid . . . anti-Semitic rants . . . [which] blighted his reputation even further." Yet so many adults and children read his books and watched movies made from his screenplays that he must have touched on something *all* people have in common (in 1990, Dahl, the "Master of Macabre" sold 2.3 million paperbacks in Britain alone). Dahl's use of violence and the surprise denouement was craftily masterful and as appealing as moral fairy-tale justice—Hansel pushes the witch into the oven, for instance. "My only moral dimension," *Entertainment Weekly* quoted Dahl, "is to teach children to read."

Dahl's own childhood was tinged with the same sort of bad luck that his fictional children experience. His Norwegian parents had left behind a farm in Oslo, and his father took up shipbroking in Wales—but died while Dahl was still a child. The family was not impoverished, and the young man attended good schools until he was 18 and joined the Exploring Society's expedition to Newfoundland. From there he joined Shell Oil and was working in Dar es Salaam, Tanzania, when World War II started. He joined the Royal Air Force immediately, eventually becoming a wing commander. In 1943 Dahl was posted in Washington, D.C., when C. S. Forester, author of the Captain Horatio Hornblower books, asked him to write some pieces about his war experiences for the *Saturday Evening Post*. After writing a book and a few collections of short stories, Dahl made his first mark with 1953's *Someone Like You*, "a collection of cleverly morbid stories," opined the London *Times*.

In 1960 Dahl and his wife, actress Patricia Neal, began writing stories for their five children. "Children are great judges of stories," *People* quoted him as saying. "Any parent who does the bedtime ritual of spinning fairy tales into nightly serials knows this only too well." *James and the Giant Peach* (which begins with James's parents being eaten by a rhino at the zoo) came in 1961, and *Charlie and the Chocolate Factory* was a huge success in 1964. The tale was eventually made into a movie starring Gene Wilder as the weird chocolate maker, Willy Wonka. Dahl disliked most of the films made from his work, and "in one instance asked for his name to be removed from the credits," according to the London *Times*. Other screen adaptations of Dahl's works include *Chitty Chitty Bang Bang*, a 1968 Walt Disney film starring Dick Van Dyke, and the James Bond spy thriller, *You Only Live Twice*, which starred Sean Connery. His contributions to television featured 22 stories specially adapted for *Tales of the Unexpected*.

Not without their setbacks, the Dahls lost one of their children, Olivia, in 1962, and Patricia suffered from debilitating strokes in 1965, the effects of which Dahl nursed her through for "a particularly grueling" three years, said *People*. They were divorced in 1983, after 30 years of marriage and six months later Dahl married Patricia's former close friend, Felicity Crosland. Dahl then "got his share of intrusive tabloid publicity," pronounced the London *Times*. Scored as having been personally unfaithful, Dahl's literature also took a beating from the critics, who declared him at different times to be antisocial, antifeminist, and certainly too violent for children. Dahl rejected these concerns and revealed the formula for his successful children's stories in the *New York Times:* portraying parents as antagonists. "It's the path to their affections . . . . Parents and schoolteachers are the enemy. The adult is the enemy of the child because of the awful process of civilizing this thing that when it is born is an animal with no manners, no moral sense at all." Some would say, then, that Dahl was especially equipped to understand children—and possibly the secret lives of adults. **Sources:** *Entertainment Weekly*, December 7, 1990; *New York Times*, November 24, 1990; *People*, December 10, 1990; *Times* (London), November 24, 1990.

Samuel Doe

Full name, Samuel Kanyon Doe; born May 6, 1952, in Tuzon, Liberia; died of gunshot wounds, September 2 (some sources report dates throughout the month), 1990, in Monrovia, Liberia. President of Liberia. Samuel Doe's reign as president of Liberia was as bloody as any of his tyrannical predecessors', but support from the United States may have allowed Doe to be a more efficient despot than the others. As a young first sergeant in the Liberian army, Doe was chosen to be part of a special group trained by the American Special Forces, or Green Berets. Liberia itself was founded as a West African colony in 1822 by freed American slaves, and became a republic in 1847. The so-called Americo-Liberians until recently led the country composed of sixteen major tribes. In Doe's lifetime, Liberia enjoyed approximately $500 million in aid; many agree that this U.S. money was used by the American government to secure the alliance of Liberia in the event of a Libyan-U.S. conflict, but that in effect, the funds were used by the Liberian goverment to support Doe's bloody domestic policies.

A member of the Krahn tribe, Doe had expressed dismay that his military career was limited because the highest officer positions were given to Americo-Liberians. After dropping out of high school, Doe entered the military in the footsteps of his father, who had been a private in the Liberian armed forces. His ties with the Marxist Progressive Alliance of Liberia (PAL) and the Movement for Justice in Africa (MOJA) were probably expressions of support for their goals of social restructuring to eliminate racism. The leaders of these two groups were given important posts in the government after the Doe-led coup of April 12, 1980. Doe claimed when taking office that his goals were to free the Liberian people from prejudice and poverty, and none of his many supporters seemed to guess that he would be as personally vulnerable to corruption and cruelty as his predecessors. The political party that was formed to support Doe and his followers was named the People's Redemption Council.

"Gruesome acts defaced the inception of his regime, continued during its entire course and signalled its violent end," said the London Times. Former president William Tolbert had been shot in his palace, and the battle with palace guards had claimed twenty-eight lives. Some sources state that the bodies were thrown into unmarked graves and that Doe had personally eviscerated Tolbert before throwing his body in a trench. Soon after the coup, Doe forces rounded up ninety officials from the previous government, and had thirteen of the most important administrators tried without representation for crimes against the Liberian people. All thirteen were shot in a public execution. Still, United States officials who promoted aid to Liberia looked on hopefully, according to Time, as Doe seemed to them to be "refreshingly simple," eschewing the traditional president's limousine for a Chevette. Time explained this lapse in political savvy in context: "This was the heyday of [United Nations representative] Jeane Kirkpatrick's theory that traditional dictatorships of the Third World were more amenable to democratization than totalitarian regimes of the left."

Doe officially became president in 1985, following pressures from the U.S. to hold free elections. Generally believed to be rigged, the election results favored him at 50.5 percent. Doe soon encountered the first of many coup attempts against his government, this one led by a former colleague, General Thomas Quiwonkpa. The London Times reported that after the general was seized and executed, "Doe later appeared in public chewing pieces of Quiwonkpa's flesh, thus ritually assuming the powers of his vanquished government." Corruption was still the rule; the World Bank suspended its operations in Liberia and was followed closely by the International Monetary Fund's withdrawal. Soon even the United States retreated, with Congress reducing aid from $76 million in 1985 to $11 million in 1990 because of tales of graft and repression.

The coup that finally overturned Doe began as a two-pronged rebellion. A former government official who had been charged with embezzlement, Charles Taylor, competed with Prince Johnson for the role of official rebel leader. Both are from the Gio tribe, and Johnson once belonged to Taylor's rebel force, the National Patriotic Front of Liberia (NPFL). While the presidential palace was under attack, Doe offered an interim administration, with elections to be held in January of 1991, but the rebels would not be appeased. He escaped briefly but was wounded and captured in a battle with Prince Johnson's forces, according to Time, which said that Doe died during interrogation. According to Time, in the last months of Doe's administration, 5,000 lives were lost in a three-way civil war. Rebel factions and Doe loyalists continued fighting after Doe's death, and many sources survey the ruins of Liberia and see no end in sight. The whereabouts of Doe's wife Nancy and their two children were not reported. **Sources:** *Chicago Tribune*, September 16, 1990; London *Times*, September 13, 1990; *Time*, August 20, 1990; September 24, 1990; October 29, 1990.

Richard Englund

Born c. 1932; raised in Seattle, Wash.; died of leukemia, February 15, 1991, in New York City. Dance company director. As the head of the Joffrey Ballet's second company, Richard Englund was a pioneer in the American regional dance movement. After his appointment as director in 1985, Englund toured the United States with the Joffrey II Dancers in the capacity of teacher and choreographer; the *Chicago Tribune* said that Englund "trained young dancers to be sensitive to nuances of style and acquainted them with anatomy, notation, dance history and stage makeup." At the time of his death, Englund was overseeing a choreographic workshop for the Joffrey.

Previous to his tenure with the famous ballet company, Englund directed the Ballet Repertory Company, the second company of the American Ballet Theatre, for 13 years. The *Los Angeles Times* reported that Englund changed that troupe "from a student organization to a respected company that toured worldwide." Englund's accomplishments as a dance coordinator began with his founding the dance department at the Governor's School of North Carolina, running the Alabama State Ballet and the Huntington Dance Ensemble. As a young man, Englund had danced with the American Ballet Theatre, the National Ballet of Canada, and the Metropolitan Opera Ballet. **Sources:** *Chicago Tribune*, February 20, 1991, February 24, 1991; *Los Angeles Times*, February 18, 1991.

Hamilton Fish

Born December 7, 1888, in Garrison, N.Y; died of heart failure, January 18, 1991, in Cold Spring, N.Y. Congressman. It is hard to imagine a politician with a more impressive pedigree, or more prominent roots in the history of the United States. A descendant of Peter Stuyvesant, the last Dutch governor of New York, Fish's great-grandfather, Nicholas Fish, was an aide to General George Washington, and his grandfather, also named Hamilton Fish, had been a governor of New York, a senator from the same state, and a U.S. secretary under President Ulysses S. Grant.

Fish assumed the politician mantle soon after his graduation from college, and was launched into a career to be distinguished by isolationist ideals and frequent clashes with four-term President Franklin D. Roosevelt. Opposed to American involvement in World War II until the Japanese attack on Pearl Harbor, Fish believed in letting Europe settle its own problems, and had lobbied for more spending on defensive weapons pointed at the Soviet Union during the Cold War. The *Los Angeles Times* recalled a speech Fish made during a Conservative party fund raiser in 1990, at the age of 101. He told his audience, "I have always opposed war, and sometimes it has made trouble for me. But I have always believed in defense, to help prevent it. I often feel I am a voice in the wilderness. But what can one man do?"

In 1914, four years after the impressive football player graduated from Harvard, Fish was elected to the state assembly, completing his term in 1916. He was commissioned on July 15, 1917, to the National Guard, and led a company of black Americans in combat in World War I. Perhaps this experience with war was to flower into isolationism, but it also made Fish a lifelong supporter of civil rights, "before there was any such things," he told the *Los Angeles Times*. Fish himself was awarded the Croix de Guerre, the American Silver Star, and was cited in the War Department general orders; he was considered a war hero when he was discharged in 1919. Fish's war record no doubt assisted his election to fill the vacancy in Congress that year made by the departure of Edmund Platt. Fish was reelected in 1920, and served until Franklin Roosevelt's last reelection in 1945. Fish was a thorn in the side of that president; Roosevelt called him "unholy" during his last campaign. Fish believed that Roosevelt had thrust the United States into World War II against its real wishes, then given away the spoils of war to Soviet leader Joseph Stalin in Eastern Europe.

Fish was also a prolific author whose last book, *Tragic Deception*, was about World War II—he completed it at the age of 95. Fish's progeny carries on the family's political tradition: Hamilton Fish, Jr., is a Republican representative from New York, and Fish's grandson, Hamilton Fish III, a former publisher of *The Nation*, unsuccessfully ran for Congress in 1988. Fish was twice widowed, divorced in his 90s, and is survived by his fourth wife, Lydia Abrogio. **Sources:** *Chicago Tribune*, January 27, 1991; *Los Angeles Times*, January 20, 1991.

Eugene Fodor

Born Jenoe Fodor c. 1906, in Leva, Hungary; died of a brain tumor, February 18, 1991, in Litchfield, Conn. Travel guide writer and publisher. The beauty of a Fodor guidebook is that it educates the traveler about the spirit of a country, not just the must-visit hotels and restaurants. A travel guide pioneer, Fodor was much imitated in his lifetime, though few guidebook compilers have reached his preeminence. In addition to his popular travel guides—which were not all actually written by their founder—Fodor wrote *On the Continent* in 1936, *Europe* in 1937, and *France* in 1951. The first particularly was a great feat of skill and included sections by playwrights and journalists. According to the London *Times,* Fodor's philosophy was that a guidebook should benefit travelers "crossing each other's boundaries in a peaceful, useful and joyous invasion."

Educated at Grenoble University in France, Fodor wanted to travel throughout Europe but was short of funds. "I wrote all the shipping lines in those days and offered my services as an interpreter and got a job with the French line," he told the *Los Angeles Times.* Fodor was fluent in six languages and considered himself "adequate" in four others at the time World War II began; he became an intelligence officer in the U.S. Army after Nazi Germany annexed the Sudetenland of Czechoslovakia. Later in his life Fodor denied charges that he had been an agent of the Central Intelligence Agency then, but conceded that he had, in fact, cooperated with the agency.

The Fodor guidebooks, which are generally held to be more budget-oriented than those offered by competitors Michelin and Baedeker, sell approximately 200 million copies a year and are often supplemented with pictorial guide videotapes. In 1968 Fodor reduced his role in Fodor's Modern Guides and sold the company; it was sold again in 1986 to Random House, at which time Fodor effectively retired. Awards for Fodor's travel books have included the 1959 French Grand Prix de Litterature de Tourisme, a special award from the 1969 Spanish International Travel Book Contest, and the 1972 British Tourist Authority Award. **Sources:** *Chicago Tribune,* February 24, 1991; *Los Angeles Times,* February 20, 1991; *Times* (London), February 20, 1991; *Washington Post,* February 20, 1991.

Margot Fonteyn

Full name, Margot Fonteyn de Arias; born Margaret Hookham, May 18, 1919, in Reigate, Surrey, England; died of cancer, February 21, 1991, in Panama City, Panama. Ballet dancer. Few names in the world of ballet are as mythically evocative as Margot Fonteyn's. A legend comparable to dancers Anna Pavlova and Alicia Markova, Fonteyn was paired most famously with Rudolph Nureyev. Before choreographer George Balanchine made his mark, ballerinas were not necessarily lithe and flat-chested; Fonteyn had a real figure, and what she lost in athleticism in her later career, she corrected with flawless expressiveness. The *Los Angeles Times* commented that "she was...extraordinarily sensitive to the musical impulse at a time when many of her rivals were distinctly amusical." Lifelong modesty and renowned poise combined in a woman who was often gently self-deprecating, yet Fonteyn saw herself objectively, and assessed her strengths and weaknesses accurately. The *Los Angeles Times* quoted Fonteyn as having written, "Great artists are people who find the way to be themselves in their art. Any sort of pretension induces mediocrity in art and life alike."

Fonteyn began ballet lessons at age four 4, encouraged by her mother, who at first wanted her to learn to tap-dance. The young prodigy danced as a snowflake in *The Nutcracker* at age 14; by 17 she was the prima ballerina of Great Britain's Royal Ballet. Her extraordinary talent came to the attention of the late Frederick Ashton, Britain's foremost choreographer, who immediately drafted her for his *Apparitions* of 1936 and composed many other works for her during her career. His final gift was *Birthday Offering,* which he composed for her 60th birthday, a few years before she retired.

When Fonteyn was nearing the traditional retirement age—for dancers—Rudolph Nureyev defected from the Soviet Union. Nureyev was, as she said, young enough to be her son, but they had a rapport on stage that was unmatched. At age 46 she danced with Nureyev in a Covent Garden, London, production of *Romeo and Juliet,* a performance that received 43 curtain calls in 40 minutes.

Some speculated that her career lasted longer than it might have because she needed the money to pay for the care of her husband. Dr. Roberto de Arias had been appointed Panamanian ambassador soon after their marriage in 1955; Fonteyn gracefully executed her diplomatic duties while still pursuing her dancing. The London *Times* reported that "when her husband fell from political favor she supported his attempts to regain power in his own country...she personally nursed her husband for 25 years until his death after he had been shot and crippled by an associate with a personal grudge."

Fonteyn herself was ill with cancer for years before her death, though she hid the fact as best she could.

Jane Hermann, co-director of the American Ballet Theater, said in the *Chicago Tribune*, "She was extremely valiant this last year, and a great lady to the end." To *People*, Hermann said, "She was part and parcel of the creation of some of the great masterpieces of our time." *People* also quoted British poet Sacheverell Sitwell, who called her "a bird of beautiful plumage taking pleasure and exulting in its wings." Margot Fonteyn spent the last years of her life on her husband's Panamanian farm, traveling often to receive tributes from around the world. **Sources:** *Chicago Tribune*, February 22, 1991, February 24, 1991; *Los Angeles Times*, February 22, 1991; *People*, March 11, 1991; *Times* (London), February 22, 1991.

Northrop Frye

Born Herman Northrop Frye, July 14, 1912, in Sherbrooke, Quebec, Canada; died of a heart attack, January 23, 1991, in Toronto, Ontario, Canada. Literary critic, theorist, and educator. Northrop Frye was perhaps the most important North American twentieth-century writer on literary criticism. As an educator he was unrivaled in making his students "think very hard." Generations of University of Toronto's Victoria College graduates idolized him. As a critic he assumed philosophic responsibilities. "The literary critic serves society," he said in the *New York Times*, "by interpreting and decoding its historical fables." Frye's key to the mystery of human history was the myth and symbol contained in the Bible, from which he also believed all literary themes sprang. While Frye's "myth criticism" enjoyed an international peak of popularity in the 1950s, his two dozen works are widely held to be the most serious, durable, and influential of modern times. The Toronto *Globe and Mail* recalled a recent reviewer's remark that Frye's "only serious rival" was Aristotle. Frye believed that literary criticism is a means "to produce out of the society we have to live in, a vision of the society we want to live in."

Frye's mother was a teacher; she taught him to read, count, and play piano before enrolling him in the fourth grade at the age of eight. "My public school career was undistinguished," he commented wryly in the *Los Angeles Times*. "I always regarded it as one of the milder forms of penal servitude." His education continued at Victoria College, where Frye was an honors graduate in philosophy and English. He went on to Emmanuel College and was ordained into the Church in 1936. His experience as a pastor in

Saskatchewan was unsatisfying, however, so he returned to school. Frye earned a master's degree in English from Oxford University's Merton College. He eventually was awarded some 36 honorary doctorates from other institutions of higher education. Despite these laurels, the scholar was often described as quiet, spare of manner, and possessing a "self-deprecating" sense of humor.

Frye's first major work—published in 1947—proposed that William Blake, the eighteenth-century visionary poet and illustrator, provided a view of mainstream western literature through symbolism that was neither freakish nor illusive, as many believed. The famous Yale University author and critic Harold Bloom said that Frye "rescued one of the great poets from scholarly misapprehensions." Frye's examination of Blake was hailed far and wide as a signal of greatness to come. Indeed, the literary world was not disappointed by Frye's second offering. The *Los Angeles Times* reported that Frye's study of Blake and his "theory of literary symbolism and Biblical analysis" had paved the way for *Anatomy of Criticism: Four Essays*, considered to be his most important critical work. Frye described his masterpiece as a "synaptic view of the scope, theory, principles and techniques of literary criticism." The work has been standard scholarly reading around the world since its publication in 1957.

Although the body of his work espoused the same or similar dominant theories, Frye's subjects were varied and the ingenuity and thoughtfulness with which he approached them was always noted. In the *New York Times Book Review* article that discussed his last book, he was called "concise and dry, his erudition compendious. The first two books expressed exactly the nature of his interests: one was an anatomy, the other laid bare a symmetry. He was always getting down to the bare bones of things while demonstrating the way they could be articulated into larger and larger structures." The same reviewer noted that the later work also detailed the "vast imaginative complex" of literature, at the center of which Frye "located the Bible." **Sources:** *Los Angeles Times*, January 24, 1991; *New York Times*, January 25, 1991; *New York Times Book Review*, March 31, 1991; Toronto *Globe and Mail*, January 25, 1991; *Washington Post*, January 24, 1991.

Rajiv Gandhi

Born August 20, 1944, in Bombay, India; assassinated, May 21, 1991, in Sriperambudur, India. Former prime minister of India. The Nehru-Gandhi dynasty probably ended with the assassination of Rajiv Gandhi during his campaign to again become prime minister of his country. His mother was Indira Gandhi, who led India from 1966 to 1977, and from 1980 until 1984, when she was shot to death by two of her own Sikh bodyguards. Rajiv's grandfather was Jawaharlal Nehru, who was India's first prime minister after the country gained independence from the British in 1947. Rajiv Gandhi (no relation to Mohandas K. Gandhi, known as Mahatma) was an Indian nationalist and advocate of non-violence, and was reluctant to enter politics, but gave up his career as an airplane pilot and entered the arena because, according to the *Los Angeles Times*, he said that "it was something Mummy asked me to do." His politically astute brother, Sanjay, was killed in a 1980 airplane accident, and Indira wanted to develop Rajiv as an heir to the leadership of India; Rajiv easily won a seat on the Indian Parliament that same year. After his mother was assassinated he was sworn in within hours as prime minister; and although such an action is not provided for in the Indian constitution, a general election confirmed his position two months later. After five years, he was ousted from the government amid suspicions of personal corruption; despite the black mark, Rajiv Gandhi's reputation was judged clean enough to afford him a probable party victory in 1991 elections. The win was predicted by a narrow margin, and some sources speculated that Gandhi would have had to forge a coalition to govern India. Following his assassination and the general bloodshed surrounding the election, however, analysts are concerned for India's future as the "largest democracy on earth." Gandhi's widow, Sonia, a naturalized Indian but Italian by birth, politely refused offers to succeed her husband; his son is only 21 years old, and similarly unwilling. However, Gandhi's 19-year-old daughter Priyanka has not ruled out a political career; and *Time* quoted a "party worker" as having said, "Give her time, and she is definitely Prime Minister material."

During his term as prime minister, Cambridge-educated Gandhi tried to modernize India, and bring it into the 21st century, efforts which earned him the name "Computerji," or "Mr. Computer." He promoted economic self-reliance and was "hailed overseas for his efforts.... He began to break down a system under which government licenses were needed for all but the smallest enterprises, stultifying the economy and fostering corruption," the *Washington Post* reported. Gandhi's campaign in 1991 was based on pledges to lower the price of essentials, build affordable housing, improve the status of women,

and set up a special police force to deal with Muslim-Hindu tensions. Hindus make up 83 percent of the nation, whereas Muslims compose only 11 percent; soon after India gained its independence, it split into two nations, Pakistan being set aside primarily for the Muslims. Six weeks before he died, Gandhi launched a campaign against the right-wing Bharatiya Janata Party, which favors the deportation of Muslims to Pakistan. A nationalist, Gandhi called it a "dangerous party for the secular traditions of our country," as reported in the *Chicago Tribune*, and many political experts believe that religious and ethnic separatism, or communalism, threatens the democratic tradition in India in the 1990s.

The village where Gandhi was killed is located 30 miles from the city of Madras in the state of Tamil Nadu, home of the Tamil ethnic group. In 1987 Gandhi sent Indian troops to quell rioting among the Tamils in Sri Lanka, and some speculate this action earned him a fatal enmity. A band of guerrillas, the Tamil Tigers, are well known for assassinating by explosives those who oppose a separate state for the Tamils. While early reports of the assassination said that a bomb, which killed 14 others besides Gandhi, was hidden in a bouquet that a young Tamil woman presented to the campaigner; it was later confirmed that plastic explosives wired to a back brace the woman was wearing were set off by remote control. Gandhi was decapitated by the blow, and guards soon sealed off the area, where some 10,000 people had gathered, to search for his remains. Just as his father had lit his grandmother's funeral pyre, so did Ruhal Gandhi light the pyre of his father several days after the assassination. Some mourners attending the funeral broke through police lines to throw sticks of incense into the flames. **Sources:** *Chicago Tribune*, May 22, 1991; *Detroit Free Press*, May 22, 1991; *Los Angeles Times*, May 22, 1991; *Time*, June 3, 1991; *Washington Post*, May 22, 1991.

Stan Getz

Born February 2, 1927, in Philadelphia, PA; died of liver cancer, June 6, 1991, in Malibu, CA. Tenor saxophonist. Stan Getz was a jazz musician who left behind a precious legacy of studio and live recordings, illustrating a popular movement in jazz, one that concentrated on melody when many jazz musicians were deconstructing tunes with be-bop. Most jazz fans will best remember his smooth sax line backing Astrud Gilberto on the bossa nova hit, "The Girl From Ipanema," in the 1960s, or his "cool" jazz of the 1950s. He never stopped playing or recording; in the 1980s he made several outstanding acoustic albums, including a song, "Anniversary," which won a Grammy. "I loved Stan Getz," jazz musician and bandleader Dizzy Gillespie told the *New York Times*. "His major contribution to jazz was melody. He's the best melody player in jazz. And an incredible soloist, but I loved his melodies. He's right up there with all of them, all the greats. You can't get better than him."

Getz's mother encouraged him to develop his early musical talents, and he started playing bass in junior high school. "I was a withdrawn, hypersensitive kid. I would practice the saxophone in the bathroom, and the tenements [in the Bronx, where Getz was brought up] were so close together that in the summertime, when the windows would be open, someone from across the alley would yell, 'Shut that kid up,' and my mother would say, 'Play louder, Stanley.'" He switched to bassoon in his first year of high school, and instead of going to Juilliard on a music scholarship, Getz left school at 15 to work as a professional jazz musician with Jack Teagarden's band. "I was inordinately quick at picking up music," Getz told Joseph Hooper of the *New York Times* in an interview shortly before the musician's death. "I had about six months of lessons, and that was it. I never studied theory or harmony."

After a few months with Teagarden, Getz worked for Stan Kenton's orchestra, until he heard Kenton say that Lester Young, the legendary saxophonist, "was too simple." Getz took his inspiration from Lester Young, and like Young, he concerned himself more with melodic improvisation rather than the overall harmonic structure of a song. After Kenton, he played with Jimmy Dorsey, then recorded his first solo in the mid-1940s with Benny Goodman's band. In 1946, he recorded his first album with Charlie "The Bird" Parker's rhythm section. There was no doubt that he was a young genius. Drug use temporarily got in his way when he was arrested for robbing a drugstore; Getz fled to Denmark in 1958, and stayed for three years.

In 1962 Getz recorded *Jazz Samba* with guitarist Charlie Byrd, and put jazzy bossa nova onto the record charts. Getz told the *Los Angeles Times* that bossa nova is "a great hybrid, the true samba blended with cool jazz...just like a man and a woman getting together." The biggest single from *Jazz Samba* was "Desafinado"—which Getz took to calling "Dis Here Finado"—a tune that became one of the sax player's signatures. He collaborated with Astrud Gilberto in 1964 on *Getz/Gilberto*, the album containing "Girl From Ipanema," which won Getz the first of his 11 Grammys.

The success of his musical life was not echoed in his private life, though he remained active and hopeful to the end. Engaged at the time of his death to a woman in her mid-twenties named Samantha, whom he met in a California health food store, Getz survived a gruesome divorce that was only resolved in 1987, seven years after he filed. Monica, his second wife, complained of years of drug and alcohol abuse and infidelities, while his son, Steve, told the *New York Times Magazine* that their home was like "a war zone." Still a heavy smoker in 1991, Getz started on hard drugs early, at 16, "because some older, decadent jazz musicians wanted to turn a nice kid on. I didn't even know that smack [heroin] was habit-forming. In two weeks I was hooked and I spent 10 years trying to get off. A good Jewish boy doesn't take drugs," he told Hooper. And yet Getz believed that he didn't sacrifice freedom or sanity to drugs; as he told Hooper, "You make it sound so depressing. Yes the drugs and the drinking caught up with me in the end, but most of that time, I did what wanted. I had a ball." **Sources:** *Chicago Tribune*, June 8, 1991; *Globe and Mail* (Toronto), June 8, 1991; *Los Angeles Times*, June 7, 1991; *New York Times*, June 8, 1991; *New York Times Magazine*, June 9, 1991; *Washington Post*, June 8, 1991.

George Gobel

Born c. 1920, in Chicago, IL; died of complications following surgery, February 25, 1991, in California. Comedian. George Gobel's own comical character provided more humorous material for him throughout his days in radio and television than other comedians could find in a closetful of celebrities. The diminutive, round-faced jester with the crew cut professed on the first episode of *The George Gobel Show* not to understand his own appeal—"Now, it's not the greatest show in the world—I mean it's not hilarious. Jocular is what it—uh, humor...well, it might just keep you from getting sullen." *People* called him a cross between "Charlie Chaplin and Charlie Brown," the *New York Times* typed him as "folksy," and the *Los Angeles Times* contrasted Gobel's "underplayed, deadpan humor...to the other TV comics of the day—such frenetic entertainers as Milton Berle and Red Skelton." Later in his life, Gobel was a favorite on the talk show circuit, and appeared many times on the *Tonight Show* and *Hollywood Squares*.

Gobel began his career as an entertainer by imitating the customers in his father's grocery in Chicago. At the age of 11, he made his debut singing on the WLS Barn Dance radio revue, and then became a regular on radio's *Tom Mix Show*, where he was the admiring kid who held the hero's horse. He enlisted in the Army Air Corps in 1943, and was made a B-26 pilot instructor (after teaching himself to fly) in Frederic, Oklahoma. "You might laugh at that," he said in the *Los Angeles Times*, "but we must have done a good job down there because not one enemy plane got past Tulsa." He polished up the jokes he had told his comrades in the army and, after his discharge, took his act to the nightclubs of Chicago.

Gobel became a regular guest in 1952 on television's *Colgate Comedy Hour* and *The Spike Jones Show* after capturing the attention of CBS's Garry Moore. He was given his own show in 1954, which earned him an Emmy for outstanding new personality. The show featured Gobel's monologues, singing or dancing guest stars, and then skits about Gobel's aggravating wife, "Spooky Old Alice," who was always played by a male actor. In fact, Gobel and Alice Humecki had a reportedly happy marriage, which lasted 40 years. The show, however, was taken off the air after ratings slipped due to its slot opposite the popular *Gunsmoke* in 1960. Gobel then made several movies and appeared on stage, as well as making regular guest appearances on television to make his signature pronouncements: "Well, I'll be a dirty bird," and "You can't hardly get them no more." **Sources:** *Chicago Tribune*, February 25, 1991; *Los Angeles Times*, February 25, 1991; *New York Times*, February 25, 1991; *People*, March 11, 1991.

Charles H. Goren

Full name, Charles Hens Goren; born March 4, 1901, in Philadelphia, PA; died of a heart attack, April 3, 1991, in Encino, CA. Bridge expert. Goren was famous for his development of point-count bidding, which made the card game of bridge more accessible to amateurs. Also known for his many tournament successes, Goren, who was originally a lawyer, wrote twenty-six books and countless articles about contract bridge. Goren first became addicted to bridge after reading a book on the subject, and his rapid devotion to the game led him to reject a proffered judgeship in his native Philadelphia and then to abandon his law practice altogether in the mid-1930s. His first big win came in 1937, when he won the National Board-a-Match Teams. He would win

again seven times within 25 years. Although he became world champion in 1950, as a member of the American team of the Bridge Olympiad, Goren considered himself an amateur and often donated his winnings to charity. "By any standard he was one of the greatest bridge players and bridge writers in the world," bridge columnist Alfred Sheinwold told the *Los Angeles Times*. "He will be sorely missed." A true celebrity, Goren was host of a long-running television show on bridge, and made the cover of *Time* with the caption "The King of Aces." Goren had played with such notable figures as Dwight D. Eisenhower, the Luces of publishing fame, Prince Aly Khan, and movie star Humphrey Bogart.

The London *Times* characterized Goren as an atypically pleasant teacher, saying that "unlike many bridge experts, Goren was patient, genial and humourous, qualities that endeared him in his books and lectures, persuading many readers to stay with a game too complicated to learn under a less sympathetic taskmaster." After suffering a stroke that impaired his memory in 1972, Goren lived with his nephew Marvin in Encino, California. Goren was joined in his column that year by the actor and dedicated bridge player Omar Sharif, who had been captain of the Egyptian team in 1960's Bridge Olympiad. Sharif said he had learned to play by reading Goren's books. Goren's classic *Contract Bridge Complete* was in its 12th edition at the time of his death. He was still actively involved in the writing of the syndicated column, often sending notes and comments on yellow legal paper to the staff. He once said, "Some hands are so difficult to bid that they should be quietly dropped on the floor and re-dealt." **Sources:** *Chicago Tribune*, April 12, 1991; *Los Angeles Times*, April 12, 1991; *New York Times*, April 12, 1991; *Times* (London), April 13, 1991.

Martha Graham

Born May 11, 1894, in Allegheny, PA; died of congestive heart failure, April 1, 1991, in New York City. Choreographer, dancer. "Martha was the biggest dancer in our century, and no one else even came close," choreographer Agnes De Mille told the *Chicago Tribune*. "She was a gigantic figure, like a Stravinsky. She started not only a whole new school of dance, but a whole new form of theater." Like De Mille, Graham was inspired to dance by Ruth St. Denis; unlike De Mille, Graham only began dancing professionally at 22. She danced until the age of 76, but her choreographing career would span a total of 70 years. Graham began to choreograph in the late 1920s and 1930s in a way that would be called "quintessential American" because of its lack of European balletic ornament, and because it possessed a natural fluidity. She established the Dance Repertory Theatre in New York City in the 1930s, and later called it the Martha Graham School for Contemporary Dance. Many critics and champions of Graham have often referred to her choreography in linguistic terms; the *Chicago Tribune*, for instance, said that "by creating dances that probed so deeply into the human psyche, Miss Graham established a new vocabulary for dance in America." Graham did more than give rise to a new dance vocabulary; she pulled a new language from the mouth of dance. "Movement is one speech that cannot lie," she said in 1958.

Graham expressed a desire not only to catch the "essence of emotion" in her dances, but to portray every possible feeling. The *Washington Post* quoted her as saying that she wanted "to move in a technically clean, clear fashion, and so passionately.... You've got to make your body do every movement; if it's the thrust of a shoulder, as if it were being done for the first time, as if you're listening to the ancestral footsteps." Critic Walter Terry described in the *Chicago Tribune* Graham's early *Lamentations* and its portrait of "a figure contracted in agony, seeking unconsciously the safe position of the fetus, pulled and twisted by visceral pains of anguish, letting the body rack itself in self-flagellation, pushing the feet into the floor, looking and reaching up to escape or to God, shrouded in the confining fabric of sorrow." Peter Sparling, once a principal dancer with the Martha Graham Dance Company, and the University of Michigan's School of Dance chairman in the early 1990s, told the *Ann Arbor News* of Graham's courage: "She was not afraid to go for the jugular. Just look at the titles of the pieces—*Cave of the Heart, Dark Meadow, Errand into the Maze*—that equate the body with a landscape of extremes of emotion."

Graham drew her inspiration from American writers such as Nathaniel Hawthorne and Emily Dickinson, but also used Greek and Native American sources. Graham's performance as the incestuous Jocasta, in her own *Night Journey* (based on the Oedipal myth) was widely acclaimed and imitated. The prototypical populist ballet *Appalachian Spring* was composed expressly for Graham by the late Aaron Copland (Also in *Newsmakers 91*). Among others who had works commissioned by Graham were Norman Dello Joio, Samuel Barber, Gian-Carlo Menotti, and William Schuma. Graham's reputation as a teacher was

unmatched. De Mille said of her in the *New York Times* that "she explained what she was doing and explained unforgettably." Her dance company produced such famous (and in turn influential) dancers and choreographers as Merce Cunningham, Anna Sokolow, Pearl Lag, and Paul Taylor. Graham's last work was her 180th, and set to the *Maple Leaf Rag* of Scott Joplin. "Our body is our glory, our hazard, and our care," De Mille remembered Graham saying. **Sources:** *Ann Arbor News*, April 7, 1991; *Chicago Tribune*, April 2, 1991; *Detroit Free Press*, April 3, 1991; *New York Times*, April 7, 1991; *Washington Post*, April 2, 1991.

Red Grange

Real name, Harold Grange; born June 13, 1903, in Forksville, Pa.; died of pneumonia, January 28, 1991, in Florida. Football player. As a running back for the University of Illinois football team and for the Chicago Bears, Red Grange was the idol of football fans everywhere for almost 60 years. Grange was a charter member of the Professional Football Hall of Fame and a member of the National Football Foundation's College Football Hall of Fame. Called "one of the game's five pioneers" by the *Los Angeles Times* and "the Babe Ruth of football" by the *Washington Post*, Grange was part of a golden era in American sports; his impressive accomplishments and sincere humility remain a standard of measure for all athletes.

Grange began his famous career with a virtual miracle: In the first moments of the 1924 game inaugurating the University of Illinois's new Memorial Stadium, Number 77 returned a kick for 95 yards to score a touchdown against Michigan for the Illini "while many people were still finding their seats," reported the *New York Times*. He scored five touchdowns that day with 402 total offensive running yards. Already dubbed "Red" for his red hair, Grange soon gained a new nickname—the "Galloping Ghost"—for his elusive and seemingly unstoppable running technique. In his 20 games with Illinois, Grange chalked up 3,637 rushing yards and 31 touchdowns before being signed with George Halas's Chicago Bears in 1925. Illinois coach Bob Zuppke, upset that the three-time All-American had been drafted before graduation, called Halas and worked out an agreement with the National Football League that ultimately regulated the drafting of collegians. The Ghost's career was not marred by this incident, however; he went on to even greater glory with the

Bears, interrupted only once by a two-season stint with the New York Yankees football team.

Quitting the gridiron in 1938 because of injuries, Grange launched a brief career as an assistant coach, then went on to sports broadcasting, commenting on college and professional football for television and radio. He covered 312 Bears games between 1947 and 1961. In his later years Grange increased his fortune as a retiree in Florida by purchasing an orange grove and an insurance agency, and investing in real estate. He had also enjoyed a brief but profitable acting career in a movie serial called *The Galloping Ghost*. The *New York Times* reported that Grange's happiest memory of football was not actually his miraculous running game against Michigan, but rather, a less remarkable task: The Illini won a game at Iowa when Earl Britton kicked a 55-yard field goal. "I held the ball for him," Grange said. **Sources:** *Chicago Tribune*, January 29, 1991; *Los Angeles Times*, January 29, 1991; *New York Times*, January 29, 1991; *Washington Post*, January 29, 1991.

Graham Greene

Born October 2, 1904, in Berkhamsted, Hertfordshire, England; died of a blood disease, April 3, 1991, in Vevey, Switzerland. Novelist. Graham Greene wrote critically of the most important facets of human existence: how human beings treat each other and think of their souls. The *New York Times* posited that Greene's "deepest concerns were spiritual: a soul working out its salvation or damnation amid the paradoxes and anomalies of 20th-century existence." His novels are considered his most important literary contributions, but because they were mainly about espionage and intrigue, they were not taken so seriously as to afford Greene a Nobel Prize for literature, though he seemed to many observers to be an obvious choice. A fellow mystery writer, John LeCarre (who had been, like Greene, employed in British Intelligence) said in the *Detroit Free Press* that Greene had been his "guiding star. He was a great and magical writer, hard to fit into any pattern." Attracted to peril as a tool for revealing true character, Greene used his own travels to color his novels, recreated the aura of danger, and captured dialogue as it occurred in such situations. He once said, "When we are not sure, we are alive."

The *Washington Post* said that Greene "focused on man at his most violent, weak and petty while still being susceptible to redemption through divine grace." The images of mayhem and death he witnessed in his travels through parts of the third world (beginning in young adulthood, and continuing throughout his life) were used as book material, and later journalistic sojourns bore fruit in successive novels. *The Heart of the Matter* was a synthesis of Greene's days in West Africa with British Intelligence in the 1940s. *The Quiet American's* material was gathered during a trip to French Indochina (now Vietnam) while Greene was a correspondent for the *New Republic*. Many accused Greene of despising Americans because of his left-wing politics and certain criticisms in *The Quiet American*, but Greene insisted that the novel reflected the facts of what he had observed. "I have to travel because I have to see the scene." he said in *Newsweek*. "I can't invent it."

Literary influences on Greene included Henry James, Joseph Conrad, and Ford Madox Ford. Greene's books were translated into 27 languages and sold more than 20 million copies in hardcover and paperback editions. Aside from his novels of intrigue, he wrote travel books, essays, short stories, two volumes of autobiography, and stories for children. Many of Greene's works were used as material for plays and screenplays. His later works were less successful than his earlier had been, receiving uneven reviews, which he attributed to his somber philosophy. Greene said, "One fails in all sorts of ways in life, doesn't one, which are much more important than writing books. In human relations and that sort of thing." Greene received the Companion of Honor in 1966 from Queen Elizabeth II, the Companion of Literature in 1984, and, in 1986, the Honor of Merit. He had seen the publication of his last work, *The Last Word and Other Stories*, two months before his death. **Sources:** *Chicago Tribune*, April 4, 1991; *Detroit Free Press*, April 4, 1991; *New York Times*, April 4, 1991, April 14, 1991; *Newsweek*, April 15, 1991.

Armand Hammer

Born May 21, 1898, in New York City; died of natural causes, December 10, 1990. International businessman. The son of Soviet parents, New Yorker Armand Hammer gleaned much from both Soviet and American culture and ideals. A consummate deal-maker—and non-practicing doctor—Hammer dabbled in numerous fields, settling into his ultimate calling relatively late in life: oil and the Occidental Petroleum Corporation. Controversial for his prestige-hungry ways—a *New York Times* editorial said he "possessed an immense ego and a gift for self-promotion"—Hammer was criticized for using his film company, Hammer Films, to document his travels, and for creating a white elephant museum in his own name, all at the cost of his shareholders. Hammer himself owned only one of the company's shares at the end of his life. The London *Times* summed up his character thus: "He was a 'builder,' but more than anything else, he was a deal-maker. 'I don't think he will ever stop,' his younger brother Victor once said. 'It's not making money. It's the question of confirming his judgment.'"

Promoting political calm between the United States and the Soviet Union was a lifelong priority for Hammer; it is no coincidence that he made many large transactions with the Soviet government to furnish goods like fertilizer. The *New York Times* opined that he could, however, be genuinely philanthropic. "He was modest about achievements that were . . . easily verifiable, as when he assembled and subsidized an international team of physicians to treat victims of Chernobyl." Hammer's fascination with the Soviet Union was passed down from his father, Dr. Julius Hammer, who had met Bolshevik leader Nikolai Lenin in 1907 and was one of the founders of the American Communist party. As a young man Armand Hammer was sent to the Soviet Union to collect fees from the Red Army, which his father's pharmaceutical firm had been supplying. The London *Times* said that "delivering the medical supplies was the closest Hammer came to practising medicine although in the East he was always known as 'The Doctor.'"

Before Joseph Stalin took power in the Soviet Union and Hammer left that country to settle permanently in New York City, he lived in a 24-room mansion in Moscow, married a Russian, and ran several business concerns, including a fur station in Siberia. *Time* magazine reported that in the late 1920s he returned to the United States with his brother, with whom he "had astutely bought a freighter load of furniture and bibelots from Russian flea markets and hotel lobbies and sold it as 'the Romanov treasure.'" Hammer's timing contributed to his success; he bought a firm that made wooden casks right before the repeal of Prohibition, and became the nation's leading supplier of beer barrels. He settled in Los Angeles in 1956, determined to retire. On a lark, he invested in oil and found himself the owner of a tiny, almost-bankrupt oil firm called Occidental. Hammer developed the firm tremendously in the roughly four decades following until it became the nation's sixteenth largest industrial company. He remained chairman until his death. That event brought international speculation that Occidental would be sold or dividends to some 450,000 shareholders cut. The *Wall Street Journal* predicted, however, that "Occidental will pare itself down," instead of splitting and selling off components. **Sources:** *Chicago Tribune,* December 12, 1990; *New York Times,* December 12, 1990, December 13, 1990; *Time,* January 28, 1991; *Times* (London), December 12, 1990; *Wall Street Journal,* December 12, 1990.

John Heinz

Born October 23, 1938, in Pittsburgh, PA; died in a plane crash, April 4, 1991, in Merion, PA. U.S. senator. John Heinz, known especially in Congress as a champion of domestic labor and the elderly, died in a plane crash which claimed the lives of six others on his plane and two on the ground. The twin-engine Piper and a helicopter collided over a school playground only fifteen minutes before recess, when the yard would have been filled with over 400 children. The senator had been en route from Williamsport to Philadelphia when the landing gear apparently jammed and a passing helicopter flew underneath the plane to assess the problem. After the collision, the vehicles burst into flame. The bulk of the debris landed 35 feet away from the playground, but some pieces landed close enough to kill two 6-year-olds. Teachers at the elementary school later received some training from therapists and trauma experts in an effort to help the students cope with the accident, but Pennsylvania was stunned by the loss of the prominent politician. "The people of the state of Pennsylvania have lost a great leader and the nation has lost a great senator," President Bush said in a statement reported by the *Chicago Tribune.*

After graduating from Massachusetts' prestigious Phillips Exeter Academy in 1956, Heinz attended Yale University, and received a masters of business administration from Harvard. He served in the Air Force, taught at Carnegie-Mellon University, worked for a family company, and won a House seat in 1971. From that year on, Heinz never lost an election. He was elected to the Senate for the first time in 1976. Heinz served on the Housing and Urban Affairs Committee and the Finance and Banking Committee, but was not known as a "major legislative figure," according to the *New York Times.* Nevertheless, the *Times* added that "the 52-year-old lawmaker left a legislative mark that was discernible and important." Heinz was among the wealthiest men in the Senate; as the heir to the H. J. Heinz food empire, he was worth between $9 million and $16 million. He was criticized in 1976 for investing $2.5 million of his own money into his election campaign.

Despite his privileged roots, Heinz was a popular choice among Pennsylvania voters for his defense of blue collar jobs. Pennsylvania's economy is dependent on an aging steel industry; the senator therefore supported legislation designed to protect Pennsylvania industry from foreign competition. Heinz was concerned about the many retirees in his state, and fought proposals, even those supported by his own party, to cut Medicare benefits. These moves did not make him the most popular of congressmen; there were reports that Heinz did not fulfill the expectations the Republican party had for him. The *Washington Post* reported that "he was eclipsed by Dick Thornburgh, who served eight years as governor and then became attorney general." Heinz was accused by some of being "aloof" and "patrician," but the prep school image was infinitely improved when George Bush took office. Senator Worth from Colorado, a friend from Heinz's days at Exeter with whom he worked on environmental issues, told the *Washington Post* that Heinz's "intense intelligence, sparkling charm and broad vision combined to make a rare and remarkable person." **Sources:** *Chicago Tribune*, April 5, 1991; *New York Times*, April 5, 1991; *Washington Post*, April 5, 1991.

Meir Kahane

Full name, Meir David Kahane; name originally Martin Kahane; born August 1, 1932, in Brooklyn, N.Y.; died of a gunshot wound in the neck, November 9, 1990, in Manhattan, N.Y. Militant rabbi, author, politician, founder of the Jewish Defense League (JDL) and the Kach Party. "I don't want to kill Arabs," Rabbi Meir Kahane was quoted in the *Detroit Free Press*, "I just want them to live happily, elsewhere." Behind these words is a racist and separatist doctrine that has incited crowds to riot and murder, and has further inflamed the delicate situation in the Middle East; Kahane's most extreme views often found receptive audiences in New York and Israel. "I say what you think," Kahane would tell his listeners. The rabbi met with a violent death (during a question-and-answer period following a speech) at the hands of an Egyptian-born Muslim. Retributive acts of racially motivated violence continued for days after the assassination; at a time when the Middle East struggles through the problems of the occupied, Arab-settled territories, Kahane's death was yet another incitement to conflict. The motto of Kahane's

JDL is "Never again," referring to 2,000 years of violence against Jews (especially the Holocaust of World War II), but his words and the legacy of the Kach Party and the JDL have insured that new atrocities against Arabs and Jews will occur.

As a young New Yorker Kahane was "steeped in right-wing Zionist [pro-Israel] tradition . . . The future rabbi joined the paramilitary Betar youth movement, training in the Catskills," according to the *New York Times*. Kahane has been described as a militant Zionist, but *People* said that his JDL eventually "repelled even hard-line Zionists in Israel." By 1963 he was living and writing his books, such as *Never Again!, Time to go Home*, and *Why Be Jewish? Intermarriage, Assimilation, and Alienation*, under the pseudonym Michael King. Within a few years he was appointed editor of the Jewish Press, a position he held until his activities on behalf of the JDL forced him to resign in 1968. Kahane left the United States in 1971 to establish the JDL in Israel. Since then, the league has escalated its militancy, and Kahane was arrested several times in Israel for promoting violent activities.

"When [Kahane] came to Israel in 1971, it was not a perfect democracy, but there were certain things that would not be said or considered, such as the use of violence against a civilian population," Dr. Ehud Sprinzak, an Israeli expert on the far right, said in the *New York Times*. Kahane and the Kach Party were barred from the Israeli parliament in 1988 because of a last minute law banning parties (specifically the Kach) that have racist platforms.

Many critics say that Kahane's murder was inevitable and that he would have approved of the vengeful beatings and deaths in New York and Jerusalem that ensued. *Newsweek* noted that "during the funeral procession in Jerusalem, young men in yellow T shirts—the signature color of Kahane's Kach movement—beat up at least four Arabs." A Palestinian couple was shot in New York in what was believed by some to be retributive violence, but may have been a robbery.

A *Maclean's* article of December 10, 1990, detailed the recent deaths in the Israeli/Palestinian conflict, and remarked on Kahane's continued influence: "His death led to an eruption of Jewish violence against Palestinians. 'Antagonism towards Arabs,' said Hanoch Smith, a veteran Israeli opinion pollster, 'is at an all-time high.'" The *Detroit Free Press* reported that the judge who issued bond to El Sayyid Nosair, Kahane's assassin, had received death threats. In these ways, the venomous legacy of Rabbi Meir Kahane takes its toll. **Sources:** *Contemporary Authors,*

Volume 112, Gale, 1985; *Detroit Free Press*, November 9, 1990, December 19, 1990; *Maclean's*, November 11, 1990; *New York Times*, November 11, 1990; *Newsweek*, November 19, 1990; *People*, November 19, 1990.

Jerzy Kosinski

Full name, Jerzy Nikodem Kosinski; born June 14, 1933, in Lodz, Poland; committed suicide by suffocation, c. May 3, 1991, in New York City. Writer. When Jerzy Kosinski was six years old, his parents sent him to the countryside of Nazi-occupied Poland with a friend, thinking that the pair could find sanctuary. The friend soon deserted the young Jewish boy, and during his wanderings Kosinski witnessed the very worst side of human nature. His first and best known novel, *The Painted Bird*, tells some of the most chilling tales ever about the Holocaust. Kosinski also brought his experiences to bear in two scholarly works (published under a pseudonym) about collective political behavior: *The Future is Ours, Comrade: Conversations With Russians* (1960), and *No Third Path* (1962). Kosinski escaped Poland (controlled by Communists after World War II) in 1957 by means of a grant to study at Columbia University, where he stayed until 1965, the year *The Painted Bird* was published. His second novel picked up the narrative of the first and detailed his abuse at the hands of repressive forces in Poland and his adjustment to "the technological society of the United States," according to the *New York Times*. Many critics felt that Kosinski's later novels never achieved the brilliance of his first two (with the exception of *Being There*, which was made into a popular movie.) *The Painted Bird* won the French literary award for the best foreign book in 1966, and *Steps* won the National Book Award in 1968.

Kosinski was struggling with illness at the time of his suicide. His wife, Katherina von Fraunhofer-Kosinski, said in the *Washington Post* that "my husband has been in deteriorating health as a result of a serious heart condition. He had become depressed by his growing inability to work, and by his fear of being a burden to me and his friends." She had found him in the bath with a plastic bag tied over his head; he had apparently committed suicide during the night.

Kosinski had spent the first six years of his life as the only child of intellectuals. His father was a classics professor and his mother was a concert pianist. After Kosinski was reunited with them and triumphed over a temporary speech impairment (he remained silent for five years), he naturally joined the academic life. Kosinski received master's degrees in sociology and history at the University of Lodz (where his father had taught) in the mid-1950s. He and his parents unsuccessfully tried for years to emigrate to Israel; eventually they were left behind when he went to the United States to study. The *Los Angeles Times* reported that Kosinski eventually effected a happy return to Poland: "In 1988, after the liberalization of Poland, Kosinski returned to the country he had fled 31 years before to a triumphal welcome. Branded since its first appearance as a traitorous work, *The Painted Bird* was being published by Poland's leading publishing house, Czytelnik. Crowds packed the auditoriums where he appeared... 'his outrageous statements, rich wordplay and puns quickly won over his audiences,' according to an Associated Press report from Warsaw." Back in the United States, Kosinski eventually taught at Yale, Wesleyan, and Princeton universities.

Kosinski's life in the United States was defined by his enormous prestige as a writer and defender of human rights. President of PEN from 1973 to 1975, Kosinski was also the director of the International League for Human Rights from 1973 to 1979, and was active in the American Civil Liberties Union. His fame also made him a target. In 1982, a cover story in the *Village Voice* accused him of false authorship (alleging that so-called "editors" authored most of his late novels) and of fabricating stories about his treatment in Poland. *New York Times* writer John Corry wrote a 6,444-word defense of Kosinski, claiming that the *Voice* had been a tool of a longtime campaign of defamation against the novelist which originated with the Communist party hierarchy in Poland. Kosinski's last novel, *The Heretic of 69th Street* (1984), an "'autofiction' in which he relentlessly lampooned his accusers and critics, was a disaster with reviewers and the public," according to the *Chicago Tribune*. The attack on his work must have seemed typical to Kosinski. "The current that runs through all of my fiction is that one can find humanity only in oneself.... These books are about confronting... a society that has a massive disregard of the individual," he once said. **Sources:** *Chicago Tribune*, May 5, 1991; *Globe and Mail* (Toronto), May 4, 1991; *Los Angeles Times*, May 4, 1991; *New York Times*, May 4, 1991; *Times* (London), May 6, 1991; *Washington Post*, May 5, 1991.

Nancy Kulp

Born in 1921; died of cancer, February 3, 1991, in Palm Desert, Calif. Actress. Nancy Kulp will be best remembered for her dead-on portrait of the always efficient, prim bluestocking Miss Jane Hathaway, Mr. Drysdale's secretary on television's *The Beverly Hillbillies*. Miss Hathaway yearned unrequitedly for hick stud Jethro Clampett—played by the robust Max Baer, Jr.—from 1960 to 1972 and then again in 1981 for the movie *The Return of the Beverly Hillbillies*, while trying to organize the affairs of the "Ozark clan" that had accidentally struck it rich in oil. Kulp was nominated for an Emmy Award in 1967, her only recognition in a business that did not often notice less-than-stunning women. Once labeled television's homeliest girl, slim and refined-looking Kulp was almost always cast as a funny but disappointed woman. Before the Jane Hathaway role, Kulp had appeared in other television programs including *The Bob Cummings Show* and *The Brian Keith Show*. Her movie roles were also usually comedic, like those in *The Model and the Marriage Broker*, *The Parent Trap*, and *Shane*.

Kulp, the daughter of an attorney and a schoolteacher, graduated from Florida State University with a degree in journalism and contributed some writing to the *Miami Beach Tropics* in the early 1940s. Kulp revealed in a *Los Angeles Times* interview that "[her] first love [had] always been journalism." After writing profiles on stars like Clark Gable and Errol Flynn, Kulp broke into a film career herself with several non-speaking parts. She found a third career late in life as a politician; Kulp had been elected to the Screen Actors Guild's board of directors in 1982, but was less successful in national politics. In 1984 she ran for Congress as a Democrat from her home district of Port Royal, Pennsylvania, but lost the race despite an endorsement from fellow actor Ed Asner. She then moved to Palm Springs and took up the cause of several charities, among them the Humane Society of the Desert, United Cerebral Palsy, and the Desert Theater League. "She was there for us when we needed her," said Theater League president Gary Walker. "She was a sweet and caring lady." **Sources:** *Chicago Tribune*, February 5, 1991; *Los Angeles Times*, February 5, 1991; *New York Times*, February 5, 1991; *Washington Post*, February 5, 1991.

Edwin H. Land

Born May 7, 1909, in Norwich, Conn.; died March 1, 1991, in Cambridge, Mass. Inventor. Land borrowed the idea for an instant camera in 1943 from his three-year-old daughter, who expressed puzzlement at the delay between the camera click and seeing the photograph. He then became determined to invent a camera that would satisfy even the most convenience-addicted consumer. The London *Times* reported Land's declaration that "within an hour, the camera, the film and the physical chemistry became so clear." He supervised research that resulted in the invention of the Polaroid Land Camera in 1948, as well as a series of related products, which Land termed "instant photography." Polaroid's market surveys revealed in the 1960s that half of America's households owned a Polaroid camera. In an age before Japanese technological advances held the camera business in a tight grasp, Polaroid owned the lion's share of the market due largely to Edwin Land's inventions. The meticulous researcher often said, "Anything worth doing is worth doing to excess."

A mostly self-taught physicist, Land held 533 patents when he retired in 1982, reflecting what he told the *New York Times* was a basic trait in inventors: "As I review the nature of the creative drive in the inventive scientists that have been around me, as well as myself, I find the first event is an urge to make a significant intellectual contribution that can be tangibly embodied in a product or process." As a young man Land was an outstanding student at Norwich Academy, where his fascination with the polarization of light was born. Though a two-time dropout from Harvard University, Land continued his research on this topic at the New York Public Library, eventually devising a light-polarizing apparatus made of iodide-quinine crystals.

Polaroid and Land ran into serious design problems in the 1970s that forever affected the company's value and reputation. The SX-70, an instant camera with complex optics, was faultily engineered, which caused a plummet in the stock valuation of the company. That disaster was followed by another: an instant moving picture system doomed by inferior design. The company, however, was financially sustained by the instamatic camera.

Land was vitally important to the success of Polaroid, which is reflected in the many positions he held there, including chairman, president, chief executive officer, chief operating officer, and director of research. He retired at the age of 73 and continued his own research in the field of lasers. He founded the Rowland Institute for Science in 1980 with a contribution from his fortune of millions. The entrepreneur, inventor, and physicist was also an adviser to the federal government on military matters; he helped utilize satellite pictures to spy on important enemy targets. Land was survived by his inspiring daughter, Jennifer, another daughter, Valerie, and his wife of 62 years, Helen Maislen. **Sources:** *Chicago Tribune*, March 2, 1991, March 3, 1991; *Los Angeles Times*, March 2, 1991; *New York Times*, March 2, 1991; *Times* (London), March 4, 1991.

Le Duc Tho

Born Phan Dinh Khai, October 10, 1911, in Dich Le Village, Ha Nam Ninh Province, Vietnam; died of throat cancer, October 13, 1990, in Hanoi, Vietnam (formerly North Vietnam). Communist Vietnam government aide. Le Duc Tho (pronounced "lay dook toe") played a crucial role in ending American military involvement (1965-1973) in the Vietnam War. The Vietnam War's roots lie in a period of colonialism, when the country was known as French Indochina and the war is essentially defined by Vietnamese resistance to invading forces. The French colonialists were forced out of Vietnam in the late 1930s by the invading Japanese, who were in turn routed when they lost World War II. The French repossessed Vietnam in 1945 and remained there until the Viet Minh forced them out in 1954, after which the United States became violently entangled with Communist factions. The American commitment in Vietnam was ill-fated for many reasons, among them: that the South Vietnamese government, with whom the United States signed military and economic aid treaties as early as 1961, was corrupt; that the South Vietnamese people were apparently sympathetic to the very effective guerrillas; and that the U.S. military was badly equipped psychologically and strategically for combat of this kind.

As an aide to the Hanoi government, Tho negotiated a treaty in 1973 to eliminate the U.S. military presence in Vietnam with President Richard Nixon's national security adviser, Henry Kissinger. Later, Tho and Kissinger were jointly awarded the Nobel Peace Prize, but Tho refused to accept it, saying that "peace had not yet been established," thus distinguishing between an end to American intervention in Vietnam and an end to the actual fighting in Vietnam. Two years after the prize was awarded, South Vietnam fell to North and Vietnam became a unified state under Communist rule.

The recent history of Vietnam has the same shape as Le Duc Tho's life—his dedication to the Communist party began early. He helped Ho Chi Minh, the future leader of North Vietnam, form the Indochinese Communist Party in 1929, when the French still ruled Vietnam. According to the *Washington Post*, Tho's "official party biography claims he was the son of peasants, [while] other sources say his father was a middle-ranking civil service official in the French colonial administration." Tho was in and out of jail in his youth for exploits such as starting anti-government riots. He held various posts in the Communist organization, eventually becoming a party executive in the south, where some sources say he orchestrated resistance to the Japanese during World War II, then later struggled against the French, and still later defied American involvement.

The secret Paris negotiations for peace in Vietnam began in 1969, with Tho and Kissinger finally reaching an agreement on January 23, 1973. Opinions vary widely as to the relative merits of the treaty, why it was signed, and what effect its terms had on the war. The treaty itself called for an in-place cease-fire and allowed North Vietnamese troops to stay in place in the south while 23,700 American soldiers evacuated. Hanoi was obliged to acknowledge Lieutenant General Nguyen Van Thieu's position as the South Vietnamese President (an office he had held since 1967) until elections could be held.

Kissinger was quoted in the *New York Times* as saying that Tho "stonewalled ingeniously for three years. And when the occasion to settle had been imposed...he did so with flexibility and speed." An expert on Asia, author Stanley Karnow, was also quoted, and revealed a different perspective of the treaty: "With tolerance for the war dwindling in the United States, Kissinger could not negotiate forever...the North Vietnamese, untrammeled by domestic dissidence, were prepared to talk endlessly." Karnow said in his 1986 book on Vietnam, *Bitter Victory*, that Tho had "craftily outnegotiated Kissinger and by ultimately gaining permission for North Vietnamese troops to remain in South Vietnam after the Americans withdrew, in effect set the stage for Hanoi's final stunning victory."

After 1973, Tho held a position of importance: No. 2 to Le Duan, the general secretary of the Communist party. Tho resigned from the party in December of 1986, as a new wave of officials took power. The hard-liner then "quietly served as senior adviser to the central committee of the party," according to the *Chicago Tribune*. He may have had a part in the 1978 Vietnam invasion of Cambodia, a neighboring country that had served as a refuge for the North Vietnamese troops in the late phases of pre-unification conflict. Shortly before his death, Tho was praised by the party General Secretary Nguyen Van Linh as an "outstanding disciple of the late president Ho Chi Minh, a staunch revolutionary fighter and an experienced leader of the party," reported the *Chicago Tribune*. Some sources said he had been married twice, but information about his personal life was scarce. **Sources:** *Chicago Tribune*, October 14, 1990; *New York Times*, October 14, 1990; *Washington Post*, October 14, 1990.

Mary Martin

Born December 1, 1913, in Weatherford, Tex.; died of cancer, November 3, 1990, in Rancho Mirage, Calif. Actress and singer. Mary Martin was the prototype Peter Pan, the funniest Nellie Forbush (of *South Pacific*), and Maria in one of the longest-running stage productions of *The Sound of Music*. Often described as "spunky," Martin weathered many misfortunes including fire, an early marriage and divorce, stage equipment accidents, car accidents, and cancer in her later years. Former First Lady Nancy Reagan's tribute to the actress (with whom she had once shared a stage) appeared in several newspapers; Reagan called her "one of the brightest stars ever . . . . She was a lady of the greatest personal courage."

Martin began her career on the Broadway stage in 1938, when she brought the house down with her suggestive rendition of Cole Porter's "My Heart Belongs to Daddy." The Texan spent several less-than-successful years in Hollywood singing in musicals, but met and married Richard Halliday in 1940. Halliday became her manager and encouraged her to go back to Broadway. In 1943 *One Touch of Venus* marked her return in a musical scored by Kurt Weill featuring the singer as a statue of Venus that comes to life. Many musical hits followed (including a touring show of *Annie Get Your Gun* that was made into a telecast) with Martin's last stage appearance being *Legends!* in which she starred with Carol Channing. Channing told the *Chicago Tribune* that she would "spend the rest of my life missing her. There's nobody like her. She's a great lady and a great presence on the stage."

Martin made her singing career debut at a fireman's ball in Weatherford, Texas, where her father was a lawyer and her mother a violin teacher. The girl had already been marked for show business—after seeing a silent screen version of *Peter Pan* at age 10, she jumped off the garage roof in an attempt to fly,

breaking her collarbone as a result. Martin married a Weatherford lawyer at age 16, but the marriage soon collapsed (some sources cite a divorce after only one year, some say five years). The happiest product of her first marriage was son Larry Hagman, best known as television's J. R. Ewing on the hit series *Dallas*.

Martin's family life did not always get the attention she felt that it deserved; her schedule and health problems in the late 1960s, she told a *Los Angeles Times* reporter, made her feel as though her life were simply "just the theater, bed; theater, bed; theater, bed. Stay in bed till 5 p.m., then do the show. It was like being in a box. I sometimes felt like a greyhound. They'd let me out for the race and that was all." At the end of the show *I Do, I Do* in 1969, Martin retired to a Brazilian farm with Halliday until his death in 1973. Busy but never ragged again, she came back to both television and the stage occasionally, wrote an autobiography in 1976, *My Heart Belongs*, and hosted a PBS talk show called *Over Easy* in the early 1980s. A car accident that proved fatal to Martin's manager and severely injured the actress and several others only slowed Martin down for a few months. Another less serious auto accident occurred on her way to Cedars Sinai Hospital where she was receiving chemotherapy for colon cancer in 1989. Syndicated columnist Shirley Eder recalled the buoyancy Martin showed to the end; when she was recovering from chemotherapy, she was excitedly planning several vacations: "I'm still taking chemo, but I told the doctors I'm going to London as planned," she told Eder. "I'll just take the stuff with me." **Sources:** *Chicago Tribune*, November 5, 1990; *Detroit Free Press*, November 5, 1990, November 6, 1990; *Los Angeles Times*, November 5, 1990.

Joel McCrea

Born November 5, 1905, in South Pasadena, Calif.; died of pulmonary complications, October 20, 1990, in Los Angeles. Movie actor. Joel McCrae was the frontiersman in all aspects of his life. He preferred the outdoors to movie sets, and was most comfortable when playing the part of the old-fashioned good-hearted cowboy. His roots reflect his close relationship with nature: his paternal grandfather, Major John McCrea, was a stagecoach driver who traveled between San Bernadino and Los Angeles, and his maternal grandfather, Albert Whipple, came to San Francisco because of the 1849 gold rush. McCrea's own father, however, had little of the Old

West romantic blood. The patriarch moved his family to Hollywood when Joel McCrea was 9 to pursue a job as a utility executive. As a young boy, McCrea was industrious and insisted on working—most of his income went to maintenance of his own horses. Ranching was his true passion, as he would list his occupation as "rancher" and his hobby as "acting." McCrea used his first acting paychecks to buy farmland, eventually becoming one of Hollywood's wealthiest landowners.

Of his 80 movies, McCrea's "most compelling performances [were] in the early 1940's," according to the *New York Times*. "He played the title role in Alfred Hitchcock's thriller *Foreign Correspondent* and a naive film director seeking out serious issues in *Sullivan's Travels*." Before McCrea's death in October of 1990, *Sullivan's Travels* had been deemed worthy of historic preservation by the Library of Congress. However, McCrea was more familiar to his public as a hero in Western films, such as *The Virginian* and *Wells Fargo*.

McCrea was often offered roles that had been refused by more popular actors, but he never revealed any bitterness. Instead, he considered among his friends such stars as Gary Cooper (from whom he gained cowboy role cast-offs) and Cary Grant (whose light comedy roles were also sometimes passed down). The actor himself would turn down parts that didn't live up to his higher principles. The *New York Times* said that "in 1945, he refused to appear in a sexy, highly publicized melodrama with Lana Turner, *The Postman Always Rings Twice*, saying: 'This character is too much of a gigolo. I don't like his moral standards.' In a 1985 interview he said he had always 'wanted to be the guy who rode off into the sunset,' to represent 'right over evil.'" McCrea could be flexible to a point, however, and allowed himself to be cast as a villain in such Westerns as *Four Faces West* and *Colorado Territory*.

Acting was as much a family activity as ranching— McCrea made several pictures with his wife, actress Frances Dee, to whom he had been married for 57 years when he died. His son Jody became an actor and played the deputy in the 1959 television series *Wichita Town*. The couple had two other sons, David, also a rancher, and Peter, a film editor. Joel McCrea was elected to the Cowboy Hall of Fame in Oklahoma City in 1958. **Sources:** London *Times,* October 22, 1990; *New York Times,* October 21, 1990; *Washington Post,* October 21, 1990.

Karl Menninger

Full name, Karl Augustus Menninger; born July 22, 1893, in Topeka, Kan.; died of abdominal cancer, July 18, 1990, in Topeka, Kan. With his father Charles and brother William, Karl Menninger founded the famous Menninger Clinic in 1919, which later became the Menninger Foundation. The importance of the clinic was noted in the citation of the Albert Lasker Group Award for 1955: "The Menninger Foundation and Clinic . . . has provided a sustained and highly productive attack against mental disease for many years. Inspired by their father . . . these brothers have developed an outstanding institution which has served as an example for other mental disease hospitals . . . the influence of the Menninger Foundation and Clinic in increasing professional and public interest in the care of the mentally ill cannot be measured, but it is indelibly recorded as a great service to mankind."

One of the first American physicians to become a psychoanalyst, Karl Menninger held certificate No. 1 from the Chicago Psychoanalytic Institute, having received his medical degree from Harvard in 1917. The most visible member of a family of philanthropists, he was to become a passionate crusader for better understanding and treatment of the mentally ill. Menninger applied his science to the world around him: he opposed imprisonment and the death penalty because of his beliefs about the human mind, and involved himself with many humanitarian associations such as the American Indian Defense Association and Planned Parenthood. The president of the American Psychoanalytic Association and a founding member of similar organizations, Menninger was honored with many awards in his life, including the Medal of Freedom in 1981.

Menninger's father (not a psychologist himself, but a personable physician who was fascinated by the problems of treating the mentally ill) said that "no patient is untreatable," according to the *New York Times*. He encouraged both of his sons to become doctors after he visited the Mayo Clinic in Rochester, Minnesota, and was inspired to staff a similar clinic with his offspring. Their clinic started out in an old farmhouse with beds for 13 patients, but grew in time to 39 buildings on two campuses with a staff of more than 1,000. The Menningers treated their patients in this supportive environment, which differed from the Freudian model of seeing patients in an office setting once or twice a week for years. They believed that this comprehensive care would cure the mentally ill more efficiently and humanely. Instead of concentrating on controlling the symptoms of emotional disturbance (and creating a "socially acceptable" person), the Menningers attempted to seek the cause of mental illness, looking often to early personal history. The three men had an open approach to mental health care, often holding conferences on individual patients and theorizing about the treatment in general.

Before Karl Menninger began writing about psychology, most Americans had almost no contact with the mentally ill, as the inflicted were confined to insane asylums. Menninger countered with the enlightened view that emotional disturbances were usually the result of some kind of abuse or emotional deficiency, such as a lack of parental support and love. He felt that most crime was a phase of mental illness. An outspoken defender of prison inmates, Menninger said that imprisonment without psychological treatment was essentially useless in reforming antisocial behavior. Menninger's many books, especially his first, *The Human Mind*, were widely read and respected in his field and by thousands of lay readers. The *New York Times* said that the book "explained psychiatry as a relatively uncomplicated method of helping the disturbed."

The Menninger Foundation has become almost synonymous with compassion and philanthropy. Karl Menninger was probably the most influential of the founders, as he trained thousands of psychiatrists (the *Los Angeles Times* estimated the amount to be five percent of the psychiatrists practicing in the United States in the early 1990s). The campaigner of the three men, he was more outspoken than his brother, and had a reputation for being fiery, thoughtless, and abrupt. His passion lent a compelling air to his writing, and his role as the Menninger Clinic and Foundation figurehead sprang mostly from his ability as an eloquent spokesman for the mentally ill. The *Los Angeles Times* quoted his book, *The Human Mind:* "The adjuration to be 'normal' seems shockingly repellent to me; I see neither hope nor comfort in sinking to that low level." **Sources:** *Contemporary Authors New Revision Series*, Gale Research, Inc., 1990; *Los Angeles Times*, July 19, 1990; *New York Times*, July 19, 1990.

Arthur Murray

Born Moses Teichman, April 4, 1895, in New York City; died of pneumonia, March 3, 1991, in Diamond Head, Hawaii. Dance teacher and entrepreneur. At the peak of his success Arthur Murray owned and operated a legendary chain of dance studios across the country. The son of poor Jewish immigrants from Austria, Murray parlayed an early talent for ballroom dancing into a lucrative business that at one time included a television series—*The Arthur Murray Party*. Aggressive advertising rapidly expanded Arthur Murray Inc.'s scope, and by the time its chief stepped down from the presidency in 1964, his studios had taught millions to dance. Among these, contended the ad copy, were Eleanor Roosevelt, The Duke of Windsor, John D. Rockefeller, Jr., Barbara Hutton, and dozens of other celebrated folk. When Murray sold the company it was grossing $5 million annually.

The dance instruction Murray invented was based on students following diagrammed footsteps to music, a technique he cannily translated to instruction books and mail-order manuals. Instructors at the Arthur Murray dance studios were told to exercise the utmost patience with all of their pupils, even the seemingly most hopeless and clumsy. Murray insisted that the studios remain spotlessly clean; the *New York Times* called him a "fanatical light bulb duster." He started out with a single studio in Atlanta, at the Georgian Terrace Hotel. A ballroom dance craze had struck the nation before the Depression, but even from the depths of poverty, Americans yearned to emulate the sophistication of movie idols like Fred Astaire and Ginger Rogers. Murray made these dreams even more tempting by promising popularity and self-confidence as side effects of dance lessons, and millions believed him. In 1939 a *New York Times* dance critic asserted that Murray's "particular slant on the dance, which would probably shock [influential nineteenth-century ballet impresario] Diaghilev, is the same as the Rockefeller perspective on oil, as the Guggenheim way of looking at the mineral kingdom."

Murray's organization was not beyond reproach, however; in 1946 Arthur Murray instructors went on strike in convicts' stripes protesting the conditions of their employment. In 1960 the Federal Trade Commission ordered the firm to cease its peculiar brand of telephone solicitation—a legendary con game that included a pop quiz the listener could hardly lose, the "prize" for which was lessons at one of Murray's studios. The implication that the lessons would be free of charge proved false. Then in 1964 Murray was arrested and held briefly on charges that a Minnesota studio was cheating clients. Although Murray and the studio did not turn out to be the actual target of the investigation itself, the dance entrepreneur found himself, nonetheless, in a position to avoid a subpoena.

Murray retired permanently in 1983 after a tennis injury. He is survived by several daughters and his wife of 65 years, Kathryn, who had been the mistress of ceremonies on Murray's eleven-year television series. According to the *Chicago Tribune*, Murray once wrote that "the man who treats the lady as though she were a china doll, holds her gently and is careful to see that she does not collide with every pillar, is more than often a man of fine sensibility." **Sources:** *Chicago Tribune*, March 4, 1991; *Los Angeles Times*, March 4, 1991; *New York Times*, March 4, 1991.

Olav, King of Norway

Born Prince Alexander Edward Christian Frederick of Denmark, July 2, 1903, at Appleton House, Sandringham, Norfolk, England; died of a heart attack, January 17, 1991, in Oslo, Norway. Monarch. Although King Olav was born in England and schooled at Oxford University's Balliol College, his Norwegian subjects called him "folke konge'—the king for all people. Norway gained its independence only two years after Olav's birth to Prince Carl of Denmark and Princess Maud, daughter of Britain's Edward VI. After his children married commoners from Norway, King Olav remarked that the family had finally become genuinely Norwegian. His 1929 marriage to his cousin, Princess Martha of Sweden, helped ease perennial tension between Norway and Sweden. The wedding ceremony was one of the first to be broadcast on radio.

When the Nazi Germany invaded Southern Denmark in 1940, Olav, then Crown Prince, his father, and assorted members of Parliament hid in the woods of the North, hoping to withstand bombing raids and the advancing army. The young monarch distinguished himself by volunteering to stay in his country and lead resistance fighters. His father and the other officials would not allow him to take the risk, however, so he spent the duration of the war making trips to the United States as envoy for the government in exile and boosting the morale of Norwegians through radio broadcasts. Olav received a hero's welcome and parade in 1945 when he returned to Norway after the allied liberation.

Prince Olav assumed the crown after his father's death in 1957. Following the example of his father's small court and simple lifestyle, he established himself as a frugal ruler. As a young man he had been an avid sportsman and an Olympic yachtsman; he was also an enthusiastic skier throughout his life. A photograph from the 1970s illustrates the populist quality that made the King such a favorite among his people. The international energy crisis of that time made public transport a necessity; Norwegians were urged to use trains and buses as much as possible, so the picture of the King on a public train carrying his own skis to the slopes set a much-admired example of self-discipline.

At the time of his death King Olav was the oldest monarch in the world and had been since the 1989 death of Emperor Hirohito of Japan. Widowed in 1954, King Olav never remarried. His heirs are Crown Prince Harald, who will succeed his father to the throne, and Princesses Ragnhild Alexandra and Astrid Maud. **Sources:** *Chicago Tribune*, January 18, 1991, January 20, 1991; *New York Times*, January 18, 1991; *Times* (London), January 19, 1991.

William S. Paley

Born September 28, 1901, in Chicago, Ill.; died of a heart attack, October 26, 1990, in Manhattan, N.Y. Broadcasting executive. William S. Paley became a media tastemaker when the world of television was in its infancy, and his power and prestige will probably never be realized again in a single person. Beginning in radio, the son of a cigar merchant made his mark producing such programs as CBS's *Hear It Now* in the 1950s, and urged legendary journalist Edward R. Murrow to give an hour-long format a try. The show was famously successful, and was parlayed into *See It Now*. Paley's idea of journalism was described by the *Chicago Tribune*: "Mr. Paley never allowed the integrity of his news division to be compromised. News, he decreed, was a public service, never to suffer interference from management, influence from advertisers or taint by the bottom-line demand that it generate profits." He ruled CBS from its purchase (then the United Independent Broadcasters) in 1928, until a hostile takeover led by Ted Turner in 1983. He was recalled in 1986 and was reelected as chairman of the board.

In transforming CBS from a faltering collection of 16 radio stations to one of the "Big Three" television networks, Paley demonstrated savvy, talent, and some luck. No one knew in the late 1920s that television would be invented, nor that it would be phenomenally profitable. Even Paley was skeptical at first, but he eventually recognized the dramatic possibilities of the medium, and invested heavily in its success. He won stars over from NBC to CBS by paying them what then amounted to fortunes; such legends as Jack Benny, Bing Crosby, and Lucille Ball made the crossover. Not only did Paley recognize star quality, but he knew which people were capable of managing it, including, according to the *Washington Post*, "Edward Klauber, a former *New York Times* editor... [who] was credited with attracting a staff whose members became household names and setting a tone of authority and restraint that stood in sharp contrast to the sensationalism that characterized much of broadcast journalism." That restraint wore well until the 1980s, when other stations surged ahead of the conservative network; the CBS evening news was ranked third through the early 1990s. Paley was married twice, first to Dorothy Hart Hearst, and then to Barbara (Babe) Cushing Mortimer, a stunning high-society beauty who died of cancer in 1978. Each marriage resulted in two children and an array of stepchildren, and Paley's reputation was tarnished by the 1990 publication of a biography by Sally Bedell Smith, which discussed these marriages in frank detail. Paley's will was amazingly complex and, according to *Newsweek*, fair to all of his children while also donating many art works to New York's Museum of Modern Art. "One Picasso from 1906," said *Newsweek*, "*Boy Leading a Horse* ... was estimated by art dealer Richard Feigen to be worth $100 million to $125 million alone." By turning this astonishing collection over to the museum, Paley again reinforced what many saw as his charitable and public-minded nature. **Sources:** *Chicago Tribune*, October 10, 1990; *Newsweek,* November 5, 1990, November 12, 1990; *Time*, November 5, 1990; *Washington Post*, October 28, 1990.

Sylvia Porter

Name originally Sylvia Feldman; born June 18, 1913, in Patchogue, Long Island, NY; died of emphysema, June 5, 1991, in Pound Ridge, NY. Financial columnist. Sylvia Porter was dedicated to educating the average person about money in layman's terms. As a woman in the world of finance, she seemed a maverick, but her advice was trusted and utilized throughout the world for decades. She was also the author of many successful books, such as 1975's *Sylvia Porter's Money Book: How to Earn It, Spend It, Save It, Invest It, Borrow It and Use It to Better Your Life*, which sold over a million copies. Porter's own financial magazine had the third largest readership in the field from 1984 until the stock market crash of 1987. The *New York Times* once ascribed Porter's success to her use of "facts, figures, broad word-pictures and succinct arguments...presented with conversational ease." The *Los Angeles Times* reported

that Porter told the *Baltimore Sun* in 1980, "I tried to combine the writing of economics with simple writing. That meant you had to know what you were talking about...which wasn't easy."

Porter was a freshman at Hunter College when the stock market crashed in 1929, marking the beginning of the Great Depression. Her mother lost $30,000 in the crash, which influenced her to change the course of her studies from English to economics. She earned a Phi Beta Kappa key and graduated magna cum laude in 1932. Porter then worked for an investment counseling firm on Wall Street and took graduate level business administration classes at night. Soon she began writing articles for financial journals, but for more than a decade, she disguised her sex in her columns by writing under the byline S. F. Porter. Although she spoke on the radio and published her books under her full name, she didn't use Sylvia in the papers until 1942.

Porter's column "S. F. Porter Says" made its debut in 1935 in the *New York Post*. By 1936 Porter was appointed financial editor of the paper. The "economist for the people" had strong ideas about justice in the financial world—she often castigated government figures for their fiscal policies and decisions, and responses varied from bouquets of flowers to outright name-calling. "When she attacked Senator Edwin Johnson of Colorado for his advocacy of silver, he called her 'the biggest liar in the United States,'" reported the *New York Times*. Porter moved her column to the *Daily News* in 1978, where it appeared under the title, "Your Money." The final version of the column was called simply "Sylvia Porter." It was printed three times a week, syndicated by the *Los Angeles Times*, and appeared in 430 newspapers around the world; 150 of the papers were in the United States, where she was read regularly by 25 million people. Her last book, published in September of 1991, is called *Sylvia Porter's Your Finances in the 1990s*. **Sources:** *Chicago Tribune*, June 7, 1991; *Los Angeles Times*, June 7, 1991; *New York Times*, June 7, 1991; *Washington Post*, June 7, 1991.

David Ruffin

Name originally Davis Eli Ruffin; born January 18, 1941, in Meridian, MS; died of a drug overdose, June 1, 1991, in Philadelphia, PA. Singer. David Ruffin was one of the early members of the pop group the Temptations, which produced such memorable hits as "Ain't too Proud to Beg," and "My Girl." The baritone left the group in 1968 to work on solo projects, and he had a hit single with "My Whole World Ended (The Moment You Left Me)." He participated in a reunion of the Temptations in 1982 and cut an album with the original members called *Reunion*. The Temptations were inducted into the Rock and Roll Hall of Fame in 1989. Ruffin had a long battle with drug abuse before an overdose of cocaine killed him in a Philadelphia crack house, according to some reports. A limousine pulled up to the University of Pennsylvania's emergency room; the driver told hospital staffers that Ruffin had overdosed and left. Ruffin's identity was not known at that point; it was only when the FBI did a fingerprint check that the singer was recognized. Fifty-five minutes after he was admitted, Ruffin was declared dead. He had been in and out of rehabilitation centers since 1967, and in 1987 was sent to jail because of a drug-related parole violation. His death became the subject of a police investigation. The Temptations attended David Ruffin's funeral, and they, along with Aretha Franklin, sang songs and hymns in his memory.

The Temptations formed in 1961 when a group called the Primes, composed of Eddie Kendricks and Paul Williams joined the Distants—Otis Williams, Al Bryant, and Melvin Franklin. They called themselves the Elgins for a while, then switched to the Temptations because of the racy connotation. Berry Gordy of Motown gave the Temptations their first gigs, and also had them sing backup for Motown's biggest stars. They never had a hit until Ruffin replaced Bryant, and stage choreography was developed for them by Cholly Atkins, who had also worked with Gladys Knight and the Pips and the Cadillacs. In 1964 the Temptations had their first big hit with "The Way You Do the Things You Do," which was written and produced by Smokey Robinson, also the author of "My Girl," their 1965 hit. "My Girl" hit number one on the charts. Norman Whitfield produced "Ain't Too Proud to Beg" in 1966, and with that hit, the group became phenomenally popular, successful in a way that would sustain them through many changes in personnel.

Ruffin was not the only casualty of the Temptations: Paul Williams was asked to leave the group in 1971 because of his problem with alcohol, and two years later, he fatally shot himself. Ruffin had been in a treatment program as recently as October of 1989, when he declared that he had recovered. **Sources:** *Los Angeles Times*, June 2, 1991; *New York Times*, June 3, 1991; *Washington Post*, June 2, 1991.

Barbara Boggs Sigmund

Born May 27, 1939, in New Orleans, La.; died of melanoma, October 11, 1990, in Princeton, N.J. Politician, mayor of Princeton, N.J. Born into a dynasty of political savants, Barbara Boggs Sigmund, the mayor of Princeton until her death, carried on a family tradition of gracefully balancing a career in public service and a family life. Friend and college classmate Phyllis Theroux eulogized Sigmund in the *Washington Post*: "All the right ingredients for public service ran in Barbara's veins and early indications pointed to easy success. Even in school—from the first grade through college—she was always elected class president. Yet despite her drive and intellectual commitment, she never successfully rose above the local level in politics." Sigmund's battle with melanoma began with the loss of her left eye in 1982 during an unsuccessful race for the United States Senate. Despite her illness, the colorful Democratic mayor kept her last years politically active and full of her family. With characteristic *savoir vivre*, Sigmund called her remaining eye "a glutton, a lecher, and a drunk," for the world around her, according to the *Washington Post*.

Her husband Paul, whom Sigmund married in 1964, is a professor of Latin American studies at Princeton University. The couple have three sons: Paul Eugene Jr., David Claiborne, and Stephen Hale, all political science majors, as are all of their cousins. Sigmund's funeral was attended by more than 2,000 people "including her son Paul, who read a letter written to him by his mother before he was born. 'As surely as I am introducing you to life,' she wrote, 'I am introducing you to death, and against this knowledge you will shape your life,'" as Theroux said in the *Washington Post*.

People explained an important part of the Boggs family history: "When Lindy Boggs [Barbara's mother] announced she would not seek reelection to her seat in Congress this year, it sent shock waves across Capitol Hill. After all, a Boggs has represented the people of New Orleans for nearly 50 years. Lindy, who succeeded her husband, Hale, in March 1973, five months after a small plane in which he was riding vanished over Alaska, said she was stepping down because of 'family considerations.'" The chief consideration was the return of Barbara's melanoma. Barbara said in a *People* interview (which included her sister, Cokie Roberts, a correspondent for National Public Radio and ABC) that "Mother cannot accept the fact that I may die before she does—it's not the natural order of things .... learning the cancer had spread was traumatic. The worst part was telling

Mother. She said, 'I wish I could rock you and make it all better.' Such a Mama thing to say."

The Boggs women are almost united in their political stances, especially when concerning adequate public housing, civil rights, and equal rights for women. A bachelor of arts degree-holder from Manhattanville College of the Sacred Heart, Sigmund's political activities and positions aside from her six-year mayoral tenure included councilwoman in Princeton, New Jersey, member of the New Jersey State Commission on Women, delegate to the Democratic National Convention in 1980, and president of the New Jersey Association of Counties. Her devotion to politics stretched to the end of her life: she was expected to run for Congress if James Courter, the Republican representative, was unsuccessful. He was, but Sigmund was suffering from her untimely relapse. "Unfortunately there is nothing much I can do except take two pills a day, run the Borough of Princeton and write poems," Barbara Boggs Sigmund told *People*. "That's the way I distill my emotions." **Sources:** *Chicago Tribune*, October 14, 1990; *People*, October 29, 1990, August 13, 1990; *Washington Post*, October 21, 1990.

B. F. Skinnner

Full name, Burrhus Frederic Skinner; born March 20, 1904, in Susquehanna, Pa.; died of leukemia, August 18, 1990, in Cambridge, Mass. Behavioral psychologist. Skinner was on the cutting edge of behaviorism, a group of theories that sets out to prove that human and animal behavior is based not so much on subjective impetus, but on reward and punishment applied to the animal. He entered the discipline in the 1920s, when it was still relatively new. Skinner's laboratory experiments were widely thought to be exciting and innovative, revealing an understanding of human behavior and logistics. The London *Times* declared that "Skinner's achievement was to create a science of behaviour in its own right." The governing principle of Skinner's brand of psychology is that of "operant behavior," according to the *Chicago Tribune*—operant meaning the specific activity that results in the desired reward or reinforcement.

The scientist's best known and most often used scientific apparatus is the Skinner box (which he called the "operant conditioning apparatus"). A soundproofed enclosure equipped with button and levers, the box is used to condition behavior with rewards of food for certain functions performed in a given order. As the functions can easily be observed

and recorded, the box provides a way for scientists to measure behavior. Skinner most often used rats and pigeons in experiments; with the Skinner box he trained his pigeons to play Ping Pong, dance, walk in figure eights, and distinguish between colors, and he taught rats to push buttons, pull strings, and press levers to receive food and drink. The psychologist applied these basic operants to humans and their responses to various environments. Many find this approach to be chilly and reductive, as a person is composed of much more than complex cause/effect equations. The *New York Times* quoted a view that Skinner was a "cold manipulator of humanity," then recalled the scientist telling an interviewer that "the ideal of behaviorism is to eliminate coercion, to apply controls by changing the environment in such a way as to reinforce the kind of behavior that benefits everyone."

His ideas were often misconstrued: the media had charged him with mistreatment of his own daughter by isolating her in a version of the Skinner box for long periods of time. Skinner replied that his daughter spent no more time than other infants did in their cribs or playpens. This box was no more than an enclosure that regulated air temperature so that a baby need not wear constricting clothing. Skinner's attempt to market the so-called "Heir Conditioner" was unsuccessful. "I find that I need to be understood only three or four times a year," Skinner had said, referring to misinterpretation of his scientific researches. The London *Times* interpreted the public's confused response to Skinner theories in this way: "A behaviorist cannot expect more than a mixed reception for presenting a view of people that is neither flattering nor comforting even if it is true."

The philosophies in Skinner's writing seemed to meet with a much more sympathetic and perceptive audience. According to *People*, Skinner's book, *Walden Two*, "became a handbook for a generation of flower children in the 1960s, selling a million copies." Translated into eight languages, the book (one of Skinner's eleven) describes a utopia in which communes of people have eradicated vice and replaced it with rewarding work and unlimited artistic self-expression. While many related these ideas to a fascistic impulse, Skinner's "was a world without punishment," according to the *New York Times*. "Though punishment worked as a negative reinforcer, it served only to produce escape or avoidant behavior that might be even more undesirable than the behavior it was designed to punish. He considered punishment ineffective in training animals, teaching children or managing public offenders."

The scientist, who as a child wanted to be a poet and novelist but "had nothing to say," became a graduate of Hamilton College in Clinton, N.Y. and of Harvard. The recipient of many awards and honors, Skinner taught at Harvard several times, once as a William James lecturer and from 1958 until his retirement in 1974 as an Edgar Pierce Professor of Psychology. Although his eyesight was quite limited toward the end of his life, Skinner continued to write and publish; his last book, *Recent Issues in the Analysis of Behavior*, was published in 1989. **Sources:** *Contemporary Authors New Revision Series*, Volume 18, Gale Research, Inc., 1986; London *Times*, August 20, 1990; *New York Times*, August 20, 1990; *People*, September 3, 1990.

Mitch Snyder

Full name, Mitchell Darryl Snyder; born c. 1944, in New York, N.Y.; committed suicide by hanging, found dead July 6, 1990, in Washington, D.C. Advocate for the homeless. One of the most insistent and controversial voices attracting attention to the problems of the homeless in the 1980s was Mitch Snyder. Steeped in controversy to the end of his life, Snyder hanged himself in a closed room in Washington D.C.'s Community for Creative Non-Violence (CCNV) shelter. A suicide note explained his despair over a failed love affair; recently he had separated from his longtime companion and fiancee, CCNV worker Carol Fennelly. The *New York Times* mentioned several other troubled aspects of Snyder's recent life, including a report that "[he had] angered some homeless advocates when he argued that the homeless should not cooperate with the 1990 census . . . . [it was] reported in recent months that his 1,400-bed shelter was plagued by widespread drug use on the part of its residents." There were also charges pending that Snyder owed tens of thousands of dollars in federal back taxes. With characteristic verve, Snyder had successfully turned the accusations into a nationwide debate on federal budget priorities.

The activist's personal life was troubled from the first; his father walked out on the family when Snyder was 9, and by his teen years, he was in trouble with the law. He served time in a reform school before dropping out of high school. Two sons were the product of the early marriage that Snyder abandoned; within a year he was arrested for theft and spent two years in a federal prison. After his release, he channeled his energy to the anti-war group that would later become the most powerful force in the fight to provide for the homeless, the CCNV. The organization was looking for a new cause, and Snyder helped define it, as he worked in a CCNV soup kitchen, drew only a minimum wage, and dressed only in donated clothing.

Snyder dramatized the desperate problems of the homeless with death-defying hunger strikes, angry speeches in Congress, and protest marches. His fasts were particularly effective, and were the means by which he acquired funds for the 1,400-bed Federal City Shelter, run by the CCNV. His flair for the dramatic was well known (his most successful fast ended two days before the 1984 presidential election), as demonstrated in a 1980 protest when participants hurled fake blood at the walls of Washington, D.C.'s District Building. His life was documented in the television movie, *Samaritan: The Mitch Snyder Story*, starring Martin Sheen, who became a close friend and is himself an champion of homeless.

The *Washington Post* quoted Haskell Carter, homeless for seven years and a resident of CCNV for several years, saying that Snyder "was very conscientious, very sincere. He was more than just an advocate." Karen Saunders, from CCNV's Women's Shelter, said at Snyder's funeral that "being homeless . . . you feel as if you are an outcast . . . . Mitch ministered to the unacceptable and sometimes he was thought of as unacceptable. But I thought of him as a rainbow," as the *Washington Post* reported. Reverend Jesse Jackson presided over the funeral, which was preceded by a public vigil attended by about 500 people. While many expressed distress that Snyder had killed himself, the *Washington Post* reported Reverend Jackson's desire that the commitments of Snyder's life not be forgotten and confirmed the responsibility of all to "recommit to the unfinished business [of helping] the homeless and hungry." Sorely missed by the residents of the shelter, who worry that an irreplaceable spark has left their cause, Snyder left his dynamic life with the same sort of agitation he lent to his crusade against homelessness. **Sources:** *New York Times*, July 8, 1990; *Washington Post*, July 6, 1990; July 10, 1990; July 12, 1990.

Danny Thomas

Born Muzyad Yakhoob, January 6, 1914, in Deerfield, Mich.; died of a heart attack, February 6, 1991, in Beverly Hills, Calif. Actor. Danny Thomas may endure as an entertainment legend more for the television shows he produced than for his actual performances, memorable though they were. As a Hollywood producer Thomas amassed a personal fortune that allowed him to become a dedicated philanthropist. Founder of the famous St. Jude's Children's Research Hospital, Thomas told the *Chicago Tribune* shortly before his death, "When I first prayed to St. Jude on that dark day in the Great Depression when my wife was expecting our first child, Marlo, I asked him to show me my way in life and I vowed to build him a shrine." Emerging from the Depression with a career in the USO, he played to overseas troops during World War II; back home he started a successful nightclub career. Eventually Thomas went on to become a television actor, producer, and virtual icon. He was father to Marlo Thomas—best known for her early work on television's *That Girl*—as well as to producer Tony, and daughter Theresa.

Thomas said his gift for storytelling came from his family. "My people are inherently storytellers," Thomas told Mervyn Rothstein of the *New York Times*. "When I was a kid, the entertainment was somebody from the old country or a big city who came and visited and told tales of where they came from." By the time he was a teenager, Thomas had changed his name to Amos Jacobs and was performing with one of his brothers, Ray, in an act called "Songs, Dances, and Happy Patter." At 16 he quit school and became a professional entertainer. The *Chicago Tribune* reported that he made a living "doing everything from small-time radio (he created the sounds of the Lone Ranger's [horse's] hooves by pounding on his chest [with two toilet plungers]) to telling slightly racy jokes at conventions." Success had to wait until Thomas was in his twenties. In the meantime, he opened his own act in a Chicago nightclub, the reputation of which was so questionable that Thomas felt compelled to change his name in the hope that his new wife, Rose Marie, wouldn't find out that he was performing there. He told the *Tribune* in January of 1991 that his "real birthday is August 12, 1940, when I opened at the 5100 Club, and I've been celebrating it every year since." By then he had gathered a faithful following, many of whom apparently mistook him for a Jewish comic. His agent at the time, Danny Newman, detailed Thomas's popularity in the *Chicago Tribune*, saying "He had a terrific following in Chicago, especially with the Jewish audiences who adored his Yiddish-flavored stories—everyone thought he was a Yiddish comic.... People would go to hear him again and again, just to hear his Old Country stories." Thomas's ancestry was actually Lebanese.

Among Thomas's landmark career moves was opening the new Sands Hotel in Las Vegas in the early 1950s, before that city had become the entertainment and gambling center it is today. Shortly thereafter he settled into Hollywood to make a long-running series, *Make Room for Daddy*—later known as *The Danny Thomas Show*—a project that closely reflected his life; it showcased the tribulations of a traveling club performer. Marlo—later married to talk show host Phil Donahue—named the show; it was what the young girl would say when her father came home from work. Tremendously successful and more colorful than its white-bread contemporaries, the program ran for over a decade and still plays in reruns. *Make Room for Daddy* was also significant in that it was one of the few family shows of the 1950s in which the father was not portrayed as a bit of a fool. It was unique too in that it contained ethnic references, like the crusty Lebanese Uncle Tonoose. Thomas's real wealth, however, was earned in production; his production company produced the enormously successful *Andy Griffith Show, Dick Van Dyke Show*, and *Joey Bishop Show*, among others.

The end of Thomas's life was distinguished by a flurry of activity. The 77-year-old entertainment industry giant had just appeared on the *Tonight Show* to promote his new autobiography, *Make Way for Danny*. He had recently appeared on *Empty Nest*, the television show produced by his son, and had been looking forward to doing a television movie with Marlo. In 1986 Thomas was awarded the Congressional Gold Medal by President Ronald Reagan for his work with St. Jude's Hospital. His death was mourned by both Reagan and President George Bush, as well as by most of Hollywood's old guard, many of whom were Thomas's close friends. **Sources:** *Chicago Tribune*, February 7, 1991; *Los Angeles Times*, February 7, 1991; *New York Times*, January 10, 1991; *People*, February 18, 1991; *Washington Post*, February 7, 1991.

John Tower

Born September 29, 1926, in Houston, TX; died in a plane crash, April 5, 1991, in Brunswick, GA. Politician, defense specialist. John Tower and one of his three daughters, 35-year-old Marian, were killed in a tragic plane crash while touring the country to promote the mid-1991 publication of his book, *Consequences: A Personal and Political Memoir*. The Republican ex-senator had weathered a shower of controversy when his nomination for defense secretary was challenged by the far right of his own party because of alleged excessive drinking and "womanizing." When a CNN reporter asked him about these accusations, the twice-divorced Tower said, according to the *Chicago Tribune:* "I'm a single man. I do date women. What is your definition of womanizing?" The same source said that his questioner then kept mum. Tower had been appointed in 1986 to head a special board that was to investigate President Ronald Reagan's role in the Iran-Contra arms-for-hostages scandal. The Tower Commission received applause for its remarkably unbiased criticism of the President and his staff, while also finding Reagan innocent of any conspiratorial crime. Despite the resulting prestige, Tower was not made the secretary of defense under President George Bush, and was retaliating by way of his revealing memoir at the time of his death. He called several powerful congressmen "less-than-brilliant," and said that others, specifically Democratic Senator Sam Nunn (See *Newsmakers 90*), had private political agendas to pursue while sinking Tower's career. Tower had only begun to enjoy his revenge when the fatal accident occurred.

Tower, who had served in the Navy during World War II, was elected to the Senate in 1961, the first Republican from Texas to do so since 1877. During his tenure in the Senate he gained the reputation of a hawk, especially reinforced in the Vietnam era. Some have summed up his contribution as a young congressman to the Senate Banking Committee as half-hearted. In 1980 he became the chairman of the Armed Services Committee and turned into, according to the *Washington Post,* "the intellectual godfather of the Reagan administration's massive defense buildup and its most skillful advocate in Congress." After Tower's retirement from the Senate in 1984, President Reagan named him as an arms negotiator to bargain with the Soviets; despite a long-term resentment of the U.S.S.R., Tower apparently worked diligently. The *Chicago Tribune* reported that Tower then had a "lucrative stint as a private defense consultant, a role that later cost him in the controversy surrounding his Defense nomination." In 1986, Tower was named to the Iran-Contra investigative panel; four years later came his unsuccessful bid for the secretaryship, during which conservative activist Paul Weyrich testified in open hearings that he had seen Tower publicly drunk on several occasions. The *Washington Post* quoted Tower's written assessment of his losses: "Lost is the fact that I was once regarded as a competent leader, worthy of trust and capable of bearing the heavy responsibilities of sensitive and demanding assignments." **Sources:**

Chicago Tribune, April 6, 1991; *Washington Post,* April 6, 1991.

Stevie Ray Vaughan

Born c. 1956 in Dallas, Texas; died in a helicopter crash, August 27, 1990, near East Troy, Wisconsin. Blues guitarist. Vaughan's first musical influence was his brother, Jimmie—when Jimmie put down his guitar, Stevie picked it up for practice time. They played in a concert together (along with Eric Clapton, Robert Cray, and Buddy Guy) the night Vaughan died in a helicopter accident. The hard-edged bluesy sound that was maturing into the Stevie Ray Vaughan trademark was tempered with jazz and rock. Buddy Guy told *People* of their last song in Vaughan's last concert: "It was one of the most incredible sets I ever heard Stevie play. I had goosebumps." Colleagues, fans, and critics alike agree that Vaughan was on the edge of mining the real wealth of his musical talent and, in the process, becoming a blues legend.

Vaughan played professionally for the first time in clubs at the age of 14; two years later he dropped out of high school to pursue a full-time music career. His path in and out of many bands is hard to follow, but he played bass for a while in the 1970s for his brother's band, Texas Storm. His career as a solo artist was the most successful; however, he was first recorded on an album by another artist: David Bowie's astonishingly successful *Let's Dance.* The six tracks he played on for that album introduced a larger and younger audience to his extraordinary, blues-born guitar. His own band, Double Trouble, became famous before they had even cut a record. At the Montreux Jazz Festival of 1982 the band stunned the crowd with a blistering set, meanwhile becoming the first group to play there without a record or a contract.

His personal life did not always follow the same upward curve as his musical career—his struggles with drug and alcohol problems ranked among the most hair-raising in a business well-known for its narcotic pitfalls. When on tour to promote his *Soul to Soul* LP, Vaughan collapsed and fell from a stage in London. Soon he was checked into the Marietta clinic for a month-long stay under the care of Dr. Victor Bloom. Friends who visited to lend him support included Jackson Browne and Eric Clapton. Later he was transferred to a Georgia treatment facility, where he made a successful recovery. *Entertainment Weekly* lauded the song "Wall of Denial" on his *In Step* album, which dealt with his drug addiction. Vaughan's appreciation for one of the rock world's saddest drug casualties, Jimi Hendrix, is documented in his many renditions of Hendrix songs. The *Village Voice* said that Vaughan was "good enough to adore [Hendrix] without embarrassing himself."

Another testimony to Vaughan's burgeoning talent was a Grammy he won for best contemporary blues recording in 1990. The last recordings he made were set for release in September of 1990, the month after his fatal accident. The first album to be released was Bob Dylan's *Under the Red Sky*, on which Vaughan and his brother Jimmie play on three tracks. The brothers released the second LP later in the month; called *Family Style*, it was recognized as far and away the best album to date for either artist. When Vaughan's untimely death was reported, the lauds poured in from around the world. Syndicated columnist Bob Greene mentioned in his obituary of Vaughan that Eric Clapton, a legend himself, had called Vaughan the greatest guitar player that Clapton had ever heard. **Sources:** *Chicago Tribune*, September 2, 1990; *Detroit Free Press*, August 30, 1990; *People*, September 10, 1990; *Village Voice*, September 4, 1990.

Irving Wallace

Born March 19, 1916, in Chicago, Ill.; died of pancreatic cancer, June 29, 1990, in Los Angeles, Calif. Bestselling author. Best known for his novels, Wallace had through the years developed an unusual forte in his fiction. He took a highly complicated subject—a Kinsey-style survey or the Nobel Prize selection, for instance—and wove it into a plot designed to hook readers with characters who have much at stake. In this way, Wallace's novels are notable for the amount of research that went into them.

Among Wallace's early fiction, *The Chapman Report* and *The Prize*, dealing respectively with the Kinsey studies of human sexual behavior and the Nobel Prize story, are the most popular. *The Chapman Report* in particular proved a highly controversial book when it first appeared in 1960, mainly because its sexual *roman a clef* elements were based on discussions Wallace had conducted with his actual neighbors at the time.

Wallace tackled no less a subject than the Bible in *The Word*. Fabricating the discovery of a new set of New Testaments written by James, brother of Jesus, was challenging scholarship, the author acknowledged. But the sense of realism he developed in *The Word* resulted in "endless letters . . . asking me if The Gospel According to James, which I had invented, really had been dug up by archaeologists, translated, and where copies might be purchased," as Wallace noted in *Contemporary Authors*. "While creating my gospel," he added, "I drew upon the best research, archeological discoveries, theories and speculations of the finest Biblical scholars." *The Word*, published in 1972, quickly attained bestseller status.

Wallace said in a 1987 interview with *Contemporary Authors* that every new bestseller excited a run on his older books—a kind of retroactive burst of popularity and sales. "All my novels are in print. What happens is that every time I get a new novel out in hardback, almost all the paperback companies reissue my old novels. Then a lot of people will go out and buy the paperbacks of the others. So the books will go on and on, and that's very exciting." Wallace believed that *The Chapman Report* and *The Word* were his most popular books.

Wallace was often derided by critics who, as the *New York Times* put it, "emphasiz[ed] that his novels were not in the tradition of Faulkner, Fitzgerald and Hemingway. But Mr. Wallace's fiction did offer a judicious sprinkling of adultery, rape, kidnapping, old-fashioned romance, suspense, babbitry, alcoholism, intrigue and assorted examples of venality."

A sometime collaborator with his wife, Sylvia Kahn, and his two children, Amy Wallace and David Wallechinsky, Irving Wallace had said that one thing was more important than the money he made: "Somebody out there loves you and respects what you do and thinks what you do may make money for them," the author was quoted in the *Chicago Tribune*. This despite his humble beginnings as the son of landed Russian immigrants—his father was a clerk in a general store. He learned the writer's trade early in life as a journalist, and even after Wallace became wildly popular (with approximately 600 million devoted readers), he lent his hand to numerous magazine articles and screenplays. **Sources:** *Chicago Tribune*, July 1, 1990; *Contemporary Authors New Revision Series*, Volume 27, Gale Research, Inc., 1987; *New York Times*, June 29, 1990.

—Obituaries by Christine Ferran

Cumulative Nationality Index

This index lists newsmakers alphabetically under their respective nationalities. Indexes in softbound issues allow access to the current year's entries; indexes in annual hardbound volumes are cumulative, covering the entire *Newsmakers* series.

Listee names are followed by a year and issue number; thus **1988**:3 indicates that an entry on that individual appears in both 1988, Issue 3 and the 1988 cumulation. For access to newsmakers appearing earlier than the current softbound issue, see the previous year's cumulation.

AMERICAN

Abbey, Edward
  Obituary **1989**:3
Abbott, Jim **1988**:3
Abdul, Paula **1990**:3
Abercrombie, Josephine **1987**:2
Abernathy, Ralph
  Obituary **1990**:3
Abraham, Spencer **1991**:4
Abrams, Elliott **1987**:1
Abramson, Lyn **1986**:3
Ackerman, Will **1987**:4
Adair, Red **1987**:3
Addams, Charles
  Obituary **1989**:1
Agassi, Andre **1990**:2
Aiello, Danny **1990**:4
Ailes, Roger **1989**:3
Ailey, Alvin **1989**:2
  Obituary **1990**:2
Ainge, Danny **1987**:1
Akers, John F. **1988**:3
Akin, Phil
  Brief Entry **1987**:3
Albert, Stephen **1986**:1
Alda, Robert
  Obituary **1986**:3
Alexander, Lamar **1991**:2
Alley, Kirstie **1990**:3
Allred, Gloria **1985**:2
Alter, Hobie
  Brief Entry **1985**:1
Anastas, Robert
  Brief Entry **1985**:2
Ancier, Garth **1989**:1
Anderson, Harry **1988**:2
Antonini, Joseph **1991**:2
Arden, Eve
  Obituary **1991**:2
Aretsky, Ken **1988**:1
Arison, Ted **1990**:3
Arlen, Harold
  Obituary **1986**:3
Armstrong, Henry
  Obituary **1989**:1
Arnaz, Desi
  Obituary **1987**:1
Arquette, Rosanna **1985**:2
Astaire, Fred
  Obituary **1987**:4
Astor, Mary
  Obituary **1988**:1

Atwater, Lee **1989**:4
  Obituary **1991**:4
Aurre, Laura
  Brief Entry **1986**:3
Axthelm, Pete
  Obituary **1991**:3
Aykroyd, Dan **1989**:3
Backus, Jim
  Obituary **1990**:1
Bailey, Pearl
  Obituary **1991**:1
Baird, Bill
  Brief Entry **1987**:2
Baker, Anita **1987**:4
Baker, James A. III **1991**:2
Baker, Kathy
  Brief Entry **1986**:1
Bakker, Robert T. **1991**:3
Baldessari, John **1991**:4
Baldrige, Malcolm
  Obituary **1988**:1
Baldwin, James
  Obituary **1988**:2
Ball, Lucille
  Obituary **1989**:3
Banks, Dennis J. **1986**:4
Barbera, Joseph **1988**:2
Barkin, Ellen **1987**:3
Barkley, Charles **1988**:2
Barr, Roseanne **1989**:1
Barry, Dave **1991**:2
Barry, Marion **1991**:1
Basie, Count
  Obituary **1985**:1
Basinger, Kim **1987**:2
Bateman, Justine **1988**:4
Bates, Kathy **1991**:4
Bauer, Eddie
  Obituary **1986**:3
Baumgartner, Bruce
  Brief Entry **1987**:3
Baxter, Anne
  Obituary **1986**:1
Bayley, Corrine
  Brief Entry **1986**:4
Beals, Vaughn **1988**:2
Bean, Alan L. **1986**:2
Beattie, Owen
  Brief Entry **1985**:2
Bell, Ricky
  Obituary **1985**:1
Belushi, Jim **1986**:2
Belzer, Richard **1985**:3

Ben & Jerry **1991**:3
Benatar, Pat **1986**:1
Bennett, Joan
  Obituary **1991**:2
Bennett, Michael
  Obituary **1988**:1
Bennett, William **1990**:1
Benoit, Joan **1986**:3
Bergen, Candice **1990**:1
Berle, Peter A.A.
  Brief Entry **1987**:3
Berlin, Irving
  Obituary **1990**:1
Bernardi, Herschel
  Obituary **1986**:4
Bernhard, Sandra **1989**:4
Bernsen, Corbin **1990**:2
Bernstein, Leonard
  Obituary **1991**:1
Bettelheim, Bruno
  Obituary **1990**:3
Bias, Len
  Obituary **1986**:3
Biden, Joe **1986**:3
Bieber, Owen **1986**:1
Bigelow, Kathryn **1990**:4
Bikoff, James L.
  Brief Entry **1986**:2
Billington, James **1990**:3
Bird, Larry **1990**:3
Bissell, Patrick
  Obituary **1988**:2
Blakey, Art
  Obituary **1991**:1
Blanc, Mel
  Obituary **1989**:4
Bloch, Erich **1987**:4
Bloch, Henry **1988**:4
Bloch, Ivan **1986**:3
Bochco, Steven **1989**:1
Boggs, Wade **1989**:3
Bogosian, Eric **1990**:4
Boiardi, Hector
  Obituary **1985**:3
Boitano, Brian **1988**:3
Bolger, Ray
  Obituary **1987**:2
Bonet, Lisa **1989**:2
Bon Jovi, Jon **1987**:4
Boone, Mary **1985**:1
Bose, Amar
  Brief Entry **1986**:4
Bosworth, Brian **1989**:1

Rosendahl, Bruce R.
  Brief Entry **1986**:4
Ross, Percy
  Brief Entry **1986**:2
Rothstein, Ruth **1988**:2
Rourke, Mickey **1988**:4
Rowan, Dan
  Obituary **1988**:1
Ruffin, David
  Obituary **1991**:4
Ruppe, Loret Miller **1986**:2
Rutan, Burt **1987**:2
Ryan, Nolan **1989**:4
Ryder, Winona **1991**:2
Saberhagen, Bret **1986**:1
Sajak, Pat
  Brief Entry **1985**:4
Salerno-Sonnenberg, Nadja **1988**:4
Sample, Bill
  Brief Entry **1986**:2
Sanders, Bernie **1991**:4
Saporta, Vicki
  Brief Entry **1987**:3
Sarandon, Susan **1986**:2
Satriani, Joe **1989**:3
Savage, Fred **1990**:1
Scalia, Antonin **1988**:2
Schaefer, William Donald **1988**:1
Schank, Roger **1989**:2
Schembechler, Bo **1990**:3
Schlessinger, David
  Brief Entry **1985**:1
Schmidt, Mike **1988**:3
Schoenfeld, Gerald **1986**:2
Scholz, Tom **1987**:2
Schott, Marge **1985**:4
Schroeder, William J.
  Obituary **1986**:4
Schwab, Charles **1989**:3
Schwartz, David **1988**:3
Schwarzenegger, Arnold **1991**:1
Schwarzkopf, Norman **1991**:3
Schwinn, Edward R., Jr.
  Brief Entry **1985**:4
Scorsese, Martin **1989**:1
Scott, Gene
  Brief Entry **1986**:1
Scott, Randolph
  Obituary **1987**:2
Sculley, John **1989**:4
Secretariat
  Obituary **1990**:1
Sedelmaier, Joe **1985**:3
Seger, Bob **1987**:1
Seidelman, Susan **1985**:4
Sharpton, Al **1991**:2
Shawn, Dick
  Obituary **1987**:3
Sheedy, Ally **1989**:1
Sheehan, Daniel P. **1989**:1
Sherman, Russell **1987**:4
Shocked, Michelle **1989**:4
Shriver, Maria
  Brief Entry **1986**:2
Sidney, Ivan
  Brief Entry **1987**:2
Siebert, Muriel **1987**:2
Sigmund, Barbara Boggs
  Obituary **1991**:1
Silber, John **1990**:1
Silvers, Phil
  Obituary **1985**:4
Simmons, Adele Smith **1988**:4
Simpson, Wallis
  Obituary **1986**:3
Sinclair, Mary **1985**:2
Skinner, B.F.
  Obituary **1991**:1

Slotnick, Barry
  Brief Entry **1987**:4
Smale, John G. **1987**:3
Smirnoff, Yakov **1987**:2
Smith, Frederick W. **1985**:4
Smith, Jeff **1991**:4
Smith, Jerry
  Obituary **1987**:1
Smith, Kate
  Obituary **1986**:3
Smith, Roger **1990**:3
Smith, Samantha
  Obituary **1985**:3
Smith, Willi
  Obituary **1987**:3
Smits, Jimmy **1990**:1
Snider, Dee **1986**:1
Snyder, Mitch
  Obituary **1991**:1
Soren, David
  Brief Entry **1986**:3
Souter, David **1991**:3
Spader, James **1991**:2
Spector, Phil **1989**:1
Spheeris, Penelope **1989**:2
Spong, John **1991**:3
Stallings, George A., Jr. **1990**:1
Steel, Dawn **1990**:1
Steele, Shelby **1991**:2
Steger, Will **1990**:4
Steinberg, Leigh **1987**:3
Steinbrenner, George **1991**:1
Stempel, Robert **1991**:3
Stern, David **1991**:4
Stern, Howard **1988**:2
Stevens, Eileen **1987**:3
Stewart, Dave **1991**:1
Stewart, Potter
  Obituary **1986**:1
Stofflet, Ty
  Brief Entry **1987**:1
Stone, I.F.
  Obituary **1990**:1
Stone, Irving
  Obituary **1990**:2
Stone, Oliver **1990**:4
Strange, Curtis **1988**:4
Strauss, Robert **1991**:4
Streep, Meryl **1990**:2
Stroh, Peter W. **1985**:2
Suarez, Xavier
  Brief Entry **1986**:2
Sullivan, Louis **1990**:4
Sununu, John **1989**:2
Susskind, David
  Obituary **1987**:2
Swaggart, Jimmy **1987**:3
Szent-Gyoergyi, Albert
  Obituary **1987**:2
Tagliabue, Paul **1990**:2
Tandy, Jessica **1990**:4
Tanny, Vic
  Obituary **1985**:3
Tarkenian, Jerry **1990**:4
Tartikoff, Brandon **1985**:2
Taylor, Lawrence **1987**:3
Taylor, Maxwell
  Obituary **1987**:3
Terry, Randall **1991**:4
Testaverde, Vinny **1987**:2
Thalheimer, Richard
  Brief Entry **1988**:3
Thiebaud, Wayne **1991**:1
Thomas, Danny
  Obituary **1991**:3
Thomas, Debi **1987**:2
Thomas, Helen **1988**:4
Thomas, Isiah **1989**:2

Thomas, Michael Tilson **1990**:3
Thomas, Michel **1987**:4
Thomas, R. David
  Brief Entry **1986**:2
Thompson, John **1988**:3
Thompson, Starley
  Brief Entry **1987**:3
Tiffany **1989**:1
Tillstrom, Burr
  Obituary **1986**:1
Tisch, Laurence A. **1988**:2
Tompkins, Susie
  Brief Entry **1987**:2
Tone-Loc **1990**:3
Toomer, Ron **1990**:1
Toone, Bill
  Brief Entry **1987**:2
Tower, John
  Obituary **1991**:4
Traub, Marvin
  Brief Entry **1987**:3
Travis, Randy **1988**:4
Treybig, James G. **1988**:3
Tribe, Laurence H. **1988**:1
Trudeau, Garry **1991**:2
Trump, Donald **1989**:2
Tucker, Forrest
  Obituary **1987**:1
Turner, Kathleen **1985**:3
Turner, Ted **1989**:1
Tyson, Mike **1986**:4
Upshaw, Dawn **1991**:2
Upshaw, Gene **1988**:1
Urich, Robert **1988**:1
Vagelos, P. Roy **1989**:4
Valente, Benita **1985**:3
Van Halen, Edward **1985**:2
Vanilla Ice **1991**:3
Varney, Jim
  Brief Entry **1985**:4
Vaughan, Sarah
  Obituary **1990**:3
Vaughan, Stevie Ray
  Obituary **1991**:1
Veeck, Bill
  Obituary **1986**:1
Vega, Suzanne **1988**:1
Vidov, Oleg **1987**:4
Vincent, Fay **1990**:2
Vinton, Will
  Brief Entry **1988**:1
Violet, Arlene **1985**:3
Vitale, Dick **1988**:4
von Trapp, Maria
  Obituary **1987**:3
vos Savant, Marilyn **1988**:2
Vreeland, Diana
  Obituary **1990**:1
Wachner, Linda **1988**:3
Waddell, Thomas F.
  Obituary **1988**:2
Waldron, Hicks B. **1987**:3
Walgreen, Charles III
  Brief Entry **1987**:4
Wallace, Irving
  Obituary **1991**:1
Wallis, Hal
  Obituary **1987**:1
Walsh, Bill **1987**:4
Walton, Sam **1986**:2
Wang, An **1986**:1
  Obituary **1990**:3
Wapner, Joseph A. **1987**:1
Warhol, Andy
  Obituary **1987**:2
Warren, Robert Penn
  Obituary **1990**:1
Washington, Grover, Jr. **1989**:1

Washington, Harold
  Obituary **1988**:1
Wasserstein, Wendy **1991**:3
Waters, John **1988**:3
Watson, Elizabeth **1991**:2
Watterson, Bill **1990**:3
Wattleton, Faye **1989**:1
Wayans, Keenen Ivory **1991**:1
Weaver, Sigourney **1988**:3
Weber, Pete **1986**:3
Wegman, William **1991**:1
Weill, Sandy **1990**:4
Weintraub, Jerry **1986**:1
Weitz, Bruce **1985**:4
Welch, Bob **1991**:3
Wells, Sharlene
  Brief Entry **1985**:1
White, Bill **1989**:3
White, Ryan
  Obituary **1990**:3
Whitmire, Kathy **1988**:2
Whittle, Christopher **1989**:3
Wigler, Michael
  Brief Entry **1985**:1
Wilder, L. Douglas **1990**:3
Wildmon, Donald **1988**:4
Williams, Doug **1988**:2
Williams, Edward Bennett
  Obituary **1988**:4
Williams, G. Mennen
  Obituary **1988**:2
Williams, Robin **1988**:4
Williamson, Marianne **1991**:4
Willis, Bruce **1986**:4
Willson, S. Brian **1989**:3
Wilson, Jerry
  Brief Entry **1986**:2
Winfrey, Oprah **1986**:4
Winston, George **1987**:1
Winter, Paul **1990**:2
Wolf, Stephen M. **1989**:3
Woodard, Lynette **1986**:2
Woodruff, Robert Winship
  Obituary **1985**:1
Woods, James **1988**:3
Woodwell, George S. **1987**:2
Worthy, James **1991**:2
Wright, Steven **1986**:3
Wynn, Keenan
  Obituary **1987**:1
Yamasaki, Minoru
  Obituary **1986**:2
Yankovic, "Weird Al" **1985**:4
Yard, Molly **1991**:4
Yetnikoff, Walter **1988**:1
Zamboni, Frank J.
  Brief Entry **1986**:4
Zanker, Bill
  Brief Entry **1987**:3
Zech, Lando W.
  Brief Entry **1987**:4
Ziff, William B., Jr. **1986**:4
Zuckerman, Mortimer **1986**:3
Zwilich, Ellen **1990**:1

ANGOLAN
Savimbi, Jonas **1986**:2

ARGENTINE
Maradona, Diego **1991**:3
Pelli, Cesar **1991**:4
Sabatini, Gabriela
  Brief Entry **1985**:4

AUSTRALIAN
Bond, Alan **1989**:2

Gibb, Andy
  Obituary **1988**:3
Gibson, Mel **1990**:1
Murdoch, Rupert **1988**:4
Norman, Greg **1988**:3
Summers, Anne **1990**:2

AUSTRIAN
Brandauer, Klaus Maria **1987**:3
Falco
  Brief Entry **1987**:2
Lorenz, Konrad
  Obituary **1989**:3
Puck, Wolfgang **1990**:1
von Karajan, Herbert
  Obituary **1989**:4
von Trapp, Maria
  Obituary **1987**:3

BRAZILIAN
Senna, Ayrton **1991**:4

BRITISH
Adamson, George
  Obituary **1990**:2
Baddeley, Hermione
  Obituary **1986**:4
Branson, Richard **1987**:1
Chatwin, Bruce
  Obituary **1989**:2
Cleese, John **1989**:2
Cummings, Sam **1986**:3
Dalton, Timothy **1988**:4
Davison, Ian Hay **1986**:1
Day-Lewis, Daniel **1989**:4
Egan, John **1987**:2
Eno, Brian **1986**:2
Ferguson, Sarah **1990**:3
Fiennes, Ranulph **1990**:3
Fonteyn, Margot
  Obituary **1991**:3
Gift, Roland **1990**:2
Goodall, Jane **1991**:1
Greene, Graham
  Obituary **1991**:4
Hamilton, Hamish
  Obituary **1988**:4
Harrison, Rex
  Obituary **1990**:4
Hawking, Stephen W. **1990**:1
Headroom, Max **1986**:4
Hockney, David **1988**:3
Hoskins, Bob **1989**:1
Hounsfield, Godfrey **1989**:2
Howard, Trevor
  Obituary **1988**:2
Ireland, Jill
  Obituary **1990**:4
Irons, Jeremy **1991**:4
Knopfler, Mark **1986**:2
Laing, R.D.
  Obituary **1990**:1
Lawrence, Ruth
  Brief Entry **1986**:3
Leach, Robin
  Brief Entry **1985**:4
Lennox, Annie **1985**:4
Livingstone, Ken **1988**:3
Lloyd Webber, Andrew **1989**:1
Macmillan, Harold
  Obituary **1987**:2
Major, John **1991**:2
Maxwell, Robert **1990**:1
Michael, George **1989**:2
Moore, Henry
  Obituary **1986**:4
Norrington, Roger **1989**:4

Olivier, Laurence
  Obituary **1989**:4
Penrose, Roger **1991**:4
Philby, Kim
  Obituary **1988**:3
Rattle, Simon **1989**:4
Redgrave, Vanessa **1989**:2
Rhodes, Zandra **1986**:2
Roddick, Anita **1989**:4
Runcie, Robert **1989**:4
Saatchi, Charles **1987**:3
Steptoe, Patrick
  Obituary **1988**:3
Stevens, James
  Brief Entry **1988**:1
Sting **1991**:4
Thatcher, Margaret **1989**:2
Tudor, Antony
  Obituary **1987**:4
Uchida, Mitsuko **1989**:3
Ullman, Tracey **1988**:3
Wilson, Peter C.
  Obituary **1985**:2
Wintour, Anna **1990**:4

BRUNEIAN
Bolkiah, Sultan Muda
  Hassanal **1985**:4

BULGARIAN
Dimitrova, Ghena **1987**:1

CAMBODIAN
Lon Nol
  Obituary **1986**:1

CANADIAN
Black, Conrad **1986**:2
Campeau, Robert **1990**:1
Cerovsek, Corey
  Brief Entry **1987**:4
Chretien, Jean **1990**:4
Coffey, Paul **1985**:4
Copps, Sheila **1986**:4
Eagleson, Alan **1987**:4
Erickson, Arthur **1989**:3
Fonyo, Steve
  Brief Entry **1985**:4
Foster, David **1988**:2
Fox, Michael J. **1986**:1
Frye, Northrop
  Obituary **1991**:3
Garneau, Marc **1985**:1
Gatien, Peter
  Brief Entry **1986**:1
Graham, Nicholas **1991**:4
Greene, Lorne
  Obituary **1988**:1
Gretzky, Wayne **1989**:2
Haney, Chris
  Brief Entry **1985**:1
Hextall, Ron **1988**:2
Hull, Brett **1991**:4
Johnson, Pierre Marc **1985**:4
Juneau, Pierre **1988**:3
Kent, Arthur **1991**:4
Lalonde, Marc **1985**:1
Lang, K.D. **1988**:4
Lanois, Daniel **1991**:1
Lemieux, Mario **1986**:4
Lévesque, René
  Obituary **1988**:1
Lewis, Stephen **1987**:2
Mandel, Howie **1989**:1
Markle, C. Wilson **1988**:1
McLaren, Norman
  Obituary **1987**:2

Cumulative Nationality Index

MALAYSIAN
Ngau, Harrison **1991**:3

MEXICAN
Kahlo, Frida **1991**:3
Paz, Octavio **1991**:2

MOZAMBICAN
Chissano, Joaquim **1987**:4
Machel, Samora
Obituary **1987**:1

NAMIBIAN
Nujoma, Sam **1990**:4

NEW ZEALAND
Campion, Jane **1991**:4

NICARAGUAN
Astorga, Nora **1988**:2
Cruz, Arturo **1985**:1
Obando, Miguel **1986**:4
Robelo, Alfonso **1988**:1

NIGERIAN
Okoye, Christian **1990**:2
Olajuwon, Akeem **1985**:1

NORWEGIAN
Olav, King of Norway
Obituary **1991**:3

PAKISTANI
Bhutto, Benazir **1989**:4
Zia ul-Haq, Mohammad
Obituary **1988**:4

PALESTINIAN
Arafat, Yasser **1989**:3
Freij, Elias **1986**:4
Habash, George **1986**:1
Nidal, Abu **1987**:1
Terzi, Zehdi Labib **1985**:3

PERUVIAN
Perez de Cuellar, Javier **1991**:3

POLISH
Kosinski, Jerzy
Obituary **1991**:4
Niezabitowska, Malgorzata **1991**:3
Walesa, Lech **1991**:2

PUERTO RICAN
Novello, Antonia **1991**:2

ROMANIAN
Ceausescu, Nicolae
Obituary **1990**:2

SALVADORAN
Duarte, Jose Napoleon
Obituary **1990**:3

SCOTTISH
Connery, Sean **1990**:4

SOUTH AFRICAN
Blackburn, Molly
Obituary **1985**:4
Buthelczi, Mangosuthu
Gatsha **1989**:3
de Klerk, F.W. **1990**:1
Duncan, Sheena
Brief Entry **1987**:1
Makeba, Miriam **1989**:2
Mandela, Nelson **1990**:3
Mandela, Winnie **1989**:3
Paton, Alan
Obituary **1988**:3
Ramaphosa, Cyril **1988**:2
Slovo, Joe **1989**:2
Suzman, Helen **1989**:3
Tambo, Oliver **1991**:3

SOVIET
Chernenko, Konstantin
Obituary **1985**:1
Dubinin, Yuri **1987**:4
Dzhanibekov, Vladimir **1988**:1
Erte
Obituary **1990**:4
Gorbachev, Mikhail **1985**:2
Grebenshikov, Boris **1990**:1
Gromyko, Andrei
Obituary **1990**:2
Molotov, Vyacheslav Mikhailovich
Obituary **1987**:1
Sakharov, Andrei Dmitrievich
Obituary **1990**:2
Smirnoff, Yakov **1987**:2
Vidov, Oleg **1987**:4
Yeltsin, Boris **1991**:1

SPANISH
Dali, Salvador
Obituary **1989**:2
de Pinies, Jamie
Brief Entry **1986**:3
Miro, Joan
Obituary **1985**:1
Samaranch, Juan Antonio **1986**:2
Segovia, Andrés
Obituary **1987**:3

SWEDISH
Garbo, Greta
Obituary **1990**:3
Lindbergh, Pelle
Obituary **1985**:4
Olin, Lena **1991**:2
Palme, Olof
Obituary **1986**:2
Renvall, Johan
Brief Entry **1987**:4

SWISS
Vollenweider, Andreas **1985**:2

SYRIAN
Assad, Rifaat **1986**:3

TIBETAN
Dalai Lama **1989**:1

VENEZUELAN
Perez, Carlos Andre **1990**:2

VIETNAMESE
Le Duan
Obituary **1986**:4
Le Duc Tho
Obituary **1991**:1

WELSH
Dahl, Roald
Obituary **1991**:2

YUGOSLAV
Pogorelich, Ivo **1986**:4
Seles, Monica **1991**:3

ZIMBABWEAN
Mugabe, Robert **1988**:4

Cumulative Occupation Index

This index lists newsmakers by their occupations or fields of primary activity. Indexes in softbound issues allow access to the current year's entries; indexes in annual hardbound volumes are cumulative, covering the entire *Newsmakers* series.

Listee names are followed by a year and issue number; thus **1988**:3 indicates that an entry on that individual appears in both 1988, Issue 3 and the 1988 cumulation. For access to newsmakers appearing earlier than the current softbound issue, see the previous year's cumulation.

Ross, Percy
  Brief Entry **1986**:2
Rothschild, Philippe de
  Obituary **1988**:2
Rothstein, Ruth **1988**:2
Sasakawa, Ryoichi
  Brief Entry **1988**:1
Schlessinger, David
  Brief Entry **1985**:1
Schoenfeld, Gerald **1986**:2
Schott, Marge **1985**:4
Schwab, Charles **1989**:3
Schwinn, Edward R., Jr.
  Brief Entry **1985**:4
Sculley, John **1989**:4
Sedelmaier, Joe **1985**:3
Siebert, Muriel **1987**:2
Smale, John G. **1987**:3
Smith, Frederick W. **1985**:4
Smith, Roger **1990**:3
Spector, Phil **1989**:1
Steel, Dawn **1990**:1
Steinberg, Leigh **1987**:3
Steinbrenner, George **1991**:1
Stempel, Robert **1991**:3
Stern, David **1991**:4
Stroh, Peter W. **1985**:2
Summers, Anne **1990**:2
Tagliabue, Paul **1990**:2
Tanny, Vic
  Obituary **1985**:3
Tartikoff, Brandon **1985**:2
Thalheimer, Richard
  Brief Entry **1988**:3
Thomas, Michel **1987**:4
Thomas, R. David
  Brief Entry **1986**:2
Tisch, Laurence A. **1988**:2
Tompkins, Susie
  Brief Entry **1987**:2
Toyoda, Eiji **1985**:2
Traub, Marvin
  Brief Entry **1987**:3
Treybig, James G. **1988**:3
Trump, Donald **1989**:2
Turner, Ted **1989**:1
Upshaw, Gene **1988**:1
Vagelos, P. Roy **1989**:4
Veeck, Bill
  Obituary **1986**:1
Vinton, Will
  Brief Entry **1988**:1
Wachner, Linda **1988**:3
Waldron, Hicks B. **1987**:3
Walgreen, Charles III
  Brief Entry **1987**:4
Walton, Sam **1986**:2
Wang, An **1986**:1
  Obituary **1990**:3
Weill, Sandy **1990**:4
Weintraub, Jerry **1986**:1
Whittle, Christopher **1989**:3
Williams, Edward Bennett
  Obituary **1988**:4
Williams, Lynn **1986**:4
Wilson, Jerry
  Brief Entry **1986**:2
Wilson, Peter C.
  Obituary **1985**:2
Wintour, Anna **1990**:4
Wolf, Stephen M. **1989**:3
Woodruff, Robert Winship
  Obituary **1985**:1
Yamamoto, Kenichi **1989**:1
Yetnikoff, Walter **1988**:1
Zamboni, Frank J.
  Brief Entry **1986**:4

Zanker, Bill
  Brief Entry **1987**:3
Ziff, William B., Jr. **1986**:4
Zuckerman, Mortimer **1986**:3

DANCE
Abdul, Paula **1990**:3
Ailey, Alvin **1989**:2
  Obituary **1990**:2
Astaire, Fred
  Obituary **1987**:4
Bennett, Michael
  Obituary **1988**:1
Bissell, Patrick
  Obituary **1988**:2
Davis, Sammy, Jr.
  Obituary **1990**:4
Dean, Laura **1989**:4
Englund, Richard
  Obituary **1991**:3
Fenley, Molissa **1988**:3
Ferri, Alessandra **1987**:2
Fonteyn, Margot
  Obituary **1991**:3
Fosse, Bob
  Obituary **1988**:1
Garr, Teri **1988**:4
Graham, Martha
  Obituary **1991**:4
Gregory, Cynthia **1990**:2
Guillem, Sylvie **1988**:2
Jackson, Janet **1990**:4
Jamison, Judith **1990**:3
Joffrey, Robert
  Obituary **1988**:3
Jones, Bill T. **1991**:4
Kaye, Nora
  Obituary **1987**:4
Lander, Toni
  Obituary **1985**:4
Madonna **1985**:2
Morris, Mark **1991**:1
Murray, Arthur
  Obituary **1991**:3
North, Alex **1986**:3
Rauschenberg, Robert **1991**:2
Renvall, Johan
  Brief Entry **1987**:4
Takei, Kei **1990**:2
Tudor, Antony
  Obituary **1987**:4

EDUCATION
Abramson, Lyn **1986**:3
Alexander, Lamar **1991**:2
Bakker, Robert T. **1991**:3
Bayley, Corrine
  Brief Entry **1986**:4
Billington, James **1990**:3
Botstein, Leon **1985**:3
Cavazos, Lauro F. **1989**:2
Cheek, James Edward
  Brief Entry **1987**:1
Cheney, Lynne V. **1990**:4
Clements, George **1985**:1
Curran, Charles E. **1989**:2
Edelman, Marian Wright **1990**:4
Edwards, Harry **1989**:4
Feldman, Sandra **1987**:3
Fernandez, Joseph **1991**:3
Futrell, Mary Hatwood **1986**:1
Giamatti, A. Bartlett **1988**:4
  Obituary **1990**:1
Goldhaber, Fred
  Brief Entry **1986**:3
Green, Richard R. **1988**:3
Gregorian, Vartan **1990**:3

Healy, Timothy S. **1990**:2
Heller, Walter
  Obituary **1987**:4
Hillegass, Clifton Keith **1989**:4
Hunter, Madeline **1991**:2
Janzen, Daniel H. **1988**:4
Jordan, King **1990**:1
Justiz, Manuel J. **1986**:4
Kemp, Jan **1987**:2
Lang, Eugene M. **1990**:3
Langston, J. William
  Brief Entry **1986**:2
Lawrence, Ruth
  Brief Entry **1986**:3
Malloy, Edward "Monk" **1989**:4
McAuliffe, Christa
  Obituary **1985**:4
Mumford, Lewis
  Obituary **1990**:2
Peter, Valentine J. **1988**:2
Rosendahl, Bruce R.
  Brief Entry **1986**:4
Sherman, Russell **1987**:4
Silber, John **1990**:1
Simmons, Adele Smith **1988**:4
Steele, Shelby **1991**:2
Thiebaud, Wayne **1991**:1
Thomas, Michel **1987**:4
Tribe, Laurence H. **1988**:1
Warren, Robert Penn
  Obituary **1990**:1
Zanker, Bill
  Brief Entry **1987**:3

FILM
Adjani, Isabelle **1991**:1
Aiello, Danny **1990**:4
Alda, Robert
  Obituary **1986**:3
Alley, Kirstie **1990**:3
Arden, Eve
  Obituary **1991**:2
Arlen, Harold
  Obituary **1986**:3
Arnaz, Desi
  Obituary **1987**:1
Arquette, Rosanna **1985**:2
Astaire, Fred
  Obituary **1987**:4
Astor, Mary
  Obituary **1988**:1
Aykroyd, Dan **1989**:3
Backus, Jim
  Obituary **1990**:1
Baddeley, Hermione
  Obituary **1986**:4
Bailey, Pearl
  Obituary **1991**:1
Ball, Lucille
  Obituary **1989**:3
Barkin, Ellen **1987**:3
Barr, Roseanne **1989**:1
Basinger, Kim **1987**:2
Bateman, Justine **1988**:4
Bates, Kathy **1991**:4
Baxter, Anne
  Obituary **1986**:1
Belushi, Jim **1986**:2
Bennett, Joan
  Obituary **1991**:2
Bergen, Candice **1990**:1
Bernardi, Herschel
  Obituary **1986**:4
Bernhard, Sandra **1989**:4
Bernsen, Corbin **1990**:2
Bigelow, Kathryn **1990**:4

Blanc, Mel
  Obituary 1909:1
Bogosian, Eric 1990:4
Bolger, Ray
  Obituary 1987:2
Bonet, Lisa 1989:2
Brandauer, Klaus Maria 1987:3
Brooks, Albert 1991:4
Brown, James 1991:4
Brynner, Yul
  Obituary 1985:4
Burum, Stephen H.
  Brief Entry 1987:2
Caesar, Adolph
  Obituary 1986:3
Cage, Nicolas 1991:1
Cagney, James
  Obituary 1986:2
Campion, Jane 1991:4
Candy, John 1988:2
Carradine, John
  Obituary 1989:2
Cassavetes, John
  Obituary 1989:2
Channing, Stockard 1991:3
Chase, Chevy 1990:1
Clay, Andrew Dice 1991:1
Cleese, John 1989:2
Close, Glenn 1988:3
Coco, James
  Obituary 1987:2
Coleman, Dabney 1988:3
Connery, Sean 1990:4
Connick, Harry, Jr. 1991:1
Coppola, Carmine
  Obituary 1991:4
Coppola, Francis Ford 1989:4
Costner, Kevin 1989:4
Crawford, Broderick
  Obituary 1986:3
Crothers, Scatman
  Obituary 1987:1
Cruise, Tom 1985:4
Crystal, Billy 1985:3
Culkin, Macaulay 1991:3
Dafoe, Willem 1988:1
Dalton, Timothy 1988:4
Daniels, Jeff 1989:4
Danza, Tony 1989:1
Davis, Bette
  Obituary 1990:1
Davis, Sammy, Jr.
  Obituary 1990:4
Day, Dennis
  Obituary 1988:4
Day-Lewis, Daniel 1989:4
De Cordova, Frederick 1985:2
Depardieu, Gerard 1991:2
Depp, Johnny 1991:3
De Vito, Danny 1987:1
Diamond, I.A.L.
  Obituary 1988:3
Diamond, Selma
  Obituary 1985:2
Diller, Barry 1991:1
Disney, Roy E. 1986:3
Divine
  Obituary 1988:3
Douglas, Michael 1986:2
Eisner, Michael 1989:2
Estevez, Emilio 1985:4
Fetchit, Stepin
  Obituary 1986:1
Fisher, Carrie 1991:1
Ford, Harrison 1990:2
Fosse, Bob
  Obituary 1988:1
Foster, Jodie 1989:2

Fox, Michael J. 1986:1
Freeman, Morgan 1990:4
Garbo, Greta
  Obituary 1990:3
Gardner, Ava Lavinia
  Obituary 1990:2
Garr, Teri 1988:4
Geffen, David 1985:3
Gibson, Mel 1990:1
Gift, Roland 1990:2
Gilford, Jack
  Obituary 1990:4
Gleason, Jackie
  Obituary 1987:4
Gless, Sharon 1989:3
Gobel, George
  Obituary 1991:4
Goldberg, Leonard 1988:4
Goldblum, Jeff 1988:1
Goodman, John 1990:3
Gordon, Dexter 1987:1
  Obituary 1990:4
Gossett, Louis, Jr. 1989:3
Grant, Cary
  Obituary 1987:1
Greene, Lorne
  Obituary 1988:1
Griffith, Melanie 1989:2
Grusin, Dave
  Brief Entry 1987:2
Hackman, Gene 1989:3
Hall, Anthony Michael 1986:3
Hall, Arsenio 1990:2
Hamilton, Margaret
  Obituary 1985:3
Hammer, Jan 1987:3
Hanks, Tom 1989:2
Hannah, Daryl 1987:4
Harmon, Mark 1987:1
Harrison, Rex
  Obituary 1990:4
Harry, Deborah 1990:1
Hayworth, Rita
  Obituary 1987:3
Heckerling, Amy 1987:2
Henson, Jim 1989:1
  Obituary 1990:4
Hepburn, Katharine 1991:2
Hershey, Barbara 1989:1
Holmes, John C.
  Obituary 1988:3
Hoskins, Bob 1989:1
Houseman, John
  Obituary 1989:1
Howard, Trevor
  Obituary 1988:2
Hudson, Rock
  Obituary 1985:4
Hunter, Holly 1989:4
Hurt, William 1986:1
Huston, Anjelica 1989:3
Huston, John
  Obituary 1988:1
Hutton, Timothy 1986:3
Ireland, Jill
  Obituary 1990:4
Irons, Jeremy 1991:4
Jillian, Ann 1986:4
Johnson, Don 1986:1
Kasem, Casey 1987:1
Kaye, Danny
  Obituary 1987:2
Keaton, Michael 1989:4
Kilmer, Val 1991:4
Kinski, Klaus 1987:2
Kramer, Larry 1991:2
Kulp, Nancy
  Obituary 1991:3

Kurosawa, Akira 1991:1
Lahti, Christine 1988:2
Larroquette, John 1986:2
Lee, Spike 1988:4
Leno, Jay 1987:1
Leone, Sergio
  Obituary 1989:4
Levinson, Barry 1989:3
Liberace
  Obituary 1987:2
Lithgow, John 1985:2
Lloyd Webber, Andrew 1989:1
Loewe, Frederick
  Obituary 1988:2
Logan, Joshua.
  Obituary 1988:4
Long, Shelley 1985:1
Lowe, Rob 1990:4
Lynch, David 1990:4
MacRae, Gordon
  Obituary 1986:2
Madonna 1985:2
Malkovich, John 1988:2
Mandel, Howie 1989:1
Markle, C. Wilson 1988:1
Marsalis, Branford 1988:3
Marshall, Penny 1991:3
Martin, Dean Paul
  Obituary 1987:3
Marvin, Lee
  Obituary 1988:1
Matuszak, John
  Obituary 1989:4
McCrea, Joel
  Obituary 1991:1
McGillis, Kelly 1989:3
McLaren, Norman
  Obituary 1987:2
Midler, Bette 1989:4
Milland, Ray
  Obituary 1986:2
Moore, Demi 1991:4
Moore, Michael 1990:3
Morita, Noriyuki "Pat" 1987:3
Murphy, Eddie 1989:2
Nelson, Rick
  Obituary 1986:1
Nicholson, Jack 1989:2
Nolan, Lloyd
  Obituary 1985:4
North, Alex 1986:3
Olin, Lena 1991:2
Olivier, Laurence
  Obituary 1989:4
Olmos, Edward James 1990:1
Ovitz, Michael 1990:1
Page, Geraldine
  Obituary 1987:4
Penn, Sean 1987:2
Peterson, Cassandra 1988:1
Pfeiffer, Michelle 1990:2
Phoenix, River, 1990:2
Picasso, Paloma 1991:1
Pinchot, Bronson 1987:4
Poitier, Sidney 1990:3
Preminger, Otto
  Obituary 1986:3
Preston, Robert
  Obituary 1987:3
Quaid, Dennis 1989:4
Radner, Gilda
  Obituary 1989:4
Redgrave, Vanessa 1989:2
Reed, Donna
  Obituary 1986:1
Reiner, Rob 1991:2
Reitman, Ivan 1986:3
Reubens, Paul 1987:2

Riddle, Nelson
  Obituary **1985**:4
Ringwald, Molly **1985**:4
Roberts, Julia **1991**:3
Rollins, Howard E., Jr. **1986**:1
Rourke, Mickey **1988**:4
Rowan, Dan
  Obituary **1988**:1
Ryder, Winona **1991**:2
Sarandon, Susan **1986**:2
Savage, Fred **1990**:1
Schwarzenegger, Arnold **1991**:1
Scorsese, Martin **1989**:1
Scott, Randolph
  Obituary **1987**:2
Seidelman, Susan **1985**:4
Shaffer, Paul **1987**:1
Shawn, Dick
  Obituary **1987**:3
Sheedy, Ally **1989**:1
Short, Martin **1986**:1
Silvers, Phil
  Obituary **1985**:4
Smirnoff, Yakov **1987**:2
Smits, Jimmy **1990**:1
Spader, James **1991**:2
Spheeris, Penelope **1989**:2
Staller, Ilona **1988**:3
Steel, Dawn **1990**:1
Sting **1991**:4
Stone, Oliver **1990**:4
Streep, Meryl **1990**:2
Susskind, David
  Obituary **1987**:2
Tandy, Jessica **1990**:4
Thiebaud, Wayne **1991**:1
Tucker, Forrest
  Obituary **1987**:1
Turner, Kathleen **1985**:3
Ullman, Tracey **1988**:3
Urich, Robert **1988**:1
Vanilla Ice **1991**:3
Vidov, Oleg **1987**:4
Vincent, Fay **1990**:2
Wallis, Hal
  Obituary **1987**:1
Warhol, Andy
  Obituary **1987**:2
Waters, John **1988**:3
Wayans, Keenen Ivory **1991**:1
Weaver, Sigourney **1988**:3
Wegman, William **1991**:1
Weintraub, Jerry **1986**:1
Williams, Robin **1988**:4
Willis, Bruce **1986**:4
Winfrey, Oprah **1986**:4
Woods, James **1988**:3
Wynn, Keenan
  Obituary **1987**:1
Zeffirelli, Franco **1991**:3

LAW
Allred, Gloria **1985**:2
Astorga, Nora **1988**:2
Baker, James A. III **1991**:2
Bikoff, James L.
  Brief Entry **1986**:2
Brown, Willie L. **1985**:2
Burnison, Chantal Simone **1988**:3
Cantrell, Ed
  Brief Entry **1985**:3
Casey, William
  Obituary **1987**:3
Dole, Elizabeth Hanford **1990**:1
Dukakis, Michael **1988**:3
Eagleson, Alan **1987**:4

Ervin, Sam
  Obituary **1985**:2
Estrich, Susan **1989**:1
Fairstein, Linda **1991**:1
Fehr, Donald **1987**:2
Florio, James J. **1991**:2
France, Johnny
  Brief Entry **1987**:1
Furman, Rosemary
  Brief Entry **1986**:4
Glasser, Ira **1989**:1
Hayes, Robert M. **1986**:3
Hills, Carla **1990**:3
Hirschhorn, Joel
  Brief Entry **1986**:1
Hyatt, Joel **1985**:3
Janklow, Morton **1989**:3
Kennedy, John F., Jr. **1990**:1
Kurzban, Ira **1987**:2
Lewis, Reginald F. **1988**:4
Lightner, Candy **1985**:1
Liman, Arthur **1989**:4
Lipsig, Harry H. **1985**:1
Lipton, Martin **1987**:3
Mitchell, George J. **1989**:3
Mitchell, John
  Obituary **1989**:2
Mitchelson, Marvin **1989**:2
Morrison, Trudi
  Brief Entry **1986**:2
Nader, Ralph **1989**:4
Neal, James Foster **1986**:2
O'Connor, Sandra Day **1991**:1
O'Steen, Van
  Brief Entry **1986**:3
Puccio, Thomas P. **1986**:4
Quayle, Dan **1989**:2
Ramaphosa, Cyril **1988**:2
Redstone, Sumner Murray **1987**:4
Scalia, Antonin **1988**:2
Schily, Otto
  Brief Entry **1987**:4
Sheehan, Daniel P. **1989**:1
Slotnick, Barry
  Brief Entry **1987**:4
Souter, David **1991**:3
Steinberg, Leigh **1987**:3
Stern, David **1991**:4
Stewart, Potter
  Obituary **1986**:1
Strauss, Robert **1991**:4
Tagliabue, Paul **1990**:2
Tribe, Laurence H. **1988**:1
Vincent, Fay **1990**:2
Violet, Arlene **1985**:3
Wapner, Joseph A. **1987**:1
Watson, Elizabeth **1991**:2
Williams, Edward Bennett
  Obituary **1988**:4
Wilson, Bertha
  Brief Entry **1986**:1

MUSIC
Abdul, Paula **1990**:3
Ackerman, Will **1987**:4
Albert, Stephen **1986**:1
Arlen, Harold
  Obituary **1986**:3
Arnaz, Desi
  Obituary **1987**:1
Astaire, Fred
  Obituary **1987**:4
Bailey, Pearl
  Obituary **1991**:1
Baker, Anita **1987**:4
Basie, Count
  Obituary **1985**:1

Benatar, Pat **1986**:1
Berlin, Irving
  Obituary **1990**:1
Bernhard, Sandra **1989**:4
Bernstein, Leonard
  Obituary **1991**:1
Blakey, Art
  Obituary **1991**:1
Bon Jovi, Jon **1987**:4
Bono **1988**:4
Botstein, Leon **1985**:3
Branson, Richard **1987**:1
Brown, James **1991**:4
Butterfield, Paul
  Obituary **1987**:3
Carey, Mariah **1991**:3
Carlisle, Belinda **1989**:3
Carter, Ron **1987**:3
Cerovsek, Corey
  Brief Entry **1987**:4
Chapman, Tracy **1989**:2
Clarke, Stanley **1985**:4
Cleveland, James
  Obituary **1991**:3
Connick, Harry, Jr. **1991**:1
Copland, Aaron
  Obituary **1991**:2
Coppola, Carmine
  Obituary **1991**:4
Corea, Chick **1986**:3
Cray, Robert **1988**:2
Crothers, Scatman
  Obituary **1987**:1
Cugat, Xavier
  Obituary **1991**:2
D'Arby, Terence Trent **1988**:4
Davis, Sammy, Jr.
  Obituary **1990**:4
Day, Dennis
  Obituary **1988**:4
Dean, Laura **1989**:4
de Passe, Suzanne **1990**:4
Di Meola, Al **1986**:4
Dimitrova, Ghena **1987**:1
Dr. Demento **1986**:1
Dolenz, Micky **1986**:4
Dorati, Antal
  Obituary **1989**:2
Eldridge, Roy
  Obituary **1989**:3
Eno, Brian **1986**:2
Ertegun, Ahmet **1986**:3
Estefan, Gloria **1991**:4
Falco
  Brief Entry **1987**:2
Foster, David **1988**:2
Garcia, Jerry **1988**:3
Geffen, David **1985**:3
Geldof, Bob **1985**:3
Getz, Stan
  Obituary **1991**:4
Gibb, Andy
  Obituary **1988**:3
Gift, Roland **1990**:2
Glass, Philip **1991**:4
Goodman, Benny
  Obituary **1986**:3
Gordon, Dexter **1987**:1
  Obituary **1990**:4
Gore, Tipper **1985**:4
Graham, Bill **1986**:4
Grant, Amy **1985**:4
Grebenshikov, Boris **1990**:1
Grusin, Dave
  Brief Entry **1987**:2
Guccione, Bob, Jr. **1991**:4
Hammer, Jan **1987**:3
Hammer, M. C. **1991**:2

Hammond, John
  Obituary **1900.2**
Hancock, Herbie **1985**:1
Harris, Emmylou **1991**:3
Harry, Deborah **1990**:1
Hart, Mary
  Brief Entry **1988**:1
Hart, Mickey **1991**:2
Heard, J.C.
  Obituary **1989**:1
Heid, Bill
  Brief Entry **1987**:2
Heifetz, Jascha
  Obituary **1988**:2
Hoffs, Susanna **1988**:2
Hornsby, Bruce **1989**:3
Horovitz, Adam **1988**:3
Horowitz, Vladimir
  Obituary **1990**:1
Houston, Whitney **1986**:3
Hubbard, Freddie **1988**:4
Hynde, Chrissie **1991**:1
Jackson, Janet **1990**:4
Jones, Quincy **1990**:4
Kaye, Sammy
  Obituary **1987**:4
Kilmer, Val **1991**:4
Knopfler, Mark **1986**:2
Kravitz, Lenny **1991**:1
Kurzweil, Raymond **1986**:3
Kyser, Kay
  Obituary **1985**:3
Lang, K.D. **1988**:4
Lanois, Daniel **1991**:1
Lauper, Cyndi **1985**:1
Lennox, Annie **1985**:4
Lewis, Huey **1987**:3
Liberace
  Obituary **1987**:2
Lloyd Webber, Andrew **1989**:1
Loewe, Frederick
  Obituary **1988**:2
MacRae, Gordon
  Obituary **1986**:2
Madonna **1985**:2
Makeba, Miriam **1989**:2
Marley, Ziggy **1990**:4
Marsalis, Branford **1988**:3
Martin, Dean Paul
  Obituary **1987**:3
McDuffie, Robert **1990**:2
McEntire, Reba **1987**:3
McFerrin, Bobby **1989**:1
McMurtry, James **1990**:2
Michael, George **1989**:2
Michelangeli, Arturo
  Benedetti **1988**:2
Midler, Bette **1989**:4
Mintz, Shlomo **1986**:2
Mitchell, Joni **1991**:4
Mutter, Anne-Sophie **1990**:3
Nelson, Rick
  Obituary **1986**:1
New Kids on the Block **1991**:2
Norrington, Roger **1989**:4
North, Alex **1986**:3
O'Connor, Sinead **1990**:4
Ono, Yoko **1989**:2
Orbison, Roy
  Obituary **1989**:2
Ormandy, Eugene
  Obituary **1985**:2
Pastorius, Jaco
  Obituary **1988**:1
Petty, Tom **1988**:1
Pittman, Robert W. **1985**:1
Pogorelich, Ivo **1986**:4
Ponty, Jean-Luc **1985**:4

Preston, Robert
  Obituary **1987**:3
Quinn, Martha **1986**:4
Raffi **1988**:1
Raitt, Bonnie **1990**:2
Rampal, Jean-Pierre **1989**:2
Rashad, Phylicia **1987**:3
Rattle, Simon **1989**:4
Reed, Dean
  Obituary **1986**:3
Rich, Buddy
  Obituary **1987**:3
Riddle, Nelson
  Obituary **1985**:4
Ruffin, David
  Obituary **1991**:4
Salerno-Sonnenberg, Nadja **1988**:4
Satriani, Joe **1989**:3
Scholz, Tom **1987**:2
Seger, Bob **1987**:1
Segovia, Andrés
  Obituary **1987**:3
Shaffer, Paul **1987**:1
Sherman, Russell **1987**:4
Shocked, Michelle **1989**:4
Sinopoli, Giuseppe **1988**:1
Smith, Kate
  Obituary **1986**:3
Snider, Dee **1986**:1
Spector, Phil **1989**:1
Sting **1991**:4
Thomas, Michael Tilson **1990**:3
Tiffany **1989**:1
Tone-Loc **1990**:3
Tosh, Peter
  Obituary **1988**:2
Travis, Randy **1988**:4
Uchida, Mitsuko **1989**:3
Ullman, Tracey **1988**:3
Upshaw, Dawn **1991**:2
Valente, Benita **1985**:3
Van Halen, Edward **1985**:2
Vanilla Ice **1991**:3
Vaughan, Sarah
  Obituary **1990**:3
Vaughan, Stevie Ray
  Obituary **1991**:1
Vega, Suzanne **1988**:1
Vollenweider, Andreas **1985**:2
von Karajan, Herbert
  Obituary **1989**:4
von Trapp, Maria
  Obituary **1987**:3
Washington, Grover, Jr. **1989**:1
Weintraub, Jerry **1986**:1
Willis, Bruce **1986**:4
Winston, George **1987**:1
Winter, Paul **1990**:2
Yankovic, "Weird Al" **1985**:4
Young, Neil **1991**:2
Zwilich, Ellen **1990**:1

POLITICS AND GOVERNMENT— FOREIGN
Akihito, Emperor of Japan **1990**:1
Aquino, Corazon **1986**:2
Arafat, Yasser **1989**:3
Arens, Moshe **1985**:1
Arias Sanchez, Oscar **1989**:3
Aristide, Jean-Bertrand **1991**:3
Assad, Rifaat **1986**:3
Astorga, Nora **1988**:2
Berri, Nabih **1985**:2
Bhutto, Benazir **1989**:4
Bolkiah, Sultan Muda
  Hassanal **1985**:4

Buthelezi, Mangosuthu
  Gatsha **1989**:3
Castro, Fidel **1991**:1
Ceausescu, Nicolae
  Obituary **1990**:2
Chernenko, Konstantin
  Obituary **1985**:1
Chissano, Joaquim **1987**:4
Chretien, Jean **1990**:4
Copps, Sheila **1986**:4
Cruz, Arturo **1985**:1
Dalai Lama **1989**:1
de Klerk, F.W. **1990**:1
Delors, Jacques **1990**:2
de Pinies, Jamie
  Brief Entry **1986**:3
Doe, Samuel
  Obituary **1991**:1
Doi, Takako
  Brief Entry **1987**:4
Duarte, Jose Napoleon
  Obituary **1990**:3
Dubinin, Yuri **1987**:4
Ferguson, Sarah **1990**:3
Finnbogadóttir, Vigdís
  Brief Entry **1986**:2
Freij, Elias **1986**:4
Galvin, Martin
  Brief Entry **1985**:3
Gandhi, Indira
  Obituary **1985**:1
Gandhi, Rajiv
  Obituary **1991**:4
Garneau, Marc **1985**:1
Gorbachev, Mikhail **1985**:2
Gromyko, Andrei
  Obituary **1990**:2
Habash, George **1986**:1
Havel, Vaclav **1990**:3
Hess, Rudolph
  Obituary **1988**:1
Hirohito, Emperor of Japan
  Obituary **1989**:2
Hume, John **1987**:1
Hussein, Saddam **1991**:1
Hu Yaobang
  Obituary **1989**:4
Johnson, Pierre Marc **1985**:4
Jumblatt, Walid **1987**:4
Juneau, Pierre **1988**:3
Kekkonen, Urho
  Obituary **1986**:4
Khomeini, Ayatollah Ruhollah
  Obituary **1989**:4
Lalonde, Marc **1985**:1
Landsbergis, Vytautas **1991**:3
Le Duan
  Obituary **1986**:4
Le Duc Tho
  Obituary **1991**:1
Lévesque, René
  Obituary **1988**:1
Levy, David **1987**:2
Lewis, Stephen **1987**:2
Livingstone, Ken **1988**:3
Lon Nol
  Obituary **1986**:1
Machel, Samora
  Obituary **1987**:1
Macmillan, Harold
  Obituary **1987**:2
Major, John **1991**:2
Mandela, Nelson **1990**:3
Mandela, Winnie **1989**:3
Marcos, Ferdinand
  Obituary **1990**:1
McGuinness, Martin **1985**:4
McLaughlin, Audrey **1990**:3

Molotov, Vyacheslav Mikhailovich
  Obituary **1987**:1
Mubarak, Hosni **1991**:4
Mugabe, Robert **1988**:4
Mulroney, Brian **1989**:2
Nidal, Abu **1987**:1
Niezabitowska, Malgorzata **1991**:3
Nujoma, Sam **1990**:4
Obando, Miguel **1986**:4
Olav, King of Norway
  Obituary **1991**:3
Palme, Olof
  Obituary **1986**:2
Paton, Alan
  Obituary **1988**:3
Paz, Octavio **1991**:2
Peckford, Brian **1989**:1
Perez, Carlos Andre **1990**:2
Perez de Cuellar, Javier **1991**:3
Peterson, David **1987**:1
Philby, Kim
  Obituary **1988**:3
Rafsanjani, Ali Akbar
  Hashemi **1987**:3
Ram, Jagjivan
  Obituary **1986**:4
Reisman, Simon **1987**:4
Robelo, Alfonso **1988**:1
Sarkis, Elias
  Obituary **1985**:3
Savimbi, Jonas **1986**:2
Schily, Otto
  Brief Entry **1987**:4
Simpson, Wallis
  Obituary **1986**:3
Slovo, Joe **1989**:2
Staller, Ilona **1988**:3
Strauss, Robert **1991**:4
Suzman, Helen **1989**:3
Tambo, Oliver **1991**:3
Terzi, Zehdi Labib **1985**:3
Thatcher, Margaret **1989**:2
Vander Zalm, William **1987**:3
Walesa, Lech **1991**:2
Wilson, Bertha
  Brief Entry **1986**:1
Ye Jianying
  Obituary **1987**:1
Yeltsin, Boris **1991**:1
Zhao Ziyang **1989**:1
Zia ul-Haq, Mohammad
  Obituary **1988**:4

POLITICS AND GOVERNMENT—U.S.

Abraham, Spencer **1991**:4
Abrams, Elliott **1987**:1
Ailes, Roger **1989**:3
Alexander, Lamar **1991**:2
Atwater, Lee **1989**:4
Atwater, Lee
  Obituary **1991**:4
Baker, James A. III **1991**:2
Baldrige, Malcolm
  Obituary **1988**:1
Banks, Dennis J. **1986**:4
Barry, Marion **1991**:1
Bennett, William **1990**:1
Berle, Peter A.A.
  Brief Entry **1987**:3
Biden, Joe **1986**:3
Boyington, Gregory "Pappy"
  Obituary **1988**:2
Brady, Sarah and James S. **1991**:4
Brown, Ron **1990**:3
Brown, Willie L. **1985**:2
Bush, Barbara **1989**:3

Caliguiri, Richard S.
  Obituary **1988**:3
Carter, Billy
  Obituary **1989**:1
Casey, William
  Obituary **1987**:3
Cavazos, Lauro F. **1989**:2
Cheney, Dick **1991**:3
Cheney, Lynne V. **1990**:4
Cisneros, Henry **1987**:2
Clark, J.E.
  Brief Entry **1986**:1
Dinkins, David N. **1990**:2
Dolan, Terry **1985**:2
Dole, Elizabeth Hanford **1990**:1
Dukakis, Michael **1988**:3
Duke, David **1990**:2
Ervin, Sam
  Obituary **1985**:2
Estrich, Susan **1989**:1
Falkenberg, Nanette **1985**:2
Farrakhan, Louis **1990**:4
Fish, Hamilton
  Obituary **1991**:3
Fitzgerald, A. Ernest **1986**:2
Florio, James J. **1991**:2
Flynn, Ray **1989**:1
Foley, Thomas S. **1990**:1
Frank, Barney **1989**:2
Galvin, John R. **1990**:1
Gephardt, Richard **1987**:3
Gingrich, Newt **1991**:1
Harriman, W. Averell
  Obituary **1986**:4
Harris, Patricia Roberts
  Obituary **1985**:2
Heinz, John
  Obituary **1991**:4
Heller, Walter
  Obituary **1987**:4
Hills, Carla **1990**:3
Inman, Bobby Ray **1985**:1
Kassebaum, Nancy **1991**:1
Kemp, Jack **1990**:4
Kennedy, John F., Jr. **1990**:1
Kerrey, Bob **1986**:1
Kerrey, Bob **1991**:3
Koop, C. Everett **1989**:3
Landon, Alf
  Obituary **1988**:1
Lansdale, Edward G.
  Obituary **1987**:2
Liman, Arthur **1989**:4
Lodge, Henry Cabot
  Obituary **1985**:1
Lord, Winston
  Brief Entry **1987**:4
Luce, Clare Boothe
  Obituary **1988**:1
Mankiller, Wilma P.
  Brief Entry **1986**:2
Martin, Lynn **1991**:4
McCloy, John J.
  Obituary **1989**:3
McKinney, Stewart B.
  Obituary **1987**:4
McMillen, Tom **1988**:4
Mitchell, George J. **1989**:3
Mitchell, John
  Obituary **1989**:2
Morrison, Trudi
  Brief Entry **1986**:2
Mott, William Penn, Jr. **1986**:1
Moyers, Bill **1991**:4
Neal, James Foster **1986**:2
Newton, Huey
  Obituary **1990**:1
Noonan, Peggy **1990**:3

North, Oliver **1987**:4
Novello, Antonia **1991**:2
Nunn, Sam **1990**:2
Oliver, Daniel **1988**:2
Orr, Kay **1987**:4
Paige, Emmett, Jr.
  Brief Entry **1986**:4
Pendleton, Clarence M.
  Obituary **1988**:4
Pepper, Claude
  Obituary **1989**:4
Perry, Carrie Saxon **1989**:2
Powell, Colin **1990**:1
Quayle, Dan **1989**:2
Richards, Ann **1991**:2
Rickover, Hyman
  Obituary **1986**:4
Robb, Charles S. **1987**:2
Robertson, Pat **1988**:2
Roemer, Buddy **1991**:4
Roosevelt, Franklin D., Jr.
  Obituary **1989**:1
Sanders, Bernie **1991**:4
Scalia, Antonin **1988**:2
Schaefer, William Donald **1988**:1
Schwarzenegger, Arnold **1991**:1
Schwarzkopf, Norman **1991**:3
Sheehan, Daniel P. **1989**:1
Sidney, Ivan
  Brief Entry **1987**:2
Sigmund, Barbara Boggs
  Obituary **1991**:1
Stewart, Potter
  Obituary **1986**:1
Strauss, Robert **1991**:4
Suarez, Xavier
  Brief Entry **1986**:2
Sullivan, Louis **1990**:4
Sununu, John **1989**:2
Taylor, Maxwell
  Obituary **1987**:3
Thomas, Helen **1988**:4
Tower, John
  Obituary **1991**:4
Violet, Arlene **1985**:3
Washington, Harold
  Obituary **1988**:1
Whitmire, Kathy **1988**:2
Wilder, L. Douglas **1990**:3
Williams, G. Mennen
  Obituary **1988**:2
Yard, Molly **1991**:4
Zech, Lando W.
  Brief Entry **1987**:4

RADIO

Backus, Jim
  Obituary **1990**:1
Blanc, Mel
  Obituary **1989**:4
Caray, Harry **1988**:3
Costas, Bob **1986**:4
Day, Dennis
  Obituary **1988**:4
Dr. Demento **1986**:1
Gobel, George
  Obituary **1991**:4
Goodman, Benny
  Obituary **1986**:3
Grange, Red
  Obituary **1991**:3
Greene, Lorne
  Obituary **1988**:1
Harmon, Tom
  Obituary **1990**:3
Houseman, John
  Obituary **1989**:1

Cumulative Subject Index

This index lists newsmakers by subjects, company names, products, organizations, issues, awards, and professional specialties. Indexes in softbound issues allow access to the current year's entries; indexes in annual hardbound volumes are cumulative, covering the entire *Newsmakers* series.

Listee names are followed by a year and issue number; thus **1988**:3 indicates that an entry on that individual appears in both 1988, Issue 3 and the 1988 cumulation. For access to newsmakers appearing earlier than the current softbound issue, see the previous year's cumulation.

Molecular biology
Gilbert, Walter **1988**:3

Monty Python
Cleese, John **1989**:2

Mothers Against Drunk Driving [MADD]
Lightner, Candy **1985**:1

Motown Records
de Passe, Suzanne **1990**:4
Ruffin, David
Obituary **1991**:4

Motorcycles
Beals, Vaughn **1988**:2
Knievel, Robbie **1990**:1

Mountain climbing
Wood, Sharon
Brief Entry **1988**:1

Moving Earth (dance company)
Takei, Kei **1990**:2

Mozambique Liberation Front [FRELIMO]
Chissano, Joaquim **1987**:4
Machel, Samora
Obituary **1987**:1

Mrs. Fields Cookies, Inc.
Fields, Debbi **1987**:3

Ms. magazine
Morgan, Robin **1991**:1
Summers, Anne **1990**:2

MTV Networks, Inc.
Pittman, Robert W. **1985**:1
Quinn, Martha **1986**:4

Multiple birth research
Keith, Louis **1988**:2

Muppets
Henson, Jim **1989**:1
Obituary **1990**:4

NARAL
See: **National Abortion Rights Action League**

NASA
See: **National Aeronautics and Space Administration**

Nation of Islam
Farrakhan, Louis **1990**:4

National Abortion Rights Action League [NARAL]
Falkenberg, Nanette **1985**:2

National Aeronautics and Space Administration [NASA]
Bean, Alan L. **1986**:2
Garneau, Marc **1985**:1
McAuliffe, Christa
Obituary **1985**:4

National Amusements, Inc.
Redstone, Sumner Murray **1987**:4

National Audubon Society
Berle, Peter A.A.
Brief Entry **1987**:3

National Cancer Institute
DeVita, Vincent T., Jr. **1987**:3
Rosenberg, Steven **1989**:1

National Center for Atmospheric Research
Thompson, Starley
Brief Entry **1987**:3

National Coalition for the Homeless
Hayes, Robert M. **1986**:3

National Coalition on Television Violence [NCTV]
Radecki, Thomas
Brief Entry **1986**:2

National Commission on Excellence
Justiz, Manuel J. **1986**:4

National Conservative Political Action Committee [NCPAC]
Dolan, Terry **1985**:2

National Education Association [NEA]
Futrell, Mary Hatwood **1986**:1

National Endowment for the Humanities [NEH]
Cheney, Lynne V. **1990**:4

National Federation for Decency
Wildmon, Donald **1988**:4

National Football League [NFL]
Esiason, Boomer **1991**:1
Gault, Willie **1991**:2
Grange, Red
Obituary **1991**:3
Kelly, Jim **1991**:4
Moon, Warren **1991**:3
Tagliabue, Paul **1990**:2

National Football League Players Association
Upshaw, Gene **1988**:1

National Hockey League Players Association [NHLPA]
Eagleson, Alan **1987**:4

National Hot Rod Association [NHRA]
Muldowney, Shirley **1986**:1

National Institute of Education
Justiz, Manuel J. **1986**:4

National Organization for Women [NOW]
Yard, Molly **1991**:4

National Park Service
Mott, William Penn, Jr. **1986**:1

National Public Radio [NPR]
Magliozzi, Tom and Ray **1991**:4

National Rifle Association [NRA]
Foss, Joe **1990**:3

National Science Foundation [NSF]
Bloch, Erich **1987**:4

National Security Agency
Inman, Bobby Ray **1985**:1

National Union for the Total Independence of Angola [UNITA]
Savimbi, Jonas **1986**:2

National Union of Mineworkers [NUM]
Ramaphosa, Cyril **1988**:2

Native American issues
Banks, Dennis J. **1986**:4
Mankiller, Wilma P.
Brief Entry **1986**:2
Sidney, Ivan
Brief Entry **1987**:2

NATO
See: **North Atlantic Treaty Organization**

Nautilus Sports/Medical Industries
Jones, Arthur A. **1985**:3

Nazi Party
Hess, Rudolph
Obituary **1988**:1
Klarsfeld, Beate **1989**:1
Mengele, Josef
Obituary **1985**:2

NBC Television Network
Tartikoff, Brandon **1985**:2

NCPAC
See: **National Conservative Political Action Committee**

NCTV
See: **National Coalition on Television Violence**

NDP
See: **New Democratic Party (Canada)**

NEA
See: **National Education Association**

Nebraska state government
Kerrey, Bob **1986**:1
Orr, Kay **1987**:4

NEH
See: **National Endowment for the Humanities**

New Democratic Party (Canada) [NDP]
Lewis, Stephen **1987**:2
McLaughlin, Audrey **1990**:3

Newfoundland provincial government
Peckford, Brian **1989**:1

New Hampshire state government
Sununu, John **1989**:2

Cumulative Newsmakers Index

This index lists all entries included in the *Newsmakers* series.

Listee names are followed by a year and issue number; thus **1988**:3 indicates that an entry appears in both 1988, Issue 3 and the 1988 cumulation.